W9-BZF-043

Ethics in Marketing

Ethics in Marketing

N. Craig Smith
School of Business Administration
Georgetown University

John A. Quelch
Graduate School of Business Administration
Harvard University

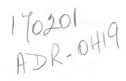

IRWIN
Homewood, IL 60430
Boston, MA 02116

© RICHARD D. IRWIN, INC., 1993

Sponsoring editor:	Steve Patterson
Project editor:	Paula M. Buschman
Production manager:	Diane Palmer
Cover designer:	Julie Smith
Designer:	Larry J. Cope
Art coordinator:	Mark Malloy
Compositor:	Impressions, Inc.
Typeface:	10/12 Times Roman
Printer:	R. R. Donnelley & Sons Company

Library of Congress Cataloging-in-Publication Data

Smith, N. Craig. 1958–
    Ethics in marketing / N. Craig Smith and John A. Quelch.
      p.   cm.
    Includes bibliographical references and index.
    ISBN 0-256-10894-3
    1. Marketing. 2. Business ethics. I. Quelch, John A.
  II. Title.
HF5414.122.S62 1992   91–41763
174'.4—dc20

Printed in the United States of America
1 2 3 4 5 6 7 8 9 0 DOC 9 8 7 6 5 4 3 2

To Professor E. Raymond Corey of Harvard Business School, in recognition of his early and continued contributions to our understanding of marketing ethics.

About the Authors

N. Craig Smith is Associate Professor, the School of Business Administration, Georgetown University. As a Visiting Professor at Harvard Business School, he developed with John Quelch the Ethics in Marketing Project, upon which *Ethics in Marketing* is based. He is the author of *Morality and the Market: Consumer Pressure for Corporate Accountability*, the coauthor of a book on research, and has contributed journal articles on a variety of marketing management and business ethics topics. He consults with firms on problems of good marketing practice, including marketing ethics.

John A. Quelch is Professor of Business Administration, Graduate School of Business Administration, Harvard University where he heads the introductory Marketing course taken by all 900 MBA students each year. He has (co)authored ten books and is frequent contributor to *Harvard Business Review* and *Sloan Management Review*. He serves as a director of Reebok International Ltd. and WPP Group plc.

Preface

In April 1987, Harvard Business School was promised one of its largest-ever donations, a gift of $23 million to fund an ethics program. John Shad, the outgoing chairman of the U.S. Securities and Exchange Commission and a graduate of the school, said about his donation: "I've been very disturbed most recently with the large number of graduates of leading business and law schools who have become convicted felons." In effect, Shad was issuing a challenge to Harvard—and other business schools—to give serious attention to ethics in their curricula. The "greed decade" of the 1980s was giving way to the "ethics era." Shad's gift was confirmation of the extent of public and corporate concern about business practices. This book, in large part, is a product of that concern and of the Harvard Business School ethics program that resulted.

Under the leadership of the senior associate dean, Thomas Piper—and before the gift was received—Harvard Business School started developing a comprehensive program on leadership, ethics, and corporate responsibility. The ethics program called for the development of a compulsory ethics module at the start of the first year of Harvard Business School's MBA program, changes in admissions procedures, the integration of ethics into required courses of the MBA program, required ethics modules in executive programs, and encouragement of faculty research and course development involving ethics. In supporting the program, Dean John H. McArthur described it as a major commitment, over 10 to 15 years, "to get a very large part of the 175 faculty to deal comfortably with issues involving values and ethics, in their courses, research, and course development."

John Quelch, head of the required introductory marketing course in the MBA program, invited Craig Smith from Cranfield School of Management, England, to help apply the school's ethics initiative within this course. In keeping with the school's broader efforts in business ethics, the aim of the Ethics in Marketing Project was to conduct research that would advance the teaching and understanding of the ethical dimensions of marketing decision making. The two-year project culminated in a three-day workshop at Harvard Business School in May 1990, "The Impacts of Marketing Decision Making: A Workshop on Ethics in Marketing." With Professor E. Raymond Corey, we brought together a group of 50 individuals representing a wide spectrum of colleges and universities, as well as businesses, regulatory agencies, and consumer groups. Employing some of the case studies and other work produced under the Ethics in Marketing Project, the workshop examined major ethical issues in marketing management and identified implications for marketing practice and public policy. Recommendations resulted for improving the coverage of the ethical dimensions of marketing decision making in marketing teaching and research.

Ethics in Marketing reflects our belief that ethical considerations are integral to marketing decision making—hence the title. This is a challenging position to adopt as a marketing manager, student, or professor. It calls into question some of the most fundamental concepts of marketing. Yet the history of the Ethics in Marketing Project illustrates the importance and necessity of this position. Much of the material in this book was developed as part of the project, including contributions specially commissioned from participants at the marketing ethics workshop.

Regardless of your position on the ethics of marketing practice, we believe you will find no easy answers to the problems presented here. The case studies, for example, have certainly stimulated our students at Harvard and Georgetown. We hope you will not only reflect on the issues raised here, but also act. As Robert Coles has noted: "A well-developed conscience does not translate, necessarily, into a morally courageous life. Nor do well-developed powers of philosophical thinking and moral analysis necessarily translate into an everyday willingness to face down the various evils of this world."

Acknowledgements

In conclusion, we would like to thank the people who helped considerably in the preparation of this book. At Harvard Business School, we are grateful to Dean John H. McArthur, Senior Associate Dean Thomas R. Piper, and Senior Research Fellow Dr. Mary Gentile for their support of the Ethics in Marketing Project. Stimulating our thoughts and efforts were our Harvard Business School colleagues in marketing and other areas, as well as the contributors to the book and other attendees at the workshop. In particular, we would mention Ray Corey, who in so many respects was a project mentor.

We would like to thank our faculty colleagues and publishers, acknowledged throughout the book, who allowed us to reprint case studies and articles, adding richness to the materials included. Professor Michael Hoffman of Bentley College Center for Business Ethics deserves a special mention for his assistance in helping Ed Petry develop such a thorough marketing ethics bibliography.

Funding as well as encouragement for our research endeavors came from the Division of Research of the Graduate School of Business Administration, Harvard University, and the School of Business Administration, Georgetown University. Our research efforts would, of course, have been frustrated without the trust and cooperation of the managers and companies who helped us develop the case studies included here. Research Assistant Elisa Morton Palter of Harvard Business School did an excellent job in keeping the book and us on track. Research Assistant John J. Brough of Georgetown University also provided valuable support. For secretarial assistance we must thank, in particular, Anna Ghonim of the School of Business Administration, Georgetown University, and Antoinette Prince of Harvard Business School—who enabled us to be productive even when we were thousands of miles distant.

Finally, we would like to thank Steve Patterson, Senior Sponsoring Editor at Richard D. Irwin, for having faith in the book. With innovation comes risk but also, we hope, rewards.

N. Craig Smith

John A. Quelch

Contents

Ethics in Marketing

Ethics and the Marketing Manager

Chapter 1

Ethics and the Marketing Manager

N. Craig Smith

THE ROLE OF ETHICS IN MARKETING MANAGEMENT

The function of the marketing manager is to manage the firm's relationships with its customers. The imperative of customer satisfaction drives all activities of the firm. As Levitt puts it: "There can be no effective corporate strategy that is not marketing oriented, that does not in the end follow this unyielding prescript: The purpose of a business is to create and keep a customer."[1] Marketing managers are primarily responsible for ensuring that this corporate purpose is realized. They act to integrate the firm's activities toward this end. In "working for customers," marketing managers are involved in:

- Selecting the target market.

- Formulating marketing strategy and developing the marketing plan.

- Developing an appropriate marketing program, incorporating decisions on:
  Product policy.
  Pricing policy.
  Distribution policy.
  Marketing communications (particularly personal selling, advertising, and sales promotions).

- Implementing plans and programs.

- Marketing organization and performance evaluation.

These activities—around which this book is structured—require the marketing manager to seek the cooperation of the other functions of the firm. In

---

[1] Theodore Levitt, *The Marketing Imagination* (New York: Free Press, 1986), p. 19.

this intermediary capacity, the marketing manager often has little direct authority; for example, to impose a production schedule that would meet the requirements of a particular customer. Moreover, the marketing manager also must mediate externally, with customers, suppliers, and other stakeholders. Developing this theme in Chapter 2.1, Ray Corey suggests "marketing managers are caught in a cross fire of conflicting pressures." Perhaps it is not surprising, given these pressures and marketing's external role, that media reports of unethical conduct in business more frequently involve marketing activities.[2]

It has become clichéd to note the widespread concern about business practices that has developed in recent years. Often, this concern focuses on unethical marketing—price-fixing, bribery, deceptive advertising, unsafe products. Marketing is seen by many as the worst offender,[3] possibly because marketing activities are more visible, but more likely because marketing people behave less ethically. As Corey argues in sharing this viewpoint, the pressures and opportunities to which marketing management is exposed are such that marketing may remain the source of most misconduct in business. This surely serves to emphasize the importance of a role for ethics in marketing, rather than to question its relevance.

Consider the alternatives: marketing without ethics or, indeed, unethical marketing. Businesspeople sometimes argue that ethical issues are not and cannot be the concern of business, that business has a different function, which would be undermined by attention to ethical issues. So, for example, doing business in South Africa has been defended as a sound business decision. Being implicated in apartheid was viewed as an unfortunate but unrelated consequence—a political, rather than a business, problem. If we ignore the evidence of corporate profits that result from apartheid,[4] the "don't mix business with

---

[2] I have only anecdotal evidence to support this claim: from newspaper cuttings and discussions with business ethicists. A 1991 search of the finance-oriented *The Wall Street Journal*, using Dow Jones Text-Search Services, found: "Marketing" appeared in 25,007 documents, "marketing" and "ethics" in 186 documents; "finance" in 27,629 documents, "finance" and "ethics" in 188 documents; "manufacturing" in 14,695 documents, "manufacturing" and "ethics" in 41 documents; "personnel" in 7,371 documents, "personnel" and "ethics" in 113 documents; "sales" in 61,012 documents, "sales" and "ethics" in 233 documents; and "production" in 28,465 documents, "production" and "ethics" in 90 documents. This superficial content analysis is supportive of the claim, though not conclusive.

[3] "The function within business firms most often charged with ethical abuse is marketing" (Patrick E. Murphy and Gene R. Laczniak, "Marketing Ethics: A Review with Implications for Managers, Educators, and Researchers," in Ben M. Enis and Kenneth J. Roering [eds.], *Review of Marketing* [Chicago: American Marketing Association, 1981], pp. 251–66). "Within the business firm, the functional area most closely related to ethical abuse is marketing. This is because marketing is the function of business charged with communicating and openly satisfying customers. Thus, marketing is closest to the public view and, consequently, is subject to considerable societal analysis and scrutiny" (John Tsalikis and David J. Fritzche, "Business Ethics: A Literature Review with a Focus on Marketing Ethics," *Journal of Business Ethics* 8 [1989], pp. 695–743).

[4] Merle Lipton, *Capitalism and Apartheid: South Africa 1910–1986* (Aldershot: Wildwood House, 1986).

politics" position can be seen to have some merit. Its more sophisticated advocates note that business may not have the right or the skills to deal with apartheid; that this is, anyway, the function of governments; and that, more fundamentally, dealing with such ethical issues would divert the firm's attention and resources away from its legitimate, revenue-generating activities. Besides, "if we don't, somebody else will"; indeed, a competitor might step in and steal an advantage on the firm choosing for ethical reasons not to do business in South Africa. In short, being ethical doesn't pay, and it conflicts with the function of the firm in a capitalist economy.

Yet, if this argument is pursued to its logical conclusion, marketing without ethics would amount to amoral business. In dismissing the "myth of amoral business," De George observes that business is integral to society, its activities, and values.[5] Trust, fairness, honesty, and respect are key values in business as well as society. Business suffers in their absence. For example, if most advertisers were not honest, there would be little point in a firm advertising, because nobody would believe its message. As De George puts it, "Business, like most other social activities, presupposes a background of morality, and would be impossible without it . . . those who buy a product expect it to be as advertised, when they take it home and unpack it."[6]

Donaldson also rejects "moral disinterest" as a necessary condition for efficient markets. He points out that economist Milton Friedman, an exponent of moral disinterest, still specifies "moral rules" that corporations should follow: compete openly, do not deceive, do not engage in fraudulent activity.[7] Donaldson develops the argument further:

> Even . . . Adam Smith believed that moral rules were necessary aspects of a society in which the marketplace could function properly and that market solutions are not always socially optimal . . . to be optimal, he believed, morality itself must be a force in the marketplace.[8]

In keeping with Adam Smith, Donaldson suggests "corporations that pursue profits are, however ironic it sounds, involved in a *moral* pursuit."[9] Perhaps surprisingly, he shares this view with Levitt. Describing profit as a requisite of business, Levitt suggests the notion of profit as a purpose of business is "morally shallow." He asks: "Who with a palpable heartbeat and minimal sensibilities will go to the mat for the right of somebody to earn a profit for its own sake?"[10]

However, Levitt and Donaldson, while both accepting a social purpose of business, do not entirely agree on the form it should take. Levitt more typically

---

[5] Richard T. De George, *Business Ethics* (New York: Macmillan, 1986), pp. 6–7.

[6] Ibid., p. 9.

[7] Thomas Donaldson, *Corporations and Morality* (Englewood Cliffs, N.J.: Prentice Hall, 1982), p. 68.

[8] Ibid., p. 107.

[9] Ibid.

[10] Levitt, p. 7.

argues in favor of the moral merits of the unfettered market system as a means of improving human welfare. On this basis and, more specifically, in the imperative of customer satisfaction, arguments that marketing is unethical may be rejected. While acknowledging Levitt's argument, Donaldson concludes that a moral "burden" remains, from which individuals and corporations cannot be excused.[11] Moral deliberation is particularly required where moral problems arise directly from corporate activity, arguably the case with apartheid. Moreover, advocates of moral disinterest concerned about the dilution of the profit motive ignore the likelihood of government intervention to curb unacceptable corporate practices, which could more seriously affect the profit motive. As Donaldson explains: "defending unadulterated profit maximization tends to generate a vicious circle. If corporations neglect moral issues, society will look outside the corporation for remedies . . ."[12]

Levitt, in suggesting that profit is insufficient as a purpose of business, concludes: "If no greater purpose can be discerned or justified, business cannot morally justify its existence."[13] The key here is acknowledgement of the social role of business. Once this is accepted, the argument for moral disinterest may be largely rejected and the debate turns on how the social role of business may be best fulfilled.[14] It is suggested here that, as part of society, business in turn has obligations and responsibilities attendant to that role and its power and status, which require business to act ethically and promote ethical conduct.

Unethical marketing, as distinct from marketing without ethics, is not founded on arguments about the appropriateness of ethical considerations within business. Unethical marketing involves a breach of ethics, the use of unethical practices within marketing to pursue corporate or an individual manager's ends. Unethical marketing also contradicts the social role of the firm, yet goes further than the amoral position of marketing without ethics. It constitutes deviant behavior and would be dysfunctional as a consequence. Bribery, for example, harms customers and competitors not involved in the practice. Similarly, the dishonest salesperson may increase commission payments by cheating customers. If undetected and unpunished, these practices benefit individuals, and perhaps their companies, at the expense of other individuals and the economic system. So the argument may be made that "it's OK if you don't get caught," at least by an individual untroubled by conscience or prepared to forsake conscience for profit.

The simple response to this crude advocacy of unethical conduct would be: "What does it profit a man to gain the whole world but lose his soul?" Yet rarely is unethical marketing so amenable to this analysis; rarely is it the result of deliberately unethical intentions, of what might be termed "evil." More

---

[11] Donaldson, p. 106.

[12] Ibid.

[13] Levitt, p. 7.

[14] Donaldson determines the social role of business on the basis of social contract theory. See Donaldson, chapter 3, for a more complete treatment of this topic.

frequently, it is the outcome of a lack of thought, of misunderstanding, or of compromise. The marketing vice president advocating "stability" at an industry association meeting and complaining of price wars that have reduced profits for all the industry's manufacturers is voicing a genuine concern. While her remarks may not constitute price-fixing—which would be illegal—they may send a signal about her company's intent. The remarks may have been made without much thought or without a full understanding of the means or effects of collusion on pricing. Alternatively, under pressure to improve margins, she may have realized the import of these remarks, with the intention being to discourage price competition, but without acting illegally. This scenario is far more likely than that of a clandestine meeting where manufacturers explicitly determine prices for the forthcoming year. It is unethical, yet it may also be understandable, at least to other marketing managers in similarly competitive industries, if not to regulators.

Faced with conflicting pressures, marketing managers may make compromises that constitute unethical conduct. Often, such decisions can be rationalized: an inadequately tested product has to be brought to market quickly to beat the competition; payments via a third party to organized crime may protect the company's employees as well as its distribution channels; a toy advertisement targeting children is entertaining as well as persuasive. A frequent rationalization is caveat emptor, buyer beware. Puffery in advertisements, incomplete sales presentations, or product performance defects unanticipated by the customer may be rationalized as acceptable if the consumer is expected to be vigilant and on guard against trickery. The caveat emptor position is discussed in more detail later.

The techniques of neutralization provide a form of rationalization that enables an individual to lessen the possible impact of norm-violating behaviors upon his self-concept and social relationships. Five techniques are typically identified within the social disorganization and deviance literature and may partly explain unethical marketing: denial of responsibility ("I couldn't help myself, I was desperate"); denial of injury ("What's the big deal? No one was hurt"); denial of victim ("If they're foolish enough to believe that, it's their own fault they were taken advantage of"); condemning the condemners ("I was only doing what others do all the time"); appeal to higher loyalties ("I did it because it was better for all concerned").[15]

In sum, arguments may be advanced to explain, if not defend, unethical conduct. Less convincing, perhaps, are arguments that attention to ethics is inappropriate, that marketing is value-neutral. Yet it is important to consider the consequences of ignoring ethics or of unethical conduct. In the long term, the firm's stakeholders will likely call to task a firm that is not ethical in its marketing: customers, for example, will go elsewhere. In the short term, this

---

[15] Scott J. Vitell and Stephen J. Grove, "Marketing Ethics and the Techniques of Neutralization," *Journal of Business Ethics* 6 (1987), pp. 433–38.

may happen, too, though the unethical and illegal action may more quickly prompt legal remedies. Unethical conduct is also likely to have repercussions on the organization: its culture, the motivation of its employees, the type of employees it can attract and retain. A company that conducts its business in a dog-eat-dog fashion is likely to encourage that mentality in its employees, with respect to the firm and each other.

Because of the repercussions of these external and internal forces, it has been argued that good ethics is good business. Often this is true. Certainly it is a useful slogan and a simple way of communicating to employees the importance of ethical conduct. However, consider situations where there is a possible trade-off between ethics and profits, as shown diagrammatically in Figure 1.

There are some marketing decisions where, even in the long term, it may be difficult to identify an ill-consequence of unethical conduct for the firm. For example, a firm that is exiting an industry may try to get away with overcharging or otherwise exploiting its customers. Or perhaps a marketing researcher, knowing the chances of detection to be negligible, interviews for a job with a company on which she is conducting a competitive analysis, to obtain confidential information. Unethical, but potentially highly profitable, these actions fall into the "risky and wrong" quadrant of the matrix—with the risks (of being caught or other ill-consequences) relatively low in these examples.

Conversely, there are marketing decisions that, though clearly ethical, have no apparent payoff in prospect. Lord Sieff, former chairman of one of Britain's most respected companies, Marks and Spencer, has commented: "Whatever we have done because we felt we had a moral obligation, turned out to be good for business within five years."[16] However, it is not clear that, for example,

---

FIGURE 1 Ethics–Profits Trade-off Matrix

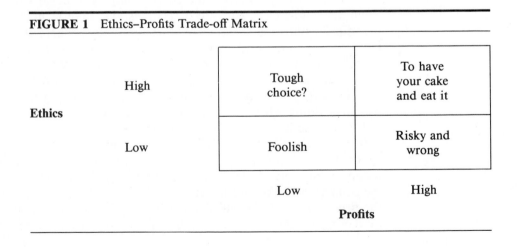

		Low	High
Ethics	High	Tough choice?	To have your cake and eat it
	Low	Foolish	Risky and wrong
		Low	High
		Profits	

---

[16] Walter Goldsmith and David Clutterbuck, *The Winning Streak* (London: Weidenfeld and Nicholson, 1984), p. 86.

a tobacco company withdrawing from the industry, because of the overwhelming evidence of the ill effects of smoking on health, is likely to profit as a result of doing so. Today's increasingly diversified tobacco companies remain dependent on tobacco revenues: Philip Morris derives less than half of its sales but more than two thirds of its profits[17] from a product that is responsible for more than one in every six deaths in the United States.[18] This industry may face problems in recruiting good people and constant legal challenges, but it remains highly profitable.

Ideally, the solution of high ethics and high profits should be sought. Yet, as the matrix illustrates, this may not always be possible. However, the pursuit of the ethical and profitable decision is to be strongly encouraged. Many companies in the case studies and news articles that follow sought this solution and, through management creativity, a good number succeeded.

An honest and realistic appraisal of the role of ethics in marketing must conclude that, while clearly desirable from many standpoints, incorporating ethical considerations within marketing decision making is certainly challenging, given the pressures and opportunities presented to marketing managers. The human and financial consequences on individuals, firms, and society, of unethical marketing or of simply ignoring ethics, constitute important but not, ultimately, sufficient arguments for ethical marketing.

How, then, can marketing ethics be advocated conclusively? The overriding force for ethical marketing is the moral precept that is basic to the human condition. (In reference to Donaldson, this was earlier described as a moral "burden.") Ethical and effective marketing managers have respect and concern for the welfare of those affected by their decisions.[19] As moral beings, ethical

---

[17] Alix M. Freedman, "New Smoke Signals at Philip Morris?" *The Wall Street Journal*, 26 March 1991.

[18] U.S. Dept. of Health and Human Services, *Reducing the Health Consequence of Smoking: 25 Years of Progress. A Report of the Surgeon General*, USDHHS, Public Health Service, Office on Smoking and Health. DHHS Publication no. (CDC) 89-8411, January 1989.

[19] A considerable body of moral philosophy supports this obligation of respect and concern for the welfare of others. For example, Kant's "categorical imperative," which, as Bowie and Duska suggest, can be summarized as two principles: 1. Act only according to that maxim by which you can, at the same time, will that it should become a universal law; 2. Act so as never to treat another human being merely as a means to an end (Norman E. Bowie and Ronald F. Duska, *Business Ethics* [Englewood Cliffs, N.J.: Prentice Hall, 1990], p. 46). Kant's categorical imperative is so fundamental to moral philosophy that MacIntyre can write: "For many who have never heard of philosophy, let alone of Kant, morality is roughly what Kant said it was" (Alasdair MacIntyre, *A Short History of Ethics* [New York: Collier, 1966], p. 190). Rawls's theory of justice (founded on his hypothesis of an "original position") provides more specific support of the rights of those affected by management decisions. As Ronald Dworkin concludes: "Rawls' most basic assumption is not that men have a right to certain liberties that Locke or Mill thought important, but that they have a right to equal respect and concern in the design of political institutions [Rawls also included corporations]. This assumption may be contested. . . . But it cannot be denied in the name of any more radical concept of equality, because none exists" (Ronald Dworkin, *Taking Rights Seriously* [Cambridge: Harvard University Press, 1977], p. 182).

considerations are an integral part of their marketing decision making. Later in this chapter, a framework is presented that will help you evaluate the ethics of marketing activities. However, it is far less important than the recognition that decisions made in your role as a marketing manager—simulated in class or in the real world—are founded on your values and how you choose to live your life. Indeed, this framework is to be interpreted and augmented by this fundamentally moral and personal starting point.

ETHICAL ISSUES IN MARKETING

Marketing ethics concerns the application of ethical considerations to marketing decision making. More simply stated: the ethical problems of marketing managers. Included, though perhaps of less interest, are legal requirements of marketing managers. Generally, what is illegal is also unethical. Breaking the law may be regarded as unethical; more important, the law acts to proscribe unethical conduct. So, for example, deceptive advertising is generally illegal. It is also unethical, because it conflicts with the principles or code of morals of the marketing profession; it is known to be "wrong" and, for instance, contradicts the American Marketing Association (AMA) code of ethics. More basically, deceptive advertising is lying and so conflicts with the social value of truthfulness.

Not all unethical conduct is illegal. Marketing managers are frequently in a position to make decisions that are legal but unethical.[20] There are areas not yet covered by the law or, because of their complexity or uncertainty about correct conduct, the law cannot or will not prescribe. So, for example, price gouging is usually not illegal, but is often viewed as unethical. The "gray areas," where conduct may be legal but is unethical or where, perhaps, both legality and ethics are uncertain, often encompass the more complex and in many respects more challenging issues. Much of the material in this book is devoted to these gray areas, where there are few easy or clear-cut answers. Finally, it must be said there are laws that govern activities often not viewed as unethical, such as Sunday trading or "blue" laws. In these cases, the law may be anachronistic and in need of change.

The coverage of marketing ethics within business ethics books has generally been limited to product safety, price-fixing, bribery, and the deception and adverse social influences of advertising. While these are important ethical issues in marketing, many more issues of concern to marketing managers also are regularly reported in the media. This chapter identifies the major issues but cautions against viewing marketing ethics as being about specific and often familiar issues. The concern, as indicated earlier, is with being ethical, which

---

[20] Some evidence suggests a shift in the law to an interpretation of unethical business acts as being thereby illegal; for example, in mail fraud statutes.

is distinct from, and more than, not being unethical. Moreover, the issues may change—and managers frequently are urged to be more adaptive to change—but ethical principles remain largely constant. This book identifies the ethical issues that tend to arise within the major activities of marketing management, often with multiple illustrations. Yet, for example, the privacy problems resulting from data-base marketing cited in the Market Selection and Marketing Research module, beginning with Chapter 3.1, would be unlikely to have been included if this book had been published prior to recent technological advances in automated dialing and data-base management.

Survey research studies have identified ethical issues in marketing. A particularly useful and thorough study by Chonko and Hunt[21] surveyed AMA members, asking: Briefly describe the job situation that poses the most difficult ethical or moral problem for you. The 10 major ethical issues identified and the frequency with which they were cited are shown in Table 1.

All these issues involve the key values of trust, honesty, respect, and fairness. Some issues are unique to the marketing function, others apply to all managers. Accordingly, some of the issues are a result of relationships inside the organization; others result from relationships outside the organization, particularly with customers. The most frequently reported ethical conflict involved attempting to balance the corporate interest against the interests of customers (28 percent of cases), followed by corporate interest versus self (16 percent), corporate interest versus society (14 percent), and corporate interest versus subordinates (10 percent). The high incidence of conflicts between the interests of the customer and the firm reflects marketing's task in the management of the firm's relationship with its customers and the conflicting pressures that characterize that role.

The concern of this book is primarily with the ethical problems of marketing managers in their *marketing* decision making. Ethical issues bearing on relationships inside the organization are mostly not unique to marketing and have been treated elsewhere. The many external issues, arising as a result of relationships outside the organization, generally have received scant coverage to date. Accordingly, the 20 major ethical issues in marketing dealt with in this book and listed in Table 2, are external and, given the role of the marketing function, mainly involve customer relationships. The list is derived from the literature and an informal survey of media reports of unethical conduct in marketing. It is structured around the "4 Ps" model of the marketing mix, the four main decision areas of the marketing manager.

There are other important ethical issues in marketing than those having effects internal to the firm (such as the treatment of marketing personnel), which fall outside the 4 Ps model. Principally, these are:

- **Market selection issues:** targeting disadvantaged consumers with "unnecessary" or harmful products whose merits they may be less able to judge; or,

---

[21] Lawrence B. Chonko and Shelby D. Hunt, "Ethics and Marketing Management: An Empirical Investigation," *Journal of Business Research* 13 (1985), pp. 339–59.

TABLE 1   Ethical Issues in Marketing Management:
Survey Findings of Chonko and Hunt ($n = 281$)

Rank	Issue (with illustrations)	Frequency (percent)
1	*Bribery* (gifts from outside vendors, "money under the table," payment of questionable commissions)	(15)
2	*Fairness* (manipulation of others, unfairly placing corporate interests over family obligations, inducing customers to use services not needed, taking credit for work of others)	(14)
3	*Honesty* (misrepresenting services and capabilities, lying to customers to obtain orders)	(12)
4	*Price* (differential pricing, meeting competitive prices, charging higher prices than firms with similar products while claiming superiority)	(12)
5	*Product* (products that do not benefit consumers, product and brand infringements, product safety, exaggerated performance claims)	(11)
6	*Personnel* (hiring, firing, employee evaluation)	(10)
7	*Confidentiality* (temptation to use or obtain classified, secret, or competitive information—as in recent Department of Defense contract cases)	(5)
8	*Advertising* (misleading customers, crossing the line between puffery and misleading)	(4)
9	*Manipulation of Data* (distortion; falsifying figures or misusing statistics or information, internally and externally)	(4)
10	*Purchasing* (reciprocity in the selection of suppliers)	(3)

Source: Lawrence B. Chonko and Shelby D. Hunt, "Ethics and Marketing Management: An Empirical Investigation," *Journal of Business Research* 13 (1985), pp. 339–59.

conversely, excluding groups of consumers from marketing efforts, because they are "unsuitable" target markets.

- Marketing research issues: in method, for example, "secret shoppers" (surveillance techniques) or "sugging" (selling under the guise of research), discussed in Chapter 3.1; in data analysis and use, for example, breaches of confidentiality.

- Fairness issues involving suppliers, competitors, and other stakeholders.

In many respects, the existence of these issues reflects areas of weakness in our economic, legal, and corporate control systems.[22] Perhaps price-fixing is

_____

[22] Ferrell and Gresham, accordingly, emphasize the importance of opportunity for unethical behavior in their descriptive model. See O. C. Ferrell and Larry G. Gresham, "A Contingency Framework for Understanding Ethical Decision Making in Marketing," *Journal of Marketing* 49 (Summer 1985), pp. 87–96.

TABLE 2   Major Ethical Issues in Marketing: 4 Ps Model

Product
- Product safety.
- "Me-toos."
- Product positioning and market segmentation.
- Ethics in the delivery of service products.
- Environmental impacts of product and packaging.

Price
- Horizontal/vertical price fixing.
- Price discrimination.
- Predatory pricing.
- Price gouging.
- Misleading pricing (e.g., non-unit pricing, bait and switch, inflating prices to allow sale markdowns).

Promotion (marketing communications)
- Deceptive/misleading advertising.
- Social harm of advertising (e.g., sex/race stereotypes).
- Questionable sales techniques and conflicts of interest in selling.
- Bribery.
- Direct marketing and privacy issues.

Place (channels of distribution)
- Exclusivity and other forms of discrimination in distribution (e.g., red-lining).
- Channel control (including franchising relationships).
- Gray marketing.
- Anti-competitive trade promotions (e.g., slotting allowances).
- Lower standards in export markets.

an inevitable result of the tension between ethics and economics, and control systems, such as the law, can only minimize, rather than prevent, this practice. The more fundamental problem, of which these issues, therefore, are symptomatic, is the incorporation of values into marketing decision making. In other words, if marketing managers were to reconcile the ethical considerations of marketing decisions, then these issues would be far less likely to arise. Attending to the ethical dimensions of marketing decision making is the concern of the remaining two sections of this chapter.

WHAT IS ETHICAL MARKETING DECISION MAKING?

In conducting their specifically marketing duties, marketing managers are involved primarily with customers, so the focus here is on the interplay of key values (honesty, trust, respect, and fairness) and the conflicting pressures within company/customer relationships. This section is concerned with understanding the desired outcome of this interplay: ethical marketing decision making. It is surprisingly difficult to pin down.

Normative ethics is the branch of moral philosophy that analyzes the criteria used to evaluate whether actions are right or wrong, good or bad. For thousands of years, philosophers have reflected on how to determine the ethics of human conduct. It would be presumptuous to attempt to summarize that work here. Some business academics have attempted to produce synopses of important theories in moral philosophy; the most useful contribution being to note the distinction between deontological and consequentialist thought. Explained below, this distinction can be readily understood by reference to simple examples. Most people are familiar with these different types of reasoning because they experience them in their daily lives.

The position adopted in this book is that ethical marketing decision making need not require an in-depth study of moral philosophy. The process of human development involves the individual becoming a moral being, capable of reflecting on and determining obligations and right conduct. Yet this is not to argue that the individual always knows innately what is right, having "learnt this at her mother's knee." While there may be agreement on common values that should be upheld—such as honesty—it is less than apparent how these values can survive the conflicts of business situations and how different obligations can be reconciled. Indeed, it is not always clear when these values are threatened and whether the business situation has been interpreted correctly. Yet every marketing decision implicitly, if not explicitly, has ethical dimensions. Accordingly, acting on values requires the marketing manager to have a keen grasp of the ethical considerations within a marketing decision.

Exposure to the different marketing situations described in this book will enable you to refine your existing thought processes as you already apply them to ethical issues in your daily life and to develop an approach that is suitable for handling the challenges of marketing decision making. The next section provides a framework specific to marketing that you can build upon in doing this. Before looking at how to evaluate marketing decisions, however, it is useful to discuss further the goal of this process: the ethical marketing decision.

Perhaps it can be argued that, as moral beings, we know what is right—at least if we are familiar with all the ethical dimensions of the marketing decision. So, for example, if a manufacturer of a food product claims on the packaging that the product is "cholesterol-free," implying that it is healthy, but does not draw attention to the product's high sodium or saturated fats (unhealthy) content, is this unethical? While ostensibly an honest claim, the implication created may have the effect of deceiving the customer. The manager might feel he can defend this action, because of obligations to the company and the need for results in a competitive environment where "everyone is doing it." Under such circumstances, he believes the intent is good, because of overriding obligations to stakeholders other than the customer.

Consider, as an alternative, the restaurant chain that continues to use plastic disposable cups in preference to paper cups, despite objections from customers who believe paper cups are more environmentally friendly. The manager responsible for this decision knows that scientists have established that a plastic cup does less harm to the environment than a paper one—paper consumes 6 times more wood pulp than the polystyrene of plastic, 12 times more steam, 36 times more electricity, and 580 times as much waste water. Moreover, it cannot be recycled because of the waterproofing resins it is treated with. Yet the consumer's perception is of unethical conduct in the use of plastic cups.

This is the sort of situation that falls within the "tough choice?" quadrant of the ethics/profits trade-off matrix of Figure 1.

The manager would be urged to seek the win-win solution. Perhaps, with creativity, it might be possible to educate consumers about true environmental impacts, or the chain may be able to switch to porcelain reusable cups for its eat-in trade. Otherwise, she is left to hope that "the truth will out" or switch to paper. If profits suffer as a result of the environmentally sound decision, the manager must consider her obligations to employees, shareholders, and other stakeholders. An important factor is whether they consent to and support the environmentally friendly policy; if not, she must weigh the relative importance of different stakeholders and the interests they represent, identifying the primary stakeholder.[23]

In attempting to explain the decision-making process for marketing problems with ethical content, Hunt and Vitell, in Chapter 9.5, incorporate consequentialist (described as teleological) and deontological evaluations. Their underlying assumption is that "people, in this case marketers, do in fact engage in both deontological and teleological evaluations in determining their ethical judgments and, ultimately, their behaviors." Deontologists employ rule-based analysis: actions are inherently right or wrong, independent of their consequences, because of the kinds of actions they are or because they conform to a formal principle. (Deontology is derived from the Greek: *deontos*, "of the obligatory.") Judeo-Christian morality, for example, is deontological, providing a body of moral rules (the Ten Commandments) and a view of what it means to be a human being and to have a set of values. As is evident from experience, Judeo-Christian morality has been absorbed into the secular life of the West and closely conforms to conventional morality in our society. From a deontological perspective, it could be concluded that, if there is deception in the "cholesterol-free" claim in the example above, this is unethical. Similarly, to deceive customers knowingly by switching to the environmentally less friendly paper cup, in a variation of the second example, would also be unethical.[24]

---

[23] In 1967, Bartels observed that "Most ethical decisions do require a balancing of numerous claims." He suggested, "Priority of some claims over others for satisfaction may be decided on the basis of such principles as rotations of claims, superiority of owner-interests in a capitalistic economy, superiority of market interests in a market economy, national interests, legal requirements, or the demands of power blocs" (Robert Bartels, "A Model for Ethics in Marketing," *Journal of Marketing* 31 [January 1967], pp. 20–26). A different approach is advocated here in the final section of this chapter.

[24] Moral philosophers might debate whether these examples are necessarily unethical from a deontological perspective. Kant, for example, has *not* argued that it would be right to lie in order to prevent serious harm to persons. However, some Kantian philosophers might adopt this position, in keeping with Kant's categorical imperative, suggesting this is a maxim that may be universally acted on in the limited situation specified. Kant himself is reluctant to embrace this approach, preferring the position that lies ought not to be spoken, come what may. See Tom L. Beauchamp, *Philosophical Ethics: An Introduction to Moral Philosophy* (New York: McGraw-Hill, 1982), p. 124.

In contrast, consequentialists hold that an action is right because of the goodness of its consequences. The utilitarianism, for example, of J. S. Mill, is consequentialist (though arguably less so in the "rule" utilitarian, rather than the "act" utilitarian, form). Under utilitarianism "an action is right if it produces, or tends to produce, the greatest amount of good for the greatest number of people affected by the action. Otherwise the action is wrong."[25] From a consequentialist perspective, it might be argued that the managers in both of the above examples are right, subject to certain assumptions about consequences. If, as has been argued, the consequence of increased health labelling is a better-informed consumer, then, despite the false implications of the "no cholesterol" claim, this is ethical. If a switch to paper cups, despite scientific evidence of greater environmental harm, is viewed positively by consumers and prompts them to recycle and reduce some of their (more substantial) contribution to the waste stream, then the action is ethical. Conversely, continuing with plastic cups and attempting to educate consumers of the environmental impacts may result in confusion or cynicism; for many years, consumers have been educated about the harm caused by plastics.

In these simple examples, it is apparent that determining the ethical marketing decision is less than straightforward. This is not surprising. Consider a classic story that moral philosophers tell: You are traveling alone in a remote corner of the world when you stumble upon a primitive tribe. You are in luck. The chief of the tribe likes you and you are fortunate to have arrived in time to partake in a tribal custom, which takes place with every full moon. As demanded by the gods, there is a sacrifice of 10 members of the tribe. The chief gives you the honor of killing one member of the tribe. Suspecting you may not be skilled with the sacrificial knife, he has suggested that there should be only one victim on this occasion. However, if you refuse the honor, he would conduct the ceremony with the full sacrifice. Your choice is to kill 1 person and save 9, or not to kill and see 10 die. You would be reluctant to offend your host by exploring other options.

A deontologist would not kill, because killing innocent people is wrong. A consequentialist, however, might conclude that the greatest amount of good would result from killing one person. As in the marketing examples, the two approaches apparently conflict on what is the ethical action. However, the purpose here is to reveal some of the difficulties of ethical analysis, not to suggest that, because either action may be defended as ethical, they are equally acceptable, or that "anything goes." The weaknesses of each approach also need to be acknowledged. Full knowledge of the facts is vital under either approach. Deontological analysis often is inflexible. Consequentialist analysis needs to be rigorously applied—it is vital to consider all consequences, though they may not all be known. Much decision making in everyday life, as well as in business, is utilitarian. Examining the two marketing examples above,

---

[25] De George, p. 44.

you likely applied a cost/benefit analysis. When laws and public policies are discussed in the media or in daily life, a similar calculus is at work. Utilitarianism does encourage, at least, a search for alternatives.

Some business writers have attempted to provide decision rules or checklists that attempt to incorporate the major theories of moral philosophy. Two useful examples are considered here. Laczniak discusses the theories of Ross, Garrett, and Rawls, presenting a synthesis of possible factors to be considered when deciding tough questions.[26] If the answer is yes to any of the questions in Table 3, then, suggests Laczniak, action A is most probably unethical and should be reconsidered. If every question can be answered negatively, then action A is probably ethical.

Despite its contribution, this framework alone is too broad in scope to be recommended to marketing managers—or to public policy or to academic analysts of marketing decision making. Consider, for example, the question, "Is the intent of action A evil?" While intent is clearly important, asking a marketing manager whether she intends evil is unlikely to be worthwhile. Rarely, in even the most infamous cases of unethical conduct in marketing, would the managers involved have admitted to themselves, let alone to others, an evil

---

TABLE 3 Laczniak's Framework for Analyzing Marketing Ethics

Does action A violate the law?
Does action A violate any general moral obligations:
  Duties of fidelity?
  Duties of gratitude?
  Duties of justice?
  Duties of beneficence?
  Duties of self-improvement?
  Duties of nonmaleficence?
Does action A violate any special obligations stemming from the type of marketing organization in question (e.g., the special duty of pharmaceutical firms to provide safe products)?
Is the intent of action A evil?
Are any major evils likely to result from or because of action A?
Is a satisfactory alternative B, which produces equal or more good with less evil than A, being knowingly rejected?
Does action A infringe on the inalienable rights of the consumer?
Does action A leave another person or group less well off? Is this person or group already relatively underprivileged?

Source: Gene R. Laczniak, "Framework for Analyzing Marketing Ethics," *Journal of Macromarketing*, Spring 1983, pp. 7–18.

---

[26] Gene R. Laczniak, "Framework for Analyzing Marketing Ethics," *Journal of Macromarketing*, Spring 1983, pp. 7–18.

intent. Even if they had, knowing evil intent would make the ethical analysis superfluous; the question is tautological. In short, these questions are too abstract to be applied meaningfully to marketing decision making.

Nash has suggested 12 questions, listed in Table 4, that draw on traditional philosophical frameworks but avoid the level of abstraction normally associated with formal moral reasoning.[27] In contrast to Laczniak, she claims "what is needed is a process of ethical inquiry that is immediately comprehensible to a group of executives and not predisposed to the utopian, and sometimes anticapitalistic, bias marking much of the work in applied business philosophy today." This seems to be a reasonable requirement.

Nash's questions can be readily recommended to a business executive and are certainly helpful in analyzing the business situations described in this book. Yet they do not in themselves, unlike Laczniak's list, attempt to identify ethical marketing decision making. They illuminate decision making, revealing the ethical dimensions of the decision. They are less abstract, though again (and this wasn't Nash's intention) they are not marketing-specific. Nash proposes the "good puppy" theory as a basis for determining what is expected of the "ethical" or "good" corporation:

> . . . here goodness consists primarily of the fulfillment of a social contract that centers on avoiding social injury. Moral capacity is perceived as present, but its potential is

---

TABLE 4   Nash's 12 Questions for Examining the Ethics of a Business Decision

1. Have you defined the problem accurately?
2. How would you define the problem if you stood on the other side of the fence?
3. How did this situation occur in the first place?
4. To whom and to what do you give your loyalty as a person and as a member of the corporation?
5. What is your intention in making this decision?
6. How does this intention compare with the probable results?
7. Whom could your decision or action injure?
8. Can you discuss the problem with the affected parties before you make your decision?
9. Are you confident that your position will be as valid over a long period as it seems now?
10. Could you disclose without qualm your decision or action to your boss, your CEO, the board of directors, your family, society as a whole?
11. What is the symbolic potential of your action if understood? If misunderstood?
12. Under what conditions would you allow exceptions to your stand?

Source: Laura L. Nash, "Ethics without the Sermon," in Kenneth R. Andrews (ed.), *Ethics in Practice: Managing the Moral Corporation* (Boston: Harvard Business School Press, 1989), p. 246.

---

[27] Laura L. Nash, "Ethics without the Sermon," in Kenneth R. Andrews (ed.), *Ethics in Practice: Managing the Moral Corporation* (Boston: Harvard Business School Press, 1989).

limited. A moral evaluation of the good puppy is possible but exists largely in concrete terms; we do not need to identify the puppy's intentions as utilitarian to understand and agree that its "ethical" fulfillment of the social contract consists of not soiling the carpet or biting the baby.[28]

Businesspeople find the analogy patronizing, but realistic (though it is problematic to moral philosophers[29]). Importantly, Nash adds, "The good corporation is expected to avoid perpetrating irretrievable social injury (and to assume the costs when it unintentionally does injury) while focusing on its purpose as a profit-making organization." Yet not all businesspeople would agree with her next statement: "Its moral capacity does not extend, however, to determining by itself what will improve the general social welfare." There are important reasons for questioning the legitimacy or capability of corporate efforts to improve general social welfare. However, this should not deny the moral capacity for such efforts or their need, particularly under circumstances where the corporation is both powerful and the last resort.[30] Social contract theory is proving increasingly influential and useful in business ethics.[31] However, the terms of the firm's contract with society—and the rights to which it, therefore, must attend—are in flux and do not preclude and may even require actions to promote good as well as to avoid causing harm.

Yet does the good puppy theory, even with the amendment suggested, constitute a satisfactory approach to determining what is ethical marketing decision making? Certainly it's a step in the right direction from a practitioner's viewpoint, particularly when illuminated by Nash's questions. Yet there is still much abstraction. The final section, which follows, proposes a less abstract, marketing-specific framework. Though not without weaknesses, it is a basis for evaluating marketing decisions, which allows for some individual adaptation. It also is consistent with and may be supplemented by the Laczniak and Nash checklists.

Perhaps the question is wrong. "How do I know my marketing is ethical?" may not be the right question or it may be too simplistic. However, this is how marketing managers frame the problem; this is the question they want to be able to answer. Increasingly, they need to be able to ask and answer this

---

[28] Ibid., p. 255.

[29] The puppy analogy is an effective rhetorical device; but it is troubling to moral philosophers, because a puppy is not a person and, therefore, not a moral agent. More important, while it is easier to make a moral evaluation based on behavior, intentions cannot be ignored, even if access to them is difficult.

[30] Invoking the "Kew Gardens Principle," Simon et al. observe: "Life is fraught with emergency situations in which a failure to respond is a special form of violation of the negative injunction against causing social injury: a sin of omission becomes a sin of commission." See John G. Simon, Charles W. Powers, and Jon P. Gunnemann, *The Ethical Investor: Universities and Corporate Responsibility* (New Haven: Yale University Press, 1972), p. 22.

[31] See, for a recent example, Thomas W. Dunfee and Thomas Donaldson, "A Theory of Social Contracts," Working Paper 91–156, Department of Legal Studies, The Wharton School, University of Pennsylvania.

question because others, including critics of the firm, are interested in the answer, too.

A MARKETING ETHICS FRAMEWORK

The concern of this book is primarily normative: By evaluating the ethics of marketing practice, we aim to determine what marketing managers should do. The research project from which *Ethics in Marketing* is largely derived attempted to answer the question: How can marketing managers determine their marketing practices are ethical? The marketing ethics framework developed to answer this question has two basic components: the ethics continuum and the consumer sovereignty test.[32] Most other marketing ethics frameworks that have been previously proposed are descriptive, rather than normative[33] (the Laczniak framework described above is one exception).

Before describing the framework and its rationale, it should be noted that its domain is limited to corporate impacts on customers. At the outset of this chapter it was established that the function of the marketing manager is to manage the firm's relationships with its customers. So this limitation is appropriate to a *marketing* ethics framework and conforms with the view that ethical issues in marketing largely involve company/customer relationships and conflicts. The framework does not, therefore, directly address marketing impacts on other stakeholders. As earlier noted, such impacts are generally not unique to the marketing function. There are more fundamental reasons for this customer impacts focus, which are explained below. However, the framework should be seen as a starting point for evaluating marketing decisions. It is necessary but not sufficient and needs to be augmented in a variety of ways, discussed at the end of this chapter.

Marketing Ethics Framework: The Ethics Continuum

Ethical relativism is not advanced here. Donaldson and Werhane, for example, ask: "Are values simply relative to the people who espouse them, or is it possible to identify universal values which apply to all?" Ethical relativism

---

[32] Derived from inductive case research and deductive theorizing, this marketing ethics framework has been discussed with a variety of different people, business executives, policymakers, students, and academics. The author is grateful for their contributions to its development and would particularly acknowledge the help of Professors John Quelch, Ray Corey, and Dr. Mary Gentile of Harvard University; Professor Tom Donaldson, Georgetown University; Professor Shelby Hunt, Texas Tech University; and attorney Steve Edwards of Davis, Markel and Edwards, New York.

[33] O. C. Ferrell, Larry G. Gresham, and John Fraedrich, "A Synthesis of Ethical Decision Models for Marketing," *Journal of Macromarketing* 9 (Fall 1989), pp. 55–64. The authors describe, evaluate, and combine three models (including the Hunt and Vitell model, see Chapter 9.5), noting they "only can *describe* the ethical decision-making process."

holds that no ethical assertion or set of assertions has any greater claim to objectivity or universality than any other. Referring to W. T. Stace, Donaldson and Werhane reject ethical relativism by noting that some values are universal, that apply without exception, and that "thoroughgoing . . . ethical relativism results in the conclusion that one cannot justify any value judgments whatsoever."[34]

The ethics continuum suggests there are different positions—founded on different values—from which marketing decisions may be evaluated. This is not to suggest they carry equal weight. Rather, the continuum presents benchmarks against which business conduct may be calibrated and understood. One position (consumer sovereignty) is advanced in the next section and an argument made to show that conformity with this position most probably constitutes ethical marketing decision making.

The continuum, shown in Figure 2, ranges from a position on the far left, where producer interests are most favored and consumer interests are least favored, to a position on the far right, where producer interests are least favored and consumer interests are most favored. Clearly, it suggests a conflict between producer and consumer interests as the basis for different positions on the ethics of marketing practice. This in turn represents a rejection of the notion that the game of the market necessarily results in a win-win outcome for consumers and producers. This is not to suggest that it is a zero-sum game; rather, it is to recognize the ideological content of the marketing concept and

---

FIGURE 2   Marketing Ethics Framework: An Ethics Continuum

- Producer interests favored.
- Consumer interests less favored.

- Producer interests less favored.
- Consumer interests favored.

Caveat emptor school:	Industry practice:	Ethics codes:	Consumer sovereignty school:	Caveat venditor school:
Profit maximization, subject to legal constraints.	In general. The best companies.	Of individual firms. Of industries. Of professional bodies (e.g., AMA).	Capability. Information. Choice.	Consumer satisfaction.

---

[34] Thomas Donaldson and Patricia Werhane, *Ethical Issues in Business: A Philosophical Approach* (Englewood Cliffs, N.J.: Prentice Hall, 1988), pp. 6–7.

to acknowledge that firms will not always be guided by the imperative of customer satisfaction. Despite the admonitions of Levitt and other marketing thinkers, the customer may not always be the starting point and priority in marketing decision making. There are three explanations for this seemingly deviant behavior:

1. The firm is not customer-oriented: The traditional explanation. Kotler writes: "Customer-oriented thinking requires the company to carefully define customer needs from the *customer point of view*, not from its own point of view. . . . The aim, after all, is to make a sale through meeting the customer's needs."[35] Firms that have not adopted marketing, perhaps pursuing a "production orientation" or a "sales orientation," have yet to recognize that it is in their best interests to satisfy the customer.

2. The firm mistakes or cannot identify customer interests: The intent is to be customer-oriented, but in practice this is difficult. Even the most proficient marketing organizations, such as Procter & Gamble, make mistakes.

3. The firm's interests are best served by not serving the customer's interests: The recognition that, under certain circumstances, customer satisfaction is not of supreme importance.

The third reason is the more interesting explanation. Unethical conduct resulting from the lack of, or difficulties in achieving, a customer orientation is to some extent excusable; the intent was probably good. More important, such actions are likely to be penalized by the market. In accordance with the ethics/profits trade-off matrix, the firm is operating within the low ethics and low profits "foolish" quadrant of the matrix. The market acts as a control mechanism to curb unethical behavior.[36] Under the third explanation, the market is an inadequate control. Customer satisfaction is a requisite of competitive markets. Without competition, customers cannot choose to vote with their feet and buy from firms that serve their interests better. It is not surprising that many ethical issues in marketing involve attempts to reduce competition—the very driving force that compels customer orientation. Consider, for example, price-fixing, predatory pricing, and exclusivity arrangements in distribution.

Many marketing activities may be understood as efforts to reduce competition. In this way, the marketing concept is ideological; it may serve the interests of producers by explaining their behavior as other-regarding—as customer-oriented. Advertising, for example, may inform and persuade the consumer; it may also serve as a barrier to entry, discouraging would-be entrants to a market. Channel management strategies involve efforts to ensure the company's products reach customers; they also attempt to "lock up" chan-

---

[35] Philip Kotler, *Marketing Management: Analysis, Planning, Implementation and Control* (Englewood Cliffs, N.J.: Prentice Hall, 1988), p. 18.

[36] A model of the social control of business highlighting the role of the market is presented in N. Craig Smith, *Morality and the Market: Consumer Pressure for Corporate Accountability* (London and New York: Routledge, 1990), pp. 87–95.

nels to deny access routes to competitors. Perhaps there is an inevitable tension between ethics and economics—ethical conduct and marketing practice. It can at least be said that competition is necessary for a customer orientation.

Kotler suggests firms need to balance company profits, consumer want satisfaction, and public interest. Under his societal marketing concept, "the organization's task is to determine the needs, wants, and interests of target markets and to deliver the desired satisfactions more effectively and efficiently than competitors in a way that preserves or enhances the consumer's and society's well-being."[37] This is appealing, but without the spur of competition this idealized view of marketing disintegrates; we are otherwise dependent on philanthropy. Paradoxically, competition creates customer orientation, yet, if competitors are defeated, would allow its elimination. A monopoly supplier has less incentive to ensure product safety or set "fair" prices, subject to legal constraints.

Caveat Emptor.   The different positions on the continuum reflect different views of the firm's obligations to its customers (or variations in the ideology of marketing or business ideology[38]). Under the caveat emptor school, profit maximization within the law is the basis for evaluating marketing practice. Providing the activity is legal and serves a business purpose (and hence is profitable), it is ethical. This excludes unethical marketing practices that are illegal, such as bribery, deceptive advertising, price-fixing, and bait and switch. However, there can be debates about the illegality of each of these practices and others.

Advertising is deceptive and, therefore, illegal when it is judged by the FTC (Federal Trade Commission) as having the capacity to deceive. Yet Ivan Preston explains that it is sometimes difficult for advertisers to identify when advertising is deceptive, subject to the perhaps inevitably vague standards of the FTC (see Chapter 8.8). Vertical price-fixing, in the form of manufacturer attempts to ensure resale price maintenance, also is illegal, as Gwen Ortmeyer explains (see Chapter 5.1). Yet, in practice, the FTC has found "efficiency-enhancing" circumstances where resale price maintenance is acceptable; for example, if there is high interbrand competition and retailers provide valuable customer service in return for some guarantee of a reasonable margin.

It can be suggested that firms should try to conform to the spirit, rather than the letter, of the law. Yet, under the caveat emptor school, it also may be argued

---

[37] Kotler, p. 28.

[38] Most managers have been said to adhere to the "classical creed," which extols the values of individualism, private property, free competition, and limited government. It has been suggested that the "managerial creed" is being increasingly adopted, under which management has a trusteeship role and a responsibility to all contributors to the firm. This creed is more frequently found in larger companies. Some writers suggest a further and more enlightened creed is also emerging. However, it seems reasonable to assume that many managers, though perhaps no longer a majority, still largely subscribe to the classical creed, wherein profit maximization is the rule.

that, without usurping the law, firms should work around it to maximize their interests, seeking loopholes if such are to be found. Firms could be said to have an obligation to test the law; so they are certain to maximize profits and not be at a competitive disadvantage.

Testing the law in this strong statement of the caveat emptor position is not advocating lawlessness; it reflects the philosophical basis of the position. Best known as a "free market" or Friedmanite philosophy, the argument is made that: "there is one and only one social responsibility of business—to use its resources and engage in activities designed to increase its profits so long as it stays within the rules of the game, which is to say, engages in open and free competition without deception or fraud."[39]

Managers are agents acting on behalf of the firm's stockholders (the principals) and, therefore, should work to increase the net present value of the firm and, hence, the principals' capital. This is a fiduciary duty of managers and, through the requirement of obedience to all reasonable directions of the principal, subject to the common law of agency.[40] Discussed in more detail later (see Chapter 2.7), Friedman's argument against social responsibility (beyond profit maximization) questions: spending someone else's money (costs of social actions are involuntarily borne by stockholders); the competing claims (ignoring the role of profit); the competitive disadvantage (resulting from social actions); management competence (to handle social actions); the fairness of management involvement in social actions; and its doubtful legitimacy (the role of government). It is rejected principally because it reflects an idealized model of capitalism that does not (and perhaps could and should not) exist: there are no truly free markets, firms are powerful, managers have discretion and moral impulses, and the separation of ownership and control provides the opportunities and often good reason to exercise this discretion.

The law is working in two ways to weaken the caveat emptor position. First, there is a trend toward allowing firms to reconcile their decisions with all stakeholders; courts have disallowed stockholder challenges to management decisions that benefit other stakeholders (such as employees).[41] Second, courts are less ready to accept "buyer beware" as a basis for allowing questionable marketing practices, as exemplified in the May Company case (see Chapter 5.3). There is a perceptible shift from caveat emptor to caveat venditor. Yet protecting the consumer in this way may be economically dysfunctional; it may diminish the consumer's incentive to search and determine the best deal and the firm's incentive to innovate and offer this. As Herbert Spencer so eloquently put it: "The ultimate result of shielding men from the effects of folly is to fill the world with fools."[42]

---

[39] Milton Friedman, *Capitalism and Freedom* (Chicago: University of Chicago Press, 1962), p. 133.

[40] Bowie and Duska, p. 70.

[41] I am grateful to Columbia University law professor John Coffee for his advice on this.

[42] Herbert Spencer, *Essays* (London: Macmillan, 1891), vol. III, p. 354.

Caveat Venditor. Positioned at the other extreme of the continuum, appropriately, is the caveat venditor school. Under caveat emptor, the firm's obligations to the consumer are limited to the constraints of the law in the interests of promoting competition and efficiency. Under caveat venditor, it is seller beware, and consumer satisfaction is the criterion against which marketing practices are evaluated. Consumer advocates are often the most frequent exponents of a caveat venditor position. Often they call on critics of capitalism, such as economist J. K. Galbraith. He suggests:

> Much exercise of power depends on a social conditioning that seeks to conceal it. The young are taught that in a democracy all power resides in the people. And that in a free enterprise system all authority rests with the sovereign consumer operating through the impersonal mechanism of the market. Thus is hidden the public power of organization—of the Pentagon, the weapons firms, and other corporations and lobbyists. Similarly concealed by the mystique of the market and consumer sovereignty is the power of corporations to set or influence prices and costs, to suborn or subdue politicians, and to manipulate consumer response.[43]

Consumers Union, the leading consumer interest group in the United States, responds to some of the concerns expressed by Galbraith. It was established in 1936, when "many of the toasters on the market were so poorly designed that you couldn't remove the toast without burning your hand . . . the marketplace was dangerous, and consumers had no power and little voice."[44] Consumers Union aims "to provide unbiased, objective information on consumer goods and services and to help improve the quality of life for consumers everywhere."[45] Recognizing that producers cannot be entirely relied upon to provide consumer satisfaction, the interest group provides information to consumers and lobbies government and industry on the consumer's behalf.

The caveat venditor position may be illustrated further by examining different views of product safety and the extent to which responsibility lies with the consumer or the producer. Velasquez identifies three theories on the ethical duties of manufacturers: the "contract" view, the "due care" view, and the "social costs" view.[46] The contract view is closely aligned with the caveat emptor position of the ethics continuum. Under the contract view, the relationship between a business firm and its customers is essentially a contractual relationship, which determines the firm's moral duties to the customer. The arguments of moral philosophers Kant and Rawls may be used to justify the basic duty of compliance with the terms of the sales contract and the secondary duties of disclosing the nature of the product, avoiding misrepresentation, and avoiding the use of duress and undue influence. (Without fulfillment of the

---

[43] John Kenneth Galbraith, *The Anatomy of Power* (London: Hamish Hamilton, 1984), p. 12.

[44] *A Look Inside Consumers Union: Publisher of Consumer Reports* (Mount Vernon: Consumers Union, 1988).

[45] Ibid.

[46] Manuel G. Velasquez, *Business Ethics: Concepts and Cases* (Englewood Cliffs, N.J.: Prentice Hall, 1988), pp. 274–90.

secondary duties, the contract would not be the "free agreement" required, for example, by Kantian analysis.) These duties may be construed as falling within Friedman's "rules of the game" and requirement to "engage in open and free competition without deception and fraud."

As Velasquez shows, these moral duties often also are legal requirements. Express and implied claims (particularly of product reliability, service life, maintainability, and safety) are incorporated within the Uniform Commercial Code, reflecting the duty to comply. There are also laws governing disclosure and the duties not to misrepresent or coerce. Velasquez notes debate about the duty of disclosure: "An agreement cannot bind unless both parties to the agreement know what they are doing and freely choose to do it . . . at a minimum, this means the seller has a duty to inform the buyer of any facts about the product that would affect the customer's decision to purchase the product."[47] As he explains, this duty reflects the idea that "an agreement is free only to the extent that one knows what alternatives are available: Freedom depends on knowledge."[48] Yet it is argued that there are costs to providing information for which consumers should pay or do without. Unfortunately, Velasquez does not offer a satisfactory resolution of this issue: "If consumers had to bargain for such information, the resulting contract would hardly be free."[49] The key lies in the extent of information provision (later discussed under the consumer sovereignty test).

Velasquez identifies three problems with the contract view. First, the frequent remoteness of the consumer from the producer; though this has not prevented consumers from taking successful legal action against manufacturers, with whom there was no direct legal agreement. Second, freedom of contract allows the consumer to assume responsibility (willingly or otherwise) for any defects that may be disclaimed by the producer and possibly overlooked by the consumer. This is also incorporated within the Uniform Commercial Code and, accordingly, disclaimers can nullify contractual duties of manufacturers. Third is the assumption of equal bargaining power of buyers and sellers. Velasquez ties this assumption directly to caveat emptor:

> Classical laissez-faire ideology held that the economy's markets are competitive and that in competitive markets the consumer's bargaining power is equal to that of the seller. Competition forces the seller to offer the consumer as good or better terms than the consumer could get from other competing sellers, so the consumer has the power to threaten to take his or her business to other sellers. Because of this equality between buyer and seller, it was fair that each be allowed to try to out-bargain the other and unfair to place restrictions on either. In practice, this laissez-faire ideology gave birth to the doctrine of "caveat emptor": let the buyer take care of himself.[50]

---

[47] Ibid., p. 278.
[48] Ibid., p. 279.
[49] Ibid.
[50] Ibid., p. 282.

He concludes that equality is more likely to be the exception, because consumers purchasing many different kinds of commodities cannot be as knowledgeable as a manufacturer specializing in particular products. The consumer, therefore, must rely on the judgment of the seller and may be vulnerable. (However, it should be noted that the consumer can often rely on the buying expertise of retailers, who are intermediaries between the consumer and the manufacturer.)

Under "due care," this vulnerability of the consumer creates a positive duty on the part of manufacturers to exercise "special 'care' to ensure that consumers' interests are not harmed by the products that they offer them."[51] Velasquez ties this view directly to caveat venditor: "The doctrine of 'caveat emptor' is here replaced with a weak version of the doctrine of 'caveat vendor': Let the seller take care."[52] This due care obligation is said to hold even if the manufacturer explicitly disclaims responsibility and the consumer accepts the disclaimer. Taking whatever steps are necessary to ensure the product is as safe as possible rests on the moral duty not to harm or injure others and the moral right to expect this duty of care. As Velasquez notes, it may be justified by Kantian and Rawlsian analysis and defended by rule utilitarians.[53] He concludes: "The judgment that individual producers have a duty not to harm or injure, therefore, is solidly based on several ethical principles."[54]

The duty of due care imposes responsibilities on the manufacturer in three areas: design, including, for example, testing the product under different conditions of consumer use; production, for example, eliminating any defective items; and information provision, for example, providing clear and simple instructions and taking account of the capacities of people using the product. The manufacturer is not morally negligent where people are harmed by a product in a manner that could not have been foreseen or prevented, or where reasonable steps have been taken to inform consumers of irremovable risks that yet result in harm due to the consumer's carelessness.

Velasquez identifies three problems with the due care view. First, the problem of knowing sufficiency of care: How safe should a product be? Can the costs of eliminating small risks of injury—which must be passed on to all consumers regardless of their exposure to the risk—be justified? A utilitarian calculation balancing actions to prevent harm with the probability of harm and the number of people affected is in any event problematic because of the difficulties of quantifying risks to health and life. Second, it is possibly paternalistic to have decisions about consumer risk exposure made by manufacturers. Third, who is to be responsible for risks not foreseen by the manufacturer? As Velasquez

---

[51] Ibid., p. 283.

[52] Ibid. Latin scholars will know that both caveat venditor and caveat vendor may be acceptably translated as "let the seller take care." Caveat venditor is the older and more classical term.

[53] "If the rule is accepted, everyone's welfare will be advanced"; Velasquez, p. 284.

[54] Ibid.

puts it: "Although manufacturers may have greater expertise than consumers, this expertise does not make them omniscient."[55]

This problem of responsibility for unforeseen risks is catered for under the "social costs" view. Going beyond the contract and due care views, this theory holds that "a manufacturer should pay the costs of any injuries sustained through any defects in the product, even when the manufacturer exercised all due care in the design and manufacture of the product and has taken all reasonable precautions to warn users of every foreseen danger."[56] It is the basis of the legal doctrine of strict liability and a clear illustration of the caveat venditor position of the ethics continuum.

The moral philosophy underpinning the social costs view of the manufacturer's duties is utilitarian. To ensure efficient allocation of resources, manufacturers should bear the social costs for injuries caused by defects in a product even where there was no negligence—the harm was not foreseen or preventable—and no contractual relationship between the manufacturer and the consumer. Efficiency results from the internalization of these costs, which are then passed on to consumers in the form of higher prices. These costs also encourage manufacturers to be wary of consumer safety and are distributed among consumers, rather than falling on individuals who may not be able to sustain the losses incurred (such as loss of employment due to serious injury).

Again Velasquez identifies three problems with this view. First, it is unfair to manufacturers and, in turn, to consumers. Second, while manufacturers may become more vigilant, consumers may become more careless. Third, the financial burden has increased the costs of insurance, which has resulted in some firms being unable to afford liability insurance or expensive liability suits and going out of business. There is, however, considerable debate about the supposed "explosion" of product liability suits and escalation of awards.

The social costs view and the legal doctrine of strict liability show how the consumer's interests may be maximized and the producer's interests minimized. As well as product safety, there are other areas where consumer satisfaction has been the basis for determining the ethics of the marketing practice. The three views of manufacturer duties with respect to product safety add to the understanding of the caveat venditor and the caveat emptor positions. Having delineated the two poles of the ethics continuum, the intervening positions may more readily be identified.

Industry Practice.   Figure 2 shows the first position beyond caveat emptor to be industry practice: the position of business in general or, more accurately, on average. As a benchmark, the basis for evaluation of marketing practice is the norms of business. Despite the attractions of Friedman's arguments, it is rare to find a firm that pursues a pure caveat emptor position. Most managers

---

[55] Ibid., p. 287.
[56] Ibid.

will exercise discretion and, for example, not make "commission payments" which, though not illegal, may constitute bribery.

The industry practice position can be expanded upon to comprise a range of different positions around the average; a variety of benchmarks, therefore, may be identified. One may be a more appropriate basis for evaluation than another. Nearest to the caveat emptor position (or perhaps to the left of it) would be the practices of the worst companies; at the other end of the range, closest to the ethics codes position (and possibly beyond it), would be the practices of the best companies. Within these boundaries, other positions include: the practices of specific industries (construction, for example, contrasted with health care), and the practices of industries or companies in different countries (American, for example, contrasted with Japanese).

Ethics Codes.   The ethics codes position recognizes that firms will not entirely conform in practice to the standards they assert in their codes of ethics, or to the codes of industries or professional bodies. These codes represent standards to which firms and individual managers aspire; even the firms with the strongest controls to ensure conformity with codes of conduct can identify abuses. Less-committed firms fail to have adequate controls, and too often codes of conduct are recognized as lip service to an ideal or as public relations devices to reduce criticism of the firm. They also serve as ways of controlling employees to prevent actions that would put the firm at a competitive disadvantage (e.g., breaches of company confidentiality) or be illegal (such as insider trading). However, this is not to deny the importance of codes in identifying ethical obligations of employees and in helping to create an appropriate corporate culture. Their importance is interesting to consider in the case studies involving Ciba-Geigy (see Chapter 2.2) and Sealed Air (see Chapter 9.2). The ethics codes position also may be viewed as an amalgam, comprising a range of different positions around a mean.

Consumer Sovereignty.   Going beyond the position established by most ethics codes is the consumer sovereignty school. Closest to caveat venditor, this position is distinct in placing a measure of responsibility on the consumer. The ethics of marketing practice are determined by the three criteria of the consumer sovereignty test: capability of the consumer, information provision, and choice. This test is discussed in detail, because this position is recommended to the marketing manager wishing to pursue ethical marketing.

The ethics continuum is an attempt to provide benchmarks for the evaluation of marketing practice. It may be used by the marketing manager to determine his position on marketing ethics. It may be used by public policymakers and academics, as well as managers, to evaluate and understand marketing managers' perspectives on their actions as well as the actions themselves. It also may be used to review marketing practices over time, because implicit in the above discussion is the belief that marketing ethics are and perhaps should be moving toward the consumer sovereignty position.

Marketing Ethics Framework: The Consumer Sovereignty Test

The appropriateness of the consumer sovereignty position will be demonstrated by briefly exploring its basis in moral philosophy. However, it can first be shown to be grounded in marketing thought and practice, which not only provides its rationale but also makes use of the consumer sovereignty test relatively straightforward for marketing managers. Unlike other business ethics frameworks, the starting point for this framework was not moral philosophy but marketing thought and practice.

In essence, the consumer sovereignty test requires marketing managers to fulfill the promise of marketing ideology, promoting as a first priority the interests of the consumer. Acknowledging, as earlier discussed, the ideological basis of the marketing concept, the consumer sovereignty test creates an obligation for marketing managers to ensure consumer capability, information, and choice, even where there is an absence of market pressure to do so. Conforming to the consumer sovereignty position, a marketing manager would establish, for example, whether a target market was fully capable of understanding the risks associated with a particular product, going beyond legal requirements and perhaps to the firm's economic disadvantage by excluding potential consumers of the product. In the Suzuki Samurai case (see Chapter 3.2), it is interesting to note that there was apparently no attempt to establish whether younger drivers buying the vehicle understood the warnings about its different handling characteristics and were capable of driving it safely. Figure 3 summarizes the consumer sovereignty test, defining the three dimensions of capability, information, and choice and, critically, establishing a basis for determining the adequacy of performance along each dimension.

Debate is possible about adequacy of performance. Yet the criteria suggested are at least preferable to the frequently advanced axiom of the Golden Rule: Do unto others as you would have them do unto you. Vulnerability factors, such as age or education, for example, or attention to individual expectations,

---

FIGURE 3   Marketing Ethics Framework: Consumer Sovereignty Test

Dimension	*Establishing Adequacy*
1. Capability: of the consumer.	• Vulnerability factors—age, education, income, and the like.
2. Information: availability and quality.	• Sufficient to judge whether expectations on purchase will be fulfilled.
3. Choice: opportunity to switch.	• Level of competition. • "Switching costs."

highlight the likely differences between the marketing manager and the consumer. These differences suggest a role for market research to establish expectations and identify vulnerabilities. The choice dimension reflects opportunity to switch: Can the consumer go elsewhere? It suggests, perhaps controversially, that, despite the intent of many marketing activities, the marketing manager should not seek to monopolize a market. The level of competition (or market share) provides one measure of adequacy of performance along this dimension. It is important to also consider "switching costs," particularly when the test is used in industrial marketing where, for example, a capital purchase can reduce the opportunity to switch. A computer purchase may "lock in" a customer to one supplier of computer peripherals if the machine has limited compatibility.

The philosophical basis of the consumer sovereignty test may be found in the philosophical foundations of capitalism. This cannot be explored in any depth here, but has been covered elsewhere; the key lies in recognition of consumer sovereignty as the rationale for capitalism.[57] Surprisingly, perhaps, one of the most convincing moral arguments for capitalism comes from the founder of modern-day economics, Adam Smith. In probably the most widely quoted extract from any economics book, he writes:

> every individual . . . neither intends to promote the public interest . . . he intends only his own gain, and he is in this, as in many other cases, led by an invisible hand to promote an end which was no part of his intention.[58]

Under the competitive model of capitalism, the individual's pursuit of self-interest results in the welfare of the community. Capitalism provides material progress, but also economic and political freedom. This is both largely achieved by and expressed in consumer sovereignty. It exists when consumers exercise informed choice, hence the dimensions of the consumer sovereignty test of capability, information, and choice.

According to economic theory, consumer sovereignty may be found when there is perfect competition. Yet few markets come close to fulfilling the requirements of perfect competition: numerous buyers and sellers, none of whom has a substantial share of the market; all buyers and sellers can freely and immediately enter or leave the market; every buyer and seller has full and perfect knowledge of what every other buyer and seller is doing, including knowledge of the prices, quantities, and quality of all goods being bought and sold; goods sold in the market are so similar to each other that no one cares from whom each buys or sells; costs and benefits of producing and using the goods being exchanged are borne entirely by those buying or selling the goods and not by any other external parties; all buyers and sellers are utility maximizers, each trying to get as much as possible for as little as possible; and,

---

[57] Smith, chapter 1.
[58] Adam Smith, *The Wealth of Nations* (London: Everyman, 1971 [1776]), vol. 1, p. 400.

finally, no external parties (such as the government) regulate the price, quantity, or quality of any of the goods being bought and sold in the market.[59]

Vickrey, while acknowledging the role of consumer sovereignty within economics, stresses its moral roots: "The acceptance of 'consumer sovereignty' as a basis for judging economic systems is fundamentally perhaps as much a matter of ethics, philosophy, and political theory as it is of economics."[60] Penz suggests consumer sovereignty is "a central normative principle in contemporary assessments of economic policies and systems . . . it has been referred to as the 'Archimedian point of reference' in economic evaluation."[61] Yet, in contrast to Vickrey and Penz, the purpose here is to consider consumer sovereignty at the microeconomic level, rather than macroeconomic level, at the level of the individual firm and the decisions of its marketing managers.

Penz is concerned with whether consumer sovereignty is an appropriate moral basis for optimizing and evaluating the design and performance of economic systems. In exploring the "interest conception of consumer sovereignty," Penz notes that, under the assumption of a "free market" (largely equivalent to perfect competition, as defined above), the interests of individuals are taken to be "the supreme determinant[s] of production and distribution . . . a morally reasonable starting point and [which] parallels the widely held notion in political philosophy that the fulfillment of the interests of individuals is 'a (. . . perhaps the) fundamental objective of the political order.' "[62] Penz's study questions whether consumer preferences are an adequate representation of human interests, proposing an alternative "objective" conception, which cannot be explored here (but may be questioned as paternalistic).

The works of many moral philosophers provide support for consumer sovereignty as the rationale for capitalism and a worthy ideal: from Cicero's discourses on the duties of merchants,[63] to J. S. Mill's espousal of individualism, to Kant's views on autonomy, and, most recently, the development of these views by writers on consent and autonomy, such as Gerald Dworkin[64] and Feinberg.[65] Yet it is surely sufficient to rely on the above discussion, which demonstrates Western society's beliefs about consumer sovereignty. The "rightness" of consumer sovereignty has a philosophical basis but, as part of a belief in the competitive model of capitalism—one of the most powerful ideologies in the West[66]—it is also well-known and understood. As Galbraith was quoted

---

[59] Velasquez, p. 182.

[60] Quoted at the beginning of G. Peter Penz, *Consumer Sovereignty and Human Interests* (Cambridge: Cambridge University Press, 1986).

[61] Ibid., p. 1.

[62] Ibid., p. 5. Penz is quoting Flathman.

[63] Cicero, *De Officiis/On Duties*, translated by Harry G. Edinger (Indianapolis: Bobbs-Merrill, 1974), Book Three, pp. 143–47.

[64] Gerald Dworkin, *The Theory and Practice of Autonomy* (Cambridge: Cambridge University Press, 1988).

[65] Joel Feinberg, *Harm to Self* (Oxford: Oxford University Press, 1986).

[66] Capitalism is set to become a global force given the collapse of communism and the dismantling at the end of 1991 of the former Soviet Union.

earlier: "The young are taught that . . . in a free enterprise system all authority rests with the sovereign consumer operating through the impersonal mechanism of the market."

Galbraith, throughout his writing, has called into question this notion of consumer sovereignty, proposing, instead, a "Revised Sequence" and identifying producer sovereignty.[67] His views have been vigorously disputed. Yet it can at least be accepted that the idea of the consumer as having absolute power—somewhat akin to that of monarchs of the Middle Ages, hence "the consumer is king"—is a free market ideal. Ludwig von Mises, for example, has written:

> The direction of all economic affairs is in the market society a task of the entrepreneurs. Theirs is the control of production. They are at the helm and steer the ship. A superficial observer would believe that they are supreme. But they are not. They are bound to obey unconditionally the captain's orders. The captain is the consumer.[68]

In the "mixed," rather than free, markets of the modern economy, there are degrees of consumer sovereignty. In other words, the captain is to some extent the consumer, but this depends principally on levels of competition (choice) and information. Accordingly, it is argued that marketing managers have an obligation to redress any power imbalance to give more weight to the consumer interest to the extent required by the adequacy of performance definitions. Clearly this obligation is rooted in the ideals of capitalism and an acknowledgement of the shortfall between the ideology of free markets and the reality of mixed markets. It is, further, not without contention, as it readily can be argued that the exercise of management discretion on the consumer's behalf is paternalism and, more fundamentally, threatens the autonomy of the consumer, which the market mechanism is intended to uphold. However, in reply, it is to be observed that the marketing manager is not asked to assume what is best for the consumer but, rather, would be encouraged to find out: through market research with consumers and consulting expert opinion. This, at least, may be preferable to inaction or government intervention.

The strengths and weaknesses of the consumer sovereignty test become more apparent when it is applied to marketing problems. It has application to many of the company/customer conflicts described in this book. Consider these examples: Cigarette advertising, which promotes an addictive drug to teenagers, or the pricing and ability to pay for the expensive AIDS drug AZT, can be assessed against the capability dimension of the consumer sovereignty test. Misleading advertising and sales puffery in personal selling can be assessed against the information dimension of the test. Trade promotions, such as slotting allowances, and channel decisions about exclusivity agreements with dis-

---

[67] John K. Galbraith, *The New Industrial State* (Harmondsworth: Penguin, 1974 [1967]), pp. 216–17.

[68] Ludwig von Mises, *Human Action: A Treatise on Economics* (London: William Hodge, 1949), p. 270.

tributors, which may restrict competition, may be assessed against the choice dimension.

In making these assessments, the marketing manager still must exercise judgment, based on her values and interpretation of the facts. In particular, she will ask: How much sovereignty is enough? The answer to this question is likely to change as society's expectations of business change. However, the consumer sovereignty test and, more broadly, the overall marketing ethics framework, focus the manager's attention on the appropriate concerns and provide some assessment criteria. When conscience signals something is not right about a marketing decision, the manager does at least have a model that can be employed to explore its ethical dimensions.

In sum, the ethics continuum provides benchmarks against which marketing practices may be evaluated. Along this continuum, you may determine your own position, based on what you consider to be an appropriate balance of the rights and interests of consumers and those of producers. There may be other stakeholders than the consumer whose interests also must be considered. However, it is at least the primary role of marketing to work on the behalf of the customer. Other functions within the firm may be expected to lobby for other interests and, therefore, appropriately constrain marketing action if out of check.

In advocating the position of the consumer sovereignty school on the ethics continuum, it is argued that this position combines the moral imperative of the human condition with the customer satisfaction imperative of the marketing role. Its origins lie in marketing and in an understanding of the function's concern with the company/customer relationship and the recognition that many ethical issues in marketing arise through this relationship. Consumer sovereignty is central to market systems, but is found to be challenged by producer sovereignty. Accordingly, an obligation of marketing managers to enhance consumer sovereignty is identified. Finally, it is noted that acting on this obligation requires a moral impulse, and the individual manager's values still play an important role in augmenting the marketing ethics framework and evaluating the marketing decision.

This chapter has explored why a marketing manager should be ethical, and it has embarked on the difficult task of establishing what constitutes ethical marketing decision making. The subsequent chapters in this book provide the opportunity for you to refine your perspective on marketing ethics and develop your own methods of evaluation.

Marketing Managers, Society, and the Environment

Marketing Managers: Caught in the Middle

E. Raymond Corey

In a recent article entitled "Cheaper Can Be Better," *Time* took aim at high-pressure tactics in drug marketing, focusing, in particular, on the "promotion and public relations hoo-ha" for the 1987 launch of TPA, a new heart drug.[1] Touted as clearly superior to the competitive product, streptokinase, TPA was also 10 times more expensive. The promotional campaign worked and the new drug became the preferred medication, so the article reported, for the majority of U.S. doctors. Four years later, research indicated that TPA was no better than streptokinase and, in fact, carried a slightly higher risk of causing strokes.

Genentech, the TPA manufacturer, according to *Time*, had "relentlessly promoted its products not to doctors and patients but to researchers as well." The article went on to cite the promotional practices of some other drug manufacturers.

- **Frequent Prescriber Plan** Wyeth-Ayerst Laboratories gives doctors 1,000 points on American Airlines' frequent-flyer program for each patient they put on the hypertension drug Inderal LA.

- **Profitable Research** As part of a "study," Roche pays doctors $1,200 if they prescribe the antibiotic Rocephin for 20 hospital patients.

- **Big-Shot Program** In return for purchasing vaccines, Connaught Labs awards points redeemable for VCRs, personal computers, and TVs.

- **Computer Freebie** A consortium of 10 drug companies provides doctors with free $35,000 computer systems if they spend 20 minutes a week reviewing "promotional messages" and "clinical information" and complete four continuing medical-education programs a year.

---

[1] See *Time*, March 18, 1991, p. 70.

- **Beachside Bonus**   Ciba-Geigy offers free Caribbean vacations to doctors in return for their sitting in on a few lectures about Estraderm, an estrogen patch.

On a much larger scale, Unisys, a major computer and defense electronics manufacturer, and Navy procurement officers were charged in June 1991 with fraud in the sale of weapons systems to the U.S. government. According to *The Wall Street Journal* report[2]:

> ... Unisys Corp. has agreed to the most expensive Pentagon fraud settlement ever—expected to total about $190 million—for its role in the bribery and influence-peddling scandal that tainted weapons purchases during the Reagan era.
>
> ... The company has agreed to plead guilty to fraud and various other felony charges, according to persons familiar with the case, of resorting to corrupt middlemen, sham consulting agreements, and other illicit schemes to try to snare defense contracts. The Unisys plea and a roughly 100-page criminal indictment spelling out a pattern of illegal corporate activities will mark the climax of "Operation Ill Wind"—the longest and most successful investigation of military procurement corruption in recent times.
>
> ... Meanwhile, federal prosecutors soon intend to seek an indictment on related charges against Melvyn Paisley, the Navy's former top purchasing official,....
>
> ... For Unisys, the guilty plea will close a costly and infamous chapter of its history. More than 10 individuals who worked for its defense operations over the years—including prominent industry consultant William Galvin and former company vice president Charles Gardner—have been convicted as part of Ill Wind and are cooperating with the investigation.
>
> ... Messrs. Galvin and Gardner, for example, have admitted to conspiring to bribe Mr. Paisley by purchasing an Idaho condominium from him in 1986 at an inflated price. In return, court documents allege, Mr. Paisley "performed official acts to benefit" Unisys and Sperry Corp., which merged with another concern to become Unisys in 1986.
>
> ... In addition, prosecutors have alleged that Mr. Gardner and several associates used a $5 million slush fund while working at Unisys to funnel bribes to Pentagon officials, make illegal campaign contributions to lawmakers, provide kickbacks to off-shore accounts they controlled, and pass on bogus bills to the Pentagon.

These are episodes in a steady flow of publicity that depicts marketers as well as purchasing managers as the "guys in the black hats." Nor do the tricks of persuasion know any bounds. They range from cash bribes, to paid vacations, to free tickets, to prostitutes.

Why is it that serious and obscene breaches of moral conduct seem frequently to arise in connection with marketing activities? What is there about marketing that seems to lead to unethical and, indeed, illegal behavior in the pursuit of making sales?

In seeking answers, we might speculate that the temptations, the pressures, the opportunities, the potential rewards—and the power—managers have to act

---

[2] *The Wall Street Journal*, June 10, 1991, p. A3.

unethically are an integral part of the market milieu. In particular, marketing managers have the potential for taking decisions that reward or punish other persons *as individuals*. A salesperson, for example, as an agent for his or her company, may be able to bribe a purchasing manager who, as an agent for his or her company, must choose between competing suppliers. The transaction may benefit both personally: the purchasing manager in receiving a bribe and the salesperson through the incentive compensation received for making the sale. It may not, however, necessarily represent an optimal contract for one or both of the companies they represent. Thus, the great potential and, indeed, the strong motivations for behaving unethically on the part of marketing managers may "go with the territory."

In what follows, we examine first the conditions that lead to unethical behavior on the part of marketing managers. Second, we identify the influences that come to bear in making moral choices. Finally, we consider ways in which top corporate executives can create an environment conducive to ethical behavior in marketing.

MARKETING'S GARDEN OF EDEN

Three conditions are inherent in marketing functions that tend to create an environment conducive to unethical behavior. First, by its very nature, marketing is cast in boundary-spanning relationships in which the goal is to negotiate and complete transactions. It relates the firm to such key external constituencies as the customer group, wholesale and retail channel members, advertising agencies, the media; sometimes regulatory agencies and other governmental bodies. The transactional nature of marketing relationships sets the stage for resorting to any means that may serve to conclude deals successfully.

Second, in their transactional roles, marketers act as agents and deal with the agents of customer firms or groups, or with the persons they represent. For this reason, the allocation of benefits mediated through transactional processes takes place at two levels: (1) the agents as individuals and (2) the firms they represent. The former may include sellers' representatives, on the one side, and on the other purchasing agents or other members of the buying decision-making unit (DMU), such as corporate officers or technicians or production managers, or such outside influencers in, say, design or engineering firms—or doctors. Thus, in the Unisys case, those individuals responsible for negotiating defense contracts between the Navy and Unisys act as agents for their respective organizations. In the example involving TPA, the new heart drug, Genentech marketing managers and sales representatives act in agency roles while the doctors may be perceived as the agents of their patients. (This thought suggests, parenthetically, that the weaker and more reliant the principals (patients) are on their agents (doctors), the more power the agents have to influence purchasing decisions for their own benefit.) Possible benefits for parties to any transactions may range from being rewarded for meeting performance goals to receiving bribes and kickbacks and other personal benefits.

Third, marketers wield economic power that may be used to reward, punish, and strongly influence customer choice. Their power is based on the ability, among other things, to advertise in mass media, to allocate scarce supplies, and, as noted, to provide personal benefits, for example, vacation trips, entertainment, and personal gifts.

These three conditions or aspects of marketing—its boundary-spanning nature, its agency role, and its capacity for the exercise of economic power—taken together may lead to severe ethical and illegal abuses. We are painfully familiar with episodes involving false and misleading advertising, product misrepresentation, monetary bribes and gift giving, and excessive and sometimes immoral forms of entertainment. In addition, the use of advertising and promotional schemes to exploit the young, the poor, and the less-educated segments of our population often provides a depressing commentary on the morals of marketing. To many of us, for example, advertising candy to young children, cigarettes to teenagers, and state lottery tickets seems to be obscene use of economic power.

It is not surprising, too, that the illicit or unethical use of power, or both, seems most often to occur in transactions where the stakes are very large and of considerable significance to both buyers and sellers. Thus, managers in such industries as defense, construction, investment banking, and aircraft manufacture seem particularly prone to engage in questionable practices. The temptation to "do what has to be done" to get a particular contract may lead—and has led in a number of cases—to paying large bribes. Once the deal is made, the pressure to make profits on these jobs, particularly ones negotiated as cost-plus arrangements, may then lead to falsifying costs. In investment banking, resorting to the use of inside information and the illegal use of financial power has been characteristic of a number of transactions involving such infamous characters as Michael Milken, Ivan Boesky, and John Gutfreund. In any industry, the pressure to get and keep large accounts may provide compelling motivation to offer bribes and other forms of pay-offs.

CAUGHT IN THE CROSS FIRE

In dealing with ethical choices, marketing managers are caught in a cross fire of conflicting pressures. Often the temptations to act unethically are strongly reinforced by the imperatives of meeting performance measures. "Making the sale" becomes imperative when, as is the case in the vast majority of sales organizations, performance goals are cast in terms of sales quotas and compensation is based on "meeting quota."

Corporate codes of conduct may represent a countervailing, sometimes confusing, and often ineffective influence on salesperson behavior. The way to close a deal may be to entertain the purchasing agents in the client organization.

The prevailing codes of conduct in his or her firm and the client organization, however, rule out granting or receiving favors, but all too often to no avail. Here is one such instance expressed in the words of the controller of Aurora-Baxter Corporation (ABC), a company that made construction materials:

> As you know, Construction Materials [an ABC business unit] does a lot of business with state governments. Among our big accounts for pipe and tile is [a large mid-western state].
>
> A couple of years ago, following a scandal in the awarding of highway contracts, the state legislature enacted some very stiff laws forbidding state purchasing officers from accepting any gifts—even free lunches. Since then our relations with state buyers have gotten a little awkward in certain respects. When our marketing guys are in the middle of negotiations with them or when they've concluded a big contract, it's natural to go out with the buyers, maybe for drinks and a nice meal. Everybody knows that each person there is supposed to pay for his or her own meal. Our guys are told that they have to make that clear. So at some point one of them will say, "OK, everybody, chip in. You know the rule." Maybe there are five of them and three of us and say the bill is $300–400. When the meal's over they've put in $2 each and we pick up the rest of the tab.
>
> In fact, on one recent occasion our sales rep for the [state] State Highway Department had concluded a big sale and our guys and their buyers went out to a restaurant to celebrate. The ABC rep put a big bowl in the middle of the table and made sure everybody saw him drop in five 10-dollar bills. When he counted the money after dinner there were three 10-dollar bills! He mentioned it to a senior buyer for the state, and the response was, "ABC is a big company; you ought to be able to find some way to buy me a dinner!"

Over and against the norms of the state purchasing agents, ABC sales representatives had to weigh the strictures of their company's Corporate Responsibility Statement, which read in part:

> The Corporation intends to comply strictly with all domestic and foreign laws which apply to its business. Employees will not be permitted to violate any law relating to the conduct of business or to engage in unethical business practices....
>
> Failure to adhere to ethical and legal standards of conduct may result in disciplinary action, including immediate suspension and eventual discharge....
>
> **Personal Gifts**. The giving or receiving of gifts, loans, favors, or other services by an employee acting on behalf of the Corporation directly or indirectly to or from anyone outside the Corporation is strictly forbidden. Such gifts are not limited to tangible or cash gifts or loans but include intangibles, such as promises for the future, valuable "tips," advantageous purchases, or other opportunities.[3]

Thus, ABC's sales representatives and its managers were caught, on the one hand, between their company code of ethics and state legislation making it illegal for government procurement managers to accept favors of any kind, and, on the other, purchasing managers "on the make" and the sales representatives' own needs, presumably, to "make quota."

---

[3] See Harvard Business School case "Aurora-Baxter Corporation" (9-578-089).

The Pressures

Complicating factors in such cases as this may include industry norms and country culture. As noted above, the construction industry, for one, has been notorious for the prevalence of large-scale bribes and kickbacks; "that's the way business is done!" As for country environment, ethical norms vary considerably in different parts of the world. Corporate managers may be caught, then, between establishing and enforcing a global code of ethics or allowing standards of business behavior to vary from country to country in accordance with the principle: "When in Rome, do as the Romans do." When Dow Corning, for example, promulgated a code of business conduct, a single code to establish the ethical guidelines for conducting business worldwide, the protests from area managers outside the United States came quickly. Dow Corning's Pacific area manager, for example, sent a memo to his superior, which stated in part:

> We may find, this time next year, that we either do business the way some American companies and the Europeans and Japanese do or we forget the Philippines market. We know we are already losing business in Korea and India by adopting a rigorous attitude to local agents' commissions. How much we can lose in Korea and still have a meaningful long-term strategy, including perhaps a manufacturing investment, is an open question. But it is one we had better ask ourselves pretty quickly. If the corporation wishes to continue to put Dow Corning at a competitive market disadvantage because of some ethical (not legal) concern, that is its prerogative. But to pressure area management, at the same time, to increase market share and leadership . . . seems inconsistent to say the least.[4]

Marketing managers are sometimes confronted, as well, with ethical dilemmas involving conflicting interests—their companies versus their customers, or one customer versus others, or one customer versus the customer set as a group. In the interest of building and maintaining loyal customers as sources of revenue, salespersons often are prone to act inside their own companies as customer-advocates, asking for customized products and services, short and often uneconomic production runs to fulfill small orders, and full product lines to meet every conceivable request. "Who does the salesperson represent, his or her company or the customer?" is a question with important ethical implications.

Finally, sales representatives are confronted with ethical choices in dealing with the several members of a customer organization who may be involved in making a purchase decision. Typically, those in the decision-making unit represent different interests, both functional and personal, a range of viewpoints, and a wide spectrum in the amount of power each has to affect the ultimate purchase choice. In industrial marketing situations, for example, sales

---

[4] See Harvard Business School case "Dow Corning Corporation: Business Conduct and Global Values (A)" (9-385-018).

representatives may seek to bypass purchasing managers to deal directly with engineering personnel. The former are perceived often as being far more concerned about price considerations and the need for preserving multiple sources of supply; the latter more interested in maintaining their relations with known vendors, with price of lesser concern. Is this ethical?

Countervailing Forces

There may be—and usually is—a high degree of tension in marketing between the external pressures on marketing managers' behavior and the inner forces affecting his or her choices. Exhibit 1 arrays these factors as an inner and outer ring. The outer ring includes many of the influences on personal behavior suggested in the above discussion and some others. To explain: in the outer ring, the determinants of behavior are, first, the prototypical norms exhibited by those in a particular function (e.g., marketing) or a particular industry (e.g., construction) or a particular part of the world (e.g., Korea or the United States). Industry and country are important dimensions of the competitive milieu. The tacit rules of competition—and commensurately the ethical content of business dealings—may vary considerably from one industry to another and from one

EXHIBIT 1

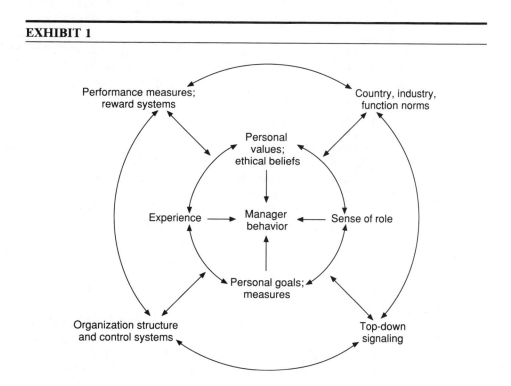

country to another, to create sometimes wrenching ethical choices for those in marketing roles.

Second, the imperatives of marketing measurement and reward systems may put compelling and sometimes irresistible pressure on sales and marketing managers to get sales by any and all means, ethical concerns aside.

Third, the way the organization is structured in terms of the multiplicity of profit centers and the number of management levels is also relevant. The more complex the structure, the more the tendency for top management to control through quantitative measures and the less their reliance on qualitative performance considerations; that is to say, the more hierarchical the organization, the more top managers are forced to control through measuring *what* was accomplished in terms of sales and profits, rather than through *how* the results were achieved, and the more managers at the operating level may be able to conceal *means* but not *end results*.

Fourth, the directions set by upper management—top-down signaling—establish the climate within which lower level managers act. Codes of conduct are only one in a complex of signals that emanate from those in charge. Codes of business conduct won't serve to support positive ethical behavior if breaches of the code are tacitly condoned by top managers, in the interests of achieving sales results. Other powerful signals may come from the pattern of promotions and what that may imply in terms of who gets rewarded for what. In addition, the corporate culture often is expressed in terms of "stories" out of the past that communicate and establish the values built up through successive generations of management.

Over and against the moral environment within which marketers act are the inner-ring factors, which are largely an expression of self. First, personal values and ethical beliefs developed from early childhood and continually evolving form a set of personal standards through which ethical issues may be screened. Second, personal goals and self-measures are powerful determinants of individual behavior, and they are likely to evolve over time. They set priorities on the relative importance of career advancement, money, power over others, personal security, and family interests. Third, experience deals out its own imperatives. Each situation with which managers are confronted may be likened to some prior experience to give direction to the manager's response to the current dilemma. Finally, managers act out of a sense of role. Dow Corning's Pacific area manager, for example, perceives that, in his role, his responsibility is primarily to increase area sales and profits. He might think differently, however, about the Pacific area's compliance with the corporate code of conduct if he were president of the firm. As president, he might well act to achieve uniformity in the way Dow Corning would do business around the world.

The two rings, inner and outer, set up what physicists and engineers may term a "force field": they are in constant tension. But not only do external pressures shape manager behavior, managers themselves often shape the moral environments in which they and others work. The extent to which they do so depends largely on their authority, their power of personality, their sense of personal security in the context of their work environment, and the economic power of their companies in their industries. As for this last consideration, the ability of Dow Corning's president to implement a corporate code of conduct that went counter to business norms in many parts of the world depended significantly on his company's position as the world's leading supplier of silicones and its reputation for the quality of its products. Those who want Dow Corning products will be inclined to do business on Dow Corning's terms.

CREATING A CLIMATE FOR ETHICAL BEHAVIOR

If corporate managers are seriously interested in creating an environment conducive to ethical behavior, it would seem that certain principles of governance are essential. First and foremost, managers at all levels must send signals that clearly underscore the importance of moral conduct. They may do this in the examples they set, in their efforts to perpetuate the "stories" that help to shape the corporate culture, and in their promotion decisions, and the reward-and-punishment patterns they establish.

Second, ethical conduct may be encouraged through developing corporate codes of conduct. In fact, if the drafting of such codes is a widely shared exercise, the process itself can be a constructive influence on behavior. Codes are worthless, however, if monitoring mechanisms are not in place and if breaches of conduct are not identified and punished.

Third, performance measures: quantitative measures per se do not encourage ethical conduct. It is essential that *how* results are achieved be taken into account. Any episodes of unethical conduct, which may have helped to achieve quantified results, should indeed be factored into performance appraisals. Ethical deviations usually are difficult to hide between a superior making the performance appraisal and the subordinate whose results are being measured. At the same time, the corporate culture must encourage "whistle blowing" if subordinates are aware of illegal or unethical behavior at higher levels of management.

Fourth, a sense of job security can go far in supporting those who, for personal reasons, want to behave ethically. It is often those who feel insecure in their positions, those measured on results alone, who are prone to act unethically or illegally.

The above precepts, insofar as they shape the climate in which managers act, would apply generally; they may be said to apply, in particular, to marketers. Marketers are the ones who are cast in boundary-spanning roles and who, as agents of their firms, deal with the agents of other firms or customer groups. They are the ones involved in large transactions, the successful outcome of which may be of critical importance to the companies they represent—and to themselves. They, in effect, are caught in the middle.

Chapter 2.2

Ciba-Geigy Pharmaceuticals: Pharma International

In August 1983, the management committee of Pharma International (PHI), CIBA-GEIGY's[1] third-world pharmaceuticals operation, had as an agenda item for its monthly meeting the decision of whether or not to approve the development and launch of a new antimalarial product in Nigeria. A lively discussion was anticipated. The product proposal had originated from the management committee of the pharmaceutical division in Nigeria (Pharma Nigeria). As was often the case, the decision involved significant commercial, ethical, and policy considerations.

Malaria was one of the leading causes of death from disease in Nigeria. Chloroquine had long been used to treat it, and in Nigeria was available as an over-the-counter (OTC) product through pharmacists, clinics, and patent medicine stores, largely as a proprietary (branded) drug. Pharma Nigeria did not have an antimalarial product and, therefore, wished to be active in this significant segment of the self-medication market. Chloroquine's extremely bitter taste had prompted Pharma Nigeria to propose a tasteless capsule form for Fevex, the new antimalarial product. It was hoped that not only would Fevex be more pleasant to take and, therefore, superior to the many other antimalarial products on the market, but that it also would have the benefits of improved compliance in completion of the full treatment and a reduced likelihood of malaria victims postponing treatment by self-medication. However, the bitter taste of chloroquine had minimized the risk of unintended consumption, particularly by children. Chloroquine's toxicity meant an overdose could be fatal.

The PHI management committee had a hard decision to make. There were considerable risks for Ciba-Geigy in launching a product that would be aggressively promoted in a third-world country. As a self-medication product, it

This case was prepared by Professor N. Craig Smith with the assistance of Professor John A. Quelch. Copyright © 1989 by the President and Fellows of Harvard College.
Harvard Business School case 9-589-108 (Rev. 7/16/90).
[1] CIBA-GEIGY is the registered company name, hereafter shown as Ciba-Geigy.

would be extensively advertised and made widely available, yet it was potentially lethal if misused. Aside from any "duty of care" obligations, Ciba-Geigy could lay itself open to criticism for marketing a dangerous product or, indeed, for wasting resources in developing and promoting a "me-too" drug. Consumer organizations had been highly critical of pharmaceutical marketing practices in the third world. The likely prospect of counterfeiting presented further difficulties. From a commercial point of view, the capsule form of Fevex was attractive, not least because it would employ underutilized capsule-filling production capacity in Nigeria. However, the necessary clinical tests would be expensive, and there was an increase in chloroquine-resistant strains of malaria. Some members of the PHI management committee firmly believed that Ciba-Geigy's strength lay in its research and development of new drugs; me-too drugs were to be avoided as a matter of policy. Prior to the meeting, a number of the committee members had already asked, "Is it really worth the effort?"

CIBA-GEIGY PHARMACEUTICALS DIVISION

In 1982, Ciba-Geigy group sales were 13,808 million Swiss francs ($6,802 million), a modest growth of only 1 percent on 1981, attributed to difficult trading conditions worldwide: uncertainty and recession, protectionism, currency instability, balance of payment deficits, and inflation. Group operating profit was 622 million Swiss francs ($306 million). Ciba-Geigy group had approximately 80,000 employees, working in 120 subsidiaries in more than 50 countries. Although headquartered in Basel, only 2 percent of sales came from Switzerland, with the rest of Europe accounting for 41 percent, North America 29 percent, Latin America 11 percent, Asia 11 percent, and Africa, Australia, and Oceania 6 percent.

The largest proportion of Ciba-Geigy's sales came from the pharmaceuticals division (Pharma), which at 4.1 billion Swiss francs ($2 billion, 30 percent of group sales, 1982), made it the second-largest pharmaceutical company in the world. Pharmaceutical sales increased 8 percent in 1982 over the previous year, well above the industry growth rate. Pharma was represented in four major areas: cardiovascular products (30 percent of sales) including beta-blockers; antirheumatics and analgesics (23 percent), including Voltaren, the 10th best-selling pharmaceutical in the world; antidepressants and drugs for treating epilepsy (15 percent); and a broad spectrum of antibiotics and other drugs for treating infectious diseases, such as tuberculosis and leprosy, certain tropical diseases, skin diseases and allergies, and bone diseases. Pharma also included a contact lens business, a division marketing self-medication (OTC) products, and the Servipharm division, which operated specifically to serve the needs of developing countries.

THE PHARMACEUTICAL INDUSTRY

The pharmaceutical industry was traditionally highly profitable, with a return on investment of around 15 percent. About 40 percent of Ciba-Geigy profits came from pharmaceutical sales. However, there were some worrying trends:

- Government attempts to reduce health care costs: At around 10 percent of GNP, the cost of health care in industrialized countries was coming under close scrutiny. There was an emphasis on lowering costs, while attempting to maintain the quality of service, through stricter price controls, restrictions on new product introductions, and limitations on doctors' freedom to prescribe (including the use of generic lists). Outside the United States, national governments paid for most drugs, though reimbursements by health insurance funds were also increasingly restrictive.

- Increasing R&D expenditures: R&D costs had been doubling every five years since 1970, due in part to rising registration costs, with regulators demanding greater evidence of economic as well as therapeutic benefits. Industry observers estimated the average cost of bringing a drug to the U.S. market to be around $100 million. Meanwhile, major technological breakthroughs were less frequent.

- Reduced patent protection: Companies depended on patents to secure a temporary monopoly in the sale of new products, and the evidence indicated that having patent-protected products had a significant impact on corporate performance. After patent expiry, brand names often would protect companies from generic competition, providing a new drug with profits for 16 years or more and real returns averaging 9–10 percent over that time. However, getting a drug approved was taking longer, and government efforts to reduce costs meant earlier substitution by generics once the drug was off-patent.

- Increasing criticism of pharmaceutical marketing practices, coupled with some questioning of the benefits provided by pharmaceuticals: There was public concern about the role of the pharmaceutical sales representative, as well as gifts provided to doctors and their expenses-paid trips to medical conventions organized by drug companies and usually in exotic locations. Promotional literature was a major source of information used by doctors when prescribing, but it did not always provide adequate detail on contraindications[2] and side effects. Pharmaceutical marketing practices in the third world had been strongly criticized. Drug use by patients always entailed some risk from the possible toxic effects of the drug (hence the industry adage "all drugs are poisons"); but this was not widely understood, and adverse patient reactions added to mistrust of drugs and the industry.

---

[2] Contraindications were situations when the use of a drug was inadvisable, for example, during pregnancy.

These trends contributed to increased industry competitiveness, but also to collaborative efforts (particularly in new fields, such as biotechnology) and to the prospect of mergers. There were also positive factors affecting the industry. The level of economic activity (at a time of recession) had little impact on drug consumption. Indeed, industry sales were expected to continue to rise at a rate in excess of 10 percent per annum. Although ethical pharmaceuticals (prescription drugs) were around 90 percent of world industry sales, the remaining OTC sector was expected to grow rapidly. Health policy was likely to attach more importance to self-therapy for the treatment of mild and transient illnesses, such as the common cold, constipation, and diarrhea, in order to reduce health care costs and inconvenience for the patient. Ciba-Geigy was attempting to increase its presence in the self-medication market, though, in 1981, 98 percent of its revenues came from ethical pharmaceuticals.

R&D prospects appeared to be improving, especially in the field of genetic engineering where Pharma was active. Ciba-Geigy spent 8.5 percent of sales on R&D. Approximately half of this was accounted for by Pharma, with an R&D expenditure of 14 percent of Pharma sales in 1982, compared to an industry average of around 10 percent. New products were expected to account for 30 percent of Pharma sales by 1986. Industry analysts had also observed a shift in industry R&D expenditures: a decline in me-too products and minor evolutionary research in the 1960s, prompted by more stringent product approval regulations; a greater interest in product differentiation, based on features promoting ease of use or patient compliance during the 1970s; with a likely focus on breakthrough R&D efforts in the 1980s, as health cost pressures reduced the prospects for drugs with minor product differences. This trend demanded good R&D management by pharmaceutical companies and broad market access to exploit R&D achievements.

Ciba-Geigy acknowledged the difficulties experienced by health services and the consequent cost pressures. In the 1982 annual report, the company noted that this "causes problems for the pharmaceutical industry, but it also presents the socially responsible, research-based enterprise with opportunities" and, further on: "Even where there is political controversy it is becoming increasingly clear that expenditure on medicines in a budget-conscious health service is money well spent. In the industrialized and developing countries alike, the provision of efficacious, high quality medicines is an important element in any health service, and one which will stand up to economic cost/benefit scrutiny . . . Ciba-Geigy offers a range of medicines for which there will always be a medical need."

Drug industry critics were not entirely convinced Ciba-Geigy was taking its social responsibilities seriously. In 1970, Japanese scientists had identified the active ingredient, clioquinol, used in Ciba-Geigy's antidiarrheal drugs as the cause of a disease known as SMON, involving paralysis and loss of sight. Following a government ban, and six years of legal action, Ciba-Geigy paid damages to Japanese victims in 1978. Two years later, a company press release claimed: "There is no conclusive scientific evidence that clioquinol causes

SMON." Ciba-Geigy policy was modified in 1982, as the annual report explained, "in the light of recent medical knowledge and experience." Ciba-Geigy had decided to gradually withdraw the problem drugs within the next five years. Critics charged that the gradual withdrawal was to save face and to avoid weakening the company's legal position. Ciba-Geigy commented: "As the demand for products of this type varies considerably, and their replacement by other treatments will take time in many countries, especially those of the third world, the wishes of the national health authorities will be respected." This criticism of Ciba-Geigy had led to a boycott by doctors and vets in Sweden, but Ciba-Geigy was not the only pharmaceutical company to be criticized for its marketing practices in the third world. It could reasonably be claimed the entire industry was under attack.

SERVIPHARM AND PHARMA INTERNATIONAL

Ciba-Geigy was changing in response to the pressures on the industry. In its 1981 annual report, Ciba-Geigy had welcomed a code of pharmaceutical marketing practice developed by the International Federation of Pharmaceutical Manufacturers Associations (IFPMA), integrating it into corporate policy. Earlier in 1977, it had formed Servipharm, a wholly owned subsidiary, specifically to provide essential drugs at economical prices to the 80 percent of the world's population in the non-OECD "industrializing" markets. Servipharm's objectives were: (1) To offer a range of pharmaceutical products that would meet the specific needs of a major portion of the world's population. (2) To ensure that its products were safe and reliable by manufacturing them according to the highest quality standards. (3) To make Servipharm products as widely available as possible by keeping them economically priced. (4) To offer to governments and institutions services in other health and health care-related areas.

Servipharm was the only company related to a major pharmaceutical manufacturer dedicated exclusively to the production and sale of high-quality essential drugs. It began operation in the "easier markets," those not requiring registration (Malaysia, smaller African markets, UNICEF tenders, etc.). It then began to develop its own registration dossiers, which were submitted to Swiss and other registration authorities, providing access to larger markets. The product range comprised branded versions of 30 basic drugs for which there was substantial demand by institutional users. One of these was Serviquin (chloroquine diphosphate), an antimalarial. The "Servi" prefix, used in all Servipharm brand names, was intended to convey a quality assurance and act as a reminder of the service orientation of Servipharm—reliable products, dependable delivery, and flexible package sizes, as well as consultancy services.

By 1983, Servipharm was active in more than 70 countries and could claim over 200 million patients had benefited from its products. It shipped over 700 million capsules and tablets in 1982 and sales had quadrupled since 1979.

Servipharm products generally were priced above those of the smaller, perhaps local, generic manufacturers and below the more expensive branded products of the major manufacturers. This pricing, Ciba-Geigy believed, reflected the quality of Servipharm products and the association with the Ciba-Geigy name, which, around 1980, began to appear on Servipharm packaging and literature.

There had been opposition to the Servipharm initiative within Ciba-Geigy. Support for generic production had been viewed as heresy; the success of the company had been built on new drugs. However, with commitment from Pharma management, the Servipharm initiative went ahead. There also had been controversy within the industry over Ciba-Geigy's sale of generics. All Servipharm products were patent-free and almost entirely non-Ciba-Geigy in origin. The major pharmaceutical companies had always viewed generic manufacturers as an external threat. Servipharm represented generic competition from within. This angered competitors.

Servipharm had, as yet, always made a loss, confirming the doubts of some within the company and the industry generally. Focusing on the institutional market avoided marketing costs, such as pharmaceutical representatives, but submitting tenders to national institutions and international organizations entailed strong price competition. Quality was an important feature of Servipharm products, but not readily established: It was not easy to show that the quality or quantity of an active substance, or the grain used (which affects absorption), would be consistently correct. The customer often would not know if a drug was effective. Servipharm and its customers could rely on the Ciba-Geigy reputation; but they had to bear the full and high associated costs of largely Swiss production, with significant quality control expenditures. Some Servipharm production took place overseas, but this, too, was expensive, because of economies of scale factors—smaller production base, cost of importing materials in smaller quantities—which in a capital-intensive industry were not offset by lower labor costs. (However, in 1982, one third of Ciba-Geigy's total pharmaceutical production came from its 20 manufacturing units in the third world.) The generic competitors, meanwhile, could source on the open market and often would have lower costs of production. In some cases, they were even supplying the active ingredient to Servipharm. Tenders by pharmaceutical companies often were assessed solely on the basis of price, but adverse experiences were encouraging former Servipharm customers to repeat purchase and pay higher Servipharm prices.

Through Servipharm, Ciba-Geigy was manufacturing some of the oldest (though essential) drugs for the poorest countries in the world, using expensive production facilities (subcontracting was minimal). Generic supply offered some potential for reasonable returns if sufficient scale were realized; Servipharm's generic competitors were largely national and smaller operations in each country. Servipharm production was also filling spare Ciba-Geigy capacity. To show a profit on Servipharm could upset third-world customers and invite further criticism from consumer organizations, so Servipharm's goal was to break even. Ciba-Geigy was taking a long-term view of its investment, believing that multinational companies increasingly would be held to account for the provision of health care to the world's poor and that public opinion on the issue would have to be satisfied. The concept of "Drugs You Can Trust ... at Prices You Can Afford" did have a strong underlying ethical purpose. Studies had shown that it was difficult for Ciba-Geigy to reach beyond the top 10 percent (in terms of income) in many third-world countries. Servipharm provided generics under the corporate umbrella with a guarantee of quality, adding value in the Ciba-Geigy name, services, and quality control. Milton Silverman, a leading drug industry critic, became one of Servipharm's strongest supporters.

Servipharm only represented about 7 percent of PHI sales. PHI generated about 10 percent of all Pharma sales, serving 120 countries in the Middle East, Far East, Eastern bloc, Mediterranean, Africa, and Latin America. Ciba-Geigy country managers were responsible for the profitability of all Ciba-Geigy activities within their countries (including Servipharm) and reported to regional managers at headquarters. Servipharm operated alongside, but separate from, Ciba-Geigy branded pharmaceutical operations.

The third world accounted for approximately 20 percent of Ciba-Geigy group sales and employees. In 1974, a corporate policy was formulated for third-world countries, shown in Exhibit 1. This governed PHI as much as any other unit in Ciba-Geigy. Ciba-Geigy believed that it was primarily the responsibility of each local government to determine a country's development policy and that aid organizations as well as transnational corporations should at most play a supporting or facilitating role, not to set the "development machine" in motion but to "contribute a drop of oil to help the machinery run a little more smoothly." Earning a "fair profit" played a part in this, though this did not preclude development aid of a charitable nature, such as, within PHI: A leprosy fund, set up to support improved diagnosis, training, treatment, and rehabilitation; a contribution of 10 million Swiss francs to the WHO Diarrheal Diseases Control Program; and the donation of drugs (that would otherwise be destroyed) to third-world countries within 24 and 12 months of their expiry dates. PHI also supported third-world public health service initiatives where its expertise could be of value.

CIBA-GEIGY IN NIGERIA

Nigeria, a West African, English-speaking country, approximately one tenth the size of the United States, gained independence in 1960. Its population was 95 million in 1983 (one in five Africans was a Nigerian) and growing rapidly at around 3 percent a year. Almost half of the population was under 15 years of age. Most Nigerians lived in rural villages, with 20 percent in the main urban areas, many in squalid shanty towns. Over half the population lived in the relatively depressed northern regions of the country. Population density was greater in the south, which included Lagos, the capital city, with a pop-

---

EXHIBIT 1   Ciba-Geigy Policy for Third-World Countries

The Fundamental Framework

- As a business organization whose activities span the globe, we wish to contribute to the economic development of the Third World. By way of
  - a far-ranging involvement in the fields of agriculture, health, and industry;
  - the international scope of our organization; and
  - our know-how and experience;
  we can help meet the basic needs of people throughout the Third World.

- Our group units are subject to the laws of the countries in which they are domiciled. We adhere to the principle of nonintervention in domestic political matters. At the same time we are aware that our presence represents an economic factor which may have an impact on the local scene.

- As a shareholder-owned enterprise we have to earn a fair profit wherever we are active. We therefore depend, in the Third World as elsewhere, on profitable operations, legally assured security and continuity, equal treatment with indigenous firms, and the unimpeded exchange of goods.

- While respecting the desire of the developing countries to foster their fledgling industries, we hold that the measures they take to this end should be economically sound and should not exclude competition.

- In national and international bodies we defend the following principles:
  - a healthy economy is indispensable to a country's development;
  - private enterprise acting in accordance with local conditions is better able to further economic development than a centrally directed system;
  - the industrialized countries should not misuse development policy and aid as instruments of intervention in the internal affairs of Third World countries;
  - developing countries and international organizations should not attach conditions to development aid which contravene the political principles of the donor countries;
  - both the industrial and the developing countries have a vital long-term interest in effective development assistance.

- We also support development aid of a charitable nature. Because this type of contribution does not form part of our organization's mission, however, we make a clear distinction between it and our business activities.

A.   *Our Commitment*

On the basis of the position outlined above, the salient features of our activities in the Third World can be summed up thus:

1. With a view to the interests of both parties, we act in partnership with the developing countries (DCs) to advance their economic potential. We observe fully the rights and duties growing out of such a partnership.
2. In making business decisions on the Third World (e.g., on products, services, technologies, investments), in addition to economic criteria we take into account the impact on the development of the host country. If a project shows a particularly strong impact, we are—considering the specific situation of the country—prepared to extend our short-range profit objectives.

EXHIBIT 1 *(concluded)*

---

3. If a DC adopts measures to protect its economy, such as import restrictions, export obligations, conditions for ownership, etc., we keep up the cooperation as long as partnership and adequate returns are not jeopardized in the long term.

4. We consider it our duty to advise our partner against undertakings if we are not convinced of their benefit for the partner (e.g., prestige projects), even if such a move proves detrimental to our short-term economic interest.

5. In the DCs we follow progressive social and personnel policies adapted to the local conditions. In particular we
   — offer employees and workers training in many fields, if necessary abroad;
   — make it possible for capable staff members to acquire international experience within our group;
   — consider nationals in filling executive positions.

6. Convinced that in the long run the pursuit of the above principles is a necessity, we shall not be discouraged by unavoidable short-term setbacks and disappointments.

B. *Philanthropic Aid*

In addition to carrying on business activities, in certain cases we also extend philanthropic support. This charitable aid is channeled through the "Ciba-Geigy Foundation for Cooperation with Developing Countries" and takes the form of:
— financial contributions;
— experts delegated to serve on development projects sponsored by the Swiss government, national and international development aid organizations, and the Ciba-Geigy Foundation itself;
— our organization's infrastructure. This assistance, made available for development aid projects, is intended to benefit particularly the poorest of the Third World.

C. *Our Public Information Policy*

We inform our employees, shareholders, the general public, governments, and international organizations fully and frankly about our Third World policy. When we can report success, we shall do so; but if setbacks occur, they will not be concealed.

Source: *Ciba-Geigy and the Third World: Policy, Facts and Examples,* a public relations brochure produced by Ciba-Geigy, Basel, Switzerland.

---

ulation of 5 million. There were vast and increasing disparities between urban and rural incomes.

Nigeria's wealth was founded largely on oil, which accounted for 97 percent of Nigeria's exports and 80 percent of government revenues in 1982. However, real GDP and disposable incomes declined in 1981 and 1982, as a consequence of reduced oil demand and inflation. Political instability also contributed to economic uncertainty. Despite the importance of oil, agriculture employed 52 percent of the labor force in 1981. A 1976 campaign, "Operation Feed the Nation," had realized some initial success. More recently, food production was barely keeping pace with population growth, as development projects were hampered by a weakening economy.

Nigeria's pharmaceutical market, having grown rapidly between 1976 and 1981, declined from N233 million ($380 million) in 1981 to N222 million ($330 million) in 1982, with a similar decline expected in 1983.[3] Around half the pharmaceutical market by value was supplied from local manufacture, though a part of this consisted merely of repackaging finished products imported in bulk. Around 20 percent of the market, institutional purchases were split 70:30 between ethicals and OTC consumer products. The private sector represented 80 percent of the market, split 80:20 between consumer and ethical products. Overall, 70 percent of the market comprised consumer products and 30 percent ethicals, so the Nigerian pharmaceutical market was characterized by heavy OTC supply.

Economic difficulties were leading to a decline in health care in Nigeria, with reduced levels of treatment and availability of drugs. Much of the rural population was not reached by the health-care network, though some popular OTC drugs were available in regions without doctors or state clinics. There were around 12,000 doctors (one for every 8,000 people); but, as they were concentrated in urban areas, the ratio was one doctor for every 50,000 people in rural areas. There were around 80,000 hospital beds (one for every 1,180 people). Nigerians suffered from high incidences of infectious disease and malaria; diarrheal diseases also were common. Distribution in Nigeria generally was highly decentralized and unsophisticated, but effective. Drugs were distributed through:

- Registered pharmacies (around 800).

- Registered patent medicine stores (15,000).

- Unregistered patent medicine stalls (10,000).

- General retail outlets also carrying OTC drugs.

- Itinerant street hawkers.

- Marketplace traders.

- Dispensing doctors (serviced by pharmacies with wholesale operations).

- Institutional outlets.

Drugs could pass through many hands before reaching the final consumer, who often purchased only a single tablet from the lowest link in the distribution chain. Patent medicine stores, little more than market stalls, were responsible for a large proportion of OTC sales. The geographical distribution of sales reflected population density and income levels; most sales were in Lagos (40

---

[3] One naira (N) = $1.485 in 1982, N1 = $1.382 in 1983 (average exchange rate). The naira was believed to be overvalued.

percent) and the east (30 percent), with 16 percent in the west and only 14 percent in the north, where half of Nigeria's population lived. There was no national pharmaceutical distribution organization. Rapid growth of the Nigerian drug market had attracted most of the major multinational pharmaceutical companies, especially in the supply of OTC products.

Ciba-Geigy and its predecessor companies had been in Nigeria since the 1950s. The Swiss Nigerian Chemical Company (SNCC) was 40 percent owned by Ciba-Geigy, with 60 percent owned by Nigerian investors, in keeping with Nigerian local ownership laws. It comprised five divisions: Ilford, Agricultural, Dyestuffs, Plastics and Additives, and Pharmaceuticals. SNCC sales in 1982 were N18.3 million ($27.2 million), of which Pharma Nigeria contributed 35 percent; net profits were N562,000 ($835,000). Pharma Nigeria employed around 100 people and was managed by Mr. Nwankwo, a Nigerian national.

Pharma Nigeria was divided into three business areas, with a marketing manager for each: ethical products; proprietary, nonprescription OTC products; and Servipharm. Ethical products had been Pharma Nigeria's main business; it had only entered the self-medication OTC market in 1983. Rapid expansion of this business area was planned under the new marketing manager, Mr. Okunmuyide, who had just joined the company after completing an MBA at Lagos University and five years as a product manager with Lever Brothers Nigeria, Ltd. Prospects in the self-medication market were particularly good at this time, because of:

- The underfunded and ill-equipped secondary and tertiary levels of the health-care delivery system.

- The need of individuals to maintain good health through the prevention and treatment of simple ailments, so they would not develop into diseases which could not be treated in the handicapped referral centers.

- The lower pricing of self-medication products relative to prescription products.

- The national health-care strategy of primary health care, which was positively disposed towards self-medication.

- The large increase in patent medicine stores, especially in rural areas otherwise inadequately served by referral health centers.

Pharma Nigeria's self-medication OTC business plan, agreed in March 1983, provided for an initial product portfolio of branded cough and cold treatments, a treatment to prevent itching, an analgesic, and an antimalarial.

MALARIA

Malaria was the deadliest of all the tropical diseases of parasitic origin. There were about 150 million cases a year worldwide, 1 percent proving fatal, and a further 600 million people were exposed to the risk of contracting malaria.

In Nigeria, in 1983, malaria was the major cause of morbidity, at 1,393 cases per 100,000 people, five times that of dysentery. It killed around 100,000 people annually. A major priority for Nigeria's primary health-care strategy was to provide increased access to treatment for malaria victims, particularly in rural areas and the urban slums.

Malaria was transmitted by about 10 percent of anopheles mosquitos. Two types of malaria were found. Malignant Malaria was an acute form that often proved fatal within a few days, especially in children. Over 1 million children died every year in Africa from this type. Tertian and Quartan Malaria was a milder and seldom fatal type, to which patients often developed a relative immunity after repeated infection.

Insecticides, such as DDT, could kill the anopheles mosquito but at the risk of contaminating the food chain. Mosquitos were less common in cities, especially in air-conditioned buildings. However, they bred easily in swamps in rural areas and in the pools of dirty water often found in shanty towns. Poor people were more frequently afflicted. But exposure to mosquitos could only be reduced, not entirely avoided. So for local people and visitors in affected areas, medical treatment often was necessary.

Chloroquine, in generic or branded forms, had been used to treat malaria for over 50 years. Prophylactic use was recommended for the 20 million or so (worldwide) visitors travelling annually to malarious areas. Chloroquine was only available by prescription in the West. It was no longer recommended for long-term prophylaxis, as use over a number of years had been linked to damage to the retina. Chloroquine was, however, on the WHO essential drug list, and was one of 26 drugs that UNIDO (United Nations Industrial Development Organization) was encouraging to be manufactured as part of its technology transfer efforts in the third world. Total demand for chloroquine phosphate from national antimalaria programs was 520 tons in 1982, 286 tons (and rising) of which went to Africa. UNIDO reported that prices fell between 1979 and 1983.

Early diagnosis and treatment of malarial infections was important. Malignant Malaria could be cured, with chloroquine sterilizing the host. Tertian and Quartan Malaria usually could only be suppressed, rather than cured, though if left untreated could be disabling and possibly fatal. Malaria relapses could occur up to 20 years after infection. It was not unusual for somebody to have three or more malaria attacks a year as a consequence of a new infection or relapse. Accurate figures on the incidence (number of new infections within a given time) and prevalence (percent of population infected) were not available.

Malaria strains resistant to chloroquine were emerging, partly because of its prophylactic use. Higher doses could overcome resistant strains. However, chloroquine's high toxicity (producing cardiac arrest) meant caution was required in using higher doses, as the margin of safety between therapeutic and toxic doses of chloroquine was very narrow, particularly in children.[4] Other

---

[4] In West Germany, child-proof packaging regulations were extended in 1982 to include chlor-

antimalarials were available, particularly multidrug combinations, which acted on resistant strains. However, they were often more expensive, with more side effects, and resistance to these alternative antimalarials also was emerging.

In the longer term, it was hoped that a vaccine against malaria would be developed. The highest annual expenditure on research and development against tropical disease by European pharmaceutical companies was on malaria, $8.1 million in 1982 out of $31.5 million. The Nigerian government's antimalaria campaign, announced in 1983 with a budget of N20 million ($29 million), was making available to each state 1.5 million chloroquine tablets (20 million in total), 1,000 liters of chloroquine syrup, and the multidrug antimalarial brand Fansidar (100,000 tablets for each state), which acted on strains resistant to chloroquine.

FEVEX

Self-medication against malaria was used extensively in the third world, though, as in Nigeria, often accompanied by warnings from health authorities about the dangers of overdose. Antimalarials were widely available as OTC products. Typically, a local Nigerian would go to a pharmacy and explain that he or she had "malaria" or "fever." The pharmacist would carry around half a dozen different brands, one or more of which the customer might know and specify. A full treatment of a pack of 10 tablets would be bought, which would bring the malarial attack to an end. It was not uncommon, however, for poorer people to buy tablets loose and in smaller quantities, according to what had worked before and what they could afford at the time. Occasionally, doctors would provide less than complete treatments at an initial visit so as to charge additional amounts for return visits. However, an incomplete treatment resulted in reduced efficacy in subsequent treatments. Free medication was available from state hospitals and other facilities; but they were usually overworked, unable to provide quick attention, and often did not have enough drugs. Some 40 to 50 percent of malarial victims in Nigeria went untreated, with kidney and liver damage as a minimum consequence. As an alternative, they might use local herbs, such as "Dogonyaro" leaves, of doubtful efficacy.

The management committee of Pharma Nigeria had proposed the launch of an antimalarial, branded as Fevex, to augment the new OTC product line. Okunmuyide had explained to the marketing manager responsible for self-

---

oquine (and 30-odd other substances) following a considerable fall in child poisoning cases after earlier regulations governing analgesics. Three percent of measures taken in children's hospitals resulted from poisoning. Acceptable pack types were those with push-through and sealed strip packs and containers with safety closures. Arguments in respect of packaging-change difficulties, stability testing in the new packs, low quantity sold, the protection of prescription-only status, or the difficulties the elderly may find, as reasons for noncompliance, were not accepted by the authorities.

medication products in Basel that the aim was "to become a key player in the antimalarial self-medication market." This was the fourth-largest segment of the self-medication market, after anti-infectives, analgesics, and vitamins. The proposed product was 250 mg. capsulated chloroquine phosphate. Capsule-presented drugs were highly regarded in Nigeria, to the point of having magical connotations in some areas, because of the relatively recent and dramatic impact of capsulated antibiotics.

Fevex faced considerable competition, with 50 brands in the N10 million market (5 million packs of 10 tablets in 1982). May and Baker's Nivaquine was the market leader, with a market share estimated at 21 percent, closely followed by Roche's Fansidar at 20 percent. Generic chloroquine phosphate, supplied to the institutional market, represented a further 20 percent. Other brands from companies, such as Bayer (Resochin), Glaxo (Paraquine), and Wellcome (Daraprim), each had 7 percent or less. Product formulation differences were essentially between chloroquine-based products and those containing sulfadoxine with pyrimethamine, such as Fansidar. Some chloroquine-based products included paracetamol to provide pain relief, such as Glaxo's Paraquine, which had a 2 percent market share. The pyrimethamine products acted against chloroquine-resistant strains of malaria; but, because of adverse reactions, were expected to be restricted to these cases only. Hence, the preference for chloroquine in Fevex.

Servipharm sales of chloroquine, branded as Serviquin, were made only to the generic institutional market segment and were 993,000 tablets in 1980; 18,600,000 in 1981; and 6,410,000 in 1982. Serviquin sales in 1983 were expected to be only 30,000 tablets.

Another difference between brands was whether they were marketed for curative or prophylactic use, though chloroquine was appropriate for either purpose. Most brands were marketed as curatives, in keeping with product usage by Nigerians. A more important distinction was between bitter and tasteless tablet brands; 80 percent had the bitter (plain) taste. Some tasteless tablet brands had been introduced but with little impact, as the film coating was inadequate to mask the bitter taste of chloroquine. An important consequence of chloroquine's galling effect was postponement or habituated partial treatment of malaria. Postponement entailed additional risk and the possibility of hospitalization. Incomplete treatment reduced the efficacy of subsequent treatments as a cumulative resistance was built up within the body. Many consumers would stop treatment after the first initial dose of four tablets. Some would hide the tablets in locally prepared food, such as Eba, Amala, or pounded yam; others would try and obtain injections of the vial form. Fevex's differentiation, and hence Okunmuyide's ambitious goal, came from overcoming this problem of chloroquine's bitter taste by using capsules. Fevex's success, however, also would depend on pricing, promotion, and distribution factors.

An added advantage of the capsule form was that it would permit local manufacture, using currently underutilized capsule-filling plants, raising utilization from 20 percent to 60 percent. It was also believed to be of strategic importance to increase local manufacturing. Pharma Nigeria was likely to request permission to export Fevex, once it was established in Nigeria.

Market research was planned to confirm pricing and promotion. However, with Fevex targeting the leading brands and the prospect of me-too launches of capsulated chloroquine by competitors, an aggressive market entry was envisaged. Nivaquine had been continuously and heavily promoted; Pharma Nigeria intended the same and more for Fevex. Marketing support amounting to 30 percent of sales was intended for the launch year, a third of which would be spent on media advertising. Television and radio advertising in English and in four local languages was proposed—a new approach for Nigerian pharmaceuticals. The first-tier sales force of five sales representatives was to be expanded and would be supported by a second-tier sales force of commission-only sales representatives; both sales forces would receive bonuses for sales above a platform target. Branded T-shirts, caps, and pens were included among the proposed promotional materials.

THE BASEL DECISION

Ciba-Geigy management in Basel was concerned about the risk involved in promoting self-medication products that depended on self-diagnosis; the responsibility—and liability—of the company was increased when a doctor was not involved. This was but one consideration for the PHI management committee reviewing the Fevex proposal. The committee had to decide whether the product would meet the needs of the patient, as well as the commercial and sociopolitical factors bearing on its success. The PHI also received input from the PEA, a Ciba-Geigy committee of detached scientists, which had to validate a drug's efficacy in the form proposed and would not sanction the launch of a drug if it did not meet the clinical and technical criteria. While clinical tests would be needed to satisfy the PEA, the PHI management committee was confident that Fevex would meet these requirements. To put it simply, the product would work from a purely technical standpoint. It was, after all, merely chloroquine in a capsule.

The management committee's "duty of care" responsibility extended beyond an acceptance of the PEA's assessment of the drug's technical performance. Would the product work and be safe in the Nigerian marketplace? Moreover, would it be profitable? If anything went wrong, what might the consequences be for Ciba-Geigy? Could such heavy promotion be defended in a third-world context? These were troubling questions for the PHI management committee when considered alongside recent criticism of the pharmaceutical industry.

McDonald's and the Environment

Society has an impression on business, as it darn well should. And business better start paying attention to society.

Shelby Yastrow, *Senior Vice President for Environmental Affairs, McDonald's Corporation*[1]

It's time to turn the golden arches green.

Fred Krupp, *Executive Director, Environmental Defense Fund (EDF), McDonald's/EDF Joint Press Conference, August 1, 1990*

This is the most flexible company on the face of the earth. We do what feels good, and if something feels different tomorrow, we'll do that.

Ed Rensi, *COO, McDonald's Corporation.*[2]

In November 1989, the McDonald's Corporation initiated a plan to recycle the polystyrene foam "clam-shell" packaging for Big Macs and other sandwiches served in its 450 New England restaurants. In early October 1990, McDonald's expanded its recycling program to Los Angeles, garnering endorsements from Mayor Bradley and other local politicians. Later that month, the company was on the verge of implementing its plastic recycling nationwide. But the Environmental Defense Fund (EDF), a nonprofit environmental lobbying group, balked. McDonald's had formed a joint task force with EDF on August 1, 1990, to study ways for the company to improve waste management. When EDF learned of the company's plan, it refused to endorse it. Edward Rensi, COO and president of McDonald's USA, called a meeting of McDonald's executives, including Shelby Yastrow, senior vice president for environmental

---

This case was prepared by Sharon Livesey, Lecturer in Communication, Harvard Business School. Copyright © 1991 by the President and Fellows of Harvard College.
Harvard Business School case N9-391-108 (Rev. 11/18/91).

[1] "The Greening of McDonald's," *Restaurant and Institutions* (hereinafter *R & I*) 100 (December 26, 1990), p. 42.

[2] Interview in "McDonald's: Company of the Quarter Century" (hereinafter "Quarter Century"), *R & I* 99 no. 18 (July 10, 1989), p. 56.

affairs. Within days, the company did an "about face": instead of expanding the recycling program, the company promised it would begin to phase out its foam sandwich packaging at all of its U.S. restaurants within 60 days.[3]

For 15 years McDonald's had withstood criticism of its use of plastic packaging, taking a high profile in the environmental debate. The company publicized its pro-plastic position in brochures, pamphlets, and in-store fliers for customers and others, in its 1989 annual report, and in interviews with the press. "We use foam packaging for the same reasons that schools, hospitals, and other restaurants do. . . . It keeps our products hot, it keeps them fresh, it's portable, and it's a safe and sanitary way to serve our product," said Yastrow.[4] As late as October 1990, Rensi criticized the critics, arguing at a conference of fast-food executives, for example, as follows: "We cannot allow ourselves to be held hostage to self-appointed saviors who are just trying to scare the American public."[5] Now the company was changing direction. Abandoning the plastic clamshells, however, meant the continued public support of EDF and its executive director Fred Krupp, who called the decision an "environmental touchdown."[6]

On October 31, 1990, word leaked out from McDonald's public relations agency, Golin Harris, that the company "plan[ned] a major news announcement [the next day] regarding the environment."[7] The rumors would produce a crush of reporters at company headquarters in Oak Brook, Illinois. The company had to decide how to announce its decision to the public and what other actions it might need to consider.

CONTEXT: BALANCING ENVIRONMENTAL AND CONSUMER CONCERNS

Environmental awareness was on the rise in America by the end of the 1980s. In the two years between 1988 and 1990, organizations such as Greenpeace and the World Wildlife Fund had sharply increased membership[8] (see Exhibit 1). A May 1989 Gallup poll showed that 75 percent of respondents considered themselves environmentalists.[9] Cambridge Reports, a Massachusetts-based

---

[3] See "McDonald's Expected to Drop Plastic Burger Box," *New York Times* (hereinafter *NYT*), November 1, 1990, p. A1; "McDonald's to Drop Plastic Foam Boxes in Favor of High-Tech Paper Packaging," *The Wall Street Journal* (hereinafter *WSJ*), November 2, 1990, p. A3; "McDonald's to Banish Foam Boxes," *Boston Globe* (hereinafter *BG*), November 2, 1990, p. 1.

[4] "McDonald's Is Urged to Alter Packaging," *NYT*, November 11, 1987, p. B2.

[5] "McDonald's Flip Flops Again and Ditches Its Clamshell," *Adweek*, November 5, 1990, p. 4.

[6] McDonald's press release, November 1, 1990.

[7] "McDonald's Expected to Drop Plastic Burger Box," *NYT*, p. A1.

[8] For example, Greenpeace and WWF grew by 50 percent and 100 percent, respectively. "The Greening of McDonald's," p. 28.

[9] Ibid.

EXHIBIT 1   Big U.S. Environmental Groups, 1989

Organization *(date founded)*	*Members* *(000s)*	*Budget* *($ millions)*
National Wildlife Federation (1936)	5,800	$85.3
National Audubon Society (1905)	550	35.0
Sierra Club (1892)	500	32.0
World Wildlife Fund (1961)	312	1.4
Wilderness Society (1935)	300	20.0
Natural Resources Defense Council (1970)	125	16.0
Environmental Defense Fund (1967)	100	15.0
National Parks and Conservation Association (1919)	95	3.8
Izaak Walton League (1922)	50	1.6
Friends of the Earth (1969)	30	2.5

Source: Burson-Marsteller.

---

company, estimated that 14 percent of Americans were "active in green organizations."[10] Publications as diverse as *Restaurant and Institutions, Fortune,* and *The Economist* were warning that corporations ignored at their peril the growing clout of these groups.[11]

Further, while marketers did not agree whether, or how, consumer beliefs would be translated into action,[12] by 1989 and 1990 some pollsters got results which showed that between one third and three quarters of consumers had made, or would make, purchasing decisions in favor of products showing an environmental advantage. In 1990, for example, Abt Associates, a Cambridge, Massachusetts, consulting company performed a study which showed that 90 percent of consumers said they would pay more for environmentally sound product, and 50 percent could cite actual purchases.[13] But some disagreed.

---

[10] "Seeing the Green Light," *The Economist,* October 20, 1990, p. 88.

[11] See ibid.; "Environmentalism: The New Crusade," *Fortune,* February 12, 1990, pp. 44–51; and "Waste Crisis," *R & I* 98, no. 20 (August 19, 1988), pp. 39–57.

[12] See "Coping with a Complicated Environment," *Progressive Grocer,* May 1991, pp. 73–80.

[13] Study cited in "Ecologists Wooed McDonald's Quietly," *Los Angeles Times,* November 9, 1990, p. D1.

Other surveys produced similar results:

In a June 1990 poll by Gerstman & Meyer, a package design company, 75 percent of respondents indicated that they would pay as much as 5 percent more for products with an environmental advantage. Study cited in: " 'Recyclable' Claims Are Debated," *NYT,* January 8, 1991, p. D5.

McDonald's Yastrow said he was convinced that most Americans did not really want to give up their plastic lifestyles: "Look at what people are doing, not what they're saying. . . . Most people who march in front of our restaurants still put their children in disposable diapers. Or they picket us, then go inside and order a sandwich."[14] Moreover, "green advertising" entailed risks; broad and misleading claims by manufacturers were promoting increased consumer cynicism and confusion.[15] Attorneys general from 10 states, backed by environmentalists, were pushing for stringent labeling and advertising guidelines.

The "greening" of America thus seemed to put McDonald's, the rest of the fast-food industry, and other users of plastic packaging, increasingly under fire. In fliers distributed by volunteers door to door, Greenpeace, for example, argued: "Industry is pushing disposability because it pays. . . . In 1989, the United States used over 12 billion pounds of plastic for packaging designed to be thrown away as soon as the package is opened. In the 1990s, this figure is expected to nearly double."[16] A 1990 survey by packaging designers Gerstman & Meyer indicated that 60 percent of respondents believed that plastic packaging was the biggest contributor to solid waste disposal problems.[17]

In fact, of the 1 billion pounds per year used in various plastic foam food-packaging applications in the United States, what ended up in the dump as plastic waste from *fast-food uses* constituted only a fraction of 1 percent of total solid waste, according to studies cited by McDonald's.[18] (See also Exhibit 2.) Further, plastic waste of all types constituted only 8 percent by weight of total municipal solid waste, much less than paper (see Exhibit 3).[19] Nevertheless, fast food had come to symbolize the "throwaway society"—convenience

---

The Michael Peters Group, another package design firm, had similar findings: 78 percent of respondents said they would pay more for a product made of recycled or biodegradable materials; 53 percent had not bought a product because of environmental concerns. Study cited in: "Some Smog in Pledges to Help Environment," *NYT*, April 19, 1990, p. D6.

A 1990 telephone survey of 400 consumers in four midwestern states conducted by Valentine-Radford, Inc., a Kansas City, Missouri, ad agency, showed that 36 percent would "very likely" change to a packaged food brand using a recycled container, while another 42 percent would be "likely" to switch. Seventy-one percent of those surveyed said they would spend 5–10 percent extra for such products. Study cited in: "There's Gold in That Garbage!," *Business Marketing*, November 1990, p. 24.

[14] "For Consumers, Ecology Comes Second: Marketers Offer New Packaging, but Buyers Balk," *WSJ*, August 23, 1989, p. B1.

[15] Environmental Research Associates found that nearly half of 1,000 adults surveyed in 1990 saw environmental claims as "mere gimmickry." Poll cited in: "Creating a 'Green' Ad Campaign Risks Making Consumers See Red," *WSJ*, December 5, 1990, Sec. B, p. 80.

[16] *Greenpeace Action*, "Plastics: An Environmental menace."

[17] Study cited in "Lever to Use More Recycled Plastics," *NYT*, August 10, 1990, p. D3.

[18] McDonald's annual report, p. 10. "All polystyrene foam *and paper packaging* used by all quick service restaurants equals only one quarter of 1 percent (¼ of 1%) of what's in a sanitary landfill [emphasis added]," said McDonald's. "Packaging: The Facts," copyright 1990 McDonald's Corporation, p. 10.

[19] Cf. Greenpeace statistics showed that plastic comprised 7 percent by weight but 20 percent by volume of municipal solid waste. "Plastic: An Environmental Menace."

EXHIBIT 2 Waste Crisis

Fast-Food Waste

Although foodservice generates only 2% of the nation's waste stream, highly visible packaging logos make the industry an easy target for recycling legislation. Following is *R&I*'s estimate of fast-food waste by product category:

Kitchen Waste = 30%		*Dining Room Waste = 70%*	
Cardboard boxes	50%	Sandwich containers	40%
Food waste	25%	Cups	35%
Plastic wraps, bags	15%	Plates, utensils	15%
Tin cans	5%	Bags, napkins	10%
Miscellaneous	5%		

Source: *Restaurant and Institutions.*

EXHIBIT 3 Thrown Away

Breakdown of the nation's garbage, in percent. Total in 1988: 180 million tons (latest available).

Paper and paperboard	40.0%
Food and yard waste	25.0
Metals	8.5
Plastics	8.0
Glass	7.0
Other	11.5

Source: Environmental Protection Agency.

---

and economy at an unacceptable environmental cost. In the words of one critic: "The earth does not deserve that burden for the sake of hamburger wrappers."[20]

As the fast-food giant, McDonald's garnered the lion's share of the criticism. Its familiar pastel polystyrofoam boxes used for Big Macs, Quarter Pounders, Egg McMuffins, breakfast pancakes, McChicken Sandwiches, and Chicken McNuggets also had made it one of the largest single users of polystyrene in the United States (about 80 million pounds per year).[21] Its actions were likely to have repercussions for the entire $2.5 billion polystyrene business.[22]

---

[20] "McDonald's Plastic Recycling Plan," *NYT*, November 27, 1989, p. D1.
[21] "Greening of the Golden Arch," *NYT*, November 7, 1989, p. A30.
[22] See "A Setback for Polystyrene," *NYT*, November 18, 1990, sec. 3, p. 14.

McDONALD'S: THE COMPANY[23]

History

McDonald's was the only restaurant business ranked with the Dow 30 Industrials. Like Disney and Coca-Cola, it dominated its industry, the $25 billion fast-food hamburger world. By 1989, the company and its franchisees employed 500,000 people, served 22 million customers per day, including roughly 8 million children, and generated sales over $17 billion. Of the 11,000-plus McDonald's restaurants worldwide, 25 percent were company-owned stores. The franchises were run by about 2,700 local operators, who typically operated three restaurants each. In 1989 alone, the company opened 600 restaurants, or one new restaurant every 15 hours.

At the end of the 1980s, however, competitive conditions in the domestic fast-food business toughened. Chicken, salads, pizza, and tacos had gained a growing place in the national fast-food palate. Market saturation and increased competition had led the hamburger houses to such strategies as discounting and menu expansion, both of which could cut heavily into margins and the bottom line. By 1990, McDonald's financial reports, although still showing consecutive double-digit profit increases, came under criticism; some analysts complained that "the quality of the earnings was terrible" because profits were based not on hamburgers but on international growth, real estate earnings (from restaurants rented or sold to franchisees), and new restaurant openings.[24] Growth in per-store sales in the U.S. operations had remained flat to negative since 1988.[25]

Ray Kroc's Success Formula: Q.S.C. & V.

Ray Kroc, McDonald's founder, had set out in 1955 with "an intense commitment to hamburgers" and a simple idea: He believed that families of Main Street America wanted Quality, Service, Cleanliness, and Value. This formula became the basis for his assembly-line cooking and fast-food concept.

The Q.S.C. & V. operating principles were instilled in managers and crew members (employees) through constant education, including videotaped messages from Ray Kroc himself, a feature of the training programs at Hamburger University at the company's Oak Brook, Illinois, headquarters. Restaurants were regularly graded on the minutiae of service: ketchup unevenly spread on

---

[23] Information in this section derives largely from "Quarter Century" *R & I* 99, nos. 18 & 22 (July 10, 1989 and August 21, 1989) and from McDonald's 1989 annual report.

[24] "Golden No More: Why McDonald's has hit a midlife crisis," *Financial World*, August 21, 1990, pp. 31–33.

[25] "An American Icon Wrestles with a Troubled Future," *NYT*, May 12, 1991, sec. 3, p. 1.

a bun was reported to have helped to earn one manager a "B."[26] Employees' obsessive concern for detail was rewarded (e.g., the "thumbless burger"—a way to fold burgers in paper without leaving a thumbprint on the bun—was called a "breakthrough" and videotaped for training managers).[27] And, to make sure executives did not lose touch with the kitchen, Kroc mandated that everyone from CEO Quinlan on down cook and clean in the restaurants on "Founders Day," a tradition still followed today in homage to Kroc.[28]

The Management Culture: The McDonald's "Family"

Strict on quality and procedural specifications, Quinlan nevertheless described the company's management style as "tight-loose."[29] The company encouraged entrepreneurship and a bottom-up approach. "Everybody at McDonald's is a president and has big responsibilities," COO Rensi said.[30] Important decisions were not the product of any one person or event. "Ray Kroc used to say that none of us is as good as all of us, and that's so true."[31]

Restaurant employees included youngsters, who worked part-time after school, young adults, and, more recently, retirees seeking to supplement their incomes with part-time work. The company also employed special groups, such as developmentally disabled individuals. The company was run through a structure of regional advisory boards to which franchisees and managers from company restaurants were elected. The 35 regional boards were, among other things, forums for sharing information and solutions to problems. McDonald's also communicated to company employees through *Crew* magazine (issued six times a year), and surveyed the stores at least once a year.

The basis of the business relationships in the McDonald's system was described as "a system of mutual risk and reward that leads independent suppliers, restaurant operators and the McDonald's corporation to work together for the good of the entire system."[32] "We develop relationships with people, not with corporations," said one McDonald's representative.[33] Franchisees, company employees, and suppliers, too, were viewed as integral parts of the McDonald's "family" where jurisdictional lines were not clearly drawn; trust and stability were at the heart of every relationship. Illustrative of this trust

---

[26] "Quarter Century," July 10, 1989, p. 38.

[27] "McDonald's Combines a Dead Man's Advice with Lively Strategy," *WSJ*, December 18, 1987, p. 1.

[28] Ibid., p. 12.

[29] Final Report of the Joint McDonald's/EDF Waste Reduction Task Force (hereinafter, Task Force Report), p. 17.

[30] "Lifelong 'Cheerleader' for McDonald's Way," *NYT*, November 5, 1990, p. D4.

[31] "Quarter Century," July 10, 1989, p. 56.

[32] Task Force Report, p. 17.

[33] "Quarter Century," July 10, 1989, p. 52.

were the well-known but still surprising "handshake deals" with suppliers who since Kroc's first days had worked without written contracts.

The Restaurants

Design and layout of the restaurants were basically the same, although stores could vary in size: customer-service counters separated from the kitchens by the food bins, computerized registers simple enough to be operated by 14-year-olds, and standardized menus displayed on lighted boards that offered breakfast until 11:00 A.M., then switched to luncheon fare. The operating procedures, designed to provide a customer with an order within three minutes of entering the restaurant, consisted of simple steps, which nonetheless needed to be carefully coordinated.[34]

For customers who wished to eat on the premises, most restaurants provided booths or plastic tables and chairs. The food for customers eating at the restaurant came wrapped as it would for take-out, but was served on a reuseable plastic tray with a paper liner, instead of in a cardboard take-out box. Customers eating in the restaurant dumped their own garbage in bins with a tray-stacking area on top. Much of McDonald's trade was take-out. Business from restaurants with drive-through windows constituted about 40 percent of McDonald's total sales,[35] and food ordered over-the-counter was also taken away.[36]

The typical restaurant generated about 238 pounds of on-premises waste per day,[37] with the large majority deriving from behind-the-counter uses. Polystyrene accounted for about 7 percent of waste by weight.[38] Thirty percent of sales at domestic chains came wrapped in some form of polystyrene.[39] In 1990, McDonald's total disposal and hauling costs were estimated at $53 million per year and were projected to increase by as much as 20 percent in 1991.[40]

Corporate Image

The Ronald McDonald clown, the company's mascot, symbolized what the restaurant was all about: entertainment and fun. A billion dollars of corporate marketing and advertising provided the fuel for making a golden public image;

---

[34] Task Force Report, pp. 21–22.

[35] "Dead Man's Advice," *WSJ*, p. 12.

[36] See, Task Force Report, p. 22, which estimated take-out at restaurants with drive-through windows at 60–70 percent.

[37] Ibid., p. 31.

[38] Ibid., p. 85.

[39] "Greening of McDonald's," p. 33.

[40] Task Force Report, p. 4.

but also central to McDonald's public appeal was its positive, proactive relationship with the community. As McDonald's senior vice president of marketing said: "Giving back to the communities is smart business, and it's the right thing to do, considering they provide us with a living."[41] Paul D. Schrage, McDonald's chief market officer, added: "Twenty years ago, we decided we wanted an image beyond food, based on strong virtues. . . . It makes us dependable. . . ."[42]

McDonald's network of community outreach activities was enormous. Corporate giving focused on children and family, but also might include programs aimed at attracting minority business people to the McDonald's system. Central to corporate efforts were the Ronald McDonald Houses (lodging for families visiting critically ill children in hospitals) and the affiliated Ronald McDonald Children's Charities, which had received a total of $24 million in support by 1989.

McDonald's dominated many high-visibility national events. For example, it sponsored the May 1990 *Life Magazine* special issue on children (at a cost of $2 million in advertising expense alone) and the World's Largest Concert, a 1989 worldwide sing-along programmed on PBS. In addition, it agreed to distribute 1 million copies of "*Newsweek* on the Drug Crisis" through its high school program and its restaurants. At the local level, McDonald's and its franchisees sponsored amateur athletic competitions, donated food at local functions, and hired and supported, with scholarships, local youth. In addition, McDonald's promoted corporate contests and achievement awards, such as the Black History Makers of Tomorrow essay contest, the Literary Achievement Awards for Black Writers, and a design competition for architectural students.

But the company also had to contend with unfavorable publicity: complaints from consumer groups about cholesterol and fat in McDonald's hamburgers and fries; charges of deceptive advertising over McDonald's claims of nutritional fare; boycotts over restaurant hiring practices in inner-city Philadelphia, where crews were paid less than those hired at suburban stores; zoning battles over siting new restaurants; questions from women's groups about the lack of female executives at the top. Some critics questioned McDonald's "values": "McDonald's fairy tales teach children moral lessons and to eat french fries. I'm concerned about values being taught merely by choices of products," said Richard Peterson, a professor of sociology at Vanderbilt University.[43]

The company saw most criticism as coming with the territory. As one trade journal put it: "McDonald's bashing is fashionable among consumer advocates, competitors, and professional skeptics."[44] "McDonald's has fostered a culture in which we're all called to lead. And when you're a leader, you'll make de-

---

[41] "Quarter Century," August 21, 1989, p. 70.
[42] "Dead Man's Advice," *WSJ*, p. 12.
[43] Ibid.
[44] "Quarter Century," August 21, 1989, p. 4.

cisions that aren't unanimously popular. We know that," said Michael Roberts, McDonald's vice president of environmental affairs.[45] McDonald's often bucked industry trends and criticism, especially when it felt that Kroc's Q.S.C. & V. principles were at stake.

The company did not see its primary mission as solving the issues of the day and thus frequently did not join industry battles that it did not perceive as pertaining to it directly (e.g., minimum wage). "We prefer to be apolitical. . . . It's not productive to get embroiled in legislation," said the company. As Rensi said, "I can't solve nuclear war, but I can run a hell of a restaurant."[46] Also, McDonald's joined industry associations carefully. For example, it did not join the National Restaurant Association until 1985; and while other manufacturers, such as Procter & Gamble and Coca-Cola USA, joined Dow Chemical and other plastics producers to form the Council on Plastics and Packaging in the Environment (COPPE), McDonald's chose not to. The company had, however, joined other packaging groups and sent representatives to joint government, nonprofit, and industry groups, such as the Council of Northeast Governors (CONEG), which looked at regional solutions to solid waste.

Educating the Public on the Environment

McDonald's took both direct and indirect steps to educate its shareholders, customers, employees, and the general public about its pro-environmental stand. The company participated with a range of nonprofit groups in environmental projects aimed at children from elementary school on. Collaborators included such organizations as the World Wildlife Fund (WWF), the Smithsonian, Conservation International, and the Royal Botanical Gardens. With WWF, for instance, McDonald's produced "Wecology," a children's educational booklet. "Environmental Action Pack," a series of classroom activities, was produced jointly by McDonald's and the Field Museum of Natural History in Chicago. In addition, McDonald's participated along with many other companies in a videotape, "Partners for the Planet," developed for Earth Day 1990 by the Environmental Protection Agency's pollution prevention office.

McDonald's also used a variety of publications to communicate to its many audiences about its environmental policies and practices. A 10-page supplement to the 1989 annual report described the company's environmental policies and waste-management practices (see Exhibit 4). To some, the report itself looked "more like an Audubon Society brochure than a financial statement."[47] Printed on recycled paper, bound by a four-page fold-out cover photograph of the forests of the Pacific Northwest, dedicated to the environment, and spread

[45] "The Green Revolution: McDonald's," *Advertising Age* 62, no. 5 (January 29, 1991), p. 32.
[46] "Quarter Century," August 21, 1989, p. 46.
[47] "McDonald's: McLeader or McFollower?", *Los Angeles Times*, March 14, 1991, p. D2.

EXHIBIT 4   Extract from McDonald's 1989 Annual Report

Agenda: Planet Earth

"Dear Sir,
   Lake Ville Elementary School is learning about our natural resources. We encourage businesses to use recyclable materials. Saving resources can stop pollution. Our junk is filling in landfills. If we stop wasting resources, our land will be clean. If we don't stop, we won't have anything left. Please help."
   Dan Getty, 11, of Davison, Michigan, sent us this letter on November 29, 1989. It's one of many letters on environmental issues McDonald's receives from students just like Dan Getty.
   We are helping, Dan.
   It is encouraging that people of all ages are asking questions about our environment, and are willing to learn and educate themselves on the issues. It is also important that people are willing to do what is environmentally sound when the responsible courses of action become clear.
   This planet has sustained life for tens of millions of years because of the unique balance of the atmosphere, the sun, and our water and land. We thrive because the range of temperature has been just right . . . the chemical elements are balanced just right . . . and the complex renewal process of our ecological systems has worked just right.
   Now we are learning that attempts to sustain five billion inhabitants on this earth are affecting this delicate balance, this system that has worked "just right" in allowing the evolution of humanity.
   And even as we are beginning to understand these complex relationships which sustain us, we are having to accommodate some 275,000 additional people on the planet each day.
   We are not surprised that Dan Getty and his fellow students are writing to us about their concerns for the future.
   We share those concerns.
   You may have heard a simple philosophy on the environment which says that we do not inherit the land from our ancestors, we borrow it from our children.
   And as we enter the 1990s, poised upon the next century, we must ask ourselves how much are we borrowing from our children, and will we be able to pay them back?
   The more we learn from around the world about the complex challenges we face, the more determined each of us must be to work together in preserving and enhancing the environment we have borrowed from the next generation.
   Scientists warn us of the possibility of global warming—climatic changes that we could be creating as our modern societies release increased amounts of carbon dioxide, methane, and other elements into the atmosphere.
   We are told the ozone layer which protects us from the sun's ultraviolet rays is being depleted by chemical reactions, and experts point out seasonal "holes" which have begun to appear in the ozone layers over the North and South Poles.
   More than 40,000 square miles of rain forests are being razed every year. Biologists tell us we are losing untold thousands of species of plant and animal life in this process, which also threatens to create massive new deserts in the band around the equator.

EXHIBIT 4 *(continued)*

Pollution of our air and water continues to plague us, threatening the quality of our lives, particularly in rapidly-growing urban areas.

And we continue to generate growing amounts of solid waste, with increasingly fewer sites available for safe disposal.

As we all learn more, we begin to wonder when we will reach the point of no return . . . the point where it will be too late to reverse the effects of our environmental changes now in progress.

It's easy for each of us to claim we're not responsible for these complex forces. But then we have to ask, "Who is?" It's easy to assert we don't have all the answers right now. But then we have to ask, "Will we ever?"

Scientist and author James Lovelock, who pioneered the "Gaia" theory of earth as a single, self-sustaining organism, says that our survival as humans in this system is up to us.

"It's personal action that counts," says Lovelock. "Any biological activation starts with a single organism."

Petra Kelley, a Green Party member of the West German Parliament, puts it this way: "Taking responsibility for our personal behavior is the only thing in this world over which we have complete control."

And that is the essence of our response to Dan Getty and his generation when they urge, "Please help."

Each of us, knowing what we have at stake, must make a commitment to a course of action that will preserve and enhance the environment we hold in trust for future generations.

We would add one more thought, based upon a precept from the late Ray Kroc, the founder of McDonald's Corporation. When we faced an organizational challenge, Ray would always remind us, "None of us is as good as all of us."

We face no greater challenge than saving the resources of this earth for the future. None of us alone will be as good in meeting the challenge as all of us together.

You can count us in.

Time for Action!

As a responsible corporate citizen, McDonald's believes we have a continuing role to play in addressing and acting upon the environmental issues that face us today.

Our environmental commitment dates from our beginning, when Ray Kroc had crew people clean up all litter within a block of each restaurant.

In the 1970s, McDonald's commissioned a Stanford Research Institute study on how different packaging affects the environment. This led to our adoption of foam packaging as a sound environmental alternative. We've also significantly improved the energy efficiency of our operations.

In the 1980s, when others determined that fully halogenated chlorofluorocarbons could harm the ozone, we voluntarily directed our foam packaging suppliers to eliminate them from the manufacturing process. We have initiated recycling efforts, including those for polystyrene foam, corrugated paper, and paper products.

McDonald's has always been committed to responsible packaging. Our actions are ongoing, and represent a good start in our commitment to be a part of the solution. We offer this report in that spirit.

We are not experts on the environment. But we have learned a great deal about

EXHIBIT 4 *(continued)*

the environmental issues that affect us—solid waste management, resource conservation and recycling. We are sharing that information to foster a broader understanding of these issues, and to promote responsible action by individuals, public officials, and corporations which will preserve and enhance a safe and healthy environment.

It is truly time to act!

1. Solid Waste Management

Disposal of solid waste materials is a key environmental issue of the 1990s, complicated by the fact that there are really two crises when it comes to solid waste.

First, there is the very real shortage of landfill capacity in the U.S. The 18,500 landfill sites in the U.S. ten years ago have dwindled to about 6,000 today. By the mid-1990s, about one-half of those sites are expected to be closed.

And second, there is a crisis of misinformation that surrounds the entire solid waste issue: its composition and the questions of its biodegradability.

According to EPA studies, quick service restaurant waste is a very small part of landfill composition. Research indicates that of total U.S. solid waste sources, all plastic, paper, and foam restaurant packaging represents less than one-third of one percent of landfill composition, according to university studies. McDonald's contribution, of course, is even smaller. By using alternatives to plastic packaging, the weight of solid waste would be 404 percent greater and the volume 256 percent greater, according to a 1987 study by the German Society for Research into the Packaging Market. . . .

The question of biodegradable products in landfills represents another misperception. Pioneering studies by Dr. William Rathje of the University of Arizona have unearthed entire newspapers, generally considered to be biodegradable, virtually intact after 20 years. And on the subject of solid waste increases, Rathje goes on to state, "No, Americans are not suddenly producing more garbage. Per capita our record is, at worst, one of relative stability."

In fact, very little biodegradation occurs in the practical lifetime of a modern landfill, which is packed densely and covered with layers of compacted dirt. Efforts to develop biodegradable packaging will benefit the environment for materials which escape the waste stream, but they will not solve the landfill crisis.

Incineration can ease the pressure on landfills, and can be more of a factor as improved technology reduces air emissions, facilitates ash disposal, and screens toxic materials.

Four critical areas of action for solid waste management recommended by the Environmental Protection Agency are: 1) reducing the amount of waste we create, 2) recycling what can be remade or reused, 3) incineration, with waste-to-energy conversion when feasible, and 4) sanitary landfill disposal. The EPA's 1992 goals for waste disposal reflect this balanced approach.

	1988	*1992*
Landfill	80%	55%
Recycling	10%	25%
Incineration	10%	20%

EXHIBIT 4 *(continued)*

McDonald's believes that the most promising long-term solutions are using less packaging, widespread recycling, and public education on our environmental challenges and the need to reduce, reuse, and recycle. And we look forward to improvements in technology which will address those challenges.

2. Resource Conservation

In a finite world, the conservation of natural resources is an essential step in maintaining the balance of the environment.

By reducing our use of scarce materials and finding more environmentally responsible alternatives, we preserve resources for future generations. Resource conservation makes sense for business, industry, and individuals for both environmental and economical reasons.

The response to the energy crisis of the 1970s, for example, represents what can be achieved when the need is clearly understood.

Energy conservation by business, industry, and individuals; development of alternative energy sources; and efficient energy usage, including down-sized cars, have resulted in dramatically reduced energy consumption. Since 1973, total U.S. energy usage has decreased 2 percent while the population has grown 20 percent.

Renewable resources, such as trees, can be maintained through careful replenishment of stocks.

U.S. forest products companies plant more than 6 million trees each day on the nation's 730 million forested acres, according to the American Forest Council.

Worldwide, however, deforestation is a major issue because this sustainability is not being maintained. According to the World Wildlife Fund, 54 acres of tropical rain forest are lost every minute, or more than 28 million acres each year.

Resources can also be conserved by consumers, by finding innovative ways to use less, or developing alternative materials.

Polystyrene plastic packaging, for example, uses less energy in its production, conserves other resources, reduces both the weight and volume of resultant solid waste, and can be recycled.

McDonald's believes that yesterday's answers are no longer adequate for today's issues. We challenge ourselves and our suppliers to continue to look for ways to conserve resources.

3. Recycling

Recycling and reuse of materials is a fundamental part of most solutions to ease pressures on the environment.

Recycling materials for productive secondary use diverts them from the solid waste disposal stream. Developing multiple uses for existing materials reduces the need to consume additional natural resources.

And recycling saves energy—you can run your television for three hours with the energy saved by recycling one aluminum can.

Most importantly, recycling is a popular concept and something that everybody can do.

Polls show that 67 percent of the American public currently favors mandatory recycling programs in their communities, and 83 percent feel that recycling can result in a substantial reduction in solid waste.

More than 1,000 curbside recycling programs have been implemented in cities in

---

EXHIBIT 4 *(concluded)*

---

virtually all 50 states. Some cities already recycle more than 25 percent of certain materials which are collected through their municipal curbside separation and collection programs.

Growth of recycling will be encouraged by new technology, more plants and companies in the recycling infrastructure, and development of new markets for recycled materials.

Associations representing the steel, aluminum, paper, glass, foam and plastics industries have all established ambitious numerical goals for increased recycling efforts in the future. The Environmental Protection Agency's 1992 target for waste disposal for all recycling in the U.S. is 25 percent.

Major advances in plastics recycling technology have opened the door for recycled plastics to play an important role in new product manufacture.

McDonald's believes that fostering recycling is a critical link toward achieving many environmental solutions, and we're firmly committed to recycling at every opportunity.

Time to Help!

This report on environmental issues is only the beginning of the story.

No one, acting alone, is capable of solving all the challenges. But everyone, acting together, can ensure the quality of the environment in which we live.

As a responsible corporate citizen, McDonald's is committed to continuing our efforts toward reducing material usage, recycling, and public education.

Our operations may represent a small portion of the challenge, but our actions can be a large part of the solution. McDonald's continues to look for opportunities to work with individuals, public officials, and other companies, as well as with the communities we serve.

We invite you to join us, to take the steps which will guarantee our children a viable and healthy world, one which they can pass on to their children.

It is truly time to help!

Here are just a few sources of information which can help you discover more about what you can do to preserve our environment:

American Forest Council, 1250 Connecticut Avenue N.W., Washington, DC 20036; National Audubon Society, Box R—Science Division, 950 Third Avenue, New York, NY 10002; The American Paper Institute, 260 Madison Avenue, New York, NY 10016; The Council for Solid Waste Solutions, Office of Community Information, P.O. Box 27599, Washington, DC 20038-7599; Environmental Action Coalition, 235 East 49th Street, New York, NY 10017; Environmental Defense Fund—Recycling, 257 Park Avenue South, New York, NY 10010; Environmental Protection Agency, Public Affairs, 401 M Street, S.W., Washington, DC 20460; The Sierra Club, 730 Polk Street, San Francisco, CA 94109; Keep America Beautiful, 9 West Broad Street, Stamford, CT 06902; Rocky Mountain Institute, 1739 Snowmass Creek Road, Snowmass, CO 81654; World Wildlife Fund, Dept. A, 1250 24th Street, N.W., Washington, DC 20037.

For more information on McDonald's packaging, write for: "McDonald's Packaging: The Facts;" McDonald's Corporation, Director of Environmental Affairs, McDonald's Plaza, Oak Brook, IL 60521.

---

throughout with nature pictures, poetry, and quotations from prominent public figures, it was a high-profile statement that the environment was part of McDonald's "commitment" to shareholders and its other constituencies.

"Packaging: The Facts" presented arguments similar to those of the annual report but was more detailed. The booklet was presented to the reader as an opportunity for McDonald's to share "some eye-opening facts" that it had discovered in its study of how packaging affects the environment.[48] Of recycling specifically, the booklet said:

> Polystyrene plastic foam is 100 percent recyclable. Polystyrene foam is easily recycled. . . . [It] is being effectively recycled in various areas throughout the United States and overseas. . . .
>
> Substitutes for foam packaging are not recyclable. The principle substitute for foam packaging would be paper or paperboard products coated with plastic, wax, or other barriers. These materials are not recyclable, as they have to be re-separated into paper and plastic, a process which is not presently commercially feasible. . . . Experts stress the use of a single, nonlaminated, or coated packaging material (glass, aluminum, polystyrene, or paper) to facilitate recycling.
>
> Biodegradable plastic packaging is suggested by some to be an appropriate substitute. However, such packaging has not yet met Food and Drug Administration standards for food packaging, and most experts believe that in order to have sufficient strength the packaging would require significantly more amounts of plastic. Finally, once such packaging biodegraded, plastic bits and dust still would remain.[49]

McDonald's also argued that "[r]egardless of where people eat and how food is packaged, the environment is affected."[50] Citing the American Public Health Association's opinion "that reusable plates, cups, and utensils are less sanitary than disposable products," McDonald's said that "Plastic packaging has important health and safety advantages."[51] Next to a graphic of a barbecue, McDonald's made the final point that:

> Polystyrene foam packaging is safer and less expensive to incinerate than paper. . . . In a modern incinerator that is properly maintained and operated, polystyrene foam produces harmless, nontoxic ash (it's mostly air to begin with), carbon dioxide, and water vapor. Because it burns so efficiently, it even acts as a secondary fuel source, making the incinerator hotter and less expensive to run and actually creates a cleaner burning process. The hotter burning also creates more energy, where incineration is used for energy generation.[52]

In addition to these publications, McDonald's had fliers and brochures available in its restaurants on such topics as ozone, the rain forests, packaging, and various nutritional issues.

---

[48] "Packaging: The Facts," p. 4.
[49] Ibid., p. 7.
[50] Ibid., p. 14.
[51] Ibid., p. 12.
[52] Ibid., p. 15.

THE GARBAGE CRISIS: SHRINKING CAPACITY, HIGH COSTS

By the mid-1980s, increasing garbage and decreasing options for disposal meant that American cities and towns had to address the waste issue. Landfills, numbered at 18,500 sites in 1980, would be reduced to 3,000 by 1995. The problems were clear, but the solutions were politically messy and subject to change with changes in technology, public policy, and public opinion.

Opening landfills was difficult, because of issues of leaching and hazardous waste. Incineration, at one time a leading alternative to landfill, raised concerns about air quality and disposal of ash. Siting and building incinerators was proving to be highly expensive and was fraught with political fights and lawsuits.[53]

By 1990, many saw recycling as an attractive disposal option, but it required putting in place an infrastructure—methods of collection, sorting centers, and reprocessing—and finding markets for the recycled material. By the end of 1990, more than 1,500 curbside recycling programs (of which 500 included plastic) in 35 states were in place. But the growing experience with recycling showed that collection and sorting methods often were cumbersome and expensive and could easily result in contamination that rendered the recycled material worthless. The technology was, in many cases, still primitive and often relied on manual labor, as well as educating and motivating people to separate their own garbage.[54] Recycling also required a sufficient, but not-too-great, supply of materials: too much material (as happened in the case of newspaper) would lead to a glut and drop in value of the recycled material and, hence, reduce the incentive to recycle; too little would mean that the recycling businesses could not meet necessary economies of scale and would not survive without subsidy from the industry.[55] While such cities as Seattle experienced success, more than meeting state-mandated goals, others, such as New York City, were threatening to delay or cancel programs.[56]

Over the long run, an integrated, long-term plan for waste was needed to ensure that various waste options did not work against each other; for example, an incineration plan could steal from materials that might otherwise be recycled. Deciding what should be done, who should pay for it, and on what basis required coordination and planning and agreement; it was not a simple task.

Local and State Response: 2,000 Pieces of Law

As dramatized by the "Mobro," Long Island's wandering garbage barge, local communities needed to act. Local legislation proliferated. From 1987 on, reg-

---

[53] See "Policies and Politics of Composting and Recycling," *BioCycle*, January 1989, p. 60.

[54] "As Recycling Becomes a Growth Industry, Its Paradoxes also Multiply" (hereinafter, "Recycling Paradoxes"), *NYT*, January 20, 1991, sec. 4, p. 6. See also, "Recycling: No Longer If, but How," *NYT*, March 31, 1991, p. 1.

[55] "Recycling Paradoxes," p. 6.

[56] "Confronting the Rising Cost of Recycling," *NYT*, November 13, 1990, p. 27.

ulators were reacting with "litter" taxes, deposits, and mandatory recycling for many disposable packaging materials. Some communities, along with environmental groups, also promoted educational programs aimed at "precycling"; that is, consumer selection of products that were environmentally benign.

Polystyrene became the focus of legislators. New York's Suffolk County was one of the first to take a strict approach, banning all plastic foam; Portland, Oregon, followed suit, but limited its ban to restaurants. Other cities, such as Berkeley, California, and Minneapolis, Minnesota, passed similar ordinances designed to discourage plastic packaging by restricting the use of materials that were not biodegradable, recyclable, or made from recycled materials. Seattle urged the state of Washington to pass a ban on nonrecyclables. During 1988 alone, 2,000 separate pieces of state and local legislation regulating solid waste had been passed or were pending in legislatures across the country. Three hundred addressed packaging issues; 206 concerned plastics, compared with only 11 which dealt with paper packaging.[57] Many of these laws directly affected restaurants in the fast-food business.

THE PLASTIC VERSUS PAPER DEBATE

Proponents of plastic used the basic arguments that McDonald's relied on in its literature: using foam "minimize[d] the number of trees cut down . . ."[58] and was environmentally superior to paper, according to "life-cycle studies" (the most recent of which was a study performed by environmental consultants Franklin Associates, Ltd., for the plastics industry in June 1990).[59] A "life-cycle" analysis measured the environmental impact of a product on from "cradle to grave," or from production to disposal. Paper and paperboard currently used for food packaging were not, as some alleged, "biodegradable." In any event, if paper decomposed, toxins from the ink on the packaging would be released in the process. "It's not earth back to earth as we would all like to believe," said a plastics industry analyst.[60] Finally, it was argued that foam could be easily recycled, in contrast to paper alternatives. Even where the infrastructure was not yet in place to support recycling, the industry view was that telling customers that a product had the potential to be recycled would nevertheless have "education value."[61] But environmentalists and consumer advocates disagreed: "Just because a polystyrene container is labeled recyclable, it does not mean much if the nearest recycling plant is hundreds of miles

---

[57] "2,000 Solid Waste Bills," *BioCycle*, February 1989, p. 68.
[58] "McDonald's Packaging: The Facts," p. 5.
[59] "McDonald's Life-Cycle Analysis Measures Greenness, but Results May Not Be Black and White," *WSJ*, February 28, 1991, p. B1.
[60] "McDonald's Is Urged to Alter Packaging," p. B2.
[61] "Some Smog in Pledges to Help Environment," p. D.1.

away."[62] "The earth does not benefit from symbolic gestures," the environmentalists said.[63]

Waste management officials described polystyrene as "one of the most intractable and difficult materials to deal with in the solid waste stream," because it did not compress easily.[64] Even proponents of plastic agreed that foam's light weight "is the major obstacle to recycling. . . . [Curbside programs] are paid by the ton of material delivered, but polystyrene takes up space without adding much weight."[65] "[T]he cost of collection and processing exceed the value of the resin," conceded the executive of a Brooklyn plastic recycling plant.[66] Contamination was also a serious problem; recycled plastic contaminated by paper and food waste would yield low-quality plastic, unacceptable to potential customers such as Rubbermaid. Finally, the recycled polystyrene offered no economic incentive: "We actually realize little or no price differential in using these resins," said a Rubbermaid spokesperson.[67] In EDF's Krupp's words: "Thus far, polystyrene recycling is more a problem-ridden theory than a proven option."[68]

Further, if burned in incinerators, foam could produce toxic by-products. Even though it was conceded that paper mills produced pollution, the production process for foam was alleged to yield hazardous chemical emissions. Perhaps most important, the blowing process for producing most polystyrene foam gave off chlorofluorocarbons (CFCs), proven harmful to the earth's ozone layer. Paper was also preferable since it would be produced from trees, considered a renewable resource. Since plastic was an "open-loop recyclable"—plastic from a foam cup could not be used to make a new cup—its production would continue to deplete irreplaceable fossil fuels.

Finally, the value of life-cycle studies, on which the plastic industry in particular relied, was in dispute. Although attempts to provide a basis for comparing paper and plastic were in development, Dr. Allen Hershkowitz, a senior scientist at the Natural Resources Defense Council said: "Right now, it is impossible to make these kinds of decisions for 95 percent of the products out there."[69] A biologist at the Environmental Protection Agency agreed: "It is certainly a goal, and it can be done in the future. But to use what is being done now for policy making would be misleading."[70]

---

[62] Ibid.

[63] " 'Recyclable' Claims Are Debated," p. D1.

[64] "McDonald's Urged to Alter Packaging," p. B2.

[65] "A Setback for Polystyrene," sec. 3, p. 14.

[66] Ibid.

[67] "Disposing of Man's Indestructible Resin: Polystyrene," *Waste Alternatives*, September 1989, p. 41.

[68] "Setback," sec. 3., p. 14.

[69] "Life-Cycle Studies: Imperfect Science," *NYT*, September 22, 1990, p. A29.

[70] Ibid.

McDONALD'S RESPONSE

The debate over plastic foam made McDonald's particularly vulnerable to regulation and to public criticism. The company saw newspaper headlines faulting its foam packaging (e.g., "[New York Mayor] Koch Faults McDonald's Packaging"),[71] while competitor Burger King sometimes picked up windfall benefits for its paperboard wrapping, which was said by some to be "biodegradable." Faced with this patchwork of local restrictions and negative publicity, McDonald's needed to act.

1987: CFC Blown Styrofoam Discontinued

Throughout the 1980s, McDonald's had taken steps to reduce its packaging volume (see Exhibit 4). On August 5, 1987, it went further, agreeing to withdraw foam packaging made with CFCs from its domestic operations. "We have made this decision with the full recognition that McDonald's packaging represents only a minute portion of total CFC usage," said a company spokesperson.[72] The company switched to a foam blown with hydrocarbon-based agents.

McDonald's believed that it had thus reasonably demonstrated that it was prepared to react aggressively to community concerns. In late 1987, however, the New York State Consumer Protection Board requested McDonald's chairman, Fred L. Turner, to "discontinue styrofoam packaging and instead expand its use of paper products made from recycled materials."[73] Further, in 1988, Citizens Clearinghouse for Hazardous Waste (CCHW), coordinating with a network of local grass roots environmentalists, started a "McToxic Campaign," including pickets at McDonald's restaurants and a mail-in of used plastic boxes to McDonald's Oak Brook headquarters.

The company considered incineration as an alternative and tested trash-to-energy on-site incinerators in McDonald's parking lots, a program referred to as "McPuff" by CCHW. That move also met with local resistance, despite McDonald's reassurances that the emissions were mostly carbon dioxide and water vapor, "less offensive than a barbecue."[74] Notwithstanding technology that improved air emissions, facilitated ash disposal, and screened toxic materials, the public was not convinced. Protests continued. In June 1989, a schoolchildren's group, "Kids against Polystyrene," which urged a boycott of McDonald's, had a member picket the United Nations dressed as "Ronald McToxic"; and in October 1990, the Earth Action Network, a radical West

---

[71] *NYT*, December 30, 1987, p. B3.
[72] "McDonald's Containers," *NYT*, August 6, 1987, p. D22.
[73] "McDonald's Is Urged to Alter Packaging," *NYT*, November 11, 1987, p. B2.
[74] "For Consumers, Ecology Comes Second," *WSJ*, p. B1.

Coast group, broke windows in a protest action at a McDonald's San Francisco store.[75]

1989 and 1990: Recycling Introduced at the Restaurants

In October 1989, McDonald's implemented a plan to recycle polystyrene plastic and corrugated cardboard trash at its 450 restaurants in the New England region. Customers, already used to disposing of their own trash, would now separate the trash into two bins—plastic and waste. The corrugated paper waste—"backdoor" items—did not involve customers. The recycled plastic would be made into pellets, which could then be re-used for making a range of items from restaurant trays and flower pots to garbage pails and plastic "lumber." It would be handled by a recycling center in Leominster, Massachusetts, the first of five plants to be put into operation by the National Polystyrene Recycling company (a plastics industry joint venture). Posters and pamphlets in the restaurants explained McDonald's rationale for the program and described what customers needed to do.

"We have set a goal of recycling 25 percent of that billion [pounds of restaurant industry plastic waste] by 1995," said Kenneth Harman, chairman of National Polystyrene.[76] Blueprints for recycling plants in Los Angeles, San Francisco, Chicago, and Philadelphia were on the drawing board, but as of 1990 most had yet to be built.[77] According to Kathleen Meade, news editor of *Recycling Times*, the jury was still out on whether the plants "were just token efforts by the affected industries or if polystyrene [would] become a recyclable plastic."[78]

Yastrow said the New England program would "reduce trash, help educate youngsters about recycling and 'is a big step toward a better environment'."[79] "My intent," said Yastrow at the news conference announcing the New England program, "is to make this permanent."[80] Harman said that many issues remained to be resolved. For instance, restaurants would be able to join the program only upon expiration of existing hauling contracts, generally long-term deals. "[T]he economics of the recycling operations were still unclear, but would include a charge to restaurants."[81]

Environmentalists' reactions to McDonald's recycling program were mixed. Some were skeptical. "[U]ntil they have the infrastructure in place to handle

---

[75] "The Greening of McDonald's," p. 36.

[76] "McDonald's Plastic Recycling Plan," p. D1.

[77] "Polystyrene defenses were too little, too late," *Chicago Tribune*, November 12, 1990, p. 3. Some environmental groups were critical of industry delays on recycling; see, for example, "McDonald's Plastic Recycling Plan," *NYT*, p. D1.

[78] "Man's Indestructible Resin: Polystyrene," p. 36.

[79] "McDonald's Plans Limited Recycling of Plastic Items," *WSJ*, October 27, 1989, p. B2.

[80] "McDonald's Recycling Plan," p. D1.

[81] Ibid.

those packages wherever they are, it is still blue smoke and mirrors," said a representative of the New York-based Environmental Action Coalition.[82] Some viewed the program as "a small step," constituting as it did only 4 percent of the company's restaurants. Moreover, because of the take-out factor, some estimated that recycling would have no more than a 2 percent net effect.[83] But others were positive, including the New England acting regional director for the Environmental Protection Agency, who said he "hoped that other large companies would follow McDonald's lead."[84]

The most critical reaction viewed McDonald's recycling as merely "a public relations ploy."[85] Further, it overlooked the issue of pollutants generated in the production of polystyrene. Recycling "just serves to legitimize increasing the use of throwaway plastics. It would be far better for McDonald's to use durable goods [reusable plates and cups], instead of promoting the throwaway society," said a representative from Massachusetts Public Interest Research Group, an offshoot of Ralph Nader's consumer lobbying group.[86] To the surprise of company officials, a customer witnessing the press conference where the program was announced spontaneously uttered words to the same effect.

In 1990, McDonald's expanded the recycling program to a few cities outside New England. Further, in April 1990, specifically addressing the need to build markets for recycled goods, McDonald's announced "McRecycle"—a commitment of $100 million, or one fourth the corporate annual building and remodeling budget, to buying recycled materials for restaurant construction, remodeling, and operations. "We challenge suppliers to provide us with these recycled products,"[87] said Rensi, who introduced the program. Newspaper advertisements announced the program as "the largest single commitment in history by anyone to buy and use recycled material." "McRecycle" was generally applauded by environmentalists.

THE JOINT TASK FORCE ON THE ENVIRONMENT[88]

The Environmental Defense Fund was a group noted for taking corporations to court, not for conferring with them. It was founded on Long Island by a group of volunteer conservationists more than 20 years ago. Under the lead-

---

[82] Ibid.
[83] "Limited Recycling," p. B2.
[84] Ibid.
[85] "McCycling: Public Service or Private Interest?" *Waste Age*, January 1990, pp. 91–92.
[86] "Limited Recycling," p. B2.
[87] "The Green Revolution: McDonald's," p. 32.
[88] Information in this section was largely derived from McDonald's/EDF joint press release, August 1, 1990.

ership of its current director Fred Krupp,[89] the organization had more than tripled its membership to 200,000, quadrupled its staff to 125, and increased its budget more than five-fold from $3 million to $16.9 million in 1990. Scientists and economists constituted two thirds of its professional staff.

EDF first won fame in the 1960s, when it managed to halt the spraying of DDT. Other accomplishments included: promoting the recall of hair-dryers with asbestos insulators (1979); providing a study to establish the link between sulfur emissions and acid rain (1984); achieving passage of a law to reduce lead additives to gasoline by 90 percent (1985); and preparing an Acid Rain Reduction Plan, which was introduced by President Bush to bipartisan support and made law in 1990. Recently, EDF had engaged in a public service campaign with the Advertising Council to promote recycling and had worked with consortia of federal, state, local, industry, and environmental groups studying the problem of solid waste. An organizational goal was to help the United States achieve 50 percent recycling by the year 2000.

EDF first approached McDonald's in the summer of 1989, sending a letter to Quinlan to request a discussion of environmental issues related to solid waste. McDonald's became interested in exploring the opportunity after Yastrow appeared on a television program opposite Krupp. Ultimately, a series of meetings between McDonald's and EDF evolved. By early summer 1990, a proposal for a six-month joint task force study was on the table.

On August 1, McDonald's and EDF task force members issued a press release and held a joint press conference to announce their "landmark" decision to pursue the waste-management study and issue a public report in about six months. Membership on the task force would include Shelby Yastrow, the director for environmental affairs of Perseco, the exclusive packaging supplier that coordinated McDonald's packaging purchases from over 100 packaging suppliers, and a cross-functional group from inside McDonald's, including representatives from operations, environmental affairs, government relations, and corporate communications. From EDF, there would be Krupp and EDF staff scientists and economists. Options to be considered would include redesigned packaging and shipping materials that used less or lighter material; increased use of materials with gentler environmental impacts, such as unbleached paper; increased recycling and use of recyclable packaging and recycled materials; composting; and increased use of reusable shipping containers and foodware items in the restaurants. McDonald's committed to implementing the recommendations "where feasible." In the short term, it agreed to suspend indefinitely its research of on-site incineration of restaurant waste.

---

[89] EDF's Krupp was chairperson of the Recycling Advisory Council and served on the boards of numerous organizations and advisory committees, including: Green Seal, Inc.; The Keystone Center; Resources for the Future; the Connecticut Fund for the Environment; Earth Communications Office; Environmental Media Association in Los Angeles; and Governor Mario Cuomo's Environmental Advisory Board. Krupp was a proponent of "Third Wave Environmentalism," an approach to environmental protection based on using market forces to achieve desired goals.

The task force was held out as an example of a way in which business and an environmental group could work together for the public interest. Krupp praised McDonald's willingness to permit "an outside independent source [to] further examine its solid waste management practices with the aim of lessening environmental impacts." EDF senior scientist and task force member Richard Denison said: "McDonald's serves 22 million people every day. There's no doubt that it has the clout and ability to make this a meaningful study and to transform the recommendations into an impressive set of actions."[90]

McDonald's Yastrow said: "EDF struck a responsive chord when they proposed to work with us. . . . This is an entirely new process for us, and evidently for businesses in general. We're taking this leadership role hoping that we are going to find new ways to improve and to reduce solid waste from our operations. This is going to be a difficult process but we want it to work."[91]

The need for each side to preserve independence was also publicly acknowledged. Each organization would be responsible for its own expenses; EDF would receive no financial support from McDonald's. More fundamentally, the parties agreed to the right to disagree with each other or with the outcome of the study. If the parties disagreed, the report could contain separate statements written by each side.

On August 2, the national press immediately gave the partnership extensive coverage: "Big Mac Joins with Big Critic to Cut Trash" said *The Wall Street Journal* on the lead page of the business section. Front-page headlines in the *Boston Globe* announced: "McDonald's Bids to Clean Up Its Reputation" and were followed with an editorial, "McSense on the Environment," on August 10. The *Washington Post* headlined its story: "The Greening of McDonald's: Fast-Food Giant to Study Ways to Reduce Its Garbage." The *New York Times* short news story on August 2 was followed a week later with a longer story entitled, "Talking Deals: Unusual Alliance for McDonald's."[92]

In the *Boston Globe* article, Krupp was quoted as follows: "It's hard to take me seriously when I say I'd like McDonald's to be garbage free. My dream is getting McDonald's to compost most of their waste, and reduce the rest of it so they don't have any garbage." McDonald's Yastrow took the position that replacing disposable utensils was not feasible, especially with take-out operations.

The Wall Street Journal pointed out the advantages and risks of the relationship to both sides: "For McDonald's, getting the EDF's blessing could help mute critics who regard it as a symbol of the disposable society." But Yastrow was quoted as conceding that if the task force disagreed on issues, "that could be an embarrassment, if it isn't handled right." EDF, on the other hand, risked criticism from fellow environmentalists. The company's continued use of polystyrene packaging was certain to be a key issue.

---

[90] McDonald's/EDF press release, August 1, 1990.
[91] Ibid.
[92] *NYT*, October 9, 1990, p. D2.

Analysts interviewed in the *Washington Post* article said that McDonald's environmental concerns reflected a genuine concern about both the environment and were consistent with its long-term commitment to community responsibility. The news story put it thus: "The agreement with EDF is part of a major move by McDonald's to position itself as an environmentally and nutritionally concerned company at a time when it has been under attack for everything from its plastic foam food containers to the beef tallow in which it until recently fried its potatoes." McDonald's Yastrow said that the firm's marketing studies did not indicate either a loss of market share or a potential market gain as a result of environmental issues but that the company was nevertheless committed to the environment.

NOVEMBER 1990: POLYSTYRENE BOXES DROPPED

By late October, nearly three months to the day after forming the partnership with EDF, McDonald's planned to expand its foam recycling program to all its U.S. restaurants.[93] But now, EDF was challenging McDonald's plan, and Rensi agreed to listen. Abruptly, the company changed its mind and decided to withdraw its polystyrene foam sandwich boxes and dismantle its plastic recycling program. In place of the plastic clamshells, it would use both quilted paper and polyethylene-coated paper wraps, which had been newly developed and tested during the summer in its Cleveland, Ohio, stores. News of the change would be released on November 1.

The new paper wraps were 70–90 percent less bulky than the foam, could be shipped using less cardboard packaging than the clamshells, and were cheaper, too.

The quilted paper, which was made of two thin layers of paper sandwiching a polyethylene quilted inner layer, would do almost the same job of containing heat and controlling condensation as the clam shell, according to manufacturers of the paper, James River. The new wrap for the Big Mac would use unbleached paper. Neither recyclable nor biodegradable, the new wraps also could not be made from recycled paper because of Food and Drug Administration restrictions on use of recycled materials in food wrapping. Nevertheless, the company indicated that a search was underway for a material that could be disposed of by composting. Based on a study it had made, EDF felt that the new paper also resulted in lower environmental impacts in respect to energy use, air emissions, waterborne waste and generation of solid waste, even assuming a highly optimistic recycling rate of 50 percent for foam containers.[94]

---

[93] This was notwithstanding the fact that by November 1990, because of high contamination of waste from McDonald's, Plastics Again had so far been able to deliver only one shipment acceptable to Rubbermaid. "A Setback for Polystyrene," Sec. 3, p. 14.

[94] Task Force Report, pp. 39–40.

The switch from polystyrene to paper wrap would affect about 75 percent of the foam packaging used by McDonald's.[95]

"The last four or five or six days around here were very intense, about whether we should make the change," Yastrow said.[96] But Rensi had been persuaded that "[a]lthough some scientific studies indicate that foam packaging is environmentally sound, our customers just don't feel good about it."[97] Now McDonald's had to position its announcement. How should it address the public, the press, and its other audiences? What would the key messages be, and how should the company deal with an apparent change of position? What should be the role of EDF, if any? Looking toward the future, how would McDonald's satisfy all its many constituencies? How would it respond to the comment: "McDonald's was the engine driving this program. . . . Without them, the whole polystyrene recycling system may collapse"?[98] And how would it respond to a recent statement from a scientist at the National Audubon Society: "Using a lot more paper means a lot more pollution. It is a mistake to make plastic the great satan and paper the great saint. Both processes generate pollution"?[99]

---

[95] Task Force Report, pp. v. and 38–39.

[96] "McDonald's to Do Away with Foam Packages," *Los Angeles Times*, November 2, 1990, p. A28.

[97] "McDonald's to Switch Packaging, Stop Using Much-Criticized Foam," *Investor's Daily*, November 2, 1990, p. 4.

[98] "Setback for Polystyrene," sec. 3, p. 14.

[99] "Packaging and Public Image: McDonald's Fills a Big Order," *NYT*, November 2, 1990, p. D5.

Chapter 2.4

The Smoke Wars

THE CASE FOR AND AGAINST THE CIGARETTE INDUSTRY

Early 1989 saw a wave of public policy activism on "the smoking issue." Ten major bills were introduced during the first month of the 100th U.S. Congress. These bills proposed to increase the cigarette excise tax, eliminate corporate tax deductions for tobacco advertising, ban smoking in federal buildings, and prohibit smoking on all public conveyances. Many corporations had imposed restrictions on smoking at work; some simply refused to hire smokers. In March 1988, the Civil Aeronautics Board banned smoking on flights of less than two hours, which was extended to six hours by February 1990. Smoking in public places was restricted in 41 states. A New York City law, put into effect in April 1988, restricted smoking in restaurants, stores, theaters, hospitals, museums, banks, and virtually all other public places.

"The new rules are sparking explosive confrontations on all fronts," reported *Time*.[1] The article added:

> Even those who like very much to quit want to do so in their own sweet time—not under a legal gun. They are sick of having glasses of water dumped on their ashtrays or ashtrays dumped on their beds. . . .
>
> Having long been segregated on scheduled flights, smokers are indignant about the outright ban. "I think it's discriminatory," says John Collins, a Los Angeles telecommunications contractor and frequent flyer. "First they put all of us smokers way in the back of the plane. We took that OK. But now they tell us that we can't smoke at all. The whole thing has been aggravating as hell, especially when I can remember

This case was prepared by Professor V. Kasturi Rangan.
Copyright © 1989 by the President and Fellows of Harvard College.
Harvard Business School case 9-590-040 (Rev. 5/22/90).
    [1] "All Fired Up over Smoke," *Time*, April 18, 1988, pp. 64–75.

when you used to get on a plane and the stewardesses were handing out five packs of cigarettes."

Signs on office walls that used to smile "Thank You For Not Smoking" now growl "If You Smoke, Don't Exhale.". . .

Smokers know, of course, that it is not quite that simple. "You can't blame people for not wanting to breathe smoke," says Kay Michael, a reporter for the Charleston, West Virginia *Daily Mail*, "but I wish the antismokers would try to understand that there is a physical addiction here. They seem to think we smoke just to mess up the air or something."

The Tobacco Institute (a tobacco industry-sponsored research and information group) offered the following perspective regarding the various restrictions on smoking:[2]

The United States Constitution imposes various restrictions on the power of the federal and state governments to regulate the lives of our citizenry. Plaintiffs who have attempted to elevate their own personal antismoking crusades against public entities to constitutional dimensions have uniformly been rebuffed. The leading case is *Gasper* v. *Louisiana Stadium*. There a group of nonsmokers sued to compel the authorities who manage the Louisiana Superdome to prohibit smoking during sports and other public events. In support of their demand, the plaintiffs claimed a constitutional right to a smoke-free environment, relying on the First Amendment (freedom of speech); Fifth and Fourteenth Amendments (due process right to life and liberty); and Ninth Amendment (which protects unspecific but so-called "fundamental" rights).

The District Court unequivocally rejected any constitutional basis for imposing restrictions on smoking in a decision that was in all respects affirmed by the Court of Appeals. Responding to the First Amendment claim, the court found that "the State's permissive attitude toward smoking in the Louisiana Superdome adequately preserved the delicate balance of individual rights without yielding to the temptation to intervene in purely private affairs." In rejecting the due process claim, the court concluded that to apply the Fifth and Fourteenth Amendments to prohibit smoking:

> *Would be to mock the lofty purposes of such amendments and broaden their penumbral protections to unheard-of boundaries. . . . To hold otherwise would be to invite government by the judiciary in the regulation of every conceivable ill or so-called "right" to our litigious-minded society. The inevitable result would be that type of tyranny from which our founding fathers sought to protect the people by adopting the first 10 amendments to the Constitution.*

Cigarette industry advocates further claimed that restrictions on the employment of smokers was a threat to black Americans. Since statistics revealed that more blacks smoked than whites, hiring bans directed at smokers, they argued, would disproportionately affect black employment. (See Figure 1 below for demographics on smokers by education, race, and age.) Research compiled by the U.S. Surgeon General showed that blacks smoked more than whites,

---

[2] "An Assessment of the Current Legal Climate Concerning Smoking in the Workplace," prepared by the law firm of Covington and Burling for the Tobacco Institute, January 1987.

FIGURE 1   The Demographics

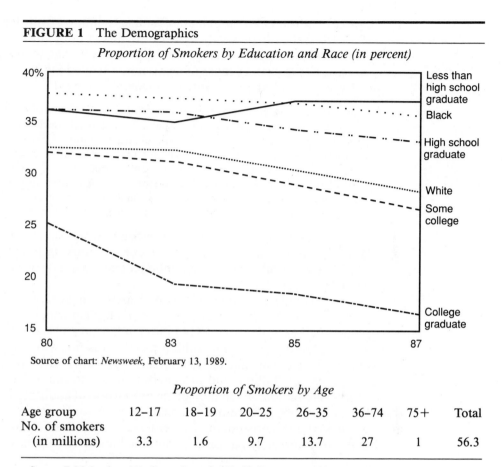

Proportion of Smokers by Education and Race (in percent)

Source of chart: *Newsweek*, February 13, 1989.

Proportion of Smokers by Age

Age group	12–17	18–19	20–25	26–35	36–74	75+	Total
No. of smokers (in millions)	3.3	1.6	9.7	13.7	27	1	56.3

Source: E. M. Lewit and D. Coate, *Journal of Health Economics*, 1982, pp. 62–87.

and that the more educated the people were, the less likely they were to smoke. *Currents* summed up the industry's case:[3]

> The signs outside personnel offices these days are very different than they were before 1964. Posters proclaiming "Blacks Need Not Apply" exist today largely only in museums as relics of a by-gone age. Yet new signs menacing to many blacks, but not mentioning race at all, are popping up across the country: "Smokers Need Not Apply." To the extent today's signs and the employment policies they represent exclude or disadvantage blacks in the work force disproportionately compared to whites, they may well be as pernicious as their predecessors.

The battle regarding restrictions on "smoking" and "smokers" was only one among several that were being fought between the advocates and foes of the

---

[3] Robert W. Ethridge and John C. Fox, "Toward a Civil Rights Approach to Smoking," *Currents*, April 1987.

cigarette industry. The problem, of course, stemmed from the fact that, since 1953, when the Sloan-Kettering Institute linked lung cancer with exposure to "tar" from cigarette smoking, scientific evidence has increasingly identified smoking as the leading cause of death in the United States. In his 1986 report, C. Everett Koop, the U.S. Surgeon General, reported:[4]

> Smoking is now known to be causally related to a variety of cancers in addition to lung cancer; it is a cause of cardiovascular disease, particularly coronary heart disease, and is the major cause of the chronic obstructive lung disease. It is estimated that smoking is responsible for well over 300,000 deaths annually in the United States, representing approximately 15 percent of all mortality. . . . It is now clear that disease risk due to the inhalation of tobacco smoke is not limited to the individual who is smoking, but can extend to those who inhale tobacco smoke emitted into the air. [This was estimated at 5,000–6,000 lung cancer deaths annually.]

To offer a perspective to this otherwise abstract statistic on smoking mortality: "Consider that the death toll due to smoking is comparable to that which would result from three jumbo jet crashes a day, occurring every single day of the year."[5]

Thus, the $35 billion (1988 retail cigarette sales) tobacco industry, which, according to a Chase Econometrics estimate,[6] contributed nearly $32 billion to the GNP, provided about $14 billion in federal and state taxes (split evenly), and employed close to one million people, was not without its detractors. Its critics pointed out that the health care costs attributed to smoking illnesses was about $22 billion, and productivity losses to the economy in the region of $30–$40 billion.[7] Even though the proportion of adult smokers in the United States had dropped from 43 percent in 1965 to 26 percent in 1988, the advocates of the antismoking movement, nevertheless, pressed on with their battle to completely banish the smoking habit from the face of the earth.

THE COMBATANTS

The tobacco lobby was represented mainly by six cigarette companies and a jointly funded Tobacco Research Institute. In 1989, the six major tobacco companies in the United States were: Philip Morris; R. J. Reynolds Tobacco (a division of RJR Nabisco); Brown and Williamson (a division of BATUS); Lorillard (a division of Loews Corporation); American Tobacco (a division of American Brands); and Liggett Group (owned by Bennett S. LeBow, a New

---

[4] The 1986 Report of the Surgeon General, U.S. Public Health Service.

[5] Kenneth E. Warner, "The Effects of Publicity and Policy on Smoking and Health," *Business and Health* 2, no. 1 (November 1984), pp. 7–14.

[6] "The Economic Impact of the Tobacco Industry on the United States Economy," Bala Cynwyd, Penn.: Chase Econometrics, 1985.

[7] James M. Shultz, "Perspectives on the Economic Magnitude of Cigarette Smoking," *New York State Journal of Medicine*, July 1985.

York-based investor). The market shares of the six competitors, and their leading brands, are shown in Table 1. Every one of these brands except Merit has been around for more than 20 years. By incurring over $2 billion dollars annually in advertising and promotional expenditure, the cigarette industry vastly outspent the antismoking group's consumer education programs (estimated to be in the region of $200–$300 million nationwide over all agencies and organizations put together). In spite of the declining demand (approximately 2 percent annually), the cigarette industry's profitability had either remained constant or improved for tobacco operations. See Table 2 for aggregate trend of U.S. tobacco shipments and prices over the last 15 years.

To continue their revenue growth, manufacturers were diversifying into other businesses and aggressively marketing cigarettes internationally. In 1985, for example, R. J. Reynolds merged with Nabisco Brands and Philip Morris acquired General Foods. Exhibits 1 to 4 provide a brief description of four leading cigarette manufacturers in the United States and their financial history for the periods 1985, 1986, and 1987.

Battling this huge and powerful monolith called the tobacco industry was an assortment of agencies and actors loosely labeled the antismoking movement.

TABLE 1 Market Shares of Leading Brands

	Market Share by Firm			
	1950	*1974*	*1979*	*1987*
Philip Morris	11.3	22.5	29.0	37.9
R. J. Reynolds	31.5	27.4	32.7	32.6
Brown and Williamson	5.2	17.4	14.5	10.8
Lorillard	5.5	8.2	9.6	8.2
American Brands	31.1	15.7	11.5	6.9
Liggett	18.6	4.6	2.7	3.6

Brand	*Company*	Market Share	
		1987	*1980*
1. Marlboro	Philip Morris	23.4	17.8
2. Winston	R. J. Reynolds	11.4	13.2
3. Salem	R. J. Reynolds	7.9	8.9
4. Kool	Brown and Williamson	5.7	8.9
5. Camel	R. J. Reynolds	4.3	4.3
6. Newport	Lorillard	4.2	3.0
7. Benson and Hedges	Philip Morris	4.0	4.6
8. Merit	Philip Morris	3.9	4.3
9. Vantage	R. J. Reynolds	3.3	3.9
10. Pall Mall	American Brands	3.1	3.9

Source: John C. Maxwell, industry analyst and Harvard Business School, "Note on the U.S. Cigarette Industry" (No. 183-046).

TABLE 2 Historic Performance of U.S. Tobacco

Product Data ($ millions)	1972	1973	1974	1975	1976	1977	1978
Value of shipments	4,204	4,624	4,996	5,854	6,461	6,756	7,381
Cigarettes	3,589	4,004	4,380	5,209	5,830	6,098	6,660
Cigars	358	350	334	317	285	256	283
Chewing/smoking tobacco	258	270	282	328	346	401	438
Value of shipments (1982$)	11,627	12,363	12,268	12,780	12,948	12,255	12,104
Cigarettes	10,314	11,061	11,034	11,627	11,874	11,189	11,044
Cigars	583	559	504	458	402	349	357
Chewing/smoking tobacco	729	743	731	695	671	717	702
Shipments price index (1982 = 100):	35.4	36.8	40.3	45.5	49.7	55.0	60.9
Cigarettes	34.8	36.2	39.7	44.8	49.1	54.5	60.3
Cigars	61.3	62.7	66.2	69.2	70.9	73.5	79.3
Chewing/smoking tobacco	35.3	36.3	38.6	47.2	51.5	56.0	62.4
Trade Data ($ millions)							
Value of imports	25.1	24.3	32.6	35.2	46.6	45.9	50.0
Cigarettes	0.6	0.7	1.7	2.1	2.6	3.1	3.9
Cigars	8.4	11.5	13.6	15.8	19.3	22.9	25.0
Chewing/smoking tobacco	16.1	12.1	17.3	17.3	24.7	19.9	21.1
Value of exports	240	289	361	401	536	637	763
Cigarettes	202	250	301	369	510	615	750
Cigars	3.0	3.7	4.0	4.6	5.7	5.5	7.7
Chewing/smoking tobacco	35.3	35.3	55.8	28.1	20.8	16.9	6.2

Source: U.S. Industrial Outlook 1988—Tobacco.

	1972	1973	1974	1975	1976	1977	1978
Average retail price per package (cents)	40.3	41.8	44.5	47.9	49.2	54.3	56.8
Average taxes (state plus federal) per package (cents)	20.0	20.0	20.0	20.0	20.0	20.0	20.0

Source: The Tobacco Institute: The Tax Burden on Tobacco 1989.

Such federal agencies as the Surgeon General's Office, Action on Smoking and Health (ASH), and the Centers for Disease Control provided smoking-related consumer education, while the National Institutes of Health, comprising agencies like the National Cancer Institute and the National Heart, Lung, and Blood Institute, provided funds for basic research.

The role of the government in regulating tobacco and tobacco products was limited; these products were specifically excluded from the Consumer Product Safety Act, the Toxic Substances Control Act, and the Food, Drug, and Cos-

1979	1980	1981	1982	1983	1984	1985	1986	1987
8,096	9,184	9,947	12,455	12,997	14,267	15,315	16,096	18,083
7,323	8,315	8,991	11,434	11,941	13,123	14,086	14,888	16,583
261	265	286	290	307	270	263	241	253
512	604	671	731	749	875	966	967	977
12,111	12,152	12,047	12,455	11,455	11,466	11,379	11,004	11,241
11,062	11,086	11,005	11,434	10,438	10,432	10,357	10,046	10,155
316	298	299	290	305	262	242	221	221
734	768	743	731	712	772	780	737	700
66.8	75.5	82.5	100.0	113.5	124.5	134.6	146.3	160.8
66.2	75.0	81.7	100.0	114.4	125.8	136.0	148.2	163.3
82.7	89.0	95.5	100.0	100.8	102.8	108.7	109.1	114.6
69.8	78.7	90.3	100.0	105.2	113.3	123.8	131.2	139.5
51.3	92.8	200	227	403	88.2	78.2	82.1	89.5
5.6	6.9	7.5	7.9	11.1	12.9	11.8	16.6	23.2
28.0	34.5	39.5	40.8	44.8	47.6	44.0	44.3	45.3
17.7	51.4	153	178	348	27.7	22.4	21.2	21.0
959	1,082	1,259	1,287	1,169	1,169	1,234	1,480	—
909	1,055	1,229	1,235	1,126	1,120	1,180	1,298	1,600
8.8	9.9	11.0	10.5	8.5	7.6	5.5	5.2	7.3
42.0	16.5	19.5	42.2	35.3	41.6	48.2	177	—
60.0	63.0	69.7	81.9	94.7	97.8	104.5	110.1	118.9
20.0	21.0	21.0	21.0	31.4	31.6	32.2	32.9	34.2

metic Act. The Federal Trade Commission, however, oversaw advertising and promotion practices and the enforcement of labeling requirements.

State and local governments also limited the distribution and use of tobacco products. Actions taken included restrictions on smoking in public places, minimum age of purchase laws, restrictions on sampling of products, and some advertising restrictions not covered by federal legislation. All 50 states and the District of Columbia added an excise tax on cigarettes, ranging from $0.02 a pack in North Carolina to $0.28 in Maine.

EXHIBIT 1   Philip Morris

Philip Morris, Inc. (PM), the market leader since 1983, was the only company to have an increase in unit volume in 1987; its 37.9 percent market share was the highest obtained by any tobacco company since the 1930s. Marlboro, PM's flagship brand, accounted for 63 percent of its sales volume in 1987.

In addition to tobacco, PM engaged in two other business segments: beer and food products. The company owned and operated the Miller Brewing Company (Miller) and General Foods (GF), acquired in 1985. In 1988, the company acquired Kraft, Inc. These two acquisitions were a continuation of the company's 25-year strategy to use corporate resources to expand its earnings base internationally and through diversification.

	1987	1986	1985
Operating revenues ($ millions):			
Domestic tobacco	$ 7,640	$ 7,053	$ 6,611
International tobacco	7,004	5,638	3,991
Food	9,946	9,664	1,632
Beer	3,105	3,054	2,914
Financial services and real estate	488	474	303
Other	—	—	816
Total operating revenues	$28,183	$25,883	$16,267
Operating income ($ millions):			
Domestic tobacco	$ 2,715	$ 2,366	$ 2,047
International tobacco	582	492	413
Food	773	741	120
Beer	170	154	132
Financial services and real estate	68	32	66
Other	20	(10)	42
Operating companies income	4,328	3,775	2,820

Source: Company annual reports.

Three major national organizations were committed to research, public education, and communication on the risks associated with cigarettes: the American Cancer Society, the American Lung Association, and the American Heart Association. These entities created the Coalition on Smoking or Health in 1982. The coalition worked on initiatives ranging from imposition of excise taxes to regulating tobacco industry advertising and promotion practices.

Other health-related organizations adopted positions on smoking. The American Medical Association, for example, advocated a total ban on cigarette advertising. There were also a variety of advocacy groups dedicated to the elimination of smoking; for example, Americans for Nonsmokers' Rights and Ralph Nader's Common Cause.

Had all this made a difference? An article in *Business and Health* argued:[8]

---

[8] Warner, "The Effects of Publicity and Policy."

EXHIBIT 2   R. J. Reynolds Tobacco

RJR Nabisco, Inc. (RJR), formerly R. J. Reynolds Industries, increased its 1987 share of domestic sales to 32.6 percent, a 3 percent change from 1986 levels. RJR's portfolio of cigarette brands included Winston, Salem, Camel, Vantage, and Doral. Doral, the largest "branded generic," was RJR's first entry into the expanding price/value segment of the market. As the only generic in the top 10 brands in the United States, it was primarily responsible for the company's 38.6 percent market share within the price/value segment.

Having undergone significant restructuring between 1985 and 1987, RJR became one of the world's largest consumer products company; it includes Nabisco Brands, Inc., Del Monte Tropical Fruit Company, and R. J. Reynolds Tobacco Company.

These businesses produced a wide range of products, including cigarettes, cookies, crackers, nuts snacks, confectionery products, processed fruits and vegetables, cereals, margarines, and fresh fruit.

	1987	1986	1985
Net sales ($ millions):			
Tobacco	$ 6,346	$ 5,866	$ 5,422
Food	9,420	9,236	6,200
Consolidated net sales	$15,766	$15,102	$11,622
Operating income ($ millions):			
Tobacco	$ 1,821	$ 1,659	$ 1,483
Food	915	820	549
Restructuring expense	(250)	—	—
Corporate	(182)	(139)	(83)
Consolidated operating income	$ 2,304	$ 2,340	$ 1,949
Net sales ($ millions):			
United States	$11,721	$11,338	$ 9,095
Canada	850	1,060	830
Europe	2,361	21,055	1,125
Other geographic areas	1,387	1,217	996
Less transfers between geographic areas	(553)	(568)	(424)
Consolidated net sales	$15,766	$15,102	$11,622
Operating income ($ millions):			
United States	$ 2,162	$ 2,026	$ 1,694
Canada	112	85	106
Europe	241	180	90
Other geographic areas	221	188	142
Restructuring expense	(250)	—	—
Corporate	(182)	(139)	(83)
Consolidated operating income	$ 2,304	$ 2,340	$ 1,949

Source: Company annual reports.

EXHIBIT 3 Brown and Williamson

BATUS was the holding company for the United States business interests of B.A.T. Industries PLC (London, England). Founded in 1980, the company operated the Brown and Williamson Tobacco Corporation (B&W), the third largest U.S. cigarette company. Kool, its flagship brand, was the fourth largest selling domestic cigarette brand. B&W brands included Kent, Lucky Strike, and Barclay, as well as several offerings in the price/value segment: Richland, a branded generic, and "GPC," an unbranded generic.

The company's two other business segments were retail and paper. Within retail, the company operated Saks Fifth Avenue, Marshall Field's, Ivey's, Brueners, and Thimbles. Appleton Papers, Inc., the world's largest producer of carbonless copy paper, manufactured specialty paper.

	1987	*1986*	*1985*
Sales (£ millions):			
UK	£ 4,179	£ 3,546	£ 3,465
Europe	5,077	5,480	4,242
North America	4,637	5,823	5,928
Australasia	531	554	485
Latin America	1,499	2,396	1,550
Asia	803	937	1,000
Africa	482	431	381
Total	£17,208	£19,167	£17,051
Profit (£ millions):			
UK	£ 295	£ 355	£ 275
Europe	223	186	113
North America	634	658	587
Australasia	36	40	31
Latin America	139	171	161
Asia	57	63	78
Africa	52	44	49
Total	£ 1,436	£ 1,517	£ 1,294
Sales (£ millions):			
Tobacco	£ 6,940	£ 8,339	£ 7,170
Retailing	3,948	4,762	4,671
Paper	1,692	1,755	1,499
Financial services	3,812	3,183	2,186
Other trading activities	816	1,128	1,525
Total	£17,208	£19,167	£17,051
Profit (£ millions):			
Tobacco	£ 722	£ 764	£ 738
Retailing	203	211	186
Paper	209	217	168
Financial services	267	291	137
Other trading activities	35	34	65
Total	£ 1,436	£ 1,517	£ 1,294

Source: Company annual reports.

EXHIBIT 4   American Tobacco Company

American Brands, Inc. (AB), was the holding company for the American Tobacco Company (ATC), the grandfather of the United States tobacco industry. Domestically, the company marketed three principal brands: Lucky Strike and Carlton, both "low-tar," and Pall Mall, a nonfilter cigarette.

In 1986, AB celebrated the 20th anniversary of its diversification strategy. Capitalizing on its marketing and distribution strengths, the company invested over $2.6 billion, to become an international holding company of packaged consumer goods and financial services. Major lines in addition to tobacco included life insurance, hardware, and security (Master Lock and Pinkerton Securities Services), distilled beverages (Jim Beam Beverages), and food products (Sunshine Biscuits).

	1987	*1986*	*1985*
Net sales ($ millions):			
Tobacco products	$6,144.0	$5,169.4	$4,390.0
Distilled spirits	599.4	254.5	249.8
Hardware	291.6	302.6	256.9
Office products	508.6	346.9	336.7
Other	1,609.3	1,179.5	972.2
Total	$9,152.9	$7,252.9	$6,205.6
Operating income ($ millions):			
Tobacco products	$ 673.8	$ 498.6	$ 519.6
Distilled spirits	68.3	35.0	40.2
Hardware	42.1	40.6	40.1
Office products	26.5	(12.1)	17.1
Other	91.5	65.4	58.3
	902.2	627.5	674.3
Financial services	168.6	176.1	174.1
Total	$1,070.8	$ 803.6	$ 849.4
Business by geographic areas ($ millions):			
Net sales			
United States	$2,815.8	$2,390.6	$2,308.7
Europe	6,250.9	4,812.6	3,845.1
Other	86.2	49.7	51.8
Total	$9,152.9	$7,252.9	$6,205.6
Operating income ($ millions):			
United States	$ 577.9	$ 434.2	$ 516.1
Europe	315.0	194.7	158.8
Other	9.3	(1.4)	0.4
	902.2	627.5	675.3
Financial services (United States)	168.6	176.1	174.1
Total	$1,070.8	$ 803.6	$ 849.4

Source: Company annual reports.

Despite all the publicity on the health hazards of smoking, some 55 million Americans engage in the habit today, and their average daily consumption of more than 30 cigarettes per smoker is at an all-time high. Collectively, Americans puff in excess of 600 billion cigarettes each year. Since the 1950s, millions of women have joined the smoking population and teenage girls have been particularly enthusiastic new recruits.

Figure 2 provides the trend of per capita cigarette consumption since the early 1900s. Only a brief chronology is offered here.[9]

RECENT BATTLES

The advocates and opponents of the tobacco lobby were locked in several major battles. While the demand for cigarettes declined nationwide, until re-

FIGURE 2   Adult per Capita Cigarette Consumption in the United States

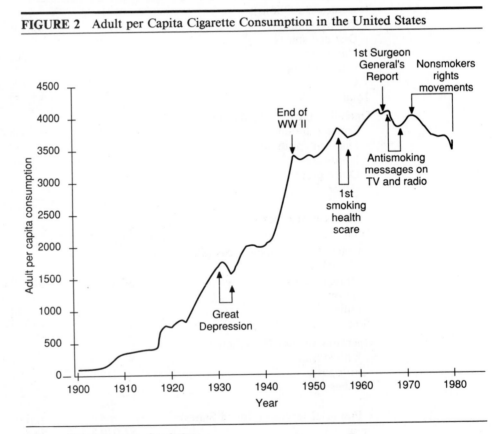

Source: U.S. Department of Agriculture.

---

[9] Information on the early history of the industry was adapted from Susan Wagner, *Cigarette Country* (New York: Praeger Publishers, 1971); Maurice Corina, *Trust in Tobacco* (New York: St. Martin's Press, 1975); and Alfred Chandler and Richard Tedlow, *The Coming of Managerial Capitalism* (Homewood, Ill.: Richard D. Irwin, 1985).

FIGURE 2 *(concluded)*

1890	American Tobacco Company formed with James Buchanan Duke as its first president.
1917 to 1919	During the First World War, per capita consumption increased from 337 to 426 cigarettes.
1939 to 1945	During the Second World War, per capita consumption soared from 1,779 to 3,457 cigarettes.
1953	Sloan-Kettering Institute linked lung cancer to cigarette smoking.
1955	Filter-tipped cigarettes introduced.
1964	U.S. Surgeon General identified cigarette smoking as a health problem and recommended health warnings and advertising restrictions. The cigarette industry adopted a voluntary code to discourage manufacturers from advertising and marketing to the youth market.
1965	Congress passed the Cigarette Labelling and Advertising Act, requiring warning labels to be printed on all cigarette packages.
1967	The Federal Communications Commission required that television and radio run anti-smoking advertising in parity with cigarette advertising.
1969	The cigarette industry voluntarily agreed to end all radio and television advertising. Congress banned these media in 1971.
1971	Low tar and nicotine cigarettes introduced. Per capita consumption started to decline steadily.
1986	Of the 55 million adult Americans who smoked, 15 million attempted to quit every year, and 1.5 million were actually successful.

---

cently, in direct confrontations between the two groups, the anti-smoking movement hardly had won any victories. This section outlines four recent battles.

The first, entitled *Free Speech or Marketing Ploy*, discusses the tobacco industry's vigorous defense of freedom of speech and advertising. The second battle, entitled *Wealth Is Not Health*, examines the tobacco industry's aggressive efforts to increase sales in global markets. The third battle, entitled *Of Mice and Men*, describes the outcome of a historic product liability suit against Liggett, a cigarette company. And finally the fourth battle, entitled *In Search of a Target*, reviews R. J. Reynolds' efforts to target new markets.

Free Speech or Marketing Ploy

Critics asserted that the cigarette industry used its marketing expertise to take advantage of unsuspecting consumers. The Health Advocacy Center reported that cigarette advertisers "prey on the insecurity of young people by providing them with sophisticated, self-sufficient role models into which they think they can transform themselves simply by smoking." Further, the advertising images and brand positions, argued critics, were becoming more appealing to young smokers. A document the FTC obtained from Brown & Williamson explored how image projection advertising could be used to attract young people:[10]

> For the young smoker, the cigarette is not yet an integral part of life, of day-to-day life, in spite of the fact that they try to project the image of a regular, run-of-the-mill smoker. For them, a cigarette and the whole smoking process is part of the illicit pleasure category. . . . In the young smoker's mind a cigarette falls into the same category with wine, beer, shaving, wearing a bra (or purposely not wearing one), declaration of independence, and striving for self-identity. For the young starter, a cigarette is associated with the introduction to sex life, with courtship, with smoking "pot," and keeping late study hours.

The tobacco industry claimed that advertising was aimed at changing current smokers' brand loyalties, not at inducing nonsmokers, especially adolescents, to begin smoking. The International Advertising Agency, supporting the tobacco industry's view, argued:

> The reasons why people start smoking are complex, and mostly concerned with the individual's psychology, background, and social context. He or she starts to smoke because of internal and external factors, which have to do with the kind of person he or she is, with the example of parents and friends, and with social influences exerted by peer groups. All that seems clear from the research that has been done. It is also clear that advertising plays no significant role in initiating the use of tobacco products. Such is the reasonable conclusion of serious, responsible researchers.

Critics disagreed:[11]

> Their lips say, "No, No," but the reality is Yes! Cigarette manufacturers *do want* young people to smoke. . . . Reality contradicts their claim. Cigarette advertisements depicting adults in their 20s in a myriad of athletic, adventurous, sexy pursuits appeal to a youthful audience. . . . One hardly needs to be an advertising executive to recognize that ads are aimed at attracting youth. Look at the *Kool* ads (and just who did they name the cigarette "Kool" to attract?) showing a male and female model, early 20s, blue jeans, and T-shirts leaning on a motorcycle looking, as the name implies, "Kool." . . . Of course, all cigarette advertising executives know of young women's obsession with their weight, and the belief many hold that smoking will help them lose weight. Yes, Virginia, they're not called "Slims" for nothing.

In 1986, there were calls for a national ban on the advertising and promotion of cigarettes in all mediums. Cigarette companies' responses were typified by Philip Morris:[12]

> We believe that such proposals ignore the constitutional rights of our industry. Further, they seek to establish a precedent that could have very damaging consequences

---

[10] W. Meyers, "The Image Makers: Power and Persuasion of Madison Avenue," *New York Times Book*, 1984.

[11] Julia Carol, "Cigarettes Advertisements and Youth," manuscript, Smoking Policy Institute Library, 1986.

[12] Philip Morris Company, *Annual Report*, 1986.

for many other products which are also legally sold, but which periodically attract public or legislative criticism. . . . We have spoken out vigorously against such prohibition, stressing the protection of commercial free speech under the First Amendment.

"Freedom of speech—a cherished freedom protected by the First Amendment of the American Constitution is indeed the very cornerstone of our democracy; an America without it would be unthinkable," wrote two crusaders of the anti-smoking movement.[13] "This kind of zealous defense of the First Amendment is commendable, but, in the context of tobacco advertising, it is terribly misguided," they argued, adding:

Commercial speech is entitled to a far different standard of constitutional protection from the forms of speech that are classically protected by the First Amendment for the purpose of preserving political liberty.

There is an excellent reason for according more constitutional protection to political speech than to commercial speech. The former relates to *ideas*, and it would be anathema to have the government tell us what ideas we may believe or listen to. We allow Nazis and Communists to speak because we know it is not possible to draw lines in deciding what are "good" and "bad" ideas. Even the most hated ideas must be tolerated to make sure that all ideas will always enjoy free expression. But commercial speech is not principally, if at all, intended to use or convey ideas. Rather, it is used to *sell* products and services. Although we do not want the government to protect us from "dangerous or unhealthy ideas," it is a fundamental duty of government to protect people from dangerous or unhealthy products. That is why it is perfectly consistent for the Constitution to prohibit Congress from passing any laws restricting freedom of speech while specifically authorizing Congress to regulate commerce, including advertising.

"Smoking is acceptable because smoking has been accepted by many individuals as a satisfying activity. Tobacco advertising is a result, not a cause of that acceptance," argued the International Advertising Association:[14]

When manufacturers of perfectly legal products are banned from advertising in certain media—or even from advertising at all—a completely different situation arises. It is the start of a process of restriction on the free flow of competitive commercial information; a form of censorship which strikes at the very basis of a free economic society.

Many civil libertarians and advertising agencies flocked to the side of the cigarette companies, and nothing much came of the move to completely ban cigarette advertising and promotion. Paradoxically, while the cigarette companies vigorously defended their right to free speech, they were not entirely tolerant of dissenters, as the following story from *Time* illustrates:[15]

---

[13] Peter Hanauer and Michael Pertschuk, "Tobacco Advertising and the First Amendment," Smoking Policy Institute Library, 1986.

[14] "Tobacco and Advertising," a document prepared by the International Advertising Association, 1986.

[15] "All Fired Up over Smoke," *Time*, April 18, 1988, pp. 64–75.

Another victim of the smoking war retired from the field last week, this one suffering from an $84 million wound. The problem began when Northwest Airlines began to air TV ads announcing that smoking would soon be banned on all its domestic flights. During the commercial, the camera pans across passengers in the Northwest cabin, stopping to focus on a solitary smoker. When an announcer's voice proclaims the smoking ban, the passengers en masse—except for the smoker—burst into applause.

Edward Horrigan, the vice chairman of RJR Nabisco, the tobacco and food giant, had a very different reaction as he watched the commercial. Considering his company's heavy involvement in cigarette manufacturing (among its brands: Camel, Winston, and Salem), Horrigan was annoyed by Northwest's tough stand against smokers. But he was enraged to learn that the spot had been created by Saatchi & Saatchi DFS Compton, the advertising agency that handled many of RJR's most familiar consumer staples, including Oreo and Fig Newton cookies and Life Savers candies.

Two top RJR executives were dispatched to Saatchi's Lower Manhattan headquarters to deliver some devastating news: RJR was firing Saatchi outright, snatching away in one swoop $84 million in annual billings and abruptly ending an 18-year business relationship. The action dramatically demonstrated, if anyone had doubts, that the tobacco companies still wield considerable clout in the public debate about smoking. RJR executives clearly regarded Saatchi's Northwest ad as an affront to the firm's basic—and most profitable—business.

Wealth Is Not Health

"Like the North American manufacturers of another dangerous product (asbestos), the American tobacco industry has been trying, successfully, to expand in overseas (and not just third-world) markets to offset a decline in sales at home," wrote *The Economist*.[16] Explaining the U.S. cigarette companies' efforts to break into export markets, the article added:

The cigarette companies' first attempts to break into the Japanese market went up in smoke. Between 1981 and 1985, the Japanese reduced the import tariff on foreign cigarettes from 90 percent to 20 percent and, at the same time, slapped on a retail tax equivalent to 41 percent of the selling price of American cigarettes.

During that time, despite $200 million spent on what is called "product development" and promotion in Japan, the Americans' market share rose from only 1.2 percent to 2 percent. That was when the tobacco industry called on its friends at the White House and in Congress to put pressure on the Japanese to open up its markets. . . .

Japan has always been lax on cigarette advertising, particularly on television, and low-key on the health risks. Packets carry the innocuous, "For your health, don't smoke too much." But Japan Tobacco, Inc., a virtual monopoly before 1980, observed a voluntary limit on its television advertising not to encourage adolescents and women to smoke. In the early 1980s, 63 percent of Japanese men smoked, but only

---

[16] "The Trade Liberalization's Dark Shadow," *The Economist*, March 26, 1988.

12 percent of women did; in South Korea the figures were 68 percent and 7 percent; and in Hong Kong 37 percent and 5 percent. To the tobacco companies, those disparities represent millions of potential female customers who do not smoke. In 1987, in America, 27 percent of adult males smoked and 24 percent of women.

The Americans brought a cigarette advertising boom to Japan. Advertisements are now frequently screened during family and children's shows, at times which would be illegal in America. . . .

Cigarette advertising, now second in value only to that for drink in Japan, seems to work. American cigarettes' market share in Japan has risen from 2 percent in 1985 to around 11 percent, worth around $3 billion in export revenues. It is still climbing. A recent survey showed that 17 percent of Japanese female college students now smoke, while only 3 percent of their mothers do.

Echoing the same theme, an article in the *National Journal* questioned, "Should the federal government's health policies jibe with its trade stance on tobacco?" The article continued:[17]

After the first Surgeon General's report on smoking issued in January 1964, the American industry responded by expanding operations in Latin America. According to Philip L. Shepherd, an expert in Latin American tobacco marketing at Florida International University in Miami, U.S. cigarette companies "conquered the Latin market in three steps." After first breaking down the barriers that restricted the sale of foreign brands, U.S. firms saturated Latin consumers with advertising. Finally, Shepherd said, after carving out a niche in the market, the U.S. companies "began to buy out and take over most of the national cigarette firms in Latin America."

According to industry critics, the principal cigarette producers, including Philip Morris International, R. J. Reynolds International, Inc., and American Tobacco, hope to repeat their Latin American successes in Asia because the potential profits in the region are enormous. At a time when fewer than 30 percent of American males smoke, the rate is 63 percent for Japan and 70 percent for China; these figures make Japan the highest per capita and China the highest gross consumers of cigarettes on the planet.

Industry spokesmen deny that American manufacturers are ramming tobacco down Asians' throats. "We are just striving to do as well there [in Asia] as we do in the United States and in Europe," said Donald Harris, director of communications for Philip Morris. "I would just point out that Japan, South Korea, and Taiwan are all producing cigarettes with no outside rivals. We're not out to convert [nonsmokers]; we're out to compete."

Washington's negotiators, echoing the stance taken by the major tobacco houses and lobbying firms, say they view tobacco exports as principally an economic issue. "All we are asking is for equal treatment. We've been quite consistent on that point," said Peter F. Allgeir, assistant U.S. trade representative for Asia and the Pacific. "We are ready to abide by any and all laws as long as they apply to the domestic brands."

According to Judith L. Mackay, the executive director of the Hong Kong Council on Smoking and Health, the trend toward franchising has already established what is essentially a "double standard of quality" in the Philippines and Indonesia. Popular

---

[17] "When Health and Trade Policies Don't Jibe," *National Journal*, April 18, 1988.

brands produced by American firms in these countries have been found to have double and triple the average tar content of cigarettes manufactured in the United States, according to studies released by the Toronto-based Addiction Resources Center.

"We are sending a message that Asian lungs are more expendable than American ones," said Representative Atkins, a member of the Foreign Affairs Subcommittee on Asian and Pacific Affairs. "Our government should not be bending over backwards to promote a product that we have *proved* leads to thousands of premature deaths every year." Atkins said that he and Levine are drafting legislation that would, among other things, require cigarette manufacturers to comply with the safety restrictions "of the country of origin." Such legislation would require all exported U.S. cigarettes to carry warning labels; it could also prohibit U.S. tobacco houses from advertising their wares on foreign television.

In a related move, as an institutional investor in tobacco company stocks, Harvard University's Advisory Committee on Shareholder Responsibility wrote the following to its corporate committee, which was in charge of managing the university's funds.[18]

Harvard's traditional view is that companies in which we own stock should consider the social consequences of their activities. Given the medical data about cigarette smoking, a company engaged in that business must give serious thought to the health consequences of their profit-seeking efforts. As to cigarettes, it is possible to argue that the United States and many other industrialized countries have addressed the issues as a matter of democratic decision. The United States, for example, bans some advertising, taxes the product heavily, engages in public education, and—perhaps most importantly (though with disputed effectiveness)—insists that health warnings appear on packages and in advertising. In many underdeveloped countries, an overburdened political process has not effectively addressed the health consequences of cigarette smoking. There is little public education about the consequences of smoking, and government does not require warning notices. These countries are the large growth market for cigarette sales. Indeed, some analysts expect sales to fall in industrialized countries in the period ahead.

We believe that companies seeking to expand sales in the Third World should address in a serious way the social consequences of their actions. We think they should tell stockholders their reasons for not placing advertisements on packages and health warnings similar to those required in Europe and the United States.

... All "truth" and "knowledge" can be questioned, but at a given time in history some "facts" are regarded as proved according to the legitimate standards. We believe there is no reputable doubt that cigarette smoking contributes to cancer and heart disease. We therefore believe that a company selling cigarettes must consider its ethical responsibilities on the assumption that use of the product contributes to disease. For example, a cigarette company should consider whether it has a duty to inform buyers of health risks even in nations that do not impose a requirement of such warnings by law.

Some members of our committee also believe that Harvard, which refuses to own stock in some companies because it does not wish to be associated with particular

---

[18] *Harvard Gazette*, October 28, 1988.

economic activities (gambling, prostitution), should consider placing the production and sale of cigarettes in that category.

Of Mice and Men

In June 1988, the anti-smoking campaign claimed its first major legal victory in years. After the tobacco industry had beaten back over 300 smoker death suits since the 1950s, without a single dime in damages, a jury awarded $400,000 to Antonio Cipollone, whose wife Rose died of lung cancer in 1984 after 40 years of heavy smoking. The following report concerning the award appeared in the *Boston Globe*:[19]

A federal jury in New Jersey last night dealt the tobacco industry a profound setback by finding, for the first time ever, that a cigarette company was liable for the death of a smoker.... It said Liggett, which produced the Chesterfield and L&M filter brands that Mrs. Cipollone smoked, misled the public through advertisements that portrayed its products as safe when it knew otherwise....

Jurors said Mrs. Cipollone bore 80 percent of the responsibility for her own death.

"The myth of invulnerability that protected the tobacco industry has been shattered," said Richard Daynard, a professor at Northeastern University Law School and a critic of smoking. "People now know tobacco companies can be held as accountable in a court of law as manufacturers of asbestos, Dalkon Shields, and other dangerous products."

"There are going to be a tremendous number of cases filed as a result of this.... It is hard for me to see how the tobacco companies can cover the eventual expenses," said Daynard.

But Charles Wall, one of 14 full-time attorneys for cigarette firms in the New Jersey case, remained upbeat: "The ruling means that the tobacco company has maintained its record in the major issues dealing with conspiracy and fraud and misrepresentation. The verdict for the defendants on those issues sends a clear message to plaintiffs and plaintiffs' lawyers that there is not going to be money found in suing tobacco companies."

Plaintiffs "spent $3 million and got back $400,000, which is a lousy return on investment," he added in a telephone interview.

Wall said damages assessed against Liggett were "a compromise. I think jurors felt they needed to give Mr. Cipollone some money, they felt anybody who spent 4½ years preparing this case and four months trying it, deserves something . . . and I think this whole thing will be overturned on appeal."

This is only the fourth smoking suit in recent years to reach a jury. But the Cipollone case was different: The widower's lawyers introduced secret tobacco company documents they said proved the firms had conspired and lied by proclaiming their products as safe when they were fully aware of the risks.

The case also had dramatic overtones: Mrs. Cipollone, who was 58, died a year after the suit was filed. Her husband, now 64, promised her he would carry on the

---

[19] "$400,000 Awarded in Death of Smoker," *Boston Globe*, June 14, 1988.

fight. And this is the first case decided since Surgeon General C. Everett Koop reported last month that cigarettes can be as addictive as heroin and cocaine.

What differentiated the Cipollone case from the 321 suits brought since 1954 was that the prior cases had been unable to demonstrate the industry's negligence in informing smokers about health risks. As a result, the cases rested on the individual's right to smoke and the personal responsibility associated with making that decision. The evidence in this case, according to anti-smoking activists, is "the first to suggest that the tobacco companies long ago privately acknowledged what they continue to deny—that is, that smoking is linked to cancer."[20] In a terse exchange, during the trial, the lawyers for the plaintiff questioned Mr. Kinsley Dey, Jr., Liggett's president, regarding an experiment in the early 1950s, where the company's researchers smeared the shaven backs of mice with tars from the cigarettes' condensed smoke. Cancerous tumors had sprouted on the mice's backs as a result.

Lawyer

What was the purpose of this?

Mr. Dey

To try to reduce tumors on the backs of mice.

Lawyer

It is nothing to do with the health and welfare of human beings? Is that correct?

Mr. Dey

That's correct.

Lawyer

How much did that study cost?

Mr. Dey

A lot. . . . Probably between $15 million and more.

Lawyer

And this was to save rats, right, or mice? You spend all this money to save mice the problem of developing tumors? Is that correct?

Mr. Dey

I've stated that we did.

In Search of a Target

R. J. Reynolds launched "Premier," a smokeless cigarette on October 1, 1988, in three test markets: St. Louis, Missouri, and Phoenix and Tucson, Arizona.[21] The price per pack was about 30 cents higher than other cigarettes. The central

---

[20] "Of Mice and Men," *The Economist*, April 16, 1988.
[21] "Smokeless Cigarette Test Turns to Ashes," *Boston Globe*, March 1, 1989.

advertising message was "Premier—the Cleaner Smoke." Marketing analysts speculated that R. J. Reynolds selected the test markets because the demographics in these cities indicated that they had numerous older, sophisticated smokers who might be trying to seek an alternative to quitting smoking. Anti-smoking activists and public health officials had denounced the new product as an attempt to numb the public to the dangers of smoking. They protested that the product went to market without being tested or approved by the Food and Drug Administration. Cigarettes were exempt from FDA regulations, except where health-related advertising claims were concerned. The FDA, however, did regulate medical devices, and critics claimed that Premier was nothing but an instrument to vaporize nicotine, an addictive drug in cigarettes.

Much to the delight of the anti-smoking lobby, R. J. Reynolds announced on March 1, 1989, that it was officially withdrawing the brand from all test markets. The cigarette company said in a statement that "while smokers are very interested in the concept, the current product has not achieved adequate consumer acceptance."

In January 1990, R. J. Reynolds attempted launching yet another new brand, "Uptown," targeted at blacks. The company chose the Uptown name because it scored highest on consumer surveys. The company planned to package the cigarettes with filters facing down instead of up, because market research showed that many blacks opened cigarette packs from the bottom. Under attack from the U.S. Secretary of Health and Human Services, Louis Sullivan, the company abandoned its plans for the product launch. Mr. Sullivan had protested, "Uptown's message is more disease, more suffering, and more death for a group already bearing more than its share of smoking-related illness and mortality."

Newsweek, March 5, 1990, reported on R. J. Reynolds' plans for yet another new product, "Dakota."

> Last week, a marketing proposal leaked anonymously to an anti-smoking group revealed that Reynolds seemed to have another target in its sights: young (age 18–24), white, working-class women.
>
> Dubbed "virile females" in a campaign recommended by a marketing agency, these are among society's most vulnerable women—and most apt to fall for the new cigarette, to be called Dakota. With little education, they work in entry-level service or factory jobs and enjoy going to hot-rod and Monster Truck events with their boyfriends, according to the marketing plan.
>
> Oriented firmly in the present, they're unlikely to have absorbed information about smoking's long-term health risks to themselves—and, if pregnant, to their unborn.

A cigarette company executive summarized her reactions, "target market selection and segmentation form the basic building blocks of the marketing concept. What we are doing is what any sensible marketeer would do!"

WHAT'S ALL THIS FUSS ABOUT ANYWAY?

People who choose to gamble with their health should at least be required to cover their own bets. Otherwise, it's very difficult to take seriously all this thumb-sucking about "soaring health costs," contend the nonsmokers. Consequently, there has been a concerted effort to increase the excise tax from about 32 cents a pack to 48 cents a pack. At an average price of about $1.35 a pack, that would represent a net price increase of a little over 10 percent. It has been argued that such an increase would encourage about 2 million persons to quit smoking or not to start. This was based on the price elasticities projected for the various age groups. It was estimated that the number of smokers in the 12–17 year group would decline by 15 percent, the 18–19 year group by 9 percent, and the rest by about 4 percent. Some economists, however, oppose the idea of "sin" taxes, because they unfairly punish the poor. They raise the question, "Why tax so heavily adult smokers who mainly harm themselves?" Nonsmokers, of course, reply "because taxpayers end up paying for it." The following excerpts from a scholarly article attempt to resolve this question of how much smokers really cost the rest of society.[22]

Is there any way to associate a monetary value, an "economic worth," to the enhanced life expectancy that comes from quitting in time or from not smoking in the first place?

There are two ways to formulate this question. They are sometimes called the prevalence approach and the incidence approach. The prevalence approach asks the question, what are the current annual costs inflicted on society, or on the economy, by the lifetime smoking practices of people who will be hospitalized this year, will be absent from work, or will die because of the consequences of current smoking. The incidence approach, on the other hand, examines the projected costs of hospitalization and other medical care, excess absenteeism, and premature death on account of current smoking practices.

The first impact is the easiest to determine. Consider the smokers who lose more days of work per year on account of illness than if they did not smoke. This results in lost production to the economy, unless employers can take up the slack with people who would otherwise work less or be unemployed; but most of what is lost to production is matched by the lost earnings of the workers. While nobody these days consumes exactly what he produces in a physical sense, most people and their families consume correspondingly more or less as their incomes go up or down. So the loss to the economy, or to the gross national product, lies mainly in the lost earnings, and, hence, consumption by those whose work schedules are impaired by their health. We may care about them and their consumption, just as we may care whether they die, but the cost falls on the economy mainly in the sense that they are themselves part of the economy. [Hence, under the prevalence approach, according to the author, there is no burden on society.]

A particular simple illustration [of the incidence approach] can be built around an unmarried male who has cancer of the lung diagnosed at the median age for lung cancer diagnosis, age 65. He has—in the absence of his lung cancer—an average life expectancy of 16 years; he dies within the year and would, on average, have lived another 15. The average 65-year-old man has already retired. He draws $6,000 from

---

[22] Thomas C. Schelling, "Economics and Cigarettes," *Preventive Medicine* 15 (1986), pp. 549–60.

a pension fund, and has some savings that yield interest or dividends, or possibly, a very modest home on which all mortgage payments have been completed. (The fraction of the labor force covered by private or government pension funds is well over half; the fraction of retired people drawing pension is smaller, but rising rapidly.) Had he lived, he would have paid $1,000 or $1,500 in federal and state income taxes and had $11,000 or $12,000 per year to spend. Dead, he relinquishes his claim to his social security and any retirement annuity. These are the transfers that he would have drawn had he lived. Discounting 15 years of these transfers at 6 percent yields at present value in excess of $100,000. The discounted value of his social security alone is $60,000. This, together with any financial assets or equity in his home, is what he leaves behind when he dies. In effect, he leaves a bequest of over $100,000 present value.

The idea that people who smoke and die 15 years early are net financial benefactors to the rest of society, by living most of a normal productive tax-paying life and dying before they can claim their retirement benefits, is momentarily surprising and somewhat paradoxical. But, we must not reverse the conclusion. If we begin by thinking that smokers in the aggregate inflict costs on the rest of us, and that is the reason why we should encourage them to quit or penalize them financially, then discovering that those who die leave behind more than they take from us might seem to suggest that we should happily let them smoke and relieve us of supporting them in their old age. But that would be a perverse and unnatural conclusion.

Not only was there increasing evidence that smokers were benefactors, not debtors, to society, recently questions had been raised regarding the net gain in life expectancy that would result as a consequence of a smoke-free society:[23]

While decreasing age-adjusted death rates, the demise of tobacco use would alter the relative mix of diseases. Chronic obstructive lung disease, currently a major source of death and disability, would become relatively inconsequential, while other pulmonary diseases, including influenza and pneumonia in the elderly, might become more common.

The dramatic decrease in lung cancers that would follow the demise of tobacco use undoubtedly would cause the age-adjusted cancer death rate to fall significantly, although it might be accompanied by increases in the (later) incidence of other cancers.

While there is little evidence to support it, a second posited undesirable health consequence of the tobacco-free society might be substitution of other stress responses, including deleterious habits ranging from alcohol or drug abuse to excessive consumption of food. The latter would bring the smoking-eating relationship full circle. . . . The net effect of freeing society from all the mortality caused by tobacco use would be life-expectancy increase of one to two years. To the lay public, this may not sound like much of a gain; to demographers and others familiar with vital statistics, it is dramatic.

---

[23] Kenneth E. Warner, "Health and Economic Implications of a Tobacco-Free Society," *Journal of American Medical Association* 258, no. 15 (October 16, 1987).

A provocative article recently suggested that "drinking," not "smoking," should be the focus of society's demarketing efforts. The authors of that article concluded:[24]

> On balance, smokers probably pay their way at the current level of excise taxes on cigarettes; but one may, nonetheless, wish to raise those taxes to reduce the number of adolescent smokers. In contrast, drinkers do not pay their way: current excise taxes on alcohol cover only about half the costs imposed on others.

Echoing this viewpoint, a *Boston Globe* editorial argued:[25]

> Smoking does not cause people to rob their neighbors to support the habit, nor beat their spouses or children in a mood-altering frenzy, nor drive crazily, nor aid international drug cartels. Smoking does not endanger neighborhoods or contribute to street crime, clog courts, or fill prisons. Smoking does not take over a person's life to the exclusion of all else.
>
> Part of the popularity of anti-smoking crusades is based on smokers, despite their perverse habit, being otherwise rational and, therefore, generally more responsive to criticism than alcoholics and drug addicts are.
>
> For the right reasons, smokers should stop. But that goal is not advanced by equating smoking with drug abuse or alcohol abuse, nor should it divert attention from those ruinous addictions.

THE HEALTH POLICE ARE BLOWING SMOKE

"Bolstered by bad science, the war on passive smoking is a trial run for a larger program of social manipulation," argued Bruce Biggs writing in *Fortune*.[26] The article added:

> The war against smoking is turning into a "jihad" against people who smoke. Smokers are being exiled from public and private places and are facing discrimination in employment. The reason, we are told, is that tobacco is deadly not only to users but also to innocents exposed to its noxious fumes.
>
> The truth is that America is suffering an epidemic of politically motivated hypochondria. Not only the liberty of smokers is threatened. Three decades ago the U.S. Public Health had apparently defeated its statutory enemy, communicable diseases, and decided to preserve itself by policing our private health. Smoking was the first target—a trial run in social manipulation. Sniffing victory in this skirmish, the feds are now turning their weapons on drinking, eating, and sex.
>
> But, you sputter, isn't the evidence conclusive that my smoke affects your health? Let me introduce you to the basics of scam science as generated for the feds. Smoking will be the example because it is the test case, but much of this mode of argumentation

---

[24] Willard G. Manning et al., "The Taxes of Sin: Do Smokers and Drinkers Pay Their Way?" *Journal of American Medical Association* 261, no. 11 (March 17, 1989).

[25] "The Smoking Equation," *Boston Globe*, May 19, 1988.

[26] Bruce B. Biggs, "The Health Police and Blowing Smoke," *Fortune*, April 25, 1988.

will be familiar to victims of the pollution, radiation, and toxic scams. All have their roots in the ambitions of the Public Health Service.

Note first the duplicitous use of words: Toxic means poisonous, but does not specify at what dose. Everything is toxic if ingested in sufficient quantity. This magazine is toxic—eat enough copies and you will get sick. Anyone who describes a substance as toxic without stating the dose level is engaging in flimflam; for example, the Surgeon General informing us that cigarette smoke is "toxic." . . .

Here's how the drill works: a toxie gets a government grant to terminate rats by all but drowning them in a suspect compound. He reports that whatzatapyrene is "carcinogenic." Because of the no-threshold principle, the feds can tell the public that "no safe dose level has been established." Next an epie gets a bigger grant to conduct a body count. He discovers that, of 87,000 watzat workers over 30 years, 46 succumbed to cancer. But the epie has calculated 22.7 "expected" deaths of the cancer in a comparable normal group, so the relative risk of whatzatapyrene exposure is 2.03. The feds tell the press that whatzateers are "twice as likely to get cancer."

Although the Public Health Service has been reticent about publicizing the fact, every study cited in support of the statement that "cigarette smoking causes cancer" reveals that a smoker is thoroughly unlikely to get cancer—only that he is statistically more likely to get it than a nonsmoker. No one can say precisely how much more likely.

Perhaps this is why people continue to smoke despite the increasingly shrill scoldings they are subject to. So lately the feds have escalated the war. Their most ingenious weapon for converting private health into public health is the "determination" that second-hand smoke—or passive smoking, or, in fed parlance, environmental tobacco smoke (ETS)—harms the public at large. . . .

More to the point, no industry is immune to the ravages of scam science. The feds are now trying to ban tobacco advertising in its surviving form. As the Surgeon General has said, "There is no safe cigarette." And no such thing as a safe automobile, a safe food, or a safe airline flight, or a safe ski, or safe cosmetic, or a safe condom. Nothing is safe as long as the authorities define private health as public health.

Barclays and South Africa[1]

By August 1985, Barclays Bank, the largest commercial bank in the United Kingdom, had been in South Africa for more than 60 years and described itself as "part of the economic fabric" of that country. However, over the previous 10 years, anti-apartheid groups had been demanding the bank's withdrawal from South Africa and the pressure had been mounting substantially in recent months on Timothy Bevan, the bank's chairman. The Barclays Group[2] employed 125,000 people in more than 80 countries; 25,000 were in South Africa. The South African subsidiary had been the group's largest overseas in terms of total assets, until it was overtaken in size by the United States subsidiary in 1981. However, Barclays' stake in South Africa remained considerable.

CAPITALISM AND APARTHEID

Apartheid in South Africa stirred many people. It was purportedly a system whereby the many races of South Africa could coexist securely and separately, different but equal.[3] Yet in effect it was a racist ideology advancing separate development of the peoples of South Africa to maintain the economic exploitation of the black majority. There were many countries whose inhabitants suffered oppression and indignities at the hands of the state; conditions were arguably as bad in some South American countries as they were in South Africa. However, as the South African government commented in a series of advertisements in the national press in the United Kingdom in 1983, "South Africa

---

This case was prepared by Professor N. Craig Smith with the assistance of Professor John A. Quelch.

Copyright © 1991 by the President and Fellows of Harvard College.

Harvard Business School case N9-592-014 (Rev. 10/4/91).

[1] This chapter is based on N. Craig Smith, *Morality and the Market: Consumer Pressure for Corporate Accountability* (London and New York: Routledge, 1990), pp. 234–41.

[2] The Barclays Group comprised Barclays Bank in the United Kingdom (around 70,000 employees) and Barclays Bank International (around 55,000 employees).

[3] The word *apartheid* is Afrikaans for separateness or segregation.

arouses more controversy than almost any other country in the world." This was due not only to the extent of the oppression in South Africa but also because of the way in which it was institutionalized.

Racism and the exploitation of the black population were firmly embodied within the culture and legislation of South Africa, with, for example, blacks unable to vote, and the Group Areas Act prohibiting people of different races from living in the same area. The immorality of such a system was judged as deeply offensive by countries of the First World (and the whites in South Africa did not wish their country to be seen as part of the Third World). Their multinational corporations operating in South Africa were, as a consequence of doing business there, seen to be implicated in apartheid.

The criticism of corporate involvement in South Africa went beyond an objection to companies remaining in a country that flouted the democratic principles cherished in the West. The economic function of apartheid and the role of business in apparently maintaining and benefiting from it suggested that those multinationals operating in South Africa had some responsibility for apartheid. It had been argued that there was a convergence of interest between business in South Africa and the upholders of apartheid—that South Africa's apartheid system had always been a mutually beneficial alliance between a minority government and private business. This was exemplified in apartheid's role in the provision of cheap labor, particularly in establishing a migratory labor system, which the U.K. government, in a white paper on South Africa, admitted, "robs the individual of the basic freedom to seek and obtain the job of his choice. It also causes grave social and family problems." Accordingly, critics of a Marxist persuasion argued that capitalism created apartheid: "Behind all the different manifestations of apartheid stands the mighty economic machine of South African capitalism. This machine absorbs cheap black labor, puts it through the wheels of industry, mining, and agriculture, and then expels it to distant reservations for the unemployed until the system requires more labor."[4]

While this reference to the role of the Bantustans or "homelands" (where many of South Africa's blacks were required to live) was largely accurate, this does not confirm a simple causal relationship between capitalism and apartheid. A study by Lipton suggested a more sophisticated analysis: "Apartheid cannot simply be explained as the outcome of capitalism or of racism. Its origins lie in a complex interaction between class interests (of white labor as well as of sections of capital) and racism/ethnicity, reinforced by ideological and security factors."[5] She argued that, while South African mining, agricultural, and white labor interests were generally served by apartheid, often the interests of manufacturing were not. The limits to black advancement also placed constraints on South African manufacturing industry.

---

[4] Charles Langford, *South Africa: Black Blood on British Hands* (London: Junius, 1985), p. 12.

[5] Merle Lipton, *Capitalism and Apartheid: South Africa 1910–1986* (Aldershot: Wildwood House, 1986), p. 365.

The debate on the extent of corporate culpability for apartheid notwithstanding, involvement in South Africa was a major issue of social responsibility in business. Continuing business operations in South Africa was defended by arguing that economic progress would necessitate the incorporation of blacks and end apartheid, but this was rejected by critics who saw little evidence of this happening. Their solution was the armed seizure of control by the African National Congress (ANC) with external pressure applied in the form of various sanctions. While condemning apartheid, Western governments and business largely resisted the pressure for disinvolvement with the South African economy, advocating constructive engagement to protect their interests.

INTERNATIONAL ECONOMIC SANCTIONS

South Africa was dependent on Western capital in the form of investment and trade. Direct investment had declined because of anti-apartheid criticism but was replaced by indirect investment. Yet, as trade and investment involved an interdependence, the West (and Britain and the United States especially) seemed committed to the stability of South Africa and, implicitly, the maintenance of apartheid, particularly as the trade with South Africa involved strategic raw materials for which South Africa was the major source of supply. This was aside from the country's political and military significance as a bastion against communism. This economic, political, and strategic interdependence made the use of effective international economic sanctions by the West unlikely. However, the increased unrest from 1984 onward and its extensive media coverage, strengthened demands for their imposition, and further measures were imposed in addition to the United Nations arms embargo and the OPEC oil boycott.[6] Business, in turn, wished to defend its economic interests and so followed the governmental line.

Four principal arguments were advanced against sanctions: the costs for those imposing them, as referred to above; that they would harm the blacks more, but then it was said that they were already suffering; doubts about their effectiveness, historically there was some support for this, particularly when countervailing measures were employed (but then why oppose them?); and, finally, constructive engagement. The latter argument, for "bridge-building" and change from within, was the most prominent. In accordance with this, corporate involvement was prescribed by codes of conduct, such as the European Economic Community (EEC) and Sullivan codes. These were voluntary but many firms complied to deflect criticism at home, and although they may have raised black living standards, they had not really challenged apartheid.

---

[6] In the United States, the Comprehensive Anti-Apartheid Act was passed in 1986. Prior to this an increasing number of state, county, and city government sanctions had appeared. In the United States and elsewhere, these regional government initiatives were often more symbolic than effective in restricting economic activity.

In 1972, when examining corporate involvement in South Africa and the constructive engagement argument, First et al. wrote:

> In their reply to the suggestion that this involvement puts a special onus on British firms to help end apartheid, businessmen generally give one of two answers: the first is that business and politics (like sport and politics) should not be mixed, and the second that apartheid may be objectionable, but that business is "doing its bit behind the scenes" to change it; the alternative to this reform-by-participation would, after all, be to try to bring down South Africa's regime and consequently her economy. So let us opt for reform through business rather than for revolution.[7]

In the United Kingdom, critics could see little evidence of constructive engagement working and, particularly with the recent unrest, it came to be seen as tacit support for apartheid. With international economic sanctions not forthcoming many consumers chose to support a consumer boycott campaign; it has been suggested that as many as one in four U.K. consumers viewed South African products as tainted (suggesting there was probably more consumer boycotting in Britain over apartheid in South Africa than any other issue). The Anti-Apartheid Movement's boycott campaign had been running for more than 25 years. Business had been attacked on other fronts as well, particularly by ethical investment, and was frequently criticized in the press for having links with South Africa, adding to the aggregate of pressure for change. A revitalized boycott campaign in the early 1980s had some successes, especially with some retail outlets and local governments, but, overall, purchases from South Africa (U.K. imports) increased rather than declined. The most well-known consumer boycott involved Barclays Bank.

BARCLAYS BANK TARGETED

Public criticism of direct investment in South Africa—through companies— and a strategy by the South African government to reduce its consequential vulnerability, reduced direct investment and brought about a trend towards indirect forms of investment. This was largely through banks, so they were soon targeted in the boycott campaign. All the major British banks lent to South Africa. The Co-Operative Bank and some other smaller banks did not. Barclays was singled out for attack because of its subsidiary in South Africa— Barclays National Bank—which was the largest bank there, with about 1,000 branches. Barclays was vulnerable in the United Kingdom because of its visibility; it had 3,000 branches on U.K. high streets. Barclays defended its involvement in South Africa using the constructive engagement argument, though its critics could see little other than cosmetic changes as a consequence of Barclays' continued involvement.

---

[7] Ruth First, Jonathan Steele, and Christabel Gurney, *The South African Connection: Western Investment in Apartheid* (London: Temple Smith, 1972).

The principal pressure group active against Barclays was End Loans to Southern Africa (ELTSA). ELTSA operated by applying what its main organizers described as "moral, public opinion type pressure and economic pressure," pressing Barclays to leave South Africa and end loans. Its materials included a glossy Shadow Report, produced on an annual basis "to chronicle details of how Barclays' presence in South Africa and Namibia helps sustain the apartheid system." Exhibit 1 lists "highlights" of 1981–84 Barclays Shadow Reports. The Shadow Board was comprised of a number of public figures, including Neil Kinnock, MP and leader of the Labour Party, and the actress Julie Christie. Many account closures were claimed, individual accounts but also those of noncommercial organizations, such as church bodies, local government authorities, and others, for example, the British Psychological Society. However, ELTSA felt the economic impact of this was low. Yet it believed this activity gave Barclays a "fairly dirty name" and contributed to the pressure on the bank to leave South Africa.

Barclays responded by producing material designed to reply to its "puzzled critics." This suggested that economic ties and investment were the only way for peaceful change—the constructive engagement argument, and the bank used this term—and that a bank cannot simply close down. While little business was said to have been lost, the criticism hurt.[8]

Yet in 1985, there seemed to be evidence of a phased withdrawal by the bank. In August, amid deteriorating economic conditions, there was an end to Barclays' majority shareholding. Pressure on the bank—presumably including the consumer boycott—was conceded as a factor in this move. One change forthcoming was an end to the use of the Barclays name in South Africa. However, the extent to which ELTSA and the boycott could claim responsibility was difficult to say at this stage. They did at least appear to have created a climate of possibility. Interestingly, the following comment was given by Sir Timothy Bevan in the chairman's statement in Barclays' 1985 *Annual Report* and reprinted in advertisements in the national press:

> It seems to me that the statement "we want to crush apartheid itself, not the victims of it" has it about right. To those who take their accounts away from us on ideological grounds, as is their right, I would pose one simple question: "Do you want us to stand back and wash our hands of apartheid or do you want us to continue to strengthen the tide of change?" Apartheid is unjust and immoral and so rightly condemned; equally it seems to me to be unjust to condemn us as supporters of the system, when in fact Barclays National is among the leaders in South Africa in opposition to it.

Barclays plc still had a 40.4 percent stake in Barclays National Bank, which it needed to defend. While, within the same statement, Sir Timothy Bevan spoke of the role of constructive engagement as above, one of the reasons given in explanation of the reduction in shareholding was, "we and many others

---

[8] The bank's reactions to the boycott were obtained through interviews with Barclays managers.

EXHIBIT 1   Highlights of Barclays Shadow Reports, 1981–84

- Barclays has constantly participated in vast international loans to South African state corporations. A United Nations study covering 1979–82 revealed it was the British bank most heavily involved in such loans.

- In 1979 Barclays bought £11 million worth of shares in Sasol, the state oil corporation, which is producing oil from coal to evade the international embargo on the one vital natural resource South Africa lacks.

- In 1976, Barclays purchased £6 million worth of South African government Defense Bonds, thereby directly funding the armed forces. The bonds were sold only after a massive international outcry.

- Barclays has run publicity campaigns specifically aimed at attracting accounts from South African troops, particularly those occupying Namibia.

- Barclays has helped finance arms sales to South Africa (although the bank says unknowingly).

- Barclays is among the largest taxpayers to the South African government.

- Barclays channels capital from black savers to the white community.

- Barclays is the largest distributor of krugerrands in the United Kingdom. These gold coins are a vital source of foreign exchange for South Africa.

- Barclays is one of the most active members of the United Kingdom–South Africa Trade Association, and is the largest financer of trade between the two countries.

- Several Barclays directors are trustees of the South Africa Foundation, a private body that disseminates South African propaganda abroad.

- In 1980, Barclays published a report called *Doing Business in South Africa*, which encouraged investment in South Africa. It took a pro-government line, and said of political unrest that "the situation is well under control and generally the labor force is content."

- Until 1980, Barclays published special reports encouraging investment in the Bantustans, which claimed that they had "meaningful self-government."

- In 1982, Barclays sacked an official of the black-consciousness Azanian People's Organization who had been convicted for putting up a poster in memory of the Sharpeville massacre. After huge protests he was reinstated.

- Barclays has dominated the banking scene in South Africa for nearly a century and is an integral part of the apartheid system.

Source: *Barclays Shadow Report 1985* (London: End Loans to Southern Africa, 1986).

deplore the slow movement of the South African government in dismantling institutionalized racial discrimination." Barclays seemed to be between a rock and a hard place: trying desperately to hold on to the constructive engagement argument to defend its remaining investment in South Africa yet at the same time trying to divest, which was extremely difficult given South Africa's instability. No doubt there was some envy of those firms, particularly American firms, such as General Electric and Pepsi, who had managed to get out.

ELTSA had not accounted for the increasing unrest in South Africa, which, during 1984 to 1986, came to be daily portrayed on television and in the press. This provided a considerable stimulus to the boycott Barclays campaign, particularly among U.K. students. Nor had it accounted for any moral dimension in Barclays' decision making on whether to stay in South Africa. The predominance over this period of the South African situation in current affairs and the pressure on Western governments to impose sanctions on South Africa highlighted Barclays' involvement there. The deteriorating economic conditions in South Africa and Barclays' planned expansion in the United States (where at this time consumer activism on South Africa was at least equal to that in the United Kingdom), added further weight to the case for a clear strategy on South Africa. It was these factors which had led to a reduction in Barclays' shareholding in its South African subsidiary and urged a complete withdrawal from South Africa.

Timothy Bevan had succeeded Sir Anthony Tuke as chairman of Barclays in 1982. Tuke had never been receptive to criticism of Barclays' involvement in South Africa, standing firm on the constructive engagement argument. Bevan, however, was said to genuinely detest apartheid and, moreover, was less susceptible to pressure from Pretoria as the relative importance of Barclays' South African operations had diminished. Neither did he have a history of long associations with white South Africans, and his views were also shared by some of the newer members of the Barclays board. These views became public when, in November 1985, Bevan mounted a critical attack on the South African regime in a speech to branch managers. Moreover, he revealed contacts with the ANC—he had met Oliver Tambo, president of the ANC, in London. The new and dynamic chief executive of Barclays National Bank, Chris Ball, also had been having meetings with black nationalists. Indeed, Ball's radical stance (for a South African business executive) was earning for Barclays National Bank in South Africa an anti-apartheid label!

Meanwhile, the corporate exodus was taking hold. *Business Week* reported that three times as many U.S. companies had halted all or part of their South African operations in the year up to September 1985, compared with the previous year. Ford, Apple Computers, and Singer were among the 18 companies disinvesting. As the *Economist* explained, also in September 1985: "The reason for the flight from South Africa is that no businessman wants to be caught propping up a government whose social policy leads to the sjamboking and shooting of people on television—so, eventually, to money-losing revolution."

WITHDRAWAL

In 1986 Bevan's stance against apartheid—for moral or commercial reasons (or both)—hardened still further. Barclays had, with the other banks, despite a request to do otherwise from the president of the Anti-Apartheid Movement, agreed to a rescheduling of South African debt in March 1986, though on tougher terms than expected by Pretoria. By the time of the May 1986 Barclays board meeting it had been decided to fully withdraw from South Africa. In November, agreement was finally reached.

Barclays sold its remaining stake in Barclays National Bank, which had a market valuation of £221 million, for £82 million (at the financial rand exchange rate) on November 23, 1986. It was bought by Anglo-American (a large South African conglomerate) and Anglo-American controlled companies. Bevan said the reasons were "basically commercial." Ball acknowledged the likely negative impact on the South African economy but was positive about the opportunities for the South African bank. It was, he said, "a unique opportunity, giving us the potential to strengthen our position both domestically and internationally." He contrasted the move with the disinvestment earlier in 1986 of multinationals, such as IBM and General Motors, by noting the bank was not dependent on outside supplies. He referred to Barclays' reluctance to take this move and explained, "they are not doing it to achieve a political objective. They are doing it because they are under political pressure."

In an editorial headed "Moral Pressure in the Market," the *Financial Times* clearly attributed the withdrawal to the boycott campaign:

> Ordinary people, revolted by what they have learned about the [apartheid] system from the news media, are not much concerned with the sometimes agonizing decisions faced by those actually involved; they want to make their opposition felt, and have proved again that they can bring effective pressure to bear on commercial organizations, even if they cannot move foreign governments. Moral pressures of this kind—whether against apartheid, whaling, the fur trade, vivisection, or even the defense industry—is an increasingly important fact of business life.

It had emerged in August 1986, from the leak of an internal Barclays document to Anti-Apartheid, that Barclays' share of the student market had dropped from 27 percent to 17 percent between 1983 and 1985. Students were a vital sector of the market for U.K. banks, because of their likely future prosperity and the high level of customer loyalty within the industry; people generally tended to stay with the bank they first joined. Chris Ball later suggested the drop was even more substantial, explaining the withdrawal as almost entirely due to this loss of business.[9] He did, however, also acknowledge the importance of Barclays' U.S. expansion plans and the limitations placed on them by involvement in South Africa. The "hassle factor" of continually hav-

---

[9] Citing a decline to 6 percent by 1986 (at the 1987 "International Conference on South Africa in Transition," White Plains, New York).

ing to respond to vociferous pressure groups also seemed to have played a part in Barclays' decision to withdraw. It may even have contributed to Barclays' lackluster performance of recent years and low morale. Sampson suggested the impact on South Africa of the departure of such a major foreign investor was considerable: "The withdrawal was perhaps the most fundamental blow so far of those that have begun to rain on the South African economy."[10] Yet it did not force great concessions out of South Africa.

The anti-apartheid groups claimed Barclays' withdrawal to be a major success. In many ways, for them, it was, although they could not claim full responsibility. It was even a victory for capitalism. As the *Financial Times* also commented:

> The whole merit of the market system is that it is the best system yet devised for recording and satisfying consumer preferences, and if these preferences rank the rights of minorities or humane farming, alongside the elegance of a design or the palatability of a strawberry flavor, it does the customers nothing but credit.

---

[10] Anthony Sampson, *Black and Gold* (Sevenoaks: Coronet Books, 1987).

Chapter 2.6

In the News

2.6.1 GOOD TAKES ON GREED*

"The secret of life," mused Groucho Marx, "is honesty and fair dealing. If you can fake that, you've got it made." Unlike Marx, companies feel the need to do more than just fake goodness in the 1990s.

It has not been a good week for the reputation of business. In America the collapse of Drexel Burnham Lambert on February 13th . . . cast a fresh spotlight on the financial excesses and crimes of the 1980s. In London the "City trial of the century" opened. Prosecuting counsel accused the former chairman of Guinness, Mr. Ernest Saunders, along with three other businessmen, Mr. Anthony Parnes, Sir Jack Lyons, and Mr. Gerald Ronson, of being "carried away with greed and ambition" during Guinness's takeover of Distillers in 1986.

Those still thirsting after anti-business amusement could watch the movie *Roger and Me*, in which General Motors is pilloried for turning Flint, Michigan, into "the unemployment capital of America" by axing 30,000 jobs there over the past decade. GM reckons it had no choice in Flint: the health of the company was at stake.

Faced with this sort of buffeting, more and more management minds are turning to questions of "business ethics." Courses on the subject have become common at business schools, and it is fashionable to attend conferences to agonise about it.

Nothing new under this sun: in 1915, Harvard offered a class on "social factors in business enterprise." Today, ethics is firmly on the Harvard Business School curriculum (its future healthily secured in 1987 by an endowment of some $20m from Mr. John Shad, then chairman of the SEC). MBA students start their ethics tuition on day one, and the ethical consequences of everything from marketing to personnel management are woven into the entire MBA syllabus.

By 1988, reckons the Ethics Resource Centre in Washington, 92 percent of America's biggest 2,000 companies had "ethical codes of practice" for their employees (compared with under half of European firms); over a third had "ethics education" programmes.

A fad? Interest in ethics seems to follow the ups and downs of society's attitude towards business: Harvard stepped up its ethics programme after the 1929 Wall Street crash. The 1990s' trend has its roots in dirt ranging from the mid-1980s' defence-contracting scandals (when companies such as General Dynamics knowingly overcharged the Pentagon) to pollution (the case of Union Carbide's plant in Bhopal, India, which negligently released toxic fumes killing over 2,500 people, is part of many MBAs' coursework) to investment in South Africa.

Cynics argue that ethics will be forgotten when the good times stop rolling. Mr. John Akers, chairman of IBM, thinks not. "Ethics and competitiveness," he says, "are inseparable . . . the greater the measure of mutual trust and con-

* This article first appeared in *The Economist*, February 17, 1990. It is reprinted with permission.

fidence in the ethics of a society, the greater its economic strength."

Trouble is, "ethics" catches too many different ideas. If it means "being seen to follow customers' non-commercial concerns," then it can clearly be good business: last August, Audi, a West German carmaker, became the first company to fit catalytic convertors as standard on cars sold in Britain (where catalysts are not yet compulsory). Thanks to that—and some slick green PR—Audi reckons its sales will climb some 40 percent this year, in an otherwise flat market.

That is quite different from "realising that your reputation forms part of the value of your brands." Perrier, combining concern for its good name with concern for its customers' health, chose to withdraw its entire worldwide stock after worries that its bottled water had been contaminated with benzene. Awkwardly, it had to contradict its initial assurances that only part of its output had been tainted. Such an issue becomes a mixture of crisis management and, ideally, crisis prevention. That is entirely different again from "behaving nicely towards your employees" (America's Polaroid pays lower-paid workers' child-care expenses) or towards a wider body of "stakeholders" (Britain's Marks and Spencer pays for social projects in its shops' local communities).

What of ethical codes of conduct? These are the closest thing to ethics as most people would understand it, since the subject applies more to individuals than to corporate entities. One of the biggest problems is preventing employees from assuming either that anything is permissible if the firm benefits or from assuming (as insider traders commonly do, for instance) that something is all right if "everybody is doing it."

The code of the Prudential Corporation, an assurance-to-property group, is typical. After pledging to work for the good of its shareholders, customers, and staff, the code notes that "in promoting its businesses the Prudential's aims are . . . to abide by the spirit of laws as well as their letter and to be a significant contributor to the development and well-being of the wider community in which we operate." Fine: but how do such well-meaning but abstract guidelines cope when the interests of the company diverge sharply from those of its employees and customers or the local community?

The answer depends on what lies behind each company's code. With no small print to tell employees what to do in specific dilemmas (such as being offered, or asked for, a bribe), and no sanctions to enforce the code, it becomes nothing more than a PR puff. Companies need to provide detailed policy on such issues as conflicts of interest, bribes and gift-giving, and relations with competitors, as well as spelling out the rights of shareholders and other stakeholders.

It also means tailoring ethics policy to each of the firm's main functions. How is the export division which deals with Saudi Arabia, where bribes are routine business practice, to act? The ethical code of Levi-Strauss, a jeans maker, forbids bribes, "whether or not prevalent or legal in the foreign country involved." In America this tough approach is gaining ground.

Souring the Sweeteners

A fifth of America's 2,000 biggest companies now have board-level ethics committees, which decide ethics policy, arrange ethics seminars for employees, and, in some firms, order regular "ethical audits." At Dow Corning, an American silicon company, that means quizzing managers on such issues as whether they have lost business because of Dow's refusal to pay bribes and whether any distribution contracts have been terminated because of a distributor's irregular business conduct. Dow reckons that auditing makes it "virtually impossible for employees consciously to make an unethical decision."

But what happens when an ethical employee is at odds with his employer? A textbook case is that of America's Morton Thiokol (now known as Thiokol), where two senior engineers gave warning, on the eve of *Challenger*'s take-off in January 1986, that the space-shuttle's O-ring gaskets (made by Thiokol) might be affected by forecast cold weather. Seven astronauts died in the subsequent disaster. Both Thiokol employees, who were praised for their action by the inquiry into the disaster, saw their careers suffer as a result of their stand.

To avoid such conflicts, around a 10th of big American companies (including past offenders like General Dynamics) have set up independent ethics offices or ombudsmen to act as a channel for whistle-blowers. Most guarantee that an employee's career is protected from the moment the whistle is blown. Sceptics are, well, sceptical.

There is a danger, thinks Professor Jack Mahoney, director of the Business Ethics Research Centre at King's College, London, that the doubters expect too much from business ethics. At best, he thinks, ethical codes and their like simply help good people to make good decisions. That, he observes, is an improvement on simple reliance on the law. Laws may limit damage, but are usually drafted only after large numbers of people have been hurt. By encouraging companies and employees to act ethically, some of that damage may be prevented.

Taking the ethical initiative, then lobbying for legislation to enshrine that in law, can help companies. Cummins Engine, a diesel-engine maker, cleaned up its engines and then lobbied for tougher pollution laws. Du Pont, the biggest producer of ozone-damaging CFC, is a vocal member of the anti-CFC lobby—partly because it thinks it is well ahead in the race for a cheap substitute. Cynical? Perhaps. But, if the 1990s are indeed more ethical, such "elevation of the level playing field" may be a popular business strategy.

2.6.2 ETHICAL SHOPPING*

Nowadays a lot of consumers want products that are "moral" as well as good value. But what do you do if your favorite peanut butter is sound on South Africa but insensitive to women?

First, a Detroit housewife launches a campaign against companies that advertise on the program *Married . . . with Children*. Then Pepsi gets roasted for its incendiary Madonna ads. Now it turns out that a New York organization called the Council on Economic Priorities has sold 200,000 copies of its handy guide to righteous supermarket behavior, *Shopping for a Better World*.

"Finally! An easy way to get in and out of the store and support companies with responsible policies," declares a happy shopper quoted on the back of the booklet, which rates the makers of 1,300 brand-name products on 10 social issues.

"Easy" is not quite the operative term. Actually, *Shopping for a Better World* is an incredibly complicated 132-page pamphlet, which lists the 1,300 products in alphabetical order, with 10 tiny boxes appearing to the right of each product name beneath such graphics as a map of South Africa and what appears to be a Christmas tree (a symbol for the environment). There are a bunch of letters, asterisks, and question marks, none of which are easy to follow, although an "X" under the graphic of a bunny rabbit clearly means that you wouldn't want to be Peter Cottontail when the company's scientists are around.

There is also a box indicating whether the company has won any awards for social consciousness, or, conversely, has participated in some particularly sinister activity, such as killing dolphins, busting unions, or not providing day-care centers for employees. The print is tiny, the graphics are enigmatic, and, if the booklet is truly "a quick and easy guide to socially responsible supermarket shopping," how come it has 15 pages explaining how to use it?

"It is pretty complicated," concedes Benjamin Corson, who helped compile it.

---

* This article by Joe Queenan first appeared in *Forbes*.

Reprinted by permission of *Forbes* Magazine, April 17, 1989. © Forbes Inc., 1989.

All the same, beams council publicist Peg Munves, "It's selling like hotcakes."

We hate to be cynical about so worthy an activity, but the Council on Economic Priorities has had some help in moving its hotcakes. The *Utne Reader*, a sort of leftist *Reader's Digest*, paid less than a dollar apiece for the 107,000 copies it mailed out with its January edition; the guides usually cost $4.95 a pop. And a lot of other copies went to public interest groups at nominal prices. Still, 200,000 remorselessly ethical shoppers is nothing for corporate America to sniff at.

Alice Tepper Marlin, who worked as a securities analyst for Burnham & Company two decades ago, is the founder and executive director of the CEP. She says that the data in the book are derived from questionnaires filled out by the companies themselves, plus material supplied by experts on corporate morality. She reports that her organization is now preparing an updated version of the booklet, to be co-published by Ballantine Books, and that it may launch a guide for ethical women, a guide for ethical kids, and a guide for ethical catalog shoppers.

What kind of impact is this having? Edwina Sanders, media director at American Cyanamid, says the firm has no reaction to being pilloried in the guide for producing—what else?—pesticides. Ted Smyth, director of corporate affairs at H. J. Heinz, is annoyed that his firm is flagged for catching dolphins in its fishing nets, but adds, "Sales have never been better."

That could be the result of burgeoning anti-dolphin sentiment, or because the guide is so hard to use. Suppose, for example, you are looking for a highly moral steak sauce. On the surface, A-1 Steak Sauce might seem like a safe bet; it gives a moderate amount to charity, has a decent record toward women, and is active in minority advancement. But reading all the way across the chart, you would learn to your dismay that A-1's parent company not only has a dismal performance in the environmental protection field but has a stake in South Africa as well. Worse still, A-1 is made by RJR Nabisco, which manufactures ecologically offensive, cardiovascularly lethal cigarettes—and uses a lot of junk bonds to do it.

Okay, so you decide to use ketchup instead of steak sauce. Heinz has a fine record in nuclear energy—something moral shoppers always look for in a condiment maker—and the company also seems decent to women. But, as noted above, these guys are gunning for Flipper. Indeed, as you wander through the aisles, you will realize that, unless you're willing to make some serious moral compromises, this is going to be one very unproductive shopping expedition.

Yuban coffee is out because the parent company makes cigarettes. The cat will have to go hungry tonight because Purina doesn't give enough money to charities. Miracle Whip is out because Kraft is accused of running misleading ads. Your woolens will have to stay dirty because the makers of Woolite don't care about blacks. And if all these decisions turn your stomach, it's no good turning to Alka-Seltzer because Miles Laboratories experiments on animals.

Actually, what the Council on Economic Priorities has inadvertently done is to put together a guide that really benefits morally degenerate consumers. Because it flags corporate miscreants in its "Alert" box, wicked consumers instinctively know to buy Velveeta, because of Kraft's misleading ads; stock up on Baggies, because Mobil is in South Africa; and get the wrinkles out of clothes the union-busting way with StaPuf. With the help of this guide, a moral leper could be in and out of the supermarket in five minutes flat.

Maybe the supermarkets could arrange their aisles not according to product but according to the moral posture of the manufacturer.

"Can you tell me where the coffee is?" a shopper would ask. "Anti-apartheid decaf in aisle 8;

Blue Mountain no-nuke, pro-whale in aisle 6," would come the reply.

Ethical double-coupon days is another idea, though an even better innovation might be moral bar-coding so that cash registers would cry out: "Grocery, $1.98, tortures bunnies, but runs an employee day care center."

Who uses *Shopping for a Better World*? Marlin insists that the people buying the guide are not just the usual crew from Greenwich Village and San Francisco, but include a surprisingly large number from such ethically suspect locales as Dallas and Denver. But when asked if he sees anybody wading through the guide when he goes shopping, Marlin's co-author, Corson, replies, "I don't. But I live out in Queens."

2.6.3 A NEW SALES PITCH: THE ENVIRONMENT*

How companies are cashing in on public concern over trash

You're socially aware. You know America is up to its eyeballs in trash, and you fret about all those nasty disposable diapers Junior goes through. Now, RMed International Inc. offers a way to throw away the guilt along with the diaper. The company sells a "biodegradable" baby wrap called Tender Care. Its pitch: "Change the world one diaper at a time."

Call it environmental marketing. Never mind that there's debate about how much "biodegradable" diapers buried deep in a landfill really degrade. Playing to environmental concern sells. Consumers are willing to pay an extra 5 percent to 10 percent for the Tender Care diaper. RMed's sales in the first six months more than doubled, to $700,000, even though it has discontinued its regular diapers.

---

* This article by Brian Bremner first appeared in *BusinessWeek*. Reprinted from July 24, 1989, issue of *BusinessWeek* by special permission, copyright © 1989 by McGraw-Hill, Inc.

With polls showing Americans growing increasingly anxious about the future of the planet, more companies are striking similar environmentally friendly poses. "The whole Green movement is moving beyond just politics," says Stephen G. Bowen, president of J. Walter Thompson USA Inc. "It's becoming a day-to-day issue for many consumers."

Feathered Friends

Of course, pitching woo to Mother Earth is nothing new to the chemical, oil, and auto industries, businesses long linked to pollution. Chevron Corporation, for example, launched its "People Do" ads three years ago. One spot relates how Chevron delayed a gas pipeline project in Wyoming so as not to upset the mating season of local grouse.

What's different now is garbage. By 1995, according to the Environmental Protection Agency, half of the nation's 5,400 landfills will be closed. That means companies not often thought of as environmental bad guys—food and consumer-products makers—are now under intense fire for the tons of paper and plastic packaging they put out. "Everybody is walking around on eggshells," says Larry Sawyer, government affairs director at General Mills, Inc. To help postpone the day that becomes a literal statement, General Mills uses recycled paper in Cheerio boxes.

For Procter & Gamble Company, the garbage glut is a particularly noisome issue. With 47 percent of the $3.7 billion disposable-diaper market, P&G is clearly concerned about biodegradable diapers. Last month, the company launched a study to back its claim that such diapers don't necessarily dissolve harmlessly into the ground. It also unveiled a pilot project to recycle regular disposable diapers into reusable pulp and plastic.

P&G alone accounts for an estimated 1 percent of the nation's solid waste, and that's one market-share number the consumer giant would dearly like to reduce. Last year, it unveiled a Spic & Span bottle that uses recycled plastic. It's also testing the idea of offering pouches of concentrated liquid detergent so consumers could refill, rather than discard, the bulky plastic bottles. The idea is already a hit in West Germany with P&G's Lenor fabric softener brand.[1]

A growing number of companies are feeling pressure to clean up their environmental acts before the government does it for them. McDonald's Corporation has long been under attack for the millions of plastic hamburger boxes it tosses out each year. In April, the Minneapolis City Council banned such plastic at food stores and restaurants. Similar measures have been passed in Berkeley, California, and Portland, Oregon.

McDonald's calls such bans a bunch of rubbish. After all, EPA figures show that paper accounts for some 41 percent of typical landfill space and plastic only about 6 percent. Still, the chain is quietly using recycled paper for its kids' Happy Meal packages and recycled plastic for some of its trays. But for now, McDonald's isn't planning any media blitz to trumpet its do-gooding. "The more we advertise it, the more we identify it as a McDonald's problem," says Shelby Yastrow, the chain's general counsel.[2]

Pulled Plug

Others are anything but reticent. Last month, Loblaw Companies, the $10 billion Canadian food distributor and grocery-store chain, launched a "Green" line of "environment friendly products" backed by a $3 million TV and print ad campaign. The 100-item line includes so-called biodegradable diapers, bathroom tissue made from recycled paper, and foam plates made without ozone-destroying gases. Early signs are that Loblaw will do well from doing good. In its Ontario stores, the chain sold $5 million worth of its Green products in June, double projected sales. The chain is thinking of introducing the line in its 100 U.S. stores, too.

Still, Loblaw has taken a few public relations lumps. A Canadian group, Pollution Probe, endorsed about 10 of the Green items but later withdrew its backing of one, the diaper, after other groups raised questions about it. "There has been a lot of sniping," admits David A. Nichol, executive vice president of Loblaw. The episode may have been an embarrassment for Loblaw, but the chain has no plans to retreat. For it and other companies, the public's growing yearning for a healthier environment offers plenty of opportunities to clean up.

---

[1] See Chapter 4.4.
[2] See Chapter 2.3.

Pharmaceutical Marketing Practices in the Third World*

N. Craig Smith
John A. Quelch

Major criticisms of pharmaceutical marketing are summarized and industry responses identified. Analysis of this industry case study highlights ethical issues in marketing and the broader problem of harnessing enterprise to ensure quality of life and public good. A social control of business model is presented and the limits of corporate social responsibility delineated.

INTRODUCTION

As part of the Harvard Business School Ethics in Marketing Project, a case study was developed on pharmaceutical marketing (Smith and Quelch, 1989a) together with a supporting note on pharmaceutical marketing practices in the Third World (Smith and Quelch, 1989b). Widespread concern about pharmaceutical marketing prompted this case development topic, though the authors' intention was not to single out the industry for specialization, not least because of the benefits provided by drugs. The focus was on learning from past experience to identify improvements in marketing practice, which have application beyond the pharmaceutical industry. The note on pharmaceutical marketing was developed from the principal secondary sources and primary sources, including interviews with pharmaceutical industry executives and discussions with some of their critics. In this chapter, we first present the principal criticisms of pharmaceutical marketing. We then analyze these criticisms in order to develop recommendations for pharmaceutical marketing practice and

---

* Reprinted by permission of the publisher from *Journal of Business Research* 23, no. 1 (August 1991), pp. 113–26. Copyright © 1991 by Elsevier Science Publishing Co., Inc.

use the industry to illustrate the requirement for social control of business and the limits of corporate social responsibility.

CRITICISMS OF PHARMACEUTICAL MARKETING

In proportion to its size, the pharmaceutical industry received more criticisms for its practices in the Third World and, indeed, the developed world, than most other industries. This was at least partially due to the nature of its business, so closely involved with life and death. Ironically, the industry's success in healing made it all the more subject to public scrutiny. A broader concern about corporate practices in the Third World readily focused on pharmaceutical corporations. As Braithwaite wrote of pharmaceutical companies: "The moral failure of the transnationals lies in their willingness to settle for much lower standards abroad than at home" (1984, p. 246). Their promotional practices received most criticism, but there was also concern about the lack of medication in the Third World, drug profits, dumping, and the testing of drugs.

Promotion in the Third World

Pharmaceutical companies were criticized for their promotional practices in the developed world. Criticisms focused on: the role of pharmaceutical sales representatives (or "detailers") and their attempts to influence prescribing habits of doctors; gifts and expenses-paid trips to conventions provided to doctors; misleading or incomplete promotional materials, which, for example, did not always give prices or adverse effects of drugs; the supply of branded pharmaceuticals rather than generics; and the associated costs of these activities. Similar, though frequently stronger charges, were also made against pharmaceutical companies for their promotional practices in the Third World. Of great concern was the promotion of drugs for a wider range of indications in the Third World than the developed world and with less disclosure of contraindications and side effects. Concern also was expressed about the availability of drugs in the Third World not available in the developed world; of variations in dosage, with higher doses often prescribed in the Third World; and the promotion of drugs as over-the-counter (OTC) products in the Third World that were only available on prescription in the developed world.

A leading and ultimately influential critic of the pharmaceutical industry was Milton Silverman, a biochemist and pharmacologist at the University of California School of Medicine, San Francisco. His *Drugging of the Americas* (1976) documented "how multinational drug companies say one thing about their products to physicians in the United States, and another thing to physicians in Latin America." He was highly critical:

> When the so-called morals of the marketplace are applied to drugs that can be invaluable when used properly, the result is not only the prostitution of science . . .

physicians and pharmacists are uninformed or misinformed ... patients are needlessly harmed (1976, p. xi).

He suggested that companies were "lying" when they claimed in their standard defense that they were not breaking any laws. Moreover, he questioned the pharmaceutical industry's arguments against regulation in the United States and the claim that the industry recognized its social responsibilities and would live up to them, law or no law. His finding of a "double standard of drug advertising" was indicative of corporate practices in the absence of laws or their enforcement. Detailed evidence was provided to support this finding. Silverman added that the practices he described were not limited to Latin America. His book was dedicated to the memory of people who had died from drugs prescribed for the treatment of minor ailments, including chloramphenicol, an antibiotic with the possible fatal side effect of aplastic anemia (bone marrow failure). Silverman contrasted the more limited indications for the drug in the United States with those given for Latin America. He also listed contraindications and side effects. Parke Davis, for example, gave no contraindications or adverse reactions (such as aplastic anemia) for its product Chloromycetin in Central America and Argentina, although a long list of both was provided in the United States.

Tables were provided by Silverman for most of the major drug categories, showing similar findings. These disparities between the information provided involved most of the large pharmaceutical companies: Squibb, Boehringer, Schering, Searle, Johnson & Johnson, Wyeth, Merck, Upjohn, Smith Kline & French, and Eli Lilly. With Ciba-Geigy, for example, nonsteroid arthritics Butazolidin (phenylbutazone) and Tanderil (oxyphenbutazone) were listed, as was Tegretol (carbamazebine), an anticonvulsant for epilepsy and neuralgia, and a Geigy anti-depressant, Tofranil (imipramine). Tables for these products showed more indications for use in Latin America and less contraindications, warnings, and adverse reactions. For Tegretol, only the *Physicians' Desk Reference* in the United States warned "since this drug is not a simple analgesic, it should not be used for the relief of trivial aches and pains." Deaths from aplastic anemia had been reported following treatment with Tegretol, but this possible adverse reaction was only given in the United States materials.

A second study by Silverman et al. (1982) compared the information provided to physicians in 27 countries in Latin America, Central Africa, and Asia, together with the United States and the United Kingdom. Again, the promotion to Third World doctors was found to be marked by exaggerated claims of efficacy and a glossing over of hazards. Interviews conducted with pharmacologists and clinical authorities in the Third World countries brought forth criticism of promotional practices, including the promotion of so-called luxury products, such as sex tonics and other vitamin combinations. The respondents had stressed the need for more basic requirements; scarce health funds could not be wasted when there were inadequate supplies for the control of such diseases as malaria, let alone food shortages.

Further studies (cited, for example, in Chetley, 1986) confirmed Silverman's work, which also caught the attention of the World Health Organization (WHO) and concerned public interest groups, such as War on Want, the International Organization of Consumers Unions, and its international information center, Health Action International. In 1981 and 1982, Social Audit, a United Kingdom public interest group, received support from these groups to lobby G. D. Searle over its marketing of Lomotil (diphenoxylate/atropine), an antidiarrheal. Social Audit produced an anti-advertisement for Lomotil that was widely distributed. The leaflet highlighted the potential dangers of Lomotil in the treatment of children, its questionable usefulness and, hence, economic waste. Lomotil was contraindicated for children under two in the United States, but recommended for infants three months old in Hong Kong, Thailand, and the Philippines. A further, and not uncommon, concern was the free availability of Lomotil over the counter. Searle promised, in response, to revise its prescribing instructions (Medawar and Freese, 1982).

Lack of Medication in the Third World

Silverman and others identified a problem of inappropriate medication. However, for many people in the Third World the problem was an absence of medication. In 1979, the International Year of the Child, an address by Senator Kennedy included the observation that over 2.5 million children would die that year from communicable diseases, such as measles and polio, because they wouldn't have access to vaccines. This was in stark contrast to the problems of overmedication in some developed countries, identified by Ivan Illich in *Medical Nemesis*, where people were too ready to view themselves as patients and, as a consequence, subject to unnecessary and expensive treatment which, of itself, could have harmful consequences. Moreover, while basic medicines were unavailable in parts of the Third World, the focus in Western medicine was on keeping people alive longer. This emphasis was reflected in R&D expenditures by pharmaceutical companies. Figures on drug consumption also were shown to be highly correlated with per capita income. Critics charged that ability to pay, rather than need, determined drug research and availability. With the Wellcome Foundation as a notable exception, R&D expenditures were far higher on drugs—deemed as less necessary—for the developed world, than R&D on tropical diseases.

Drug Profits

The shortage of medicines in the Third World added weight to the more general criticism that drug companies made substantial profits out of sickness, as high prices were blamed. More radical critics questioned the appropriateness of private enterprise involvement in health care, though they could not point to

Eastern bloc pharmaceutical development and production as representing a better approach. Others sought evidence of inadequate competition, but, with no one company having more than 5 percent world market share, this was difficult to establish. It could be shown, however, that the uniquely international character of the industry created barriers to entry, with no new drug companies emerging among long-established leaders in the industry. There were also concentrations by product; reaching a readily identified global market segment with a patent-protected product could be highly profitable, as Glaxo found with Zantac and Hoffman-La Roche with Valium Diazepam.

Simple comparisons between the cost of chemical ingredients and drug prices suggested blatant profiteering. However, this ignored substantial R&D costs. Ciba-Geigy estimated that, of 10,000 preparations synthesized and tested, only one would become a drug sold, some 12 years later, in the marketplace. The risks and costs associated with R&D provided the rationale for patent protection. But there was only limited evidence of these factors causing financial difficulty; drug profits remained high and critics charged that too much R&D was on "me-too" products. ICI and Dow Chemical, for example, generated the highest level of earnings from their pharmaceutical activities in 1981 (ICI: 24 percent of profit, at 22.1 percent margin), though they made up less than 6 percent of the sales of either company (Tucker, 1984). The industry cited the absence of financial difficulty as proof that the system worked. Not surprisingly, therefore, pharmaceutical companies opposed price control efforts, including the use of generic lists.

Studies suggested that doctors preferred brand names (Tucker, 1984, p. 133). Generic names could be a mouthful and difficult to remember, so doctors chose to behave as consumers, and brand names acted as a guarantee of quality. Pharmacists also were resistant to substitute a generic equivalent for a prescribed brand as it increased their liability in the event of an adverse reaction. Attempts by Third World countries, such as India, Pakistan, and Sri Lanka, to control drug costs by generic sourcing and local manufacture had limited success. Doctors were uncertain about quality, and generic substitution gave little incentive to the large pharmaceutical companies to research tropical diseases if they were to be denied the profits from such endeavors. Ciba-Geigy withdrew from Pakistan in 1973, apparently in protest at generic substitution. This project failed, allegedly due to pressure from the pharmaceutical companies. Sri Lanka was more successful. Although there were quality problems, the United Nations Industrial Development Organization reported a 65 percent savings in Sri Lanka's drug bill for 1974. An equivalent to Roche's patented Diazepam, for example, had been sourced at 4 percent of the original price (Braithwaite, 1984, pp. 270–74).

Differential pricing also was criticized. The 1967 U.S. Congress Select Committee on the pharmaceutical industry cited Schering's Meticorten (100 $\times$ 5 mg tablets), listed at \$17.90 in the United States, \$22.70 in Canada, \$12.26 in Mexico, \$5.30 in Brazil, and \$4.37 in Switzerland. While on average 15 percent of a country's health expenditure was on drugs, the figure was estimated by the World Bank in 1980 to be 25 percent for a typical Third World country; some sources put it higher still. However, this was at least partly explained by the lower salaries for health workers in those countries. The proportion of health spending taken up by drugs in the developed world was declining.

Dumping

Consumer organizations, suspicious of pharmaceutical companies, often would ask whether a drug available in the Third World also was available in the developed world. Dumping was the fear. Dowie, writing in 1979 in *Mother Jones*, identified Upjohn's Depo-Provera and A. H. Robins' Dalkon Shield as two examples (Braithwaite, 1984, p. 258). Depo-Provera, an injectable drug preventing conception in women for three to six months, was not even approved for human testing in the United States, but was available without prescription in Central America. The Dalkon Shield IUD had been recalled after the death of at least 17 women users in the United States, but then subsequently was provided to Third World countries through the United States government's Office of Population. However, under Chapter 8 of the U.S. Food, Drug, and Cosmetic Act of 1938 (and subsequent amendments), pharmaceutical companies could not export drugs not approved for marketing within the United States. (A 1986 amendment relaxed this regulation for exports of drugs for tropical diseases.) Dowie identified a range of dumping strategies used to avoid prohibitive regulations, including: the name change; dumping the whole factory; the formula change—a minor change to avoid detection by scanning devices; the skip—exporting via countries with little regulation (e.g., Guatemala) to those that insist drugs are approved for use in the country of origin; and the ingredient dump—exporting ingredients separately to a recombining facility.

Braithwaite (1984, pp. 259–60) confirmed this list. He also identified a double standard of manufacturing quality, where large pharmaceutical companies granted licenses to manufacture to Third World companies with questionable quality standards. He suggested that the most common form of dumping was of products whose shelf life had expired—possibly exported immediately prior to expiry. Quality problems resulting from these and other practices, such as smuggling, could readily be blamed on counterfeiters.

Testing of Drugs in the Third World

The testing of pharmaceutical products could entail substantial risks and so pre-clinical development involved extensive testing on animals. This, of itself, was not above controversy in the West. Human testing in clinical trials also was controversial, particularly with new drugs for killer diseases (Chase, 1989). There was debate, for example, about whether there should be a randomly assigned control group receiving a placebo, which would be scientifically desirable, when testing a drug for a fatal disease such as AIDS. Did those receiving the placebo not have a right to the best treatment available?

Testing new products on humans was governed by the Helsinki Declaration, published by the World Medical Association in 1964, which took over from the Nuremberg Code, developed at the end of World War II. Both guidelines required voluntary, informed consent of drug trial participants. The Food and Drug Administration refused to grant licenses to new drugs if these and other conditions were not met during testing. However, critics charged that informed consent was not always evident in the testing of new drugs in the Third World, which often were regarded as having risks too high for testing in developed countries.

In *Poor Health, Rich Profits*, a review of drug companies in the Third World, Heller (1977) suggested the most "flagrant" abuse was in the development of contraceptives. The first oral contraceptives were given large-scale clinical trials in 1953 in Puerto Rico, by G. D. Searle. Subsequent tests took place in Haiti and Mexico and, when first tested in the United States, on women of low-income groups, 84 percent were of Mexican extraction. Other methods of contraception were also first tested in Third World countries. Heller (and others) concluded different valuations on human life figured alongside practical considerations, such as the reduced possibility of legal action in the event of side effects and the costs of testing in developed countries.

PHARMACEUTICAL INDUSTRY RESPONSES TO CRITICISMS

The pharmaceutical industry had some difficulty understanding the charges leveled against it. There was also surprise. The Thalidomide disaster in the early 1960s had caused outrage and prompted more stringent regulation of the industry, specifically in testing requirements prior to the registration and approval of new drugs. However, this disaster could be viewed as an aberration. But by the mid-late 1970s, it was apparent that the industry itself was under attack. This was despite clear evidence of the benefits of drugs. Chain, the Nobel Prize-winning biochemist, had said drugs were "one of the greatest blessings—perhaps *the* greatest blessing—of our time."

It was in the laboratories of the dye producers for the textile industries that the discovery was made of "magic bullet" drugs. Paul Ehrlich, working in the Hoechst laboratories in 1907, came up with salvarsan, which attacked the spirochete that caused syphilis. Unlike most drugs at that time, it attacked the causes of disease without harming the patient, rather than ameliorating the symptoms. Ehrlich coined the term *chemotherapy* to describe his approach, prior to which drugs were often little more than quack medicine, with some exceptions, such as morphine (isolated from opium in 1817) and aspirin (discovered in the mid-19th century and available as an analgesic from the 1890s). The chemotherapeutic revolution brought rapid progress against disease. With the discovery of penicillin (by Fleming in 1928) and later antibiotics, the prevention or cure of killer diseases became possible; polio, malaria, typhoid, tuberculosis, cholera, diphtheria, pneumonia, and influenza could be eradicated. The importance of the benefits provided by drugs was such that the pharmaceutical industry could claim that everybody was a customer at some time in life. This was yet another reason for industry claims to uniqueness—that this was, as an OECD report put it, "an industry like no other" (Tucker, 1984).

Nonetheless, the industry was the outcome and a part of private enterprise. It was, therefore, also subject to normal commercial pressures and used commercial methods such as advertising and personal selling. Sales representatives, as well as selling, were required to provide information, fulfilling a useful role in this capacity; advertising, likewise, the industry would explain. It was argued that gifts and conventions in exotic locations did not influence prescribing practice by doctors. More recent cost-containment pressures were seen as misguided when directed against pharmaceutical companies. The industry argued that drugs were the most cost-effective therapy, that increased availability would lower costs, and that the best way to contain costs was through drug development. It was emphasized that drugs represented only about 10–15 percent of health care costs, with around 5–8 percent going to drug producers. Hence, the social responsibility of pharmaceuticals was more innovation, and that of the authorities was the provision of the right regulatory frameworks and not to unduly delay drug introductions (which could take as long as eight years in such countries as Germany).

The industry had been secretive; this was changing (see, for example, Leisinger, 1988). There was increasing openness about the risks associated with drug use and an effort to provide more information to patients as part of a broader effort to involve patients in decisions about their health care. It had come to be recognized that risk assessment had a subjective element: an unacceptable risk to one patient might be deemed acceptable by another patient who might be less willing to tolerate pain or inconvenience (Stearns, 1987). Pharmaceutical companies also were becoming involved in public policy discussions about the trade-offs to be made in using expensive, high-technology products, drugs or equipment (Tucker, 1984).

The Third World situation was more complex; but industry critics did not always appreciate this, the pharmaceutical companies argued. Much illness could only be eradicated with the provision of adequate sanitation, clean water, and food. The success of the developed world in fighting disease in the early 20th century was due as much to the provision of these basic requirements and access to fresh air and sunshine as it was to drugs. Moreover, given these basics, many areas of the Third World still did not have primary health care; in some of these countries, 70 percent of the population had never seen a doctor or a hospital. Distribution difficulties presented further obstacles to improved health care and, with the shortage of health-care facilities, provided the incentive for OTC supply, as ready access to drugs was deemed preferable to no access at all. The industry also cited, in its defense, difficulties in controlling subsidiary operations in remote locations, the requirement to obey local laws, and pressures to serve the interests of the minority elite found in some Third World countries. It felt unfairly targeted for problems that were not and could not be its responsibility. With increased world tension, defense spending had risen and health spending decreased, yet the World Health Organization had set the goal of "Health for All by the Year 2000." It seemed as if many of the industry's critics were really asking fundamental questions about capitalism.

The International Federation of Pharmaceutical Manufacturers Associations (IFPMA) code of pharmaceutical marketing practice was developed in 1981, and is summarized in Exhibit 1. A supplementary statement added in March 1982 indicates that "information given in Third World countries should be consonant with what is being done in the companies' markets in the developed world"—which was a clear response to Silverman's work. The Third World countries themselves had also taken measures to build production facilities and centralized buying. The WHO in 1977 had, with UN support, developed an essential drug list (225 drugs) to support these and other initiatives. Efforts also were being made to harmonize regulations governing drug testing and approval. By 1986, Silverman et al., reporting a third study of drug promotion in the Third World, were able to confirm improvements:

> Many of the pharmaceutical firms were found to be showing more restraint in limiting their claims in the Third World to those which can be supported by scientific evidence, and far more willingness to disclose serious hazards. The companies discarding a double standard in doing promotion have apparently not suffered any significant loss of profits. There is, however, evident need for further improvement by both multinational and domestic companies (Silverman et al., 1986).

The mid-late 1980s were witnessing a shift in approach by pharmaceutical companies. The low profile of the industry was, with fewer pharmaceutical breakthroughs and greater expressions of public concern about drug risks, giving way to more openness. There were efforts to make practices more uniform, drug use more controlled, and to communicate drug risks to the public, including a more complete understanding of risk. There was, for example, misunderstanding about the coexistence of old and new drugs for the same treatment, often assumed to be the result of poor practice. Yet there was a tradeoff to be made by the patient under these circumstances: The new drug might offer greater efficacy, but there was more knowledge of the old drug. A drug's development did not stop with its market launch. Postmarketing surveillance, a continual monitoring throughout a drug's useful life, was intended to identify undesirable side effects that could emerge under the widely differing conditions of drug use by many different people. It also could identify additional uses for a drug. However, more openness entailed acknowledgement of the role of postmarketing surveillance and the problems in claiming drug safety: that there may always be the possibility of a new combination of factors coming together

---

EXHIBIT 1   IFPMA Code of Pharmaceutical Marketing Practice 1981: Summary of Main Principles

1. Information on drugs to be:
   a. Accurate, fair, and objective.
   b. Based on an up-to-date evaluation of all available scientific evidence.
   c. Communicated consistently with regard to safety, contraindications, side effects, and toxic hazards.
2. Promotional material to be:
   a. Withheld until required approval for marketing of the drug is obtained.
   b. Based on substantial scientific evidence (cf. (1)*b*) and have clearance by medical authorities or pharmacists.
   c. Couched in terms that avoid ambiguity, exaggeration of claims, and unqualified use of the word "safe."
   d. Inclusive of information on the active ingredients of the products, at least one approved indication for use, dosage, and method of use, and a (succinct) statement on side effects, precautions, and contraindications.
   e. Limited in frequency and volume of mailing so as not to be offensive to health-care professionals.
3. Medical representatives (detailers) to be adequately trained and sufficiently knowledgeable to present drug information accurately and responsibly.
4. Symposia, congresses, et cetera, to be principally focused on scientific objectives. Entertainment and other hospitality to be consistent with those objectives.

Notes:
1. The code included a clause saying that samples may be supplied to the medical profession, but did not specify limits to this practice.
2. It is pointed out that the clauses on information are not intended to restrict the flow of progress reports to the scientific community, to the public, and to stockholders in the company.

Source: David Tucker, *The World Health Market*, p. 154.

---

in the use of a drug, with undesirable side effects. Information exchange efforts were increased to try and ensure, for example, that awareness of new contraindications or side effects was rapidly communicated to Third World operations.

DISCUSSION

This industry case study provides evidence of poor practice and misconduct which, following criticism, led to some improvements. Yet pharmaceutical companies still face significant challenges in addressing concerns about their marketing practices in the Third World, particularly given the complexity of the industry and the uncertainty about who is ultimately responsible for health care. The case highlights some of the major ethical issues in marketing, such as product safety and misleading advertising, illustrating the ethical dimensions of marketing decision making. If only because of the consequences of doing otherwise, as examples above confirm, an ethical and effective marketing manager must exhibit respect and concern for the welfare of those affected by his or her decisions. This is more than the "good ethics is good business" argument—there is a moral imperative governing all human behavior, including that of managers.

Further Recommendations for Improvements in Marketing Practice

Additional measures could be taken by pharmaceutical companies, beyond those given above. Promotional practices could be improved further by pharmaceutical companies having centralized monitoring and control functions to ensure consistent standards globally. This would present political problems in some organizations, especially the more decentralized, though they would surely not be insurmountable. The aim would be to provide sufficient information for informed choice by physicians, including prices, as well as full details on side effects and contraindications. The industry's self-regulation efforts also could be made more exacting, not just in the terms but also the enforcement of the IFPMA code. It currently has no teeth, with "embarrassment" the main penalty for offenders. This also would help provide a level playing field for competitors, ensuring that social responsibility does not entail a competitive disadvantage. The trend of increased OTC supply may demand a separate code or new provisions to deal specifically with issues raised by marketing directly to the consumer.

As for the availability of medication issues, continued openness on risks should be encouraged, together with public education efforts; for example, supporting materials for physicians to provide to patients. More Third World initiatives, particularly in distribution and R&D, also should be encouraged. On product testing, informed consent may not be enough. Unlike the testing of contraceptives example, it would seem more appropriate if new products were tested on the target market.

More generally, closer control and monitoring of subsidiaries and greater cooperation with the UN/WHO and similar agencies would seem to be in order. Finally, in comparing the Third World with the developed world, the apparent gross inequities may even dictate acceptance and legitimation of the need to subsidize Third World activities. Such a position would be in recognition of a "special case" status of Third World markets and greater social responsibility requirements of companies operating therein. This is further discussed below.

Many more specific suggestions could be made, according to the issue at hand. Broader issues remain, however, for which there are no easy answers:

- The provision of information versus persuasive communication.

- Innovation versus social control. The industry is an outcome and part of private enterprise—does this mean that innovation and competition, vital though they would seem to be, are inevitably on occasion in conflict with the public interest?

- Who is ultimately responsible for health care? Should pharmaceutical companies merely act to serve their own interests, or do they have a far broader responsibility for health care?

- Are the changes adequate and permanent? Why did they come about? Would they have occurred without the criticisms of marketing practice?

The Social Control of Business

The case study illustrates the requirement for social control of business, an observation that extends beyond the pharmaceutical industry. Yet this control must not come at the expense of diminished innovation. The problem is one of harnessing enterprise to ensure public good. As the issues raised indicate, the profit incentive alone is insufficient; social control of business is required to give direction and set parameters. The forms of social control of business can be summarized in a simple model, based on an understanding of power (Smith, 1990, pp. 87–95). Table 1 gives the model, incorporating pharmaceutical industry examples and the weaknesses of each form of control.

TABLE 1   Social Control of Business: A Simple Model

Form of control	Type of power (exerted by society)	Weaknesses	Examples (discussed in the chapter)
Legislation (government intervention)	• Coercive • Force • Condign	• Overloaded • Limited effectiveness • Threat to market system	• FDA regulations • Criminal charges in Thalidomide case
Market forces	• Remunerative • Inducement • Compensatory	• Insufficient	• Profits from successful products, e.g., Zantac (Glaxo) • Consumer boycotts of "irresponsible" firms; e.g., Lomotil, following anti-advertisement
Moral obligation (including deliberate self-regulation efforts)	• Normative • Manipulation • Conditioned	• "Unfair"/elitist • Inadequate	• IFPMA code • Voluntary disclosure of drug risks

Source: N. Craig Smith, *Morality and the Market: Consumer Pressure for Corporate Accountability* (London and New York: Routledge, 1990), p. 88.

The Limits of Corporate Social Responsibility

How much can and should a firm or industry do to alleviate social problems in fulfilling its obligations to society? Very little, is the classic Friedmanite response to this question. As Friedman explains:

> There is one and only one social responsibility of business—to use its resources and engage in activities designed to increase its profits so long as it stays within the rules of the game, which is to say, engages in open and free competition, without deception or fraud (1962, p. 133).

Friedman's arguments against social responsibility beyond profit maximization are more sophisticated than his critics allow, and tend to be ignored. They are worth reviewing. In essence, he identifies six problems in social responsibility beyond profit maximization:

1. Spending someone else's money.
   —The costs of social actions are borne involuntarily by shareholders, customers, or others.
2. Competing claims—the role of profit.
   —Other claims involve the deliberate sacrifice of profits or at least muddy decision making.
3. Competitive disadvantage.
   —Social actions have a price.
4. Competence.
   —How are firms to know what their social responsibilities are? Do firms have the skills to deal with social issues?
5. Fairness—domination by business.
   —Do we want corporations playing God?
6. Legitimacy—the role of government.

The counterarguments to the Friedman position outweigh the above, though these are important considerations. The case itself presents compelling evidence of the inadequacy of unfettered profit maximization. The main counterarguments are:

1. Inaccuracy of (Friedman's) competitive model of capitalism. Markets just don't work in the way neoclassical economists would wish.
2. Managerial discretion in practice.
3. Extent of corporate power.
4. The "moral minimum"—where you have to draw the line.
5. Relationship between enlightened self-interest and long-term profitability.

Accepting social responsibility beyond profit maximization presents problems in identifying what and how much is socially responsible. Ethicists identify three levels of duties to which people and, hence, managers in organizations are obligated: (1) avoid causing harm, (2) prevent harm (caused by others), (3) do good. Negative duties are stronger than positive duties. It seems reasonable to expect businesses not to cause harm and to make efforts to prevent harm, insofar as that is within their control. More wide-ranging efforts to prevent harm and efforts to do good are less justifiably advocated. Four criteria have been identified that can be helpful (Simon et al., 1972, p. 22). There is an obligation to act when these conditions are present: (1) critical need, (2) proximity, (3) capability, and (4) last resort.

Because of the danger of assuming someone else will act when others are present, or because one is trying to find out who is the last resort, or because of the possibility of pluralistic ignorance (not acting because no one else is and the situation, therefore, seeming less serious), there may be a situation in which no one acts at all. This suggests that the criterion of last resort is less useful, and there should be a presumption in favor of taking action when the first three criteria are present. These criteria and their usefulness are readily understood in the context of "The Parable of the Sadhu" (McCoy, 1983), in which a group on a climbing expedition have difficulty choosing between reaching the summit, realizing important personal goals, and possibly failing in this quest by stopping to help a holy man (the Sadhu), whose life is in danger. The criteria clearly are also useful in determining responsibilities in pharmaceutical marketing in the Third World.

Within the above framework, four positions delineate the limits of corporate social responsibility (Smith, 1990, pp. 56–60):

1. Profit maximization and social irresponsibility.
   —Firms may do good through profit maximization (Adam Smith's "invisible hand") but may also cause harm, would not act to prevent it, and are only doing good as a result of serving their self-interest.
2. Profit maximization tempered by the "moral minimum," operating through self-regulation.
   —This is avoiding causing harm. Most firms/managers are at this position.
3. Profit as a necessary but not sufficient goal, with affirmative action extending beyond self-regulation.
   —Some firms/managers make efforts to not only avoid causing harm but also prevent harm and possibly do good. Johnson & Johnson is the classic example (Smith and Tedlow, 1989).
4. Profit as a necessary but not sufficient goal, with social responsibility extending beyond self-regulation and affirmative action to include the championing of political and moral causes unrelated to the corporation's business activities, perhaps even including gifts of charity but only as long as profitability permits.
   —Gifts of charity here refer to genuine philanthropy, rather than that which is primarily PR-driven. Few firms reach this position of actively doing good as well as not causing and preventing harm (which many would argue is not a bad thing, because of the fairness and legitimacy concerns identified by Friedman). Many firms do not have sufficient resources for the championing of political and moral causes. Classic examples of firms at this position are Ben and Jerry's and the Body Shop.

The pharmaceutical industry case study refers to many firms at positions 1 and 2, the inadequacy of which is apparent, particularly within the Third World context. Where are pharmaceutical companies today? Where should they be? We would argue they should at least be at position 3. We conclude with two important questions to consider if position 4 is advocated: Should pharmaceutical companies aim to achieve more than break even in their Third World operations? Would efforts to "do good," social actions way beyond the corporation's conventionally defined business activities, be fair (whose values would be imposed?) and legitimate?

REFERENCES

Braithwaite, John. *Corporate Crime in the Pharmaceutical Industry.* London: Routledge and Kegan Paul, 1984.

Chase, Marilyn. "Patient's Death in AIDS Test Fuels a Debate." *The Wall Street Journal*, June 28, 1989.

Chetley, Andrew. "Not Good Enough for Us but Fit for Them—An Examination of the Chemical and Pharmaceutical Export Trades." *Journal of Consumer Policy* 9 (1986), pp. 155–80.

Friedman, Milton. *Capitalism and Freedom.* Chicago: University of Chicago Press, 1962.

Heller, Tom. *Poor Health, Rich Profits.* Nottingham: Spokesman Books, 1977.

Illich, Ivan. *Medical Nemesis.* Calder and Boyars, 1975.

Leisinger, Klaus M. "Sound Ethical Practices Make Good Business Sense." *CIBA-GEIGY Journal* 3 (1988).

McCoy, Bowen H. "The Parable of the Sadhu." *Harvard Business Review* 61 (September–October 1983), pp. 103–108.

Medawar, Charles, and Barbara Freese. *Drug Diplomacy.* London: Social Audit, 1982.

Silverman, Milton. *The Drugging of the Americas.* Berkeley: University of California Press, 1976.

Silverman, Milton; Philip R. Lee; and Mia Lydecker. "The Drugging of the Third World." *International Journal of Health Services* 12, no. 4 (1982).

Silverman, Milton; Philip R. Lee; and Mia Lydecker. "Drug Promotion: The Third World Revisited." *International Journal of Health Services* 16, no. 4 (1986).

Simon, John G.; Charles W. Powers; and Jon P. Gunnemann. *The Ethical Investor: Universities and Corporate Responsibility.* New Haven: Yale University Press, 1972.

Smith, N. Craig. *Morality and the Market: Consumer Pressure for Corporate Accountability.* London and New York: Routledge, 1990.

Smith, N. Craig, and John A. Quelch. "CIBA-GEIGY Pharmaceuticals: Pharma International." Harvard Business School Case Services #9–589–108 (1989a).

Smith, N. Craig, and John A. Quelch. "Note on Pharmaceutical Marketing Practices in the Third World." Harvard Business School Case Services #9–589–039 (1989b).

Smith, Wendy K., and Richard S. Tedlow. "James Burke: A Career in American Business (A), (B)." Harvard Business School Case Services #9–389–177 and 9–390–030 (1989).

Stearns, Beverly. "RAD-AR: Homing in on Risk." *CIBY-GEIGY Journal* 2 (1987).

Tucker, David. *The World Health Market*. London: Euromonitor, 1984.

Market Selection and Marketing Research

Ethical Issues in Researching and Targeting Consumers

N. Craig Smith
John A. Quelch*

Marketing research aids management understanding of customers, competitors, channels, and the company's marketing activities. It is a basic component of the marketing information system and, thereby, marketing decision making. Reliable estimates of the size of the marketing research industry are difficult to obtain, because it is highly fragmented and includes substantial in-house expenditures; however, the combined revenues of the top 50 U.S. marketing/advertising/public opinion research organizations (research activities only) was $2.83 billion in 1990.[1] Marketing research is an industry and activity that has received considerable attention within the marketing ethics literature; some sources suggest it has received the most attention.[2]

Much of the attention given to the ethics of marketing research has been prompted by the self-interest concerns of the industry. In particular, there has been the realization that consumer goodwill is vital for most market research; unethical practices lessen the likelihood of consumer cooperation in an activity that rarely yields any direct benefit to the individual respondent.[3] Accordingly, codes of conduct have been developed and efforts made to "professionalize"

* The authors gratefully acknowledge the research assistance of John J. Brough in the preparation of this chapter.

[1] Jack Honomichl, "Spending for Research Shows 3.5% Real Growth," *Marketing News,* May 27, 1991, p. H2.

[2] John Tsalikis and David J. Fritzsche, "Business Ethics: A Literature Review with a Focus on Marketing Ethics," *Journal of Business Ethics* 8 (1989), pp. 695–743. Patrick E. Murphy and Gene R. Laczniak, "Marketing Ethics: A Review with Implications for Managers, Educators and Researchers," in *Review of Marketing,* ed. Ben M. Enis and Kenneth J. Roering (Chicago: American Marketing Association, 1981), pp. 251–66.

[3] Kenneth C. Schneider, "Subject and Respondent Abuse in Marketing Research," *MSU Business Topics,* Spring 1977, pp. 13–19.

marketing research. An early American Marketing Association (AMA) code explicitly acknowledges the importance of consumer goodwill: ". . . marketing management is more and more dependent upon marketing information intelligently and systematically obtained. The consumer is the source of much of this information."[4]

The more detailed and comprehensive codes of conduct have been developed by the Professional Marketing Research Society of Canada (PMRS),[5] the International Chamber of Commerce and the European Society for Opinion and Marketing Research (ICC/ESOMAR),[6] and the Council of American Survey Research Organizations (CASRO).[7] More perfunctory codes are provided by the Marketing Research Association (MRA),[8] the AMA (as quoted above), the New York chapter of the AMA,[9] and the American Association for Public Opinion Research (AAPOR).[10] The PMRS code is provided as Exhibit 1. The codes are structured according to the rights and obligations of the different stakeholders of marketing research.

---

[4] The AMA no longer actively promotes this 1962 code. It is reprinted in various texts, including Donald S. Tull and Del I. Hawkins, *Marketing Research: Measurement and Method* (New York: Macmillan, 1990), pp. 724–25.

[5] "Rules of Conduct and Good Practice" (Toronto: Professional Marketing Research Society, 1984).

[6] The "ICC/ESOMAR International Code of Marketing and Social Research Practice" is widely recognized in Europe. In keeping with the code of the U.K. Market Research Society, it is detailed and comprehensive. The code is reprinted in *Consumer Market Research Handbook,* ed. Robert M. Worcester and John Downham (Amsterdam: North-Holland, 1986), pp. 813–26.

[7] The 1981 "Code of Standards for Survey Research" is mandatory for all CASRO members. It is reprinted in H. Robert Dodge, Sam Fullerton, and David Rink, *Marketing Research* (Columbus: Charles E. Merrill, 1982), pp. 375–78.

[8] The MRA "Code of Professional Ethics and Practices" lists nine principles and is reprinted in various texts, including Dodge et al., *Marketing Research*, p. 374. The MRA (of Rocky Hill, Connecticut) has a Professional Standards Committee, which will intervene and, if necessary, hold hearings on breaches of ethics ("AMR Interviews Burt Kramer on Professional Standards," *Applied Marketing Research* 29, no. 1 (Winter 1989), pp. 3–5). The MRA code serves as a sign of professionalism—though it specifically prohibits use of membership of the MRA as proof of competence—and provides a basis for settling conflicts. However, it has been suggested that the MRA modify the code to produce accountable standards that are clear, enforceable, and consistent (see Stephen B. Castleberry and Warren A. French, "Reviewing the MRA's Code of Ethics," *Journal of Data Collection* 27, no. 2 (Fall 1987), pp. 42–48).

[9] This "Personal Code for Practicing Market and Opinion Research" is a four-page "pledge." It is a "promise I make to myself and to those I deal with. It makes an explicit and public statement of my commitments to scientific practice, honest research, fair business dealings and the public interest." The AMA New York chapter qualifies the 1980 code by stating it is "a personal code of ethics, with no requirement of acceptance or penalty for nonadherence." Among its provisions: "I will resist temptations to shade results." It is reprinted in various texts, including Dodge et al., *Marketing Research,* pp. 371–73.

[10] The "Code of Professional Ethics and Practices" of the American Association for Public Opinion Research is reasonably comprehensive but lacks detail, at least as of the 1960 version provided in Sidney Hollander, Jr., "Ethics in Marketing Research," in *Handbook of Marketing Research,* ed. Robert Ferber (New York: McGraw-Hill, 1974), p. 123. AAPOR is to release a new code in September 1991.

EXHIBIT 1   Rules of Conduct and Good Practice of the Professional Marketing
Research Society of Canada (1984)

Introduction

This document is currently divided into two chapters: Chapter A—For The General
Professional Marketing Research Society Membership, and Chapter B—For The Qualitative Research Division Membership. Within each chapter are a number of sections
and each section may include two types of statements:

(1) *Rules of Conduct* are considered mandatory: their violation could result in disciplinary action on the part of the Society as per the Constitution.

(2) *Good Practice* guidelines represent an *ideal* toward which members should strive.

In the reading of this document, and for all purposes thereof, all references to and use
of the masculine gender shall be deemed to be referenced to and use of the feminine
gender where appropriate in the course of the affairs of the Society.

The acceptance of marketing and social "research" as a reliable source of information
and, hence its growth as a profession, depends upon the confidence of the business
community and the public in the integrity of those professionally engaged in this type
of work.

Membership in the Professional Marketing Research Society (P.M.R.S.) implies acceptance of—Chapter A Rules of Conduct and Good Practice, and membership in the
Qualitative Research Division implies acceptance of both Chapter A and B. *Members
of the Society undertake to refrain from any activity likely to impair confidence in
marketing research in general and to comply with whatever general professional practices
may be laid down from time to time by the Society.*

(A) FOR THE GENERAL P.M.R.S. MEMBERSHIP

I. The Responsibility of the Members to the Public

Most marketing research depends on the cooperation of "respondents" either in their
personal or in their business capacity. Marketing researchers, therefore, have a direct
responsibility to ensure that respondents are in no way embarrassed or hindered in
other ways as a result of any "interview." The purpose of interviewing respondents
shall be limited to the finding out of information or observation of reactions relevant
to the research problem at hand. Every possible attempt should be made by members
to ensure a continuing climate of goodwill, responsibility and trust. A meticulous standard of good manners with respondents should be maintained and everything should
be done to leave respondents positively disposed to marketing research.

Rules of Conduct

1.1   Interviewing may not be used as a disguise for selling or developing sales leads,
nor for deliberately influencing the opinions of those interviewed.

1.2   Any statement or assurance given to a respondent in order to obtain cooperation
shall be factually correct and honoured.

1.3   No procedure or technique shall be used in which the respondent is put in such
a position that they cannot exercise their right to withdraw or refuse to answer

---

EXHIBIT 1 *(continued)*

---

at *any stage* during or after the interview. Any request of the respondent to terminate the interview must be granted and, if he so requests, any information already given must be deleted.

1.4 The interviewer should explain to all respondents at the commencement of the interview, when applicable, the presence and purpose of any 1-way mirror or audio/visual monitoring equipment.

1.5 The identity of individual respondents shall not be revealed by the "practitioner" to the "client" or anyone other than persons belonging to the organization of the practitioner concerned (either by supplying lists of individual respondents or by passing on answers to questions linked to the names of the individual respondents even when the client has supplied the original list of potential respondents) and members are entitled to give respondents such an assurance.

Exceptions to the aforesaid rule may be made in the following instances:

(i) if the consent of respondents has been obtained before revealing their names to the client,

(ii) if disclosure of these names is essential for the data processing, for verification of the original research, or to carry out further research. In such instances, however, the practitioner responsible for the original interview must insist that all the Rules of Conduct in this document are observed by all parties involved, via appropriate instructions in writing.

1.6 Interviewers must carry with them identification from the organization they represent for all face-to-face interviewing. Interviewers must identify themselves by name and organization in an introductory statement on *all* interviews. If requested by the respondent, the interviewer should provide the name, address, and/or telephone number of the organization they represent. This information should be clearly indicated on any questionnaire handed out to respondents.

1.7 No respondent should be pressured into testing products which he does not want to try. Product information, such as ingredient lists and instructions including the name, address, and/or telephone number of the practitioner, should be available where possible.

1.8 Before children under the age of 12 are *interviewed,* or asked to complete a questionnaire, the permission of a parent, guardian, or other person responsible for them, such as a teacher, shall be obtained. In obtaining this permission the interviewer shall allow the responsible person to see or hear the questions which will be asked or, if this is not practical, shall describe the nature of the *interview* in sufficient detail to enable a reasonable person to reach an informed decision (e.g., not only should the subject matter of the *interview* be described, but any sensitive, embarrassing or complex questions should also be brought to the attention of the responsible person).

1.9 If computerized telephone interviewing techniques (e.g., collecting data or conducting an interview via taped message with no human interviewer) are employed, the type of machinery that automatically disconnects or "frees the line" when the respondent hangs up the phone must be used.

EXHIBIT 1 *(continued)*

Good Practice

1.10 A potential respondent who has initially refused to take part in a study should not be contacted for the same study on more than one subsequent occasion in person or by telephone. Any second call should be conducted by a specially trained interviewer or (field) supervisor (i.e., *not* the original interviewer).

1.11 It should be recognized that when communicating with any member of the public it is important that the materials used are appropriate in terms of content and wording to that particular public.

1.12 "Overly long questionnaires" should be avoided at all costs. If the respondent asks, interviewers should indicate to the respondent a reasonably accurate estimate of the duration of the interview. When appropriate, interviewers should make appointments for interviews in advance when interviewing representatives of companies or other organizations.

1.13 The practitioner should inform the local authorities (e.g., police, security, etc.) before carrying out interviews under circumstances or about topics which might make the public suspicious or cause them to report the interviewer's activities.

1.14 If a respondent is interviewed as part of a study, the practitioner should not deliberately seek an additional interview with this specific respondent unless re-interviewing is required by the study's design or unless the respondent's permission was obtained during the initial interview (and each subsequent interview).

1.15 Incentives should be avoided where possible for quantitative studies. Even when incentives are used, they should be offered as a small token appreciation (e.g., lottery tickets and small gift items).

1.16 When interviewing 12 to 15 year old respondents discretion should be used when addressing sensitive subject matter or information (e.g., delete "household income" question, etc.).

II. The Responsibility of Clients to Practitioners

Rules of Conduct

2.1 In some instances potential clients ask for competitive bids from two or more practitioners, and, when properly done, such practice is completely within the Rules of Conduct. However, certain conditions are essential to meet the standards of proper practice. These include:

(i) Whenever a client asks more than one practitioner for a "proposal" or "cost estimate," this fact and the number of proposals or cost estimates being requested must be communicated to the practitioners concerned. For any study, *the practitioner is then entitled to indicate in advance that he will request payment for the cost of preparing such a proposal or cost estimate.*

(ii) During and following the proposal or cost estimate process, both the client and the practitioner must respect the confidentiality of each party's technical input or ideas. Specifically, in a competitive situation, no unique technique or idea included in a practitioner's proposal may be used by the prospective client in conjunction with another practitioner unless an appropriate payment has been made. (See 2.1 (i) above.) Additionally, in a competitive situation, all unaccepted

EXHIBIT 1 *(continued)*

proposals in whole or in part remain exclusively the property of the originating practitioner unless an appropriate charge has been made. (See 2.1 (i) above.) Conversely, no unique technique or idea included in a prospective client's specifications during the proposal or cost estimate process may be offered to other prospective clients by the practitioner without the originating client's approval.

2.2   Reports provided by a practitioner are the property of the client and are normally for the use within the client company or associated companies (including the client's agents). If a wider circulation of the results of the study either in whole or in part is intended, the following minimum standards of disclosure should be adhered to in order that there will be an adequate basis for judging the reliability and validity of the results reported:

(i) The client should ensure that dissemination of the study findings will not give rise to misleading interpretations and that the study findings will not be quoted out of their normal context.

(ii) If a practitioner's name is to be used, he must be consulted prior to dissemination of findings and is entitled to refuse permission for its name to be used in connection with the study until the practitioner has approved the exact form and contents of the dissemination.

(iii) For all reports of survey findings the client has released to the public, the client must be prepared to release the following details on request: sponsorship of the survey; dates of interviewing; methods of obtaining the interviews (in home, telephone, or mail); population that was sampled; size of sample; size and description of the sub-sample, if the survey report relies primarily on less than the total sample; exact wording of questions upon which the release is based; an indication of what allowance should be made for sampling error; and the percentage upon which conclusions are based.

2.3   Unless otherwise agreed and provided that the practitioner has followed the stipulated procedures and all reasonable precautions have been taken, the client is responsible for any damages sought by the public as a result of using any product or material supplied by the client. Additionally, when testing products or materials, proper usage instructions will be provided by the client and any cautions necessary for normal sale, must be highlighted (e.g., possible allergic reactions) and a listing of ingredients will be made available by the client where it is appropriate.

Good Practice

2.4   Clients have a responsibility to provide practitioners with enough information about a project for the latter to do a professional job. Specifically, clients should provide insight, preferably in writing, into the following areas:

(i) A statement of the research problem or, if unable to define the research problem, a perspective on the problem in terms of its general background.

(ii) A statement of the type of decision(s) that is likely to be influenced by the research results or the uses to which the research results will be applied.

(iii) A broad indication of the budget available.

EXHIBIT 1 *(continued)*

2.5 When requesting proposals some indication should be provided about how the successful proposal will be determined. Factors which might be used to determine the organization selected could include:

(i) Innovative approaches to solving the problem under review.

(ii) Ability to provide the necessary information-gathering and analysis resources—personnel, facilities, equipment, etc.

(iii) Relevant experience of the research firm.

(iv) Background/experience of individuals to be assigned to the work.

(v) Recognition of the limitations of the research.

(vi) Cost.

2.6 Clients should provide a prompt notification to all proposers once a selection has been made on a proposal or cost estimate.

2.7 Clients should only request a reasonable number of competitive proposals or cost estimates (e.g., 2 to 4) on any given project.

2.8 Clients should not assume that the contingency cost range included in some research proposals or cost estimates (e.g., $+/- \times\%$) may be applied to changes in the research specifications. Changes in specifications may be justification for revising the original estimate.

III. The Responsibility of Practitioners to Clients

Rules of Conduct

3.1 Research specifications, such as background, objectives, and technical approaches or ideas, provided by a client or potential client remain the property of the client and contents may not be revealed to third parties without the client's permission. (See Section 2.1.)

3.2 Unless authorized by the client, the practitioner will not reveal to respondents, interviewers, or any other person not directly concerned with the study, the identity of the client, including the fact that he had undertaken or considered undertaking research in a particular area, confidential material relating to the study, or the results of any study commissioned exclusively for that client.

3.3 If any aspect of a project is to be subcontracted to another practitioner, the originating practitioner is obliged to inform the client before committing to the project.

3.4 When the same project is carried out on behalf of more than one client, or two or more projects are combined in one interview, the practitioner is obliged to inform each client concerned that another client exists and to inform each client of the *generic* subjects addressed by the other client's project before the client commits to the project.

3.5 "Primary" and "secondary" records are the property of the practitioner. The practitioner is entitled to destroy primary records 1 year from the end of the fieldwork (providing secondary records are adequate to enable reconstruction of the results) and to destroy secondary records 2 years from the end of the fieldwork without reference to the client. The preferred method of destruction is shredding

EXHIBIT 1 *(continued)*

on premises. If the client wishes exceptions to this, he must make special arrangements with the practitioner. The practitioner must provide reasonable access for the client on nonsyndicated studies, to the completed questionnaires or data forms, cards/tapes provided the client bears the reasonable cost of preparing any duplicates or masking individual identity.

3.6   Unless otherwise specifically made clear that this practice will not be followed, the practitioner will automatically "verify" or "monitor" a minimum of 10% of each interviewer's completed interviews.

The practitioner will inform the client, prior to commencement of the study, the proposed nature of the verification or monitoring, including the proportion of each interviewer's interviews to be covered. Upon request from the client, the practitioner is obliged to disclose the result of the verification. If verification of an interviewer's completed interviews suggests problems, verification must be done until there is firm evidence of either valid or invalid work. If the interviews appear to be invalid, 100% of the interviewer's interviews must be either rejected or replaced. In this case, the practitioner is obliged to inform the client immediately of these problems with verification.

3.7   For each survey, a practitioner will provide the following information, where applicable, to the client (either in a report or in supporting documentation if a formal report is not being prepared):

(i) Copy of questionnaire, interviewers' instructions, and visual exhibits.

(ii) The name of organization for which the study was conducted and name of organization conducting it, including subcontractors.

(iii) The specific objectives of the study.

(iv) The dates on or between which the fieldwork was done and the time periods of interviewing.

(v) The universe covered (intended and actual), including details of the sampling method and selection procedures.

(vi) The size and nature of the sample and details of any weighting methods used.

(vii) The contact record based on the last attempt to obtain an interview, with the exception of mall surveys and quota samples where it is not appropriate.

(viii) The method of recruitment when prior recruitment of respondents is undertaken.

(ix) The method of field briefing sessions.

(x) Weighted and unweighted bases for all conventional tables, clearly distinguishing between the two.

(xi) A statement of response rates, how they were calculated, and a discussion of possible bias due to nonresponse.

(xii) The method by which the information was collected (e.g., mall intercept, telephone, etc.).

(xiii) The details of any incentives provided to respondents.

(xiv) Sources of desk research.

EXHIBIT 1 *(continued)*

(xv) An adequate description of verification or monitoring procedures and results of the same.

(xvi) The detail of any special statistical methods used in the analysis of the results.

3.8 The practitioner will limit the information supplied to prospective clients regarding their experience, capacities, and organization to a factual and objective description.

3.9 When changes are made to the specifications of a study by either the practitioner or the client, the practitioner should inform the client of any fee changes at the time the specifications are revised.

3.10 A practitioner will conduct a study in the manner agreed upon. However, if it becomes apparent in the course of a study that changes in the plans should be made, the practitioner is obliged to make his views (including cost estimates) known to the client immediately.

3.11 A practitioner is obliged to allow clients to verify that work performed meets all contracted specifications and to examine and be present at all operations of the practitioner's organization relevant to the execution of the study.

Good Practice

3.12 The practitioner should make known any current involvement in the same general subject area before accepting a project. However, exclusive use of a practitioner over a given time period may be established only by special arrangements between client and practitioner.

3.13 When reporting findings of a study in either written or oral form, the practitioner should make a clear distinction between the objective results and their own opinions and recommendations.

3.14 The practitioner should provide to the client in the report or a supporting document to fieldwork, tables, etc., in addition to the items listed in 3.7:

(i) A discussion of any aspects of the research which may bias the results.

(ii) An assessment of the reliability of the sources used in desk research.

(iii) The name(s) of the individual(s) responsible for the study and report.

(iv) A list of sampling points used in the study (upon request).

3.15 The practitioner will assist the client in the design and execution of effective and efficient studies. If the practitioner questions whether a study design will provide the necessary information, the practitioner should make his own reservations known.

3.16 During and following the proposal or cost estimate process, cost quotations may be made public without the practitioner's permission, as long as an individual quotation cannot be associated with a given practitioner.

3.17 A practitioner will not use the names of clients in promotional material without the express permission of the client.

EXHIBIT 1 *(continued)*

IV. General Rules of Practice for Members

Rules of Conduct

4.1 Members shall not try to turn to account or to use the fact of their membership in P.M.R.S. as evidence of particular professional competence, except insofar as membership implies the member subscribes to the Rules of Conduct and Good Practice.

Unless authorized by the executive, members, when talking to the "press" or media representatives, should request that their membership in P.M.R.S. not be included in any subsequent articles or media reports to avoid their personal views or opinions being confused with those of P.M.R.S.

4.2 Members recognize that marketing and social research is more an art than a science. It, therefore, follows that what is practical, sound, and useful to clients is frequently more a matter of judgment than of definite rules and regulations.

It is because such judgment follows from experience within the field that members of the Society believe they have a responsibility to their respective clients and management to point out the limitations of marketing research as appropriate.

Members of the Society will do everything possible to extend and maximize the use of marketing and social research. They will also discourage research which, in their best judgment, is considered inadequate, inappropriate, or subject to providing misleading information for the problem at hand.

4.3 Members commissioning market or social research work with a practitioner known not to be bound by these Rules of Conduct and Good Practice, shall ensure that the practitioner is familiar with its content and agrees in writing to abide by them.

Good Practice

4.4 When considering interviews with small populations that are likely to be of interest to other researchers, members should be especially careful to minimize the total number of interviews conducted to avoid "over researching" such populations. For the same reason, members interested in such populations should attempt to undertake syndicated research projects within those populations.

(B) FOR THE QUALITATIVE RESEARCH DIVISION MEMBERSHIP

V. Responsibility to the Public

Rules of Conduct

5.1 Any statement or assurance given to a respondent in order to obtain cooperation shall be factually correct and honoured.

5.2 The respondent shall be allowed to remain anonymous or, in special circumstances where this is not possible, the respondent should be informed, when being recruited, that his responses may not be anonymous.

5.3 Qualitative interviews must not be used for selling or developing sales leads, and, for this reason, surnames and/or addresses and telephone numbers may not be

EXHIBIT 1 *(continued)*

supplied to the client. The interview itself should not be used by the client to deliberately try to influence the opinions of those interviewed.

5.4 Most marketing research depends upon the cooperation of the respondents. All persons involved in a qualitative research project, therefore, have a direct responsibility to ensure that respondents or potential respondents are not embarassed in any way.

5.5 Members must not harass, badger, grill, or belittle any member of the public either while trying to recruit for or during the conducting of any qualitative study. Clearly, behaviour cannot be precisely defined but sincere and consistent efforts to show respect to the respondents are, nevertheless, a mandatory requirement of the Society's Rules of Conduct and Good Practice.

5.6 The respondent's right to withdraw, or to refuse to cooperate at any stage, shall be respected.

5.7 The *moderator* must explain to all respondents at the commencement of the interview (group or individual in-depth), where appropriate:

(i) The presence and purpose of the 1-way mirror.

(ii) The presence and purpose of the video-camera.

(iii) The presence and purpose of the tape recorder.

(iv) The confidentiality of the respondent's names and addresses.

Good Practice

In conjunction with the above Rules of Conduct:

5.8 The *client* has a particular responsibility to ensure that the moderator does not (or is not asked to) exceed "acceptable" limits of "harassment" of respondents. The client has an equal responsibility for their own attitude and behaviour (and that of other persons present at the invitation of the client) not only in front of the respondent but also when watching the interview in a separate location. In addition, if exposed to the respondent, the client should be careful not to introduce unsuitable bias by their reactions or comments.

5.9 It is the responsibility of the recruiter to ensure that the respondent is properly qualified for inclusion in the study. Recruiters also have a responsibility to explain to participants in the study exactly what is expected of them; for example, the importance of punctuality, the likely full length of the interview period, the date, time, and exact location (with details of parking, nearest public transit stop, etc.), whether they will be asked to taste food or beverages, the payment (and any associated terms), whether or not smoking will be allowed during the group. It is a good idea if this information is confirmed in writing or through a follow-up reminder telephone call.

5.10 The moderator has a responsibility to keep the session within the time limits specified to respondents on the occasion of their recruitment.

The moderator also has the responsibility of ensuring that all respondents have an equal opportunity to participate in the discussion. If the offensive language or behaviour of one respondent inhibits other respondents from fully participating,

---

EXHIBIT 1 *(continued)*

---

the moderator may have to ask the offending participant to leave.

5.11 No respondent should be pressured into taste-testing any products which he does not want to try. Ingredient lists should be available if requested.

5.12 The issue of payment to participants who arrive too late to be included in the discussion should be clarified by recruiter, moderator, and/or client prior to commencement of the study. Since the fault is often not solely that of the respondent, it is suggested that some payment should always be made. (How much and who actually picks up that cost is a matter for negotiation between parties involved; it is suggested that at least half the promised amount be paid.)

VI. Other Responsibilities of the Recruiter

Rules of Conduct

6.1 The following Rules of Conduct are *assumed to be in operation* for any qualitative research undertaken by members of QRD, *unless changes* to any or all of the Rules have *been discussed and agreed to by all parties involved in the research study:*

(i) All respondents must meet usage/trial/ownership standards, including type of brand, frequency of use/trial or other time limits specified for the study.

(ii) All respondents must meet demographic specifications for the study, including marital status, age, sex, income, occupation, household composition, etc.

(iii) No respondents (nor anyone in their immediate families or households) may *work* in an occupation that has anything to do with the topic area (whether wholesale, retail, sales, service, or consultant) nor in advertising, marketing, marketing research, public relations, or the media (radio, television, newspaper, etc.) nor *may respondents themselves ever have worked in such occupations.*

(iv) No respondent may be recruited who has attended, *in the past five years,* a focus group discussion or in-depth interview on the *same general topic* as defined by the moderator.

(v) No respondents should be recruited who *know each other* for the same study, unless they are in *different groups, or interviews, that are scheduled back-to-back.*

(vi) No respondent may be recruited who has attended a group discussion or in-depth interview *within the past year.*

(vii) No respondent may be recruited who has attended *five or more* focus groups or in-depth interviews ever, *unless he or she has not attended a group discussion/ in-depth interview in the past five years.*

(viii) At least *one half* of the respondents recruited for each group/study involving in-depth interviews must never have attended a group discussion or in-depth interview before.

(ix) All respondents must have been living in the specified market area for at least the past two years.

(x) All respondents must be able to speak and read in the language of the group or study being conducted.

EXHIBIT 1 *(continued)*

Good Practice

6.2   Before accepting a project, it is important that the recruiter clearly understands the moderator's (or client's) specifications; the recruiter has a responsibility to query any points of confusion and to highlight potential problems.

Once accepted, instructions should be followed explicitly. No changes to the agreed-upon questionnaire should be made without prior approval from the moderator or client. Any information given to respondents (e.g., the topic, whether there will be taste testing, etc.) must have been approved beforehand.

If problems in recruiting arise, the moderator (or client) should be advised immediately.

6.3   Recruiters have a responsibility to make every effort to ensure that all recruited respondents comply with specifications detailed for the project and that they turn up at the correct place, at the right time, being fully aware of what is expected of them. Confirmatory/reminder rescreening should, where possible, be conducted by someone other than the original recruiter.

Screening questionnaires used in the recruitment should be made available to the moderator in advance of the research sessions.

VII. Other Responsibilities of the Moderator

(A) To the Recruiter

Rules of Conduct

7.1   To protect the respondents, persons recruited for a specific study should be used by the moderator only for that study and not be recalled to participate in another qualitative study without permission of the initial recruiter.

Good Practice

7.2   The moderator should clearly define (preferably in writing) the complete specifications for the study to the recruiter (e.g., specific usage/trial/ownership standards; demographic specifications, etc.) as well as what, if anything, the respondent can be told about the topic, or session, in advance. In addition, the moderator should obtain confirmation that the recruiter will follow the accepted Recruiting Guidelines of the Qualitative Research Division.

(B) To the Client

Rules of Conduct

7.3   When responsible for recruiting, the moderator must obtain agreement from the client regarding recruitment specifications, supervise the recruiting for the study, and ensure that recruitment goals are met (or provide an explanation when they are not met).

7.4   *Unless otherwise agreed,* the client can assume that the moderator will listen to taped interviews, or work from "transcripts," when preparing the analysis.

7.5   Each report should include a standard statement emphasizing the non-projectability of the results. Specifically, reports should not include precise percentaged

---

EXHIBIT 1 *(continued)*

---

results, unless it is made clear at that point in the report that the result applied only to those respondents and is not necessarily true of the population at large; proportions may be used (e.g., one third).

7.6 Each report should also contain a copy of the recruiting questionnaire and details of respondent qualifications together with a copy of the discussion outline and, if possible, any materials used as stimuli during the interview.

7.7 All material relating to clients must remain confidential to persons wholly or substantially employed by the moderator, unless otherwise authorized by the client.

Unless authorized to do so by the client, the moderator should not reveal to recruiters or respondents nor any other person not directly concerned with the work of the study the name of the client commissioning the study.

Good Practice

7.8 The moderator must ensure that the client understands the non-projectability of qualitative research to the population at large before embarking upon the project.

7.9 The moderator has responsibility to ensure that he has a clear understanding of the problem and the reasons why the research is being undertaken. A discussion outline should be provided for perusal by the client well in advance of the first session.

However, flexibility should be demonstrated when moderating the sessions in order to pursue areas which emerge as possibly meaningful but have not been included in the preliminary discussion outline.

The moderator should check with the client before dismissing the group to ensure no areas of special concern have been missed.

7.10 The moderator must remain objective and observe rigorous neutrality (except when playing the devil's advocate) while conducting the group session and when preparing the report/analysis.

VIII. Other Responsibilities of the Client

Note: In some circumstances, the client may directly arrange for the recruiting. In such circumstances, the "client" is required to assume the responsibilities to the recruiter outlined in Sections 3.1 and 3.2.

Good Practice

8.1 *One* person at the *client* company should take responsibility for final liaison with the moderator.

8.2 The moderator should be given every opportunity to understand the problems to be researched and should be included as early as possible in the planning stages of the project.

8.3 An outline of the research objectives and the immediate use to which the qualitative research learning will be put should be provided, in writing, for the moderator. This briefing document should be approved by *all* members of the client team before being given to the moderator.

EXHIBIT 1 *(continued)*

It is helpful if key members of the client team (e.g., product managers, agency personnel, as well as marketing research personnel) can be available for follow-up discussion of this briefing. Examples of all stimuli to be used (e.g., product, advertising, packaging, etc.) should ideally be available for review well in advance of the first interviewing sessions.

Specifications regarding the screening criteria should be agreed upon and, preferably, confirmed in writing.

8.4　Response to the moderator's suggested "discussion outline" should be provided as quickly as possible to allow time for further discussion. The client should ensure that all issues currently under evaluation are included in the discussion outline.

8.5　The client has a responsibility, in agreeing to the proposed cost of the study, to ensure that the moderator understands:

(i) whether a written analysis is required, and by what date;

(ii) whether the client expects to be given tape recordings of the proceedings;

(iii) whether the client requires transcripts of proceedings;

(iv) whether simultaneous translation is required for groups in a language other than English;

(v) how many copies of the report/presentations of the results, etc., are required.

8.6　The client with responsibility for the study (see 8.1 above) should, wherever possible, watch all qualitative research sessions. Where this is impossible, the client should attend the first session so the moderator can obtain clarification of any unexpected issues.

Clients watching qualitative research sessions should do so with appropriate seriousness and decorum.

APPENDIX

Definitions

(1)　"Research" refers to any examination or collection of information.

(2)　The term "respondent" refers to any individual, organization or group or persons to whom the practitioner approaches either directly or indirectly to collect information.

(3)　The term "interview" refers to any form of contact intended to generate information from a respondent (see #2 above).

(4)　The term "client" shall be understood to include any individual organization, institution, department, or division—including any belonging to the same organization as the practitioner—which is responsible for commissioning a research project.

(5)　The term "practitioner" shall be understood to include any individual, organization, department, or division, including any belonging to the same organization as the "client" (see #4 above), which is responsible for or acts as a consultant on all or part of a research project.

EXHIBIT 1 *(concluded)*
_____

(6) An "overly long questionnaire" may vary in length of time depending on variables, such as subject matter, the number of open-ended questions, and the frequency of use of complex scales. As a general guideline, the following are generally considered "overly long":

A personal interview in-home	over 60 minutes
A telephone interview	over 30 minutes
A mall-intercept interview	over 30 minutes

(7) The term "proposal" refers to a practitioner submission that requires his recommendations on technique, sampling, or other design facets, as well as a cost estimate.

(8) The term "cost estimate" refers to a practitioner's submission that provides a cost estimate based on specifications provided by the client.

(9) The term "primary records" refers to the most comprehensive record of information on whch a research project is based (e.g., completed questionnaires, taped recordings of interviews, etc.).

(10) The term "secondary records" is any record of information on which a research project is based, apart from primary records (see #9 above) (e.g., computer input, coding and editing instructions, etc.).

(11) The term "records" refers to both primary and secondary records collectively (see #9 and #10 above).

(12) The term "verify" refers to the process of recontacting an original respondent to confirm that the interview was in fact done and that selected aspects of the interview were carried out in the manner prescribed by the questionnaire and instructions.

(13) The term "monitor" refers to the process of a supervisor listening to an interviewer interview a respondent.

Reprinted with permission of the Professional Marketing Research Society of Canada.

Market research primarily involves the researcher, research subjects (consumer respondents), and research users (client sponsors). As subjects of research investigations, consumers may be exposed to techniques ranging from observation to experimentation. From a consequentialist perspective, it may be argued that respondents ultimately benefit from product and service improvements resulting from market research insights. Respondents also may receive more direct benefits: monetary or other compensations for their participation and the intrinsic psychic rewards from involvement in the study. However, as the discussion below indicates, these techniques may impinge on rights of respondents, emphasizing the importance of a deontological perspective, too.

This chapter will focus on market research and the consumer; however, it will identify the ethical issues arising for other stakeholders in market research: respondents in companies, the research sponsor, the researcher—and their respective organizations—and the research profession and society. With the broader activity of marketing research, which includes research of competitors, distributors, and the client's marketing organization, the number of stakeholders increases further. The ethical issues involving each major stakeholder and possible solutions are discussed in turn.

Understanding the market enables the firm to identify groups of customers that it may target most appropriately. Subsequent modules of this book examine each element of the marketing program which may be formulated to appeal to these market segments: product policy, pricing, distribution policy, and marketing communications. However, market selection, while a basic prerequisite of the marketing program, is not above ethical controversy. Market selection implies the exclusion of certain groups from marketing activities. It also means targeting certain groups, which can be problematic if this involves stereotyping or, with potentially harmful products, may suggest the group is being victimized.

CONSUMER RESPONDENTS AS STAKEHOLDERS IN MARKETING RESEARCH

Tybout and Zaltman suggest market research subjects have the right to choose, to safety, and to be informed, in keeping with President Kennedy's 1962 address outlining the Consumer's Bill of Rights.[11] Churchill, in a more recent review of marketing research ethics, adds the right to be heard and the right to redress.[12] Table 1 lists eight ethical issues arising as a result of possible violations of respondent rights. Much of the following discussion of consumer respondents in research is based on the Tybout and Zaltman/Churchill analysis. Added to their schemas are the rights to privacy and respect. The privacy right is included because, in contrast to Tybout and Zaltman, failure to preserve participant's anonymity is viewed as a violation of the right to privacy rather than the right to safety (granted that safety concerns may conceivably arise if the privacy right is violated).[13] The right to respect is included because it is self-evident that a fundamental obligation of market researchers toward respondents is respect for human dignity within the research process, particularly given the voluntary cooperation of respondents.

---

[11] Alice M. Tybout and Gerald Zaltman, "Ethics in Marketing Research: Their Practical Relevance," *Journal of Marketing Research* 11 (November 1974), pp. 357–68.

[12] Gilbert A. Churchill, *Marketing Research: Methodological Foundations* (Hinsdale, Ill.: Dryden Press, 1991), pp. 53–65.

[13] Ibid, p. 54. Churchill states: "Maintaining subjects' anonymity ensures that their identity is safe from invasions of privacy."

TABLE 1.   Major Ethical Issues Involving Consumer Respondents

Ethical Issues	*Rights Violations*	*Rights Compensation*
1. Preserving participants' anonymity.	Right to privacy.	
2. Exposing participants to mental stress.	Right to safety.	Right to be heard. Right to redress.
3. Use of special equipment and techniques.	Right to privacy. Right to safety. Right to choose.	Right to redress.
4. Involving participants in research without their knowledge.	Right to be informed. Right to privacy.	Right to redress.
5. Use of deception.	Right to be informed.	Right to be heard. Right to redress.
6. Use of coercion.	Right to choose.	
7. Selling under the guise of research ("sugging").	Right to be informed.	
8. Causing embarrassment, hindrance, or offense.	Right to respect.	Right to redress.

Source: Based on Gilbert A. Churchill, *Marketing Research: Methodological Foundations* (Hinsdale, Ill.: Dryden Press, 1991), p. 54, Table 2A.4.

Rights overlap with respect to any specific issue and other, perhaps more fundamental, rights may be identified, such as honesty or trust. However, in dealing with the major ethical issues involving consumers as research respondents, the expanded list of seven rights, presented here, works well.

Preserving Anonymity

All seven codes of conduct referred to above contain provisions preserving respondent anonymity. However, as with other provisions, the codes vary in detail, strictness, and usefulness. Extracts from each code on respondent anonymity are provided in Exhibit 2, both to illustrate the issue and to show, more generally, the range of adequacy of the different codes. The more adequate codes of ICC/ESOMAR, CASRO, and PMRS (see Exhibit 1, provisions 1.5 and 1.14) require absolute anonymity of respondents except under certain, specified circumstances. Acknowledging that research design or validation, for example, may require some limitation of respondent anonymity, these codes describe these contingencies and explain how they should be managed.

EXHIBIT 2 Preserving Anonymity: Provisions of Marketing Research Codes of Conduct

---

- **MRA**

  To protect the anonymity of respondents and hold all information concerning an individual respondent privileged, such that this information is used only within the context of the particular study.

- **AMA**

  If respondents have been led to believe, directly or indirectly, that they are participating in a marketing research survey and that their anonymity will be protected, their names shall not be made known to any one outside the research organization or research department, or used for other than research purposes.

- **AMA New York Chapter**

  I will protect the right to privacy by guarding the identity of individual respondents.

  I will not release the names of respondents to anyone for any purpose other than legitimate validation, because the guarantee of anonymity is the respondent's only insurance against the disclosure of personal matters.

- **American Association for Public Opinion Research**

  We shall protect the anonymity of every respondent. We shall hold as privileged and confidential all information which tends to identify the respondent.

- **ICC/ESOMAR**

  Article 2

  Subject only to the provisions of Article 3, the informant shall remain entirely anonymous. Special care must be taken to ensure that any record which contains a reference to the identity of an informant is securely and confidentially stored during any period before such reference is separated from that record and/or destroyed. No information which could be used to identify informants, either directly or indirectly, shall be revealed other than to research personnel within the researchers' own organization who require this knowledge for the administration and checking of interviews, data processing, etc. Such persons must explicitly agree to make no other use of such knowledge. All informants are entitled to be given full assurance on this point.

  Article 3

  The only exceptions to the above Article 2 are as follows:

  (a) If informants have been told of the identity of the client and the general purposes for which their names would be disclosed and have then consented in writing to this disclosure.

  (b) Where disclosure of these names to a third party (e.g. a subcontractor) is essential for any purpose such as data processing or in order to conduct a further interview with the same informant (see also Article 4). In all such cases the researcher responsible for the original survey must ensure that any third parties so involved will themselves observe the provisions laid down in this code.

  (c) Where the informant is supplying information not in his role as a private individual but as an employee, officer or owner of an organization or firm, provided that the provisions of Article 5 are followed.

EXHIBIT 2 *(continued)*

Article 4

Further interviews, after the first, shall only be sought with the same informants under one of the following conditions:

(a) in the course of carrying out normal quality control procedures, or

(b) if the informants' permission has been obtained at a previous interview, or

(c) if it is pointed out to informants that this interview is consequent upon one they have previously given and they then give their permission before the collection of further data, or

(d) if it is essential to the research technique involved that informants do not realize that this interview is consequent upon one they have previously given, but they do give their permission before the collection of further data.

Article 5

If the informant is supplying information not in his role as a private individual but as an employee, officer or owner of an organization or firm, then it may be desirable to list his organization in the report. The report shall not however enable any particular piece of information to be related to any particular organization or person except with prior permission from the relevant informant, who shall be told of the extent to which it will be communicated.

• **CASRO**

Confidentiality

1. Survey research organizations have the responsibility to protect the identities of respondents and to insure that individuals and their responses cannot be related.

2. This principle of confidentiality is qualified by the following exceptions:

(a) Respondent names, addresses, and/or telephone numbers obtained in the course of an interview may be used during or immediately following completion of a study by those research professionals responsible for supervising the survey for purposes of: (1) validating the fact that the interview was conducted by the interviewer; (2) substantiating or amplifying the nature of one or more specific responses; and/or (3) determining an additional fact of analytical importance to the study. In these cases respondents must be given a sound reason for the re-inquiry. In all cases a refusal by a respondent to continue must be respected.

(b) Respondent names, addresses, and/or telephone numbers for a study may be maintained in a confidential file by a company and accessed for later use under these conditions only: (1) when study design requires measured recourse to original respondents as in the use of panels or other types of longitudinal studies; and/or (2) when to meet the study purpose it is desirable to match survey data about individual respondents with data about the same individuals from a different source.

3. The principle of confidentiality includes the following specific applications:

(a) Restricting the company's own personnel from the use or discussion of respondent-identifiable data beyond legitimate internal research purposes.

(b) Accepting the responsibility for seeing that subcontractors (interviewers, interviewing services, validation, coding, and tabulation organizations), as well as contractually hired consultants, are aware of and agree to adhere to the principle of respondent confidentiality.

(c) Denying requested access to respondent-identifiable opinion or fact (in question-

---

EXHIBIT 2 *(concluded)*

---

naires or other survey documents) on the part of the client, sponsor, or any other organization. Care should be exercised, when there is a legitimate reason to produce questionnaires (with respondent names deleted) for findings, documentation, or the like, that there are no other means throughout the body of the questionnaire that permit identification of the respondent. Two exceptions to the above requirement are permitted: (1) client validation of interviews is permitted if this does not result in harassment of respondents through multiple validation contacts, and if the survey research organization is convinced that the client is capable of conducting the validation in a fully professional manner. The maintenance of respondent confidentiality, however, should be agreed upon by the client in writing. (2) Where different survey research organizations are conducting different phases of a multistage study (i.e., a trend study), requiring recontact of respondents, it is desirable to have respondent identification pass directly from one research organization to another, but it is permissible for the client to be an intervening agency. The maintenance of respondent confidentiality should be agreed upon in writing by all parties involved. Guiding these exceptions is the understanding that all use of respondent-identifiable information outside the original survey research organization is permissible only if the survey research organization gives permission and obtains in writing a statement of the purpose and a description of how the information is to be used and written assurances that the principle of confidentiality will be maintained.

(d) Rejecting the use of secretly identified mail questionnaires to connect respondent answers with particular individuals.

(e) The use of survey results in a legal proceeding does not relieve the survey research firm of its ethical obligation to maintain in confidence all respondent-identifiable information or lessen the importance of respondent anonymity. Consequently, survey research firms confronted with a subpoena or other legal process requesting the disclosure of respondent-identifiable information should take all reasonable steps to oppose such request, including informing the court involved of the factors justifying confidentiality and respondent anonymity and interposing all appropriate defenses to the request for disclosure.

Respondent-identifiable information obtained during market research could be useful to a client; however, if, for example, this information were to be obtained and used by the sales force, it could be in breach of the obligation of respondent anonymity. The CASRO code explains how survey research organizations can avoid letting clients pursue this temptation. While a client may wish to introduce a secondary purpose to a research study in obtaining customer-specific data for sales purposes, this would violate the individual's right to privacy and discredit the survey organization and marketing research. This may be permissible if the respondent provides informed consent (by approving in writing the use of the information by the client's sales force). However, repeated use of this tactic may be questioned by respondents.

Secondary uses of market research data may extend beyond the research or client sponsor organizations. Credit card companies have sold data on card users, including information about transactions, without their permission or compensation. This practice is in breach of a 1973 Code of Fair Information Practices developed by the U.S. Department of Health, Education, and Welfare. The code states: "There must be a way for individuals to prevent information about themselves obtained for one purpose from being used or made available for other purposes without their consent."[14]

Courts have generally not found it necessary to compromise the anonymity of survey respondents. However, in a recent case involving the Exxon Valdez oil spill, the Superior Court of Alaska ordered limited-access release of confidential survey data obtained during interviews of 600 households in towns affected by the spill. The research organization, CASRO, and the AMA expressed concern at this breach of research confidentiality. However, a spokesperson for Exxon, which obtained the data, commented that the "court guaranteed confidentiality of sensitive, personal information." Only appropriate legal counsel, experts, and witnesses were to be allowed to see the data. This violation of the respondents' right to privacy was said to be justified by the exceptional nature of the case.[15]

Tybout and Zaltman note that the degree of anonymity provided in a study may affect subject responses and that violations of promised anonymity can bias data and willingness to participate in future research. They identify several methods that may be used to protect respondent anonymity: subjects in short-term studies can be assigned identifying numbers and the original identifying data destroyed, and "link" systems may be used in longitudinal studies. The more recent increase in telemarketing activities, enabled by significant improvements in information technology, has led to growing public concern about invasions of privacy and the drafting of privacy legislation. Consumers apparently do not make the distinction between telemarketing and marketing research surveys by telephone, even though this often exists.[16] The result is likely to be greater skepticism about respondent anonymity in research studies as well as greater consumer reluctance to participate in marketing research and telemarketing, and possibly legislative restrictions, too.

Exposing Participants to Mental Stress

Research studies may be stressful to participants simply by, for example, testing knowledge they believe they are expected to have, or, in taste tests, exposing an inability to distinguish a preferred brand from others. The CASRO code

---

[14] James A. Senn, *Information Systems in Management* (Belmont, Calif.: Wadsworth, 1990), p. 724.

[15] Howard Schlossberg, "Court Allows Exxon to See Confidential Research Data," *Marketing News,* June 24, 1991, p. 1.

[16] Jack Honomichl, "Legislation Threatens Research by Phone," *Marketing News,* June 24, 1991.

states: "Research organizations are responsible for developing techniques to minimize the discomfort or apprehension of respondents and interviewers when dealing with sensitive subject matter." Tybout and Zaltman suggest subjects who find research settings stressful may avoid participating in research, which would introduce sample bias. Subjects who do participate may provide contrived responses to questions they cannot answer. Tybout and Zaltman recommend protecting subjects from stress by pretesting the level of stress, employing procedures that limit the stress evoked, and relieving stress that does occur. They suggest disclaimers, such as "there are no correct responses, we are only interested in your opinion," may reduce stress. Where stress does occur, perhaps as a requirement of the research design, debriefing sessions may be used to reassure subjects and allay any fears and misgivings.

Churchill, following Tybout and Zaltman, suggests exposing participants to mental stress violates the right to safety. He suggests the right to be heard requires that participants are allowed to ask questions during and after the research procedure or to voice anxieties and misgivings. The right to redress emphasizes restoration to an original or comparable position. Debriefing as part of a research study evoking participant stress would be a compensatory measure in keeping with rights to be heard and to redress. The ethical principles and guidelines adopted by psychologists are particularly relevant to this ethical issue and are discussed in some detail below. However, a reply to Tybout and Zaltman suggested they overstated the amount of stress that occurs in most marketing research.[17]

Use of Special Equipment and Techniques

The PMRS, ICC/ESOMAR, and CASRO codes require that participants have advance knowledge of observation and recording techniques, including one-way viewing rooms and audio/visual recording or monitoring devices. The ICC/ESOMAR code suggests an exception to this requirement exists when actions or statements of individuals are observed or recorded in public places (such as a store or a street) and the individuals could reasonably expect to be observed or overheard by other people present. However, under these circumstances the code requires fulfillment of at least one of two conditions: (1) all reasonable precautions are taken to ensure that the individual's anonymity is preserved; (2) the individual is told immediately after the event that his actions or statements, or both, have been observed or recorded or filmed, is given the opportunity to see or hear the relevant section of the record, and, if he wishes, to have it destroyed or deleted. Hence, this provision acknowledges the respondent's rights to privacy and to redress.

---

[17] Robert L. Day, "A Comment on Ethics in Marketing Research," *Journal of Marketing Research* 12 (May 1975), pp. 232–33.

A study by Crawford found a significant minority of a sample of 400 marketing executives condoned the use of hidden tape recorders and one-way mirrors. However, this study was reported in 1970 and may not reflect current attitudes.[18] A replication of this study by Akaah, reported in 1990, appears to support this view, suggesting reduced approval of such techniques.[19]

Tybout and Zaltman view "unobtrusive measures" as a violation of the respondent's right to choose. They suggest this practice might prompt subjects to avoid environments where unobtrusive measures may be made. As a solution they support informed consent procedures, similar to those advanced in the ICC/ESOMAR code. Churchill views the use of special equipment and techniques as a threat to the right to safety. This is more likely to be the case where, as he suggests, projective techniques attempt to circumvent the need for subjects' consent or physiological measures involve some risk of physical harm.

Involving Participants in Research without Their Knowledge

This ethical issue overlaps with the use of special equipment and techniques, but is more specifically concerned with informed consent and, hence, the right to information. The ICC/ESOMAR code (in keeping with the PMRS code,

---

[18] Crawford asked respondents to approve/disapprove of three situations involving violations of privacy including: (1) "In a study intended to probe rather deeply into the buying motivations of a group of wholesale customers by use of a semi-structured personal interview form, the M.R. [Marketing Research] Director authorized the use of the department's special attache cases equipped with hidden tape recorders." Of research directors, 33 percent approved, 67 percent disapproved. Of line marketers, 26 percent approved, 71 percent disapproved. (2) "One product of the X Company is brassieres, and the firm has recently been having difficulty making some decisions on a new line. Information was critically needed concerning the manner in which women put on their brassieres. So the M.R. Director designed a study in which two local stores cooperated in putting one-way mirrors in their foundations dressing rooms. Observers behind these mirrors successfully gathered the necessary information." Of research directors, 20 percent approved and 78 percent disapproved. Of line marketers, 18 percent approved and 82 percent disapproved. For both situations some respondents pointed out that the techniques were unnecessary; the data could be obtained without subterfuge. Both situations contravene the codes of ICC/ESOMAR, PMRS, and CASRO. The third situation examined by Crawford, involving a violation of privacy, was the use of ultraviolet ink to enable the identification of respondents to an "anonymous" questionnaire. Also contravening the codes, this situation was approved by 29 percent of research directors. See C. Merle Crawford, "Attitudes of Marketing Executives toward Ethics in Marketing Research," *Journal of Marketing* 34 (April 1970), pp. 46–52.

[19] Akaah was primarily interested in differences in research ethics attitudes among marketing professionals in Australia, Canada, Great Britain, and the United States. Instead of asking for approve/disapprove responses, he asked for responses on a five-point scale ranging from disapprove (coded 1) to approve (coded 5). Of his total sample ($n = 127$), the mean evaluation was 1.8 for the hidden tape recorder situation (with a standard deviation of 1.4); the mean evaluation was 1.4 for the one-way mirror situation (standard deviation 1.1). He found that the marketing professionals of the four countries did not differ in terms of research ethics attitudes. See Ishmael P. Akaah, "Attitudes of Marketing Professionals toward Ethics in Marketing Research: A Cross-National Comparison," *Journal of Business Ethics* 9 (1990), pp. 45–53.

provisions 1.2 and 1.3) requires that "Any statement made to secure cooperation and all assurances given to an informant, whether oral or written, shall be factually correct and honored."

In identifying this issue, Churchill is more specifically concerned about participant observation, observing people in public places, and withholding benefits from control groups. Incognito participation avoids the "control effect" likely when people know they are being observed. If required for research validity, Churchill suggests respondents might be allowed to read the final report on their activities and, thereby, refuse to participate after the fact, upholding the right to redress. Solutions suggested by Churchill to the problems in observing people in public places are: (1) posting a notice in the area stating it is under observation by researchers; and (2) asking for permission of subjects after the data has been collected and, in keeping with the right to redress, providing an opportunity to refuse to participate. Use of control groups requires an assessment of the benefit to the participants (not provided to the control group) and the crucial nature of the information to be provided by running the study. The use of "blind" control groups is particularly problematic where the research is of a product such as a life-saving drug. Under these circumstances a "double-blind" procedure is often used where both respondents and researchers are unaware of the identity of the control group and this procedure is fully understood and accepted by the respondents.

Use of Deception

The PMRS and ICC/ESOMAR codes require researchers to identify themselves and their organizations to respondents. However, both codes also permit client confidentiality. They do not require the disclosure of the study sponsor, though this may be required if respondent identity is to be disclosed to the client (see Article 3 of ICC/ESOMAR code above). Again the right to information of the respondent has to be weighed against the threats to the validity of the research. Informing respondents of a study's sponsor may bias responses. However, research validity concerns would be insufficient to justify many acts of deception; for example, college professors performing commercial market research under the guise of academic research, particularly where respondents are competitors of the professor's client.

Tybout and Zaltman suggest alternatives to the various kind of deception often found in market research: role playing, forewarning respondents that all facets of the study cannot be revealed in advance, and simulations. Pilot studies that anticipate informed consent may be used to screen experiments involving deception. Debriefing can counter any potential harmful effects of deception.

Use of Coercion

The PMRS, ICC/ESOMAR, and CASRO codes each address coercion to varying degrees. The PMRS code has provisions relating to the right to withdraw or refuse to participate in a research interview; pressure to test products; and interviews with children, who may be more susceptible to coercion (see provisions 1.3; 1.7; 1.8; and 1.16). The ICC/ESOMAR code, Article 7 states:

> The informant's right to withdraw, or to refuse to cooperate at any stage of the interview, shall be respected. Whatever the form of the interview, any or all of the information given by the informant must be destroyed without delay if the informant so requests. No procedure or technique which infringes this right shall be used.

The CASRO code has a similar provision and also notes: "The voluntary character of the interviewer-respondent contact should be stated explicitly where respondent might have reason to believe that cooperation is not voluntary." CASRO does permit an element of persuasion, allowing: (1) explaining the purpose of the research project; (2) providing a gift or monetary incentive adequate to elicit cooperation; and (3) recontacting an individual at a different time if the individual is unwilling or unable to participate during the initial contact. Unlike PMRS and ICC/ESOMAR, CASRO does not offer guidance on interviewing children.

Tybout and Zaltman note that consent to interviews and experiments is often obtained on the basis of little or no information about what participation entails. Hence, the codes emphasize a right to withdraw from a study at any time. Yet, because the study is conducted within a social situation, researchers can capitalize on the sense of obligation developed within respondents and place highly personal questions at the end of the study. To ensure the respondent's right to choose, Tybout and Zaltman suggest informed consent procedures, including an explanation of the study being undertaken and the right to withdraw at any time.

Churchill suggests coercion may be found when there is the use of captive subject pools, persistent harassment, or an abuse of the status position of the researcher. Captive subject pools include, for example, company employees who think their success in the company may depend on compliance, such as sales representatives interviewed via their managers; and interviews of members of church groups, where the church receives a donation for each interview obtained. With telephone interviewing as the most popular data collection technique, the potential for harassment of respondents—at relatively low economic cost—is high. While nonresponse bias is a legitimate concern in ensuring survey research validity, this should not lead to the harassment and possible coercion of subjects. It also could result in biased data if respondents are unwilling participants. Finally, as an expert and authority figure, the researcher may be tempted to use this status position to secure participation through intimidation; children and elderly, uneducated, or disadvantaged people may be particularly vulnerable to this tactic. Under the Privacy Act of 1974, government agencies and research suppliers under government contracts must make clear to potential research respondents that compliance is purely voluntary; information must never be extracted from an individual without securing "his informed, expressed consent."[20]

Selling under the Guise of Research

"Sugging" is more accurately viewed as an unethical selling practice than an unethical research practice. However, it is specifically prohibited under the PMRS code (provisions 1.1 and 5.3) and the AMA code. The ICC/ESOMAR code Article 9 requires that, if a research design involves a selling or simulated selling situation, the experimental nature of the selling situation be explained after completion of the research and any money passed over by the respondent be reimbursed.

Sugging is illegal in the United States,[21] but it is still encountered. A recent example comes from the United Kingdom, where the Director General of Fair Trading attacked the practice of luring customers into time-share presentations by pretending to carry out bona fide market research. Approached in the street or over the telephone, respondents answered questions about leisure or holidays and were then told they had won a prize. When they went to collect the prize they had to sit through a timeshare presentation.[22] A recent study found MBAs more willing to use a sales presentation under the guise of research than their counterparts of earlier years.[23] Consumer confusion of telemarketing and marketing research, earlier noted, has prompted many research companies to tell respondents outright at the beginning of an interview that they are not selling anything. However, pressure for legislation to curb privacy abuses is growing.[24]

---

[20] Cynthia J. Frey and Thomas C. Kinnear, "Legal Constraints and Marketing Research: Review and Call to Action," *Journal of Marketing Research* 16 (August 1979), pp. 295–302.

[21] Ibid.

[22] "We Woz Sugged!" *Investors Chronicle,* June 14, 1991. p. 27.

[23] George M. Zinkhan, Michael Bisesi, and Mary Jane Saxton found in a longitudinal study at a major southwestern university that, over the course of the 1980s, there had been a decrease in the MBA students' use of moral idealism when making decisions about morally difficult marketing decisions, particularly in marketing research. One of the 14 scenarios was: "You are a sales manager in an encyclopedia company. A common way for encyclopedia representatives to get into homes is to pretend they are taking a survey. After they finish the survey, they switch to their sales pitch. This technique seems to be very effective and is used by most of your competitors. What would you do?" In 1981, fewer than 35 percent of respondents said they would engage in this activity; by 1987, over 50 percent favored this action (and another marketing research scenario involving the use of a false marketing research company name). Accordingly, "MBA students in the late 1980s seem more willing to engage in quasi-ethical (allowing the ends to justify the means) marketing research practices than their counterparts in the early 1980s." See Zinkhan et al., "MBAs' Changing Attitudes toward Marketing Dilemmas: 1981–1987," *Journal of Business Ethics* 8 (1989), pp. 963–74.

[24] Howard Schlossberg, "Right to Privacy Issue Pits Consumers against Marketers, Researchers," *Marketing News,* October 23, 1989.

Causing Embarrassment, Hindrance, or Offense

Research respondents have a right to respect, which, because they are not involved in an exchange relationship, must at least be equal to that of consumers in general. Respondents typically receive nothing in return for their voluntary participation in research studies, so there is a strong obligation on the part of researchers to respect respondents' time, feelings, dignity, and right to self-determination. Accordingly, the PMRS code discourages "overly long interviews" (provision 1.12 and definition 6), suggests wording and other content be appropriate to the audience (1.11), and has various provisions governing embarrassment and harassment (e.g., 1.10; 5.4; 5.5; 5.8; 5.10).

Article 6 of the ICC/ESOMAR code requires "all reasonable precautions" to ensure respondents and their associates are not "adversely affected or embarrassed" as a result of any interview. The CASRO code has provisions governing unnecessary and unwanted intrusions and harassment, the convenience of interview timing, the length of interviews, and the need to minimize discomfort or apprehension of respondents and interviewers when dealing with sensitive subject matter. While the MRA, AMA, and the AAPOR codes have nothing specific on this issue, the pledge of the AMA New York chapter does at least take a position:

> I recognize that my research may intrude on the time and privacy of those who give me information. But I will make every effort to minimize their discomfort . . .
>
> I will do research without harming, embarrassing, or taking unfair advantage of respondents.
> — I believe that, with care and imagination, participation in an honest and productive survey can be made a positive experience for most respondents, and I believe this can be accomplished without compromising the interests of the sponsor, or the scientific integrity of the research.
> — I will not drain the public's goodwill and cooperation through unnecessarily long interviews or poorly designed questioning procedures. And I will not tolerate those who use the pretense of conducting research to get money from, exploit, propagandize, or otherwise take advantage of people.

Churchill refers to a right to choose and a right to redress where participants are deprived of their right to self-determination. He suggests this might occur when subjects are substantially changed by the research experience. This may be overstating the impact of marketing research experiences. It does at least require an exceptional study and respondent for this to happen. There may also be similar skepticism about his concerns for participants asked questions detrimental to their self-interest. His example of respondents asked about the acceptability of price levels, said to be in violation of the right to safety, is unconvincing. More realistically, perhaps, researchers should respect respondents' rights to be circumspect or not to answer questions on this topic. Where deception is used to obtain this information, the concern is more appropriately with the use of deception than the right to self-determination. In any event, the fairness of any price, established as a result of the research, is subject to evaluation by the market.

It should be noted that agreement to participate in research does create some obligation on the part of the respondent to answer questions accurately and avoid yea-saying or other behaviors that threaten the reliability of the data. This obligation is increased when respondents are paid to participate or receive another form of compensation.

APPLYING MORE STRINGENT GUIDELINES TO CONSUMER RESEARCH

Day's comments on the Tybout and Zaltman paper attributed their concerns to a lack of real-world research experience.[25] While not accepting this charge in their reply, Tybout and Zaltman did stress that their paper addressed experimental as well as survey research, noting the increased use of laboratory and field experiments and in-depth interviews. They also referred to the broadening of marketing and, hence, its involvement with many potentially sensitive issues in such fields as family planning or health care. They reiterated their findings.[26] As the above discussion shows, the more detailed marketing research codes, developed subsequent to the Tybout and Zaltman critique, address many of their concerns. However, some of the concerns applying more specifically to experimental research and in-depth interviews are more satisfactorily covered in the code of the American Psychological Association (APA).

It is useful to bear in mind controversial psychological studies, such as the Milgram obedience experiments, when reviewing the APA code. Milgram showed that subjects were willing to inflict electric shocks of up to 450 volts on other "subjects." These recipients of the shocks were actors working for the experimenter and, under the research design, protested, claimed heart trouble, cried out, and were held down by the experimenter to receive the (simulated) shock, administered to the 450 volts level by at least a third of all subjects.

APA Guidelines

Psychology researchers often conduct studies similar to those of market researchers, also with limited direct benefits for respondents. Members of the APA are required to adhere to its ethical principles, including Principle 9:

---

[25] Day, "A Comment on Ethics . . ."

[26] Alice M. Tybout and Gerald Zaltman, "A Reply to Comments on 'Ethics in Marketing Research: Their Practical Relevance,'" *Journal of Marketing Research* 12 (May 1975), pp. 234–37.

Research with Human Participants.[27] Principle 9 comprises 10 subprinciples governing: the decision for or against conducting a given research investigation; fairness and freedom from exploitation in the research relationship; exceptions to the obligation of obtaining informed consent to participate; ensuring freedom from coercion to participate; protection from discomfort, harm, and danger; responsibilities to research participants following completion of the research; and anonymity of the individual and the confidentiality of data. In addition to the explanation of these subprinciples, the APA Committee for the Protection of Human Participants in Research has provided detailed guidelines to supplement Principle 9.[28] Principle 9 states:

> The decision to undertake research rests on a considered judgment by the individual psychologist about how best to contribute to psychological science and human welfare. Having made the decision to conduct research, the psychologist considers alternative directions in which research energies and resources might be invested. On the basis of this consideration, the psychologist carries out the investigation with respect and concern for the dignity and welfare of the people who participate and with cognizance of federal and state regulations and professional standards governing the conduct of research of human participants.

The first part of the principle represents a consequentialist perspective. In the introduction to the APA's guidelines to this principle, the inevitability of conflicting ethical considerations in psychological research is noted alongside the obligation to use "research skills to extend knowledge for the sake of ultimate human betterment." The committee concludes psychologists' "underlying ethical imperative, thus, is to conduct research as well as they know how." In deciding whether to conduct a research study, the psychologist must weigh its contribution to knowledge against its effects on research participants: "The obligation to advance the understanding of relevant aspects of human experience and behavior will, at times, impinge upon well-recognized human rights."[29] So the second part of the principle represents a deontological perspective, acknowledging the rights of study participants. Two general considerations are proposed in the guidelines:

> First, given the initial ethical obligation of psychologists to conduct the best research of which they are capable, conflict is sometimes unavoidable. The general ethical question always is whether a negative effect upon the dignity and welfare of the participants is warranted by the importance of the research. Second, in weighing the pros and cons of conducting research that raises ethical questions, priority must be

---

[27] American Psychological Association (APA), "Ethical Principles of Psychologists (Amended June 2, 1989)," *American Psychologist* 45, no. 3 (March 1990), pp. 390–95.

[28] Committee for the Protection of Human Participants in Research (Committee), *Ethical Principles in the Conduct of Research with Human Participants* (Washington: American Psychological Association, 1982), pp. 25–74.

[29] The APA also was concerned with the uses of psychological research: "Scientific knowledge and techniques that can be used for human betterment can be turned to manipulative and exploitative purposes as well" (ibid., p. 16).

given to the research participant's welfare. The fundamental requirements are that the participants have made a fully informed and competent decision to participate and that they emerge from their research experience unharmed—or, at least, that the risks are minimal, understood by the participants, and accepted as reasonable.

It is also suggested participants should enjoy some benefit and, as a result of their experience, would willingly participate in further research.

The extent to which market researchers use psychological research techniques is a measure of the importance of adherence to Principle 9 in marketing research. The APA guidelines add to the codes specifically governing marketing research and may be particularly useful in the more troubling examples of experimental research with consumers. The purely commercial purpose of marketing research would suggest that some research techniques used within psychology—involving, for example, extensive manipulation or deception of respondents—are not permissible in market research.

Much marketing research involves what the APA describes as "minimal risks" to respondents. However, participant rights will always to some extent be at risk in a market research study. Moreover, as earlier noted, in many studies some deception of respondents is viewed as necessary to obtain meaningful results. The committee notes that deception "might offend the participants or damage their self-esteem, lower the level of the participants' confidence in the quality of their relationships with others, or provide the participants with a bad example on which they might model their behavior." This applies equally to market research. The market researcher, however, also will attend to the rights of the client. It may be concluded that, for example, some deception of participants may be necessary to fulfill the researcher's obligation to the client to conduct a meaningful study in the most efficient manner. Clearly, such a decision needs to be reached explicitly, with care, and will likely result in a study involving rigorous consent procedures and possibly remedial action, too.

Adapting the APA Guidelines to Market Research

APA Principle 9 establishes the rights of research participants as a determining factor in decisions on whether and how to conduct psychological research. Given the discussion in Chapter 1 of marketing's obligations to the consumer, it is entirely fitting that market researchers should endorse Principle 9 and consider consumers to be the primary stakeholders in the research process.

Although the concern is mainly with individual consumers as research participants, some consideration also must be given to the larger group of consumers who should benefit from product improvements arising from research. However, the rights of individual research participants must take precedence over consumers benefiting from the research. This deontological position could be contrasted with a utilitarian analysis, which might indicate a net gain as a result of small benefits for a large group at the expense of harm to a small group of people. But moral philosophers generally do not find this analysis convincing, even from a utilitarian perspective (the analysis has not fully considered all consequences).

The CASRO code (within its privacy provisions) makes an oblique reference to a requirement to weigh the benefits of the research against the threat to respondent rights, to some extent echoing APA Principle 9: "Survey research organizations have a responsibility to strike a proper balance between the needs for research in contemporary American life and the privacy of individuals who become the respondents in the research." As the earlier review of marketing research codes indicates, the benefits of a market research study need to be balanced against a much broader array of respondent rights. Hence, a necessary revision to all marketing research codes should be the explicit acknowledgement of respondent rights and the requirement for judgment by the marketing researcher of whether the contribution of the study intended warrants the effects on respondent rights and, accordingly, whether the study design minimizes or compensates for these effects.

More detailed prescriptions, within codes and to be adopted by marketing research organizations, may also be suggested. From a consequentialist perspective, the researcher should be encouraged to conduct a means/ends analysis:

- Are the means (specific techniques/use of deception, etc.) necessary and justified by the ends (commercial improvements)?

- Would respondents willingly participate in another, similar research study? (An important question which addresses consequences for the research industry as well as the respondent.)

- What respondent benefits result directly from the study?

From a deontological perspective:

- Do the research techniques violate respondent rights—to privacy, confidentiality, and the like?

- Can these violations be avoided? Has the best study design been chosen?

- If unavoidable, how may these violations be minimized?

- Have respondents given informed consent to their participation in the study—knowing of the rights violation?

- Are respondents entirely free to withdraw themselves or the data provided from the study at any time?

- Are remedial actions intended which remove the consequences of any harm caused?

CLIENT SPONSORS AS STAKEHOLDERS IN MARKETING RESEARCH

The concern of this chapter is primarily with the ethical issues involving consumers that may arise in market research and selection. However, as the foregoing discussion indicates, there are ethical issues in marketing research involving other stakeholders and, moreover, the concerns of these parties directly influence research decisions that affect consumers. However, the ethical issues involving other stakeholders will be more briefly discussed.

Hunt et al., in survey data of 254 practicing marketing research professionals, found that the most often reported ethical conflict of marketing research agency respondents was attempting to balance responsibilities to a client outside the company against company responsibilities. Similarly, the most often reported ethical conflict of in-house researchers was attempting to balance the researcher's self-interest against the researcher's responsibilities to clients within the company. Table 2 shows the frequency of the major ethical issues identified.[30]

By total frequency, more than half of the responses identifying the "most difficult ethical or moral problem" involved the researcher/client relationship and the issues of research integrity (33 percent), treating outside clients fairly (11 percent), and research confidentiality (9 percent).

Under research integrity, Hunt et al. include deliberately withholding information, falsifying figures, altering research results, misusing statistics, ignoring pertinent data, compromising the design of a research project, and misinterpreting the results of a research project with the objective of supporting a predetermined personal or corporate point of view. One in-house researcher commented: "It is tough to be in a position where you criticize management. Much marketing research is only 'eye wash' for the wholesale buyers to convince them that the product is indeed needed and will sell in volume—almost a 'fraudulent' situation." This comment would find support from Day. In questioning Tybout and Zaltman's concerns about respondent rights, he suggested: "There are few fields of scientific activity that are as susceptible to fraud as some aspects of consumer research. In many cases what is really being paid for by a client is an interpretation of detailed data; the temptations that beset the researcher in such a situation are very real."[31]

The second-ranked ethical issue in the Hunt et al. study was treating outside clients fairly. This issue predominantly involves fairness in pricing: "hidden charges" passed on to the customer; cutting corners on validation requirements because costs are running higher than estimated; the use of (more expensive) retainer-type services rather than fixed-price contracts.

Confidentiality arises as an ethical issue for in-house researchers when balancing the interests of different clients/subsidiaries of the same corporation or

---

[30] Shelby D. Hunt, Lawrence B. Chonko, and James B. Wilcox, "Ethical Problems of Marketing Researchers," *Journal of Marketing Research* 21 (August 1984), pp. 309–24.

[31] Day, "A Comment on Ethics . . ."

TABLE 2 Ethical Issues in Marketing Research: Survey Findings*

Issue	In-House Researchers' Frequency[†]		Agency Researchers' Frequency[†]		Total Frequency[†,‡]	
	No.	Percent	No.	Percent	No.	Percent
1. Research integrity	62	31%	37	37%	99	33%
2. Treating outside clients fairly	15	8	16	16	31	11
3. Research confidentiality	15	8	12	12	27	9
4. Marketing mix social issues	17	9	6	6	23	8
5. Personnel issues	14	7	6	6	20	7
6. Treating respondents fairly	17	9	2	2	19	6
7. Treating others in company fairly	11	6	1	1	12	4
8. Interviewer dishonesty	1	1	9	9	10	3
9. Gifts, bribes, and entertainment	6	3	2	2	8	3
10. Treating suppliers fairly	8	4	—	—	8	3
11. Legal issues	8	4	—	—	8	3
12. Misuse of funds	5	3	1	1	6	2
13. Other	17	9	7	7	24	8
	$n=196$	102	$n=99$	99	$n=295$	100

* Response to open-ended question: "In all professions (e.g., law, medicine, education, accounting, marketing, etc.), managers are exposed to at least some situations that pose a moral or ethical problem. Would you please briefly describe the job situation that poses the *most difficult* ethical or moral problem for you?"

[†] Though respondents were asked to describe only one ethical problem, 38 respondents described two coequal problems and one respondent described three coequal problems. Therefore, *n* is the number of problems described by all valid responses (i.e., 254 respondents described 295 problems: *n* = 295).

[‡] Issues are ranked by total frequency. Spearman rank order correlation=.09 *n.s.*

Source: Shelby D. Hunt, Lawrence B. Chonko, and James B. Wilcox, "Ethical Problems of Marketing Researchers," *Journal of Marketing Research* 21 (August 1984), pp. 309–24.

in deciding whether to release competitive intelligence forwarded by an unethical employee in a competitor organization. For agency researchers, confidentiality issues arise regarding the interests of different clients: Where does background knowledge stop and conflicts exist, as a result of work with a previous client? Can data from one project be used in a related project for a competitor? And, if so, should the second client be charged the same amount for this data as the first?

Some of the earliest contributions to the literature on marketing research ethics highlight the issues above. Bogart described the researcher's dilemma as involving constant conflict between professional/scientific aspirations and business/commercial obligations.[32] Figure 1 shows how this conflict interacts with what Bogart terms *means* and *ends* decisions. Also nearly 30 years ago, Blankenship commented on "standing up for the right approach," "handling confidential information," "handling competitive assignments," and other conflict-of-interest problems.[33] Both authors referred to the recently developed AAPOR code and the potential of codes and other attempts to "professionalize" marketing research as solutions to the industry's ethical problems. Accordingly, the AMA, MRA, and AAPOR codes are concerned predominantly with researcher obligations to the client. Similarly, the "pledge" of the AMA New York chapter has three of its four pages addressing these obligations, under the headings of: ("my commitment to") "scientific practice," "honest research," and "fair business dealings."

The ICC/ESOMAR code has provisions governing the confidentiality of the study and client. Research integrity concerns are covered under reporting standards. The researcher is required to make a clear distinction between study results and the interpretation of them and recommendations. The code lists information to be provided in any research report on the study background, sample, data collection, and results. This includes, for example, details of the sampling method and of any weighting method used, and the method of recruitment used for informants and the general nature of any incentives offered to them to secure their cooperation. Similar provisions are included in the CASRO and PMRS codes (see Exhibit 1, section III).

The researcher has a clear responsibility to appraise the client of the reliability of research findings and the limitations of the analysis and any recommendations that are made on the basis of the findings. Ignoring this responsibility could result in legal action, as the marketing research firm of Yankelovich, Skelly, and White found. The firm's client, Beecham, filed suit because of a 1985 study by Yankelovich on Beecham's new cold-water wash,

FIGURE 1   The Researcher's Dilemma and "Means" and "Ends" Decisions

	Means	*Ends*
Professional orientation	Craftsmanship goals	Scientific goals
Business orientation	Bureaucratic goals	Corporate goals

Source: Leo Bogart, "The Researcher's Dilemma," *Journal of Marketing* 26 (January 1962), pp. 6–11.

---

[32] Leo Bogart, "The Researcher's Dilemma," *Journal of Marketing* 26 (January 1962), pp. 6–11.
[33] A. B. Blankenship, "Some Aspects of Ethics in Marketing," *Journal of Marketing Research* 1 (May 1964), pp. 26–31.

Delicare. The study predicted the product would become the industry leader, but it only achieved half the projected market share. Settled out of court with a blackout on details, in August 1988, it is known that Yankelovich blamed the deficiency on poor advertising by Beecham and did not admit to any failings of its research methods. However, the research industry interpreted the case as a signal to qualify research findings, make assumptions more explicit, and revise contracts to caution against undue reliance on research findings.[34]

Al Ossip, writing as director of corporate services at General Foods, had the following suggestions for researchers in response to the research integrity concerns raised in the Hunt et al. study:

— Your role is to be objective, to present the data as you see it even if it is counter to company position. I would suggest that this aspect of your role be put in writing and you seek acceptance of it by the groups you work with.
— Set an example for your subordinates if you are a senior person. Stray once or twice into an unethical territory, and the people working for you may more easily lose some of their backbone.
— Face up to your goofs. Apply the same standards to yourself as you do to the actions of others.[35]

RESEARCHERS AS STAKEHOLDERS IN MARKETING RESEARCH

Researchers and their organizations are the third major stakeholder group in marketing research. Ethical problems involving harm to researchers result mainly from their relationships with clients. A survey of 420 marketing research firms by Bezilla et al. identified five possible "client transgressions":[36]

1. "Holding out the carrot" proposals.
   The promise of a more substantial program following an initial study which would be very competitively priced.
2. Fulfilling corporate purchasing requirements.
   A research buyer may know that firm A will be used to conduct the study, but seeks bids from firms B and C to meet purchasing policies.
3. Unauthorized request for proposals.
   Research proposals may, for a variety of reasons, be sought without the client representative having the authority to allocate the funds to implement them.

---

[34] Ted Knutson, "'Marketing Malpractice' Causes Concern," *Marketing News,* October 10, 1988, pp. 1, 7.
[35] Al Ossip, "Ethics—Everyday Choices in Marketing Research," *Journal of Advertising Research* 25 (October/November 1985), pp. RC-10–12.
[36] Robert Bezilla, Joel B. Haynes, and Clifford Elliot, "Ethics in Marketing Research," *Business Horizons,* April 1976, pp. 83–86.

4. Pseudo-pilot studies.

"Pilot studies" which prove to meet all client requirements, but have been costed by the researcher on the assumption of a more comprehensive study.

5. The consultant's ploy.

Implementation of a research firm's proposal and/or methodology by another firm or in-house, resulting in expert advice at cut-rate prices.

Similar issues were studied by Laroche et al. in a survey of Canadian marketing researchers.[37] Their findings of perceptions of frequency of client-initiated abuse are shown in Table 3. Despite the provisions of codes of conduct, most abuses of researchers occurred at least occasionally. More than half of the respondents indicated that "fairly or very often" researchers are asked to bid on projects they have no chance of securing, because of client purchasing policies. However, these transgressions are not unique to the marketing research industry and may, for example, be found in management consulting.

Client sponsors may be less familiar with or committed to codes governing marketing research. The ICC/ESOMAR code states: "Any person or organization involved in, or associated with, a marketing research project and/or proposal is responsible for actively applying the rules of this code." This code has detailed provisions on researcher property rights governing proposals and techniques. For example, "prospective clients shall not communicate the proposals of one researcher to another researcher except where the latter is acting directly as a consultant to the client on the project concerned."

The CASRO code has few provisions relating to the protection of the researcher, perhaps in recognition of their likely limited effectiveness. It does, however, address the issue of inaccurate reporting of research findings. Research organizations are to seek agreements from clients that they will be able to review and clear any findings publicly disclosed and be able to make their own releases to clarify any incorrect disclosures. The PMRS code has detailed provisions relating to public disclosure of findings and client requests for research proposals (see Exhibit 1, section II). Bezilla et al.'s remedies for client abuse of researchers in requesting proposals go beyond all of the marketing research codes.[38] They suggest: partial payment for proposals, total payment or consultation fees, a strong professional association to "police" illegitimate behavior of research buyers or suppliers, and monitored opening of sealed bids. These suggestions may be overkill or ignore market realities. They do, however, indicate the strength of industry feeling on client practices and suggest client sponsors need to be more careful in soliciting research proposals.

---

[37] Michel Laroche, K. L. McGown, and Joyce Rainville, "How Ethical Are Professional Marketing Researchers?" *Business Forum,* Winter 1986, pp. 21–25.

[38] Bezilla et al., "Ethics in Marketing Research."

TABLE 3   Perceptions of Frequency of Client-Initiated Abuse

	Never	Rarely	Occasionally	Fairly Often	Very Often	Regularly
1. How frequently or infrequently are research proposals solicited from several firms only to have the best features of each combined into the one actually performed by the low bidder or an in-house research department?	0%	29%	53%	12%	6%	0% (n=73)
2. How frequently or infrequently are researchers asked to bid on projects they really have no chance of securing, but are asked to do so for purely technical compliance with a company's purchasing policy for obtaining competitive bids for proposed studies?	0%	15%	32%	38%	14%	1% (n=74)
3. How frequently or infrequently do clients approach research organizations on a full proposal basis when there is no reasonable probability that the project under consideration actually will be commissioned?	0%	45%	40%	13%	1%	1% (n=73)
4. How frequently or infrequently is a phony marketing research approach used in order to help sell products door to door or over the telephone?	7%	22%	38%	15%	9%	9% (n=69)
5. How frequently or infrequently are research proposals solicited from several firms where the client's sole purpose is to generate ideas, with no intention of accepting any of them?	6%	53%	26%	6%	8%	1% (n=72)
6. How frequently or infrequently are research proposals evaluated solely on their merit, unless other criteria (size or special capabilities of the research firm) are made known in advance?	4%	14%	29%	27%	26%	0% (n=70)
7. How frequently or infrequently do clients knowingly portray research findings in a biased or distorted fashion when publishing them?	0%	39%	46%	8%	7%	0% (n=70)

Source: Michel Laroche, K. L. McGown, and Joyce Rainville, "How Ethical Are Professional Marketing Researchers?" *Business Forum*, Winter 1986, pp. 21–25.

OTHER STAKEHOLDERS IN MARKETING RESEARCH

Other stakeholders in marketing research include respondents other than consumers, such as employees, suppliers, or distributors; the research profession; competitors; and society. They generally are given less attention within the marketing research literature and codes.

Societal interest in marketing research results in two ways: first, when consumers benefit from product and service improvements developed as a result of research and second, when research findings are publicly disclosed. The results of much market research are only disclosed (and are confidential) to the client. However, the client may wish to use the research to support marketing communications; for example, as evidence of product superiority in comparative advertising or in trade promotions to retail buyers. Indeed, a significant amount of research is commissioned for this purpose, particularly as the Federal Trade Commission requires substantiation of product claims in advertising (see Chapter 8.8). Accordingly, society as a stakeholder in marketing research requires integrity in the practice and reporting of research; nonobjective research or incomplete or misleading reporting would conflict with the public's right to the honest reporting of scientific practice.

The fourth-ranked major ethical issue in the Hunt et al. study is social issues in the marketing mix (see Table 2). The concerns expressed by the survey respondents were not specific to marketing research, relating more accurately to product or advertising decisions. For example, there was concern regarding research on "trivial" products or products with health hazards, such as cigarettes. Research on advertising to children would also be seen as an ethical problem by many marketing researchers, but again is a societal issue arising within the advertising rather than the research domain of marketing ethics (see Chapter 8.9).

Article 16 of the ICC/ESOMAR code requires that "no one shall knowingly disseminate conclusions from a given research project or service that are inconsistent with or not warranted by the data." This code also prohibits the misrepresentation of an activity as marketing research that has other purposes and, in particular, threatens privacy, including:

- Enquiries whose objectives are to obtain personal information about private individuals per se, whether for legal, political, supervisory (e.g., job performance), private, or other purposes.

- The compilation of lists, registers, or data banks for any purposes that are not marketing research.

- The acquisition of information for use by credit rating or similar services.

- The collection of debts.

- Direct or indirect attempts, including the framing of questions, to influence an informant's opinions or attitudes on any issue.

The codes emphasize the professional nature of marketing research. Interestingly, the PMRS code does not go so far as to suggest it is an entirely scientific activity, describing research as "more an art than a science" (see 4.2 in Exhibit 1). The notion of a marketing research profession emphasizes the researcher's obligation to other researchers. The research profession is a stakeholder in marketing research and, indeed, the codes may be viewed as rules to protect marketing researchers from possible misconduct by each other. Poor research or public misreporting of research does a disservice not only to society but also to the marketing research profession. Accordingly, the profession is protected by specific provisions, too. For example, Article 14 of the ICC/ESOMAR code states: "Researchers shall not misrepresent themselves as having any qualifications, experience, skills, or access to facilities which they do not in fact possess." Similarly, provisions in the codes cover a variety of potential ways by which researchers may abuse their position as skilled professionals; for example, in meeting respondent selection criteria in qualitative research (see Exhibit 1, 6.1). Various provisions discourage involvement in unnecessary research (see Exhibit 1, 3.15).

Research of competitors is necessary for effective marketing. For instance, a company can identify product improvements by researching consumer reactions to competitors' products. However, competitor intelligence gathering can quickly become problematic, ethically and legally. It would be unfair and probably illegal for a company to obtain information about competitor bids prior to submitting its own bid in a sealed bidding arrangement. Accordingly, the ICC/ESOMAR code prohibits the misrepresentation of marketing research as "industrial, commercial or any other form of espionage." This topic is discussed in detail in Chapter 3.7. The ICC/ESOMAR code also prohibits unjustified criticism and disparagement of competitors in research.

Finally, it should be acknowledged that not all research respondents will be consumers. To a large extent these respondents will have identical rights. However, there may be circumstances where the relationship between the researcher and respondent changes the nature of the obligations involved. For example, research involving the company's sales representatives may require more caution in seeking cooperation because of the difficulty these respondents would have in refusing to participate. Conversely, if the interviews are conducted during work hours, there may be justifiably less concern about the use of the respondent's time. Insofar as research with nonconsumer respondents is, fundamentally, research involving human participants, the APA guidelines may again be useful.

RESOLVING ETHICAL ISSUES IN MARKETING RESEARCH

Industries are often prompted into self-regulation by the threat of government intervention and legislation. Frey and Kinnear issued a "call to action" to marketing researchers, noting: "Unchecked abuses of individual firms eventually will cause the entire industry to be dragged into the legal arena. The ensuing struggle not only would discredit the industry in the eyes of the public, but would result in governmental regulation, which frequently encompasses more than just the original problem."[39] Similar concerns were expressed by Murphy and Coney.[40] Unless it is argued that Frey and Kinnear's call was heeded, their 1979 prediction that "the problem will soon be out of the industry's control" seems unfulfilled. Pressure currently is growing for legislation governing threats to privacy, but major legislative constraints have not been imposed on marketing research.

There are some indications that industry standards have not improved.[41] Perhaps, however, there has been some level of positive response to the more comprehensive codes of conduct discussed above. A variety of sources have argued in favor of codes of conduct as a way of resolving ethical issues in marketing research. Some sources have also suggested the codes need to be enforced and be accompanied by the accreditation of marketing research "professionals." Others have argued that codes are insufficient and attention to other factors influencing unethical behavior is required.

Taking a controversial stand, Coe and Coe argued that marketing research activity does not meet the criteria for professionalism, in comparison with, for example, law or medicine.[42] The criteria they employ are:

1. Rendering of essential services to society.
2. Requirements for admission regulated by law.
3. Governance through a code of ethics and disciplinary procedures for violation of [the] code of ethics.
4. Specialized body of knowledge acquired through formal education and a specialized language unique to the body of knowledge.

The first criterion is substantive. Coe and Coe suggest marketing research does not meet this criterion, because it is "typically performed to benefit private interests, rather than public interests. While . . . some marketing research activities lead to eventual goods and services which benefit the public interest . . . these activities are directed toward the development of profitable goods and services with little recognition given to the public good." Coe and Coe note that identification of public responsibility implies the development of an

---

[39] Frey and Kinnear, "Legal Constraints . . ."

[40] John H. Murphy and Kenneth A. Coney, "Accreditation of Marketing Researchers?" in *Marketing: 1776–1976 and Beyond,* ed. Kenneth L. Bernhardt (Chicago: American Marketing Association, 1976), pp. 260–65.

[41] A 1984 survey of 500 marketing researchers by Washington Researcher Limited found the use of unethical marketing research techniques was common and on the rise (cited in Steven J. Skinner, O. C. Ferrell, and Alan J. Dubinsky, "Organizational Dimensions of Marketing-Research Ethics," *Journal of Business Research* 16, no. 2 (1988), pp. 209–23).

[42] Ted L. Coe and Barbara J. Coe, "Marketing Research: The Search for Professionalism," in *Marketing: 1776–1976 and Beyond,* ed. Kenneth L. Bernhardt (Chicago: American Marketing Association, 1976), pp. 257–59.

enforceable code of ethics to protect that interest. Perhaps it is not surprising that research practitioners have questioned the seriousness researchers place on professionalism.[43] The Canadian survey by Laroche et al., meanwhile, found that a significant minority (27 percent) of respondents did not perceive a need for a formal or standardized ethical code; they enforced a personal code of ethics in their marketing research practice.[44]

Murphy and Coney suggest that a marketing research accreditation program would be a necessary and desirable development in the evolution of the marketing profession.[45] It could (1) protect both clients and respondents, (2) reduce the threat of government action, (3) represent a positive step by the AMA in providing leadership in the advancement of science in marketing, (4) make competition among contractors more equitable, and (5) support the development of a professional marketing research ethic. The benefits are shown in more detail in Figure 2. Likewise, Schneider, noting that it is the practicing marketing researcher who allows unethical practices to exist, suggests that it is insufficient to rely on these individuals to solve the problem, that codes and certification are required. He advocates research to identify practices of concern to society, which then would form the basis of a code for which it would be

FIGURE 2   Benefits of the Accreditation of Marketing Researchers

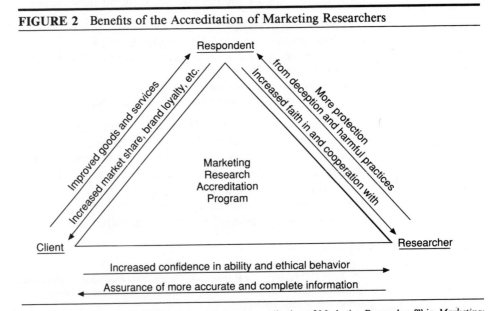

Source: John H. Murphy and Kenneth A. Coney, "Accreditation of Marketing Researchers?" in *Marketing: 1776–1976 and Beyond,* ed. Kenneth L. Bernhardt (Chicago: American Marketing Association, 1976), pp. 260–65.

[43] Margaret R. Roller, "Research Has Far to Go to Achieve Professional Status," *Marketing News,* September 12, 1986.

[44] Laroche et al., "How Ethical Are . . . Researchers?"

[45] Murphy and Coney, "Accreditation of Marketing Researchers?"

possible to demand adherence and to censure nonadherents. He also suggests public awareness efforts: to demonstrate to consumers the value of research and how they may benefit in becoming "better consumers" as a result of participation. Consumers would be encouraged to report misconduct.[46]

Day suggested that codes "can only serve as very broad, wide-mesh fences to discourage the most obvious wrong-doers."[47] Empirical studies support this recognition of the limits of codes, but not necessarily Day's conclusion about the individual's personal set of values ensuring the highest standards. Hunt et al. concluded that "the presence of either corporate or industry codes of conduct seems to be unrelated to the extent of ethical problems in marketing research."[48] This, however, may have been due to the limitations of the existing codes. Hunt et al. did find that top management actions make a difference: "When top management lets it be known that unethical behavior will not be tolerated, marketing researchers experience fewer problems." But codes are not useless; they provide the guidelines that management can use as starting points in delineating acceptable and unacceptable behavior.

Ferrell and Skinner have suggested that codes of ethics, "the most obvious device to improve ethical behavior," may not have been fully utilized.[49] Skinner et al. propose that the behavior of referent others (colleagues) and opportunity to engage in unethical behavior are better predictors of unethical behavior within marketing research organizations than is the individual's own ethical belief system.[50] As earlier noted, there is considerable opportunity for unethical behavior in marketing research. However, a survey of 1,500 researchers by Kelly et al. found that levels of (unethical) "opportunistic behavior" varied between different types of research organizations. The long-term relationship between a corporate research department employee and his or her organization made opportunistic behavior less likely than among the employees of data subcontractors, who experience relatively short-term interorganizational relationships. More important, Kelley et al. found an inverse relationship between ethical climate and opportunism. This suggests, in keeping with other studies, that corporate culture is an important factor in ethical behavior, a finding which can be acted on.[51]

It has been suggested that the demographic characteristics of researchers influence ethical behavior. For example, Kelley et al., in keeping with other studies, found that female researchers rate themselves as more ethical than males.[52] Older marketing researchers and researchers holding their present job

---

[46] Schneider, "Subject and Respondent Abuse . . ."

[47] Day, "A Comment on Ethics . . ."

[48] Hunt et al., "Ethical Problems . . ."

[49] O. C. Ferrell and Steven J. Skinner, "Ethical Behavior and Bureaucratic Structure in Marketing Research Organizations," *Journal of Marketing Research* 25 (February 1988), pp. 103–9.

[50] Skinner et al., "Organizational Dimensions . . ."

[51] Scott W. Kelley, Steven J. Skinner, and O. C. Ferrell, "Opportunistic Behavior in Marketing Research Organizations," *Journal of Business Research* 18 (1989), pp. 327–40.

[52] Scott W. Kelley, O. C. Ferrell, and Steven J. Skinner, "Ethical Behavior among Marketing

for more than 10 years also rated their behavior as more ethical. While far from conclusive, further research of this type may indicate some desirable characteristics of leaders of research projects.

In conclusion, the more comprehensive codes of conduct offer greater potential in providing remedies to unethical behavior in marketing research. It was proposed, however, that even these codes require strengthening, by incorporating provisions from the APA guidelines. The codes (a code?) must also be universally adopted and enforced, to be meaningful. Additional research—and input from those to be governed by the codes—may be required to confirm the appropriateness of their provisions. However, codes alone are insufficient. Senior management and project leaders of research organizations or departments must demonstrate their commitment to the code employed and, by example and enforcement of the code, promote an ethical climate.

INCLUSION AND EXCLUSION ISSUES IN MARKET SELECTION

Identifying market segments—through market research—and selecting target markets is a logical consequence of the marketing concept. In one of the most widely used marketing texts, Kotler explains:

> A company that decides to operate in some broad market . . . normally cannot serve all customers in that market. The customers are too numerous, dispersed, and varied in their buying requirements. Some competitors will be in a better position to serve particular customer segments of that market. The company, instead of competing elsewhere, often against superior odds, needs to identify the most attractive market segment that it can serve effectively.[53]

Ethics in Marketing shows that some of the most fundamental concepts in marketing, when looked at afresh, raise important ethical issues. Market selection, though so clearly basic to marketing thought and practice, is problematic because of the way in which it directs marketing programs to explicitly include or exclude groups of consumers.

Target marketing is increasingly more focused. Markets have fragmented, requiring programs to target smaller and more elusive groups of consumers. However, technological improvements have permitted greater sophistication in identifying and reaching these groups. In some industries in the 1990s,

---

Researchers: An Assessment of Selected Demographic Characteristics," *Journal of Business Ethics* 9 (1990), pp. 681–88. Kelley et al. also found the higher the respondents' level of education, the less ethical they rated themselves. This conflicted with the finding of Laroche et al. (see footnote 37). However, Laroche et al. did find experience positively related to ethical behavior, in keeping with Kelley et al.

[53] Philip Kotler, *Marketing Management: Analysis, Planning, Implementation and Control* (Englewood Cliffs: Prentice Hall, 1991), p. 262.

marketing practice has evolved to "segments-of-one" marketing or "customized marketing," where programs are directed at the ultimate narrow target: the individual consumer.[54] For example, a consumer receiving a certain number of collect phone calls will be approached directly by MCI Communications, pitching its personal 800-number product. Waldenbooks has enrolled 3.7 million members, at $5 each, in a program that rewards frequent book buyers with discounts and extra service. If a member shows an interest in certain kinds of books, Waldenbooks will send information about new titles in that area. However, Merrill Lynch chooses not to use customer financial information it has on file in its mailings, because it does not want clients to feel as if their files are open to just anyone. This privacy concern is only one example of inclusion issues raised by targeting consumers.

Star argues that, despite this "microsegmentation" of consumers, mass marketing remains the predominant mode.[55] While acknowledging that the marketer develops a program "to coincide, to the greatest extent possible, with the attributes of the consumer target group," he suggests there is often a significant misfit between market segment, program target, and program audience. This is shown in Figure 3. He concludes this has innocent origins and is inevitable, but also problematic: "the marketing concept . . . is burdened by process constraints that limit, in implementation, the achievement of its promises . . . the lack of congruence among segments, targets, and audiences seems a significant cause of consumer distraction and frustration." Advertising messages will reach and frustrate people for whom they are not intended: consumers and their children may have a strong desire for the expensive toys advertised on Saturday morning television, but not the resources to pay for them. Star advocates greater efforts to fix some of the misfits and alleviate some of the discontents. This is one illustration of exclusion issues raised by targeting consumers.

Inclusion Issues

In contrast with microsegmentation, more broadly defined and larger groups of customers make up the segments targeted in mass marketing. This imprecision, as Star suggests, can result in marketing effort reaching beyond the target segment and distracting, irritating, or frustrating other consumers. Yet it also can create problems with consumers within the target segment. While necessarily similar on some dimensions, members of a target segment may overall be highly heterogeneous. To capture similarities and simplify messages, marketers may resort to undesirable stereotypes: the traditional "housewife"

---

[54] Kathleen Deveny, "Segments of One," *The Wall Street Journal,* March 22, 1991, p. B4.
[55] Steven H. Star, "Marketing and Its Discontents," *Harvard Business Review,* November–December 1989, pp. 148–54.

FIGURE 3 Marketing Effort and Consumer Discontent

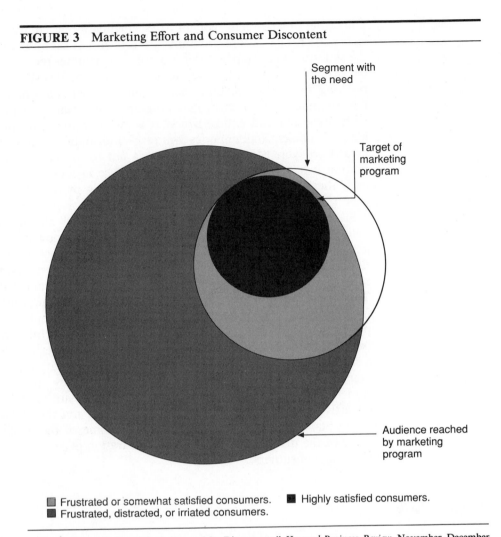

Segment with
the need

Target of
marketing
program

Audience reached
by marketing
program

Frustrated or somewhat satisfied consumers.   ■ Highly satisfied consumers.
■ Frustrated, distracted, or irriated consumers.

Source: Steven H. Star, "Marketing and Its Discontents," *Harvard Business Review,* November–December 1989, pp. 148–54.

and mother whose greatest concern is dirty laundry (when around two thirds of American women work and more than a quarter of all households are one person).

Sex-role stereotypes in advertising influence sex-role formation through socialization processes.[56] Traditional portrayals of women in advertising gener-

---

[56] See, for example, Phyllis A. Katz, "The Development of Female Identity," *Sex Roles* 5, no. 2 (1979); Joyce Jennings (Walstedt), Florence L. Geis, and Virginia Brown, "Influence of Television Commercials on Women's Self-Confidence and Independent Judgement," *Journal of Personality and Social Psychology* 38, no. 2 (1980).

ally are said to have diminished. This is partly due to feminist criticism, but also to the recognition that these stereotypes are often invalid and that advertising is likely to be less effective if it insults its intended audience. Some studies question whether there has been much improvement. Lazier-Smith found 72 percent of the advertisements in *Time, Newsweek, Playboy,* and *Ms.* magazines portrayed women as sex objects or in traditional roles, a figure comparable to that found in a 1973 study, 15 years earlier.[57] She concluded women still tend to be portrayed "as idiots, bimbos, and basically sex objects," despite gains in employment, earnings, and job advancement. Ferguson et al., in a 15-year content analysis of *Ms.*, found that the portrayal of women as subordinate to men or as merely decorative decreased over time, but advertisements showing women as alluring sex objects increased.[58] However, the study highlights the difficulties of measuring sexism, a complex construct that changes over time.

Advertisers have been seeking the advice of women's groups. But there is some disagreement over what is sexist. Most feminists find sex in advertising acceptable, if the woman is "in control of her sexuality," rather than shown passively or as a victim.[59] Reverse sexism, with men shown as sex objects, developed during the 1980s, as in advertisements by Sansabelt: "What women look for in men's pants."[60] Feminists generally agree that, like the beer advertisement with bikini-clad models, this also is dehumanizing.

Anheuser-Busch claims its beer advertisements at least meet the approval of its customers.[61] Similarly, an executive on the Valvoline advertising account justifies the use of "girlie calendars" for mechanics by noting: "It may offend some groups—but they aren't your customers."[62] Outside the target segment, some people may be exposed to offensive advertising. In a 30-year content analysis of industrial advertising, Reese et al. found about 40 percent of 1980s advertisements with decorative portrayals of women showed them inappropriately dressed.[63] This figure was an improvement on the 1970s; men also were found to be increasingly used in decorative portrayals. However, the proportion of males shown as authority figures increased in the 1980s, and women are still almost always portrayed as demonstrators or users. Attitudes

---

[57] Reported in "Ads' Portrayal of Women Today Is Hardly Innovative," *Marketing News,* November 6, 1989, p. 12.

[58] Jill Hicks Ferguson, Peggy J. Kreshel, and Spencer F. Tinkham, "In the Pages of *Ms.*: Sex Role Portrayals of Women in Advertising," *Journal of Advertising* 19, no. 1 (1990), pp. 40–51.

[59] Joanne Lipman, "Sexy or Sexist? Recent Ads Spark Debate," *The Wall Street Journal*, September 30, 1991.

[60] Lynn G. Coleman, "What Do People Really Lust After in Ads?" *Marketing News,* November 6, 1989, p. 12.

[61] "Sex Still Sells—But So Does Sensitivity," *Business Week,* March 18, 1991, p. 100.

[62] Lipman, "Sexy or Sexist? . . ."

[63] Nancy A. Reese, Thomas W. Whipple, and Alice E. Courney, "Is Industrial Advertising Sexist?" *Industrial Marketing Management* 16, no. 4 (November 1987), pp. 231–40.

are changing: Lotus Development recently canceled a marketing brochure that showed a busy woman in a revealing T-shirt.[64]

Similar arguments surround the use of race or age stereotypes. Advertisers are increasing expenditures in minority media to address undertargeting of earlier years. Messages are tailored accordingly. However, sensitivity may become patronizing if the execution is poor, which has prompted some companies to use minority agencies. Meanwhile, elements of minority cultures, such as rap music, are becoming more prevalent in mainstream advertising.[65] Consumers have to be reached via media and messages they would wish to be addressed through. This means minorities or the elderly should not be viewed as a homogeneous group. Advertisers should ask: Which are they first, Hispanic or professional, elderly or golf enthusiasts? The key is to use variables that cut the segmentation for the particular product category.

Among the companies using advertising campaigns focusing on minorities are those producing products that may cause harm. Targeting market segments is as legitimate a marketing technique for cigarettes as it is for bank services. If marketing is to be permitted for these products, it is to be expected that companies will direct their marketing efforts efficiently and effectively. However, with increases in minority targeting of cigarettes, alcohol, and sneakers have come criticism from organized and vocal minority groups.

In July 1991, G. Heileman Brewing Company was forced to abandon its newly developed PowerMaster malt liquor product, following an outcry by community activists. The beer was targeted at low-income, inner-city blacks, who suffer disproportionately from alcohol-related diseases. The Bureau of Alcohol, Tobacco, and Firearms insisted the company drop the word "power" from the brand name, which communicated the product's high potency (a 5.9 percent alcohol content, compared to 3.5 percent for regular beer). Pressure against the $500 million malt liquor category is likely to increase as the bureau is further pressed to impose restrictions on other brewers promoting their products' high firepower. Complaints are not limited to marketing communications. Discounting of popular malt liquors by 50 percent (to around 99¢ for two 16-oz. cans) has also brought criticism: "What makes the beer promotion so insidious is that they have targeted ethnic communities. We don't see these kinds of promotions for the same products in other neighborhoods," commented the San Francisco health commissioner.[66]

Similar criticisms were experienced by R. J. Reynolds with the Uptown cigarette, also targeted at blacks, and withdrawn from test marketing in January

---

[64] "Sex Still Sells . . ."

[65] Peg Masterson, "Should Marketers Target Blacks More?" *Advertising Age* 61, no. 27 (July 2, 1990), p. 20.

[66] Alix M. Freedman, "Heileman, under Pressure, Scuttles PowerMaster Malt," *The Wall Street Journal*, July 5, 1991, p. B1; Alix M. Freedman, "Malt Advertising that Touts Firepower Comes under Attack by U.S. Officials," *The Wall Street Journal*, July 1, 1991, p. B1; Perry Lang, "Hard Sell to Blacks of Potent Malt Brew Called 'Irresponsible,'" *San Francisco Chronicle*, November 3, 1990.

1990 (see section 3.6.3). In Chicago, Rev. Michael Pfleger, an inner-city Roman Catholic priest, made use of a "necessity defense" to win acquittal on property-destruction charges after he defaced neighborhood billboards advertising tobacco and alcohol. Noting that complaints to advertisers and city government had proved fruitless, Pfleger commented: "When they force us into a corner, we can come out with a paintbrush." His vandalism was intended to prevent a greater harm: the sale of potentially addictive products to young blacks. R. J. Reynolds later announced it had removed billboard ads for tobacco products from Chicago's predominantly black and Hispanic neighborhoods.[67]

The more general backlash against alcohol has prompted an industry emphasis on moderation, promoting "responsible drinking," to the approval of Mothers Against Drunk Driving. Concerned about the effects of a target market on other people, the brewers have reduced marketing programs targeting students during spring break. Resort communities have banned beer-sponsored beach parties. Acknowledging concern about underage drinking, Anheuser-Busch has provided booklets to help bartenders identify fake driver's licenses. While critics question brewers' claims that they do not target underage drinkers, Miller has put out a campaign: "Good beer is properly aged. You should be too."[68] The targeting of children is controversial in other ways, as Paine discusses (see Chapter 8.9).

Reynolds also came under fire for its plans to target young, poorly educated, blue-collar women. The Dakota brand, positioned to appeal to the "virile female," was to target one of the few remaining growth sectors of the cigarette market. Dakota was shelved. Existing brands targeting women have prospered; unit sales of Eve increased 8.4 percent in 1989, while industry shipments dropped 6.6 percent. Anti-smoking activists have, in turn, targeted female brands. Such groups as the National Organization for Women have adapted a Virginia Slims advertising campaign in getting across the message: "You've come the *wrong* way, baby." In this example, again, organized and vocal interest groups, claiming to represent a market segment, have pressured companies to stop target marketing.[69]

Targeting creates victims of market segments when the products involved are harmful. In some cases, however, it has been suggested that the products are not the problem. With sneakers and with alcohol, the more fundamental problems of minority neighborhoods—unemployment and poor education, housing, and health care—are said to be to blame. Suggesting black endorsers

---

[67] Christina Duff, "Priest Who Defaced Billboards Acquitted," *The Wall Street Journal,* July 5, 1991; "R. J. Reynolds Pulls Some Cigarette Billboard Ads," *Marketing News,* September 30, 1991.

[68] Jill Abramson, "Alcohol Industry Is at Forefront of Efforts to Curb Drunkenness," *The Wall Street Journal,* May 21, 1991; Marj Charlier, "Big Brewers Will Be among Wallflowers at the 1991 'Spring Break' Beach Parties," *The Wall Street Journal,* March 13, 1991.

[69] Alix M. Freedman and Michael J. McCarthy, "New Smoke from RJR under Fire," *The Wall Street Journal,* February 20, 1990; Peter Waldman, "Tobacco Firms Try Soft, Feminine Sell," *The Wall Street Journal,* December 19, 1989.

of sneakers are "exploiting an ethos of mindless materialism," Rev. Jesse Jackson commented: "Our youth are trapped with economic depression, with zero-based self-esteem ... [they] cover up [their] inadequate feelings with $200 tennis shoes."[70]

Targeting also raises privacy concerns. Some 300,000 telemarketing agents make some 18 million calls a day, but "junk calls" irritate consumers. Public concern resulted in 1,000 new state bills to curb telemarketing in 1991. Among the laws already passed are restrictions on auto-dialers in 20 states and "don't call me" lists, which telemarketers must honor.[71] Consumers are concerned about invasions of privacy: "Scavenging for the personal details of people's lives is today a high-tech, billion-dollar industry. It is the invisible engine of junk mail and junk phone calls. And it has been instrumental in the erosion of personal privacy."[72] Direct marketing is more effective when campaigns are based on detailed consumer profiles. Consumers have objected. Blockbuster Entertainment Corporation denied that it intended to sell household-specific video rental lists, after the story appeared in the press. A Gallup poll found 76 percent of respondents would take their tape-rental business elsewhere if that happened.[73] The poll also found 45 percent "very concerned" about the information marketers may have gathered about them without their knowledge; 33 percent were "somewhat concerned."

Lotus Development Corporation dropped plans to sell Marketplace, its software product with shopping habits and personal data about 120 million U.S. households. When the company offered to delete data about anyone who called or wrote, it was flooded with 30,000 requests. Developed with the consumer information company Equifax, the disk would not have contained data not already available to direct marketers. Equifax has suggested that surveys find consumer privacy concerns are diminished when the benefits of direct marketing are explained and when made aware of services that delete their names from mailing lists. However, consumers still object to storage of information without their consent. As Alan Westin, a privacy expert, puts it, "the individual perceives that some of his or her uniqueness has been appropriated."[74]

Exclusion Issues

While some consumers are concerned about the privacy issues raised by direct marketing, others may be concerned by being excluded. This is discussed by

---

[70] Bill Brubaker, "Athletic Shoes: Beyond Big Business," *Washington Post,* March 10, 1991.

[71] Michael W. Miller, "Lawmakers Are Hoping to Ring Out Era of Unrestricted Calls by Telemarketers," *The Wall Street Journal,* May 28, 1991.

[72] Michael W. Miller, "Data Mills Delve Deep to Find Information about U.S. Consumers," *The Wall Street Journal,* March 14, 1991.

[73] Jack Honomichl, "Legislation Threatens Research by Phone," *Marketing News,* June 24, 1991.

[74] Michael W. Miller, "Lotus Is Likely to Abandon Consumer-Data Project," *The Wall Street Journal,* January 23, 1991; Mary J. Culnan and John A. Baker, "An Issue of Consumer Privacy ... and Corporate Retreat," *New York Times,* March 31, 1991.

Cespedes (see Chapter 6.1). A related topic is "redlining" (see Chapter 6.5). An important consequence of this exclusion is that not only may certain groups not receive products and services, but they may have to pay more for those they do receive.

Reviewing research on whether the poor pay more, Andreasen concluded that prices in disadvantaged areas for both durables and nondurables are higher than in nondisadvantaged areas.[75] A 1991 survey by New York City's department of consumer affairs confirmed that food prices are highest where customers are least able to afford it.[76] Stores in impoverished inner-city neighborhoods were also fewer in number and were smaller and poorly stocked, with inferior foodstuffs and poor service. A low-income shopper would pay 8.8 percent more, or at least $350 more each year, for a family of four. The same basket of goods at an A&P store in Harlem was 13 percent more than at an A&P store in middle-class Queens.

As Andreasen concludes, a substantial portion of the price difference is attributable to market structure: "Disadvantaged areas have more small, higher-cost independent supermarkets and mom-and-pops than nondisadvantaged areas, which more often have low-cost supermarkets." Smaller stores carry less high-margin items, such as film or beauty aids, because of space constraints. They lack the bulk purchasing power of large chains and the technology, such as scanner systems, to provide sales information that allows the larger stores to maximize sales per foot. They also may have higher shrinkage costs. As evidence of exclusion, the New York study found one store for every 9,400 people in Manhattan's poor zip codes, against one outlet for every 5,800 people in the Upper East Side. With suburban areas saturated, there is some indication that supermarket chains may return to inner-city neighborhoods. However, the chairman of one chain commented: "Part of the reluctance of big chains to go into minority areas is the fact that the minorities themselves want to have their own people open independent stores and keep the money within the community." This comment may be self-serving. Exclusion simply may be a result of prejudice. It has been suggested that gays represent a viable segment that could be targeted by condom manufacturers. The failure to exploit this opportunity has been attributed to "homophobia."[77]

In conclusion, while market selection may be a logical consequence of the marketing concept, it raises ethical issues about which consumers are included and how they are targeted, as well as which consumers are excluded and the benefits they are denied. As the examples above show, these issues involve an intriguing interplay of the rights of different stakeholders and demand sensitivity of the marketing manager.

---

[75] Alan R. Andreasen, *The Disadvantaged Consumer* (New York: Free Press, 1975), p. 166.

[76] Alix M. Freedman, "The Poor Pay More for Food in New York, Survey Finds," *The Wall Street Journal*, April 15, 1991.

[77] Franklin B. Krohn and Laura M. Milner, "The AIDS Crisis: Unethical Marketing Leads to Negligent Homicide," *Journal of Business Ethics* 8 (1989), pp. 773–80.

Suzuki Samurai: The Roll-Over Crisis

"Never a dull moment" was the theme adopted for the advertising of the Suzuki Samurai, the four-wheel-drive vehicle marketed by American Suzuki Motor Corporation. This positioning concept seemed to have worked well and the Samurai had achieved outstanding sales levels, especially among younger drivers, since its launch in November 1985. The introduction of the Samurai to the United States was widely viewed as the most successful model launch of any Japanese automobile manufacturer. However, in June 1988, Suzuki and the Samurai had a positioning problem of a different kind. Consumers Union, the highly respected consumer interest group and publisher of *Consumer Reports*, was to hold a press conference the next day, June 2, naming the Samurai as unsafe because of its tendency to roll over. It would be demanding that the 160,000 or so Samurais already sold should be recalled. Suzuki managers were concerned about the effects of the press conference and how they should respond.

AMERICAN SUZUKI MOTOR CORPORATION

The Suzuki Motor Company, Ltd., was founded in Japan, in 1909, by Michio Suzuki. It began exporting motorcycles to the United States in 1964 and subsequently other products, such as outboard motors, generators, and water pumps. American Suzuki Motor Corporation (ASMC) comprised the motorcycle division, the marine division, and the automotive division, which had been established in 1985. It was based in Brea, California.

ASMC started selling the Suzuki Samurai in November 1985. This vehicle, also known as the SJ413, was a derivative of Suzuki's SJ410, of which over

---

This case was prepared from public sources by Professor N. Craig Smith with the assistance of Professor John A. Quelch.

half a million had been sold throughout the world since its introduction in 1960. Both models were mini, four-wheel-drive, off-road vehicles; but the SJ413 was an upgraded model, designed for the U.S. market, with a 1,324 cc engine, compared to the less powerful 1,000 cc engine of the SJ410. The SJ413 was also more comfortable. It was marketed as the Samurai in the United States, as in Canada, and was available in convertible and hardtop versions, pictured in Exhibit 1.

Suzuki's hopes of becoming established in the U.S. automobile market were pinned on the Samurai. Suzuki SJ410s, imported without the company's authorization, had proved popular in Florida. The Samurai seemed to have substantial appeal and it soon proved to be a success story. In the first six months, ASMC sold 14,833 Samurais, well in excess of the target of 10,500 Doug Mazza, ASMC general manager, had set, and more than double that initially set by Suzuki's Japanese management. By the end of May 1988, ASMC had sold 160,749 Samurais and had 210 dealers throughout the United States (none of whom, however, were exclusively Suzuki). Exhibit 2 shows market size and share data. Two new vehicles were to be launched in September 1988: the Sidekick, a larger and more comfortable four-wheel-drive vehicle than the Samurai, which had an automobile chassis, rather than a truck chassis, and the Swift, a sporty subcompact car.

SUZUKI SAMURAI POSITIONING

The Samurai had been positioned to appeal to buyers of sport utility vehicles, compact trucks, and subcompact cars, rather than any one of these specific categories. Indeed, it was intended that the Samurai should fall within a category of its own: "as a unique, exciting, fun vehicle ('alternative to small-car boredom') that stands in a class by itself" (a Suzuki communications objective). Ninety accessories were available to add to the vehicle, allowing customization as buyers saw fit. The Samurai was inexpensive, both to buy and to run. Mazza commented in November 1987: "The Samurai presents buyers with an unbeatable combination of low purchase price, great fuel economy, and rock-solid reliability, as well as the all-weather versatility of four-wheel drive." The launch price of the Samurai was $6,550 for the soft-top and $6,700 for the hardtop. The price in 1988 was $7,995 (soft-top) and $8,095 (hardtop).

Samurai advertising and the presentation of the vehicle was unconventional, reflecting this positioning.[1] However, the vehicle was never shown in a com-

---

[1] In *Positioning: The Battle for Your Mind* (McGraw-Hill, 1986), Al Ries and Jack Trout observe that "positioning starts with a product . . . but positioning is not what you do to a product. Positioning is what you do to the mind of the prospect. That is, you position the product in the mind of the prospect" (p. 2). "You concentrate on the perceptions of the prospect. Not the reality of the product. 'In politics,' said John Lindsay, 'the perception is the reality.' So, too, in advertising, in business, and in life" (p. 8). Accordingly, Mazza, in March 1988, commented on the Samurai: "The key to its success has been to look at it not from what it was but from what it could be."

EXHIBIT 1   Samurai Hardtop and Convertible

Convertible JA 4-passenger
Convertible JX 4-passenger
Convertible JA 2-passenger
Convertible JX 2-passenger

Hardtop JA 4-passenger
Hardtop JX 4-passenger
Hardtop JA 2-passenger
Hardtop JX 2-passenger

Source: Suzuki Samurai owner's manual.

promising situation—with its wheels off the ground or its occupants not wearing seat belts. Television advertisements showed, for example: the Samurai undergoing and successfully completing a test to break through the "dull barrier"; an anniversary vehicle, produced after 16 weeks of sales; and a comparison between a stretch limousine and a Samurai. Exhibit 3 summarizes the TV advertisements for the Samurai shown between November 1985 and May 1988. A 1988 consumer brochure shows, on consecutive pages, the Samurai under the following headings:

- "I found the perfect first 'car' and it's not even a car!"
  Convertible Samurai shown with young people on a beach and as a graduation gift. Copy stresses fun, versatility, value for money, and fashionable appeal of the Samurai. Endorsement from young woman reads: "It's great looking and I look great in it, and it could've been a boring box—I love it! Now, if I could only get my friends to let me drive it."
- "Our family's new 'second car' is now our first choice."
  Samurai convertible with deluxe, removable top and other accessories shown with young family in a nature reserve and, inset, crossing a stream. Copy stresses fun, cost, and other advantages of the Samurai over pickup trucks, compact vans, and second-hand wagons. Variety of uses suggested: taking kids to school, shopping, collecting garden supplies, camping. Endorsement from a park ranger reads: "Seems like the folks that buy them respect my forest. I respect that."
- "We went looking at pickup trucks, and picked up something better."
  Basic Samurai hardtop shown with father and (adult) son on a farm and, inset, at a gas station. Copy stresses Samurai as workhorse: reliable, tough, economical, and maneuverable, a superior alternative to other trucks or a used pickup. Fun aspect not excluded: also shown pulling a small boat and driven alongside a young woman on a horse, under which the endorsement reads: "It's built rugged, and it's too good-looking to be ignored. Especially, when I'm out rounding up ... a date."
- "Taxi, bus, or blow my budget? I'll take the Samurai."
  Samurai convertible with canvas top and alloy wheels shown outside a dance studio in a fashionable city street and driven by a young woman; inset picture shows ease of parking in a small space. Copy stresses advantages of Samurai over high-priced town car or the aggravation of public transport, including its style, status, practicality, and versatility. Endorsement from woman passenger: "Whether we're driving to work, out on the town, or just out shopping, I can't help but notice how much we're noticed."

This brochure, in keeping with the entire Samurai marketing communications mix, emphasized the vehicle's multiplicity of applications, its dependability and quality engineering, its economy, and its style. The appeal was fun with value, reliability, and versatility. The promise was never a dull moment. The brochure included a disclaimer at the bottom of the list of the vehicle's specifications: "Please be advised the Samurai handles and maneuvers differently than a passenger car. Avoid sharp cornering, abrupt maneuvers, and always wear your seat belt. For specific information, read your Owner's Manual." This notice also appeared in smaller print in Suzuki's print advertisements.

EXHIBIT 2 Market Size and Share Data

Market Size

1. **Total U.S. Industry**

	1985	1986	1987
(A) Car	10,979,362	11,404,463	10,188,892
(B) Truck	4,436,441	4,622,709	4,688,023
(C) Total	15,415,803	16,027,172	14,876,915
(D) Percent change		4%	−7.2%

2. **Japanese Imports***

	1985	1986	1987
(A) Car	2,170,896	2,339,506	2,136,272
(B) Truck	815,443	959,270	899,305
(C) Total	2,986,339	3,298,776	3,035,577
(D) Percent change		10.5%	−8%

Market Share (Percent)/Sales

	1985	1986	1987
1. Japanese total market share	19.4	20.6	20.4
2. Sport utility industry market share	3.5	3.7	4.7
3. Sport utility sales	540,158	600,392	696,641
4. Subcompact market share	12.5	14.4	15.8
5. Subcompact sales	1,920,718	2,302,677	2,344,030
6. Import truck market share	4.6	4.7	4.1
7. Import truck sales	702,892	760,339	610,639
8. Samurai market share	0.5	8.0	11.7
9. Samurai sales	2,646†	47,732	81,349

* Figure includes domestic dealers selling Japanese imports under their name plate.
† Represents sales figures of November and December.

CUSTOMER SATISFACTION

Many Suzuki customers were first-time buyers. Of registered Samurai owners in 1988, 34 percent were female and 66 percent were male. The average age of the Samurai owner was 28. Twenty-three percent were under 25, 44 percent were between the ages of 25–34, 22 percent were 35–44, and 11 percent were 45 or over. Twenty to 30 percent of Samurai customers were college graduates. For many owners, the Samurai was a "statement of image": of individuality, of an outgoing personality, of someone who looked for alternatives.

An independent study by automotive analysts at J. D. Power and Associates, conducted in March and published in April 1988, indicated a high customer satisfaction index (CSI) for the Samurai. The Samurai ranked fifth in the compact sport utility segment, with a CSI of 116, coming after the Toyota 4-Runner

EXHIBIT 2 *(concluded)*

Sport Utility Segment: Sales and Market Share

1. Import

		1985		1986		1987	
(A)	Toyota 4-Runner	18,879	3.5%	35,722	5.9%	35,058	5.0%
(B)	Toyota Landcruiser	4,740	0.9	4,475	0.7	5,008	0.7
(C)	Nissan Pathfinder	N/A	N/A	6,901	1.2	34,313	4.9
(D)	Isuzu Trooper	25,844	4.8	36,893	6.1	42,693	6.1
(E)	Mitsubishi Montero	2,707	0.5	6,673	1.1	10,924	1.6
(F)	Dodge Raider	N/A	N/A	4,768	0.8	19,539	2.8
(G)	Suzuki	2,646	0.5	47,732	8.0	81,349	11.7
	Import total	54,816	10.1%	143,164	23.9%	228,884	32.9%

2. Domestic

		1985		1986		1987	
(A)	Chevrolet S-10 Blazer	187,234	34.7%	159,820	26.6%	153,064	22.0%
(B)	GMC S-15 Jimmy	42,239	7.8	39,027	6.5	38,841	5.6
(C)	Ford Bronco II	104,934	19.4	103,020	17.2	120,905	17.4
(D)	AMC Jeep CJ	37,956	7.0	18,414	3.1	N/A	N/A
(E)	AMC Cherokee	98,877	18.3	107,225	17.9	111,945	16.1
(F)	AMC Wagoneer	14,102	2.6	12,800	2.1	12,289	1.8
(G)	AMC Wrangler	N/A	N/A	16,853	2.8	30,713	4.4
	Domestic total	485,342	89.9%	457,169	76.1%	467,757	67.1%
	Total industry	540,158		600,323		696,641	

N/A means not available.

Source: Trade figures.

(a CSI of 134), the Nissan Pathfinder (118), the GMC S-15 Jimmy (118), and the Mitsubishi Montero (117). There were seven other vehicles listed below the Samurai. With the exception of the Isuzu Trooper II (CSI of 105), they were all from domestic manufacturers: the Dodge Raider (115), the Chevrolet S-10 Blazer (109), the Ford Bronco II (87), the Jeep Wagoneer (84), the Jeep Cherokee (77), and the Jeep Wrangler (56). The Samurai also scored higher than five out of the six vehicles in the full-size sport utility segment: the Ford Bronco (102), the Dodge Ramcharger (99), the Chevrolet Blazer (93), the GMC Jimmy (79), and the Jeep Grand Wagoneer (68). Top of the full-size segment was the Toyota Land Cruiser, with a CSI of 117.

The Samurai also fared well in comparison with the CSI for the total compact, compact van, and compact pickup markets. Its high index was attributable to product reliability, in which it led the sport utility segment and performed far better than the average for the other segments. For example, only 33 percent of consumers having dealer service/repair experience reported two or more repair problems with the Samurai, compared with 49 percent for all compacts, 40 percent for compact pickups, 61 percent for compact vans, and 54 percent for compact sport utility vehicles. However, service evaluations

---

EXHIBIT 3   Samurai Television Advertising

---

1. **History Ad (1985)**
   Samurai shown driving towards the camera on an empty desert road under turbulent sky. Voiceover introduces the Samurai as "The next major turning point in the history of all mankind." Ad ends showing four young people in the vehicle, waving to the camera and after tooting the horn, saying "hi." Price ($6,550) given together with toll-free telephone number.

2. **Anniversary Vehicle (1986)**
   SJ410 shown (briefly) in a studio and then first Samurai sold in the United States, followed by limited edition Samurai produced to celebrate 16 years of sales of the former outside the United States and 16 weeks of sales of the Samurai within the United States. Actor has cake with candles. "Never a dull moment" strapline included.

3. **Dull Barrier (1986)**
   Convertible Samurai containing four young people seen breaking through the "dull barrier" in "scientific" test. Attributed to MPPV (Multi-Purpose Passenger Vehicle) and "proof that there is never a dull moment in the Suzuki Samurai."

4. **Prince and Princess (1986)**
   Demonstration of Samurai accessories in a story about a prince (young contemporary male) trying to appeal to a princess (young contemporary female) by being the athletic sort, fitting a rack and a surfboard; the sporty sort, fitting alloy wheels; and the rugged sort, fitting off-road accessories. The prince ultimately gives up!

5. **Dull People (1987)**
   Lambasting of Suzuki and Samurai at conference of "Dull People of America" for "flaunting fun." Film to the conference of "dullards" includes young people in the "1987 Samurai," Samurai breaking the "dull barrier," young couple getting out of a Samurai with the young woman undressing to a bikini, and the toll-free telephone number.

6. **Test Track (1987)**
   A parody of the typical automobile test track advertisement. Concludes with an "off-road test:" a picnic lunch for the Samurai's four young occupants by the side of the track.

7. **Off-Road/City (1987)**
   Young male shown driving a Samurai hardtop around suburban streets. Young female shown anxiously looking at her watch while clearly awaiting the Samurai driver, who forgets to collect her. Voiceover: "The 4 × 4 Suzuki Samurai, taking you there, anywhere, even places you forgot to go."

8. **Fun-Crazed (1987)**
   Special edition Samurai in studio adjacent to map of the United States. Forty-year-old male presenter explains that America has 240 million "fun-crazed Americans" who would all like to own a Suzuki Samurai. Noting there are not enough Samurais to go around, he concludes: "This one's mine!"

EXHIBIT 3 *(concluded)*

9. **Trail Crossing (1988)**
   Wildlife park scene, accompanied by dramatic music, shots of brown bears and other animals. Appearance of Samurai on the trail, music mellows, the vehicle's young adult occupants wave and say "hi." No voiceover. Ends with "Never a dull moment" strapline.

10. **Born to Be Wild (1988)**
    Samurai and four young male and female occupants shown moving quickly along country and suburban roads, accompanied by the (Steppenwolf) song "Born to Be Wild." Stop outside ice cream store from where the vehicle's occupants return carrying ice creams, to which they sing "Born to Be Wild." No voiceover. "Never a dull moment" strapline included.

11. **Most Popular (1988)**
    Studio shot of Suzuki Samurai presented, after a fanfare, as America's "most popular convertible" alongside a second Samurai and presenter who says, after second fanfare, "And here is America's least expensive convertible." He feigns surprise. Voiceover: "The Suzuki Samurai, most popular, least expensive, cheerful."

12. **What It's Like (1988)**
    Young black* male actor imitates driving a Samurai, sitting on a chair, from getting in and closing the door, to the engine noise, to the operation of the windscreen wipers. Ends with a studio shot of him in a Samurai at the wheel and the familiar two toots of the horn, followed by a wave and "hi." Includes "Never a dull moment" strapline.

13. **Limo (1988)**
    Voiceover: "Some people go to great lengths to make driving more fun," accompanies shot of stretch limousine, which, at the rear, is seen to contain three young adults having a party. Followed by shot of Samurai containing two adults and the voiceover, "Others take the short cut." Strapline included.

14. **Quotes (1988)**
    Studio shot of Samurai followed by quotes, as voiceover and shown in black and white, from Samurai test reports: "We gave the Samurai good points for maneuverability, engine performance, and chassis balance" (*Off-Road*, October 1986); "The Samurai's dependability has been quite impressive" (*4-Wheel and Off-Road*, April 1987); "The Samurai's turning ability is steady and responsive" (*Truckin'*, December 1985); "If you want a rugged four-wheel driver for the minimum amount of money, the Samurai is the only game in town" (*Car and Driver*, January 1986). Voiceover concludes: "In the last 17 years over ½ million Suzuki 4 × 4s have been sold in over 100 countries." Toll-free number shown.

15. **Road to Hana (1988)**
    Endorsement from 30- to 40-year-old Samurai owner shown driving the road to Hana, where he lives, in Hawaii. Suzuki never let him down over 300 trips of 30 (difficult) miles, when moving to his home. No strapline; toll-free number shown.

* All other advertisements show white actors.

were below average, though improving on the previous year (attributed to the completion of dealership facilities). The percentage indicating they would definitely repurchase the same make was also below average, at 26 percent for Suzuki, compared with 36 percent for total compacts, 37 percent for compact pickups, 36 percent for total compact vans, and 34 percent for total compact sport utility vehicles. The report concluded:

> If service evaluations continue to climb at the rate they have over the past year, and product reliability problems remain low, the Suzuki Samurai will become a major contender for having the most satisfied owners in the segment. Currently, vehicle satisfaction is high, with 6 to 10 owners (64 percent) indicating they are very satisfied with their vehicles. However, only half this number (29 percent) are very satisfied with their dealers. With this in mind, dealerships must continue to implement programs to improve service satisfaction if Suzuki is to lead the segment in customer satisfaction.

Roll-over accidents in the Jeep CJ5 had led, in 1984, to the National Highway Traffic Safety Administration (NHTSA) insisting on warning stickers being fitted to the driver's door of vehicles of this type. A warning sticker was prominently displayed on the driver's door of all Samurais. This read:

> WARNING: This is a multipurpose vehicle which will handle and maneuver differently from an ordinary passenger car, in driving conditions which may occur on streets and highways and off-road. As with other vehicles of this type, if you make sharp turns or abrupt maneuvers, the vehicle may roll over or may go out of control and crash. You should read driving guidelines and instructions in the owner's manual and WEAR YOUR SEATBELTS AT ALL TIMES.

The owner's manual included a section of two-and-a-half pages under the heading "Safe Driving." The owner's attention was drawn to this section in the manual's foreword, where it was noted: "Your Suzuki multipurpose vehicle is designed and built to be capable of performing both on pavement and off road. You should, therefore, remember that your vehicle is distinctly different from ordinary passenger cars in handling as well as in structure." The safe driving section contained further information on four-wheel-drive vehicle handling characteristics, notably:

- An advantage of the higher ground clearance is a better view of the road allowing you to anticipate problems. They [multipurpose vehicles] are not designed for cornering at the same speed as conventional 2-wheel-drive vehicles any more than low-slung sports cars are designed to perform satisfactorily under off-road conditions. If at all possible, avoid sharp turns or abrupt maneuvers. As with other vehicles of this type, failure to operate this vehicle correctly may result in loss of control or vehicle rollover.
- Without these essential differences—higher ground clearance, shorter wheelbase, and narrower body width and track—your vehicle could not provide you with excellent off-road driving performance. However, it is also true that on-pavement driving, handling, and steering will be different from what drivers experience with a conventional 2-wheel-drive vehicle.

- Since you will often use your vehicle on paved roads, you should learn these guidelines for your on-road driving: Know your vehicle. . . . Wear your seatbelts at all times. . . . Slow down in crosswinds. . . . Slow down and use caution on slippery roads. . . .
- Your vehicle is designed primarily for off-road driving . . . off-road conditions call for different driving techniques from paved roads: Steep inclines require caution. . . . Do not drive across the side of hills. . . . Wear your seatbelt at all times. . . . Avoid sudden reactions in mud, ice, or snow. . . .
- Do not let anyone else drive your vehicle unless they are also aware of the handling differences described above.
- It is good policy to never loan your vehicle to anyone unless you accompany them.

NBC CRITICIZES THE SAMURAI

Suzuki already had experienced adverse publicity on the safety of the Samurai prior to hearing of the Consumers Union press conference on the vehicle. In early 1987, the Insurance Institute for Highway Safety, a trade group, had announced that utility vehicles with wheelbases of 100 inches or less had the highest occupant death rate of any category of vehicle, at 5.7 for every 100,000 vehicles. The Samurai, which had a wheelbase of 79.9 inches, was not included in the report because of insufficient accident data. But in December 1987 and January 1988, reports appeared on television of high insurance rates for sport utility vehicles, which specifically referred to the Suzuki Samurai. In one report, a Samurai was shown, driven by the reporter. However, it was a Jeep dealer who commented, in reference to the Jeep Wrangler:

> Jeep builds this vehicle as safe as they can build it. Built-in roll bar, reinforced in the back, also in the front. We have the full seat belt, the strap. If the people don't use protection as provided, then we can't hardly help them.

The reporter expressed concerns about the advertising for sport utility vehicles, noting that "the Center for Auto Safety [a consumer group founded by Ralph Nader] says it's misadvertising because the companies are targeting young people and these are probably the more inexperienced drivers." Another report suggested that the Samurai had been blacklisted by some insurance companies. A representative of Nationwide Insurance said this included "the type [of vehicle] like the CJ5, the CJ7, Suzuki Samurai, because they have a high center of gravity, a short wheelbase, and could be subject to rollovers more than other vehicles." A Suzuki spokesperson commented that a Suzuki survey of insurance companies had found very few would not insure the Samurai, but did say insurance rates were high. A Samurai owner interviewed on the news program was quoted $75 a month to insure her Samurai, compared with $25 a month for a standard sedan. The reporter concluded: "Next time you're out shopping for a car, don't just kick the tires, check what it will cost to insure."

Two newspaper articles also appeared specifically on the Samurai's safety record. A letter from Ron Rogers, the president of Rogers and Associates, a public relations firm retained by Suzuki, published in reply to the newspaper's report on the Samurai, said that criticisms of the safety of the vehicle were unfair and based on broad generalizations about sport utility vehicles. He contended that government data showed the Samurai to be at least as safe as other sport utility vehicles. Rogers referred to Suzuki's "deep sense of responsibility" to its customers and a faith in the reliability and safety of the Samurai.

More significantly, the safety concerns which had prompted the higher insurance premiums formed the basis for a petition for defect investigation lodged with NHTSA by the Center for Auto Safety (CAS). Exhibit 4 is the CAS petition, dated February 23, 1988. Soon after, Suzuki learned that some NBC stations planned to air a three-part news report showing vivid footage of a Samurai roll-over. On February 28, Suzuki issued a press release, reproduced as Exhibit 5. Exhibit 6 is the transcript for the NBC program. However, also aired was a new television commercial developed by Suzuki in anticipation of the program. Exhibit 3 includes an outline of the "quotes" advertisement used by Suzuki and the subsequent "Road to Hana" endorsement advertisement. The first advertisement ran during the NBC news programs and for two weeks thereafter. Rogers explained its purpose in an interview with *Adweek* in early March: "Their [NBC's] information was incomplete, so no conclusions can be drawn . . . we believe there is no problem and that's what our advertising is meant to counter." Exhibit 7 reproduces a newspaper article reporting Suzuki's response.

Trade and other commentators praised Suzuki's handling of the crisis, noting a marked contrast between Suzuki's approach and the way in which Audi, the German automobile manufacturer, had handled a similar crisis:

- Rather than taking a low profile when bad news breaks, Suzuki of America Automotive Corporation speaks out strongly when its interests are at stake. . . . Unlike Audi, which allowed reports of sudden acceleration to blossom into a major crisis, Suzuki immediately went on the offensive, sending out a press release disputing the NBC report before it aired. (*Automotive News*, March 7, 1988.)
- The company's effort to maneuver around the negative publicity follows other cases in which auto makers have been hurt after safety questions drew public attention. For example, the Audi 5000, which had been highly regarded, suffered a plummet in sales during the past two years after allegations that models with automatic transmissions were prone to sudden acceleration. The charges ultimately led the automaker, a subsidiary of Volkswagen, to recall a quarter million cars. The Center for Auto Safety, no longer affiliated with Nader, was among those most critical of the Audi. . . . Thomas F. O'Grady, analyst with Integrated Automotive Resources in Wayne, Pennsylvania, said he was aware of no evidence that the Samurai had a safety defect. . . . He asked: "When does use end and abuse begin?" . . . O'Grady said adverse publicity about the Samurai could hurt Suzuki in two ways: by encouraging lawsuits and by cutting into sales. "I'm certain they [the consumer group] are trying to do good, and that they are going after

things they think are very important to society," the analyst said. "I just hope they're very careful." (*Los Angeles Times*, February 29, 1988.)

- "Suzuki did the right thing, responding the way they did," said Chris Cedergren, senior auto analyst for J. D. Power and Associates. "They're looking over their shoulders to prevent an Audi situation from developing [sales of Audi's 5000 series plunged after reports that the car had accidental acceleration problems]. If things heat up, though, they will have to directly address the problem." (*Adweek*, March 7, 1988.)

WHAT NEXT?

Suzuki's roll-over problem had not gone away, though. It had to contend with criticism from Consumers Union, the leading consumer interest group in the country. A Consumers Union publication described the organization's purpose: "To provide unbiased, objective information on consumer goods and services and to help improve the quality of life for consumers everywhere." Under the heading "Consumer Reports Magazine," it reads, "Each month, *Consumer Reports* publishes results of tests on a variety of products. . . . Products found unsafe, defective, or clearly not capable of performing their advertised task are rated 'Not Acceptable'."[2] Consumers Union was to announce that the Samurai would be classified as "Not Acceptable" in the July issue of *Consumer Reports*, the first time a vehicle had received this rating in 10 years. Suzuki now had to survive the inevitable storm following the Consumers Union press conference.

EXHIBIT 4 Center for Auto Safety Petition

CENTER FOR AUTO SAFETY

February 23, 1988

Diane Steed
Administrator
National Highway Traffic Safety Administration

PETITION FOR DEFECT INVESTIGATION

Dear Ms. Steed:

Although the Suzuki Samurai has only been sold in this country for two years, tremendous concern over the questionable safety of this vehicle has developed in light of a trend of roll-over accidents. With only 132,000 Samurais sold as of December 21, 1987, the Center has already received 11 roll-over accident reports causing 8 injuries and 3 deaths. The Center has also received reports of three injuries and one death in four roll-over accidents involving variants of the Samurai, such as the SJ410. What is even more disturbing is that many of these roll-overs are

---

[2] Further information on Consumers Union is presented in Exhibit 8.

EXHIBIT 4 *(concluded)*

occurring during normal, foreseeable use of the vehicle in everyday driving conditions. Moreover, the accidents reported to the Center are just the tip of the iceberg, as far more are reported only to Suzuki and fatal accident reporting systems.

The handling characteristics of the Samurai play an important role in this vehicle's tendency to roll over. Because of its high ground clearance, short wheelbase, narrow track, and stiff suspension, the Samurai becomes tricky to handle and behaves abnormally in accident avoidance maneuvers. For example, when Ann Aires of Beverly Hills, California, suddenly applied the brakes on her 1987 Samurai, the vehicle rolled over, causing her serious injury. Similarly, the Samurai's propensity to roll over can be demonstrated by an accident in Virginia Beach, Virginia, when Jennifer Jennings hit a patch of ice at 35 MPH in her 1987 Samurai and upon striking pavement again the vehicle rolled. The enclosed accident reports clearly show the existence of a defect causing Samurais to lose control and roll over, especially in accident avoidance situations.

The Samurai is being marketed and sold as a vehicle not for off-road use, but instead for highway use. Since it is in the price range of a compact car buyer, Suzuki is focusing its advertisements on the *car* buying public by representing the Samurai as a great vehicle for highway trips and commuting to work. Clearly, a vehicle with such a high center of gravity and unstable handling characteristics is not fit for such driving.

A case in Colorado demonstrates this quite well. The District Attorney in Denver dropped vehicular homicide charges against the driver of a Samurai that flipped over and killed the passenger. The unstable nature of the Samurai (something the driver could not control) was found to be a major factor in the accident.

NHTSA requires Suzuki to place a sticker inside the Samurai to warn drivers of the roll-over and handling dangers of this vehicle. Yet, since its introduction, the Samurai has quickly developed a roll-over accident rate that clearly demonstrates the failure of the sticker to prevent deaths and injuries in roll-over accidents. Even though owners are warned, there is nothing they can do in many instances to prevent the vehicle from rolling over in an accident. As with any vehicle on the highway, sharp turns or accident avoidance maneuvers are inevitable, but in the Samurai they can be lethal.

NHTSA's involvement in this problem is vital since the rate of Samurai roll-over accidents continues to rise, killing more people and increasing public awareness of the defect. The Center for Auto Safety, therefore, petitions the National Highway Traffic Safety Administration to open a defect investigation and recall all 1986–88 Suzuki Samurai and its variants, such as the SJ410. In responding to this petition, NHTSA should analyze all available databases, including FARS and NASS, as well as its consumer complaint file and accidents reported to Suzuki.

Sincerely,

Samuel H. Cole
Vehicle Safety Staff

EXHIBIT 5 Suzuki Press Release

FOR IMMEDIATE RELEASE

CONTACT:
Ron Rogers
Rogers & Associates

SUZUKI OF AMERICA OPENS INVESTIGATION
INTO INACCURATE CLAIMS AGAINST COMPANY, PRODUCT

BREA, California (February 28, 1988)—Suzuki of America Automotive Corporation today announced that it has begun an investigation into companies and organizations making erroneous and inaccurate claims about the company and its product, the four-wheel-drive Suzuki Samurai.

Suzuki of America, which began selling the Samurai in November of 1985, quickly became the most successful Japanese automotive company in the United States in a launch year, selling more than 47,000 Samurais in calendar year 1986. More than 140,000 of the popular sport utility vehicles have been sold to date.

The investigation was triggered by claims made by the Center for Auto Safety, a consumer group, that the Samurai is an unsafe vehicle. Subsequently, Suzuki received inquiries from several media sources, including NBC News, questioning the Samurai's safety.

According to Suzuki, the statements made by the Center for Auto Safety are misleading and without substance or foundation.

Suzuki believes the Center's claims may have been instigated in part by trial lawyers seeking to foster public opinion against Suzuki and perhaps the entire sport utility industry.

In a letter to the National Highway Traffic Safety Administration, the Center for Auto Safety calls into question the safety of the Samurai allegedly because it has a high center of gravity. According to Suzuki, this approach could also call into question all multipurpose passenger vehicles and other commonly used vehicles with high centers of gravity, including school buses, pick-up trucks, ambulances, vans, and motorhomes.

The Center for Auto Safety has confirmed it is basing its claims about the Samurai's safety on 11 reports of incidents involving Samurai roll-overs. The Center did not conduct independent investigations on the incidents and does not have the capability of vehicle testing.

Suzuki believes it has been targeted because the Samurai is the leading imported sport utility vehicle from Japan and has gained tremendous media attention due to its unique styling, reliability, and affordable price.

Seemingly as a result of the allegations by the Center for Auto Safety, Suzuki said NBC News' Stations Division in Washington, D.C., has developed and is preparing to broadcast a segment on Samurai safety. Suzuki indicated that the NBC segment relies upon data obtained from NHTSA's Fatal Accident Reporting System (FARS). The data, also obtained by Suzuki, outlines some details of accidents involving Samurais, but is insufficient to reach a conclusion about the cause of the reported

---

EXHIBIT 5 *(concluded)*

---

accidents. Suzuki stated that NBC does not take into account certain information contained in the FARS data, including the fact that the data indicate that approximately 50 percent of the accidents involved drunk drivers and 60 percent involved occupants who were not wearing seat belts. NHTSA has issued no analysis of the FARS data.

NBC told Suzuki it hired a professional driver who rolled the Samurai under what NBC described as "normal driving conditions." According to Suzuki, the driver's maneuvers were erratic and in no way indicative of normal driver reactions. Further, a University of Michigan study conducted for NHTSA concluded that almost any vehicle can be made to turn over as a result of maneuvers similar to those of NBC's professional driver.

Suzuki stated that the Samurai was thoroughly tested for stability and handling prior to its introduction in the United States. Further, Suzuki said that statements made to NBC by so-called "experts" in its report are inaccurate, erroneous, and misleading.

Despite numerous requests by Suzuki to the Center for Auto Safety and NBC for details of the reported incidents involving Suzuki roll-overs, both organizations have refused to provide such details.

Suzuki said it will conduct its investigation to determine the original source of the allegations and why the company is being singled out. Suzuki will utilize every available means of halting the allegations, including any appropriate legal action.

Suzuki concluded that the Samurai is a safe and stable vehicle and was thoroughly tested for stability and handling prior to its introduction in the United States. The vehicle meets or exceeds all federal regulations for this type of sport utility vehicle.

EXHIBIT 6 NBC Program Transcript

DATE	February 28, 1988
TIME	11:00–11:30 PM
STATION	WKYC-TV
LOCATION	Cleveland
PROGRAM	Channel 3 News Nightside

Tom Sweeney (anchor)

It is not often that a new vehicle hits the market and becomes an overnight success. But that is the case with the little Suzuki Samurai, a little truck that's zooming to near cult status coast to coast. Steve Handelsman now reports on the first part of a special investigation: prominent safety experts are warning that the Suzuki Samurai could be more dangerous than most other vehicles on the road.

EXHIBIT 6 *(continued)*

Steve Handelsman (reporting)

It's small and it's cute. A four-wheel driven on- and off-road vehicle that looks like a Jeep and costs as little as eight to nine thousand dollars.

Suzuki owner

I think it's a cool car. I don't care what anyone has to say about it.

Handelsman

Even though all of its U.S. dealerships are not yet in place, the Samurai is already a sales phenomenon. Already it's the number one selling imported light utility vehicle. Already it's the best selling convertible in America. But as young people have been grabbing up more than one hundred thousand Samurais, safety experts like Brian O'Neal of the Insurance Institute for Highway Safety have become increasingly alarmed at the Samurai's high center of gravity and narrow width.

Brian O'Neal

It's comparable to vehicles like the old Jeep CJ5, which is the vehicle that had the highest fatality rate for roll-overs than any other vehicle documented so far.

Handelsman

July 20, last year, on this freeway in Los Angeles in her new Suzuki Samurai, Ann Aires was headed home from work. Police say she was cut off.

Ann Aires (Suzuki Samurai owner)

My Samurai, I swerved it to the left, avoided hitting the center divider and swerved back over again, and it flipped over on the left-hand side and skidded about thirty feet.

Handelsman

Her arm was trapped underneath the rolled Samurai.

Aires

I glanced over at my arm and it was just. . . . I started screaming. I couldn't help it.

Handelsman

Anne's thumb was sewn back on, but she faces further plastic surgery.

Aires

It hurts, it really hurts. I was lucky and very fortunate, more fortunate than others.

Handelsman

Denver, Colorado . . . August 1986. Around this freeway exit from I-70 to I-25, came two people in a Samurai like this one [visual of Suzuki Samurai]. Police say driver Kathy Vangon was drunk and she lost control, but instead of sliding, the Samurai flipped over several times. Twenty-five-year-old Robbie Pierce, wearing no seatbelt on the passenger side, was thrown out in the wild roll over

---

EXHIBIT 6 *(continued)*

---

and killed. Vangon was charged with vehicular homicide. But to one investigator, the Samurai appeared to have turned over easily. Then an outside expert said there would have been no roll-over death if Robbie Pierce hadn't been in a Samurai.

The prosecutor here in Denver dropped the homicide charges, saying, in effect, Vangon shared the guilt for Robbie's death with the Suzuki Samurai.

Marti Pierce (Robbie's mother)

It was just a very unsafe vehicle to be in.

Handelsman

Marti and Roger Pierce feel they'd still have their son Robbie today if he hadn't been in a Samurai.

Roger Pierce (Robbie's father)

They never would have wrecked. They never would have turned over.

Mrs. Pierce

If Robbie can be an example for someone else not to get killed, then maybe there's been some good come out of this after all. I hope so.

Handelsman

Can the Samurai roll over in emergency maneuvers at city driving speeds on dry roads? The answer is yes. [Test done.] Suzuki officials who've seen this footage say their Samurai does not have a roll-over problem; that it's safe and stable. But, tomorrow, two experts show how a Samurai can tip over in ordinary emergency maneuvers. In East Liberty, Ohio, this is Steve Handelsman, Channel Three News.

Sweeney

Steve Handelsman's special report on these Suzuki Samurais continues tomorrow night here on Channel 3 at eleven o'clock.

DATE	February 29, 1988
TIME	11:00-11:30 PM
STATION	WKYC-TV
LOCATION	Cleveland
PROGRAM	Channel 3 News Nightside

Leon Bidd (anchor)

Just two years after being introduced, the little four-wheel-drive Suzuki Samurai is already the best-selling import in its class, but an investigation by Channel 3's Steve Handelsman reveals the Samurai can roll over if it swerves even at city driving speeds. Here's part two of Steve's report.

EXHIBIT 6 *(continued)*

Steve Handelsman (reporting)

Billy Peterson is an engineer/test driver at Automotive Safety Testing, East Liberty, Ohio. Our project: to run ordinary emergency maneuvers in the phenomenally popular Suzuki Samurai to shed light on Samurai roll-over accidents since its introduction two years ago. Our Suzuki is stock. Outriggers are mounted to protect us without affecting the Samurai's handling.

Billy Peterson (engineer/test driver)

In our case here, I think we're actually lowering the center of gravity.

Handelsman

So it should improve the handling?

Peterson

It should improve it.

Handelsman

The first maneuver, a hard left turn. This is low highway speed.

Peterson

City driving. J-turn at thirty-five miles an hour. [Visual of Samurai roll-over.]

Handelsman

It didn't even feel like it was leaning that much and suddenly, right over she went.

Peterson

All of a sudden, it just tripped. Starts to roll.

Handelsman

Another run at forty miles per hour. [Visual of Samurai roll-over.] This time accident expert Ben Kelley is aboard. He's our paid consultant.

Ben Kelley (auto safety consultant)

It was a horrifying experience.

Handelsman

Without protective outriggers, Kelley and Peterson say they could've suffered more than a scare.

Kelley

Yes, the likelihood of emerging from that kind of crash in the roll-over you just saw, without being killed or very seriously injured, would be very remote.

Handelsman

Did the Samurai ever fail to roll over in this maneuver on dry pavement? Yes, two times out of five. [Visual of a Samurai not rolling over.] A second maneuver simulates what might happen at low speed if something suddenly gets in your way.

EXHIBIT 6 *(continued)*

Kelley

A kid runs out in front of you. It's a residential area driving speed and you crank the wheel real hard to get out of the way.

Handelsman

Then you return quickly to your lane. It's called an S-turn. [Visual of Samurai roll-over.] Billy, what's been your experience with similar vehicles to this, doing this very ordinary accident avoidance maneuver?

Peterson

Well, I have driven utility vehicles through very similar maneuvers and nothing happened. You were able to correct without rolling over.

Kelley

It was built this way. So anyone buying it from a dealer, is buying a vehicle that will do exactly what we've just been through here and that is to, without any warning, get into a terrifying situation and possibly roll over on top of you and kill you or injure you. And that's the way the manufacturers make it and that's the way the dealers sell it as far as I can see. [Visual of Samurai roll-over.]

Handelsman

At Suzuki of America Headquarters in Brea, California, general manager Douglas Mazza watched the handling demonstration and contended:

Douglas Mazza (Suzuki of America)

I don't think there's a vehicle on the road today that you could not find conditions under which they would roll over. We would like to be able to evaluate what the conditions were for this particular vehicle. But there are no vehicles that cannot be made to leave a four-wheel stance.

Handelsman

Suzuki experts later stated that almost any vehicle can be made to turn over under the circumstances of this demonstration. [Visual of Samurai roll-over.] Tomorrow, the Samurai safety record on the highway. In Brea, California, this is Steve Handelsman, Channel 4 News.

Bidd

Steve Handelsman's special report on the Suzuki Samurai continues tomorrow night at eleven o'clock.

DATE   March 1, 1988
TIME   11:00-11:30 PM
STATION   WKYC-TV
LOCATION Cleveland
PROGRAM   Channel 3 News Nightside

EXHIBIT 6 *(continued)*

Leon Bidd (anchor)

The Suzuki Samurai is the best-selling imported light truck in America; but as we've been reporting this week, some experts say it rolls over too easily. In the final part of his report, Channel 3's national correspondent, Steve Handelsman, looks at the Suzuki Samurai's fatality numbers and at what Suzuki says is its defense.

Steve Handelsman (reporting)

After our demonstrations of emergency handling in the Samurai, two experts suggested that the Suzuki has a tendency to roll over. Test driver Billy Peterson:

Billy Peterson

Well, my opinion is that this is one of the worst that I have put through these types of maneuvers.

Handelsman

At Suzuki of America headquarters, general manager Douglas Mazza says the Samurai has been thoroughly tested for safety and handling.

Doug Mazza (Suzuki General Manager)

I'm very confident in the safety record and in the ability of our company to deliver a very safe and stable vehicle to the United States.

Handelsman

Here at the National Highway Traffic Safety Administration, NHTSA, in Washington, 1987 fatality statistics for the Suzuki Samurai are nearly complete. A top official here says it would appear the rate for the Samurai will be about forty deaths per hundred thousand vehicles. Forty percent of those will be roll-overs. That's not as high as the notorious Jeep CJ5, but it is according to the Insurance Institute for Highway Safety, about typical of the class of light utility vehicles, the vehicles which have the highest fatality rates. And it's about double the rate for all passenger vehicles.

Like other Jeep-type vehicles, each Samurai must carry a warning sticker saying, "If you make sharp turns or abrupt maneuvers, the vehicle may roll over." Is that true about the Samurai?

Mazza

In any motor vehicle.

Handelsman

Test driver Peterson says that's wrong.

Peterson

Any vehicle, you should be able to take that type of maneuver without rolling. At the very worst, the vehicle would skid.

Handelsman

Spin out?

Peterson

Spin out.

EXHIBIT 6 *(concluded)*

Handelsman

On February 23rd, the Center for Auto Safety formally petitioned the Highway Agency NHTSA, to recall all Samurais for what the center calls this vehicle's tendency to roll over. NHTSA was already preparing to test the Samurai and other vehicles as part of a massive project officials say could result for the first time in federal safe handling standards for all vehicles. Insiders here warn that process could take years. Meanwhile, Suzuki says it's selling more than five thousand Samurais every month. In Washington, this is Steve Handelsman, Channel 3 News.

Bidd

The president of the Insurance Institute for Highway Safety said Samurai owners do not understand the risks involved with the vehicle, and he said they assume a roll-over just will not happen to them.

EXHIBIT 7   Press Report on Suzuki Response

SUZUKI THREATENS LEGAL ACTIONS TO HALT COMPLAINTS ABOUT SAMURAI SPORT VEHICLE

By Joseph B. White
Staff Reporter of The Wall Street Journal

The U.S. sales arm of Suzuki Motor Company doesn't want to hear any complaints that its Suzuki Samurai sport vehicle may be unsafe, and is threatening legal action to squelch them.

The Japanese auto maker's announcement, issued by its Brea, Calif.-based U.S. arm Sunday and again yesterday, came in reaction to a complaint filed with little fanfare last week by the Center for Auto Safety, a Washington D.C.-based consumer group.

The group said it has evidence of 11 accidents in which a Samurai rolled over after a skid or a sharp turn. The accidents resulted in three deaths and injuries to eight other people, the group said in a petition filed last week with the National Highway Transportation Safety Administration.

But Suzuki, in an unusually combative response, said the consumer group's charges that the Samurai's high center of gravity made it too easy to tip over were "instigated in part by trial lawyers seeking to foster public opinion against Suzuki and perhaps the entire sport utility industry." The company said the Samurai is safe, and added that it will conduct an investigation to determine the source of the charges and "utilize every available means of halting the allegations, including any appropriate legal action."

Among the complaints lodged with the consumer group was one from John Moschetto, a retired New York City motorcycle patrol officer. Mr. Moschetto said in an interview yesterday that a Samurai he rented on a vacation in Aruba last July tipped over on its side after he skidded on wet pavement and hit the curb in a traffic circle. Mr. Moschetto said that he was traveling at less than 25 miles an hour when the accident occurred, and that he hadn't

---

EXHIBIT 7 *(concluded)*

been drinking. "I couldn't believe what was happening," he said. Mr. Moschetto's daughter and another passenger were injured in the crash.

Complaints about roll-overs aren't new to the sport utility vehicle industry. A number of lawsuits filed in the early 1980s charged that the Jeep CJ5 vehicle was prone to roll-overs because of its high center of gravity. American Motors Corporation ultimately stopped producing the CJ series at the end of 1984.

Suzuki and its public relations agency, Rogers & Associates of Los Angeles, put "quite a bit of thought" into the pros and cons of reacting to the consumer group's petition, a spokeswoman for Rogers & Associates said. "It was important for the company to make sure its point was well made, (and) I think it was," the spokeswoman said.

Suzuki said its investigation will seek to "determine the original source of the allegations and why the company is being singled out."

Source: *The Wall Street Journal,* March 1, 1988.

EXHIBIT 8 Consumers Union

What Is Consumers Union?

A half century ago, many of the toasters on the market were so poorly designed that you couldn't remove the toast without burning your hand. Refrigerators were often inadequately insulated, and many electric irons were made so shabbily that they were—literally—shocking. Even drugs and patent medicines that claimed to *improve* health contained ingredients that actually *threatened* it. The marketplace was dangerous, and consumers had no power and little voice.

Our organization was created in 1936 to help fill that void. Within a few months, our monthly magazine, now known as *Consumer Reports,* was reaching consumers, legislators, and businesspeople. We've been testing products and reporting our findings ever since.

Today we evaluate videocassette recorders and microwave ovens instead of "six-tube" radios and "mechanical" refrigerators. But while many things have changed over the decades, our goals have remained constant: To provide unbiased, objective information on consumer goods and services and to help improve the quality of life for consumers everywhere.

We're proud of our independence and of our international reputation for delivering information that consumers don't get from advertisers—and, in most cases, from anywhere else. In addition to testing, researching, and rating products and services, we report on dubious business practices, unsafe product design, inadequate labeling, and health quackery.

Consumers Union's Impartiality

We're nonprofit, beholden to no commercial interest, and responsible only to our subscribers and members. (*Consumer Reports* subscribers can become members by voting in the annual election for our Board of Directors.)

EXHIBIT 8 *(concluded)*

Our income is derived solely from the sale of our publications and from a few nonrestrictive, noncommercial grants and contributions—we decline commercial contributions and grants. We accept no free product samples; every product we test is bought at retail. *Consumer Reports* takes no outside advertising.

To further protect our reputation for independence and objectivity, we never grant permission for commercial use of any of our test results or other material, nor for any commercial use of the name of Consumers Union, *Consumer Reports*, or any of our other publications and products. If advertisers use our ratings without our permission, we take all steps open to us to stop them.

Consumer Reports Magazine

Consumer Reports magazine—the nation's preeminent product-test and consumer advisory publication—reaches more than 3 million subscribers.

Each month, *Consumer Reports* publishes results of tests on a variety of products, from major purchases, such as automobiles and appliances, to everyday items, such as foods and cleaning supplies. Its articles not only tell you what you need to know to be a smart shopper, they name names—brand names. Products found unsafe, defective, or clearly not capable of performing their advertised task are rated Not Acceptable.

How CU Tests a Product

Virtually all our testing takes place at our testing laboratories in Mount Vernon, New York, and at our Auto Test Center in Orange, Connecticut.

In deciding which products and services to evaluate we consider many factors, including reader requests. Expensive products, such as automobiles or major appliances, are tested on a regular schedule. Other products are tested as often as is appropriate and feasible.

Once a product category has been selected, our market information specialists analyze the marketplace and recommend brands and models to be tested. Then we go shopping, using our staff shoppers in Mount Vernon or calling on our network of more than 90 part-time shoppers in 65 cities throughout the United States. The shoppers—who don't disclose their affiliation with Consumers Union—visit stores just as you do, and pay the same price you would. The products are then brought or shipped to our laboratories.

Under the scrutiny of our engineers, products are evaluated for their performance, convenience, safety, and economy of operation. Many of the tests are those prescribed in industry or government standards, but, not infrequently, our engineers develop their own—and even invent their own test equipment. After thorough testing, the technical experts work with *Consumer Reports* editors to prepare articles for publication.

Source: *A Look Inside Consumers Union: Publisher of* Consumer Reports (Mount Vernon, N.Y.: Consumers Union, 1988).

Chevron Corporation: Corporate Image Advertising

INTRODUCTION

The 1970s had been a tumultuous period for U.S. oil companies. OPEC had united and exercised considerable pressure on world oil markets. In both 1974 and 1979, Americans suffered tenfold gasoline price spikes and endured shortages at the pump. The U.S. oil industry, already distrusted by the American public, emerged from each period with a severely tarnished image. Exhibit 1 summarizes consumer attitudes toward the U.S. oil industry between 1974 and 1990. During this time, Chevron's public opinion research captured Americans' attitudes toward the U.S. oil industry, as well as their opinions of Chevron. Favorable attitudes toward Chevron were consistently higher than those toward the industry in general; however, the company's image rose and fell with that of the industry.

Chevron withdrew all corporate advertising during 1979–81 because the public opinion environment was extremely hostile as a result of the supply and price difficulties. By late 1981, the strongly negative public opinion environment had ebbed enough that effective communications seemed possible.

In early 1982, Chevron's public affairs department began systematic research to understand the factors behind Americans' attitudes toward the company and to design a communications program to either improve attitudes, as a best case scenario, or at least to forestall any further deterioration.

COMPANY BACKGROUND

Chevron Corporation, headquartered in San Francisco, was an integrated petroleum company. It was involved in all aspects of the energy business: ex-

---

This case was prepared by Aimee L. Stern under the direction of Professor John A. Quelch.
Harvard Business School case 9-591-005 (Rev. 7/12/91).

EXHIBIT 1 Attitudes toward the U.S. Oil Industry

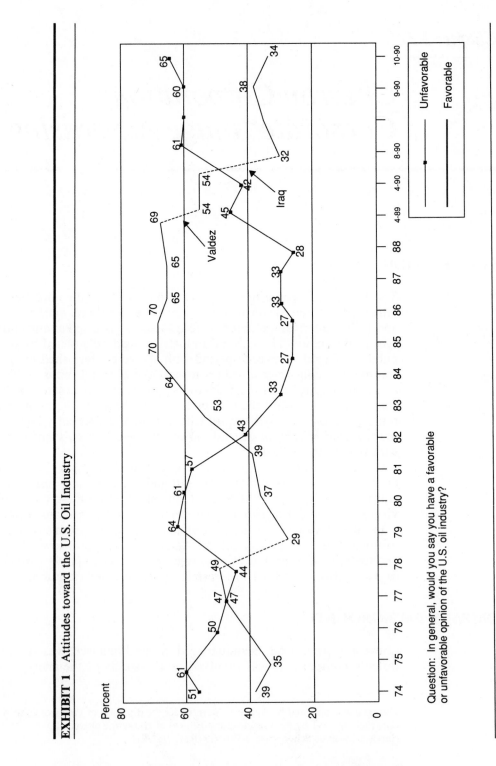

Question: In general, would you say you have a favorable
or unfavorable opinion of the U.S. oil industry?

Source: Chevron Public Opinion Monitor.

ploration, production, manufacturing, transportation, marketing, and research. Chevron was the largest refiner and marketer of petroleum products in the United States. The company's origins dated to 1870, when Fredrick Taylor, a wildcatter, drilled the first wells at Pico, California, just north of Los Angeles. Taylor's Pico No. 4 well became the most productive well in the state. Soon, his Pacific Coast Oil Company caught the eye of John D. Rockefeller and, in 1900, Rockefeller's Standard Oil Company (New Jersey) acquired the firm. Rockefeller commenced a decade of capital infusion and dramatic expansion. When the Supreme Court dissolved the Standard Oil Trust in 1911, Standard Oil (California) had oil fields, refineries, pipelines, and tankers. Since those early beginnings, the company had grown consistently, particularly in California, where the Chevron gasoline brand had long been a market leader and where the company sold about 25 percent of its products. Chevron's 1984 revenues totaled $27.8 billion; by 1989, revenues totaled $31.9 billion.

ADVERTISING HISTORY

Chevron had long been committed to advertising in support of its product marketing. Yet only in the 1970s, as a result of the energy crisis, did Chevron venture into corporate or image advertising. During the mid-1970s, Chevron's corporate campaign featured an animated dinosaur and focused on a much-needed conservation theme. In the early 1980s, J. Walter Thompson began acting as Chevron's advertising agency. It appeared that the public opinion climate had become more favorable toward Chevron, and executives believed that a new communications effort could further this progress. Together, Chevron's public affairs department and the J. Walter Thompson account team began to investigate some strategic communications questions, specifically:

- Could a new corporate advertising campaign bolster favorable public attitudes toward Chevron?

- Who should be targeted for this advertising?

- What should be the key message of such communications?

OPINION RESEARCH

Lewis Winters had been appointed Chevron's manager of public opinion research in the early 1970s. Winters, a Ph.D. in psychology and a specialist in advertising research, had established the Chevron Public Opinion Monitor study in 1974, to monitor overall attitudes toward the industry, Chevron, and its competitors. The monitor also assessed public attitudes toward Chevron across a variety of "image" attributes. Exhibit 2 shows the 16 attributes that

---

EXHIBIT 2   Oil Company Attributes Measured

Do you agree or disagree that Chevron:

- Contributes money to meet the health, education, and social welfare needs of the community?
- Shows concern for the public interest?
- Pays its fair share of taxes?
- Contributes money to cultural, music, or cultural arts organizations?
- Sponsors radio and television programs on PBS, the Public Broadcasting System?
- Provides good service at its stations?
- Would be a good company to work for?
- Is a good stock investment?
- Charges fair prices for its products?
- Makes too much profit?
- Makes high-quality products?
- Is seriously concerned with protecting the environment?
- Cares about how people feel about them?
- Makes public statements that are truthful?
- Is making efforts to develop alternative forms of energy?
- Is making efforts to find new sources of oil and gas, including drilling offshore?

Source: Chevron Public Opinion Monitor 1981–1982.

Chevron measured in the 1981–82 annual survey. Winters had a strong interest in personal values and their role in shaping public opinion. During the late 1970s, work at SRI International in Menlo Park, California, had captured his attention. A new program called "VALS" (the Values and Lifestyle Program) had been developed under the guidance of sociologist Arnold Mitchell. In Mitchell's vision, the VALS program would be a way to "psychographically" segment the public based on their values. Values segments would help researchers to understand the underlying motivations for attitudes and behaviors of various segments of the population.

Winters believed that VALS could offer important insights for Chevron's pending corporate communications efforts. In 1983, Chevron began to apply the VALS segmentation to respondents in its Public Opinion Monitor. The results revealed important preliminary information, which would ultimately guide the selection of Chevron's target audience. Exhibit 3 describes the various VALS segments. Exhibit 4 reports Chevron's 1984 Public Opinion Monitor results by VALS segments. The attributes are grouped and ordered from high to low, based on further data analysis discussed below.

EXHIBIT 3   The VALS™ Typology

The VALS typology, developed by the VALS Program at SRI International, is a unique and widely used segmentation tool. The typology characterizes groups within the U.S. adult population on the basis of their values, attitudes, needs, wants, beliefs, and demographics. The VALS typology is divided into three major categories, with a total of nine lifestyle types.

The Need-Drivens

The Need-Drivens are people so limited in resources, especially financial resources, that their lives are driven more by need than by choice. Their values center around survival, safety, and security. Such people tend to be distrustful and dependent, unlikely to make plans. Many live unhappy lives focused on the immediate specifics of today, with little sensitivity to the wants of others and little vision of what could be. They are furthest removed from the cultural mainstream and least aware of the events of their times.

VALS divides the Need-Driven category into two lifestyles: Survivor and Sustainer.

Survivors

Survivors are the most disadvantaged people in American society by reason of their extreme poverty, low education, old age, infirmity, and limited access to the channels of upward mobility. They are oriented to tradition, but marked by despair and unhappiness. While some may once have lived lives associated with higher levels of the VALS hierarchy, others may have been ensnared in the so-called culture of poverty.

Sustainers

Sustainers are struggling at the edge of poverty. They are better off and younger than Survivors, and many have not given up hope. They are angry, streetwise, and determined to get ahead. Many are thought to operate in the underground economy.

The Outer-Directeds

The Outer-Directeds conduct their lives in response to signals—real or fancied—from others. Consumption, activities, attitudes—all are guided by what Outer-Directeds think others may think. Psychologically, Outer-Direction is a major step forward from the Need-Driven state. The Outer-Directed perspective on life has broadened to include other people, a host of institutions, and an array of personal values and options far more complex and diverse than those available to the Need-Driven. In general, the Outer-Directeds are the most content of Americans, being well-attuned to the cultural mainstream—indeed creating much of it.

VALS has defined three Outer-Directed lifestyles: Belonger, Emulator, and Achiever.

Belongers

Belongers are the solid, comfortable, middle-class Americans that are the main stabilizers of society and the preservers and defenders of the moral status quo. Belongers tend to be conservative, conventional, nostalgic, sentimental, puritanical, and conforming. Their key drive is to fit in—to belong—and not to

EXHIBIT 3 *(continued)*

stand out. The Belonger's world is well-posted and well-lit, and the road is straight and narrow. Family, church, and tradition loom large. Belongers know what is right, and they adhere to the rules.

Emulators

Emulators have aims wholly different from those of Belongers. Rather than drift with events like many Belongers, Emulators are striving to get ahead. They are trying to burst into the upper levels of the system—to make it big. The object of their emulation is the Achiever lifestyle (though many Emulators are not truly on the track to becoming Achievers). They are ambitious, upwardly mobile, status-conscious, macho, and competitive. Many see themselves as coming from the "other side of the tracks" and, hence, are intensely distrustful, angry, and skeptical that "the system" will give them a fair shake.

Achievers

Achievers include many leaders in business, the professions, and government. Competent, self-reliant, hard-working, and efficient. Achievers tend to be materialistic, oriented to fame and success, and comfort loving. These are the affluent people who have created the economic system in response to the American dream. As such, they are the defenders of the economic status quo. Achievers are among the best adjusted of Americans, being well-satisfied with their place in the system.

The Inner-Directeds

In contrast with the Outer-Directeds, Inner-Directeds conduct their lives primarily in accord with inner values—what is "in here" rather than what is "out there." Thus, concern with inner growth is a cardinal characteristic. Inner-Directeds are self-expressive, person-centered, impassioned, individualistic, and diverse.

VALS has defined three Inner-Directed lifestyles: I-Am-Me, Experiential, and Societally Conscious.

I-Am-Me's

I-Am-Me is a short-lived stage of transition from Outer-to-Inner-Direction. Values from both stages are much in evidence. Typically, I-Am-Me's are young, fiercely individualistic, contrary, narcissistic, impulsive, and exhibitionistic. People at this stage are confused and full of emotions they do not understand; hence, they often define themselves better by their actions than by their statements. Much of their Inner-Direction shows up in great inventiveness, and in often-secret inner exploration that may later crystalize into lifelong pursuits.

Experientials

At this stage of Inner-Direction, the psychological focus has widened from the intense self-centeredness of the I-Am-Me to include other people and many social and human issues. Experientials want direct experience and vigorous involvement. They are attracted to the exotic (such as Oriental religions), to the strange (such as parapsychology), and to the natural (such as organic gardening and home-baking). The most Inner-Directed of any VALS type, Experientials also are probably the most artistic, the most passionately involved with others, and the most willing to try anything once.

EXHIBIT 3 *(concluded)*

Societally Conscious

The Societally Conscious are mature, prosperous, and highly educated people who have extended their psychological focus beyond the self and others to the society as a whole, to the globe, or even, philosophically, to the cosmos. A sense of societal responsibility leads these people to support such causes as conservation, environmentalism, and consumerism. They tend to be innovative, active, impassioned, and knowledgeable about the world around them. The Societally Conscious seek to live lives that conserve, protect, and heal. Inner growth remains a crucial part of their lives.

Source: Reprinted with permission from SRI International.

DETERMINATION OF THE TARGET AUDIENCE AND MESSAGE

The particular VALS segment that intrigued Chevron was the Inner-Directed segment. Cross-tabulated data from the 1984 Public Opinion Monitor showed this group to be significantly more negative toward Chevron. Moreover, their ratings of Chevron across the 16 image attributes also were lower than those of the Outer-Directed population segment. This was even more evident in Chevron's home state of California. To further understand the Inner-Directed, Winters and his staff began to explore the associations between Inner-Directeds' overall negative opinion of Chevron and their ratings of Chevron on specific company attributes. The answers to such an analysis, it was thought, could help to guide the message for the campaign. After all, the evidence of the 1970s suggested that more emphasis should be placed on improving negative attitudes than on buttressing the opinions of more favorable segments, such as the Outer-Directeds.

Two types of statistical analysis proved useful in understanding the 1984 Public Opinion Monitor data. Factor analysis was used to discover the underlying "dimensions" in the collective response patterns of the entire sample and to simplify long attribute lists into a subset of "factors" (groups of attributes). The factor analysis performed by Chevron revealed three factors, to which Winters assigned the following labels:

- Marketing/business conduct.

- Environmental/social conduct.

- Corporate contributions.

Winters knew that multiple regression analysis could shed light on the relationship between each respondent's score on each of the three factors and his or her opinion of Chevron. In other words, it was possible to learn which of the three factors was most associated with a favorable or unfavorable opinion of the company. Further, regression analysis could be undertaken separately

EXHIBIT 4   Public Opinion Monitor Results (1984)

Do You Agree or Disagree That Chevron . . .	Total* (N=605)	Inner-Directeds (N=162)	Outer-Directeds	
			Achievers (N=152)	Belongers (N=202)
Factor 1: Marketing/Business Conduct				
Makes high-quality products?	80%†	75%	84%	82%
Provides good service at its station?	69	66	67	74
Would be a good company to work for?	52	37	59	68
Is a good stock investment?	60	43	60	64
Factor 2: Environmental/Social Conduct				
Shows concern for the public's interest?	23	(4)	44	33
Pays its fair share of taxes?	10	(6)	16	24
Is seriously concerned with protecting the environment?	15	(14)	34	32
Cares about how people feel about them?	43	42	55	47
Makes public statements that are truthful?	34	19	43	38
Charges fair prices for its products?	28	27	28	36
Makes too much profit?	34	33	10	40
Factor 3: Corporate Contributions				
Contributes money to meet the health, education, and social welfare needs of the community?	22	(1)	31	29
Contributes money to cultural, music, or cultural arts organizations?	41	33	49	40
Contributes to PBS, the Public Broadcasting System?	48	44	54	46

* Results from the regionally stratified sample were adjusted to reflect the U.S. population.
† Percentages reported are "Net Agreement"—the total percent agree minus the total percent disagree. Parentheses reflect negative scores (i.e., a net disagreement).

Source: Chevron Public Opinion Monitor.

for each VALS segment—perhaps, for instance, the negative attitudes toward Chevron indicated by Inner-Directeds were associated with a different factor than the more positive Outer-Directed segment? Exhibit 5 chronicles the results of the multiple regressions by VALS segment. To summarize, for the total sample, marketing/business conduct was the most influential of the three factors. Environmental/social conduct ranked second and corporate contributions was a distant third. However, when the same analysis was performed separately on the VALS inner-directed and outer-directed segments, inner-directeds placed more importance on the environmental/social conduct factor. These data, combined with Chevron's knowledge of the high concentration of inner-

EXHIBIT 5   Unstandardized Regression Coefficients for Three Factors on Overall Favorability toward Chevron

Group	Factor			Adjusted R²	Constant	Average Favorability Rating
	Marketing	*Social Conduct*	*Contributions*			
Inner-Directeds	0.16	0.93	0.06	0.31	1.13	
(N=90)	3.96*	3.21	3.56			4.97†
Outer-Directeds	0.45	0.39	0.01	0.20	2.05	
(N = 434)	4.11	3.58	3.76			5.25

* Mean value of attributes in factor on original 5-point disagree to agree scale.
† On 7-point scale indicating unfavorable to favorable attitude toward Chevron.

Source: Chevron Corporation.

EXHIBIT 6   Population Breakdowns by VALS Segment

	Total United States (percent)	California (percent)
Need-Drivens		
Survivors	4%	2%
Sustainers	6	7
Outer-Directeds		
Belongers	39	26
Emulators	10	20
Achievers	21	25
Inner-Directeds		
I-Am-Me	3	5
Experiential	5	7
Societally Conscious	12	17

Source: MRI/VALS.

directeds in California (28 percent of the California population versus 20 percent of the whole United States, as indicated in Exhibit 6), proved key in the selection of the advertising campaign theme and target audience for Chevron's new corporate campaign. The next step was to develop the specific commercials to improve favorable attitudes toward Chevron among the Inner-Directeds.

DEVELOPMENT OF THE "PEOPLE DO" CAMPAIGN

Based on the research findings, David Soblin, Chevron's account director at J. Walter Thompson, organized six creative teams to design potential commercials targeted at California's Inner-Directeds. After considerable refinement, six 30-second animatics (rough TV commercials) were presented to Chevron. Scripts of these animatics appear in Exhibit 7.

Chevron, like many major advertisers, had a history of testing its advertising before committing its considerable media budget to a new campaign. For the past several years, Chevron had submitted both marketing and corporate commercials to a multisponsored pretest developed by McCollum-Spielman. McCollum-Spielman advertising pretest methodology involved inviting 100 respondents into a theater-like setting, seating them in groups of 25 around television monitors, and asking them to view what they were told were excerpts from pilot television programs. Several key measures—among them attitudes toward test-sponsors and purchase behavior—were collected before the programming began. Then, as on normal television, the new programming was interspersed with several commercials, among them a Chevron test commercial.

Chevron committed to testing the animatics developed by J. Walter Thompson. For this research, respondents were prescreened to learn whether they were Inner-Directed or Outer-Directed. The tests were conducted in July–August 1984 in two California cities, since the final campaign would air only in that state, at least initially.

The McCollum-Spielman test was predicated on the assumption that advertising has three distinct functions to perform:

1. Generate awareness—the consumer should know what company or product was sponsoring the ad.
2. Communicate a message—the intended message of the ad should be understood and capable of "playback" by the viewer.
3. Motivate—the ad should have a positive influence on either product purchase disposition or attitudes toward the company.

As summarized in Exhibit 8, the six test ads reviewed via the McCollum-Spielman procedure received good measures on all three criteria. Importantly, the commercials scored well in an absolute sense against McCollum-Spielman's norms for competitive corporate advertising *and* in a relative sense, as compared to previous Chevron campaigns. Among the target Inner-Directed segment, one animatic, "Water," was especially effective. It scored particularly strongly among the societally conscious subsegment of the Inner-Directeds. Consequently, the overall approach of "Water," which gave a specific example of Chevron's commitment to the environment, was determined to be the right approach. "Water" utilized a very emotional or "soft" tone to tell a story of how concern for the environment was of the utmost importance to Chevron.

The successful pretest of the "Water" animatic led ultimately to the development of a corporate advertising campaign named "People Do." In 1985 Chevron began running the first few "People Do" commercials on television—using carefully selected media buys to ensure a large Inner-Directed audience. The commercials were shown during news programming and in magazines oriented toward Inner-Directeds. The storyboard and script for one of the first "People Do" commercials is presented in Exhibit 9.

EXHIBIT 7   Six Chevron Animatics: 1984

---

1. Go Softly and Gently

Video

Scene of Alaskan or Yukon landscape. An owl or a hawk flies into frame. Cut to deer grazing, a stag and a fawn. Cut to stag's head next to Chevron oil pipeline. Follow stag's head as he looks up. Reveals Chevron pipeline disappearing into landscape.

Cut to close-up on fish's eye. As he swims away we realize that we're underwater looking up at bottom of boat. Camera travels up to view two scientists in boat (still seen from just under the surface). Cut to close-up of scientist's hand holding vial of crystal-clear water.

Cut to aerial view of man walking in wilderness. He is being dwarfed by large bird's shadow. Angle to see man looking up at owl or hawk. He has Chevron logo on his jacket. Cut back to aerial view as owl (hawk) flies into camera, obscuring our view.

Focus on Chevron logo on flag being blown by stiff breeze.

Audio

Singers (children's chorus with organ-like mood music):

> Go soft and gently upon the land,
> With what you build and what you plan.
> Don't spite the tiny for the grand.
> Go soft and gently upon the land.
>
> Go soft and gently upon the deep.
> Take only that which one should reap.
> And guard that which was meant to sleep.
> Go soft and gently upon the deep.
>
> Go soft and gently into the sky.
> Leave it pure to fill the eye,
> With sights that soar and dreams that fly.
> Go soft and gently into the sky.

2. Kids

Voice: Chevron asked some very important people, "Why do we need clear air?"

1st Kid: If we had a bad atmosphere, then we'd have to move to Venus or someplace like that.

2nd Kid: It's nice. I could, you know, fly kites, airplanes.

3rd Kid: It's better for your body to breathe clean air.

4th Kid: I wouldn't like bad air.

5th Kid: Because when you breathe through their lungs they don't get, they get, they need oxygen.

Voice: These are a few *big* reasons why Chevron works for clean air today. And a few *small* reasons why we'll be doing the same tomorrow.

6th Kid: I like it.

EXHIBIT 7 *(continued)*

3. Water

Video

Water pouring into something we cannot see as a shape . . . the water sparkles as it pours . . . and gradually our TV set seems to fill up with water.

The filling is completed and the water sits there for a moment. It looks very clean to us.

A stickleback fish swims into view.

Another comes in. Then a third. Then a fourth.

Pull back to see tank in lab. Worker peers through to see that fish are doing okay.

Chevron hallmark.

Audio

Voice: The water you are looking at came from an oil refinery where it was used to help turn crude oil into gasoline. It got pretty dirty doing that.

Before it goes back into the bay where it came from, the traces of the work it has done have to be removed.

Who makes sure of that? Our final inspectors . . . Oscar . . . Fred . . . Susie . . . Miranda. . . . After all, they have to live in it.

Do people really go to all that trouble to make sure that you don't hurt the fish? Some people do.

4. Friends

Voice: Chevron asked some *very* important people, "What makes a good neighbor?"

1st Kid: A good neighbor makes a good friend.

2nd Kid: You should really like them especially and they should really like you a lot, too.

3rd Kid: You buy me ice cream and stuff.

4th Kid: It's someone to talk to, to make you feel better.

Voice: At Chevron we think the most neighborly thing to do is to act like a friend.

5th Kid: You mean, like, tomorrow you're going to say that (you) think that they trust in you, like to pick a flower for them.

5. Rabbit

Video

A farmer, plowing a field at sunset, discovers a nest of rabbits . . . and plows around it.

Superimpose: Chevron logo.

EXHIBIT 7 *(concluded)*

Audio

Song: Tomorrow's getting closer
It's almost here today
Just in time to see that we
Don't let the good things get away.

The good things all around us
Keep 'em safe for one and all
For all creatures
Great and small.

Voice: The Chevron Corporation believes that industry has a responsibility to
conduct itself in such a way that the future is secure for all creatures, great
and small.

6. Color It

Video

Child drawing a landscape.

Begin to move in on drawing.

Picture begins to transform into reality.

Once the landscape is real, a man walks into the picture leading the child who made
the drawing by the hand.

Super Chevron logo and "Let's Make it Happen."

Audio

Music: Color it fresh . . .
Color it new . . .
Color it magical . . .
Color it true . . .
See with the eyes of a child . . .
But dream the dreams of man . . .
Make your dreams come full to life by doing all you can . . .

Voice: The Chevron Corporation believes that a future worth working for begins
with a vision of the world we want our children to live in. Let's make it
happen.

GAUGING COMMERCIAL EFFECTIVENESS

The artificial environment of commercial "pretest" research did not convince
Chevron's management that the $5 million annual investment in the "People
Do" corporate campaign was paying off. So, to gauge commercial effectiveness,
Chevron used the "Communicus" methodology pioneered by Jack Moore. The
"Communicus" approach involved benchmark interviews with "target audi-

EXHIBIT 8   McCollum-Spielman Pretest Results

	Clutter/Awareness*		Main Idea†		Attitude‡	
	Total (%)	Inner-Directeds (%)	Total (%)	Inner-Directeds (%)	Total (%)	Inner-Directeds (%)
"Go Softly"	46%	45%	39%	46%	+18%	+16%
"Kids"	42	36	35	35	+14	+11
"Water"	37	44	29	45	+32	+36
"Friends"	34	47	24	38	+5	−9
"Color It"	39	32	20	15	+12	+1
"Rabbit"	47	45	35	35	+3	−14
Norm for 30-second corporate ads by oil companies	46	31	+16			
Range from which norm derives	(11 to 87)	(7 to 75)	(−4 to +33)			

* *Clutter/Awareness:*   This score is the percent who mentioned seeing a Chevron commercial after one exposure to the commercial. The unaided measure is taken about 30 minutes after seeing the commercial. The Chevron commercial was embedded in a clutter of seven commercials—the other six were non-oil company commercials.

† *Main Idea:*   This score represents responses to the question "other than getting you to buy their products, what would you say were the main ideas they were trying to get across in the commercial?" Again, this was after just one exposure to the commercial in a clutter of seven commercials.

‡ *Attitude:*   This score is calculated after two exposures to the commercial, when respondents are asked, "Did the Chevron commercial change your feelings about Chevron as a company in any way?" Those who said, "yes, more unfavorably" are subtracted from those who say, "yes, more favorably" to arrive at the commercial effect (attitude) score.

ence" respondents in advance of the campaign, followed by natural exposure to the campaign for a designated period (usually a year) and then a reinterview of the same respondents to gauge (1) campaign awareness, (2) sponsor identification, and (3) commercial effect on either gasoline purchase, or, in the case of "People Do," favorability of attitudes toward Chevron. Generally, Chevron's senior management required a positive reading across these measures to continue campaign funding. Exhibit 10 presents data from year 1 of the "People Do" campaign in California, comparing consumers who were unexposed to any of the commercials to a second group who had viewed and successfully identified Chevron as the sponsor of at least one of the commercials during the period. Here again, "People Do" met its objectives, especially among the Inner-Directed target.

Chevron produced and aired six executions of the "People Do" campaign between 1986 and 1988. All emphasized Chevron's concern for the environment and the protection of endangered species of wildlife. Chevron's 1988 tracking study found that 57 percent of respondents (65 percent of Inner-Directeds) could recall an ad from the campaign and correctly identify Chevron as the advertiser. When asked to name the oil company that exhibited the

EXHIBIT 9 "People Do" Advertisement

1. (MUSIC) ANNCR: This eagle could land in trouble.

2. The high point he might decide to rest on

3. could be dangerous.

4. Unaware that 13,000 volts await him,

5. he heads toward it and lands,

6. unharmed.

7. Wooden platforms above power lines now keep him above danger.

8. They were developed and put there by

9. a lot of people whose work brings them

10. to this remote area.

11. Do people really reach that high to protect a natural wonder?

12. People do. (MUSIC OUT)

EXHIBIT 10   Impact of the "People Do" Campaign

(A)   **Proven awareness of 1986 "People Do" campaign.**

	Net Campaign Awareness		
Proven Aware	*Total (Percent)*	*Inner-Directeds (Percent)*	*Outer-Directeds (Percent)*
Any ads	41%	47%	41%
1–2 ads	22	15	27
3 or more ads	19	32	14

(B)   **"People Do" campaign effectiveness: attitude change toward Chevron as a company among VALS Inner-Directeds (California), January 1987 versus January 1986.**

Attitude Change toward Chevron (1986–87)	*Unaware of Chevron Ads (N=47) (Percent)*	*Aware of Chevron Ads (N=41) (Percent)*	*Advertising Effect (Percent)*
Favorable	+7%	+15%	+8%
Unfavorable	−3	−5	+2
Net	+10	+20	+10

(C)   **"People Do" campaign effectiveness: purchase impact among total sample and VALS Inner-Directeds (California)**

	Advertising Awareness				Advertising Effect	
	Unaware		Proved Aware			
Brand Bought Last Was Chevron	*Total (N=146) (Percent)*	*Inner-Directeds (N=47) (Percent)*	*Total (N=103) (Percent)*	*Inner-Directeds (N=41) (Percent)*	*Total (Percent)*	*Inner-Directeds (Percent)*
January 1986	24%	26%	9%	10%		
January 1987	26	21	19	27		
Net	+2	−5	+10	+17	+8%	+22%

greatest environmental responsibility, 31 percent of respondents (30 percent of Inner-Directeds) mentioned Chevron; Arco was second, cited by 10 percent. Nevertheless, despite all Chevron's efforts, there remained a hard core 25 percent of Inner-Directeds who were unconvinced by the advertising even if aware of it.

FUTURE CHALLENGES

Chevron's polling in 1988–90 revealed important changes in public attitudes toward the environment. Specifically, environmental protection had been democratized. Polls by Chevron and major nonpartisan groups, such as Gallup, Roper, and Cambridge Reports, traced the phenomenal growth of the environmental movement. By 1990, over 75 percent of Americans identified themselves as environmentalists. Further, environmental attitudes were beginning to translate into changed behavior. As of September 1990, nearly 75 percent of Americans claimed to recycle paper, cans, and bottles. Researchers at Chevron believed that these changes were based on shifts in personal values. It seemed that the 1980s' emphasis on personal health and safety was being projected to environmental concern. A movement that in the 1970s was largely tied to aesthetic concerns and values (green, open space; trees; restrictions on land development) appeared to be touching a much more central chord for Americans—survival of future generations.

Winters and others at Chevron questioned how the widespread concern for the environment would impact the effectiveness of the "People Do" campaign. They wondered if the target should be broadened beyond Inner-Directeds. In March 1989, the Exxon Valdez oil spill in Alaska "focused" public attention once again on the alleged shortcomings of the U.S. oil industry. Even though Chevron was not related to Exxon, what would that spill do to efforts by Chevron to convince the public of its environmental concern? Would the "People Do" campaign serve Chevron well, should there be another fast run-up in gasoline prices, supply shortages as occurred in the 1970s, or a conflict in the Middle East causing severe instability in world oil markets?

Optical Distortion, Inc. (C): The 1988 Reintroduction

On June 14, 1988, Don Lambert stopped by the office of his former first-year marketing professor at the Harvard Business School to tell him about his new job, selling contact lenses for chickens.

Optical Distortion, Inc., had been founded in 1969 by David Garrison. He determined that chickens fitted with contact lenses designed to distort their vision were less inclined to peck at each other in hen houses. As a result, no pecking order emerged and cannibalism was reduced. Less trauma also resulted in additional egg productivity and greater feeding efficiency. Garrison estimated that these savings would more than offset the cost of the lenses and their installation. The potential market was huge (in 1969 about 500 million chickens were raised on around 400,000 farms in the United States) but chicken farmers were not easily persuaded to adopt the innovation. In addition, two problems emerged that forced the company to withdraw the lenses from the market in the late 1970s; eye irritation and an unacceptably low retention rate. After nearly 10 years, the problems were solved and the company was again ready to begin marketing its product.

Lambert brought his former professor up to date with recent developments at the company:

> The lenses have changed quite a bit. They no longer distort the chicken's vision. We found out that red tint was enough. So now, they are simply red lenses. The technology is still proprietary. We have a new patent pending, and we're the only ones who can make them. Some people had tried putting red lights in the hen houses, but it didn't work. The hen houses had to be sealed up so that no other light entered, and that caused serious ventilation problems. Besides, the farmers couldn't work in the hen houses in that light. Once we solved the irritation and retention problems, the lenses were clearly the best solution.
>
> All birds still have to be debeaked because cannibalism starts even before they reach maturity, and, therefore, before the lenses can be inserted. But debeaked chick-

This case was prepared by Professor Patrick J. Kaufmann.
Copyright © 1988 by the President and Fellows of Harvard College.
Harvard Business School case 9-589-011 (Rev. 7/17/90).

ens still kill each other, and the hard part is that, even when the lenses are used in conjunction with debeaking, the benefits are so great you get the reaction that it's too good to be true. But it is! Over the past few years, extensive tests have been conducted at a university farm on thousands of birds and the results are fantastic. The red lenses really make the chickens calm; calm chickens don't kill each other, and they eat less while egg production stays the same or increases slightly. With farm operations currently running at a break-even level or worse, a $0.30–$0.50 per bird profit with lensed birds is incredible. It just seems too good to be true.

When asked how they intended to market the lenses, Lambert handed the professor a box; the cover read, "Warning: What's inside this box will make you laugh, then it will make you money." Inside was a professional glossy brochure, a videotape, and a tube containing 10 pairs of red lenses. The brochure explained the product in detail (including economic analysis), and asked the farmers to try the lenses on 10 of their birds. The videotape demonstrated how they were to be inserted.

As you know, 80 percent of the chickens in the United States are owned by only 3 percent of the producers. I sent these packages to some of the large producers and am following up with personal visits. The real problem is getting the producers to believe the numbers. We've got great data from the university test, but we need a large commercial test, a whole hen house—50 thousand chickens. The funny thing is that once the farmers believe in the numbers everybody is going to want lenses, and we're going to have trouble supplying them. These farmers work on such tight margins it's incredible, and the egg market is intensely competitive. So, everytime anyone finds a way to cut costs, prices drop and the others either follow along or go out of business. For example, there was a problem because debeaked birds used to throw their food around. Well, someone invented a kind of worm gear which moves food slowly down the trough. The side of the gears prevent the chickens from tossing their head from side to side and solves most of the food waste problem. Once one farmer adopted it and prices started to drop, everyone had to have it.

The producers don't share cost savings information, because industry cost savings just lead to price cuts. If a producer has an edge, it wants to keep it as long as it can. Information about new techniques spreads through university extension agents, whose job it is to gather and disseminate information on technological solutions to common problems. The extension agents are very highly respected and important to the farmers. But, in order to get information from the agents, the producers have to be open with them, or the next time the farmer calls the agent he'll be "too busy" to return the call.

Lambert elaborated on the competitiveness of the egg production market:

I'll tell you how fierce the competition is. A few years ago a group of southwestern farmers sued a huge midwestern producer for pricing too low and dumping eggs on the market. They lost the suit, but emotions still run high. I've talked to that huge midwestern producer and they're quite interested in the lenses. They are the second largest producer in the country and by far the largest producer in their region, controlling about one sixth of all U.S. production. They are very scientific and run a highly efficient operation. I've heard that their goal is to continue doubling in size every two years. If they decide to run a test, I'm sure they'll end up placing an order for their entire flock. If that happens, we're home free.

Lambert thought for a moment and said:

I know I could use the fact that that particular producer is interested in the lenses to influence other farms to test the product. That producer's behavior is of great concern to them. I don't feel really comfortable doing that. The real problem would be if that producer does place an order for their whole flock, it will eat up our entire capacity for a year. Even if the others wanted to use the lenses, we couldn't supply them. With the prices that producer could charge for eggs, a lot of the smaller farms could never survive. Last year alone about 500 of the 3,000 commercial producers went out of business anyway.

I really don't know what I should do. I can either spend my time trying to finalize the deal in the Midwest, or keep trying to convince the smaller farms to place orders now so that we can reserve some capacity for them. Since there's only me, I can't be everywhere at once.

TABLE 1 A Sample Farm Income Analysis*

Summary of economics (optimistic)		Normal Debeak ($)	Lenses plus Debeak ($)
Revenue:	Revenue/bird	$ 10.76	$ 11.08
	Total revenue	10,759,595	11,078,290
Cost:	Bird cost (each)	2.70	2.70
	Feed cost/bird	6.17	5.81
	Lens cost/pair	0	0.15
	Miscellaneous cost	1.87	1.92
	Total cost/bird	10.74	10.58
	Total cost	10,738,650	10,577,269
Profit:	Profit/bird	0.02	0.50
	Total profit	20,945	501,021

* Mortality, feed cost, and egg production effects vary under different local circumstances. In this example, revenue and costs reflect reasonable but optimistic levels of both decreased mortality and increased egg production, and assumes a 1 million layer operation and a cage system with five birds to a cage.

Chapter 3.5

Secret Shopper Program

In April 1990, Linda Douglas, a marketing professor at a major state university, received an unsolicited letter (Exhibit 1) from the director of marketing of *SportStyle* magazine. The letter invited applications from second year marketing students interested in participating in *SportStyle*'s Secret Shopper Program. A description of this program was attached to the letter (Exhibit 2) along with a student application form (Exhibit 3).

Douglas's familiarity with secret shopper programs was limited. She was aware of a consumer electronics manufacturer that used secret shoppers to check on the selling practices of its independent retailers, particularly the level of retail discounts being offered to customers and the prevalence of bait-and-switch practices.

It was unclear whether the *SportStyle* program had a similar purpose. Douglas was cautious. Before announcing the program to her students, she wanted more information. She began to develop a list of questions that she would ask the director of marketing when he called.

EXHIBIT 1   Letter to Douglas

SportStyle magazine, a Fairchild publication, is the leading trade publication servicing sport retailers in the active industry. We are interested in recruiting one marketing student from your university to conduct small surveys for major sports manufacturers at local sporting goods stores.

Your marketing student—known as the *SportStyle* Secret Shopper—will conduct in-person retailer surveys that provide merchandising information to companies like Nike, Adidas, Penn, et al. The Secret Shopper will go into local sport stores and ask a few questions about a particular product. The Secret Shopper's feedback will give manufacturers immediate information on how their product is being sold. The Secret Shopper Program is a merchandising plan that *SportStyle* offers our advertisers. A detailed outline of the program is attached.

This case was prepared by Professor John A. Quelch.
Copyright © 1990 by the President and Fellows of Harvard College.
Harvard Business School case N9-590-095 (Rev. 5/28/90).

EXHIBIT 1 *(concluded)*

SportStyle is looking for one second-year marketing student with an interest in sports. In order to qualify, the candidate must complete the attached questionnaire and return it to us.

We will contact you to see if you would like to participate in this program.

Sincerely,

Director of Marketing

EXHIBIT 2   Program Description

SportStyle's Secret Shopper program is a merchandising value-added program designed for advertisers.

College students function as Secret Shoppers. They go into sport stores posing as consumers wearing a *SportStyle* cap and inquire about a particular product or brand. The questions the students ask have been designed by the manufacturer/advertiser.

Students from all across the United States forward their brief reports of these shopping trips to *SportStyle. SportStyle* combines all the results and submits a complete report to the manufacturers.

Students are given approximately two weeks to make store visits. Each store visit should take 15 to 20 minutes. We estimate that two to four store visits would be completed for each assignment.

Students are paid $7 for each store visit/report.

EXHIBIT 3   Application Form

Students interested in participating in the program should fill out this form and return it to:

> Director of Marketing
> SportStyle
> 7 E. 12 St.
> New York, NY 10003

STUDENT NAME:

STUDENT ADDRESS:

HOME PHONE:

EXHIBIT 3 *(concluded)*

SCHOOL NAME:

SCHOOL ADDRESS:

FRESHMAN: _____   JUNIOR: _____

SOPHOMORE: _____   SENIOR: _____

GPA: _____

MAJOR: _____

<u>INTERESTS</u>

HOBBIES:

SPORTS:

MAGAZINES & NEWSPAPERS READ:

Chapter 3.6

In the News

3.6.1 MISERY MARKET: WINOS AND THUNDERBIRD ARE A SUBJECT GALLO DOESN'T LIKE TO DISCUSS*

NEW YORK—In the dim light of a cold February morning, a grizzled wino shuffles into the Bowery Discount liquor store muttering, "Thunderchicken, it's good lickin.'" Fumbling for some change, he says: "Gimme one bird." Raymond Caba, the store clerk, understands the argot and hands over a $1.40 pint of Thunderbird, the top seller in what he calls "the bum section."

The ritual is repeated a thousand times a day in dead-end neighborhoods across the country. Cheap wines with down-and-dirty names—and an extra measure of alcohol—are the beverage of choice among down-and-out drunks. But winos are a major embarrassment to the big companies that manufacture these wines. With rare exceptions, they aren't eager to acknowledge their own products.

Thunderbird and Night Train Express are produced by the nation's largest wine company, E. & J. Gallo Winery, though you'll not learn that from reading the label on the bottle. MD 20/20 is made by Mogen David Wine Corporation, a subsidiary of Wine Group, Ltd., which refuses to talk about its product. Richards Wild Irish Rose Wine, the very best seller in the cat-

egory, is produced by Canandaigua Wine Company. Canandaigua is volubly proud of the wine but quick to point out that it enjoys wide popularity with people who aren't alcoholics.

People concerned about the plight of street alcoholics are critical of the purveyors of dollar-a-pint street wines made with cheap ingredients and fortified with alcohol to deliver the biggest bang for the buck. At 18 percent to 21 percent alcohol, these wines have about twice the kick of ordinary table wine, without any of the pretension.

The consumption of alcohol in the United States is declining in virtually every category, but the best selling of the low-end brands keep growing, in large part because customers can't stop drinking. Says Paul Gillette, the publisher of the *Wine Investor* in Los Angeles: "Makers of skid-row wines are the dope pushers of the wine industry."

Vintners generally try hard to filter their wines through the imagery of luxury and moderation, stressing vintage, touting quality. So they are understandably reluctant to be associated in any way with what some call a $500 million misery market.

Suppliers deny that the most popular street wines sell as well as they do because they appeal to dirt-poor, hard-core drinkers. Companies contend that their clientele is not like that at all, and, besides, any alcoholic beverage can be abused. (The wine people say they face stiff competition from high-alcohol malt liquor and 200-milliliter bottles of cheap vodka.) The future for the high-proof business, vintners say, isn't particularly rosy in any case. The wine category they call "dessert" or "fortified"—sweet wines with at least 14 percent alcohol—has lost favor with drinkers.

Wino wines are inexpensive to produce. They come in no-frills, screw-top packaging and require little or no advertising. Although they generally aren't the major part of vintners' product lineups, they are especially profitable. All told, net profit margins are 10 percent higher than those of ordinary tables wines, Canandaigua estimates. Gallo says that isn't true for its products, but it won't say what is true.

The wines are also a rock-solid business. Of all the wine brands in America, the trade newsletter *Impact* says, Wild Irish Rose holds the No. 6 spot, Thunderbird is 10th, and MD 20/20 is 16th. In contrast to the lackluster growth of most other wine brands, unit sales of the leading cheap labels, Wild Irish Rose and Thunderbird, are expected to be up 9.9 percent and 8.6 percent, respectively, this year, *Jobson's Wine Marketing Handbook* estimates.

So unsavory is this market that companies go to great lengths to distance themselves from their customers. If suppliers are willing to talk about the segment—and few are—they still don't acknowledge the wino's loyal patronage. Gallo and Canandaigua leave their good corporate names off the labels, thus obscuring the link between product and producer.

"This is the market with no name," says Clifford Adelson, a former executive director of sales at Manischewitz Wine Company, which once made low-end wines and was recently acquired by Canandaigua. "It's lots and lots of money, but it doesn't add prestige."

Cheap wines typically aren't even sold in many liquor stores. For instance, Frank Gaudio, who owns the big Buy-Rite Twin Towers Wine & Spirits store in New York's World Trade Center, doesn't stock any of these brands, though many homeless alcoholics spend their days just outside his door. "We don't want that clientele in our store," he says. "We could sell fortified wines and probably make money, but

we don't." The wines, however, are staples of the bulletproof liquor stores of low-income neighborhoods. While you can't say the whole market for items like Thunderbird and Night Train consists of derelicts, down-and-outers do seem to be its lifeblood. Fifty current and reformed drinkers interviewed for this article claim to have lived on a gallon a day or more of the stuff.

"The industry is manufacturing this for a select population: the poor, the homeless, the skid-row individual," says Neil Goldman, the chief of the alcoholism unit at St. Vincent's Hospital in Manhattan's Greenwich Village.

Dawn finds a small bottle gang near the Bowery, chasing away the morning shakes with a bottle of Thunderbird they pass from hand to hand. Mel Downing tugs up the pant leg of his filthy jeans to reveal an oozing infection on his knee. He is drinking, he says, to numb the pain of this "wine sore" and other ones on his back before he goes to the hospital later in the morning. "We're used to this stuff," the 39-year-old Mr. Downing quickly adds. "We like the effect. We like the price."

A cheap drunk is the main appeal of the wines that winos call "grape" or "jug," but most often just "cheap." Winos say that these wines, even when consumed in quantity, don't make them pass out as readily as hard liquor would.

Walter Single, a recovering alcoholic, recalls that on a daily diet of nine pints of Wild Irish Rose, he still was able "to function well enough to panhandle the money he needed to drink all day and still have enough left for a wake-up in the morning."

Some drinkers say the high sugar content of the wines reduces their appetite for food, so they don't have to eat much. Others say they still can drink wine even after their livers are too far gone to handle spirits. Still others appreciate the portability of pint bottles.

"I feel more secure with a pint," explains Teddy Druzinski, a former carpenter. "It's next to me. It's in my pocket." Canandaigua estimates that low-end brands account for 43 million gallons of the dessert category's 55 million gallons and that 50 percent is purchased in pints.

Many people in the wine industry eschew producing skid-row wines. "I don't think Christian Brothers should be in a category where people are down on their luck—where some may be alcoholics," says Richard Maher, the president of Christian Brothers Winery in St. Helena, California. Mr. Maher, who once was with Gallo, says fortified wines lack "any socially redeeming values."

"The consumers are we alcoholics," agrees Patrick Gonzales, a 45-year-old wino who is undergoing a week of detoxification at a men's shelter on New York's Lower East Side: "You don't see no one sitting at home sipping Mad Dog MD 20/20 in a wine glass over ice."

Major producers see their customers otherwise. Robert Huntington, the vice president of strategic planning at Canandaigua, says the Canandaigua, New York, company sells 60 percent to 75 percent of its "pure grape" Wild Irish Rose in primarily black, inner-city markets. He describes customers as "not supersophisticated," lower middle-class and low-income blue-collar workers, mostly men.

Daniel Solomon, a Gallo spokesman, maintains that Thunderbird "has lost its former popularity in the black and skid-row areas" and is quaffed mainly by "retired and older folks who don't like the taste of hard products."

According to accounts that Gallo disputes, the company revolutionized the skid-row market in the 1950s after discovering that liquor stores in Oakland, California, were catering to the tastes of certain customers by attaching packages of lemon Kool-Aid to bottles of white wine. Customers did their own mixing at home. The story goes that Gallo, borrowing the idea, created citrus-flavored Thunderbird. Other flavored high-proof wines then surged into the marketplace. Among them: Twister, Bali Hai, Hombre, Silver Satin, and Gypsy Rose. Gallo

says that the Kool-Aid story is "a nice myth," but that Thunderbird was "developed by our wine makers in our laboratories."

Vintners advertised heavily and sought to induce skid row's opinion leaders—nicknamed "bell cows"—to switch brands by plying them with free samples. According to Arthur Palombo, the chairman of Cannon Wines, Ltd., and one of Gallo's marketing men in the 1950s and 60s, "These were clandestine promotions." He doesn't say which companies engaged in the practice.

Today, such practices and most brands have long since died out. Companies now resort to standard point-of-sale promotions and, in the case of Canandaigua, some radio and television advertising. There still is an occasional bit of hoopla. In New Jersey, Gallo recently named a Thunderbird Princess, and Canandaigua currently is holding a Miss Wild Irish Rose contest. But to hear distributors tell it, word of mouth remains the main marketing tool.

The market is hard to reach through conventional media. Winos will drink anything, if need be; but when they have the money to buy what they want, they tend to hew to the familiar. (Sales resistance may help to explain why the handful of low-end products that companies have tried to launch in the past 20 years mostly have bombed.) Besides, "It would be difficult to come up with an advertising campaign that says this will go down smoother, get you drunker, and help you panhandle better," says Robert Williams, a reformed alcoholic and counselor at the Manhattan Bowery Corporation's Project Renewal, a halfway house for Bowery alcoholics.

Companies see no reason to spend a lot of money promoting brands they don't want to be identified with. "Gallo and ourselves have been trying to convey the image of a company that makes fine products," says Hal Riney, the president of Hal Riney & Associates, which created the TV characters Frank Bartles and Ed Jaymes for Gallo's wine cooler. "It would be counterproductive to advertise products like this."

Richards Wild Irish Rose purports to be made by Richards Wine Company. The label on a bottle of Gallo's Night Train reads "vinted & bottled by Night Train Limited, Modesto, Ca." Gallo's spokesman, Mr. Solomon, says "The Gallo name is reserved for traditional table wines."

Industry people chime in that it isn't at all uncommon for companies to do business under a variety of monikers. But they also agree with Cannon's Mr. Palombo: "Major wine producers don't want to be associated with a segment of the industry that is determined to be low-end and alcoholic."

Winos have their own names for what they buy, Gallo's appellations notwithstanding. When they go to buy Night Train, they might say, "Gimme a ticket." They call Thunderbird "pluck," "T-Bird," or "chicken." In street lingo, Richards Wild Irish Rose is known as "Red Lady," while MD 20/20 is "Mad Dog."

If skid-row wines are cheap to market, they are even cheaper to make. They are generally concocted by adding flavors, sugar, and high-proof grape-based neutral spirits to a base wine. The wine part is produced from the cheapest grapes available. Needless to say, the stuff never sees the inside of an oak barrel.

"They dip a grape in it so they can say it's made of wine," says Dickie Gronan, a 67-year-old who describes himself as a bum. "But it's laced with something to make you thirstier." Sugar probably. In any event, customers keep on swigging. Some are so hooked that they immediately turn to an underground distribution system on Sundays and at other times when liquor stores are closed. "Bootleggers," often other alcoholics, buy cheap brands at retail and resell them at twice the price. The street shorthand for such round-the-clock consumption is "24–7."

At nightfall, Mr. Downing, the member of the bottle gang with the leg infection, is panhandling off the Bowery "to make me another jug," as he puts it. As his shredded parka attests, he got into a fight earlier in the day with his buddy, Mr. Druzinski, who then disappeared. Mr. Downing also got too drunk to make it, as planned, to the hospital for treatment of his "wine sores."

A short while later, Mr. Druzinski emerges from the shadows. He has a bloodied face because he "took another header," which is to say he fell on his head. Nevertheless, in the freezing darkness, he joins his partner at begging once again.

"I'm feeling sick to my stomach, dizzy, and mokus," Mr. Downing says. "But I still want another pint." He scans the deserted street and adds: "Another bottle is the biggest worry on our minds."

3.6.2 RISKY BUSINESS: MARKETERS MAKE A BEELINE FOR THE NATION'S SCHOOLS*

Welcome to the wonderful world of educational "partnerships." Brand loyalty always gets an A-plus

When Whittle Communications launched its Channel One commercial television network for high schools last year, the storm of outrage was almost palpable. Parent-teacher groups and school officials from New York to California denounced Whittle chairman Chris Whittle as a crass despoiler of young minds.

Since then, Whittle has been roundly criticized for failing to anticipate public reaction, but surely that can be forgiven. After all, what's so new about targeting the schools? Whittle might have gotten the headlines, but exploiting America's students for brand share is a very old business.

_____

* By Laurie Petersen, of *Adweek's Marketing Week*, May 14, 1990. Reprinted with the permission of *Adweek* magazine.

But now that exploitation has reached new—and gluttonous—heights. Major marketers of products consumed by children are targeting the schools with tie-in and advertising programs that raise sensitive issues of educational standards, ethics, and taste. The sheer throw-weight of in-school advertising and marketing gimmicks virtually guarantees a strong public backlash. In-school marketers, who generally have proven incapable of restraining themselves, inevitably will face the scrutiny of hostile legislators and regulators.

The origins of the marketing community's commercialization of the schools are obvious enough. Media clutter and the rush of new product introductions have made it more difficult to reach parents and children through traditional media. With the average U.S. household now consisting of two working parents, children are either home alone or out at the malls for longer times, making buying decisions their parents used to make.

Meanwhile, federal aid to education has barely kept pace with inflation. Home-owner revolts against rising school taxes are spreading across the country. Education officials, with varying degrees of enthusiasm, have turned to the business community to fill the vacuum left by decreased government support. But are in-school couponing programs for breakfast cereals and candy or promotions that tie purchases of peanut butter to support for education the answer to what ails America's schools? Probably not. Increasingly, as the number of such programs proliferates, the American public will conclude that it is marketers who ail America's schools.

Coca-Cola Foods' Minute Maid, for example, publishes a summer-fun guide touting the joys of selling lemonade—Minute Maid's brand, of course. Pepsi distributes a space-shuttle poster to science classes that serves as a billboard for the Pepsi logo. To promote its movie, *The Bear*, last year, Tri-Star Pictures compiled wall charts and study guides for elementary schools. Edu-cation is surely perverted if "study guides" to movies can be considered valid curricula.

Some programs sponsored by other corporations have won praise. Merrill Lynch created a Scholarship Builder program to inspire inner-city first-graders to aim for college. American Express set up a National Academy Foundation to provide job experiences to high school students. The Exxon Education Foundation is funding an experiment on new teaching methods. Polaroid's Project Bridge helps employees switch careers to become math or science teachers.

These programs share a concern that, if business doesn't help students today, there won't be an educated work force tomorrow. Such enlightened self-interest generates good press and is not ruled by short-term returns on investment.

But more often than not, the current situation is ripe for exploitation. An audience of more than 45 million students enrolled in 102,000 elementary and secondary schools is too tantalizing to ignore. Quality Education Data of Denver estimates 12,000 companies and individuals are trying to reach these kids through their needy schools.

The appearance of corporate-sponsored materials in schools is hardly new. Since 1915, American children have learned about nutrition from the National Dairy Council. A 1929 National Education Association report turned up 82 commercial items in just *one* New England city classroom from sponsor companies whose products ranged from cereal to insurance. And most baby boomers can remember boring school-day filmstrips, courtesy of major corporations, electric utilities, and national trade associations.

Today educational marketing suppliers use data bases to target programs based on region, income, race, and other variables. These firms design programs to acquaint students with branded products and services. No company, it seems, is immune. Even Scholastic, Inc., once a respected educational publisher with strong recognition in the schools, is slowly transforming itself into an aggressive in-school marketing service. (See the following: "Business Is Booming . . .")

Mava Heffler, a vice president at Glendinning Associates of Westport, Connecticut, developed Johnson & Johnson's Shelter Aid, a program widely regarded as a model of "marketing with a social conscience." The program set up a hot line for victims of domestic violence through UPC code collection and coupon redemptions.

Heffler feels it's naive to think marketers will develop school programs that do not contribute to a company's bottom line. "Schools are definitely the next frontier. As long as they are open for targeting, they will and should be pushed by marketing entities," she says. "And manufacturers aren't going to be happy unless there's something in it for them."

Business Is Booming for In-School Middlemen

In the courtship between needy schools and hungry marketers, there is no shortage of matchmakers.

Roberta Nusim, a former high school English teacher, makes the connections with Lifetime Learning Systems of Fairfield, Connecticut. Nusim founded the company 13 years ago to develop classroom-ready curricula for corporate sponsors. She says more than 46 million students from preschool through college use Lifetime programs each year. "Our client base has been growing steadily since the early 1980s," says Nusim, who estimates Lifetime has produced more than 600 programs since its inception.

Sampling Corporation of America, a Glenview, Illinois-based distributor of in-school marketing programs, works mostly with packaged-goods firms. Founded in 1979, SCA has a waiting list of 4,000 schools that want its materials, according to executive vice president Steven Kaplan.

Kaplan says SCA in 1989 reached about 70 percent of students aged 6–12 and 85 percent of teens in high school. And he claims the company will distribute three times as many programs this year.

While Nusim speaks knowledgeably about the need for fresh school curricula, her company saves its most persuasive pitches for prospective clients.

"Let Lifetime Learning Systems take your message into the classroom, where the young people you want to reach are forming attitudes that will last a lifetime," the company's sales kit urges. The brochure calls school hours "prime time" for young people. "Whatever your objective, we can help you meet it," the kit promises.

Apparently, the kit delivers. More than 92 percent of packaged-goods samples handed out in schools with a Lifetime Learning program make their way into students' mouths or their parents' homes. When General Mills wanted to introduce Fruit Roll-Ups to preschoolers and their parents, Lifetime worked up a kit of booklets, growth charts, and product samples. Teachers themselves became the hucksters, passing out more than a million samples to preschoolers.

For Lederle Laboratories' Centrum Jr. multivitamins, Lifetime created a teaching kit on vitamins and minerals. A survey showed 98.6 percent of the teachers involved used the kit and more than 80 percent gave their students literature to take home.

To increase turnout for Paramount Pictures' teen movie, *The Breakfast Club*, Lifetime created teaching kits discussing the film for selected markets. The company claimed audience increases of almost 70 percent in those markets.

Lifetime employs former teachers and educational publishing veterans to design its curricula, and programs are screened by a panel of educators before they hit schools. Nusim argues her company benefits teachers starved for fresh materials on such topics as energy conservation and AIDS and notes that 130,000 new teachers sign up for Lifetime's programs each year.

As for charges of undue commercialism, Nusim claims teachers will only permit programs of intrinsic educational value into their classrooms. "We get phone calls daily from teachers who have come to view us as a resource for things they know are unavailable anywhere else," she says. Yet the curricula are limited to schools targeted by their sponsor.

SCA's operation makes little pretense of offering "educational curricula." It applies conventional coupon distribution systems and contests. For example, its flagship program is a safety kit distributed every Halloween in conjunction with the National Safety Council. Safety literature is wrapped around a sheet featuring coupons for the sponsors' products. Participating sponsors can distribute product samples and coupons to children along with the safety literature.

SCA's latest efforts include customized client programs, such as an elementary school poster about computers for Kool-Aid. Accompanying the material is a collect-and-save program. It urges kids to buy Kool-Aid and save proof-of-purchase "points." That way, they'll earn merchandise from the Wacky Warehouse and computer equipment for their schools.

Publisher Scholastic, Inc., Learns to Sell Itself

For 70 years, Scholastic, Inc., the publisher of *Scholastic News* and 30 other respected school periodicals, has described itself as "the most trusted name in learning." Now Scholastic is aggressively repositioning itself as the most trusted in-school vehicle for marketers.

Scholastic, the largest publisher of printed materials for children in the English-speaking world, reaches 23 million students and 1 million teachers in 85,000 schools nationwide. Scholastic's partnership with teachers and school administrators has always been strong.

But lately that relationship is taking a backseat to the publisher's partnerships with marketers such as AT&T, Minute Maid, and M&M/Mars.

"We are very careful to make sure that what we are doing doesn't compromise our constituency," says Michele Magazine, senior vice president of Scholastic's fledgling Education Marketing Group. With the company for just 10 months, she is intent on building business and education "partnerships" through Scholastic.

The former publisher of *Lear's*, Magazine started by jazzing up Scholastic's marketing materials to showcase the company's powerful distribution network. A slick look and a compelling sales message have combined to create spectacular results, she says: "On 80 percent of our first calls, something happens. There is always interest."

For AT&T, Scholastic literally drew a map. A map of Eastern Europe, that is, tracking the rapidly unfolding events there and providing a lesson plan to go with it. It was only the latest in a series of in-class image-builders that Scholastic has produced for AT&T. Designed around the theme of communications, the series—which starts in the first grade with comic books and the AT&T Adventure Club—will eventually follow students through their elementary school years.

Kathleen Redmond, youth market manager for AT&T Consumer Communication Services, says she selected Scholastic to develop the Adventure Club because of the company's reputation and access to schools. "If you're going to spend a lot of money, you want to be sure the program gets in," says Redmond. "Scholastic brings that to the table. They have an incredible distribution channel."

While tastefully produced, many of Scholastic's programs offer strange partnerships. A nutrition program created by Scholastic for fifth- and sixth-graders, for example, is sponsored by the M&M/Mars candy company.

"This is an education company," Magazine says. "We are not an advertorial publisher. We have walked away from clients who just want us to distribute coupons. We won't do a program unless we know teachers need it and will use it."

But Scholastic isn't unalterably opposed to coupons. This month, in a summer reading program sponsored by Minute Maid to benefit the Reading Is Fundamental (RIF) literacy group, Scholastic will distribute 3.7 million posters in schools and to retailers. Those given to elementary school kids just before they start vacations will have Minute Maid coupons attached.

"If this were not a cause-related program, I might be concerned about distributing coupons in classrooms. But there is a definite benefit to RIF," says Judy Goodfarb of Saatchi & Saatchi Promotions in New York, who helped develop the promotion. Minute Maid has committed $50,000 to RIF, and the program has been endorsed by First Lady Barbara Bush.

RIF director of development Wade St. Clair has no qualms about a little coupon-clipping if it motivates kids to read. "It's up to the individual teacher whether they want to participate," he says. "It's a local call."

Magazine bristles at suggestions her job requires the exploitation of children. After all, she once worked for Ralph Nader. "I really am interested in programs that work for consumers. If they work there, they'll work for everybody."

P&G's New Math: A Dime for Every Pound of Jif

In January, Procter & Gamble offered elementary schools a no-strings-attached deal: the more Jif peanut butter sold, the more P&G would contribute to each school that signed up with the company.

It sounded pretty good. For every pound of Jif Peanut Butter sold in the United States between February 1 and April 30, 10 cents went into the Jif Children's Education Fund. There would be no restriction on how the schools spent their money. P&G expected to split $4 million in July among the schools that registered.

If anything, the program was too successful. Since the fund was announced, nearly one of every three elementary schools in the United States has signed up. A $4-million pot translates into just less than $200 for each of the 21,600 schools enrolled—enough to buy a few basketballs.

The Jif fund is just one of a number of programs that tie product sales to corporate gifts to education. In fact, the field seems to be attracting more interest all the time.

Campbell Soup Company ran one of the first partnership promotions in 1973 with its Labels for Education. Four years ago, Scott Paper Company launched Learning Tools for Schools. Apple Computer has teamed with retailers to offer computers in exchange for the collection of cash register receipts from participating supermarkets. Sears plans a national launch in schools this fall of its Great Payback program, which features various packaged-goods manufacturers. Del Monte Corporation will make free software available to school systems this fall through proof-of-purchase and redemption programs.

Critics contend that all such programs teach children is a bit of Latin: quid pro quo. In "Hucksters in the Classroom," a 1979 report from the Center for Study of Responsive Law, Liam Ronney, an Evanston, Illinois, elementary school teacher, blasted his school's support of the Campbell program: "The idea of conditioning youngsters to use a product . . . for purposes totally unrelated to the product, to me indicated our staff's placing a high value on non-thinking, something-for-nothing, support-your-brand-names behavior."

More important to marketers, such plans lack brand-building sense. They signal that the designated product is not worth the consumer's loyalty for its own sake. If the promotions are meant to develop associations with a young audience, the last thing that is needed is a mixed message.

David Ryan, president of Ryan Partnership, a promotion consulting agency in Westport, Connecticut, says such programs try "to spur product trial or create a halo effect for the brand." But a poorly run partnership promotion could backfire badly, he warns: "If on a per-school basis, you have to go through an awful lot to get not a lot, it leads to disappointment and can add to skepticism about the brand."

Making the Cafeteria the Next Marketing Frontier

They are the butt of an entire subspecies of jokes and where kids learn to refine their play with food. But school cafeterias, serving 30 million meals a day, are a natural arena for manufacturers of branded food products to win over the hearts and stomachs of children.

Marketers are now running perhaps as many as 100 programs a year in school cafeterias. And though all food promotions are screened by nutritionists for the American School Food Service Association, there are still no solid rules defining the limits of the promotions.

To introduce kids to its yogurts, Dannon tested a four-week cultural literacy promotion in 23 elementary schools in six test markets. Cafeteria displays and accompanying lesson plans featured a cartoon "Culture Vulture" who led the youngsters on educational adventures. Cafeteria staff charted the actual yogurt consumed—an average of just under 60 percent of students sampled the product. A control test indicated that the promotional materials helped increase the children's consumption by 8–10 percent.

Last year, Kellogg launched a four-week "Game of the States" promotion. The game was created after a National Geographic Society survey found Americans ranked nearly last in an international geographic literacy test. Not incidentally, the program touted Kellogg brands and impeded other cereals' penetration into elementary schools.

Grade schools had to schedule one additional "Kellogg's Cereal Day" for each week of the promotion, guaranteeing Kellogg product exclusivity. In return, they received posters and maps for each student. Each week, cafeteria staff distributed a sticker sheet to apply to one of four U.S. regional maps. Students had to put the right stickers in the right states. Participation levels determined the winning schools.

The grand prize? A thousand dollars for trips to the state capital, where the educator Tony the Tiger greeted the kids.

3.6.3   AFTER UPTOWN, ARE SOME NICHES OUT?*

R. J. Reynolds Tobacco Company's withdrawal of plans to test market a cigarette aimed at blacks—following intense public pressure—may make targeting certain consumer groups more difficult for tobacco and even liquor companies.

The company late Friday announced that it was dropping plans to begin test marketing its new cigarette, Uptown, after the cigarette generated a firestorm of protests in the black community and drew a blistering attack last week by Health and Human Services Secretary Louis W. Sullivan.

The cigarette, in slick black and gold packaging, was the first produced by any tobacco company that was to be explicitly targeted at blacks. In its decision to drop test-marketing plans in Philadelphia next month, the RJR Nabisco, Inc., unit said it couldn't get accurate re-

---

* By James R. Schiffman, staff reporter of *The Wall Street Journal*, January 22, 1990. Kenneth H. Bacon contributed to this article. Reprinted by permission of *The Wall Street Journal* © 1990 Dow Jones and Company, Inc. All Rights Reserved Worldwide.

sults from the test market under such adverse conditions. It won't say whether it will attempt to roll out the cigarette elsewhere or target it to a wider audience.

The company's announcement that it would scuttle the planned test market came as a shock to some marketing experts. "When big companies are challenged by consumer groups, they almost always stick to their guns," says Al Ries, chairman of Trout & Ries, a marketing consulting firm in Greenwich, Connecticut, "This shows the enormous power that consumer public opinion" can have.

He and others predicted that the Uptown fiasco would only make it increasingly difficult in the future for tobacco and liquor companies to target their brands to minorities, women, and youth. "I think they are all going to have to be careful that they don't target a specific gender or group," Mr. Ries says.

RJR's decision to back away from Uptown is sure to fuel the campaigns of those who want to prevent tobacco companies from using seductive pictures in advertisements, anti-smoking activists say. Also, groups from the American Cancer Society to the Junior League recently have been trying to counter the tobacco industry's efforts to market certain cigarettes specifically to women, and Dr. Sullivan has spoken out against such products as well.

As a result of the Uptown debacle, Michele Bloch, a physician who is director of the Washington-based Women vs. Smoking Network, says the group will intensify efforts against targeting cigarettes at women and will contact Dr. Sullivan for help in coordinating the attack.

RJR's decision against testing Uptown could also spur attempts in inner cities to remove or limit black-targeted billboard advertising for cigarettes and alcoholic beverages, such as malt liquors, says Michael Pertschuk, co-director of the Washington-based Advocacy Institute. And it could spill over into campaigns against exporting cigarettes to developing countries in Asia and the third world, where tobacco markets are growing by leaps and bounds.

In the tobacco industry, targeting is vital because the percentage of Americans who smoke is steadily dwindling. So cigarette makers increasingly have been trying to come up with new brands aimed at specific groups in order to gain market share.

For RJR, this has been especially true. The food and tobacco giant has been losing ground to archrival Philip Morris Companies in recent years. Its tobacco business has suffered from successive management shakeups both before and after the record-setting $25 billion leveraged buy-out of RJR by Kohlberg Kravis Roberts & Company last year.

The company's major brands, Winston and Camel, particularly, have suffered from not being sufficiently targeted to specific-enough audiences, marketers say. And many believe the future vitality of RJR's tobacco business depends on the company's ability to come up with clever, specifically aimed new products. James W. Johnston, who became chief executive officer of RJR's domestic tobacco unit last May, has said that RJR, despite a heavy debt load, will be aggressive in introducing new products.

But Uptown is a dubious start, especially following so soon after the failure of Premier, the revolutionary and expensive "smokeless" cigarette developed by Mr. Johnston's predecessors. RJR pulled Premier from test marketing in March after the cigarette proved difficult to light and draw smoke through. That product, too, drew unexpected controversy from health advocates and anti-smokers.

Premier was much more expensive than Uptown. Over the years, it cost more than $300 million to develop and test market, according to internal estimates. The cost of Uptown is more toward the low range of the $2 million to $10 million RJR generally spends on new products, according to an industry executive.

But Uptown could be a bigger public relations debacle, some say. "Premier was just a marketing miscalculation. This one is considered an insult by the black community," says Mr. Ries, the consultant.

Not that tobacco companies haven't marketed to blacks in the past. They have, but they've been more subtle about it. While saying, for instance, that menthol brands are aimed at the general public, tobacco companies have pitched the products in black publications, on billboards in black neighborhoods and by sponsoring black events.

Marketing specialists and anti-smoking activists agree that Reynolds's big mistake was in its blatant declaration that Uptown was aimed at blacks. In fact, that move enabled disparate black groups for the first time to forge an alliance on the issue, says Mr. Pertschuk of the Advocacy Institute.

RJR says it had simply decided to be upfront about its intentions. "We're an honest company, what do you say when the audience is going to be predominantly black?" says a company spokesman. In a statement, the company said that pressure from anti-smoking "zealots" succeeded in limiting choices for black smokers, resulting in "a further erosion of the free enterprise system." The spokesman says the company doesn't consider the Uptown experience a new-product failure. "We don't expect every brand we take to test market to succeed," he says.

Uptown was conceived in late 1988, in response to problems with the company's menthol Salem brand, its most popular brand among blacks. Salem was losing market share to rival menthol Newport, made by Loews Corporation's Lorillard tobacco subsidiary. RJR concluded Salem's menthol was too strong for some black smokers, the company spokesman says. Blacks are very important to tobacco companies; according to Mr. Pertschuk, their rate of smoking is declining more slowly than among whites and is increasing among young, poor, uneducated blacks.

So the idea for Uptown, a lighter menthol, was hatched. Partly because of the Premier fiasco, the company was under great pressure to do test marketing that produced meaningful results, says an industry executive. Since Uptown was to be a cigarette for blacks, executives decided testing had to be done exclusively among blacks.

The company's marketers debated whether to be straightforward or subtle in their approach. They decided, finally, that they would be accused of being underhanded and devious if they didn't explicitly say the brand was aimed at blacks, says the executive. In some of the Philadelphia areas to be tested, Reynolds was planning to sell Uptowns packed with their filters down, because Reynolds found that many blacks open cigarettes from the bottom, the executive says.

The company expected controversy from the Philadelphia test market, according to the executive, but it never anticipated the denunciation from Dr. Sullivan. "Uptown's message is more disease, more suffering, and more death for a group already bearing more than its share of smoking-related illness and mortality," Dr. Sullivan said, in a speech at University of Pennsylvania last week.

Dr. Sullivan signaled that he is prepared to take a leading role in the fight against smoking. Dr. Sullivan has long opposed smoking and his criticism of the Uptown cigarette also fits in with his goal of promoting health among minority groups.

His actions also illustrated a more aggressive approach against smoking. Scott Ballin, a vice president of the American Heart Association, said last week that Dr. Sullivan's attack is the strongest he can remember by a public official against a specific cigarette company. He said the "harsh letter" the HHS chief sent to R. J. Reynolds is symptomatic of the tougher tactics that smoking opponents are using against the tobacco industry. "Finally, we're beginning to beat them at their own game," he said.

Dr. Sullivan said he was "elated" at the RJR decision to cancel Uptown. "I would hope this spells the end of Uptown," he added.

A spokesman for HHS said that Dr. Sullivan's criticism of Uptown didn't presage a campaign against any other brands. But he did say that Dr. Sullivan intended to press an anti-smoking message in the black community. The spokesman said that Dr. Sullivan was especially cheered that local groups in Philadelphia, where Uptown was to have been test marketed, had opposed the cigarette. Dr. Sullivan hopes other community groups around the country begin anti-smoking campaigns, the spokesman added.

The spokesman added that this was the first time a secretary of HHS had ever singled out a cigarette brand for criticism.

The proposal by Dr. Sullivan wasn't discussed by the senior White House staff, nor was the proposal sent to President Bush, according to a senior White House official. "This was Sullivan's baby," he said, adding that there hasn't been any criticism of the secretary for his decision, either beforehand or afterward.

The Uptown dispute fits a pattern of growing resistance to smoking, making it increasingly difficult for politicians to defend the tobacco industry. Last year, Congress banned smoking on most domestic airline flights and among pending anti-smoking legislation is a broad proposal by Sen. Edward Kennedy (Democrat, Mass.). The bill would give the federal government authority to regulate the additives in cigarettes and the way tobacco products are labeled. Among its provisions, the bill would prevent companies from sponsoring sporting events in the name of a tobacco product, blocking such events as the Virginia Slims tennis tournaments sponsored by Philip Morris.

3.6.4 MAKING A PHONE CALL MIGHT MEAN TELLING THE WORLD ABOUT YOU*

Number identification service is a dream for marketers but a threat to privacy

Whether you like it or not, they've got your number:

American Express. J. C. Penney. Various oil companies. Insurance salesmen. Mail-order catalogs. Stockbrokers. People selling magazines. Banks. Bill collectors. Fund-raisers. Even your nosiest neighbors.

Now they can know it is you who is calling—often even before they answer the phone. Many companies automatically take down the caller's phone number for future marketing purposes. Across the country, American Telephone & Telegraph, MCI Communications, and US Sprint Communications are offering business customers a new service, known as automatic number identification, that renders up callers' phone numbers. The seven regional Bell companies are pushing automatic number identification for local calls. Buyers of the service can trace incoming calls, and much faster than the police used to do it in the movies.

Using a computer match-up with a customer list or some other data base, number-identification helps retrieve and display the name and address of the caller—and perhaps also the caller's credit history, income, marital status, number of children, you name it.

Faster Service

When the phone rings at certain J. C. Penney catalog offices, for instance, callers immediately are known by their phone number and are instantly identified with detailed account information on a service representative's computer screen. J. C. Penney says the technology affords faster service to customers and reduces Penney's very big phone bill.

In Red Bank, New Jersey, Florence Bahr rigged up her telephone with a black speaker

* By Mary Lu Carnevale and Julie Amparano Lopez, staff reporters of *The Wall Street Journal*, November 28, 1989. Reprinted by permission of *The Wall Street Journal*. © 1990 Dow Jones & Company, Inc. All Rights Reserved Worldwide.

the size of a paperback book; the gizmo, being tested by Bell Communications Research, identifies and announces the name of each caller a split second after the phone rings. Ms. Bahr, a real estate agent, says she likes to amaze her friends by greeting them by name. "They ask, 'How did you know it was me?' " she says. "I usually just say I was thinking about them."

A cream-colored plastic device sold by Bell Atlantic and also available in electronics stores stands sentinel next to florist Daniel Dachille's telephone. By flashing his callers' phone numbers, much as a paging device might do, the gadget helps Mr. Dachille spot credit-card fraud (because it reveals the calling number) and guard against nosy rivals. "I can tell when it's my competitors calling to check on my prices," says the owner of La Rose Florist in North Bergen, New Jersey.

Endangering a Life

Eileen Hahm is one person, however, who regards the new call-tracing services as a threat to her life. The New Jersey social worker counsels disturbed patients, some of whom are violent. She does not want to call a client and, by doing so, divulge her unlisted home phone number.

The call-tracing services are certain to change the way consumers and businesses regard their telephones. One calling from home no longer has any way to preserve his anonymity, no way to make an anonymous call to the police or the child-abuse hot line, no way to escape the embrace of aggressive salesmen. On the other hand, the services can safeguard one from heavy breathers, obscene callers, and total strangers making cold-calls at the dinner hour to pitch investment opportunities. If you don't recognize the number (or perhaps if you do), you don't have to answer. So this new privacy-invader is two-edged, a mixed blessing.

The potential for abuse, however, feeds debate over telephones and privacy rights. At the heart of it is this question: Does a public utility—the phone company—have the right to release phone numbers, particularly unlisted ones, to individuals and institutions willing to pay a fee for the information?

Of Computers and Glass Houses

"We'll be living in a glass house," says Gary T. Marx, a professor of sociology at Massachusetts Institute of Technology, when businesses "can find out where we live and who we are just because we made a simple call seeking information."

Hundreds of businesses across the nation already have been paying long-distance companies for computerized phone listings of everyone who calls their 800 or 900 numbers. Each month, the phone companies deliver the lists on tape, which can be loaded into a company's computer and matched with other information at hand in a data bank.

USA Today, for example, uses the computer-tape service on its national weather hot line. As it is giving callers a weather report, the newspaper also surreptitiously records their phone numbers for possible marketing use.

American Express service representatives use an AT&T number-tracing system in order to provide faster service. When an American Express Card customer calls about his account, a service representative usually has the client's name and account information up on a video screen before even answering the phone.

For a short time, American Express would answer the phone by greeting customers by name. But that practice spooked so many people it was stopped.

For big companies that get millions of customer calls a year on their 800 lines, number identification can reduce costs and help them do better by their clientele. A caller to Goodyear's 800 line who is looking for the nearest tire dealer, for instance, gets an answer within seconds. The company that answers Goodyear's phone, AT&T's American Transtech telemarketing unit, has been testing a system that captures the caller's number and matches it with the nearest retail outlet for this or that consumer product.

The system is said to pare 12 seconds from the average call and thereby save a company 3.6 cents. Agents are able to field about 7 percent more calls, according to Todd Stephenson, an American Transtech manager. A company that gets a million calls a month, he figures, could save about $432,000 in phone charges a year.

Big businesses obviously aren't the only ones intrigued by the possibilities. Residential and small-business customers have their own reasons to want to know, when the phone rings, who is on the line. The Bell companies have a service to sell them, too, but just for local calls. Using a small device like Mr. Dachille's or direct transmission into a company's own telephone system, the Baby Bells can show where the call is coming from, though they can't display calls from outside the region. New Jersey Bell undertook the first local test a year ago and is now rolling out the service throughout the state.

An Answering Service

In addition to displaying callers' numbers, the Bell companies' Caller I.D. box also can store up to 64 phone numbers. With the push of one button, the client gets the machine to flash the phone numbers of everybody who has called while he was out. Sharon T. Moran, the owner of a small apparel business in New Jersey, says that feature can be extremely helpful when callers don't leave a message on her answering machine, which many people are averse to doing.

"If people call after hours and don't leave a message, I can call them back and see what they needed," she explains. "Every time someone hangs up on my machine, I can't help but think, 'There goes business.' "

Even so, she admits, calling people out of the blue who don't know that you know they phoned you can create some bad feeling. Callers who didn't leave a message or a return number aren't always all that pleased with a call-back. Indeed, they sometimes are shocked, embarrassed even, to hear from Ms. Moran. "They couldn't understand how I knew they had called," she says. "When I explained, they were ashamed because they had hung up."

Forward behavior of this sort, she says, has warded away some business. "I've learned not to push. If they say they didn't call me, I apologize and hang up," she explains. "But at least *I know* who has called me."

Data Galore

Once a person or company has possession of a name and address, hundreds of data banks can be drawn on for demographic information, a credit history, mortgage figures, police records and other salient facts. So a company with this new technology—and some good data banks—could match a person's phone number with the story of his life—although most marketers are thrilled merely to have a name and address.

Telematch, a division of Times Journal Company in Springfield, Virginia, says major retailers, credit-card companies, and fund-raisers are particularly keen to pair phone numbers with names and addresses. "People are just beginning to identify all the applications," says Ruth Baker, a Telematch sales executive. Marketers, she says, want to pinpoint potential customers so they don't end up "sending lawnmower ads to apartment dwellers or trying to sell tractors to people who live in the city."

With nothing to go on but a reporter's home phone number, the Telematch computer swiftly spits out her husband's name, address, and the fact that they live in a single-family home in a city neighborhood where household incomes generally exceed $55,700.

Acutely aware of the privacy issue, Ms. Baker stresses that only listed numbers are matched and that the stuff is hardly intimate. "Privacy becomes an issue when you start coming up with more specific information, such as credit history or exact household income," she argues.

Brian Rivette, the director of marketing for Call Interactive, an American Express–AT&T telemarketing partnership whose customers include the cable television rock-music channel MTV, says, "Getting the basic information—the name and address—is what's most important to sponsors."

Omaha-based Call Interactive has been working on number ID technology both to speed calls and to tailor-make recorded messages for its customers' 800 and 900 hot lines. With its data base and your seven digits, the service knows what car you own and the names and addresses of your nine closest neighbors, if not friends.

"From a marketing standpoint, the service is phenomenal because it can link and fine-tune data bases," says H. Skip Weitzen, a consultant who teaches business courses at the University of Maryland. "The frightening part is that consumers don't know their personal information is being collected, sorted, stored, and sold." Perhaps they soon will.

Indeed, J. C. Penney acknowledges that it doesn't make a point of telling people it has their number. A spokesman says the company doesn't want to make customers uncomfortable or to distort the testing of its systems. Besides, J. C. Penney, unlike some companies, doesn't sell the information it gathers about its customers.

Into the Bargain

Despite assurances from phone companies and enthusiasts of call-tracing that they won't abuse their powers, some people do object. Edward Martone, the executive director of the American Civil Liberties Union of New Jersey, fears that consumers will be misled into believing they are getting free information on the weather, stocks, or consumer goods when, in fact, they are giving more than they are getting, certainly more than they have bargained for. "These phone numbers will just be a front," warns Mr. Martone.

Indeed, Ms. Hahm, the New Jersey social worker with the unlisted home phone number, says that since the service was introduced in her area six months ago, she has noticed a marked increase in phone solicitations. "This is a clear example of technology gone mad," she says. "It really stinks."

But phone calls from fund-raisers and hucksters are the least of her worries. Because she works with mentally disturbed patients and domestic-violence cases, she is concerned about her very safety. Recently she phoned a client from her home and was shocked to have the woman return the call though she hadn't left her number. She never leaves a number, as a precaution against menacing and obscene calls. It is bad enough, she says, that clients have called her at work, threatening to kill her. Now they can get her at home.

And short of making night calls from phone booths, there is not much she can do to prevent it. Paying extra for an unlisted number doesn't buy her protection. "Do I not have any rights?" she asks.

Not in New Jersey, not in this regard. Ms. Hahm has complained to the state's Public Utilities Commission and to New Jersey Bell, which is part of Bell Atlantic Corporation. But both say there's nothing they can do to help her.

A Boon to Some

Of course, call-tracing offers a measure of protection from harassment and strangers talking dirty. But consumer activists don't buy the line. They argue that phone customers should have the right to keep their numbers from being recorded if they wish. And if they can't prevent it, the consumerists say, the telephone company should be obliged to provide the caller with a short warning message that his number is about to be given out.

New Jersey Bell maintains that blocking would ruin the service and kill the business. And state regulators concluded that protections, even for the 25 percent of phone customers who pay extra for unlisted numbers, are uncalled for.

As telephone companies seek to introduce call-tracing in other states, similar fights are brewing between consumer groups and phone companies. In Pennsylvania, Bell of Pennsylvania and regulators have been debating the matter.

The state's Public Utilities Commission staff vehemently opposed call-tracing and in September issued a 123-page recommendation against it, claiming it would violate Pennsylvania's wiretap laws, which forbid telephone trap-and-trace devices and the interception of wire or oral communications. Despite the urgings of its staff, the commission earlier this month approved the phone company's plan to offer its Caller I.D. service.

Still, some people—individuals, not consumer advocates—believe in call-tracing as a protector of their privacy and something of a friend. Paul Gibbons of North Bergen, New Jersey, uses the service to screen his calls when he is relaxing at home. "If I don't recognize a phone number, I let my answering machine pick it up so I can decide later whether I want to talk," says Mr. Gibbons, a 37-year-old shop owner. "I value my free time."

Capt. Earl Stutzman of the Westfield, New Jersey, police department says a number identification system that gives dispatchers not just the phone number but the address of the caller speeds response time and saves lives. "Not long ago, a woman who had ingested a large amount of pills called us." he recalls. "She was incoherent. But we had her address and were able to send a police car and an ambulance."

3.6.5 FOR THESE MBAs, CLASS BECAME EXERCISE IN CORPORATE ESPIONAGE*

Graduate students in Professor Terry Wilson's Marketing 321 class got a first-hand look last year at the cutthroat competitive world of business.

The West Virginia University students engaged in what one terms "industrial espionage." They swallowed ethical concerns, misled companies by telling half-truths, and, for their efforts, got passing grades in the course. "It makes me shudder to think about it," says Mark Wheatley, one of the students.

The tale of Marketing 321 is an extreme example of what can go wrong when business schools go to work for corporate America. In general, educators praise the growing bond between the two worlds. But, they say, it's all too easy for faculty and students to confuse the real-world goals of big business with the more rarefied aims of academia.

Columbia and Edelman

Indeed, the problems of collaboration are being seen with increasing frequency. At Columbia University, corporate raider (and adjunct professor) Asher Edelman last fall offered $100,000 to any business student in his class who could provide him with information leading to a successful takeover. According to Columbia, cash incentives are inappropriate in a learning environment, and it rescinded his offer.

In another instance, Eastman Kodak Company got the University of Rochester to bar the enrollment of an employee from Fuji Photo Film, Inc., a Kodak rival. The university rein-

* By Clare Ansberry, staff reporter of *The Wall Street Journal*, March 22, 1988. Reprinted by permission of *The Wall Street Journal*. © 1990 Dow Jones & Company, Inc. All Rights Reserved Worldwide.

vited the student but only after its actions became publicly known.

To critics, the problem is largely one of balance. "There's an increasing school of thought that universities should serve the corporation," says Leonard Minsky, director of the National Coalition for Universities in the Public Interest. That, he says, is worrisome: "If the ethics of the corporation become the ethics of the universities, then we're really in trouble."

Even now, university business programs "walk a lot thinner line regarding ethics than they used to," says Charles Hickman, director of projects and member services for the American Assembly of Collegiate Schools of Business.

But in the case at West Virginia University's College of Business and Economics, the students not only walked the line. They jumped over it.

In theory, Marketing 321 is typical business school fare. The class calls for master's degree candidates to go into the field and work for real clients, applying marketing concepts learned in earlier courses. Usually the end results are highly speculative, and for most of Professor Wilson's students, that was the case. But not for the two groups who conducted research on behalf of two Caterpillar heavy-equipment dealerships—H. O. Penn Machinery Company in Armonk, New York, and Yancey Bros. in Atlanta, Georgia.

These dealerships wanted the students to conduct competitive analyses on actual competitors. The dealers provided names of competitors and even suggested what questions to ask.

"I thought I was doing them a favor," says Milton Long, marketing manager of the H. O. Penn dealership. His group of four students, he says, was "ill-prepared" to act without his advice. So advise them he did.

And the students delivered. They were able to obtain and analyze information on competitors' inventory levels, sales volumes, advertising expenditures, and even potential new product introductions.

Indeed, the competitors were surprisingly candid. And why not? The students never mentioned their Caterpillar connections. They identified themselves only as university students working on a class project and, when corresponding with the dealers, used university marketing department stationery.

Says Mr. Wheatley, who worked for H. O. Penn: "We were really telling half-truths."

Professor Wilson says he told his class he had just two rules: no invading privacy and no lying. "If [competitors] asked, they should be told about the client," he recalls instructing his students. But since that situation never arose, Professor Wilson feels none of his students actually lied. They just kept to themselves information not asked for directly. It is, he says, the smart thing to do: "If [a dealer's competitors] know you work for a specific client, they give specific answers. It biases answers."

Exactly, says Alan Stith, senior vice president of Atlanta-based Stith Equipment Company, one of Yancey Bros.' surveyed competitors. And, unlike Professor Wilson, he's concerned about it. People let their guard down when dealing with students, he says, making them perfect "disguises" for information-hungry clients. "That's not ethical in my mind," he says.

Some students agree. "I felt kind of like, 'Gee, we're out here spying,'" says Herman Flinder, who worked for H. O. Penn.

Some even received little gifts—pocket calendars and toy replicas of heavy equipment—from the dealers. "It was bad enough to be doing what we were doing," says one of the five students on the Yancey project. "But when they started passing out gifts, I felt lower and lower."

Even so, they kept on doing as bid. One reason: Professor Wilson had a consulting agreement with Caterpillar and the students assumed, if they didn't deliver what the dealers requested, they might get in dutch with their professor. As Mr. Wheatley puts it: "We weren't worried about ethical issues. We were worried about getting through the course."

But none of the students ever discussed the consultancy issue with Professor Wilson. And Professor Wilson maintains that his work for Caterpillar was unrelated to his students' work for its dealers.

Once the students finished getting the information, they had to consider the issue of naming names.

In the Yancey Bros. project, dealers got confidentiality only if they requested it—and few did. "They thought only the professor would see it," says one student. "They had no idea what was going on."

Yancey Bros. spokesman Goodloe Yancey IV says if the students did anything unethical, he didn't know about it nor would he have condoned it.

In the H. O. Penn project, the competitors were promised confidentiality whether they asked for it or not. "Your name and company will remain anonymous. The results of your survey will be combined with other results to generate a profile of heavy equipment dealers and distributors in your area," a letter to them said.

Yet the results were kept anything but confidential. One student, Donna Buntack, says she tried to protect the competitors' identities by referring to them as A, B, C, and so on in the final written report. But, following an oral presentation to H. O. Penn, she and the rest of her group provided the names. They say their client left them little choice. "There was pressure and we succumbed," says Mr. Wheatley.

Penn's Mr. Long denies pressuring the students or receiving competitors' names.

Professor Wilson says his students should not have divulged confidential information to their clients. He also says that, as graduate students, they should have known better: "They'll be facing these issues every day in their career. They have to learn to deal with them. I tell them to think through the trade-offs."

Proprietary Information?

Still, Professor Wilson says, the information the students got wasn't proprietary. His final assessment: no harm done.

But that's not the assessment of Gary Clark, an executive vice president of W. I. Clark Company in Wallingford, Connecticut, and one of H. O. Penn's competitors.

He says some of his answers could have been obtained through normal channels. But not all. For example, the inventory levels of new, rented, and used pieces of equipment isn't readily available, nor is his projected increase in business. Says Mr. Clark: "I wouldn't give out that type of stuff if I knew it was going to someone other than students."

Professor Wilson, after being questioned about the class project by this newspaper, says students no longer will undertake outside business projects for his class—even though he insists neither he nor his charges did anything improper.

Cyril M. Logar, dean of the university's College of Business and Economics, says he plans to meet with his executive committee to discuss the ethics issue.

And what do the students in the class think of the entire experience? Despite some misgivings, Mr. Flinder says he found the project worthwhile. It expanded his understanding of how business actually works. "You learn," he says, "that the boss has the final say in everything, that you get things done or forget it."

Corporate Policy and the Ethics of Competitor Intelligence Gathering*

Lynn Sharp Paine

Top management's ethical leadership role requires continuing attention to the changing nature of the marketplace. New businesses and business practices often raise novel ethical questions and introduce new areas of ethical vulnerability. Interpreting or reinterpreting ethical standards in light of the changing business environment, alerting employees to the new ethical issues and pressures they may face, and providing guidance and institutional structures that support appropriate responses are important aspects of managers' role.

The purpose of this chapter is to highlight the need for management to address the ethics of competitor intelligence gathering. Recent developments in the business environment have generated increasing interest in competitor intelligence, information that helps managers understand their competitors. Although information about rival firms has always been a valued and sought after commodity, competitor intelligence gathering only recently has begun to be systematized and legitimated as a business function. While understanding the competition is an important part of running a business, there are ethical limits: on the types of competitor information that may be acquired, on the methods that may be employed to acquire it, and on the purposes for which it may be used. To date, however, few managers or management educators have addressed the ethics of intelligence gathering.

* An earlier version of this paper was presented at the European Business Ethics Network conference held in Barcelona in September 1989. The author, Associate Professor at Harvard Business School, is grateful to members of that group for their criticisms and suggestions. She also wishes to thank Professor J. Ron Fox for his detailed comments on a version of the paper and Gary Edwards, executive director of The Ethics Resource Center, for discussions of intelligence-gathering practices and for making the center's resources available for research. In addition, the staff at the Defense Industry Initiative Clearing House were most helpful.

This chapter will focus primarily on methods of acquiring competitor information. Separating legitimate from illegitimate approaches to information acquisition is, in practice, the central ethical issue for intelligence-gathering specialists. Although important questions surround the issue of what types of information, if any, should be treated as private or confidential to a firm, and thus off-limits for intelligence gatherers, these questions can in practice be minimized, though not eliminated, by respecting certain ethical principles in the selection of acquisition techniques. By examining some questionable but commonly used intelligence-gathering practices, this chapter will identify the ethical principles at issue, discuss the risks of failure to respect these principles, and suggest steps managers can take to encourage ethically sound intelligence-gathering activities.

GROWTH OF COMPETITOR INTELLIGENCE GATHERING

Evidence of the growth of interest in competitor intelligence is abundant. A 1985 study, which looked at the intelligence-gathering budgets of 25 Fortune 500 companies, found that all had increased substantially over the preceding five-year period.[1] Five years earlier, one third of the companies had not had intelligence-gathering departments at all. Respondents to a 1986 study of 50 firms anticipated a dramatic increase in their intelligence-gathering budgets and almost all foresaw rapid growth in the staff assigned to intelligence gathering over the succeeding five-year period.[2] The findings of a recent Conference Board study of more than 300 U.S. firms were similar. Nearly all respondents said that monitoring competitors' activities is important, and more than two thirds expect their monitoring efforts to increase.[3] The trend is not confined to the United States. British companies, too, are increasingly setting up systems to collect competitor intelligence.[4] The Japanese reputation for careful intelligence gathering is well-established.

In-house formalization of the intelligence-gathering function has been accompanied by the growth of consulting firms specializing in competitor information collection.[5] Some consultants have prospered by offering seminars for employees of smaller companies that cannot afford separate intelligence-

---

[1] Information Data Search, Inc., *Corporate Intelligence Gathering, 1985 and 1986 Surveys* (Cambridge, Mass., 1986), p. 24.

[2] Ibid., p. 6.

[3] Howard Sutton, *Competitive Intelligence*, Conference Board Report no. 913 (New York: The Conference Board, 1988), pp. 6–7.

[4] "Competitor Intelligence: Present & Growing in UK," *The Fuld & Company Letter*, Summer 1989, p. 1.

[5] Elizabeth Tucker, "Corporate Gumshoes Spy on Competitors," *Washington Post*, March 30, 1986, p. F1.

gathering departments.[6] Data bases, newsletters, and self-help books have proliferated as well. National membership in the Society of Competitor Intelligence Professionals has grown to nearly 900 in its first three years.[7]

Although the value of competitor intelligence has long been appreciated, it appears that systematic efforts of collection are on the increase.[8] This is understandable, given the sheer proliferation of available information and the advantages that can flow from knowing what rivals are up to.[9] Knowledge about rival firms' strategies, research and development efforts, products, customers, expansion plans, work force, costs, pricing, and so on can translate into competitive advantages for the short if not the long term.[10]

THE DARKER SIDE

There is, however, a darker side to the growth of intelligence gathering. It is reflected in the use of ethically questionable techniques for collecting information, the increase in trade secret litigation and information crimes, and the increase in the resources devoted to corporate security. One expert on trade secret law estimates that court rulings on theft and misappropriation of information have increased fourfold over the past decade to more than 200 a year, and that the actual problem of information misappropriation is at least 10 times as large.[11] Another reports a surge in information crimes.[12] The American Society for Industrial Security, which includes both outside consultants and in-house security groups, was reported in 1986 to have 24,000 members and to be gaining 5,000 new members a year.[13]

Explanations for the increase in information disputes are varied. Some commentators point to the rising costs of research and development associated with today's advanced technology. It is simply cheaper to get ideas from a

---

[6] Small firm interest in competitor intelligence is described in Mark Robichaux, " 'Competitor Intelligence': A Grapevine to Rivals' Secrets," *The Wall Street Journal*, April 12, 1989, p. B2.

[7] Information provided by the Society of Competitor Intelligence Professionals in Washington, D.C.

[8] The current growth of interest appears to be the continuation of a trend. See Jerry L. Wall, "What the Competition Is Doing: Your Need to Know," *Harvard Business Review*, November–December 1974, p. 22.

[9] Intelligence-gathering stories with happy endings can be found in many news articles. See, for example, Brian Dumaine, "Corporate Spies Snoop to Conquer," *Fortune*, November 7, 1988, p. 68.

[10] The 1988 Conference Board study reports the types of competitor information considered most useful by executives. Sutton, *Competitive Intelligence*, p. 16.

[11] Roger Milgrim quoted in "Information Thieves Are Now Corporate Enemy No. 1," *BusinessWeek*, May 5, 1986, p. 120.

[12] The surge in information crimes is noted by Donn B. Parker of SRI International as reported in "Information Thieves," ibid.

[13] Alan D. Haas, "Corporate Cloak and Dagger," *Amtrak Express*, October/November 1986, pp. 19–20.

competitor than to invest in research.[14] Other commentators point to the inadequacy of law in the face of advancing technology: the law is just not keeping up.[15] Still others suggest that the increase in information disputes is simply a reflection of the sheer increase in the volume of information now available through information technology. While there may be some truth to all these explanations, it is doubtful that all the turmoil can be laid at the door of developing technology. Many well-documented information disputes have arisen over questionable intelligence-gathering practices unrelated to modern information technology in industries that are decidedly low-tech. Trash surveillance in the casket industry,[16] cookie recipe espionage in the food industry,[17] and employee piracy in the car rental business,[18] for example, have all given rise to information litigation.

Moreover, a close look at information quarrels in high-technology industries shows that they frequently involve intelligence about marketing strategies or costs and pricing, rather than new technologies. Charges that resulted from the "Ill Wind" investigations of the defense industry, for instance, center on the bribery of public officials to obtain information about competitors' bids.[19] Similarly, marketing information was at issue in the dispute that arose when an advertising agency seeking the business of software manufacturer MicroSoft hired account executives who had worked on the account of MicroSoft's main rival, Lotus Development Corporation, at a competing agency. In a letter to MicroSoft, the agency touted its access to information about Lotus: "You see, the reason we know so much about Lotus is that some of our newest employees just spent the past year and a half working on the Lotus business at another agency. So they are intimately acquainted with Lotus's thoughts about MicroSoft."[20]

These examples, and others described in the press and recent court decisions, show that the increase in information litigation cannot be explained solely by

---

[14] See judge's introductory comments in *Fortune Personnel Agency of Ft. Lauderdale, Inc.*, v. *Sun Tech, Inc., of South Florida*, 423 So. 2d 545 (Fla. Dist. Ct. App. 1982): "As the cost of research and development increase the theft of trade secrets becomes a lucrative, although somewhat immoral, alternative to the expenditure of one's own funds."

[15] See, for example, "Information Thieves," p. 120.

[16] Robert Johnson, "The Case of Marc Feith Shows Corporate Spies Aren't Just High-Tech," *The Wall Street Journal*, January 9, 1987, p. 1.

[17] Nabisco, Keebler, and Frito-Lay were all accused of stealing cookie secrets from Procter & Gamble's Duncan Hines. J. Neiman, "Cookie Makers Deny Swiping P&G Secrets," *Advertising Age*, June 25, 1984, p. 2.

[18] A dispute between Hertz and Avis arose when the president of Hertz departed to become head of Avis. See Tamar Lewin, "Putting a Lid on Corporate Secrets," *New York Times*, April 1, 1984, sec. 3 front page.

[19] Tim Carrington and Edward T. Pound, "Pushing Defense Firms to Compete, Pentagon Harms Buying System," *The Wall Street Journal*, June 27, 1988, p. 1.

[20] Quoted in Gary Putka, "Lotus Gets Order Barring Ad Agency from Telling Secrets," *The Wall Street Journal*, December 14, 1987, p. 16. See also Cleveland Horton, "Ethics at Issue in Lotus Case," *Advertising Age*, December 21, 1987, p. 6; and Chapter 7.4, Rossin Greenberg Seronick and Hill (A).

increasingly complex and costly technology. The increase also reflects growing use of questionable techniques to gain access to ordinary business information generated by or about competing firms. The use of these techniques may evidence a general decline in ethical standards or a decline in resourcefulness and creativity. It may also be a by-product of increased competition and the competitor orientation of current thinking about business strategy.[21]

ETHICS AND THE COMPETITOR ORIENTATION OF STRATEGY

Within the competitive strategy framework, competitor information and analysis are essential to strategy formulation. There is nothing inherently wrong with such an approach to business strategy. Indeed, much can be said for it from the point of view of efficiency. However, the approach raises broad ethical questions about ideals of competition and the spirit in which it is undertaken, as well as more specific questions about the methods and limits of information acquisition.

Traditionally, the highest and best form of competition was thought to reflect a striving for excellence by each competitor. Interfering with a rival's efforts, or even taking advantage of his or her weaknesses, was regarded as a departure from this ideal. Motivated by a vision of excellence, each competitor was thought to be engaged in an independent, constructive, and positive effort to attain the objective in question. As Adam Smith said, "In the race for wealth . . . [a person] may run as hard as he can, and strain every nerve and every muscle, in order to outstrip all his competitors. But if he should jostle, or throw down any of them . . . it is a violation of fair play."[22] The traditional view is reflected in the common law of unfair competition and in antitrust law, both of which prohibit certain business tactics whose motive is to drive out competition.

The traditional ideal recognizes a fine but important distinction between using competitor information constructively to guide strategy formulation and using it destructively to undo the competition. This distinction is largely a matter of the attitude or spirit in which economic rivalry is undertaken, rather than its results. Contrary to the traditional ideal, much current thinking recommends explicit consideration of how best to undermine the competition. Some of the tactics recommended by competitive strategy specialists directly conflict with the ideal and would very likely violate competition law.[23]

---

[21] See, for example, Michael Porter, *Competitive Advantage: Creating and Sustaining Superior Performance* (New York: Free Press, 1985).

[22] Adam Smith, *The Theory of Moral Sentiments*, II.ii.2.2, first published 1759 (p. 83 in 1976 Oxford University Press edition).

[23] The antitrust law implications of tactics recommended by Porter in his *Competitive Strategy* and *Competitive Advantage* are discussed in Vance H. Fried and Benjamin M. Oviatt, "Michael Porter's Missing Chapter: The Risk of Antitrust Violations," *The Academy of Management EXECUTIVE* 3, no. 1 (1989), pp. 49–56.

To the extent that firms adopt the competitor orientation of current thinking about strategy, their need for information about their competitors increases. Along with new incentives for employees to gather competitor information come new pressures and opportunities for unethical conduct. As competitor analysis becomes the order of the day and the premium on competitor information rises, management can expect the use of questionable intelligence-gathering tactics to spread unless ethical limits are articulated and widely understood.

QUESTIONABLE METHODS OF ACQUIRING INTELLIGENCE

While surveys have examined people's willingness to engage in specific questionable practices, and at least one author has provided a list of ethical and unethical intelligence-gathering techniques, the ethical principles at issue in this area generally have not been made explicit.[24] However, a review of studies of questionable practices, judicial opinions, news reports, popular articles, and the writings of intelligence-gathering experts reveals that the most prevalent methods of questionable intelligence gathering fall into three broad ethical categories:

- Those involving deceit or some form of misrepresentation.

- Those involving attempts to influence the judgment of persons entrusted with confidential information, particularly the offering of inducements to reveal information.

- Those involving covert or unconsented-to surveillance.

Norms prohibiting practices in these categories appear to be weaker than norms prohibiting theft of documents and other tangible property—a fourth category of ethically problematic intelligence gathering.

In contrast to intelligence gathering relying on information that firms have disclosed to public authorities or to the general public, or which is available through open and aboveboard inquiry, questionable techniques are generally employed to obtain information that the firm has not disclosed, is not obligated to disclose, and probably would not be willing to disclose publicly. But most of these techniques would be objectionable—whatever type of information they elicited—because they offend common standards of morality calling for honesty, respect for relationships of trust and confidence, and respect for privacy. While stating these principles does not resolve difficult and disputed questions concerning their interpretation and application, some of which are discussed

---

[24] For lists of ethical and unethical techniques, see William Johnson and Jack Maguire, *Who's Stealing Your Business?: How to Identify and Prevent Business Espionage* (New York: AMACOM, 1988), pp. 12–15.

below, understanding the principles can contribute to clearer thinking about the factors distinguishing legitimate from illegitimate practice. Several indicators point to the use of techniques that violate or call into question these principles.

Misrepresentation

Opinion research indicates that many employees say their companies condone, and they themselves approve of, the use of various forms of misrepresentation to gather competitor intelligence.[25] For example, 45.9 percent of the respondents to a questionnaire administered to 451 participants in seminars on intelligence gathering approved of getting information by posing as a graduate student working on a thesis.[26] A striking 85.6 percent of the respondents believe their competitors would use this method of intelligence gathering.

The same study found that 46.8 percent felt comfortable posing as a private research firm, and that 38.4 percent approved of posing as a job-seeking college student. The study showed a close correspondence between respondents' level of approval for various practices and their perceptions of their employers' approval. The study concluded that practitioners seem to align their views of what is acceptable with what they perceive to be company standards, although the authors were not sure who influenced whom.[27]

The use of misrepresentation can take many forms: conducting phony job interviews,[28] hiring students to gather intelligence under the guise of doing academic work,[29] posing as a potential joint venturer, supplier, or customer.[30] The prevalence of phony interviews has led at least one marketing manager to remind his people that "a job interview may be a total sham, a way to get intelligence."[31] The victims of deceit may be rival firms, themselves, their suppliers and customers, or other parties with access to valuable information.

In a recently litigated case, a marketing manager and his firm were found liable for damages incurred by a competitor that had revealed confidential information to the manager and another employee when they posed as a po-

---

[25] William Cohen and Helena Czepiec, "The Role of Ethics in Gathering Corporate Intelligence," *Journal of Business Ethics* 7 (1988), pp. 199–203.

[26] Ibid., pp. 200–1.

[27] Ibid., p. 202.

[28] Steven Flax, "How to Snoop on Your Competitors," *Fortune*, May 14, 1984, p. 31.

[29] Clare Ansberry, "For These M.B.A.'s Class Became Exercise in Corporate Espionage," *The Wall Street Journal*, March 22, 1988, p. 37. (Reprinted in Chapter 3.6.)

[30] In a 1987 lawsuit, Service Corporation International alleged that Hillenbrand Industries had posed as a prospective supplier in order to deceive Service Corporation into divulging confidential information. "Service Corp. Is Suing Hillenbrand, Alleges Theft of Trade Secrets," *The Wall Street Journal*, March 4, 1987, p. 7.

[31] Sutton, *Competitive Intelligence*, p. 15.

tential customer.[32] The marketing manager, whose branch office was failing to meet its sales quotas and who personally was failing to meet his own quotas, arranged to have a new-hire who had not yet joined the firm pose as a potential customer for the competitor's software. The manager attended the software presentation as a friend and consultant of the supposed customer, but without identifying himself or his employer. As a result of the misrepresentation, the pair had been given a detailed demonstration of the software, in-depth answers to their questions, and access to the competitor's sales manual. They made unauthorized copies of critical information in the manual and successfully developed a competitive software program within a short time. In testimony reported in the court's opinion, the marketing manager referred to himself as a "scoundrel," but explained that market pressures had led him to this tactic.

Improper Influence

A second category of questionable techniques centers on attempting to influence potential informants in ways that undermine their judgment or sense of obligation to protect confidentiality or to act in their employer's best interests. Frequently, the attempt involves offering inducements or the possibility of certain advantages to those who may be able to provide valuable information. In its crudest form, this technique is bribery, the offering of something of value in exchange for the breach of a fiduciary duty. In the recent Pentagon scandals, consultants to defense contractors offered large sums of money to government officials in exchange for revealing information they, as fiduciaries, were legally obliged to protect. In more subtle cases not involving legal obligations of confidentiality, the inducement may work to compromise the potential informant's judgment. The source may decide to reveal information that is not, strictly speaking, confidential, but whose revelation is contrary to the employer's interests.

The inducement to disclose need not be cash, it may be a better job. The hiring of a rival's employee to gain access to confidential information appears to be a widely used and approved intelligence-gathering technique. Surveys conducted in 1974, 1976, and 1988 all found that many executives would use the practice.[33] Fifty-one percent of the smaller companies and 37 percent of the larger ones surveyed in 1974 said they expected employees hired from

---

[32] *Continental Data Systems, Inc.,* v. *Exxon Corporation,* 638 F. Supp. 432 (E.D. Pa. 1986). In addition to actual damages, the court awarded the competitor punitive damages. The court found that it would be unfair to permit the firm to use its formal written "policies" to avoid corporate liability where the evidence allowed the jury to infer that these formal "policies" were not the actual operational understanding at the branch in question.

[33] Wall, "What the Competition Is Doing," pp. 32–34; Steven N. Brenner and Earl A. Molander, "Is the Ethics of Business Changing?" *Harvard Business Review,* January–February 1977, p. 57; "Industry Ethics Are Alive," *Advertising Age,* April 18, 1988, p. 88.

competitors to contribute all they knew to the new job, including the competitor's trade secrets.[34] And the Conference Board found that nearly half the respondents to its 1988 survey regard former employees of competitors as a very or fairly important source of information.[35] About half the executives responding to the 1976 study said they would try to hire a rival's employee to learn about an important scientific discovery that could substantially reduce profits during the coming year.[36]

In 1988, *Advertising Age* asked its readers whether it was ethical to hire an account supervisor from a competitor to gain information about the competitor's client. Seventy-three percent of the 157 professionals responding—advertisers, agency personnel, media people, consultants, and "others"—said the practice was ethical.[37] The Center for Communications posed the same hypothetical question to professors and students of marketing. Fifty-nine percent of the 626 students responding said the practice was ethical, and 70 percent said they would do it.[38]

The hiring of employees with access to valuable competitor information has been the subject of numerous recent lawsuits and threatened lawsuits. When Wendy's International decided to substitute Coke products for Pepsi products in its restaurants, Pepsi threatened to sue Coke for pirating executives to gain information about Pepsi's contract and programs with Wendy's and for tampering with contractual relationships.[39] Similar issues have arisen in litigation between Johns-Manville and Guardian Industries,[40] Avis and Hertz,[41] and AT&T and MCI.[42]

Sometimes the inducement to reveal valuable information is not an actual job but the possibility of a job or some other commercial advantage. As reported in *Fortune*, Marriott recently hired a headhunter to gather competitor information from regional managers of five competing economy-hotel chains. The managers were told the truth: that no jobs were available at the time of the interview but that Marriott might have jobs in the future.[43]

These sorts of inducements are designed to give competitors' employees incentives to talk. Some of the more subtle uses of this technique do not introduce new incentives for disclosure but play on the existence of relation-

---

[34] Wall, "What the Competition Is Doing," p. 38.

[35] Sutton, *Competitive Intelligence*, p. 19.

[36] Brenner and Molander, "Is the Ethics of Business Changing?" p. 57.

[37] "Industry Ethics Are Alive."

[38] The results noted here are available from the Center for Communications, a nonprofit educational organization located in New York City.

[39] "Pepsi to Sue Coke over Wendy's," *Washington Post*, November 13, 1986, p. E1.

[40] *Johns-Manville Corp.* v. *Guardian Industries Corp.*, 586 F. Supp. 1034, 1075 (E.D. Mich. 1983), aff'd, 770 F.2d 178 (Fed. Cir. 1985).

[41] Lewin, "Putting a Lid on Corporate Secrets."

[42] "Information Thieves," pp. 122–23.

[43] Dumaine, "Corporate Spies Snoop to Conquer," p. 76. According to the article, Marriott eventually hired five or so of the competition's managers.

ships of dependence or on natural human propensities. Customers, for example, may be willing to reveal confidential information about a competitor to maintain an advantageous supply relationship. Conversely, a competitor's supplier may talk if he or she thinks it will lead to new business. A competitor's technical people may divulge sensitive information in the course of describing their achievements at scientific meetings, particularly if they are asked the right questions in the right way.[44] Plying a competitor's employee with drinks at a trade meeting, a technique approved of by nearly 60 percent of the respondents to a survey mentioned earlier, is yet another way of undermining the judgment of a potential source.[45]

These techniques are ethically problematic because they involve attempts to undermine relationships of trust and confidence. In many cases, the information-seeker deliberately creates a conflict of interest in hopes that self-interest will overcome the potential informant's sense of obligation to protect his employer's confidential information or to act on his behalf. One must assume that the offering of valuable inducements reflects the fact, or at least the information-seeker's belief, that the information is not publicly available and can only be acquired, or can be acquired more cheaply, by attempting to induce a breach of confidence or to otherwise influence the judgment of those acting on behalf of the rival firm.

Part of the effectiveness of these inducements is explained by employees' uncertainty about what information may and may not be disclosed. While most firms treat some information as freely available to the public and other information as strictly confidential, there is a great deal of information that could be quite valuable to a competitor and whose confidentiality status is ambiguous in the minds of many employees, suppliers, and customers. For example, a firm may regard certain information shared with a supplier as confidential, while the supplier sees it as public knowledge. The annals of trade secret litigation contain many examples of this sort of discrepancy. Indeed, there may be in-house discrepancies about what information is confidential and what may be revealed. The use of disclosure incentives in these cases may be the decisive influence tipping the potential informant's judgment in the direction of disclosure.

Ethical judgments about particular intelligence-gathering practices in this category are complicated by these same uncertainties. Still, legitimate questions about the scope of employees' obligations of confidentiality do not remove the moral difficulty that attaches to offering inducements deliberately intended to undermine a person's judgment or sense of obligation.

---

[44] These techniques are discussed in Flax, "How to Snoop on Your Competitors," p. 31.

[45] Cohen and Czepiec, "The Role of Ethics in Gathering Corporate Intelligence," p. 200–02. See also Richard F. Beltramini, "Ethics and the Use of Competitive Information Acquisition Strategies," *Journal of Business Ethics* 5 (1986), pp. 307–11.

Covert Surveillance

Covert surveillance, another category of ethically problematic intelligence gathering, includes electronic espionage as well as other unconsented-to forms of observation, such as eavesdropping and aerial photography. This category, perhaps the most difficult to define, raises questions about the legitimate scope of corporate privacy. When covert surveillance involves trespass or theft of tangible property, there is a convenient legal label for condemning it. But when it involves eavesdropping in public places or observation from afar using sophisticated technology, the wrong is most readily described as a violation of corporate privacy. Although the prevailing view is that corporations have no legal right to privacy, the idea persists that businesses and their employees should be able to assume they will not be observed or listened to in certain situations.[46]

The techniques of covert surveillance are varied. They range from planting a spy in a competitor's operation—a technique that also involves deception and perhaps inducing actual employees to violate duties of confidentiality—to strategic eavesdropping in the bar and grill favored by a competitor's employees.[47] A widely discussed case of covert surveillance, which resulted in an award of damages for the target company, involved aerial photography of an unfinished manufacturing plant.[48] Clever gadgets of various types are available to assist covert observation: binoculars that hear conversations up to five blocks away, a spray that exposes the content of envelopes, a gadget that can read computer screens some two blocks away by picking up radio waves emitted by the machine.[49] Inspecting the competition's trash is another type of unconsented-to surveillance that has received attention in the press and has been litigated in at least one case.[50]

Covert observation, like misrepresentation and improper influence, is yet another way to obtain information that a rival does not wish to divulge. Ethical assessments of various forms of undisclosed observation may be controversial, since privacy expectations are quite variable, as are judgments about the legitimacy of those expectations.

---

[46] For general discussion, see Anita L. Allen, "Rethinking the Rule against Corporate Privacy Rights: Some Conceptual Quandaries for the Common Law," *John Marshall Law Review* 20 (Summer 1987), p. 607.

[47] Both practices are described in Flax, "How to Snoop on Your Competitors," pp. 28, 32.

[48] *E.I. du Pont de Nemours* v. *Christopher*, 431 F.2d 1012 (5th Cir. 1970), *cert. denied*, 400 U.S. 1024 (1971).

[49] "New Ways to Battle Corporate Spooks," *Fortune*, November 7, 1988, p. 72.

[50] *Tennant Co.* v. *Advance Machine Co.*, 355 N.W.2d 720 (Ct. App. Minn. 1984). The appeals court upheld a verdict awarding compensatory and punitive damages to Tennant, the victim of trash surveillance. Under California law, said the court, "an owner retains a reasonable expectation of privacy in the contents of a dumpster 'until the trash has lost its identity and meaning by becoming part of a large conglomeration of trash elsewhere.' " Tennant had disposed of its documents in sealed trash bags put into a covered dumpster used only by Tennant. For another example of trash surveillance, see Johnson, "The Case of Marc Feith."

Covert observation in or from public places is especially problematic. For example, it may be possible to ascertain the volume of product that competitors are shipping by observing from public property the number of tractor-trailers leaving the plant's loading bays and by noting the size of the product in relation to the size of the trailers.[51] Opinions vary about the legitimacy of this practice. One might say that the firm has consented to observation by not putting a fence around the property. And yet, just as it is unseemly to peer through an open window into the neighbors' living room while walking down the sidewalk, we may think observation to be an invasion of the firm's privacy.

Likewise, we may raise eyebrows at the Japanese practice of surreptitiously employing students to record the conversations of competitors' employees as they commute to work on the train, and at the same time wonder why employees would discuss sensitive matters in such crowded public places.[52]

Unsolicited Intelligence

The questions raised by covert surveillance are closely related to those raised by the receipt of unsolicited information. Disgruntled former employees of rival firms have been known to offer highly confidential technical information as well as more general information to competitors. Two recently litigated cases involved disputes about valuable information acquired as a result of a rival's mistake. In one case, a coded customer list inadvertently was left in the memory of a computer that had been purchased at an auction by a competitor. The rival gained access to the codeword from an unwitting computer operator.[53] In another case, a dealer list was accidentally left in the store of a dealer who later became a competitor.[54]

There is no question of deceit or improper influence in these cases. The ethical question centers on whether unsolicited or inadvertently revealed information should be respected as private to the competitor. If intelligence gathering is governed by respect for the competitors' voluntary disclosure decisions, then information acquired through accident or mistake, or a former employee's breach of fiduciary duty, should not be examined and utilized. Indeed, this is the view reflected in the Uniform Trade Secrets Act.[55] Some courts and commentators, however, have taken the position that privacy is forfeited if information is accidentally revealed.[56]

---

[51] Discussed in Flax, "How to Snoop on Your Competitors," p. 33.

[52] This practice is described in Sutton, *Competitive Intelligence*, p. 17.

[53] *Defiance Button Mach. Co.* v. *C & C Metal Products*, 759 F.2d 1053 (2d Cir. 1985).

[54] *Fisher Stoves, Inc.*, v. *All Nighter Stove Works*, 626 F.2d 193 (1st Cir. 1980).

[55] *Uniform Trade Secrets Act with 1985 Amendments*, sec. 1(2)(ii)(c), in *Uniform Laws Annotated* 14 (1980, with 1988 Pocket Part).

[56] *Fisher Stoves; Defiance Button.* See also *Kewanee Oil Co.* v. *Bicron Corp.*, 416 U.S. 470, 476 (1973) ("A trade secret law . . . does not offer protection against discovery by fair and honest means, such as by . . . accidental disclosure . . .").

The forfeiture view has some plausibility when disclosure is the result of a rival firm's carelessness: It is not unreasonable to expect a firm to suffer some loss if it acts carelessly. The view has less merit, however, when a third party, such as a supplier, inadvertently discloses a rival's valuable information. Still, in a survey discussed earlier, nearly half the marketing professionals questioned said it would be ethical to use information acquired as the result of a supplier's mistake.[57] In the survey vignette, a marketing professional is accidentally given slides prepared for a direct competitor's final presentation in a competition in which both are participating. Having examined the slides before returning them to the embarrassed employee of the slide supply house, the marketer must decide whether to use the information to alter his presentation and attack the competitor's recommended strategy.

Marketing students were more guarded than the professionals about the propriety of using the information, but nearly two thirds said they would use it, despite their ethical judgment to the contrary. While 73 percent said it would be unethical to use the information, only 31 percent said they would refrain from doing so.[58]

THE DEARTH OF CORPORATE GUIDANCE

Despite the growing importance of intelligence gathering and the occurrence of unethical and questionable practices, top management has not yet faced the issue squarely. Only a handful of corporations offer employees practical guidance on intelligence gathering in their codes of conduct or ethics policies.[59] While codes of conduct are not the only, or even the most important, index of a corporation's ethical standards, they do provide some indication of ethical issues thought by the code's authors to merit attention.[60]

Among approximately 480 nonconfidential corporate codes of conduct on file at The Ethics Resource Center, Inc.,[61] and the Defense Industry Initiative

---

[57] "Industry Ethics Are Alive."

[58] Survey results received from the Center for Communication, New York City.

[59] This research was conducted in March–April 1989. It is quite possible that many corporations do not include intelligence gathering in their companywide code of conduct, but, instead, provide employees in the most relevant areas—marketing, for example—with ethical guidance in the form of a specific policy statement on intelligence gathering. I have not attempted to locate specific policy statements beyond those available in the collections assembled by the Ethics Resource Center and the Defense Industry Initiative Clearing House, both described in notes below.

[60] As illustrated in the *Continental Data Systems* case, discussed at footnote 32, written codes do not always reflect the actual operational understanding of a firm's employees.

[61] The Ethics Resource Center, Inc., is a nonprofit educational organization in Washington, D.C. Its library contains corporate codes of conduct gathered over the past seven years in the course of four major research studies involving Fortune 500 companies, major defense contractors, and most recently a varied sample of 2,000 American corporations. Besides those involved in these studies, other companies interested in furthering the center's research efforts also have contributed codes.

Clearing House in Washington, D.C.,[62] only five could reasonably be expected to be useful to an employee looking for ethical guidance on intelligence gathering.[63] These five codes make explicit mention of general governing principles and provide specific illustrations of their application. They mention acquisition methods that are to be avoided, kinds of information that are off bounds, and, in some cases, objectives that are improper. For instance, one code explains that "improper means include industrial espionage, inducing a competitor's personnel to disclose confidential information, and any other means that are not open and aboveboard."[64] However, none of the five explicitly addresses all four types of ethically problematic practice discussed above (p. 264).

Another 19 codes provide little practical guidance but at least alert employees that intelligence gathering is an area of ethical vulnerability. These codes typically contain a conclusory statement or general principle cautioning employees about improperly seeking proprietary information of a competitor or admonishing them to ensure that data collection is proper and legal. However, the codes offer little or no advice about what specific practices are improper or illegal.

Thirteen other codes contain one or two provisions prohibiting specific practices, such as industrial espionage, using confidential information of former employers, or mishandling government information. These narrowly drawn provisions, however, are not backed by general principles that could be helpful in thinking about other intelligence-gathering practices. Six companies warn employees not to accept the confidential or proprietary information of others. Although relevant for intelligence gathering, these provisions appear to address the problem of unsolicited submissions of confidential information of others, rather than deliberately undertaken data collection.[65]

The code of ethics adopted by the Society of Competitor Intelligence Professionals in 1987 targets two areas for specific mention.[66] It requires intelligence professionals to make full disclosure of their identity and organization prior to interviews and to respect requests for the confidentiality of information. Otherwise, the code's provisions express general commitments to acting eth-

---

[62] The Defense Industry Initiative Clearing House has on file the codes of conduct of some 45 defense contractors. All these contractors are signatories of the Defense Industry Initiatives on Business Ethics and Conduct, a voluntary industry effort undertaken in 1986 in response to the report of President Reagan's Blue Ribbon Commission on Defense Management, better-known as the "Packard Commission."

[63] Another study of ethics policies gathered from 67 Fortune 500 companies found only one that covered intelligence gathering. Robert E. Hite, Joseph A. Bellizzi, and Cynthia Fraser, "A Content Analysis of Ethical Policy Statements Regarding Marketing Activities," *Journal of Business Ethics* 7 (1988), p. 771.

[64] Hewlett Packard Company, *Standards of Business Conduct.*

[65] For discussion, see Arthur H. Seidel, "Handling Unsolicited Submission of Trade Secrets," *The Practical Lawyer* 30 (March 1984), pp. 43–52.

[66] The code is available through the Society of Competitor Intelligence Professionals in Washington, D.C.

ically, legally, and in accordance with the policies of the professional's employer.

Top management is not alone in neglecting the ethics of intelligence gathering. In the Conference Board's ethics survey of 300 companies worldwide, intelligence gathering was not included among the list of topics posing ethical issues for business.[67] Only slightly more than one quarter of the respondents to a survey on ethics education in accredited U.S. graduate and undergraduate business programs say they cover intelligence gathering.[68]

EXPLAINING CORPORATE SILENCE

Corporate failure to provide guidance may reflect an assumption that intelligence gathering is adequately covered by the corporation's commitment to honesty, integrity, or legal compliance. Many company codes begin by asserting that the firm's business is to be conducted in accordance with the highest standards of law and ethics. Quite apart from evidence that much intelligence gathering is not conducted according to the highest standards of law and ethics, such highly general statements are of little practical value when the requirements of law and ethics are unclear to employees or when they conflict with other corporate demands.

Compliance with conclusory general standards like these depends on employees' abilities to recognize when legal and ethical principles might be relevant to their work and to interpret the relevant principles in the particular context at hand. It is quite implausible, however, to assume that employees are familiar with the general principles of law governing confidential information or with their interpretation in the courts. Variation in ethical sensibilities and intellectual capacities, coupled with legitimate disagreement about the ethical status of certain practices, require that management provides more specific guidance. It may be too much to expect the average employee under pressure to collect information to make the connection between the company's policy of conducting business ethically and the particular intelligence-gathering practices he or she may consider, especially if the company's evaluation system favors the practices.

An alternative explanation for corporate failure to address the ethics of intelligence gathering is management's desire not to hamstring its intelligence operations. By remaining silent, management perhaps can benefit from questionable practices without explicitly condoning them. This is a risky policy,

---

[67] Ronald E. Berenbeim, *Corporate Ethics*, Conference Board Research Report no. 900 (New York: Conference Board, 1987), p. 4.

[68] Lynn Sharp Paine, *Ethics Education in American Business Schools*, a report of the Ethics Resource Center (Washington, D.C.: February 1988), pp. 16–17. Among MBA program respondents, 32 percent cover intelligence gathering. Only 23 percent of the responding undergraduate programs discuss the ethics of intelligence gathering.

as well as a costly one, in the long run. It also violates management's respon-sibility to alert employees engaged in intelligence gathering to the legal and ethical risks associated with their job. Few employees engage willingly and without reservation in legally questionable activities for their employers. But if management does not address the ethics of intelligence gathering, employees may unwittingly find themselves in legal difficulty.

RISKS OF CORPORATE SILENCE

The most immediate risk of neglecting to address the ethics of intelligence gathering is the risk of litigation invited by the use of questionable practices. Under the general principles of trade secret law, intelligence gathering may be actionable if it involves misrepresentation, theft, bribery, breach or inducement of a breach of a duty to maintain secrecy, espionage, or other improper means.[69] Although liability is limited to cases involving acquisition of trade secrets, the definition of "trade secret" is quite broad in many jurisdictions and quite vague in others.

In some jurisdictions, for example, a trade secret must be "continuously used in one's business."[70] Thus, the date of a new policy or information about a particular proposed event or a key executive's health problems would not qualify. In other jurisdictions, information need only afford a competitive advantage and be subject to reasonable efforts to maintain its secrecy to qualify as a trade secret. While manufacturing methods, processes, and chemical for-mulations generally are accorded trade secret status, other types of information have received different treatment in different courts. Customer lists, marketing plans, bidding procedures, identities of suppliers, and operations information, for example, have been protected in some cases but not in others.[71]

Given jurisdictional variation and the uncertainty surrounding interpreta-tion of trade secret principles, it is difficult to know precisely what information enjoys legal protection and what does not. Moreover, the outcome of trade secret cases seems to be influenced by the court's analytical starting point. In theory, liability for misappropriation of a trade secret depends on finding both that the information in question is a trade secret and that it was acquired by improper means. However, one commentator has observed that protection is less likely if the court's inquiry focuses on the trade secret question than if it focuses on the means of acquisition. It seems that courts are reluctant to deny trade secret protection if they find the use of "improper means" to gather information.[72]

---

[69] *Uniform Trade Secrets Act*, sec. 1(1).

[70] The requirement of continuous use was written into the Restatement of Torts (First), but is not part of the Uniform Trade Secrets Act definition of a trade secret.

[71] For a readable discussion of treatment of different types of information, see Robert Alan Spanner, *Who Owns Innovation?* (Homewood, Ill.: Dow Jones-Irwin, 1984).

[72] Spanner, *Who Owns Innovation?*

"Improper means" is, itself, a somewhat indefinite and expanding category. The well-known case of *Du Pont* v. *Christopher* shows that courts are willing to go beyond the standard legal classifications of prohibited means in finding liability.[73] The question in the case, a novel one under Texas law, was whether aerial photography was an "improper means" of discovering trade secrets. The Christophers had taken aerial photographs of a Du Pont plant which, because it was still under construction, was exposed to view from above. Analysis of the photographs revealed a secret, but unpatented, process for producing methanol, which Du Pont contended was a trade secret. Even though aerial photography did not fall within the usual legal categories of "improper means," the court held that, under the circumstances, it was improper. The court reasoned that it would be unfair to permit a rival to reap the benefits of the process developed by Du Pont and that it would be unreasonable to expect companies to protect themselves against espionage of this sort.

The legal picture is further complicated by the possibility of other theories of recovery, such as inducing a breach of fiduciary duty or a breach of confidence. Even if information gathered from an informant is not protected as a trade secret, legal action for inducing a breach of confidence may be possible. Thus, information about the impending appointment of a key executive, although treated as confidential within the firm, might not count as a trade secret. Still, someone who revealed that information might be in violation of a duty of confidentiality.

As a practical matter, the risks of litigation and legal liability can best be minimized by avoiding intelligence-gathering activities in the ethically problematic categories discussed above: misrepresentation, improper influence, unconsented-to surveillance, and theft. Admittedly, the threat of legal reprisal for engaging in these practices may be minimal in certain situations. Victims of unethical practices may not know they are being targeted, or they may lack evidence to prove their case in a court of law. Moreover, the law does not provide a remedy for every violation of ethics. If the victim of misrepresentation is not individually harmed, for example, she will have no legal recourse against the intelligence gatherer. And even if substantially harmed, the victim may have no remedy if the information acquired does not qualify as a trade secret or if the target firm has not taken adequate steps to protect the information in question.

From a management perspective, however, it is quite impractical to instruct employees to fine-tune their use of questionable practices on the basis of the legal risk in particular situations. Not only is it difficult to undertake an objective assessment of legal risk when under everyday performance pressures, but the legal risk of using unethical practices depends on consequences that are difficult, if not impossible, to anticipate in advance: the kind of information

---

[73] *E.I. du Pont de Nemours v. Christopher*, 431 F.2d 1012 (5th Cir. 1970), *cert. denied*, 400 U.S. 1024 (1971).

that will be obtained, the use to which it will be put, the harm that the target will suffer, the adequacy of the target's security measures, the likelihood of discovery, and the evidentiary strength of the target's case. What is known in advance is that certain types of practices—namely those involving misrepresentation, theft, improper influence, and covert surveillance—can provide the necessary foundation for legal liability. Even from the narrow perspective of legal costs, there is a good case for instructing employees to avoid questionable practices altogether, rather than attempt to assess the fine points of legal risk.

INCREASING SECURITY NEEDS

More costly, perhaps, than the litigation and liability risks involved in the use of questionable practices are the increased security needs these practices generate over the long term. Every user of unethical practices must recognize his contribution to a general climate of distrust and suspicion. Insofar as individuals are more likely to engage in unethical conduct when they believe their rivals are doing so, unethical intelligence gathering contributes further to the general deterioration of ethical expectations. As the recent growth of interest in information security illustrates, declining ethical expectations translate into intensified programs for self-protection.[74]

Firms that expect to be subjected to intelligence gathering through covert surveillance, deceit, and various forms of improper influence—especially when legal recourse is unavailable or uncertain—will take steps to protect themselves. They will tighten information security by building walls, installing security systems, purchasing sophisticated counter-intelligence technology, and instituting management techniques to reduce the risks of information leakage. Although some degree of self-protection is necessary and desirable, security can become a dominant consideration and a drain on resources.

Besides their out-of-pocket cost, security activities often introduce operational inefficiencies and stifle creativity. Avoiding use of the telephone and restricting access to information to employees who demonstrate a "need to know" impose obvious impediments to the exchange of information vital to cooperation within the firm. When researchers, for instance, are denied information about the projects they are working on and about how their work relates to the work of others, they are cut off from stimuli to creativity and useful innovation.

---

[74] The 1985 Hallcrest Report documents the growth of employment and expenditures for private security, including information security, in the 1970s and projects continuing growth in security-related sectors of the economy. The report's authors link this growth with increased crime in the workplace and with increased awareness and fear of crime. See William C. Cunningham and Todd H. Taylor, *Private Security and Police in America: The Hallcrest Report* (Portland, Ore.: The Chancellor Press, 1985), pp. 105–16.

Employee morale and public confidence also may be at stake. Information systems designed to ensure that employees do not know enough to hurt the firm if they depart, like the dissemination of information on a "need to know" basis, proceed from a premise of distrust that can undermine employee morale. Even more clearly, information protection programs encourage an attitude of distrust toward outsiders. Employees are trained to be suspicious of public inquiries and to be wary of talking to or cooperating with outsiders who do not have security clearances. Overrestrictions on public access to information and excessive corporate secrecy generate public suspicion and hostility.

Although questionable intelligence-gathering practices may offer short-term advantages, they contribute, over the longer term, to a climate of distrust and the need for costly expenditures to tighten information security. These expenditures represent a diversion of management resources from more productive activities. Moreover, it is doubtful that firms can effectively protect their own valuable information if they encourage or tolerate loose ethical standards in acquiring competitor information. As the 1985 Hallcrest Report on private security in America concluded from studies of employee theft, "[E]ffective proprietary security programs . . . must emanate from a . . . strong sense of organizational ethics in all levels of the organization."[75]

SUGGESTIONS FOR MANAGERS

There are compelling reasons for management to address the ethics of competitor intelligence gathering. In the absence of clearly communicated standards of propriety in this field, as in others, some employees will be uncertain about what is expected of them. They may feel that management expects them to engage in acts of misrepresentation, improper influence, and covert surveillance to gain information. Or they may be unsure what conduct constitutes misrepresentation, improper influence, or covert surveillance. As found in one study discussed earlier, there is a close correspondence between the intelligence-gathering practices that employees find acceptable and those that they perceive to be in line with company standards.[76] It also appears that employees are more willing to engage in questionable practices if they believe their competitors are doing so.[77] Given the general prevalence of questionable and unethical practices, it is risky for management to remain silent on the ethics of intelligence gathering.

Managers can take various steps to discourage ethically questionable intelligence-gathering practices. The first is to work toward developing a shared commitment to the ethical standards that should govern intelligence gathering.

---

[75] Ibid., at p. 41.
[76] Cohen and Czepiec, "The Role of Ethics in Gathering Corporate Intelligence," p. 202.
[77] Ibid.

Essential to this process is the involvement of employees, particularly those who are active in the intelligence function, to promote open discussion of the opportunities and pressures encountered in the field as well as discussion of the "gray areas" where the requirements of ethics may be unclear.

Managers may choose to create a written code or other document to express the governing standards and to provide guidance on their application, but more important than such documentation is sustaining a commitment to these standards in practice. Various activities beyond the initial process of developing standards may be useful in building and sustaining commitment: monitoring the pressures and gray areas employees encounter and providing a forum for discussing them, including ethics in orientation and training for all intelligence personnel, and encouraging managers to ask employees about the ethical questions they encounter and to be responsive when employees raise such questions.

For such efforts to be taken seriously, however, it is critical that performance evaluation and, more generally, the firm's system of rewards and incentives, be compatible with the ethical standards espoused. Employees who govern their activities by these standards should not be penalized for doing so; nor should employees be rewarded for successes achieved at the expense of ethics. An evaluation and reward system that ignores the ethical dimensions of performance can breed cynicism and outright hostility to well-intentioned efforts to promote ethical practices, unless there is a strong culture of ethical commitment already in place.

CONCLUSION

Managers who remain silent or fail to incorporate their "official" ethics policies into day-to-day management practice run the risk that they, their employees, and their firms will be involved in costly litigation over questionable intelligence-gathering tactics. More important, they jeopardize their own information security and run the risk of contributing further to the increasing demand for information protection. This demand represents a costly diversion of resources from the positive and creative aspects of doing business, a drag on innovation, and an impediment to good public relations. By supporting a competitive system that respects the principles of common morality and the right of rivals not to divulge certain information, management supports its own vitality and the vitality of the competitive system.

Product Policy

Ethical Issues in Product Policy

Melvyn A. J. Menezes

Effective product policy decisions are critical to successful marketing management. A firm's choice of products and services affects all significant dimensions of the marketing program such as decisions on distribution channels, promotional media and messages, and physical distribution arrangements. There are four elements of product policy where managerial decisions raise significant ethical issues: design and positioning, packaging and labeling, product recalls, and the product and the environment. By ethical issues I mean issues that involve doing what is "right," even if it means going beyond what is required by the law, beyond what the lawyers advise, beyond even what customers want and are willing to pay for, and beyond what a short-term profit objective would seem to suggest. This chapter will focus on the significant ethical issues involved in each of these four elements of product policy.

PRODUCT DESIGN AND POSITIONING

Product Design

A product's design is often crucial in determining whether the product functions properly and safely. Allegations of design problems lie at the heart of a number of tragic and well-publicized product failures, such as the Ford Pinto automobile and the "O rings" Morton Thiokol manufactured for the space shuttle *Challenger.*

Companies clearly bear a responsibility for safety when designing their products. Although consumers want and expect safe products, they don't actively seek safety, tending instead to make their choices for other reasons (Nelson-Horchler, 1988) They assume that the government will assure product safety and that manufacturers and retailers would not sell unsafe products. From a manufacturer's point of view, designing a safer product usually results in higher costs. But in most cases, promoting safety features, which are often incorporated at significant expense, does not help sell the product (Nelson-Horchler, 1988).

Product design must also take into account legal considerations and, in particular, liability law, which in the 20th century has moved toward the doctrine of strict liability. That is, the product itself (rather than the intentional actions of management) is examined. Almost independent of management behavior, the manufacturer is strictly liable for harm caused by the product.

One pragmatic approach manufacturers can take to avoid or at least reduce potential liability expenses is to design safer products, with a sense of legal minima (i.e., how to reduce product liability and avoid getting sued). Regina Corporation, for example, a small appliance manufacturer, equips its home spa products with an immersion detection circuit interrupter that protects users from electrical shock if they accidentally drop an appliance in the water. Despite the immersion detection circuit interrupter's extra cost and Regina Corporation's inability to get credit for it with the consumer, the company includes it in the product primarily to reduce potential liability expense (Nelson-Horchler, 1988).

Organizational changes can also help the company cope with product liability. Downs and Behrman (1986) propose a product liability coordinator who can generate, process, and disseminate relevant information and oversee corporate strategic decisions that might result in product liability. This person would coordinate and monitor the product design activities of the engineering, manufacturing, marketing, and legal departments that relate to product liability.

A third approach to avoiding liability problems is to hire more and better lawyers. Silverstein (1987), for example, suggests that attention to the changing legal environment will help managerial decision making, especially when profit maximization and social welfare conflict. Businesses often take a static rather than a dynamic, view of the legal environment. Lawyers, he asserts, would hold a dynamic view of the law, rather than just the legal requirements of the day. The company could then act preemptively to keep itself out of trouble. He suggests that management should be guided by present laws and the prospect of future laws.

An ethical issue facing firms is to what extent are they responsible for designing safety into a product when consumers are unwilling to pay a higher price for the increased safety. Firms that have tried to emphasize safety haven't had much success. For example, children's pajamas traditionally have been purchased on the basis of price, color, softness, and attractiveness. However, the material was highly inflammable; Sears tried to sell "safe" pajamas made from nonflammable material and promoted it heavily, but was not rewarded (Nelson-Horchler, 1988). The Consumer Product Safety Commission eventually was forced to mandate a sleepwear flammability standard, because there was no economic incentive to provide pajamas that were highly nonflammable.

Furthermore, highlighting safety features can have unintended negative consequences, causing customers to question what they previously had assumed was a safe product. Consider again Regina Corporation. Despite the enhanced safety of its product, the company does not advertise this feature, believing that to mention the possible accident would frighten potential buyers (Nelson-Horchler, 1988).

In some industries, the role of ethical considerations in decisions of design safety has been questioned. In the automobile industry, for example, safety has been a long-time concern, yet its idea of safety may have differed from that held by the rest of society. Its approach was to ensure that, if an accident occurred, the fault was "the nut behind the wheel." Almost no consideration was given to providing that "nut" and his or her passengers more protection in an accident. In 1955, Robert McNamara, the Ford division chief, took a unique approach to marketing autos by focusing on safety features. The response shocked him. Executives of other car companies protested that McNamara was giving the entire industry a bad name by implying that its products were unsafe. The advertising campaign was soft-pedaled, and Ford took a beating from Chevrolet's new models. That episode confirmed the industry's belief that "safety doesn't sell."

As we enter the 1990s, however, "safety does not sell" is being re-examined; safety is beginning to sell better, especially when it fits into customers' lifestyles. Also, attitudes in several industries are changing, and there is certainly a greater consciousness in some companies that ethical considerations are an important component of the managerial decision-making process. But in marketing new safety features, such as antilock braking systems, manufacturers will continue to face the dilemma of cost versus sales volume (Moskal, 1988b).

An important consideration is where the responsibility for safety does and should reside in an organization. In most cases, it appears to rest in either the engineering or legal departments; marketing appears to play a very small role in deciding safety issues. In today's business environment marketing should play a larger role by *(a)* identifying ways in which consumers might misuse the product and as a result encounter some safety problems; *(b)* participating in the firm's trade-off decisions, such as safety versus other features, and safety versus cost; and *(c)* deciding the level and type of communication needed.

A final ethical issue in product design is the extent to which manufacturers have a responsibility to do what's good for customers, even if customers do not want it. For example, even when seat belts became standard equipment, a majority of motorists refused to wear them. When equipment to reduce exhaust emissions turned out to also reduce engine efficiency, thousands of car owners disconnected it. What happens when those "benefits" push up the price of the product? On the flip side, what about when consumers want and are willing to pay for something that does not affect the product's performance but which the company believes is not very good for the consumer? Should that be incorporated into the product? For example, how should cereal producers respond to children's preference for high sugar levels in cereals? Sales probably will increase if the sugar content of the cereal is increased. But the issue is, should that be done?

Product Positioning

Product positioning involves distinguishing the product from its competitors to gain a competitive edge. Firms spend considerable amounts of time and money to decide on product positioning, because it could impact not only sales but also how customers perceive and use the product.

How a product is positioned and how this is communicated can have a major impact on how the product is used, which in turn affects the likelihood of safety-related problems. Consider two examples. First, in the case of the Suzuki Samurai, critics charged that the way in which the vehicle was positioned was partly responsible for the manner in which it was used and the subsequent safety problems. In February 1988, the Center for Auto Safety filed a complaint with the National Highway Traffic Safety Administration, charging that the Suzuki Samurai was unsafe. They said they had evidence of 11 accidents in which a Samurai rolled over after a skid or a sharp turn; three people died and eight others were injured. In June 1988, Consumers Union announced that the Samurai had failed its track test and asked that all the 150,000 Suzuki Samurais sold be recalled (Treece, 1988, and see Chapter 3.2). In a second case, a feeder auger manufacturer stated in a promotional brochure that "even a child can do your feeding." The brochure had a photograph of the auger with its safety cover removed, the intent being to show the product's inner workings. A young boy was injured while using the feeder auger with the safety cover removed. In the subsequent court case, the jury found that the promotional brochure was misleading in terms of the safety of the product and operating conditions (Downs and Behrman, 1986).

An important issue facing marketers is trying to identify the conditions under which product positioning and target marketing might become unethical. Often, there is much confusion about whether the product itself is unethical, or whether the group being targeted is unable to think rationally through the information and, therefore, will make an uninformed or poor choice. This explains why, for example, some people believe that the Uptown cigarette and products targeted at children may be unethical (see Chapter 3.6). Manufacturers need to consider whether the positioning strategy that is good from the point of view of differentiation and sales may influence the way in which a consumer uses the product and, consequently, impact the customer's safety.

PRODUCT PACKAGING AND LABELING

A second element of product policy in which ethical issues often are raised is packaging and labeling. In addition to its traditional role of holding, protecting, and transporting goods, packaging can provide an effective communications and promotional medium for the supplier. Packaging has become an important management concern for many product categories in recent years. As more products are sold on a self-serve basis, the package plays an increasingly important role in capturing attention, communicating the product concept, and enumerating product benefits, ingredients, and uses. Ethical issues in packaging have been highlighted by the Tylenol and Contac product-tampering cases, as well as by numerous lawsuits regarding inadequate product warning labels. There are three main areas of ethical concern in packaging and labeling: misleading information on labels, warning labels, and packaging waste.

Misleading Information on Labels

Concern about inadequate and misleading labeling, especially for food products, is growing. Most food products require nutritional labels, and many companies have been accused of providing misleading health information to promote their products (Miller, 1989). For example, there are questions about the nutritional values given on labels, and the word *natural* appears to have escaped the regulatory attention given to ingredient listings and advertising claims. The term is so broadly used that it can mean almost anything the manufacturer wants it to mean (Carlson, 1984).

Similarly, manufacturers increasingly are using *informational* labels concerning the environmental impact, recyclability, and the like, of their products for promotional purposes. It appears that much of the information on labels, while technically correct, can be misleading. According to a recent *Business Week* article (April 23, 1990) , ". . . who can believe the label? 'Recycled' paper is often made from fiber trimmings at paper plants instead of paper that was once used. Products advertised as free of CFCs often contain butane, an air pollutant."

Warning Labels

Warning labels differ from instructions in that warning labels call attention to a danger, while instructions describe procedures for effective and reasonably safe product use. The purpose of warning labels is to signal a danger to consumers and to provide them with the information they need to use the product safely and, consequently, to reduce the firm's possible exposure to product liability suits. This area attracts considerable attention because of the product liability concerns of manufacturers.

Some manufacturers put a warning on any product that may cause an injury, as well as warning when in doubt. This leads to an overuse of warning labels. Manufacturers need to be concerned about how best to present risk related information to consumers (Bettman, Payne, and Staelin, 1986). As the number of warnings increases, consumers may not take the time or be able to differentiate the relative magnitude of the risks between products, and, consequently, they will ignore the risk (Schwartz and Driver, 1983). In fact, on-product warnings are often ignored or not seen, and there is little empirical evidence to suggest that they influence behavior (Driver, 1987). One way to improve this situation would be to use on-product labels in a more discreet manner, only for those products where it can be reasonably determined that labels are an appropriate method of communication.

Warning labels are more effective when consumers pay sufficient attention to them. The attention paid to labels has been found to depend on a number of factors, one of which is the individual's information-processing objectives. Although people could invoke many specific information-processing objectives, the two most frequently used are *memory-set*, in which people attempt to remember as much information as possible from a given set of instructions, and *impression-set*, in which people attend to information with the goal of evaluating the information to form an opinion or impression. Consumers who use a memory-set processing objective (compared to an impression-set processing objective) tend (1) to devote more time to examining the label, (2) to recall more information from the label, (3) to perceive the products as safer, and (4) to be more likely to comply with safety recommendations (deTurck and Goldhaber, 1989).

Other factors influencing the use of labels are consumers' familiarity with and frequency of use of the products. Frequent users of a product tend to pay less attention to warning labels/signs, and are more likely to engage in risk-taking behaviors with a product. Also, as consumers learn more about a product, they suffer from the "familiarity effect" (i.e., they become less concerned with safety information) (Goldhaber and deTurck, 1988).

There is considerable legal literature on the role of product warnings in strict liability law (Madden, 1988). Clearly, manufacturers need to attend to this to ensure they are staying within legal requirements. However, in the literature very little attention is paid to the ethical implications of these decisions. As Driver (1987) points out, "By omitting discussion of it [ethical issues] in this article, I do not mean to imply that the question of whether an organization has a duty to warn is not important."

An ethical concern is how much emphasis the firm should give to the warning. Many firms believe that a prominent warning will discourage product use. On the other hand, a warning placed inconspicuously will meet legal requirements but not affect the product's sales. For warning labels to be effective as communication tools, companies need to pay careful attention to what information goes into labels, how they are written, and where the labels are placed (Velotta, 1987). Warning labels should have some signs or symbols to grab consumers' attention. For example, safety labels could include a signal word, a hazard alert symbol, a specific color, a hazard identification, or a description of the result of ignoring the warning. To serve their purpose, labels should be clear, concise, forceful, descriptive, easy to read, and well organized. The design of a warning label also should take into consideration the ways in which such human factors as motor skills, perception, attention, comprehension, and memory can be incorporated into the warning (Clement, 1987). It is probably best to write warning labels by taking a pessimistic view of users' behavior; if it's possible to make a mistake in using the product, at least a few people will do so.

In spite of taking all possible precautions, not all risks can be avoided, of course. Companies often compare the benefits of eliminating the risk to the cost involved. A risk management approach using the estimated benefits of warning (avoidance of major injuries, avoidance of minor injuries, perception of the company as oriented toward user safety, reduced cost of liability insurance) and the costs of warning (increased costs of instructions, costs of warning decals, perception of the product as being unsafe, perception of the product as requiring outside maintenance) can help assure that costs both to the manufacturer and to society are at their lowest possible level (Clement, 1987).

Packaging Waste

Companies must pay attention to growing societal concerns about packaging. First, there are charges that packaging is often excessive and can raise prices; sometimes the package costs more than the contents. Second, the concern about shortages of paper, aluminum, and other packaging materials puts pressure on the industry to reduce its packaging. Third, packaging, which accounts for about 40 percent of the total solid waste in the United States, creates a major environmental problem in solid waste disposal. Marketers need to be sensitive to these concerns, otherwise they may have to face increased regulation.

A related packaging issue involves tampering. Many products require packaging that is difficult to tamper with and, if it has been tampered with, this should be evident to consumers. Yet no package is completely tamper-proof (Crossen, 1986); it can be made tamper-resistant, but a determined criminal cannot truly be stopped (Peters, 1983).

Organizations realize that making the packaging more tamper-resistant increases the cost, and often this cost cannot be passed on to the consumer. Thus, an ethical issue facing organizations is how much to improve packaging, given that this typically results in lower margins and no obvious returns for the investment. However, firms should recognize their responsibility to provide consumers with safe products and, consequently, with packaging that is not easy to tamper with. OTC (over-the-counter) drugs and food marketers have, for example, initiated steps to develop better protective packaging for their goods. On a more pragmatic level, firms must consider the extent of liability they could face in the event of a major problem. To better protect themselves against liability problems, firms must develop packages that minimize the possibility of unnoticed tampering, elicit cooperation of all channel members to guard against tampering opportunities, and educate consumers about how to identify packages that have been violated or modified (Morgan, 1988). Morgan asserts that companies must closely monitor developments in packaging, packaging regulations, and pending legislation, use state-of-the-art packaging, meet FDA regulations, be as protective as reasonably possible, and anticipate some attempts at tampering. Managers would do well to follow these guidelines, because it probably costs less to make packaging meet these criteria than it does to lose a lawsuit.

Packaging raises other ethical issues as well. For example, do manufacturers deliberately design product packaging to encourage incomplete use or waste of the product? Examples might include toothpaste tubes and cleaners that spray more cleaner into the air than on the cleaning surface. Another issue is "slack fill" (i.e., packages being only partially filled with the product). In some cases this may be to protect the product (potato chip bags) or because of product settling (cereals), but suspicions are raised when the consumer sees two similar-sized boxes of products, within the same category, that contain different amounts. Solid deodorants provide another example, where the consumer typically purchases a large box half-filled with a plastic tube, which in turn can only be partially used. Are consumers deceived by the size of the box? Is the intent to deceive consumers and look bigger than the competition? Or does it have to do with shipping considerations, or designs for gaining shelf space? What are the ethical implications of the excessive environmental waste generated by these practices?

PRODUCT RECALLS

The advent of consumerism and product liability legislation has restricted the flow of flawed products into the marketplace. However, despite the best efforts of a firm to design, develop, manufacture, and market safe and reliable products, flawed products, and sometimes dangerously flawed products, can still reach the market. Some flaws may reside in the product itself, while other flaws may be caused by people external to it such as users or tamperers. Often these products turn out to be harmful in unanticipated ways. Whether anticipated or not, these products could result in harm to consumers, leading to product liability damages and substantial drops in the product's sales and the firm's reputation. If not handled appropriately and promptly, this could have severe financial implications for the firm.

Companies have to deal with a series of complex trade-off decisions when determining if a recall program is worthwhile. These decisions obviously must consider the economic implications and legal requirements of the firm. Decisions on whether to inform consumers of the problem, repair or modify the product, or recall it can have dramatic effects on company and consumer alike. Such decisions typically are made on the basis of economic and legal considerations, but often without the usual amount of time and information that typically accompany other major business policy decisions. These decisions often raise significant ethical issues.

Companies vary quite dramatically in terms of how they respond to situations in which the product is found to be potentially dangerous. Some companies, on realizing the danger posed by a product, immediately inform consumers and distribution channels and carry out a quick and complete withdrawal of the product from all retail and wholesale outlets. This, of course, can be an extremely expensive choice. In 1986, for example, Tylenol capsules were tampered with at the retail outlets by a person outside the company or its normal distribution channels. Johnson & Johnson, manufacturer of Tylenol, decided to recall all Tylenol capsules and destroy the unsold capsules at a cost (including recall and destroying) of about $150 million (*Time*, 1986; *Business Insurance*, 1986). In September 1980, Procter & Gamble halted production and withdrew its Rely tampon from retail and wholesale shelves when its use was linked to toxic shock syndrome. The total after-tax cost of this withdrawal was $75 million (Davidson and Goodpaster, 1983c).

Other firms respond by denying the problem and refusing to take any blame for the product failure: Firestone in the case of the steel-belted radial 500 tire, Audi in the case of the 5000-S model, A.H. Robins in the Dalkon Shield case, and Ford in the case of the Ford Pinto. Firestone first argued that there was no hard data to support the contention that its steel-belted radial 500 tire was defective (Davidson and Goodpaster, 1983b). Five years after it started receiving complaints from its dealers—after several investigations by the National Highway Traffic Safety Administration, congressional hearings, legal complications; after years of vigorously defending the safety of the tire; and after 41 deaths and more than 65 injuries were linked to the product—Firestone recalled approximately 10 million of its steel-belted radial 500 tires. Firestone estimated that the after-tax cost of the recall was approximately $135 million (Davidson and Goodpaster, 1983b).

Owners of the Audi 5000-S model complained that the cars lunged out of control when they shifted into drive or reverse (Weinstein, 1987). Audi blamed the drivers. This led to slumping Audi sales in late 1986 and 1987, as well as to faltering company credibility (Weinstein, 1987). Audi took steps to rebuild its tarnished image and boost sales by a combination of cash incentives and rebate programs, as well as a $30 million, six-month media campaign (Moskal, 1988a). Critics contend that Audi seriously mismanaged the crisis, and Audi owners were angered by the company's insensitivity and its position of blaming drivers for the problem.

Ethical issues also are raised by the manner in which companies prepare for and deal with problems that will be encountered as machines and equipment age. Consider aging commercial aircraft and the Aloha Airlines accident of April 28, 1988. In that accident, the top half of a fuselage section was lost during flight at an altitude of 24,000 feet, resulting in the loss of one life and injury to 69 passengers. An important consequence of this accident was a call for reevaluating standards for inspection, surveillance, and design, which are issues of importance to the aging fleets of all airlines. Aloha Airlines decided to retire four 737-200s with the greatest number of flight cycles. The reason given by Aloha Airlines was: "We are not trying to pass judgment on older aircraft. . . . We don't want our passengers to wonder about the aircraft they are in" (O'Lone, 1988).

Some firms may be hesitant to pull products, because recalls are often extremely expensive in terms of the cost of withdrawal or modification, diminished reputations, and as a signal of unanticipated quality problems to consumers (Hartman, 1987). But these signals are usually product-specific, with no evidence of cross-product effects. It has been found that, while there are serious short-term drops in demand following "severe" recalls (i.e., involving more than 20 percent of the model's stock), the impact on product demand is "transitory" for most recalls (Reilly and Hoffer, 1983). Consider the resale automobile market. Recalled vehicles are not excessively penalized, but, instead, recalls lower the resale value to the degree appropriate to the problem (Hartman, 1987). The market differentiates recall signals by type of defect (brake, engine, and other) and severity of recall (major and minor). The market also responds fairly quickly to the new quality information; a recall in fall 1981 affected the resale price by fall 1982 (Hartman, 1987).

Product recalls also affect security prices, which have been found to react to nonautomotive product recall announcements for approximately two months following the initial press release (Pruitt and Peterson, 1986). The results for the automotive industry are conflicting; and one may conclude there is no evidence that shareholders are affected by automotive recalls. Automotive recalls were approximately twice as many as all other recalls combined during the period 1968–1983 (Pruitt and Peterson, 1986), thus leading to one other possible explanation: recalls are simply a regular cost of doing business in the automotive industry and are already discounted for.

There are some recalls that come under federal regulations, with five federal agencies involved with the majority of recalls in the United States (Jackson and Morgan, 1988). However, it is critical that ethical responsibilities are an equally important consideration in the decision. What principles should guide these recall decisions? And how should those ethical principles be weighted against possibly conflicting legal and economic considerations?

Three different approaches to product failure and possible product recall are often suggested (Jackson and Morgan, 1988). The first approach involves taking a strict economic view of response to product failure and is based on calculating the costs and benefits of recall. Many of the costs of such a program (cost for upgrading quality control, increasing communication with distributors, periodic goods recall drills) can be estimated. But the savings related to the recall program (how does this reduce the probability of recall, cost to the firm if a recall occurs, value of damaged corporate reputation, cost of defending and settling claims) are more difficult to estimate, according to Jackson and Morgan. They suggest considering the likelihood and severity of harm. A few mild cases of food poisoning will be painful, but are unlikely to be seriously harmful to consumers. Certain death due to possible brake failure is a much more dangerous matter. The authors suggest making the recall decision based on a calculation of expected values: "Expected values can be computed by combining the seriousness of the problem and its probability of occurrence, assuming the marketer can and is willing to estimate the cost of an injury or death."

A second approach calls for doing the "right" thing by recalling the product regardless of cost factors. Such a viewpoint may not be cost-justified; but some would suggest it might be an appropriate external posture to adopt, even if management behaves otherwise when not under scrutiny.

The third option is to contest vigorously the need for the recall, particularly if the product is crucial to the firm's success and is closely identified with the firm's name. This reaction is nonetheless risky, possibly unethical, and can be successfully implemented only by firms with very loyal customers. Because recalls are expensive in terms of diminished reputation and the cost of taking goods back, this approach views recalls as a course of action that is to be taken only if and when forced by the government or dictated by enlightened economic self-interest.

Kotler and Mantrala (1985) provide a framework for managers facing problems with a product failure. To decide whether it makes sense to withdraw a product, they suggest a firm should ask:

- Is there a flaw in the product?

- If so, is the flaw dangerous to customers and/or our reputation?

- If so, is the flaw removable and can the cost of removing the flaw be covered?

- If not, can the customer be educated to use the product safely?

- If not, withdraw the product.

This approach does imply some ethical responsibility for customer safety; but "is the product dangerous?" is sufficiently hazy to provide much room for interpretation. It is also interesting to note that Kotler and Mantrala place the one screening factor with real ethical consequences (consumer safety) in the same question as the screening factor for economic consequences (is it dangerous to our reputation). Although stated as an and/or question, no guidance is provided about how to reconcile conflicts between the two.

Why do firms handle major product failures so differently? One explanation lies with the economic implications that a product recall might have on the firm's bottom-line results. For example, the estimated after-tax cost of Firestone's recall of the steel-belted radial 500 tire was $135 million, which was 123 percent of its after-tax earnings of $110 million. On the other hand, the estimated after-tax cost of Procter & Gamble's withdrawal of Rely tampons was $75 million, which was less than 15 percent of its after-tax earnings of $512 million. This financial explanation, however, does not cover Ford's reluctance to recall the Ford Pinto. The estimated after-tax cost of that recall was $20 million, just 1 percent of the firm's after-tax earnings of $1,500 million (Davidson and Goodpaster, 1983a).

I suggest that attribution theory might better explain why firms differ in how they respond to product failures. There are two important dimensions: locus of control, which refers to whether the cause of the problem is internal or external to the firm; and controllability, which refers to whether the problem is controllable. When a problem is perceived to be caused by an agent external to the firm and to be relatively uncontrollable (e.g., Tylenol case in 1986), then it is easier for the firm to take the ethical high ground and recall the product. On the other hand, when the problem is perceived to be the result of something internal to the firm (e.g., design in the Ford Pinto, or product positioning in the Suzuki Samurai) and controllable, then the firm is likely to take on a harder stand and resist the recall.

Managing product safety problems obviously raises ethical issues and challenges, in addition to economic and legal considerations. Analysis of a recall also must take into account the cost (in terms of sales, earnings, or company reputation) of further delays or nonaction on the part of the company. From a marketing standpoint, an important consideration is the consumer's perception of the risk involved. For example, when people fly they realize that there is a small probability that a crash will occur and that the consequences are likely to be fatal. On the other hand, consumers had never considered any risk when buying a pain reliever capsule, such as Tylenol. Consequently, any consumer uncertainty over the safety of the product would be unacceptable to consumers and the manufacturer and would demand immediate attention. Questions that might help decision making in these situations are:

1. Can the product cause harm that the consumer does not know about?
2. Can the product cause harm that the consumer cannot reasonably avoid?
3. Can the product pose an unacceptable level of risk?

Recalls are discussed further in Chapter 4.7.

THE PRODUCT AND THE ENVIRONMENT

The fourth area of product policy that raises major ethical issues is the product and the environment, a rapidly growing concern affecting not just the consumers of the product but society at large. In fact, many believe that the 1990s will be the "earth decade" or the "decade of the environment." According to Gary Miller, a public policy expert at Washington University: "In the Nineties environmentalism will be the cutting edge of social reform and absolutely the most important issue for business" (Kirkpatrick, 1990). At the World Economic Forum annual meeting in February 1990, 650 industry and government leaders ranked the environment as the number-one challenge facing business (*Business Week*, 1990).

Consumers are becoming deeply concerned about potential environmental damage caused by products and packaging. Being "green," as the environmentally concerned are known in Europe, is now becoming popular in the United States and is having a significant impact on consumer attitudes. In a poll conducted in 1990 by the *New York Times* and CBS, in response to a very strong statement: "Protecting the environment is so important that requirements and standards cannot be too high, and continuing environmental improvements must be made regardless of cost," as many as 79 percent agreed and only 18 percent disagreed. The corresponding percentages in 1981 were 45 percent and 42 percent, respectively (Kirkpatrick, 1990).

It is as yet unclear how many consumers are willing to back their beliefs with a change in buying habits. Some may be willing to give up convenience (e.g., disposability) to buy environmentally responsible products. In a 1990 *Advertising Age*/Gallup poll, as many as 43 percent of the 1,029 people surveyed said that they favor a ban on sales of disposable diapers (*Advertising Age*, 1990). Some consumers might even be willing to spend more to achieve the same result. But some businesses have found that consumers are unwilling to pay a higher price for environmentally safe products, even though they say that they support them. A service station in New Bedford, Massachusetts, for example, installed sophisticated equipment to reduce the amount of fumes escaping into the air. The station increased its price of gasoline by 3 cents and explained to its customers that the new equipment would lead to a cleaner environment. The result was a drop in sales, as customers went to the competitor next door who was priced lower by 3 cents a gallon!

The 1990s is seeing the emergence of the "green" marketing movement (i.e., firms using consumers' environmental concerns to help sell products). Some firms expect that green products will be to the 1990s what "lite" products were to the 1980s. Consequently, such companies as Colgate-Palmolive, Mobil, Procter & Gamble, and Kimberly-Clark are turning out "environmentally friendly" products. Kimberly-Clark, for example, is introducing Hi-Dri paper towels made from 100 percent recycled paper (Winters, 1990). However, despite efforts to use recycled and recyclable components whenever possible, it isn't always easy to use environmentally friendly products and to simultaneously satisfy customer perferences. For instance, "softness is a key attribute that consumers look for in a premium tissue, and only virgin fiber provides the necessary level of softness," according to a Kimberly-Clark official (Winters, 1990).

In several industries, such as soft drink and fast food, packaging is emerging as a major environmental concern. Coca-Cola Company and Pepsi-Cola Company both have announced plans to introduce recycled plastic bottles in 1991. These would be the first recycled plastic packages that come in direct contact with the food consumed. In 1991, Kraft Microwave Entrees will come in recycled trays, Heinz ketchup in recycled plastic bottles, and Fuji film packaged in paper canisters instead of plastic ones (Winters, 1990). Bottles made from recycled material would cost the firm more than those made from virgin plastic. But Coke, Pepsi, and Heinz have indicated that they will absorb the cost increases and not charge consumers more for the recycled products (*The Wall Street Journal*, 1990). As Beth Adams, manager of public communication for Heinz USA put it: "Consumers won't buy a product for the package alone, but we expect to gain customers for Heinz ketchup because it is a quality product in an environmentally safe package" (Winters, 1990).

Other companies are responding to the changing emphasis on the environment as well:

1. Procter & Gamble is attempting to cast its products in an environmentally friendly light, in line with public opinion against conspicuous waste. For example, it is redesigning its Crisco oil bottles to use 28 percent less plastic and is compressing Pampers into smaller plastic packs. It also is test marketing Downy fabric softener in refillable carton containers. The softener has to be mixed with water in a used plastic Downy bottle to make 64 ounces of the fabric softener. An appeal to the environment is prominently displayed on the package: "Better for the environment . . . . less packaging to throw away." The package is 75 percent smaller, and the refill costs 10 percent less than the regular Downy (Kirkpatrick, 1990, also see Chapter 4.3).

2. Wal-Mart has asked suppliers for more recycled or recyclable products and was the first retailer to state that it would give special in-store merchandising support to marketers trying to help prevent lasting environmental problems. Wal-Mart says that it is receiving tremendous responses from consumers and vendors, and that several vendors are making plans to change the packaging or the contents of their products (Hume and Strnad, 1989). Kmart Corporation disclosed a similar program with a full-page advertisement in *USA Today* (Hume and Strnad, 1989).

3. McDonald's is not only taking active steps to reduce waste at the source, it is also educating consumers about environmental issues. By making its straws 20 percent lighter, McDonald's eliminated 1 million pounds of waste per year (Kirkpatrick, 1990). It also tested recycling in 450 New England outlets, separately collecting polystyrene waste and recycling it. It made great efforts to describe its efforts and explain recycling on the paper liners on customers' trays (see Chapter 2.3).

4. 3M is investing in pollution controls to an extent that is well beyond what is required by law. New federal regulations require replacement or improvement by 1998 of underground storage tanks for liquids and gases. 3M has decided to comply by 1992 and to have all tanks worldwide in compliance by 1993 (Kirkpatrick, 1990). The estimated cost to 3M of this is more than $30 million. 3M management sees it is worthwhile to reduce the emission of a number of materials that might otherwise trigger further regulation.

5. Du Pont is pulling out of businesses that may harm the earth's atmosphere. Du Pont has announced that based on new evidence it believes that chlorofluorocarbons (CFCs) might be seriously depleting the earth's ozone layer. Consequently, it has decided to voluntarily suspend all production of CFCs, a $750 million-a-year business in which it leads the industry, by the year 2000 or sooner if possible (Kirkpatrick, 1990).

These varied responses of some leading firms are based on very different views about how the firm should adjust its products to respond to the green movement. Three views dominate.

First, consumer attitudes about the environment are changing dramatically and, in turn, this impacts their preferences. As good marketers, companies should adjust to take advantage of these changes. Firms that use their response to environmental concerns to differentiate themselves may well enjoy some competitive advantage, with potentially substantial improvements in market shares and profits for the first movers. One firm that has successfully exploited the green boom is the German battery manufacturer Varta. It was the first to market mercury-free batteries in the United Kingdom and its market share rose from 2 percent to 13 percent (Rice, 1990). This view can be seen as following customers' noncommercial concerns and clearly makes good marketing and business sense. In this view, what is ethical is also what is the most profitable.

A second view is that, given the growing public concern about the environment, if industry does not change quickly enough, regulation likely will increase. Hence, companies will have to change their ways sooner or later. In many respects it may be better to move sooner, rather than later, to reduce the likelihood of regulation, and, in fact, to influence regulation if it is to come about. This approach proposes that one must maximize profits but operate within the law, and, if possible, try to influence the law.

A third view involves making environmental considerations a part of all business and product policy decisions. This may strengthen the firm even though profits may suffer in the short term. Du Pont's CEO Edgar Woolard holds this view (Kirkpatrick, 1990). He is certain that the new emphasis on the environment will strengthen the company, but he admits that profits will suffer from those efforts over the next few years. This view has the potential of raising a host of ethical issues for the operating manager, because in this case doing the ethically right thing is not the most profitable. Implementing this view needs conviction and courage.

A major issue facing firms is how to handle the trade-off between doing what is best from an environmental point of view versus what is best from a profitability point of view. In some situations (view 1 above) this is easy, because there is no conflict. However, in a large number of situations (primarily view 3 and to some extent view 2), this can be a serious and difficult problem. Under what conditions is it better for the manager to put the environment ahead of the firm's profits?

CEOs continuously must weigh the long-term benefits, to society, of preventing pollution and, to the firm, of avoiding liability, all against the pressures for short-term returns. It probably will be several years or even decades before management decisions on air and water pollution, disposal of toxic chemicals and nuclear wastes, safety of new drugs and food additives, and exposure to toxic chemicals in the workplace will be proven to be adequate or lacking. At present, a few highly visible companies seem determined to do the right thing. It is one task to trade off profits for more environmentally appropriate behavior when the firm is making profits of billions of dollars. It is quite another task to make the same trade-off when the firm is running at a loss or making a small profit. Most firms are in fact in these latter groups. It will be interesting to see if smaller businesses (which account for a very large share of pollution) can follow the lead given by some of the large global organizations, especially given their typical lack of funds, profits, and technical know-how. The issue is, Can we expect and should we expect these smaller firms to make decisions that help the environment and at the same time adversely impact their bottom-line results?

A final major issue of concern in this area is what a company should do to avoid the potential backlash if it is viewed as exploiting the environmental concern for profit making. Consumers in general would like companies to be environmentally conscious and take steps to protect the environment. However, it is uncertain that consumers will sit back and accept exploitation of their environmental concerns. Overzealous marketers with overextending green-marketing campaigns in Britain and Canada have been attacked by environmentalists for unsubstantiated and inappropriate claims (Kirkpatrick, 1990). In the United States, the Federal Trade Commission started investigating environmental product claims in March 1990. Shortly thereafter, Mobil, for example, stopped claiming that its Hefty waste bags were biodegradable.

CONCLUDING COMMENTS

Marketers face an expanding variety and number of ethical issues in making product policy decisions. With the increasing competitiveness of markets and the growing complexity of products, this trend is likely to continue. Given the present emphasis on short-term profitability, managers are under intense pressure to focus on profitability without giving adequate attention to ethical considerations. Clearly, including ethical considerations in decision making will be helpful to society at large—but, in many cases, will be helpful to the firm as well—in the long run.

Some of the ethical issues in product policy deal with product and the environment, an area that is new, different, and likely to become even more important over the next few years. Marketers need to think carefully about whether the approaches used to address other issues can be used effectively to deal with environmental issues. It is an area that deserves much attention, because it affects not just the firm and those who deal with it or its products but society in general.

From a research point of view, product policy raises several extremely complex, interesting, and highly relevant issues that need to be addressed. The challenge facing researchers is how to address these rather complex, and in many ways rather different, issues with the research tools currently available and employed. Theory building, experimental testing of hypotheses, and sound field-based research may need to be combined to address any given issue. Very substantial rewards await researchers and managers who are able to address these issues appropriately.

REFERENCES

"The Best of Advertising Age/Gallup." *Advertising Age*, December 24, 1990, p. 22.

Bettman, James R.; John W. Payne; and Richard Staelin. "Cognitive Considerations in Designing Effective Labels for Presenting Risk Information." *Journal of Public Policy and Marketing* 5 (1986), pp. 1–28.

Carlson, K. O. "Natural Foods—The Consumer's Perspective." *Nielsen Researcher* 1 (1984), pp. 13–20.

Clement, David E. "Human Factors, Instructions and Warnings, and Product Liability." *IEEE Transactions on Professional Communication* PC-30, no. 3 (September 1987), pp. 149–56.

Crossen, Cynthia. "Tamperproof Packaging: Inventors Say It Can't Be Done—But They Keep Trying." *The Wall Street Journal*, February 26, 1986, p. 27.

Davidson, Dekkers L., and Kenneth E. Goodpaster. "Managing Product Safety: The Ford Pinto." Harvard Business School Case #383-129 (1983a).

————. "Managing Product Safety: The Case of the Firestone 500." Harvard Business School Case #383-130 (1983b).

————. "Managing Product Safety: The Case of the Procter & Gamble Rely Tampon." Harvard Business School Case #383-131 (1983c).

deTurck, Mark A., and Gerald M. Goldhaber. "Effectiveness of Product Warning Labels: Effects of Consumers' Information Processing Objectives." *Journal of Consumer Affairs* 23, no. 1 (Summer 1989), pp. 111–26.

Downs, Phillip E., and Douglas N. Behrman. "The Product Liability Coordinator: A Partial Solution." *Journal of the Academy of Marketing Science* 14, no. 3 (Fall 1986), pp. 58–65.

Driver, Russell W. "A Communication Model for Determining the Appropriateness of on-Product Warnings." *IEEE Transactions on Professional Communication* PC-30, no. 3 (September 1987), pp. 157–63.

Goldhaber, Gerald, and Mark deTurck. "Effects of Consumers' Familiarity with a Product on Attention to Compliance with Warnings." *Journal of Products Liability* 11 (1988), pp. 29–37.

"The Greening of Corporate America." *BusinessWeek*, April 23, 1990, pp. 96–103.

"A Hard Decision to Swallow." *Time*, March 3, 1986, p. 59.

Hartman, Raymond S. "Product Quality and Market Efficiency: The Effect of Product Recalls on Resale Prices and Firm Valuation." *Review of Economics and Statistics (Netherlands)* 69, no. 2 (May 1987), pp. 367–72.

Hume, Scott, and Patricia Strnad. "Consumers Go 'Green'." *Advertising Age*, September 25, 1989, pp. 3, 92.

Jackson, George C., and Fred W. Morgan. "Responding to Recall Requests: A Strategy for Managing Goods Withdrawal." *Journal of Public Policy and Marketing* 7 (1988), pp. 152–65.

Kirkpatrick, David. "Environmentalism: The New Crusade." *Fortune*, February 12, 1990.

Kotler, Philip, and Murali K. Mantrala. "Flawed Products: Consumer Responses and Marketer Stategies." *Journal of Consumer Marketing* 2, no. 3 (Summer 1985), pp. 27–36.

Madden, M. Stuart. "The Duty to Warn in Products Liability: Contours and Criticism." *Journal of Products Liability* 11 (1988), pp. 103–79.

Miller, Thomas J. "Food Advertising and Health Claims: Everything You Read Is Not Always Good for You." *Journal of State Government* 62, no. 3 (May/June 1989), pp. 107–10.

Morgan, Fred W. "Tampered Goods: Legal Developments and Marketing Guidelines." *Journal of Marketing* 52 (April 1988), pp. 86–96.

Moskal, Brian S. "Can Audi Make It Back?" *Industry Week* 236, no. 3 (February 1, 1988a), pp. 49–50.

————. "When Will Safety Sell?: Antilock Brakes Could Be a Competitor's Edge." *Industry Week* 237, no. 8 (October 17, 1988b), pp. 33, 36.

Nelson-Horchler, Joani. "Safety: A Tough Sell." *Industry Week* 236, no. 1 (January 4, 1988) p. 24.

O'Lone, Richard G. "Safety of Aging Aircraft Undergoes Reassessment." *Aviation Week and Space Technology*, May 16, 1988, pp. 16–18.

Peters, James, W. "We Can't Stop a Really Determined Nut." *Package Engineering*, March 1983, p. 7.

Pruitt, Stephen W., and David R. Peterson. "Security Price Reactions around Product Recall Announcements." *Journal of Financial Research* 9, no. 2 (December 1986), pp. 113–22.

"Recycled Plastic Wins Converts: Coke and Pepsi." *The Wall Street Journal*, December 5, 1990, pp. B1, 5.

Reilly, Robert J., and George E. Hoffer. "Will Retarding the Information Flow on Automobile Recalls Affect Consumer Demand?" *Economic Inquiry* 21 (July 1983), pp. 444–47.

Rice, Gillian. "Being Green: U.S. Marketers Begin to Respond." *Academy of Marketing Science News*, April 5, 1990.

Schwartz, V., and R. W. Driver. "Warnings in the Workplace: The Need for a Synthesis of Law and Communication Theory." *University of Cincinnati Law Review* 52, no. 1 (1983), p. 60.

Silverstein, David. "Managing Social Responsibility in a Changing Legal Environment." *American Business Law Journal* 25 (1987), pp. 523–66.

Treece, Jim. "If It Has Wheels and Carries People, Shouldn't It Be Safe?" *BusinessWeek*, no. 3057 (June 20, 1988), p. 48.

"Tylenol Decision to Cost J&J about $150 Million." *Business Insurance*, February 24, 1986, pp. 2, 18.

Velotta, Christopher. "Safety Labels: What to Put in Them, How to Write Them, and Where to Place Them." *IEEE Transactions on Professional Communication* PC-30, no. 3 (September 1987), pp. 121–26.

Weinstein, Fannie. "One Foot in the Junkyard." *Advertising Age* 58 (October 19, 1987), p. 92.

Winters, Patricia. "Cola Giants Take Packaging Lead." *Advertising Age* 53 (December 17, 1990), p. 30.

Black & Decker Corporation: Spacemaker Plus[1] Coffeemaker (A)

"My Black & Decker Spacemaker Plus coffeemaker has just set itself on fire," said the California caller to Black & Decker's customer service "800" number on December 1, 1988. Fortunately, as the caller calmly explained, the fire had been confined to the unit and was quickly extinguished. As he was preparing to paint his kitchen, he was not concerned about the smoke damage, though he did want a replacement coffeemaker. Black & Decker's concern was to get the unit back to the Household Product Group's (HPG) Shelton, Connecticut, headquarters as soon as possible to establish the cause of the fire in its new "Cadillac product."

With sales exceeding the same period in 1987 by more than 20 percent, the 1988 holiday season orders were strong for HPG. By December, it had succeeded in shipping all it could produce of the Spacemaker Plus line, including over 80,000 coffeemakers, in time for the peak holiday buying period. Launched mid-1988, the Spacemaker Plus line was a "key introduction" for HPG in the United States, illustrating Black & Decker's commitment to innovation and the development of quality new products with design appeal. A product recall would be a big professional and personal disappointment to HPG president Dennis Heiner. It could not automatically be assumed that a product involved in a fire would need to be recalled; it would need to be established whether the product was the cause or the victim of a fire. However, customers already had reported steaming problems with the Spacemaker Plus coffeemaker prior to the December 1 fire call. One of HPG's main competitors recently had settled out of court a product liability suit involving a fire hazard in one of its coffeemakers, at a figure around $40 million. But the prospect of litigation was only one of many considerations likely to influence Heiner's decision about a recall.

This case was prepared by Professor N. Craig Smith.
Copyright © 1990 by the President and Fellows of Harvard College.
Harvard Business School case 9-590-099 (Rev. 7/16/90).
[1] Spacemaker Plus is a trademark of the General Electric Company, U.S.A.

BLACK & DECKER CORPORATION

In 1910, Duncan Black and Alonzo Decker started their Baltimore machine shop. The name Black & Decker was soon to become synonymous with power tools after the company obtained a patent, in 1917, on the world's first portable power drill with pistol grip and trigger switch, virtually inventing an industry. Seventy years later, Black & Decker was "a global marketer and manufacturer of quality products used in and around the home and for commercial applications." It was the world's largest producer of power tools but had also become a leading supplier of household products, such as irons and toaster ovens. Marketing its products in over 100 countries, there was worldwide recognition of its brand name and a strong reputation for quality, value, and innovation. In fiscal 1988,[2] Black & Decker sales were $2.28 billion, generating net earnings of $97 million and a return on equity of 14.1 percent. These figures constituted a turnaround after some years of poor performance and were a credit to the leadership of Nolan Archibald, CEO since 1985, and his management team. In 1987, Alonzo Decker, Jr., the 80-year-old son of the company's cofounder, was able to say to Archibald: "Nolan, I want you to know this is the best Christmas I've had in 10 years."

Much of the success of the turnaround was attributed to a transformation in the corporate culture, with a customer orientation replacing a complacent manufacturing mentality such that "being market driven is more than a catch phrase; it defines [the] entire organization." This was a vital part of Black & Decker's efforts to reverse a persistent decline in market share to foreign competition, such as Makita of Japan and Bosch of West Germany. There was also a major restructuring, involving a $215 million write-off in 1985, five plant closures and downsizing of others, streamlining of the distribution system, and a 10 percent reduction in the number of employees to 20,800 by 1988. Under this "cut and build" strategy, globalization in manufacturing and marketing also came to be emphasized. With many of its products based around small electric motors, Black & Decker had been using 100 different motors worldwide. Rationalization and globalization reduced that number to less than 20. A global product strategy allowed Black & Decker to have common products worldwide that were customized to suit individual markets.

By 1988, Black & Decker had also digested its 1984 acquisition of the General Electric (GE) Housewares Division. Under the terms of the acquisition, Black & Decker had been permitted to manufacture and market appliances under the GE name until 1987. A marketing program was developed which successfully transferred the Black & Decker name to the GE small appliance lines, increasing market share from 27 percent to over 30 percent by 1988. The slower growth rate of the power tool market and increased foreign competition, as

---

[2] The Black & Decker fiscal year end was September 30. A calendar fiscal year was adopted as of 1990.

well as the success of its Dustbuster[3] rechargeable hand-held vacuum cleaner, had prompted Black & Decker to significantly increase its presence in the housewares market, with the GE acquisition providing greater access to housewares buyers. Further acquisitions were likely: to expand the earnings base and exploit a substantial tax loss carryforward. A hostile bid for American Standard, attractive to Black & Decker because it included a plumbing products business, had proven unsuccessful in 1987.[4]

In 1988, 52 percent of Black & Decker sales were in the United States, 33 percent in Europe, and 15 percent in other countries. Following the GE acquisition, Black & Decker had been formed into two key business units: power tools and small household appliances. The Power Tools Group was responsible for power tools (42 percent of worldwide sales), accessories (11 percent), and outdoor products (8 percent). Power tools included portable electric and cordless electric drills, screwdrivers, saws, sanders, and grinders; car care products; Workmate[5] Workcenters (a workbench with vices); and stationary woodworking tools. Accessories included power tool accessories and fastening products. Outdoor products included hedge and lawn trimmers, electric mowers, cordless brooms, and chain saws. The Household Products Group (33 percent worldwide sales) was responsible for products used inside the home: cordless vacuums, irons, food preparation products (such as mixers), coffeemakers, toasters, toaster ovens, and lighting, heating, and fire safety products. HPG sales grew by 14 percent in fiscal 1988. Supporting both groups was Black & Decker's service operation (6 percent worldwide sales), comprising 244 company-owned service centers (120 in the United States) and several hundred authorized independent outlets.

SPACEMAKER PLUS

Industry analysts described the flow of new products as probably the single most critical factor in Black & Decker's growth equation. In 1988, 40 percent of HPG sales came from products three years old or less. At the housewares trade exhibition in January 1989, Black & Decker planned to display 12 new small appliance lines. Archibald had said, "There are no mature markets, only mature managements." Heiner believed the way to sell a product as mature as an iron was to add something like an automatic shut-off feature; similarly,

---

[3] Dustbuster is a registered trademark of Black & Decker Corporation.

[4] In April 1989, Black & Decker acquired the larger Emhart Corporation, a diversified multinational producer of industrial and consumer products, including fastening products, and information and electronic systems. Annual revenues would be doubled; but industry analysts had doubts about the acquisition, with the more favorable commenting that this would be "an interesting story in the long term." A bid to acquire Sunbeam/Oster from the bankrupt Allegheny International had fallen through earlier in 1989.

[5] Workmate is a registered trademark of Black & Decker Corporation.

blenders became cordless and Dustbuster vacuum cleaners became more powerful. Average industry returns on sales were low, at 3–4 percent, in the price-sensitive domestic appliance market. (It had yet to attract much interest from Japanese competition.) Some companies serving narrow niches in the market realized 8 percent; HPG had done better still, realizing an operating income in excess of 10 percent of sales in 1987 and 1988. But achieving growth and high levels of profitability through innovation was certainly a challenge for HPG.

Black & Decker's household product sales were $749 million worldwide in 1988, the majority of which were in the United States. Heiner aimed to significantly increase U.S. sales over the next five years by concentrating on the five core business areas where Black & Decker felt it had sustainable competitive advantage: irons, vacuum cleaners, toaster ovens, coffeemakers, and toasters. While some of this growth probably would be through acquisitions, much of it would need to be internally generated. In keeping with Black & Decker's market-driven philosophy, HPG's mission was "to provide superior customer satisfaction as the dominant brand of high-quality, innovative household products." Heiner was striving to develop a total quality culture with a commitment to customer care within HPG. He believed this approach would enable the group to realize its ambitious sales targets.

In a composite market share estimation, Black & Decker dominated the U.S. small domestic appliance market in 1988, with around a 30 percent share by volume and value, compared to the roughly 10 percent share held by each of its nearest rivals, Proctor Silex and Sunbeam. Table 1 shows Black & Decker and competitor composite quarterly market shares 1987–88. Table 2 shows Black & Decker and leading competitor market shares by product category for July–September 1987 and 1988. Table 3 shows Black & Decker and competitor quarterly market shares for drip coffeemakers 1987–88.

The new Spacemaker Plus line was described in the annual report as a "major product highlight of 1988." As well as offering new products, this line was able to command the better profit margins HPG was keen to secure: its "contribution margin" (effectively, gross profit) was substantially higher than the 40 percent average of all HPG lines. Black & Decker had inherited the Spacemaker concept from GE. An under-the-cabinet electric can opener had been launched in 1982, followed in 1983 by the addition of a toaster oven, a drip coffeemaker, a mixer, and an electric knife sharpener to the Spacemaker line. However, while off the countertop, these products remained bulky and saved little space in their vertical configuration. Lower-priced competitive imitations had also appeared.

In the product line evaluation after the GE acquisition, Black & Decker decided the Spacemaker line needed to be completely redesigned. An integrated development team—comprising former GE and Black & Decker designers, engineers, and manufacturing experts—was responsible for the project from conception to production. Focusing on the coffeemaker, the product development team sought to reduce its size and bulk, making it as horizontal as

TABLE 1 Composite Quarterly Market Shares by Volume and Value: Small Domestic Appliances, 1987–88

Core Categories*	1987 By Volume				1988				By Value	
	Jan.–Mar.	Apr.–June	July–Sep.	Oct.–Dec.	Jan.–Mar.	Apr.–June	July–Sep.	Oct.–Dec.†	July–Sep.	Oct.–Dec.†
Black & Decker	25.0%	25.9%	26.1%	27.4%	27.3%	29.0%	29.0%	32.2%	28.6%	31.1%
Hamilton Beach	7.8	7.8	7.4	8.1	7.8	7.9	7.4	7.1	6.1	5.3
Proctor Silex	9.5	10.3	10.7	9.5	11.4	10.4	11.2	9.0	8.3	6.6
Sunbeam	10.7	10.1	10.5	10.7	10.0	9.8	10.2	9.4	9.4	8.4
Norelco	8.0	7.1	6.6	5.0	5.1	4.1	3.5	2.8	2.6	2.2
Toastmaster	5.5	5.2	5.5	5.3	5.4	5.4	5.3	4.6	4.5	3.7
Other	33.5	33.6	33.2	34.0	33.0	33.4	33.4	34.9	40.6	42.6

Columns may not total 100 percent due to rounding error.
† Estimated.
* Core categories are: irons, rechargeable hand-held vacuum cleaners, rechargeable stick vacuum cleaners, toaster ovens, toasters, drip coffeemakers, food processors, food choppers, portable mixers, can openers, electric knives, and blenders.

Source: Black & Decker Corporation.

possible and a genuine spacesaver. A new "book-shaped" water reservoir that inserted like a video cassette was developed, and much of the volume of the housing of the coffeemaker was kept to the rear of the cabinet, significantly reducing actual and, from a standing position, perceived size. An innovation stemming from consumer research, the use of a thermal carafe eliminated the requirement for a "keep-warm plate," reducing space and size but also manufacturing and assembly costs. Design featured strongly in Black & Decker's strategy of leveraging low-cost manufacturing with aggressive marketing.

Launched to praise from many quarters in June 1988, the Spacemaker Plus line comprised five models: the PDC403 coffeemaker, with digital clock for preset brewing (suggested retail price $112); the PDC401 coffeemaker, without clock ($80); the PEC90 can opener, with knife sharpener ($37); the PEC60 can opener, without knife sharpener ($32); and the PLA100 kitchen accessory light ($24). In contrast to the dark colors of the original Spacemaker line, these products were in white and, together, made a cohesive visual scheme, encouraging consumers to combine units, as shown in Exhibit 1. Said to resemble a Danish stereo, Spacemaker Plus met the approval of the Industrial Designers Society of America, winning its Design Excellence award in August 1988; the "design's elegant restraint is exquisite," said the jurors. In October 1988, *Appliance Manufacturer* magazine named Spacemaker Plus the first-place winner in its annual award competition for appliance products, based on its aesthetic appeal, functionality, ease of use, and engineering execution. Spacemaker Plus soon was "making inroads in a market that swooned over Krups and Braun," commented the *New York Times*. Until December 1988, at least, it was a Black & Decker success story.

THE FIRE INVESTIGATION

When the fire call came in, David Wildman, manager of the HPG Product Safety and Liability Group, had been immediately alerted. This group was responsible for safety. It had reviewed the design and initial prototype of the coffeemaker and arranged for its testing in Black & Decker's laboratories when approval had been given for the production of larger numbers of prototypes. A failure mode effect analysis had not indicated a safety problem arising from any of the three primary causes of injury: fire, shock, or cut hazard. However, the coffeemaker's new design meant there were no established standards. The normal industry practice for small appliances was to have them certified as safe by Underwriters' Laboratory (UL), an independent testing service. This was not mandatory, but it was required of manufacturers by many retailers. It was Black & Decker company policy not to sell a product unless it met, if not exceeded, UL requirements. The Spacemaker Plus exceeded the UL requirement for coffeemakers of a single temperature cut-off (TCO), which shuts the unit off in the event of overheating. Black & Decker fitted two TCOs to all its coffeemakers, believing that the fire and consequent liability problems

TABLE 2 Volume Market Shares by Product Category, 1987 and 1988

Product Category	Company (rank ordered)	Percent Market Share by Volume	
		July–September 1987	July–September 1988
Irons	Black & Decker	47.4%	47.7%
	Proctor Silex	13.6	18.3
	Sunbeam	18.9	18.0
Can openers	Rival	30.6	29.2
	Black & Decker	22.6	23.3
	Sunbeam	11.2	11.3
Rechargeable hand-held vacuum cleaners	Black & Decker	79.8	74.4
	Hoover	2.1	15.0
	Eureka	8.6	5.6
Toaster ovens	Black & Decker	45.7	59.7
	Toastmaster	16.0	13.8
	Proctor Silex	19.9	13.4
Portable mixers	Black & Decker	27.2	35.0
	Sunbeam	28.7	23.0
	Hamilton Beach	7.9	10.0
Food choppers	Black & Decker	14.5	27.0
	Sunbeam	13.9	23.9
	Cuisinart	21.2	16.2
Food processors	Sunbeam	30.5	22.4
	Hamilton Beach	15.1	12.5
	Black & Decker	8.2	9.5
Drip coffeemakers	Mr. Coffee	21.3	21.6
	Black & Decker	11.3	16.4
	Proctor Silex	13.6	15.3
Toasters	Toastmaster	32.8	30.7
	Proctor Silex	25.7	25.9
	Black & Decker	12.0	12.6
Rechargeable stick vacuum cleaners	Black & Decker	N/A	37.6
	Eureka	32.6	32.7
	Regina	62.4	29.7
Rechargeable "lites"	First Alert	35.2	31.3
	Black & Decker	34.7	24.7
	Houseworks	5.0	20.4
Smoke alarms	First Alert	38.2	38.4
	Southwest Labs	2.1	20.0
	Family Gard	23.0	17.6
	Black & Decker	7.1	11.6

TABLE 2 *(concluded)*

Product Category	Company (rank ordered)	Percent Market Share by Volume July–September 1987	July–September 1988
Stand mixers	Sunbeam	50.0	45.7
	Kitchen Aid	15.3	34.3
	Hamilton Beach	10.6	7.1
	Waring	13.5	5.2
	Krups	8.5	5.2
	Black & Decker	0.0	0.5
Electric knives	Hamilton Beach	34.2	37.0
	Black & Decker	30.7	31.4
	Regal/Moulinex	16.9	11.1
Regular blenders (excluding hand blenders)	Oster	44.6	45.7
	Hamilton Beach	37.5	34.0
	Waring	16.0	10.4
	Black & Decker	2.0	7.1
Hot air corn poppers	West Bend	36.8	32.1
	Presto	36.4	31.3
	Wearever	22.0	19.9
	Hamilton Beach	3.4	8.5
	Black & Decker	1.4	6.5

N/A means not available.

Source: Black & Decker Corporation

experienced by a competitor with one of its coffeemakers might have been avoided if a second cut-off had been included in the unit. The PDC401 and PDC403 coffeemakers were both fitted with two TCOs.

Wildman spoke with the California customer about possible causes of the fire and arranged for the immediate collection of the coffeemaker by a courier service. Within 24 hours the damaged coffeemaker was in Shelton and investigations began immediately. Working round the clock, it was concluded on December 3, less than 48 hours after the fire had been reported, that the unit was responsible and external sources or misuse could be ruled out. The precise cause of the fire had yet to be established. However, a laboratory test, which involved clamping the feed from the reservoir to the heater element, starving the unit of water, had produced overheating and fires in new units, despite the TCOs. Accordingly, all units could be considered potentially faulty and, therefore, fire hazards. Wildman informed Heiner, who was then in Australia and promptly curtailed his trip to return to Shelton.

A manufacturer was obligated under the United States Consumer Product Safety Act to recall a product where there was knowledge of a substantial product hazard. Although telephone calls to California had led Wildman to

TABLE 3 Drip Coffeemakers: U.S. Market Shares by Volume and Value, 1987–88

Company (ranked order)	1987								1988							
	Jan.–Mar.		Apr.–Jun.		Jul.–Sep.		Oct.–Dec.		Jan.–Mar.		Apr.–Jun.		Jul.–Sep.		Oct.–Dec.*	
	By Volume	By Value	By Volume	By Value	By Volume	By Value	By Volume	By Value	By Volume	By Value	By Volume	By Value	By Volume	By Value	By Volume	By Value
Black & Decker	12.0%	(14.9)%	12.8%	(15.1)%	11.3%	(12.8)%	14.3%	(14.8)%	12.8%	(13.6)%	16.7%	(16.8)%	16.4%	(16.2)%	22.0%	(23.3)%
Mr. Coffee	21.9	(17.6)	19.4	(15.5)	21.3	(16.9)	21.6	(17.6)	19.0	(15.2)	19.3	(15.4)	21.6	(16.3)	20.8	(15.2)
Braun	7.8	(9.6)	9.2	(11.6)	10.5	(13.9)	12.0	(15.5)	11.7	(15.7)	11.6	(15.8)	12.2	(16.5)	13.0	(17.4)
Proctor Silex	11.4	(7.5)	13.3	(8.8)	13.6	(9.4)	14.0	(9.5)	17.7	(12.6)	16.6	(11.6)	15.3	(10.0)	11.9	(7.4)
Krups	8.3	(13.6)	9.7	(15.2)	9.4	(14.4)	6.8	(10.0)	7.1	(11.5)	8.1	(13.2)	9.3	(15.6)	9.4	(15.0)
Norelco	18.3	(14.3)	15.6	(12.2)	15.0	(11.8)	13.3	(10.7)	12.6	(10.1)	8.9	(7.1)	7.3	(5.7)	7.2	(5.8)
All other	20.3	(22.5)	20.0	(21.6)	18.9	(20.8)	18.0	(20.0)	19.1	(21.4)	18.8	(20.3)	17.9	(19.6)	15.7	(15.7)

Columns may not total 100 percent due to rounding error.
* Estimated.

Source: Black & Decker Corporation.

EXHIBIT 1 Spacemaker Plus Coffeemaker, Can Opener, and Accessory Light

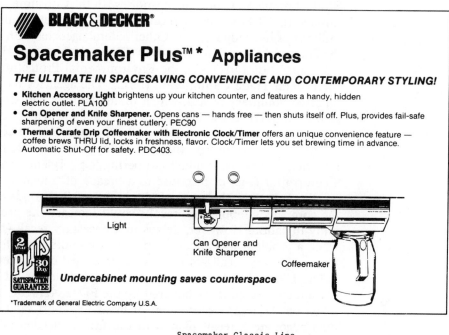

BLACK & DECKER®

Spacemaker Plus™ * Appliances

THE ULTIMATE IN SPACESAVING CONVENIENCE AND CONTEMPORARY STYLING!

- **Kitchen Accessory Light** brightens up your kitchen counter, and features a handy, hidden electric outlet. PLA100
- **Can Opener and Knife Sharpener.** Opens cans — hands free — then shuts itself off. Plus, provides fail-safe sharpening of even your finest cutlery. PEC90
- **Thermal Carafe Drip Coffeemaker with Electronic Clock/Timer** offers an unique convenience feature — coffee brews THRU lid, locks in freshness, flavor. Clock/Timer lets you set brewing time in advance. Automatic Shut-Off for safety. PDC403.

Light

Can Opener and
Knife Sharpener

Coffeemaker

Undercabinet mounting saves counterspace

*Trademark of General Electric Company U.S.A.

Spacemaker Classic Line

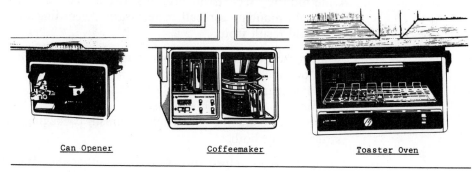

Can Opener   Coffeemaker   Toaster Oven

Source: Black & Decker Corporation.

suspect the fire had something to do with the customer not fully inserting the water reservoir drawer, he did believe there was some prospect of a legal requirement to recall the coffeemaker. In the event any product liability claims emerged, these would have to be met by the company because Black & Decker was self-insured.

PRODUCT RECALLS

Product recalls were not uncommon, with the Consumer Product Safety Commission (CPSC) overseeing more than 100 product recalls annually, involving millions of individual items. Other federal agencies with recall authority were the Food and Drug Administration (FDA), the National Highway Traffic Safety Administration (NHTSA), the Environmental Protection Agency (EPA), and the Federal Trade Commission (FTC). The agencies relied primarily on self-reported voluntary recalls, which manufacturers had strong incentives to organize; but NHTSA could mandate recalls and had forced automobile manufacturers to undertake major recall programs. Recalls could result from poor design or manufacturing, although many arose from faults that developed in unanticipated ways. Product tampering (e.g., Tylenol case) or legal action by a competitor (e.g., in response to a breach of trademark) could also prompt recalls. As well as the costs of obtaining recalled goods and possible harm to the company's reputation, recalls could increase the prospect of product liability litigation. However, delays to a necessary recall—by not acting quickly when a problem was apparent, or not responding to a federal agency request for a voluntary recall—could have severe legal consequences.

The CPSC, created in 1972, was responsible for all goods used by final consumers, except those covered by the FDA, NHTSA, and EPA. The agency relied on the legal requirement of firms to report safety problems. It would then negotiate a recall plan with the firm if needed. The firm then had to provide monthly reports on progress of the recall. Black & Decker believed CPSC could mandate a recall if necessary. According to CPSC, a dangerous defect could result from:

1. A fault, flaw, or irregularity that causes weakness, failure, or inadequacy in form or function.
2. Manufacturing or production error.
3. A product's design or materials.
4. A product's contents, construction, finish, packaging, and warnings or instructions, or both.

Guidelines also helped to determine whether the safety problem was substantial:

1. The nature of the risk of injury the product presents and the severity of the risk (i.e., the seriousness of the possible injury and the likelihood that an injury could occur).
2. The necessity for the product, its utility, and the ways it can be used or misused.
3. The number of defective products, and the population group exposed to the products.
4. The physical environment within which the defect manifests itself.
5. Case law involving health, safety, and product liability.

6. The CPSC's own experience and expertise as well as other relevant factors.

Recall return rates varied greatly. NHTSA recalls for automobiles reportedly achieved correction rates of 15–70 percent. Many CPSC recalls achieved return rates under 10 percent, particularly with the difficulty in contacting owners of inexpensive but harmful products. A study of CPSC recalls,[6] obtained by HPG, had examined factors influencing the three conditions necessary for a successful recall:

- Product availability—in the distribution channel or at least still in the possession of consumers (determined by the average age of the product and its average useful life).

- Distributor and consumer awareness of the recall.

- Benefits of compliance with the recall exceeding perceived costs of time, effort, and lost product services.

The CPSC study outlined a model for predicting likely recall return rates, highlighting these variables:

- The number of months separating end of distribution and the start of the recall.

- The percentage of products owned by consumers who are notified of the recall directly by mail.

- The percentage of items (produced) in retail inventory. (Distributors and retailers had strong incentives to comply with recalls, because of concern for their reputations and the prospect of liability suits; their costs of compliance were usually relatively low and they could be relatively easily reached.)

- The percentage of items (produced) in the hands of consumers. (Return rates are typically lower for products with consumers than those in the distribution channel. Factors said to influence consumer compliance include the severity of the safety hazard, the value of the product—higher benefit of compliance with more expensive products—and the type of remedy provided.)

- Whether a repair at home is offered to the consumer (relative to more inconvenient alternatives).

While the CPSC study reported an average correction/return rate of 54.4 percent over the sample of 128 recalls between 1978 and 1983, there was considerable variance, largely explained by the above variables. In the experience of Black & Decker personnel, return rates of products distributed to consumers were historically low, with a domestic appliance industry average said to be around 5 percent and anything over 22 percent "doing excellent."

---

[6] R. Dennis Murphy and Paul H. Rubin, "Determinants of Recall Success Rates," *Journal of Products Liability* 11 (1988), pp. 17–28.

HPG had not previously recalled a product, though the GE Housewares Division had recalled an electric fan some years ago and Black & Decker had recalled some of its power tool products in the past. The GE fan recall had also involved a fire hazard. The low response rate of 6 percent was attributed to the late announcement of the recall; negotiations with the CPSC had delayed the announcement to November, when few consumers were thinking about fans. Return rates on Black & Decker outdoor products had been as low as 3 percent.

In the opinion of Ken Homa, vice president of marketing at HPG, most manufacturers would try to avoid recalls but, should they arise, had few incentives to pursue high return rates. The conventional wisdom was that recalls were difficult to do effectively; they increased the possibility of product liability litigation, the regulatory agencies were cumbersome to deal with, and a high return rate would set a precedent for future recalls. The cost of recalls and the potential damage to the company's brand name were also considerations. As a consequence, established procedures were limited and, as Gael Simonson, director of brand marketing and strategy development, put it: "There was a precedent to be passive."

HEINER'S DECISION

On December 5, Wildman informed the CPSC that there had been a fire in a Spacemaker Plus coffeemaker, which was being investigated, and that shipments of the product had stopped. He also advised the corporate legal department. The next day at a meeting with Heiner, Homa, and other senior management, Wildman reported his investigations. While not certain of the cause of the starvation problem, he suspected it was due to incomplete closure of the reservoir drawer. "You'd have to try hard to get the reservoir in the wrong way" was one exasperated reaction at the meeting.

Heiner was told that about 25,000 units were with consumers in virtually any of the 90 million households in the United States. About 10 percent of these owners were believed to have returned warranty cards, supplying their names and addresses. Black & Decker had distributed 88,400 Spacemaker Plus coffeemakers, the majority through major retailing chains, such as Sears, Penney's, Best Products, and Service Merchandise, with the remainder through small local appliance and department stores and some within Black & Decker. The precise number of units sold through to consumers could not be ascertained, but was believed to be about 30–35 percent of units distributed. In some recalls, consumers were provided with a similar or superior model to replace the faulty product; but HPG did not have a suitable replacement for the Spacemaker Plus coffeemaker. Most worrying for the HPG management team was the likelihood of the safety problem arising when the product was unattended. Both versions of the coffeemaker operated automatically; the PDC403 had a 24-hour digital clock/timer, so consumers could preset the machine at night to start at a selected time and wake in the morning to fresh-brewed coffee. Around 40 percent of HPG sales were during the pre-Christmas season and many of these units, therefore, were wrapped as gifts.

HPG was facing increased pressure on margins, with rising costs of raw materials. The corporate safety manager from Black & Decker's Towson, Maryland, headquarters had suggested a 15–20 percent return of units with consumers would probably meet the letter of the law. It had been estimated that with a 25 percent consumer return rate the recall would cost around $4 million (excluding opportunity costs of lost sales). Table 4 shows recall cost estimates. The corporate safety manager explained that the procedure, in the event of a recall, was to notify CPSC and develop a recall program. These negotiations usually took about four to six weeks.

Heiner had informed Archibald of the safety problem. But it was Heiner's decision as to what HPG should do next.

TABLE 4 Recall Cost Estimates*

Consumer Recall

Approximate
$ millions

- 25,000 units sold @ 25 percent response — 6,250 units returned.

Option 1 Replacement coffeemaker when available at (current) manufactured cost of $40 (PDC403) and $30 (PDC401). PDC403 sales were approximately twice those of PDC401.

$$PDC403 \quad 6,250 \times \tfrac{2}{3} \times 40 = \$166,667$$

$$PDC401 \quad 6,250 \times \tfrac{1}{3} \times 30 = \underline{\quad 62,500\quad}$$

$$\$229,167 \qquad \$0.230$$

Option 2 Cash refund at suggested retail prices:

$$PDC403 \quad 6,250 \times \tfrac{2}{3} \times 112 = \$466,667$$

$$PDC401 \quad 6,250 \times \tfrac{1}{3} \times \quad 80 = \underline{\quad 166,667\quad}$$

$$\$633,334 \qquad \$0.635$$

- Freight, labels, administration:

  Approximately $100/unit returned $0.625

Retail Recall

- Return of 63,400 units for refund (and to be reworked).
  Lost margin, at an average of $30/unit:

  $$63,400 \times 30 = \$1,902,000 \qquad \$1.900$$

- Freight, refunds on joint promotions, administration, and the like:

  Estimated at $500,000 $0.500

- Rework of returned units for later sale.
  Best estimate, unless major work required, of $10/unit:

  $$63,400 \times 10 = \$634,000 \qquad \underline{\$0.635}$$

Total cost approximately (with cash refund to consumers) $4.3M

---

* Cost and margin data have been disguised, but estimates provided here are useful for analysis.

The Procter & Gamble Company: The Lenor Refill Package

In July 1987, Kathy Stadler, assistant brand manager for Lenor, Procter & Gamble GmbH's (P&G Germany) profitable fabric softener brand, was preparing for an upper-level management meeting to discuss the proposal for the national launch of a Lenor refill package. The refill package represented an innovative solution to West Germany's growing environmental concerns by promising to reduce by 85 percent the packaging materials used in Lenor's standard plastic container. Management hoped that this line extension would help stem Lenor's eroding sales volume and market share.

Stadler recalled a memo written two years earlier by Rolf Kunisch, the general manager for P&G Germany, in which he advocated "moving the company's attitudes from defensive thinking in environmental terms towards offensive and successful approaches." While Stadler felt that the Lenor refill package met this mandate, she was uncertain about the consumer response. Stadler knew that the refill package would not address many German consumers' concerns over the product's chemical content. A biodegradable version of Lenor still needed several years of development. The refill package seemed to offer an interim solution. Would the public hail it as an attempt to protect the environment? Or would they view it as an effort to sidestep the "real" issue of water pollution from Lenor's chemical contents?

Stadler's brand manager, Leonard Phillippe, felt that an aggressive promotion of an existing concentrated formula of Lenor, which used less packaging materials than the more-popular fully diluted version, would be less risky than the refill package introduction. Stadler, however, believed that this strategy would not stem Lenor's eroding sales volume. Nevertheless, she knew that both options would be hotly debated at the forthcoming meeting with Rolf Kunisch.

This case was prepared by Julie L. Yao under the direction of Professor John A. Quelch and with the assistance of Professor Minette E. Drumwright. Certain data and names have been disguised. Copyright © 1991 by the President and Fellows of Harvard College. Harvard Business School case N9-592-016 (Rev. 9/11/91).

THE PROCTER & GAMBLE COMPANY

In 1987,[1] the Procter & Gamble Company (P&G), a leading consumer products company, had more than $13.7 billion in assets, generated $17 billion in worldwide revenues, and delivered $617 million in pretax earnings. P&G sold products in 125 countries, marketing more than 100 brands of laundry, household cleaning, personal care, food, and beverage products. International operations, which included Europe, South America, and Asia, accounted for over 30 percent of P&G's 1987 sales and earnings. In 1987, international sales grew 38 percent, almost five times as much as U.S. domestic sales.

P&G had a long-standing reputation for superior products, marketing expertise, talented employees, conservative management, and high integrity in its business dealings. A strong corporate culture pervaded the firm. The 1987 annual report stated the company's philosophy as follows:

> We will provide products of superior quality and value that best fill the needs of the world's consumers. We will achieve that purpose through an organization and a working environment which attracts the finest people; fully develops and challenges our individual talents; encourages our free and spirited collaboration to drive the business ahead; and maintains the Company's historic principles of integrity and doing the right thing. Through the successful pursuit of our commitment, we expect our brands to achieve leadership share and profit positions and that, as a result, our business, our people, our shareholders, and the communities in which we live and work, will prosper.

To develop these superior products, P&G relied on continual product development. In 1987, more than 3.3 percent of its revenues were spent on research. In addition, P&G believed in extensive product and market testing. P&G frequently took two to three years to test a new product and its marketing strategy before a major launch.

Procter & Gamble GmbH

Procter & Gamble GmbH was established in 1963 following the acquisition of a local detergent manufacturer. By 1987, P&G Germany generated DM 1,037 million in revenues.[2] P&G Germany sold more than 30 brands, including Ariel, a top-selling detergent, and Lenor, West Germany's leading fabric softener. Seventy-seven percent of its revenues and 60 percent of its earnings came from the Laundry and Cleaning Division, which included detergents, cleaners, and fabric softener.

---

[1] P&G operated on a July 1 to June 30 fiscal year basis; at the time of this case, P&G had just entered its 1988 fiscal year. Unless otherwise specified, all company data are on a fiscal year basis.

[2] One U.S. dollar was equivalent to 1.9 deutschmarks (DM).

P&G Germany's 6,700-person subsidiary comprised four divisions: Laundry and Cleaning, Paper, Beverages, and Health and Beauty Care. Each division had sales, finance, manufacturing, and product development organizations. Every major P&G Germany product also had its own brand management team, which developed and implemented the brand's marketing strategy against sales and profit targets approved by top management. A brand team generally consisted of a brand manager, an assistant brand manager, and one or two brand assistants, who all worked closely with the division's other departments as well as with staff groups specializing in advertising services, management information systems, and personnel.

A 320-person sales force marketed P&G Germany products to the retail trade. Key account managers called on the headquarters of the large retail grocery chains year-round, while field salespeople serviced both independent stores as well as chain outlets.

P&G Germany manufactured most of its products locally. While some production was outsourced, P&G Germany generally preferred to manufacture its own products to ensure the highest level of quality control.

The Fabric Softener Industry

Fabric softener products first appeared during the 1950s to combat the harsh effects of detergents; when added to the wash, fabric softener produced soft, scented, and static-free clothes. It was particularly popular in Europe, where hard water washing conditions were common. In 1987, consumers could purchase fabric softener in one of three forms: a diluted liquid; a concentrated liquid, three or four times more concentrated than the dilute; and woven sheets that were used while machine-drying. The regular user's average purchase cycle was two months. Dosage varied according to the type and volume of laundry, but an average washload required 100 milliliters of dilute or 30 ml to 40 ml of concentrate.

Fabric softener liquids combined 5 percent softening ingredients, called *cationic tensides*, with 95 percent water. Fabric softener concentrates included 15 percent softening ingredients. Fabric softeners were packaged in hard, high-density polyethylene (HDPE) plastic containers. Users added liquid fabric softener during a washing machine's wash cycle or poured it into a convenient special dispenser built into the machine before the start of the wash.

Like many other household chemical products, fabric softeners, with 2 percent inert non-biodegradable ingredients, were considered by some environmentally conscious consumers to be unnecessary water "pollutants." An increasing number of consumers believed that a buildup of non-biodegradable chemicals could damage their water supply. Many felt that the benefit delivered by fabric softener was superfluous.

Environmental Concern

In the mid-1980s, public anxiety about environmental problems escalated in Europe. A 1986 survey of 11,800 Western European consumers revealed that 72 to 79 percent were "somewhat" or "very" concerned about ecological problems, such as acid rain, toxic waste, and the greenhouse effect. The media attributed these concerns to Europe's high population density and its centuries-old exploitation of natural resources.[3]

West German attitudes were consistently "greener" than those of neighboring countries. In 1987, an opinion poll entitled "Sorrows of the Nation" found that 53 percent of West Germans surveyed were concerned with the protection of the environment, up from 16 percent four years earlier. Concern for the environment ranked as their second most common concern, behind unemployment. Environmental issues also affected the German political arena, as evidenced by the rising popularity of the pro-environment Green Party.

A 1987 opinion poll showed that 47 percent of German households agreed that they used fewer environmentally problematic goods than previously, versus 21 percent who agreed with the same statement in 1985. Both consumer awareness of environmentally controversial products and the percentage of consumers claiming a willingness to pay more for environmentally friendly packaging had increased. In practice, however, consumers traded off price against environmental safety; there was a limit to the price premium they were prepared to pay. In addition, many consumers indicated that they were not willing to give up product quality for the environment. Nevertheless, environmentally uncontroversial products, such as phosphate-free detergents, had become increasingly popular.

In 1984, a West German federal government agency publicly denounced allegedly environmentally harmful products, including P&G Germany's laundry booster, Top Job. A consumer boycott to force the removal of these products from the market caused Top Job's sales volume to drop by 50 percent in the following year. In 1986, the government passed the Waste Avoidance, Utilization, and Disposal Act, which gave authorities the power to restrict or even ban materials with content toxicity or waste volume that were considered excessively environmentally problematic.

The West German government also supported a nationwide eco-labeling initiative called the "Blue Angel" program, to promote environmentally compatible products through labeling. By 1987, more than 2,000 products in 50 categories bore the Blue Angel seal; fabric softener products had never qualified. By 1987, the Blue Angel seal was recognized by 80 percent of West German consumers.[4] Industry experts believed that products "blessed" with the Blue Angel seal enjoyed increased sales of up to 10 percent.

---

[3] A. Hussein, *Eco-labels: Product Management in a Greener Europe* (Environmental Data Services, Ltd. Finsbury Business Center), p. 53.

[4] Lori K. Carswell, *"Environmental Labeling in the United States—Background Research, Issues, and Recommendations,"* draft report, Applied Decision Analysis, 1989, p. 10.

Though public and media attention centered more on a product's contents and less on its packaging, the issue of solid waste reduction was growing in importance. Land was scarce; West Germany burned 34 percent of its trash, compared to only 3 percent in the United States. Municipalities charged citizens for garbage collection based on volume. By 1985, West Germans recycled more than one third of their paper, glass, and aluminum waste; however, plastic recycling was limited.

Market Size and Trends

The average West German homemaker used eight different products, such as bleach and fabric softener, for washing and cleaning. The German fabric softener consumer enjoyed "fresh" clothes, which combined the characteristics of a soft touch, "clean" smell, and bright appearance. A 1986 P&G Germany market research study concluded that fabric softener usage and dosage were relatively uniform across all age groups, irrespective of brand. Fabric softener users, however, spent more effort on pretreating and prewashing their laundry than nonusers.

In 1987, West Germany was the largest fabric softener market in Europe, with retail sales totaling DM409 million ($215 million), compared to $4 billion in the U.S. market, with a population four times West Germany's. Although the value of retail sales had increased due to price rises, market volume had fallen from a peak of 18,200 MSUs in 1983 to 16,700 MSUs in 1987.[5] Forecasters predicted further volume decreases of 1 to 3 percent per year.

Research had shown that this decline was attributed to a shrinking base of fabric softener users. Table 1 shows usage trends from periodic diary studies:[6]

TABLE 1   Fabric Softener Usage Trends (percentage surveyed)

	1982	1984	1986
Fabric softener users	89%	84%	72%
Total wash loads softened*	72	67	57
Wash loads softened among users†	75	73	74

* Percentage of all wash loads recorded in diary study that had fabric softener added.
† Among fabric softener users, percentage of wash loads that had fabric softener added.

[5] An MSU, or thousand statistical units, was a standardized P&G measure that permitted comparison of products on the basis of an equal number of uses. Consequently, a 1-liter bottle of 4:1 Lenor concentrate and a 4-liter bottle of Lenor dilute were equivalent on an MSU basis because both gave the consumer the same number of uses. Costs and unit volumes are presented per SU (abbreviation for statistical unit) for comparison purposes.

[6] Each participant was asked to keep a diary of his or her usage habits during a two-week time period, from which results were tabulated.

Results from a 1986 telephone survey found that many consumers had ceased using fabric softener due to environmental concerns highlighted by the news media. Research revealed that West German consumers were more concerned about the environmental effects of using supplementary household chemicals such as fabric softener than consumers in other West European countries. Exhibit 1 presents key results from this study.

Competition

In 1987, four competitors sold 80 percent of the volume in the West German fabric softener market.[7] P&G Germany's Lenor led the market with a 39 percent volume share, followed by Colgate-Palmolive's Softlan (19 percent), Unilever's Kuschelweich (Snuggle) (12 percent), and Henkel's Vernel (8 percent). Generic and private-label brands accounted for the remaining 22 percent of the market.

All four firms sold fabric softener in most West European markets. Each competitor promoted similar product benefits: freshness, softness, ease of iron-

EXHIBIT 1   Selected Results from Fabric Softener Usage Monitoring Studies

	June 1985	*February 1986*
Percentage of respondents who were:		
Fabric softener users*	60.0%	60.0%
Nonusers	40.0	40.0
Percentage of homemakers aware that fabric softener allegedly harms the environment:		
Fabric softener users	55.0	74.0
Nonusers	66.0	70.0
Percentage of fabric softener users claiming to:†		
Use less fabric softener per load	18.0	24.0
Soften fewer loads	16.0	14.0
Total (unduplicated)	26.0	27.0
Percentage of reasons nonusers never used/stopped using fabric softener:		
Environmental reasons	42.0	48.0
Softness dissatisfaction	26.0	13.0
Effects on skin	29.0	23.0
Drying on clothesline	20.0	29.0

* Fabric softener users had used the product at least once in the previous three months before the interview; nonusers had not.
† Seventy-two percent of the users who used less softener or softened fewer loads claimed to be doing so for environmental reasons.

---

[7] All market share figures were based on statistical unit (MSUs) volume.

ing, and elimination of static cling. Lenor's distinctive, 4-liter blue container appeared in the mid-1970s and quickly became the standard package size and shape imitated by competitors. By 1987, all brands were sold in both diluted and concentrated formulas, in 4-liter and 1-liter sizes, respectively. In addition, in 1987 Henkel and P&G introduced dryer sheets, which accounted for less than 1 percent of market volume. All brands were broadly distributed throughout the retail trade.

Vernel followed a low-budget advertising strategy. Softlan, on the other hand, was aggressively advertised through the media. Kuschelweich gained high consumer awareness through its "stuffed bear" advertising mascot. In newspaper and handbill copy, Lenor led in feature share (42 percent for May/June 1987), followed by Softlan (21 percent), Kuschelweich (15 percent), and Vernel (5 percent).[8]

The materials cost for each brand varied due to different chemical formulations. Table 2 shows selected relative costs and pricing for the top four brands of diluted fabric softener in 1987.

Consumers perceived little differentiation among fabric softener brands except on the basis of price and scent. Consequently, fabric softener brands were frequently involved in price and promotion wars to defend or capture market share, which depressed manufacturer and trade margins. For example, the average profit margin realized by retailers on Lenor declined from 12.7 percent in 1984 to 2.5 percent in 1986.

Henkel, a prominent German household products company with 1987 sales of DM 9.9 billion, rapidly imitated innovative product ideas and marketed them globally. Henkel also strongly emphasized environmental protection, spending nearly 25 percent of its DM 285 million research budget on these

TABLE 2   1987 Indexed Costs and Prices for Leading German Fabric Softener Brands

	P&G	*Colgate*	*Lever*	*Henkel*
Brand name	Lenor	Softlan	Kuschelweich	Vernel
Packaging	100	106	106	106
Chemicals	100	85	93	92
Media expenses	100	136	85	40
Total costs	100	105	94	82
Average retail price	100	87	88	85

Note.   The index is based on a 4-liter package of dilute.

---

[8] Feature share, calculated from a survey of 200 West German newspapers and 2,000 grocery handbills, represented the percentage of times a particular brand was featured in retail trade promotions for fabric softeners.

issues in 1987. Colgate-Palmolive (DM 10.6 billion in 1987 sales) and Unilever ($57 billion) devoted less than 2 percent of their revenues to R&D.

In early 1987, Henkel acquired Lesieur-Cotelle S.A., a French detergent manufacturer that produced Minidou, a fabric softener concentrate sold in 250-ml flat, plastic pouches. Minidou users emptied the pouch's contents into any 1-liter container and then diluted the concentrate with water. Some P&G executives suspected that Henkel might try either to extend the successful Minidou concept, which had captured 29 percent of the French market by 1987, to other markets or to license the use of the technology to Colgate-Palmolive, which was pursuing lower-cost packaging alternatives.

Distribution

Fabric softener was sold through West Germany's highly concentrated retail market; five major chains together controlled more than 75 percent of total grocery sales (DM 127 billion in 1987). Each retailer sold products through several classes of trade: mass merchandisers (more than 53,800 sq. ft. in size), hypermarkets (16,100–53,800 sq. ft.), supermarkets (8,600–16,100 sq. ft.), convenience stores (under 8,600 sq. ft.), and discounters (various sizes). West German consumers shopped for fabric softener in all types of stores, although it was less likely than other grocery items to be purchased in convenience stores.

Fierce competition meant that grocery retailers achieved total after-tax profit margins of only 1 to 1.5 percent. Because they focused increasingly on the direct product profitability (DPP) of their stock per linear foot of shelf space, retailers were especially keen on high-margin, space-efficient products with rapid turnover. The emphasis placed on DPP resulted in a selective product assortment; only the large mass merchandisers and hypermarkets maintained a complete selection of brands and package sizes for any product category. Supermarkets kept a full range of brand names, but with limited size selection, whereas convenience stores and discounters sold only one or two brands. All classes of trade, except for convenience stores, also sold their own private-label brands in many high-turnover categories.

Every August, manufacturer account representatives negotiated with each major retailer the following year's major target purchase levels, volume discounts, and new product listing agreements. Manufacturers needed a retailer's listing for each new product, even for product line extensions; individual retail stores could purchase products only from their chain headquarters' approved list. Although manufacturers could introduce new products throughout the year, listing agreements were easier to obtain during the August meetings. Approved products generally reached store shelves within two weeks of an order being placed. In addition to account representatives, each manufacturer also had field salespeople who serviced individual stores, both chain-owned and independents, by taking stock orders, suggesting shelf arrangements, and implementing local sales promotions.

To minimize handling and reshelving costs, many retail stores sought to display products in their original shipping cartons and stressed convenient packaging to the manufacturers. A set of product packaging guidelines, known as the "ten commandments," was developed by a retail trade association for manufacturers. These guidelines defined the dimensions, weight, and appearance of the shipping cartons that retailers preferred. Few products met all 10 guidelines.

Advertising and Promotion

In 1987, most television advertising reached German consumers via the two state-run national channels. Each September, manufacturers reapplied for time slots; the television stations then allocated specific commercial spots to each firm for the upcoming year. P&G Germany would then allocate the time slots it had been granted among its brands.

Regulations limited the consumer promotions that West German manufacturers could use. Coupons and refund offers were not permitted; the value of on-pack and in-pack premiums (gifts attached to or included in product packages) could not exceed DM 0.30 in value. Bonus packs, which gave consumers extra volume of product for the same price, were difficult to implement on liquid products such as Lenor. Price packs (products with a lower-than-normal recommended retail price preprinted on the package) were allowed but were rarely used due to trade opposition. Some manufacturers did run sweepstakes and contests though they were tightly regulated by government agencies.

Volume discounts and trade promotion allowances for each product were traditionally negotiated with individual retailers. However, P&G Germany instituted account-specific promotion plans based on total sales volume rather than the sales of each brand. This approach was considered more effective in building trade relationships because it gave retailers more flexibility in what they promoted.

LENOR FABRIC SOFTENER

Lenor, launched in West Germany in 1963, was the first nationally marketed brand of fabric softener. By 1987, Lenor had achieved 98 percent store penetration. More than half of Lenor's total volume was sold through mass merchandisers, as indicated in Exhibit 2. Sales revenue and unit volume in 1987 were DM 228 million (29 percent of division sales) and 6,200 MSUs, respectively.

At first, Lenor was sold as a specialty item in small, 500 ml containers, at a price nearly 10 times higher than the 1987 inflation-adjusted price for the

EXHIBIT 2 Lenor Sales Volume by Store Type in 1987

Store Type (by size)	Number of Stores	Percent Number of Stores	Grocery Market Turnover* (billion DM)	Percent Market Turnover	Lenor Volume Breakdown†	
					4-Liter Dilute	1-Liter Concentrate
Mass merchandisers	412	0.6%	17.2	13.6%	62.0%	36.0%
Hypermarkets	1,195	1.6	17.2	13.6	20.0	20.0
Supermarkets	2,542	3.5	18.6	14.7	9.0	13.0
Convenience stores	64,409	88.2	59.9	47.3	6.0	16.0
Discounters	4,442	6.1	13.8	10.9	3.0	14.0
Total	73,000	100.0%	126.7	100.0%	100.0%	100.0%

* Market turnover is defined as sales volume times retail value. 1.9 DM = US$1.
† Percentages are based on statistical unit volume for the first six months of 1987.

same quantity. In 1965, P&G Germany broadened Lenor's appeal by lowering its price and developing a highly successful advertising campaign that remained in use for the following 18 years.

The 1-liter Lenor concentrate (Lenor CT) joined Lenor dilute on retail shelves in 1983. By 1987, 30 percent of Lenor's volume was sold in this 3:1 concentrated form.[9] Brand management believed that some fabric softener users regarded the concentrate's performance as inferior to the dilute's, although laboratory tests demonstrated no difference in efficacy. These users questioned whether "so little could perform as well." One P&G executive explained, "Although the concentrate is less awkward to carry home from the store, many consumers are wedded to the 4-liter package." Dryer sheets, introduced in the spring of 1987, sold to a limited market (0.4 percent of Lenor's 1987 sales volume) because 75 percent of West German households line-dried their laundry rather than using electric clothes dryers.

P&G Germany promoted Lenor heavily to the retail trade and consumers, spending 20 percent of the product's yearly manufacturer's sales on television and radio advertising, consumer promotions, trade promotions, and indirect brand support.[10] Table 3 below indicates the percentage breakdowns of Lenor's advertising and promotion expenses for 1986 and 1987. Approximately 30 percent of the brand's total marketing budget was allocated to the concentrate.

In 1987, liquid Lenor was available in the package sizes and prices shown in Exhibit 3. Recommended retail prices were at least 10 percent higher than

---

[9] The consumer was required to mix the concentrate with three times the volume of water before use.

[10] Indirect brand support included development costs for advertisements and commercials, production expenses associated with store displays, and other expenses incurred for consumer and trade promotions.

TABLE 3 Percentage Breakdown of Advertising and Sales Budget

	Dilute 1986	Dilute 1987	CT 1986	CT 1987
Media	20%	23%	20%	21%
Consumer promotion	4	1	1	1
Trade promotion	74	74	77	75
Indirect brand support	2	2	2	2
Total	100%	100%	100%	100%

EXHIBIT 3 Lenor Liquid Package Sizes and Prices, 1987

Formulation	Size	Number of Units per Case	Number of Stat. Units per Case*	Suggested Retail Price (DM)	Average Feature Price (DM)	Suggested Retail Price per SU (DM)	Average Feature Price per SU (DM)	Percent Lenor Sales Volume
Dilute	4 L.	4	0.68	5.53	4.64	32.53	27.29	70%
Concentrate (3:1)	1 L.	16	2.01	4.75	4.08	37.81	32.48	20%
Concentrate (3:1)	2 L.	8	2.01	8.38	6.98	33.35	27.78	10%

* Statistical Units (SUs) convert different sizes and products to an equivalent use basis. Thus, two items with the same number of SU will deliver an equivalent number of uses to the consumer.

those of its competitors. However, Lenor was a popular loss leader among retailers.[11] Ninety percent of Lenor dilute volume and 25 percent of concentrate volume were sold by retailers at feature prices in 1987.

Between 1984 and 1986, Lenor's sales volume had declined by 7.5 percent annually, with an actual loss of more than 1,000 MSUs. Brand management attributed this loss to increasingly aggressive competitive price promotion, which eroded Lenor's market share, and to a shrinking market due to unfavorable consumer sentiment. Lenor brand management had to develop a marketing strategy that would combat Lenor's eroding sales and market share in the face of consumers' increasing environmental concerns.

LENOR'S STRATEGIC OPTIONS

Stadler reviewed the strategic options her brand management team had developed in the last few months.

---

[11] Loss leaders, products retailers sold at prices below cost to attract consumers, were usually popular brands in frequently purchased product categories.

Relaunch the 3:1 Concentrate

One option explored was the aggressive relaunch of Lenor concentrate, promoting waste reduction benefits similar to those of a refill package. The 1-liter concentrate used approximately 45 percent less packaging materials than the 4-liter bottle on an equivalent use basis. Lenor's 1988 advertising and promotion budget (DM 45.6 million) could be increased by DM 2.85 million and be reallocated so that 40 percent would be spent on the dilute and 60 percent on the concentrate. Brand management estimated that this change would generate 60 percent of the total volume increase expected from the launch of the refill package. It would increase the concentrate's sales by 780 MSUs but 400 MSUs of this volume would result from cannibalization of the dilute.

The Lenor Refill Package

A second option was introducing Lenor concentrate in a refill package. Consumers would pour the concentrate into an empty 4-liter Lenor dilute bottle at home and add water. The Lenor brand group believed that the waste reduction benefits gained both from packaging reduction and bottle reuse would appeal to environmentally conscious consumers. The refill idea was not new to West Germans; many shoppers purchased milk packaged in flat, plastic bags that were then slotted inside a permanent container at home. Stadler also felt that "German consumers were ready to bear the extra trouble associated with refilling to help their environment."

Preliminary Research.   In the fall of 1986, P&G conducted two focus group interviews of 8 to 12 fabric softener users to explore their attitudes toward a refill concept and determine how to market such a product. Several users expressed interest in trying a refill product that they felt would reduce waste through container reuse. When asked how they would sell this idea to their neighbors, many said that they would stress waste reduction.

Next, a consumer panel test explored the acceptance of specific refill package ideas. Participants used different types of trial refill Lenor packages for four weeks, and afterward answered a survey about their likes, dislikes, and purchase intentions. From the results, researchers concluded that the refill concept had significant business-building potential.

Package Design.   In the spring of 1987, P&G Germany explored two specific refill package options. Technical researchers suggested two designs: (1) a laminated cardboard milk carton and (2) a stand-alone, soft plastic package, known as a "doypack" pouch, already used in West Germany to sell single servings of fruit juice. The technical staff believed that it could expand the size of this package to hold fabric softener concentrate.

In March 1987, P&G Germany tested these refill options in a consumer panel test. Participants were asked to test one of two package designs for Lenor concentrate: a 1-liter laminated "milk" carton and a 1-liter doypack pouch. Users rated the laminated carton highest for its environmental compatibility, ease of use, and convenience; the doypack pouch ratings followed closely behind. Messiness was also a significant factor in preference for either package; participants who spilled the product when transferring it into the larger container rated both packages lower in terms of handling. Exhibit 4 summarizes the test results.

Laminated Cartons versus Doypack Pouches. Brand management investigated further the advantages and disadvantages of the two refill package designs. Both designs promised the same 85 percent reduction in package materials volume.

Laminated Cartons. Laminated carton technology had existed for 20 years. The cartons rarely leaked and consumers spilled a minimum of product during refill tests. Retailers could easily display the rigid carton on their shelves; the product would not require a customized shipping case. Each case would hold ten 1-liter cartons of Lenor.

P&G Germany currently had no in-house facilities that could produce the laminated cartons. In-house production would cost P&G Germany DM 4.2 million per 2,100 MSU of annual capacity, assuming two shifts, and would take six months to establish. The one major West German supplier that could produce and fill the cartons could guarantee P&G Germany 100 MSUs production per month. The supplier could provide the 400 MSUs initial stock needed to fill P&G's trade pipeline for a September launch, but at a premium of DM 1.00/SU. Any orders beyond 100 MSU monthly production would also incur this premium.

West German safety regulations, focusing on the potential for accidental misuse of products, strongly discouraged packaging nonfood substances in containers generally used for food items. Consequently, P&G Germany ran some risk of government intervention if it used the laminated carton for its refill package. In addition, although the general public considered the carton as environmentally friendly, environmental experts regarded the wax-coated cardboard material as difficult to recycle.

Doypack Pouch. Adapting the doypack pouch to Lenor's requirements proved difficult; the largest pouch size previously produced was 500 ml, half the size needed for Lenor. The first prototypes leaked and more than 30 percent of the packages burst when dropped. Furthermore, a product-handling test in June 1987 revealed spillage difficulties. Participants in studio tests were asked to open the pouch and pour its contents into a 4-liter Lenor container. Although the least spillage occurred after the doypack's entire top was cut off with scissors, researchers found that users preferred to clip off only a corner of the package top. Lenor's brand management was concerned that the refill package would prove to be too messy for many consumers.

EXHIBIT 4   Consumer Panel Results, March 1987

	1-liter Carton	1-liter Doypack
Number of users	205	205
Percentage of participants who would buy the alternative regularly at 4.98 DM	53	49
Percentage of favorable/unfavorable comments on handling	88/33	88/41
Percentage of reused containers that were "smeary" after transfer	10	28
Percentage of packaging ratings:		
Ease of opening	57	52
Transferability of product	63	46
Environmental friendliness	74	65
Ease of disposal	79	75
Percentage of incidence of spillage	8	25

EXHIBIT 5   Cases of Doypack Refill Pouches

P&G Germany would need to produce customized shipping containers that would display the product attractively while following the stringent criteria determined by retailers. A picture of the doypack and the proposed case design are presented in Exhibit 5.

Given a target launch date of September 1987, P&G would need to outsource doypack pouch production. No subcontractor could mass produce the 1-liter doypacks. One subcontractor was willing to accommodate P&G Germany by building a new factory that could produce 200 MSUs per month when fully operational. According to Henry Horst, the technical head for Lenor, "We would need a tremendous effort to get this factory up and running to P&G's standards by September. We can only guarantee production of 300 MSUs by then." The subcontractor advised that P&G Germany would have to contribute DM 360,000 toward the investment in the new factory and commit to purchasing 800 MSUs in doypack orders. A penalty of DM 1 million would be imposed if P&G broke the contract before full-scale production began. In-house packaging by P&G Germany, requiring an investment of DM 3.2 million for 1,900 MSUs of annual capacity, would not be possible until January 1988.

Comparative Production Costs. The laminated carton and doypack pouch would achieve respectively 5 percent and 14 percent cost savings per SU over Lenor dilute, due to reduced package materials and lower delivery costs. Exhibit 6 shows a detailed cost breakdown for the proposed and existing Lenor product line. Lenor's allocated fixed costs were approximately DM 68 million per year.[12] The first 400 MSUs would cost an extra DM 4.00/SU and DM 4.56/SU for the carton and doypack, respectively.

EXHIBIT 6   1988 Breakdown of Direct Materials and Manufacturing Costs (DM per statistical unit)

	1-liter Carton*	1-liter Doypack*	4-liter Dilute	1-liter Concentrate
Fabric softener chemicals	DM4.60	DM4.60	DM4.69	DM4.77
Packaging materials	1.84	1.82	3.40	2.72
Manufacturing	3.33	3.19	2.93	2.60
Delivery	0.86	0.76	1.79	1.01
Contractor expense†	1.52	0.65	—	—
Total direct costs (DM)	12.15	11.02	12.81	11.10
Cost index (Lenor Dilute = 100)	95	86	100	87
SU per container	0.17	0.17	0.17	0.126
Total costs/container (DM)	2.06	1.87	2.18	1.40

* P&G Germany expected that the first 400 MSU produced would cost DM4.00/SU and DM4.56/SU more for the carton and doypack, respectively, due to initial start up costs.

† These payments to manufacturing subcontractors (covering their profit margins and delivery costs) would be eliminated if P&G Germany moved all manufacturing in-house.

---

[12] Fixed costs included general sales/marketing, administrative, and distribution costs (80 percent of total), fixed manufacturing (17 percent), and product research and development costs (3 percent).

Pricing.   Exhibit 7 shows the breakdown of 1987 proposed prices and trade margins for the Lenor product line. Brand management wanted the suggested retail price for the refill package to be at least DM 1.5/SU lower than that for the 4-liter dilute to reflect packaging cost savings. This would provide the price incentive needed to motivate consumers to buy the refill packs. The savings represented 5 percent of manufacturer's list price.

Volume Forecasts.   The brand group forecast a 10-month (remainder of FY1988) sales volume of 1,500 MSUs for the refill pouch; however, the team predicted that 60 percent of the refill package sales would come from cannibalization of existing Lenor sales. The finance department was less optimistic, forecasting an 80 percent cannibalization rate and a 10-month volume of 750 MSUs, resulting in only a 150 MSU net increase in total sales. For the launch, P&G would need 400 MSUs to stock 70 percent of West Germany's retail chain stores.

Promotion and Advertising.   Brand management proposed a 6 percent increase over its original 1988 advertising and promotion budget, with DM 6.5 million to be allocated specifically to the refill package relaunch. At estimated refill sales of 1,500 MSUs, this budget equaled DM 4.31/SU. Table 4 breaks down the Lenor marketing budget with and without the refill package introduction.

The Lenor brand group proposed to focus all Lenor advertising on the refill package for the first three months after launch. P&G Germany's advertising

---

EXHIBIT 7   1988 Proposed Retail Price and Trade Margins

	1-liter Refill	4-liter Dilute	1-liter Concentrate
Expected retail price (DM)	5.49	5.79	4.89
Expected retail margin (percent)	9.00%	0.00%	9.00%
Manufacturer's selling price (DM)	5.04	5.79	4.49
SU per container	0.17	0.17	0.126
Retail revenues (DM/SU)	32.29	34.06	38.90
Manufacturer's revenues (DM/SU)	29.63	34.06	35.63

TABLE 4   Alternative 1988 Advertising and Promotion Budgets

	Without Launch	With Launch	Difference
Media	DM 10,849	DM 12,227	DM 1,378
Consumer promotion	1,957	1,976	19
Trade promotion	29,830	31,350	1,520
Indirect brand support	2,546	2,565	19
Total	45,182	48,118	2,936

agency developed and tested two commercials called *Splish-Splash* and *Perspectives*, based on the doypack pouch option (see Exhibits 8 and 9). *Splish-Splash* and *Perspectives* achieved unaided recall ratings of 37 percent and 47 percent, respectively, exceeding P&G Germany's 35 percent average unaided recall score for acceptable new copy.[13] Product labeling would highlight the environmentally friendly packaging, in particular the 85 percent volume reduction in packaging materials, and would carry the phrase *refill pack*. Stadler hoped that the refill package would qualify for a Blue Angel label, which could help increase Lenor's sales, but felt uncertain that the improved packaging alone would overcome the Blue Angel program's objection to fabric softener products.

Proposed sales literature emphasized reductions in the retailer's warehousing (48 percent less), transportation (72 percent), and handling costs (70 percent) compared with the 4-liter Lenor dilute. The case container designs for both the carton and the doypack met 8 of the trade's 10 commandments, more than

---

EXHIBIT 8 Advertising Copy for Lenor Pouch: *Splish-Splash* Commercial

(Music begins, with young male and female dancers, brightly dressed, dancing while holding Lenor containers and the Lenor pouch.)

Singing to the 1960's tune of *Splish-Splash*:

Splish, Splash,
We're up-to-date,
Use Lenor in the refill pouch.

Just take your empty bottle,
Refilling is not difficult.
Just add water

Splish, Splash,
You feel it immediately,
Everything April-fresh and soft.
New Lenor in the
Environmentally safe refill pouch.

Splish, Splash,
The pouch is great,
Makes itself really small for the garbage

Splish, Splash,
Be up-to-date,
Use Lenor in the refill pouch.

---

[13] Day-after recall testing measured communication effectiveness. Consumers who had watched television at the time when a test commercial spot was being shown were interviewed by telephone the following day. Unaided recall occurred when a consumer remembered the brand and message content of the test commercial without prompting. Aided recall involved prompting.

EXHIBIT 9 Storyboard for *Perspectives* Commercial

1. **Husband:** I love housework.

2. **Wife:** Klaus, I still need the Lenor bottle.

3. **Husband:** Do we get the deposit back? Here, what do you want with it?

4. **Wife:** To use it again. **Husband:** Huh?

5. **Wife:** With the new refill pouch...

6. ...From Lenor.

7. **Husband:** Lenor in a bag?

8. **Wife:** Yes...

9. ...Pour it in the top...

10. ...Add water... ...Finished!

11. **Husband:** Smells just like Lenor.

12. **Wife:** Softens like Lenor...

13. ...And that is for the garbage.

14. **Husband:** My wife really has perspective.

15. **Offvoice:** Lenor, soft and april-fresh...

16. ...Now in the environmentally safe pouch.

19

any existing P&G Germany product. Finally, brand management felt that the opportunity to realize higher retail margins than could currently be obtained on the heavily promoted 4-liter dilute (9 percent versus 0 percent) would also appeal to the trade.[14]

An Integrated Marketing Option

As Stadler pondered the pros and cons for the refill package, Daniel Knower, the assistant brand manager for Vizir, P&G Germany's liquid detergent brand, stopped by her office to discuss a new marketing concept he wanted to pursue. He said, "You know, we are struggling with the same environmental issues. I think that this refill concept is great and could be expanded to other brands, such as Vizir. We could market the products more efficiently under a new brand name, such as *Eco-pak*. Advertising copy could focus on the refill package as a product form that spanned multiple brands—Lenor, Vizir, and other liquid products." Realistically, both Stadler and Knower speculated that the manufacturing complications, larger marketing scope, and increased coordination associated with such a strategy would add at least three months to the Lenor refill package's September introduction date. However, both felt that the idea merited discussion with their respective brand managers.

CONCLUSION

At the next day's meeting, Rolf Kunisch discussed several issues with the Lenor brand management team. First was the possibility that any effort P&G made to address environmental issues could backfire. The public relations department had warned of "waking a sleeping dog." P&G had many highly visible products that might attract opposition from environmentalists. Although the Lenor refill package might raise the firm's profile as an environmentally conscious corporate citizen, it might also draw attention to other P&G products for which environmentally friendly and cost-effective improvements were not readily available.

Kunisch also was concerned about the rapidity with which brand management had developed the refill package proposal. Had the product been tested enough? Were there hidden issues that might have been missed in the rush to launch? Was there really an urgent need for action? No other German consumer goods company had addressed environmental issues through innovative packaging. With such a novel and relatively untested idea, what risks would P&G Germany run as the first to market?

---

[14] Retail trade margins of 0 percent were due to the frequent use of the Lenor 4-liter dilute as a loss leader. Retail margins on Lenor sold at feature prices were often negative.

Several other P&G country managers in Europe had scoffed at the "crazy German ideas about the environment," seeing little applicability of the refill package idea to their own markets. Kunisch wondered if P&G Europe headquarters would also conclude that P&G Germany was overreacting to the environmental concerns of some West Germany consumers. Stadler left the meeting, uncertain of the final outcome for the refill package's future.

After the meeting, Lenor's brand manager, Phillippe, asked Stadler to prepare a revised set of recommendations for Lenor, addressing some of Kunisch's concerns. Stadler continued to be positive about the new packaging concept; however, she realized that the internal sell would be tougher than she had anticipated.

Kodak and Polaroid: Consumer Compensation

Between 1976 and 1985, Eastman Kodak Company (hereafter Kodak) sold 16.5 million instant cameras, but, in 1985, sales were abruptly stopped. Polaroid, Kodak's major competitor in the instant camera market and the inventor of instant photography, won a patent infringement suit, which forced the withdrawal of Kodak instant film and cameras from the shelves. Immediate remedies proposed by the company for the millions who had purchased Kodak cameras now rendered obsolete were rejected by a class action suit lodged in the Circuit Court of Cook County, Illinois. Only after a costly legal battle was a compensation plan devised that was acceptable to the courts, consumers, and the company. Thus ended the largest successful class action suit in U.S. history in terms of the number of people who ended up receiving compensation.

PATENT INFRINGEMENT

On April 20, 1976, Kodak announced its entry into the instant photography market, which had been monopolized for 28 years by Polaroid Corporation. At a press conference in New York City, Walter A. Fallon, president of Kodak, demonstrated two new cameras and an instant film that had "remarkable color quality." He also stated that Kodak, in a departure from tradition, would license other companies to manufacture cameras that could use its instant film. The Kodak instant camera comprised over 250 parts, compared to the 12 snap-together pieces that made up the Polaroid instant camera. On the same day as Fallon's announcement, Polaroid issued a statement: "We have had a chance to make a brief comparison between the Polaroid instant picture system and the new Kodak system. The comparison renews our confidence that our

This case was prepared by Professors John A. Quelch and N. Craig Smith.
Copyright © 1991 by the President and Fellows of Harvard College.
Harvard Business School case N9-591-015 (Rev. 3/22/91).

leadership in the field of instant photography remains unchallenged." One week later, however, Edwin Land, founder, director of research, and chairman of the board of Polaroid, announced that the company had filed suit in federal court charging Kodak with the infringement of 12 Polaroid patents. Fallon responded: "We believe that our patent position is sound. We don't knowingly infringe anybody else's valid patents."

In 1986, Kodak stopped selling its instant cameras and film. After losing the infringement suit, Kodak announced a program offering previous purchasers (who no longer could obtain film for their cameras) three alternative forms of compensation if they wished to return them: one of its newly launched disk cameras, $50 in Kodak coupons, which could be used toward the purchase of Kodak products, or one share of Kodak stock valued on the day of the announcement at $44.375. This plan was not challenged by overseas purchasers, but the Cook County class action lawsuit blocked the implementation of the plan in the United States. Those filing the suit charged that Kodak knew during the seven-year product development process prior to 1976 that it was vulnerable to a challenge from Polaroid for violating patents. Basic commercial law insured consumers that products were free from patent lawsuits.

According to Burton Weinstein, an attorney representing those who brought the class action suit, the central issue was cash. "People wanted cash. They didn't want to be bound to Kodak products." But camera owners like William Allbach of Waynesville, North Carolina, suspected that Kodak had instigated the suit in the hope that further delay would cause more owners to discard their cameras. A court order prevented Kodak from sending letters to owners explaining the reason for the delay in settlement.

On May 16, 1988, a preliminary settlement of the class action suit was announced, under which Kodak set up a $150 million fund to compensate owners of its instant cameras through a combination of cash and coupons redeemable for Kodak products. Kodak agreed to reserve $108 million for cash payments, $42 million for the value of coupons redeemed (assumed to be one third of the value of coupons issued), and $8 million for administrative and advertising expenses.

As of May 16, 4.3 million owners had registered their claims, many of them through a toll-free 800 number, which Kodak had established at a cost to the company of $17 million over two years. Kodak management estimated that about 10 percent of the claims were mistakenly filed by owners of Polaroid instant cameras. The preliminary settlement gave owners until September 9 to register their claims. The percentages of each consumer's settlement that would be cash versus coupons depended on how many valid claims eventually were filed; the fewer the number of valid claims, the higher the proportion of cash.

Letters explaining the settlement were mailed to consumers who had previously identified themselves as Kodak instant camera owners by calling Kodak's toll-free number. By September 9, 1988, Kodak instant camera owners had to verify their ownership both by completing a certificate included in the letter they received following their toll-free phone calls, and by attaching their camera's nameplate. Those who had not called could clip a certificate from an advertisement that appeared in 100 major U.S. newspapers on May 22 and in *Parade* magazine on June 19, 1988 (see Exhibit 1). A maximum of three exchanges per household was permitted. Consumers who received their instant cameras as promotional give-aways could also qualify. The final tally showed that only 3.4 million camera owners submitted valid claims that enabled them to participate in the exchange program. This represented just over one quarter of the 16.5 million who had purchased Kodak instant cameras and, therefore, were eligible for the rebate program.

A modified version of the preliminary settlement finally was approved by the courts on September 27, 1988. Kodak would pay owners of the cameras between $50 and $70 in cash and coupons, depending on the type of camera owned. The objective was to provide each owner with cash compensation greater than the market value of his or her camera at the time Kodak withdrew from the market. Owners of basic models would receive about $20 in cash and $30 in coupons, while owners of more expensive models would receive about $50 in cash and $20 in coupons. The coupons would have to be redeemed by January 31, 1990, for Kodak film, cameras, batteries, or a slide projector. Kodak management expected one third of the coupons to be redeemed. The final cost to Kodak was $193 million.

REFERENCES

Ansberry, Clare. "At This Rate, When the Suit Ends the Cameras Will Be Collectibles." *The Wall Street Journal*, February 8, 1988.

————. "Kodak Settles Suit by Owners of 'Instants.'" *The Wall Street Journal*, August 27, 1988, p. 47.

Berg, Eric N. "Kodak Pact on Payouts Is Cleared." *New York Times*, September 27, 1988.

Collingwood, Harris. "Kodak Settles with Sore Shutterbugs." *BusinessWeek*, May 30, 1988.

Feder, Barney J. "Kodak to Compensate Instant Camera Owners." *New York Times*, May 17, 1988.

"Kodak Set to Mail Rebates to Settle Suit over Camera." *The Wall Street Journal*, September 27, 1988.

Merry, Glenn W., and Norman Berg. "Polaroid-Kodak." Harvard Business School case 376-266, 1976.

Porter, Michael E., and Mark B. Fuller. "Polaroid-Kodak Addendum." Harvard Business School case 378-165, 1978.

EXHIBIT 1   Kodak and Polaroid: Consumer Compensation

Print Advertisement Outlining May 16 Settlement

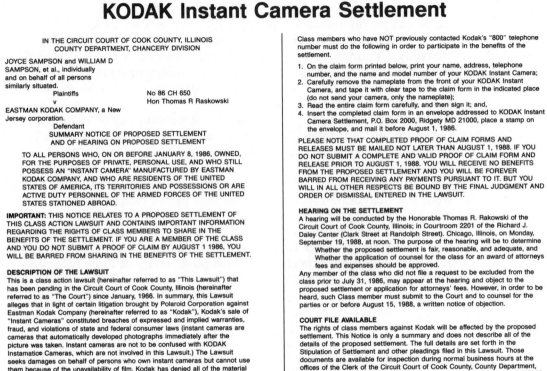

KODAK Instant Camera Settlement

IN THE CIRCUIT COURT OF COOK COUNTY, ILLINOIS
COUNTY DEPARTMENT, CHANCERY DIVISION

JOYCE SAMPSON and WILLIAM D
SAMPSON, et al., individually
and on behalf of all persons
similarly situated.
          Plaintiffs   No 86 CH 650
          v   Hon Thomas R Raskowski
EASTMAN KODAK COMPANY, a New
Jersey corporation.
          Defendant
          SUMMARY NOTICE OF PROPOSED SETTLEMENT
          AND OF HEARING ON PROPOSED SETTLEMENT

TO ALL PERSONS WHO, ON OR BEFORE JANUARY 8, 1986, OWNED,
FOR THE PURPOSES OF PRIVATE, PERSONAL USE, AND WHO STILL
POSSESS AN "INSTANT CAMERA" MANUFACTURED BY EASTMAN
KODAK COMPANY, AND WHO ARE RESIDENTS OF THE UNITED
STATES OF AMERICA, ITS TERRITORIES AND POSSESSIONS OR ARE
ACTIVE DUTY PERSONNEL OF THE ARMED FORCES OF THE UNITED
STATES STATIONED ABROAD.

IMPORTANT: THIS NOTICE RELATES TO A PROPOSED SETTLEMENT OF
THIS CLASS ACTION LAWSUIT AND CONTAINS IMPORTANT INFORMATION
REGARDING THE RIGHTS OF CLASS MEMBERS TO SHARE IN THE
BENEFITS OF THE SETTLEMENT. IF YOU ARE A MEMBER OF THE CLASS
AND YOU DO NOT SUBMIT A PROOF OF CLAIM BY AUGUST 1 1986, YOU
WILL BE BARRED FROM SHARING IN THE BENEFITS OF THE SETTLEMENT.

DESCRIPTION OF THE LAWSUIT
This is a class action lawsuit (hereinafter referred to as "This Lawsuit") that
has been pending in the Circuit Court of Cook County, Illinois (hereinafter
referred to as "The Court") since January, 1966. In summary, this Lawsuit
alleges that in light of certain litigation brought by Polaroid Corporation against
Eastman Kodak Company (hereinafter referred to as "Kodak"), Kodak's sale of
"Instant Cameras" constituted breaches of expressed and implied warranties,
fraud, and violations of state and federal consumer laws (instant cameras are
cameras that automatically developed photographs immediately after the
picture was taken. Instant cameras are not to be confused with KODAK
Instamatic Cameras, which are not involved in this Lawsuit.) The Lawsuit
seeks damages on behalf of persons who own instant cameras but cannot use
them because of the unavailability of film. Kodak has denied all of the material
allegations of the various complaints held in this Lawsuit and it continues to
deny any fault, liability, or wrongdoing of any kind.

THE PROPOSED SETTLEMENT
The Plaintiffs in this Lawsuit and Kodak have reached an agreement on
settlement. The proposed settlement will provide benefits to the class in excess
of Two Hundred Fifty Million dollars ($250,000,000.00), consisting of cash,
rebate coupons and the payment of expenses of this Lawsuit and of
implementing the settlement. The proposed settlement will dismiss this Lawsuit
with prejudice and release Kodak from any liability in the Class arising out of
Kodak's sale of instant cameras as or out of its proposed Exchange Program
with respect to the instant cameras.

PARTICIPATION IN THE SETTLEMENT
The following class has been certified in this Lawsuit
          All residents of the United States of America, its territories and
          possessions, as well as all active duty personnel of the armed forces of
          the United States stationed abroad, who on or before January 8, 1986,
          owned for the purposes of private personal use and who still possess an
          "Instant Camera" manufactured by Defendant Eastman Kodak Company.
          The Court has ordered that claims forms be sent to every member of this
          class that has been identified by telephoning Kodak's "800-Number"
          telephone system. Thus, ALL CLASS MEMBERS THAT HAVE
          TELEPHONED KODAK'S "800-NUMBER" TELEPHONE SYSTEM NEED
          DO NOTHING FURTHER UNTIL THEY RECEIVE THEIR CLAIM FORMS.

Class members who have NOT previously contacted Kodak's "800" telephone
number must do the following in order to participate in the benefits of the
settlement.
1. On the claim form printed below, print your name, address, telephone
   number, and the name and model number of your KODAK Instant Camera;
2. Carefully remove the nameplate from the front of your KODAK Instant
   Camera, and tape it with clear tape to the claim form in the indicated place
   (do not send your camera, only the nameplate);
3. Read the entire claim form carefully, and then sign it; and,
4. Insert the completed claim form in an envelope addressed to KODAK Instant
   Camera Settlement, P.O. Box 2000, Ridgety MD 21000, place a stamp on
   the envelope, and mail it before August 1, 1986.

PLEASE NOTE THAT COMPLETED PROOF OF CLAIM FORMS AND
RELEASES MUST BE MAILED NOT LATER THAN AUGUST 1, 1988. IF YOU
DO NOT SUBMIT A COMPLETE AND VALID PROOF OF CLAIM FORM AND
RELEASE PRIOR TO AUGUST 1, 1988. YOU WILL RECEIVE NO BENEFITS
FROM THE PROPOSED SETTLEMENT AND YOU WILL BE FOREVER
BARRED FROM RECEIVING ANY PAYMENTS PURSUANT TO IT. BUT YOU
WILL IN ALL OTHER RESPECTS BE BOUND BY THE FINAL JUDGMENT AND
ORDER OF DISMISSAL ENTERED IN THE LAWSUIT.

HEARING ON THE SETTLEMENT
A hearing will be conducted by the Honorable Thomas R. Rakowski of the
Circuit Court of Cook County, Illinois; in Courtroom 2201 of the Richard J.
Daley Center (Clark Street at Randolph Street). Chicago, Illinois, on Monday,
September 19, 1988, at noon. The purpose of the hearing will be to determine
          Whether the proposed settlement is fair, reasonable, and adequate, and
          Whether the application of counsel for the class for an award of attorneys
          fees and expenses should be approved.
Any member of the class who did not file a request to be excluded from the
class prior to July 31, 1986, may appear at the hearing and object to the
proposed settlement or application for attorneys' fees. However, in order to be
heard, such Class member must submit to the Court and to counsel for the
parties or or before August 15, 1988, a written notice of objection.

COURT FILE AVAILABLE
The rights of class members against Kodak will be affected by the proposed
settlement. This Notice is only a summary and does not describe all of the
details of the proposed settlement. The full details are set forth in the
Stipulation of Settlement and other pleadings filed in this Lawsuit. Those
documents are available for inspection during normal business hours at the
offices of the Clerk of the Circuit Court of Cook County, County Department,
Chancery Division, Room 802, Richard J. Daley Center, Chicago, Illinois 60602,
under the number 86 CH 650. Additionally a more complete notice has been
mailed to all identified class members.

If you believe that you are a class member and have any questions about this
Notice you may direct such questions to the attorneys for the Class by writing
them at the following addresses

          Perry M. Berke, Esq.
          Burton I. Weinstein, Esq.
          William J. Harte, Esq.
          Judah I. Labovitz, Esq.
          Counsel for the Class
          P.O. Box 64629
          Chicago, Illinois 60664-0629

          APPROVED BY ORDER OF

          Hon. Thomas R. Rakowski
          Judge of the Circuit Court of
          Cook County, Illinois

PLEASE DO NOT TELEPHONE THE JUDGE OR THE CLERK OF THE COURT

IF YOU HAVE REGISTERED WITH KODAK'S TOLL-FREE "800-NUMBER"
TELEPHONE SYSTEM, YOU DO *NOT* NEED TO DO ANYTHING UNTIL YOU
RECEIVE A PRE-PRINTED CLAIM FORM IN THE MAIL. WHEN YOU RECEIVE
THE CLAIM FORM, PLEASE COMPLETE IT AND MAIL IT BEFORE AUGUST 1,
1988. *PLEASE DO NOT CALL THE "800" NUMBER*

EXHIBIT 1 *(concluded)*

KODAK Instant Camera Settlement
P.O. Box 2000
Ridgely, Maryland 21688

Please fill out the information below and tape your KODAK Instant Camera nameplate where indicated. If you have already responded to this request, there is no need to contact us again.

BY SIGNING THIS FORM AND SUBMITTING THIS CLAIM THEREBY RELEASE AND FOREVER DISCHARGE EASTMAN KODAK COMPANY AND ITS OFFICERS DIRECTORS AND EMPLOYEES FROM ANY AND ALL CLAIMS AND LIABILITY ARISING OUT OF OR CONNECTED WITH THE SALE OR MY OWNERSHIP OF THE KODAK INSTANT CAMERA DESCRIBED ABOVE

UNDER THE PENALTIES AS PROVIDED BY LAW PURSUANT TO SECTION I 109 OF THE ILLINOIS CODE OF CIVIL PROCEDURE ILL REVSTAT CH 110 I 109 THE UNDERSIGNED CERTIFIES THAT THE STATEMENTS SET FORTH IN THIS PROOF OF CLAIM INCLUDING THOSE SET FORTH IN THE CLAIM STATEMENT ARE TRUE AND CORRECT

Signature
Name

Address

City State Zip

Daytime Telephone # (   )

Kodak Instant Camera Model

CLAIM STATEMENT
By signing and submitting this Proof of Claim Form I am stating, under penalty of perjury, that (1) my correct name, address and telephone number are set forth above, that (2) on or before January 8, 1986 I owned the KODAK Instant Camera described above for purposes of private, personal use, that (3) I still have that camera in my possession, that (4) I have removed the nameplate from that camera and have attached it to this form, and that (5) I and my immediate family have NOT submitted proofs of claim for more than three (3) KODAK Instant Cameras.

LIMITATIONS
KODAK Instant Camera nameplate is the only acceptable proof of ownership. No more than three (3) exchanges per household, group, or organization. Requests in excess of this limitation will not be acknowledged or returned. Do not return cameras or accessory items. Valid only for residents of the United States, its territories, possessions and military personnel. Sellers of Kodak products are excluded. Camera nameplate must be mailed directly by owners without brokers or other third parties. Any other use of this offer is invalid. We are not responsible for submitted entries lost, damaged or destroyed in the mail. *Instant Camera nameplate must be postmarked no later than August 1, 1988.*

TAPE YOUR NAMEPLATE HERE, FACE UP, USING CLEAR TAPE.
DO NOT SEND YOUR CAMERA, ONLY THE NAMEPLATE.
The nameplate of a KODAK Instant Camera is attached with a light adhesive and can be easily removed.
Carefully lift a corner of nameplate with tweezers and gently pull off. A hair dryer will help loosen the glue if needed.

In the News

4.5.1 PROTECTIONIST THE DOLPHINS*

Man is still trying to communicate with dolphins, but neither species has reason to sound enthusiasm for last week's move by the big sellers of tuna in the United States. Led by H. J. Heinz Company (Starkist brand), three canners with a huge share of the market capitulated to environmentalists who demanded they quit netting the big tuna that often swim under the lovable water mammals.

Greenpeace and its cohorts had launched a boycott of tuna to protest the deaths of dolphins caught up in the fishing boats' nets. Heinz, after what it called marketing studies, said its customers would be willing to pay extra for younger yellowfin, which don't frolic with dolphins, or for bigger tuna caught in oceans where the mysterious symbiosis isn't observed.

In line with its newfound consciousness, Heinz now wants the government to put a lid on imported tuna ruled "dolphin-unsafe." Hmmm. Protectionist the dolphins.

Come to think of it, even without the lid on imports, the instant consensus among competitors to offer only more costly tuna might excite some curiosity among the reinvigorated trust-busters at the Federal Trade Commission. After all, even consumers who haven't turned green will be laying out the green.

_____

* Editorial, *The Wall Street Journal*, April 17, 1990. Reprinted by permission of *The Wall Street Journal.* © 1990 Dow Jones & Company, Inc. All Rights Reserved Worldwide.

One group that has more than curiosity at stake is the U.S. tuna fleet, which mostly sails out of San Diego. It unloads the bulk of its catch in Puerto Rico and American Samoa. If fishermen can't find an economic way to make a living under the new rules—and their spokesmen say they may not be able to, given how the loss of nets will cut the catch in what is already a difficult business—it's going to further shrink a fleet that's already diminished by two thirds since 1981. How many workers will now suffer at Heinz's clean hands is a guess.

Many Americans may care more about porpoises than fishermen. If so, then they especially should realize the magnitude of progress in tuna-netting practices, gains that may be stalled or lost by last week's action. Since the *Journal*'s Roy Harris, Jr., detailed the development of dolphin-sparing tuna techniques in a front-page article 13 years ago, the kill rate has been about halved. Last year the toll in the U.S.-fished region was under 13,000. Half the time the boats drop one of their purselike nets, they kill none of the average 650 dolphins swept up. The Marine Mammal Protection Act of 1972, combined with the fact that dolphin kills only detract from tuna yields, has spurred the United States to remarkable achievements.

In the international marketplace, love for Flipper isn't universal. Greenpeace is not usually so effective when it goes calling on Mexico City or Seoul. So now the Pacific region off the Americas may belong to foreign fishing vessels, who are likely to kill more dolphins than the San Diego boats they replace.

If the industry is correct in saying that younger tuna will now be fished out before they can reproduce, the agreement will also be bad for the tuna. We might face a depletion scare, such as one that prompted tuna-conservation controls on the West Coast fleet 20 years ago. Saving the tuna will come second to saving the dolphin, but it will come, and kids may then be condemned to cheese sandwiches. We wonder what cows would think of that.

4.5.2 THE POISONING OF AMERICA

McDonald's Beefs About Anti-Fat Ads*

McDonald's Corporation is leaning on newspapers that ran ads accusing the fast-food giant of "poisoning America" with foods too high in fat.

In letters to major U.S. newspapers, including *USA TODAY*, McDonald's disputes claims made about its hamburgers, French fries, and milkshakes in ads paid for by businessman Phil Sokolof.

McDonald's hints that it might sue newspapers that run any more Sokolof ads. "Any further publication without . . . corrections would have to be considered malicious," the letter says. Courts usually have required proof that publications acted maliciously before finding them guilty of libel.

Sokolof, a wealthy Omaha businessman, has used similar ads to attack the makers of packaged foods containing tropical oils and countries exporting those oils to the U.S.A. Eating too many fatty foods can increase cholesterol levels and the risk of heart attack.

His ad [shown on page 344], which ran in 15 U.S. dailies on April 4, was "shoddy and deceitful," the company says. McDonald's says its hamburgers are "leaner than . . . the ground beef most people buy in the supermarket."

None of the newspapers that ran the ad attempted to verify Sokolof's fat-content numbers with the company, says McDonald's Chuck Ebeling.

Says *USA TODAY* publisher Cathleen Black: "There's no way we can verify the information. If he takes a position he wants to share with the country, that's his right. It's between Sokolof and McDonald's."

Thursday, Sokolof refused to say where his fat numbers originated. "I don't want to get involved in technicalities, [such as] who did my testing."

4.5.3 GE REFRIGERATOR WOES ILLUSTRATE THE HAZARDS IN CHANGING A PRODUCT†

Firm Pushed Development of Compressor Too Fast, Failed to Test Adequately

LOUISVILLE, Ky.—General Electric Company began making a new refrigerator model in 1986—and thought it had a breakthrough. Its engineers had designed a revolutionary compressor and a futuristic factory to make it.

GE was so certain the new product would leapfrog Japanese rivals that it staked its entire $2 billion refrigerator business on the innovative design of the compressor—the pump that creates cold air, as crucial to a refrigerator as an engine to a car. The old compressor was scrapped. At the appliance division's headquarters here, managers were setting out to prove that America could still be a world leader in manufacturing.

But today, the very managers who had defiantly refused to buy compressors from overseas rivals are doing exactly that. Now, when GE assembles refrigerators at its plants in

* By James Cox, *USA TODAY*, April 13, 1990. Reprinted with permission.

† By Thomas F. O'Boyle, staff reporter of *The Wall Street Journal*, May 7, 1990. Reprinted by permission of *The Wall Street Journal* © 1990 Dow Jones & Company, Inc. All Rights Reserved Worldwide.

Courtesy of National Heart Savers Association, Phil Sokolof, President.

Louisville, Indiana, and Alabama, it uses compressors purchased from six suppliers, five of them foreign.

"Nightmare Come True"

The project, says Roger Schipke, the division's former chief, "was your worst nightmare come true. I don't even want to think about it anymore." Mr. Schipke now is the president of Ryland Group, Inc., a Columbia, Maryland, home builder.

GE's new compressor flopped so badly that the company had to take a $450 million pretax charge in 1988. And since early last year, it has voluntarily replaced nearly 1.1 million defective compressors.

At first, it was changing 5,000 a week. Even now, the process goes on. In a kitchen in rural Beaver County near Pittsburgh, serviceman Paul Jackson yanks a defective compressor from the back of an almond-colored refrigerator. He replaces it with one made in Italy. The changeover takes 90 minutes. Still to be repaired: as many as 200,000 refrigerators, many of which can't be located.

The full story of GE's fiasco has never been told. After interviews on the matter with more than 30 current and former GE employees, the tale that emerges offers a lesson for all manufacturers.

GE's travails don't show that America should stop trying to compete with the Japanese—who, as GE later discovered, had similar troubles with the same compressor design. Rather, the story illustrates how even a company with GE's vast resources and formidable skills can fall into trouble if it goes too far, too fast. Pioneering new technology carries great risks along with the possibility of great rewards, and the risks may indicate that a manufacturer should phase in a new product gradually.

Missing Balance

"You have to have that magical balance between getting it right and getting it fast. Ob-viously, we didn't have that," says Stephen Holmes, who was one of several GE managers that supervised the refrigerator's design and who now is a vice president at rival Whirlpool Corporation. Adds Dietrich Huttenlocher, a former GE technical trouble-shooter who was part of the research team that investigated the failure: "GE learned a hard lesson: Don't cut corners on the testing."

Blunders were committed at practically every level. In designing the compressor, engineers made some bad assumptions and then failed to ask the right questions. Managers, eager to cut costs, forced the engineers to accelerate "life testing" of the compressor, curtailed field testing, and rushed into production.

Ultimately, the problems stemmed from poor corporate communication. Several low-level salaried employees at GE—the technicians who did the actual preproduction testing—say they suspected that the compressor might be defective and told their superiors. But senior executives, six levels removed, heard only good news.

An Afterthought

In retrospect, Richard Burke, the appliance division's current chief of technology and manufacturing, says he would have done it differently. "I'd have gone and found the lowest damn level people we had . . . and just sat down in their little cubbyholes and asked them 'How are things today?'"

How could such errors be made at GE, widely acclaimed for its management?

From the start, GE was under pressure. In the fall of 1981, when the compressor saga began, the appliance division's market share—and profits—were falling.

What's more, GE was using antiquated methods to make refrigerators, the core of the appliance group. GE's compressor plant—Building 4 in the Appliance Park complex that employs 12,300 in Louisville—was relying on 1950s technology and lots of manpower. Making a single piston took 220 steps. Even simple grinding operations were done by hand. GE took 65 minutes of labor to make a compressor. Rivals in Japan and Italy made theirs in just 25 minutes and, because of lower labor rates, at half the cost.

Ira C. Magaziner, a Providence, Rhode Island, consultant brought in for advice, handed down a somber verdict: either buy compressors abroad or find a way to build better ones. (Mr. Magaziner's findings are recounted in his 1989 management book, *The Silent War*, which praised GE's efforts to build the new compressor.)

After a fierce internal debate, appliance-division executives decided to build their own. On September 1, 1983, Mr. Schipke and two senior engineers flew to Connecticut to sell the idea to GE chairman Jack Welch. (Mr. Welch declined to be interviewed.) The division executives proposed that GE commit $120 million to build a factory in Columbia, Tennessee, about 50 miles south of Nashville. The factory would make a newly designed compressor—the rotary—a technology that GE had invented but used only in air conditioners.

"We told them it wasn't a moonshot. We knew how to make rotaries. We'd made 12 million of them in air conditioners," Mr. Schipke recalls. Mr. Welch agreed. So did directors at GE's next board meeting.

In reality, though, the rotary *was* a moonshot in refrigerators. At first glance, the new design seemed ideal. It weighed less and was more energy-efficient than old-fashioned reciprocating compressors, which had three times as many parts. The new design and new factory would halve GE's compressor-production costs.

But Peter Davey, a former chief design engineer for refrigerators, cites "a whole lot of reasons you don't go into a rotary compressor fast." Mr. Davey, who retired in 1981, and others had long argued that rotaries weren't good in refrigerators.

Rotaries run hotter than traditional compressors. That isn't a problem in most air conditioners; fast-flowing coolant cools the compressor. But in a refrigerator, which typically runs four times as many hours as an air conditioner in a year's time, coolant flows one 10th as fast. And excessive heat can kill a compressor.

Even in air conditioners, moreover, rotaries aren't perfect. Introduced in 1957, they initially caused trouble. Gradually, the bugs were worked out. But in the mid-1970s, GE had to abandon rotaries in its big air conditioners. The compressors broke down in hot climates; failures in Saudi Arabia and Arizona eventually persuaded management to return to reciprocating compressors in the big units.

Despite these portents, GE's refrigerator managers and engineers were fixated on other issues. One was noise. Fearful that the rotary's high-pitched whine would spook consumers, executives argued over ways to mask it. Managers and consumer test panels spent hours listening to the new refrigerators.

Another time-consuming issue concerned manufacturing. The new design required the key parts to work together at a friction point of 50-millionths of an inch—about 100th the width of a human hair. Nothing had ever been mass produced at such an extreme tolerance.

The manufacturing engineers, led by Tom Blunt, felt sure they could do it. But they needed a little help—and the design engineers, working across the hall, provided it. The compressor that GE ultimately manufactured was nearly identical to the rotary used in air conditioners. There was one change, though, and it turned out to be disastrous.

A New Material

Two small parts inside the compressor were made out of a new material, powdered metal, rather than the hardened steel and cast iron in air conditioners. Powdered metal—made by fus-

The Saga of the Rotary Compressor

FALL 1981: GE appliance division in Louisville, Ky., hires consultant Ira Magaziner to investigate its refrigerator business.

MAY '82: Chief design engineer John Truscott assembles team to design a new compressor, the rotary.

SEPT. '83: Mr. Truscott, fellow engineer Tom Blunt, and division head Roger Schipke present idea to GE chairman Jack Welch and get authorization for $120 million factory.

FALL '84: Twenty top executives convene for meeting; they review test data and, finding no failures, authorize production.

MARCH '86: Full-scale production starts.

JULY '87: First failure in Philadelphia.

DEC. '87: Mr. Schipke announces decision to drop the compressor and use purchased units, mostly foreign made.

JAN. '88: Changeover to purchased compressors begins.

SUMMER '88: Investigators figure out the cause of the problem.

MARCH '89: GE reveals $450 million pretax charge for fixing the compressor.

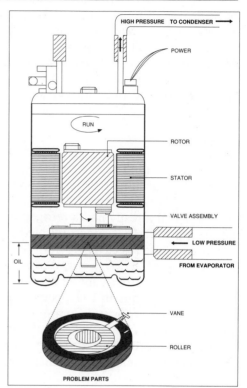

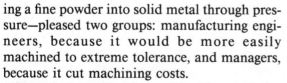

PROBLEM PARTS

ing a fine powder into solid metal through pressure—pleased two groups: manufacturing engineers, because it would be more easily machined to extreme tolerance, and managers, because it cut machining costs.

However, powdered metal had been tried a decade earlier in air conditioners and "didn't hold up," says Burr Stanton, an evaluation engineer who supervised tests on it in the early 1970s. He and others say that information was passed on to the design engineers. But they didn't listen, he says. "The guys who were designing it were new to compressors. They figured they were smarter and thought it wouldn't happen to them," Mr. Stanton explains.

The engineers who did the actual design were assembled by the appliance division's chief design engineer, John Truscott. Before coming to Louisville, Mr. Truscott was considered one of GE's top technologists; he had been, for example, on an aerospace team involved in the breaking of the sound barrier.

Now, he and the engineers on his team believed, GE would show that it still could be a world leader in manufacturing. But, like him, his engineers were new to compressors. "John figured you didn't need previous compressor-design experience to design a new compressor," one associate says. Mr. Truscott, who retired last year, declined to be interviewed.

Help Rejected

Moreover, the team he assembled was convinced that it didn't need outside help. Mr. Magaziner, the consultant, had recommended that the design be joint-ventured with a Japanese producer that already had a refrigerator rotary on the market. Mr. Truscott rejected that idea.

The team also rejected help from Milton Kosfeld, who, as a GE design engineer in the 1950s, had invented the rotary for air conditioners. He left GE in 1969, but, in 1983, before joining his present employer, Bristol Compressors of Bristol, Virginia, he offered his consulting services to the design team. They declined, writing him that "they had sufficient technical expertise," he says.

Limited testing of a compressor prototype began in 1982. Within a year of getting the board's final go-ahead in September 1983, the evaluation engineers had "life tested" about 600 compressors. In the fall of 1984, when 20 senior executives met to review the test data, there wasn't a single documented failure. "It looked too good to be true," recalls James Lehman, a finance official who attended the meeting.

It was. If they had known what some technicians knew, they wouldn't have been so sanguine. Though the compressors hadn't failed, they didn't look right, either, according to one of the technicians, Paul Schank. He had worked in the Louisville testing lab for more than 30 years—and knew compressors. After running the compressors continuously for about two months—under temperatures and pressures supposedly simulating five years' operating life—Mr. Schank would disassemble them and inspect the parts.

About 15 percent of them, he says, were suspect: Copper windings on the motor were discolored, a sign of excessive heat. Bearing surfaces appeared worn. And some small parts had a black, oily crust—evidence, he thought, that high heat was breaking down the sealed lubricating oil.

Mr. Schank's direct supervisors—a total of four in three years—discounted the findings and apparently didn't relay them up the chain of command. They believed in the basic air-conditioner design and thought the tests far exceeded field conditions. But Mr. Schank contends that the supervisors didn't have the proper technical background to ask the right questions and didn't want to do anything that might derail so big a project.

"The bottom line was that GE would save massive sums of money on each new compressor, and, if they brought the project in on schedule, they'd look like heroes," he says. Adds Robert Derman, who worked with Mr. Schank: "The pressure to get this project done was enormous. It was an awfully big task, and there just wasn't enough time to do it right."

Others involved in the project dispute that, but nearly all agree that the pressure to produce influenced the test results. Although GE offered a five-year warranty on the refrigerator's cooling system, it couldn't wait for five years of testing. But "life testing"—simulating harsh conditions—can be a tricky guide to a new product's future reliability. In the past, GE had always supplemented such estimates with extensive field testing. This time, field testing was curtailed. The original plan, to put models in the field for two years, was revised to about nine months as managers raced to keep up with their schedules.

"Nobody liked the idea that we weren't getting the proper field exposure," one engineer says. "But it would have taken a lot of courage to tell Welch that we had slipped off schedule."

Meanwhile Mr. Stanton, the retired engineer, was hired as a consultant to evaluate the testing. He considered the tests suspect, he says, because only one compressor had failed in two years—an extraordinarily low number. He says he recommended to a management committee that the test conditions be intensified. But "they didn't want to embark on a new program at that point," he says.

Schedule Met

In the end, the schedule was met. By March 1986, some 2½ years after board approval, the Tennessee factory was turning out rotary compressors at a rate of one every six seconds, an amazing feat given the manufacturing tolerances. Later that year, Mr. Blunt, the chief manufacturing engineer, passed out coffee mugs to hundreds of Louisville colleagues to commemorate production of the 1 millionth compressor.

Consumers, too, were pleased. They snapped up the new models, which featured other innovations, such as a refreshment center in the door. In 1986, GE's market share in refrigerators shot up two full percentage points to about 30 percent, its best showing in years.

But in July 1987, a bad omen: The first refrigerator—in an unventilated closet in Philadelphia—failed after little more than one year. At first, executives thought it was a fluke. Then, they got reports of failures in Puerto Rico. A team of technicians investigated. By Labor Day, Louisville knew it had a big problem. Over the next few months, as the toll of failed refrigerators mounted, GE engineers worked furiously, often through the night, trying to diagnose the malady.

By December, they still lacked satisfactory answers. So, Mr. Schipke, then the appliance-division chief, pulled the plug on the new compressor. The news, one manufacturing engineer says, literally made him sick. "How do you think the engineers at Thiokol felt when the *Challenger* blew up?" he asks.

GE scoured the globe for compressors. They weren't easy to find. Ultimately, GE had to persuade one U.S. manufacturer that had quit the business, Tecumseh Products Company, to get back into it. And it provided Tecumseh with GE-built motors, airlifted from Singapore. GE also had to fly Japanese compressors to Louisville.

Culprits Found

Perhaps just as disheartening, the new factory worked fine. Only the design had failed. By the summer of 1988, the team investigating the failure rendered its verdict: The two powdered-metal parts were wearing excessively, burning up the oil, and eventually choking off all cold air to the refrigerator.

With the problem identified, managers acted swiftly to correct it and, in the process, sidestepped a potentially devastating blow to GE's refrigerator business. Buyers of the refrigerators—some units cost $2,000—were made whole; the compressors were replaced, usually even before the customers knew anything was wrong.

So far, the company says, not a single lawsuit has been filed against it. In fact, GE's U.S. market share in refrigerators rose during the 1980s, according to *Appliance* magazine, as the company widened its lead over no. 2 Whirlpool. The Tennessee factory was kept running, though at half its rated capacity, through a contract to supply Fedders Corporation with air-conditioning compressors.

Meanwhile, GE has redesigned the compressor, abandoned powdered-metal parts, and developed new lubricants. It also changed its testing procedures. GE says it plans to bring the new compressor back into limited production this fall.

The man now in the hot seat, division engineering manager Mark Schreck, says he's "absolutely convinced we've got a high-quality compressor. Wouldn't you be in my circumstances?"

Incorporating a Consumer Safety Perspective into the Product Development Process

Fred W. Morgan

INTRODUCTION

The process by which new products reach the marketplace varies from firm to firm, although certain similarities have been observed.[1] Larger organizations generally take a more formal view of this process, leading commentators to develop a series of steps to describe the new product development sequence.[2] These various stages, beginning with the generation of ideas and ending with product commercialization, have been widely reviewed and discussed by practitioners and academicians alike.

While they seem to agree about the nature of the activities required to bring a new product to market, product development experts uniformly spend little time discussing the ethical and legal aspects of new product development. Such a viewpoint might be acceptable were it not for the publicity caused by lawsuits involving faulty products and injured consumers or by product recalls initiated

---

This review chapter was prepared by Fred W. Morgan, professor of marketing, College of Business Administration, University of Oklahoma.

[1] See, for example, Robert D. Hisrich and Michael P. Peters, *Marketing Decisions for New and Mature Products*, 2nd ed. (New York: Macmillan, 1991).

[2] The product development process includes from five to eight steps, depending upon the way the analysts conceptualize the sequence. See, for example, Hisrich and Peters, ibid. (five stages, with subsets); J. Paul Peter and James H. Donnelly, Jr., *A Preface to Marketing Management*, 4th ed. (Plano, Tex.: Business Publications, 1988) (six steps); Philip Kotler, *Marketing Management: Analysis, Planning, Implementation, & Control*, 7th ed. (Englewood Cliffs, N.J.: Prentice Hall, 1991) (eight steps).

by firms, either voluntarily or at the request of regulatory agencies. Litigation and recalls clearly raise questions about product safety that were not fully considered prior to these products appearing in the marketplace.

Perhaps the insufficient concern with regard to safety issues indicates that managers take too much of a reactive stance when it comes to product safety. Possibly the ethical/legal environment of marketing really does not get fully discussed during the new product development process. Such an attitude might be described as "Wait until something happens, then let the legal department deal with the problem."

This is an inappropriate perspective, because product safety concerns and issues have been with us for many years.[3] A more enlightened view would be to try to anticipate safety-related problems associated with the introduction of a new product prior to the product's commercialization. Once a product is made available for sale, the firm is left with a series of undesirable alternatives—negative publicity, recalls, litigation—if a product that turns out to be dangerous is used in unexpected ways. If such actions can be minimized through proactive product development, the firm can retain much more control over its marketing activities. Thus, the purpose of this discussion is to present a view of the product development process that incorporates a broader concern for consumer safety as the product is being prepared for entry into the marketplace.

THE PRODUCT DEVELOPMENT PROCESS

Generation of New Product Ideas

At the outset of the product development process, legal counsel has no role to play. In the idea generation stage, participants are encouraged to be very creative—a "no holds barred" situation. One of the keys to successful generation of truly new ideas is to reserve criticism of them and their originators until the brainstorming, focus group, problem solving, or whatever structure is utilized, is finished. Thus, any attempt to assess legal viability or vulnerability in this stage might hinder the desired spontaneity. In reality, this is the only stage where legal implications should be given little consideration.

Of course, a firm's research and development department also has a very significant role to play in this stage as it works on the technology frontier. This group should not yet be utilized to assess the ideas of others, but, instead, should supply new product ideas from the viewpoint of being technically possible.[4]

---

[3] For an overview discussion, see E. Patrick McGuire, *The Product-Safety Function: Organization and Operations* (New York: Conference Board, 1979); see also, Sheila A. Miller, "Liability Prevention: Corporate Policies and Procedures," *Personnel Administrator*, February 1986, pp. 47–56.

[4] See, for example, Richard T. Hise, Larry O'Neil, A. Parasuraman, and James U. McNeil, "Marketing/R&D Interaction in New Product Development: Implications for New Product Success Rates," *Journal of Product Innovation Management* 7 (June 1990), pp. 142–55.

Screening New Product Ideas

Here the purpose is to reduce the diverse set of ideas to a workable number of new product ideas that might be successful. Various types of models and rating schemes have been developed, some of which were introduced more than 20 years ago.[5] These approaches typically weigh a variety of product, company, and environmental factors to supply an estimate of the product's likely success. Yet safety factors are routinely excluded from such analyses.

At this stage, legal counsel, in conjunction with others on the research team, can begin to provide a useful overview of the safety implications of new product ideas. "High exposure" ideas, those that can readily lead to dangers for the consumer, might be identified early enough so that further investment of time and money is forestalled. For example, the dangers and ensuing litigation associated with the use of motorized, three-wheeled, off-road vehicles might have been avoided if a "safety/liability" factor had been evaluated during idea screening. Someone familiar with automobile roll-over litigation, especially arguments about center of gravity, might well have concluded that the intended use for these off-road machines would result in safety problems.

More generally, product liability attorneys can comment about any legal trends, either underway or likely to begin, which might affect new product ideas. Has anyone at the Federal Trade Commission made a recent statement indicating a special interest in certain product classes? Has the attorney general's office in, say, Michigan, begun to take action against particular sellers? Though such information might not be conclusive, it could alter the rankings of various new product ideas. If nothing else, management would be aware of the possible legal implications of continuing with certain new product ideas.

Formally including legal counsel in the product development process at this stage might appear unnecessary, given that no new product has yet evolved to be marketed. Yet one of the long-standing views about new product development is that a broad cross-section of affected organizational departments should be designated as part of the new product team.[6] As long as the legal representative is qualified to render opinions about product safety issues, he or she can come from either the firm's legal department or outside counsel.

Developing and Evaluating the Product (from Concept to Test Version)

At this point, product ideas are transformed into product concepts, which include consideration of the various uses for products, the benefits they will

---

[5] See, for example, David B. Lerner, "DEMON New Product Planning: A Case History," *Proceedings*, American Marketing Association, 1965, pp. 489–508; Glen L. Urban, "SPRINTER: A Tool for New Product Decision Makers," *Industrial Management Review* 8 (Spring 1967), pp. 43–54; Gert Assmus, "NEWPROD: The Design and Implementation of New Product Model," *Journal of Marketing* 39 (January 1975), pp. 16–23.

[6] E. Patrick McGuire, *Evaluating New Product Proposals* (New York: Conference Board, 1972).

supposedly provide, and the target markets that might be interested. From the standpoint of consumer safety, each of these concerns is relevant.

One of the truly pivotal issues in a dispute involving a consumer injured by an alleged faulty product is the way in which the product was being used at the time of the accident. To avoid liability today, it is not enough for the company to claim that the consumer was using the product in an unintended manner, maybe even in a clearly dangerous way. The marketer might even be able to prove that the product was being used inappropriately. If the jury can be convinced that the so-called misuse should have been anticipated by the selling organization, the plaintiff has taken a big step toward establishing seller liability.

The problem becomes one of trying to predict all of the strange ways in which a product might be used. Suppose a company markets a series of scented candles accompanied by decorative candle holders. Obviously other candles can be purchased as replacements for the originals, then placed in the candle holders. To counter this and to encourage additional sales, the firm develops a process by which the candle holder can be used to burn only two or three candles. The holder slowly melts, disintegrates, or in some fashion becomes unusable. So consumers will then purchase additional sets, which include both the candle and the base.

What is the likelihood that some purchasers will try to utilize the candle holder too many times? With tens of thousands of buyers, you can practically guarantee that overuse will occur. Suppose a fire results from this overuse; the subsequent consequences are predictable and grave. This kind of misuse very likely will be determined in a court of law to be foreseeable. But the seller claims that warnings, clearly stated and obvious, were included, putting buyers on notice that the candle holder should not be used more than twice. Not good enough. It will be easy to present evidence that such warnings are unlikely to be read. Besides, who would think that a candle holder is unsafe for continued use?

Many similar examples can be found in the transcripts of reported litigation. Even more examples could be found in the confidential outcomes of cases that were filed but settled prior to jury decisions. Thus, all of the really odd and unsafe uses for a product must be pondered and handled through product design or warnings. Even then, there are no assurances; but, at least, the product development team must systematically consider the various misuse possibilities.

A useful perspective in terms of identifying product uses is to look at all of the possible benefits the product provides. What benefits will someone get from using this product? The value of asking consumers this question should be apparent. Often, consumers will find unexpected uses for products, uses that are simply beneficial in ways not apparent to the seller. For example, a compound intended to be sprayed on a cloth for use in dusting furniture may include a fragrance that freshens the smell of a recently dusted room. Would someone consider using the compound as a freshener for clothing by spraying some into a clothes dryer? How will the compound react under such high-heat conditions? Does it matter if the dryer is electric- or gas-powered? This chain of events might appear far-fetched to managers of the firm that developed the dusting compound, but it is the logic of the consumer, not management, that matters.

A related issue is the various groups of consumers that are likely to come in contact with the proposed product. Which prospective consumers are going to be using the product? Are any others, not really within the target markets for the item, likely to come in contact with the product? An instructive example here is children's toys. New toy products may be aimed at very specific age groups, but these products may well find their way into homes with children younger than intended users. Are such youngsters going to have access, perhaps without adequate supervision, to these toys? Does an attractive new toy have any small, removable pieces that might pose a danger to preschoolers? If the sequence suggested here might appear reasonable to a jury, management must take steps to prevent the unfortunate conclusion from occurring. Moreover, by taking the consumer's perspective, the innovative firm may be able to identify truly endearing features of prospective new offerings.[7]

Planning the Accompanying Marketing Program

Once the new product has been formulated into a working physical prototype, attention should be turned to other marketing activities, which eventually will be utilized to present a safe total offering to consumers. Proposed introductory advertising programs, in addition to catching the attention and interest of buyers, must encourage the proper use of the product. Subsequent advertising campaigns must continue to discourage improper use once the product has been accepted. For example, American Motors Corporation found itself in a series of lawsuits resulting from a number of roll-over accidents involving the Jeep four-wheel-drive vehicle.[8] Apparently, management was aware of the Jeep's propensity to roll over during ordinary use; yet an advertising campaign showed the vehicle being operated aggressively over hilly terrain. One court noted that the advertising, particularly the sound track, was "intentional incitement to unlawful conduct" and upheld a punitive damages award against American Motors.[9]

Salespersons' activities also can lead to unsafe use of an otherwise carefully designed product. If salespeople fail to reinforce warnings or instructions for

---

[7] See, for example, Michael W. Lawless and Robert J. Fisher, "Sources of Durable Competitive Advantage in New Products," *Journal of Product Innovation Management* 7 (March 1990), pp. 35–44.

[8] *Judge* v. *American Motors Corporation* (1990), 908 F.2d 1565 (11th Cir.); *Anson* v. *American Motors Corporation* (1987), No. 1-CA-CIV-7625, slip op. (Ariz. Ct. App.); *American Motors Corporation* v. *Addington* (1984), No. 82-CA-2624-MR, slip op. (Ky. Ct. App.).

[9] *Leichtamer et al.* v. *American Motors Corporation* (1981), 67 Ohio St.2d 456, 424 N.E.2d 568, 21 Ohio Op.3d 285.

correct product use, customers might also ignore such materials.[10] An even more serious problem arises for the seller if a salesperson explicitly tells a consumer not to bother with certain precautions. Here the buyer's point-of-purchase experience actually has negated the hoped-for impact of warnings.[11] Of course, the assumption so far is that salespeople do not intentionally misrepresent their offerings. The firm likely will be held responsible if products are used incorrectly due to salespeople knowingly making false statements.[12]

Warnings and labels should be developed to apprise users of the level of care necessary for safe product use. One of the essential trade-offs here is minimum legal compliance versus provision of information that will be noticed. Labels that meet statutory or administrative law requirements for disclosure, but which contain trademarks and promotional slogans, may not actually provide adequate warnings to consumers about safe product use. Numerous judicial opinions have focused upon the question of warning adequacy, with such issues as size and type of print, number of words, technical nature of wording, coloration of label, competing promotional language, method of delivery, and literacy of target market being discussed.[13]

The last safety issue to be addressed at this stage is packaging, for the protection of both the buyer and the product. If the product eventually will be ingested by humans, the issue of product tampering must be considered. Technology now makes it possible to reduce the likelihood of someone intentionally adding a foreign substance to a product. Certain goods, most notably over-the-counter pharmaceuticals, are obvious examples. Other products, however, are candidates for tampering, including many food items and personal grooming supplies. The firm must make the difficult judgment of whether an addition to one of these product categories will be sufficiently attractive so that somebody might be inclined to alter it, especially if novel packaging is an integral part of the offering.

Test Marketing the Product

A complete test market of the new product would involve studying all of the factors considered in the prior sections—product design, various product uses,

---

[10] See, for example, Karl A. Boedecker, Fred W. Morgan, and Jeffrey J. Stoltman, "Legal Dimensions of Salespersons' Statements: A Review and Managerial Suggestions," *Journal of Marketing* 55 (January 1991), pp. 70–80.

[11] See, for example, *In re First Commodity Corp. of Boston* (1987), 119 F.R.D. 301 (D. Mass.); *Wooderson* v. *Ortho Pharmaceutical Corp.* (1984), 235 Kan. 387, 681 P.2d 1038.

[12] See, for example, *Scott* v. *Mid Carolina Homes, Inc.* (1987), 293 S.C. 191, 359 S.E.2d 291 (S.C. App.).

[13] For a discussion of consumer responses to print warnings, see Jacob Jacoby and Wayne D. Hoyer, "The Comprehension/Miscomprehension of Print Communication: Selected Findings," *Journal of Consumer Research* 15 (March 1989), pp. 434–43; see, also, Karl A. Boedecker and Fred W. Morgan, "A Legal Perspective on the Importance of Product Warnings," *Proceedings*, Western Marketing Educators' Association, 1990, pp. 62–66.

different customer groups, and supplemental marketing activities. But the usual concerns regarding test marketing come into play: How thoroughly do we test, so we learn about market reactions without providing too much information to our competitors? Moreover, some questions simply cannot be answered in a short-term market test. For example, the variety of consumer misuses of a product may not manifest themselves except over the many years a product is available and being used. Clearly, however, test marketing provides an excellent opportunity, without exposing all those who will eventually be targeted consumers, to assess the efficacy of product safety planning to date.

The increasingly popular approach of simulated test marketing also provides a way for marketers to query consumers about product usage.[14] But the laboratory-like setting of a simulation, although useful for assessing generic product preferences, may not allow firms to evaluate possible product misuses. Thus, there may be no substitute for small-scale, limited test marketing to learn about a product's latent dangerous features.

Product Commercialization

Safety awareness should continue unabated into the product commercialization stage. As the product is introduced, the firm should be looking carefully for any indications that consumers are being exposed to unanticipated risks. Are customers reporting, either directly back to us or through our distribution network, any product-related problems? Are certain geographic markets experiencing more complications than others—an indication of defects in certain manufacturing lots? Is merchandise moving off retail shelves fast enough so spoilage (if useful product life is an issue) is avoided?

Ideally the firm should have contingency plans in place to respond quickly if any of the above or other situations occur. If the safety issue is not life-threatening, perhaps the immediate use of new warning labels or package inserts will suffice.[15] If not, a product recall may have to be initiated.[16] The value of having a recall plan in place well in advance of its use can readily be appreciated. If the product-related defect is potentially fatal, the firm must respond instantly—taking even a day or two to organize a recall is unacceptable.

---

[14] Leslie Brennan, "Meeting the Test," *Sales & Marketing Management* 142 (March 1990), pp. 57–60, 63–65.

[15] The postsale duty to warn is a well-established common law concept. See, for example, *Lewy* v. *Remington Arms Co.* (1988), 836 F.2d 1104 (8th Cir.); *Tetuan* v. *A. H. Robins Co.* (1987), 241 Kan. 441, 738 P.2d 1210.

[16] For a discussion of product recalls, see George C. Jackson and Fred W. Morgan, "Responding to Recall Requests: A Strategy for Managing Product Withdrawals," *Journal of Public Policy & Marketing* 7 (1988), pp. 152–65. Also see Chapter 4.7.

SUMMARY AND CONCLUSIONS

The overriding message here is to incorporate a product safety perspective into the product development process. The foundation for this is a management culture that explicitly supports and values product safety—clearly extending well beyond mere public statements indicating a concern for safety. Those involved in new product development, at a minimum, must be concerned for the legal impact of their work. In addition, these people must be concerned about the moral acceptability of the products they develop and the impact of these products on consumers.

Of particular importance here is the immediacy of impact of decisions on new products. Research suggests that people are less concerned about consequences that occur in the distant future and that do not impact them directly.[17] Management must discourage this tendency and encourage a "do the right thing" mentality within the organization.

While management does not want to hinder the spawning of new product ideas, these ideas should be evaluated very early for potential product safety problems. At one level, people with exposure to and understanding of the legal environment of marketing (i.e., practicing attorneys and academics who study this area) can provide the appropriate viewpoint.

One might be tempted to oppose the involvement of legal specialists on the grounds that "what we don't know can't be held against us." This kind of thinking is doubly wrong! First, it rather blatantly minimizes the importance of making genuinely safe products available for sale. Second, the legal theory of strict liability is not fault-based but, instead, deals with the quality (including safety) of the product. Typically the manufacturer/marketer of a product is considered to be a collective expert on its product lines, particularly in comparison with consumers. The seller will be held to the standards befitting an expert, even if the seller chooses to remain ignorant of critical product-related information.

Firms that are safety conscious and legally proactive, however, may find themselves in an intriguing and perhaps paradoxical situation in the long run. Such firms presumably will develop safer products than their unconcerned competitors and will be involved in less litigation because of their sound products. These same firms, because of their documented research on and concern for product safety, will help to elevate the safety standards for their industries. Society at large and consumers of these safer products arguably will be better off, but these firms will be under continual pressure to maintain and improve their safety records. As these firms expend greater sums to develop even safer products, the upward cost/safety spiral becomes apparent.

In addition, truly safety-conscious firms may observe their less-careful counterparts profiting by not taking a leading position on safety, but merely adopting

---

[17] Thomas M. Jones, "Ethical Decision Making by Individuals in Organizations: An Issue-Contingent Model," *Academy of Management Review* 16, no. 2 (1991), pp. 366–95.

safety innovations when possible. Some firms may gamble that their customers will not be injured, even though their products are dangerous in some insidious fashion. This cost versus safety ethical dilemma is a fundamental one and is not clearly focused, because of the difficulties in estimating all of the costs involved, as well as all of the consequences of varying product safety levels.

Ultimately, an organization's commitment to product safety must be operationalized, not just verbalized. From a marketing perspective, safe products do not simply happen; instead, they must be planned. And the planning of safe products should not be a last-minute afterthought as products are being readied for national roll-out. Instead, the entire product development sequence should incorporate an active awareness of the importance of product safety.

Managing Product Recalls

N. Craig Smith
John A. Quelch

Since product safety cannot be totally assured in the new product development process, any company may at some time face the prospect of a costly and potentially damaging product recall. The safety concerns that drive most recalls and the possibility of human tragedy, or at least injury and inconvenience, highlight the importance of marketing ethics. The defective Pfizer heart valve, for example, is said to be responsible for 261 deaths and, therefore, considerable anxiety as well as inconvenience for the 86,000 people who were fitted with the valve between 1979 and its 1986 recall.[1]

Recalls are increasing. Consumer product companies are required by U.S. law to report product safety problems to the Consumer Products Safety Commission (CPSC). Recalls involving the CPSC have about doubled over the last 10 years; in 1989, the agency supervised 260 recalls, covering more than 37 million products. Food and Drug Administration (FDA) recalls also about doubled over the same time period, with 2,183 recalls in 1989. Statistics from other federal agencies, such as the National Highway Traffic Safety Administration (NHTSA), also indicate an upward trend. Product recall insurance has become more expensive and difficult to obtain as a consequence.

Recalls are not limited to automobile and pharmaceutical products. They can and do occur in any industry, and even companies in industries with substantial recall experience may be ill-prepared as recall circumstances change. The challenges of a recall—and the potential for mismanagement—are considerable and often underestimated.

Consider the Perrier recall.[2] Benzene discovered in Perrier's bottled water in early 1990 resulted in a worldwide recall of 160 million bottles at a direct

---

[1] Jeff Bailey, "Fears over Pfizer Heart-Valve Fractures Lead to Patients' Suffering and Lawsuits," *The Wall Street Journal*, June 21, 1990.

[2] The principal source used is: "When the Bubble Burst," *The Economist*, August 3, 1991, pp. 67–68.

cost in excess of $30 million. The benzene concentration was less than that of non-freeze-dried decaffeinated coffee, and health officials reported that it did not constitute a serious health risk. However, Perrier's "purity promise" had been broken, and sales have not recovered to their pre-recall levels.

One of the many challenges of recall implementation is resolving the logistics problems created by the return of large numbers of products. Illustrative of these problems is the experience of Perrier in the United States, which faced legal action resulting from "stolen" milk crates used for the storage and return of the recalled bottles. In the United Kingdom (U.K.), disposal of the 40 million bottles returned created an outcry when it was announced that only half would be recycled. Despite the limited demand for green glass in Britain, Perrier was subsequently able to arrange for all the bottles, their caps, and packaging to be recycled. Few companies have the necessary expertise and resources in-house to deal with recall logistics problems: tracking products, persuading customers and channel intermediaries to return products, establishing customer information and other systems, and creating a return/repair organization—including appropriate arrangements for the storage, transport, and disposal of the recalled product.

While prompt in ordering the recall, the company's subsequent handling of it damaged the brand image—the basis of differentiation for what is essentially a commodity product. With little international coordination, explanations of the source of the benzene differed: Perrier in the United States said the contamination was limited to North America; Perrier in the U.K. said it did not know what happened; in France, meanwhile, Perrier announced that the source of the benzene was a cleaning fluid mistakenly used on the North American bottling line and that the source of Perrier water was unaffected by pollutants. February 14, 1990, three days later, the company established the true cause, a failure to replace charcoal filters used to screen out impurities in the natural gas present in the Perrier source. At a press conference announcing a global recall, the company finally admitted that it routinely filtered out several gases, including benzene. Not only had Perrier tried to deceive the public about the cause of the contamination, but, when obliged to explain why an entire six months' production was affected, had to reveal that its purity promise was imperfect.

The consequences of this mismanagement were severe for Perrier. Despite the rapidly growing sparkling water market, Perrier group sales declined 18 percent in 1990, while profits fell by 21 percent and the share price dropped one third by the end of the year. In the United States, Perrier's market share fell from 13 percent in 1989 to 9 percent in 1991. In Britain, the fall was from 49 percent to less than 30 percent. Gustave Leven, Source Perrier's chairman and founder, resigned.

Elsewhere in this book, you will find further examples of companies faced with a possible recall requirement: Suzuki, during the Samurai roll-over crisis (Chapter 3.2); Black & Decker, after receiving a report of a fire in its award-winning Spacemaker Plus coffeemaker (Chapter 4.2); General Electric Company, after its "breakthrough" rotary compressor refrigerator broke down (Chapter 4.5); bookstores, who received bomb threats after displaying the controversial Salman Rushdie novel, *The Satanic Verses* (Chapter 6.3 and Chapter 6.4); and, finally, Audi, following problems of "unintended acceleration" with its Audi 5000 (Chapter 8.4).

Given the increase in product recalls and the ethical issues involved, this chapter reviews product recall management. Recalls typically are difficult to manage and can have devastating effects, as examples in this book show. These factors prompt three critical questions for senior management:

1. What is the organization doing to reduce the likelihood of a recall requirement?
2. Are recall procedures established?
3. How easily and quickly can these procedures be implemented?

Each question is examined in turn below.

REDUCING THE LIKELIHOOD OF RECALLS

A recall may be required for reasons other than a safety problem—for example, the 1987 recall of poor quality toys by Marks and Spencer, because of the British retailer's desire to protect its quality image; and, for preventive maintenance, the 1987 recall of 150,000 GM Chevette and Pontiac engines. Recall requirements also extend beyond what is generally understood as product quality. For example, a Kraft General Foods sales promotion contest was cancelled when the number of winners proved to be many times the number the company had budgeted for; and where there is a legal infringement, as in Bausch and Lomb's Hypocare, which breached the trademark of Allergan's Hydrocare. A patent infringement prompted the recall described in the Kodak and Polaroid case (see Chapter 4.4). Accordingly, recalls are here defined as involving the return, repair by the manufacturer, and/or removal from sale of products in the distribution channels and with consumers, because of some actual or perceived safety or quality problem or some legal infringement.[3] In essence, recalls constitute "reverse marketing."

Despite the diverse reasons for recalls, the root cause is often a quality problem. The best insurance against a recall is a quality product. Generally, quality standards are rising, though even Japanese quality leaders are having

---

[3] The CPSC prefers the term *corrective action plan* to recall. It offers this definition: "The term *corrective action plan* (CAP) is used to describe any type of corrective action measure taken by a firm. It could be a recall and return of the product to the manufacturer, importer, distributor, or retailer. Or it could be a product warning. Likewise, it could involve the repair of the product by the consumer, retailer, or manufacturer; the exchange of the product for a product without the defect; or a cash refund of the purchase price"; Consumer Product Safety Commission, *Recall Handbook* (Washington, D.C.: CPSC, 1988), p. 1.

problems. *BusinessWeek* recently reported that MITI (the Japanese Ministry of International Trade and Industry), following "a wave of product recalls" involving televisions, automobiles, and computers, issued an administrative guideline directing TV manufacturers to change their quality control measures immediately. Factors affecting Japanese product quality were said to include: imported components, lack of adequate product testing, and less dedication among younger workers.[4] More fundamental factors militating against quality and, thereby, increasing recalls are: shorter product life cycles; the trade-off between product testing and securing market leadership, with competitive forces often shifting the balance toward the latter; and high-tech design and engineering. With innovation there is always risk, not least because new concepts and designs cannot be as well tested and understood as their more established antecedents.

A manager who supervised the development of the GE rotary compressor refrigerator commented: "You have to have that magical balance between getting it right and getting it fast." GE went too far, too fast: declining market share and profitability (the old compressor was 1950s technology, costing twice as much to produce as Japanese and Italian units) created enormous pressures to complete the project on time. Corners were cut—life-testing was accelerated, evidence of technical problems ignored. Because of poor communications, and a fear of admitting failure, senior executives, too removed from the project, only heard good news.[5]

At the same time that products and production processes have (despite solid state electronics) generally become more complex, the technical and mechanical sophistication of the typical consumer has decreased. More complicated products available to mass markets of less well-educated consumers result in product misuse or abuse. Retail salespeople often cannot be relied on to educate consumers how to use the product or advise of safety precautions. One solution had been to design products to be "childproof," regardless of the age of the likely user. Products also are designed to "fail-safe" in the event of consumer misuse. Consumer and industrial goods manufacturers also provide "toll-free" customer service telephone services, to assist customers in operating equipment, because retailers or other suppliers are unable or unwilling to help.

The shift from caveat emptor toward caveat venditor[6] has increased consumers' expectations of protection, including cases where products have failed due to consumer misuse. This has contributed to the increase in product recalls and efforts to reduce their likelihood. Consumers also have come to expect protection from abuse of the product by others, with or without malicious intent. Product tampering, as in the well-known Tylenol and Contac cases, is a particularly troubling concern for food, beverage, and pharmaceutical com-

---

[4] "Now Japan Is Getting Jumpy about Quality," *BusinessWeek*, March 5, 1990, pp. 40–41.
[5] See Chapter 4.5, "GE Refrigerator Woes . . ."
[6] Discussed in Chapter 1.

panies. Manufacturers who fail to make their products "tamper-resistant" face the prospect of legal action as well as a recall.

A recall requirement may arise from problems for which the company does not think it is responsible. In the extreme, this could be as a result of terrorist activity or a "direct action" by a radical pressure group. The 1989 withdrawal from sale of *The Satanic Verses* by major U.S. book chains is an example. Similarly, in 1984, the claim by the Animal Liberation Front in the U.K. to have poisoned Mars candy bars. The action, protesting Mars's use of animals in tooth decay research, was a hoax. Nevertheless, it involved the company in the costs both of a recall and of restoring consumer confidence and lost market share.[7] Preventive measures to avoid recalls can usefully involve attempts to estimate and reduce potential vulnerability to product tampering, direct action by pressure groups, and terrorist acts.

Total quality programs, introduced in many organizations in recent years, can ensure that products are comprehensively tested before launch and are consistently manufactured to specifications, so any safety defects are identified before shipment. Comprehensive testing includes, for example, tests conducted under all geographic and climatic conditions under which the product would be used. Product testing in company laboratories can rarely fully simulate product use by customers. Increased home-use testing programs by consumer goods companies, prior to and after product launches, have helped companies avoid recalls as well as provide information about possible product improvements. Consumer misuses of products that create safety hazards or quality problems can be identified and then addressed through education efforts at the consumer or, possibly, retailer level.

Product safety needs to be explicitly considered throughout the new product development process, even at the early stages of concept development and testing. Product safety should not act as a brake on creativity but as a necessary condition to be addressed through creativity. Ensuring product safety—and avoiding recalls—does not end when the product has been fully developed and shipped. As the founder of Matsushita Electric has stated: "We are responsible for our products until they are disposed of by the ultimate consumer."

An active responsibility for product safety rests with the firm throughout the product life cycle, from development through to retirement. This may mean that products which have become "safety-obsolescent," as safer alternatives have become available, should be retired and their inventory scrapped, despite the prospect of further sales (perhaps in less attentive international or Third World markets). This "early retirement" of products ideally should be marked by the introduction of a superior replacement from the same company. Product safety responsibility continues throughout the product's useful life, which may be many years for manufacturers of industrial equipment or durable consumer goods and long after the company has ceased the product's manufacture. This

---

[7] David Hearst, "'Spiked' Sweet Eaters Unscathed," *The Guardian*, November 19, 1984.

responsibility diminishes over time or if owners do not take reasonable care of the product and conduct regular maintenance, but it does not entirely disappear until the product's safe disposal. Increased environmental concern has heightened this responsibility for safe disposal.

Total quality programs will reduce the likelihood of recalls, not only due to physical defects in the product but also for such diverse reasons as errors in labeling or packaging or even, perhaps, the legal department not keeping current with, and communicating, legal requirements of product performance and safety. Total quality programs should not overlook the organizational pressures, evident in the GE example, which may ultimately lead to product defects.

Planning in anticipation of a recall requirement is likely to give more credence to these preventive measures. Organizations prepared for recalls are also able to respond more quickly and effectively if and when a recall is required.

THE RECALL PLAN[8]

The management of a recall can have significant impacts on customers, channel intermediaries, and employees, as well as involving major ethical, legal, and financial considerations. Yet evidence suggests that recalls frequently are not taken seriously. Many companies seem satisfied with low recall response rates—many achieve less than a 10 percent return—which, while meeting the letter of the law, may leave many consumers dissatisfied if not endangered. A satisficing approach suggests that expressions of consumer care, when put to the test, are lip service to a notion the firm is not prepared to deliver. Poorly administered recalls also harm channel relationships and employee morale.

If recalls are to be taken seriously, all firms should have a recall plan in place before any requirement for its use emerges. A plan permits a speedy and effective response that could mean averting a fatality. A preplanned recall will certainly, for all foreseeable contingencies, be less costly than a recall that has not been planned for, at least minimizing duplication of effort. This is aside from any costs or other risks resulting from legal proceedings due to product liability or negligence charges. The plan itself may constitute part of a good faith legal defense.

Any recall plan or manual should cover six areas: company philosophy, management, decision making, communications, logistics, and evaluation.

---

[8] As well as field research (primarily with Black & Decker), the discussion of recall planning and implementation draws on the following sources: Lowell A. Ledbetter, "Product Recall Plan Guidelines for Manufacturers and Sellers of Industrial Products," *Professional Safety*, March 1989, pp. 18–23; Ashutosh Riswadkar, "Product Recall Program," *Professional Safety*, August 1988, pp. 19–22; Pete Mateja, "The Marketing Nightmare," *Marketing News*, May 8, 1987; David L. Malickson, "Are You Ready for a Product Recall?" *Business Horizons*, January–February 1983, pp. 31–35; George Fisk and Rajan Chandran, "How to Trace and Recall Products," *Harvard Business Review*, November–December 1975, pp. 90–96; CPSC, *Recall Handbook*.

Multiple plans may be required in large organizations with many product lines. The content of the plan is briefly discussed below. Details of particularly crucial elements in planning are discussed under recall implementation.

- **Company Philosophy**
  This is a statement of the company's commitment to product quality and safety and what this means for all employees. It could be derived from a detailed corporate values statement; for example, the Johnson & Johnson Credo.[9] It conveys the intent to treat recalls seriously, acknowledging obligations where recall situations do not involve product quality or safety, such as a terrorist action.

- **Management**
  The plan covers recall responsibilities and organization. It specifies who has overall responsibility for product recalls, including preventive measures, coordinating recalls, and regularly auditing and updating the recall plan. Because recalls are intrinsically linked to customer relationships, primary recall responsibility should rest with the company's most senior marketing executive. The marketing VP will have the customer outreach experience and skills and, as a senior line manager, is able to command multifunctional resources and make final decisions. She or he is likely to designate a recall coordinator. The responsibilities of other departments and personnel may also be assigned, including external agencies retained by the company, identifying an ongoing recall committee.

  The marketing VP, with assistance from the recall coordinator and the recall committee, identifies and includes in the plan: recall scenarios; recall procedures of relevant government agencies (e.g., CPSC); liaison with legal counsel to ensure the recall program meets legal obligations (and the plan itself does not create legal difficulties); financing methods (funded internally or by product recall insurance); and recall program test procedures (mock recalls). She or he also ensures the plan is circulated within the organization and organizes regular meetings of the recall committee. Meetings cover recall procedures and roles of committee members and periodic reviews of customer complaints and new products.

- **Decision Making**
  The plan provides guidance on the circumstances under which a recall may be needed, without substituting for the judgment of senior management who make the recall decision. An obvious decision rule would be that a product must be recalled if, due to a manufacturing defect, there is a high probability of both product failure and serious injury resulting. Other decision rules are specified within government agency guidelines.

---

[9] See Richard S. Tedlow and Wendy K. Smith, "James Burke: A Career in American Business (A)," Harvard Business School case no. 9–389–177 (1989).

- **Communications**

   The plan covers information procedures necessary to identify a recall requirement and to trace products to be recalled, as well as notification procedures in the event of a recall. The recall committee reviews information procedures to ensure the company knows as early as possible of the first instance of any defect. Where serious—perhaps after screening by the recall coordinator—this information should be rapidly communicated to the marketing VP. Traceability requires that the company can quickly isolate a product defect by batch, plant, process, or shift. Once isolated, the cause of the defect can be more readily identified and the affected products requiring recall pinpointed and restricted in number. This minimizes recall costs and customer inconvenience.

   Notification is the communication of the recall once the cause of a defect has been identified and a recall requirement determined. The recall plan uses marketing plans to specify how customers and channel intermediaries may be reached most cost effectively. Notification procedures for reaching other interested parties (such as regulatory agencies, the media, stockholders, and employees) are also included.

- **Logistics**

   The plan identifies a field response program—the physical location, movement, storage, and repair/disposal of the recalled product, together with the information system necessary for this to happen. A management information systems (MIS) manager is responsible for maintaining or, in the event of a recall, promptly compiling a data base of owners of products by unique product identifiers (such as serial numbers). The MIS manager is a member of the recall committee.

- **Evaluation**

   The recall plan specifies how recalls are evaluated and the conditions under which the product is relaunched. The plan shows how evidence of the recall's effectiveness is to be established and maintained in the event of any legal proceedings, as well as for control and learning purposes.

   Table 1 identifies 10 important questions senior management should ask to determine recall readiness.

RECALL IMPLEMENTATION

The recall plan covers all foreseeable contingencies, providing broad guidelines on appropriate responses. However, a recall is typically complex, requiring a tailored plan developed to meet each specific situation. The following discussion of recall implementation is roughly chronological in structure, covering each important decision and action in turn. However, the safety concerns that prompt most recalls require swift action; hence many recall activities are conducted simultaneously.

TABLE 1   Are You Ready for a Recall? Ten Questions to Ask

1. What programs are in place to reduce the likelihood of a recall requirement, such as, total quality programs, product safety audits?
2. Are product recalls explicitly considered throughout the new product development process and in the design and development of logistics systems and company data bases?
3. Does field monitoring include reviews of the safe performance of older products—perhaps no longer made by the company—and their safe disposal?
4. How quickly and from whom would senior management learn of a recall requirement?
5. Does the company have a comprehensive recall plan or manual, identifying recall scenarios and appropriate responses? Is the plan reviewed regularly?
6. Who is the senior executive responsible for product recalls?
7. How quickly could a recall be implemented? (Is this response time confirmed by mock recalls?)
8. Do the company's products, packages, and shipping containers carry easy-to-read identifiers that designate the product's date and place of manufacture?
9. Where possible, do customer and end-user records show sales by product identifiers?
10. How would a recall be funded?

The CPSC suggests: "Consumers believe they enjoy a safer, better product as a result of a recall. . . . Successful product recalls in the past have often rewarded companies with continuing consumer support."[10] This outcome requires sound recall implementation, with attention focused on the factors responsible for recall effectiveness and success.

Recall return rates vary greatly. NHTSA recalls for automobiles reportedly achieve correction rates of 15–70 percent. Many CPSC recalls achieve return rates under 10 percent, particularly with the difficulty in contacting owners of inexpensive but harmful products. A study of CPSC recalls[11] examined factors influencing the three conditions necessary for a successful recall:

- Product availability—in the distribution channel or at least still in the possession of consumers (determined by the average age of the product and its average useful life).

- Distributor and consumer awareness of the recall.

- Benefits of compliance with the recall exceeding perceived costs of time, effort, and lost product services.

The CPSC study outlined a model for predicting likely recall return rates, highlighting these variables:

---

[10] CPSC, *Recall Handbook*, p. 8.
[11] R. Dennis Murphy and Paul H. Rubin, "Determinants of Recall Success Rates," *Journal of Products Liability* 11 (1988), pp. 17–28.

- The number of months separating end of distribution and the start of the recall.

- The percentage of products owned by consumers who are notified of the recall directly by mail.

- The percentage of items (produced) in retail inventory. (Distributors and retailers have strong incentives to comply with recalls, because of concern for their reputations and the prospect of liability suits; their costs of compliance are usually relatively low and they can be relatively easily reached.)

- The percentage of items (produced) in the hands of consumers. (Return rates are typically lower for products with consumers than those in the distribution channel. Factors said to influence consumer compliance included the perceived severity of the safety hazard, the value of the product—higher benefit of compliance with more expensive products—and the type of remedy offered.)[12]

- Whether a repair at home is offered to the consumer (relative to more inconvenient alternatives).

While the CPSC study reported an average correction/return rate of 54.4 percent over a sample of 128 recalls between 1978 and 1983, there was considerable variance, largely explained by the above variables. In the experience of Black & Decker personnel, return rates of recalled products distributed to consumers were historically low, with a domestic appliance industry average said to be around 5 percent and anything over 22 percent "doing excellent." A GE Housewares Division electric fan recall, involving a fire hazard, only achieved a response rate of 6 percent. This low response was attributed to the late announcement of the recall; negotiations with the CPSC had delayed the announcement to November, when few consumers were thinking about fans.

Measures of effectiveness are confounded by discarded units; a company can never be certain how many of the recalled products are in use. An accurate measure of effectiveness, if it could be obtained, would be the number of units returned as a percentage of those units remaining with consumers that will be used in the future.

Initial Actions

Preliminary actions and decisions are often required within a few hours of receiving information that might prompt a recall or more rapidly when safety concerns are paramount. If time is essential, early information about a possible recall requirement and a recall manual to guide the process can be critical.

---

[12] A related consideration not covered in the CPSC study is the percentage of items bought as gifts. It may be assumed that a high percentage of gift purchases would lower recall response rates.

Information that may prompt a recall comes from a variety of sources: field monitoring by the sales force, field service engineers, customer service, and market research; customer complaints and other customer-initiated contacts, such as the call to Black & Decker's toll-free number (see Chapter 4.2); government agencies, such as the CPSC; and through the legal department. As part of the recall program audit, the marketing VP should look for ways of speeding up the process of relaying information—solicited or unsolicited—about a possible recall requirement, and check for incentives or disincentives that influence whether she receives this information. In a "shoot the messenger" culture, employees may feel discouraged from reporting product defects. But a recall requirement identified early on—certainly before product liability charges—is likely to be less serious, more manageable, and may mean the saving of life and the survival of the firm. Relevant information should be funneled to the recall coordinator, who informs the marketing VP of any situation which, as specified in the recall manual, might conceivably require a recall.

1. Meeting of the Recall Committee. Once notified, the marketing VP assembles the recall committee as quickly as the seriousness of the situation and the availability of committee members allow. In many recalls, this first meeting, when the decision whether to recall will be made, is going to involve all senior management, including the CEO. When immediate action is required and the decision is clear-cut, the decision to recall will have already been made by senior management, and the marketing VP can inform the recall committee of this mandate.

The recall committee more typically will include representatives of marketing, PR, customer service, sales (if separate from marketing), dealer relations, manufacturing, engineering/R&D, personnel (to arrange temporary hires), MIS, transportation, legal counsel, finance, and management accounting/control. The marketing VP chairs the committee and establishes the smaller recall task force, which meets on a daily basis and is responsible for the operation of the recall. As most departments contribute to the recall in some capacity, involvement of all at the outset is useful.

In the early days of the recall, the marketing VP should be fully accessible and meeting daily—probably morning and night—with the task force. Roles of each member of the task force, including the designated spokesperson, need to be clearly established. Recall operations are time-consuming. Members of the task force should not be expected to perform their normal daily duties; the marketing VP should arrange with department heads for these duties to be covered by other personnel. A dedicated task force avoids the requirement for other executives and staff to be involved and, hence, distracted from the company's day-to-day operations; arguably, in crisis situations, such as the early days of the Tylenol recall, perhaps everyone should be distracted by a companywide effort to meet the challenge. The task force provides regular written reports on the recall's progress, circulated to the recall committee, probably on a daily basis for the first one to two weeks.

Once a decision has been made to recall a product, the recall committee will determine the extent to which production, distribution, advertising, and sale of the product should be suspended. Further information will be requested to maximize the potential traceability of the product and to assess resource requirements.

2. The Recall Decision.   Determining a recall requirement and the appropriate response is the first task of the recall committee. In most recalls, the principal factors determining a recall requirement are the severity and likelihood of harm occurring, which in turn are related to the probability of product failure. The principal role of the recall then is to ensure that injury is prevented by removing unsafe products or eliminating the hazard in some other way. Immediate steps must be taken where serious injury is likely. A consideration, which may complicate the decision, is whether the hazard results from a product defect or consumer misuse. This is illustrated in Figure 1. A problem that develops in normal use of the product, and has potentially serious consequences, clearly requires a recall.

Factors determining a recall requirement and the appropriate response are:

- Probability of product failure.

- Probability of harm resulting.

- Severity of the consequences (property damage as well as injury).

- Number and location of products involved (totals and percentages likely to be defective).

- Nature of the defect, including the obviousness of any hazard.

- Cause of the defect (internal/company or external responsibility?)—or early guesses.

- Legal, statutory, or regulatory obligations.[13]

FIGURE 1   Determining Recall Requirement by Product Use and Consequences

Product Use			
	Improperly	No recall	Probable recall
	Properly	Possible recall	Definite recall
		Minor	Major
		Consequences	

---

[13] See CPSC, *Recall Handbook*, for example.

- Impacts on company image, reputation, and customer confidence.

- Estimate of costs of the recall (allowing for insurance coverage or claims against suppliers of faulty materials or components).

- Validity/accuracy of information received.

The largely objective factors listed above sometimes count for little when the public perceives a significant safety hazard. In the case of the recalls of the Audi 5000 and the Rely tampon, for example, evidence did not conclusively identify a product problem.[14] There may need to be a management predisposition to act and recall even when there is only a remote hint of company responsibility, because of the firm's image exposure. The Suzuki Samurai case is interesting to consider in this regard (see Chapter 3.2).

Table 2 provides examples of recall situations which, moderated by their seriousness and other situation-specific factors, prompt one of the range of responses identified. For example, good traceability may permit a selective recall strategy; the bulk of the product and the nature of the defect may dictate a repair on site; a trademark infringement, perhaps in package design, may only require the recall of products in the distribution channel. Recalls may be contested by the company but this is likely to test customer loyalty and will involve legal action if the recall has been mandated by a government agency.[15]

A factor militating against a recall decision is the company's liability exposure. In a litigious society (there are more than 1 million lawyers in the United States), the law can act dysfunctionally. Unfortunately, recalls can be a double-edged sword. While delaying the recall of an unsafe product may increase the size and number of potential claims against the company, announcing a recall serves notice of the company's admission of a problem and may open the door to a flood of lawsuits. Between 1978 and 1988, the number of product liability actions filed in U.S. federal courts increased by 758 percent to 17,140, compared with a 62 percent rise in the total number of tort suits. While many actions do not come to trial and, indeed, are often without merit, the average value of jury verdicts in liability cases increased by 370 percent over the same time period. However, the General Accounting Office disputes the "explosion" in product liability cases seemingly evident from these figures.[16] There has been a steady rise in awards made and the cost of liability insurance.[17]

---

[14] The Audi recall is briefly described in Chapter 8.4, "Audi of America Inc." The Rely tampon recall is described in "Managing Product Safety: The Procter & Gamble Rely Tampon" in John B. Matthews, Kenneth E. Goodpaster, and Laura L. Nash, *Policies and Persons: A Casebook in Business Ethics* (New York: McGraw-Hill, 1985).

[15] George C. Jackson and Fred W. Morgan, "Responding to Recall Requests: A Strategy for Managing Goods Withdrawal," *Journal of Public Policy and Marketing* 7 (1988), pp. 152–65.

[16] The General Accounting Office notes that much of the increase is due to litigation involving asbestos, pharmaceuticals, and motor vehicles (45 percent of cases), and that a large proportion of cases involve a small number of firms. This response does not satisfy insurance and business

TABLE 2   Recall Situations and Responses

Examples of Recall Situations	*Seriousness Categories**	*Range of Responses*
• Product safety or quality in doubt, due to flaw in design, components/raw materials, or manufacture. • Hazards or quality problems resulting from improper use, misuse, or abuse of product by consumers. • Inadequate or incorrect product use instructions or labelling. • Product tampering. • Infringement of copyright or trademark. • Terrorist threats.	• Class A: Death/grievous injury/ illness is likely or very likely. Serious injury/illness is very likely. • Class B: Death/grievous injury/ illness is not likely, but is possible. Moderate injury/illness is very likely. • Class C: Serious injury/illness is not likely, but is possible. Moderate injury/illness is possible.	• Full recall. • Selective recall: By product (model, batch, and the like). By customer (geographic or other segmentation variables). • Repair/retrofit: Product returned or in situ. By the customer/owner or by company service engineers. • Silent recall: Announcement of recall limited to minimum legal requirement. • Optional recall: At customer's discretion. • Cease or change production and distribution. • Cease or change production only. • Issue advisory/warnings. • Refute: Contest recall mandated by government agency (or advice of legal counsel).

* This categorization is used by the CPSC. It is limited to safety hazards, ignoring, for example, legal infringements. A similar scheme is used by the FDA.

Recalls can have other negative impacts, as well as raising liability exposure. Image exposure increases, as the recall typically identifies quality problems that may be attributed to all the company's products and harms its reputation—this impact will be more critical if the brand name is also the company name. Inconvenience is created for channel intermediaries, who are required to stop selling and return recalled products, may need to deal with consumers wishing

interests, whose lobbyists have been promoting a product liability bill in Congress in an attempt to establish a cap on product liability awards and clearer and more consistent standards in court rulings. For a review of the product liability reform debate, see: Frances E. Zollers and Ronald G. Cook, "Product Liability Reform: What Happened to the Crisis?" *Business Horizons*, September–October 1990, pp. 47–52.

[17] For example, chemical industry liability premiums have risen as much as 500 percent since 1985. Awards may be high; the average payment was close to $500,000 in 1985 and large product liability claims have increased 150 percent over the last 10 years. Settled claims against the Manville Corporation's asbestos personal-injury trust, set up as part of a bankruptcy court reorganization plan, amount to almost $1 billion.

to return products, and will be looking for alternative sources of supply. Direct costs of the recall are likely to be substantial, encompassing consumer refunds (at retail prices); trade reimbursements; and notification, product rework, freight, and administration costs. Indirect costs may be greater, when the opportunity costs of lost sales and efforts to regain market share are included.

3. Early Notification.   Early notification of the recall decision should be given to the board, the legal department (if not already involved), and any regulatory agency governing the industry. Consumer product companies, for example, are required to notify the CPSC within 24 hours of learning of a product defect that creates a "substantial product hazard." The agency will wish to review the subsequent corrective action plan. Companies may wish to institute a recall even where this is not required or advised by a regulatory agency. The agendas of government agencies and the firm may differ; in the 1982 Tylenol recall, the FDA was particularly concerned about the implications of giving in to the terrorism implied in product tampering by recalling the product. Johnson & Johnson management had to weigh this public policy concern against the threat to its customers and the firm, too.[18]

4. Plan Announcement, Adjustment Offer, and Logistics.   While the first concern of most recalls is to stop the use of a hazardous product, the recall announcement also must explain which products are affected, how they are to be returned, and the compensation offered in exchange. If a replacement part or product is involved, supplies need to be secured and provided to service centers or channel intermediaries, preferably before the announcement is made. The understanding and cooperation of distribution channels throughout the recall require that they ideally be consulted (by telephone or fax) in advance of the recall announcement. A system for tracking returned products also needs to be established, based on product identifiers.

Announcement

Since silence suggests guilt, the company should announce the recall publicly as soon as possible after the recall decision. Effective announcement is critical to the success of the recall. Table 3 lists some reasons why consumers say they do not respond to recalls, according to a *Consumer Reports* survey. Some of these factors are controllable by the company; they are influenced by the adjustment offer, the field response program, and, as important, the aggressiveness of the recall communications program. Announcement of the recall should not only aim to reach as many affected consumers as possible but also persuade them to respond.

---

[18] See Richard S. Tedlow and Wendy K. Smith, "James Burke: A Career in American Business (B)," Harvard Business School case no. 9–390–030 (1989).

TABLE 3   Why Consumers Don't Respond to Recalls

- Too much trouble:
  Inconvenience of leaving a product at a service
  center or waiting while it is repaired.
  Returning products to distant service centers.
  Shipping paid but packaging not provided.
- Lack of incentive:
  Defect not seen as serious.
  Inadequate adjustment offer.
- Doubts about the fix:
  Service center won't fix the defect properly or will cause other defects.
- Problem solved another way:
  Product discarded.
  Product used less frequently or more carefully.
  Defect fixed by the consumer or an independent agent.

Source: "The 'Failure' of Product Recalls," *Consumer Reports*, January 1981, pp. 45–48.

The recall announcement should be agreed in advance with the CPSC (or other relevant agency). The urgency of some recall situations may prompt senior managers to question this bureaucratic procedure or seek instant approval. The agency aim is to avoid consumer confusion. Companies must ensure that recall announcements comply with regulatory agency guidelines (which should be included in company recall manuals).

Announcement decisions include:

1. Timing.   Urgency may dictate an immediate announcement. Otherwise, the time or even the day chosen will be determined by media schedules, for example: afternoon to fit with evening TV newscast deadlines; Federal Express collection times; or media "off" news days, such as Sundays and holidays, to maximize exposure.

2. Traceability and Audiences.   For many industrial products and some (typically higher-value) consumer products, all owners are more likely to be known and can be reached by telephone, fax, or mail. The company then may not need or wish to publicly broadcast the recall. Traceability is the key to determining what audiences need to be communicated with and how they may best be reached. Ensuring good traceability is an important element of planning in anticipation of a recall. Table 4 provides traceability checklists.

The traceability of owners of low-value consumer goods is unlikely to extend to records that identify specific individuals who can be reached directly. Under these circumstances, careful attention must be paid to profiling likely owners; and a wider range of audiences will have to be reached, including stockholders, who may be concerned about the publicity necessary to reach owners. Figure 2 shows potential audiences of a recall.

TABLE 4   Traceability Checklists

Market segmentation is a vital ingredient of sound marketing programs. Similarly, traceability is vital to the reverse marketing involved in product recalls. With both, the aim is to identify specific products with particular customers. Good traceability reduces:

- Possible explanations for the defect, by isolating specific causes.
- The number of products to be recalled, avoiding a "blanket recall."
- The number of customers to be notified of the recall, minimizing costs and inconvenience to customers and channel intermediaries.
- The company's product liability exposure, by strengthening its defense.

1. Scope of Documentation

Good traceability requires accurate records which span the entire life of the product, from initial designs through to disposal. Proper documentation enables the approximate date of manufacture to be established and the defect attributed to the responsible operation, or faulty component or materials, or some interference with the product in the distribution channel. Many of these documentation activities form part of a product safety audit. They cover:

- Design records, including details of "critical parts," which form part of the data base by product.
- Sourcing of raw materials and component parts, such as supplier records.
- Production records, including the product identifiers used (tags, plates, indent stamps, ink stamps).
- Quality control records.
- Distribution records, such as shipping papers and invoices.
- Channels; to know which products are in which channels, the progress of products through distribution channels is recorded and retained, establishing a "trail" that forms part of the data base by customer; product identifiers attached before shipping and during distribution also are included in the data base, such as SKU or contract numbers.
- Sale to the final customer, with suppliers to these customers encouraged to keep records if this is impractical for the manufacturer.
- Owner registration cards (ORCs), including worthwhile incentives for their return (product updates, extended warranties, cash rebates); retail salespeople may be encouraged to assist customers to complete ORCs.
- Product resale, information on new owners obtained via service center records or ORCs included in packaging for subsequent owners.
- Complaints handling and service/repair operations.

2. Document Control and Retention Policy

The document control system and policy specifies who is responsible for record retention and which records are to be retained. Record retention policy covers:

- Duplicate records—stored off-site on microfilm, protected from damage.
- Length of retention—the expected life of the product plus a minimum of 30 years for many industrial products.
- Review procedures to test product traceability.

TABLE 4 *(concluded)*

---

3. Optimizing Traceability

Traceability can rarely be maximized, given its costs. Factors determining optimum traceability include:

- Likelihood of recall.
- Product's inherent risk of injury/economic loss (products with significant loss potential are: inherently dangerous or are used in dangerous activities, easily misused, have a long service life or deteriorate after prolonged use or over time, or can cause severe injuries or high economic losses when failures occur).
- Product complexity and number of critical parts.
- Unit cost—the greater the cost, the greater the need to minimize the number recalled, avoiding the recall of nondefective products.

Sources: *Recall Handbook* (Washington, D.C.: U.S. Consumer Product Safety Commission, 1988); Lowell A. Ledbetter, "Product Recall Plan Guidelines for Manufacturers and Sellers of Industrial Products," *Professional Safety*, March 1989, pp. 18–23; Ashutosh Riswadkar, "Product Recall Program," *Professional Safety*, August 1988, pp. 19–22; and E. Patrick McGuire, *The Product-Safety Function: Organization and Operations* (New York: Conference Board, 1979).

Recall communications may be guided by the product marketing plan and other information on marketing communications used in promoting the product. For example, in announcing the 1980 recall of the Rely tampon, Procter & Gamble specified a reach objective of 90 percent of women in the target audience (i.e., the percentage receiving at least one message of the recall). This was seven percentage points higher than Rely advertising's normal reach and higher than that of any other tampon brand. The campaign ran for four weeks on all key media: in 203 television areas (covering virtually all households with televisions), 350 radio stations (87 percent of households), and 1,200 newspapers.

The recall decision should be telephoned to the sales force, other field operations, and channel intermediaries. Instructions on their roles in the recall should be sent in a subsequent letter or fax, detailing: receiving, collecting, transporting, storing, replacing, repairing, and disposal functions. Incentives to fully participate may include: commission payments otherwise lost by the sales force, company efforts to minimize the role and inconvenience of channel intermediaries, and a quick restocking of retailers with the relaunched product.

Dealers, retailers, and service centers should be asked to cease the sale of the product, to return all inventory, to post notices of the recall (at store entrances and exits, where the product is routinely sold, at check-out and customer service centers), and to supply any lists of affected customers. Their personal contact with customers may be vital in explaining the recall and maintaining customer confidence. Company employees need to be able to answer questions on the recall and internal fact sheets and posters may be useful. Unauthorized responses to inquiries from customers should be pro-

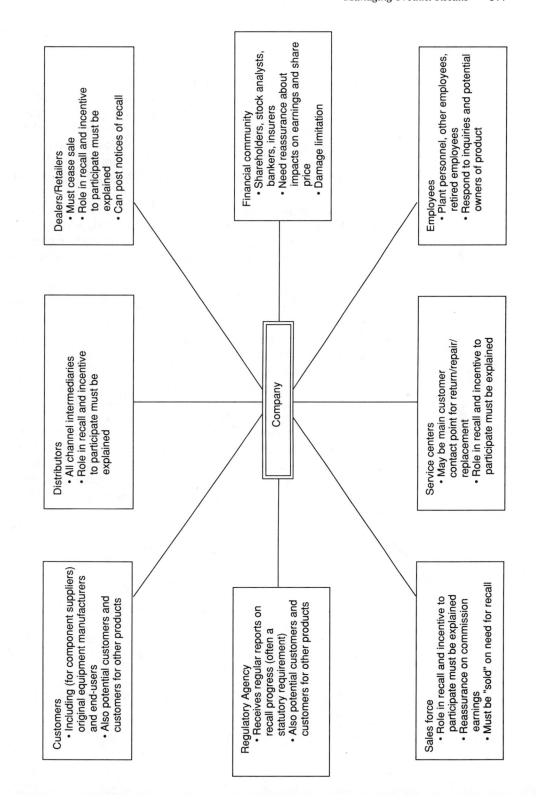

Dealers/Retailers
• Must cease sale
• Role in recall and incentive to participate must be explained
• Can post notices of recall

Financial community
• Shareholders, stock analysts, bankers, insurers
• Need reassurance about impacts on earnings and share price
• Damage limitation

Employees
• Plant personnel, other employees, retired employees
• Respond to inquiries and potential owners of product

Distributors
• All channel intermediaries
• Role in recall and incentive to participate must be explained

Company

Service centers
• May be main customer contact point for return/repair/replacement
• Role in recall and incentive to participate must be explained

Customers
• Including (for component suppliers) original equipment manufacturers and end-users
• Also potential customers and customers for other products

Regulatory Agency
• Receives regular reports on recall progress (often a statutory requirement)
• Also potential customers and customers for other products

Sales force
• Role in recall and incentive to participate must be explained
• Reassurance on commission earnings
• Must be "sold" on need for recall

hibited; employees should be advised to forward inquiries to the toll-free customer service number handling the recall.

3. Media. Media employed vary according to such factors as the type of product, seriousness of the recall, location and number of products involved, and the nature and size of the audience. Creativity is important in media selection. The support of representatives of the broadcast and print media can be particularly helpful in ensuring favorable and low-cost coverage, as examples of recalls in this book illustrate. Table 5 lists the communication techniques that can be used to reach owners of recalled products and channel intermediaries.

In product safety recalls, letters to customers should be sent as certified or registered mail. A return card should be enclosed, which the consumer can check to indicate what has been done with the product. Records of letters sent and their receipt are a valuable defense in the event of product liability suits.

4. Message. Message content covers three areas: how customers should identify if they are affected by the recall; what to do if affected; and who to contact for further information. If the recalled product cannot be easily identified by the consumer, a blanket recall may be required. Some wrong models and competitor products inevitably will be returned; but clear product identification at least minimizes this. Table 6 lists the information to provide.

There is an underlying tension to recall communications. While seeking to minimize the likelihood of a product hazard causing harm (which also may result in product liability suits), the company will wish to avoid undue negative publicity, which harms the brand and the company's reputation. Some communications will be needed for damage control to combat adverse publicity, striking a balance between the notification requirement and the need to reassure all the company's customers and channel intermediaries, shareholders, and employees. Crisis communications techniques may be useful, even if a crisis, such as a fatality, is averted by the recall. Table 7 provides a crisis communications checklist.

Adjustment Offer

Customer orientation is fundamental to the reverse marketing of product recalls. The adjustment offer must provide customers with sufficient incentive to comply with the recall, as well as maintain (perhaps increase) their loyalty and that of the trade. Turnkey logistics minimize customer and channel inconvenience. Factors to consider include:

- Product type (particularly durable or nondurable), age, and weight (heavy or difficult to transport/mail).

- Retail prices (current and previous).

TABLE 5   Notification Checklist I: Ways of Reaching Consumers

For a Class A hazard, the CPSC recommends "immediate, comprehensive, and imaginative corrective action measures by the company,"* including:

- A joint news release issued by the CPSC and the company; extensively circulated, including TV and radio networks, periodicals on CPSC lists (such as *Consumer Reports*), major metropolitan newspapers, and news wires (AP, UPI).
- Direct mail, using ORCs or other owner information, such as rebate return cards, service contract names, consumer requests for spare parts.
- Purchase of mailing lists of suspected product owners, to augment direct mail campaign.
- Use of "bill stuffer" enclosures.
- Paid advertisements in nationally and regionally distributed newspapers and magazines reaching suspected owners of the product.
- An "800" toll-free telephone line to receive calls (question-and-answer sheets prepared in advance).
- Incentives, such as "bounty" money, gifts, and premiums.
- Point-of-purchase posters at retail outlets and service centers.
- Notices in product catalogs, marketing newsletters, other sales materials.
- Notification to groups and trade associations for whom the product recall may have particular concern.

Other creative ways of reaching consumers include:

- Providing recall notices with complementary products; for example, in tins of coffee in a coffee percolator recall, in packaging of other products in the product line.
- Communication networks particular to the target market; for example, electronic mail to reach computer users, agricultural newsletters to reach farmers, trade association newsletters.
- PR campaigns providing stories to the media created around the recall; for example, an unusual gift or attractive "bounty" offered in return for the recalled product, and, after initial announcements, a campaign targeting "low performance" geographic areas describing their surprising failure to respond to the recall.
- Public safety announcements, provided in the form of videos, audio tapes, and scripts for local radio and TV stations, where they are often used as fillers; an interesting story line and quality of presentation is critical.
- Spokespersons available at short notice to join radio and TV talk shows.
- Trade shows that provide an opportunity for presentations to the media.
- Poster campaigns in locations specific to the target market; for example, waiting rooms of pediatricians and maternity clinics in the recall of a baby's crib, and, in geographically focused recalls, at local post offices, on bulletin boards of large local employers.
- Creative development of mailing lists. To illustrate: all parents of children under 21 months, using birth registration data, in the crib recall; contestants in competitions where the recalled product was a prize; callers to company toll-free numbers, inquiring about the recalled or related products; credit card records of purchases (contacted via the credit card issuer); retailer scanner data and other store records of purchases of the recalled or related products.

TABLE 5 *(concluded)*

- All ways used to promote the product before the recall should be reviewed, suggesting further possible avenues for reaching consumers.

* *Recall Handbook* (Washington, D.C.: CPSC, 1988), pp. 4–5.

TABLE 6   Notification Checklist II: Information to Provide

The CPSC suggests* notification of recalls by letter, press release, or poster should be specific and concise and individualized to the target audience (consumer, retailer, distributor). Typically, less information is required in the recall of nondurable goods. Information required includes:

- "Important Safety Notice," prominently displayed on envelopes and letters.
- Statement that the recall is for safety reasons.
- The nature of the hazard; for example, fire.
- Name of the product and the manufacturer.
- Suggested retail price.
- Description of the product and its intended use.
- Product identifiers: model and serial numbers of the product, batch or date code, and where this information may be found on the product.
- Dates and times of product availability.
- Names of major national stores or chains selling the product.
- Description of the hazard and when it was identified (the date the CPSC was first notified).
- Recommended actions and guidelines for the customer, distributor, or retailer; for example, immediately disconnect and stop using the product.
- Directions about how consumers may return the product and obtain refunds/ replacement/repair.
- Toll-free telephone contact number and name to ask for.
- Photograph or line drawing of the product.

* *Recall Handbook* (Washington, D.C.: CPSC, 1988), pp. 5–6.

- Original and current distribution channels.

- Whether the product/model has been discontinued.

- Availability of equivalent models from the company, not subject to recall.

- Product guarantees.

- Customer inconvenience in being without the product.

1. One-for-One Exchange.   The simplest option is often to replace the faulty product with an equivalent. However, the company must decide whether it also needs to compensate the customer for effecting the exchange, perhaps by

---

TABLE 7   Crisis Communications Checklist

In keeping with effective crisis communications/strategies, companies should:

- Ensure credibility and honesty at all times.
- Provide factual, consistent, and timely communications.
- Have an expert spokesperson available and authorized to be interviewed, who is well-trained—and capable of sensitivity, compassion, and concern—armed with the facts, and can field questions in a way that is credible and respected.
- Be creative, to deal with "media fatigue."
- Deal with the "garbled word" and other confusions or misinterpretations of reporters by providing question-and-answer sheets, toll-free telephone numbers, and issuing corrections and amplifications in response to confused reports.
- Make immediate announcements of important developments, so the media knows and reports the company's stance.
- Seek third-party support; for example, independent scientists.
- Recognize the importance of—and communicate with—both professional and consumer audiences.
- Hold press briefings prior to major events, such as the recall announcement.
- Recognize that irresponsible reporting, including articles in tabloids, such as the *National Enquirer*, can be influential.
- Determine, in advance, planned media coverage, so media and the company spokesperson have the right information.
- Aim to increase the likelihood of balanced media coverage, by establishing the company as an objective, accessible source of reliable information about the product, its testing, and the company itself.

Source: Christopher P. A. Komisarjevsky, "Trial by Media," *Business Horizons*, January–February 1983, pp. 36–43.

---

providing a superior product or an additional free gift. Alternatively, a one-for-one exchange may be too generous if the item is costly and the consumer already has enjoyed the use of it for some time.

2. Repair.   Costly or complex products with recalled or defective components, such as durable consumer goods and industrial equipment, are most likely to require repair. Again, such factors as the age or size of the product will determine whether it should be repaired on site or in company service centers or factories, and whether the company will organize the collection of the product or whether its return is required of the customer. Under some circumstances, the company may require some payment from the customer; for example, where an expensive repair is required to an older product, upgrading it beyond merely fixing the defect.

3. Refund of Full Purchase Price.   While heavy products are expensive to exchange if they are to be replaced by mail, this still may be less costly than a full refund, because the company has to make the refund at purchase price. Customers may not reasonably be expected to furnish receipts when a recall is involved, so the refund will need to be at the suggested, rather than the actual, retail price. In the Rely recall, Procter & Gamble not only bought back purchased products but also offered to buy back $10 million of promotional samples. Where the customer has received considerable use from the product, a prorated cash refund may be possible, but may test customer loyalty and reduce compliance with the recall.

4. Combination Offers.   Combinations of exchanges, gifts, cash refunds, and discounts on other company products may also be made.

Communication of the adjustment offer must be clear and, once made, cannot be changed easily. Complex adjustment offers, based, for example, on the age of the product, are likely to confuse customers and increase correspondence, which may be considerable when millions of products are recalled. Recalls subject to regulatory agency controls may require agreement of the terms of the adjustment offer with the agency.

The decision to stop using an unsafe product ultimately rests with the customer. Aside from the company's concern about harm occurring, the company should be aware that notice of the recall provided to the customer only reduces and does not eliminate liability. The company is still to some extent responsible for defective products in customers' hands. It is a marketing task to ensure maximum compliance with the recall, involving attention to all the elements of the marketing mix, from pricing (the refund) to logistics (effecting the exchange). The terms of the adjustment offer can reduce "recall resistance."

Field Response Program

The field response program encompasses adjustment fulfillment and the operation of the recall from its announcement through to its conclusion. The field response program aims to maximize compliance with the recall, while minimizing trade and consumer inconvenience at the lowest cost to the company. The program includes:

1. Adjustment Fulfillment.   Adjustment fulfillment requires adequate supplies of the replacement part or product with the responsible company service centers, dealers, or retailers. Alternatively, the company may rely on the postal service. As well as ample supplies, channel members should be able to provide any customer compensation (credit notes or vouchers) and also may receive compensation for assisting in the time-consuming administration of a recall.

2. Logistics.   Recall logistics are more complex than reversing the existing distribution system. Even if existing channel intermediaries are used to manage the return of the product, additional facilities and systems may be required. Many distribution systems only permit a one-way flow, from the manufacturer to the consumer. Even where recycling entails some reverse flow, a two-way system is difficult to manage. A major problem is simply ensuring that recalled products do not get mixed up with sound products or end up being redistributed. To avoid any mix-up of the new and the recalled product—by distributors, retailers, and customers—product identifiers on the product and its packaging must, as a minimum, be different. One common method is to use stickers on preprinted packaging.

Separate assembly locations may be required to accumulate volume loads for shipment back to a central point. Once collected, recalled products may be destroyed, repaired, or stripped of useful components. Controls must ensure they are not shipped out again through salvage operators.

3. Tracking. Tracking is critical to the logistics system. This requires the planning and design of reporting forms to be completed by customers, service centers, distributors, and retailers. These data, an input to the recall data base, enable the company to track the return of products and locate those units still to be returned. These units may be targeted in a second or subsequent wave of communication campaigns. In the event of product liability suits, the data base can also serve as an audit trail and produce lists of customers notified of the recall and their responses.

4. Monitoring and Reporting. Monitoring should continue throughout the recall. Each repaired unit or unit returned from consumers and distributors/retailers should be recorded. Return rates indicate whether—and where—further announcements of the recall are required. Recall expenses should be identified and reported to a central control center (probably the recall coordinator). They are tax deductible and may be claimed against recall insurance. They can be used to calculate the cost effectiveness of different communication efforts used in the recall program.

Progress reports are required by regulatory agencies, such as the CPSC. Internal reports will be required of the recall task force, which is likely to be meeting daily after the announcement of the recall until recall procedures are firmly in place and known to be working as anticipated. These reports may be circulated to employees, distributors, customers, and the media, as well as the recall committee.

Review and Relaunch

Toward the conclusion of the recall (as the rate of returned units diminishes), the company needs to review its effectiveness and make plans to relaunch the product, if possible. The effectiveness of the recall should be reviewed by somebody outside the recall task force. This audit should review the recall return rate, customer attitudes toward the company and its products, including customers not affected by the recall, and whether the fix worked. A lack of interest in such review procedures may reduce the opportunity to learn from the recall and indicate to the product liability courts that the recall has not been taken seriously.

Determining what to do with the recalled brand depends, in part, on the causes of the defect. Options include:

- Reintroduce the product, with corrections, under the same brand.
- Offer an improved version, under the same brand.
- Offer the relaunched product as another line.
- Discontinue the line.

IN CONCLUSION

Despite the potential costs and other possible adverse consequences of a recall, this may be the only responsible course of action when a company is faced by a product safety problem. The goal must be to create a positive out of a negative. Effective management of the recall can ensure this opportunity is realized. Table 8 lists the 10 most important questions to be asked of recall management.

Avoiding harm to consumers by maximizing the prompt return of defective products ensures recall effectiveness. A successful recall, however, has a broader

---

TABLE 8   Making Recalls Work: Ten Questions to Ask

Faced with a recall requirement, senior management should ask:

1. How serious is the recall situation—Class A, B, or C—and how quickly does the company need to respond?
2. What recall procedures are established in the recall plan, manual, or company practice? Are they appropriate to this situation?
3. Who has overall responsibility for managing the recall, and who else will serve on the recall task force?
4. To what extent is the company responsible for the problem? If the problem has external causes, is the company the best or only agent capable of managing it?
5. What type and scale of response is required—full, selective, or optional recall? On-site repair? Cease production, distribution, and issue advisory?
6. How can customers and channel intermediaries be alerted most quickly and effectively to the recall?
7. Is the recalled product readily identifiable?
8. What adjustment offer should be made which will persuade customers and channel intermediaries to return the recalled units and maintain their confidence and loyalty?
9. What logistics arrangements will minimize inconvenience to customers and channel intermediaries at lowest cost and disruption to the firm?
10. What will the company do differently next time?

effect. Treated seriously and well-managed, a recall can succeed in maintaining the firm's good relationships with all its stakeholders. Customer relationships especially are threatened. Where recalls involve product safety, the company's concern for the welfare of consumers and others who may be harmed by the product should be paramount and evident. More broadly, the company must be seen to be living up to the promise of quality after the sale, enhancing the company/customer relationship. Customer satisfaction with the handling of the recall, therefore, should achieve at least the same level as that established for other customer service operations.

Similar concerns should direct efforts to maintain relations with trade customers, with the added requirement to protect channels from competitors. A well-managed recall is likely to minimize the opportunity for competitive disparagement. Within the organization it is also going to communicate to employees that quality and customers count. In a well-managed recall, the company succeeds in looking good—as well as doing good.

Pricing Policy

Ethical Issues in Pricing

Gwendolyn K. Ortmeyer

Ethical issues in pricing can be separated into two broad categories. Anticompetitive pricing has its roots in the legal and economic literatures, this being a result of the conflict between pricing decisions and antitrust law. Issues in anticompetitive pricing include price-fixing and other price conspiracies, predatory pricing, and discriminatory pricing. The critical legal assessment, for each of these pricing practices, is the extent to which the practice inhibits free competition.

The second category, fairness in consumer pricing, focuses on the effects of pricing actions on the *end consumer*. Potentially misleading pricing tactics, which influence the consumer's ability to interpret and compare prices, as well as unit pricing, which is meant to facilitate price comparisons, are examples of ethical issues in consumer pricing. In addition, this discussion includes recent efforts to uncover the consumer's view of what constitutes fair versus unfair pricing tactics.

ANTICOMPETITIVE PRICING: PRICE CONSPIRACIES, PREDATORY PRICING, AND DISCRIMINATORY PRICING[1]

Pricing is an element of the marketing mix that is closely watched by antitrust enforcement agencies. Antitrust law, as it applies to pricing, is motivated by two primary objectives. The first is protecting "fair competition," and, in particular, protecting the small businessperson from being "run out of business" by larger competitors. This objective is at the heart of legislation that addresses predatory pricing and discriminatory pricing. The second objective

---

[1] This section borrows heavily from Chapter 5 of Louis W. Stern and Thomas L. Eovaldi, *Legal Aspects of Marketing Strategy: Antitrust and Consumer Protection Issues* (Englewood Cliffs, N.J.: Prentice Hall, 1984). Greater detail on each of the issues addressed in this section can be found in this text, which includes comprehensive discussions of the antitrust law that governs each issue and the significant cases that determine legal precedent.

of antitrust law is to protect buyers from being treated unfairly by sellers conspiring to fix prices and includes horizontal and vertical agreements, the latter of which typically are referred to as resale price maintenance agreements. For some issues, such as predatory pricing, there is continuing controversy over whether the legislation in fact meets the objective for which it was designed. Also, there are pricing behaviors not governed by antitrust law, which nonetheless appear to be unfair to smaller competitors, particularly in the case of complex, long-term bidding situations.

Price Conspiracies: Price-Fixing, Exchanging Price Information, Parallel Pricing, And Price Leadership

Price conspiracies, including both explicit and implicit agreements to fix price, are covered by Section 1 of the Sherman Act, which stipulates that efforts by competitors to collude on price are anticompetitive and are thus prohibited. Charges of price-fixing often have been levied against major airlines and oil companies, the latter with regard to their oil production activities in particular. One of the more recent price-fixing investigations undertaken by the Justice Department has involved allegations that 55 private schools have engaged in price-fixing agreements that have resulted in overly high student fees. The outcome of the investigation, as of March 1991, had not yet been determined.

An explicit agreement by competitors to fix price is considered a *per se* violation and, thus, is distinguished from such practices as the exchange of price information and forms of parallel or uniform pricing, such as price leadership, which may lead to implicit agreement among competitors to fix prices. These latter two practices are subject to the *rule of reason*, as explained by Stern and Eovaldi:

> The per se doctrine labels as illegal any practice to which it applies, regardless of the reasons for the practice and without extended inquiry as to its effects. Under a per se rule, it is only necessary for the complainant to prove the occurrence of conduct falling within the class of practices that are "so plainly anticompetitive" that they are subject to per se prohibition. This is in contrast to the "rule of reason" doctrine, which calls for a broad inquiry into the nature, purpose, and effect of any challenged arrangement before a decision is made about its legality. When applying the rule of reason, the courts examine the facts peculiar to the contested practices, their history, the reasons why they were implemented, and their competitive significance.[2]

Thus, agreement to fix price—that is, the existence of an agreement in the form of a contract, combination, or conspiracy—is considered so blatantly anticompetitive as to be "just plain wrong." However, if competitors are engaged in price signaling and no explicit agreement exists, then *implicit* agreement must be established. In this case, the courts look for evidence of a motive by com-

---

[2] Ibid., pp. 238–39.

petitors to collude on price and, correspondingly, do not rely solely on the outcome, which is uniformity in pricing across competitors, to determine wrongdoing. Similarly, when competitors agree to exchange price information with no further explicit agreement regarding the setting of prices, it must be established that the competitors nonetheless priced in a coordinated manner. Parallel pricing—that is, uniformity in pricing across competitors—is common to oligopolistic industries and is also subject to review for evidence of implicit agreement. In this case, an effort is made to distinguish the cause of the uniformity in prices: is uniformity a result of market conditions or implicit agreement?

Price leadership in an oligopolistic industry with large and small competitors is an example of parallel pricing that has been deemed acceptable by the courts as long as there is no explicit agreement to fix prices and no evidence of coercion. In such a situation, the smaller competitors often follow the price established by the industry leader. What is critical is the motive for following the industry leader—in this case, the uniform pricing in the industry is considered fair, because the smaller competitors must match the prices of the leader to compete, along with the leader, for business.

The legal precedent surrounding the establishment of implicit agreement to fix prices is quite complex for those without legal training. Highly competitive, oligopolistic, commodity markets, where much of the differentiation across competitors is on the price dimension, are particularly problematic. The practitioner in such industries should recognize the potential difficulties that may arise from efforts to improve prices through price leadership or price-signaling tactics, or both. The intent of the legislation is to prohibit those actions that may inhibit free competition, thereby protecting buyers from being overcharged.

This intent may be at odds, however, with market forces when the prices in a commodity market have deteriorated, through overcapacity and aggressive price competition, to such an extent that most competitors cannot cover their fixed costs. Such is the case, for example, in the electrical equipment industry, which sells primarily to electric utility companies.[3] With little product differentiation and a history of periodic overcapacity, attempts to exert price leadership are often advocated, this being considered one of the ways of establishing more profitable prices. While uniformity of pricing, in such a situation, would likely be deemed acceptable by the courts, the practitioner must recognize first the clear illegality of explicit agreement. Second, the practitioner must carefully assess the effects of such a pricing policy on competition from an industrywide perspective, considering, for example, whether uniform pricing in the industry can be justified as smaller competitors following the prices of the market leader.

---

[3] See, for example, "Federated Industries (A)," HBS case no. 585–104, for a detailed description of the highly competitive capacitor industry.

Resale Price Maintenance

Section 1 of the Sherman Act also governs resale price maintenance, or vertical price-fixing, whereby the manufacturer specifies the minimum and the maximum prices the retailer or wholesaler, or both, may charge. Before 1975, state fair trade laws exempted such vertical price agreements from federal antitrust law, because the intent of the state regulations, which was to protect small "mom-and-pop" retailers from price competition by larger chains and discount stores, was consistent with federal concerns. However, in 1975, with only 22 states still enforcing fair trade laws, Congress repealed the Miller-Tydings and the McGuire Acts, which had provided for the exemption. These changes reflected greater concern for the end consumer by state and local regulators and specifically recognized that the consumer benefited by the lower prices charged by discounters and mass merchants. Thus, as of 1975, explicit agreements between manufacturers and their intermediaries on resale price were viewed as inhibiting free competition and, therefore, prohibited.

While there is no doubt about the clear illegality of explicit vertical agreements to fix resale prices, there has been a good deal of controversy recently regarding allegations of wrongful termination of discounters. The controversy focuses on determining the competitive effects of the manufacturer's agreement with its dealers to terminate price-cutters. Taken from an intrabrand perspective, agreements to terminate price cutters clearly inhibit price competition across dealers, thereby hurting the end customer. However, when looked at from an interbrand perspective, such agreements may enhance competition, because they will lead to improved service competition by correcting for potential free-rider problems. The latter occur when retailers with lower prices and little service benefit by the service offered by the higher-priced retailers operating in the same trading area.[4] A potential result of such a scenario is an overall deterioration in service for the brand as the high-end retailers are forced to lower price and correspondingly decrease service to meet the prices of the low-priced dealer. Durable goods, such as electronics, appliances, and computers, with well-known and widely available brand names, are particularly subject to free-rider problems due to the heavy informational preselling that is required.

Recent court decisions in this area have involved dealers who have brought suit against former suppliers for being cut off. In one example, the *Business Electronics* case, the terminated dealer maintained that, along with his termination, there was an implicit agreement on price between the supplier and the remaining dealers. A number of dealers had complained about the price-cutting tactics of the intermediary that Sharp, the manufacturer, agreed to terminate. The judge in that case stipulated that, in the absence of any explicit

---

[4] In this case, one might also question the intentions of the consumer who goes to one retailer for information and other presale service, then goes to the lower-price retailer to purchase.

agreement on price between the complaining dealers and the supplier, the agreement to terminate would be judged under the rule of reason doctrine, thus balancing the procompetitive interbrand effects against the anticompetitive intrabrand effects to resolve the issue of wrongful termination.[5]

Predatory Pricing

Attempts to monopolize by predatory pricing are governed by Section 2 of the Sherman Act. Stern and Eovaldi explain predatory pricing and its corresponding effects on industry competition as follows:

> Simply put, predatory pricing involves cutting prices to unreasonably low or unprofitable levels in markets where competition is encountered in order to drive others from those markets. The losses that are incurred and/or the profits foregone by the price cutter are accepted in the expectation that they will be more than made up at a later date by the monopoly profits that can be obtained after the competitive threat from other firms is ended. Thus, the predator's motivation is presumably to secure a monopoly position once rivals have been driven out, enjoying long-run profits higher than they would be if rivals were permitted to survive.[6]

Predatory intent is often difficult to determine when, for example, a competitor with dominant market share can price substantially below the marginal costs of smaller or new entrants due to its lower cost structure. As well, the realities of the competitive marketplace may demand pricing at levels that are below marginal or average cost. Interestingly, there is an extensive body of literature in economics that maintains predatory pricing is not an effective tool for gaining monopoly power.[7] The intuition given for this assertion is that the dominant firm, seeking to monopolize by cutting prices, will face substantial losses on its large volume of business. As a result, the dominant firm, if successful, must charge a monopoly price for a substantial time to recoup its losses. The ability to charge a monopoly price over an extended period, in turn, depends upon barriers to entry. Yet, such barriers are unlikely to exist since, if one firm could enter, one presumes that others could also, particularly given the assets left available by the failed firm(s). Thus, economists taking this position conclude that no rational manager of a dominant firm would seek to gain monopoly power through predatory pricing. These arguments, as well as those below, concerning the definition of a predatory price, are representative of the ongoing controversy that surrounds this issue.

A critical issue in the determination of predatory behavior is defining what constitutes unreasonably low or unprofitable prices. The current standard used

---

[5] See Patrick J. Kaufmann, in Chapter 6.6, for a more detailed presentation of the *Business Electronics* case and other recent developments in this area.

[6] Stern and Eovaldi, *Legal Aspects . . .* , p. 257.

[7] This issue is more extensively covered in B. S. Yamey, "Predatory Pricing: Notes and Comments," *Journal of Law and Economics* 15 (1972), pp. 129–47.

by most courts is the Areeda-Turner test, a cost-based rule that defines predatory pricing as prices set below average variable or marginal cost, whichever is lower. It may be difficult, however, to determine the relevant costs. As well, this rule does not address those situations in which a competitor prices above variable costs but, nonetheless, sets a low price with *predatory intent*. A second standard that has been proposed looks at the intent of the firm as well as the actual prices set relative to costs. Related to this standard is the view, consistent with the discussion above, that the courts ought to evaluate carefully the barriers to entry in the industry. If barriers to entry are low, it is unlikely that the dominant firm will recoup the losses it incurs in predatory pricing, thus making predatory intent highly improbable.

Other standards that have been offered include an output rule offered by Williamson that looks at the post-entry output of the dominant firm and rules that specify investigation of the long-run welfare implications of the pricing behavior.[8] Scherer, for example, favors the latter view and has suggested that one way of investigating the long-run welfare implications is to look for evidence of the intent of the dominant firm.[9]

Charges of predatory pricing often have been levied against major oil companies in connection with their retail gasoline operations. In particular, the major oil companies that are fully integrated have been accused of predatory pricing to drive out smaller independents that operate only at the retail level. In recent years, Japanese companies exporting to the United States have been accused of predatory pricing, for example, in the semiconductor memory chip industry. American manufacturers, in addition to petitioning for relief from the courts, have taken a number of actions in response to the below-cost pricing by the Japanese, including selling to technical, rather than purchasing department, personnel in customer companies and adding to product and packaging differentiation through value-added and application specific features.

Often, in long-term contract bidding situations involving complex and changing product specifications, larger firms may price below cost to obtain the initial bid, hoping to make up the lost margin over the course of the contract as the bid gets updated. This sometimes happens in defense contracting, for example, when the bid is for a long-term, multiphased project in which the bid is updated periodically. Smaller competitors bidding for the project are often at a disadvantage, because their size and financial position prohibit them from pricing below cost initially in order to "buy in" to the contract. While this type of predatory behavior by the larger firms is not strictly prohibited by law, it is unfair to the smaller firms who are unable to operate in this fashion. Furthermore, such behavior places pressure on the large firm, over the long run, to make potentially excessive revisions to the bid so as to make up the

---

[8] Oliver E. Williamson, "Predatory Pricing: A Strategic and Welfare Analysis," *Yale Law Journal* 87 (1977), pp. 284–340.

[9] F. M. Sherer, "Predatory Pricing and the Sherman Act: A Comment," *Harvard Law Review* 89 (1976), pp. 901–3.

lost margin. The Defense Department and other governmental agencies that face this problem recognize this and have developed comprehensive guidelines for potential suppliers that prohibit such behavior.

Discriminatory Pricing

As noted above, there is substantial controversy surrounding predatory pricing, both in rationalizing it as a means of gaining monopoly power and in determining what constitutes a predatory price. There is perhaps even greater controversy surrounding the Robinson-Patman Act, the antitrust legislation that addresses price discrimination. This act, for the most part, deals with price discrimination as it might occur in business-to-business selling situations, suppliers to retailers, for example. Specifically, Section 2(a) of the act states that it is unlawful for a company to price discriminate in selling or purchasing a commodity "of like grade and quality," with several exceptions. The two most notable of these acceptable justifications for price discrimination are that the price differences reflect differences in manufacturing, selling, or delivery costs, or all, and that the price differences result from an effort to meet a competitor's prices. In determining if products are of like grade and quality, the courts have ruled that product differences may include perceived differences that are attributed to the promotional and advertising efforts of the higher-priced product.

The Robinson-Patman Act stipulates that price discrimination is subject to the rule of reason, and, therefore, upon evidence of price differentials, the court goes further to determine their effect on competition. The courts investigate the impact of price discrimination on three levels of competition. The primary level of competition concerns those relatively infrequent cases in which price discrimination by a seller affects competition at the seller level. For the most part, however, these cases would be addressed by predatory pricing legislation and not the Robinson-Patman Act. The more common level of competition considered is the secondary level, when price discrimination by the seller affects competition among the buyers. The concern, at the secondary level of competition, is that a seller may offer a better price to a favored buyer, thereby giving an unfair competitive advantage. Finally, the courts may look at the effects of a seller's price discrimination on competition among the customers of its buyer. This may be the case, for example, when a manufacturer price so discriminates among its wholesalers that competition at the retail level is affected.

Much of the controversy surrounding the Robinson-Patman Act focuses on its ultimate effect on competition. As initially adopted in 1936, the act was meant to prevent large firms from gaining advantage over smaller competitors by obtaining lower prices from suppliers. Many critics of the legislation argue, however, that it protects *competitors* rather than *competition*. These critics argue that the courts have used harm to one or more competitors as direct evidence of harm to competition industrywide. It should be noted that the

Federal Trade Commission is not active currently in enforcing the Robinson-Patman Act. Consequently, most cases brought are private lawsuits.

CONSUMER PRICING

The discussion above makes apparent the rich history of political and legal interest in pricing decisions and their impact on market competition. Thus, in discussing these issues, we typically appeal to antitrust legislation and the ruling of the courts in enforcing the legislation. In discussing the ethics of pricing policies from the consumer's perspective, however, the legislative view is not as clearly represented, nor is there a rich history in legal precedent. Typically, when the courts get involved in issues of fairness in consumer pricing, they have to do with pricing policies that mislead consumers. Not surprising, research in consumer behavior plays a particularly strong role in identifying misleading pricing tactics, as will be discussed below. A discussion of experimental work undertaken to begin understanding how consumers view fairness in pricing concludes this overview of ethical issues in pricing.

Unit Pricing And Item Marketing

In the early 1970s, legislative efforts designed to increase and improve the information provided to the consumer at point of purchase led to the passage of unit pricing laws in many states, including Massachusetts, Connecticut, Maryland, and Rhode Island. Unit pricing laws stipulate that product prices must be provided on a per-unit weight or volume basis and are most applicable in the packaged goods categories. Providing this information, in addition to the item price, is meant to facilitate price comparisons, thus helping the more price-vigilant customers find the best value. Additionally, it was thought that those consumers who are more brand-conscious might find this additional economic information useful, because it would facilitate price comparisons across brands of different package sizes. Low-income consumers, in particular, were predicted to benefit by this additional information.

Controversy surrounding unit pricing has focused on two key issues. The first concerns the retailer's costs in implementing unit price systems. One of the arguments against enforced unit pricing is that the cost of implementation and the specific implementation actions required are prohibitive to independent retailers and small chains. In studies reported by Carman[10] and by Monroe and LaPlaca,[11] retailers who adopted unit pricing found the cost of installing

---

[10] James M. Carman, "A Summary of Empirical Research on Unit Pricing in Supermarkets," *Journal of Retailing* 48 (Winter 1972–73), pp. 63–71.

[11] Kent B. Monroe and Peter J. LaPlaca, "What Are the Benefits of Unit Pricing?" *Journal of Marketing* 36 (July 1972), pp. 16–22.

and maintaining the system to be relatively constant per store, regardless of store volume. As noted by Monroe and LaPlaca:

> Thus, unit pricing could be a prohibitive cost to small, independent stores which do not have sufficient sales volume to absorb the costs. To the extent that small, independent stores are located in urban, low-income areas, some of the potential benefits of unit pricing for low-income shoppers are diminished.

Still, those retailers in the study that tried unit pricing reported it led to some operational improvements.

A second source of concern about unit pricing centers on consumer processing of the added price information. Monroe and LaPlaca, for example, report that the differing labeling methods and the terminology used by retailers to provide unit prices made it difficult for consumers to decipher the added information.[12] However, in another study, Houston reported that value-conscious consumers were better able to determine the most economical alternative when shopping at a store that provided unit prices.[13] Other studies have sought to determine if low-income shoppers take advantage of the new information. Isakson and Maurizi, for example, found that low-income subjects were less likely to use unit price information than middle- or high-income subjects. They used their results to suggest that unit pricing needs to be accompanied by educational efforts specifically targeted at lower-income households.[14]

Item marking has become a more recent topic of debate as the number of grocery stores converting to electronic scanning checkout systems has increased. Such systems make item marking—a stamped price on each item—unnecessary from an operational perspective. However, consumer advocates maintain that providing only shelf prices reduces consumer awareness of prices and generally will make shopping more time-consuming. Zeithaml studied consumer awareness in particular and found that item marking increased subjects' exact recall of prices as well as their certainty in the accuracy of their recall. This study suggests that the cost benefits gained by retailers in removing item price tags should perhaps be balanced against negative effects of their removal on consumer decision making.[15]

Misleading Pricing

Concerns about misleading pricing have been raised in the context of a number of retail pricing practices, including sale pricing, the use of price comparisons,

---

[12] Ibid., p. 22.

[13] Michael J. Houston, "The Effect of Unit Pricing on Choices of Brand and Size in Economic Shopping," *Journal of Marketing* 36 (July 1972), pp. 52–69.

[14] Hans R. Isakson, and Alex R. Maurizi, "The Consumer Economics of Unit Pricing," *Journal of Marketing Research* 10 (August 1973), pp. 277–85.

[15] Valerie A. Zeithaml, "Consumer Response to In-Store Price Information Environments," *Journal of Consumer Research* 8 (March 1982), pp. 357–69.

and the provision of manufacturer's suggested retail prices. Of these practices, retail promotional practices recently have come under particularly close scrutiny. At issue are the intensive, almost every day "sale" events, and sale-priced merchandise currently offered in retail categories that include department stores, general merchandise, fine jewelry, furniture, appliances, and home electronics. Under such a policy, which is referred to as "high-low pricing" by the trade, a retailer sets prices at an initially high level for a brief time, then discounts the merchandise from the so-called original or regular price for the bulk of the selling season. Typically, very little of the merchandise priced this way is sold at regular price. The question raised by such a policy is whether the consumer understands that the "sale" price is, in fact, the price at which most of the goods are sold. Many state and local agencies, in particular, argue instead that the consumer uses the artificial regular price as a reference, and thus the consumer assumes that the sale price represents a real saving. If such is the case, these agencies argue, then the pricing policies are deceptive.

The Code of Federal Regulations of Commercial Practices for 1990 includes, in Part 233, the Federal Trade Commission's "Guides Against Deceptive Pricing" (initially adopted in 1964). One could assume, therefore, that the Federal Trade Commission might be the agency that investigates such policies. However, according to Barry J. Cutler, director of the FTC Bureau of Consumer Protection, the FTC is not currently playing a major role in enforcing deceptive pricing laws and instead has left enforcement to state "mini FTC" agencies.[16]

In a recent example involving a court case concluded in May 1990, a Colorado state court found the pricing practices in the housewares department of May D&F (a division of May Department Stores), to be deceiving. The pricing practices in question, which occurred prior to August 1989, stipulated that in certain sections of the store, items were marked at an "original" or "regular" price for 10 days, then dropped to a sale price for the rest of the six-month selling season. In addition, over the six-month selling season, further limited time discounts were taken off already reduced prices. This case is notable in that it is one of few that has not been settled out of court. The judge ruled that May D&F's pricing practices were deceptive, noting in particular that it was not apparent that May D&F had made a "good faith effort" to sell at the advertised regular or original prices. Evidence of a good faith effort, according to the FTC Guides, is indicated if the regular or original price was in effect for a "reasonably substantial" period or if a substantial amount of merchandise was sold at that price. Other retailers who have been or currently are involved in similar suits include J. C. Penney Company, Nordstrom, John Wanamaker, and Montgomery Ward & Company. In general, these lawsuits are resolved out of court, with the retailer paying a fine and agreeing not to price deceptively in the future.

---

[16] Hal Taylor, "FTC Gives States Job of Policing Ad Price Claims," *Women's Wear Daily*, October 3, 1990, p. 29.

Research that addresses the consumer's use of reference prices suggests that they are skeptical of "manufacturer's list price," "list price," and "regular price" designations but are influenced by such information nonetheless. Fry and McDougall[17] and Liefeld and Heslop[18] each concluded that consumers were skeptical of regular prices reported in store advertisements. Sewall and Goldstein came to a similar conclusion, in the context of catalog showrooms' use of manufacturer's list price as a reference price.[19] However, other researchers have argued that, even though they are skeptical of retailers' advertised reference prices, consumers are nonetheless influenced by them in assessing the value of a sale offering. Blair and Landon, for example, showed, through an experimental study, that, even though subjects generally were suspicious of such reference prices, they still used the information to infer greater savings than if reference prices were not presented.[20] In another study, Urbany, Bearden, and Weilbaker found a similar result.[21]

On the other hand, retailers that employ such pricing policies argue that consumers are indeed skeptical, having been exposed to a promotion-intensive environment for quite some time. Thus, they are able to understand the value they are getting when they buy on sale. In addition, retailers have argued that few states provide concrete guidelines for the amount of time the merchandise must be at regular price or the volume of merchandise that must be sold at regular price. Of those that do, Massachusetts regulations, for example, stipulate that sale prices are legitimate if the retailer has sold at least 30 percent of the sale-priced item at the regular price *or* the regular price must be in effect for at least 15 days initially, and then, over an 180-day period, the merchandise must be offered at the regular price at least 55 percent of the time. Finally, the retailers who have been challenged appeal to the notion of a "level playing field" and argue that, if any one retailer is singled out as the only competitor that must cut back on promotional pricing, it will lose considerable volume to retailers with similar policies who have not yet been challenged. This issue promises to be an ongoing controversy if the promotion intensity in the retail environment continues.

Comparative pricing, when a retailer compares its prices against those of its competitors, is an issue that concerns retailers, particularly in highly compet-

---

[17] Joseph N. Fry and Gordon H. McDougall, "Consumer Appraisal of Retail Price Advertisements," *Journal of Marketing* 38 (July 1974), pp. 64–74.

[18] John Liefeld and Louise A. Heslop, "Reference Prices and Deception in Newspaper Advertising," *Journal of Consumer Research* 11 (March 1985), pp. 868–76.

[19] Murphy A. Sewall and Michael H. Goldstein, "The Comparative Price Advertising Controversy: Consumer Perceptions of Catalog Showroom Reference Prices," *Journal of Marketing* 43 (Summer 1979), pp. 85–92.

[20] Edward A. Blair and E. Laird Landon, Jr., "The Effect of Reference Prices in Retail Advertisements," *Journal of Marketing* 45 (Summer 1981), pp. 61–69.

[21] Joel F. Urbany, William O. Bearden, and Dan C. Weilbaker, "The Effect of Plausible and Exaggerated Reference Prices on Consumer Perceptions and Price Search," *Journal of Consumer Research* 15 (June 1988), pp. 95–110.

itive, branded product categories. With the proliferation of model numbers and exclusive merchandise agreements among manufacturers and retailers, it becomes difficult for a customer to compare the prices of comparable merchandise across retailers. Furthermore, when retailers offer a guarantee to match the prices of competitors, exclusive model numbers for essentially similar products make the benefit of such a guarantee suspect. In response to this problem, many retailers develop extensive lists of their competitors' "derivative" model numbers that are included in the price guarantee claim. Comparative price advertising has come under investigation by state and local agencies as well, particularly when a retailer claims to be the lowest-priced competitor.

Retailers, perhaps recognizing the potential for continued litigation over promotional policies and comparative pricing, have undertaken efforts at self-regulation under the auspices of the National Advertising Review Board and the Council for Better Business Bureaus. The latter, in particular, has been working with a number of major retailers to develop a code of advertising that includes guidelines on price comparisons with competitors, sale pricing, price matching, and lowest-price claims. The guidelines for using comparisons to former prices, for example, are similar to those offered in the FTC Guide and stipulate the following:[22]

> An advertiser may claim a savings from its own former price if it can demonstrate that its former price is a bona fide or genuine price; that is, a price from which a reduction represents a genuine savings to the customer. A former price is bona fide when "reasonably substantial sales" were made at or above the price in the recent regular course of business. While it is reasonable to expect that a retailer's nonsale prices will usually result in sales of the product, there will be occasions where the nonsale prices do not produce substantial sales. The bona fides of a former price may also be established where a few or no sales were made only if the advertiser openly and actively offered the merchandise honestly and in "good faith" for a "reasonably substantial period of time" in the recent regular course of business.

Fairness In Pricing From The Consumer's Perspective

The discussion of misleading prices above highlights the effect of certain pricing policies on the consumer's ability to process price information and use it to judge the fair value of the offering, particularly in comparison to the seller's former and competitors' current prices. Researchers have gone further to begin understanding what consumers view as fair and unfair pricing policies. Kahneman, Knetsch, and Thaler, for example, have developed a number of "community standards of fairness for the setting of prices," by posing many pricing

---

[22] *Code of Advertising*, draft form, as of March 1991, developed by the Council of Better Business Bureaus and several of its national retail members.

scenarios to subjects, via telephone surveys.[23] After presenting a scenario, subjects were asked whether the pricing action was fair. Generally, subjects accepted price increases if they were related to changes in the cost of the good, but found increases unfair if these were a result of changing market conditions. In particular, subjects considered a price increase acceptable if it was done to pass on increases in costs and thereby protect the seller's profits. On the other hand, subjects generally did not expect sellers to pass on the savings when the costs of the product decreased. However, subjects did view higher prices in times of shortage to be unfair. In addition, subjects found price increases prompted by increases in monopoly power to be unfair.

The authors used these standards for fairness in pricing to elaborate on Okun's argument that fairness explains why consumer markets, in contrast to standard economic theory, sometimes fail to clear.[24] For example, consumer concern over price increases in times of shortage is consistent with empirical observations that prices tend not to rise in times of severe shortages. The authors' data are also consistent with the observation that sporting tickets are not offered at market-clearing prices, even though there is variation in demand for them, depending on the teams playing and their relative standing.

This work, and ongoing efforts to determine the consumer's view of fair pricing policies, has immediate relevance for companies faced with limited supply conditions. Oil companies, for example, often are criticized for price-gouging at the retail level during periods of crude oil supply shortages. Such has been the case most recently in the fall of 1990, when Iraq's invasion of Kuwait prompted concerns about shortages in crude oil supply that led to increases both in the price of crude oil and the retail price of gasoline. Many argued that the major oil companies used these events to generate windfall profits, particularly since retail prices were raised on gasoline that had been produced from crude oil acquired before the crisis began. The allegations made in the popular press are consistent with the results of the research reported above, that consumers consider price increases prompted by shortages to be unfair.[25]

Price-gouging claims have also been levied against major airlines during peak travel periods and when a particular market is dominated by a major airline. Pharmaceutical companies, as well, have been accused of price-gouging with respect to life-saving drugs of limited supply, as in the case of an AIDS treatment, for example. The continuing experimental research by Kahneman, Knetsch, Thaler, and others promises to be instrumental in explaining consumer response and guiding public policy in such situations.

---

[23] Daniel Kahneman, Jack L. Knetsch, and Richard H. Thaler, "Fairness as a Constraint on Profit Seeking: Entitlements in the Market," *The American Economic Review* 76 (September 1986), pp. 728–41.

[24] Arthur Okun, *Prices and Quantities: A Macroeconomic Analysis* (Washington, D.C.: The Brookings Institution, 1981).

[25] See, for example, Silvio O. Conte, ". . . Or Tax Excess Profits," *New York Times*, September 10, 1990, p. 23.

CONCLUSION

The study of ethical issues in pricing has focused historically on questions about the use of pricing actions to affect competitors, industrywide competition, and channel relationships, with less attention placed on the effects of pricing actions on the end consumer. This reflects an emphasis, in antitrust legislation and enforcement, on the protection of the small competitor, thus enabling "free competition." More recently, however, the consumer's point of view has become important as consumer groups and regulatory authorities have become more concerned over the interpretability of price information. Thus, standards regarding how prices should be communicated appear to be evolving as the retail environment becomes more competitive. As well, fair pricing in times of shortage, and the apparent lack of acceptance for the market mechanism to address such situations, promises to be an ongoing topic of debate and empirical investigation.

PRICING BIBLIOGRAPHY

Anticompetitive Pricing

1. **General Review of Anticompetitive Pricing Issues**
   Stern, Louis E., and Thomas L. Eovaldi. *Legal Aspects of Marketing Strategy*. Englewood Cliffs, N.J.: Prentice Hall, 1984.

2. **Price Conspiracies**
   a. **Price-fixing—horizontal:**
   Posner, Richard A. *Antitrust Law: An Economic Perspective*. Chicago: University of Chicago Press, 1976.
   Scherer, F. M. *Industrial Market Structure and Economic Performance*. 2nd ed. Chicago: Rand McNally, 1980.
   b. **Price-fixing—vertical—resale price maintenance:**
   Kaufmann, Patrick J. "Dealer Termination Agreements and Resale Price Maintenance: Implications of the Business Electronics Case and the Proposed Amendment to the Sherman Act." *Journal of Retailing* 64 (Summer 1988), pp. 113–24.
   Marves, Howard P., and Stephen McCafferty. "Resale Price Maintenance and Quality Certification." *Rand Journal of Economics* 15 (Autumn 1984), pp. 346–59.
   Posner, Richard A. "The Next Step in the Antitrust Treatment of Restricted Distribution: Per Se Legality." *University of Chicago Law Review* 48 (1980), pp. 6–26.
   Springer, Robert F., and H. E. French III. "Deterring Fraud: The Role of Resale Price Maintenance." *Journal of Business* 59 (July 1986), pp. 433–49.

3. Predatory Pricing

Areeda, Philip, and Donald Turner. "Predatory Pricing and Related Practices under Section 2 of the Sherman Act." *Harvard Law Review* 88 (1975), pp. 720–32.

McGee, John S. "Predatory Pricing Revisited." *Journal of Law and Economics* 23 (October 1980), pp. 289–329.

Scherer, F. M. "Predatory Pricing and the Sherman Act: A Comment." *Harvard Law Review* 89 (1976), pp. 901–3.

Williamson, Oliver E. "Predatory Pricing: A Strategic and Welfare Analysis." *Yale Law Journal* 87 (1977), pp. 284–340.

Yamey, B. S. "Predatory Pricing: Notes and Comments." *Journal of Law and Economics* 15 (1972), pp. 129–47.

4. Discriminatory Pricing

Asch, Peter. *Economic Theory and the Antitrust Dilemma.* New York: John Wiley & Sons, 1970.

Grether, E. T. *Marketing and Public Policy.* Englewood Cliffs, N.J.: Prentice Hall, 1966.

Scherer, F. M. *Industrial Market Structure and Economic Performance.* 2nd ed. Chicago: Rand McNally, 1980.

Consumer Prices

1. Unit Pricing

Carman, James M. "A Summary of Empirical Research on Unit Pricing in Supermarkets." *Journal of Retailing* 48 (Winter 1972–73), pp. 63–71.

Friedman, Monroe P. "Consumer Price Comparisons of Retail Products: The Role of Packaging and Pricing Practices and the Implications for Consumer Legislation." *Journal of Applied Psychology* 56 (1972), pp. 439–46.

Houston, Michael J. "The Effect of Unit Pricing on Choices of Brand and Size in Economic Shopping." *Journal of Marketing* 36 (July 1972), pp. 52–69.

Isakson, Hans R., and Alex R. Maurizi. "The Consumer Economics of Unit Pricing." *Journal of Marketing Research* 10 (August 1973), pp. 277–85.

Monroe, Kent B., and Peter J. LaPlaca. "What Are the Benefits of Unit Pricing." *Journal of Marketing* 36 (July 1972), pp. 16–22.

Ziethaml, Valerie A. "Consumer Response to In-Store Price Information Environments." *Journal of Consumer Research* 8, (March 1982), pp. 357–69.

2. Misleading Prices

Blair, Edward A., and E. Laird Landon, Jr. "The Effect of Reference

Price in Retail Advertisements." *Journal of Marketing* 45 (Spring 1981), pp. 61–69.

Della Bitta, Albert J.; Kent B. Monroe; and John M. McGinnis. "Consumer Perceptions of Comparative Price Advertisements." *Journal of Marketing Research* 18 (November 1987), pp. 416–27.

Fry, Joseph N., and Gordon H. McDougall. "Consumer Appraisal of Retail Price Advertisements." *Journal of Marketing* 38 (July 1974), pp. 64–74.

Liefeld, John, and Louise A. Heslop. "Reference Prices and Deception in Newspaper Advertising." *Journal of Consumer Research* 11 (March 1985), pp. 868–76.

Posch, Robert Jr. "Comparative Advertising Yesterday and Today." *Direct Marketing*, May 1982, pp. 106–11.

Sewall, Murphy A., and Michael H. Goldstein. "The Comparative Price Advertising Controversy: Consumer Perceptions of Catalog Showroom Reference Prices." *Journal of Marketing* 43 (Summer 1979), pp. 85–92.

Urbany, Joel E.; William O. Bearden; and Dan C. Weilbaker. "The Effect of Plausible and Exaggerated Reference Prices on Consumer Perceptions and Price Search." *Journal of Consumer Research* 15 (June 1988), pp. 95–110.

3. Fairness in Pricing

Kahneman, Daniel; Jack L. Knetsch; and Richard H. Thaler. "Fairness and the Assumptions of Economics." *Journal of Business* 59 (1986), pp. 285–300.

_____. "Fairness as a Constraint on Profit Seeking: Entitlements in the Market." *American Economic Review* 76 (September 1986), pp. 728–41.

Kaufmann, Patrick J.; Gwendolyn K. Ortmeyer; and N. Craig Smith. "Fairness in Consumer Pricing." *Journal of Consumer Policy* 14 (1992) (forthcoming).

Monroe, Kent B. *Pricing: Making Profitable Decisions.* New York: McGraw-Hill, 1979.

_____. "Buyers' Subjective Perception of Price." *Journal of Marketing Research* 10 (February 1973), pp. 70–80.

Okun, Arthur. *Prices and Quantities: A Macroeconomic Analysis.* Washington, D.C.: Brookings Institution, 1981.

Taylor, Bernard, and Gordon Willis, eds. *Pricing Strategy.* Princeton, N.J.: Brandon/Systems, 1970.

Thaler, Richard H. "Mental Accounting and Consumer Choice." *Marketing Science* 4 (Summer 1985), pp. 199–214.

_____. "Toward a Positive Theory of Consumer Choice." *Journal of Economic Behavior and Organization* 1 (March 1980), pp. 39–60.

Retail Promotional Pricing: When Is a Sale Really a Sale? (A)

The U.S. retail environment has become increasingly promotional over the past 10 years, as exemplified by aggressive double couponing in the grocery trade, price discounting, rebating and special financing in retail auto sales, and nearly daily advertised sales events by general merchants, department, and specialty stores.[1] Over 60 percent of department store sales volume in 1988 was sold at sales prices, for example.[2] The intensive promotional policies of department stores, general merchandisers, and certain types of specialty stores, in particular, have come under close scrutiny by state and local agencies, who argue that the policies practiced by many of these retailers result in deceptive pricing to the end consumer. These pricing practices, often referred to as high-low pricing by the trade, entail setting prices at an initially high level for a brief time, then discounting the merchandise from the so-called original, former, or regular price for the bulk of the selling season. In this case, these price designations are referred to collectively as the *reference price* against which a sale price is compared. Typically, in-store signage and the item price tags continue to display the reference price along with the discounted price, so customers can "compare the savings." Under such a pricing policy, very little of the merchandise is sold at reference prices.

The question raised by such promotional pricing is whether the consumer understands that the "sale" price, is, in fact, the price at which most of the goods are sold. Many state and local agencies have argued that customers overestimate the true value of merchandise priced this way, because they com-

---

This case was prepared by Professor Gwendolyn K. Ortmeyer.
Copyright © 1991 by the President and Fellows of Harvard College.
Harvard Business School case N9-591-111 (rev. 7–1–91).

[1] Sears and Montgomery Ward are the most notable general merchants. These retailers carry both soft goods including clothing, jewelry and accessories, housewares and linens, and hard goods including home appliances, tools, and electronics. In contrast, department stores tend to focus on the soft goods categories, often including furniture and some electronics as well.

[2] Dudley R. McIlhenny, "Introducing the NRMA Retail Market Monitor," *Retail Control*, November 1989, pp. 9–14.

pare the reference price to the sale price and interpret the latter as representing a real savings. This case documents the ongoing controversy, and presents a particular court case, the *State of Colorado* v. *The May Company.*

BACKGROUND

The increased promotional activity by department stores, as well as other classes of retail trade, can be traced to a number of industry changes, most notably increased competition. Continued expansion by department stores, the growth of specialty stores, such as the Gap, the Limited, Toys 'R' Us, and the movement upscale by discount stores, such as Target, has produced a dramatic increase in the number of retail options available to customers and, in many cases, has resulted in markets that are over-stored relative to the available retailer business. As competition has increased, many retailers have experienced modest or no sales gains in existing stores. Thus, to boost sales volume, and often to match the regular and sale prices of a broad range of competitors, retailers, across classes of trade, have resorted to incessant and extensive sale events. Most recently, many highly leveraged retailers, including the Federated-Allied chain, Macy's, and Carter Hawley Hale, have faced added pressure to boost sales volumes due to their debt-laden balance sheet. The result has been a further increase in promotional intensity in markets in which they operate.

Coinciding with the increased promotional activity has been an increase in the margins of retail list prices before they are reduced for sale events. These margins, termed *initial markup* by department stores and calculated as a percent of the original selling price, have risen from an average of 47.5 percent in 1979 to 50.9 percent in 1988. Over the same time period, department store markdowns, which are the dollar reductions from the originally set retail prices and are calculated as a percent of net sales, have risen from an average of 10.43 percent in 1979 to 16.27 percent in 1988.

Most product categories carried by department stores are susceptible to high-low pricing. For example, in the women's coat business, a seasonal category, department stores have resorted to more sales events and sale-priced merchandise, partly in response to competition from coat discounters, such as the Burlington Coat Factory. The women's coat business traditionally has had an annual Columbus Day preseason event with perhaps the most popular coat in a number of lines promoted for the event, but the rest of the coats offered at full price. More recently, however, with increased competition, more sales events are offered throughout the season, with a much greater proportion of merchandise offered early in the season at allegedly reduced prices. Fine jewelry is a product category that is well-known for high-low pricing, with 40 and 50 percent discounts off the reference prices being nearly a continuous event for many retailers, including department stores, jewelry stores, and catalog merchants.

Often the reference prices vary across retailers. For example, *The San Francisco Chronicle* reported the following in "Why Buyers Should Beware of 'Sale' Prices" (Wednesday, July 18, 1990):

> A random survey of "sale" and "original" prices in Bay Area furniture stores found a difference of $1,680 between the highest and lowest "original price" for a single Henredon sofa.
>
> Model No. 8670, with identical "E-grade" upholstery, was advertised at Noriega Furniture, a small furniture retailer, at an "original price" of $2,320, on sale for $2,170. A major department store offers the same sofa for $2,500—"35 percent off" the "original price" of $4,000. A major furniture chain advertised the same model, originally priced at $3,009 "on sale at 20 percent off" for $2,749. Another small furniture retailer in Marin County offers the same sofa at $2,476, 20 percent off its original price of $3,095.

Some department stores, Dillard's for example, are trying to reduce their reliance on sales events and sale-priced merchandise. In a speech to the American Apparel Manufacturers Association on October 18, 1989, James W. Sherburn, Jr., chairman of Dillard's Fort Worth Division, reported that the chain had "eliminated five major sale events this year to reinforce to our customer our commitment to sell merchandise at regular price," and had instituted a policy of pricing goods at "the prevailing market price." In the women's coat category, Macy's Northeast adopted everyday low prices in the fall of 1989, and in its advertisements promised to "cut through all the confusing sales, special buys, and clearances out there" by offering the lowest prices on an everyday basis. Like many retailers who have tried everyday low pricing on a limited basis, however, and have experienced significant short-term decreases in sales volume, Macy's reinstituted sale pricing in the coat category in the 1990 season.

REGULATORY PERSPECTIVE

Existing Federal and State Legislation

At the heart of the controversy surrounding high-low pricing policy is the claim made by an increasing number of state and local authorities that such pricing policies are deceptive. The FTC Guides against Deceptive Pricing, initially adopted in 1964 and currently included, as Part 233 in the FTC's *Code of Federal Regulations of Commercial Practices*, provide the Federal Trade Commission's guidelines about what constitutes deceptive pricing policies (see Exhibit 1 for an excerpt from the Guide's Part 233.1 that addresses comparisons to former prices specifically). The FTC is not currently playing a major role in enforcing deceptive pricing laws, however, and instead has left enforcement to state and local authorities. Barry J. Cutler, director of the FTC's Bureau of Consumer Protection, in an interview with Hal Taylor of *Women's Wear Daily*

EXHIBIT 1   FTC's Code of Federal Regulation of Commercial Practices, 1990, Volume 16

Part 233—Guides against Deceptive Pricing

§ 233.1   Former price comparisons.

(a) One of the most commonly used forms of bargain advertising is to offer a reduction from the advertiser's own former price for an article. If the former price is the actual, bona fide price at which the article was offered to the public on a regular basis for a reasonably substantial period of time, it provides a legitimate basis for the advertising of a price comparison. Where the former price is genuine, the bargain being advertised is a true one. If, on the other hand, the former price being advertised is not bona fide but fictitious—for example, where an artificial, inflated price was established for the purpose of enabling the subsequent offer of a large reduction—the "bargain" being advertised is a false one; the purchaser is not receiving the unusual value he expects. In such a case, the "reduced" price is, in reality, probably just the seller's regular price.

(b) A former price is not necessarily fictitious merely because no sales at the advertised price were made. The advertiser should be especially careful, however, in such a case, that the price is one at which the product was openly and actively offered for sale, for a reasonably substantial period of time, in the recent, regular course of his business, honestly and in good faith—and, of course, not for the purpose of establishing a fictitious higher price on which a deceptive comparison might be based. And the advertiser should scrupulously avoid any implication that a former price is a selling, not an asking price (for example, by use of such language as, "Formerly sold at $——"), unless substantial sales at that price were actually made.

(c) The following is an example of a price comparison based on a fictitious former price. John Doe is a retailer of Brand X fountain pens, which cost him $5 each. His usual markup is 50 percent over cost; that is, his regular retail price is $7.50. In order subsequently to offer an unusual "bargain," Doe begins offering Brand X at $10 per pen. He realizes that he will be able to sell no, or very few, pens at this inflated price. But he doesn't care, for he maintains that price for only a few days. Then he "cuts" the price to its usual level—$7.50—and advertises: "Terrific Bargain: X Pens. Were $10. Now Only $7.50!" This is obviously a false claim. The advertised "bargain" is not genuine.

(d) Other illustrations of fictitious price comparisons could be given. An advertiser might use a price at which he never offered the article at all; he might feature a price which was not used in the regular course of business, or which was not used in the recent past but at some remote period in the past, without making disclosure of that fact; he might use a price that was not openly offered to the public, or that was not maintained for a reasonable length of time, but was immediately reduced.

(e) If the former price is set forth in the advertisement, whether accompanied or not by descriptive terminology such as "Regularly," "Usually," "Formerly," etc., the advertiser should make certain that the former price is not a fictitious one. If the former price, or the amount or percentage of reduction, is not stated in the advertisement, as when the ad merely states, "Sale," the advertiser must take care that the amount of reduction is not so insignificant as to be meaningless. It should be sufficiently large that the consumer, if he knew what it was, would believe that a genuine bargain or saving was being offered. An advertiser who claims that an item has been "Reduced to $9.99," when the former price was $10, is misleading the consumer, who will understand the claim to mean that a much greater, and not merely nominal, reduction was being offered. [Guide I]

(October 3, 1990), offered the FTC's position, stating that deceptive pricing claims are "a hot topic among the states," and that he felt "it would not be a good use of our resources to duplicate their efforts."

Many states have instituted regulations that correspond with the FTC Guides against Deceptive Pricing. Others have statutes that specify compliance with the FTC rules and regulations is "a complete defense" to allegations of deceptive pricing. Critical in the FTC Guides, as well as in the state statutes, are statements of what is acceptable as a reference price. These definitions, which use various terms for the reference price against which the sale price is compared, include, for example:

Former price as "the actual, bona fide price for which the article was offered to the public on a regular basis for a reasonably substantial period of time." (FTC Guides against Deceptive Pricing)

Regular price as "the price . . . at which the seller of merchandise has sold or offered to sell such merchandise for a reasonably substantial period of time in the recent, regular course of the seller's business." (Hawaii's Office of Consumer Protection—Rules on Unfair or Deceptive Prices in Advertising)

Reference price as the "price at which the person, in the regular course of its business, made good faith sales of the same or similar goods or, if no sales were made, offered in good faith to make sales of the same or similar goods." (Administrative Rules of Oregon Department of Justice)

What is common to most of the definitions is that the reference price is legitimate if it has been offered for a reasonable amount of time *or* if it has resulted in significant sales. (Significant sales at the reference price are not appropriate as the *sole* indication of a legitimate regular price, since retailers, on occasion, make buying mistakes, which necessitate heavy discounting to clear out unpopular merchandise.) Neither the FTC Guides, nor many of the state statutes, however, give concrete definitions of what constitutes "a reasonably substantial period of time" or what percentage of the overall sales of an item correspond to "good faith sales" at the reference price. Some states have provided concrete guidelines as listed in Exhibit 2. Most recently, for example, Massachusetts, in May 1990, adopted retail advertising regulations stipulating that a reference price is legitimate if at least 30 percent of sales occur at that price *or* if the regular price is established for at least 15 days prior to the sale reduction and the item is not "on sale" for more than 45 percent of a 180-day period.

This lack of a concrete standard in most jurisdictions has created a great deal of confusion for retailers seeking to comply with federal and state regulations. Still, some in the industry maintain that "you know phony pricing when you see it" and suggest that if retailers offer merchandise at regular everyday prices that represent a realistic and not inflated initial margin, they will almost certainly be operating within both federal and state regulations.

EXHIBIT 2 State Standards Regarding the Legitimacy of Regular Prices

State	Time Period for Reference Price	Percent of Total Sales That Were at Reference Price
Connecticut	At least four weeks over the previous 90-day period.	No standard given.
Massachusetts	At least 15 days (unless seller discloses the original offering period) and over an 180-day period, the higher reference price must be offered at least 55 percent of the time.	Thirty percent of the items sold at reference price.
Minnesota	Thirty days preceding the comparison.	No standard given.
Missouri	Reference price must be in effect for some number of days initially, and in effect for 40 percent of the time during a period not less than thirty days, nor more than 12 months.	Ten percent of items sold at reference price.
Wisconsin	At least 4 weeks during any 90-day period prior to the comparison.	No standard given.

Some retailers have added disclosures to their sale advertising that state the reference price may not have resulted in actual sales. For example, an East Coast department store includes the following statement in small print at the bottom of its print ads:

Regular, Original*, and Former prices reflect offering prices which may not have resulted in actual sales. Advertised items may be offered in future sale events. *Intermediate price reductions may have been taken.

Another department store on the East Coast uses a similar disclaimer in its print ads:

Regular and Original prices are offering prices only and may or may not have resulted in sales. Advertised merchandise may be available at sale prices in upcoming sales event. Intermediate markdowns taken.

Recent Litigation

Many states, including California, Georgia, New York, North Carolina, Pennsylvania, and Colorado, currently are active in prosecuting deceptive advertising claims against department stores. For example, in 1989, the Philadelphia-based John Wanamaker department store chain was accused, by the Pennsylvania attorney general, of advertising special sales of 14-karat gold jewelry in late 1988 and early 1989—even though the sale prices were the same as the store's normal prices. The Georgia Governor's Office of Consumer Affairs has made similar allegations of deceptive pricing of jewelry against Macy's South and Rich's. Typically, such cases are resolved out of court, with the retailer not admitting any guilt but still paying a fine and agreeing not to advertise sale prices unless the reference price can be substantiated. Such agreements, as a rule, apply only to the category of trade that has been investigated. In some cases, local authorities have prosecuted retailers that have local stores in their jurisdictions. For example, the Los Angeles district attorney, in 1990, settled a suit against Nordstrom, the headquarters of which was in Seattle, in which the retailer was charged with "making false or misleading statements of facts concerning the existence and amounts of price reductions." These and other recent examples of retailers prosecuted for deceptive pricing policies are included in Exhibit 3.

Retail Efforts at Self-Regulation

In response to both the increased investigation and tougher legislation by state and local authorities, a group of major retailers, under the auspices of the Council of Better Business Bureaus, has proposed a Code of Advertising for Comparative Price Advertising. The retailers involved included Sears Roebuck, K mart Corporation, Ames Department Store, Circuit City Stores, F. W. Woolworth Company, Goodyear Tire & Rubber Company, Home Depot, J. C. Penney Company, May Department Stores Company, Montgomery Ward, Service Merchandise Company, Best Products Company, Dayton Hudson Corporation, Federated Stores/Allied Stores Corporation, Marshalls, Mellart Jewelers, R. H. Macy & Company, Saks Fifth Avenue, and Woodward and Lothrop. The code, proposed in September 1989, provides guidelines for a range of comparative pricing tactics that includes comparisons to former selling prices and list prices, comparisons with the prices of competitors, and the use of terms such as *factory to you, emergency* or *distress sale, imperfects, irregulars,* and *seconds.* The code also sets out some guidelines for price matching and lowest-price claims. Violations of the code, once approved, would be handled by the Council of Better Business Bureaus either through its local offices, or, in the case of national advertising, by the council's National Advertising Division. In either case, the council would ask the retailer to discontinue any inappropriate behavior and, if necessary, notify the appropriate state or local regulatory agency for further action.

The section of the code that addresses comparisons with *former selling prices,* its term for reference prices, stipulates that: "An advertiser may claim a savings from its own former price if it can demonstrate that its former price is a bona

EXHIBIT 3 Some Recent Litigation Regarding Deceptive Pricing

State	Retailer(s)	Product Category	Status
California—Los Angeles district attorney	Nordstrom	Men's clothing	Settled out of court in August 1989 with Nordstrom paying a $200,000 fine.
California—Sacramento County district attorney	Montgomery Ward & Co.	Paint	Settled out of court in February 1990 with Montgomery Ward paying a $160,000 fine.
Georgia—governor's office of consumer affairs	Macy's South and Rich's	Jewelry	The cases were settled in 1989. Both stores denied the allegations, but paid $37,500 each in fines and signed assurances saying they would refrain from "original/sale" price comparisons unless they could substantiate the reference prices.
Massachusetts—state attorney general	Hit-or-Miss; Casual Corner; Anderson-Little; Caren Charles; Cherry, Webb & Touraine; Chess King; Cummings; and the Limited	Clothing	In May 1985, all retailers but the Limited agreed to pay fines, ranging from $500–$12,000, and to refrain from deceptive pricing tactics in the future.
North Carolina—state attorney general	Rhodes, Inc.	Furniture	Settled out of court in April 1987 with Rhodes paying a $10,000 fine and agreeing to refrain from deceptive pricing tactics in the future.
Pennsylvania—state attorney general	John Wanamaker	Jewelry	In August 1989, Wanamaker's settled, paying $10,000 in fines and agreeing to refrain from deceptive pricing tactics in the future. They denied wrongdoing, however.
North Carolina—state attorney general	J. C. Penney	Jewelry	No settlement reached as of May 1990.

fide or genuine price, that is, a price from which a reduction represents a genuine savings for the consumer." The criteria for establishing that a former price is genuine are similar to those offered in many of the state statutes and in the FTC Guides. Either "reasonably substantial sales" must have occurred at the former price *or* the retailer must have made a "good faith effort" to sell the merchandise at the former price. The latter is most often indicated by the time period over which the former price is in effect but could also be indicated by other factors, including the initial margin relative to the retailer's customary margin (see Exhibit 4 for the section in the proposed code that addresses comparisons with former prices).

The proposed code is reasonably specific about the appropriate time period for a legitimate reference price, stating: "The offers of products at the former price for at least a majority of time during the relevant selling period presumptively meets the 'reasonably substantial period of time' criterion, although lesser periods may meet this criterion depending on the circumstances." The code is not specific, however, in suggesting the percentage of overall sales that must be accomplished at reference prices.

In proposing the code and publicly committing to it, the major retailers involved in its development hoped to prompt other retailers to agree to it as well, thus creating a level playing field for all with a return to reasonable initial margins and less-frequent sales. The concept of a level playing field is critical to any retailer's decision to discontinue high-low pricing. If competitors continue to promote aggressively and consumers remain responsive to sales, the retailer that reduces promotional activity risks losing substantial sales volumes. This fear has kept many retailers from attempting to stabilize their prices on an everyday basis and is often used as a defense when state and local agencies question high-low pricing policies.

THE STATE OF COLORADO VERSUS THE MAY DEPARTMENT STORES COMPANY

In June 1989, May D&F, a unit of the May Department Stores operating 12 department stores in Colorado, was charged with engaging in deceptive advertising practices in its Home Store department by the state attorney general's office. The Home Store department at May D&F includes housewares, cookware, mattresses, linens, textiles, small appliances, and electronics. The state alleged that, since 1986, May had used fictitious or exaggerated reference prices as a basis for comparison against its sale prices. These reference prices included price designations, such as "original" and "regular" price. The Colorado attorney general gave several examples of suspect pricing, including:

- Bedding sheets that had remained on sale for eight months.

- A cutlery set advertised and displayed "on sale" for two years.

- A new style of luggage offered at its special "introductory price" indefinitely.

The case against May D&F, in contrast to most lawsuits alleging deceptive pricing by retailers, was not settled out of court. It went to trial in May 1990,

---

EXHIBIT 4   Excerpt from Council of Better Business Bureau's Code of Advertising

1. Comparative Price, Value, and Savings Claims

Advertisers may offer a price reduction or savings by comparing their selling price with:

1. Their own former price.
2. The current price of identical merchandise offered by others in the market area.
3. The current price of comparable merchandise offered by others in the market area.
4. A manufacturer's list price.

When any one of these comparisons is made in advertising, the claim should be based on, and substantiated in accordance with, the criteria set forth below. Savings claims should be substantiated on the basis of evidence existing when the claim is made, or, if the advertising must be submitted in advance of publication, a reasonable time prior to when the claim is made.

Most consumers reasonably expect that claims of price reductions expressed in terms of a percent "off" or a specific dollar "savings" are reductions or savings from an advertiser's own former price. Accordingly, unless the savings claim is in fact based on the advertiser's own former price, the basis for the reduction (item 2, 3, or 4 above) should be affirmatively disclosed, such as, "Buy from us and save $50. Sold elsewhere at $199. Our price $149." For example, it would be misleading for an advertiser, without explanation, to claim a savings from a "ticketed price" if the advertiser could not establish that the "ticketed price" was a genuine former price.

a. Comparison with Own Former Price

1. An advertiser may claim a savings from its own former price if it can demonstrate that its former price is a bona fide or genuine price, that is a price from which a reduction represents a genuine savings for the customer.

   A former price is bona fide when "reasonably substantial sales" were made at or above the price in the recent regular course of business. While it is reasonable to expect that a retailer's nonsale prices will usually result in sales of the product, there will be occasions where the nonsale prices do not produce substantial sales. The bona fides of a former price may also be established where few or no sales were made only if the advertiser openly and actively offered the merchandise honestly and in "good faith" for a "reasonably substantial period of time" in the recent regular course of business. A more detailed discussion of these criteria is set forth in (3) and (4) below.

2. If the former price was the price in effect immediately prior to the savings claim, the following usual and customary trade usages may be used to describe a former price: "Regularly," "Usually," "Formerly," "Was," "You Save $____," and "Originally." If, however, the former price was not the price in effect immediately prior to the reduction, the advertiser should disclose this fact clearly and conspicuously by indicating that immediate markdowns have been taken. Appropriate ways to do so include: "Originally $400, Formerly $300, Now $250"; or "Originally $400, Now $250, Intermediate markdowns taken." If the former price is one that was last used at a remote point in time, for example, more than six months earlier, the advertising should also indicate the

---

EXHIBIT 4 *(continued)*

---

time period in which the former price had been applicable. For example, "Now $250, Originally $400 in Fall 1988, Intermediate markdowns taken."

3. Establishing the bona fides of a former price through reasonably substantial sales.

   When substantiating a former price on the basis of reasonably substantial sales, the appropriate time period for evaluating the claim may vary depending on the product in question. If the product is seasonal, the "season" may be the appropriate time period in which to evaluate whether substantial sales were made at or above the former price. If the product is staple, up to a year could be an appropriate period for measurement.

   An advertiser that establishes a uniform price over a national or regional trade area may rely on sales made at the price throughout that national or regional trade area in order to substantiate the bona fides of that price.

4. Establishing the bona fides of a former price through a "good faith" offer to sell.

   The offers of products at the former price for at least a majority of time during the relevant selling period presumptively meets the "reasonably substantial period of time" criterion, although lesser periods may meet this criterion depending on the circumstances. If the product is seasonal, the "season" may be the period for measuring conformance with this criterion. If the product is staple in nature, up to one year could be an appropriate measurement period. In any event, the period during which discontinued products are permanently reduced for clearance or closeout from the advertiser's inventory should not be counted in measuring conformance.

   A former price is not necessarily fictitious merely because "substantial sales" were not made at that price. In these situations, however, the advertiser should be especially cautious to assure that its former or offering price was a good faith offer to sell and not a price that has been inflated or exaggerated merely to show a large reduction.

   Factors an advertiser may rely on in substantiating its good faith include, but are not necessarily limited to:

- Whether the advertiser had a reasonable expectation of selling the product at the offering price, based on demonstrated facts, such as prior experience with sales of the same or comparable merchandise, and the appropriate time at or above the former price.

- Whether the offering price is realistic (i.e., whether it generally fell within the range of prices that the advertiser reasonably believes to be bona fide in the market area for the same or substantially similar products).

- The extent to which sales of the product were made at the former price, even if not "substantial," taking into account the nature of the merchandise.

- Whether the offering price is based on a markup that does not significantly exceed the advertiser's usual and customary retail markup for similar merchandise.

EXHIBIT 4 *(concluded)*

- Whether the product was openly and actively offered in the recent, regular course of business such as by devoting reasonable display space to the product during the period(s) in which it was at the offering price, maintaining reasonable inventory during former price periods, or advertising the product at the offering price, etc.

---

with the Colorado attorney general asking Denver District Court Judge Larry Naves to establish a standard for the proportion of overall sales volume that must occur at the reference price and to apply that standard in ruling on the legitimacy of May D&F's pricing policies. (See Exhibit 5 for *The Wall Street Journal* article published at the start of the trial.)

May D&F's Pricing Policy: June 1986–August 1989[3]

During this time period, May D&F's pricing, specifically its *comparative price advertising*, the term used to reflect the retailer's promotional pricing, was dictated by the "Comparative Price Advertising" policy developed in 1986. This 1986 policy required that merchandise in the Home Store be offered at the so-called original price for at least 10 days at the beginning of each six-month selling season. Thereafter, the merchandise was discounted and advertising, in-store signage, and item price tickets indicated that it had been reduced from its original price. In addition, over the course of the six-month selling season, the merchandise could be discounted further for various sales of limited duration, including "15-Hour Sales" and "Three Days Only" sales events. After any such sale, prices were returned to the first discount level and not to the original price. At the end of the six-month selling season, the original prices were restored for a 10-day initial period.

More specifically, May D&F pricing was the responsibility of its buyers, who also were responsible for the advertising within their departments. Buyers set two prices when ordering merchandise: an initial markup price and a promotional markup price. The initial markup price reflected May D&F's usual

---

[3] Prior to the 1986 policy, in October 1982, May D&F had entered into an "Assurance of Discontinuance" with the Colorado attorney general, whereby it agreed to certain comparative advertising standards for a period of five years. Among these standards, according to May D&F, was the stipulation that an initial offering period for the reference price was an appropriate standard for judging the price's legitimacy. This offering period corresponds to the number of days, at the beginning of the selling season, that the merchandise is at regular or original prices. May D&F, on February 6, 1984, also received a letter from the Colorado attorney general's office to all Colorado retailers advising them "to consider the enclosed copy of the Federal Trade Commission's 'Guides against Deceptive Pricing' when developing your advertisements . . ."

EXHIBIT 5   Press Report at the Start of the Trial

STORE'S CONCEPT OF 'SALE' PRICING
GETS COURT TEST

By Francine Schwadel
Staff Reporter of The Wall Street Journal

When is a sale truly a sale?

A state court judge in Denver could provide a precedent-setting answer in a widely watched case scheduled to go to trial today. The Colorado attorney general is asking Judge Larry Naves to define a standard for determining when a retailer promotes legitimate discounts.

Among the criteria suggested by the state: Retailers can advertise discounts only from higher prices at which goods actually were sold—not just offered for sale.

Any ruling would apply only to the Denver-based May D&F unit of May Department Stores Company, which stands accused of misleading Colorado consumers. But it could send shock waves throughout the retailing industry. The Colorado attorney general's suggested criteria are among the most detailed in the nation. And the defendant is the nation's largest operator of department stores.

"The decision is going to dictate how the states act in enforcement and how the retailers are going to advertise," predicts Clayton Friedman, an assistant attorney general in Missouri.

The Colorado case also provides a rare glimpse at how retail price promotions really work. The state alleges that May D&F deceives consumers by artificially inflating its "original" or "regular" prices, then promoting discounts from those prices to create the illusion of offering bargains on cookware, linens, and other household goods. May denies the charges, claiming in part that its practices don't violate Federal Trade Commission guidelines.

But rather than settling out of court as other retailers have done in similar cases, May publicly is explaining how it establishes "original" and "regular" prices.

The case also comes as the Federal Trade Commission is taking its first comprehensive look at the subject in more than a decade. The agency is mulling comments on voluntary advertising guidelines drawn up recently by May and other big retailers, who are anxious to head off new state regulations. The FTC's current guidelines, which date from 1964, require that goods be offered for sale at regular prices "for a reasonably substantial period of time . . . honestly and in good faith and not for the purpose of establishing a fictitious higher price."

Sales are coming under more scrutiny today because they have become so common. As competition intensified in the 1980s, stores sought an edge by running more and more specials. That attracted the attention of state attorneys general, who investigated the claims, started writing more stringent rules, and sued some of the most trusted names in retailing. Cases now are pending in other states against Sears, Roebuck & Company, J.C. Penney Company, and other big retailers.

Colorado prosecutors are cutting to the heart of the debate by suggesting that May be held to a standard of actually selling merchandise at the higher price. "That's a very important question," says Steven Cole, general counsel of the Council of Better Business Bureaus.

Neither prosecutors nor lawyers for May D&F would comment on the Colorado case. A spokesman for the parent company, based in St. Louis, also declined to comment.

EXHIBIT 5 *(concluded)*

In court documents, the Colorado attorney general argues that an actual sales standard is necessary to make any injunction against May enforceable and to match consumers' perceptions about what constitutes a special deal. The state says the majority of 400 Colorado consumers surveyed in March believed that at least 25 percent of a retailer's sales were made at the "original" or "regular" prices. The average consumer in the survey understood the terms "regular" and "original" to mean prices that were charged on 50 of the last 90 days, the state says.

In court documents, May D&F acknowledges that, before last August, it made few sales in its Home Store departments at what it called "original" prices. At the time, the company says its policies required that household goods be offered for sale at an "original" price for at least 10 days at the beginning of each six-month season. After the 10 days, May says its policies allowed promotions touting discounts from the "original" price.

May changed its policies in August (two months after it was sued by the state) "to eliminate any doubt as to the legitimacy of its advertising," according to the company's court filings. Under the new policy, May says it establishes "regular" prices by offering Home Store merchandise for sale for at least 28 of every 90 days. And it says it instituted a "Satisfaction Guaranteed" program allowing shoppers to return merchandise for a full refund.

The company defends its new policy, contending it reduced the so-called reference prices the company uses to calculate discount claims on most Home Store merchandise. The price used to calculate discounts on a 12-cup Braun coffeemaker, for example, slid to $64 from $69 as a result of the policy change.

May also says in court documents that it now makes "many sales" at its "regular" prices. In the six months ended in March 1990, May says it sold anywhere from less than 1 percent to more than 25 percent of the 55 best-selling Home Store items at its "regular" prices. Still, those levels may not be high enough to satisfy the state.

The company maintains that consumers aren't misled by its practices. In court documents, it cites surveys showing the majority of consumers understood the term "original" to mean "the first price of the season" and that 90 percent didn't care whether there were actual sales at that price.

May also argues in its filings that an actual sales standard is unworkable and would impede price competition. "May D&F cannot control how many products it will sell at a given price," the company says. "This will vary by the type of product, expectations of consumers about whether they might be able to obtain the merchandise on sale, the competitive environment for a given product, the economy" and other factors.

Source: *The Wall Street Journal*, May 15, 1990.

or planned margin and was calculated using a formula that considered the cost of goods, the cost of doing business, and the company's profit goals. Merchandise was discounted to this price after being at the "original price" for 10 days. Thus, the initial markup price was the price for an item for the bulk of the selling season. The promotional markup price was significantly greater than the initial markup price and was used as the "original price," in effect for 10 days at the beginning of the season. Buyers set this price by taking into account competitors' prices, manufacturers' suggested retail prices, the quality, popularity, and brand name of the merchandise, and other subjective factors. Buyers who testified at the trial reported that this "original price" was a price at which some sales were expected, but they did not expect substantial sales at this price, nor could they provide a definition of what constituted substantial sales.

May D&F's Policy: After May 1989

In August 1989, May D&F introduced a new comparative price advertising policy. Promotional markup prices were lowered, though they were still determined subjectively, and were presented as "regular prices" on in-store signage and advertisements, rather than as "original prices." In addition, these "regular prices" were to be in effect 28 out of each 90 selling days, with the 10 days at the beginning of the selling season counting toward the 28 days. This 28 out of 90 day standard was derived from the standards required by Connecticut and Wisconsin (see Exhibit 2). Customers who bought merchandise at the regular price also were able to return merchandise for a full refund under the store's new "Satisfaction Guaranteed" program, even though prices had been subsequently reduced. Finally, May D&F hired a manager of consumer affairs in April 1989 to monitor and ensure the credibility of May D&F's advertisements.

May D&F reported that, between October 1989 and March 1990, Home Store sales done at "regular price," for 55 top-selling items, ranged from 1 percent to more than 25 percent of total unit sales. However, in a sampling of 5,340 household items sold by May D&F between January 1989 and March 1990, done by an investigator for the Colorado attorney general, over 97 percent of the items were sold at sale prices. For example, of total sales of 2,257 units of a Braun coffeemaker, 79 units were sold either at its "original price" of $49.99 or its subsequent "regular price" of $46.99, and 2,178 were sold at the "sale price" of $35.24. Of total sales of 324 units for a Magnalite pot, one sold at the "original price" of $155, two sold at the subsequent "regular price" of $149.99, and the remaining 321 units sold at $99.99 or less.

Specific Allegations Made by the State Attorney General

The Colorado attorney general's office claimed that May D&F's comparative pricing policies, including both the 1986 and the August 1989 policies, violated the Colorado Consumer Protection Act, specifically the section dealing with deceptive trade practices. This section, 6-1-105 reads as follows:

6-1-105 Deceptive Trade Practices: (1) A person engages in a deceptive trade practice when, in the course of his business, vocations, or occupation, he:

(i) Advertises goods, services, or property with the intent not to sell them as advertised;

(ii) Makes false or misleading statements of facts concerning the price of goods, services, or property; or for the reasons for, existence of, or amounts of price reduction; and

(iii) Fails to disclose material information concerning goods, services, or property which information was known at the time of an advertisement or sale if such failure to disclose such information was intended to induce the consumer to enter into a transaction.

Assistant attorney general James Lewis presented the state's position in the closing arguments of the trial saying, "May D&F violated the law every day for the last four years." "These were false, fictitious prices set not for the purpose of selling the items but for setting subsequent discounts," and "Consumers don't know what the original price of the item was nor the actual savings, if any, of the marked down sales item." The state asked the judge to award up to $20 million in civil penalties and to place new limits on the comparative price advertising used by May D&F.

State attorneys provided, along with other evidence, the testimony of customers, included as Exhibit 6, and expert witness testimony by associate professor Joel Urbany of the University of South Carolina, a specialist in consumer behavior. Professor Urbany reported the results of a survey of Denver consumers he conducted for the attorney general. The executive summary from his study is given in Exhibit 7. Most notably, Professor Urbany's study indicated that, when an "original" or "regular" price was advertised along with the sale price, respondents generally perceived greater savings and showed greater intention to purchase than when the advertisement contained no reference price. In addition, the majority of the respondents believed that "regular" or "original" priced merchandise represented at least 25 percent of the unit sales of a product in the previous 90 days, and that the "regular" or "original" price was the price charged for the majority of the selling period. The Colorado attorney general argued that both the customer testimony and the survey results showed that consumers had been deceived by May D&F comparative pricing.

May D&F Defense

Attorneys for May D&F denied that the retailer had engaged in any deceptive advertising or trade practices and offered among a number of defenses the following:

1. Colorado law is vague on the issue of comparison advertising standards.

EXHIBIT 6   Summary of Testimony by Four Customers*

Consumer A had been watching ads for a Farberware rotisserie, and, when it was "on sale" for "4 days only" at 40 percent off the "regular price" (stated as $119.99), she bought it at $71.99. She did no comparative shopping in advance. While shopping in a discount store, she saw the identical product in that store at $59.97 with a comparison price of $79.99 and a regular price of $64.97. She was angry. She checked a May D&F competitor and found a regular price of $74.99. She called the manufacturer in New York and found the suggested price was $109.99, $10.00 less than May D&F's "regular price."

Consumer B purchased a Scanpan saucepan at 25 percent off the regular price of $99.99, or $74.99, and then saw it in three competitor stores at a regular price of approximately $74.00. When she complained, May D&F gave her a full refund.

Consumer C had been watching some glasses priced at $15 and a set of mugs at $10. When she received a coupon with those glasses and mugs, it claimed "25 percent Off Last Sold Price with Coupon Only." At the store, the $15 glasses were now $21.99, the set of mugs, $13. Twenty-five percent (25%) off the glasses would be $16.50 on sale versus $15 before for the glasses and $9.75 versus $10 for the set of mugs.

Consumer D had been watching Krups coffee machines. Prior to January 1990, each time she checked they were at $79.99. In that month, when they were advertised at 30 percent off, she found that the 30 percent off sale price was $79.99 and the regular price was either $109.99 or $119.99.

* As reported in *Retailing Today*, January 1991, edited by Robert Kahn.

Specifically the Colorado Consumer Protection Act (CPA) does not contain language requiring either an offering period during which the regular or original price must be in effect, or a standard for the percentage of sales that must be done at regular or original prices.

2. May D&F's compliance with the FTC Guides pre-empts the CPA.

3. May D&F's ads were not misleading and caused no injury.

4. The standards proposed by the Colorado attorney general would hurt consumers and competition. Specifically, they argued that imposing any standard either regarding the proportion of time merchandise must be at regular price or the proportion of sales that must be done at reference price and applying that standard only to May D&F would place the retailer at a competitive disadvantage against retailers who continued to promote without such restrictions.

May D&F attorneys cited two consumer surveys, done for them by Leo Shapiro, a Chicago-based market research firm, as evidence that their ads were not misleading. In the first, done in October 1989, a random sample of 500 Denver households were surveyed by telephone to assess May D&F's reputation among area retailers and some specific advertising practices. A summary of the findings of this survey are reported in Exhibit 8. In a second survey, conducted in April 1990, 331 individuals were surveyed in a number of malls

---

EXHIBIT 7   Executive Summary and Selected Results from "Comparative Price Advertising Effects in the Denver Market," Prepared by Joel Urbany, Ph.D., April 23, 1990

Study Description

- This paper reports the results of a study of whether/how comparative price advertising affects consumer perception and behavioral intentions. The study was conducted during the period March 19–28, 1990, in the Denver, Colorado, SMSA.

- The study involved mall intercept interviews of 400 Colorado consumers. Respondents were asked to examine and evaluate an advertised sale offer from the May Department Stores Company ("May D&F" or "May Company"), although the company name was removed from the ad. Of those surveyed, 46 percent said they recognized that the ad was from May D&F.

- Actual ads from two products recently advertised on sale by May D&F were used in the study: a Hoover canister vacuum cleaner and a Revereware fry pan.

- To examine whether the comparative prices (i.e., the "regular" or "original" prices stated in the ad) had any influence on consumer perception of savings and purchase intentions, half of the respondents were shown ads in which the comparative prices had been removed (these respondents are referred to as the "control" group).

- To examine consumer perception of comparative pricing terminology, respondents were additionally asked to explain their understanding of the terms *regular, original,* and *intermediate markdowns have been taken.*

Selected Results

	Vacuum Cleaner		Frying Pan	
	Sale Price Only in Ad	*Sale and Regular Price in Ad*	*Sale Price Only in Ad*	*Sale and Regular Price in Ad*
Percent Who Agreed:				
"I'll save a lot if I buy from the advertising store"	11%	35%	29%	44%
"The product is a bargain at the advertised sale price"	14	27	29	44
"The retailer reduced the price a lot for this sale"	11	35	13	41
Choice:				
Percent who would consider buying today, rather than comparison shopping	3	13	5	9
Chance:				
Percent perceived chance of buying from the advertised retailer	22	36	43	46

EXHIBIT 7 *(concluded)*

Note: When the regular price was included, the sale price represented a 30 percent savings for the vacuum cleaner and a 35 percent savings for the frying pan.

Conclusion:

1. The presence of the comparative price (i.e., regular) in the advertisements significantly increased both perceived savings and purchase intentions (the "comparative price effect").
2. This comparative price effect occurred in both the vacuum cleaner and frying pan product categories and for those respondents who knew that May D&F was the advertiser.
3. The majority of respondents believed that at least 25 percent of the products sold by the advertiser in the previous 90 days had been sold at the regular or original price.
4. Respondents believed that the terms *regular* and *original* referred to the price that was charged for the product when it was not on sale.
5. Respondents generally believed that the *regular* or *original* price is charged by the retailer the majority of the time during a given selling period.
6. The majority of respondents believed that, after the sale was over, the price would return to the regular or original level stated in the ad.
7. When respondents were asked the meaning of the term *intermediate markdowns have been taken*, the most frequent answer was "don't know."

---

in Denver. Respondents in this survey were asked a number of questions designed to show what the term *original price* meant to them and whether respondents' perceptions of the term were influenced by the amount of merchandise actually sold at that price. The results of the second survey are also provided in Exhibit 8.

Finally, May D&F attorneys presented some mitigating circumstances that they hoped the judge would consider in determining penalties if he ruled that May D&F had violated the Colorado Consumer Protection Act. These included that May D&F, in August 1989, adopted a new policy for comparative price advertising that included a standard offering period for the regular price of 28 out of 90 days, which was consistent with the standard offered by the state of Connecticut, one of the few states offering a specific standard. Also cited as mitigating circumstances was the hiring of a consumer affairs director to monitor the chain's advertising and the establishment of the store's "Satisfaction Guaranteed" program. They also mentioned that the Home Store had operated at a net loss for the past three years.

Closing arguments for the case concluded on May 24, 1990. Retailers, state regulators, and state consumer protection agencies across the country had watched the progression of the case and were keenly interested in the judge's decision, particularly as it applied to the establishment of standards for the legitimacy of the reference prices used in sale advertising. As noted by Clayton

Friedman, an assistant attorney general in Missouri in *The Wall Street Journal* accounting of the case (see Exhibit 5): "The decision is going to dictate how the states act in enforcement and how retailers are going to advertise."

EXHIBIT 8 Summary of the Findings of Two Surveys Done for May D&F by Leo Shapiro and Associates, Inc.

Survey 1, October 1989

Survey Responses

- "And, on balance, do you feel that May D&F's advertised prices are generally higher or lower than the other stores in your area who sell the same things?"
  May D&F's advertised prices are higher   72% responding
  May D&F's advertised prices are lower   6% responding
  May D&F's advertised prices are the same   20% responding

- "Specifically, when you see an advertisement from May D&F that says 50 percent off, do you believe that the item advertised from May D&F is going to be priced lower than any of the other stores in your area that sell the same thing?"
  No   70% responding
  Yes   25% responding

- "By the way, sometimes a store like May D&F will have a particular item or items that you can almost always find on sale in their store and in their ads. Do you believe that such an item from May D&F is going to be priced lower than any of the other stores in your area that sell the same things?"
  No   70% responding
  Yes   21% responding

Experts' Conclusions

- The reputation that May D&F has among the retailers who serve Denver area households can be described as a store whose prices are relatively high while offering good quality products and good service to its customers.

- Denver area households expect May D&F to advertise specials and sales which bring its prices more in line with other area retailers; however, a majority believe that May D&F advertised sales prices generally are higher than those of other area merchants.

- When confronted with a claim for 50 percent off in a May D&F ad, nearly three in four (70 percent) report that they do not believe that this means May D&F is priced lower than other area retailers.

- When asked how they felt about items which are almost always offered on sale in their advertisements and in their store, a similar majority (70 percent) report that these items are not lower priced than can be found at other area retailers.

- Taken collectively, the results of this survey indicate that May D&F advertising is not misleading for households in the Denver metropolitan area. In fact, few households believe that May D&F advertised prices are better than those which

---

EXHIBIT 8 *(continued)*

---

they can find at other area retailers, even when advertising claims (e.g., 50 percent off) are for substantial reductions.

Survey 2, April 1990

Selected Results

Respondents were shown a graph which showed the price at which May D&F offered a Cuisinart Mini-Mate for sale over a three-month period (see Exhibit 9). They were then asked the following questions:

- "Please take a look at this chart. It shows what the price was that a department store charged for a specific item over the course of three months. Thinking about the advertising where they show the original price for an item and then show the sale price, please point to or read aloud the price or point on the graph where the price is what you would consider to be the original price for this item."

$49.99	56% responding
39.99	19% responding
37.49	8% responding
34.99	9% responding
33.49	3% responding
29.99	4% responding
Other	1% responding

- "And when you consider what they mean by the original price, does it make a difference to you how much merchandise, if any, they had sold at that price?"

No	88% responding
Yes	12% responding

- "Thinking about advertising for bedding, clothing, household appliances, jewelry, home electronics, and other things for your home and family, about how often do you check the ads before you shop for items like this?"

All of the time	41% responding
Some of the time	31% responding
Not much at all	17% responding
Never	11% responding

- "Thinking about the way stores advertise, when you see an ad, how can you tell whether the price of an item is really very good? What tells you this is a really super price for something?"

Compare to other stores	47% responding
I know the price/previous experience	31% responding
Compare to the original price	12% responding

Expert's Conclusions

- Consumers have a very clear idea of what the word *original* means when looking at department store advertising. When shown the actual prices at which a typical May D&F housewares product was offered for sale by date, over a three-month period, a majority of consumers report that the price which they themselves would

EXHIBIT 8 *(concluded)*

judge to be the *original* price was, in fact, the price which the May D&F advertisement said was the *original* price.

• In addition, when asked whether or not it makes any difference in their assessment if any products are sold at the original price point, 9 out of 10 consumers report that it does not make any difference whether any sales occur at that price.

• It is also clear from this study that most Denver-area consumers feel that the most important thing to look for when trying to judge a price is to compare that price with other stores, while few feel that the store's reference or original price holds great importance for them.

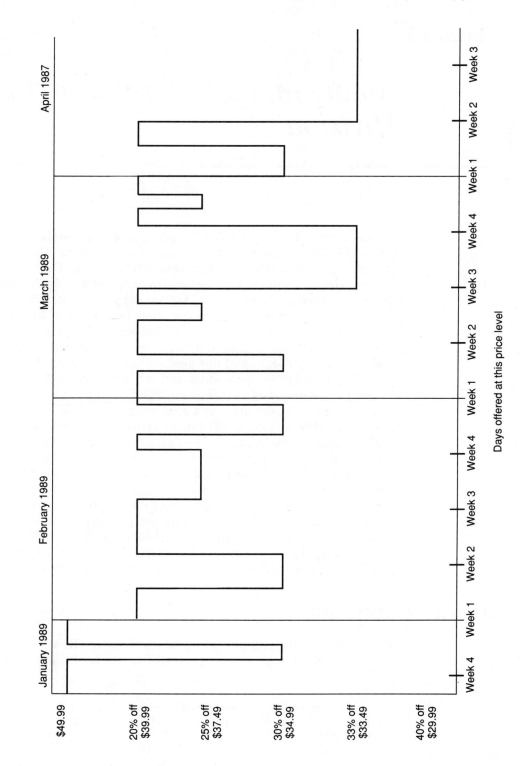

Amalgamated Aluminum Alloy Division

In March 1987, Dr. Gwendolyn Harper, a staff metallurgist at the Alloy Division (AD) of Amalgamated Aluminum, darted into the research and development vice president's office to announce, "Hot dog! The new alloy works, but only over a small range of tensile strength. We still don't know why that cheap alloy mixture does the job, but we suspect it's because of an unusual eutectic structure at that point in the phase diagram. The important thing is that we can get major cost savings at that segment of our product line and, perhaps, if we can develop an understanding of the metallurgy, we can expand it to cover a larger section of our product line. When I was an undergraduate at Tuskegee, one of my professors told me about the high I'd feel from discovering something useful. It is a real high!"

By January 1989, the alloy was confirmed to have the previously believed properties. AD's process development team had developed a commercially viable process for producing it. The commercial development customer contact people had arranged for a few initial customer tests, with excellent results! Harper had, in fact, discovered a new useful alloy for the AD product line. She now led a team of metallurgists and material scientists in an effort to understand the metallurgy and broaden its applicability. It was understood by all involved that this would take years and perhaps a decade.

Meanwhile, Andrew McAndrews, product manager for high-strength aluminum alloys, began to develop a marketing plan for GH 1000, the working designation of the new alloy. First on his list of decisions was a price.

THE PRICING DECISION

The 7000 series of aluminum alloys, which included GH 1000, contained zinc, often magnesium, and sometimes smaller amounts of copper and chromium.

This case was prepared by Professor Benson P. Shapiro and Barbara Feinberg.
Copyright © 1988 by the President and Fellows of Harvard College.
Harvard Business School case 9-589-035 (rev. 2/89).

They were generally of high strength and hard, with good weldability. Primary applications were high-strength structures, cryogenics, missile components, keys, gears, and a variety of aircraft and aerospace products. Sixty percent of AD's tonnage of products in this series eventually went to military and space products; the other 40 percent were widely spread in a variety of commercial applications.

The relationships among material cost, processing cost, price, and tensile strength for the series are shown in Exhibit 1. Lower-strength alloys, which were still quite strong relative to other types of aluminum alloys, were less expensive to produce because both material cost and process cost were lower. Prices also were lower than for the more costly alloys in the series.

There was a break point in the materials cost at a tensile strength index of about 1000 because of a shift in alloying ingredients. Over 1000, additional tensile strength was more expensive than equal increments below 1000. Processing costs tended to rise gradually with tensile strength.

The alloy business was an oligopoly, with six major North American players and a variety of foreign manufacturers. Prices did not vary a great deal from one company to another; all offered volume discounts and negotiated large contracts at favorable prices. Prices were very sensitive to the balance between capacity and demand. However, during the mid-1980s, despite soft pricing in the general aluminum market, because of overcapacity and weak demand, alloy prices had been fairly firm because of the U.S. military buildup. AD, with the largest share and most extensive R&D program, tended to be the price leader in this part of the industry, but its flexibility was severely limited by the industry environment.

GH 1000 was less expensive than the products it replaced in raw material cost, as shown in Exhibit 1. Processing cost was not changed. All commercial development and R&D data indicated that GH 1000 would perform no differently from the grades it would replace.

About 80 percent of the tonnage for AD products directly competitive with GH 1000 in tensile strength went eventually to the U.S. government for military and space programs. Most of the rest went into high-strength products for commercial aviation and cryogenic containers for liquefied gases. Seven corporate customers accounted for 75 percent of AD's sales in that product range, although this comprised many plants, programs, and operating units of the customers. All seven were major customers for Amalgamated Aluminum's corporate product line. And all were part of the corporation's corporate accounts program, which provided "special care and treatment" to Amalgamated's 18 most strategic corporate customers.

The largest single purchaser of AD's GH 1000-strength products accounted for 23 percent of tonnage.

The R&D vice president had assured McAndrews that no competitor currently had a product comparable to GH 1000. He warned, however, that other competitors were likely to be hard at work to accomplish the same thing. He continued: "Because we have a larger R&D effort in general, and a far larger

EXHIBIT 1 Amalgamated Aluminum Alloy Division

Cost and Price Data (graph form)

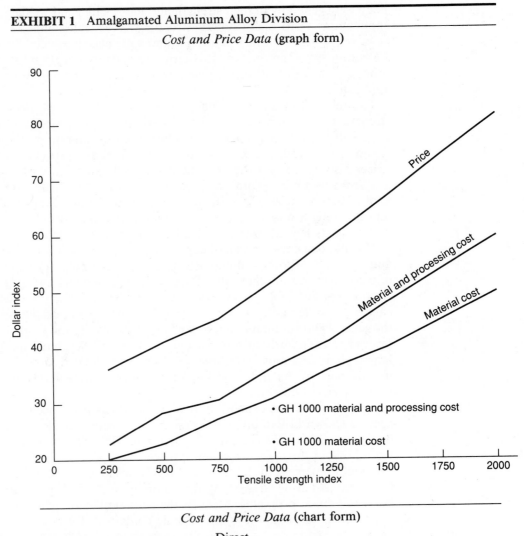

Cost and Price Data (chart form)

Tensile Strength Index	Material Cost Index	Direct Processing Cost Index	Total Cost Index	Price Index	Contribution Index
250	20	3	23	36	13
500	23.3	4	27.3	41.3	14
750	26.7	5	31.7	46.7	15
1000	30	6	36	52	16
GH 1000	23	6	29	☐	☐
1250	35	7	42	59.5	17.5
1500	40	8	48	67	19
1750	45	9	54	74.5	20.5
2000	50	10	60	82	22

one in this area than our competitors, they are not very likely to be able to replicate this product. Gwen knows this area of metallurgy better than anyone else alive, and she is confused by the strange behavior of the alloys. Surely, someone else will be baffled!"

The R&D vice president, the general counsel, and the outside patent attorney had all told McAndrews that patent protection for GH 1000 was almost assured, although they warned that the protection would be limited to this particular alloy combination and closely related ones. If a competitor developed a product with the same properties based on a different alloy combination, AD's patent would not cover it.

As McAndrews pondered the pricing issues, he thought about the following:

1. Profit implications.
2. Potential cannibalization at low prices.
3. Volume impact.
4. Competitive responses.
5. Relationship to volume discounts and contract prices.
6. Relationship to the corporate accounts program.

He was particularly perplexed by the CEO's 1988 year-end directive to be more "customer driven." The CEO's letter, which went to all Amalgamated management personnel, stated in part:

> We have seen that, where we have deep and close relationships with our most important customers, we thrive and they thrive. We are committed to sacrificing short-term gains for long-term profitability based on unique products and enduring customer relationships. We want to be the vendor of choice and the preferred supplier to all our most important customers. *Each decision we make will be measured against its impact on our most strategic customers.*
>
> Of course, we must constantly strive to maintain maximum return to our shareholders. At no time is that more important than during the unsettled period we face in 1989.

Car-Rental Collision Damage Waivers

> *Consumer advocates have long criticized the (collision damage) waiver for being too expensive. . . . "Pure and simple, it's a rip-off."*[1]

On January 1, 1989, the State of Illinois limited rental drivers' damage liability to $200 and thus eliminated the incentive for drivers to purchase collision damage waivers (CDWs). One year later, this ban had resulted in increased car-rental prices, more restrictive rental agreements, and less consumer choice of car-rental companies as smaller operations folded. Small, independent car-rental companies complained bitterly that, "if they could not go after the customer's insurance company, they were too small to self-insure and this bill would put them out of business."[2] Was the CDW a necessary charge that helped car-rental companies recoup their car repair costs? Or was it really disguised "revenue padding?"

INDUSTRY BACKGROUND

The $8 billion U.S. car-rental market, growing at 13 percent annually since 1982, was divided into three segments: business travel (48 percent of revenues), leisure travel (32 percent), and replacement rentals (20 percent). Ninety-five percent of business and leisure rentals originated from airports. The leisure market was growing twice as fast as the business markets.

Business travelers were more concerned with fast, dependable service. Leisure travelers were more price conscious and retained vehicles, on average,

---

This case was prepared by Julie Yao under the direction of Professor John A. Quelch.

Copyright © 1990 by the President and Fellows of Harvard College.

Harvard Business School case N9–591–020 (rev. 7/26/90).

[1] Jonathan Dahl and Christopher Winans, "States, Car Rental Firms Collide over Damage Waivers," *The Wall Street Journal*, August 14, 1989, p. B1.

[2] Barbara Tzivanis Benham, "Riding the Rocky Road of CDWs," *Best's Review* 89, no. 6 (October 1988), p. 67.

for longer periods. According to a 1988 *Consumer Reports* survey, leisure travelers preferred companies that disclosed a car rental's full cost upfront. Over 50 percent of vacation travelers rented their automobiles at some discounted or special rate.

The car-rental industry included four types of competitors: large national players; smaller, regional companies; franchisees; and independent operators. As indicated in Exhibit 1, four large competitors—Hertz, Avis, National, and Budget—dominated the business segment, with each deriving over 75 percent of its revenue from short-term business rentals in 1988. Smaller independent car-rental companies, such as Alamo and American International, targeted the rapidly expanding and price-sensitive leisure market. The aggressive growth strategy of these independents eroded the four largest companies' market share over 20 percent in five years, from 97 percent market share in 1982 to 77 percent in 1987. In the late 1980s, both large and small players in the industry were tarnished by scandals involving false or overstated car repair charges and misleading advertising that failed to fully disclose rental charges to customers.

Car-rental base rates varied widely, even within an individual company; such factors as the pickup location, metered versus unlimited mileage, length of rental time, or the length of advance reservation time affected the price a consumer paid. Car-rental companies frequently added several fees that could cumulatively double this base cost, such as young driver fees, fuel surcharges, airport fees, one-way drop charges, additional driver fees, and CDWs (or loss damage waivers). Car-rental companies often charged well over cost for these

EXHIBIT 1 Car-Rental Industry Statistics: 1988

Company	Number of Locations	Market Share*	Fleet Size	CDW Cost
Avis	1,400	27.2	125,000	$ 9.95
Budget	1,220	17.6	112,000	9.99
Hertz	1,500	30.9	160,000	10.95
National	1,000	16.4	100,000	9.95
Alamo	82	NA	60,000	11.99
American International	104	NA	NA	8.95
Dollar	740	5.6	NA	10.95
General	28	NA	NA	10.99
Thrifty	369	NA	40,000	8.95
Value	23	NA	NA	10.95

NA means not available.
* Based on on-airport revenues.

Source: Research reports and *Consumer Reports*.

extra services; one company charged a car renter $10 a day for an infant car seat worth $50.

Before 1986, car-rental companies grew profits through fleet-size expansion since larger fleets reaped greater tax depreciation benefits. After the 1986 Tax Reform Act greatly reduced these benefits, rental companies turned their attention to profit margin improvement. To reduce costs, many car-rental companies increased the customer's damage liability for rental vehicles. In the early 1980s, a car-rental customer typically had a maximum liability of $500; by 1987, this liability had increased to $10,000 or $15,000, effectively making the customer financially responsible for the car's full value.

COLLISION DAMAGE WAIVERS

A CDW released a car-rental customer from any financial liability for damage to the car during a rental period. Car-rental companies generally charged a CDW fee on a per day basis, which a customer accepted by initialing a section of the rental contract. The actual coverage provided by a CDW varied from firm to firm; in some cases, the CDW became invalid if the customer was considered "negligent." In addition, the CDW often excluded coverage of damaged glass or tires. Exhibit 2 reproduces the text of a typical CDW.

A customer who refused to buy the CDW was liable for full damages on the rental vehicle. In addition, car-rental companies frequently charged the customer the company's opportunity costs associated with the loss of the car's

---

EXHIBIT 2   Sample Language on Rental Car Contract

Optional Collision Damage Waiver (CDW).   If I accept optional CDW, I will pay the rate per day even if I have the car only part of a day. CDW is not insurance. Law of State of rental may modify or prohibit these CDW provisions.

Loss or Damage to the Car.   If I *decline* the CDW, I'll pay you for all loss, damage, or loss of use of the car regardless of who is at fault. You may have limited liability to the amount printed on the front. If the car cannot be repaired, I'll pay the retail value of the car before it was damaged, less any amount you get for salvage. (State Law may limit allowable recovery). If I *accept* CDW, I won't have to pay anything, unless I or an authorized driver:

(1) intentionally caused the damage or engaged in willful and wanton misconduct; (2) was legally intoxicated or under the influence of illegal drugs; (3) was in a speed contest or race; (4) rented the car based on my false or fraudulent information; (5) used the car in the commission of a felony or other criminal activity; (6) used the car to carry people or property for hire, or to tow or push anything; (7) left the ignition key in the car and the car was stolen or vandalized; or (8) drove the car outside the U.S. and Canada without written consent. I will visit the nearest . . . office to report any accident involving the rental car.

---

use during its repair. Often, however, a customer had alternative coverage. Personal insurance policies, coverage from credit card companies, and direct corporate agreements with preferred rental companies often reduced a customer's exposure. Insurance experts estimated that 55–60 percent of car insurance holders held policies that covered their car-rental risk. A car renter's true liability was difficult to ascertain, since it varied significantly depending on the extent of his or her liability responsibility to the rental company and the individual's own alternative sources of coverage. For instance, some credit card companies fully covered a cardholder's liability, while others only fulfilled any financial obligation unsatisfied by corporate agreements or personal insurance.

Approximately 30 percent of car renters accepted the CDW. Some wished to avoid any hassle with car agencies trying to recoup a damaged car's repair costs. Others feared increased car insurance rates resulting from claims filed on a rental car. Some worried about the "loss of use" risk that their insurance policies did not pay for. Others bought the CDW because they could not afford to wait for a reimbursement claim on potential repairs that a car-rental agency would require them to cover immediately. On the other hand, many employers advised their employees on business trips not to purchase the CDW.

The price of a CDW more than quadrupled during the 1980s, with rates rising from $2–$3 per day in 1980 to $8–$12 per day by 1990. On an annualized basis, the daily premium charged was higher than the equivalent private auto insurance coverage; private insurance typically cost $1 per day versus the $10 CDW charge. In 1987, renters spent an estimated $500 million on CDWs, covering $260 million in vehicle damage. One regional car-rental company made $2 million a year in profits from CDW revenue in the Boston area alone. When car renters began to receive more liability coverage from other sources, rental companies tried to recoup their revenue losses with price increases. When American Express offered collision coverage to all cardholders using its credit card for rental transactions, Hertz and Avis responded with price increases of 2.5–5.0 percent, while Alamo raised prices 20.0 percent.

Several media investigations unearthed high pressure tactics used by car-rental companies and their agents to persuade customers to accept the CDWs. One car-rental company required any customer refusing the CDW to sign another waiver that warned him or her about the potentially negative consequences stemming from such a refusal. Another agency handed out contracts with the CDW accept box precircled for a customer's initials. Some car-rental companies placed a several thousand dollar hold on each customer's credit card to cover potential damages. Other firms encouraged acceptance of CDWs by broadening a customer's financial responsibility to include a car's theft or vandalism. Some firms even demanded immediate payment for repairs. One incident reported in *The Wall Street Journal* described how some travelers were prevented from boarding their plane until they financially compensated for car repairs.

REGULATION OF CDWs

Regulators had long debated the appropriateness of CDWs. In 1986, the National Association of Insurance Commissioners (NAIC) tried to gain broad acceptance of voluntary guidelines to regulate CDW charges. In 1988, large CDW price increases and frequent reports of CDW price gouging by car-rental companies finally prompted state legislators to introduce bills regulating or banning the sale of CDWs. Many felt that car-rental companies used CDWs to unfairly subsidize low car-rental rates. In June 1988, the Illinois legislature passed a bill limiting a car renter's collision damage liability to $200. That August, California introduced legislation that placed a $9 ceiling on the daily CDW charge car-rental companies could demand. By 1989, over 20 states were considering similar rulings, although many states later modified or dropped these rulings in response to industry pressure.

Regulators also began to question the advertising techniques used by car-rental companies and their agents. The National Association of attorney generals passed advertising guidelines in March 1988 requiring companies to disclose prominently extra charges in their advertising. As one attorney general said, "It sets a real price for consumers so they can shop car-rental agencies."[3] Such guidelines paved the way for suits against several companies for false advertising. For instance, in 1988 the FTC negotiated a consent decree with Alamo, after charging that "the company was too sporadic in telling customers who reserved by phone that they had to pay a mandatory fuel fee."[4]

The proposed regulations divided the car-rental industry. The four major car-rental companies, after initial disapproval, supported these initiatives and encouraged the elimination of CDWs. As one industry executive said, "Rather than have regulation, we chose to support elimination (of CDWs)."[5] Some, such as Hertz, placed advertisements stating their positions (see Exhibit 3). Smaller companies, such as Alamo, lobbied intensively against the proposed regulations, which they believed would place them at a competitive disadvantage to the major firms. Larger firms, they felt, had deeper financial pockets with which to cover car-repair costs. In addition, these smaller independents believed that they would incur greater revenue losses than the larger firms, since the independents served disproportionately more of the price-sensitive leisure rental market.

---

[3] Johnnie R. Roberts, "States Seek a Crackdown on Deceptive Car-Rental Ads," *The Wall Street Journal*, December 8, 1988, p. B1.

[4] Johnnie R. Roberts, "FTC Cracks Down on Car-Rental Firms after Similar Efforts by State Officials," *The Wall Street Journal*, December 30, 1988, p. B1.

[5] Buck Brown, "Rental Car Firms Change Stance on Collision Waivers," *The Wall Street Journal*, June 5, 1990, p. B1.

EXHIBIT 3 Hertz Newspaper Advertisement

Car Renters'
BILL OF RIGHTS

When you rent a car, assert your rights. You are entitled...

To be treated fairly and honestly in all aspects of your car rental experience and to a prompt redress from the car rental company if it fails to live up to your standard for service.

To rent a clean, well-maintained car.

To be advised in advance through the advertised price and quoted rate of the total cost of the car rental, exclusive of state and local sales taxes. Not to be confronted later with add-on charges such as mandatory gas charges or airport fees that were not included in the advertised quoted price.

To a full and honest explanation in advance of all restrictions that apply to the car rental price or terms of rental, such as geographic or mileage limitations.

To know that you can obtain comparative car rental information from your professional travel agent enabling you to decide which company offers the best value.

To a well-informed professional rental transaction. To be advised by the car rental company of the facts that benefit you. For example, you may not need collision damage waiver if your personal auto insurance provides adequate car rental coverage.

To have a free choice regarding car rental options without encountering transaction delays or penalties resulting in cash deposits.

Hertz believes these truths should be self-evident.

When you rent a car, you should know exactly what you're getting into.

This car renters' bill of rights, which has been endorsed by ASTA, the American Society of Travel Agents, will ensure that you do. After you read it, you'll know when you're being treated fairly, and when you're not.

If you feel your rights as a car renter have been violated, contact your rental car company or the Better Business Bureau. So the next time you rent a car, assert your rights. Because now that you know what they are, you'll have a much easier time standing up for them.

ASTA Hertz is a member of the American Society of Travel Agents (ASTA), the world's largest travel trade association representing over 20,000 members in 129 countries, each of whom subscribes to the ASTA Professional Code of Ethics. Hertz and ASTA are leading advocates for the safety, convenience, and comfort of the traveling public.

Hertz

Source: *The Wall Street Journal*, January 17, 1989, p. C28.

REGULATION ALTERNATIVES

By 1989, legislators in many states were considering regulatory options that included CDW elimination, imposition of price ceilings, mandatory liability coverage through personal insurance, and increased regulation of promotional techniques.

Elimination of CDWs.   The alternative adopted by Illinois completely prohibited the sale of CDWs. This placed the liability burden completely on the car-rental companies. "Prohibiting CDWs may work better than regulation without causing us any more work," explained one government insurance regulator.[6] Advocates argued that this alternative would (1) require insurance costs to be borne by the rental company, (2) eliminate the need for regulators to police car-rental firms, (3) affect prices minimally as competition would restrain companies from increasing their rates excessively, (4) eliminate the opportunity for car-rental companies to inflate repair bills to renters, and (5) force companies to advertise car-rental prices more reflective of final charges. On the other hand, such a regulation would reduce a driver's incentive to care for his or her rental vehicle. It could also place smaller companies at a disadvantage since they would be unable to secure insurance at rates as low as those obtained by the major car-rental companies. If insurance costs were included in the general rental charge, this would penalize careful customers less likely to be involved in collisions as well as those already covered by alternative sources.

Price Regulation of CDWs.   Placing price ceilings on CDWs, it was argued, would reduce price gouging and allow car-rental companies to directly recoup some of their repair costs. Many legislators, however, were concerned about the monitoring and enforcement costs of such regulations. Others questioned the ability of legislators to determine a fair price for CDWs. For instance, small companies catering to higher-risk renters would be at a disadvantage if their CDW price ceilings were not high enough.

Mandatory Coverage by Personal Insurance.   Some states, such as New York, considered bills that would require all auto owners to retain provisions within their personal auto policies that covered damages to rental vehicles. Such legislation tried to clarify the ambiguity surrounding an individual's personal insurance coverage as applied to car rentals. A complication, however, was how to cover the many car renters who did not own vehicles and, therefore, did not have auto insurance.

---

[6] Meg Fletcher, "NAIC Advises States to Bar Sale of CDWs," *Business Insurance*, June 20, 1988, p. 1.

Truth-in-Advertising. Advertising guidelines requiring disclosure of CDW charges aimed to ensure that customers would not be surprised by unexpectedly high costs at the time of a car pick-up or check-in. Proponents argued that this would allow the customer to make a more informed choice, while forcing the car-rental companies to compete on a level informational playing field. However, some legislators questioned the outcome of this approach and debated how prominently CDW rate information should be displayed in car-rental advertising.

THE SITUATION IN 1990

In February 1990, 13 months after the Illinois bill went into effect, *The Wall Street Journal* reported that "Car-rental prices (in Illinois) in some cases have risen more than expected (up to 35 percent), rental companies are growing wary of whom they'll rent to, and some of the smaller companies that used to offer competitive rates are folding."[7] Unable to sustain the insurance costs, some car companies were delaying repairs on vehicles, creating a safety hazard "time-bomb" for future renters. Several companies also reported an increase in the frequency of collisions, allegedly because drivers realized they were no longer liable for damages.

Increased repair claims also changed the policies of credit card companies that since 1987 had offered additional collision damage coverage as a benefit to their cardholders. In April 1990, American Express ceased offering car-rental collision insurance to corporate cardholders working at major companies. While American Express insisted that the insurance was dropped since these corporations already had their own coverage, some experts believed that the real reason behind the move was the service's unexpectedly high costs.

SOURCES

Benham, Barbara Tzivanis. "Riding the Rocky Road of CDWs." *Best's Review* 89, no. 6 (October 1988), pp. 64–68.

Brown, Buck. "Rental Car Firms Change Stance on Collision Waivers." *The Wall Street Journal*, May 16, 1988.

"Car Rental Companies: The Best and the Worst." *Consumer Reports*, July 1989, pp. 477–80.

Dahl, Jonathan. "American Express Drops Corporate Card Car Insurance." *The Wall Street Journal*, June 5, 1990, pp. B1–B2.

————. "Car Rental Firms Leave Drivers Dazed by Rip-Offs, Options, Misleading Ads." *The Wall Street Journal*, June 1, 1990, pp. B1, B10.

---

[7] Christopher Winans, "Laws to Trim Car-Rental Cost Due for Tuneup," *The Wall Street Journal*, February 8, 1990, p. B1.

Dahl, Jonathan, and Christopher Winans. "States, Car Rental Firms Collide over Damage Waivers." *The Wall Street Journal*, August 14, 1989, p. B1.

Fletcher, Meg. "NAIC Advises States to Bar Sale of CDWs." *Business Insurance*, June 20, 1988, p. 1.

Roberts, Johnnie R. "Credit Card Firms Expand Role in Car-Rental Insurance." *The Wall Street Journal*, December 30, 1988, p. B1.

————. "FTC Cracks Down on Car-Rental Firms after Similar Efforts by State Officials." *The Wall Street Journal*, December 30, 1988, p. B1.

————. "States Seek a Crackdown on Deceptive Car-Rental Ads." *The Wall Street Journal*, p. B1.

"The Collision over Collision Waivers." *Business Week*, May 1, 1989, pp. 96, 100.

Thomas, Charles M. "Rental Car Industry: A Tumultuous Giant." *Automotive News*, March 27, 1989, pp. 1, 78.

Winans, Christopher. "Laws to Trim Car-Rental Cost Due for Tuneup." *The Wall Street Journal*, February 8, 1990, p. B1.

Chapter 5.5

In the News

5.5.1 SANDOZ CORPORATION'S CLOZARIL TREATS SCHIZOPHRENIA—WHO IS GOING TO PAY $8,944?*

For 10 years, Ann Jones believed she was God and thought she controlled the weather. Diagnosed as schizophrenic, she was in and out of hospitals 35 times and was put on just about every anti-psychotic drug available.

Then, last year, she began taking a drug whose brand name is Clozaril and, finally, something worked for her. Her delusions disappeared. She hasn't been inside a mental hospital since. In the fall, the 37-year-old Ms. Jones plans to take courses toward a teaching degree. The change in her life, she says, "is really wonderful."

The drug, known generically as clozapine, is the most significant advance in anti-psychotic drugs in 20 years, and it offers hope to at least 200,000 people in the United States—many of them locked away in mental wards or roaming homeless in city streets—for whom conventional treatment has failed. But few of them are getting the drug or are likely to get it anytime soon. The reason is money: Clozapine costs $8,944 a year, and nearly everyone who stands to benefit from it is poor.

---

* By Ron Winslow, staff reporter of *The Wall Street Journal*, May 14, 1990. Reprinted by permission of *The Wall Street Journal*, © 1990 Dow Jones & Company, Inc. All Rights Reserved Worldwide.

Rich Man's Drug

In many states, mental health agencies and Medicaid programs, strapped for cash, can't—or won't—pay for clozapine. Some private insurers are balking at coverage. Even where money is available for initial treatment, physicians are reluctant to prescribe the medicine without assurance that patients will be able to go on taking it.

"Clozapine is a rich man's drug for a poor man's disease," says Larry Lehmann, associate director for psychiatry at the U.S. Department of Veteran's Affairs in Washington.

The drug spotlights—much as the costly AIDS drug AZT has—the conflicts that arise between companies seeking to market and profit from new medicines and the welfare of patients who need them. It raises tough questions about trade-offs necessary when beneficial treatments also have potentially devastating side effects. And in the near-term, at least, it poses an economic challenge to a health care system already saddled with huge costs. Lawyers around the country are contemplating legal action to require states to make clozapine available to those who might benefit. At the current price, that could cost somebody $2 billion.

As a consequence, the nation's mental health system, which already spends more than $7 billion a year to treat schizophrenia, has been in an uproar ever since Sandoz Pharmaceuticals Corporation introduced the drug on February 5. The company packages the drug along with a mandatory and expensive blood-monitoring system designed to detect a side effect that could otherwise be fatal to as many as 2 percent of patients. Without its proprietary system, Sandoz says, some patients will die and the drug will inevitably be pulled from the market.

The blood monitoring is the more expensive part of the package and, because of it, critics say, few will be able to afford the drug, anyway. So state mental health leaders, Medicaid officials, pharmacists, members of Congress, and the secretary of veterans affairs have mounted an intense, and thus far unsuccessful, effort to force Sandoz to uncouple the drug from the blood-testing program—or at least itemize the costs—and cut the price. The issue is the subject of a major forum today at a meeting of the American Psychiatric Association in New York.

"People are desperate to use this drug," says Mona Bennett, the deputy commissioner for mental health in Massachusetts. "We can't *not* use it." But treating the state's eligible patients would cost $5 million, "which we simply do not have."

Millions of Sufferers

Schizophrenia is a mysterious, little-understood mental disorder that typically strikes people in their late teens and early 20s. It affects about 1 percent of the population, or about 2.5 million Americans. On any given day, schizophrenics occupy 25 percent of the nation's hospital beds, according to a study by John Talbott, a psychiatrist at the University of Maryland.

Its victims suffer from paranoia, hallucinations and delusions—they hear voices, converse with telephone poles, send brain waves through televisions and radios, and believe secret agents, presidents, or aliens are out to kill them. Psychiatrists call these the "positive" symptoms. The "negative" symptoms include apathy, lack of motivation, and physical and emotional withdrawal.

About 25 percent of schizophrenics suffer only infrequent psychotic episodes, and another 50 percent can be treated adequately with such drugs as Thorazine, Haldol, Mellaril, and Prolixin. These medicines, however, usually don't alleviate the negative symptoms that rob schizophrenics of their ambition, and they cause nasty side effects—stiffness and restlessness in more than 60 percent of patients, and more severe twitching and involuntary body movements, called tardive dyskinesia—in about 20 percent of patients.

The remaining 20 to 25 percent—perhaps as many as 500,000 people—don't respond to any conventional medication, or develop side effects so severe that they can't take the drugs. Considered "treatment resistant," they live lives that amount to "a roller-coaster ride through hell," as one patient describes it.

The trip sometimes starts in private institutions, where costs can amount to $200,000 a year or more and can thus quickly deplete insurance benefits and family resources. Unable to hold even menial jobs, patients often end up on public assistance. Many are either confined in state mental hospitals or admitted so frequently that the wards become a second home. As many as 20 percent attempt suicide.

Sandoz is the U.S. subsidiary of Sandoz Ltd., the Swiss drug giant, which first developed clozapine in 1961 and introduced it in Europe 10 years later. The drug sparked a great deal of interest in the United States in 1988, when Herbert Meltzer, a psychiatrist at Case Western Reserve University in Cleveland, John Kane of Long Island (N.Y.) Jewish Hospital, and other researchers published a study showing that the drug worked far better than traditional treatments for many hard-to-treat schizophrenics—and essentially without debilitating side effects.

For the first time, a drug relieved the negative symptoms of schizophrenia, giving patients back their interest in the world around them. Many have been able to live independently and hold jobs. "They come out of the woodwork," says Dr. Meltzer. "They want to experience pleasure. That is one of the key advantages to this drug. It's definitely a medical breakthrough."

But it isn't a cure. At least 40 percent of the targeted patients don't respond or can't take it; for the lucky 30 percent to 60 percent, levels of improvement vary widely. The drug must be taken indefinitely. And nearly all patients need intensive psychotherapy and social and vocational rehabilitation if they are to re-enter society. "One patient compared herself to Rip van Winkle," Dr. Meltzer says.

The drug's biggest drawback is that it can kill people. Sandoz learned that the hard way in 1975, when several patients in Finland died, victims of virulent infections that developed after clozapine induced agranulocytosis, a condition that blunts the body's ability to produce infection-fighting white blood cells. Sandoz yanked the drug from the market temporarily. Clinical trials in the United States were canceled.

In the mid-1980s, the FDA agreed to reconsider clozapine. And, on the basis of the "amazing" results of the 1988 study, says Paul Leber, director of the agency's neuropharmacological drug division, the FDA took steps to approve it despite the danger. Through the mid-1980s, Sandoz says, 43 patients died among 112 who developed agranulocytosis worldwide. (More recently in the United States, 18 of 1,800 users developed the condition; but it was successfully reversed in each case when patients were taken off the drug.)

"Everyone involved understood that there would probably be deaths," Dr. Leber says. "The question was, is the bang big enough to make it worth this kind of risk. The [FDA's expert advisers were] fairly convinced that this was a dramatic thing."

The agency was even more enthusiastic when Sandoz decided that the drug would be dispensed only in concert with a monitoring system. In approving the drug last October, the FDA says it didn't designate a specific approach, but to Sandoz, there is only one—its own Clozaril Patient Management System—and that is at the heart of the furor.

The company negotiated exclusive contracts with Baxter International, Inc.'s Caremark home care division to take weekly blood samples from each patient and to dispense the drug, and with Roche Biomedical Laboratories, Inc., a subsidiary of Hoffmann-La Roche, Inc., to analyze the blood for white cells. No other company, agency or hospital can deliver the medicine, and each patient has to submit to a blood test each week. "The motto is: 'No blood, no drug,'" says a Caremark employee.

The price—no matter how much of it the patient is taking or where in the United States he lives—is the same nationwide: $172 a week, $8,944 a year. At that price, annual revenue could ultimately reach at least $600 million. Sandoz's annual U.S. pharmaceutical sales currently total $750 million.

Sandoz says the drug will eventually save states thousands of dollars per patient over the $66,000 it costs on average to treat hospitalized schizophrenics for a year. But states maintain that any savings are long-term at best. Vacated beds will be filled with other patients. "To save money, we have to close a wing," one official said. And patients on clozapine will need new therapy, housing, and rehabilitation, all of which cost money too.

"This is the most expensive treatment we've encountered," says Dr. Stephen Shon, medical director of California's mental health department. "We don't have any history with a drug that has a whole laboratory attached to it," adds Norwood Knight-Richardson, assistant director of the state psychiatric institute in Alaska, where winter storms are a daunting problem for home care teams heading to remote villages to draw blood and dispense clozapine.

In Oklahoma, the cost of treating eligible patients would exceed the state's total mental-health budget. Texas, which ranks 48th among the 50 states in per capita spending for the mentally ill, would have to budget almost $100 million a year. For California, it could be $300 million. In South Dakota, despite Sandoz's one-price-fits-all policy, officials say they are contending with Caremark over transportation costs to reach patients in remote areas.

Critics charge that there is more marketing than medicine in the "system," that it is a clever ploy that helped speed regulatory approval and that will camouflage hefty profit in a package price—before the company's exclusive right to market the drug runs out in 1994. While they agree that blood monitoring is necessary, they maintain the Sandoz system is unnecessary and much too expensive. Doctors and hospitals routinely monitor patients on other medicines—including AZT and some cancer drugs—at least as life-threatening as clozapine. The VA's Dr. Lehmann says his agency can do the blood work for $1.86. Doctors and pharmacists also say the system pre-empts their clinical judgment.

Moreover, Sandoz sells the same drug in Europe at prices as low as $20 to $32 a week, according to several reports, and without requiring the same blood-monitoring frequency. "We think we're getting the short end," says Tom Ahrens, senior consulting pharmacist for Medi-Cal, California's Medicaid program. "The whole country is."

Sandoz has rebuffed all efforts to negotiate. The VA, for instance, proposed its own monitoring system, with a computerized "lock-out" to prevent the dispensing of the drug to patients whose blood hasn't been tested. Medi-Cal said it would pay $117 a week for the package. Sandoz said no to both. The company has also refused to itemize the costs of the package, thus confounding insurers, Medicaid programs, and other payers, which usually consider medication, home care, doctor visits and lab fees separately in determining how much to pay in reimbursement.

For its part, Sandoz says its aim is to protect patients and the drug. The different pricing and monitoring in Europe reflect local regulatory costs, policies, and price controls. Besides that, in the United States, "we want to and can meet a higher standard of patient safety," says Gilbert Honigfeld, Sandoz's director of scientific communications, who has supervised clinical research on clozapine since 1973.

But Sandoz stands firm on its U.S. price. The company, Mr. Honigfeld argues, deserves a fair return on a drug it pursued despite long odds against marketing approval. "People forget we're a business," he said, "we're not a charity."

Sandoz won't sanction other monitoring systems, he added, because it would be liable for their quality under the FDA-approved labeling. A strict system is necessary, the company and some psychiatrists say, because schizophrenic patients are particularly hard to track, and many state mental health programs are already understaffed. Even in carefully designed clinical trials, some patients inadvertently went several weeks between blood checks, Mr. Honigfeld says, which is evidence that no matter how conscientious a hospital, certain patients will slip through the cracks.

"If there were a number of deaths, we would feel compelled to take Clozaril of the market," Mr. Honigfeld says. "It would be a tremendous loss for the many other patients who don't develop this problem."

Stuck in the crossfire are the patients. Hardly thrilled with the price, the National Alliance for the Mentally Ill, an advocacy group—mainly patients' families—is reluctant to criticize the company. "I don't know whether the company has priced this fairly," says Laurie Flynn, executive director of NAMI. "I just want it to be available." And she thinks the cost controversy raises another issue.

"The Medicaid system is willing to spend $50,000 a year on kidney dialysis," per patient, she says, "but they don't want to spend $9,000 on schizophrenia. We feel there is a stigma, that there's a feeling these people aren't worth it."

Currently, about 4,000 patients are on clozapine, including 1,500 who began the treatment as clinical research subjects. Sandoz is continuing to carry the research patients "while the states are getting their act together," Mr. Honigfeld says. So far, about 15 state Medicaid programs pay for the drug, and 23 mental health agencies have earmarked funds for it.

Sandoz projects its first-year sales at 8,000 to 10,000 patients. While the total market ultimately depends on how much those who pay the bills can afford, Mr. Honigfeld sees it topping out at about 70,000.

Some students of the subject think that estimate is too low. Dr. Meltzer, a champion of the drug who supports Sandoz's view of the controversy, says that at least 300,000 people in the United States could benefit from it. "I would hope that if it gets scaled up, the price could come down," he says.

As the first of a new class of drugs, clozapine may lead to better drugs without such potentially dire side effects—or expensive monitoring systems. Scientists and major drug firms already are working with sister compounds that look promising. But products are at least three to five years from the marketplace.

For now, the standoff has created questions so vexing that some doctors think it is unethical to treat impoverished patients with clozapine. For instance, New York state has budgeted $2 million of mental health funds for clozapine, mostly for patients confined to hospitals. Those who get well enough to leave the hospital would look to Medicaid for coverage. But so far, it won't pay. Even if it did, patients who find jobs could quickly earn enough money to lose their Medicaid eligibility—and then not be able to afford to buy the drug that keeps them well enough to work. Says John Oldham, chief medical officer for New York's mental health agency: "The result you want from this drug puts you in a tremendous dilemma."

5.5.2   U.S. PROBES WHETHER AIRLINES COLLUDED ON FARE INCREASE*

Amid mounting concern about rising air fares, the Justice Department's antitrust division is investigating whether some airlines might have colluded on a fare increase earlier this fall.

The department has asked several major carriers to turn over internal information about how ticket prices are set.

The scope of the federal investigation isn't known, but officials at several major carriers privately confirmed that they are complying with the request for documents. The airline executives said the Justice Department appears to be focusing on a fare increase announced by AMR Corporation's American Airlines on September 18. The fare increase, which went into effect September 29, was quickly adopted throughout the industry.

Amy Brown, a Justice Department spokeswoman, said prosecutors sent documents known as civil investigative demands to carriers "within a short period of time after" the September 29 fare hikes. She said the investigation is to determine whether "there was any agreement among two or more of the airlines in connection with the September 29, 1989, increase in airline ticket prices." She declined to identify the airlines targeted "or any other specifics," including what action prosecutors are considering.

American Airlines said it had complied with the U.S. request. A spokesman added: "There was absolutely nothing to indicate that there was any impropriety."

---

* By Asra Q. Nomani, staff reporter of *The Wall Street Journal*, December 14, 1989. Paul M. Barrett contributed to this article. Reprinted by permission of *The Wall Street Journal*, © 1989 Dow Jones & Company, Inc. All Rights Reserved Worldwide.

The probe has caused some alarm among airline executives, who say it isn't clear to them what the government suspects.

The rapid consolidation of the airline industry in recent years has raised concerns in many quarters about declining competitive forces and the increased potential for collusion. Several congressmen have criticized the way carriers appear to move in lockstep with many price increases.

Besides American Airlines, Pan Am Corporation's Pan American World Airways also officially confirmed that it is cooperating with the inquiry.

In addition, industry people said most other carriers are complying with the demands, too. They include: UAL Corporation's United Airlines, NWA, Inc.'s Northwest Airlines, Trans World Airlines, Delta Air Lines, Texas Air Corporation's Continental Airlines, and Midway Airlines.

Officials of those companies couldn't immediately be reached for comment.

USAir Group, Inc., is also believed to be part of the investigation, but refused to comment last night.

The specific fare increase under scrutiny was an American Airlines-led boost pegged to the number of days tickets are purchased before departure: 14 days, $10 to $20; seven days, $30 to $80; and two days, $60 to $80.

The next day, September 19, American's competitors saw details of the proposal in a computer tariff data base they rely on for fare information. On September 20, Midway and TWA boosted their fares in line with the American Airlines plan. On September 21, Delta, Pan Am, and Continental followed suit. Over the next several days, United, Northwest, and USAir matched.

This price-setting pattern is exactly the type of behavior that has become increasingly controversial in recent months. It would be illegal if such a fare increase occurred because the airlines colluded in some way.

The American Airlines spokesman denied that any collusion had taken place. "We make our decisions independently. What other carriers do is their business," the spokesman said.

Some congressional leaders and antitrust experts have asserted that such behavior by the airlines suggests that they are colluding—not necessarily in person, but by signaling each other through the sophisticated computer networks they have developed. "They don't wink, blink, or nod, but what they're doing looks like tacit collusion," says William E. Kovacic, a former antitrust attorney at the Federal Trade Commission.

Details about the Justice Department's inquiry have unfolded in recent weeks as airline officials complied with the department's demands for all data related to their pricing actions around the time of the American Airlines' proposal.

The Justice Department's demands relate to how the airlines determined daily fare changes during the period in question. In response, airlines chronicled their pricing changes and included related financial or market studies, memos, and personal notes, according to airline executives.

The airlines also were asked to identify the names, positions, and job descriptions of staff and executives in pricing departments. They also are providing names of superiors in the chain of command.

Initially after deregulation, fares fell sharply. But the impetus for lower fares was a wave of young discount carriers that put pressure on the industry to lower costs. Today, few such carriers remain, and the consolidation of the industry has given powerful market clout to a few major competitors.

In the past few years, the trend has been toward higher fares. Although fares have risen only slightly this year, concern about the potential effects of industry consolidation remain.

There have been several recent fare-related federal studies. Most, led by the General Accounting Office and the Transportation Department, have centered on whether airlines tend to gouge customers after building fortress hubs of operations. But most of those have been studies, rather than investigations.

Until now, the government hasn't paid much attention to the way that airlines go about setting their prices. In this Justice Department inquiry, several airline executives said that they are being asked for detailed pricing action that they've never been forced to provide before.

According to people familiar with the Justice Department probe, it's possible that the department may be trying to piece together whether the country's airlines are acting improperly by using their daily fare changes as signals about how they plan to set their prices or as devices to prompt rivals to price their seats a certain way.

This sort of case is difficult to prove, and even antitrust attorneys and policymakers are divided on what is unlawful. Some argue that industry use of signaling would suggest only tacit collusion, at the most.

The Justice Department probe is markedly different from one in 1982, when it investigated the possibility of price collusion at American Airlines. In that case, the company settled—without admitting or denying guilt—charges stemming from a call that chairman Robert Crandall had made to Braniff's top officer. In that call, Mr. Crandall offered to increase his airline's fares 20 percent if Braniff followed suit. Braniff provided the Justice Department with a tape recording of the conversation.

The Bush administration's interest in the pricing issue was flagged September 20 during a Senate aviation subcommittee hearing. There, James F. Rill, chief of the Justice Department's antitrust division, testified that his department was conducting an airline investigation that included charges of predatory pricing, a practice that involves slashing fares below cost in order to drive rivals out of a market. The status of that investigation couldn't be learned last night.

The continuing inquiry into the fare increase initiated by American Airlines is considered a separate investigation that doesn't involve predatory pricing.

5.5.3 DEMAND FOR RUBBER GLOVES SKYROCKETS— PROFITEERING DURING AIDS CRISIS SUSPECTED*

NEW YORK—The medical glove market, already stretched thin, is getting even tighter.

Reflecting the acquired immune deficiency syndrome crisis, prices for such gloves, and for the latex they're made of, have bounced as high as three times year-ago levels.

A growing number of producers, distributors, traders, and consumers also suspect that the surge in prices reflects profiteering in the markets for gloves and for raw latex tapped from rubber trees.

Demand, of course, accounts for much of the pricing pressure, as a wide variety of workers—from municipal employees to police and health service workers—have increased their use of gloves because of fear of transferring infection to other patients or to themselves.

"Nurses can wear an average of 8 to 10 pairs a day," says Edward Sun, vice president for marketing for the New York unit of Taiwan's General Pacific Corporation, which brokers and supplies rubber gloves and other medical equipment.

10 Billion Gloves a Year

Because of such ballooning demand, the United States may now use as many as 10 billion latex

---

* By Peter Truell, staff reporter of *The Wall Street Journal*, June 9, 1988. John Berthelsen in Singapore and Helen White in Thailand contributed to this article. Reprinted by permission of *The Wall Street Journal*, © 1990 Dow Jones and Company, Inc. All Rights Reserved Worldwide.

and vinyl examination gloves a year, compared with about 2 billion annually just a couple of years ago, estimates Joe Fleming of New Jersey medical distributor Med Mark.

That's led to higher prices for gloves and for latex, headaches for purchasing agents, and complaints of suspected profiteering, price gouging, and other unethical practices. "It's been terrible. I feel like calling the attorney general about it," says Renatte Hechenberger, director of materials at New York Infirmary–Beekman Hospital's procurement department. "From what I see there's profiteering going on."

Recently, the hospital has been paying about $75 a case for a thousand single latex or vinyl examination gloves, compared with about $55 or $60 a case a year ago. "Other places are having to pay $90 to $100 a case," says Ms. Hechenberger, who is spared such higher prices for the moment because she has long-term contracts. Beekman uses 100,000 exam gloves a month, compared with 20,000 a month a couple of years ago, she says.

In Phoenix, Arizona, Art Mires of medical supply company Medical Companies of America says he is paying 10 cents or 11 cents a glove (or $100 to $110 a case), compared with 5 cents to 6 cents a glove (or $50 to $60 a case) a few months ago.

Fearing infection from an accidental scratch or cut, surgeons, who wear more expensive latex gloves, now increasingly add to the growing demand by donning two or three pairs of gloves before an operation, hospital officials say. Beekman now goes through 5,000 pairs of surgeon's gloves a month, compared with half that number a couple of years ago.

Beekman recently had to pay $264 for a case of 200 pairs of surgeon gloves on the open market, compared with its long-term contract prices of $83 and $64 a case, because of a temporary shortage.

Outstrips Demand for Condoms

Many analysts originally expected a sharply rising market for condoms in the face of the AIDS

threat. While there's been some increase, demand for rubber gloves has caused the largest problem. "There's an incredible immediate shortage because of the crisis of AIDS. Usage has increased phenomenally," says Mr. Mires.

Med Mark's Mr. Fleming says he no longer has to deliver medical gloves; customers are so eager to get supplies that they rush to pick up gloves when he calls them.

U.S. producers also report a tight market for gloves. "Our Texas manufacturing operation [which makes latex exam and surgical gloves] is running 24 hours a day, 365 days a year," says Jeff Leebaw, a spokesman for Johnson & Johnson, New Brunswick, New Jersey. In response to the demand surge, the company is adding two new machines and has canceled sales to a majority of its nonmedical and industrial customers.

A spokesman for Baxter Travenol Laboratories, Inc., Deerfield, Illinois, which makes well over a billion gloves a year, said the situation has been difficult for about a year. "We have been increasing capacity, but that takes a year or so," he said. A new Baxter plant in Malaysia will soon begin production; a second new plant is set to begin production next year.

Some distributors say market shenanigans are more common with smaller, recently arrived suppliers and with some of the newer foreign suppliers. The big U.S. manufacturers "have behaved well," says Buddy Dortch, vice president of a unit of Durr-Fillauer Medical, Inc., a big medical distributor based in Montgomery, Alabama. He says he's only experienced small and understandable price increases from the big U.S. manufacturers.

"We certainly haven't been able to get all the gloves we want. We've tried to supplement with imports from China and some other places," Mr. Dortch says. But unlike many others in the rubber glove market he believes "demand has peaked."

"Flakes" Enter Market

Such demand has attracted all sorts of buyers and sellers. "You've got a lot of flakes coming into the market. There's false reliability, and goods tend to go to the highest bidder," Medical Companies of America's Mr. Mires adds. He says he has lost money on letters of credit that he has paid to arrange but which have lapsed because suppliers haven't honored delivery commitments, preferring to take higher offers from opportunistic bidders.

A General Pacific official says prices for raw latex have risen to about $2,200 a metric ton, compared with only $600 a ton last August. She notes that the Taiwan press has suggested that the governments of Thailand and Singapore recently interrupted latex shipments, leading to suspicions of a latex cartel in the making.

Traders in the latex markets in Southeast Asia categorically deny such intentions. As one senior trader says, "demand has actually outstripped supply because it caught everyone unaware." Part of the problem is that an increasing amount of latex is diverted to local production of goods, such as tires and rubber sheeting. Local consumption of latex in Malaysia has increased over the past two years to an expected 115,000 tons this year from 100,000 tons in 1987 and from 80,000 in 1986, the head of one of the country's biggest rubber producing companies says.

More latex plants will soon be built. There are now 116 permits pending in Malaysia to build disposable rubber glove factories, according to a senior executive at one large local conglomerate. Indonesian and Chinese manufacturers also are racing to meet the rush in demand.

Industry sources in Thailand confirm the sharp increase in latex prices to $2,000 a ton from $800 to $850 a ton in January. The rise, they say, is due to the winter season, when sap production falls, and to the tremendous increase in demand, particularly in the United States, for latex for rubber glove production. To ensure local supplies, some Thai latex users have tried unsuccessfully to pressure their government into banning latex exports, local industry sources said.

The latex shortage in Thailand and other big latex-producing countries probably won't diminish quickly. Trees take seven years to reach maturity, and chemical stimulation of older trees hasn't been that successful. To help ease the problem, some latex now used elsewhere can at least be diverted to glove manufacture, some Southeast Asian industry officials said. For example, some substitution can occur with synthetic rubber replacing latex to make tires and some other products.

5.5.4 WHO WINS WITH PRICE-MATCHING PLANS?*

It seems as though it should be good news for shoppers: Big retailers increasingly are promising to match the lowest advertised price a shopper can find.

But there's a cloud in all this silver lining. The marketing pitches are largely a boon to the stores, drawing customers by giving them what can be a false sense of security.

When a store pledges to match a competitor's advertised prices, it isn't promising that all its prices are the lowest in town. What's more, such stores expect only a small percentage of shoppers to try to collect on price-matching promises.

"Retailers have gone into the business of selling price insurance," says Leo J. Shapiro, a market researcher in Chicago. A price-matching pledge, he adds, amounts to "an insurance policy that shoppers won't feel foolish."

Benefits for a Select Few

Critics question the fairness of the policies, which allow merchants to cut special deals with only the most conscientious comparison shop-

---

* By Francine Schwadel, staff reporter of *The Wall Street Journal*, March 16, 1989. Reprinted by permission of *The Wall Street Journal*, © 1990 Dow Jones & Company, Inc. All Rights Reserved Worldwide.

pers. "That's the deceptive part," says Robert Kahn, an industry consultant and newsletter publisher who often criticizes retailing practices. "Retailers don't really have an intent to sell for lower prices [than competitors] or they would meet that price for everybody."

Ivan Png, a pricing specialist at the Graduate School of Management at the University of California at Los Angeles, says price-matching policies actually give merchants "a way to keep prices a little higher for the loyal customers, while giving a lower price" to new customers the store is trying to attract. "It's a way to make more money," he adds.

Price-matching pledges proliferated in the early 1980s, as retailers responded to heavier competition and a growing bargain consciousness among shoppers. The tactic was first used in the cutthroat consumer-electronics, auto-supply, and general discount-store businesses, but it spread. So many stores began using the policies as a marketing pitch that mainstream merchants had little choice but to start making the claim, too.

Late last year, Montgomery Ward & Company expanded its price-matching policy from its electronics and auto-supply departments to all items in its stores. And on March 1, Sears, Roebuck & Company, the nation's largest retailer, instituted a similar pledge as part of its move to a competitive policy called "everyday low pricing."

"We think it would be uncompetitive not to have a price-matching policy when many of our competitors do," says Thomas E. Morris, vice president of marketing at Sears's merchandise group. Sears, he says, considers its pledge a way "to communicate to the customer a confidence that the prices are good throughout the store."

Price-matching policies typically require shoppers to produce a competitor's ad showing a lower price for an identical item. Most stores also offer to match or beat their competitors' advertised prices for 30 days after a purchase.

Retailers say they are responding to the fact that consumers nowadays compare prices more often than in the past and wait for sales to make purchases, particularly with big-ticket items. Offering to match a competitor's price gives merchants "a way of intercepting these shoppers," says Sid Doolittle, a partner in the Chicago retail consulting firm of McMillan Doolittle. "It's an important sale-closer."

But retail industry executives and consultants readily concede that few shoppers actually bother to collect on the price guarantees.

Some companies claim that this is because their prices are truly competitive. But others acknowledge that most shoppers simply don't want to go to the trouble of doing the necessary research to get what they believe will be only a small price differential. "I don't think the average person has the time to go out seeing if they got the very lowest price in town," says Sears's Mr. Morris.

John Gray, a 41-year-old Chicago banker, is typical. "There may have been something that was $10 cheaper," he says of his purchases in recent years of a video-cassette recorder and a television. "But on a $200 or $300 purchase, my time is worth more than that."

Mr. Doolittle agrees. Last December, he bought a 13-inch RCA color television from Montgomery Ward for $239. After convincing himself that that was "the best price" he could find at the time, he says, "I didn't look back. . . . It's too much trouble to read ads for a month. That's a lot of bookkeeping."

Price-matching policies are also more limited than they first appear, because they usually apply only to "identical" items. Appliances and electronic goods are among the easiest merchandise to compare. But clothing and household goods often carry private labels, meaning they are made exclusively for one store. Sears, for example, still sells mostly house brands, though it is adding national brands at a furious pace.

Advertising a price-matching policy apparently does work, though. In surveys during the past year, Mr. Shapiro's Leo J. Shapiro & Associates found that offering to match a competitor's prices made a store seem more attractive to as many as two out of three consumers.

Special Attraction Is Lost

Still, the offer can lose its value as a marketing tool if it's made by too many stores. In Southern California, Carter Hawley Hale Stores, Inc., took down signs describing the price-matching policy at its Broadway department stores about a year ago, because its competitors had adopted similar policies. "It was one thing when we first started doing it," in 1982, a spokesman for the chain says. "But it became an accepted practice, so you don't need to advertise it anymore. The customer knows that everybody does it."

Some stores try to gain an edge by offering to refund more than the difference between their prices and any lower prices their competitors may advertise. Sears's Tire America chain promises to refund 125 percent of the price difference.

Ultimately, merchants may need a new message, however—like selection, service, or convenience. "What many leading retailers have discovered," says Paul A. Koenigsberg, an executive with the Management Horizons retail consulting unit of Price Waterhouse, "is that you don't have to have the very lowest price."

Why Do Companies Succumb to Price-Fixing?*

Jeffrey Sonnenfeld
Paul R. Lawrence

When Ben Franklin wrote *Poor Richard's Almanac* and the words, "A little neglect may breed great mischief," he did not have price-fixing in mind. To the 47 executives in companies in the folding-box industry convicted of price-fixing, however, the words must seem tailored to fit. In those companies convicted under antitrust laws in 1976, there were not enormous incidents of collusion in which the executives were involved, but, rather, small incidents involving junior managers and salespeople who were unaware of or unaffected by top management's policies about illegal profits. The authors of this article review those external and internal pressures that endanger a company's ethical standards. They extensively quote folding-box executives to illustrate the industry and company conditions that are a natural breeding ground for collusion. The most critical factor in preventing collusion is that managements unambiguously foster the kind of professional pride that is repulsed by any form of illegal profits.

CAUGHT IN THE LAW WEB

Down the centuries social analysts have frequently charged, "Laws are like spiderwebs, which may catch small flies but let wasps and hornets break through." As more and more corporations have been caught in the web of price-fixing laws, however, this charge has lost its punch. Senior business managers in industries that have never before known these problems, as well as previous offenders, are probably more concerned now about their corporate exposure to being indicted and convicted of price-fixing than they were in any other recent period.

The reasons are not hard to find. As federal agencies, the courts, and Congress respond to the heightened post-Watergate expectations of the public, the law enforcement net has been substantially strengthened.[1] Instead of hearing protests over the legal immunity granted to the large and powerful, one now hears the anguish coming from the reverse direction. One can regularly read about prominent individuals and organizations that are overwhelmed by the stiff penalties they have incurred for behavior which may have been customary business practice in the past but which now violates social and legal standards.[2]

The costs of violating price-fixing laws are very high: lawyers' fees, government fines, poor morale, damaged public image, civil suits, and now prison terms. Justice Department statistics indicate that 60 percent of antitrust felons are sentenced to prison terms.[3] Thus, for very pragmatic reasons as well as for personal convictions, America's top executives are searching for fail-safe ways of meeting legal requirements. While top executives strongly complain about increasing government interference, they also acknowledge, "We operate through a license from society which can be revoked whenever we violate the terms of the license."

Executives in large decentralized organizations, however, find it increasingly difficult to carry through on their intentions. The considerable time and money corporations spend developing positive public images can be wasted by the careless actions of just one or two lower-level employees. At the same time that organization size and complexity increase, top executives find that the law imposes on them additional responsibility for the business practices of their subordinates.

Executives tremble over what may be going on in the field despite their internal directives and public declarations. One CEO well expressed the frustration common to executives in convicted companies:

> We've tried hard to stress that collusion is illegal. We point out that anticompetitive practices hurt the company's ethical standards, public image, internal morale, and earnings. Yet we wind up in trouble continually. When we try to find out why employees got involved, they have the gall to say that they "were only looking out for the best interests of the company." They seem to think that the company message is for everyone else but them. You begin to wonder about the intelligence of these people. Either they don't listen or they're just plain stupid.

---

[1] "Carter Trust Busters," *Newsweek*, September 26, 1977.

[2] *United States* v. *Park*, 421 U.S. Court 658 (1975); Tony McAdams and Robert C. Miljus, "Growing Criminal Liability of Executives," *Harvard Business Review*, March–April 1977, p. 36.

[3] Timothy D. Schellhardt, "Price-Fixing Charges Rise in Industry Despite Convictions," *The Wall Street Journal*, May 4, 1978, p. 31.

Some executives we interviewed in researching this article believe, with the CEO quoted, that their employees who collude in price-fixing are just not listening or are plain stupid. In our view it is less likely that the employees are deaf or stupid than that many well-meaning, ethical top managers simply are not getting their message down the line to loyal alert employees.

To better understand this lack of communication as well as other forces contributing to employees committing unlawful acts, we thought that it would be enlightening to look at the unfortunate experience of the forest products and paper industry in the midst of antitrust litigation. Looking just at antitrust cases in 1977, one can see that the paper industry was hit with separate prosecutions for price-fixing in consumer paper, fine paper and stationery, multiwall bags, shopping bags, labels, corrugated containers, and folding cartons. In early 1978, over 100 suits have been filed against the industry.

In addition, a U.S. grand jury has been gathering information on competitive practices in the industry at large—which many suspect is part of a probe into industry collusion to restrain supply.[4] In fact, *The Wall Street Journal* recently stated that the paper industry is gaining the reputation as the "nation's biggest price-fixer."[5]

The folding-box litigation has, by far, been the most damaging (see Exhibit 1). The Justice Department has described this case as the largest price-fixing one since 1960. It is hard to understand how socially responsible companies could ever have found themselves in such a nightmarish situation. To find out, we discussed the various pressures and conditions in this industry with 40 senior, division, and middle-level executives. Our investigation concentrated on the predicament of the large forest products companies that derive about 4 percent or 5 percent of their total company sales from folding-carton revenues.

The shock for those companies, with strong and well-publicized ethical positions, is perhaps most severe. In case the reader is skeptical, our interviews with the senior people in these companies left us without a shred of doubt about the sincerity and completeness of their personal commitment to legal compliance. In fact, the top people we spoke to in the major forest products companies desperately want to know how and why they got on the wrong side of the law, so they can be sure it never happens again.

HOW IT CAN HAPPEN

Before we discuss the factors that create a price-fixing prone industry and organization, we would like to point out that the various problematic situations

---

[4] "13 Paper Concerns Face Price-Fixing Charges," *New York Times*, December 23, 1977, p. D5; "Two Paper Firms Are Convicted in Price-Fixing," *The Wall Street Journal*, November 27, 1977, p. 3; "Indictment Cites 14 Paper Makers for Price-Fixing," *The Wall Street Journal*, January 26, 1978, p. 3; Morris S. Thompson, "Aides of Box-Making Concerns Sentenced to Prison, Fined in Price-Fixing Case," *The Wall Street Journal*, December 1, 1976, p. 4.

[5] Schellhardt, "Price-Fixing Charges Rise," p. 1.

EXHIBIT 1   Costs of Ambiguous Policies

In late 1976, a federal judge imposed fines, probation, or jail terms on 47 of 48 executives in 22 companies charged with and found guilty of price-fixing violations in the folding-carton industry. In terms of the numbers of defendants, this case was the largest price-fixing one since 1960.

Of those convicted, 15, including chief executive officers, were sentenced to brief prison terms, from 5 to 60 days, and were individually fined as much as $35,000. Of the remaining executives, 17 were fined from $500 to $30,000 and placed on probation. The remaining 15 executives were fined between $100 and $2,500. The 22 companies were initially fined $50,000 each, the maximum fine for a misdemeanor violation. The maximum fine now for a felony violation of antitrust law is $2 million for each violating company.

Following these criminal convictions, the companies faced 45 civil suits filed by customers seeking damages for alleged overcharges. Over the past two years, many of these same companies have been inundated with charges of criminal price-fixing involving felony and misdemeanor violations in virtually every one of the converting ends of the business. One chief executive officer reported that his folding-carton division's past five years' earnings had been surpassed by just the legal fees involved in this case. The cost to image and company morale is incalculable.

---

that contributed to this unhappy end are certainly not unique to the paper industry. One can easily draw parallels between the paper industry's difficulties and the situations leading to price-fixing in other very different industries. For such a comparison, we will at times glance at the 1960 electrical contractors' conspiracy. We hope, too, that no one will read this article without reflecting on his or her own company's situation.

Price-Fixing Prone Industry

Many economists would consider the folding-carton industry to be one of the least likely to spawn a price-fixing conspiracy. The industry's very diffuse structure is the complete antithesis of the tight-knit oligopoly, which, economists tell us, breeds collusion. Of the over 450 box-making companies, the larger ones control only from 5 percent to 7 percent of the market; only one company controls near 10 percent.

With this number of companies, one would think that the rivalry among them would be so intense that it would preclude any mutual understandings and tacit agreements. Yet companies representing 70 percent of the $1.5 billion in annual industry sales were convicted.

In fact, the number of companies in the industry is one of the factors that tempted some businessmen to abandon the rugged competitor role and adopt "a more statesmanlike attitude toward competitors," as one executive euphemistically puts it. The market was, simply, badly crowded. Other pressures toward collusion were the job-order nature of the business and the fact that the products were undifferentiated.

Crowded and Mature Market

In the late 1950s and early 1960s, as the expansion of prepackaged and frozen foods kept the market growing at about 7 percent a year, the folding-carton business attracted new entrants. With low barriers to entry, competitors of all sizes saw this area as a great opportunity. Traditionally dominated by small family-run box-making shops, the industry became attractive to very large forest products companies, which integrated forward. These large companies first supplied the paperboard for box making and then began to compete with their customers further down the line in making the actual boxes themselves.

The tendency toward overcapacity in paperboard production tempted these large paper companies to look on folding boxes as a way to unload excesses. Some blamed the softening of the box market on this attitude, claiming that "the big companies did not care about box prices because they were making their profit back at the paperboard mill."

Also harmful to the market in the intervening years was the halt of super-market expansion as well as the growth of the use of substitute containers, such as plastics, which eroded the market share for paper containers. The industry is now very mature and has even suffered revenue as well as profit declines.

These declines place great pressure on middle-level managers who are keenly aware that the constant use of existing capital equipment is the way to drive down unit costs. One general manager commented:

> Large volume is important because we didn't make the investment in more efficient equipment we should have years ago. We could have brought on more sophisticated equipment and been more efficient in the use of labor and style of production. However, we can't get the money now. Too much was invested in the paperboard mills and nothing in folding-carton plants. Financial analysts look at these past bad investments and the bad earnings here and refuse to look on this industry with a favorable eye. It's a bad cycle we're caught in.

Some say a shakeout is long overdue; others complain about vicious customers. Some managers in folding-box companies complain of the predatory influence of the large companies they supply. One division manager stated:

> This sector has been ripped off by big customers for a long time. Anything this industry has done has been more in defense than offense. Business is really dwindling, and we are even more dependent on pleasing the big customers we depend on. You really can't do a profitable business with a customer buying $30 million from one carton manufacturer. They will destroy you. . . . No one here is making much in this industry anymore. Now the pressures are not to make more money but to keep from going under. Price discussions between competitors are important just to keep from going broke. Our customers should be investigated instead.

When a manager feels his or her division's survival is in question, the corporation's standards of business conduct are apt to be sacrificed. In the 1960 electrical contractors' case the issue was also survival. A convicted General Electric division vice president explained:

> I think we understood it was against the law. . . . The moral issue didn't seem to be important at that time . . . it was a period of trying to obtain stability, to put an umbrella over the smaller manufacturers. . . . I've seen the situation change, primarily due to overcapacity, to almost a situation where people thought it was a survival measure. . . .[6]

Job-Order Nature of Business

In the folding-box industry cost-cutting practices are also hampered by the nature of the production process. Boxes generally are manufactured for short job orders. One general manager said:

> Those guys up in headquarters think making boxes is like making paper, but papermaking is just following recipes. No two boxes are the same for us. Even with soap boxes, there are diverse product specifications.

Each of these jobs is costed and priced individually. Since each order is custom made, the pricing decisions are made frequently and at low levels of the organization. One salesman illustrated how a job-order business exposes a company to low-level price collusion:

> Every order is a negotiation, even when we've got a contract. Dialogue on prices is always on your mind. Any time I've met with a competitor, whether at a trade association meeting or in a customer's waiting room, one of us will eventually crack a smile and say, "You son of a bitch, you're cutting my prices again. . . ." Sometimes things go on from there and sometimes they don't. I think our company has been stupidly naive. It is impossible not to have talked price at some time.

Undifferentiated Products

Finally, while job specifications vary greatly between orders, the skills and equipment are fairly undifferentiated between companies. Several executives we interviewed concur with the following statement from one vice president:

> Part of the problem is that we're not competing with a unique article here. Our bags and boxes aren't really any better or worse than those of our competitors. You don't really go out and sell the product. Salespeople don't have any special product to sell. The only way to get a buyer is to sell at a lower price. Thus competitors may think that the only way to make it is to get together and fix prices.

---

[6] John Herling, *The Great Price Conspiracy* (Washington, D.C.: Luce, 1962), p. 241.

With such factors as a crowded and mature market, declining demand, difficulty in cutting costs, and no company product differentiation, it is not surprising that profits have been bad. Lately, folding-carton profits, at best, have been running between 3 percent to 6 percent of sales. Several companies have folding-carton divisions that have not seen a real profit in years. Just in the time in which we conducted this research, three large box makers announced they were either selling out or closing up.

Collusion then may take place despite economists' doubts that it will succeed and despite company statements that legal compliance is mandated.[7] When we try to empathize with someone fighting for the survival of a sick business, we realize that the problem may be greater than employees that don't listen or are just plain stupid. Perhaps these people really believe that they are committed to the company's best interests. We heard one convicted executive explain in a quivering voice:

> The unhealthy state which characterizes this industry has of course afflicted this company as well. We're not vicious enemies in this industry, but rather people in similar binds. I've always thought of myself as an honorable citizen. We didn't do these things for our own behalf. It was presumably done for the betterment of the company.

It seems that the recognition of common goals can be shared within a large group of diverse competitors as well as within a close-knit oligopoly. Certainly not all industries face such adverse conditions. But many other industries face some combination of these circumstances, and management complacency in the face of these conditions could be very costly.

Price-Fixing Prone Organization

Our interviews clearly reveal that not all the factors contributing to price-fixing come from the industry, economic, and technical factors we have considered. Some come directly from the companies themselves and the subculture of the industry; some are built into personnel, pricing, sales, and legal staff practices.

Culture of the Business. In the electrical contractors' conspiracy, there were strong pressures to enforce the anticompetitive norms. A GE vice president describing the type of coercion placed on an executive who resisted the norms of collusion stated, "We worked him over pretty hard, and I did too; I admit it." One GE executive who was a target of this pressure from his colleagues

---

[7] W. Bruce Erickson, "Price-Fixing Conspiracies, Their Long-Term Impact," *Journal of Industrial Economics*, March 1976, p. 200; Almarin Phillips, *Market Structure, Organization and Performance* (Cambridge: Harvard University Press, 1962). The belief is that, as the number of companies increases, the probability of mutual understanding and anticompetitive agreement will decrease.

committed suicide.[8] In one recent folding-box case, some executives threatened others with physical violence if they resisted raising prices.[9]

Executives in the paper industry point out that people in the folding-carton business are not necessarily evil but are just people who have worked in a system with a history of very different ground rules. A convicted executive claimed that price-fixing was common practice in his business:

> Price agreements between competitors was a way of life. Our ethics were not out of line with what was being done in this company and, in fact, in this industry for a long time. I've been in this industry for 32 years, and this situation was not just a passing incident. That's just the way I was brought up in the business, right or wrong.

Another factor encouraging price-fixing arises when a company with one culture acquires another with a quite different one. In several companies convicted of price-fixing, senior executives acknowledge that rapid vertical integration brought their forest products companies into secondary converting businesses, which were little and poorly integrated.[10] One division vice president of a convicted company conceded:

> Our folding-carton units were like a bunch of geographic "left outs." The geographic separation was fantastic. The 15 individual plants were poorly coordinated and poorly managed. We just came along with our acquisition drive and then sent top management attention elsewhere.

The parent companies often naively assumed that business practice and ethics in the two companies would automatically be congruent even if there were no common heritage. As an illustration of the sort of side practices that may come with a business acquisition, the management of one large forest products company learned to its shock that the box-making company it had just acquired had been running a house of prostitution as a customer service for years. One vice president stated:

> The guys at the core of this conspiracy were acquired people from acquired companies and not part of our culture. That is just not the way we do business. Questions of ethics were never raised. We assumed that people do business ethically at our company. Apparently that was a simple-minded assumption.

Personnel Practices. On top of any other influences, the personnel practices used in many companies seemed actually to encourage people to engage in price-fixing.[11] In a number of the companies convicted, management almost

---

[8] Herling, *The Great Price Conspiracy*, p. 249.

[9] Schellhardt, "Price-Fixing Charges Rise," p. 1.

[10] The recent acquisition spree may exacerbate this problem. See "The Great Takeover Binge," *BusinessWeek*, November 14, 1977, p. 176.

[11] Gilbert Geis, "White Collar Crime: The Heavy Electrical Equipment Antitrust Case in 1961," in *Criminal Behavior Systems: A Typology*, eds. Marshall B. Clinard and Richard Quinrey (New York: Holt, Rinehart & Winston, 1967), p. 150. Here it is explained that structural factors are

exclusively appraised individual performance on the basis of profits and volume. And not only advancement but also bonuses and commissions, which often exceeded 50 percent of base salary, were dependent on these measures. A division manager spelled out these practices:

> In the folding-carton division, our local salesmen have all been compensated with a base salary and a commission. Some bonus programs account for 60 percent of someone's compensation. People have been evaluated on the basis of profit and how forcefully they can execute a price increase. Thus, if he does this by price agreement with competitors, he'll build profit and price credits and get a reward.

So, instead of seeing the top people explicitly and officially acknowledge the difficult industry conditions, many of the lower officials see only strong pressures and inducements to "get the numbers no matter what." As one executive of a convicted company sadly acknowledged, "We've definitely run into some problems from jamming our corporate targets down everyone's throats."

It is not surprising that junior managers perceive such company-induced pressure as conveying top management's intent. One sales manager explained that any other corporate messages that came down from other company executives were only from ". . . staff guys and were not related to my evaluation and advancement. If it is known that the operating chief of your area wants business conducted in a certain way, it seems that is what really counts."

One chief executive officer who spent a lot of time thinking over his company's involvement in the recent conspiracy summed up the effect of these kinds of pressures:

> I think we are particularly vulnerable where we have a salesman with two kids, plenty of financial demands, and a concern over the security of his job. There is a certain amount of looseness to a new set of rules. He may accept questionable practices, feeling that he may just not know the system. There are no specific procedures for him to follow, other than what other salesmen tell him.
>
> At the same time, he is in an industry where the acceptance for his product and the level of profitability are clearly dropping. Finally, we add to his pressures by letting him know who will take his job from him if he doesn't get good price and volume levels. I guess this will bring a lot of soul-searching out of an individual.

Pricing Decisions. Another area that caused vulnerability in companies convicted of price-fixing was their decentralized price-setting mechanism. A GE division manager jailed for price-fixing made this point before a senate subcommittee 15 years ago:

> I think decentralization exposed the flanks a great deal more. It made the exposure greater. . . . It has put more pressure on the manager because he has complete re-

---

major contributing elements to criminal behavior. Executives who were uncooperative with price-fixing training were transferred by the company. These issues are more fully discussed in: Laura Shill Schrager and James J. Short, Jr., "Toward a Sociology of Organizational Crime," presented at the American Sociological Association meeting, Chicago, August 1977.

sponsibility in a smaller organization. Yes, I think decentralization has certainly contributed to the forces that tend to make [conspiracies] a reality.[12]

Descriptions of this earlier conspiracy indicate that the job-order nature of this equipment business increased the frequency of these decisions and the degree of competitor contact.

In the paper industry, we found that senior managers assumed pricing was done as it was for commodity products, where any changes were large, rare, and received top management attention. The prices for folding boxes, however, like other job-order business, are heavily influenced by very junior managers and salespeople. This was true even though a general manager was nominally held responsible for pricing. Because managers made pricing decisions frequently, the number of diffuse influences on these decisions are great. As a result, one salesman explained:

> Everyone gets his nose into pricing issues. You're nothing unless you get into the pricing mechanism. There are maybe 10 guys that can get involved in every decision, including clerks, plant managers, cost estimators, and salespeople. Yeah, the responsibility rests ultimately with the general manager but that's horseshit! Everyone wants a piece of the action and an awful lot of people get their hands into prices unnecessarily.

Thus, people can get involved in pricing issues for status reasons alone and can be tempted to use their influence to impress and help friends in other companies. It is also clear that the more decentralized pricing decisions become, the more difficult it will be for top managers to control collusion.

Trade Associations. Over two centuries ago, Adam Smith, the dean of free market economics, warned: "People of the same trade seldom meet together, even for merriment and diversion, but the conversation ends in a conspiracy against the public, or in some contrivance to raise prices."[13]

In keeping with this prediction, a sales manager of a convicted paper company complained that industry trade association activities can directly contribute to a company's involvement in conspiracy:

> You must limit the occasion of sin. You can't put yourself in a position of contact with competitors. I've dropped contact with personal friends in competing companies since this prosecution started, and I should have dropped such contacts sooner. I don't go to industry meetings at all. Now, finally, this whole company frowns on industry bullshit!

Though many executives will not now talk to old friends in competitive companies, some general managers disagree with these assessments. They feel that there may be truth to the suspicion that these trade meetings give an

---

[12] "Administered Prices," Hearings before the Subcommittee on Anti-trust and Monopoly of the Committee on the Judiciary, U.S. Senate, April 12 to May 2, 1961, p. 17065.

[13] Adam Smith, *The Wealth of Nations.*

opportunity for price-fixing; but as one manager argued: "Just the same, these associations have a great value, and it's too bad to see them in trouble. A lot of lobbying relevant to the industry happens there. Perhaps participation has been too liberal . . . it's just a big party."

Virtually all the senior managers surveyed agree "that it's hard to talk about the costs of production without discussing prices." An executive at one of the relatively uninvolved companies proudly stated that his company has sharply curtailed the number of company employees participating in trade association meetings:

> I think that trade associations have some value, but the risks are fairly high. We've cut back dramatically, and now only one or two people per division attend the meetings. The trade meetings are limited to the top people. Some second echelon employees just loved to go to these meetings and take their wives. They wanted to be entertained. I've always believed that familiarity breeds attempt [sic]. For each point on the asset side, trade associations have two points on the liability side.

Similarly, executives in the electrical contractors' case condemned the collusionary influence at the trade association meetings. In 1960, a GE vice president stated to a congressional committee:

> The way I feel about it now, sir, the way my company . . . has been damaged, the way my associates and their personal careers have been damaged and destroyed, the way my family and myself have been suffering, if I see a competitor on one side of the street, I will walk on the other side, sir.[14]

Corporate Legal Staff.   Several corporate lawyers reluctantly acknowledge that their performance was related to their company's convictions. While in many companies antitrust memoranda and periodic legal lectures became more frequent after the landmark 1960 electrical contractors' conspiracy, legal departments in the paper companies still tended to react to problems, rather than to anticipate them. The corporate counsel at one of the convicted paper companies explained: "In the past, we practiced what we thought was our proper role, and that was to respond to legal questions. We sometimes did big group things like lectures, but we never sat down to talk the subject through with small groups of managers."

Similarly, another vice president of legal affairs conceded that, although his department is quite heavily involved in antitrust education now, "We've only really become anticipatory since the folding-carton case."

Thus, the lawyers did not serve as a source for legal advice to avoid problems but allowed people to navigate to the brink of prosecution. A division manager in one of the convicted companies summed this up by giving his impression of the performance of the legal division: "I can tell you that the lawyers here are a damned smart bunch of guys who can get you out of trouble once you've gotten into it. But we sure need more of an active force."

---

[14] "Administered Prices," p. 16663.

HOW TO AVOID IT

We have examined both the industry and the company factors that contributed to one industry being so badly caught up in price-fixing. It is time to take stock of the implications of our inquiry for managers who are resolved to avoid such traumatic experiences. How should managers respond to this predicament? The lessons are, in fact, fairly easy to perceive but at times very difficult to put into practice.

It is obvious but not trivial to say that managers in competing companies who would be fail-safe should move to the opposite poles from each and every one of the contributing factors we have identified. (Exhibit 2 lists these factors and their opposites.) But, of course, recognizing danger signs provides no more than a start toward solving the problem. Which factors are relatively controllable and which are not? What specific practices have we identified in our study that were helpful? What ideas and concepts can be useful in achieving compliance?

Managing the Market Conditions

Certainly very little in the market environment is under management's direct control. One may conclude that the conditions of the folding-carton industry are sufficiently hostile that a company would be justified in leaving the business entirely. Since four large companies have left the business over the past year,

---

EXHIBIT 2   Danger and Safety Zones of the Factors Contributing to Price-Fixing

Industry Characteristics

Danger zone	*Safety zone*
Overcapacity	**Undercapacity**
Undifferentiated products	**Differentiated products**
Frequent job-order pricing	**Infrequent commodity pricing**
Contact with competitors	**No contact with competitors**
Large, price-sensitive customers	**Small, price-insensitive customers**

Company Characteristics

Danger zone	*Safety zone*
Collusion culture	**Top management modeling and training**
High rewards for profits	**Multidimensional rewards**
Decentralized pricing decisions	**Centralized pricing decisions**
Widespread trade association participation	**Constrained trade association participation**
Reactive legal staff	**Anticipatory legal staff**
Loose, general ethical rules	**Specific ethical codes with auditing**

---

obviously some involved executives have reached that very conclusion. In our interviews, senior managers at one forest products company expressed sheer relief at being "liberated."

Those who have remained are striving for cost control and product differentiation to allow for longer runs and greater pricing freedom. Only a few have as yet succeeded in this effort. Many executives complain that their company could never remove itself from the brutal paper carton market unless top management made a really major commitment to a new strategy. Most are unable to free themselves from the tradition of trying to be all things to all people. A vice president of legal affairs in one convicted company pointed to the superficial nature of some attempts to affect the market and shows how they can backfire:

> Everyone here is competing for the same sales. We wanted to somehow differentiate ourselves, so through the 1950s and the early 1960s we developed over 300 minor patents. These patents weren't really worth the time, but that was the way we competed then. Customers would insist that at least one other box maker be licensed under the patent so they wouldn't be so dependent on one supplier. That's how we then got involved in pricing discussions. When discussing royalties, prices became important issues.

A sales manager of one of the convicted companies reported that the larger companies did seriously try to segment the market into such areas as frozen food, beverages, cosmetics, and so forth.

But, said this manager, "Some independents would just continue to treat their businesses like general printing shops, and the large companies could never organize the market." Such a market allocation could, of course, still violate antitrust legislation.

Only a handful of companies seem to have succeeded in a product differentiation strategy. But the fact that a few have is not insignificant, and we will return to this point later.

Managing the Company Culture

As we talked to executives in the forest products industry, we of course asked about their experience with management methods that could help control the price-fixing problem. One of the consistent and early points that came up was the example set for the company by the behavior of top management. We found one of the most frequent approaches senior management uses to encourage legal compliance is to cite its record in regard to social responsibility.

Psychological research on obedience,[15] business research on employee morality, and common sense all indicate that the behavior of those in authority

---

[15] Stanley Milgram, *Obedience to Authority: An Experimental View* (New York: Harper & Row, 1974).

serves as important role models to others.[16] Unless top management projects consistent and sincere company commitment, operating practices will not change.

This commitment, however, is a necessary but not a sufficient factor to ensure compliance. The major forest products companies where we interviewed have a long-standing reputation for the expression of public interest commitment by senior executives. Each company has its own internal maxim for, "We believe that ethics start at the front office." Unfortunately, these statements tend to stop here as well. A vice president of a convicted paper company explained:

> When we were small enough and in a stable environment, people all knew each other by first names. We could communicate informally, and we were successful in molding behavior through modeling. People could resolve gray areas of decision making by reflecting on how their superiors would handle such an issue. But, with our very explosive growth of the last decade and a half, this old approach has become problematic. Can we still communicate corporate standards to a lot of people in the same way we communicated to a few?

A number of companies are actively developing some promising ways to go beyond the example of the front office.

General Management Signals.   Some executives talked very explicitly about the problem of changing the culture of a problem division. Having been burned in the past, the financial vice president of a convicted company has adopted a preventive approach. He has communicated new acquisition criteria to his investment brokers. He is now at least as interested in information about a company's ethical practices as in its financial performance. One chief executive officer said that he and his top managers learned the hard way from troubles soon after making an acquisition. He felt that retraining management is helpful:

> Managing these disparate cultures in the face of institutional transition is difficult. You have to change the self-perpetuating norms. Given our hard-charging acquisition policy, maintaining our corporate beliefs is hard. We have to move in and go with the old management still in place. Managing newly acquired divisions is like trying to raise adopted kids. An adopted child after age five may still need his new parents to teach him when to go to bed and when to get up.

Some companies find that, just as training acquired personnel is helpful to reorient business practices, training salesmen to sell product features rather than to sell for price alone also helps change practices. If a company manages to develop special mechanical packaging systems, special graphic design abil-

---

[16] Raymond Baumhart, *An Honest Profit* (New York: Holt, Rinehart & Winston, 1968). This survey, based on 1,710 subscribers responding to a *Harvard Business Review* poll, found most subordinates ultimately accept the values of chief executives. See also Archie B. Carroll, "Managerial Ethics: A Post Watergate View," *Business Horizons*, April 1975, p. 75.

ities, or some other means of differentiation, salesmen must be given the knowledge needed to sell these features. Well-trained salesmen often can find ways to compete in terms of special delivery services, inventory aids, and design suggestions. As one sales manager put it, "Only lazy sales managers rely on commissions to get their salesmen to sell."

Another tool of general management is the evaluation and rewards system. The companies that were least involved in the price-fixing conspiracy compensate their sales forces on straight salary and evaluate on the basis of volume, rather than of price level or profit. Several companies convicted of price-fixing have now adopted this method and are in the process of learning to evaluate people along broader dimensions.

Price Decision Procedures.   One of the factors contributing to price-fixing we cited previously was the practice in some of the companies studied of allowing specific price decisions to be influenced by salespeople and others below the general management level. In effect, because of bonus and commission arrangements, junior people were acting almost as profit center managers. Since these were the same people who might well see their competitors' sales representatives in the customers' waiting rooms, the scene for illegal action was set.

Some managers in the companies we studied have been reviewing their practices in this regard and making tighter definitions of who can legitimately take part in pricing decisions. It takes careful analysis of the multiple sources of relevant information concerning prices as well as an explicit commitment procedure to make such rules both workable and prudent.

Code of Ethics.   Attempts to move beyond top-level role modeling have led some executives to prepare codes of ethics on company business practices. In some companies this document circulates only at top levels and, again, the word seems to have trouble getting down the line. Even those documents that were sent to all employees seemed to have been broadly written toothless versions of the golden rule. One company tried to get more commitment by requiring employees to sign and return a pledge. A senior vice president in this company complained that even though a copy of the law is also sent along:

> This stuff isn't all that valuable. In the first place you're only sending the employee what the law says and you're not telling him or her anything new. Second, it's not signed in blood! You haven't committed him to any behavior; he just recognizes that he has to sign the card to work.

An employee convicted of price-fixing agreed with these comments and questioned the view that price-fixers can be helped by ethical statements:

> A code of ethics doesn't do anything. I thought I had morals. I still think I do. I didn't understand the laws . . . not morals. What might to me be an ethical practice might have been interpreted differently by a legal scholar. The golden rule might be consistent with both views.

For codes to really work, substantial specificity is important. One executive said his company's method was successful because the code was tied in with an employee's daily routine:

> There is a code of business conduct here. To really make it meaningful, you have to get past the stage of endorsing motherhood and deal with the specific problems of policy in the different functional areas. We wrote up 20 pages on just purchasing issues.

Auditing for Compliance.   Once these more specific codes of business conduct are distributed, top managers may want more than a signed statement in return. Individuals can be held responsible if they have been informed on how to act in certain gray areas. The company can show its commitment to the code by checking to see that it is respected and by then disciplining violators.

Several companies are developing ways to implement internal policing. Some executives think that audits could hold people responsible for unusual pricing successes as well as for failures.[17] Market conditions, product specifications, and factory scheduling could be coded, put on tables, and compared to prices. High variations could be investigated. One division vice president also plans to audit expense accounts to see that competitor contact is minimized.

Legal Training.   As we noted earlier, executives in the convicted paper companies acknowledge that the lack of contact between them and company lawyers makes it hard to apply the law. Direct contact between operating managers and members of the legal staff seemed to be less frequent in the companies that were more heavily involved in the conspiracy. The legal division must overcome at least three barriers to take this more anticipatory stance.

The first barrier is a negative image. As advisers, lawyers must accept being seen as holier-than-thou naysayers. One general manager complained:

> I'm very critical of legal people in big corporations. Most corporate counsel is negative on any level of risk. They say don't take chances in new areas, when we should. They tell us not to sue, when we should. They don't want us to cause any waves because it's easier for them. If it were up to them, they'd say don't even get out in the market.

This statement indicates how important it is for operating managers to understand the legal constraints on their plans and for the lawyers to be sensitive to the pressures of operating managers. Senior management must take the initiative to legitimize both perspectives.

The second barrier, limited interaction, is a problem for lawyers when they play the detective role, which they must at times. In one convicted company

---

[17] William D. Hartley, "More Firms Now Stress In-House Auditing, but It's Old Hat at GE . . . Staff Doesn't Spare Top Brass Keeping Antitrust Vigil," *The Wall Street Journal*, August 22, 1977, p. 75.

we often heard comments such as: "Lawyers only come around when they're invited. That's only when we're in trouble. We could really use a lot more of a missionary effort from the legal department with more frequent visits."

Lawyers also complain that meeting people at infrequent lectures and formal visits rarely gives them the information that they seek.

Part of this problem is owing not only to the frequency of the visit but also to the level of the people visited. At many companies lawyers often meet with only top-level managers who are expected to spread the word through the organization. Unfortunately, the word rarely reaches the people in an organization who are the most vulnerable and who need to hear it most. One convicted sales manager explained:

> If you want to face facts, we never got any indication from above that what we were doing was wrong. I was never asked to attend any of the lectures our legal division gave. I guess only the general managers did. If any applicable information had ever been passed down to me or if there had been any support to ask questions from above, I don't know what I would have done. You can bet that, at the least, I would have begun to ask some questions.

The third barrier, boredom, stems from the educator role that the corporate counsel must assume. One lawyer in one of the convicted companies complained, "We really don't know how to teach this stuff without sending people off to the coffeepot." Another lawyer complained that only now, because the costs of prosecution have been so severe, are people starting to listen.

Some companies have developed successful legal programs by fostering very close contact between the general managers and the legal division. In one such program there are two lawyers who specialize in traveling around and meeting the general managers. The chief legal counsel added:

> Any whistle-blowing probably comes through the lawyers. This style of communication is essential in getting the point across. We try to be serious and sincere. Also the approach is important. A lot of smart legal departments used to start off with the first line of vice presidents and work up in their education program. However, these people often think that they're smarter than the lawyer; or else they may not have very good communication with their subordinates, so we try to get close to the danger line. If nothing happens in five years, they say we're paranoid, but with top management support we can continue.

Thus, even a successful program has problems of its own. If it works, people may not believe it was needed in the first place.[18]

Executives in another company, which was not involved in the conspiracy, agree with the need to tailor a program to the danger line of the organization. Outside counsel is extensively involved on two levels. First, attorneys meet

---

[18] These sorts of frustrations are frequently heard in legal conferences; for example, see Allen D. Choka, "The Role of Corporate Counsel," presentation at the Eighth Annual Corporate Counsel Institute, Northwestern School of Law, October 8 and 9, 1969.

with each salesman on a one-on-one basis. The lawyer digs up expense reports and other files and grills the salesman. This same procedure is then repeated at group and general manager meetings.

At the general manager and vice president levels, the legal staff puts on a simulated grand jury inquiry. In these dramatizations even the president sits on the witness stand to defend himself on the basis of documents prepared by his vice presidents. There is a great deal of tension surrounding these mock trials. The president of this company cited this trial as:

> . . . one of the most important ways we've sought to keep the organization sensitive to legal issues. We identify several hundred people with point-of-sales exposure and talk to a large percentage of that group. We're trying to get the lawyers to prepare a dossier and challenge each of these people. This confessional situation is a very intensive experience.

This procedure helps management spot problems so it can clear up misunderstandings before they become more serious. The possible interpretations of employee words and actions are made very clear. The president said that this sort of investigation on top of the usual lectures is needed to bring the message across:

> We've had attorneys giving their fire and brimstone talks to large groups for 10 to 15 years, and we have simply concluded that isn't strong enough medicine for this ailment. Our experiences in other parts of the company convinced us that this thoroughness is vital.

Several members of this same company told us that they feel more comfortable discussing these issues with outside counsel, as this plan provides. They prefer speaking to someone who represents broader legal expertise and who is not immediately tied in with the corporate hierarchy and internal pressure. The interrogation by a fresh outsider seems to bring more reality to the investigation.

Most of the managers in the company believe that communication with counsel is protected by attorney-client privilege, but recent court decisions suggest that, should the interests of the corporation differ from those of any executives, it is the corporation, in the name of the shareholders, not management, which really has the right of attorney-client privilege. Unless shareholders abdicate this right, management cannot be categorically protected in such communication.[19] The use of safeguarded channels of communication, however, whether they be lawyers or general ombudsmen, is important for individuals trapped by the questionable practices of superiors.[20]

---

[19] Howard E. O'Leary, Jr., "Criminal Antitrust and the Corporate Executive," *American Bar Association Journal,* October 1977, p. 1389; "Attorneys Privilege," *U.S. Law Week, Bureau of National Affairs* 46 (February 28, 1978), p. 2435.

[20] Helen Dudar, "The Price of Blowing the Whistle," *New York Times Magazine,* October 30, 1977, p. 41.

PROFESSIONAL PRIDE

Many industries share the exposures to price-fixing we have highlighted. And the problems of ensuring compliance increase in complexity as the list of contributing factors grows. Our review of the specific compliance methods that are being used in the forest products companies with the better records provides a good start toward the development of a fail-safe approach. In our interviews we also were searching for a promising general approach—perhaps a philosophy of management—that could infuse a company and serve as an antibody to thoughts of price collusion.

We believe we did find such a condition in one company. The evidence we saw was largely indirect, but it can probably best be characterized as professional pride. This company is one of the handful that is largely successful in developing a differentiated set of products. It is no accident. Even in the face of all the industry difficulties we have cited there exists a very strong belief that "if we're not smart enough to make reasonable profits without resorting to any form of price-fixing, we'll simply get out of the business."

This belief is translated at the individual level into "I'd rather quit than stoop to getting my results that way." In effect, this company's executives are making an old-fashioned distinction between clean, earned profits and rigged, dirty profits. It is literally unthinkable for them to want to make money the latter way. They have too much self-esteem.

Although executives and salespeople in this company widely share the strong code of behavior, it is not clear exactly how it has been disseminated throughout the organization. The best evidence is that when top managers emphasize professional pride and the distinction between clean and dirty profits, the commitment to achieve profits through legal means is clearly driven down the line. Such emphasis cuts out ambiguous signals that lead to junior people second-guessing top management's intentions.

Distribution Policy

Ethical Issues in Distribution

Frank V. Cespedes

"Distribution" typically refers to the ways in which a product or service reaches its end users. Some goods and services are sold directly to their ultimate buyers, while others pass through one or more intermediary (or indirect) channels of distribution on their way to end users. A common channel arrangement is:

Manufacturer → Wholesaler → Distributor → Retailer → Consumer

During the past two decades, the share of sales volume attributable to distribution intermediaries has grown significantly in many industries. According to U.S. Commerce data in the *Census of Wholesale Trade* reports of various years, wholesalers increased their share of total sales volume from about 50 percent in 1972 to 58 percent in 1982 (the latest year for which these data are available), while sales via manufacturers' direct sales forces declined from 37 percent to 31 percent during that period. During the 1980s, wholesale trade real growth increased faster than real growth in GNP in the United States and, according to many observers, will continue to do so at least through the 1990s. A number of factors account for this growth in distribution volume, including the increased costs of personal selling, the ancillary impacts of just-in-time inventory management systems on channels networks, the capital requirements and economies of scope inherent in the computerization of many distribution activities, and a concentration trend among distributors themselves.[1] In turn, these developments have meant a general escalation in the scale and complexity of channels relationships for many marketers, changes in the balance of power between suppliers and resellers in many industries, the emergence of new channel entities and modes of going to market, and the increased salience of distribution relations as a component of effective marketing at numerous companies.

---

[1] For a fuller discussion of these trends and their implications, see Frank V. Cespedes and E. Raymond Corey, "Managing Multiple Channels," *Business Horizons* 33 (July–August 1990), pp. 67–77.

These developments also raise a number of current and potential ethical issues in distribution that receive increasing attention by both managers and students of management. Specifically, the channel topics that have received the most attention in this regard are: (1) *direct marketing* practices (including direct mail, telemarketing, and direct-response channels of various sorts); (2) *trade promotion* practices, especially the increased prevalence of so-called slotting allowances in consumer goods channels; and (3) the allied channel topics of what are often synonymously referred to as *gray markets*, *diverting* practices, and *parallel imports*. This overview provides a brief introduction to the potential ethical issues embedded in each of these topics, while also outlining certain issues that are typically fundamental in channel relations and, hence, important to recognize in discussions of what is and is not ethical behavior in distribution.

DIRECT MARKETING

Direct mail, telemarketing, and new electronic direct-response channels have, in recent years, probably been the most salient area for raising issues of distribution ethics. The reasons for this attention are twofold.

One reason is the growth in the use of direct-marketing channels over the past decade. According to Roberts and Berger,[2] for example, by the mid-1980s U.S. companies as a group began spending more money on direct-mail vehicles than on network television advertising. According to the Simmons Market Research Bureau,[3] total mail order sales grew by about 15 percent annually from 1984 to 1990, while the number of direct mail shoppers in the United States rose by more than 42 percent. In 1989, about 91 million Americans—slightly more than half of the total adult population—shopped at least once by phone or mail. In the same year, telemarketing was an estimated $42 billion expenditure in the United States, with about half that amount spent for outgoing telephone sales calls and the other half representing incoming calls for purchases and customer-service activities. Finally, various kinds of broadcast, electronic media, and on-line information systems also are growing rapidly in availability and usage. Hence, the different distribution vehicles usually referred to by the term *direct marketing* now represent a large and growing portion of marketing attention, talent, and money.

A second reason for the interest in the ethics of direct marketing is the increased power and declining costs of the information technologies and consumer data bases that form the infrastructure for these channels. Progress in computer technology during the 1980s made it more economical for more entities to develop data bases, while the development of relational data base

---

[2] Mary Lou Roberts and Paul Berger, *Direct Marketing Management* (Englewood Cliffs, N.J.: Prentice Hall, 1989), pp. 11–15.

[3] See the data cited in "Delivering New Strategies," *Apparel Merchandising*, May 1990, p. 21.

techniques and structured query languages in software have made it much easier to cross-classify information. In addition, passing information between organizations is easier as computer networks and interorganizational systems become more common. Further, as personal computers and local area networks have diffused throughout industry, information search and transfer costs have often declined. These technological developments have allowed companies to create proprietary data bases of customers' demographic and shopping characteristics.

In turn, these technological developments are both supported by, and accelerate an interest in, so-called micromarketing campaigns or other forms of personalized target marketing. Major consumer packaged goods companies, for example, now use information from redeemed coupons and rebate forms to create data bases for targeted marketing of additional products. The goal here is to apply the new technology to create more targeted vehicles for reaching (ultimately, at the household level) customers deemed particularly attractive because of their shopping patterns and long-term profit potential. A recent publication by the Boston Consulting Group labels such efforts "Segment-of-One Marketing" and provides a representative summary of the vision behind many companies' direct marketing activities:[4]

> "Segment-of-One Marketing" brings together in a working relationship two formerly independent concepts: information retrieval and service delivery. On one side is a proprietary data base of customers' preferences and purchase behavior; on the other is a disciplined, tightly engineered approach to service delivery that uses the information base to tailor a service package for individual customers.
>
> Other options [besides data bases] for personalized communication are beginning to proliferate. Selective binding technology that makes it possible to customize magazines to individual subscribers is on the drawing boards. Videotext, point-of-purchase communication, and targeted co-op mailers are beginning to be available. Addressable cable TV is a technical, if not yet a commercial, reality.
>
> These new options will force marketers to come to grips with personalized communications. But they will work most powerfully for those who employ them in the context of an integrated Segment-of-One strategy.
>
> A successful Segment-of-One strategy involves more than experiments with data bases and direct mail—although these can be first steps. It requires a broad rethinking of the values a company provides to its customers and the way it approaches them. . . .
>
> From a competitive point of view, the implications will be dramatic. Economies of scale in production or product volume have eroded in many industries. Segment-of-One marketers will reestablish powerful scale economies in information, information management, service, and distribution. As a result, competitive advantage will tilt to those companies that simultaneously "own" the market and are able to satisfy individual customer needs.

The ethical issues raised about direct marketing channels tend to focus on issues of privacy, confidentiality, and intrusion.[5] According to the Direct Mar-

---

[4] Richard Winger and David Edelman, "Segment-of-One Marketing," *Perspectives*, no. 305 (Boston: Boston Consulting Group, 1989).

[5] For a detailed discussion of these issues, as well as a suggested framework for analyzing many

keting Association, for example, an estimated 7 million Americans receive automated telephone sales messages *daily*. Credit bureaus use data from their files to create new data bases, from which mailing lists of names and addresses are sold for micromarketing purposes. In related developments, several firms have developed businesses based on the cross-referencing of several credit bureau data bases as well as additional sources of information (e.g., motor vehicle records) about individuals. In the money-lending process, many banks routinely gather information about an individual's credit history; and much of this information, now made available to prospective creditors, is often also used for target marketing campaigns. These developments raise increased tensions between the dynamics of direct marketing channels and what Louis Brandeis in 1890 termed "the right to be left alone."

One result is that, by 1990, there were an estimated 500 pieces of legislation dealing with direct marketing pending in state legislatures, and at least two bills in Congress to curb telemarketing activities and the transfer of information in the credit industry. Further, increased consumer awareness of these issues has also prompted more self-examination (usually in the form of guidelines and "codes of ethics" intended to promote self-regulation) among marketers that develop and utilize such channels.[6]

However, one might also suggest that another set of ethical issues about direct marketing concerns the potential for exclusion, rather than individual intrusion, in this form of marketing channel. Here, I refer to the potential that, based on cross-tabulations of demographic information with individuals' shopping behavior and zip codes, certain groups can become isolated from increasingly important sources of product information, buyer-seller exchanges, and economic incentives. This issue is implicit in the potential scale and scope of direct marketing efforts in the 1990s; and it may ultimately reflect the logic of market segmentation in what many call an "information society" and its potential social consequences.

As an example, consider developments at Citicorp POS Information Services, a relatively new business unit in the Consumer Banking Division of Citicorp. For a number of years, Citicorp has been gathering information on the supermarket shopping habits of over 2 million households. The bank does this by working with retailers to hook up store checkout scanners to software programs that perform multiple functions, such as check/credit authorization and electronic funds transfer. Then Citicorp recruits shoppers to sign up for its electronic rebate program called "Reward America." The shopper completes

---

of the ethical implications, see H. Jefferson Smith, Jr., *Managing Information: A Study of Personal Information Privacy*, DBA dissertation, The Graduate School of Business Administration, Harvard University, 1990, from which I have borrowed the examples in this paragraph.

[6] For a sampling of industry views about the ethical issues involved, see Jo Anne Parke, "5 Marketers Speak Out," *Target Marketing* 13 (April 1990), pp. 22–24; Dan Fost, "Privacy Concerns Threaten Database Marketing," *American Demographics* 12 (May 1990), pp. 18–21; and John Stevenson, "Eavesdropping on the Privacy Issue," *Direct Marketing* 51 (July 1988), pp. 111–12.

a short survey that asks for demographic data and then receives a card that he or she can present to the grocery cashier each time that customer shops in participating stores. In the process, this customer becomes eligible for instant discounts (called "electronic coupons") or cash awards that can be used toward future purchases. The shopper also receives a monthly, mailed statement, and the individual's shopping "file" is fed into a computer at a Citicorp facility. By 1995, Citicorp POS (point-of-sale) expects 40 million households in its data base (for comparison purposes, note that this is about half of what the U.S. Census Bureau has in its computers); and the business goal is to utilize such information with the information it gathers in the course of banking activities (e.g., Citicorp has one of the leading credit card businesses in the world) to develop marketing and promotion vehicles for companies interested in more refined micromarketing campaigns.

Richard Braddock, the head of Citicorp's Consumer Banking division, notes that, "from a marketing point of view, our objective is to create a data base of household-specific buying patterns. . . . When integrated into a 'single source' presentation, taking into account the advertising and promotions consumers have been exposed to, this data base will allow us to satisfy the needs of three sets of customers—retailers and marketers as well as consumers."[7] Braddock notes a number of the benefits of such a data base (e.g., many consumers will get better targeted offerings as well as more individually relevant and convenient economic savings). He also notes one danger: "All this technology creates the potential for invasion of customer privacy. However, banks have long experience in collecting and packaging information and keeping it confidential. . . . We always make sure that customers understand their purchases will be recorded and used for marketing purposes."[8]

Beyond issues of privacy and confidentiality, however, a data base containing the purchasing patterns of individual households and utilized for various purposes by financial institutions, manufacturers, marketers, and retailers is a powerful tool. By definition, targeted campaigns exclude as well as include certain groups. People may have more or less access to the electronic coupons, rebates, information, and other economic advantages depending upon their incomes, zip codes, or any other criteria that users of such data develop. The danger is that exclusion from such exchanges may be unwittingly systemic (e.g., the danger that certain ethnic groups may be substantially under-represented in targeted campaigns),[9] widening the gulf between lower- and upper-

---

[7] Richard S. Braddock, "Keeping the Customer at the Fore," a speech delivered at the Conference Board's 1989 Marketing Conference (New York: The Conference Board, 1989), p. 10. For additional information, see Bill Purcell, "Citicorp's Super Info," *The Marketer*, September 1990, pp. 22–27.

[8] Ibid., p. 11.

[9] See, for instance, the views expressed in Peg Masterson, "Should Marketers Target Blacks More?" *Advertising Age*, July 2, 1990, p. 6; and Howard Schlossberg, "Hispanic Market Strong, but Often Ignored," *Marketing News*, February 19, 1990, pp. 1, 12.

income groups in society. This is particularly a danger, it would seem, with marketing channels so intimately connected to information technology: If individuals in lower-income areas have fewer opportunities to use computers and to access the relevant information services, this can lead to a new kind of marketplace illiteracy and disadvantage. Conversely, target marketing based on past purchasing patterns and tied to future discounts and other economic incentives can be a self-fulfilling prophecy, targeting "up-scale" consumers for economic incentives while excluding poorer groups from these sources of product information and exchange.

In one sense, such activities are merely a logical continuation of a longer-term trend in marketing: In broad terms, the story of consumer goods marketing in the United States in the 20th century is a story of continually increased market segmentation as targeted divisions in the market have become the primary focus of companies' efforts, rather than a single homogeneous market for a standardized brand or product form (e.g., the Model T in cars or Coca-Cola in soft drinks).[10] This trend has generally increased consumer choice and often resulted in more efficient distribution of goods and services; especially in competitive markets, the benefits for consumers usually have been permanent while the abuses have been real but temporary. Developments in direct marketing channels in the 1990s, however, are potentially on a much wider and more powerful scale than in the past. In banking, one controversial form of target marketing has long been known as "redlining." What is the potential for a more subtle but broader form of information redlining in the evolution and use of direct marketing channels in the 1990s?

TRADE PROMOTIONS

Another area of distribution in which ethical issues often are raised concerns trade promotions and, in particular, the practice of paying "slotting allowances" (often known as "street money")—that is, fees paid to retailers for allocating warehouse space or shelf space to manufacturers' products. As in the case of direct marketing channels, the level of activity in this aspect of channels relations increased significantly during the 1980s. In 1978, advertising accounted for 42 percent of marketing budgets at U.S. consumer packaged goods firms; by 1988, ad spending was 31 percent against 69 percent for promotions, and trade promotions accounted for nearly three quarters of this shift.[11] According to some published reports, a number of major packaged goods firms were reportedly selling 80–90 percent of their volume on deal (i.e., via specific trade promotions rather than manufacturer's list price) by the later

---

[10] See Richard S. Tedlow, *New and Improved: The Story of Mass Marketing in America* (New York: Basic Books, 1990).

[11] Donnelley Marketing, *Eleventh Annual Survey of Promotional Practices* (Stamford, Conn.: 1989).

1980s; and much of this product volume was placed via slotting allowances paid by the manufacturer to the retailer. Slotting allowances and other trade promotion practices raise issues concerning channel efficiency and consumer welfare as well as the uses made of increased channel power by different firms in supplier-reseller networks.

One issue is the extent to which these practices are (to use the dichotomy of one article on this subject) legitimate "incentives" or less-savory "ransoms." Most retailers clearly view these payments as incentives for dealing with the estimated 2,000 new items and 3,000 line extensions introduced annually in grocery stores by manufacturers. Each item means purchasing, stocking, labeling, and other transaction costs incurred by the store. In effect, many retailers claim, slotting allowances and other trade-promotion practices justly subsidize the retailers' costs and in effect act as a price-based market-clearing mechanism for allocating space. Many manufacturers, on the other hand, often view such payments as ransoms demanded by an increasingly concentrated and powerful retail trade that, in fact, often does not pass on these deals to consumers in the form of lower prices.

A second issue concerns the impact of these practices on new products and smaller firms at the supplier level of the channel. In 1989, for example, grocery store chains in the New England area reportedly were requiring slotting allowances of from $15,000 to $40,000 for each new-product introduction—fees required *in addition to* the more traditional trade allowances, such as cash discounts, free goods, or other terms and conditions. In other areas, fees of $70,000 or more were reportedly required to get a truckload's worth of a new product (with 6 SKUs—stock-keeping units) into just one 50-store chain.[12] Many smaller packaged goods manufacturers have argued that such practices discourage new-product introductions and innovation and, ultimately, work to suppress competition and consumer choice. Larger manufacturers, some claim, are better able to spread such costs and often can avoid paying slotting allowances because retailers know those companies can back their product introductions with multimillion-dollar advertising campaigns.

Finally, a third issue concerns the net impact of these practices on distribution efficiency, prices, and consumer welfare. One study has estimated that the increase in manufacturer and distributor costs in 1988 from trade promotions (including forward-buying and other practices as well as slotting allowances) amounted to about 2.5 percent of total retail sales.[13] This is a very substantial amount and, to the extent that these costs are passed on to consumers, represents added costs in the supply chain from manufacturer through retailer to consumer.

---

[12] Lois Therrien, "Want Shelf Space at the Supermarket? Ante Up," *BusinessWeek*, August 7, 1989, pp. 60–61.

[13] Robert D. Buzzell, John A. Quelch, and Walter J. Salmon, "The Costly Bargain of Trade Promotion," *Harvard Business Review* 68 (March–April 1990), pp. 141–49.

As with many other areas of distribution, trade promotion practices are especially complex. They have a legal dimension: as of 1990, the Federal Trade Commission was studying slotting allowances and use of the Robinson-Patman Act to prohibit this form of trade promotion was a possibility. They have a consumer-behavior dimension: consumers with the time and inclination to shop for bargains have probably enjoyed lower prices as a result of trade-promotion practices, while those whose shopping time is more constrained have probably paid somewhat higher prices on items affected by the increased distribution costs. They have a channel power dimension which, from one point of view, is the latest chapter in a half-century story of the "politics of distribution" among suppliers, wholesalers, and grocery retailers.[14] But as payments ultimately required and made by individual managers at various companies, slotting allowances and other trade-promotion decisions also have an ethical dimension that should not be ignored in analyses of their legal, marketing, and competitive impacts.

GRAY MARKETS

Gray markets involve the selling of products through channels of distribution that are not authorized by the trademark holder. It can involve unauthorized distribution of goods either *within* a market or *across* markets. Gray marketing occurs within a market when a manufacturer's authorized distribution-channel members sell the trademarked goods to unauthorized intermediaries who, in turn, distribute the goods to customers within the same market area. (In the consumer packaged-goods business, this practice is often called "diverting.") When gray marketing occurs across markets—and especially across international markets—it is called "parallel importing." Manufacturers increasingly produce and market products in more than one country, often establishing distribution networks in each country. Parallel importing occurs when goods intended for one country are diverted into an unauthorized distribution network, which then imports the goods into another country.

It is important to distinguish between gray market activity and the selling of counterfeit products, a distinction sometimes confused in discussions of distribution dynamics. Counterfeit products are not genuine and do not originate from the trademark owner. In the United States, such goods are subject to the provisions of the Lanham Act that cover trademark infringement. Counterfeit goods are illegal. In the case of gray market/diverting/parallel import activity, however, what is at stake is the legitimacy of the means by which the

---

[14] For a historical perspective on supplier-retailer relations in food retailing (and other channels of distribution), see Joseph C. Palamountain, *The Politics of Distribution* (Cambridge, Mass.: Harvard University Press, 1955).

products are distributed, not the product itself, which (in gray markets) is a genuine trademarked product.

Many well-known products have been sold through gray market channels: IBM personal computers, Seiko watches, Olympus cameras, Duracell batteries, Mercedes-Benz automobiles, and even Caterpillar tractors and excavators. Given the nature of the activity, exact figures concerning the scale of gray markets are clearly unavailable. Further, in what is essentially a form of product-market arbitrage (i.e., buying an asset in one market to sell it in another and thus profit from pricing discrepancies), individual gray markets tend to rise and fall depending upon changing market conditions. Nonetheless, estimates indicate that anywhere from $10–15 billion worth of goods flow annually through gray market channels in the United States alone. In consumer packaged goods markets, regional or "local" marketing programs have often increased diverting opportunities as products bought on deal in one market are transshipped to another part of the country. Internationally, exchange rate fluctuations coupled with global marketing programs that may produce standardized products (often, with multilingual labels and instructions) make parallel importation easier to sustain. In many industrial marketing situations, quantity discounts or negotiated "bid" prices, or both, significantly lower than manufacturers' book prices, are common. Bid customers can buy in large quantities and may sell some of the merchandise to gray marketers, who in turn sell to other customers who would otherwise have to buy at the higher book price.

As with the topic of slotting allowances, however, whether or not gray markets are fundamentally an ethical issue (as opposed to one that is more usefully discussed in terms of pricing strategies or buyer power) often depends upon what level of the distribution channel becomes the focus of discussion. Most manufacturers and many distribution intermediaries often regard a gray market as a breach of ethics as well as an economic disruption. For the manufacturer and its authorized distributors, a gray market usually poses several difficulties:

1. It upsets pricing policies in the channel and can conflict with prices on direct sales, perhaps eroding them as well.

2. If prices and margins erode, the manufacturer usually finds it harder to maintain dealer support and point-of-sale services.

3. For many industrial goods in particular, after-sale service is a prime source of revenues and profits, often yielding much higher margins than the sale itself. A gray market, however, tends to trigger unbundling of product sales from service income (i.e., the manufacturer's warranty and other service terms usually apply only to purchases through authorized channels of distribution), causing an eventual drain on the product's revenue stream.

4. A gray market can create customer dissatisfaction. While caveat emptor might seem to be a justified attitude for manufacturers to take toward buyers of gray market goods, competitive realities often mean that any product problems encountered by these buyers are still brought to the manufacturer's door.

Most discussions of gray markets have been focused on the problems they present to the manufacturer and its authorized resellers. As Duhan and Sheffet point out,[15] one reason for this focus is that

> ... most, if not all, of the legal and regulatory appeals about gray marketing practices have been filed by manufacturers and their authorized channel members. Additionally, they have formed a trade group called COPIAT (Coalition to Preserve the Integrity of American Trademarks) to fight gray marketing practices. Hence, the agenda for the debate of gray marketing activities has been set by entities seeking to have the practices eliminated. Even the use of the term "gray market" reflects the point of view that there is something "almost black market" or tainted about such practices.

By contrast, many intermediaries (i.e., those who would not otherwise have access to certain brands) and some consumer groups view gray markets as another form of cutting channel costs and lowering end-user prices. Having a product available from both authorized and unauthorized intermediaries may indeed erode distributor support, but it also puts downward pressure on prices. In addition, an economist might point out that a gray market is often one market mechanism for implementing price discrimination and market segmentation theory: Gray marketers (selling at lower prices and usually without ancillary support services) typically appeal to more price-elastic segments of a market than do the authorized distribution channels.

Nonetheless, when it develops, gray market activity tends to generate intense discussion among various channel members. The following issues concerning gray markets are often viewed as having important ethical implications for those involved:

- **Free-riding problems**. In a gray market situation, authorized channels are often put in the position of educating consumers about product features and usage while watching the customer eventually purchase the product from a lower-priced, unauthorized reseller. Authorized resellers often offer important services like advertising, product demonstrations, and point-of-sale as well as post-sale services. These functions involve time and expenses on the part of the authorized reseller. Gray marketers, however, enjoy a free ride on these customer-education and market-development activities. Indeed, many gray marketers, recognizing this, even honor manufacturers' discount coupons and try to coordinate their activities with manufacturers' advertising and promotion campaigns as a means of skimming the benefits of the authorized channel's marketing efforts.
- **Destruction of brand and channel equity**. Because the manufacturer and its authorized resellers have adopted these higher-priced/higher-service terms and conditions, they have built over time a certain amount of brand and channel equity. But this equity, perhaps built over a number of years, can be "unfairly" destroyed by free-riding gray marketers. An example concerns the

---

[15] Dale F. Duhan and Mary Jane Sheffet, "Gray Markets and the Legal Status of Parallel Importation," *Journal of Marketing* 52 (July 1988), p. 75.

situation facing IBM and its authorized personal computer (PC) dealers a few years ago. In the early 1980s, when PCs were new and unfamiliar products for most potential customers, IBM imposed relatively stringent requirements on its authorized dealers. They had to allocate a certain amount of store space for product demonstrations, keep a certain number of store personnel trained in its equipment (a not inconsiderable expense when product technology is developing rapidly), and maintain stock parts sufficient to sustain certain levels of service and repair. IBM's aim was to build a store of value in its PC product franchise and, through these point-of-sale services, encourage brand preference and win repeat business. Meanwhile, unauthorized retailers (perhaps the best-known example being 47th Street Photo in New York City) did not meet IBM's conditions. As consumers became more familiar and comfortable with the product, these unauthorized resellers' low-service/low-price selling operations essentially appropriated a portion of the brand value accumulated by IBM and its authorized channels of distribution.

• **Consumer protection issues.** Some gray market resellers (e.g., 47th Street Photo) offer their own warranty. But most diverters typically do not offer warranties. Further, because they have bought through unauthorized channels and, therefore, did not complete warranty cards or other required documents, these consumers often are not included in any subsequent product recalls or other notices from the manufacturer. Again, one may cite "caveat emptor" as the rule of the game for such buying practices. But, in practice, many gray market consumers simply do not realize that they lack warranty protection, or that a product defect has resulted in a recall by the manufacturer, until they have a problem with the product. Further, if the consumer does learn of a defect and recall, the consumer may also find that authorized dealers refuse to perform repairs or service for the gray market good.

• **Impact on channel relationships.** Finally, a fourth issue is what might be called the quality and "tone" of channels relationships. More than many other elements of marketing, distribution arrangements tend to involve longer-term commitments on the part of both supplier and reseller. As a result, personal relationships and trust tend to be especially important components of an effective, viable distribution network. A gray market, however, involves a series of unauthorized "shadow marketing"[16] transactions that, in turn, can set in motion a kind of ethical Gresham's law where bad behavior drives out good, lowering ethical standards across a broader range of supplier-reseller exchanges in the distribution channel. An example of this perspective is found in the following comments by an experienced observer of consumer-goods marketing practices:

> Twenty years ago, diverting was not regarded as respectable and was confined largely to HABA (health and beauty-aids) and coffee items. But today . . . almost all dis-

---

[16] I borrow the term from Sidney J. Levy and Gerald Zaltman, *Marketing, Society, and Conflict* (Englewood Cliffs, N.J.: Prentice Hall, 1975).

tributors are involved in buying from the diverting system. Previously, there were ethical restrictions associated with participating in the system. However, these have largely vanished because those that do not participate find themselves at a competitive disadvantage.

The future of diverting looks positive. An expanded infrastructure (i.e., electronic diverting networks) is now being put in place. Today there are at least three networks around the country where you can make a market in diverted products electronically and instantly. Five years ago, a diverting operation looked like a bookie joint—lots of phones, papers, a very confusing situation. But today you see big bucks, lots of incentive, and a new entrepreneurial opportunity.[17]

From a strategic point of view, gray markets often reflect a common set of dynamics as a market matures and a product category becomes familiar to buyers.[18] As customers become more confident about the details of product usage, they tend to place less value on the support programs offered by the manufacturer and its authorized distributors. What they once purchased as a system of product and ancillary support, they often unbundle into discrete purchases and then seek channels that sell on price while furnishing little product support. A gray market often signals the emergence of this group of customers. Meanwhile, both the manufacturer and its authorized distributors usually have significant investments and interests in continuing to market the full package of product and support through a more selective distribution network that excludes the low-price/low-support channels. The manufacturer has received important point-of-sale support services through this arrangement (especially important for any planned product introductions in many categories), and the authorized distributors receive some assurance, through the limited intrabrand competition of exclusive or selective distribution, that their point-of-sale efforts will be rewarded through sales at their location rather than that of a lower-priced competitor. Any move the manufacturer makes at this point is risky. If, for example, it wants to sell direct to large, increasingly price-sensitive buyers, it will run headlong into the interests of its existing authorized channels. If (as is common) these same distributors handle other important items of that manufacturer's product line, actions taken to deal with the gray market product can have reverberations for placement, support, and technical or merchandising assistance across the line.

One result is that, while gray markets ultimately reflect pricing policies, distribution policies, channel evolution, and changes in buyer behavior, they also often generate much animosity among the parties involved. Manufacturers often feel that the unauthorized distributors are "stealing" their brand franchise but that the authorized distributors are not "aggressive" enough in pursuing

---

[17] Willard R. Bishop, Jr., "Trade Buying Squeezes Marketers," *Marketing Communications*, May 1988, pp. 52–53.

[18] For an analysis of gray markets in the context of longer-term buyer and channel dynamics, see F. V. Cespedes, E. R. Corey, and V. K. Rangan, "Gray Markets: Causes and Cures," *Harvard Business Review* 66 (July–August 1988), pp. 75–82.

more price-sensitive segments of the market. For their part, the authorized distributors often view the gray marketers as the business equivalent of pirates, but also view the manufacturer as "ungrateful" for the distributor's past market-development efforts in that product category. In the gray market context, some of these charges are undoubtedly calculated by each party—an instance of the "adversarial collaboration" (see below) that characterizes supplier-reseller relations. And if business were entirely a matter of marginal-cost pricing in the context of supply-and-demand dynamics, then one could presumably "settle" gray market problems through some optimal combination of pricing and channel structures.[19] But since business (and especially the business of distribution) is handled by people who, over time, develop certain expectations, norms, biases, and implicit or explicit assumptions about duties and responsibilities, these economic "facts" inevitably (and, in my view, legitimately) become enmeshed with charges and countercharges concerning the ethics of these distribution practices.

CHANNEL POWER AND CHANNEL RELATIONS

In its official code of ethics (included in this volume as Appendix C), the American Marketing Association cites, in the area of distribution, the following responsibilities of the marketer:

• Not manipulating the availability of a product for purpose of exploitation.

• Not using coercion in the marketing channel.

• Not exerting undue influence over the resellers' choice to handle a product.

  This code becomes especially interesting when considered in the context of the construct that has guided much academic channels research for the past three decades. I refer to the notion of "channel power," defined in one of our best and most representative distribution textbooks as follows:

> Power is the ability of one channel member to get another channel member to do what the latter would not otherwise have done. Power is the inverse of dependence: the more highly dependent one channel member is on another, the more power the latter has relative to the former. Available to channel members are several power bases they may use to evoke change or gain continued cooperation; these include rewards, coercion, expertness, reference, and legitimacy. They are almost invariably used in combination. There is a cost associated with their use, however, which must be an integral part of the analysis in the development of interorganization management programs.[20]

---

[19] For an example of such an approach, see R. Howell, R. Britney, P. Kuzdrall, and J. Wilcox, "Unauthorized Channels of Distribution: Gray Markets," *Industrial Marketing Management*, November 1986, pp. 257–63.

[20] Louis W. Stern and Adel I. El-Ansary, *Marketing Channels*, 3rd ed. (Englewood Cliffs, N.J.: Prentice Hall, 1988), p. 302.

Further, the typical measures of channel power in the distribution literature concern activities that are aimed precisely at one channel member's attempts to "exert undue influence" over another channel member's business practices. In the case of manufacturers, these measures refer to the manufacturer's ability (through the use of the "power bases" mentioned above) to wield some control over: reseller pricing, the choice of reseller location, the reseller's minimum order size, the product mix ordered, amount of reseller advertising, the provision of credit to consumers, the reseller's ability to buy from other suppliers, the physical layout of the reseller's location, and reseller selling policies, including territorial and customer restrictions.[21]

In recent years, the academic theory of channel power (and the behavioral science constructs that have guided this research for many years) has received increased scrutiny.[22] But in this brief overview of potential ethical issues in distribution, I want to make three concluding observations that are independent of the important theoretical questions concerning channel power.

First, the AMA Code of Ethics seems to suggest a broad moral condemnation of many practices that, in the channel power literature, are discussed as legitimate ends and means of various parties in a channel relationship. (Indeed, depending upon how one interprets "exploitation," the first statement in the Code—"Not manipulating the availability of a product for purposes of exploitation"—might implicate many common and economically important forms of exclusive distribution arrangements between suppliers and intermediaries.) This potential anomaly is noteworthy, and one perspective on this situation is that voiced some years ago by a noted scholar of distribution:[23]

> The "power system"—the efforts of one or more members to bend the channel will to its will, and the unique effects this may have on the micro units (firms) and the macro unit (channel)—has received particular attention in the literature. [However] . . . the power discussions have been limited to such "value-less" topics as the measurement of channel power, the managerial uses of channel power, the concept and theory of channel power, the sources of channel power . . . and so on. Little attention has been given to such "value" questions as: Is it good for society? Is it fair and equitable? Is it exploitative?

As this author also noted, this situation is fairly common in discussions of distribution, which probably has received less attention in terms of ethical questions than other areas of the marketing mix, such as product policy, pricing, or advertising.

Second, in thinking about ethical issues in distribution, however, it is important to recognize that certain facts typically condition supplier-reseller re-

---

[21] See ibid., p. 417, for a representative list of practices and outcomes typically cited as measures and sources of channel power.

[22] See, for a still-pertinent review of the constructs, John F. Gaski, "The Theory of Power and Conflict in Channels of Distribution," *Journal of Marketing* 48 (1984), pp. 9–29.

[23] Bruce Mallen, "Channel Power: A Form of Economic Exploitation," *European Journal of Marketing* 12 (1978), p. 195.

lationships, making channel relations exercises in "adversarial collaboration."[24] On the one hand, the fact that exchange takes place between supplier and reseller means that each has something deemed valuable by the other, and thus both have mutual interests in maximizing the sales or margins of the supplier's product. On the other hand, channels relations also involve each party in an implicit struggle to retain a larger share of the profits and control concerning the product or service in question. Also, the goals and operating constraints of manufacturers and resellers are often very different, leading to conflicts in the implementation of marketing programs.

Because suppliers and resellers simultaneously have mutual interests and inherent conflicts, the rhythm of these relationships is analogous to an ongoing tug-of-war, as illustrated earlier in their differing perspectives concerning slotting allowances and gray markets. Exhibit 1 emphasizes this aspect of channels relations via the "seesaws" used to depict the comparative interests and goals of a supplier and its channel intermediary.[25]

Suppliers selling through intermediaries must develop capabilities at two levels: as sources of product and revenues for those intermediaries and as the locus of brand preference with end users. In the former role, suppliers try to act as "marketing partners" with their distributors, building levels of trust and influence that motivate resellers to stock and actively support that supplier's product(s) rather than the many other products typically carried by a reseller. In the latter role, however, suppliers seek to have their products specified by end users, and this often requires terms and conditions that can conflict with resellers' preferences.

Conversely, resellers act simultaneously as selling agents for suppliers and as sources of supply for certain groups of customers. In the former role, resellers seek to develop with individual suppliers marketing programs that can build demand for particular brands. In the latter role, however, resellers typically seek to assemble a package of products that will serve particular customers' desires for purchasing convenience or lower transaction costs. This latter goal often motivates distributors to give preference, first, to the generic package of products appropriate to a customer segment and, secondly, to the selection and promotion of particular brands capable of completing the package.

How these seesaws tip in a given channel relationship will depend on various factors, including the profit margins available to each party through one or another mode of distribution, the supplier's ability to build and maintain brand "pull" with user customers, and the distributor's other sourcing options in the product category. In practice, moreover, most suppliers and resellers are usually members of multiple—often competing—channels systems. Suppliers often sell through a number of intermediaries, while resellers often carry the products

---

[24] See E. R. Corey, F. V. Cespedes, and V. K. Rangan, *Going to Market: Distribution Systems for Industrial Products* (Boston: Harvard Business School Press, 1989), pp. 281–82.

[25] This discussion of channel relations is borrowed from Frank V. Cespedes, *Organizing and Implementing the Marketing Effort* (Reading, Mass.: Addison-Wesley, 1991), chapter 5.

EXHIBIT 1   Channel Relations

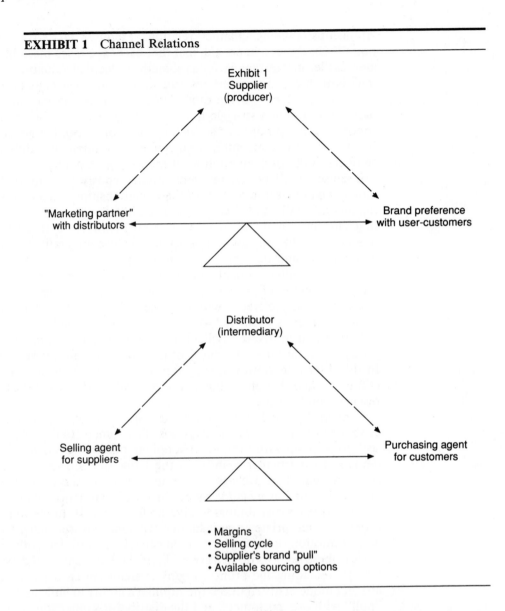

of competing manufacturers. Hence, the tug-of-war also occurs within the context of a set of entangling alliances between suppliers and resellers. One result is a series of shifting incentives for conflict or cooperation during the course of supplier-reseller relations, and this fact of life should be a working assumption in discussions of channels ethics.

A third observation concerns the legal framework relevant to distribution decisions in the United States. Compared to many other countries, U.S. laws relevant to channel relations leave much more room for bargaining, negotiations, and ongoing give-and-take between individual suppliers and resellers. Specific terms and conditions of distribution are, in the United States, typically negotiated by suppliers and resellers; in many other countries (e.g., Japan and, historically, many European countries), these same terms and conditions are often specified by law, not marketplace negotiations. This legal framework has been an important condition for a relatively responsive, flexible, and vital distribution infrastructure in the United States over the past century. But one might also suggest that concerns for equity, fairness, and ethical behavior must become more important in such a framework, compared to an industrial sys⁺ tem where laws and regulations occupy a bigger part of the space between channel members.

This is particularly true because both supplier and reseller often make substantial and irreversible commitments when they become part of a channel system. For a supplier, a certain channel of distribution represents a commitment to certain market segments and, over time, the development of certain marketing capabilities to the exclusion of others. For the intermediary, relations with suppliers represent a substantial commitment of working capital and, often, a certain "identity" in the local marketplace. In this situation, each party's actions have substantial impact on the other. Such supplier-initiated actions as increasing distribution intensity in a trading area, establishing captive branches in areas served by franchised independent distributors, or reclassifying reseller accounts as direct "house" accounts when they grow in sales volume can depreciate and sometimes destroy the reseller's investment in the channel system. Conversely, reseller actions can have a similar effect on suppliers. One example is "bait and switch" tactics, in which a reseller attracts customers on the basis of a given supplier's advertising and other investments, only to substitute private-label merchandise at the point of purchase. Another example is the gray market and diverting situations described earlier in this chapter, actions that can disrupt and sometimes destroy years of work by suppliers in building and supporting a channel network.

Further, the situation facing channel entities is also complicated by the perennial possibilities for what some have labeled "opportunistic" behavior in vertical systems.[26] No distribution agreement, however detailed, is likely to foresee with actionable precision all of the many situations encountered by supplier and reseller over the course of the agreement in a dynamic, competitive marketplace. Inevitably, important aspects of channel relations effectively become joint "promises" rather than strictly legal, contractual obligations. Again, this is especially true when, as in the United States, more room is left to marketplace bargaining rather than a codified body of legal restrictions concerning supplier or reseller rights and obligations. However, broken promises are, of course, a common event in life, and so the possibilities for op-

---

[26] The seminal discussion of this topic is Oliver Williamson, *Markets and Hierarchies: Analysis and Antitrust Implications* (New York: Free Press, 1975).

portunism make channel systems potentially fragile affairs despite the commitments involved.

By their very nature, moreover, distribution arrangements are constantly being besieged and redefined by larger competitive and macroeconomic changes. And these changes often mean that either supplier or reseller *do* lose a store of accrued value; that promises and personal relationships *are* nonetheless broken under the pressures of new market conditions, which require different terms of exchange; that "consistency" in channels relations can often become inertia in the face of new competitive realities. No less than other facets of a market economy, distribution systems are part of the process that Schumpeter called "creative destruction," and his phrasing nicely captures the orthogonal forces inherent in channel relations. Further, this combination of factors—the legal framework, the relative room it leaves for the use and abuse of channel power, and the ongoing process of creative destruction in a market economy—makes distribution an especially complicated but also particularly important area for research and discussion of marketing ethics.

Sorrell Ridge: Slotting Allowances

Carol Pressman, Allied Old English VP marketing and sales, arrived at the offices of Bromar of Southern California on June 5, 1987, expecting to close a deal. Pressman believed that California's second largest food broker had already decided to represent the company's best-selling brand, Sorrell Ridge spreadable fruit. Sorrell Ridge sales had grown from $720,000 in 1982 to $5.9 million in 1986 as a result of the appeal to increasingly health conscious consumers of its all-fruit products over sugared jams.

Bromar's president, vice president, and five account managers listened to Pressman's proposal, then gave their response. They informed Pressman that Allied Old English would have to pay "slotting allowances in up-front cash of around $250,000" to obtain supermarket shelf space for Sorrell Ridge. Bromar also suggested Sorrell Ridge would have to distribute 2 million 50-cents-off coupons through free standing inserts in Los Angeles newspapers as part of the introductory marketing program and also launch a boysenberry conserve, a new product for Sorrell Ridge, but currently fashionable in California.[1] In return, the broker committed to securing distribution for Sorrell Ridge in stores accounting for 90 percent of grocery volume within three months of the introduction.

Surprised by Bromar's requests, Pressman returned to Allied Old English's head office in Port Reading, New Jersey, to consult with president Fred Ross. While wanting to employ Bromar and be the first to enter the California market with an all-fruit product line ahead of their key competitors, J. M. Smucker and Polaner, Pressman and Ross felt they had to consider these options:

1. Find another broker. However, the largest broker in southern California was already representing a competitive brand.
2. Propose a less expensive launch program to Bromar and hope that they would still agree to represent the line.

This case was prepared by Aimee L. Stern under the direction of Professor John A. Quelch. Proprietary data have been disguised.

Copyright © 1990 by the President and Fellows of Harvard College.

Harvard Business School case N9-590-112 (rev. 6/12/90).

[1] Bromar expected a 3–4 percent coupon redemption rate, with production, distribution, and retailer and clearing house handling costs amounting to 60 cents per redemption.

3. Sell through grocery distributors or a middleman who would take title to the product. However, this approach would cause the retail price to be 25 percent higher.

COMPANY BACKGROUND

Fred Ross was heir to Allied Old English, a small family business, which specialized in duck sauce and blackstrap molasses. The firm was founded by Ross's father in 1951 and distributed products primarily through health food stores. When Ross took over day-to-day operations in 1975, Allied Old English had sales of about $2.5 million, 75 percent in private label and institutional products sold to restaurants, hospitals, and schools, and 25 percent in brand names, such as China Pride and Dai-Day. Realizing that sales of branded products were more profitable and dependable, he concentrated on growing his existing brands and acquiring others, including Mee Tu Noodles (1977), Sorrell Ridge (1982), Hot Cha Cha (1983), and Gathering Winds (1984). He expected sales of $19 million by 1990, 93 percent of which would be from brands owned by Allied Old English.

Ross purchased the Canadian jam company Sorrell Ridge in February 1982 for $75,000. In the prior year, the company had sold 15,000 cases of honey-sweetened jam through U.S. and Canadian health food stores.

In 1982, all jams and jellies on the market were sweetened with honey, cane sugar, or corn syrup. The jams of the market leader, J. M. Smucker Company, comprised 6 percent fruit, 60 percent corn syrup and sugar, and 34 percent water from fruit and corn syrup. Ross substituted white grape juice concentrate for honey and started promoting Sorrell Ridge as a product made entirely of fruit. Sorrell Ridge spreadable fruit consisted of 50 percent fruit and 50 percent water from fruit and was made in the company's existing Port Reading plant.

Ross originally cooked fruit in small open kettles, brought it to a boil, then packed and cooked Sorrell Ridge in jars. The process was primitive and the product was often overcooked, resulting in loss of flavor and color. Ross invested about $800,000 in state-of-the-art manufacturing equipment that cooked the product at a consistent 130 degrees Fahrenheit and cooled it quickly, improving quality substantially.

Ross changed Sorrell Ridge's packaging to make it stand out on store shelves. Most jams were packaged in squat, round 10- to 18-ounce jars with red, purple, or orange labels. Ten- and 12-ounce jars were the best-selling sizes. Ross used tall, thin, 10-ounce jars with light green labels and matching bottle caps. Sorrell Ridge was available in 20 flavors, including the best-selling strawberry, blueberry, orange marmalade, raspberry, apricot, and peach.

The commercial jam, jelly, and preserve market originally consisted of six types of fruit spreads: jellies, jams, preserves, conserves, marmalades, and fruit butters. Definitions were as follows:[2]

---

[2] Source: *Packaged Facts*, "Jams, Jellies & Preserves Market, 1986."

Jellies—made by combining strained fruit juices with sugar and cooking until the mixture reaches a clear consistency. Popular flavors: apple, crab apple, grape, black raspberry.

Jams—made of finely sliced fruits cooked with sugar until the mixture becomes slightly jellied. Popular flavors: grape, strawberry, peach, apricot.

Preserves—made by cooking whole or cut-up fruits in a sugar syrup until clear. Popular flavors: apricot, gooseberry, peach, plum, strawberry.

Conserves—jam-like spreads made from a mixture of two or more fruits, often combined with nuts or raisins.

Marmalades—contain shreds of citrus fruits suspended in clear syrup. Popular flavors: lemon, orange, grapefruit, ginger/lime.

Fruit butters—made from fruit pulp and sugar cooked together.

Jellies accounted for a quarter of the total volume, while jams, preserves, and conserves combined accounted for almost 70 percent.

Traditional distinctions among product types blurred over the years, and the terms *jams, preserves*, and *conserves* often were used interchangeably. In 1982, Ross referred to the product line as Sorrell Ridge conserves but, when competitive all-fruit brands entered the market, he changed the product description to Sorrell Ridge spreadable fruit.

Sorrell Ridge products enjoyed an average 18-month shelf life; but lighter fruits, such as peach and apricot, were sensitive to heat and turned brown in the jars after 6 months. Sales of jams and jellies were highest in the fall and winter and lowest in the spring and summer. Sales of premium-priced gourmet items increased during the pre-Christmas shopping season.

Ross initially, in 1982, sold Sorrell Ridge through 20 percent of the 6,000 U.S. health food stores. Most of Sorrell Ridge's outlets were in the Northeast. Total health food store retail sales of jams and jellies were $4.5 million in 1982. A dozen small brands, including R. W. Knudsen, Cascadia Farms, and Whole Earth, competed in the category. Two national health food distributors serviced 50 percent of health food retailers with their own brands.

Ross, therefore, had to sell through health food distributors. These distributors marked up each case of twelve 10-ounce jars by about 25 percent, and the health food stores then retailed each jar for 40 percent more than they paid for it. In 1984, Sorrell Ridge retailed for an average of $2.59 per jar in health food stores. That year, Sorrell Ridge achieved a 60 percent market share in health food stores nationwide. Health food stores accounted for about $2.3 million of the brand's $2.8 million in wholesale sales. Ross decided that, to expand further, he had to distribute through supermarkets, which accounted for 86 percent of all retail jam and jelly sales. He approached Smucker to explore a joint selling and distribution arrangement. However, Smucker was not interested. Ross recalled the chairman of the company, saying, "We merely want to own your niche in health food stores." Smucker executives did not believe the 100 percent fruit concept had "mass marketability."

SUPERMARKET EXPANSION

Ross first introduced Sorrell Ridge to New York area supermarkets in 1984 because local distributors who handled the company's Chinese food line could obtain supermarket placement. The New York metropolitan area, which consisted of the five boroughs of New York City, Long Island, Westchester County, and northern New Jersey, represented about 9 percent or $60 million of national jam and jelly retail sales through supermarkets.

Ross hired Carol Pressman, a 35-year-old sales representative with a health food distributor, Island Natural Health Foods, to help with the rollout because her firm was outselling all of Sorrell Ridge's health food distributors. A working mother who had never finished college, Pressman had outstanding sales skills. She and Ross developed an aggressive presentation for New York food brokers and supermarkets. She filled an empty jam jar with sugar and a few plastic raspberries and opened her sales pitch by placing the "sugar jar" on the buyers' desks. She told them, "This is what you're buying." Pressman then explained how stocking Sorrell Ridge would help build sales in a declining category. Exhibit 1 is drawn from the merchandising flyer used in the sales presentation.

Sorrell Ridge had to use food brokers to distribute its products to supermarkets since it did not have its own sales force. Brokers worked exclusively with one manufacturer in each product category they represented. For a new principal like Sorrell Ridge, a food broker typically would help to develop the initial marketing program (including the introductory trade deal) and present it to trade buyers. In addition, the broker merchandised the brand, planned its placement on supermarket shelves, provided labor for restocking, and sometimes price-ticketed the product at retail. The broker also processed retail orders and sent them to the manufacturer. Food brokers typically received a 5 percent commission on the net selling price to the trade after trade allowances.

The New York market was controlled by three major supermarket chains, which accounted for 42 percent of New York jam and jelly sales. Shop Rite was the largest with 180 stores, followed by Pathmark with 125, and Waldbaum with 110. In November 1984, Ross approached Shop Rite. He agreed to provide Shop Rite one free case per store per flavor as an introductory slotting allowance. The chain accepted six flavors. Starting in February 1985, Shop Rite sold 50–75 cases per week per flavor of Sorrell Ridge during its first six months on the market. In total, Ross provided New York supermarkets free goods worth $150,000 to gain distribution. One year after the introduction, Ross paid New York supermarkets additional slotting fees of two free cases per additional flavor per store to attain his minimum goal of 6–8 flavors in each store. This cost Ross an additional $50,000 in fees during 1985.

In 1984, supermarket prices for jams varied according to flavor. A 10-ounce jar of strawberry jam sold for an average of $1.39 at retail, while less heavily demanded fruits like raspberry sold at 20–30 cents more per jar. Ross suggested a single retail price of $1.99 for all flavors of Sorrell Ridge. He reduced the

EXHIBIT 1   Excerpt from Merchandising Flyer

The fruit. And nothing but the fruit.

suggested retail selling price in 1986 to $1.79 as his sales and production volume increased. The main competitors, Smucker and Polaner, followed his lead and also introduced line pricing, a standard price for each jar size regardless of flavor.

In March 1985, Sorrell Ridge launched a $175,000 spot television campaign in New York, which ran for four weeks. The advertisement pictured sugar jam competitors and, most prominently, a fat jar of Smucker's jam adrift in a desert of sugar with a voiceover by actor Burl Ives. Exhibit 2 provides a storyboard of the advertisement. Smucker sent a blistering letter to all three

---

EXHIBIT 2   Sorrell Ridge Storyboard 1985

ANNCR. (VO): Sorrell Ridge would like to challenge — the giant in the jam industry. — Their preserves have mostly corn syrup,

refined sugar, — and just some fruit. — Sorrell Ridge has no corn syrup.

No refined sugar. — Just 100% fruit and fruit juice. Maybe it's about time someone knocked the giant down to size. — Sorrell Ridge. With 100% fruit, it has to be better.

networks plus the Federal Trade Commission in Washington demanding that the "misleading" commercial be taken off the air. The letter suggested that Sorrell Ridge was harmful to diabetics. Ross countered with a press conference in July of 1985, which featured actor Tony Roberts, a board member of the Juvenile Diabetes Foundation. They handed out letters from doctors and food chemists stating that Sorrell Ridge could be included in diabetic diets. The dispute and the associated publicity helped Ross to achieve distribution in New York supermarkets accounting for 90 percent of grocery volume by the end of 1986.

Sorrell Ridge used intensive in-store sampling to persuade consumers to try the product. Sorrell Ridge hired an independent product demonstration service to conduct the program. About 300 major stores received demos.

From New York, Sorrell Ridge expanded into nearby markets, such as Boston, Philadelphia, and Buffalo. The brand also made minor inroads in Chicago, Denver, and Cincinnati. Ross spent most of 1986 preparing for a major new market expansion in 1987.

THE MARKET IN 1986–87

By 1986, Sorrell Ridge factory sales had reached $5.4 million and, as indicated in Exhibit 3, accounted for over half of Allied Old English's total sales. An income statement for the Sorrell Ridge brand is shown in Exhibit 4. Sorrell Ridge's media advertising expenditures of $150,000 in 1986 compared to national spending levels of $5.3 million for J. M. Smucker, $2.1 million for Welch

EXHIBIT 3 Sorrell Ridge: Slotting Allowances

		Sorrell Ridge Sales: 1982–87		
Year	*Sorrell Ridge Sales*	*Percent of Company Sales**	*Sorrell Ridge Case Sales†*	*Number of Flavors*
1982	$ 720,000	14.4%	40,000	10/HS‡
1983	1,500,000	21.4	105,000	8/HS, 8/FO
1984	2,800,000	32.9	200,000	8/HS, 12/FO
1985	4,800,000	50.0	360,000	15/FO
1986	5,400,000	51.0	430,000§	20/FO
1987e	6,500,000	55.1	520,000	20/FO

* Percentage of total Allied Old English sales.
† A case comprised a dozen 10-ounce jars.
‡ HS = honey-sweetened; FO = fruit only.
§ 70 percent of cases were distributed through supermarkets, 30 percent through health food stores.
e means estimated

Source: Company records.

EXHIBIT 4   Income Statement 1986 ($000)

Manufacturer sales	$5,356
Cost of goods	2,700
Shipping and warehousing	120
Brokers fees	206
Slotting allowances	80
Other sales promotion	300
Advertising	150
Fixed overhead	1,600
Profit before taxes	200

Source: Company records.

EXHIBIT 5   Jam and Jelly Retail Sales and Market Shares: 1986

	Retail Sales ($millions)	Share of Retail Sales (Percent)
J. M. Smucker	$312	31%
Welch Foods	123	12
Kraft	84	8
Borden	46	5
Polaner	18	2
Private label	76	8
Other (including gourmet brands)	341	34

Source: *Packaged Facts*, "Jams, Jellies, & Preserves Market, 1986."

Foods, and $900,000 for Polaner. National retail sales and market shares for these and other competitors are reported in Exhibit 5. Market shares along with case volume and dollar sales in New York City for 1985 and 1986 are shown in Exhibit 6.

Retail sales for jams and jellies in 1986 in the United States were about $800 million. Jam and jelly retail sales had declined at a compound annual rate of 3 percent between 1981–85, due partly to consumer health concerns. Jams and jellies were laden with sugar and many adults switched to low-sugar or diet spreads. Supermarkets devoted, on average, eight feet of shelf space to the jam and jelly section, which often also included peanut butter and honey. Six jar facings of Sorrell Ridge fit in one linear retail foot of shelf space. Less than 1 percent of total supermarket sales came from this category, yet over 100 brands competed for the limited shelf space available.

Children aged 2–17 years were above-average consumers of jams and jellies. According to a product usage survey by *Progressive Grocer* magazine, 44 percent of jam and jelly consumers were single brand users.

EXHIBIT 6 Brand Sales and Shares in the New York City Jam and Jelly Market: 1985–86

Brand	Case Sales (12 units per case)	Dollar Sales ($000)	Dollar Share of Category	Percentage Change	
Kraft	1985—176,263	1985—$ 2,899	1985— 8.3%	Cases —	1%
	1986—152,666	1986— 2,579	1986— 7.1	Dollars +	12.4
Sorrell Ridge	1985— 50,238	1985— 1,120	1985— 3.2	Cases +	14
	1986—120,861	1986— 2,632	1986— 7.2	Dollars +	135
Smucker	1985—724,087	1985— 12,463	1985—36.0	Cases —	2
	1986—713,115	1986— 12,769	1986—35.2	Dollars +	2.4
Polaner	1985— 48,199	1985— 956,070	1985— 2.3	Cases —	73
	1986— 27,810	1986— 512,482	1986— 1.8	Dollars —	86
Welch Foods	1985—408,401	1985— 7,266	1985—20.8	Cases —	2.2
	1986—399,469	1986— 6,799	1986—19.6	Dollars —	7

Total New York City jam sales retail: Total New York City case sales:
  1985–$34,847,000   1985–2,172,000
  1986–$36,225,000   1986–2,254,000

Source: Company records.

Higher-priced gourmet jams were gaining popularity among young urban adults. Premium-priced preserves retailed at $4 to $5 per jar. The leading brands were Knotts's (upscale) Berry Farm line and Tiptree by Wilkin & Sons, Ltd.

Polaner introduced its 100 percent fruit jam called All-Fruit to East Coast supermarkets in late 1985. Smucker followed with Simply Fruit in early 1987. From 1985 to 1987, domestic jam and jelly retail sales grew at a 3 percent annual rate, largely due to the introduction of all-fruit brands. Smucker only sold Simply Fruit in markets where Sorrell Ridge was a major contender, because it was concerned about losing share for its sugared jams.

By the first half of 1987, all-fruit brands represented about 3–4 percent of national jam and jelly sales through grocery stores and were expected to increase their share to 26 percent by 1992. In early 1987, Sorrell Ridge held 60 percent of retail sales in the all-fruit segment. All-fruit jams were distributed in only 40 percent of the country's supermarkets, with the majority of sales concentrated in the Northeast.

PLANNING THE SOUTHERN CALIFORNIA LAUNCH

Early in 1987, Ross and Pressman discussed which market they should enter next. Pressman was convinced that growing health consciousness made California the ideal target.

Pressman noted that the number two food broker in southern California (which included Los Angeles, San Diego, and surrounding counties) had ceased to represent the leading regional jam manufacturer, Knotts Berry Farm, in December 1986. Knotts wanted to reduce Bromar's commissions from the standard 5 percent to 2.5 percent but Bromar had refused. The number one food broker represented Smucker. There were several other smaller food brokers in the market whom Pressman could also approach.

A top food broker was an asset when trying to acquire supermarket distribution. Bromar handled large-volume accounts, including Starkist Tuna, Campbell Soup Company's Prego spaghetti sauce line, and Arrowhead Water, the number one regional brand of bottled water. It had a staff of 400 people, including 25 account executives, 325 merchandising and field managers, and 50 administrative workers. As a result, Bromar could provide complete and frequent coverage of grocery stores in the market. Each Bromar customer was assigned an account executive, who managed the product line and worked with supermarket chain buyers, merchandisers, and store managers to customize merchandising and marketing plans for each store.

In addition to brokers, there were six distributors in southern California that sold supermarkets low-turnover items, which were not sufficiently important or profitable for supermarkets to stock in their own warehouses. These included gourmet foods, pantyhose, and women's hair goods. Distributors took a 25 percent margin. California supermarkets expected to earn at least a 20 percent retail margin whether they bought from a distributor or direct from a manufacturer. By 1987, they expected slotting fees as well as the standard off-invoice allowance of 15 percent on their initial orders.

Pressman resolved to introduce Sorrell Ridge to southern California supermarkets in the summer of 1987 and to enter northern California early in 1988. "It was very important to me that I convince a broker to take us on," Pressman said. "I wanted every rollout that I did to be successful. We did not have the resources to make mistakes and did not have the budget cushion for failure."

In 1986, 1,793,000 cases of jams and jellies were sold in southern California, a decline of 21 percent from 1981. Exhibit 7 shows 1986 market shares by brand and by flavor in southern California. Exhibit 8 provides price information on selected items.

The southern California grocery retail sector was concentrated, with six chains accounting for 82 percent of grocery volume. One of the six, Certified Grocer, was a wholesale cooperative servicing 2,000 small, independently owned and operated grocery stores. The sizes and strategies of the six chains are summarized in Exhibit 9.

For reasons of ethics and legality, Pressman wanted to approach all six buyers with the same opening deal. However, if those chains that depended more heavily on a strong price appeal to attract their consumers pressed for more generous terms, she would have to rethink this objective. She anticipated first-year sales of 90,000 cases, of which half would be sold under the terms of the initial orders. The price per case was set at $17.16 before allowances, 31 cents

EXHIBIT 7 Brands, Shares, and Flavors of Jams, Jellies, and Preserves: Southern California Market 1986

Brand	1982 Cases Sold	1986 Cases Sold	Percent +/(−)	Percent 1986 Share of Market
Smucker	394,398	415,318	+ 5.3%	23.2%
Smucker Low Sugar	90,096	109,370	+21.3	6.1
Private label/generic	489,155	367,172	(− 2.5)	20.5
Knotts	236,140	226,259	(− 4.2)	12.6
Tropical	221,706	176,244	(−20.5)	9.8
Kerns	354,869	141,447	(−60.1)	7.9
Welch's	184,868	145,299	(−21.3)	8.1
King Jelly	103,449	82,055	(−20.6)	4.6
Miscellaneous (including gourmet brands)	86,319	129,836	+50.4	7.2
Total	2,161,000	1,793,000	(−17.0%)	

Top Flavors

Flavors	Percent
Strawberry	33.0%
Grape	22.9
Orange marmalade	8.9
Boysenberry	6.7
Red raspberry	6.5
Apricot	4.9
Apricot/Pineapple	4.4
Blackberry	2.5
Peach	1.7
Plum	1.3
Miscellaneous	7.2

Source: Bromar.

higher than in the Northeast, to partially offset freight and warehousing costs of 75 cents per case. Shipping costs to California reduced Sorrell Ridge's margin by 50 cents per case.

Pressman had heard that Smucker and Polaner also planned to introduce their all-fruit products in Los Angeles in the summer of 1987. Smucker's line included 6 flavors and Polaner's 12. Both manufacturers expected to secure additional shelf space at the expense of private labels and weaker brands, rather than through substitution for the slower-moving items in their existing lines. Smucker's suggested retail price for a 10-ounce jar of Simply Fruit was $1.69,

EXHIBIT 8 Prices of Selected Jams, Jellies, and Preserves in Southern California: 1986

Package Size			Factory Case Price	Factory Unit Price	Retail Price: Independent Grocery Store	Retail Price: Supermarket Chain
No. of Jars	Ounces	Brand and Item				
12	16	Knotts red raspberry	$18.24	$1.52	$2.03	$1.98
12	16	Knotts strawberry	16.79	1.39	2.04	1.99
12	16	Knotts boysenberry	18.75	1.56	2.24	2.19
12	12	Smucker red raspberry	13.32	1.11	1.62	1.57
12	18	Smucker strawberry preserves	17.35	1.44	2.14	2.09
12	12	Smucker boysenberry preserves	13.56	1.13	1.65	1.60
12	18	Welch's grape preserves	11.63	0.97	1.31	1.26
12	32	Welch's grape preserves	13.65	1.13	1.90	1.85
12	32	Private label strawberry preserves	10.55	0.87	1.34	1.29

Source: Key Price Book/*Packaged Facts, Inc.*

while Polaner planned to retail All-Fruit at $1.79. Bromar's research had uncovered some details of their launch programs, as reported in Exhibit 10.

SLOTTING ALLOWANCES

For decades, grocery products manufacturers provided the trade with an introductory deal at the time of any new product launch. Typically, such deals took the form of temporary off-invoice case allowances on the trade's initial orders or, alternatively, free goods (e.g., 1 case free with 10). Slotting allowances emerged in the early 1980s as an added administrative charge of $25 to $50 per new item per store to cover the costs of entering the new item on the retailer's computer system and of making a slot available for the product in the warehouse and on the retail shelf.

Over time, these nominal charges escalated, especially in the Northeast and in refrigerated and frozen product categories where shelf space was at a premium (see Exhibit 11). Retailers justified increased slotting allowances on the grounds that the costs of the buyer's time in reviewing and accepting a new product and, subsequently, notifying individual store managers of its listing should also be covered. However, manufacturers soon argued that the slotting charges greatly exceeded the costs involved. One consultant's report estimated that only 30 percent of slotting allowances could be attributed to the costs of the services provided. Another estimated that one third of the $19 billion grocery manufacturers would spend on trade promotion in 1988 would be accounted for by slotting allowances.

The escalation of slotting allowances reflected the increasing power of the grocery trade. As the editor of *Supermarket Business* put it: "The way I heard it, a retailer named an outlandish fee and was as surprised as anyone else when

EXHIBIT 9   Six Principal Grocery Chains in Southern California: 1987

Store group	Percentage of Grocery Volume	Number of Stores	Marketing Approach
Vons/Pavilions/Tianguis	24%	350	Operates on a high/low* pricing philosophy. All three chains target an upscale clientele. Vons doubles manufacturer coupons up to $1.
Lucky/Alpha Beta/Advantage	24	350	Pursues a low retail price strategy and does not offer double value coupons.
Ralphs	14	138	Operates on a high/low philosophy. Offers to double value of manufacturer coupons. Upscale target market.
Certified Grocers	12	2,000	The largest wholesale grocer in southern California. Debt services charges incurred by major chains help independents continue to compete on price.
Albertson's/Grocery Warehouse	8	113	Aggressive expansion in southern California. Market share expected to grow in 1988.
Stater Brothers	7	100	Largest independent grocery chain. The company passes on 100 percent of manufacturers' promotion allowances to consumer. Everyday low prices.
Other	11	200 plus	

* Under a high/low pricing policy, a supermarket offered a selection of items at deep discount that changed weekly.

Source: Company records.

the manufacturer paid it. Once retailers realized how much manufacturers would pay, they just kept raising the fees." Some manufacturers believed that acceding to excessive slotting allowance demands would place them in violation of the Robinson-Patman Act, which required that equivalent allowances be offered to all trade accounts in any market area. Exhibit 12 summarizes the principal clauses of the act. As the vice president of sales for a leading packaged goods manufacturer stated: "Retailers are talking out of both sides of their

EXHIBIT 10   Introductory Trade Promotion Expenditures Proposal: All-Fruit Jams—Southern California

Company	Date of Introduction	Case Discount	One-Time Slotting Fee	Coupons	Advertising	In-Store Sampling
Sorrell Ridge	July 1987	$2.80 off $17.16 case price. Available July and August.	Three free cases per flavor per store.	50 cents off 2 million FSI* planned for October 11	$150,000 TV ads. Three flights over six months.	$30,000 to $40,000
Simply Fruit	August 1987	$2.65 off $16.94 case price. Three weeks beginning August 24.	One free case per flavor per store.	25 cents off 2 million FSI planned for mid-Sept.	$1 million national advertising.	None announced.
All-Fruit	September 1987	$1.50 off $18.93 case price. One month beginning November.	Unknown	Unknown	Unknown	None announced.

* Free standing inserts
Note: All three brands were sold in cases of twelve 10-ounce jars.

Source: Company records.

EXHIBIT 11   Promotion Expenditures and Slotting Fees by Product Category

Product Category	Advertising and Promotion Allocations	Slotting Fees— per Slot ($)
Frozen/Refrigerated foods	1987—12% advertising, 18% consumer promotion, 70% trade promotion	1982—$ 1,000 1987— 10,000 1992— 20,000(e)
Candy/Snacks	1987—37.5% advertising, 27.5% consumer promotion, 35% trade promotion	1982— 300 1987— 3,800 1992— 6,000(e)
Prepared foods	1987—16% advertising, 24% consumer promotion, 60% trade promotion	1982— 1,000 1987— 8,000 1992— 11,000(e)

e means estimated

Source: Clayton/Curtis/Cottrell, Inc. Data based on store groups averaging 50 stores per chain.

mouths; on the one hand, they say, 'Treat us all the same!' But then they turn around and say: 'You've got to give me my own special program.' "

The cost of a slot varied from one retailer to another according to such criteria as the number of stores in the chain, the aggressiveness of the retail buyer, the perceived strength and turnover rate of the new product, and the

---

EXHIBIT 12   Summary of the Clayton Act as Amended by the Robinson-Patman Act (1936), 15 U.S.C. Section 13

Section 2(a)

Prohibits discrimination of price between two or more customers in sales of commodities in interstate commerce where the effect may be substantially to lessen competition with the seller (primary line) or the favored buyer (secondary line) or customers of the latter (tertiary line).

Contains a defense based on different costs in serving different customers. Also includes a defense based on disposal of perishable or obsolete goods.

Section 2(b)

Permits a discrimination that is otherwise unlawful if it results from a seller's good-faith meeting of competitive prices.

Section 2(c)

Prohibits a seller from paying *and a buyer from receiving* a brokerage fee or allowance in a sales transaction unless services are rendered that result in cost savings to the seller. Competitive injury is not an element of this offense, and neither cost justification nor meeting competition are defenses.

Sections 2(d) and (e)

Prohibits sellers' discrimination among customers with respect to promotional allowances [*Section 2(d)*] and services [*Section 2(e)*]. Competitive injury is not an element of the offense; meeting competition is a defense, but cost justification is not.

Section 2(f)

Prohibits buyers from knowingly inducing and receiving unlawful *price* discrimination. Must be a seller violation of *Section 2(a)*, including absence of defenses, and buyer must reasonably be charged with knowledge of that violation. Receipt of illegal promotional allowances and services not covered by *Section 2(f)*.

---

promised level of media advertising and promotion support. No retailer published a schedule of slotting charges or publicly stated what a slot bought in terms of initial order size or the length of time the slot would be maintained before the new product's sales performance was evaluated (though 60 or 90 days appeared to be the norm).

Smaller manufacturers claimed that slotting allowances constituted a barrier to entry, especially when the trade demanded them in the form of up-front cash payments, rather than free goods or credits against the invoices on new product orders. Larger manufacturers with established brands and good new product track records were better able to resist trade demands for slotting allowances and could promise to place substantial advertising support behind their new product introductions.

For its part, the grocery trade pointed to after-tax profit margins of only 1 percent as one reason for their aggressive pursuit of promotional allowances, including slotting fees, from manufacturers. In addition, the grocery trade complained about the proliferation of new item introductions from around 2,700 in 1980 to 9,000 in 1987. Some 90 percent of these new products failed and were withdrawn within a year. The trade viewed slotting allowances as one way to discourage manufacturers from launching new brands and line extensions almost indiscriminately as they tried to maximize their share of shelf space in a slow growth market characterized by an increasing percentage of in-store purchase selections by consumers.

In an effort to control slotting allowances, Campbell Soup Company proposed failure fees as an alternative. These would be paid to the trade after the launch period if a new product failed to sell at a predetermined rate. The manufacturer would buy back any unsold product and compensate the trade for the opportunity cost associated with use of the shelf space, adjusting for actual sales performance. The major grocer chains rejected this proposal.

SLOTTING ALLOWANCES AND SORRELL RIDGE

Sorrell Ridge had paid slotting allowances when it entered New York supermarkets in 1985, but the fees had risen sharply by 1987. In New York, Ross had paid a slotting charge of one free case of product per flavor per store. To break into southern California, Bromar told Ross he would have to offer three free cases per flavor per store as well as an off-invoice case allowance.

In one Midwest market, Sorrell Ridge had paid a slotting fee to a chain for placement in the produce section. A month later, the supermarket chain moved the Sorrell Ridge line from the produce section to another area of its stores. The retailer asked Ross to pay a second slotting charge for each flavor. Ross agreed, because the chain controlled 60 percent of the market. "Slotting fees are a cost of doing business in supermarkets," said Ross. "We knew we had to pay them. We didn't realize the fees would become so high. If Sorrell Ridge was starting out today as a small company trying to break into the market, we wouldn't be able to afford the charges."

The Satanic Verses (A)

In February 1989, the B. Dalton/Barnes & Noble and Waldenbooks bookstore chains removed Salman Rushdie's novel, *Satanic Verses,* from their shelves. The two store groups held a 27 percent share of the $5 billion market in retail book sales. Rushdie's story of a fictional prophet called Mahound was considered blasphemous by Islamic fundamentalists. On February 14, Iran's spiritual leader, Ayatollah Ruhollah Khomeini, ordered Muslims to "assassinate Salman Rushdie, his publisher Viking Penguin, and anyone else involved in the distribution of the novel." A bounty of $2.6 million was placed on Rushdie's head if the avenger was Iranian, $1 million if he was not. Rushdie went into hiding with his family.

A CONTROVERSIAL AUTHOR

In 1947, Salman Rushdie was born to a wealthy Kashmiri Muslim couple. At the age of 13, he left home in Bombay, India, to study at an English prep school and later at Cambridge University. Rushdie was born a Muslim but later rejected the faith; the traditional Muslim punishment for an apostate was death. Rushdie's first novel was published with little fanfare; but his second work, *Midnight's Children*, created an international sensation and sold roughly a half-million copies worldwide. In 1981, *Midnight's Children* won the Booker Prize, England's most prestigious award for fiction.

In the 547-page novel, *The Satanic Verses,* two middle-aged Indian actors miraculously survived a terrorist-induced explosion of a jetliner over the English Channel and were "born again." The prophet Mohammed was represented by "Mahound," an Islamic term for devil. Rushdie retold the Islamic legend in a whimsical, sometimes outrageous style through dreams within dreams. The most sensational episode of the novel took place in a brothel when a dozen prostitutes adopted the names and identities of Mahound's wives

This case was prepared from public sources by Aimee L. Stern under the direction of Professors N. Craig Smith and John A. Quelch.
Copyright © 1990 by the President and Fellows of Harvard College.
Harvard Business School case N9–591–013 (rev. 3/5/91).

and enhanced business. In another bitterly disputed passage, Mahound was tempted by Gibreel (a reference to the angel Gabriel) to cut a deal with his enemies and tolerate worship of three goddesses alongside one God. Gibreel told Mahound the idea came from Satan.

REACTIONS TO RUSHDIE'S NOVEL

The Satanic Verses was not published in the United States until February 13, 1989. Its earlier release in Europe already had provoked reaction. In January, Pakistani immigrants in Bradford, England, had nailed copies of the novel to a stake and burned them outside the town hall. This was followed by a demonstration in Hyde Park, London, involving 8,000 Muslims who vowed court battles against *The Satanic Verses.*

On February 13, several thousand Muslims marched on the American Cultural Center in Islamabad, Pakistan, that nation's capital. Six people died and over 100 were wounded as police fired on demonstrators. The ayatollah's edict was issued on the following day.

Mindful of the impact of bold statements on the fate of Americans held hostage in Lebanon, the U.S. government's response to the ayatollah's edict was muted. A few days later, the 12 European Community nations agreed to recall top diplomats from Teheran, suspended high-level official visits, and considered further restrictions on the movement of Iranian diplomats stationed in their capitals.

The Canadian government halted further imports of *The Satanic Verses* while it decided whether the novel violated Canadian laws against hate literature.

Rushdie issued a statement from hiding: "I profoundly regret the distress that publication has occasioned to sincere followers of Islam. The book that is worth killing people for and burning flags for is not the book I wrote." Khomeini said devout Muslims should kill the author even if he "repents and becomes the most pious man of all time."

THE REACTION OF BOOKSELLERS

Viking Penguin initially printed 50,000 copies of *The Satanic Verses* for distribution to U.S. bookstores, with a suggested retail price of $19.95. The Waldenbooks division of K mart Corporation purchased 15 percent of total copies for its stores, and B. Dalton/Barnes & Noble, a 1,100-store unit of B.D.B., Inc., purchased 10 percent. These chains had gradually been increasing their market share at the expense of the 10,000 independent book stores to which the remaining copies from the print run were shipped.

Following Ayatollah Khomeini's statement, anonymous bomb threats were received by Viking Penguin and by both the headquarters and individual stores of the major booksellers. Forty-four Islamic countries threatened to ban sales of all Viking books. Two independent bookstores in California that were carrying the book were firebombed. On February 16, Waldenbooks became the first major chain to pull *The Satanic Verses* from shelves, though stores could contrive to sell it from their stockrooms. Bonnie Predd, executive vice president of Waldenbooks, said: "We've fought long and hard against censorship. But when it comes to the safety of employees, one sometimes has to compromise." Waldenbooks had about 15,000 employees. The cost of providing security at all Waldenbooks stores was considered prohibitive. B. Dalton/Barnes & Noble stopped selling *The Satanic Verses* the next day. Leonard Riggio, chief executive officer of B. Dalton cited similar arguments: "We have never before pulled a book off our shelves. It is regrettable that a foreign government has been able to hold hostage our most sacred First Amendment principle. Nevertheless, the safety of our employees and patrons must take precedence."

The fear of retaliation muted public opposition to the ayatollah's edict and its effects. An attempt by the editor of *Publishers' Weekly* to persuade publishers to sign a letter of protest foundered. When the Wayne State University bookstore in Detroit withdrew *The Satanic Verses* from its shelves, faculty members who drew up a petition calling for a boycott of the store in protest were surprised to find few colleagues willing to sign.

Increasingly, however, independent bookstore owners spoke out against the withdrawal of the book by the major chains. Those that still had copies contrived to sell them, but many independents had run out and were awaiting further shipments from Viking Penguin. After its stock was depleted, the Harvard Book Store used the window display space formerly devoted to *The Satanic Verses* to display books on freedom of expression.

Gradually, momentum turned in favor of public rejection of the ayatollah's threats. On Wednesday, February 22, members of PEN American Center, including Norman Mailer and Susan Sontag, held a public reading of excerpts from *The Satanic Verses* in New York. The National Writers Union set up informational picket lines outside B. Dalton, Barnes & Noble, and Waldenbooks stores in six cities and also demonstrated outside the Iranian mission to the United Nations. The NWU stated that "removal of the book from the shelves sent a message any credible threat can banish, if not ban, a book." The NWU was apparently close to calling for a consumer boycott of the three major book chains.

Also on February 22, a full-page advertisement (Exhibit 1) was placed in the *New York Times* by the American Association of Publishers, the American Booksellers Association (which represented 80 percent of U.S. bookstores), and the American Library Association. The advertisement did not detail the locations, officers, or members of the three associations but announced that they would ensure that the book would be made available.

Late that same afternoon, B. Dalton announced that *The Satanic Verses* would be on sale again in B. Dalton and Barnes & Noble stores "as soon as it is available from the publishers." Viking Penguin had announced that a

---

EXHIBIT 1   *New York Times* Advertisement

**Today is the publication date of
Salman Rushdie's book**

THE SATANIC VERSES

FREE PEOPLE WRITE BOOKS

FREE PEOPLE PUBLISH BOOKS

FREE PEOPLE SELL BOOKS

FREE PEOPLE BUY BOOKS

FREE PEOPLE READ BOOKS

**In the spirit of America's commitment to
free expression we inform the public that this book
will be available to readers at bookstores and
libraries throughout the country.**

**Association of American Publishers
American Booksellers Association
American Library Association**

---

second printing of 100,000 copies would reach bookstores easily the following week. B. Dalton said the resumption of sales was decided on "at the urging of the overwhelming majority of our store managers."

Executives at Waldenbooks had to reconsider their options. They had to decide whether to stock *The Satanic Verses* and, if they decided to stock it, whether to advertise and display it or merely to have it available on request. Also at issue was whether to establish a chainwide policy or to delegate these decisions to individual store managers. A statement would have to be issued to the media promptly.

SOURCES

Ibrahim, Youssef M. "European Community Nations Reply to Khomeini." *New York Times*, February 21, 1989, pp. A-1, A-8.

"Furor over *Satanic Verses* Puts a Halt to Iranian Talks on European Lending." *The Wall Street Journal*, February 24, 1989, p. A-9.

Rosenblatt, Roger. "Zealots with Fear in Their Eyes." *U.S. News & World Report*, February 27, 1989, pp. 8–11.

"Satanic Strategy." *New York Times*, February 22, 1989.

"Satanic Times for Stores and Statesmen." *The Wall Street Journal*, February 22, 1989, p. B-1.

Sharkey, Joe. "B. Dalton to Sell *The Satanic Verses* as Writers Protest." *The Wall Street Journal*, February 23, 1989, pp. A-1, A-3.

Smith, William E. "Hunted by an Angry Faith." *Time*, February 27, 1989, pp. 28–33.

Watson, Russell. "A 'Satanic' Fury." *Newsweek*, February 27, 1989, pp. 34–39.

The Satanic Verses (B)

On Friday, February 24, 1989, Waldenbooks placed full-page advertisements (such as Exhibit 1) in nine major newspapers. Waldenbooks decided that it would resume selling *The Satanic Verses* but would "continue to use discretion in displaying the book." A second printing of 100,000 copies by Viking Penguin began to arrive in bookstores the following week.

By March 5, *The Satanic Verses* had reached second place on the *New York Times* Book Review fiction best-sellers list. On March 26, it assumed first place.

The Rushdie affair had an aftermath in the book publishing industry. In May, the *New York Times* criticized on its editorial page the participation of American publishers in the Iranian Book Fair held that month. On May 8, John Wiley & Sons, Inc., one of the participating publishers, sent a letter to its authors signed by the company chairman and president defending its position (Exhibit 2).

EXHIBIT 1 Waldenbooks Newspaper Advertisement

Waldenbooks' Position Regarding

THE SATANIC VERSES

A Statement of Fact in Troubled Times

1. We have never taken the book off sale and have completely sold all copies. (The publisher ran out of stock and it will be back in print within the next two weeks.)
2. We will continue to sell the book when it comes back in stock at the publisher.

This case was prepared from public sources by Professor John A. Quelch. Copyright © 1990 by the President and Fellows of Harvard College. Harvard Business School case N9-591-014 (rev. 3/5/91).

EXHIBIT 1 *(concluded)*

3. We will continue to use discretion in displaying the book.
4. We deplore the many threats of violence made against our stores and our people.
5. We admire the courage of our people who have gallantly performed in the face of bomb threats and unfair castigation.
6. Waldenbooks is a staunch supporter of First Amendment Rights.

Harry Hoffman
President & CEO
Waldenbooks

EXHIBIT 2   John Wiley & Sons Letter to Authors

Recently The New York Times reported in its news columns, and then also commented on its editorial page, on participation in the May Iranian Book Fair by a number of European and American publishers. John Wiley and McGraw-Hill were named as American publishers who had chosen to participate in the event.

Two elements of The Times's pieces raised questions we would like to discuss with you.

The Times said that Wiley and McGraw-Hill had "broken ranks" with other U.S. publishers on the question of participation in the fair. There was in fact no industry or trade-association position on this issue. Indeed, there were no ranks to be "broken."

Additionally, The Times asserted that Viking Penguin had appealed to Wiley, McGraw-Hill, and other publishers not to participate in the event. No such appeal was made to Wiley at any time; we are informed that no such appeal was made to McGraw-Hill.

The Iran Book Fair has proved not to be a legitimate international fair, and both Wiley and McGraw-Hill have withdrawn their participation. Nonetheless, we believe it useful to explain why it is Wiley's policy to exhibit books at all legitimate book fairs.

Like all other major international scientific and technical publishers, Wiley was invited many months ago to exhibit books at the Teheran Book Fair in May. Shortly thereafter, we—like most if not all of our colleagues—shipped a number of books to Iran to be displayed.

When—much later, and in an entirely unrelated development—Salman Rushdie was threatened by Iran, we vigorously supported him, his publishers, and the right of his book to be sold and read. A Wiley vice chairman who is president of the International Publishers Association led that organization in worldwide support of those same goals. Another vice chairman of Wiley is an officer and director of the Association of American Publishers, which with the American Booksellers Association supported with advertising Salman Rushdie and the freedom of authors and publishers to write and publish without fear or censorship.

EXHIBIT 2 *(concluded)*

We did not withdraw the Wiley books that had been shipped to Teheran. For one thing, the books had been delivered and were no longer under our control. But more important was our belief—a belief we strongly hold—that our policy of displaying our authors' books at international fairs is consistent with the very rights that we insisted should be afforded Salman Rushdie and his book.

Wiley and others have been criticized for "greed" in being willing to display books at such fairs. Anyone who knows the international book trade, particularly as it exists in Third World countries, knows that this is nonsense. There is in fact no immediate profit to be earned from such activities. The results are not likely to be felt for years to come, if ever.

Publishers distribute books worldwide because such distribution is part of the social contract of being a publisher. While it can be considered a long-term investment, it can more aptly be described as an expression of the belief that materials printed in the free world stimulate the sort of thinking that may ultimately lead to a world in which information can easily cross boundaries.

This belief must not be dismissed as visionary. It has happened in this decade. Nations once as fiercely hostile as Iran to outside ideas have in recent years dramatically changed their attitudes. Books published in the United States are now welcomed in countries where the very possession of such a book was once considered a crime against the state. Seeds of freedom do indeed travel with books.

We believe that authors must be free to write what, how, and when they choose. And we believe that publishers must be free to distribute the books written by their authors anywhere and everywhere. We reject the notion that a publisher or a nation should respond to censorship with more censorship.

That belief is also part of U.S. international policy, which excludes printed materials from trade boycotts of nations. Our nation exempts newspapers, periodicals, and books from trade embargoes because Americans believe that a free flow of information not only preserves freedom in our country but also stimulates it abroad.

We will continue to uphold the right of Salman Rushdie and all other authors to write unafraid and uncensored, without restriction or censorship. At the same time we will continue to support the principle that a publisher must be free to exhibit the work of its authors without restriction.

We see no conflict here; we believe that in both instances, the freedom of ideas is the issue. Since our founding in 1807, we have been in the forefront of these rights—the freedom of ideas to travel across our country and throughout the world.

Chapter 6.5

In the News

6.5.1 BENETTON IS ACCUSED OF DUBIOUS TACTICS BY SOME STORE OWNERS*

Karle Falkenberg, a blond model who adores clothes, wanted to run her own boutique. She didn't have any business experience, but she says a representative for Benetton, the trendy Italian apparel chain, told her that she had something more important: Young and vivacious, she had "the Benetton spirit."

So the former pro-football cheerleader entered into a handshake deal—but not a written contract—with the Benetton representative. In December 1984 at a Madison, Alabama, mall, Mrs. Falkenberg began selling the brightly colored knitwear that has made Benetton S.p.A. one of modern retailing's biggest success stories, a family company that started as a sweater maker in 1965 and now claims about 4,500 stores worldwide.

But Mrs. Falkenberg's dream of running her own business soon turned into a nightmare, and today she is enmeshed in a messy dispute with Benetton's U.S. subsidiary over bills totaling $1.2 million.

Many Complaints

She complains that, although her store was in the Deep South, much of her first shipment was

* By Teri Agins, staff reporter of *The Wall Street Journal*, October 24, 1988. Reprinted by permission of *The Wall Street Journal*, © 1988 Dow Jones and Company, Inc. All Rights Reserved Worldwide.

heavy wool sweaters. Benetton repeatedly sent damaged merchandise and refused to take anything back, she says, and in 1986 it shipped her $80,000 worth of clothing she didn't order. The Benetton representative, Gilberto Casagrande, pressured her into opening three more stores nearby by saying that otherwise he would find someone to open competing outlets in those locations, she charges. She adds that none of her five stores ever turned a profit.

Mrs. Falkenberg isn't the only store owner complaining. Earlier this year, she organized a meeting, in Birmingham, Alabama, of 15 store owners representing 40 Benetton outlets all around the country. Their conclusion, she says: "Benetton didn't care anything about us."

Small-business people who own dozens of Benetton outlets accuse the company of questionable marketing tactics. At least four civil lawsuits allege that the company or its representatives engaged in, among other things, fraud, extortion, and various financial misrepresentations. Some of the suits charge that Benetton is violating laws designed to protect small businesses from abuses by franchisers and that it, in fact, is run as a franchise operation but has failed to meet registration and disclosure requirements.

Company's Position

However, Benetton S.p.A. says, "For the few dissatisfied shop owners, there are 4,500 shop owners who run successful businesses and who

Benetton is very proud to work with." The number of U.S. Benetton outlets now totals 693.

Moreover, the Federal Trade Commission, which enforces federal franchise regulations, and regulators in states with their own statutes say they haven't received any complaints about Benetton. Franchise agreements in many industries have sparked litigation in recent years.

Some Benetton store owners say they are afraid to complain. Operating without contracts, they believe that they don't have any legal recourse. Benetton recently reinforced that perception when it sent store owners an "authorization" to sign. Despite the company's aversion to lawyers and contracts, the document says any disputes between store owners and Benetton are to be settled by the courts in Treviso, Italy. A cover letter defended the document on the ground that Benetton was "restructuring and merging."

"It's the classic case of David versus Goliath," says David Slater, an attorney and former owner of the Mister Donut of America, Inc., franchise chain. "They know people have their life savings tied up in these businesses and they can't litigate forever."

Benetton denies all charges on the specific accusations by unhappy store owners and steadfastly maintains that it isn't a franchise operation and thus isn't subject to franchise requirements. Store owners, it says, are licensees because they own their stores and don't pay royalties to Benetton, as franchisees typically do. Although it acknowledges that a few store owners have complained, it blames any problems on the owners themselves or on its field representatives who deal directly with them.

Benetton disclaims any responsibility for the representatives because, it says, they also are independent business people, not Benetton employees. Aldo Palmeri, the managing director of Benetton Group S.p.A., acknowledges that among Benetton's 70 representatives worldwide "there are some who are not the very best

that we can have. We can change them in some cases. . . . But in 99 percent of the cases, the system works perfectly."

In addition, Mr. Casagrande specifically denies Mrs. Falkenberg's allegations. "The reality is that she received merchandise that she didn't pay for," he says. "I am responsible for her bills; I have to pay the money to Benetton. I think that it is something unfair when people owe me money and turn around and try to sue me."

Federico Minoli, the general manager of Benetton Services Corporation, the U.S. subsidiary, minces no words about Mrs. Falkenberg and other griping store owners: "No matter what has happened, we don't think we owe them anything." He says only about 20 U.S. stores closed last year, for various reasons.

He adds, however, that he "fired" Mr. Casagrande this summer after getting many complaints from Southern store owners. Mr. Casagrande replies that Mr. Minoli didn't fire him and that Mr. Minoli is saying that "for legal reasons." Mr. Casagrande adds that he is still serving as a "consultant" for Benetton's office in New Orleans. Mr. Minoli denies that.

Clearly, not all Benetton store owners are disgruntled. Ival Goldstein says he has put up with the Benetton's quirky habits since he opened a store in Chattanooga, Tennessee, last year because he is getting plenty of business and making money. In Tampa, Florida, Frank Garcia owns 22 stores and says he plans more. "I've made a lot of money with Benetton," he says.

Shari Johnson, who owns two North Dakota stores, also says she is content, but she adds that she feels "totally at Benetton's mercy. I know they would stop shipping to me if I did something they didn't like."

The breakneck speed at which Benetton became the McDonald's of knitwear is already a retailing legend. In 1965, Luciano Benetton and his sister Guiliana began making sweaters they sold through Italian department stores. Three years later, the Benettons were penetrating Italy and the rest of Europe with a chain of studio-size Benetton boutiques, often clustered close together. By the end of 1982, the Ponzano Veneto, Italy, company had expanded to 1,800 outlets.

Move into U.S.

After saturating Europe, the company invaded the U.S., aided by ubiquitous "United Colors of Benetton" ads showing multiracial crowds swaddled in layers of Benetton knitwear. Today, Luciano, Guiliana, and two brothers run a $1.2 billion empire headquartered in a magnificent 17th-century villa.

Helping propel this phenomenal growth is a novel distribution strategy. Instead of opening its own outlets—a risky, costly proposition—Benetton has representatives who scout out small investors to open stores. Each representative supervises the stores in his territory and gets a commission on merchandise the stores order. The store owners can sell only Benetton clothes and must follow the Benetton marketing plan.

Benetton's strategy also reflects the unorthodox ideas of Luciano Benetton, considered the company's spiritual leader. A stately six-footer, Mr. Benetton jaunts around the world in a private jet preaching the Benetton philosophy, a curious sort of laid-back, utopian optimism.

"We have caused a [new] type of retailer to become important who, until the day before, was perhaps a florist or a hairdresser. His prior career was of no importance, but he had to have the right spirit to work in a Benetton shop," Mr. Benetton told an interviewer preparing a Harvard Business School case study.

A Matter of Faith

In a lengthy profile published in the *New Yorker* magazine in 1986 and often used by Benetton representatives to help sign up recruits, Mr. Benetton pontificated on Benetton's supposedly unique ties with its store owners. The retail pacts were devoid of lawyers and contracts, he noted, possessing instead "a rapport made up

of handshakes and understanding and knowledge on a human level and also of extreme faith, total faith."

To meet the FTC's definition of a franchise, three conditions must be satisfied: A company must distribute goods or services identified by a trademark; offer significant assistance and exercise control over the franchisees' operations; and require a franchise fee or payment of $500 or more in the first six months of operation.

Since 1979, the FTC has required franchisers covered under the rule to furnish disclosure documents to prospective franchisees. In addition, 15 states require state registration of franchisers, with all but two of them requiring their regulators to review disclosure documents. Among such documents are audited financial statements of franchisers; the names and addresses of at least 10 franchisees nearest to the proposed location; litigation and bankruptcy disclosures by the franchiser and key executives; and details about the franchise relationship (including any financing assistance, expansion plans in the area, information about franchisees that have been terminated, and conditions under which the relationship can be ended).

Like other store owners, Tony Joudi, who opened a Benetton store in El Paso, Texas, two years ago, says he never signed a formal contract with his representative or Benetton. Nor did he get any financial-disclosure statement. Instead, he received a promotional package consisting of favorable news articles about Benetton.

Some Early Surprises

But once Mr. Joudi was in business, he says what happened was a far cry from what his representative had told him. "It was like they were playing a trick on you," he says. His start-up costs were $138,000, more than twice what he says that his representative had predicted. They included fixtures required by the company and the salaries and expenses of four assemblers who flew in from Italy to set up the store.

Mr. Joudi's first order, which his representative placed, came several weeks late, and he got clothes that he recognized from "two or three seasons ago" that Mr. Joudi wanted to mark down immediately. But his representative told him his selling price: 2.7 times the wholesale price.

"They sent me a note to tell me that I couldn't sell on discount unless it was approved by Benetton," Mr. Joudi says. Jacques Chahbazian, the representative, says the letter was "for the good of the retailer." Mr. Chahbazian disputes Mr. Joudi's description of the arrangement. He says store owners could choose "American sources" as well as Italian ones to get the fixtures. And he denies shipping Mr. Joudi clothes that he didn't order.

By getting heavily involved in the stores' marketing and other operations, Benetton frequently acted just like a franchiser—a heavy-handed one at that. Store owners regularly received memos from their representatives telling them how to run their businesses. One April 1987 memo advised stores on hiring sales help: "Please skip over [women with] makeup, long nails, fat bodies." Another banned eating and smoking in the stores because the odors could penetrate the clothing.

Twice a year, some stores were billed for at least $50 worth of Benetton mail-order catalogs that they were told to display. Store owners say they were shocked to discover that the catalogs directly competed with them—the mail-order goods were priced a few dollars cheaper, and the revenues went straight to Benetton.

Pushing a Book

To show the Benetton spirit, some store owners were also asked to buy a shipment of Luciano Benetton's "Benetton Color Style File." The book, with a suggested retail price of $20, promised in the introduction to be "a celebration of color, sometimes serious, sometimes irreverent, but always inspiring." Sherry Cupit, a Laurel, Mississippi, store owner, reluctantly bought $700 worth of the books at her representative's behest. She hasn't sold one.

Benetton denies that all this makes the company a franchiser. Mr. Minoli says the company doesn't get any revenue from the sale of Benetton-approved store fixtures because they are made by other companies. And although Benetton representatives once told store owners the prices at which they could sell, they no longer do. Nor are the owners still expected to buy the mail-order catalogs.

Mr. Minoli blames the current problems on store owners who are "bad managers" or "bad retailers." Store owners, he says, should put their faith in their representatives to supervise them but, at the same time, should stand up to representatives who sell aggressively. "It is up to the store owner to make the right buy," he adds.

But Harold Brown, a Boston attorney who often represents franchisees, says Benetton's argument that its representatives are acting on their own is dubious. "Benetton is giving the representatives apparent authority over its operations, which puts them in the womb of the [franchise] law," he says.

Although the FTC hasn't taken an official position on whether Benetton is a franchiser, Craig Tregillus, its chief of franchise enforcement, comments that Benetton's requirement that store owners buy company-approved fixtures could constitute a franchise fee.

Some Other Cases

Benetton isn't the first foreign-based retailer that has set up dealerships to avoid the franchise identity. The seven Rive Gauche boutiques that sell designer clothes by Yves St. Laurent in the United States "function like franchises, but we don't like to call them that," concedes Ari Hoffman, a marketing vice president of Paris Collections, Inc., which owns the U.S. license.

In 1986, KIS Corporation, the U.S. operation of a French company, sold some photographic minilabs to about 100 Wisconsin investors under a licensee arrangement, and state regulators accused the company of operating an unregistered franchise operation. KIS successfully avoided trouble because Wisconsin regulators failed to prove that KIS actually "prescribed" a marketing plan. After losing a decision in an administrative hearing conducted by state securities regulators, the state broadened its franchise law to envelop marketing plans that are "suggested" as well as prescribed.

Among Americans taking grievances against Benetton to court is Frances Robertson, a former owner of two Oregon stores. She says she was long afraid to draw attention to her problems because her representative warned that Benetton would "stop shipping to store owners who cause trouble." Finally, last month, Mrs. Robertson and her mother sued Benetton in Oregon federal court, alleging, among other things, that the company violated Oregon franchise and sales laws. The women also contend that the representative threatened to revoke their license and halt deliveries in order to get them to accept unwanted merchandise.

Robert Spirito, Mrs. Robertson's representative, denies her allegations and says he didn't threaten her. He adds: "If they expect to go months and months without paying [Benetton] and without establishing a letter of credit, how can I continue to ship to them?"

Louisiana Suit

In another suit, filed last February in Louisiana state court, Gloria Frost alleges that her Benetton representative, Mr. Casagrande, urged her to open a Sisley shop, another Benetton chain, next to her Benetton store in Lafayette.

After Mrs. Frost declined to open a new store, the suit says, Mr. Casagrande himself opened a Sisley shop directly across from her "with the specific purpose and intent to drive [Mrs. Frost] out of business." Mrs. Frost's attorney obtained an affidavit, which was filed in court, from a New Orleans customs broker who says that he held up a shipment of Benetton merchandise to her on orders from Mr. Casagrande. But Mr. Casagrande comments, "There's nothing true in any of that."

Two other suits have been filed. Stephen S. Iandolo, a former Chicago store owner, sued Benetton in 1986 in an Illinois federal court seeking damages "in excess of $250,000." Among the allegations, the suit charged that Benetton enforced pricing schedules, under its right to cease supplying merchandise and to terminate store owners for any reason.

The other suit, a counterclaim, was filed in 1987 against Benetton's Minneapolis representative by Linda Dossey in a Washington state court. The suit charges, among other things, that the representative misrepresented the financial condition of four Seattle stores that she agreed to buy.

Mr. Minoli, the U.S. general manager, says Benetton recently dropped its strategy of saturating the market with small stores. Now, it is concentrating on "professionalism" and the servicing of existing stores, he says. New stores will be larger outlets, called United Colors, that will offer a much broader range of merchandise. Benetton plans to have 10 United Colors shops operating in the United States by next spring. Mr. Minoli also estimates that as many as 100 smaller Benetton stores may close in the next five years.

But with Benetton not owning the stores, what will cause them to go out of business? "The forces of demand in the market," Mr. Minoli says.

Meanwhile, Mrs. Falkenberg and Mrs. Cupit, the Mississippi store owner, have taken down their Benetton logos and are selling other brands of clothes. "We have no choice," Mrs. Falkenberg says. "We are stuck in leases and we've built up a following; so, we might as well stay in business selling clothes."

6.5.2   THE BANKS: REDLINING AND RHETORIC*

Within a matter of weeks, Boston's headlines should be simmering and news broadcasts brimming with charges of redlining and racism, as two controversial reports on bank-lending practice in low-income neighborhoods are released.

The studies, one conducted by the Boston Redevelopment Authority (BRA) and one by the Boston Federal Reserve Bank, both due out this summer, are almost certain to verify earlier reports that bank policies are biased against people living in poor neighborhoods. And they're almost certain to set off a chain reaction of rhetoric among those in the thick of housing policy and politics in Boston.

Housing advocates and politicians will charge that the banks are guilty of blatant mortgage-lending discrimination against low-income people—which is true. The banks will claim that the studies don't represent the complete picture of mortgage lending in low-income areas—which is also true. And the Federal Reserve Bank, which regulates local banks, will more than likely offer a truism of its own: if limited access to housing is to change in Boston, banks will have to do something constructive very soon.

Right now, bankers are engaging in less-than-constructive business policies in minority neighborhoods.

"The banks don't deal with realtors in black neighborhoods, they don't provide the same types of services and mortgages they do in other

neighborhoods, and they don't market in black neighborhoods," says Mary O'Hara, president of the Massachusetts Urban Reinvestment Advisory Group (MURAG), which monitors bank adherence to the Community Reinvestment Act (CRA), the federal law that requires that lenders respond to community credit needs.

The evidence is overwhelming. Boston has the widest gap between wages and housing prices of any metropolitan area in the country. The rate of black homeownership as a percentage of white homeownership is lower here than in 47 other major metropolitan areas, according to a survey conducted by the Joint Center for Political Studies in Washington, D.C. If low-income people, minorities, and indeed, the average Boston resident—who earns less than $25,000 a year—are to gain any access to the area's soft but still wildly inflated housing market, something radical in the way banks do business is going to have to change.

"A family needs an income of over $60,000 to afford the typical Boston-area home, which costs $181,000, but the average wage is less than $25,000," says Peter Dreier, director of housing for the BRA. "In terms of expanding the American Dream, that is a recipe for disaster."

Indications that Boston banks might be engaging in a 1980s version of redlining—refusing to lend mortgage and home-rehabilitation money in areas deemed poor financial risks—surfaced in January of this year, when preliminary results of a Federal Reserve Bank study were leaked to the *Boston Globe*. The paper's report that the Fed study concluded that bank lending was racially biased in Boston touched off cries of outrage among activists and politicians and claims of unfairness and inaccuracy among bankers.

The BRA immediately hired Minnesota-based economist Charles Finn, who has conducted redlining studies throughout the country, to begin a similar study here. And bankers started an informal campaign to discredit the preliminary results of the Fed study as well as Finn's reputation for objectivity. Late in May, for example, the Massachusetts Bankers Association held a special session for reporters in which it outlined what it considers potential weaknesses in the study.

Bankers insist that both the authors of the initial Fed study and Finn (in his work in other cities and his preliminary inquiries here) misrepresent the true picture of access to mortgage money in minority neighborhoods by tracking only bank lending in the neighborhoods. Mortgage companies and homeowners provide most of the mortgages in those neighborhoods, they point out, rendering access to credit easier than the two studies make it seem. Bankers also note that the studies use census data that are more than 10 years old and that they include figures from 1986, an atypical lending year when interest rates were low and a number of homeowners refinanced their home loans.

According to a source close to the banking community, the bankers tried to use their claims of inaccuracy to convince Fed president and chief executive officer Richard Syron to deep-six plans to produce a more in-depth housing study than the one leaked to the *Globe*. But Syron wouldn't have it. Instead, he called for a thorough study of local lending (the one slated to be released this summer) and a series of forums to look at banking-access problems. The Massachusetts Bankers Association eventually signed on to co-sponsor the forums.

Congress enacted the CRA in 1977 to ensure that banks meet the credit needs of low- and moderate-income people who live in the communities they serve. Under the original tenets of the law, banks weren't required to prove they were meeting local credit needs unless they were challenged by a community group when they attempted to expand, limit, or merge their banking services.

MURAG, for one, challenged a number of banks and received a number of concessions for Boston-area communities throughout the 1980s, including a 1980 deal with the Bank of New England—one of the first CRA agreements

in the country—whereby the bank offers a certain number of mortgages that are more accessible than average to low- and moderate-income homebuyers.

Even as local banks have been forced to comply with CRA regulations, though, they've fallen behind banks in other cities in demonstrating a significant commitment to meeting the needs of the entire city.

A few local financial institutions—most notably State Street Bank, the Shawmut Bank, and the Bank of New England—have been active in the Boston Housing Partnership, which has worked to help build or rehabilitate 2,000 units of affordable housing worth more than $150 million. But that partnership was founded and nurtured by an individual banker—State Street chairman William Edgerly—and it doesn't fulfill the banks' obligations under the CRA.

Few Boston banks have initiated the kinds of bold affordable-housing programs and consortiums now common in other cities. These include Chase Manhattan's $200 million commitment, announced last week, to finance housing and economic development in poor New York neighborhoods; the relatively small Wilmington Savings Bank of Wilmington, Delaware's $25 million loan pool that will serve homebuyers in low- and moderate-income neighborhoods; the Harris Bank of Chicago's $35 million low-income loans program; and the Atlanta bankers' consortium that's set up a $65 million loan fund that allows qualified applicants lower interest rates and closing costs.

At the same time, Boston banks have engaged in what some call a disinvestment policy in poor and minority neighborhoods.

During the 1980s, deregulation allowed banks to expand their scope and services at an unprecedented clip, and they stumbled over one another to get into new lines of business—including the kind of rampant and speculative lending to condominium developers that is now showing up on bank ledgers as a wash of red ink.

At the same time, banks were competing to open branches in the suburbs and to lend money to ill-conceived, high-end condo projects, such as the now-bankrupt Paragon Park, they were pulling out of minority neighborhoods at an alarming pace.

Half the local bank branches in Boston's predominantly minority neighborhoods—Roxbury, Mattapan, North Dorchester, and the South End—have closed within the past 10 years. At the same time, the number of branches in mostly white East Boston, West Roxbury, and Hyde Park have grown. According to a *Globe* survey, Boston's 12 largest banks maintain five times as many offices in the city's white neighborhoods as they do in minority areas. Automated teller machines (ATMs) are rarities in minority neighborhoods as well.

"What this does is make us go to armbreakers for our banking needs," says Diana Strother, a Roxbury resident who co-chairs the Massachusetts Affordable Housing Alliance's Homebuyers Union. "We have to go to check-cashing joints, which charge a lot of money to cash a check, or to Bradlees or Zayre, which have a minimum amount."

Because they often don't have local banks, many people in Strother's neighborhood don't have checking and savings accounts. Without those, they have no track record or line of credit with a bank if they want to apply for a mortgage or a housing-rehabilitation loan. Absent those loans, they're unable to buy or fix up homes in their neighborhood. And so in this Catch-22, Boston minority neighborhoods remain the kind of run-down, rapidly deteriorating place banks making mortgage loans tend to avoid.

Banking and housing-market observers in Boston offer different explanations for the banks' reluctance to jump eagerly into the community reinvestment fray.

"What you got right around the time the CRA was passed was new emphasis among banks on profitability," says the well-placed banking-community observer. "The market was forcing them to become more competitive. They knew they had to obey the law. But no one was telling young loan officers to be aggressive about it—because it isn't profitable."

Some community activists admit their efforts at bank monitoring have in the past been scattershot and not particularly effective. For years, they say, the housing-advocacy community allowed MURAG to take the lead in battling with the banks to get them to fulfill their responsibilities to their communities, even though several activists disagreed with some of the principles and politics of MURAG chairman Hugh McCormack. (In 1986, for instance, a coalition of housing activists opposed a move by an out-of-state bank to acquire Capitol Bank, which had financed scores of speculative condominium conversions that were displacing tenants in places like Allston-Brighton. McCormack didn't.) It is only recently that local organizations, such as the Greater Roxbury Neighborhood Authority, have vowed to do their own bank monitoring.

Whatever the reasons for it, the banks' reluctance to engage actively in community-based lending has helped create what activists like Marvin Martin of the neighborhood authority sees as a two-tiered social system in this city.

"Homeownership is something that has always been considered a right in this country," Martin said at a June 22 Fed forum on housing. "Right now, a whole class of people is being denied that right."

Federal bank regulators took a few steps toward helping to ensure the right to decent housing in March, when they announced revisions to the Community Reinvestment Act, calling on banks to live up to their "affirmative responsibility to treat the credit needs of low- and moderate-income members of their community, consistent with sound banking."

But a beefed-up CRA is not enough. Since revisions to the act were announced, some banks have attempted to ease their mortgage requirements slightly, so more moderate-income people can qualify for home loans. The Bank of Boston, for instance, in May announced a $50-million first-time mortgage program that lends to homebuyers at a below-market interest rate and requires them to pay minimal closing costs.

The bank's program is certainly a welcome one in the third-highest-priced housing market in the United States. But the bank made a critical mistake by announcing it at its Dudley Square branch. For while the mortgage program will be useful to people who earn $35,000 to $40,000 a year, it will be well out of reach of most residents of the Dudley Square area, whose average income is $15,000.

The banks don't know the needs of low-income neighborhoods, and, because they don't know them, they don't understand them. For any real change in bank lending practices to take place, the "culture and intent and focus" of lending institutions will have to change, according to the Reverend Charles Stith, one of Boston's most prominent black leaders.

"Folks in banks who are doing deals are going to have to go and look at Roxbury," Stith said in a phone interview last week. "You can't make a decision about Roxbury if all you know about it is what you read in the papers. People die of old age in Roxbury. There are streets with trees and kids that play and folks that are happily married. It's crazy that the buck now stops at the Roxbury line."

There is growing political pressure on the banks to stop passing the buck. The Federal Reserve Board recently denied the Chicago-based Continental Bank's request to buy a small bank in Arizona because Continental had not fulfilled its obligations under the CRA. The U.S. House of Representatives has passed amendments to Congress's $157 billion bailout of the corrupt and bankrupt savings-and-loan industry, sponsored by Congressman Joe Kennedy (D-Massachusetts), that would require lending institutions to release data on race, gender, and income of all applicants for home

mortgages. And last week, three Boston city councilors introduced a measure that would encourage banks to reinvest profits in local neighborhoods.

A handful of Boston bankers acknowledge the problem of low-income lending in the city is a critical one. Boston Fed head Syron is one. Bank of New England chairman Richard Driscoll is another. Speaking to a room full of bankers and community activists at the Fed forum, Driscoll noted that "certainly banks have to stop saying, 'We've never done it this way before,' or 'Our policies prevent us from doing that,' or . . . 'give it [the job of financing low-and moderate-income housing] to the government.' "

But the more-progressive bankers will have to recognize that more than cathartic forums are needed. As Strother, of the Homebuyers Union, puts it, "It's all well and good to have a forum. What I want to know is, where's the action?"

Because Boston has lagged behind other cities in meeting community credit needs, it can look to a number of models for progressive ideas on how to proceed to catch up. Alan Fishbein, general counsel to the Washington-based Center for Community Change, which works with low-income groups on community reinvestment, points to a number of successful community-reinvestment agreements.

"Banks are looking for safe, cookie-cutter loans," he says. But there are many things banks can do to increase credit access besides offering low-interest loans. "They can have active small-business outreach programs," Fishbein says. "They can be flexible in their underwriting: if people can't afford a down payment, they can require 3 percent as a down payment. They can offer special rehab loans, and give someone the extra $25,000 they need to fix up a deteriorating property."

Community groups, such as the Community Investment Coalition, an umbrella group formed recently to try to pressure banks to help create affordable housing, offer a number of suggestions for improving access to credit for low-income Boston residents. They can offer "lifeline" no-charge checking and set up credit-information programs. They can do things as simple as printing information about home loans in Spanish, Portuguese, and Creole French. They can hire loan officers familiar with non-profit housing-development groups, which are increasingly putting together projects, such as limited-equity housing cooperatives, that banks are wary of because they're unfamiliar with them.

Banks that reach out to low-income customers, says Fishbein, "bring in new people and open a new market niche for a bank. Their loans are steady, safe-type loans. By and large, the banks find their experience with them is equal to or better than other parts of the bank's portfolio."

6.5.3   GROWTH OF MUSEUM SHOPS STIRS DEBATE ON TAX STATUS*

Tucked in among Bloomingdale's, the Gap, and other traditional stores at an upscale New Jersey mall is an artful newcomer to the retailing business. Selling fancy cards and gifts, it may look like a boutique found anywhere—only this one doesn't pay taxes.

The Short Hills, New Jersey, store is the recently opened gift shop of the Metropolitan Museum of Art. The venerable New York museum has a sister shop at a Stamford, Connecticut, mall and another within R.H. Macy's flagship store in Manhattan.

---

* By Teri Agins, staff reporter of *The Wall Street Journal*, February 27, 1989. Reprinted by permission of *The Wall Street Journal*, © 1989 Dow Jones and Company, Inc. All Rights Reserved Worldwide.

The Met's march beyond its portals is one of the most aggressive examples of a growing trend: Museums are becoming merchandisers.

For ages, museums have sold post cards, T-shirts, and other souvenirs, but such trifles are only for starters these days. In satellite stores like the Met's, through mail-order catalogs, and in expanded shops within their exhibition halls, museums are broadening their inventories, selling items ranging from jewelry to antique furniture. The popularity of the shops has spawned at least one major for-profit imitator, the 19-store Nature Company retail chain specializing in items on wildlife and nature.

But as museums ring up sales, they are coming under scrutiny from both the government and tax-paying retailers irked at the tax-free edge their new competition enjoys. Specifically, a congressional subcommittee is looking into nonprofit organizations' retail ventures and, in the end, some rules could be changed. Meanwhile, last year the Internal Revenue Service audited the American Folk Art Museum in New York. Although the museum has been without a gallery space since 1986, it has continued to operate a retail shop selling crafts and even opened a second store last year. A museum spokesman says it received "a clean bill of health."

Hard pressed for funds, many museums say they have little choice but to promote their retailing activities. They are looking for "creative ways to generate capital," notes Beverly Barsook, executive director for the Museum Store Association, a trade group with 1,300 members.

The Metropolitan Museum says income from its endowment has shrunk to 16.6 percent of its annual budget from 62.2 percent in 1967. Last year retailing contributed about $5 million, or 8 percent, of the Met's budget, up from about $4 million, or 4 percent, in 1985. The Museum Store Association adds that for most of its members—which tend to be far smaller than the Met—profits are only a fraction of that amount.

The majority earn less than $150,000 a year, it says.

Museum shops also insist that, although they've become more aggressive sellers, they're making an increased effort to relate their inventory to their operations. To tie in with its Machine Age exhibition in 1986, the shop at New York's Brooklyn Museum sold art deco kitchenware and vintage radios that were specially purchased during a museum-shop buying trip to New Orleans.

Among the items for sale at Old Salem, a historic Germanic settlement in Winston-Salem, North Carolina, is some old-fashioned Delft chinaware specially commissioned by the museum. "In the last eight years, we've transformed from being just another nice general gift store to a store with historical reference to the museum," a spokeswoman for Old Salem says.

At the Exploratorium, a science and industry museum in San Francisco, that means selling Silly Putty in special educational packages that explain the stretchy, bouncy toy's scientific properties. Binney & Smith, Inc., which makes Silly Putty, provided the special packaging because "it sheds some new light on the product as an educational product," says a company spokesman.

Still, nonprofit museum shops have gone far enough afield to raise eyebrows. The Metropolitan Museum of Art, for example, has licensed its name to two home-furnishings manufacturers to allow them to sell "museum collections" of sheets and fabrics. Then there is the Smithsonian Institution, which has nine shops in Washington and sends out mail-order catalogs to more than five million people a year. The institution—whose shops made $6.6 million on sales of $43.5 million in 1987—recently announced that it will begin selling video-cassettes, the first being an educational tape about whales.

That annoys Kenton Pattie, who runs a business distributing videotapes and is a spokesman for the Coalition for Unfair Competition, which represents 27 trade groups. The Fairfax, Virginia, businessman says museum shops are part of a larger problem with merchandising by nonprofit institutions. Mr. Pattie charges that many nonprofit institutions, including hospitals and universities, "are enjoying lower postal rates and avoiding business taxes at the expense of tax-paying" enterprises.

The House Ways and Means Committee is expected to soon consider proposals to tax nonprofit groups on items they sell that are unrelated to their businesses. A spokesman for the Subcommittee on Oversight, which prepared the proposals, says they include taxing museums on sales of reproductions and artifacts whose value exceeds $50, unless they are "educational materials." Museum T-shirts and mementos under $15 would be tax-free, but royalty income not tied to the museum's educational efforts—the Met's bed-sheet licensing business, for example—would be subject to income tax.

Such new rules seem only fair to Mr. Pattie, who complains that big retail enterprises like the Smithsonian's "are channeling their profits not just to the museum but into selling more products."

Dealer Termination Agreements and Resale Price Maintenance*

Patrick J. Kaufmann

INTRODUCTION

It is difficult to imagine an area of the law that elicits stronger disagreement between suppliers[1] and retailers than the prohibition against resale price maintenance. From the 1911 Supreme Court decision in the *Dr. Miles* case to the present there has been an ongoing debate about the wisdom, effect, and dimensions of that prohibition. [*Dr. Miles Medical Co.* v. *John D. Park & Sons Co.*, 220 US 373 (1911).] In recent years, however, this debate has intensified, and the executive, legislative, and judicial branches have never been farther apart in their views on the matter. Two recent events: the introduction in Congress of an amendment to the Sherman Act, and the Supreme Court decision in the *Business Electronics* case bear directly on that debate. [*Business Electronics Corp.* v. *Sharp Electronics Corp.*, 56 LW 4387 (1988).] Both focus on the termination of price-cutting dealers and, therefore, raise issues critical to suppliers, dealers, and consumers.

In this chapter I examine the three most important issues addressed by the proposed amendment and the Supreme Court's decision: (1) the *per se* treatment of resale price maintenance agreements; (2) the evidence sufficient to allow a jury to infer a dealer-supplier conspiracy; and (3) the proper dividing line between *per se* resale price maintenance agreements and rule of reason

---

* This chapter first appeared as "Dealer Termination Agreements and Resale Price Maintenance: Implications of the *Business Electronics* Case and the Proposed Amendment to the Sherman Act," *Journal of Retailing* 64, no. 2 (Summer 1988), pp. 113–24. Reprinted by permission of the *Journal of Retailing.*

[1] Supplier here is used to refer generally to a party that sells to another for resale. The comments would apply equally to manufacturer or wholesaler.

nonprice restraints. In order to appreciate the current state of the law concerning resale price maintenance (generally, and as it applies specifically to dealer termination), we examine each of these issues in light of the recent action by Congress and the Court. In the concluding section some implications are drawn for retailers and suppliers.

PER SE TREATMENT OF RESALE PRICE MAINTENANCE

Resale price maintenance is prohibited as a "contract, combination . . . or conspiracy, in restraint of trade" under section 1 of the Sherman Act. It falls within the general category of vertical restraints; along with territorial restrictions, customer restrictions, and other vertical nonprice agreements. It differs from other vertical restraints because of its direct effect on price, and consequently has come to be treated differently by the courts. [Sherman Antitrust Act, 15 USC 1]

Although the Sherman Act appears to prohibit all concerted activity in restraint of trade, early in its history it was interpreted by the Supreme Court to apply only to unreasonable restraints. [*Standard Oil Co.* v. *United States*, 221 US 1 (1911).] The reasonableness of a questioned restraint is tested by examining its history, nature, intent, and expected competitive effect in a process of industry analysis known as the "rule of reason." However, some classes of restraints (e.g., agreements between competitors to fix prices) have been identified as having such a "pernicious effect on competition" that there could be no justification for engaging in them. [*Northern Pacific Railway* v. *United States*, 356 US 1 (1958).] They are illegal *per se* (i.e., illegal in and of themselves). For those classes of restraints, therefore, rule of reason analysis is not necessary. Once an agreement is classified as falling into one of the *per se* classes of restraints, there is no reason to examine its intent or effect; it is presumed anticompetitive. *Per se* treatment of a particular type of agreement, therefore, is significant in that it precludes the defendant from arguing any extenuating circumstances that might prove the agreement reasonable, including the fact that it actually increased competition.

Since the *Dr. Miles* case in 1911, resale price maintenance has been considered one of those classes of obviously anticompetitive restraints. In other words, contracts, combinations, or conspiracies that restrict resale price are presumed to be always reasonable and are illegal *per se*.

In the landmark *GTE Sylvania* case in 1977, the Supreme Court ruled that nonprice vertical restraints were not illegal *per se* and must be examined under the rule of reason. [*Continental T.V., Inc.* v. *G.T.E. Sylvania, Inc.*, 433 US 36 (1977).] The Court was persuaded that nonprice vertical restraints are often designed to protect full-service dealers from free riding, and thereby induce greater investment in promoting the brand. Under such restraints, intrabrand competition is restricted to increase interbrand competition.

To test the reasonableness of vertical restraints, therefore, the anticompetitive intrabrand effects of the questioned restriction must be balanced against any procompetitive interbrand effects. If, on balance, the restriction promotes overall competition, it is permitted. For example, a supplier could legally terminate a dealer under an exclusive territory agreement, even if the termination reduced competition on the supplier's brand, as long as the overall effect of the agreement was to strengthen competition among different brands. In fashioning this test, the Supreme Court clearly indicated that the primary concern of antitrust law was interbrand competition.

Using reasoning similar to that expressed in *Sylvania*, a number of lawyers and economists (including officials in the Antitrust Division of the Justice Department) have argued that the rule-of-reason test should also be applied to vertical price maintenance agreements (Posner, 1981). Although critics of that position charge that resale price maintenance permits the efficient creation and control of suppliers' and dealers' cartels, proponents of the rule-of-reason test argue that it is just as likely that suppliers will use vertical price agreements to promote interbrand competition. Because it is not possible to ascertain the true intent or competitive effect of the restriction on its face, they believe the court should invoke the rule of reason and examine all of the relevant facts to determine what the intent and effects might be. The resale price maintenance agreement ultimately might be found to be anticompetitive, but the defendant supplier would be given the opportunity to demonstrate its procompetitive intent and effect.

The Justice Department's disapproval of *per se* treatment for resale price maintenance agreements has led to several recent clashes with Congress. The fact that the Antitrust Division has filed only one resale price maintenance case since 1981 (a case originating during the Carter administration and subsequently dismissed by the Division) is seen by some in Congress as an indication of unwarranted tolerance of resale price maintenance (U.S. House of Representatives Committee on the Judiciary, 1987; U.S. Senate Committee on the Judiciary, 1988). The disagreement between Congress and the Justice Department over the appropriate treatment of resale price maintenance became manifest in 1984. In a civil case before the Supreme Court, the Antitrust Division filed a friend of the court brief on behalf of the defendant asking the Court to abandon the *per se* rule for resale price maintenance agreements. [*Monsanto Co.* v. *Spray-Rite Service Co.*, 465 US 752 (1984).] Although the Court declined to address the issue, Congress responded by adding an amendment to the Justice Department's 1984 appropriation bill, which explicitly precluded the Antitrust Division from continuing to seek to overturn or alter the *per se* rule for resale price maintenance. In 1985, the Justice Department issued its Vertical Restraint Guidelines, which appeared to Congress to narrow the application of the *per se* rule in vertical price maintenance cases. Congress again responded with appropriations restrictions and a resolution labeling the guidelines as an inaccurate representation of the current law and congressional intent.

In order to make explicit their intention that resale price maintenance be treated the same as horizontal price fixing, both houses of Congress have introduced identical proposed amendments to the Sherman Act.[2] HR 585 and S. 430 specify that an agreement between buyer and seller to establish the resale price is sufficient to constitute concerted action to set, change, or maintain prices in violation of the Sherman Act (and thus, by implication, be unreasonable *per se*). HR 585 was passed by the House of Representatives by voice vote on November 9, 1987. Its companion bill in the Senate, S. 430, was reported favorably out of the Judiciary Committee in February 1988 and at this writing awaits action by the full Senate.

For its part, the Supreme Court has maintained a distinction between the rule-of-reason approach afforded nonprice vertical restraints and the *per se* treatment of vertical price restrictions. Although the Court's current application of the *per se* rule to resale price maintenance agreements is consistent with HR 585 and S. 430, codification would insure that a change in the makeup of the Court would not lead to a reconsideration of the issue and an extension of the *Sylvania* rationale to price related vertical agreements.

EVIDENCE SUFFICIENT TO PROVE A CONTRACT, COMBINATION, OR CONSPIRACY

Even if the *per se* rule for resale price maintenance agreements remains intact, the courts still must determine whether the manufacturer or supplier has acted independently or whether there has been sufficient evidence of concerted action (i.e., a contract, combination, or conspiracy) between the supplier and one or more of its dealers. The courts then must determine the nature of that concerted action; that is, does it constitute resale price maintenance or should it be categorized as a nonprice vertical restriction and subject to rule-of-reason treatment? Specifically, the trial courts require guidance on what evidence is sufficient to prove, or to allow a jury to infer, a price-related agreement in restraint of trade.

Typically, these questions arise when a price-cutting dealer is terminated by a supplier pursuant to complaints by other dealers. The first issue for determination is whether the supplier acted independently or conspired with the complaining dealer. Under the narrow but long-standing Colgate doctrine [*United States* v. *Colgate & Co.*, 250 US 300 (1919)], a supplier can terminate a price-cutting dealer without liability if the supplier is acting independently. In that instance the concerted activity required by the Sherman Act is missing. It is not always clear, however, whether there has been concerted activity or not. Often direct evidence of an agreement is lacking and the jury must infer

---

[2] Horizontal price fixing has long been considered a clear example of an unreasonable restraint and treated as illegal *per se*. [*United States* v. *Trenton Potteries Co.*, 273 US 392 (1927).]

concerted activity based on indirect evidence. In the trial of such a case, a threshold level of evidence of concerted activity must be reached for the judge to allow the jury to make the determination. If the judge does not think the evidence which has been introduced would be legally sufficient, even if believed, he or she will not allow the jury to infer the conspiracy, and will enter summary judgment for the defendant.

Prior to 1984, some lower courts held that a complaint from a dealer followed by the supplier's termination of a price-cutting competing dealer was sufficient for a jury to infer the concerted action necessary for a violation of the Sherman Act (see Jacobson, 1982–83). Suppliers who had received complaints about price-cutting dealers, therefore, were unable to terminate them without facing the unenviable task of proving that the decision to terminate was completely independent of the complaints (that they were not working in concert with the complaining dealer). In the *Monsanto* case the Supreme Court ruled that complaints and subsequent termination were not enough for a jury to infer conspiracy between the supplier and the complaining dealers. "Something more" by way of evidence was necessary, or summary judgment would be entered in favor of the defendant supplier. What that "something more" could consist of remained unclear. However, if the only evidence of a conspiracy was the fact that a competing dealer complained and the price-cutting dealer was terminated, under *Monsanto* the judge would decide as a matter of law that the jury could not reasonably find a conspiracy, and judgment would be entered for the defendant supplier.

Congress became concerned with some of the language in the *Monsanto* case, which appeared to place too great a burden on the plaintiff (Senate Committee on the Judiciary 1988, p. 5). For example, the Court implied that, in order to avoid summary judgment for the defendant supplier, the terminated dealer must introduce evidence that "tended to exclude the possibility" that the supplier had acted independently. Consequently, in addition to the sections equating resale price maintenance with horizontal price-fixing, Section 8(a) of HR 585 and S. 430 addresses the evidentiary issues raised in *Monsanto*. Essentially, the proposed amendment declares that evidence showing that (1) a defendant supplier had received a request from a dealer to curtail or eliminate price competition by terminating the plaintiff dealer and (2) that request had been a major contributing cause of the subsequent termination was sufficient for a jury to infer a conspiracy (see Exhibit 1).

THE LINE BETWEEN RESALE PRICE MAINTENANCE AND NONPRICE AGREEMENTS

Proving concerted action on the part of a supplier and one or more of its dealers fulfills the Sherman Act's requirement for a contract, combination, or conspiracy. The question remains about whether agreements to terminate price-cutting dealers should be classified as resale price maintenance agree-

---

EXHIBIT 1   Section 8(a) of HR 585 and S.430

Sec. 8. (a) In any civil action based on section 1 or 3 of this Act, including an action brought by the United States, or by a state attorney general, or by the Federal Trade Commission under section 5 of the Federal Trade Commission Act, which alleges a contract, combination, or conspiracy to set, change, or maintain prices, if there is sufficient evidence from which a trier of fact could reasonably conclude that a person who sells a good or service to the claimant for resale—

   (1) received from a competitor of the claimant an express or implied suggestion, request, or demand, including a threat to discontinue an existing business arrangement, that the seller take steps to curtail or eliminate price competition by claimant in the resale of such good or service, and

   (2) because of such suggestion, request, demand, or threat terminated the claimant as buyer of such good or service for resale or refused to supply to the claimant some or all of such goods or services requested by the claimant,

then the court shall permit the trier of fact to consider whether such person and such competitor engaged in concerted action to set, change, or maintain prices for such good or service in violation of such section. A termination or refusal to supply is made "because of such suggestion, request, demand, or threat" only if such suggestion, request, demand or threat is a major contributing cause of such termination or refusal to supply. (S. 430, 100th Congress, 2'd Session.)

---

ments and held to a *per se* standard or as nonprice vertical agreements subject to the rule of reason. In other words, is an agreement between a supplier and a complaining dealer to terminate a price-cutting dealer sufficient to invoke the sanction against resale price maintenance, or is it also necessary to have a specific agreement to maintain prices? The Supreme Court addressed this issue directly on May 2, 1988, in *Business Electronics* v. *Sharp.*

In the *Business Electronics* case there was evidence of a complaint by one of two local dealers of Sharp calculators about the below-list pricing of its competing dealer, Business Electronics Corporation. Sharp agreed to terminate the price cutter, leaving the complaining dealer as the exclusive Sharp outlet in that market. The Supreme Court found that the agreement to terminate the low-price dealer was a nonprice vertical restraint and should be tested under the rule of reason. It stated that only terminations which took place in conjunction with a further agreement on the price or price levels to be charged by the remaining dealer would give rise to *per se* treatment. The Court distinguished between horizontal agreements (i.e., between competitors) which constitute price-fixing *per se* even though they don't specifically set prices, and vertical agreements (i.e., between channel members) which must set prices to receive *per se* treatment.

It would appear that the Court's decision in *Business Electronics* is inconsistent with the proposed amendment to the Sherman Act. Under HR 585 and S. 430, an agreement to terminate a price-cutting dealer because of another dealer's suggestion, request, or demand that the supplier take steps to curtail or eliminate price competition would be sufficient for the jury to find concerted action to "set, change or maintain prices . . . in violation of [the Sherman Act]," and thus, be deserving of *per se* treatment. Although both the House and Senate committee hearings and reports were completed prior to the Court's decision in *Business Electronics*, in speaking about the aftermath of the *Monsanto* case, the Senate Judiciary Committee report anticipated the *Business Electronics* decision:

> Some decisions have suggested, for example, that even if the termination was directly caused by the price-related complaints of a competing dealer, accompanied by economic duress, coercion, and threats, the plaintiff could not get to the trier of fact unless it also offered independent proof of a resale-price arrangement between the supplier and the complaining dealer. These requirements are too severe, and S. 430 is intended to remedy these problems. (Senate Committee on the Judiciary, 1988, p. 5.)

If the Senate follows the House of Representatives and passes the proposed amendment as it presently stands, the standard for *per se* treatment contained in *Business Electronics* arguably will be overturned. Juries would be allowed to infer resale price maintenance agreements based on a termination designed to curtail or eliminate price competition without independent evidence of a specific agreement between the supplier and remaining dealers to set prices.

SOME CONCLUSIONS AND IMPLICATIONS

Although the proposed amendment to the Sherman Act may significantly alter the evidentiary standards for *per se* resale price maintenance, for the present the test specified in *Business Electronics* will determine the legality of suppliers' terminations of price-cutting dealers. If there is no specific agreement on price between the complaining dealers and the supplier, the reasonableness of an agreement to terminate will be determined by balancing the anticompetitive intrabrand effects against any procompetitive interbrand effects.

Assessing the competitive effects of vertical restrictions requires extensive analysis of the dynamics of the consumer market for the particular good or service (Zelek, Stern, and Dunfee, 1980; Cady, 1982). Nonprice vertical restrictions allow prices to rise by protecting dealers from direct price competition on the focal brand. For example, territorial restrictions rely on a combination of distance between dealers and consumer travel costs to protect the dealers from direct price competition. At the margin, competition from other brands will limit those price increases. However, the effectiveness of territorial restrictions in reducing intrabrand price competition also depends on other factors, including the size of the territory, the type of product, and the cost consumers attach to travel.

Termination of price-cutting dealers is a much more direct restriction of intrabrand price competition. Moreover, by using this type of vertical restraint, the supplier does not sacrifice intensive market coverage because the price protection offered dealers does not rest on market allocation. There are, however, costs associated with termination agreements that do not apply to other forms of vertical restraints. Because agreements between a supplier and its dealers to terminate price cutters are reactive in nature, they are more likely to introduce conflict and disruption into the distribution system than proactive territorial restrictions. Nevertheless, terminations can be extremely effective and are probably second only to specific resale price maintenance agreements in reducing intrabrand price competition.

In fact, the effectiveness of concerted termination agreements in reducing intrabrand price competition is due primarily to their similarity to specific resale price maintenance agreements. Resale price maintenance (under *Business Electronics*) consists of an explicit agreement by dealers to maintain a price or price range specified by the supplier. Concerted systematic termination of price-cutting dealers implies (1) a tacit agreement between full service dealers about what price levels are inappropriately low and should elicit complaints, (2) an acquiescence in that categorization by the supplier, and (3) enforcement through termination. Together, these three elements form an extremely tight restriction on intrabrand price competition.

This is not to say that competition in the business sense necessarily would be reduced by concerted systematic price-cutter termination, merely that intrabrand price competition would be effectively curtailed. In fact, the reduction of intrabrand price competition is often motivated and/or justified by an expected increase in customer service (including investment in repair facilities, highly trained personnel, and dealer inventory), which strengthens the brand's position against other brands. If the *quid pro quo* for intrabrand price protection is an agreement by the dealer to differentiate the brand through increased service at the retail level, interbrand competition could increase (Zelek, Stern, and Dunfee, 1980). Although such increases in interbrand competition may not lead directly to lower prices, they do provide consumers with a wider selection of product-service combinations.

In order to avoid direct price competition with other outlets of the same brand, dealers are often anxious to differentiate their services, segment the market, and target particular customer groups. Some become low-cost, low-service, low-price dealers and target highly price-sensitive consumer segments. Others invest heavily in service and attract those customers willing to pay more to attain it. Because each strategy competes only on the margin with other strategies, it is generally to the supplier's and dealer's advantage to have a system comprised of various types of dealers. Through such a structure the supplier enjoys maximum market coverage, and the dealer avoids direct price competition with dealers focused on the same consumer segment. Because of the advantages of segmentation, therefore, termination of a dealer simply for following a low cost, low price strategy would not be in the interest of the supplier. Of course, a reduction in the number of competitors would normally benefit remaining dealers even if the terminated dealer primarily was targeting another segment. Nevertheless, if the terminated low-cost, low-price dealer were replaced by a full-service dealer, existing full-service dealers could find themselves worse off because of the termination.

It seems clear that the real danger to a distribution system (i.e., to suppliers, dealers, and consumers) comes not from price cutting or discounting but, rather, from free riding. Free riders compete unfairly with other dealers because they offer high service together with low cost and low price. They do so by appropriating the service provided by high-cost dealers.

Faced with free riding, dealers following a high-cost, high-price strategy lose their incentive to invest in service, and over time the supplier's distribution system will cease to provide the service necessary to attract service-conscious customers. If it were simply a case of terminating those dealers that intentionally engaged in free riding behavior, the test for reasonable terminations would be straightforward. Unfortunately, low-cost, low-price dealers are naturally allied with consumers (unconcerned with the long-term effects of their actions), who are more than willing to assist them in the appropriation of service provided by high-price dealers.[3] Moreover, the low-price dealers (let alone the supplier or other dealers) may have no idea of the degree to which they are free riding on other high-service dealers. Supplier termination of low-price dealers, therefore, may be a solution to a real free rider problem, or it may merely reduce the number of alternatives available to potential customers.

In those markets where services important to the consumer are not easily susceptible to free riding, such as in after-sales service and repair, full-service dealers will make investment decisions that allow them to compete most effectively with other brands and other dealers. In that case, concerted selective termination of price cutters would appear to reduce intrabrand competition without the likelihood of corresponding increases in interbrand competition. Complaints from full-service dealers could best be explained as an attempt to protect a profitable strategy, perhaps found to be somewhat ill-suited to current market demand, by depriving the consumer of a low-cost, low-price alternative. Supplier acquiescence would most likely reflect either tacit interbrand collusion or the existence of a powerful dealer cartel. In short, where free riding is unlikely, there seems little justification for concerted price-cutter termination.[4]

On the other hand, where services important to the consumer are easily susceptible to free riding, such as in presale education, all low-price, low-service dealers will become free riders through the process of rational consumer shopping behavior. In those instances, all else being equal, concerted systematic termination of price cutters can promote overall competition. Under this approach, two of the most important issues to be examined by the court in

---

[3] The example of the camera customer being educated by a full-service dealer's salesperson only to buy the camera at a discount outlet is likely to be familiar to the reader, because most have engaged in some variation of that process.

[4] This, of course, does not take into account those instances where the product's price conveys an image of quality important to the positioning of the brand.

determining the reasonableness of a termination would be the nature of customer service used to compete with other brands, and the availability of any other less restrictive means of preventing consumers from transferring that service from one dealer to another.

It is unlikely that consumers will alter their behavior, because of an appreciation of the fact that, in the long run, free riding discourages investment in services they value. Low-cost, low-service dealers will continue to be the willing recipients of transferred service. Although the Court and Congress agree on the complete unacceptability of specific resale price maintenance as a method of controlling this transfer, they apparently disagree on whether a supplier-dealer agreement to terminate a low price dealer could ever be a reasonable response. Because the issue is one of statutory, not constitutional, interpretation, Congress will have the last word. Passage of HR 585 and S. 430, therefore, could have significant impact on suppliers, dealers, and consumers alike.

REFERENCES

Cady, John F. "Reasonable Rules and Rules of Reason: Vertical Restrictions on Distributors." *Journal of Marketing* 46, no. 3 (1982), pp. 27–37.

House of Representatives Committee on the Judiciary. *Report on HR 585, the Freedom from Vertical Price-Fixing Act of 1987*, Report 100–421 (1987).

Jacobson, Jonathan M. "On Terminating Price-Cutting Distributors in Response to Competitor's Complaints." *Brooklyn Law Review* 49 (1982–83), pp. 677–711.

Posner, Richard A. "The Next Step in the Antitrust Treatment of Restricted Distribution: *Per Se* Legality." *University of Chicago Law Review* 48 (1981), pp. 6–26.

Senate Committee on the Judiciary. *Report on S. 430, the Retail Competition Enforcement Act of 1987*, Report 100–280 (1988).

Zelek, Eugene F.; Louis W. Stern; and Thomas W. Dunfee. "A Rule of Reason Decision Model after Sylvania." *California Law Review* 68 (1980), pp. 13–47.

Marketing Communications: Personal Selling and Sales Management

Ethical Issues in Personal Selling and Sales Force Management

Robert J. Kopp

INTRODUCTION

If business ethics, in general, have come under increased public scrutiny recently with the insider trading and savings and loan scandals, the personal selling profession has long been criticized by the public. Arthur Miller's searing portrayal, in *Death of a Salesman*, of personal selling as an immoral profession prompted the Sales Executive Club of New York to demand that the television version be followed by an epilogue describing the "joys and rewards of salesmanship" (Nelson, 1970). In a *Journal of Marketing* article in 1965, Mason implied that personal selling's "low prestige" had and would continue to adversely affect salesperson recruiting on campuses. As evidence, the author cited a survey, published under the title "Selling Is a Dirty Word," which revealed college students' skepticism of the ethics of personal selling. History, however, has not borne out Mason's fears. Currently, personal selling accounts for the majority of all entry level marketing positions offered to U.S. students graduating with a bachelor's degree (College Placement Council, 1991).

Ethical conflicts are inherent in the salesperson's job. In this author's view, four factors combine to explain this phenomenon: the organizational pressure typically exerted on salespeople to "make the numbers;" the sales force's boundary-spanning position; its autonomous operation; and the salesperson's role as a paid advocate of company doctrine.

Organizational Pressure. Salespeople are on the front line of any business. In competitive markets there is always pressure on the sales force to close the

Acknowledgements: The author would like to thank the editors, John A. Quelch and N. Craig Smith; and Ross Petty, assistant professor of law, Babson College, for their helpful suggestions.

sale and "make the numbers." Where the payoff is large, and the chances of detection small, a purely economic decision model yields a large incentive to cut ethical corners to make the sale. The sales force's position is such that the pressure felt by top management to achieve financial objectives is inevitably transferred, via organizational gears and levers, down to the sales force, sometimes with negative consequences. For example, recently Dun & Bradstreet's credit unit was plagued by a rash of unethical sales and marketing practices. Partly to blame was sales pressure brought to bear on the division by company headquarters (see Chapter 7.5).

Boundary Position.   From an organizational perspective, the salesperson occupies a boundary-spanning role between the company and customer. That is, to be successful, the salesperson must be regarded by each party as a strong and loyal advocate for its respective cause. Because it is usually impossible to maximize simultaneously the payoff to both the company and customer, the salesperson is plagued by a "constantly shifting focus of identification" (Belasco, 1966). Salespeople often encounter ethical dilemmas when fulfilling the expectations of one party serves to penalize the other.

Autonomous Operation.   The field sales force tends to operate more autonomously than other corporate departments. Removed from the corporate culture and continuous supervision, the salesperson often operates akin to an independent entrepreneur; as such, he or she usually is accorded a level of resources and decision-making authority, creating opportunities to engage in unethical practices.

Advocacy Role.   Ethicists argue that personal selling, as well as advertising, is inherently unethical because these forms of promotion cause the individual to promulgate what he or she is *paid* to believe, rather than what is truly believed. Under these conditions, the argument goes, real trust between parties is not possible (Gowans, 1984; Oakes, 1990). College students have criticized personal selling on this point, maintaining that selling requires the individual to convey a pretense of sincerity (Thompson, 1972).

Incorporating these factors, which help explain the ethical conflicts inherent in personal selling, this chapter is organized according to four sets of interfaces—that is, company/customer, company/salesperson, salesperson/customer, and salesperson/competitor (see also Anderson, Hair, and Bush, 1988, pp. 550–52). This framework is useful, but it is not without definitional problems. For example, when ethics are breached in dealings with the customer, it may be difficult to assign blame. Did the salesperson initiate the unethical action? Or did sales management prompt the behavior? If the latter, was sales management's action, in turn, ordered (or expected) by the firm's top management? Sales force management texts discuss the breaking of federal, state, and local laws as an ethical problem of the sales force. Nevertheless, it is difficult to envision the widespread practice of such acts as bribery, collusion, and price discrimination without top management's knowledge. In fact, when companies are prosecuted for anticompetitive practices, top management is almost always named in the suits although lower echelon managers may also be cited (Hughes and Singler, 1983, p. 153).

Following this train of logic, classified under the *company/customer* interface, are illegal (and, hence, unethical) activity in the breaking of federal, state, and local statutes intended to protect consumers and to prohibit anti-competitive activity. Industrial espionage and competitive harassment ("dirty tricks") are covered under the *salesperson/competitor* interface; illegal and unethical activities in the areas of persuasion, misrepresentation of claims, and account discrimination are discussed under the rubric of the *salesperson/customer* interface. The *company/salesperson* interface discusses policies and activities, internal to the company, which affect the firm's ability to direct sales force activity toward ethical goals and the salesperson's ethical behavior toward the company. Subsequent to this discussion, separate sections will address *situational influences on ethical behavior* and *corporate codes of conduct*, two topics that cut across the four interfaces. Research findings are reported throughout as appropriate. In addition, this chapter draws on interviews conducted with one sales manager from each of four companies: Johnson Controls, NCR Corporation, the Nestlé Company, and the Norton Company.

COMPANY/CUSTOMER INTERFACE

A number of federal, state, and local laws govern the interface between customers and companies and, therefore, have important implications for sales force ethics. These laws, described, for example, in Hughes and Singler (1983), have been enacted over the years to preserve fair competition and to protect consumers. The Sherman Act (1890) prohibits monopolies and price collusion, thus calling into question the exchange of price information between competitive salespeople.

The Clayton Act (1914), as amended by the Robinson-Patman Act (1936), forbids price discrimination that tends to lessen competition. Acceptable defenses of price discrimination include discounts on perishable or obsolete goods, discounts to meet competition, and discounts based on a cost differential (e.g., quantity discounts). Generally, the practice of offering one or more competing retailers special discounts not offered to the others is considered, prima facie, price discrimination, which lessens competition. Thus, salespeople selling to competing distributors and retailers must take care *not* to offer special promotional incentives or price breaks to *individual* customers. Likewise, retailers are forbidden by Robinson-Patman to pressure salespeople to provide special deals or "street money." The interview research with salespeople confirmed that pressure-for-results directed at the sales force can represent a significant incentive to salespeople to offer special deals to close sales. Robinson-Patman also prohibits predatory pricing—that is, pricing below cost—for the purpose of lessening competition.

Several laws prohibit companies and their salespeople from engaging in power tactics with retailers and end-customers. Tying arrangements, such as "full-line forcing," may run afoul of the Clayton or Sherman Acts. Thus, salespeople cannot threaten retailers with the withdrawal of the company's line for the purpose of gaining the retailer's agreement to stock additional items. Vertical price-fixing, or the manufacturer's dictating retail prices, was apparently outlawed in the 1960s and 1970s by the abolishment of fair trade laws. Today, however, legal interpretations during the 1980s have made vertical price-fixing a "grey area" of the law. In the 1970s, if a manufacturer refused to deal with a discounter, the discounter would be, typically, successful in claiming that the manufacturer had violated antitrust laws. The Reagan Supreme Court, however, moved to reaffirm the notion that businesses should be free to deal with whom they choose. Consequently, today a terminated dealer bears the heavy burden of proving that a price-fixing agreement exists between the manufacturer and other dealers. Simple termination of dealers, who happen to be discounters, no longer satisfies that burden. In sum, the manufacturer, as represented by its sales force, may retain its ability to discourage discounting as long as certain legal requirements are strictly adhered to.

The Federal Trade Commission Act (1914), as amended by the Wheeler-Lea Act (1938), prohibits unfair trade practices, such as deceptive selling, misrepresentation, and high-pressure selling. Bribery is proscribed by state criminal laws and may violate the FTC Act, while the Foreign Corrupt Practices Act (1977) makes it a criminal offense to bribe foreign government officials to gain sales. The paying of "push monies" to retailers and distributors is legal as long as the payment is offered on an equitable basis to all competing accounts.

At the state level, the Uniform Commercial Code is a set of guidelines adopted by most states to govern sales contracts, warranties, shipping terms, and the like. Court actions under this code usually concern misrepresentation of claims and overpromising by salespeople (Anderson et al., 1988). The Green River Ordinances, adopted by most major metropolitan areas, require nonresidents to obtain a license to sell door-to-door. Closely related to these laws is the three-day "cooling-off rule," enacted by the FTC after it received years of complaints about high-pressure sales tactics (Anderson et al., 1988). This rule allows customers of door-to-door salespeople to rescind a sales contract within three days.

In an oft-cited study, Chonko and Hunt surveyed marketing managers and sales managers about ethical problems they faced. Bribery was mentioned by 41 percent of the sample as the most difficult ethical problem. In their comments, respondents implied that often bribery was *not* initiated by the salespeople themselves but, rather, was part of a pattern of selling employed by the company or commonly found in the industry, or both. In a study by DeConinck and Good (1989), both sales managers and student respondents rated bribery as the most unethical of three sales scenarios, the other two involving dishonesty and competitive sabotage. While the use of gifts and entertainment in selling generally are condoned, the determination of when these inducements constitute a bribe is a difficult one. To address the issue many companies have set specific dollar limits on the size of business gifts that can be given or received by employees.

As an alternative to laws and regulations, there are free market solutions to unethical business practices. Customers may refuse to do business with unethical sellers. Thus, through a process of natural selection, the more ethical enterprises would flourish and the less ethical would wither. Companies may accelerate this process by calling customers' attention, via personal selling and advertising, to competitors' unethical activities. In sum, any discussion of the laws and regulations affecting personal selling should address the issue of why free market solutions have (apparently) proven inadequate.

COMPANY/SALESPERSON INTERFACE

Ethical issues surrounding the company/salesperson interface will be addressed from two standpoints. First, the means by which the company may direct sales force activity toward ethical goals will be discussed using a model of sales force management—that is, recruiting and selection; training; evaluation and compensation; supervision and control; and territory allocations. Next, the salesperson's ethical obligations to the company will be covered.

Recruiting and Selection.   The 1964 Civil Rights Act set up the Equal Employment Opportunity Commission, which forbids discrimination in hiring except on the basis of clearly performance-rated criteria. In the interview research, none of the sales managers disagreed with the principle of nondiscrimination. However, they suggested the company's *customers* may possess ethnic and gender prejudice, which is not as easily set aside, and the minority salesperson's odds of success on the job may be lessened. They added that they try to inform the minority applicant that he or she may face prejudice; as long as the individual is aware and feels he or she can deal with the situation, sales managers no longer regard this as a hiring barrier.

In a similar vein, sales managers said the company has an ethical obligation to present the possible disadvantages of the particular sales position to applicants. One way to do this is to invite the applicant to spend a day working with a regular salesperson. In the words of one sales manager, "I expect applicants to be open and honest with me about their own strengths and weaknesses. In return I invite them to spend a day in the field, and I tell the regular salesperson: 'Don't do anything special and you can say anything you want about your job and the company.'" Another sales manager said: "Be honest to your employees and they will be honest to you—and it all starts with the job interview." The commitment to honesty has a tangible payback to the company: fewer new-hires leave, and recruiting and training costs are held down. A Scott Paper Company manager estimates the costs of recruiting and initial training to total one to one and one-half the employee's annual salary (Futrell, 1988, p. 333).

Training.   Training is critical in establishing the ethical tenor of the sales organization. Sales management instructs the sales force regarding the company's ethical standards not only through formalized training but also through setting an example on field visits. Sales manager respondents confirmed that, in sales training programs, more time is being devoted to ethical issues—such as going over the company's code of ethics—than was the case as recently as five years ago. One sales manager said that difficult ethical situations were a standard part of sales training role-play exercises.

Evaluation and Compensation.   A salesperson's overall job performance rating and compensation usually are based on *outcome measures*, such as sales volume, or *behavior measures*, which capture more intangible performance dimensions, such as new business solicitation, supporting retailers, training activities, and the like. Robertson and Anderson found that, compared to the use of outcome measures alone, the addition of behavioral measures results in a higher level of ethical behavior (see Chapter 7.6).

According to the interview research, top sales producers vying for promotion may be trapped in a classic Catch-22 situation. Excellence in generating sales *is* usually a key criterion for promotion to higher job levels; but this factor may cause the sales manager—who also has a quota to meet—to be reluctant to promote the top producer out of the manager's area of responsibility. One respondent said that he had seen this happen in his company. As a means of averting the situation, he recommended that personnel evaluations be carefully reviewed by sales management superiors and human resources personnel. Another manager said this practice was self-defeating because "promotable people who are held back are more likely to leave the company."

Supervision and Control.   These systems can be used to monitor sales force performance against ethical standards. Conversely, an absence of supervision and control may constitute tacit approval of unethical selling practices. One respondent said that her company's control system ensured that a salesperson would have "no way of getting reimbursed for an unethical or illegal use of company funds." Less encouraging, another respondent said that the failure on the government's part to enforce regulations would lead, "naturally," to his company's de-emphasis of these regulations in its internal control system.

Territory Allocations.   Where the salesperson's compensation is based on sales volume, his or her income depends to a great extent on: the territory assignment—territories may differ markedly in terms of sales potential; the split of business between territory accounts and house accounts[1]; and on the allocation of the pool of promotional monies across territories. Traditionally, salespeople complain that these decisions are not always made in a manner that is fair and above board (Futrell, 1988, p. 752). One sales manager said that splitting territories was an ever-present problem. A solution, practiced by his company, is to reward salespeople on the degree of sales *growth*, a measure that generally favors the smaller territory. Even so, he said that the salesperson who has fought to develop a territory usually opposes a split because he or she continues to see "great sales potential" in the future.

Ethical Obligations to the Company.   In general, the salesperson's obligations to the company are no different than those of other employees. However, owing to their relatively autonomous and unsupervised operation, field salespeople probably have more of an opportunity for such unethical acts as misuse of company assets, falsifying reports and sales records, breaking company policies, and even moonlighting. Clearly, salespeople have a greater opportunity than most employees to pad expense accounts, to misappropriate company supplies or equipment for personal use, and to conduct personal business on company time. Because much sales force compensation may be earned through commissions, bonuses, and sales contests, there is an incentive for salespeople to cheat through such tactics as "overloading" customers. One sales manager interviewed said that loading customers with more product than they required could easily lead to a breakdown in trust between the parties, with negative consequences for future sales. Another sales manager said that the pressure to load *does* get communicated from management to the sales force; when volume is needed, salespeople are implicitly asked to cash in some of the "chips" they have accumulated with the customer. (For a more complete discussion of this topic, see Futrell, 1988, pp. 756–57; and Anderson et al., 1988, p. 550).

SALESPERSON/CUSTOMER INTERFACE

Where ethical problems occur at the customer interface, it is often difficult to allocate blame among top management, sales management, and the individual salesperson; accordingly, some of these problems have already been discussed. This section will deal with personal selling techniques aimed at psychological manipulation, account discrimination, and the topic of misrepresentation and breach of warranty. These three ethical issues readily fall within the domain

---

[1] A "house account" is a customer that is serviced directly from company headquarters (or regional sales headquarters), even though the account may be geographically located in a regular sales territory. Generally, house accounts are established to provide better service to large, important customers. In effect, house accounts lower the sales potential of the regular territory, and, therefore, salespeople will feel cheated to the extent they view the house account mechanism as penalizing their own income.

of the salesperson/customer interface, because they may be relatively difficult to detect via the company's normal control procedures.

Psychological Techniques for Persuasion.   The nature of the salesperson's interactions with the customer is the focal point of a historical and widespread social criticism of the personal selling profession. Like advertising, personal selling has been assailed for "creating needs" and for employing psychological manipulations to convince people to buy what they do not need or to choose a particular brand. The question of whether the marketing profession in general serves to *respond* to market demand or to *create* demand (unnecessary demand for the sole benefit of the company) is a philosophical issue which has long defied clear resolution. In Chapter 7.2, David Namer, a career salesperson, suggests that needs-creation is the salesperson's *raison d'être:*

> Man is ignorant of change; he does not recognize the beneficial value of it. He must be sold, sold on an idea, sold on a product, sold on a service. This is why the salesman is so important in society today and has been since the beginning of time.

Namer implies that the ends—that is, fueling change and economic growth—justify the means: high-pressure sales tactics. Clearly not everyone would agree. In one study of college students, among the top 10 words associated with the term *salesman* were "fast talker" and "high pressure." Another study of college students uncovered the general opinion that, to be successful, salespeople must lie and deceive and must conduct themselves in an "arrogant and overbearing" manner (both studies reported in Thompson, 1972).

Ethical issues are raised by any situation in which a customer's free will to choose is abrogated by illusion or psychological ploys. Advertising texts openly present distraction techniques, such as humor and sex appeals, as a means of overcoming the buyer's natural perceptual defenses (Ray, 1982). Personal selling and sales force management texts describe a similar (though not equivalent) set of methods under the heading of sales closing techniques. For example, Kurtz, Dodge, and Klompmaker (1988) describe a number of common "closes," including the "standing room only" technique, in which a product shortage is threatened. Yalch (1979) reviews uch closing techniques as "foot-in-the-door," "door-in-the-face," and "eve a-penny-helps," which have a theoretical basis in social psychology. For example, in the foot-in-the-door technique, the salesperson endeavors to close a relatively small sale in order to condition the buyer psychologically to accede to a larger purchase. Again, many "closing techniques" share the basic goal of creating persuasion by setting psychological traps for the buyer as opposed to appealing to his or her inherent needs for the product. The topic raises clear ethical issues (see Oakes, 1990, and Gowans, 1989).

On the other hand, sales closes that obtain buyer assent based on the demonstration of the product's real benefits would appear to be ethically sound. The popular FAB approach, in which the salesperson informs the customer of the product's Features, Advantages, and Benefits, is an example of such a closing technique (see Johnson, Kurtz, and Scheuing, 1986, pp. 72–73).

Account Discrimination.   This occurs when certain customers are given more favorable treatment than others: receiving product delivery in times of shortages; receiving lower prices or higher discounts (generally forbidden by the Robinson-Patman Act); being made aware of new products in a "timely" fashion; being accorded services, such as the picking up of damaged goods and the restocking of shelves at the retail level. Reciprocity, or giving favorable treatment to customers who are also suppliers, is another common form of account discrimination. Such actions are most serious when they upset the competitive balance within the customer's or the seller's industry. Sales managers themselves regard account discrimination as a serious ethical problem (Dubinsky and Gwin, 1981), and such practices may violate federal laws, such as Robinson-Patman (discussed earlier).

Misrepresentation and Breach of Warranty.   Misrepresentation and breach of warranty are grounds for legal action under which the injured party (customer) seeks damages. Breach of warranty is proscribed by the Uniform Commercial Code (Section 2–312–318). Misrepresentation is a common law tort, and it may qualify as a deceptive selling practice forbidden by the FTC Act. Intentional misrepresentation is considered fraud, and the injured party may sue for damages and for rescinding the contract. If misrepresentation is found to be unintentional, customarily redress is limited to cancellation of the contract. The FTC does not need to prove intent to issue a cease and desist order prohibiting further misrepresentation, but can only order consumer redress for knowingly dishonest conduct.

While misrepresentation and breach of warranty differ in the burden of proof required and the types of damages that may be awarded, both can occur when a salesperson makes erroneous statements or false promises. *Puffing* consists of statements that are so obviously exaggerated or subjective (e.g., "We are the best!") that customers are not misled by them. Such sales rhetoric is expected in society and is excluded from the definition of misrepresentation. Although the company is *usually* blamed, the salesperson *can* be held legally accountable for all claims of a factual nature that relate to product performance. As an example, a sales representative sold heavy industrial equipment with the promise that the machinery would "keep up with any other machine then being used, and that it would work well in cooperation with the customer's other machines and equipment." Later, the customer sued, claiming that the sales literature and the sales representative had made false statements. The court ruled in the customer's favor, rejecting the defense that the salesperson's statements were nonactionable opinions made in good faith with no intent to deceive (Futrell, 1988, p. 759). From a legal standpoint the salesperson may be held strictly accountable for statements made to the customer. Beyond legality, lying and misrepresentation are unethical if only because they interfere with the customer's right of free consent in purchase decisions (Cooke, 1990).

SALESPERSON/COMPETITOR INTERFACE

Any unethical action, undertaken to build sales or lower costs, has a negative, if indirect, consequence for competitors. In addition, there are a number of unethical sales force actions that pose a clear and direct hazard to a competitor's well-being. Anderson, Hair, and Bush (1988, p. 552) have identified four categories of unethical sales force behavior toward competitors:

Disparaging the Competition. Falsely exaggerated disparagement falls into the same category as misrepresentation (see above) and may result in a lawsuit. The practice is self-limiting to the extent that the buyer views disparagement as unfair, as an indication of the seller's own weakness, or as a sign that the salesperson, in a similar way, may disparage the buyer's company at some later time.

Disturbing Competitor's Products and Displays. It is unethical, and sometimes illegal, to tamper with a competitor's products, shelf facings, or displays. For example, Kleenex salespeople were found to be removing the cardboard ovals from display boxes of Scott tissues so the pop-up package feature on the Scott products would fail to work (Dalrymple, 1985, p. 544).

Spying on Competitors. According to Anderson, Hair, and Bush (1988, p. 552) salespeople may use many guises to obtain competitive information: "For example, they may pump competitors' salespeople at social gatherings, encourage customers to put out phony bid requests to get information on competitors' offerings, or pretend to be customers at professional conferences, at trade shows, or on plant tours." In addition, trade secrets may be obtained by such methods as hiring away competitors' employees for this express purpose. While the above practices may not be serious enough to violate criminal laws, they do invite civil lawsuits for damages inflicted.

Unreasonably Exclusionary Behavior. This refers to unreasonable attempts to lessen competition. For example, if a company's goal is to spoil a rival's new product introduction, unreasonably exclusionary actions might include special deals, "fighting brands," and "flying squadrons." (A "fighting brand" is a new product temporarily placed on the market to neutralize a competitor's innovation. "Flying squadron" refers to a sales force blitz program specifically aimed at loading customers, such as with fighting brands.) Such actions may violate federal antimonopoly laws. However, the complainant must show the exclusionary conduct has occurred within an industry structure, which in itself poses significant threats to free competition.

Some would argue that harassing competitors is simply part of the business game, since "nearly everybody does it" (Anderson, Hair, and Bush, 1988, p. 552). Empirical research indicates that unethical actions aimed at *competitors* are generally viewed as *less odious* than similar actions involving *customers*. Dubinsky, Berkowitz, and Rudelius (1980) found that "gaining information about competitors by asking purchasers" was seen as ethically questionable by only 25 percent of field sales respondents and was ranked last out of 12 scenarios in terms of seriousness as an ethical issue (see Table 1). In another study, Dubinsky and Gwin (1981) found this issue to be ranked by salespeople as 11th out of 11 scenarios in terms of seriousness. In this same study, however, purchasing agents ranked this scenario as the *most* serious ethical question, thus indicating their own discomfort at being asked to provide competitive information. DeConinck and Good (1989) uncovered sales managers' views that employing entertainment and alcohol to extract sales plans from competitive salespeople was less offensive ethically than bribery or lying about a delayed order. On the other hand, in the same study, *students* considered competitive sabotage to be more serious than lying and less serious than bribery. Overall, it appears that harassing competitors is considered to be less serious than several other potential ethical problems in selling. On the other hand, the fair treatment of competitors is often explicitly mandated in company ethics codes (see Table 2).

SITUATIONAL INFLUENCES

In several studies, researchers have identified extrinsic or situational variables that were hypothesized (in the studies) to influence the nature of the ethical situation or the means of its resolution. Bellizzi and Hite (1989) found that sales managers were likely to be less harsh in disciplining unethical behavior to the extent that the offending salesperson was a *high performer* or *male*, or both, and to the extent that the *expected* consequences of the ethical breach were judged to be less serious.

Robertson and Anderson (see Chapter 7.6) measured the relationship between 11 situational variables and reported ethical behavior of salespeople. Their major hypothesis was that unethical behavior would increase to the extent that the company's control system focused on outcome measures (e.g., sales volume) as opposed to behavior measures (e.g., ethical conduct). This hypothesis was confirmed, indicating that the type of control system selected by the company does affect ethical behavior of the sales force. In addition, the following factors were hypothesized to increase the incidence of unethical actions: larger order quantities, greater industry competitiveness, more cold calling, fewer repeat sales, shorter time horizon for expected tenure in territory and with company, greater isolation from other employees, less seniority, and male gender. However, only two of these variables, industry competitiveness and salesperson seniority, were found to have a significant influence on ethical

TABLE 1 Evaluation of 12 Sales Situations or Practices

Situation or Practice	An Ethical Question?		Respondents replying "definitely yes" or "probably yes"			
			Have Stated Policy Now?		Want a Stated Policy?	
	Rank	Percentage	Rank	Percentage	Rank	Percentage
1. Allowing personalities—liking for one purchaser and disliking for another—to affect price, delivery, and other decisions regarding the terms of sale.	1	52%	3	47%	3	57%
2. Having less-competitive prices or other terms for buyers who use your firm as the sole source of supply than for firms for which you are one of two or more suppliers.	2	50	2	52	1	61
3. Making statements to an existing purchaser that exaggerate the seriousness of his problem in order to obtain a bigger order or other concessions.	3	49	7	31	6	44
4. Soliciting low-priority or low-volume business that the salesperson's firm will not deliver or service in an economic slowdown or periods of resource shortages.	4	42	6	34	5	46

5.	Giving preferential treatment to purchasers to whom higher levels of the firm's own management prefer or recommend.	41	10	28	8	40
6.	Giving physical gifts, such as free sales promotion prizes or "purchase-volume incentive bonuses," to a purchaser.	39	1	56	2	60
7.	Using the firm's economic power to obtain premium prices or other concessions from buyers.	37	5	37	7	42
8.	Giving preferential treatment to customers who are also good suppliers.	36	8	30	10	33
9.	Seeking information from purchasers on competitors' quotations for the purpose of submitting another quotation.	34	9	29	9	39
10.	Providing free trips, free luncheons or dinners, or other free entertainment to a purchaser.	34	3	47	4	55
11.	Attempting to reach and influence other departments (such as engineering) directly, rather than going through the purchasing department when such avoidance increases the likelihood of a sale.	29	12	22	11	30
12.	Gaining information about competitors by asking purchasers.	27	11	29	11	30

Source: Alan J. Dubinsky, Eric N. Berkowitz, and William Rudelius, "Ethical Problems of Field Sales Personnel," *MSU Business Topics*, Summer 1980, p. 14.

TABLE 2   Excerpts from NCR's Code of Ethics

Gifts and Favors

Giving and receiving gifts in our business dealings can create conflicts of interest; such situations require careful thought.

The purpose of gifts and favors is generally to create goodwill. If they do more than that, and unduly influence judgment or create a feeling of obligation, we should not give or accept them.

We may not give or receive business-related gifts even of nominal value if they create even the slightest conflict. We should decline such gifts and tell the giver that company policy prohibits their acceptance.

Of course, we may pay for or accept business entertainment, such as meals, if the expense is reasonable and directly related to NCR's business . . .

Selling and Servicing NCR Products

NCR people compete vigorously, but always fairly. Those of us whose jobs involve direct contact with NCR customers should find these guidelines helpful.

Do not misrepresent our products. Where silence about a fact could be misleading to a customer, NCR people must clearly disclose significant information. We simply don't stretch or hide the truth. Likewise, if we recommend solutions to meet a customer's needs, we should understand those needs and the customer's capabilities. We never knowingly oversell or undersell a customer. In short, we treat our customers with candor and respect . . .

Competitive Comparisons

When selling against competitors, we don't disparage or unfairly compare the competitor's products. It's always wrong to spread rumors about the competitor's financial stability in order to make a sale. Our products are good enough to stand on their own.

It is also wrong to try to unhook a competitor's sale . . .

Source: "Code of Business Conduct," produced by Stakeholder Relations Division, NCR Corporation, Dayton, Ohio, 1990. Used by permission.

---

behavior. While not confirmed by the Robertson and Anderson study, sales managers interviewed said that, by its very nature, *relationship selling*, which involves repeat sales and a long-term relationship with the customer, must be more ethical generally than *transaction selling*, or "one-shot" deals.

Two studies have examined the relationship between the salesperson's role conflict and ethical behavior. Dubinsky and Ingram (1984) hypothesized that the salesperson's "ethical conflict" would be greater to the extent that he or she had greater role conflict, shorter time in present job, shorter time in sales, more education, and fewer commission sales, and to the extent that the industry was less competitive. However, no significant correlations were found.

In a study of three types of sales personnel—sales representatives, sales managers, and sales support personnel—Chonko and Burnett (1983) employed multi-item scales to measure four types of role conflict: ethical, customer relations, family, and job conflict. Ethical conflict included such issues as truthfulness in sales presentations and the use of high-pressure selling tactics. Customer relations conflict measured the agreement between salesperson and customer on such issues as providing product training and maintenance services, and the salesperson's overall availability to the customer. Ethical conflict was rated by all three groups as the most troublesome of the four conflict types.

CODES OF CONDUCT

In a 1988 *Wall Street Journal* survey, senior executives cited three factors as important in upgrading or maintaining ethical conduct in business (in order of importance): ethics codes, more humanistic business school curricula, and legislation (Bellizzi and Hite, 1989). In a 1980 content analysis of ethics codes, the most commonly prohibited behaviors were: extortion, gifts, kickbacks, conflicts of interest, illegal political payments, use of insider information, bribery, falsification of corporate accounts, violation of antitrust and other laws, moonlighting, illegal payments abroad, violations of secrecy agreements, ignorance of work-related laws, fraud, deception, and justification of means by goals (Chatov, 1980). Research among salespeople found that they prefer to have ethical guidelines spelled out in formal documents (Dubinsky, Berkowitz, and Rudelius, 1980; Dubinsky and Levy, 1985), and the sales force management literature generally argues for the adoption of company or industry ethical codes (Dalrymple, 1985; Stanton and Buskirk, 1987). All of the companies interviewed for this chapter had established ethics codes (see example in Table 2).

Some authors are less sanguine about the impact of codes (Anderson, Hair, and Bush, 1988, p. 556). Chonko and Hunt (1985) found no significant correlation between the existence of corporate or industry ethics codes and the extent of ethical problems among marketing managers. On the other hand, the same study found that *top management* actions, through power of example, were a strong predictor of ethical behavior. One manager interviewed said that she was well aware of top management's expectations regarding employee ethics: "Don't do anything you can't defend before family, neighbors, and co-workers." Codes will probably be most effective if they are specific (rather than vague) in describing infractions, and if they are supported by top management and enforced through a system of rewards and punishments (Anderson, Hair, and Bush, 1988). (Note that the NCR Code in Table 2 contains some very specific language regarding ethical issues commonly encountered by the sales force.)

IN CLOSING

Personal selling and sales management are rich in ethical issues. Conceptual frameworks to be employed in analyzing ethically charged situations are covered by Smith (see Chapter 1) and Hunt and Vitell (see Chapter 9.5), and in Laczniak (1983) and Cooke (1990). While personal selling has evolved away from Arthur Miller's Willy Loman toward greater professionalism, so, too, it appears that companies are concerned, to an increasing degree, with the ethics of their sales and marketing operations. Many businesses have established codes of ethics and the precepts thus set forth are reinforced in sales force training programs. At the same time, the literature points to a rather broad range of ethical problems in which the company's sales function may be involved. Such factors as organizational pressure and the sales force's autonomy and boundary position combine to create ethical dilemmas for salespeople and their managers.

Laws and regulations, intended to foster competition and protect consumers, have important implications for personal selling. While it can be shown that such strictures have been, on balance, to society's benefit, free market remedies to ethical breaches do exist. These should be considered, along with regulations, in discussions of society's response to unethical selling practices.

The topic of ethics in personal selling and sales force management is inextricably linked to business ethics in general and this, in turn, to the moral tenor of society. Personal selling represents a powerful competitive force. For example, by controlling the information available to buyers, salespeople can aid or hinder the buyer's right to free and informed choice. Breaches of ethics at the sales force level potentially have an adverse effect on many stakeholders including customers, competitors, and the company's owners. Last, but not least, from the standpoint of the individual sales representative, unethical behavior may cause some very uncomfortable pangs of conscience.

REFERENCES

Anderson, Robert E.; Joseph F. Hair, Jr.; and Alan J. Bush. *Professional Sales Management*. New York: McGraw-Hill, 1988, pp. 550–52.

Belasco, James A. "The Salesman's Role Revisited." *Journal of Marketing* 30 (April 1966), pp. 6–11.

Bellizzi, Joseph A., and Robert E. Hite. "Supervising Unethical Salesforce Behavior." *Journal of Marketing* 53 (April 1989), pp. 36–47. The authors cite a survey published under the title "Ethical Behavior," *The Wall Street Journal*, January 18, 1988, p. 13.

Caywood, Clarke L., and Gene R. Laczniak. "Ethics and Personal Selling: *Death of a Salesman* as an Ethical Primer." *Journal of Personal Selling & Sales Management*, August 1986, pp. 81–88.

Chatov, Robert. "What Corporate Ethics Statements Say." *California Management Review* 22 (Summer 1980), pp. 20–29, cited in Anderson, Hair, and Bush (1988), p. 556.

Chonko, Lawrence B., and John J. Burnett. "Measuring the Importance of Ethical Situations as a Source of Role Conflict: A Survey of Salespeople, Sales Managers, and Sales Support Personnel." *Journal of Personal Selling & Sales Management*, May 1983, pp. 41–47.

Chonko, Lawrence B., and Shelby D. Hunt. "Ethics and Marketing Management: An Empirical Examination." *Journal of Business Research* 13 (1985), pp. 339–59.

College Placement Council, *Salary Survey*. Bethlehem, Penn., 1991. This is a national sample of job offers extended to bachelor's degree candidates in the period September 1, 1990, to March 8, 1991. Of a sample of 758 job offers in marketing, 65 percent were for sales positions, followed by buyer/merchandising (13 percent), brand/product management (9 percent), market research (5 percent), distribution (4 percent) purchasing (2 percent), and advertising (2 percent).

Cooke, Robert A. "Ethics in Business: A Perspective." Review article written for and published in 1990 by Arthur Andersen & Company, Center for Professional Education, St. Charles, Ill.

Dalrymple, Douglas J. *Sales Management: Concepts and Cases*, 2nd ed. New York: John Wiley & Sons, 1985, chapter 12, p. 544.

DeConinck, J. B., and D. J. Good. "Perceptual Differences of Sales Practitioners and Students Concerning Ethical Behavior." *Journal of Business Ethics* 8 (1989), pp. 667–76.

Dubinsky, Alan J.; Eric N. Berkowitz; and William Rudelius. "Ethical Problems of Field Sales Personnel." *MSU Business Topics*, Summer 1980, pp. 11–16.

Dubinsky, Alan J., and John M. Gwin. "Business Ethics: Buyers and Sellers." *Journal of Purchasing and Materials Management*, Winter 1981, pp. 9–16.

Dubinsky, Alan J., and Thomas N. Ingram. "Correlates of Salespeople's Ethical Conflict: An Exploratory Investigation." *Journal of Business Ethics* 3 (1984), pp. 343–53.

Dubinsky, Alan J., and Michael Levy. "Ethics in Retailing: Perceptions of Retail Salespeople." *Journal of the Academy of Marketing Science* 13, no. 1 (Winter 1985), pp. 1–16.

Futrell, Charles. *Sales Management*. 2nd ed. Chicago: Dryden Press, 1988, chapter 18.

Gowans, Christopher W. "Integrity in the Corporation: The Plight of Corporate Product Advocates." *Journal of Business Ethics* 3 (1984), pp. 21–28.

Hughes, G. David, and Charles H. Singler. *Strategic Sales Management*. Reading, Mass.: Addison-Wesley, 1983, p. 153.

Johnson, Eugene M.; David C. Kurtz; and Eberhard E. Scheuing. *Sales Management: Concepts, Practices, and Cases*. New York: McGraw-Hill, 1986, pp. 72–73.

Kurtz, David C.; H. Robert Dodge; and Jay E. Klompmaker. *Professional Selling*. 5th ed. Plano, Tex.: Business Publications, 1988, chapter 11.

Laczniak, Gene R. "Framework for Analyzing Marketing Ethics." *Journal of Macromarketing*, Spring 1983, pp. 7–18.

Mason, John L. "The Low Prestige of Personal Selling." *Journal of Marketing*, October 1965, pp. 7–10. Mason cites a three-part series of articles published, with no author given, by *Sales Management*: "Selling Is a Dirty Word," 89, no. 8 (October 5, 1962), pp. 44–47; "People Shouldn't Be Forced to Buy," 89, no. 9 (October 19, 1962), pp. 44–47; "Salesmen Are Prostitutes," 89, no. 10 (November 2, 1962), pp. 46–54. The articles were based largely on a survey of college students conducted for *Sales Management* by Crossley Surveys.

Nelson, Benjamin. *Arthur Miller, Portrait of a Playwright.* New York: David McKay, 1970. Cited in Caywood and Laczniak (1986).

Oakes, G. "The Sales Process and the Paradoxes of Trust." *Journal of Business Ethics* 9 (1990), pp. 671–79.

Ray, Michael L. *Advertising and Communication Management.* Englewood Cliffs, N.J.: Prentice Hall, 1982, chapter 12.

Stanton, William C., and Richard A. Buskirk. *Management of the Sales Force.* Homewood, Ill.: Richard D. Irwin, 1987, chapter 23.

Thompson, Donald L. "Stereotype of the Salesman." *Harvard Business Review*, January–February 1972, pp. 20–36.

Yalch, Richard F. "Closing Sales: Compliance Gaining Strategies for Personal Selling." In *Sales Management: New Developments from Behavioral and Decision Model Research*, ed. Richard P. Bagozzi. Cambridge, Mass.: Marketing Science Institute, 1979, pp. 187–201.

David Namer: An Interview with a Professional Salesman

In February 1975, a professor of business administration and two of his students were researching the ethics of salesmanship. In the course of their research, they met and interviewed David Namer, a professional salesman for 14 years, vice president of a marketing research organization, and author of a manuscript entitled *The People Business*. In his manuscript, which was intended to be a training manual, Mr. Namer was deeply concerned with salesmanship as a profession. He wanted to change the image of the salesman and provide what he felt were the basic tenets of salesmanship.

The following is an edited transcript of the interview, wherein Mr. Namer is asked to answer specific questions about how his manuscript relates to the many "gray areas" encountered in the day-to-day pursuits of the professional salesman. As stated, the interview was edited, and, in several instances, passages from Mr. Namer's manuscript have been included to clarify his responses.

The exhibits include two "hard-sell" pitches provided by Mr. Namer, wherein he illustrates common sales techniques used in door-to-door encyclopedia sales.

Question: Mr. Namer, your book entitled *The People Business* puts the sales profession on a very high plane. It appears that you are saying salesmanship is practiced to some degree by everyone.

Namer: Everyone, all of us, is involved in the people business. But what is the people business? Nothing less than the day-to-day contact and involvement of people, which I call selling. From the first days of Adam and Eve, people have been trying to sell others ideas, beliefs, viewpoints, or services. Eve was

This case was prepared by Ladd Cutter and Brad McKean under the direction of Associate Professor Jeffrey A. Barach. The casewriters would like to acknowledge the help and cooperation of David Namer, without whom the case could not have been produced.

the first salesman when she sold Adam on the idea of eating the apple. And what a salesman she was! Here was Adam, all the comforts of paradise and no worries, and yet Eve convinced him that he would have a *"better"* life if he ate the apple.

One would think that man could recognize on his own what is beneficial and what is necessary for his betterment or for his existence, but he really can't.

Man is resistant to change; he will resist change, and will fight change all the way down the line. Man is ignorant of change; he does not recognize the beneficial value of it. He must be sold, sold on an idea, sold on a product, sold on a service. This is why the salesman is so important in society today and has been since the beginning of time. He will probably continue to be no matter how far man progresses.

Question: Do you feel then that, for instance, this is why the artist and the writer, who are both innovators, are attacked by society? Do you mean that the consumer is too dumb to know what is good for him?

Namer: I don't mean that they're dumb in the sense of not being educated or not knowing what's going on around them. What I am saying is that they're ignorant about the *new things* going on around them—about the changes being made.

The fundamental aspects of persuasion are suggestion and logical reasoning—suggestion taking precedence and probably more important than logical reasoning. The human species is not essentially a reasoning creature. In fact, most people scarcely reason at all. All of their actions are usually the result of imitation, habit, or suggestion. Most of their actions, and psychologists will bear this out, are only reactions. The average person accepts as true every idea or conclusion that enters his mind unless a contradictory idea blocks this acceptance. Additionally, the average person will act according to an idea of action which enters his or her mind unless it is blocked by a physical obstacle or a contrary idea. This is the principle upon which the foundation of most of our modern-day advertising is based; the fact that statements which are repeated and not denied will tend to be accepted. The salesman uses those principles during the presentation and close. The salesman will fill out the order, thereby suggesting an act of writing. When he hands the prospect a pen with the suggestion "Please okay this agreement at the X or where indicated," the prospect will generally go along with this idea.

Question: Something disturbs me here, and that is the targeting of your book. A Peace Corps worker in South America trying to teach Indians to drink only water that has been boiled would be less inclined to pick it up than would be a less-scrupulous type who wishes to utilize persuasion to sell me something I didn't need.

Namer: I take issue with that. When I sat down to write the book, I reflected on my 13 years in sales; I really like sales. During that time, my mind was constantly thinking of ways to improve the occupation, of upgrading it, of making it more professional. I wanted to bring salesmanship out of the "drummer" image and to spread that professionalism to all salesmen regardless of what they are selling. That is why I named my book *The People Business.* The Peace Corps worker would be just as apt to pick it up as would the vacuum cleaner salesman.

Originally, the book was to be targeted at salesmen; however, as it developed it turned out to be applicable in all phases of life. As I've said before, I feel that I've compiled something that can be used by everyone. My main contention is that everyone is selling in day-to-day interactions with other people. I'm selling my ideas to you and vice versa. Whether or not I get my ideas across to you determines the success of my presentation, whether or not I make the sale.

Question: Many people have the wrong impression of salesmen, through either naiveté or bad experiences, actual or perceived.

Namer: The best example of what you are talking about has occurred in the insurance industry. In the last 15 or so years there was a time when people had a definite image of an insurance salesman. The sloppy, shirt-sleeved person driving through rural sections, banging on doors to get people to buy insurance through high pressure. Threatening people with out-and-out coercion, loss of life, limb and/or property; the last thing people wanted to see was the insurance salesman. The industry spent, therefore, great sums of money promoting the image of the neat, trained professional counselor.

Question: Do you feel that salesmanship is inherent? Are there born salesmen?

Namer: There are no, or at least very few, born salesmen. To be an efficient, successful salesman one must be trained. This training doesn't only consist of attending a seminar and listening to someone who is successful tell of his achievements. Selling is individualistic; when one hears how a salesman makes a sale, that particular strategy may or may not apply to him. What works for you may not work for me. The concepts of selling are universal. Unlike the means, they must be formulated, nurtured, and grasped—then the means will fall into place, just like a puzzle.

Question: What selling experiences have you had?

Namer: I've sold just about everything: encyclopedias, magazines, coffee; recently I've been selling commodities, including flour, rice, wheat, cement, lemon oil, etc., all in bulk lots.

Question: What about product knowledge? I think it would be difficult to sell cement without specific knowledge about its applicability.

Namer: Absolutely, the salesman must have working knowledge of his product; he must have all the answers for anticipated questions. I followed my own advice and researched each item. I don't have an engineering degree in structural concrete, but I know what, where, and how to produce a product to meet desired specifications. I also listen a lot. One must listen to customers and people around him. It's fine to talk, but if you don't get a dialogue going it's almost impossible to get indications of your progress—feedback, as it were.

Question: What about the sales pitch itself? There are some encyclopedia companies that entice a customer by promising a "free" set of encyclopedias as a neighborhood demonstration unit. The only catch to this is that the customer must furnish a letter extolling the virtues of the encyclopedia to the company and must keep the encyclopedia up to date for 10 years with yearbooks, which add up to the full cost of the encyclopedia.

Namer: I can continue that! You know, Mr. Jones, that works out to less than one half the price of a pack of cigarettes a day for a year. Now you know, $70 a year for 10 years, that's kind of ridiculous. Sending a check out every year, that's time-consuming for both of us. Tell you what I'm going to do. If you will agree to pay the $720 or the $20 a month over a period of three years, we will give you, tonight, this beautiful bookcase, unlimited research service on the subjects of your choice, and so on. Isn't that fair?

Question: That's what I had in mind. Is it successful?

Namer: Absolutely. It's a beautiful pitch. By far it and its many variations are highly successful.

Question: In this light, then, are people dumb or ignorant? Why do they fall for it?

Namer: I don't think people are dumb. I don't think they're ignorant either. I think people are unaware. They are ignorant in that they're not exposed to the business atmosphere. They don't know how things are done. In other words, a salesman can enter the home and create the illusion that you're getting something for nothing. There is a little bit of larceny in everyone. Realistically, if people thought they could do something and get away with it, they would do it 99 percent of the time. In fact, even if they had only a fairly good chance of pulling it off they'd try.

Question: Well, do you think that this is fair play? Would you use that pitch?

Namer: No. That is not fair, in the sense that you are taking advantage of people who are unaware or are less aware than you are. You are using your experience and your knowledge.

Question: Could you possibly provide us with an example of what you consider to be an unscrupulous sales pitch? What I'm looking for is an expansion of the pitch that you just gave us.

Namer: Certainly. As a matter of fact, I have an example in my files and will send it to you.[1]

Question: You agree with what you wrote in your book? You stress honesty.

Namer: Yes—honesty and straightforwardness. To be truthful, however, I have used this pitch in my early selling days with both encyclopedias and magazines. I like to consider those early days, tinged with deception and dishonesty, as being my learning period. The latter portion of my career has been dedicated to honesty and legitimacy.

---

[1] **Note:** The pitch, as supplied by Mr. Namer, is included in its entirety as Exhibit 1.

EXHIBIT 1   Encyclopedia as Advertising-Premium Pitch

AT DOOR

(KNOCK ON DOOR)

Hello! I'm Dave Namer with the Marketing Division of the Intercontinental Encyclopedias, Inc.* What is the family name here? (GET NAME.)

Mr. (or Mrs., depending on who answers the door) _____, I'm not here to sell you anything. In fact, I am part of an advertising and promotional campaign making a survey of *your* neighborhood's ideas on education. If I may step in, I can better explain to both you and your _____(wife or husband) what this is all about. (STEP TOWARD THE DOOR. IF ONLY ONE SPOUSE IS PRESENT, RESCHEDULE TO COME BACK WHEN BOTH ARE THERE.)

INSIDE

(POSITION YOURSELF SO YOU ARE SEATED NEXT TO YOUR PROSPECTS; MAKE SURE THAT TV AND STEREO ARE OFF, THEN PROCEED.)

Mr. and Mrs. _____, as I previously stated, I am taking a survey of your neighborhood. The purpose of this survey is to select one qualified family to participate in a rather unusual offer.

You see—Intercontinental has just come out with a new edition of its educational library. After many years of planning and over $30 million investment, we are now ready to market and sell our library. In order to make the salesman's job a lot easier, we have decided to place our library in the home of a selected family. This is done at no cost or obligation to the qualified family.

(SHOW A PICTURE OF SET AND EXPLAIN.)

Now, I know what you must be thinking. No one comes into your home and gives away over $500 worth of merchandise for nothing. There has to be a catch, right?

Well, Mr. and Mrs. _____, there is a catch. See, we realize the value of word-of-mouth advertising, especially between friends and neighbors. Therefore, as you use your library, you will be so impressed that you will tell your neighbors and friends about it. This will increase sales. But—equally important—when our salesmen are out in the field, they can use you as a testimonial for our set.

In order to accomplish this, we will require three things from you:

First, 60 to 90 days after you have received the library and had a fair chance to look it over, we ask you to write us a letter giving your frank and honest opinion of the library. A letter of testimony, so to speak.

Second, the company reserves the right to photostat this letter and use it as sales material. You see, they're going to send their regular professional sales staff into your community in three or four months, and experience tells them the first question asked them is who actually owns a library of this type here in town. Now, if they can truthfully tell these people the Browns over here and the Jones

---

* Fictional company name.

EXHIBIT 1 *(continued)*

over there already own a library of this kind and can show them a letter of recommendation—well, you can get the sales psychology behind this, I am sure.

Third, that you keep the set up to date with our yearbooks. Remember that your neighbors will be coming to see your set. We want them to see, and for you to have, an updated set. You understand. (EXPLAIN YEARBOOK AND BRING OUT PICTURE.) After all, if we *gave* you a Cadillac, would it be too much to ask you to buy the gas from our station? (GET A VERBAL "NO" FROM BOTH.)

Exactly the way that we feel about it, too. The yearbooks cost us $50 a year, which is the cost of a daily newspaper, and that is all that we will charge you. All we ask is that you maintain your set current for 10 years. Isn't that fair? (DO NOT WAIT FOR AN ANSWER; CONTINUE. . . .)

Needless to say, to do our work properly, we must make placements intelligently. We must place these libraries with families who have a genuine use and appreciation for material of this type in their home. After all, if we place this library with families who have accepted it only because it was something for nothing, and stored it in the attic or used it as a doorstop, it would defeat the advertising purpose completely.

So, I would have to ask another question: If we could extend to you the invitation, would you and your family appreciate material of this type in your home? In other words—if there was nothing else involved and they would send you a complete 24-volume library and even pay the shipping expenses to get it here, would you be willing to give them the advertising help they ask for by writing a letter of testimony? (GET COMMITMENT FROM BOTH.)

(IF ANSWER IS IN AFFIRMATIVE). . . . Well, is this something that you and your family would use and appreciate over the years as well as now if you had it in your home? (GET COMMITMENT FROM BOTH.)

In summary, then, folks, all that we ask in return for this magnificent free library is that you:

1. Send us a testimonial letter.
2. Give us permission to use and reproduce it.
3. Agree to keep your set current for the next 10 years.

In order to help you with the yearbook we will send you an Intercontinental Calendar Bank. (EXPLAIN BANK.) By saving 15¢ a day, the cost of a daily newspaper, you can keep your set up to date.

Quite frankly, though, Mr. and Mrs. _____, the only objection that we've run into is that nobody wants to fool with 15¢ a day for 10 years. Not to mention the cost of bookkeeping and accounting that we would incur by this.

Therefore, we have another proposition that will benefit both of us. If instead of taking 10 years, you would pay for the yearbooks in 3 years, you would not have anything to pay for the other 7 years. Also, you would save us 7 years of bookkeeping costs.

So, if you will do this—prepay the yearbooks in 3 years—we will pass on our accounting savings to you by way of extra merchandise.

If you agree, we will send to you, at no cost, the following:

1. 15-volume Junior Set (EXPLAIN).
2. 10-year Research Service (EXPLAIN).
3. Bookcase (SHOW PICTURE).

EXHIBIT 1 *(concluded)*

Thus, for your advertising cooperation and your agreement to pay for the yearbooks in 3 years rather than 10, you will receive:

1. 30-volume Intercontinental Encyclopedia.
2. 15-volume Junior Set.
3. Bookcase.
4. 10-year research service.
5. Yearbooks for 10 years.

Now, if I can get some information from you, I will see if your family qualifies for this program. (FILL OUT AGREEMENT AND CREDIT APPLICATION.)

Well, Mr. and Mrs. _____, from all the preliminary information, your family qualifies. If you will fill out this Registered Owner's Card, then OK the application here (PUT "X" ON SIGNATURE LINE OF AGREEMENT), I will submit it to the home office for final approval.

Now all I need is ten dollars to cover the shipping charge, and we will process your application.

(PACK UP MATERIALS WHILE THEY WRITE CHECK OUT. AFTER BEING HANDED THE CHECK, STAND UP, . . . WALK TO DOOR, . . . AND SAY:)

Congratulations, and welcome to the Intercontinental Family of Library Excellence. (WALK OUT OF DOOR.)

Question: There is no one more vehement about honesty than a reformed thief! Now, can you draw a line as to what is good and evil, black and white, so to say? The pitch that we've been talking about is obviously over the line, but you are not going to go completely the other way—for example, here are the issues, here are the pluses and minuses. That would constitute a judicial approach—your approach would seem to be more advocative.

Namer: I don't think you can draw a line. Each case must be approached individually. It depends on the product you are selling and the needs of the people to whom you are selling. Suppose I was selling quality encyclopedias to a family who could afford it. Assume that their children need and want the set. In this case I would apply pressure to the extent that I wouldn't normally use. I wouldn't take the approach that the children would grow up ignorant, that they will fail in society, that they won't complete high school, or will never get into college, etc. What I would say is that the children would not have the advantages of their peers. In the schools today, given the overcrowded classrooms, teachers do not have time for individual instruction. They tend to give class projects. They say, "Go home and look this up in your reference set," assuming that all families have reference sets. Now, sure you can look that up in the public library if one is available. But can you see 30 or 40 people descending upon a single reference volume all at once? What usually happens is that after five or six people, someone gets tired of waiting around the library and rips out the page for home study. What does your child do then?

I deliberately referred to *any* reference set as opposed to my own set because I didn't want to imply that without my set the kids will grow up ignorant. It's a case of semantics. You are doing something that you believe is beneficial for that family. You know that sooner or later someone is going to sell them a set of encyclopedias. That salesman could be selling a "flimflam" product, so I feel that it would be to their advantage to get something of quality, something that the family can make good use of.

Question: OK. We will include what you consider to be an unethical sales pitch in the case, but we don't have any idea of what you consider to be a fair approach. Can you give an example of what you consider to be within the bounds of ethical behavior? What I want is something to demonstrate how you would handle the sale of a set of encyclopedias today; perhaps a hard-sell situation, given the rules of conduct by which you govern yourself.

Namer: That's not difficult. Instead of a canned approach, let me give you a scenario which will demonstrate quite graphically, I hope, the dynamics of the sale, the events leading up to it, how I would handle objections, and several closes which I would use.[2]

Question: Do you have to have absolute faith in your product before you step in the door? Have you sold items you didn't believe in?

Namer: At one time, when I was a lot younger, I was able to sell something I wholeheartedly didn't believe in, or that I thought was inferior. I think, and my ego confirms this, that I can sell anything to anyone because I'm a very good salesman. But morally, now, I wouldn't sell if I didn't perceive a genuine benefit to the purchaser.

Question: Many products sold door-to-door are first-rate, top of the line, and, therefore, expensive. Why are lower- and middle-class neighborhoods preferred by salesmen? Is it right to sell a quality $10 knife to a housewife in a ghetto?

Namer: Let me tell you something about selling quality products in the ghetto. That woman will purchase a shoddy knife for a dollar. Two weeks later, that knife will break, she'll have to purchase another, and so on. Over a period of time she will have invested more money in knives than the $10 she could have if she had bought quality. This would have benefited her.

Question: In the case of an insurance salesman who convinces someone that he needs a policy and sells a quality product, how does this fit in? Perhaps after the sale the guy becomes dissatisfied with the premium and gives the salesman a lot of grief. How does the salesman handle this?

Namer: The salesman must consider himself in a positive light. He must believe in the beneficial aspects of his product. Sure, the premiums are a bit of a drag now, but look at the future—the customer will soon have something of value, probably more than he would have had if he had tried saving alone.

---

[2] **Note:** The scenario as given by Mr. Namer was quite lengthy and, therefore, is included as Exhibit 2.

EXHIBIT 2   Encyclopedia Sales Scenario

Namer: OK. Let me set it up this way. Take the Braswells, Joan and Ted, who live in a lower-middle-class neighborhood, comprising mainly one-story, single dwellings. The homes have wash on the line, automobiles and pickup trucks occupy cluttered carports, and toys and young children fill most front yards. Ted holds a decent job as day-shift foreman at a local manufacturing plant; his salary barely covers month-to-month expenses. Joan helps out with the monthly budget occasionally by taking in wash and working part time for a caterer. They have two children, Anne, 10; and Ted, Jr., 8.

Several weeks earlier Ted noticed an appealing coupon insert in a national magazine, filled it out, and mailed it. The advertisement promised a free booklet entitled "Views of Tomorrow," which offered hitherto unimagined worlds to its recipient in print, in glorious color photographs, and in illustrations.

The postage-free card arrives in the national sales headquarters of Intercontinental Encyclopedias, Inc. (IEI). We'll use a phony company so we don't step on any toes. It is catalogued and then sent to the regional sales director in charge of the territory where the Braswells reside.

Mike McNamara, our fictitious salesman, receives the card as a lead, after paying a modest service charge to the company. Mike is an independent sales agent who contracts with IEI to market their encyclopedias in his territory. Mike telephones the Braswell home to make an appointment.

"Hello, Mrs. Braswell. My name is Mike McNamara. I'm a representative of IEI. We received a request that you made for some information regarding the special offer we have on the Intercontinental Encyclopedia set. I'm calling to find out the best time to get together with you and your husband to show you the details of this special program. I was wondering if perhaps you had time this evening; or possibly Friday or the weekend would be better for you?"

At this point Mrs. Braswell replies that they wouldn't be home that evening.

Mike continues, "I see. Well, how about Saturday—will your husband be home then?"

Joan answers in the affirmative.

"Aha, great; how about if we make it this Saturday at eleven o'clock, or say between eleven and eleven-thirty? Is that OK?"

Joan agrees.

"Great, I'll be looking forward to seeing you then. Thank you."

Mike is punctual. At 11 on Saturday, he parks his car at the curb, walks to the front door, and rings the bell.

Ted Braswell answers the door. Mike takes two steps backward and introduces himself.

"Mr. Braswell? Hi, I'm Mike McNamara from IEI. I have come to deliver the booklet you requested several weeks back depicting the wealth and knowledge and pleasure available to you from Intercontinental."

Ted scowls and says that he didn't expect any salesman, only the booklet.

Mike continues, "Mr. Braswell, Intercontinental is so excited about their new edition that they asked me to bring you free and without obligation their 60-page colorful and informative booklet entitled "Views of Tomorrow," and complete details. . . .

EXHIBIT 2 *(continued)*

Ted interrupts, saying that he is not interested.

Undeterred, Mike goes on, ".... and complete details on how to receive this magnificent set direct from the publisher on the special monthly payment plan."

Ted asks if there is any way that Intercontinental could put the booklet in the mail.

Mike responds, "Yes sir, there is. In fact, we do have a booklet that we can mail out to you. Unfortunately though, there is nothing contained in that book that will probably give you the specific information that you are looking for. In other words, information on the quality of the bindings, the prices, and so on and so forth. This is why the company has requested that I take about 15 to 20 minutes of your time to give you a review of what we've come out with. I feel that this would be 20 minutes of your time well invested insofar as your future and the future of your family is concerned. Whether you buy the set or not, at least you would have a more enlightened view of the set; and in the future, when you do get ready to buy, you'll be in a better position to make a decision."

Ted indicates that he has no intention of buying a set at this particular time, and apologizes for causing bother and inconvenience to Mike.

"Well, Mr. Braswell, it is my job to show this set on a public relations basis. Whether you buy it or not is up to you; in other words, all I ask is that you look at it. If you like it, you buy it; if not—I thank you for your time.

"I feel that by showing it to you, it will not only give you an awareness of just what Intercontinental is but also will help to dispel a lot of rumors which may or may not crop up about Intercontinental. It will also make you a very good representative of our company. When someone comes to you and starts talking about encyclopedias, you will be able to give them the benefits of your education in that field."

Ted raises no further objections and, still skeptical, grudgingly allows Mike to enter the room. Mike requests that Mrs. Braswell be present for the demonstration. Ted goes toward the rear of the house to summon Joan.

The most outstanding features in the room are an imposing leatherette bar grouping, a new 25-inch color television set, and a huge leatherette lounge chair. The rest of the furniture is old and scratched; both the sofa cover and the curtains are tattered chintz.

Mike hears Ted Braswell's loud voice from the rear of the house, which indicates that he is venting his frustrations on Joan for granting the interview in the first place. Shortly thereafter, the Braswells enter the room.

Mike reintroduces himself to Joan, "Hi, Mrs. Braswell. I'm Mike McNamara. I spoke to you on the phone the other day."

Joan reacts pleasantly, noting that the soothing voice that she recalled from the phone call is attached to a well-dressed, handsome young man.

Ted mumbles that it is about time to get "this thing" over with and sits down in the lounge chair. Joan follows suit on the edge of the sofa. Mike kneels down and delves into his presentation case.

First he brings a sample volume of the encyclopedia out of the presentation case and hands it to Joan Braswell. She accepts the book with the rich, dark brown leather binding and gives it an admiring gaze. She starts thumbing through the volume while paying close attention to Mike.

"Mr. and Mrs. Braswell, as I indicated earlier, the reason I'm here is to demonstrate IEI's new edition, which we feel is a real breakthrough in the field of

EXHIBIT 2 *(continued)*

encyclopedias. We sincerely believe that no other reference set can touch this new edition and Intercontinental is so excited about it that they have decided to introduce the set, complete with convenient credit terms, so that everyone can take advantage of our offer."

Mike proceeds carefully, step by step, in company-approved fashion. His pitch is intentionally slow and deliberate, eliciting favorable responses from Mrs. Braswell at the close of each train of thought. Ted Braswell occasionally nods or grunts, but remains generally silent.

Mike describes the bindings and paper as the finest available. Joan agrees and passes the sample volume to Ted, who glances at it, flips it over twice, and then tosses it on the table. Mike continues unperturbed. He then emphasizes the star-studded panel of contributors, scientists, professors, businessmen, etc., who have lent their expertise to IEI's new edition. It is a lengthy and impressive list. Mike then goes on to describe the attention to detail inherent in the set; the time it took to collect and assemble the data; and the cost to finally produce the new edition. The figure is staggering.

Mike then begins to explain some of the valuable services that IEI provides for owners of reference sets. He decides that he will start to work on Ted Braswell.

"Perhaps some day, Mr. Braswell, you might want to go into business for yourself. The Intercontinental research staff is at your disposal to answer any questions that might come up, be they on engineering, management, merchandising, taxes, accounting, or any other subject. At any rate, any technical question you might have about your present job would gladly be handled by IEI, too. Don't you think this could be very helpful to you?"

Ted replies that it might come in handy sometime. Mike goes on, "Mrs. Braswell, we can help you in the home to save time, steps, and money—three things I'm sure you're very interested in. Also, we'll help you with your outside activities. For example, if you were on the entertainment committee of the PTA, write and tell us how big your group is; what kind of budget it has; what kind of things were done in the past; and we'll supply you with information on what other groups like yours have done in other parts of the country." Joan nods enthusiastically and adds that such a service could be "invaluable" to her. Ted maintains his silence.

Mike keeps the pitch moving. "Incidentally, are your schools crowded in this neighborhood like they are everywhere else?" Joan replies that they "sure are." Mike continues, "Then you know that the brighter child has just as much a problem as the child who gets behind. It seems that our schools are geared only to the average. But, with our service, your children can use this excellent learning tool to pursue their own interests and to help them if they have difficulty with any particular subject. You know, the curiosity of our children is probably our nation's most important asset. If we don't help them to find out how to get the right answers and encourage them to keep their interests in things, how will our country ever get the doctors, scientists, and leaders that we so desperately need?"

Joan Braswell responds immediately, "I want the very best for my children and this encyclopedia set could be the key to their future. If Anne and Ted, Jr., could grow up to be rich and famous, I'd pay almost anything."

At this point, Mike briefly outlines the credit terms which IEI offers. Neither Ted nor Joan objects to the payment plan he presents. Mike now has qualified his clients, created a need for the product, and arranged reasonable financial terms—the three key elements of a successful close. He then makes his first move toward

EXHIBIT 2 *(concluded)*

wrapping up the sale. "Let me ask you, can you folks see how our encyclopedia set and services could be a great benefit to the future of your family?"

Ted Braswell replies, after a slight pause, "Well, it looks like a pretty good deal, but I don't think I want to spend the money right now. Why don't you come back in a few months."

Mike begins to push, "Mr. Braswell, let me ask you just three questions before I go. Do you think your family would use and enjoy our encyclopedia set?" Ted nods yes. "Do you feel that IEI's $600 selling price is fair?" "Yes, I guess so," Ted answers. Mike counters, "You guess so, sir. Do you feel we're being excessive with the charges?" "No, not really. It seems to be a fair price," Ted finally replies. Mike then pops the most crucial question, "Can you afford the set?" Ted, a bit indignant answers, "Yeah, we can afford it, but I just don't want to buy it."

Mike then thinks he has them and starts to push harder. "Mr. Braswell, you've just informed me that you feel your family will use and enjoy the set, that the set is worth it to you, and that you can afford it. I really don't think it would be fair of you to deprive your wife and children of this educational opportunity any longer. The price is bound to increase if you delay because of inflation. Besides, we're both here now. You've given me your time; I've given you my time and knowledge." Mike then decides to use what he hopes will be the clincher. "Mr. Braswell, if I could bring into your home a magician who could give you access to 10,000 of the world's greatest minds, who could recreate 10,000 of the world's greatest historic moments—all at your personal request—would you want him?" Ted says, "Sure, why not?" Mike quickly proceeds. "The magician has only one drawback. You must give him a pack of cigarettes once a day. Wouldn't it be worth it to you to be able to have this magician for only one pack of cigarettes?" "Yeah," Ted answers, "but it's not the same as a bunch of books sitting in a corner."

Joan Braswell suddenly blurts out, "Ted, you're being stubborn. You're hurting the future of this family. If you won't come up with the money for this, I don't know what I'll do!"

Mike glances around the living room, eyeing the new bar set and the big color TV. He is forced to play his ace in the hole. "There are only two basic reasons why a person won't buy this encyclopedia set. One, that person is absolutely destitute, completely broke. And looking around this room, I'd have to say you're living pretty comfortably. I think you'll agree with me there. The second reason is that the person is plain ignorant! But, I don't think you're ignorant either. In fact, I believe you're an intelligent man. I think this encyclopedia is something you want, something your family wants, and particularly something your wife wants. Now, you don't want her to cut you off, do you? You're the one that's got to live with her. . . . I really believe you'd be helping your family by taking this reference set."

"I guess you're right," Ted eventually answers.

Mike brings out his order pad while Joan and Ted whisper to each other. The details of the credit terms are easily worked out within a few minutes. Mike feels that he has performed another mutually profitable transaction. As he gathers up his possessions, Mike thanks the Braswells for their courtesy and adds, "Thank you for the order. I'll be on my way to get things moving on it properly. You should have the complete set by dinnertime tonight. Welcome to the IEI family!"

If you do something deceitful, it is difficult to visualize yourself as beneficial. If you view yourself as beneficial, it is easy to live with criticism.

Question: Periodically, there are times in order to close a deal you must use every . . .

Namer: You have to border on things which might be construed to be devious, sly, or cunning—but I hate to use those words.

Question: Taking another tack, then, nobody has ever spoken to me the way door-to-door salesmen have, except my mother. Why is it when that salesman leaves the door, the sweat is pouring off your forehead?

Namer: I think it is important to delineate between a warm prospect who comes to you with the realization of need for your product and service and a cold one whom you approach and is completely in the dark as to who you are and what you have. The guy who approaches you has a need, a problem, and is seeking help. This is problem solving. The cold prospect doesn't know he has need of your product or service. A mental trauma takes place in the cold prospect; chances are that he went all through his life without knowing or caring that he needed a set of encyclopedias. The moment you hit him, you have thrown cold water on him. The way in which you arouse his awareness has a profound effect upon the outcome of your presentation.

Question: Why then do so many door-to-door salesmen prefer less-affluent neighborhoods? Is it because we can consider those people to be more susceptible to a given pitch?

Namer: You must realize that you're dealing with individuals. You cannot stereotype people. You can't go into a home with the feeling that those people are dumb or less worldly or more susceptible. Look at the Beverly Hillbillies!

Question: On another track, there are times when a salesman has built up the customer to the point of purchase—you say you can sell anything, disregarding ethical practices. At that point, to what extent is the customer begging the salesman to help make the purchase decision? Is the fact that the customer was dumb enough to set himself up reason to rip him off—the way the tennis player who refuses to come to the net asks to be "chopped" at?

Namer: I don't think that people should be taken advantage of, unless they are aware of the rules. Tennis is a win-lose situation; when you enter the court you intend to take advantage of every weakness your opponent possesses, subject to strict and unbending rules.

Question: You have stated in your book that life is a game, that America is competitive, as is selling. How far towards the tennis court do you feel the salesman should go?

Namer: You are right, but the rules and boundaries must be clearly stated to all contestants. You must be sure that all contestants play by the same set of rules. This is one of my major points. It's all right to take advantage—this might be a quirk of my thinking—of someone to whom you have clearly stated the rules. If you use a rule or fine print but you've made him aware that the fine print exists, he has the equal opportunity of using that against you.

Question: Give me an example.

Namer: Take a company purchasing agent and a salesman. When a contract is written it clearly states the rules whereby the product is delivered and under what conditions. Generally there exist penalty clauses. The purchasing agent specifies a delivery date. The seller accepts, knowing that he cannot deliver on time, but he needs that contract. The buyer has covered himself, knowing that the penalty clause will cover his company and ensure speedy delivery. Each has taken advantage of the other.

Question: Who is responsible for the sucker? What about the guy who has got to have something for nothing? Does this give license to the salesman to teach this guy a lesson?

Namer: It is not the duty or place of a salesman to teach the customer a lesson. The sole function of the salesman is to sell his product, period. He may, by his function as product advocate, teach the customer a lesson, but subsequent bad publicity may be detrimental to him and his product. The salesman must pay heed to public relations, despite the fact that he's dealing with a complete idiot. He must maintain a professional approach, similar to that of a physician dealing with a hypochondriac. He will generally give that patient the benefit of the doubt.

Question: What about the obligation of the buyer?

Namer: The buyer has no obligation to the salesman. The obligations of the sale rest solely on the shoulders of the salesman.

Question: What about the buyer who elicits a great deal of time, technical drawings, surveys, etc., from the seller? Don't you think he has created an obligation in his own part? He is stringing him along, in effect stealing the salesman's time, which is incidentally his stock in trade.

Namer: Why is the salesman allowing this to happen?

Question: To make a sale, obviously.

Namer: Precisely. If there was no sale involved, would the salesman allow himself to be taken advantage of? The salesman allows this only because he foresees taking advantage of the buyer when the sale is made.

Question: If you, the salesman, did allow yourself to get strung along too far, you would have overlooked selling's tenet number two—qualify your client. You went too long with a nonproductive client.

This brings me to a very interesting point. When industrial sales are made, big-ticket items are moved. Corporate salesmen do a lot of entertaining, some involving large gifts and the like. Do the ends justify the means using these sales techniques? Do kickbacks fall within the same category?

Namer: I would say that kickbacks do fall within the same category. My contention, as I've stated before, is that the buyer's role is to get what he wants at the lowest possible price. Any means that he has of achieving that is completely justified on the part of the buyer. The salesman is the professional. It is his business to distinguish what constitutes a legitimate buyer from a phoney or unqualified buyer. If he cannot, he doesn't belong in the business.

Question: What if the salesman encounters evidence of collusion or price-fixing? What if, in a client's office, he spots a competing bid on the desk which indicates price collusion?

Namer: That is of no concern to the salesman. That is a top-management affair.

Question: I worked for a used-car dealership and when asked about speedometer settings we were told to respond, "As far as I know, they were not set back." What are your thoughts on this aspect?

Namer: My book covers the fact that the salesman must know his product, and every step in the production of that product.

Question: What about cribbing information on your customers? When I used to sell, I would look across the client's desk and, if I saw competing bids, I would try to read the quotes.

Namer: That's not unethical. You have to know what other people are doing in order to compete. It's a dog-eat-dog world out there; they're doing it to you. You also need to know about your competitors so as to judge your own product.

Question: Many firms consider salesmen to be their intelligence-gathering force. What about the ethics of divulging privileged information?

Namer: It's the duty of the salesman to scout out his competition. If you see something on my desk, it is public because I made no effort to hide it. If you rifle my desk, or if I tell you that something is off the record, it would be unethical of you to divulge it. However, the salesman is almost morally obligated to utilize any information obtained ethically to his benefit. Observance is not dishonest, nor is it unethical.

Question: How about handling receptionists and secretaries? Is it ethical to woo them or to bribe them from time to time with little gifts?

Namer: When you go into a firm, the first person you meet is a secretary or a receptionist. You must woo this girl to get her on your side. She helps you with your sale by making the buyer more accessible. I don't believe that is unethical or immoral. You are selling yourself and that is a very good quality. I make a strong point in my book on how to handle receptionists and secretaries. That falls neatly into the category of intelligence gathering.

Question: Let's consider retail selling for a moment. When a customer is trying to decide between two items, what is the salesman's role here, and how does he avoid losing the sale because the customer can't make up his mind?

Namer: Three things come into play here. First, the salesman must be an astute listener. He must sense which way the customer is leaning. Second, he must give the customer greater confidence to make up his own mind. And in order to do this, the salesman must be able to adapt to the customer's needs.

Question: Can you expand on the role of adaptability in selling?

Namer: I have found that adaptability is a trait that all salesmen must possess. The salesman must always be ready to confront new selling situations and be able to cope with them. He must realize that he cannot change people, that people change only when they want to, that he must change himself first, and that he must always be positive in his mental outlook.

Question: How does self-confidence fit in?

Namer: As I state in my manual, the basic principle on which the world of selling is founded is confidence or trust. Therefore, it is the salesman's job not only to exude these qualities but also to create a trusting relationship with his customer.

There's another aspect to self-confidence, and that is pride and the desire to feel important. All of us want to be appreciated and to be complimented. Not only must a man feel that he is of some importance, but he craves recognition from his fellows. An appreciation of this very human trait makes it natural for the salesman to use indirect methods in place of the often offensive direct method. It's more tactful to use indirection because this recognizes the right of the other person to feel important. We, therefore, merely suggest instead of dictate. We all resent backseat drivers. The prospect must be made to feel that he did the buying, that he made a wise decision of his own free will.

Question: In other words, you are saying that adapting to the customer's viewpoint is part of the process of building his confidence in his decision. That's an important point. Can you give us an example of how this would work in practice?

Namer: OK. Let's see what happens when Bob Simon walks into Lookwell Clothing Store and is approached by a salesman. Bear in mind that, unless the customer and salesman have met before, there is no association and each appears neutral to the other.

If salesman Art is inexperienced or untrained, the encounter might go something like this:

Art

"Good morning, sir; can I help you?"

Mr. Simon

"Yes. I'm looking for a suit."

Art

"Right this way, sir; these suits are just the thing for you. I think that they will look very well on you."

At this point, Art has committed himself. Mr. Simon, on the other hand, might find the suits undesirable by virtue of their price or appearance and thus would tend to hold Art in the same undesirable light or lose respect for Art's suggestions.

This would be the end of the sales attempt in the majority of cases, for even if Mr. Simon found a suit that he liked, there would be an inconsistency between his like for the suit and dislike for the salesman.

If, on the other hand, Salesman Art is experienced and more skillful, the encounter would be different.

Art

"Good morning. My name is Art. Can I help you?"

Mr. Simon

"Yes. I'm Bob Simon and I'm looking for a suit."

Art

> "Right this way, Mr. Simon. Is there anything in particular that you are looking for and what price range?"

By not at once revealing his own preferences, Art has allowed Mr. Simon to look over the possibilities and express his taste. When Mr. Simon likes something, Art will hasten to agree, thus making Art consistent with Mr. Simon's attitude and way of thinking. When Mr. Simon criticizes, Art will hasten to agree, again making him consistent with his customer. This establishes Art as a man of good taste consonant with Mr. Simon's attitudes.

At this point, Art can use his new position to suggest a suit which might be mildly negative to Mr. Simon, and use this position to change Mr. Simon's mind about it as follows:

Art

> "Mr. Simon, I know that this suit is slightly more than you wanted to pay, but I think that it is just what you are looking for."

Mr. Simon

> "Yes, Art, I think that you're right. I'll take it."

Art has successfully eliminated the inconsistency in Mr. Simon's mind created by the higher cost of the suit and his preference for that suit. This resulted in the sale.

Of course, the salesman's expressions of agreement with a customer's taste, after that taste has already been expressed, are somewhat suspect because of their obvious instrumentality. If the salesman has an alert mind and if the customer's choices follow some pattern, he will be able to anticipate and project ahead to another suit. This will be stronger than after-the-fact association. This consistency principle is the basis of what we, in sales, call the *depth theory* of selling.

The principle recognized in depth selling is that often the buyer approaches the salesman with a need or want before it is expressed in terms of a specific product or service. Through conversation the salesman can assist the buyer in exploring and focusing on his need and can also explore his own capacity in terms of goods or services to satisfy this need. This interchange of ideas leads to a clarification of the buyer's problem and also to an understanding of how the salesman can help solve it.

Question: Should a salesman push a sale in light of obvious dysfunction? How hard should a salesman push a higher-ticket item despite the fact that it appears incongruous with the customer's appearance?

Namer: Yes, the sole function of the salesman is to make a sale, within the ethics and morality of sound business practice. Anything he does to make that sale befits his function in life. A customer that comes in and wants to spend his money should be able to, and if the salesman can coax him to spend more than intended, that's fine. This really is a gray area of ethical behavior. Usually, if the salesman can convince the customer to buy, that is sufficient justification [of the idea] that the customer wants the product. It's the customer's, not the salesman's, taste that matters. Sometimes, of course, it is more important in the long run for the salesman to be sure that the customer gets what he really needs. This is particularly true in industrial selling, where the salesman is trying to solve the buyer's problem, and if he doesn't do it, he will lose the business to the salesman who can.

Question: OK. Let's continue that train of thought. I'm concerned with the buyer's right to control his destiny when he walks into a store. Generally, the buyer's aim is to get the best possible deal, regardless. If, for instance, I went to a camera store selling many brands and ask for advice, suppose the salesman recommends a certain brand of camera because he is paid "push money" by the manufacturer. Now, I would have to have a good working knowledge beforehand to know what was the best camera for the money. Is push money ethical? Again we return to the judicial versus the advocacy (by virtue of the push money) approach.

Namer: I would say that this would be an ethical approach to sales, if taken in the light that, even though the store sells many brands, it tends to specialize in one. Furthermore, if a person enters a store, asks for a specific model item, is satisfied with the price as quoted, you, the salesman, are justified in making that sale regardless of the underlying motivations inherent in that sale.

Question: OK. Here is the final question. If, for instance, I am not mentally ready, not all fired up to lead a marketing class case discussion, what is lost? When I do my damnedest to present a case, what is the value added in the difference between low-pressure, judicial teaching and high-pressure, advocative teaching—am I really selling?

Namer: Yes, I think you are. You're selling yourself and your ideas. What you're interjecting into the situation is a touch of realism, humanity, and warmth. You're getting away from the mechanistic process where you say this is A, B, C, etc.; choose any one, all, or none. Just because the facts are stated in black and white doesn't mean there isn't a human element in there somewhere. You're placing yourself in the role of human being by expressing this humaneness, this enthusiasm. By doing so, you are conveying your thoughts; you are imputing to your listeners your excitement and enthusiasm; and you are drawing them out of their apathy, their blaséness. They get excited—maybe not to the point of agreeing with you, but even if you get them to the point that they disagree, you will have brought out their spirit. You have them thinking, you have them using what makes them unique, God's gift—their brains.

Petite Playthings, Inc., 1984 (A)

After Harold Cassady received his MBA in June 1984, he joined Petite Playthings, Inc., of New York City. He expected to work for six months as a marketing analyst and then to be assigned to a sales territory for one to two years. Following that, he would return to New York in a sales or marketing management position.

Petite Playthings—a large children's-wear manufacturer by industry standards, with sales of $50 million—employed 25 salespeople who were paid a straight commission of 4 percent of sales. As was typical in the industry, all salespeople reported to the national sales manager, Beth Rodgers.

In early September 1984, Ed Autry, the salesperson who covered Texas, died suddenly. During the fiscal year July 1983 to June 1984 the territory had shipped slightly over $1,750,000 in sales. Ed had been a long-term employee of Petite Playthings and had a good reputation within the sales force for sales skill and servicing ability.

When news of Autry's death reached headquarters, Beth Rodgers asked Cassady to take Autry's territory. Hal Cassady perceived this as an excellent opportunity. First it shortened his training period. Second, it gave him a territory considerably better than most new hires, since the commissions for the past year had been over $70,000. Third, it was a territory with good potential for growth.

Beth Rodgers explained that, since she was about to leave for a two-week trip to Europe, Hal Cassady would have to introduce himself to the territory. This was regrettable since she preferred to introduce Cassady to the major accounts.

On Sunday, September 9, Cassady flew to Texas to get settled and to begin covering the territory. On Monday and Tuesday he traveled the suburban and exurban areas around a large city. He had arranged to meet his second-largest customer—the children's-wear buyer for a large department store—for dinner on Tuesday evening. In reviewing his orientation to the territory on his way

This case was prepared by Professor Benson P. Shapiro.
Copyright © 1984 by the President and Fellows of Harvard College.
Harvard Business School case 9-584-080 (rev. 8/87).

to dinner, Cassady was pleased with the approach he had taken. He had begun to learn about his accounts, and in these early stages he had been successful in developing rapport with some smaller accounts. These experiences made him feel confident about meeting Jim Carson, the buyer, who had purchased over $200,000 worth of merchandise from Petite in the 1983–1984 fiscal year—accounting for $8,000 in commissions to Autry.

Cassady was anxious to discuss the upcoming winter line as well as to find out how the fall line was selling. Although he wanted to discuss business, he did not want the dinner conversation to become too "weighty."

Rossin Greenberg Seronick & Hill, Inc. (A)

Looking through the latest issue of *Computer Reseller News*, Neal Hill, president of the Boston advertising agency Rossin Greenberg Seronick & Hill (RGS&H), came across a story indicating that Microsoft Corporation was conducting an agency review. Two days later, November 5, 1987, Hill wrote to Martin Taucher, at Microsoft, Redmond, Washington, suggesting he consider RGS&H. This was an account the agency was keen to secure.

"OUR AMBITION IS YOUR OPPORTUNITY"

RGS&H had been established in 1983. Four years later it had billings of around $25 million and was described in the trade press as the "hottest agency in New England." Yet it was still comparatively small, employing 45 people. Hill would not find it easy to convince the West Coast software company, which had sales of just under $200 million in 1986, that it should transfer its $10 million account to RGS&H. The agency had, however, recently recruited two new creative people, Jamie Mambro and Jay Williams, who had computer industry experience.

In his letter, Hill posed the question: "Why should you even think about an agency in Boston that you've probably never heard of?" He gave four reasons in response:

1. We turn out a wonderful creative product (which has won much more than its share of national and regional awards) and have a tremendous fund of experience in marketing PC-related products, both hardware and software. (That means we do some great advertising, because it's both on target and creatively powerful. *One specific fact*: I've included the recent Lotus insert

This case was prepared by Professor N. Craig Smith with the assistance of Professor John A. Quelch.

because *the creative team which produced it and the rest of Lotus's work over the past year joined this agency last Monday*.)

2. We're just under five years old, and billing just over $25 million annually. (Translation: we're old enough to be "real," and large enough to have terrific resources in creative, marketing, media, and production. It also means that we're young enough and small enough to move quickly and intelligently—to still be *very* hungry to do the kind of work that explodes off the page and screen. Just a note: Lotus's agency is just down the road from us in Providence, Rhode Island, and is the same size we are.)

3. We already handle large national accounts—our clients include Hasbro, Dunkin' Donuts, Fidelity Investments, Clarks of England, and British Telecommunications—and have several concrete ideas for eliminating any problems posed by the (perceived) distance between Redmond and Boston. (This demonstrates that we know how to work with advertising needs on the scale of yours . . . and that we'd love to fly out to show you some of our work and explain some of our logistical approaches.)

4. We are intent on becoming a nationally recognized advertising agency—and doing a bang-up job with one or more Microsoft products would take us a good way down that road. (Which means that our ambition is your opportunity.)

A week later, Hill called Taucher and established that his letter should have been sent to Rob Lebow, director of corporate communications, to whom it had been forwarded. On November 16, Hill wrote to Lebow enclosing further samples of work done by the agency's staff: a Lotus direct-mail brochure, an advertisement for Charles River Laboratories, and an advertisement for software by a company no longer active in the U.S. market. His key message was: "We are an awfully good agency, with a great deal of knowledge of Microsoft's industry, competition, and products. And we would kill to do even a project for you."

Follow-up calls were not returned, so Hill decided to send a further sample of artwork to Microsoft: a 12 × 9 inch brochure promoting RGS&H and containing a plane ticket for a trip to Boston. This specially produced "flier" was mailed by overnight express to Lebow on November 20. On the front, in white letters against a dark background, it simply stated: "You probably haven't thought about talking to an agency in Boston." The interior of the flier is shown in Exhibit 1.

ENCOURAGING NEWS

On November 23, RGS&H received a "no thanks" letter from Lebow. As this was dated November 16, Hill was not too disappointed. A call the following day established that Lebow was out of the office for the next week. On November 30, Hill was told that Lebow "certainly took notice of the mailed piece" and that he should call back December 4, when Lebow would be available. Hill wrote a further letter to Lebow expressing his delight at securing some attention with the flyer and explaining "what we wanted to do was to demonstrate simultaneously our creative approach to messaging and our aggressive approach to marketing—in this case, marketing ourselves." He included an extract from *Adweek* (New England) which discussed RGS&H; its commitment to sophisticated office automation and how it pitched against New York agencies for the Playskool print account. Hill also explained that the agency would be interested in a single product or limited-term project instead of the entire account: "We just want a chance to show you what we can do for you."

EXHIBIT 1 RGS&H "Flier"

In the News

7.5.1 ON THE TAKE*

There are parallels between bribery and nuclear weapons. A bribe can win a contract, just as a nuclear bomb can win a war. But to offer bribes and to make nuclear weapons invites rivals to do the same. When all companies bribe, none is sure of winning the contract, but each must pay so as not to be outdone. As bribers bid against each other, the cost rises; bribery's effectiveness does not. All companies—and the countries whose officials are corrupted—would gain from an agreement to scrap bribes.

In 1975, the United Nations began work on an international ban on bribery. Progress is even slower than on arms control. Frustration has bred an urge for unilateralism; but here the nuclear comparison stops. Unilateral nuclear disarmament would hardly serve the interests of a country like the United States. But America is bribery's unilateralist, and its experience indicates that renouncing bribery need not damage the fortunes of a country's businessmen.

In 1977, America passed the Foreign Corrupt Practices Act, which forbids American companies from making payments to foreign officials. Companies are liable to a fine of $1 million for each violation; individuals to a fine of $10,000 and five years in jail. Prison terms are the more powerful half of the deterrent, since the potential revenues from some bribes make a $1 million fine look like loose change. The

PEMEX scandal in the 1970s, in which Mexico's national oil company received bribes from a Texan businessman, involved contracts worth $293 million.

After the antibribery legislation was passed, American businessmen complained that they were losing orders to Japanese and European competitors for whom bribery was sometimes not merely legal but tax free, since it could be counted as a business expense. Business lobbyists have repeatedly demanded that the act be repealed or diluted, citing the country's $150 billion trade deficit as a reason for urgent action.

America's law suffers from being vague. It does not, for instance, forbid "facilitating payments" to government employees "whose duties are essentially ministerial or clerical." Only a handful of companies have been prosecuted under the Foreign Corrupt Practices Act. But though the act has its faults, damage to American exports is apparently not one of them.

Studies by Mr. John Graham of the University of Southern California and Mr. Mark McKean of the University of California at Irvine suggest that the businessmen's cries of pain are exaggerated. Using information from American embassies in 51 countries that together account for four fifths of America's exports, Mr. Graham divides the countries into two groups: one where bribery is endemic, the other where it is not. He then checks the embassies' impressions against American press reports of bribery, which broadly confirm the corrupt/noncorrupt classification. He has found that in the eight years after the Foreign Corrupt Practices Act was passed, America's share of the imports of

---

* From *The Economist*, November 19, 1988. Reprinted by permission of The Economist Newspaper Group Inc.

corrupt countries actually grew as fast as its share of the imports of noncorrupt ones (see table). His findings are convincing even though, over the period studied, a few of the baddies may have become goodies (and vice versa).

Shady Folk in Sunny Places

The need to pay bribes to win business is, it seems, overestimated. Bribes are awkward to distribute: it is not always clear in a foreign country whom should be bribed, or with how much. "Commissions" are sometimes not passed on. Sometimes they are, but the enriched official then awards the contract on the basis of merit. Costs are incurred, and risks are run for uncertain benefits. As well as being expensive, bribes can be embarrassing if exposed. Many man-hours are, therefore, spent fudging accounts and keeping things quiet. Low prices and high quality are often an easier way to win contracts.

The success of the Foreign Corrupt Practices Act ought to have encouraged other governments to copy America's virtuous example. None has: nearly all countries have laws against the bribing of their own officials, but only America forbids the bribing of other people's.

Virtue Rewarded

	U.S. Share of Imports of Corrupt Countries, Percentage	U.S. Share of Imports of Uncorrupt Countries, Percentage
1977	17.5%	13.8%
1978	17.8	13.6
1979	18.6	12.9
1980	18.6	13.7
1981	19.1	14.8
1982	18.9	14.8
1983	18.7	14.6
1984	18.2	14.4

Source: John Graham and Mark McKean.

Despite the evidence from America, bribery is still thought of as a necessary part of doing business in the third world. Anthropologists' studies of gift-giving are wheeled in to show that bribery is part of the culture of many poor countries: nonbribers are presented as cultural imperialists as well as naive businessmen. The way share-ownership is becoming more international is cited as another reason for business managers to bribe freely: whatever their personal moral scruples, they should not impose them on shareholders to whom such morals might be alien.

Such attitudes once prevailed in America, too. Lockheed, an American aircraft manufacturer, admitted in 1975 that it had paid out $22 million in bribes since 1970; but it protested that: "Such payments . . . are in keeping with business practices in many foreign countries." Yet the Lockheed scandal—along with the humiliating revelations of corrupt political practices that came with the Chilean-ITT and Watergate hearings—helped to bring about a change of mood among America's politicians, even if not among its businessmen.

In 1977, the Senate was told that the Securities and Exchange Commission had discovered that more than 300 American companies had paid bribes abroad. The image both of American government and of American business was suffering, and so were America's relations with friendly foreign governments. Lockheed's bribes to Mr. Kakuei Tanaka when he was Japan's prime minister in 1972–74 led to his arrest in 1976 and a protracted trial that has still not been completed. The Senate report also made a point that has grown with the fashion for laissez-faire economics. A free-market economy is based on competition—which corruption subverts.

The report's result was the Foreign Corrupt Practices Act. Far from being patronising, the act's proponents argued, it enforced American compliance with other countries' anti-corruption laws. Even Saudi Arabia, renowned for the lush bribing that goes on there, has anti-corruption legislation on its books. Indeed, it may often be developing countries' standards that are brought down by multinational firms, rather than the other way round.

Innocents Abroad

Two researchers from the University of Western Ontario, Mr. Henry Lane and Mr. Donald Simpson, argue that foreign businessmen on brief visits to Africa presume corruption too easily, and so make it worse. If they fail to win a contract, they prefer to believe that the rivals won with larger bribes than that their own products were not up to scratch. Once sown, rumours of corruption spread quickly among the expatriates of an African capital. This leaves Westerners with the impression that they have little choice but to bribe: the rumours are self-fulfilling.

The style of Western business also encourages bribery. Executives from head office spend fleeting days in a poor country's capital. Few know their way about, or understand the workings of the cumbersome local bureaucracy. The foreignness of foreign cities makes it hard to resist the speakers of excellent English who hang around the hotel bars: a Westerner gets conned, and quickly spreads the news that the city is corrupt. Alternatively, his lack of time makes him impatient with local bureaucratic rules. The simplest solution, so it seems, is to cut through the rules with bribes.

Mr. Lane and Mr. Simpson base their views on private talks with officials and businessmen. None, for obvious reasons, wants to be named, so the theories cannot be checked. But they fit with Mr. Graham's conclusions. First, the moral justification for bribery abroad—that it is part of local custom—is sometimes spurious. Second, the business justification does not stand up either: since bribery is not expected of foreign firms, contracts can be won without it. Yet European governments show no signs of heeding such research and legislating against bribery abroad.

Their mistakes need not be repeated by European companies, which could also learn from their counterparts in the United States. More and more American companies are telling their employees to act ethically as well as profitably. Managers have three standard weapons in their armoury. Company codes of practice lay down general ethical guidelines. These are fleshed out with training courses, based mainly on case studies. Then there are ways of catching offenders by encouraging colleagues to report them. One is to create an ethics ombudsman to whom employees may report anonymously. Another is IBM's "skip level" management reporting, whereby everybody spends periods working directly for his boss's boss, and so has a choice of two familiar superiors to report to.

According to the Ethics Resource Centre, a Washington-based research group, 73 percent of America's largest 500 companies had codes of ethics in 1979; by 1988, the figure had risen to 85 percent of the 2,000 biggest. In 1980, only 3 percent of the companies surveyed had ethics training for their managers; now 35 percent do. In 1985, the centre knew of no company that had an ethics ombudsman; by 1987 more than 1 in 10 had created the post.

Most American business courses now include a training course in ethics. At Harvard nearly a quarter of the business school students opt for the ethics course. More European business schools are also starting to teach business ethics. Last year an umbrella body, the European Business Ethics Network, was set up in Brussels.

Down to Self-Defence

Yet the fight against corruption remains a peculiarly American concern. The Europeans and Japanese (whose own country is pretty corrupt) hurt themselves by their complacency, but they hurt developing nations more. In the end it is up to poor countries to defend themselves from foreigners' corruption—as well as from their own.

Sheer poverty makes this hard to do. By 1900, Britain had beaten the worst of its corruption. But in 1900, the average Briton had a yearly income (GDP per person in today's prices) of $4,000—more than 10 times that of the average person in the developing world today. Britain had acquired a middle class, whose belief in reward for hard work was the antithesis of corruption. Few of today's poor countries have a sizable middle class; the rest are sat upon by elites accustomed to acquiring money through inheritance and other gifts.

Poverty goes with a weak state, which makes corruption worse. If the state cannot enforce laws, nobody will respect it. Disrespect quickly breeds disloyalty among civil servants: corruption seems eminently sensible, since it involves robbing from the state in order to give to relatives and friends who provide the security that the state is too feeble to deliver. Thus impoverished, the state's strength diminishes further; the rival authority of the clan is consolidated.

Though hampered by their poverty, developing countries can dent the worst of their corruption. The first step is to **admit corruption exists**. It hides behind respectable masks. Mexican policemen ask for "tips." Middlemen in business deals demand "consultancy fees" and "commissions." A favourite trick in Pakistan is for the post-office teller to be out of stamps. Terribly sorry, but there happens to be a street vendor just outside the post office who sells them—at a premium. Not everybody guesses that half the premium goes to the teller.

It is also necessary to admit it is damaging. The Mexican policeman gets the national minimum wage (a bit over $3 a day), so it may seem natural that he should supplement his pay. The bribes accepted by an official before he awards a government contract do not necessarily distort competition among rival tenderers: sometimes, all are accompanied by a similar bribe, which serves as an entry fee. Equally, a judge may offer the plaintiff with justice on his side the first chance to make a "contribution." For businessmen, a modest bribe may seem an efficient way to secure a licence quickly.

Even these apparently mild examples of corruption are harmful. Mexican policemen refuse to investigate crimes reported by those who cannot afford to pay the tip: access to public services, which should be equal, is thus restricted to the better off. While refusing to investigate crimes that do not pay, the Mexican police assiduously tackle noncrimes that do: innocent motorists are stopped to extract a bribe.

The poor and innocent suffer, but there is wider damage, too. The tip for a quickly issued licence encourages officials to invent new licences. The tangle of lucrative red-tape strangles would-be entrepreneurs—and the economy suffers. The state's venality diminishes its standing in the eyes of its citizens. No sane Mexican respects the police. South Africa's supposedly independent homelands are made all the more despicable because their rulers are thieves.

By weakening the state, corruption can even prompt—or at least provide the excuse for—political violence, as when Nigeria's president Shehu Shagari was deposed in 1984. Honest regimes, by contrast, are generally strong enough to get even their unpopular policies accepted. Ghana's flight-lieutenant Jerry Rawlings, who overthrew his civilian predecessors because of their corruption, has imposed an awesome dose of economic austerity on his people, but still survives in power.

Once corruption's harmfulness is acknowledged, **train civil servants to spot and stop it**. The polite silence that surrounds corruption often blocks the passing on of useful tips on how to tackle it. The story is told of an engineer responsible for an irrigation system in India. The rich farmers in the area bribed a local politician, who in turn ordered the irrigation engineer to divert water from poor farms to rich ones. The engineer agreed to do as he was told, so long as the politician would speak his order into the engineer's tape recorder: whereupon the politician backed down. If this was made a case study for trainee water engineers, India's water might be better managed.

As well as instructing the virtuous on how to beat corruption, training should explain to the not-so-virtuous why corruption is so damaging. It may not be a bad idea to explain the benefits to a country of an honest civil service, much as student lawyers learn some jurisprudence. The same goes for businessmen. Some Latin countries—Mexico, Chile—are making ethics training part of their business school curriculums, which should make businessmen aware of the harm that corruption does to the economy, and to the standards of their firms.

Next, let **journalists and other snoops** help in exposing corruption. It is not enough for governments to break their silence on the subject; general openness is essential for having corruption discussed. In the Soviet Union, parts of which are pretty poor, Mr. Mikhail Gorbachev is allowing more press freedom than before, partly in order to expose the corruption that festered under the secretive rule of Leonid Brezhnev.

Greater openness is the first step towards increased accountability. Mr. Gorbachev also wants some party officials to be exposed to elections, so they can be judged on the records that *glasnost* has made known. Elections are one good way of holding people to account. Another is the separation of powers. Independent executives, judiciaries, and legislatures can keep tabs on each other.

Even strong and open states have difficulty retaining civil servants' loyalty, so the wise ones **reduce bureaucrats' discretion**: fewer licences will mean fewer bribes. In famously corrupt Indonesia, the government's economic-reform programme includes the burning of red tape. To build a hotel only one licence is now required; once, an entrepreneur needed 33.

In particular, do away with economic controls that create black markets. If the state fixes the exchange rate artificially high, foreign currency will be scarce, and distributing it will be the task of bureaucrats. Bribes will flow, because businessmen who need to import spare parts will pay generously for dollars or import quotas. The same happens when state food-marketing boards force farmers to sell their crops at artificially low prices: farmers are encouraged to bribe the board's officials to overlook their grain, and then to bribe customs officials to allow it across the border into a country where it will fetch more. Five years ago, Ugandan coffee could be sold in Kenya for 10 times its domestic price.

Slimming down the state will make possible the next corruption-beating move that is sometimes needed: **pay public employees more**, so they no longer depend on "tips." The Indonesian government is likely to find its anti-corruption policies damaged by the freeze it has put on civil servants' pay. It may do wonders for Indonesia's budget, but it will probably encourage civil servants to find pay of their own. Along with better training, better pay will improve morale. The more pride that officials take in working for their governments, the less likely they are to subvert them by accepting bribes.

Another way to raise the professional morale of bureaucrats is to make the civil service **meritocratic**. Competitive entry examinations and promotion on merit helped diminish corruption in 19th-century England. In Mexico today, the relatively high professional standards of the Finance Ministry, Bank of Mexico, and Foreign Ministry go with their relatively clean reputations. The Indian civil service has competitive examinations but, in some states at least, civil service jobs are known by the size of bribe needed to obtain them. So long as that persists, those who do the jobs will see them as an instrument of plunder, not as a chance to serve the state.

Tolerated, corruption spreads easily. The civil servant who buys his job will reimburse himself corruptly. In the Philippines, corruption has even infected the body investigating corruption under the country's deposed ruler,

Mr. Ferdinand Marcos. Because it is so hard to beat, and because all societies and institutions develop taboos against snitching on colleagues, corruption is too often met with defeatism or indulgence. That is an unkindness to bureaucracies and businessmen, whether poor or rich.

7.5.2   DAMAGE CONTROL AT DUN & BRADSTREET*

It's cleaning up the credit unit's billing abuses, but once-hefty profits seem sure to suffer

The decision made Dun & Bradstreet Corporation an information giant—and may haunt it for years. In 1975, Richard F. Schmidt, a former McKinsey & Company consultant whom D&B had hired as a top executive, was assigned to analyze D&B's strategy. After a year of study, Schmidt devised a plan. He felt that D&B could profit immensely with new products developed by repackaging the vast credit records it maintained on American businesses. Harrington Drake, D&B's chief executive at the time, agreed. He ordered that all the information sprinkled throughout D&B be rounded up and stored in a central computer—the key to the new approach.

The plan worked. Spurred by the credit unit, D&B's overall sales doubled by 1980, to $1.4 billion. They have climbed about 15 percent a year since, as credit unit profits funded a $700 million buying spree—without new debt. But the strategy also put unrelenting pressure on the credit unit, creating distortions in a 148-year-old culture that traced its roots to such former employees as Abraham Lincoln. "We became a cesspool," says a 30-year D&B West Coast salesman.

---

* By Jeffrey Rothfeder and Stephen Phillips. Reprinted from November 27, 1989, issue of *BusinessWeek* by special permission. Copyright © 1989 by McGraw-Hill, Inc.

Tarnished Image

Indeed, the new strategy set off a chain of events that could hurt D&B well into the 1990s. About three dozen lawsuits, plus articles in *The Wall Street Journal*, have alleged that in the 1980s D&B salespeople cheated customers and misled them into buying more reports and services than they needed. D&B may not lose business: It sells 90 percent of all corporate credit reports, and competition is scarce. But without admitting guilt, the company has quietly doled out millions to settle with such customers as IBM and American Telephone & Telegraph Company. It also has agreed, in a class-action settlement negotiated in a Cincinnati federal court, to make major changes in the way it is run.

Can D&B recoup? In a series of wide-ranging interviews with *Business Week*, key D&B officers opened the company's files and, for the first time, gave their account of what had gone wrong and why. They also outlined the steps D&B is taking to try to restore its reputation.

Besides paying back customers, D&B is easing the pressure on salespeople by making their compensation depend less on commissions. It is developing a simpler pricing system and setting up hotlines for customers. James K. Murray, Jr., the credit unit's new president, has jettisoned 10 percent of D&B's 700-member sales force and has rewritten job descriptions so that salespeople spend more time advising customers than selling. And now, D&B employees take classes in ethics. "It's a wrenching cultural change," says Murray, and it's costing $100 million.

The financial effect will be worse than that. With salespeople hustling less, the credit division's revenues may fall in 1990 and again in 1991. Its net margins will drop to about 10 percent from 30 percent. The credit unit also will hurt D&B's overall revenues, even though it produces only a third of them. Analysts expect D&B's sales to be flat in 1989, at $4.27 billion, and to grow by only 4 percent in 1990. The company is likely to prop up profits, analysts

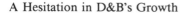

A Hesitation in D&B's Growth

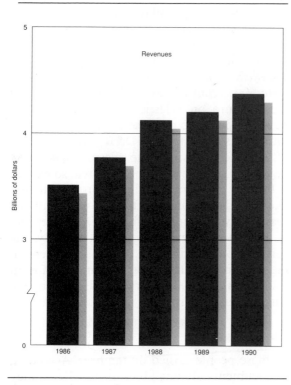

Data: Company and Analyst Reports.

say, with accounting changes and interest income on its $650 million in cash. Still, Wall Street is alarmed. Since August, D&B's stock has dropped 10 points from its postcrash high of 60.

Ironically, Drake's move to computers was meant to avoid slow growth. At the time, credit reports were done on paper and kept in local offices. Some could take weeks to get—and customers complained. Beyond that, Drake felt that growth would suffer if D&B remained a one-product company. Computers solved both problems.

Cash Cow

Today, more than 70 percent of D&B's credit reports are sent via PCs, fax, or voice mail. And D&B has more than 100 credit products. The basic report is an accounting of a company's business, its recent financial activities, its number of employees, and its dealings with other companies. D&B has spun off from these such products as Dun's Financial Profiles, which compare a company's balance sheet with others in the same industry. Developed for $200,000 in 1979, by 1981 Financial Profiles was bringing in revenues of close to $5.5 million, and other new products soon followed.

D&B had found its cash cow, says Paine-Webber, Inc., analyst Kendrick J. Noble. And it milked it. Partly because of the credit unit's growth, D&B's stock outpaced the market. In 1984, this made it easy to buy A. C. Nielsen Company for $1.3 billion in stock. Soon, in addition to Moody's Investors Service, D&B's lineup included software maker McCormack & Dodge, pharmaceuticals researcher IMS International, and business credit insurer American Credit Indemnity.

But by then, the price of these gains was starting to show. In the late 1970s, D&B's management had begun to pressure the credit division for 15 percent annual gains. "We were told this was a key to D&B's expansion plans," says a former West Coast regional vice president.

The credit division responded. First, it changed the way it billed. For decades, customers had paid up front each year for reports they predicted they would need. Then in 1977, D&B switched to selling voucher-like units— like carnival tickets for rides. One unit bought a basic report. Two bought the report delivered via computer. A more thorough analysis could run nine units. The system wasn't devious initially, says Harold T. Redding, former senior vice president and still a D&B consultant: It was "the most efficient way to price" D&B's varied line.

But it was also the most confusing. Before long, D&B had more than 200 separate services, each with a different price. Customers who underestimated the number of units they would need were charged big premiums to buy more

How D&B Is Changing Its Ways

Dozens of customers have sued Dun & Bradstreet for alleged overcharges by its business-credit unit. About 40 of these suits were settled out of court. The rest are included in a class action settlement. Here are the details of that settlement.

- D&B must pay a total of $18 million, minus legal fees and court costs, to as many as 45,000 customers that choose to participate in the settlement

- The company must ease the pressure on its sales staff to produce huge sales—and thus to cheat customers. This involves raising base salaries for salespeople and lowering their commissions

- D&B must end unit pricing and attach a dollar price to each service instead. Previously the company sold its services under prepaid one-year contracts priced according to how many "units" of service a customer required. This pricing mechanism was so confusing that few customers could tell how many units they had used—and D&B did not provide a clear accounting. The company must now also provide a hotline for customers to monitor their accounts by computer and modem or touchtone phone

- The company must reduce the premium that customers pay if they use up their prepaid allotment of D&B services and need to buy more before their one-year contract is up. Previously, D&B induced customers to sign one-year contracts by charging higher prices for services bought without a contract

---

Data: Dun & Bradstreet Corporation.

in midcontract. And, incredibly, D&B never told customers how many units they had left. "We were penalized for the confusion that D&B instigated," charges Allen Farber, director of credit at Metro Factors of New Jersey, Inc. Customers complained, to no avail. "This was arrogance," says Murray. But also smart. It let a management obsessed with growth "make sure that revenue goals were met," says a former D&B manager who now works at Standard & Poor's Corporation, a McGraw-Hill, Inc., subsidiary.

D&B salespeople played on the confusion, warning customers of having too few units to cover D&B's stream of new products. Salespeople had to book 18 percent more revenues each year for commissions to kick in—and those were 60 percent of pay. "The unit system and the pressure on salespeople were a one-two punch intended to increase sales, not cheat customers," says a former D&B vice president. "But the feeling was, if the salesman got a little aggressive and the customer suffered, so what?"

Initially, customers mainly heard "white lies, like: 'You got awful close to your unit limit last year,'" says Al Brown, a former D&B salesman in Rochester, New York. But ultimately, according to D&B insiders, up to 15 percent of the sales force realized that customer confusion could turn a $50,000 salary into a six-figure one and get them on the fast track, too.

Forged Signatures

So these people turned up the heat. According to documents obtained by *Business Week*, they sold subscribers expensive supplemental units they didn't need. They forged customers' signatures on rewritten, higher-priced contracts and even charged customers for thousands of credit reports without authorization. D&B critics say such tactics cost customers tens of millions of dollars. Salespeople who objected were "told to mind their own business," says a 30-year D&B veteran in the Midwest. That was because bonuses for district managers depended on revenues from their offices. "The activities of the salespeople were lining the managers' pockets as well," says Cindy Starr, a former D&B saleswoman who quit last April, she says, after internal auditors ignored her complaints about sales abuses. D&B refuses to comment.

At least for a while, the man most in the dark may have been John P. Kunz, who became credit division chief in 1984. "Kunz had a mercurial temper, and he could chop your head off if you brought him bad news," says a Northeastern district manager. So no one did. Moreover, as a newcomer to the credit division, Kunz didn't know its sales methods, though certain statistics were hard to miss: Revenues ballooned year after year, but customer usage never kept pace. A former regional vice president says that Kunz, who declined to be interviewed for this article, tried to ignore this: "The last thing he wanted to do was tell D&B's board that the cash cow was sick."

That would have been heresy indeed. CEO Charles W. Moritz, who took over from Harrington Drake in 1985, has told analysts that D&B's 100-plus units are individual companies run by "disciplined entrepreneurs" with one goal: meeting revenue targets. Throughout the scandal, Moritz leaned on this to keep himself and his directors at arm's length. "He told Kunz to clean it up quietly and quickly," says a Kunz associate.

What was happening couldn't be hidden forever, though. By late 1987, a regional vice president told Kunz of suspicions that Frederick Paley, D&B's lead salesman to IBM, had charged Big Blue upward of $100,000 for reports it hadn't ordered. An internal audit confirmed this. Paley denies toying with IBM's account, but says he "can't explain how IBM's usage figures got elevated." In January 1988, Paley was fired—and D&B paid IBM back.

As word spread of the IBM deal, more customers complained, and Kunz tried to quell the revolt. In 1988, he let dozens of salespeople go, according to D&B insiders, and began settling with clients. Customer sources say that AT&T received more than $1 million, including thousands of low-priced units into the 1990s. Subscribers got quarterly-usage statements. Salespeople signed an ethics code. And reacting to complaints of inaccurate credit reports, Kunz devised a quality-control system to monitor virtually all of D&B's reports. Now, D&B says, 95 percent of its reports are on the mark.

But change came too late. "Kunz's mistake was to keep the problem inside D&B, instead

of going public and making a clean breast of it," says a former D&B vice president. "I would've done things differently," asserts Murray, who took over last May when Kunz was let go.

Since then, Murray has been as outspoken as Kunz was silent. Strong on style, one of his first acts was to issue a brochure that trumpets the founding of "a new company." And Murray is apt to pop up anywhere. He drops in on customers and D&B district offices or calls up the new 800 customer hotline—all to find out what subscribers are saying.

No Rivals

Because of the class-action settlement, he's making other changes, too. By 1991, the unit pricing system will be dropped for a dollar price on each product. Already, customers get monthly-usage statements—and can get them by phone any time. To discourage cheating, base pay has been raised for salespeople, and commissions lowered. Sales quotas are gone. Commissions are based on how much customers use, and, uniquely, on the results of a new market research program that measures customer satisfaction. Adds Murray: "Anybody that manhandles customers will be thrown out, no questions asked." Indeed, he recently told a companywide sales meeting that 25 percent of those on hand would be unable to fit into the new system and be gone in a year.

Murray has time for the changes to work, if only because D&B has little competition. TRW, Inc., its closest rival, has begun a direct-mail campaign to D&B customers, claiming that its own reports are cheaper and collected from third parties and public records, not from the company the report is about. Still, analysts say that TRW has only about 8 percent of the market, mainly because customers feel that its data bank is too small. Says Roger Green, a credit manager at a New Jersey drug company, which last year got $200,000 back from D&B: "We need D&B because they know much more about our prospective customers than we could find out anyplace else."

Still, for Murray the hard work has just begun. By replacing gamesmanship with salesmanship, his reforms will stifle the credit division's growth, perhaps for years. Murray insists that as D&B rebuilds customer confidence, subscribers will decide that they need the higher-priced, specialty products that Drake's repackaging strategy created. Maybe, maybe not. But for the first time in years, one thing seems likely: The only dollars the credit division will be raking in should be honest ones.

OUTRAGEOUS FORTUNE? TWO GUYS FROM D&B CASH IN

Thomas Paley and George J. Thomas are in business to make Dun & Bradstreet pay for cheating customers. Since March 1988, when the two former D&B salesmen formed Credit Advisors, Inc., they've been advising the information giant's customers on what to look for when suing it for alleged overcharges. So far, three dozen D&B customers have taken the Bound Brook (N.J.) company's advice. With the help of a law firm retained by CAI, these customers have recouped nearly $10 million—half of which they've paid to CAI for its help.

Paley can advise customers, since he understands how they were misled. He was fired just before forming CAI because, according to D&B, he sent a letter under a false signature saying his client had used up more buying units than it actually had. Paley, whose father, Frederick, also was fired by D&B, doesn't deny the company's charges: "From what I've seen, I wasn't half as bad as a lot of the other guys at D&B." Thomas quit D&B in 1986, disgusted, he says, with its sales tactics.

Now, CAI is fighting the clock. Last August, D&B tried to contain the suits against it by negotiating an $18 million class-action settlement. Customers wishing to sue D&B separately must opt out of the class by November 28. And Paley and his staff of 15 in three CAI offices around the country are urging them to do so. It's a matter of numbers. Says Paley: "Divide $18 million among 45,000 customers, and each one gets an average of $400." That doesn't begin to pay back what D&B customers lost, he says. Some, he claims, were overcharged by more than $1 million over eight years. CAI's pitch is apparently working. According to Paley, more than one third of the customers are thinking of not participating in the class action. D&B refuses to comment on that.

D&B could be hurt if CAI is right. The company's strategy, say D&B insiders, is to get most of its customers to join the class action. Then, if some minor cases are still kicking around, D&B could settle them quietly. If this plan fails, D&B has an out. If more than 5 percent of eligible customers don't buy in, D&B can cancel the settlement and, if it chooses, avoid planned reforms in its business practices.

Short Life

Although the settlement might save D&B money, its main goal is simply to end the dispute and put distance between itself and the scandal. That's why, in a Newark federal court last month, D&B argued that CAI is undermining the class-action settlement. D&B tried to prove this by subpoenaing CAI's records, including correspondence and notes of conversations with D&B customers. No ruling has yet been made. Says Paley: "We gave D&B what we had. If they push us any further, we'll defend ourselves" by challenging D&B in court.

Paley and Thomas are acutely aware that CAI's business has a short life, and that one day they'll need new ways to make money. But Paley says CAI has a chance to rake in more than $20 million during the next couple of years just by being a thorn in D&B's side. And for a couple of out-of-work New Jersey salesmen, that's the type of payoff that normally isn't found north of Atlantic City.

7.5.3 DON'T LET BAD COMPANY MANNERS HURT GOOD PRODUCTS*

A recent display ad in this newspaper described an appealing new mutual fund. After reading the copy through twice, I decided to find out more about the fund.

There was a coupon to be mailed for further information, or, if the reader preferred, an 800 number. After I dial the 800 number, a woman answers.

"I am calling about your ad in today's *Wall Street Journal.* I would like more information on your new fund."

"Are you calling about a bond fund or a stock fund?" the woman asks.

"I'm calling about your ad in today's *Journal*—the new fund described there."

"Are you calling about a bond fund or a stock fund. I can't help you unless you tell me which."

"Well, it appears to be a stock fund."

No human response. However, the sounds of telephone switching gear are heard clicking, and in a half-minute another female voice says, "This is Linda. May I help you?"

"Yes, Linda, I am calling about the new fund you have advertised in today's *Journal*. Could you tell me—"

"What is your zip code?"

"I'm not sure you'll need my zip code. I don't know yet whether I want you to send me a prospectus. All I want is to ask a couple of questions about the fund."

"I'll have to have your zip code," says Linda.

She now has my zip code and I resume my quest for information. "What I would like to know," I say, "is whether—"

"Give me your name," she cuts in. "Last name first, then first name, then middle initial, if any. Begin by spelling your last name."

Further recital of my discussion with Linda is unnecessary. Suffice it to say she never got my name (first, last, or middle initial); I never got the information I was after; and Linda's company will never have me for a customer.

The point of this anecdote has absolutely nothing to do with poor Linda. She was doing her job exactly as she believed it should be done. She correctly surmised that at the end of the day her work performance would be judged on a single factor: The completeness and accuracy of the computer printout she turned in, with each caller's zip code entered on the first line and his last name on the second line.

Rather, the moral of the story is this: No matter how good the product or how brilliant the marketing plan, it all comes to naught if there is a breakdown at the most critical interface in all of business—the point at which the customer comes in contact with the company.

Some executives never seem to grasp this precept. They assume that the task of attracting customers is strictly a responsibility of the sales department. Managers of successful organizations, however, recognize that each employee, whether a service technician, an installation mechanic, a receptionist, or a parts clerk, personifies the company when he or she comes in contact with a customer.

When an IBM technician shows up to repair a typewriter or replace an electronic board, in the eyes of the customer that technician is IBM while he remains on the customer's premises. It is no mere happenstance, then, that IBM technicians, in addition to being skilled in their special area of expertise, are also usually solicitous of customer needs and concerns. They have been trained to be sensitive to the nuances of customer worries.

---

* By Howard Upton, "Manager's Journal," *The Wall Street Journal*, April 11, 1988. Mr. Upton is a trade association consultant in Tulsa. Reprinted with permission of *The Wall Street Journal* © 1988 Dow Jones and Company, Inc. All rights reserved.

In his book *Further Up the Organization,* former Avis president Robert Townsend writes: "When you're off on a business trip or a vacation, pretend you're a customer. Telephone some part of your organization and ask for help. You'll run into some real horror shows."

Good advice. A friend of mine, who is marketing vice president of a major bank, decided to follow Mr. Townsend's suggestion. He had a woman acquaintance call his bank (while he listened in on an extension line) to inquire about obtaining an automobile loan.

"It was terrible," he says. "We are a bank. Making loans is our business, and auto loans are very profitable. But the woman who made the call to ask about borrowing money for the purchase of a new car was treated with thinly veiled disdain at every step along the way.

"I don't mind telling you," my banker friend fumed, "that if I had been the prospective customer making the call, and had been treated as that woman was treated, I would have taken my business elsewhere. . . . We've got some serious attitude changing work ahead of us."

Satisfied customers represent the principal intangible asset of any company, regardless of its products or services. Every working day there are scores of situations in which customers interface with people in the company, from the president on down to the newest file clerk. Above all else, the manner in which these customer/company contacts is handled determines the ultimate success of the company.

Does Opportunity Make the Thief?: How Control Systems Influence an Industrial Salesperson's Ethical Behavior[1]

Diana C. Robertson
Erin Anderson

Pressures abound in sales. The field salesperson has to meet the demands of both the firm and the customer, demands that are not always compatible. The salesperson often operates alone, with few guidelines from the firm, except, of course, the necessity of making the sale. Purchasing agents may demand special considerations, ranging from entertainment activities to gifts that constitute outright bribery. Dubinsky (1985) argues that ethical conflicts such as these create tension, frustration, and anxiety among salespeople. They also require that salespeople engage in a continuous process, perhaps unconscious, of decision making about ethical issues.

Because salespeople are likely to work independently, they may feel that they are working for themselves, rather than their employer. This perception may lead salespeople to deceive their role partners, such as sales managers and customers ("opportunistic" behavior). This effect has been demonstrated by Hunt, Wood, and Chonko (1989) among marketing managers and by Anderson (1988) among industrial salespeople. In addition, the more risk that the salesperson assumes in regard to compensation (depending on commission,

[1] A more detailed treatment of this chapter is found in "Control System and Task Environment Effects on Ethical Judgment: An Exploratory Study of Industrial Salespeople," by Diana C. Robertson and Erin Anderson, *Organization Science*, forthcoming. The authors gratefully acknowledge the financial support of the Reginald H. Jones Center for Management Policy, Strategy and Organization, The Wharton School, University of Pennsylvania.

rather than on being paid a salary), the less cooperative is the salesperson's attitude toward management (John and Weitz, 1988).

Sales managers also encounter situations that are ethically troublesome. Sales managers' rewards generally are tied to salespeople's sales success. For this reason managers may tend to overlook ethics infractions on the part of their salespeople, particularly when the salespeople are performing well (Bellizi and Hite, 1989). Along these lines, Caywood and Laczniak (1986) indicate that sales managers may be sending a mixed set of ethical signals to salespeople by ignoring questionable behavior.

Our particular interest is in determining, first, what types of behavior in response to ethical issues salespeople find most and least acceptable, and second, what factors in their organizations influence the ways in which they respond to these ethical issues. With these objectives in mind, we surveyed 301 industrial field salespeople and 145 sales managers to assess their responses to a series of 14 scenarios or vignettes involving ethical issues. Our sample consists of salespeople around the country, 85 percent of them male, with the largest concentration involved in manufacturing sales (28 percent), followed by wholesale trade (16 percent), business services (15 percent), retail trade (10 percent), transportation, communication, and utilities (10 percent), and the remainder fairly evenly distributed throughout other specializations.

COST/BENEFIT DECISION MAKING ON ETHICAL ISSUES

One approach to decision making about ethical issues suggests that individuals weigh in advance the expected costs and benefits of behaving unethically, and that they focus on the consequences of their actions both for themselves and for others affected (Fritzsche and Becker, 1984; Bellizi and Hite, 1989). This calculation of costs and benefits or "expected profit" suggests that, if the utility of the expected costs of behaving unethically outweighs the utility of expected benefits, the individual makes an "ethically appropriate" decision. But when expected profit is positive, the individual may "bend the rules" and behave unethically.

This cost/benefit or "expected profit" approach is heavily oriented toward opportunity. The individual calculates not only the expected profit or loss of the behavior but also the likelihood of the expected profit or loss occurring. For example, a salesperson might calculate that the expected cost ensuing from cheating a customer is the loss of the account; but the salesperson would also be calculating the likelihood that the customer detects the cheating. Thus, an element of risk of detection is also present in the salesperson's calculations. The opportunity to engage in unethical behavior has been shown to have a powerful effect on behavior (Zey-Ferrell and Ferrell, 1982; Ferrell and Gresham, 1985).

ETHICAL ISSUES IN SALES

Prior to constructing our questionnaire, we conducted three focus groups, consisting of salespeople and sales managers within a company. We were interested in determining the types of ethical issues encountered in day-to-day selling, how these issues are handled, and any commonalities among salespeople selling industrial products and those in consumer products. One of the first things we discovered in the focus group context was that salespeople are reluctant to talk about ethics at all, particularly their own ethics, a phenomenon Bird and Waters (1989) refer to as "moral muteness." The comfort level increases only when ethics is cast in the third person, and the ethical issues that "someone else" faces are discussed.

The favorite third person to surface in these groups is the salesperson from a competing firm. Such a person is not only likely to face lots of ethical issues but is also, according to our focus group members, likely to resolve them in an unethical manner. Purchasing agents' ethics are also questionable; our focus group participants encountered ethical pressures from purchasing agents on a regular basis. These salespeople cited examples of purchasing agents demanding "special considerations," including entertainment, such as tickets to sporting events, and gifts in exchange for their business. (Of course we don't know what the purchasing agents would have to say in their own defense, or what aspersions they might cast on the ethics of salespeople.) Such sentiments are consistent with business ethics research, which has found that most respondents believe themselves to be more ethical than their peers (Ferrell and Weaver, 1978; Newstrom and Ruch, 1975).

A number of reasons for greater ethical pressure in today's selling environment emerged from the focus groups. A great deal of agreement exists that, as one salesman expressed it, "It's a whole lot easier to be ethical in a good year than in an off year." Pressure for sales creates greater pressure for unethical behavior. "It's harder to maintain your ethics in an entrepreneurial atmosphere," expressed another salesperson. The implication was that the entrepreneurial atmosphere encourages leniency about ethics and is focused only on results, not on the means used to achieve these results. The entrepreneurial atmosphere can also mean less loyalty on the part of the customer, so the salesperson has to work harder to develop customer loyalty. Again, it may be tempting to do whatever is necessary to fuse that bond. This reasoning is consistent with business ethics research linking performance pressures and unethical behavior (Posner and Schmidt, 1987; Carroll, 1975).

The focus groups elicited a number of ethical issues common to several industries. We then used these issues, along with examples from the marketing and sales force literature, to construct 14 projective vignettes—sales scenarios that invite the respondent to recommend what action a sales colleague in the same firm would take. A similar approach was used by Kellaris and Dabholkar (1989), who developed 20 sales scenarios in which sales professionals and students rated which response was most ethically appropriate for the sales-person in the scenario.

Much of the ethics literature addressing marketing issues has used surveys to establish "how ethical" an action is considered to be by some population. This approach has been particularly prevalent in sales force management (Dubinsky, 1985), where the populations surveyed include salespeople, sales managers, and purchasing agents. This literature identifies what behavior is considered more (rather than less) ethical by a substantial segment of the population being studied. In the development of our vignettes, we chose problems in which large numbers of respondents would consider one response to be more ethical than its opposite response. "More ethical" is taken to mean here (1) consistent with recognized societal norms (such as fair play and honesty) and (2) endorsed as more ethical in research describing the attitudes of salespeople, purchasing agents, or corporate managers.

PROJECTIVE VIGNETTES

As we discovered in our focus groups, one of the greatest difficulties in studying ethical attitudes and behavior is the respondent's desire to give a socially acceptable answer, rather than a candid one. One technique for overcoming respondent reticence to answer sensitive questions candidly is projective questioning, in which respondents are not asked about themselves but are asked, instead, to imagine someone else and forecast what that person might do, feel, or think. It is hoped that respondents "project" their true intentions, feelings, or beliefs onto the imagined person, thereby bypassing self-defense mechanisms and revealing themselves with greater candor than they would under direct questioning.

A useful way to pose projective questions is to embed them in a "vignette," in which a business situation involving an ethical issue is presented to the respondent (Cavanaugh and Fritzsche, 1985). The specificity of the situation tends to elicit greater candor than more generally worded questions, because the respondent can relate more to the situation, and because the respondent can usually see trade-offs involved in giving the prescribed ethical answer. Hunt and Vitell (1986) note that scenarios or vignettes have been used to a limited extent in studying marketing ethics: Subjects are typically asked to judge either whether or not the action taken in the scenario is ethical or if the action is commonly observed.

We combined these two ways to elicit answers, projection and vignettes, to develop "projective vignettes." Projective vignettes ask the subject *what someone else should do in the situation.* Projective vignettes combine the advantages of vignettes (concrete situations, respondent interest, and involvement in the story presented) with the advantages of projective questioning (depersonalizing the issue to elicit candor). To give a projective dimension, the set of vignettes was preceded by the following narrative:

A close friend of yours, John, used to work with you but was transferred to another region, still working for your company. John calls to ask your advice about the following . . .

"Close friend," "used to work with you," and "still working for your company" were designed to maximize involvement and similarity so that the respondent would project his or her intended behavior more accurately.

SALES FORCE RESULTS

As Table 1 indicates, there is a considerable range of what salespeople would advise "John" to do. We have divided the vignettes into three categories: deceiving the customer, cheating (or deceiving) one's own firm, and terms and conditions of the sale (behavior other than deceiving the customer that is designed to clinch the sale; for example, providing a "gift" to the purchasing agent).

Evaluating the responses to the vignettes strictly from the point of view of violation of an ethical standard leads to some puzzling results. For example, the two vignettes that respondents are least likely to advise, "Unnecessary Features" and "Expense Account," would not seem to be to us as flagrantly unethical as "Gratuity," which some could interpret as bribery.

We believe that the cost/benefit approach to decision making may help to explain why these two behaviors are deemed the ones to be avoided. Deceiving the customer may well lead to ultimately losing the customer, particularly if the customer is apt to discover the deception. In "Unnecessary Features," such a discovery seems likely over time. "Expense Account" constitutes a somewhat blatant violation of expense account procedures. In contrast, the gift mentioned in "Gratuity" is made to sound like standard procedure—"John has heard that the only way to get an order from this buyer is to offer the purchasing agent a gift." The cost/benefit approach argues that, the more routinized the sales-person perceives the activity, the less risk of both detection and punishment he or she perceives.

If the risk of deceiving the customer is discovery of the deception and a displeased customer, one would expect vignettes containing the most "dis-coverable" deceits to be those least advised by the respondents. Our results provide some indication of this. The behavior in "Tie-in Sale" is probably not likely to be uncovered by the customer. On the other hand, the wording of "Negotiation" indicates that the deceit inevitably will come to the surface, yet respondents are significantly more likely to advocate this behavior than they are the deception in "Unnecessary Features" or "Customer Ignorance." These results suggest that potential discovery of the deceit by the customer is one, but not the only, factor influencing the responses of our salespeople.

Similarly, in the vignettes concerned with cheating the firm, the risk-of-detection argument is plausible, but does not provide a full explanation of the range of responses. The behavior in the "Defective Merchandise" vignette may

---

TABLE 1   Responses of 446 Field Salespeople and Sales Managers to 14 Projective
Vignettes

The following questions were scaled so that the answer more likely to violate a
moral standard has the larger value.

Salespeople responded by circling a number on this scale:

Definitely should not						*Definitely should*
1	*2*	*3*	*4*	*5*	*6*	*7*

Scenarios	*Mean*
Deceiving the customer	
Unnecessary Features: John is selling a number of office machines to a small service firm. The firm is ready to order the top-of-the-line machine, even though as far as John can see the firm has no possible use for any of the extra features of this machine and would be much better off with a less expensive model. Should John say nothing?	2.0*
Customer Ignorance: John sold one of his major customers a large order, which was delivered to the customer about two weeks ago. John has just discovered that the merchandise delivered is a slightly less sophisticated, less expensive model than the one ordered. John can't believe it, but he thinks that the customer just didn't notice. Should John say nothing?	2.1
Negotiation: John is negotiating the final details of a large order. The customer is insisting on one minor point about service that John doesn't think he'll be able to provide. John knows he can clinch the sale by agreeing now; if necessary, he can blame his company later for not being able to come through. Should John say that he thinks his company can provide the service upon which the customer insists?	2.4
Customer Problem: John has found that by exaggerating the seriousness of a customer's problem he can get the customer to place a larger order. Should he pursue this sales tactic?	3.0
Tie-in Sale: John has one product that is selling like the proverbial hotcakes. John has developed a strategy in which he insists that he won't sell the customer this "hot" product unless the customer also buys other items in the product line. In fact, John is bluffing. Assuming it works, should John continue using this strategy?	3.4

TABLE 1 *(continued)*

Scenarios	Mean
Cheating the firm	
Expense Account: John is a relatively inexperienced salesperson who is having some difficulty living on what he perceives to be a less than adequate salary. John occasionally takes his wife out to dinner and charges the company. John reasons that he works hard and deserves to enjoy some company benefits. Should John continue his practice?	2.0
Defective Merchandise: One of John's longstanding accounts has suffered a temporary financial setback. The customer wants to place a fairly large order with John and asks John to give him a break by submitting a claim that 5 percent of the merchandise the customer received was defective. John's company does not require the return of defective goods before processing a claim. Should John tell the customer that he will submit the claim?	2.1
Mistaken Credit: John's sales manager mistakenly believes that John deserves the credit for landing a major new customer and has privately praised John for this. In fact, a rookie salesperson who has since left the company was largely responsible. Should John say nothing?	2.3
Exaggerated Sales Calls: John's boss is a real stickler for reporting procedures and for making lots of sales calls. John hasn't been able to convince his boss that John is much more effective making fewer, more targeted calls. Should John keep his boss happy by exaggerating the number of calls he's making?	2.6
Terms and conditions of the sale	
Differential Pricing: John is charging more to his buyers for whom he is the sole supplier than he does in a similar sale where he is competing with other suppliers. Should he do this?	3.1

TABLE 1 (concluded)

Scenarios	Mean
Gratuity: John's manager is pressuring him to "crack" a large account which has never made any substantial purchases from John's company. John has made several calls on this account and has gotten nowhere. John has heard that the only way to get an order from this buyer is to offer the purchasing agent a gift. Should John try this approach?	3.2
Friendship: John has one purchaser whom he especially likes. Their wives are friends, too, and their children go to school together. John finds that he is giving this purchaser special considerations on price and delivery that John doesn't give to his other customers. Should he continue this practice?	3.3
Competitor Bashing: One of John's largest steady customers is just about to place an order with a competitor of John's (and your) company. John knows the people working for the competitor, knows their capabilities, and doesn't believe that they can possibly make the delivery date they are promising. Should John tell the customer that, in his opinion, the competitor won't be able to make the promised delivery date?	5.1
Pulling Strings: John is excited because he's been working on a big sale to a major corporation. Ed, a personal friend of yours and John, works at this corporation. Ed told John that, when it comes time to make the decision about the sale, Ed will not be part of the decision for appearance's sake. However, Ed will work behind the scenes to make sure that John gets the business. Should John encourage Ed to help him get the sale?	5.5

* Any differences in means of 0.2 or greater are statistically significant at $p < 0.05$.

well constitute fraud, so the egregiousness of the behavior itself accounts for respondents' reluctance to advocate it.

"Competitor Bashing" and "Pulling Strings" contain the two behaviors most likely to be condoned by respondents. It is entirely possible that these two vignettes involve issues that respondents perceive as having nothing to do with ethical principles. In "Competitor Bashing," no moral standard of honesty is violated. The vignette makes it very clear that John would be telling the truth about his competitor's limitations. The ethical issue here is a much more subtle one of "fair play." Salespeople may not see the situation in "Pulling Strings" in ethical terms, but they may perceive that such behavior follows prevailing industry practice.

These responses provide some indication of how salespeople react to ethical issues. Our interpretation of the responses suggests that it is not merely a question of whether or not a moral standard is violated that determines how salespeople view these issues. There is first of all a question of perceiving the behavior in ethical terms, then there is a question of calculating the likelihood of certain outcomes, and finally there is the question of weighing the expected profit versus the expected cost of the behavior. Our results serve to corroborate the complex nature of decision making about ethical issues, and suggest the need for further research on the decision-making process itself.

SALES FORCE GOVERNANCE

We were particularly interested in how the control system of the organization affects a salesperson's recommended approach to these dilemmas. The firm's control system includes: (1) the way in which salespeople are compensated (salary versus commission), (2) the extent of supervision, (3) how much contact takes place between the salesperson and his or her supervisor, and (4) objective versus subjective methods of evaluation. A firm's sales force control system may be described along a continuum anchored by two opposite ideal types: "outcome control" and "behavior control" (or "input control").

In an outcome control system, salespeople essentially are left alone to achieve results as they see fit. Monitoring is minimal and the supervisory style is "hands off." Salespeople are compensated in proportion to their measurable results (outcomes); for example, growth in revenue.

The opposite system, behavior control, entails close supervision of salespeople's activities, interventionist supervision by the manager, and performance evaluation on subjective bases (such as telephone manner and selling style). These "inputs" or behaviors are thought by management to contribute to the company's goals. Of course, most sales forces are "governed" by systems which combine elements of behavior *and* outcome control.

We measured each of the four elements of the control system with a separate scale. And we used the scales to determine how closely a respondent's own job situation resembled either of the two ideal types, behavior or outcome control.

We created statistical profiles of the work environment and background of the salespeople prone to advise John to act ethically, and, in contrast, those more likely to advise him to act unethically. One of our most significant findings was that older, more senior salespeople tend to advise John to take the high road more often. This finding corroborates the results of other business ethics studies.

Our results show that the extent of supervision and amount of contact with a salesperson's immediate supervisor have a significant impact on how field salespeople tell John to resolve the problems sketched in our 14 scenarios. Salespeople who are closely monitored are more likely to give ethical responses. This finding suggests that independence translates to opportunity, and opportunity to temptation. It also suggests that immediate supervisors may be exerting pressure to act ethically, rather than unethically, as previous studies have found. Since the previous studies were questioning individuals about the ethics of their actions, it may well be that blaming the supervisor is a convenient way to rationalize the necessity for one's less ethical actions.

Interestingly, when we separated the method of compensation (salary versus commission) from the extent of supervision, we found that how salespeople are paid did not have much impact. Although autonomy and commission tend to go hand in hand, the effects of autonomy are more significant than those of compensation method. In industrial selling, the importance of word of mouth in a sales territory is substantial, so salespeople quickly develop reputations that can either support or hinder their sales efforts. Perhaps these reputation effects restrain commission-based salespeople, whose future income is directly proportional to their future sales, from taking ethical shortcuts. This speculation is supported by our additional finding that salespeople who rely most heavily on repeat business are more likely to recommend observing ethical standards in their selling behavior.

Salespeople who see themselves operating in a cutthroat environment are prone to less ethical responses. Again, this may be a rationalization, since our scale of competitiveness consisted of items measuring respondent perceptions of competition and did not use objective indicators of the competitiveness of the environment. In other words, a salesperson who engages in less ethical action could blame the competitive environment for the necessity of doing so. This is further compounded by our focus group perception that the competition is unethical. If a salesperson believes that the selling environment is highly competitive, and also believes, as some participants in our focus group did, that his or her competitors are "cheating" to get sales, then he or she may feel pressured to match the competitors' tactics. "Everybody's doing it" is a familiar (albeit weak) justification for less than ethical behavior. This suggests that managers whose salespeople are complaining about competition more than usual may be witnessing a rationalization for ethical breeches on the part of their salespeople.

CONCLUSION

This study has assessed salesperson responses to a set of vignettes involving ethical issues in sales. The responses to the vignettes indicate that some behaviors are more tolerated than others. We have suggested that acceptance of a behavior is not totally dependent on its conformity with ethical principles but also on perceptions about how it fits with prevailing industry practice, perceptions of the likelihood of the behavior leading to certain outcomes, and calculations of the profits and costs of those outcomes.

Our sales force governance findings suggest that particular attention be paid to the opportunities present in the firm for unethical behavior. If employees tend to work autonomously in a decentralized setting, then extra efforts to instill the importance of ethical behavior need to be undertaken. If employees work in a highly competitive atmosphere, where competition is stemming either from competitive firms in the industry or from employees in their own firm vying for promotion, or both, again a corporate emphasis on ethics is necessary to counter the effects of the competition. If a firm's transactions tend to be major ones, in which employees perceive their careers to be on the line, then clearly it is vital that the message *must* get through to them from senior management that unethical behavior will not be tolerated, despite the importance of the transaction.

REFERENCES

Anderson, Erin. "Transaction Costs as Determinants of Opportunism in Integrated and Independent Sales Forces." *Journal of Economic Behavior and Organization* 9 (Fall 1988), pp. 247–64.

Bellizi, Joseph A., and Robert E. Hite. "Supervising Unethical Sales Force Behavior." *Journal of Marketing* 53 (April 1989), pp. 36–47.

Bird, Frederick B., and James A. Waters. "The Moral Muteness of Managers." *California Management Review*, Fall 1989, pp. 73–88.

Carroll, Archie B. "Managerial Ethics: A Post Watergate View." *Business Horizons* 18 (April 1975), pp. 75–80.

Cavanaugh, Gerald F., and David J. Fritzsche. "Using Vignettes in Business Ethics Research." *Research in Corporate Social Performance and Policy*, vol. 7. Greenwich, Conn.: JAI Press, 1985, pp. 279–93.

Caywood, Clarke L., and Gene R. Laczniak. "Ethics and Personal Selling: *Death of a Salesman* as an Ethical Primer." *Journal of Personal Selling and Sales Management* 6 (August 1986), pp. 339–59.

Dubinsky, Alan J. "Studying Field Salespeople's Ethical Problems: An Approach for Designing Company Policies." In *Marketing Ethics*, Gene R. Laczniak and Patrick E. Murphy, (eds.). Lexington, Mass.: Lexington Books, 1985, pp. 41–54.

Ferrell, O. C., and Larry Gresham. "A Contingency Framework for Understanding Ethical Decision Making in Marketing." *Journal of Marketing* 49 (Summer 1985), pp. 87–96.

Ferrell, O. C., and K. M. Weaver. "Ethical Beliefs of Marketing Managers." *Journal of Marketing* 42 (July 1978), pp. 69–73.

Fritzsche, David J., and Helmut Becker. "Linking Managerial Behavior to Ethical Philosophy." *Academy of Management Journal* 27, no. 1 (1984), pp. 166–75.

Hunt, Shelby D. and Scott Vitell. "A General Theory of Marketing Ethics." *Journal of Macromarketing* 2 (Spring 1986), pp. 5–16.

Hunt, Shelby D., Van R. Wood, and Lawrence B. Chonko. "Corporate Ethical Values and Organizational Commitment in Marketing." *Journal of Marketing* 53 (July 1989), pp. 79–90.

John, George, and Barton Weitz. "Salesforce Compensation: An Empirical Investigation of Factors Related to Use of Salary versus Incentive Compensation." *Journal of Marketing Research* 26 (February 1989), pp. 1–14.

Kellaris, James J., and Pratiba A. Dabholkar. "The PSE Scale: A Scenario-Based Approach to Assessing the Ethical Sensitivity of Sales Students and Professionals." *Journal of Personal Selling and Sales Management* 9 (Summer 1989), pp. 60–70.

Newstrom, J. W., and W. A. Ruch. "The Ethics of Management and the Management of Ethics." *MSU Business Topics* 23 (Winter 1975), pp. 29–37.

Posner, Barry Z., and Warren H. Schmidt. "Ethics in American Companies: A Managerial Perspective." *Journal of Business Ethics* 6, no. 5 (1987), pp. 383–91.

Zey-Ferrell, Mary, and O. C. Ferrell. "Role-Set Configuration and Opportunity as Predictors of Unethical Behavior in Organizations." *Human Relations* 35, no. 7 (1982), pp. 587–604.

Marketing Communications:
Advertising and Sales Promotions

Ethical Issues in Advertising and Sales Promotion

Minette E. Drumwright

Advertising is perhaps the most publicly visible and the most criticized aspect of marketing.[1] Much of the criticism revolves around ethical issues. By the age of 21, the average American has been exposed to an estimated 1 to 2 million advertising messages.[2] In 1989, U.S. advertising expenditures were $123.93 billion in the nine media tracked for the McCann-Erickson U.S. advertising volume reports[3]—newspapers, magazines, farm publications, television, radio, yellow pages, direct mail, business papers, and outdoor.[4]

Ubiquitous as it is, advertising is not the largest marketing communications expenditure. Media clutter and the escalating costs of advertising, along with an emphasis on short-term profits, have prompted many companies to divert communications expenditures from advertising to sales promotions.[5] In 1989, U.S. sales promotion expenditures of $135.5 billion, excluding $24 billion for

---

[1] The American Marketing Association defines advertising as "any paid form of nonpersonal presentation of ideas, goods, or services by an identified sponsor."

[2] See Christopher Gilson and Harold W. Berkman, *Advertising: Concepts and Strategies* (New York: Random House, 1980), p. 3. This estimate is based on generally accepted industry figures of 50 to 200 exposures to advertising messages per day, with allowances of gradually increasing exposures from age 3 to age 16.

[3] The McCann-Erickson U.S. advertising volume reports represent all expenditures by U.S. advertisers—national, local, private individuals, and so on. The expenditures include all commissions as well as the art, mechanical, and production expense that are part of the advertisers' budgets.

[4] Robert J. Coen, "Little Ad Growth: Industry Forecaster Sees Recovery at Yearend," *Advertising Age* 62 (May 6, 1991), pp. 1, 16.

[5] The Council of Sales Promotion Agencies defines sales promotions as "couponing, refunds and rebates, sweepstakes and contests, allowances, education programs, promotional public relations, meetings, premiums and incentives, promotional packaging, point-of-purchase and display, and trade shows."

trade deals, exceeded advertising expenditures by more than 9 percent.[6] Despite the substantial expenditures on sales promotions, they have not been subject to as much criticism or controversy as advertising, perhaps because they are more varied, less intrusive, less repetitive, and, thus, both less aggravating and less salient than advertising. For this reason, the focus of this chapter will be directed more to advertising than to sales promotions.

Advertising and sales promotions, in their many and varied forms, frequently are combined with other marketing tools. For example, advertising often is used to communicate sale prices, product quality, and warranty information. Likewise, sales promotions often play an important role in distribution strategy. Thus, ethical issues related to advertising and sales promotion are also dealt with in other sections in this book.

IDENTIFYING ETHICAL ISSUES

Ethical issues are implicit in almost every advertising and sales promotion management decision. To identify and wrestle with ethical issues, one must consider how and why marketing managers use such communications tools as advertising and sales promotions. We will use an example to highlight some of the ethical issues involved in advertising management.

Take the Massachusetts Lottery, a legal form of state-sponsored gambling (see Chapter 8.2). What is the purpose of its advertising? Is it to create demand for the lottery, to influence and persuade people who do not gamble to engage in gambling? Or, conversely, is the purpose of the advertising merely to inform the public of this opportunity to gamble and capture the clientele of the casinos in Atlantic City and Las Vegas? To some degree, the purpose can be inferred from the ad itself. Does it inform in the manner of a classified ad in a newspaper or a listing in the Yellow Pages, or does it use emotional appeals and attractive images to persuade?

In addition, one must consider the manner in which advertising managers choose to communicate the ad content. Considering again a Massachusetts Lottery ad; is it truthful, creating an accurate impression of the odds of winning, the prizes the winners receive, and any contingent conditions, such as the payment schedules or the income taxes owed? Or is it misleading and deceptive, omitting key facts that an individual would need to make an informed decision to purchase a lottery ticket or to refrain?

Other issues lottery managers must grapple with include who to target. Should the target be people in low-income neighborhoods, who can more readily be lured with the prospects of winning megabucks? Or should the target be affluent professionals, for whom the expense of a lottery ticket is trivial?

---

[6] Russ Bowman, "Sales Promotion Continues to Outpace Media in the Race for Marketing Dollars," *Marketing & Media Decisions* 25 (July 1990), p. 20.

The target audience selected is a major factor in determining where and when the advertisements will appear.

Finally, there are more global issues regarding advertising's effects. For example, does advertising create or influence the values of individuals and of society at large, or does it merely reflect them? Does the Massachusetts Lottery advertising create values by making gambling more acceptable or materialism more attractive, or does advertising merely reflect values that already exist?

And what if the "product" was something other than the Massachusetts Lottery? What if it was something more or less socially desirable—preventing drug abuse or advertising cigarettes? Would the answers to some of the questions raised regarding the appropriateness of influencing versus informing or creating versus reflecting values be different?

As the example of the Massachusetts Lottery indicates, the ethical issues involved in advertising and sales promotion are multifaceted and complex. What follows is an attempt to provide an overview of the types of ethical issues being dealt with through two discourses that have been occurring among various groups of professionals.

TWO DISCOURSES

Ethical issues in advertising and sales promotion are of two ilk. On the one hand, there are the ethical issues embedded in the practice of advertising and sales promotion. Most of these issues involve manifestations of truthfulness—avoiding deception and staying free of fraud. These issues, which usually become translated into law, bound advertising and sales promotions, setting parameters around what marketers can and cannot do. They involve such questions as, "What are marketers' rights? What can they do and what must they do to avoid deception and fraud?" The discourse regarding these issues is based on two fundamental assumptions: first, that advertising and sales promotion are worthwhile from economic and social perspectives; and second, that marketers have the right to persuade. Many of the participants in this discourse are lawyers and regulators, and their debate will be referred to as the *legal discourse.*

On the other hand, there are ethical issues involving the essence of advertising and sales promotion themselves, their appropriateness socially and economically, and their potentially harmful effects on individuals and on society at large. Participants in this discourse, who are primarily philosophers and ethicists, make a distinction between "having a right" and "the right thing to do." They raise broad and far-reaching questions regarding what advertisers should do. For example, should advertisers target children as an audience, and should advertisers attempt to persuade inner-city young people to buy sneakers priced at more than $170 a pair? This discourse is not based on the assumption that persuasion is a right that necessarily should be exercised by advertisers.

Because it deals with the morality of advertising and sales promotion, this debate will be referred to as the *moral discourse*.

It is unfortunate that these two discourses, which usually reflect radically different perspectives, do not inform each other more than they do. Participants in the legal discourse fail to raise the broader questions, and participants in the moral discourse have difficulty bringing their discussion to the practical level of empirical investigation. I will review issues representative of those raised in each of the two discourses and then speculate about why the participants often appear to be talking past each other.

THE LEGAL DISCOURSE

Legal issues are an important subset of ethical issues. Laws are ultimately a reflection of ethical judgments. We often make illegal what we consider to be most unethical. Therefore, debates about the law are debates about ethics.

The major thrust of advertising regulation has been to deal with deception—false representations, material omissions, and other deceptive acts or practices—with the goal of enhancing the amount and accuracy of information available to purchasers. The Federal Trade Commission (FTC) has been a major force, if not the major force, in advertising regulation through its mandate from Congress to prevent "unfair or deceptive acts or practices" and "unfair methods of competition."

For a particular advertisement to be determined deceptive by the FTC, it must have the tendency or capacity to deceive a significant number of consumers relating to facts that are important in purchasing decisions. Proof that consumers actually were deceived is not required. The representation may be made expressly or by implication, and literal truth is not a defense to a representation that as a whole conveys a false impression. The advertiser's knowledge of the false representation and the advertiser's intent to deceive are irrelevant to finding that deception has occurred. The determination that an advertisement is deceptive may be made by the FTC on the basis of its expertise; no empirical proof is required.[7]

Advertising issues attracting substantial attention from regulators and the courts with respect to deception include puffery, children's advertising, demonstrations and mock-ups, endorsements and testimonials, and price advertising, while sales promotion issues include fraud in coupons, sweepstakes, contests, and games.

---

[7] For a fuller discussion of advertising and the FTC, see Louis W. Stern and Thomas L. Eovaldi, *Legal Aspects of Marketing Strategy: Antitrust and Consumer Protection Issues* (Englewood Cliffs, N.J.: Prentice Hall, 1984), pp. 369–411.

Puffery

In tone and style, advertising spans a wide spectrum from factual information to overstatement and exaggeration, known as puffery. The legal definition of puffery is advertising or other sales representations that praise the product or service with "subjective opinions, superlatives, or exaggerations, vaguely and generally, stating no specific facts."[8] The characteristics "puffed" must actually exist; statements claiming that something exists when it does not are not puffery. The following are a few examples of what is known as "permissible (i.e., legal) puffery":

The legendary marque of high performance (Alfa Romeo).

The lightest, most compact cellular phone on earth (Motorola).

A perfect partner for American business (Sunkyong).

We do more to keep you at the top (Credit Suisse).

The right fund at the right time (Dreyfus).

Critics of puffery claim that it does not provide relevant information, and instead makes claims that are not factually true. For example, William Prosser notes that "the 'puffing' rule amounts to a seller's privilege to lie his head off, so long as he says nothing specific. . . ."[9] Ivan Preston refers to puffery as "soft core" deception and asserts that its "continued existence in the mass media shows that advertisers think it effective with a substantial portion of the public in obtaining reliance and altering purchase decisions."[10]

Nonetheless, the FTC has found puffery generally acceptable. The key legal distinction regarding puffery involves that between falsity and deception. While falsity and deception may seem to be synonymous, they are not. Deception is a characteristic that is subjectively interpreted as injurious to consumers and, therefore, illegal, while falsity is an objective characteristic that may or may not be deceptive and illegal. The legal question regarding puffery, then, is not whether it is false, but whether or not it is deceptive.

The FTC and the courts view puffery as nondeceptive on three grounds. First, they presume that purchasers do not rely upon a positive expression of opinion by the seller regarding the seller's product. Second, the FTC recognizes that, because certain general statements of praise are not likely to be relied upon by reasonable consumers, they do not have the capacity to deceive. Third, there is no objective way to establish that general statements of praise are false.[11]

---

[8] Ivan Preston, *The Great American Blow-Up: Puffery in Advertising and Selling* (Madison: University of Wisconsin Press, 1975), p. 17.

[9] William Prosser, *Handbook of the Law of Torts*, 4th ed. (St. Paul, Minn.: West Publishing, 1971), p. 723.

[10] Preston, *The Great American Blow-Up*, p. 29.

[11] For a fuller discussion of the defense of puffery, see Stern and Eovaldi, *Legal Aspects of Marketing Strategy*, pp. 375–77.

The FTC's tolerance for puffery is easier to understand when one recalls that the goal of much regulation is to preserve and encourage competition and the attendant benefit to consumer welfare. Thus, the FTC's position on puffery seems to favor advertisers and reflect the notion of caveat emptor: "Let the buyer beware." The obligation to be cautious is placed on the buyer, which permits the competitive market to work. The notion of caveat emptor, which has its roots in common law in post-medieval Europe, was adopted from English law by American courts desirous of bolstering the affairs of business in the early days of this country.[12] Reflecting this sentiment, Walter Hamilton writes that in the 19th century in this country "judges discover[ed] that caveat emptor sharpened wits, taught self-reliance, made a man—an economic man— out of the buyer, and served well its two masters, business and justice."[13]

Regulators' historical tolerance toward puffery reflects another deep-seated American political and legal value, that of the right to unfettered speech. Oliver Wendell Holmes elegantly explains the value of unfettered speech:

> But when men have realized that time has upset many foundations of their own conduct, that the ultimate good desired is better reached by free trade in ideas—that the best test of truth is the power of the thought to get itself accepted in the competition of the market. . . . That at any rate is the theory of our Constitution.[14]

Legally, commercial speech is not guaranteed the same protection as political speech under the First Amendment. Nonetheless, the basic notion that the antidote to false speech in the marketplace of ideas is more speech, rather than censored or regulated speech, seems to have influenced views regarding commercial speech.

Children's Television Advertising

Concern regarding children's television advertising has been the focus of consumer activism since the early 1970s (see Chapter 8.9).[15] A group of mothers in the Boston area organized Action for Children's Television in the late 1960s, which has lobbied against children's television advertising for more than two decades. The Council on Children, Media, and Merchandising (CCMM) focused on food products being advertised to children and was also an early catalyst for the issue. Both groups petitioned the Federal Communications

---

[12] For a discussion of the roots of caveat emptor, see Preston, *The Great American Blow-Up*, pp. 30–57.

[13] Walter H. Hamilton, "The Ancient Maxim Caveat Emptor," *Yale Law Journal* 40 (1931), p. 1186.

[14] *Abrams* v. *United States*, 250 U.S. 616 (1919), p. 630.

[15] For a discussion of the history of the issue, see Richard P. Adler, "Children's Television Advertising: History of the Issue," in *Children and the Faces of Television*, ed. Edward L. Palmer and Aimee Dorr (New York: Academic Press, 1980) pp. 237–72.

Commission (FCC) and the FTC, calling for reform. They had four primary concerns:[16]

1. That children were being exposed to advertising for products (e.g., heavily sugared cereals) that could be harmful to them if misused.
2. That certain television techniques (e.g., program hosts selling products) may be deceptive to children lacking the skills to evaluate them properly.
3. That advertising to children is de facto bad in that it exploits their vulnerabilities (e.g., naive conceptions of time and money).
4. That the long-term cumulative exposure to television advertising may affect adversely the development of children's values, attitudes, and behaviors.

As public pressure built, two industry groups, the National Association of Broadcasters and the National Advertising Division of the Council of Better Business Bureaus, both developed codes regarding children's advertising in the early 1970s. The codes identified specific advertising practices (e.g., selling of products by program hosts) that are unacceptable, but, not surprisingly, they reflected the broad value judgments that advertising to children is a legitimate social and economic activity.

During the 1970s, the FCC and the FTC considered a variety of proposals restricting children's television advertising. The FCC concluded that broadcasters have a special responsibility to children and that special safeguards may be required against possible advertising. However, the FCC did not adopt any of the proposed rules or require any specific changes. Likewise, the FTC made no progress regarding specific proposals. Both the FCC and the FTC apparently had decided in favor of industry self-regulation, reflecting another deep-seated American political value: that government that governs best governs least.

Despite the lack of support from the FCC and the FTC, children's television advertising remained an active issue among consumers and reform groups, who continued to lobby for legislation. As a result, the Children's Television Act of 1990 was passed by Congress and enacted.[17] The bill required commercial television licensees and cable operators to limit the advertising in children's programming to not more than 10.5 minutes per hour on weekends and not more than 12.0 minutes per hour on weekdays. In addition, it required the FCC to determine how well every television station has served the "educational needs" of the young as a condition of its license renewal. Finally, the act required the FCC to define and determine how to treat program-length commercials.

---

[16] R. P. Adler, B. Z. Friedlander, G. S. Lesser, L. Meringoff, T. S. Robertson, J. R. Rossiter, and S. Ward, *Research on the Effects of Television Advertising on Children* (Washington, D.C.: United States Government Printing Office, 1977).

[17] Harry F. Waters, "Watch What Kids Watch: New Legislation Hopes to Channel Children's TV in a Healthier Direction," *Newsweek*, January 8, 1990, pp. 50–52.

Program-length commercials are shows based on popular children's toys, like G.I. Joe, He-Man, and ThunderCats. By 1990, there were 70 programs based on commercial products.[18] Lobbyists who pushed for the legislation argued that these programs should be considered commercials subject to the new time limits, though they would permit shows that had been on the air for two years to license their characters without being subject to the time-limit restrictions. To their disappointment, the FCC defined "program-length commercial" in such a way to permit the toy-based shows to continue. To be unacceptable as a "program-length commercial," a show about a particular toy must have a paid commercial about the toy aired within it. However, a paid commercial about the toy may appear in the programs before or after the show based on the toy.

Use of Mock-Ups and Demonstrations[19]

What looks like ice cream in a television commercial may really be mashed potatoes. The photograph of the frothy head on a mug of beer most likely was created with soap suds. What appears to be coffee in the steaming mug probably is wine.

Each of the above substitutions is a mock-up, the artificial alteration of a product to get a photograph of it. In contrast to puffery and children's advertising, mock-ups have been rather tightly regulated. The acceptability of mock-ups depends upon the purpose of the substitution and the product characteristics portrayed. For example, assume that mashed potatoes are substituted for ice cream, which melts too quickly under the photographer's lights to enable effective photography. If the commercial emphasizes the enjoyment of eating ice cream, then most likely no deception would be found by regulators. If, on the other hand, the commercial emphasizes the texture of the ice cream or the fact that it melts more slowly than competitive products, deception most likely would be found. In one well-known case, the FTC condemned the Campbell Soup Company for photographing its vegetable soup with clear glass marbles in the bottom of the bowl, which forced the solid parts to the top and created the impression of a stew-like substance. Without the glass marbles, the company's advertisers found the vegetables sank to the bottom of the bowl, out of camera sight, leaving the appearance of a clear broth. This outcome understated a positive product attribute and may even be said, by the company's advertisers at least, to have misled consumers. Nonetheless, the FTC deter-

---

[18] Patrick J. Sheridan, "FCC Sets Children's Ad Limits," 1990 Information Access Company, vol. 119, no. 20, p. 33.

[19] The sections on mock-ups and demonstrations, endorsements and testimonials, and price advertising draw heavily from Stern and Eovaldi, *Legal Aspects of Marketing Strategy*, pp. 389–99, which provides greater detail on each of the issues as well as discussions of significant legal cases.

mined that when an advertisement portrays a photographic characteristic of a product, the real thing must be used.

Demonstrations, which emphasize the superiority of a product, have proliferated since the advent of television as a way to show the product in action. In one well-known case, the Colgate-Palmolive Company created a television commercial demonstrating the superiority of its shaving cream. The shaving cream appeared to be applied to sandpaper, after which the sand was quickly and easily shaved off. Actually, sandpaper was not used; sand was sprinkled on clear plexiglass. The FTC and the Supreme Court found the commercial to be deceptive and determined that, if an advertiser created the impression that the consumer was seeing a demonstration, the demonstration must be real or the consumer must be informed otherwise.

Endorsements and Testimonials

Do Madonna, Michael Jackson, Tina Turner, and Lionel Richie really prefer Pepsi to Coke? Is Jim Palmer's glowing opinion of Jockey brand underwear objective, or does he have a vested interest in the product or the company? Is the individual who appears to be randomly selected to testify regarding the merits of Tide detergent really a paid actor?

An endorsement is defined as an advertising message that "consumers are likely to believe reflects the opinions, beliefs, findings, or experience of a party other than the sponsoring advertiser."[20] The FTC makes a distinction between an endorsement (usually by well-known individuals) and a testimonial, an ordinary commendation of the sponsor by unfamiliar people, who most likely will be perceived to be communicating the sponsor's views.

Two types of endorsements are common—celebrity and expert. The FTC has stipulated that endorsements by celebrities, who usually are entertainers or sports stars, must meet several requirements. First, they must reflect the honest opinion or experience of the endorser. Second, the endorser must not make claims that the advertiser cannot substantiate. Third, if the endorser is portrayed as a user of the product, the advertiser must have good reason to believe that the celebrity continues to be a user of the product each time the advertisement is run. In addition, the FTC requires that any potentially biasing connections between the advertiser and the endorser, such as financial interests in the firm or its products, must be disclosed; ordinary payments for services are not considered biasing connections.

An expert endorser is "an individual, group, or institution possessing, as a result of experience, study, or training, knowledge of a particular subject, which knowledge is superior to that generally acquired by ordinary individuals."[21]

---

[20] Federal Trade Commission, *Guides Concerning Use of Endorsements and Testimonials in Advertising*, 16 C.F.R. Part 255 (1982), referred to hereafter as *FTC Guide*.

[21] Ibid., Part 255.0(d).

Expert endorsements typically communicate the results of tests, surveys, and studies and must meet three requirements. First, the product qualities being endorsed must be within the endorser's expertise. Second, the endorsement must be based on product characteristics that are actually available to typical consumers. Third, the endorsement must be based on actual use of the expert's knowledge, and his or her conclusions must be portrayed accurately. Again, biasing connections must be revealed.

Testimonial ads in which consumers talk about favorable experiences with the product must represent a "typical" consumer experience with the product, not an exceptional or unusual one. In addition, testimonial ads should use actual consumers, rather than actors, unless a disclaimer that the actors are being paid is presented.

Advertisements Based on Price

The FTC is concerned about the accuracy of pricing claims that are made through the media because of the emphasis that consumers are thought to place on price. For example, the results of price surveys reported in advertisements to show that one competitor's prices are lower than others must be restricted to the items actually compared and may not be generalized to other items.

Regulators, state attorneys general in particular, recently have become concerned about the accuracy of the price reduction claims that accompany the advertising of sales, which have become almost an everyday occurrence. As the article entitled "As Retailers' Sales Crop Up Everywhere" (see Chapter 8.7) explains, regulators are concerned about inflated "regular" prices that deceptively convey the impression of a markdown sale price. The chapter on ethical issues in pricing reports recent legal developments (see Chapter 5.1, also Chapter 5.3).

Another area of concern regarding price advertising is a tactic known as bait-and-switch advertising. This involves the advertising of an unusually low price, often on a brand that will draw consumers to the store, combined with personal selling tactics that discourage the purchase of the advertised item and encourage the purchase of a higher priced and more profitable item. Often the personal selling tactics involve disparaging the advertised product or informing the customer that the advertised item is out of stock. The disparagement practices have been condemned by the FTC, and retailers are required to have a sufficient quantity of the advertised product to meet reasonably anticipated demand unless the advertisement clearly states that supply is limited. If adequate quantities were ordered, but unavailable because of shipping difficulties or excessive demand, the bait-and-switch rule is not violated. The retailer, however, must provide a "raincheck" permitting the item to be purchased in the near future at the advertised price. Failure to provide a raincheck is considered a violation of the rule. The Audi case (see Chapter 8.4) presents an example of alleged bait-and-switch tactics in which Audi management mailed 400,000 certificates offering a $4,000 rebate when only 5,500 cars qualifying for the rebate were available. At the time of the promotion, dealers, who received no incentive to sell the promoted model, were offered a $2,000 per unit incentive to sell two other models—allegedly the "switch" models.

Coupon Fraud[22]

Coupons are the most frequently used consumer promotion tactic for packaged goods companies. The face value of coupons in 1989 averaged 50 cents, and the dominant medium for distribution was free-standing newspaper inserts. Coupon fraud accounts for an estimated $400–$500 million in losses to manufacturers annually.[23] Coupon redemption often is a complex process requiring retailers to forward coupons to a clearinghouse, a redemption agency, or the manufacturer. Fraud or misredemption occurs when coupons were not accepted during a retailer's normal course of business for the specified product. Fraud can happen at any point in the coupon cycle, from printing to distribution to redemption. Although misredemption can be the result of dishonest or misinformed consumer behavior, most coupon fraud schemes require the participation of the retailers or their employees. For example, cashiers can exchange coupons for cash for people who did not buy the product; or coupon entrepreneurs, who may have stolen the coupons, can sell them directly to stores or submit the coupons for redemption in the name of the stores.

Precautions such as inspecting all of the coupons that come to the manufacturer and compiling a computerized list of bona fide retailers, which includes their redemption histories, can help control coupon fraud. In addition, some companies, such as American Express, print coupons that are serially numbered with a special ink on a special stock as a security measure.

Fraud in Sweepstakes, Contests, and Games

Sweepstakes, contests, and games of chance are a popular promotional strategy for generating excitement for a product and eliciting consumer involvement. Contests require considerable involvement from consumers, who must submit something for judging. In contrast, sweepstakes require only that participants fill out entry blanks and mail them in or leave them at a store. Games of

---

[22] Trade promotions, which often play an important role in distribution strategy, are dealt with in the overview of ethical issues in distribution (see Chapter 6.1).

[23] Robert G. Blakey, "Coupon Fraud Capers," *Security Management* 32 (September 1988), p. 139. For more discussion of coupon fraud, see "Come to Grips with Coupon Fraud," *Security Management* 31 (November 1987), pp. 44–51; and Paulette Fernholz, "The Coupon Caper," *Security Management* 31 (March 1987), p. 45.

chance typically involve the distribution of game pieces at specified retail outlets. Prizes are awarded to the lucky few of the many participants in sweepstakes, contests, and games.

Sweepstakes and games of chance are particularly vulnerable to being classified as lotteries, a form of gambling that is illegal in most states. The FTC considers all lotteries to be unfair or deceptive unless permitted by state law.[24] A sweepstake or game is classified as an illegal lottery if it has three characteristics: (1) a prize is offered; (2) winning a prize depends on chance, rather than skill; and (3) the participant is required to give up something of value to participate (e.g., requiring the participant to buy something). Most sweepstakes and games have the first two characteristics, but they fall short of being classified as lotteries because they lack the third characteristic. (Hence the often used statement: "no purchase necessary.") Because sweepstakes and games resemble lotteries, some industry observers believe that state-run lottery games (e.g., the Massachusetts Lottery) have given increased public confidence in sweepstakes and games, legitimizing them.[25]

Unethical conduct in sweepstakes, contests, and games can involve unfair operations, such as rigging the awarding of prizes or promising prizes that are never awarded. The FTC enacted a rule regulating games in the food retailing and gasoline industries, and state and local governments have enacted similar legislation regulating other industries. The FTC rule requires game operators to make disclosures, including the exact number of prizes and the odds of winning; the geographic area and the total number of outlets participating in the contest; the game termination date; and, if the game extends longer than 30 days, the unredeemed prizes valued at $25 or more and the revised odds of winning.

"Charity" sweepstakes, sometimes referred to as "bonanza" sweepstakes, are particularly vulnerable to unethical conduct (see Chapter 8.7). These sweepstakes are promoted as fund-raising for various types of medical research, and often have names resembling respected organizations, such as the American Heart Disease Prevention Foundation, which could be confused with the highly credible American Heart Association. In some cases, only a tiny fraction of the millions of dollars in donations have gone to the designated causes; the vast majority goes to running more sweepstakes. Sometimes, little of the donations go to prizes as well.

Marketers can take precautions to reduce fraud by being in control of sweepstakes, games, and contests from the initial printing of materials through prize presentation. The precautions include supervision of game piece production, to avoid duplication and theft and to ensure a random mix of game pieces, and using videotaping or registered mail for the delivery of prizes.

---

[24] For more discussion, see Stern and Eovaldi, *Legal Aspects of Marketing Strategy*, pp. 445–47.

[25] David Enscoe, "Sweepstakes Are Addictive," *Target Marketing* 13 (March 1990), p. 14.

THE MORAL DISCOURSE

Philosophers and ethicists make a distinction between the legality of advertising and its ethical propriety. That is, even if advertisers have a legal right to advertise in nondeceptive ways, philosophers and ethicists assert that it is not necessarily the right thing to do.

The question for philosophers and ethicists then becomes how to determine "the right thing to do." Opinions regarding the right thing to do are as varied as advertising's critics themselves. The critics range from conservative groups affiliated with the so-called Moral Majority, who contend that advertising contributes to the moral breakdown of society, to left-wing groups with a Marxist philosophy, who assert that advertising's false promises "buy off" potentially revolutionary groups of working people. Many assert impassioned and well-stated positions. However, determining the right thing to do necessitates a systematic analysis and critique well grounded in principles and theories, as opposed to individual ideology and predilection. Much of the moral discourse seems to consist of ad hoc arguments and statements of personal beliefs that lack the rigor of systematic ethical reasoning. If there is a theme to the moral criticisms of advertising, it is that advertising creates false needs among consumers, which result in unnecessary and often harmful demand. According to the Moral Majority, advertising creates an unhealthy demand for sex. From the perspective of the opponents of advertising to children, advertising creates unnecessary demand for sugared foods. In *The Affluent Society*[26] and *The New Industrial State*,[27] John Kenneth Galbraith attacks the role of advertising in creating demand that is not independently derived from consumers' wants and needs and, thus, can distort the market system. Galbraith's work represents one of the few attempts to ground criticisms of advertising in theory.[28] Most of advertising's critics, however, focus on the effects of advertising rather than on the principles and theories underlying the criticisms.

Philosophers and ethicists raise a broad spectrum of far-reaching questions regarding advertising's effects. For example, "Does advertising violate the individual's autonomy by manipulating or controlling behavior?", "Is advertising certain products in certain ways to certain target groups moral?", "Does advertising pollute the psychological and social environment?", and "Does advertising create or reflect society's values?"

The diversity of the criticisms makes it difficult to present a succinct summary that addresses the full range of concerns. Some representative issues will be dealt with in sections on determining the morality of advertising and identifying the negative effects of advertising.

---

[26] John Kenneth Galbraith, *The Affluent Society* (Boston: Houghton Mifflin, 1958).

[27] John Kenneth Galbraith, *The New Industrial State* (Boston: Houghton Mifflin, 1967).

[28] For elaboration on Galbraith's criticisms of advertising, see William Leiss, Stephen Kline, and Sut Jhally, *Social Communication in Advertising: Persons, Products, & Images of Well-Being* (New York: Methuen Publications, 1986).

Determining the Morality of Advertising

Various criteria have been asserted as appropriate for determining the morality of advertising. These criteria involve assessing the product, the media, the advertiser's conduct, the message, and the target market.

Burton Leiser asserts that moral ads are those about products or services that are essential and useful, while immoral ads are about those things that people do not need or that are harmful to them.[29] Consumers supporting a ban of tobacco and alcohol advertising (see Chapter 8.7), on the grounds that these products are health hazards, are making judgments on this basis. Likewise, individuals use this criterion when they object to even highly informative and accurate ads about the Massachusettes Lottery (see Chapter 8.2), because they view lotteries as regressive taxes that burden lower-income groups.

In addition to making what are often difficult judgments about the harmfulness of certain products and services, Leiser's approach requires determining a need for various individuals. Do people really need expensive Rolex watches; aren't Timex watches adequate? And does everybody need the same thing? Are not insurance and financial planning needed by some but not by others. The problems are at least twofold: (1) how advertisers or anyone else can determine the genuine needs of various individuals and (2) how a message can be confined just to people who need it.

Paul Santilli challenged criteria, such as Leiser's, by asserting that morality should be determined by the truthfulness of the message, rather than by the worthiness of the product or service, the correctness of the media, or the conduct of the advertiser.[30] He distinguished between moral problems with making and selling a product, as opposed to informing the public of the product, a distinction that has been made in defense of tobacco advertising. Using an argument that often is cited in defense of free speech, Santilli said that truthful advertising of immoral products in immoral media by immoral individuals should be welcomed as a way of revealing enemies rather than censored in an attempt to quiet them. Santilli's criterion for determining the truthfulness of advertising is based on the style and content of the advertisement—all forms of persuasive advertising are immoral; all forms of informative advertising are moral. Santilli's perspective implies that persuasion undermines the rational cognitive processes by which people determine what their needs really are. The result is that advertising violates individual autonomy, in that people are acting on desires that are not their own.

From a practical standpoint, Santilli's stance against persuasion is problematic for several reasons. First, sometimes it can be difficult to make a distinction

---

[29] Burton Leiser, "Beyond Fraud and Deception: The Moral Uses of Advertising," in *Ethical Issues in Business*, ed. Thomas Donaldson and Patricia Werhane (Englewood Cliffs, N.J.: Prentice Hall, 1979) pp. 59–66.

[30] Paul C. Santilli, "The Informative and Persuasive Functions of Advertising: A Moral Appraisal," *Journal of Business Ethics* 2 (1983), pp. 27–33.

between information and persuasion. Many advertising messages appear to combine information and persuasion. Second, often we want persuasion regarding social causes, such as the prevention of AIDS, drinking and driving, and drug abuse. Should people preparing advertisements for these causes be denied their most effective tool, persuasive fear appeals, and limited to straightforward pronouncements regarding these causes? Most likely, few ethicists would say "yes." For less noble causes, one must ask what is wrong with persuasion? Is it harmful because of its medium, mass media advertising? Is persuasion in other forms, such as personal selling, wrong as well?

A final criterion for determining the morality of advertising involves the target audience. Some people assert that advertising is harmful and immoral even if truthful, when those receiving the information are unable to respond in a normal, mature manner. Children often are cited as an example of such an audience (see Chapter 8.9).

Identifying Advertising's Negative Effects

Critics have asserted that advertising's negative effects include creating conflict between parents and children, polluting the psychological and social environment, influencing its audiences to become worse persons, and making our society more materialistic.

Advertising has been shown empirically to be harmful to children, in that it precipitates parent-child conflict when parents refuse to purchase the child's request.[31] Children also suffer unhappiness when products fail to fulfill their advertising-induced performance expectations, and when they are exposed to commercials portraying possessions and lifestyles more affluent than their own.

John Waide is among those who claim that advertising pollutes our psychological and social environment.[32] He places much of the blame on associative advertising, which "induces people to buy (or buy more of) a product by associating that market product with such deep-seated nonmarket goods as friendship, acceptance and esteem from others, excitement, and power, even though the market good seldom satisfies or has any connection with the nonmarket desire."[33] Stuart Ewen points to a transition period in the 1920s when advertisers switched from a focus on products to a focus on the social and psychological meanings of products, which quickly became the dominant mode of advertising.[34] Critics assert that associative advertising influences its audi-

---

[31] See Charles K. Atkin, "The Effects of Television Advertising on Children," in *Children and the Faces of Television*, ed. Edward L. Palmer and Aimee Dorr (New York: Academic Press, 1980), pp. 287–305.

[32] John Waide, "The Making of Self and World in Advertising," *Journal of Business Ethics* 6 (1987), pp. 73–79.

[33] Ibid., p. 73.

[34] Stuart Ewen, *Captains of Consciousness* (New York: McGraw-Hill, 1976).

ence to be worse persons by encouraging the neglect of the nonmarket cultivation of virtues and the substitution of market goods instead.

Fred Inglis also views consumption based on associative advertising as harmful:

> Attainment of the values is signalled by acquiring the appropriate objects, using them, throwing them away, and acquiring replacements. Continuous and conspicuous consumption is the driving energy of this fiction. . . . The objects advertised are drenched in a certain light and smell. They give off the powerful fragrance of the very rich and, instead of leaving the object in an intelligible domestic world, remove it to a fantastic one.[35]

Implicit in Inglis's contrast between "an intelligible domestic world" and a "fantastic one" is an objection to giving objects social and symbolic meanings apart from their functional uses.

In addition to their effects on individuals and advertisers, Waide claimed that associative advertisements have a collective effect that bombards our culture and infuses our society with an ideology of acquisitiveness that asserts, "You are what you own." This ideology was illustrated by a Renault television commercial in the mid-1980s in which a man announced that "you are what you drive," and as he continued speaking he was transformed into the automobile that he had been describing. This blurring of the distinction between products and people is viewed as troublesome by some. Judith Williamson expresses her concern with this aspect of advertising:

> There is nothing "wrong" about symbols as such—obviously systems of signification are necessary and inevitable. . . . [But] there is a danger in having people involved as part of the currency in these systems. When people become symbols they need not be treated as human beings. . . . Women are especially liable to this phenomenon. But in all areas of life it is clearly very dangerous to see only what people "mean" (e.g., a threat, a status symbol), rather than what they are.[36]

In a similar vein, some symbols in advertising create and perpetuate negative stereotypes. Everyone can think back to examples of blatantly negative stereotypes in advertising, many of which have been removed. Perhaps more interesting are the more subtle forms of stereotypes. For example, Erving Goffman asserted that advertisements typically portray women not only as subordinate to men but as children.[37] For example, women's hands are often shown barely touching an object, as though they are not in control of it, while men's hands are shown grasping and manipulating objects. Women are more often portrayed in childish poses, lying down suggesting a position of weakness, or drifting off mentally while under a man's protection. Both Williamson and Goffman con-

---

[35] Fred Inglis, *The Imagery of Power: A Critique of Advertising* (London: Heinemann, 1972), p. 17.

[36] Judith Williamson, *Decoding Advertisements* (London: Marion Boyars, 1978), p. 169.

[37] Erving Goffman, *Gender Advertisements* (New York: Harper & Row, 1979).

tend that, through their selective portrayal of people and symbols, advertisements can create new meanings that influence society at large.

An ideology of acquisitiveness that blurs people and products prompts people to work to consume. Richard Pollay describes this ideology saying, "Advertising's most fundamental impact may be that it induces people to keep productive in order to keep consuming, to work in order to buy."[38] Michael Schudson acknowledges that "advertising may influence cultural life in the large even when it is not doing much to sell goods piece by piece."[39] These scholars base their criticisms on the assumption that advertising at least influences and perhaps creates society's values, rather than reflects them.

The notions regarding advertising's negative effects on its audiences seem to be substantiated anecdotally by criticisms of the athletic shoe companies.[40] The advertising of such pricey sneakers as the Nike Air Pressure and the Reebok Pump, originally priced at about $170 a pair, has been criticized for exploiting inner-city youth and adversely affecting their values and their well-being. Critics have blamed the companies' advertising practices for the extreme brand loyalty, resulting in inner-city youth killing each other for their sneakers. Critics also have asserted that advertising plays a part in luring young people into illegal drug trade, which they engage in to make money to buy the status symbols, such as the sneakers that they see advertised. Criticisms like these, along with discontent with Nike's minority employment record, precipitated a boycott of Nike by Operation PUSH, the Chicago-based civil-rights organization, during the summer of 1990.

THE LEGAL VERSUS THE MORAL DISCOURSE

It is curious that the legal and moral discourses are separate, dealing independently with different issues without engaging each other. The differences in the discourses reflect differences in the mindsets, training, and professional orientations of the participants. Both the differences in the discourses and ways of bringing them together are worthy of consideration.

The perspectives of the participants in the legal discourse reflect a debate over narrow definitions of deception that fails to raise the broader questions characteristic of the moral discourse. The legal debate is heavily influenced by deep-seated American political and legal values, such as caveat emptor, the extent of First Amendment rights to free speech, and the notion that govern-

---

[38] Richard W. Pollay, "The Distorted Mirror: Reflections on the Unintended Consequences of Advertising," *Journal of Marketing* 50 (April 1986), p. 25.

[39] Michael Schudson, *Advertising, The Uneasy Persuasion: Its Dubious Impact on American Society* (New York: Basic Books, 1984), p. 10.

[40] See "Has Sneaker Madness Gone Too Far?" *Newsweek*, December 18, 1989, p. 51; and "When Games Turn Nasty: Nike and Operation PUSH Square Off in a Boycott that Turns up the Heat on the Sneaker Industry," *Newsweek*, August 27, 1990, pp. 44–45.

ment that governs best governs least. Participants are tolerant of persuasion in advertising, perhaps because First Amendment rights to free speech presume the right to persuade. As a matter of law, legislation that comes close to infringing on rights that are perceived to be fundamental—such as freedom of speech and persuasion—is required to be narrowly tailored to address clearly identifiable and particular harms. Laws should not be vague or overly broad. They should be specific and the least restrictive as possible. As noted earlier, commercial speech does not, as a matter of law, have the same protection as political speech and persuasion. However, because persuasion in the commercial arena is so akin to our notions of free political speech, there is an ethic of regulating only at the level of deception in its least ambiguous form. In addition, many of the participants in the legal discourse are lawyers, who by their training are predisposed to the right to persuade. After all, a part of the professional legal ethic is that even the murderer is entitled to a persuasive defense. Though we may understand why the legal discourse is so narrow, it need not be. Many areas of the law reflect sophisticated attempts at regulating social problems.

The American Association of Advertising Agencies' Creative Code reflects the legal discourse, rather than the philosophical one. Its members pledge to not knowingly produce advertising that contains the following:

a. False or misleading statements or exaggerations, visual or verbal.
b. Testimonials that do not reflect the real choice of a competent witness.
c. Price claims that are misleading.
d. Comparisons that unfairly disparage a competitive product or service.
e. Claims insufficiently supported, or which distort the true meaning or practical application of statements made by professional or scientific authority.
f. Statements, suggestions, or pictures offensive to public decency.

Thus, it appears that ethics to professionals in the advertising industry is largely synonymous with legality. If we truly care about ethical behavior, this is not enough.

Participants in the moral discourse largely have relegated the determination of deceptiveness to regulators and have made eloquent arguments regarding the morality of advertising and its potential negative effects. While these arguments are indeed articulate and impassioned, they seem to represent a casual empiricism. Few of the alleged effects have been directly observed or documented empirically.[41] For example, there have been no studies of the effects of a lifetime of exposure to associative advertising or of years of exposure to advertising for luxury goods, expensive cars, jewelry, wines and the like. While it may be appropriate to hold positions that are not empirically based, the assertions philosophers make largely are hypotheses in need of empirical in-

---

[41] There have, however, been empirical studies to determine gender bias and the effects of advertising on children. See, for example, Goffman, *Gender Advertisements*, regarding gender bias and Atkin, "The Effects of Television Advertising on Children," regarding children's advertising.

vestigation. Absent empirical investigation, there is little hope that the important ethical considerations will be taken seriously by those who can effect change. Change will come in two ways: by law, and by moral suasion. In a liberal society, law often only reflects the least common denominator of morality. To do more, legislators and regulators often need evidence, or at least plausible justification to impose legal restrictions. Likewise, industry may be persuaded to behave in more ethical ways, but it is unlikely to do so without solid empirical evidence.

Empirical work is needed not only to test the hypotheses in the moral discourse but also to help identify deception for purposes of the legal discourse. Neither attorneys nor philosophers are trained to do empirical work or to be particularly appreciative of it. Empirical work is the contribution that marketing scholars and social scientists can make to the legal and ethical discourses. However, this work must be truly integrative. Marketing scholars must fully understand the more complicated constructs that philosophers deal with as well as the subtleties of legal issues.

The Massachusetts Lottery

It's a chance to make your dreams come true.

The Massachusetts State Lottery was created by a legislative act in September 1971, "to provide a source of revenue for the 351 cities and towns of the Commonwealth." Its first lottery product, a 50-cent weekly game, was introduced the following year and referred to as "The Game" to establish the image of the lottery as being "fun" rather than gambling. The Game realized total revenues of $56 million in 1972, and, in its first full calendar year of operation, $72 million in 1973. In subsequent years, the lottery continued to grow, increasing its revenues and offering a variety of games. By 1988, total revenues were $1,379.2 million, around $235 per capita, generating net revenues distributed to the state of $434.8 million. Chairman Robert Crane, in the lottery's 1987 annual report, commented: "Modern marketing techniques and the most up to date electronic equipment enable Massachusetts to be the leader among state lotteries." The lottery had become one of the largest commercial enterprises in the state. Yet state lotteries, and particularly their advertising, were subject to criticism. An editorial in *The Economist*, July 1989, observed:

> Governments have no duty to stop people from spending their money foolishly. But they do have a duty not to encourage people to spend their money in that fashion. On both counts, the role of government in America's current state-lottery frenzy is wrong. Egged on by $400 million a year in fantasy-inducing government-paid advertisements, Americans now spend more than $15 billion a year—up from $2 billion a decade ago—on ever-smaller chances of winning ever-larger sums of money.

STATE LOTTERIES

In 1988, 29 states were operating lotteries, generating total revenues of $15.6 billion, $93.73 per capita; with 48 percent distributed as prizes, 15 percent covering operating costs, and the remaining 37 percent, $5.74 billion, consti-

This case was prepared from public sources by Professors N. Craig Smith and John A. Quelch with the assistance of Ron Lee.

tuting total net revenues to the states. As Table 1 shows, California had the highest total revenue, with Massachusetts ranked fifth, though having the highest per capita revenue. On average, 3.3 percent of own-state revenues were generated by lotteries.[1] Half of the states operating lotteries earmarked net revenues entirely for specific public services (education in 50 percent of cases); the remainder added the revenues to general funds.

As well as generating revenue, state lotteries also were intended to provide an alternative to illegal gambling and, hence, help curb the associated organized crime. A 1972 report by the Fund for the City of New York recommended legalization of the numbers game and betting on sports. Noting that the illegal numbers game was widely played by the poor, the Fund concluded:

1. The primary objective of any legalized gambling should be the elimination of illegal operations.
2. Legal gambling should be seen as a tool of law enforcement, rather than a substitute for law enforcement.
3. The purpose of the legal game should be to attract current players, not to create new players.

Yet, in 1989, *The Economist* was urging the privatization of lotteries: "legal private competition would help the consumer. It would quickly drive up the prizes on lottery tickets beyond the current chintzy 48 cents on the dollar. Private lotteries could well put state lotteries out of business completely." Unlike state lotteries, private lotteries and their advertising would also come under Federal Trade Commission jurisdiction.

In December 1988, when the prize for the New York Lotto had reached $45 million, the largest in the lottery's history, 80 percent of the state's adult residents bought tickets. Massachusetts claimed more than 60 percent of its adult

TABLE 1   The Lottery Industry: The Leading Players, State by State, Ranked in Order of Their Annual Revenues

State/Year Started	Total Revenues ($ million)	Percent Change ('88–'87)	Revenues per Capita	Prize as Percent of Total Revenues	Operating Expense as Percent of Total Revenues	Net Income ($ million)	Percent of Revenues to State
California/1985	$2,106.4	49%	$74.78	49%	13%	$804.0	38%
New York/1967	1,632.0	8	91.17	47	9	725.6	44
Pennsylvania/1972	1,461.0	9	121.48	50	10	592.9	40
Ohio/1974	1,411.0	31	129.78	48	14	545.6	38
Massachusetts/1972	1,379.2	8	234.92	59	10	434.8	31

Source: "Lottomania," *Forbes*, March 6, 1989.

---

[1] Own-state revenues exclude state borrowings and federal grants and reimbursements.

population regularly bought lottery tickets. Yet research findings suggested a small proportion of participants accounted for most lottery sales. *The Wall Street Journal* cited a study by Duke University economists Charles Clotfelter and Philip Cook, which found that the 10 percent betting most frequently accounted for around 50 percent of the total wagered, with the most frequent 20 percent accounting for 65 percent. Characteristics of lottery players and participants in other types of commercial gambling (legal and illegal) also were reported:

- Sex: men generally gamble more than women, but almost equal numbers play lotteries.

- Age: generally young people gamble the most, but in lotteries the under-25 and over-65 age groups play less frequently and less heavily than the in-between ages.

- Education: gambling generally rises with education, but lottery play falls steadily as formal education increases.

- Occupation: laborers play the lottery the most and professionals the least.

- Race: blacks and Hispanics outplay non-Hispanic whites.

- Income: dollar amount wagered is fairly constant at all income levels, but proportionately higher amounts of household income are therefore wagered by lower income players.

A California survey reported in *US News and World Report* found that "the poor" wagered 2.1 percent of their income on lotteries, compared with the 0.3 percent expenditure of "the rich." *Money* calculated that the typical player's household income was $25,000. Some poor had become rich, with 800 people winning at least $1 million in 1987, though they represented only 0.000008 percent of the 97 million who played the lottery annually. Sheelah Ryan, a 63-year-old mobile home resident in Florida won the biggest lottery jackpot in North American history in 1988. She commented: "This is the first time I've ever won $55 million!" However, the odds of winning were greater in other forms of commercial gambling. In comparison to the 50 percent payout in lotteries, prizes averaged 81 percent of the total amount wagered in horse racing, 89 percent in slot machines, and 97 percent in casino table games.

LOTTERY MARKETING[2]

In *Selling Hope*, Clotfelter and Cook questioned whether the businesslike orientation of state lotteries was in the public interest. They attributed much of the success of state lotteries to the use of sophisticated marketing:

---

[2] This section is based on Charles T. Clotfelter and Philip J. Cook, *Selling Hope: State Lotteries in America* (Cambridge: Harvard University Press, 1989).

Unlike virtually every other operation of government at any level, but very much like most suppliers of consumer products, lottery agencies pay attention to details of product design, pricing, and promotion. This marketing is motivated by the lotteries' objective of maximizing revenue and made possible by their unusual degree of independence. . . . With the help of . . . specialists and experienced advertising agencies, the lotteries have set about to increase their revenues by stimulating the demand for their products.

State lottery marketing was "not as an afterthought but as a deliberate policy." Clotfelter and Cook quote one lottery director as having commented: "To survive and prosper, it is essential that lotteries practice the business techniques of the private sector, particularly in the area of marketing."

As monopoly suppliers of legal lottery games, the state lotteries realized their objective of maximizing revenue by strategies of recruiting new users or stimulating increased usage, rather than growing market share. Increasing usage was the dominant strategy, so, for example, Maryland lottery's advertising plan stated: "All advertising programs for the lottery must develop regular participants of the games, not casual impulse sales." Accordingly, target marketing, based on regular marketing research to identify the characteristics and preferences of market segments, was well established. So Arizona, using data collected from winners, found that games involving future drawings were more attractive to older people than to younger ones. Heavy users were targeted in particular, with market segments often geographically defined so that neighborhoods were identified with the highest relative rates of participation for each lottery game. Lottery advertisements in Spanish were commonplace in California and New York, though the targeting of minority groups had become controversial in some states. There had even been a boycott organized of the Illinois lottery, following charges that it devoted special attention to sections of Chicago populated by poor blacks.

According to lottery consultant John Koza, psychographic segmentation as well as demographic segmentation was important. "Belongers," one of nine distinct lifestyle groups in the VALS (Values and Lifestyles) typology, although not inherently attracted to gambling activities, was a substantial group of participants in lotteries because they were government-sanctioned. As Koza put it, for this segment "If the government says 'it's ok,' then it's ok." The "societally conscious" group, however, gambled considerably less than average and, accordingly, was less likely to be targeted. Having segmented the market, lotteries would then put together appropriate marketing mixes.

Product design encompassed play value, prize structure, the variety and the complexity of games. Instant "rub-off" games, for example, added play value to an otherwise passive game by incorporating elements of choice and suspense.[3] A mix of prize structures often was used to appeal to different players; though a study showed that neither players nor nonplayers knew the odds of

---

[3] Rub-off games had hidden symbols revealed by rubbing a coin over the surface of the card.

winning the Washington state's lotto game, the awareness of large prizes, rather than the odds, was the overriding concern. Price considerations not only included the ticket price but also the expected value of prizes. However, lottery managers were often constrained by state legislation specifying payout rates or setting minimum rates; though some states, such as Massachusetts, provided the flexibility to vary the payout rates among games. Yet awareness of this variation was often low, as Clotfelter and Cook conclude, "players generally appear to be ignorant about basic parameters of the lottery games in which they participate."

Convenience of purchase was important in reaching impulse buyers, especially for instant games. Convenience stores, supermarkets, liquor stores, drugstores, newsstands, and lottery ticket kiosks were the main outlets used. Vending machines sometimes were utilized in high-traffic areas. Enlisting the support of retail agents was an important place consideration, as Clotfelter and Cook suggest: "A cashier who asks, 'Would you like a lottery ticket with that quart of milk?' may have a significant role in determining a lottery's success in maximizing sales." Promotion considerations encompassed advertising, sales promotions, publicity, and personal selling. Sales promotions included "buy one, get one free" offers; free ticket coupons in newspapers, which achieved high redemption rates; and joint promotions with retailers, such as McDonald's. Lottery sales representatives played an important role—in dealing with retail agents—as well as favorable publicity. Clotfelter and Cook write: "Imagine how delighted most companies would be if their main product were featured on television news shows and newspaper front pages. For lotteries this kind of publicity has become routine." All lotteries employed public relations specialists.

Advertising was largely on television (an estimated 57 percent of state lottery budgets allocated to specific media in 1988), but radio (16 percent) was also important, as were point-of-sale advertisements (11 percent), print advertisements (7 percent), and transit signs and billboards (5 percent). Selective data analyzed by Clotfelter and Cook suggested the time devoted to lottery advertising was about three fourths the total amount for all state advertising, such that "most state citizens see lottery ads far more often than virtually any other message put out by the state." A survey by Maryland found that those most likely to be aware of lottery advertisements were young adults, blacks, television watchers, and lottery players. Attention was paid to the timing of advertising, particularly to coincide with paydays. The advertising plan for Ohio's Super Lotto specified: "Schedule heavier media weight during those times of the month when consumer disposable income peaks."

Clotfelter and Cook's content analysis of a sample of advertisements provided by 13 of the largest lotteries identified 8 primary messages, split equally between the "largely informational" and the "basically thematic." Informational advertisements included announcements of a new lottery game; direct appeals to buy tickets (in California: "Watch it grow! Play Lotto 6/49"); information about how to play a lottery game; details about winners; and, notably in brochures, information on rules of the game, prize structures, and the odds of winning. Many advertisements featured a reminder of the lottery's contribution to the state: "Thanks to you, everybody wins" (District of Columbia), "Our schools win, too" (California). Only a few advertisements were devoted to this purpose, though a series on this theme was developed by Maryland:

> One of the most dramatic of these was a television spot depicting a little boy wandering away from his family's campsite in the woods. In the gathering darkness the frightened boy wanders through the woods crying for his mother and father while the worried parents describe their son to police officers. A state police helicopter spots the boy with a searchlight, and a voice-over points out that the state lottery contributed $300 million in funds for public service, part of which was set aside for this police helicopter. As a sobbing mother is notified that her son is safe, the ad intones: "The Maryland state lottery pays off in ways you may not even know about."

Thematic advertisements employed humor and fantasy, with themes of the fun and excitement of the lottery; the dual message that anyone can win and that winning can change your life, such as "before-and-after" advertisements; a focus on wealth and luxury, "The rich. Join them" (Michigan); and a focus on money itself, such as coins being minted. Clotfelter and Cook reported that many advertisements portrayed wealth, leisure, gracious living, excitement, romance, and fame. A California advertisement featured dreams of possibilities created by winning, from a carefree retirement to establishing a father-son business. Advertisements tended to show wholesome surroundings and players younger and more affluent than the typical lottery player. Clotfelter and Cook described lottery advertisements as "among the most clever and appealing shown on television today."

Omissions from lottery advertisements formed the basis of some of the strongest criticisms. A consistent overstatement of the true value of prizes was said to result from not disclosing that large prizes were typically paid out over a 20-year period and that the stated prize was the sum of the payments not its present value, that large prizes only applied to single winners, and that jackpots were subject to taxation. Clotfelter and Cook found only 20 percent of the advertisements in their sample gave any information on the odds of winning, and usually only the probability of winning any prize as opposed to the grand prize. They suggested that with over 50 percent of the advertisements mentioning the dollar amount of prizes, there was an emphasis on prizes over probabilities giving a distorted impression of the probability of winning and increasing players' "subjective probability" of winning.

Missouri, Virginia, and Wisconsin attempted to restrict lottery advertising, viewing it as an inducement to gamble. This was in keeping with a wide-ranging National Association of Broadcasters code of conduct which, if it had not been ruled anti-competitive, would have questioned many lottery advertisements because of specific provisions on lottery advertising practice which, for example, said advertisements should not "indicate what fictitious winners may do, hope to do, or have done with their winnings."

Clotfelter and Cook believed that, while those running the lottery were well-intentioned and professional, there were legitimate concerns about their marketing practices, notably the use of misleading advertising and, largely as a consequence, the undermining of the credibility of state government. As California's attorney general commented, "People look to the government to be honest and straightforward and not to be using suckering kinds of techniques."

THE MASSACHUSETTS LOTTERY

The legislation governing the Massachusetts lottery specified revenue distribution such that a minimum of 45 percent was to be paid out in prizes, operating expenses were not to exceed 15 percent (from this amount a 5 percent commission and 1 percent bonus was paid to the sales agents who sold the tickets), and the balance was to be distributed to the Local Aid Fund for the benefit of the 351 towns and cities of the Commonwealth. The lottery itself assumed no responsibility for determining how much each city or town was to receive. The department of revenue was responsible for disbursement of revenue, according to each city or town's population. The cities and towns were then free to use their share of the revenue as they saw fit. The lottery produced around 3.8 percent of Massachusetts's revenues generated within the state.

After The Game was established in 1972, the Massachusetts State Lottery Commission pioneered the Instant Game. In this game, the player purchased a rub-off ticket with a pre-printed prize structure that allowed the buyer to know immediately if he or she was a winner. Prizes ranged from a free Instant lottery ticket to $100,000 a year for life. Despite its initial success, the Instant Game suffered a decline in popularity in 1977 and 1978. To encourage sales, the prize structure was readjusted to devote a greater portion of the prize money to the lower-tier prizes, which could be paid "instantly" by the sales agents. In 1987, sales were over $425 million and the Instant Game became Massachusetts's most popular lottery. In 1976, the lottery established the Numbers Game in order to allow players to participate more actively through selection of their own four-digit number, type of bet (with variation of the amount and which combination of digits in the four-digit number were bet on) and length of time they wished to play (between one and six days). The second objective of the Numbers Game was to challenge illegal gaming through an attractive and honest numbers game.

Megabucks, a number selection game whose jackpot grew until it was won, was established in 1982. Six numbers were to be chosen from a field of 30, which was later increased to a field of 36. In 1984, three drawings that failed to produce a winner ended by producing a jackpot of $18.2 million. Megabucks was the fastest-growing game in the history of the Massachusetts State Lottery, beginning with weekly sales of $50,000 in 1982 and growing to over $7 million a week in 1987.

Exhibit 1 shows an advertisement for Mass Millions. Launched in 1987, this game was designed to respond to public interest in very large jackpots. Though the Megabucks game routinely produced jackpots of $2 to $6 million, the jackpot did not reach $10 million or more unless no one won the jackpot for three or four drawings. Mass Millions was structured to produce larger, but less-frequent, jackpots than Megabucks. Players selected six numbers out of a field of 46, with each bet costing $1. Players matching all six numbers were guaranteed a minimum jackpot of $1 million. Players who matched five of the six winning numbers plus the "bonus" (or seventh) number won $50,000. The odds of winning the smallest prize ($2), were one in 47; the odds of winning the jackpot were one in over 9 million.

MASSACHUSETTS LOTTERY ADVERTISING

Massachusetts lottery advertising and promotion expenses in 1988 were just under $11.5 million, with around 38 percent on television advertising, 38 percent on radio, 20 percent on press, and 4 percent on point-of-sale materials. Agents selling lottery tickets provided flyers giving information on the odds and prize structures for games. Exhibit 2 shows an example of a flyer for a $1 instant game. Around 250,000 flyers were produced for each instant game (there would typically be seven different games in a year).

Criticism of lottery advertising was not uncommon. Writing in *Adweek* in March 1989, John Carroll suggested the advertising by the Massachusetts lottery "rivals professional wrestling in its egregious manipulation of people's baser instincts." He referred, for example, to the "ESP" campaign:

> Remember the "ESP" campaign? The television spot asked you to pick a number from one to five, then superimposed a number on the screen. (I think there were five versions of the spot.) If you were right, the spot went on to say, you *might* have ESP. Admittedly, that would come in handy when filling out your lottery slip. Unfortunately, though, there are no lottery games in this state that have one-to-five odds. If you really did have ESP, you'd probably have a better chance of making money from the *National Enquirer*.

EXHIBIT 1   Advertisement for Mass Millions

EXHIBIT 2   Instant Game Point-of-Sale Flyer

Front	*Rear*

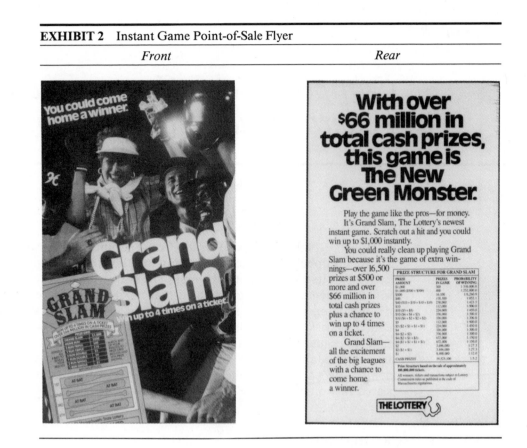

Campbell Soup Company and the Federal Trade Commission

In January 1989, the Federal Trade Commission (FTC) issued a complaint against Campbell Soup Company charging the company with deceptive advertising of its Campbell brand soups. The controversy centered on Campbell print advertisements, which claimed that its chicken noodle soup and "most of" the company's other soups were low in fat and cholesterol and helped reduce the risk of heart disease. The FTC said the advertisements were misleading because they failed to disclose the high sodium content in Campbell's soups that could potentially increase the risk of heart disease. The advertisements were part of Campbell's "Soup Is Good Food" campaign, which appeared in women's service magazines throughout 1988.

COMPANY BACKGROUND

Campbell Soup Company was a $5 billion sales, food manufacturer, based in Camden, New Jersey. It had over 48,000 employees worldwide. Soup accounted for 30 percent of Campbell's 1988 sales and an even higher percentage of its profits.

Campbell's market share of the $2.3 billion retail U.S. soup market declined from 80 percent in the early 1970s to 60 percent in 1988. The share loss was attributed to consumer interest in healthy and natural products and to increased competition. To stem the erosion, Campbell launched a series of line extensions, including Special Request soups, with a lower sodium content, and Golden Classics for the premium-priced segment. Unit sales of Campbell's Chunky ready-to-eat soups dropped 6 percent in 1987 and sales of the flagship red-and-white soup line fell 5 percent during that same period.

This case was prepared from public sources by Aimee L. Stern under the direction of Professors John A. Quelch and N. Craig Smith.
Copyright © 1990 by the President and Fellows of Harvard College.
Harvard Business School case N9-591-017 (rev. 3/8/91).

Throughout the 1980s, Campbell pursued a product diversification strategy. It acquired several food companies, including Mrs. Paul's Kitchens, which processed and marketed frozen prepared seafoods; Vlasic Foods, Inc., distributor of salad dressings, pickles, and cheese spreads; and Swift-Armour, a producer of fresh and canned meat products. Campbell also owned other strong nonsoup brands, such as Pepperidge Farm cookies, Prego spaghetti sauce, and Godiva chocolates.

CAMPBELL SOUP

Campbell spent $202.5 million on television and print advertising in 1988. Advertising and promotion were a critical part of Campbell's marketing strategy for its soup products. The core of Campbell's 1988 advertising continued to be the Soup Is Good claim. Magazine ads with the tag line "At the bottom of it all soup is good food" ask in bold headlines, "What's at the bottom of a bowl of Campbell's soup?" The accompanying print copy claimed that Campbell's soups were a "delicious source of fiber" and that "most" were low in fat and cholesterol. The next sentence referred to the results of scientific research that a diet high in fiber and low in fat and cholesterol may help reduce the risk of some forms of cancer and heart disease. A further claim was made that Campbell's tomato, cream of mushroom, and cream of celery soups were a "delicious source of calcium."

Campbell's advertising had attracted the attention of regulators before 1989. For example, in 1969, the FTC criticized Campbell for adding marbles to the bottom of bowls of vegetable soup to make the soup appear chunkier in photographs used in advertising. Campbell eventually agreed to stricter standards for product photography. In 1984, the New York state attorney general's office called into question Campbell advertisements in its "Soup Is Good Food" campaign, which referred to soup as "health insurance." The company paid $25,000 for the state's legal expenses and, in an out-of-court settlement, agreed to certain changes in the content of its advertisements.

In 1988, attorneys general in nine states alleged that Campbell's claims of high calcium content in its tomato soups were misleading. The attorneys general argued that most of the calcium came from milk that was added to the condensed soups in heating. They also complained about advertisements that noted a high fiber content in Campbell's bean and pea soups but showed pictures of chicken noodle soup, which was low in fiber. These advertisements referenced National Cancer Institute findings that a high-fiber, low-fat diet could reduce the risk of cancer. Campbell withdrew the NCI references and later agreed to pay $315,000 to cover the cost of the state investigations. Campbell also agreed to comply with guidelines proposed by the attorneys general that stated that any advertisements focusing on one type of soup as the source of a nutrient could depict other soups only if they also contained that nutrient. They stated further that, if an advertisement featured a nutrient in a recipe using a soup product, but the nutrient was not in the product itself, then the source of the nutrient had to be disclosed. Campbell discontinued the "Soup Is Good Food" campaign and reinstated its traditional "M'm, M'm Good!" theme in late 1988.

CONSUMER PROTECTION

The majority of complaints filed against Campbell and other food companies were generated by the Center for Science in the Public Interest (CSPI), a consumer watchdog group based in Washington, D.C. CSPI was founded in 1971 by three scientists, who wanted to apply their knowledge of science to health and nutrition issues. It was supported by 80,000 dues-paying members, the sale of educational publications, and foundation grants.

According to its brochure, CSPI "routinely disclosed deceptive marketing practices, dangerous food additives or contaminants, conflicts of interest in the academic community, and flawed science propagated by industries concerned solely with their profits . . . CSPI strives to halt corporate practices that undercut the nation's health."

Responding to growing consumer health consciousness during the 1980s, food manufacturers increasingly emphasized nutritional claims in their product advertising. At the same time, the FTC shifted from a pro-regulatory stance to an economic orientation. "The FTC believed virtually any advertisement provided useful information to the public," said Charles Miller, a senior staff attorney with CSPI. "They had an exaggerated faith in the market to act as a corrector of abuse." The FTC and the courts judged the propriety of an advertisement according to whether it was unfair or deceptive. Unfairness was a standard that the FTC rarely applied. Deception, however, was more clearly defined. False and misleading claims were always considered deceptive. A decision about whether an advertisement was deceptive was based upon the "net impression" of the entire advertisement. Even if every statement made was literally true, an advertisement was considered deceptive if the overall impression left with the consumer was misleading. Any ambiguity was construed against the advertiser.[1]

CSPI filed several complaints with the FTC against food manufacturers. For example, CSPI criticized Kellogg for promoting its Rice Krispies cereal as a product loaded with B vitamins for extra energy. CSPI also complained about Quaker Oats print advertisements, which implied consumers could reduce heart disease by 20 percent if they ate the cereal. The FTC disallowed both complaints. The state of Texas ultimately filed a lawsuit citing that Quaker had broken the state's deceptive trade practices law. Increasingly, state governments assumed the role of policing advertising campaigns in light of the FTC's hands-off policy.

---

[1] Hall, Dickler, Lawler, Kent, and Friedman (New York), "What Is Unfair and Deceptive," *Advertising Law Handbook.*

In 1988, the FTC finally did take up a 1985 complaint by CSPI, which accused Kraft of inflating the calcium content of its Singles cheese slices in product advertisements. Kraft stated that a Singles slice contained the same amount of calcium as five ounces of milk. The company did not mention that 30 percent of the calcium was lost in the processing of the cheese. The advertisements were discontinued.

CAMPBELL'S DILEMMA

In issuing the January 1989 complaint, William MacLeod, director of the FTC's Bureau of Consumer Protection, said the heart disease claim was "undermined" by the failure to disclose sodium levels:

> This case stands for the proposition that when you advertise a particular quality or characteristic of your product, you should disclose facts that tend to undermine or refute the specific claim you have made. The message here is that the commission takes health claims seriously and will police the advertising of these claims.

In a separate statement to *Advertising Age*, MacLeod commented further:

> If there's no heart-healthy claim, then there's no [FTC] order. But what we're saying is that, if you advertise a soup as heart-healthy, here's the disclosure you have to make. It's important to note this case is not an attempt to make advertisers say what's bad about their products whenever they say what's good about them.

The FTC stated that, if it found Campbell violated "truth in advertising" laws, it might order the company to notify consumers of the sodium content of its soups in advertisements. It said disclosure might be required on any can of soup with more than 500 milligrams of sodium per 8-ounce serving. Most Campbell soups had a sodium content of 400–600 milligrams per eight-ounce serving, including the Special Request line, which was promoted as containing "one-third less sodium." The National Research Council recommended an adult intake of 1,100 to 3,300 milligrams of sodium per day, though the minimum daily requirement was only 200 milligrams.

A Campbell spokesman complained that the company was being unfairly singled out, since Campbell was the only major soup manufacturer to list sodium content on the labels of the 5 billion cans of soup it sold each year. He indicated that the company would defend itself against the complaint. The company had 30 days to prepare its response.

SOURCES

Colford, Steven W., and Judann Dagnoli. "FTC Attacks Campbell Ad Health Claim." *Advertising Age*, January 30, 1989.

Freedman, Alix M. "FTC Alleges Campbell Ad Is Deceptive." *The Wall Street Journal*, January 27, 1989.

"Just How Healthy Are Campbell Soups?" *The Wall Street Journal*, March 1, 1989.

Saporito, Bill. "The Fly in Campbell's Soup." *Fortune*, May 9, 1988.

Chapter 8.4

Audi of America, Inc.

On March 19, 1986, the Center for Auto Safety, a Washington-based group founded by consumer activist Ralph Nader, and the New York state attorney general submitted a petition to the National Highway Traffic Safety Administration (NHTSA) claiming that 1978–86 Audi 5000s equipped with automatic transmission were unsafe and demanding that they be recalled. A number of incidents involving injury and death had been reported, in which Audi 5000s had surged out of control when the drivers shifted from park to drive or reverse. Unintended acceleration problems had been reported on other cars but not nearly as often as with the Audi 5000. The Audi, like many other European cars, placed the brake and gas pedals closer together than in many American designs, so a driver could move faster between pedals in high-speed emergencies. It was not, however, immediately clear that this was the cause of the problem.

THE RECALL

In July 1986, Audi of America, Inc., agreed to recall 132,000 1984–86 models to replace the idle stabilization valve and to relocate the brake and gas pedals. Audi management subsequently decided that installing a shift lock, which required the driver to depress the brake before shifting into gear, would be preferable. The cost of the recall to Audi was estimated at $25 million.

By January 1987, Audi had installed the shift lock in 70,000 cars. In that month, Audi decided to recall another 120,000 Audi 5000s sold between 1978 and 1983 for the same retrofit. Unfortunately for Audi, unintended acceleration incidents began to be reported on cars equipped with the shift locks. By May 1987, the Center for Auto Safety recorded the toll taken by unintended acceleration of Audi 5000s at 1,700 incidents, 1,500 accidents, over 400 injuries, and 7 deaths. In addition to product liability suits filed by victims of unin-

This case was prepared from public sources by Professor John A. Quelch.
Copyright © 1990 by the President and Fellows of Harvard College.
Harvard Business School case N9-590-114 (rev. 1/11/91).

tended acceleration, a class-action suit seeking compensation from Audi was initiated on behalf of existing Audi owners whose cars' resale values were depressed by the problem.

SALES IMPACT

The unintended acceleration problem had a devastating effect on Audi sales. In 1985, Audi of America enjoyed record sales of 74,000 units. In 1986, sales dropped to 60,000. The rate of decline accelerated following coverage of the Audi safety problem in November 1986 on the CBS Show, *60 Minutes*. Audi management complained that reports of unintended acceleration increased dramatically following the broadcast. In January 1987, sales fell to 1,439, or 3.5 units per dealer, from 2,072 in January of the previous year.

By March, Audi management faced a 248-day supply of 5000 models, compared to a normal inventory of 60–65 days. Hence, Audi announced a $5,000 rebate from April 1 to June 30, 1987, on the purchase or lease of any 5000 series model. The rebate represented a 23 percent discount off the dealer list price. Close to 120,000 coupons were mailed; 18,000 cars were sold or leased under the program. An Audi survey showed that only 6 percent of coupon recipients would have bought a car had the rebate been $4,000.

In the absence of the promotion, Audi of America sold only 41,300 vehicles in 1987, despite a new advertising campaign launched in the summer with a spending level double that in 1986. In addition, Audi introduced the more aerodynamically styled Audi 80 and 90 to replace the Audi 4000 series, a smaller and less expensive companion line to the 5000. Worldwide Audi sales rose 14 percent in 1987, despite the problem in the United States, which accounted for only 6 percent of the total.

THE VALUE ASSURANCE PLAN

January 1988 sales were only half those in January 1987. The new Audi 80s and 90s were not selling as well as had been expected. Audi management believed that consumer concern over the resale value of new Audis was restraining sales. They, therefore, conceived and launched in February 1988 a value assurance plan on all Audi 80s, 90s, and 5000s.

Under the plan, Audi promised to refund the difference between any new Audi's resale value and the resale value of comparable models sold by BMW, Mercedes-Benz, and Volvo. The Audi had to be resold between two and four years of the purchase date, and the value would be determined by the National Automobile Dealers Association (NADA) used car guide. A hypothetical example was cited in a February 1988 issue of *Automotive News*: assume a 1988 model Audi sold three years after the date of purchase was worth, on average, 56 percent of its $25,000 value. If the average price of the designated competitive models was 60 percent of their original prices, there would be a difference of 4 percent in resale value. Audi then would multiply the $25,000 purchase price by 4 percent—an equation worth $1,000 to the owner. Under the program, the Audi 80 and 90 were considered comparable to the Mercedes-Benz 190-E, BMW 325i, and Volvo 740. The Audi 5000S and Quattro were lined up against the Mercedes 269-F, the BMW 528e, and the Volvo 760 GLE. The Audi 5000 CS Turbo and Turbo Quattro were compared with the Mercedes 300-E, BMW 535i, and Volvo 760 GLE Turbo.

THE 1988 REBATE

The value assurance plan had a positive but limited impact on retail sales. Frequent media reports on the progress of lawsuits filed against the company by victims of unintended acceleration did not help. Audi management looked forward to September, when the 5000 series would be replaced by the new Audi 100 and 200 models that were already sold in Europe. Meanwhile, 1988 sales were still running at only half those in 1987.

Hence, Audi management conceived a second rebate program whereby 400,000 certificates were mailed to current and former Audi owners offering a $4,000 rebate on those Audi 5000s with automatic transmissions still in stock. These vehicles carried a dealer sticker price of $22,180. The rebate offer was good from May 1 through August 31. An existing $2,500 per unit dealer incentive on remaining Audi 5000s was curtailed in favor of the consumer promotion.

It soon became apparent that only 5,500 qualified vehicles were available at Audi dealerships. In June 1988, Costa N. Kensington filed a $76 million class action suit claiming that the Audi promotion represented bait-and-switch advertising with the intent of selling Audi 80s and 90s which, at the time, carried a $2,000 per unit dealer incentive. Mr. Kensington stated: "It is clear that the plan was not intended to benefit Audi customers but to jump-start sluggish sales of Audi's newly introduced automobiles."

Federal Trade Commission regulations required a retailer to have "a sufficient quantity of the advertised product to meet reasonably anticipated demands unless the advertisement clearly and adequately discloses that the supply is limited." Audi officials pointed to a sentence on the back of the rebate coupon that read "The availability of eligible vehicles is limited." Attorney general offices in Pennsylvania and Connecticut contended that this warning was inadequate because it did not specify the average number of cars at each dealership.

The Wall Street Journal reported on June 22, 1988, that Audi executives had told their dealers to expect 24,000 interested buyers to visit showrooms as a result of the offer. Responding to a question regarding the gap between supply and demand of the Audi 5000, Audi's general sales manager, Joe Tate, said that the company's projection of 24,000 was inflated to generate enthusiasm among dealers and corporate members. "If anything," he said, "we have pulled a bait-and-switch in the minds of our dealers. We may have hyped our numbers to excite a retail organization . . . so we could be certain to sell out the 5000s we had left. It was an attempt to build their confidence." In a memo dated May 2, 1988, Tate told the dealers that the program had been devised "to present attractive purchase alternatives" to coupon holders "who discover that the new 80 and 90 series vehicles may be a better solution to their driving needs." In the company newsletter of the same month, Tate expanded on the company's intentions pointing out that "Hopefully we can send some of the excess [Audi] 5000 customers toward the 80 and 90 line. What we're trying to do is jump-start Audi sales."

Separately, Dick Mugg, president of Audi America, commented: "In the past, I expected total commitment from the dealer to the product. Now I realize that is a totally unfair expectation. The industry has changed over the years—and probably for the better. We're no different from Procter & Gamble. We've got to earn shelf space; we've got to earn dealer share of mind every day."

Having already suffered allegations of mechanical failure, Audi shuddered at the prospect of a marketing plan that would compound criticism. An unidentified Audi executive commented: "It's frightening to think that just after we've enraged customers with the whole sudden-acceleration issue, we can come back with something that could be construed as bait-and-switch and cause another whole public relations blowup."

FUTURE PLANS

Audi executives were concerned that their plans for launching the Audi 100 and 200 in August 1988 might be derailed by the accusations of bait-and-switch. In addition, Audi of America faced over 100 product liability suits and the class-action suit by Audi owners seeking compensation for the loss in resale value of their cars had yet to be resolved. Management planned to launch a new program called the Audi Advantage program that covered almost all normal maintenance and repairs for three years or 50,000 miles on any new Audi. Free roadside assistance was also included. Audi's agency had proposed an advertising campaign that claimed: "Audi introduces a better car to own. And a better way to own a car."

SOURCES

"Audi 5000 Carries Discount of $4,000." *Automotive News*, April 18, 1988.

Kahn, Helen. "Audi Tries to Settle Class Suit." *Automotive News*, June 13, 1988.

Naj, Amal Kumar. "Audi of America Agrees to Recall 5000 Model Cars." *The Wall Street Journal*, January 16, 1987, p. 2.

Schwartz, Bradley A. "Audi Agrees to Give Owners of Its 5000 Rebate toward Future Audi Purchases." *The Wall Street Journal*, June 8, 1988.

————. "VW's Audi Unit in the U.S. Draws Fire over Controversial Incentive Programs." *The Wall Street Journal*, June 22, 1988, p. 7.

Sundstrom, Geoff. "NHTSA Won't End Audi Probe." *Automotive News*, June 27, 1988.

Versical, David. "An Anatomy." *Automotive News*, May 4, 1987.

————. "Audi Guarantees Resale, Offers Dealer Rebate." *Automotive News*, February 15, 1988.

————. "Mugg—Audi Healer." *Automotive News*, May 30, 1988.

PepsiCo and Madonna

INTRODUCTION

In April 1989, PepsiCo, Inc., the number two soft drink manufacturer in the world, announced that it was cancelling a two-minute television commercial starring pop singer Madonna. Pepsi had already paid Madonna close to $5 million for a product endorsement contract that included several advertisements and joint promotion of her upcoming concert tour. A Pepsi executive argued that viewers might confuse the advertisement with a promotional video that first aired the following day and also featured Madonna's new song "Like a Prayer." A Pepsi executive told *The Wall Street Journal*, "We knew she was making a video in a church with a choir. We didn't know the video featured burning crosses, priests, and religious figures."

CELEBRITY ENDORSEMENTS

Pepsi was one of the first companies to use rock stars as commercial endorsers to reach young soft drink consumers. In 1984 and 1987, Pepsi signed multimillion dollar promotional deals with Michael Jackson to support the launch of his *Thriller* and *Bad* albums. Pepsi also signed up such rock musicians as Tina Turner, Lionel Richie, and the Spanish group Menudo to promote its brands.

Pepsi's contract with Madonna was announced in January 1989. Around the same time, Coca-Cola signed pop singer George Michael. Some commentators questioned Madonna's appeal. A study released by Marketing Evaluations TVQ, Inc., found that Madonna was recognized by 88 percent of respondents but liked by only 25 percent, compared to an average of 21 percent

---

for female singers. The corresponding figures for George Michael were 80 percent, 48 percent, and 22 percent.

PEPSI VERSUS COKE

Coca-Cola's unsuccessful launch of New Coke gave Pepsi an opportunity to strengthen its position as the preferred youth-oriented brand of cola. Coke was forced to drop its popular "Coke is it" campaign because of consumer confusion between its two brands, Classic Coke and New Coke. Coke replaced "Coke is it" with what some analysts saw as a less appealing slogan, "Can't beat the feeling."

In 1988, Pepsi held a 30.7 percent share of overall sales in the $20.7 billion U.S. soft drink market. Coke had a 40.5 percent share. That year, however, Pepsi surpassed Coke in supermarket retail sales for the first time. Industry analysts partially credited Pepsi's advertising for this success.

Between 1985 and 1987, Pepsi increased its U.S. advertising budget from $116.7 million to $135.8 million, while Coke's advertising spending declined from $159 million to $141 million. The vast majority of these budgets were spent on network television.

Pepsi's advertising was considered by analysts to be more creative than Coke's. It consistently outperformed Coke in consumer advertising recall tests. Based on recall scores, Market Facts, Inc., calculated that the cost per week of having 1,000 television viewers remember an advertisement was $9.97 for Coke but $8.19 for Pepsi.

"MAKE A WISH"

The two-minute "Make a Wish" advertisement was aired in prime time on March 2, 1989, during the first commercial break of "The Cosby Show." On the same day, the advertisement was shown in 40 countries around the world and viewed by approximately 250 million people. This represented one of the largest single-day media buys in history. Pepsi planned to air 30- and 60-second versions of the advertisement in a continuation of the campaign. A series of additional advertisements with Madonna was also planned.

The advertisement was Madonna's first commercial endorsement. It was described by *Adweek* as a blend of *It's a Wonderful Life* and *Peggy Sue Got Married*. It opened with Madonna watching a black-and-white home movie facsimile of her eighth grade birthday party. The younger version of the singer joined the older Madonna in a song and dance fest. The ad concluded as the older Madonna (in color) viewed her younger self (in black and white) blowing out her birthday candles. She urged the young girl to "Go Ahead, Make a Wish." An *Advertising Age* review described the advertisement as "the best commercial of its genre—the perfect balance of entertainment and sell," noting that the Pepsi name was visible 11 times before the closing logo shot.

"LIKE A PRAYER"

The "Like a Prayer" video was aired on MTV (Music Television Videos) on March 3. Both the advertisement and the video featured Madonna's new song "Like a Prayer," which was also the theme song for her upcoming concert tour. The video depicted Madonna wearing a black negligee receiving the stigmata of Christ. The commercial contained no footage from the video.

THE REVEREND DONALD WILDMON

American Family Association director, Reverend Donald Wildmon, was considered the primary reason Pepsi withdrew the advertisement. Wildmon headed a Christian advocacy group with approximately 380,000 members in hundreds of local chapters. In 1989, his organization had a budget of $5 million, funded primarily through small donations. He threatened a boycott of all Pepsi products if the company continued to air the advertisement and received public support from several individual Catholic bishops. Some Pepsi executives feared that this might be followed by a potentially damaging statement from the U.S. Catholic Conference.

Wildmon's aim was to clear the airwaves of anti-Christian material. His primary targets were not the broadcast networks but the corporations who supported sexually explicit advertisements and television programs. In 1986, he convinced Southland Corporation to remove sexually explicit magazines from its company-owned 7-Eleven stores. In 1989, he convinced General Mills to stop running advertisements on NBC's "Saturday Night Live," a program that Wildmon considered "vulgar."

The association's monthly journal contained headlines such as "Boozing Priest on Show Bought by RJR Nabisco, Pfizer" and "Kellogg, Sara Lee Promote Christian Buffoons on ABC." Wildmon commented that television sex, "done affectionately, with love and within the bonds of marriage, doesn't bother me. But . . . some things you do privately."

PEPSI'S REACTION

Wildmon's first confrontation with Pepsi occurred in the fall of 1988 over its promotional sponsorship of the videocassette release of *ET*. The movie was produced by MCA/Universal, the same studio that had released *The Last Temptation of Christ*. Wildmon asserted that Pepsi's willingness to deal with

MCA/Universal implied that the company supported what he viewed as sacrilege in this film. Pepsi refused to cancel the *ET* project.

Wildmon called the Madonna video "one of the most offensive things I've ever seen." Pepsi's initial reaction to Wildmon's threatened boycott was a denial that it would pull the commercial. A few days later, a Pepsi spokesperson announced "a temporary hold on the commercial until we see a reaction to the video." In particular, Pepsi substituted other commercials on MTV after MTV began airing the video. The spokesman said the company was concerned that consumers might confuse the commercial and the video. He stated that Pepsi wanted to see the video gain recognition before it expanded the commercial campaign. Two other religious groups protested and Pepsi received complaint letters and calls from consumers. A month after the advertisement debuted, Pepsi canceled its affiliation with Madonna in the United States, including the sponsorship of her U.S. concert tour. However, Pepsi continued to run the advertisements in Europe and Asia. Wildmon then announced an end to the boycott of Pepsi products.

Pepsi executives told reporters that they had not seen the video before it aired and had not been informed that it would air so soon after the commercial. Entertainment marketers speculated that Madonna would not have agreed to any preview even if Pepsi had asked.

Advertising and beverage industry executives expressed outrage that religious groups could pressure Pepsi to censor creative advertising. A Pepsi spokesperson said the Madonna flap generated "a tremendous amount of publicity." However, Russell Klein, senior vice president of Seven-Up Company, told *The Wall Street Journal*: "I find it very difficult to believe Pepsi would find this current mistake acceptable because of the public relations they received. I don't think they're sitting in their offices smiling."

ADVERTISING RECALL

A tracking study by *Advertising Age* and the Gallup Organization found that Pepsi led in unaided advertising recall in March 1989. One thousand consumers were asked: "Of all the advertising you have seen, heard, or read in the past 30 days, which advertisement first comes to mind?" The three most frequently mentioned advertisers at the end of February and March 1989 were:

	February Rank	*March Rank*
McDonald's	1	2
Pepsi-Cola	2	1
Ford	3	4
Coca-Cola	4	3

Pepsi was the most frequently recalled advertiser among all groups, except consumers aged 65 or more. The strongest recall was among respondents aged 25–34. When asked "which soft drink advertiser first comes to mind?" the percentages of mentions were:

	February	*March*
Pepsi-Cola	37.6%	40.9%
Coca-Cola	32.5	29.6
Diet Coke	9.4	8.9

SOURCES

Garfield, Bob. "Pepsi Should Offer Prayer to Madonna." *Advertising Age*, March 6, 1989, p. 76.

Hume, Scott. "Pepsi Tops Ad Recall after Madonna Flap." *Advertising Age*, April 24, 1989, p. 12.

McCarthy, Michael J. "Pop Go the Soda Wars: Pepsi Signs Madonna to Appear in Ads." *The Wall Street Journal*, January 26, 1989, pp. B1, B5.

Schiffman, James R. "PepsiCo Cans TV Ads with Madonna, Pointing Up Risks of Using Superstars." *The Wall Street Journal*, April 5, 1989, p. B11.

"Soft Drinks: Pepsi's 'New Generation' Takes Over." *Adweek*, March 6, 1989, p. 38.

Ticer, Scott. "The Cola Superpowers' Outrageous New Arsenals." *Business Week*, March 20, 1989, pp. 162–63.

Waldman, Peter. "This Madonna Isn't What the Reverend Really Had in Mind." *The Wall Street Journal*, April 7, 1989, pp. A1, A8.

Winters, Patricia. "Pepsi Won't Cut Ties with Madonna." *Advertising Age*, March 6, 1989, p. 74.

Chapter 8.6

Anheuser-Busch

In January 1987, Anheuser-Busch (A-B) launched an internal investigation to determine if senior executives had accepted gifts and kickbacks from a company handling A-B's sales promotion. This investigation would not only examine the kickback charges but also help A-B evaluate its gift-receiving practices in the wake of the recent scandal that had "rocked" the firm. One A-B executive later stated that gifts were so numerous at the largest U.S. brewer's headquarters that they lined both sides of the corridors.

SALES PROMOTION AND THE BREWING INDUSTRY

Analysts suggested it was common practice for executives in the beer industry to accept gifts from outside suppliers. Some sales promotion and advertising agencies believed that gifts were necessary to obtain business, and brewers did not always dissuade these firms in their gift-giving practices. It was illegal for brewers to give gifts or payments to retailers to obtain shelf space or preferential treatment. However, many in the business believed these gift-giving practices occurred, and in 1984, Miller, Adolph Coors, and Stroh Brewery paid the Bureau of Alcohol, Tobacco & Firearms $280,000 in fines following allegations that they attempted to influence beer brand selection at various major league baseball parks across the country. The fines were paid without admission of any wrongdoing. This was not the first incident of its kind within the beer industry.

Many observers believed that the temptation to accept illegal payments had increased because advertising and promotion budgets in the brewing industry had risen substantially in recent years. Beer companies' advertising expenditures doubled between 1978 and 1983. Furthermore, beer company spending patterns had shifted. In 1978, 15 percent of the total media budget was allocated

This case was prepared from public sources by Jonathan D. Hibbard under the direction of Professors N. Craig Smith and John A. Quelch.
Copyright © 1989 by the President and Fellows of Harvard College.
Harvard Business School case 9-590-021 (rev. 5/17/90).

651

to sales promotion rather than advertising; by 1983, this figure had grown to 40 percent. Advertising spending by brewers tripled from 1983 to 1987, and the sales promotion allocation continued to expand, increasing from 40 percent to 45 percent of total media budgets. Exhibit 1 lists recent media spending by leading brewers. Top company executives dealt with a company's advertising agencies, but lower-level managers typically worked with a brewer's sales promotion suppliers. Since the sales promotion area was where most of the gift giving occurred, these lower-paid managers were more vulnerable to the temptation of illegal rewards and kickbacks.

Analysts believed that, while sales promotion agencies were improving their auditing systems, clients needed accountability from their employees. One analyst commented: "The Anheuser illegal gift problem could only have happened because somebody at A-B was not checking what was going on well enough. You have to delve into the backgrounds of the companies you employ. You can't allow sales promotion to be handled on a lower management level and then not monitor the situation." Another analyst stated: "As long as companies bring in agencies on projects where the fee is predicated on how much you sell, you're open for trouble. Allowing junior-level managers to oversee millions of dollars raises the possibility for temptation."

THE A-B GIFTS SCANDAL

As the nation's largest brewer, A-B's marketing budgets were substantial, and this may have made the temptation to accept gifts even greater. A-B, head-

---

EXHIBIT 1   1987 U.S. Beer Brand Information ($ millions)

	Number of Combined Brands*	Measured Media Spending	Percentage of All Beer Sold
Anheuser-Busch brands:			
Budweiser	9	$168	23.5%
Michelob	5	92	11.7
Busch	2	27	3.5
Other A-B beers	4	9	1.3
A-B totals	20	$296	40.0%
Other leading brands:			
Miller	9	$152	22.0%
Coors	9	83	12.0
Strohs	7	25	4.0
Old Milwaukee	3	17	2.5
Lowenbrau	2	12	1.7
Molson	7	10	1.4

* "Combined brands" references a beer's line extensions, such as Bud Light for Budweiser.

quartered in St. Louis, dominated the beer promotion and advertising market, typically spending 25–50 percent more than its closest rivals. A-B spent $339 million in 1987 on advertising, placing it 10th on a list of the U.S. leading national advertisers. Its nearest beer competitor, Miller, spent $260 million in 1987. A-B's 1987 market share climbed to 39.8 percent, an increase of 1.8 share points from 1986; the increase was widely attributed to its heavy advertising expenditures. Sales were $9 billion and net earnings were $615 million, a 19 percent increase over 1986 net earnings. This was A-B's fourth consecutive year of double-digit earnings growth.

The kickbacks allegedly took place between 1981 and 1983, when Marvin Cotlar, the former chief executive of sales promotion agency Hanley Worldwide, overbilled A-B for advertising and promotional services. This overbilled amount—totalling about $240,000 from several invoices—was then split between Hanley and several A-B executives. The illegal payments might not have surfaced had Hanley not filed for bankruptcy in December 1983. The bankruptcy proceedings showed that Hanley maintained lavish offices in St. Louis and New York City to service its accounts though the company was only operating at about break-even. According to rival sales promotion industry executives, Hanley had a reputation for producing topnotch creative work while Cotlar was viewed as a sharp and aggressive manager who hired good people.

The bankruptcy investigation revealed that Cotlar had been convicted of embezzling and sentenced to eight years in prison in September 1971. He was released on parole in July 1973 and founded Hanley in 1974. Some of the illegal payments were discovered because Hanley had listed those payments to A-B as deductions on its tax documents. The Internal Revenue Service statutes allowed deductions for "ordinary" and "necessary" business expenses, and some firms included kickback payments within these deductions. A former Hanley employee stated: "Hanley operated on two ethical levels. On one hand, staffers were expected to produce top quality work for clients. But at the same time, staffers were aware of 'interesting' bookkeeping and billing practices." In 1986, the bankruptcy trustees for Hanley filed several lawsuits aimed at recovering nearly $1 million paid out by Hanley in illegal payments before it filed for bankruptcy. One of those suits asserted that Hanley paid a car-leasing company $13,000 to subsidize the purchase of a new Porsche for A-B's sales promotion manager, John Lodge.

As a result of A-B's internal investigation, four A-B executives resigned or were fired: Dennis Long, president of A-B; Joseph Martino, vice president—national sales; Michael Orloff, vice president—wholesale operations; and William Glickert, international marketing manager. Many analysts believed the flap forced the resignation of Long because he chose to take responsibility for the scandal. Others felt it was because the investigation revealed that A-B had channeled about $6 million in promotions business to Worldwide Products, Inc., another St. Louis-based marketing firm that was run by relatives of Long. However, no wrongdoing on Long's part was uncovered in the investigation.

Martino and Orloff attempted to exercise their accumulated A-B stock options but found that the company had frozen their accounts. These executives then filed countersuits, alleging they did not "consent or authorize" any illegal payments from Hanley, and requested $14 million in damages because they were forced to resign from A-B and not allowed to cash in their stock options.

GIFT PRACTICES ON TRIAL

In April 1988, after a year-long investigation, a federal grand jury convened in St. Louis to decide whether Hanley had paid illegal kickbacks to the Anheuser-Busch executives. Payments and gifts (cash, crystal, cellular phones, computers, and TV sets) were allegedly funneled through Hanley. These officers failed to report the gifts on company conflict-of-interest forms to A-B's corporate ethics committee, as well as to the Internal Revenue Service.

With the grand jury trial less than a week away, many industry followers were assessing the case. Although the 19-count indictment listed the former A-B executives and a promotion agency head, analysts believed it was beer marketing and promotional practices that would be on trial. On one hand, there seemed to be indisputable proof that these executives had accepted gifts and favors from Hanley. However, some saw the situation as reflecting normal business practice in the beer industry that a few managers may have taken too far. One defense lawyer stated, "In the sales promotion industry, the practice of making gifts is commonplace."

ASSESSING THE IMPACT

August A. Busch III, Anheuser-Busch's chairman, realized A-B had received significant negative coverage as a result of the widely publicized kickback allegations. With the upcoming trial, A-B was sure to continue to remain in the public spotlight. Although the company had "safeguards" against taking gifts in place, Busch recognized that the A-B system may have allowed a few executives to take advantage of their positions. The current safeguards were that A-B gave its employees a business ethics manual when they began their employment with the firm, and they also required each employee to sign a "statement of compliance" once a year. This statement dealt specifically with gift-receiving and other questionable business practices.

Whatever the result of the trial, August Busch wanted to make certain that this type of situation did not repeat itself. After the resignation of Dennis Long, Busch decided to take on the additional responsibilities of president, in order to stay closer to A-B's operations and to oversee a possible overhaul of the company's gift policies.

Chapter 8.7

In the News

8.7.1 FOES CLAIM AD BANS ARE BAD BUSINESS*

As pressure mounts to restrict tobacco and alcohol advertising, the ad industry is doing more than just wrapping itself in the First Amendment. This time it plans to counterattack with a different weapon: economics.

Ban tobacco advertising and send 7,904 newspaper jobs packing, while killing 165 magazines, according to a new study. End beer and wine advertising on television, and there go another 4,232 jobs, plus an enormous chunk of network sports programming. Without ads for hard liquor, another 84 magazines would fold, including many for blacks.

The yearlong study, to be released today, comes from the Leadership Council on Advertising Issues. Made up of media and advertising executives, the group is hardly unbiased: Its stated mission is "to preserve and enhance the right and freedom to advertise."

Still, the study's authors say they hope the results will add the possible economic impact to the debate over ad bans. "The costs of these types of activities—whether it's tax or regulation—hadn't been put on the table," says William Lilley III, president of Policy Communications, Inc., and a former CBS executive, who co-wrote the study with Rudolph Gerhard Penner, a senior fellow at the Urban Institute, a think tank. The costs, he says, should "become part of a political calculus when the decision is made."

The study no doubt will be met with resistance from various groups pushing for further restrictions on smoking and alcohol advertising. After all, even though the study presents some eyecatching figures of jobs lost and media outlets demolished, the other side can play the same game at least as well. Just last week, Louis Sullivan, secretary of Health and Human Services, released a report saying that smoking costs the country over $52 billion a year in lost work time, health claims, and other costs.

The new study also "doesn't consider what new forms of advertising might replace" lost beer, alcohol, and tobacco ads, says Michael Pertschuk, co-director of the Advocacy Institute, which works with anti-smoking and other advocacy groups. "When one advertiser disappears, new ones step forward. [The study] assumes the marketplace is static, that you lose those advertisers and nobody else steps in." The study's authors say their model takes into account some substitutions.

The study reaches some interesting conclusions. Perhaps the most unexpected: A ban on beer ads would lead to enormous reductions in network TV sports programming—and fuel a resurgence in pay cable, leading to a 39 percent increase in sports viewing on pay cable over current projections.

Beer ads account for over 15 percent of all ad spending on network sports. Without beer ads, the study says, the networks would have far less money to spend on sports programming. In 1993, it predicts, the networks would slice

*By Joanne Lipman, *The Wall Street Journal*, February 27, 1990. Reprinted by permission of *The Wall Street Journal*, © 1990 Dow Jones and Company, Inc. All Rights Reserved Worldwide.

spending by 16.4 percent, or $146 million, from current projections.

Some major sporting events, meanwhile, would move to pay cable. Pay-per-view might also benefit, Mr. Lilley says. (The study assumes viewers would be willing to pay to see some of the events they now get for free.) Minor sports, on the other hand—such as auto and boat racing and Ivy League football—could lose TV exposure altogether, the study suggests.

A ban on beer ads, which account for 4.4 percent of all network ad spending, would also hurt general TV programming. Without beer ads, "certainly, the quality of programming will be affected," says Mr. Penner. With less ad revenue, he says, the networks would have no choice but to reduce spending on programs—presenting either fewer new programs or lower-quality programs.

Banning liquor and tobacco ads would have similar, if less dramatic, effects on magazines and newspapers. Tobacco, for example, accounts for 6.1 percent of all advertising in general-interest magazines. Without it, magazines would have to raise prices, leading to circulation declines, the study says. The magazine industry would lose 4,130 jobs along with 165 publications. Especially hard hit would be magazines such as *TV Guide, McCalls, Redbook,* and *Sports Illustrated,* all of which drew 10 percent or more of their 1988 ad revenue from tobacco ads, the study says.

A ban on liquor ads, meanwhile, would hit magazines aimed at minorities, the study says. An earlier study, which the two authors finished last summer, found that, when ad spending in general declines, minority outlets are hit harder than their mass-market counterparts. If ad spending is 5 percent lower than expected through 1993, for example, the number of all radio stations would decline 2.1 percent—but the number of black and Hispanic radio stations would drop 4.1 percent and 5.6 percent, respectively, that study found.

Reginald Brack, chief executive officer of Time Inc. Magazines, a unit of Time Warner, who also is co-chairman of the Leadership Council, says the impact on minority media would be the "most significant" result of any ad cutback. "The more marginal the media," he says, "the more devastating it is. It's alarming to all of us. [But] it's going to have more effect on them than it will on Time Warner or CBS."

Ad-ban proponents often insist that a ban wouldn't hurt the media business, and they point to 1971, when cigarette advertising was banned on television, as proof. At that time, "you could find all these predictions that there would be all these losses of TV jobs, and of course none of that happened," the advocacy group's Mr. Pertschuk says.

But the study's authors say the media business is so different and so much more complex now than it was 20 years ago that those comparisons aren't valid. Twenty years back, pay cable, special-interest magazines, and pay-per-view weren't a factor. But now, if networks bring in less ad revenue because of an ad ban, they'll spend less on programming and lose viewers to other media, the authors say. "It's a very vicious cycle," Mr. Lilley says. "In 1971, you didn't have that kind of competitive media marketplace that you have now."

8.7.2 AS RETAILERS' SALES CROP UP EVERYWHERE, REGULATORS WONDER IF THE PRICE IS RIGHT*

It seems everything is on sale these days, and regulatory officials aren't buying it.

The number of sales and markdowns at retail stores has exploded in recent years, leaving consumers perplexed about pricing tactics and

---

*By Teri Agins, staff reporter of *The Wall Street Journal,* February 13, 1990. Reprinted by permission of *The Wall Street Journal,* © 1990 Dow Jones and Company, Inc. All Rights Reserved Worldwide.

wondering whether they are really getting bargains. Responding to a rising tide of consumer complaints, regulators are closing in.

"The key issue is how do you go about judging whether a sale price has market validity," says Steven Cole, vice president of the Council of Better Business Bureaus. "Was [the regular price] a good faith price or a fictitious one set up just for the purpose of having a future sale?" The council has been meeting with a group of big retailers and attorneys general from six states to come up with new advertising standards.

One of the most closely watched regulatory changes is coming in Massachusetts. This May, the state will put into effect a law that regulators consider among the toughest to govern retailers on matters such as price comparison claims, price and quality disclosure, and the availability of merchandise advertised as marked down. Also under the rule, sales advertised in retail catalogs, which are printed months in advance, must disclose that the so-called original price is really only a reference price and not necessarily the actual former selling price.

Campeau Accelerates Trend

Sales have become more suspect simply because they're so commonplace. Once confined mostly to end-of-the season clearances, markdowns now are a year-round promotional tactic. The trend snowballed as competition intensified between department stores and off-price retailers, which have been gaining market share in recent years.

Markdowns seem to be occurring faster and faster. Last month, Spiegel, Inc., mailed out its spring catalog filled with seasonal fashions, including a floral sundress "you'll wear long after dark." The price: $68. Just a couple of weeks later, Spiegel sent out another catalog featuring the very same floral sundress. The price: $54— on sale.

Many industry watchers considered this past Christmas season perhaps the most promo-

tional ever. That's partly because of troubled Campeau Corporation, which slashed prices at its department stores to generate cash, prompting other stores to follow suit. "Campeau was the catalyst and had other stores insecure enough to follow, which exaggerated that trend," says Bruce Missett, an analyst at Oppenheimer & Company. As a result, many analysts say stores are hurting their profit margins because they've gone so overboard with sales.

While shoppers bagged plenty of bargains during the holiday season, they were wary. "I caught almost all of my Christmas gifts on sale," says Martelle Shaw, a Long Island, New York, teacher who treated herself to a raccoon coat marked down 50 percent. But she was suspicious: "I don't really think all of those sales were for real."

There's also a feeling of frustration among consumers. "All the price-cutting has made people anxious that they aren't getting the absolute best price," says Leo Shapiro, chairman of a retail consulting firm that interviewed 300 Chicago-area shoppers after Christmas. He says 82 percent of those shoppers believed they could probably have found even better deals "if they had just looked a little harder."

For their part, regulators aren't so sure all advertised bargains are such good deals. Last December, the New York state attorney general filed suit against Sears, Roebuck & Company, charging that the company's "everyday low price" strategy has created a "false impression" that Sears' prices represent significant discounts from former prices. Sears, which adopted the policy to try to kick the habit of constant sales, has denied the charges.

A similar lawsuit was filed by New York City's Department of Consumer Affairs against Newmark & Lewis, Inc., a consumer electronics chain based in Hicksville, New York, that also adopted a so-called lower-pricing strategy last year. Newmark & Lewis has denied the charges that it engaged in deceptive advertising.

Last August, three St. Louis furniture stores agreed to pay $352,000 in restitution to consumers under settlements negotiated by the Missouri attorney general's office. The state alleged that the stores had boosted the manufacturer's suggested retail price when advertising their sale prices. Under the settlement, about 2,500 consumers were refunded, on average, about $150 each on furniture they had purchased earlier from the stores.

Industry watchers are anxiously awaiting the outcome of a suit that Colorado filed against May Department Stores, Inc.'s May D&F unit. Among the allegations in that case, which is slated to go to trial in May, the Colorado attorney general charged that May D&F misled consumers on offering sale prices for a limited time only, when such prices are offered "continuously throughout most calendar periods." The state also alleged that May used pre-printed price tags with inflated regular prices, which "deceptively convey the impression" that those prices were "genuine regular selling prices." A May spokesman declined to comment on the suit.

Determining value has gotten tougher lately because stores are selling more private-label merchandise, often putting them on sale at 50 percent off or more. Even though a shirt with a store's own label looks like a great deal when marked down, the retailer still makes a healthy profit, says George Hechtman, a partner at McMillan & Doolittle, retail industry consultants. Unfortunately, private-label sales make comparison shopping almost impossible. "With Liz Claiborne you know what it is worth by shopping at different stores," says Mr. Missett, the Oppenheimer analyst. "But with private-label merchandise you have no standard to judge by."

The same kind of problems can occur with discount stores specializing in electronic goods like stereos and VCRs. Their advertising dares customers to find lower prices on comparable merchandise, when, in fact, in some cases the goods were specially made for the store, so identical items don't exist elsewhere.

Some stores say they are backing off on sales as a marketing strategy. Dayton Hudson Corporation says that last year it cut storewide sales promotions by a third. The Minneapolis-based chain says the move has allowed it to focus on selling its full-price merchandise. And Toys "R" Us, Inc., says that, because it constantly adjusts prices, it doesn't need to advertise sales to generate traffic.

But industry sources believe most retailers continue to play the markdown game because customers have come to expect discounts on everything. "Once you start doing this, you're on a treadmill," says Robert Buchanan, an analyst with Alex. Brown & Sons. "And I don't see how they're going to get off."

8.7.3 A CRACKDOWN ON "CHARITY" SWEEPSTAKES*

In December, the Iowa attorney general's office sent a van to a private mail-processing concern in the town of Red Oak and hauled away thousands of letters containing an estimated $125,000 in checks made out to the Pacific West Cancer Fund.

Pacific West set up a forwarding address in Kansas. Then the federal government stepped in. Since January 30, when U.S. postal inspectors got a court order in Topeka halting delivery, the letters have been piling up.

The seizure and delivery halt are part of a crackdown by state and federal officials against a number of self-described charities that use vaguely worded "bonanza sweepstakes" letters to raise money—purportedly for health-related

---

*By Rhonda L. Rundle, staff reporter of *The Wall Street Journal*, March 6, 1989. Reprinted by permission of *The Wall Street Journal*, © 1990 Dow Jones and Company, Inc. All Rights Reserved Worldwide.

Some Watson & Hughey Clients: Where the Money Went

	Year	Revenue	Management and Fund Raising	Lobbying	Education*	Grants and Programs
American Heart Disease Prevention Foundation	1987	$ 1,262,266	$ 808,137	N.A.	$ 619,191	$ 35,000
Cancer Fund of America†	—	—	—	—	—	—
Pacific West Cancer Fund‡	—	—	—	—	—	—
Project Cure Inc./ Center for Alternative Cancer Research	1987	3,593,820	1,150,321	1,069,524	1,068,523	N.A.
United Cancer Council	1987	10,762,501	6,300,638	N.A.	3,809,512	302,641
Walker Cancer Institute	1987	109,779	168,813	N.A.	36,853	None

N.A. means not available.
* Includes postage, mailing lists, printing.
† Required to file its first financial statement by May 31.
‡ Required to file its first financial statement by June 30.

Source: Connecticut Attorney General's Office report, December 1988.

causes. The sweepstakes drives—most of which are handled by Watson & Hughey Company an Alexandria, Virginia, direct-mail concern founded in 1981—have garnered millions of dollars in donations, but only a tiny fraction has gone for medical research, authorities say. Most of the money appears to go back into more sweepstakes mailings.

The wording of the sweepstakes letters often leaves the impression that the recipient has already won a prize and has only to send in a donation to collect, authorities say. "People have the idea that they have actually won or have a very good chance of winning $5,000" when they receive a Pacific West letter, says Iowa attorney general Tom Miller. Most winners get "a grand total of 10 cents, if that," he says, "and virtually none of the money donated goes to . . . cancer research."

House Panel Plans Hearings

Complaints from consumers, watchdog groups, and state regulators have flooded Washington. A House transportation subcommittee is expected to hold hearings next month to decide whether federal laws are needed to clamp down on charity fund-raising abuses. While some federal statutes may be applicable in some cases, such regulation currently is left mostly to the states. But few states have statutes as tough as Iowa's.

At least six states, including Iowa, have sued Watson & Hughey and some of its clients, charging them with violating various consumer-protection and charity laws. Iowa's suit, filed January 4 in state court in Des Moines, charges Pacific West, Watson & Hughey, and Robert R. Stone, an attorney who signed the fund's sweepstakes letters, with consumer fraud and deceptive practices.

In a telephone interview, Byron C. Hughey says only that he and his partner, Jerry C. Watson, believe "we haven't done anything wrong." He declines to comment further.

Mr. Stone, an attorney whose Virginia license was suspended in 1983 for misconduct related to alcohol abuse and who currently faces disciplinary charges by the District of Columbia bar, answered his telephone but said he couldn't talk then and would call back. He never did, and couldn't be reached again. Pacific West's administrator, Donald Tarver, didn't return phone calls.

Financial reports for Pacific West aren't available because the 16-month-old organization isn't required by the states in which it operates to submit information until later this year. However, in a deposition filed last month in the Iowa court, Mr. Tarver said the fund's only charitable activity in the past year consists of "our direct-mail campaign to build a donor base." He did outline a number of cancer-treatment projects that Pacific West plans to support in the future, but it's unclear how much support the fund intends to give.

Pacific West has no staff, according to the deposition. The fund's board consists of Mr. Tarver, his son, and his daughter. A company owned by Mr. Tarver gets $60,000 a year to manage Pacific West, the Iowa attorney general's office says.

Besides Pacific West, other Watson & Hughey clients that have used sweepstakes include the American Heart Disease Prevention Foundation, Project Cure Inc./Center for Alternative Cancer Research, the Walker Cancer Institute, United Cancer Council, and Cancer Fund of America. None of the groups meets philanthropic standards set by the Better Business Bureau—because they are too new, haven't provided clear information about their charitable activities, or spend more than 50 percent of their income on fund raising and administrative expenses, some as high as 98 percent. The established American Cancer Society, by contrast, uses less than 25 percent of its income for these purposes.

Many donors mistakenly believe they are helping established charities, such as the American Heart Association, by giving to groups with similar-sounding names.

Charles L. Israel, an 81-year-old retired San Diego resident and longtime Red Cross worker, twice sent off $7 last year to the American Heart Disease Prevention Foundation. "I have a heart condition myself, and I thought this group was part of the [American] Heart Association," he says.

The letters Mr. Israel received contained a black-ruled box with three names, including his, printed inside. "The three individuals named in the cash disbursement box below are Grand Finalists in the $5,000 Cash Bonanza Sweepstakes," the letters said. To claim a prize he had "already won," according to the letters, Mr. Israel was asked to send a check for $7. The letters went on to say that some finalists would receive prizes early in March.

Where do the donations go? According to its 1987 financial report, the American Heart Disease Prevention Foundation had a deficit of about $200,000. It raised $1,262,266, spending $699,000 for fund raising, $109,000 for management and general expenses, and $654,000 for program services. A breakdown of the last category shows that $257,000 went for postage and shipping; $139,000 for printing and publications; $223,000 for miscellaneous expenses; and $35,000 to the Kenneth L. Jordan Heart Foundation—an organization that uses the same Montclair, New Jersey, address as the American Heart Disease Prevention Foundation.

This is an example of "creative allocation of costs," says Larry Campbell, registrar of charitable trusts in the California attorney general's office.

The American Heart Disease Prevention Foundation's executive director, Marvin L.

Bierenbaum—who is also a board member of the Jordan foundation—concedes that the organization only allocated 3 percent of donations to charitable causes in 1987, but he says that share grew to "over 10 percent" last year. He also says his organization decided to use a sweepstakes only after other fund-raising efforts failed. He adds that the foundation's board decided in January to terminate its contract with Watson & Hughey because of "all of the legal challenges by attorneys general." He says he isn't sure which states have filed suits against the foundation or how many suits are pending.

Some state officials say blue-chip charities themselves are partly to blame for the questionable tactics of the lesser-known groups. "The legitimate charities are frightened to death that the public might discover that there is such a thing as fund-raising costs," says David Ormstedt, a Connecticut assistant attorney general.

Accounting-Rule Change

The accounting profession, at the urging of many major charities, adopted a rule change in 1987 that permits some fund-raising expenses to be allocated to "public education," Mr. Ormstedt says. This makes it hard to determine what percentage of donations actually goes for fund raising. Many charities using sweepstakes allocate 50 percent to 70 percent of their contest costs to this category, he adds. Often the only thing educational is a line or two in sweepstakes letters telling people to "maintain ideal weight," or some such advice.

Established charity groups also have fought states' efforts to restrict how donations are spent. In 1984, the U.S. Supreme Court ruled unconstitutional a Maryland law restricting the percentage of donations that can be used for fund raising. Last year the high court also struck down a North Carolina law that required charities to disclose to donors what part of their contribution went to good works. Independent Sector, Inc., a Washington, D.C., umbrella group of 650 national charities, had rallied opposition to both laws.

For now, the biggest hope in stopping the spread of charity sweepstakes letters lies in the federal action against Pacific West, Watson & Hughey, and Mr. Stone. On March 16, postal-service attorneys will argue in a hearing before an administrative law judge in Washington that the defendants engaged in a scheme to obtain money through the mail by means of false representation and an illegal lottery. The outcome will decide the fate of Pacific West's undelivered Kansas mail.

"This is, in effect, a test case," says Timothy Mahoney, a postal inspector who has handled the investigation. "If it succeeds, there might be others." But he says he isn't overly confident. "It isn't a black-and-white case."

Relating Research on Deceptiveness Law to Ethics in Advertising

Ivan L. Preston

To discuss my research on advertising law in a program on ethics has required subduing an incongruity not nearly so thorny as it first appeared. I study how society tells advertisers what they *must* do, while ethics involves decisions about what they need not do yet feel they *should*. How, then, can legal research contribute to the development of ethics?

The answer begins with the fact that ethical choices *can* be made with respect to the law—not about being subject to it, but about coping with that subjection. An advertiser may decide that a first ethical step is to choose voluntarily to learn and know the law, so as to obey it and to take full competitive advantage of all actions permissible within it.

A problem, however, is that deceptiveness law is obscure to the advertisers, as demonstrated by their unpreparedness and lack of understanding in numerous cases. How, then, do they carry out an ethical choice to know the law when it is overly difficult to understand? And for that matter, need one feel ethically bound to obey a law that one cannot sufficiently comprehend?

An appropriate ethical choice might be that parties subject to law are bound to know it and must make whatever effort is required, no matter the difficulty. The study of such a topic certainly seems ripe for an ethicist to pursue, but I am not a scholar in that area. My work, rather, aims at eliminating the need for such pursuit by eliminating the obscurity in the first place.

The problem has been created, ironically, through the agencies' and courts' admirable diligence in conducting so many cases. I am referring principally to the Federal Trade Commission (FTC) and to Lanham Act cases brought privately by advertisers in federal courts. Actions by the states are not unimportant, but are fewer than at the FTC and typically reflect the latter. The self-regulatory activities of the Better Business Bureau appear potentially significant but produce informal reports of too little detail to permit fruitful study.

As the addition of individual trees eventually creates a deep forest, the regulators and Lanham courts compile case records that reach formidable proportions. But they do not compile, at least not publicly, road maps to help travelers navigate through their forests. The result leaves observers in the dark on many issues—for example, guidelines would be useful for the types of evidence needed to show what claims are conveyed by ads.

The specific interest of FTC watchers in knowing the requirements for acceptable surveys has been illustrated by their frequent mention of a set of factors from a 1975 decision (Bristol-Myers, 1975, p. 744). Despite its being old, outdated, incomplete, and explicitly represented as applying no more broadly than "in reaching this decision," the list has been valued by observers because it's the only one there is. Nothing illustrates the need for updated guidelines more than the forced reliance on that list.

There are also the numerous spectacles of advertisers, and sometimes the FTC staff, too, making frivolous attempts to defend or prosecute their positions. I am referring not to the first time a point has occurred but, rather, to points missed from previous cases or other obvious sources—for example, the attempt by Listerine (Warner Lambert, 1975) to prove it could prevent and cure coughs and colds through a study done on guinea pigs. The animals being untrained in gargling, the product was directed through tubes into their stomachs, a test the company then swore under oath was a reasonable basis for confirming Listerine's effect in human throats (pp. 1451–52, 1507). Another rejected test was on rabbits, which inhaled the formula for four to six hours, resulting in far more exposure to the product than humans would receive (pp. 1451, 1507). A third among other rejected items was marketing evidence showing that consumers *thought* Listerine was effective (pp. 1495–96).

This illustrates the general problem of "equivalence," meaning proof can come only from evidence examining what is claimed (Preston, 1987a, pp. 287–89, 292; 1989b, p. 549). Although the point was not made in previous FTC cases, it was obvious to experts in the relevant scientific area. And following the Listerine case were others in which this point now established on the FTC record was nonetheless again missed. Anacin was tested on post-partum pain while the advertising claims were for headache pain (American Home Products, 1975, pp. 381–83). It also was tested in a study of a formula only similar but not identical to Anacin's commercially available form (p. 382).

Sterling Drug (1983, pp. 771–72) also had a test rejected for not using Cope's exact formula. And it compared Cope against nothing but a placebo, which could not support a claim of superiority over other analgesics (p. 772). Studies for Anacin (American Home Products, 1981, pp. 304–05), Bayer (Sterling Drug, 1983, p. 765), Bufferin (Bristol-Myers, 1983, p. 340), and Aspercreme (Thompson Medical, 1984, pp. 744–45) showing speed and amount of absorption of analgesics into the bloodstream were held irrelevant as measures of claimed speed and degree of relief they provide.

Lanham cases also demonstrate the equivalence failure. One involved the absorption problem (Ciba-Geigy, 1985), while in another a pain reliever and its competitor were never actually compared, although the ad claim was comparative (American Home Products, 1978). Another pain reliever study was of grip strength and joint stiffness, even though the ads made no claims about those benefits (American Home Products, 1978). A study involved a version of a product sold in Italy but not in the United States and was done inappropriately on animals (Upjohn, 1986). A study testing effects at prescription dose levels had no relevance for effects claimed for the nonprescription version, and other tests examined all side effects lumped together and so could not substantiate a claim about one side effect in particular (American Home Products, 1987).

These and other instances of nonequivalence represent only one of various areas in which advertisers' defenses have been frivolous, perhaps not in the legal sense, but certainly frivolous in that the companies should have known of their likely failure on the prior bases of both expert scientific practice and legal precedent. When they do not know what they ought to know, it may happen because advertising law is obscure and difficult to comprehend.

Of course, frivolous arguments may not always be pressed in ignorance. Some advertisers may know that their evidence fails to prove, or even disproves, their claims. They may be hoping proof can be deemed established by the mere existence of scientific-appearing evidence, whether or not actually scientific. Even in such cases, however, the advertisers fail to know something they ought to know, which is that the ploy doesn't work. They may know what the words of preceding cases say, but not believe they really mean it.

The role of my legal research, then, has been to make deceptiveness law clear and its outcome undeniable. My working assumption has been that the various points are not unclear because they are really unclear, but only because they are deeply embedded. There are many cases, often lengthy, up to 300-plus pages, and when I started there was no index to them.

Michelangelo once remarked, it's said, that the sculpture was already there, inside the block of granite; all he did was cut away the excess stone to reveal it. That is a good way of describing what my analyses are meant to do. The analogy is not quite apt, because you need not cut away the outside pages of a decision to see the inside. Yet somehow the embedding is happening, and people are not seeing the content; it's as if it's really hidden.

Points are discussed in a bewildering number of places, and with different language and sometimes in contradictory ways. Thus, the need is not only to locate the different comments but to reconcile them into a summary that is richer than any of its parts. I have found the contradictoriness usually to be more apparent than real, and the patterns obscure only because they were embedded. Identifying categories and using them to classify content permits the creation of those missing roadmaps to the deceptiveness forest.

Exhibit 1 is helpful in explaining how I have worked. The three items in the center are the three areas of evidence required to prove deceptiveness. The FTC or plaintiff advertiser must first show what the ad or other item of commercial speech consists of, meaning its explicit content. Next it must show

EXHIBIT 1

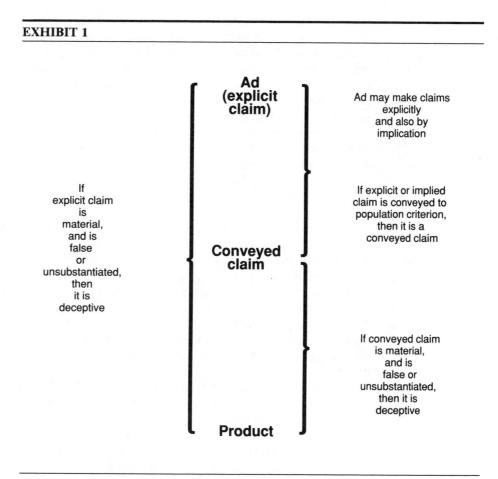

what claims that content conveys into consumers' heads, often including more than what is explicitly stated. Finally it must show the facts about the product or other advertised item that are relevant to the conveyed claims.

Next come decisions about the relationships between these items, indicated by the brackets, each linking a different pair of the three. The bracket on the left may seem intuitively the path to deceptiveness, but it involves only the explicit content. If that content is discrepant from the product, there can be a violation; but such analysis fails to incorporate all the possible conveyed claims, including the implied. Thus, the proper analysis is represented by the two brackets on the right, going from ad to product by detouring in two steps through the conveyed claim. First, the conveyed claim must be determined, then its relationship to the product facts must be determined.

My research has focused on the areas where disputes occur. They do not occur over what the ads explicitly say, which is easy to determine. But the other two types of facts are much less easily confirmed and have produced arguments going on for page after page in the published decisions.

The evidence used to determine conveyed meanings is of two sorts, intrinsic, meaning nothing more than the ad itself, and extrinsic, meaning any other evidence of consumers' perceptions of the message. The FTC is privileged by law to use nothing but intrinsic evidence to identify any and all conveyed meanings, including implied ones. One of my analyses (Preston, 1986), therefore, examines all the case facts and decisions leading to the commission's acquisition of that right. The study also examines the FTC's decision to forego that right and insist on extrinsic evidence in certain circumstances. In addition, rules compel the commission to recognize valid extrinsic evidence when advertisers introduce it, even though it might wish to decide on intrinsic evidence alone.

These are important points for advertisers, because sole reliance on intrinsic evidence gives the commission great scope to rule as it pleases about what message is conveyed. Also, unopposed valid extrinsic evidence gives a great advantage to whichever party holds it. This means advertisers should possess, preferably before running their claims, valid extrinsic evidence for possible later use, or, if that cannot be done, they should know it early enough to consider prudently tempering their use of the claim. Undoubtedly the most important thing advertisers need to know in the entire area of deceptive advertising is what claims they are conveying, or if they do not, to realize they do not.

Another of my analyses (Preston, 1987b) is on the types of extrinsic evidence used in FTC cases, and on what makes each type valid or invalid, or better or worse than some opposing evidence. Valid consumer surveys make the best extrinsic evidence because they examine the precise ad under challenge. Expert testimony is reliable when supported by evidence about the specific ads, but less well-supported opinion from experts or from other sources, such as textbooks or dictionary definitions, often has little influence because it is based on messages generally, rather than the challenged message in particular.

What is at stake here is the error, which the records show occurs frequently, of relying on findings about consumer response that are later invalidated, often for being based on surveys whose methods are invalidated. My synthesis is that surveys are thrown out for two reasons: they are irrelevant or methodologically faulty. While the latter is a matter of expertise in behavioral study, the irrelevance occurs because the evidence is not chosen to fit the legal requirements. In all of my work I have tried to emphasize the role of consumer research in the context of legal proceedings, because it is so common a mistake to assume it should be handled in court the same way it is handled in contexts where consumer researchers typically function.

The analysis of extrinsic evidence is one of several I call "catalog" articles, because they involve reading every decision and collecting and synthesizing all comments into summaries and generalizations intended to remove the material from its former embedded state. Because any single comment may give a misleading conclusion about how the given point is handled generally, I felt sampling would not suffice. When the overall record is in hand, the synthesis usually shows the conclusions to lean predominantly in a certain direction. For example, although the expert opinion referred to above has been successful as evidence of conveyed meaning, the total record demonstrates that its use overall has not been a reliably good way to win points.

A further project on the topic of surveys developed because the state of the art shows different experts reasonably disagreeing on aspects of method (the nature of samples, for instance, or formulation of coding schemes). Because of this, opposing counsel have long since learned that, instead of directly disputing their opponents' findings, they may take the prior step of disputing how they arrived at them. To eliminate the method means never having to cope with the findings. Accordingly, the case records are full of fights over the acceptability of a variety of methodological choices.

Because of these disagreements, another analysis (Richards & Preston, 1987) has explored the possibility of a dispute resolution procedure by which participants would negotiate, prehearing, on how to collect evidence. They would then agree at least informally to make no later objection to those choices. There has been at the FTC at least one instance of such cooperation. The advertiser upon seeing the survey results consented to the FTC's allegations and waived its right to a hearing, which could mean it saved considerable time and work that would have led to the same result, anyway. The cooperation was accomplished through informal contacts, however, whereas our analysis has proposed formal procedures to be publicized widely and so incorporated into many advertisers' planning at an early stage.

While the research items to this point have involved how conveyed messages are determined, another catalog analysis (Preston, 1989a) has examined what those messages are. Explicit messages typically are found to be conveyed and, therefore, rarely are disputed. Attention, thus, was turned to the more controversial question of the implied meanings conveyed. The FTC has never recognized implications as coming in separate types, and, in fact, it has frequently failed to identify whether particular messages were conveyed explicitly or implied.

Nonetheless, it has been possible to identify 15 types of implications prosecuted by the commission. The typical process starts with a true explicit claim, but, because consumers have a natural tendency to see additional content implied, and because they expect advertisers to make strong claims, they see an additional claim conveyed by implication. Although such implications may be true, the ones singled out by the FTC, of course, are held to be false.

There is the "proof implication," for example, in which the ad explicitly mentions a test or survey for the product claim, leading consumers to see implied that such evidence *proves* the claim. Merit cigarettes claimed explicitly that 60 percent of surveyed consumers found them equal or better than Triumph. Omitted was that 24 percent said equal while 36 percent said better. The remaining 40 percent said Triumph was better, meaning 64 percent called

Triumph equal or better. Triumph thus won, which Merit had not explicitly denied. But Merit was held to have claimed by implication to have won, because of the way in which consumers will naturally expand a message.

Classifying implications into types enhances ability to predict in advance what messages ads are likely to convey. Advertisers may say they don't know what implications they are creating and, therefore, should not be responsible for them. My analysis suggests the opposite view—that in most cases advertisers can compare their explicit content to what has produced false implications in the past, and so have a high degree of predictability about the implied messages their new ads are likely to convey.

As in all of my research, I am striving to enable advertisers to know the past and so predict the future with confidence. There is the possibility that advertisers will feel inconvenienced by my recognition of types of implications, since it undercuts the chance for them to claim they cannot predict consumer response with certainty. But in the longer run it should be beneficial for them, because they will no longer *have* such uncertainty.

The American Association of Advertising Agencies (AAAA) sponsored an analysis of conveyed meanings (Jacoby, Hoyer, & Sheluga, 1980) which argued that implied meanings should be blamed on consumers, because they are not literally in the ads but exist solely within consumers' heads through miscomprehension of the ads' literal content. They are not the fault of the advertisers and, therefore, should not be called deceptiveness and so not be violations of law.

Two analyses (Preston & Richards, 1986, 1988) have been done in rejoinder to that argument, the first of which points out flaws in the AAAA's argument. My co-author and I expressed sympathy for the misfortune of blaming advertisers for claims they didn't intend to produce and didn't know they had produced. However, we suggested the AAAA should search for a better argument, because its proposal was defective. For one reason among several, fault is legally irrelevant; long-established procedure allows the law to prohibit claims, even when advertisers made them in complete innocence. For another, advertisers are not necessarily faultless in regard to consumer behavior if they can predict such behavior in advance and then write ad content that will cause consumers to see the additional implied meanings.

Later, an economic analysis of deceptiveness law (Craswell, 1985) argued that advertisers should not have to bear the high monetary cost of correcting false claims unless the benefits outweighed the costs. We (Preston and Richards, 1988) expressed appreciation for the general need for benefits to exceed costs, which regulators may not always have appreciated. But we invoked our earlier analysis of miscomprehension to argue that correction costs would typically not be high. We pointed out that, since advertisers seem at times to use carefully contrived messages to induce miscomprehension, at a probable high cost in copywriter time, there should be no monetary cost (perhaps even a net gain!) for them simply to write claims with full clarity in the first place.

Turning to the burden of facts about the product, another catalog analysis (Preston, 1987a) examined FTC cases involving the use of tests and surveys to establish such facts. It did not involve all cases where product facts must be established; however, while many such efforts are easy and uncontroversial, those involving formal types of factfinding are the ones where controversy occurs.

A factor complicating the area is that ads refer in different ways to evidence for their claims. An ad can show a test or demonstration in progress, which can tell consumers they are actually seeing the claim being proved. Or the ad can cite the existence of a test or survey, thus conveying that proof exists. The ad can show items—such as laboratory instruments, people with white coats, and the like—that imply formal types of proof without saying so explicitly. Finally, the ad can simply make a factual claim, which, although adding nothing explicitly or implicitly about evidence, is held by the FTC to mean to consumers that evidence appropriate to prove the claim, of whatever sort it might be, existed when the ad was first made.

The area also is complicated because the type of evidence necessary for proof varies among claims and products. If a test or survey or other evidence is demonstrated or referred to in the ad, or alluded to by indirect means, then that type must exist to avoid a violation. If the conveyance to consumers is merely that the appropriate evidence exists, then the type must be what experts in the given product field find suitable. The latter is a messy area, in that the type of evidence suitable for testing automobile tires, say, will differ from that for testing wine or aspirin or detergent or cola preference.

Nonetheless, synthesis of the entire body of cases reveals generalizations across all or many products. The question of equivalence discussed earlier, for example, represents a widely applicable standard. While tests of tires on one road surface may not prove claims for overall performance on all surfaces, so may a test of a detergent on one type of clothing be equally lacking as evidence of overall performance. The products are different, the tests are different, the required experts are different, and so on, but the principles of evidence are quite the same.

What is at stake for advertisers is that the predictability of such principles may help them avoid thinking wrongly that they were sufficiently covered. Just as they may find that their supposed proof of claims conveyed or not conveyed is rejected, so may their evidence that presumably proves those claims be rejected. The record shows the advertisers often naively uninformed about the quality of evidence required for substantiation.

The latest catalog analysis (Preston, 1989b) did an omnibus job of examining Lanham Act cases in the manner of all the previous analyses, which had covered only the FTC. The smaller number of Lanham cases made coverage in a single article feasible. Although Lanham and FTC differ in important ways, notably in procedural matters, they are so similar in my interest areas that the various topics and conclusions will not be rediscussed here.

My most recent analysis (Preston, 1990) presents a definition intended to include all steps required to define deceptiveness legally. Its 500-plus words contrast it greatly to two definitions debated at the FTC, which call an ad deceptive if "there is a representation, omission, or practice that . . . is likely to mislead consumers acting reasonably under the circumstances, and . . . is material" (Cliffdale, 1984), or if there is "a tendency or capacity to mislead a substantial number of consumers in a material way" (Cliffdale, 1984; Bailey dissent). The new formulation defines the steps not only conceptually, but also operationally. The latter is not typical in the law literature, yet, in practice, if there are no operations there can be no legal conclusions.

The contribution I am attempting with the definition, as with all my other analyses, is simply to inform. All of it is work that the FTC could do, and doing it would carry out its congressional mandate to *prevent* deceptiveness. I am grateful to have been left a vacuum to work in, but I am concerned about not reaching as many people as an official statement would. The best results would come if the FTC, and the advertising industry also, played major roles in disseminating these roadmaps of the forest.

REFERENCES

American Home Products, FTC Decisions 98 (1981), pp. 136–427.

American Home Products v. *Johnson & Johnson*, 577 F. 2d 160–72 (1978).

American Home Products. v. *Johnson & Johnson*, 654 F. Supp. 568–92 (1981).

Bristol-Myers, *FTC Decisions* 85 (1975), pp. 688–754.

Bristol-Myers, *FTC Decisions* 102 (1983), pp. 21–394.

Ciba-Geigy v. *Thompson Medical*, 672 F. Supp. 679–98 (1985).

Cliffdale, *FTC Decisions* 103 (1994), pp. 110–202.

Craswell, Richard A. "Interpreting Deceptive Advertising." *Boston University Law Review* 65 (1985), pp. 657–732.

Jacoby, Jacob; Wayne D. Hoyer; and David A. Sheluga. *Miscomprehension of Televised Communications.* (New York: American Association of Advertising Agencies), 1980.

Preston, Ivan L. "Data-Free at the FTC? How the Federal Trade Commission Decides Whether Extrinsic Evidence of Deceptiveness Is Required." *American Business Law Journal* 24 (Fall, 1986), pp. 359–76.

————. "Description and Analysis of FTC Order Provisions Resulting from References in Advertising to Tests or Surveys." *Pepperdine Law Review* 14, no. 2 (1987a), pp. 229–312.

————. "Extrinsic Evidence in Federal Trade Commission Deceptiveness Cases." *Columbia Business Law Review*, 1987 (No. 3), pp. 633–94.

————. "The FTC's Identification of Implications as Constituting Deceptive Advertising." *Cincinnati Law Review* 57, no. 4 (1989a), pp. 1243–1310.

————. "False or Deceptive Advertising under the Lanham Act: Analysis of Factual Findings and Types of Evidence." *Trademark Reporter* 79 (July–August 1989b), pp. 508–53.

————. "The Definition of Deceptiveness in Advertising and Other Commercial Speech." *Catholic University Law Review* 39, no. 4 (1990).

Preston, Ivan L., and Jef I. Richards. "Consumer Miscomprehension as a Challenge to FTC Prosecutions of Deceptive Advertising." 19 (Spring 1986), pp. 605–35.

————. "Consumer Miscomprehension and Deceptive Advertising: A Response to Professor Craswell." *Boston University Law Review*, 69 (March 1988), pp. 431–38.

Richards, Jef I., and Ivan L. Preston, "Quantitative Research: A Dispute Resolution Process for FTC Advertising Regulation." *Oklahoma Law Review* 40 (1987), pp. 593–619.

Sterling Drug, *FTC Decisions* 102 (1983), pp. 395–806.

Thompson Medical, *FTC Decisions* 104 (1984), pp. 648–844.

Upjohn v. *Riahom*, 641 F. Supp., 1209–27 (1986).

Warner-Lambert, *FTC Decisions* 86 (1975), pp. 1398–1515.

Children as Consumers: The Ethics of Children's Television Advertising*

Lynn Sharp Paine

Television sponsors and broadcasters began to identify children as a special target audience for commercial messages in the mid-1960s.[1] Within only a few years, children's television advertising emerged as a controversial issue. Concerned parents began to speak out and to urge the networks to adopt codes of ethics governing children's advertising. By 1970, the issue had attracted the attention of the Federal Trade Commission (FTC) and the Federal Communications Commission (FCC).† The FCC received some 80,000 letters in support of a proposed rule-making "looking toward the elimination of sponsorship and commercial content in children's programming."[2] Public attention to the controversy over children's television advertising peaked between 1978 and 1980 when the FTC, under its authority to regulate unfair and deceptive advertising, held public hearings on its proposal to ban televised advertising directed to or seen by large numbers of young children. More recently, Congress and regulators have focused on limiting the quantity of advertising in children's programming, particularly on so-called program-length commercials or entire programs created to sell children's toys.[3]

As this brief chronology indicates, children's television advertising has been a continuing focus of controversy. In this chapter I propose some explanations for why this is so and argue that there are good ethical reasons for the criticism of child-oriented advertising. In the process of this investigation, I will nec-

---

* A longer version of this paper appeared in the *Business and Professional Ethics Journal* 3, nos. 3 & 4 (Spring/Summer 1984), pp. 119–45.

† Action for Children's Television (ACT), a Cambridge, Massachusetts, nonprofit organization founded by Peggy Charren in 1968, was largely responsible for putting children's television and children's advertising on the agendas of these agencies.

essarily turn my attention to the role of consumers in a market economy, to the capacities of children as they relate to consumer activities, and to the relationships between adults and children within the family. First, however, a few points of clarification are in order.

It is important to bear in mind that the ethical propriety of children's advertising is distinct from its legality. Even if advertisers have a constitutional right to advertise lawful products to young children in a nondeceptive way, it is not necessarily the right thing to do. In this chapter, I take no position on the scope of advertisers' First Amendment rights to freedom of speech or on the desirability of particular proposals to regulate children's advertising.[4] I am primarily interested in the ethical questions raised by this practice. The fact that constitutional, political, or administrative considerations make it impossible or unwise to impose legal restrictions on children's advertising does not eliminate the underlying ethical questions or shield advertisers from responsibility for addressing them.

The term *children's advertising* refers to advertising targeted or directed to young children, particularly children under the age of eight.[5] Generally speaking, these are the children who lack the conceptual abilities required for making consumer decisions.[6] Through commercial messages, advertisers attempt to persuade young children to want and, ultimately, to request their products. Although current voluntary guidelines prohibit advertisers from explicitly instructing children to request that their parents buy advertised products,[7] child-oriented advertising is designed to induce favorable attitudes that result in such requests.

Frequently, child-oriented advertisements utilize themes and techniques that appeal particularly to children: animation, clowns, magic, fantasy effects, superheroes, and special musical themes.[8] Usually, they involve such products as cereals, sweets, and toys.[9] The critical point in understanding child-directed advertising, however, is not simply the product, the particular themes and techniques employed, or the composition of the audience viewing the ad, but whether the advertiser intends to sell to or through children. Advertisers routinely segment their markets and target their advertising.[10] The question at issue is whether young children are appropriate targets.

CHILDREN AS CONSUMERS

Child-oriented advertising challenges traditional assumptions about the proper role of young children in the marketplace. At common law, for example, children are permitted to disaffirm or avoid most contracts because of their lack of business sophistication and vulnerability to exploitation. A different view is reflected in the argument supporting children's advertising advanced by the Association of National Advertisers (ANA), the American Association of Advertising Agencies (AAAA), and the American Advertising Federation (AAF):

Perhaps the single most important benefit of advertising to children is that it provides information to the child himself, information which advertisers try to gear to the child's interests and on an appropriate level of understanding. This allows the child to learn what products are available, to know their differences, and to begin to make decisions about them based on his own personal wants and preferences. . . . Product diversity responds to these product preferences and ensures that it is the consumer himself who dictates the ultimate success or failure of a given product offering.[11]

Supposed benefits to children are a central aspect of this argument. Equally significant is the depiction of children as typical market actors. They are represented as a class of consumers distinguished primarily by their product preferences. That children may require messages tailored to their level of understanding is acknowledged, but children's conceptual abilities are not regarded as having any other special significance. Advocates of children's advertising argue that it gives children "the same access to the marketplace which adults have, but keyed to their specific areas of interest."[12]

Viewing young children as simply a segment of the market obscures the problematic nature of advertising to them. Indeed, it appears almost unfair to deprive children of televised information about products they might want. But this view neglects significant differences between adults and young children. These differences, which go far beyond product preferences, affect children's capacities to function as responsible consumers and suggest several arguments for regarding advertising to them as inappropriate. For purposes of this discussion, the most critical differences are young children's conceptions of self, time, and money.

Child development literature generally acknowledges that the emergence of a sense of one's self as an independent human being is a central experience of childhood that continues through adolescence.[13] This vague notion, "having a sense of one's self as an independent human being," encompasses a broad range of capacities gradually mastered in the normal course of maturation: recognition of one's physical self as distinct from one's mother and acceptance of responsibility for one's actions, for example. While mastery manifests itself as self-confidence and self-control in an ever-widening range of activities and relationships, it depends more fundamentally on the emergence of an ability to see oneself as oneself. The reflexive nature of consciousness—the peculiar ability to monitor, study, assess, and reflect on oneself and even on one's reflections—underlies the ability to make rational choices. It permits people to reflect on their desires, to evaluate them, and to have desires about what they desire. It permits them to see themselves as one among others and as engaging in relationships with others. Young children lack, or have only in nascent form, this ability to take a higher-order perspective on themselves and to see themselves as having desires or preferences they might wish to cultivate, suppress, or modify. They also lack the self-control that would make it possible to act on these higher order desires if they had them.

Closely related to the sense of self, if not implicit in self-reflection, is the sense of time. Children's understanding of time as it relates both to their own existence and to the events around them differs from that of adults. Young children have limited abilities to project themselves into the future and to imagine themselves having different preferences in the future. Besides having extremely short time horizons, children are struggling with time in a more fundamental sense. Intrigued with "time" questions, they are testing conceptions of time as well as learning to gauge its passage by conventional markers.[14] Young children's developing sense of time goes hand in hand with their developing sense of self. Their capacities for self-reflection, for evaluating their desires, and for making rational choices are intimately related to their understanding of their own continuity in time.

Finally, young children lack facility in the skills of calculation and do not understand the value of money.[15] In my experience, many young children are stymied by the fundamentals of arithmetic and do not understand ordinal relations among even relatively small amounts, let alone the more esoteric notions of selling in exchange for money.[16] Young children, moreover, do not engage in "counter-argument" when faced with commercial messages.[17] Unlike mature viewers who regard advertising critically, noting possible exaggerations and incomplete information, young children are quite credulous.[18] They place indiscriminate trust in the commercial characters who present products to them,[19] and they are overly optimistic about the satisfaction advertised products will bring them.[20]

All of these differences point to serious problems with the advertisers' claim that children's advertising enables children "to learn what products are available, to know their differences, and to begin to make decisions about them based on [their] own personal wants and preferences."[21] Ignore, for the moment, the fact that existing children's advertising, which concentrates so heavily on sugared foods and toys, does little either to inform children about the range of available products or the differences among them.[22] Even if children's advertising were more informative, the critical difficulty would remain.

Because of their immature conceptions of self, time, and money, children know very little about their own wants and preferences—or about rational mobilization of their economic resources to satisfy them. Lacking the capacity for critical reflection, they are unable to assess, modify, or even curtail their felt desires for the sake of more important or enduring desires that they have or expect to have in the future. Moreover, they lack the conceptual wherewithal to research and deliberate about the relative merits of alternative expenditures in light of their economic resources.[23] There is thus a serious question whether advertising has or can have much at all to do with children beginning "to make decisions about [products] based on [their] own personal wants and preferences."[24] It is doubtful that advertising actually delivers or could deliver to children the benefits described in the advertisers' claims.

CONSUMER SOVEREIGNTY AND ADVERTISING TO CHILDREN

Although the advertisers' argument appeals initially to advertising's benefits to children, it appeals ultimately to the principle of consumer sovereignty.[25]

Of venerable heritage, this principle reflects the twin sources of the market's moral justification: respect for the individual and welfare maximization. According to its supporters, children's advertising can "ensure that it is the consumer himself [the child] who dictates the ultimate success or failure of a given product offering."[26] Under the principle of consumer sovereignty, it is consumers' preferences that should determine what products succeed in the marketplace. But *who* is the "consumer" when children's products are at issue? Are children's preferences the only ones that should count? Children may eat the candy or play with the toys advertised to them, but does this qualify them to be the arbiters of the success of these products?

The view that young children should be seen as sovereign consumers implies for parents a rather minimal role in their children's consumer activities. They become, as one marketer put it, their children's "purchasing agents."[27] Anyone who agrees that children's conceptions of self, time, and money do not equip them to make responsible consumer decisions and who respects the interlocking interests of parents and their children will find the notion of children as sovereign consumers—and the parental role it implies—problematic.

When parents buy products for their offspring it is much more accurate to regard both parent and child as the relevant consumers. Both have interests in the purchase. Not only does the parent supply the funds and make the decision to buy while the child uses the product, but the parent derives satisfaction from the child's enjoyment of the product. As a consequence of the common and interlocking interests of parents and children, a product that is well-priced, wanted by the child, and wanted by the parent for the child is much more satisfactory than a product desired by the child but not by the parent. Whether we view the child alone as the relevant consumer, or include the parent as well, can make a significant difference in which products we regard as successful and which as unsuccessful. It will also make a difference in our assessment of the contribution children's advertising makes to consumer satisfaction.

Children's advertising has been most commonly challenged by appeals to general ethical principles requiring veracity, fairness, respect for persons, and avoidance of harm.[28] A somewhat different critique can be grounded on the principle of consumer sovereignty, the very principle implicitly invoked by advocates of children's advertising. Rather than enhancing consumer well-being, however, I suggest that children's advertising, like misleading advertising, may actually diminish it. Taking a realistic view of children's decision-making capacities and acknowledging the interdependence of children's and parents' desires and preferences will lead, I think, to this conclusion. To develop this suggestion, it is necessary to review how children's advertising works.

HOW CHILDREN'S ADVERTISING WORKS

According to a recent textbook on marketing, the purpose of advertising is to "communicate information, imagery, and purchasing incentives" to prospective buyers.[29] As applied to children's advertising, this statement is not quite accurate. Typically, the prospective buyers of products advertised to children are adults, who may never see the advertisements, and not the children to whom the information and imagery are communicated. In contrast to advertising addressed to adults who will themselves decide whether to purchase the advertised product, child-oriented advertising provides purchasing incentives to individuals who can influence, but who cannot make, the ultimate purchase decision. The desire for the product and the decision to buy lie with different individuals.

Although advertising through children poses the problem of linking children's desires with their parents' purchase decisions, it is apparently effective to sell certain products. From the frequency with which advertisements for sugared foods and toys, for example, are targeted to children, we can infer that some companies believe they sell more toys and sweets by advertising to children than by advertising to adults.[30] This must mean that many children ask their parents to buy toys and sweets they see advertised on television and that a significant number of parents accede to these requests.[31] The effectiveness of children's advertising, thus, is apparently based on children requesting advertised products they would not otherwise request and on parents purchasing items they would not otherwise purchase—either because they would not have known about the products or they would not have purchased them had they not been requested by the child.

Children's suggestibility and indiscriminate enthusiasm for the products they see on television can be attributed to their immature concepts of self, time, and money discussed earlier, as well as their failure to understand economic exchange, the motives of sellers, and the difference between television fantasy and reality.[32] Parents' responsiveness to children's requests is attributable to parents' affection for their children and the positive value of shared emotional experiences. Generally speaking, parents want to please their children and enjoy sharing their immediate and obvious delight at receiving something they want. A parent may buy what he regards as a worthless or overpriced item when requested by his child, provided it is not too costly in absolute terms and its purchase would not seriously interfere with other parental desires, when he would not buy the product on the basis of its merits assessed independently of the child's wishes.[33] Parents' inclinations to see their children's immediate desires satisfied may operate quite independently of their concern for their children's abiding interests over the longer term. Sometimes parental desires for children's immediate pleasure and for their long-term well-being conflict. Rational, responsible parenthood may require parents to refuse certain requests for the sake of their children's own longer-term or future desires.[34]

Advertising directed to children affects the consumer decisions faced by parents in two main ways. It increases the number of requests to which they must respond, and it alters the factors relevant to their purchase decisions. Every purchase decision that parents face requires consideration from several points of view: the family budget, other comparable products, the interests and needs of various family members. But when a child initiates a purchase decision by making a request, a new factor is introduced. In addition to all the considerations that would be relevant had the potential purchase come directly to the parent's attention, the parent must also take into account the child's express desire for the item and the parent's own predisposition to satisfy that desire. The child's potential unhappiness over the denial of the request is not the critical factor, although, by the same token, the strength of the child's desire for the product cannot be totally ignored.

For purposes of this discussion, a parent's purchase rationales may be classified into two broad categories. *Child-satisfaction* reasons are those stemming from the parent's desire to satisfy the child's request. *Product-related* reasons are those which would govern the parent's purchase decision in the absence of the child's request. Product-related reasons are not necessarily unrelated to the child. This category might include the product's value for developing the child's interests and capacities, or the parent's belief that the child would like the product, as well as more general financial considerations.

Employing this vocabulary, we can now say that the effectiveness of children's advertising can be attributed, in part, to parents' child-satisfaction motivation. Even when parents have no product-related motivation to purchase a product, their child-satisfaction desires may be strong enough to supply the motivation to buy. Children's advertising may also promote sales by channeling to parents information that would not otherwise reach them. Parents may buy items they hear of through their children for product-related reasons and not only for child-satisfaction reasons.

Given the variety of consumer preferences, we can assume that both of these explanations for the success of children's advertising are operative. Certainly there may be occasions on which parents are glad to learn of products their children point out and willingly buy them for product-related reasons. However, it would be unwarranted to assume that most, or even a large proportion, of the sales resulting from children's advertising can be explained by children's drawing attention to products their parents want to buy for product-related reasons. Parents' natural inclinations to enhance their children's welfare and to satisfy their children's desires guarantee that they will be generally attentive and receptive to consumer goods available to express those dispositions. It seems much more likely that the effectiveness of children's advertising is in large measure attributable to the child-satisfaction motivations supplied by children's requests.

CHILDREN'S ADVERTISING AND CONSUMER SATISFACTION

This analysis suggests that the products advertised to children are ones that would not sell as well if advertised directly to their parents. They are likely to be products many parents would not buy solely for product-related reasons, presumably because product considerations alone are not sufficiently compelling. It also suggests that parents who would not buy if not spurred on by their children are the critical market for children's advertisers. If parents would buy without the motivations provided by their children's requests, advertising to parents should be just as effective as advertising to children.

Parents in the critical group face a difficult decision when advertising arouses their children's interests in consumer products. They must choose between acting on their product-related judgment and on satisfying their child's requests. As Figure 1 shows, if they do not or cannot buy, they will frustrate their children's express wishes and their own wishes to please their children. On the other hand, yielding to their children's desires puts them in the position of acting against their own better judgment.

From the perspective of maximizing consumer satisfaction, the parents' product-related judgment ought to have the greatest weight. Presumably informed by relevant knowledge of product characteristics and by appreciation of the child's longer-term and future interests, the parents' product-related judgment more closely approximates an evaluation of the product's contribution to consumer satisfaction than does the child's desire for the product. Because of the limitations described earlier, it is unlikely that the child's desire represents a reliable judgment of the product's worth to him.

From the perspective of their child's immediate and intense desires, however, parents may be inclined to grant the child's request. Parents who exercise their best consumer judgment and decline to buy may find that their child experiences unhappiness, anger, or disappointment as a result.[35] Parents, thus, face a difficult choice: acting on their product-related judgment may maximize satisfaction over the longer term, but immediate consequences may favor satisfying the child's request.

From the standpoint of consumer satisfaction, child-oriented advertising is quite problematic. Adam Smith's invisible hand hypothesis suggests that profitability or sales may be a good indicator of a company's relative success in satisfying consumers. Whether or not this is true as a general matter,[36] it is

---

FIGURE 1   Child-Oriented Advertising

	Parent's Product-Related Desires	Parent's Child-Satisfaction Desires	Child's Desire for Product
The parent chooses not to buy for product-related reasons	S	U	U
The parent buys the product to satisfy the child but would not buy on product-related grounds	U	S	S

S = Satisfied
U = Unsatisfied

not clear that sales achieved through child-oriented advertising reflect increased consumer well-being. Sales generated by child-focused advertising represent increased consumer satisfaction when parents' product-related judgments correspond with their children's requests. But when, as may frequently be the case, parent's purchase decisions are motivated solely by child-satisfaction reasons, the resulting sales have little to do with enhancing children's and parents' well-being as consumers. In these cases, the merits of the products themselves are relatively unimportant. Whatever positive value is associated with fulfilling the child's wish must be seen as quite incidental to the product, since children can be primed to want or desire a great variety of goods through advertising and other persuasive techniques.[37]

Moreover, child-oriented advertising introduces sources of family conflict and frustration that would not exist if children's products were advertised to adults or not advertised on television at all. For significant numbers of parents, children's advertising has the effect of increasing the occasions on which they rationally and ethically ought to deny their children's requests. Without child-focused advertising, parents would less frequently face the necessity to choose between their children's consumer requests and their own consumer judgments. While it is true that children may develop desires for products they see in advertisements not directed to them, the likelihood is greatly enhanced when the advertising is child-focused.[38]

Some supporters of children's television advertising argue that parental opposition is based on parents' weakness or their reluctance to stand up to their children. They argue that children would be better off if parents refused their children's requests.[39] While urging parents to deny their children's requests is sound advice in a world where children's advertising exists, it is not a satisfactory response to the argument that children's advertising should not encourage the requests in the first place. As Figure 1 suggests, child viewers and their parents would be better off still if there were no child-focused advertising. Moreover, the proffered advice to parents puts advertisers in the morally questionable position of deliberately stimulating in children desires which they acknowledge ought to be denied.

The effects of children's advertising extend far beyond child viewers of commercials and their parents. We have seen that when child-oriented advertising works to the advantage of advertisers, it does so in part because some parents act contrary to their product-related judgments and comply with their children's purchase requests. These purchases contribute to the advertiser's sales goals, but they are not reliable indicators of consumer satisfaction. Indeed, it may be argued that children's advertising contributes ultimately to the misallocation of society's resources. Resources that otherwise would be utilized to produce goods of greater value to consumers are channelled into the production of less desirable goods sold through children.

CHILDREN'S ADVERTISING AND BASIC ETHICAL PRINCIPLES

This evaluation of children's advertising has proceeded from the principle of consumer sovereignty, a principle specific to the market system. As noted earlier, children's advertising has also been criticized from the standpoint of more general ethical principles requiring veracity and fairness and prohibiting harmful conduct. These principles, rooted in our common social life, are what are sometimes called principles of "common morality."[40] Before concluding, it may be useful to mention these critiques.

The principle of veracity, understood as devotion to truth, is much broader than a principle prohibiting deception. Both critics and defenders of children's advertising agree that advertisers should not intentionally deceive children by making false factual statements. Nevertheless, the particular nature of children's conceptual worlds makes it exceedingly likely that child-oriented advertising will lead to false beliefs or to highly improbable product expectations.[41] The central issue is how far advertisers should go to insure that children are not misled by their advertisements.

The fact that children's advertising benefits advertisers while at the same time nourishing false beliefs and unreasonable expectations among children calls into play principles of fairness and respect. Critics have said that advertisers take advantage of children's limited capacities and their suggestibility. According to Michael Pertschuk, former chairman of the FTC, advertisers "seize on the child's trust and exploit it as weakness for their gain."[42] To employ, as the unwitting means to the parent's pocketbook, children who do not understand commercial exchange, who are unable to evaluate their own consumer preferences, and who consequently cannot make consumer decisions based on those preferences fails to respect children's limitations as consumers, and instead capitalizes on them.[43] In the language of Kant, advertisers are not treating children as "ends in themselves" but solely as instruments for their own gain.[44]

Another principle to which appeal has been made by critics of television advertising is the principle against causing harm. Researchers have pointed to such harms as parent-child conflicts over refusals to buy requested products, children's unhappiness and anger when their parents deny their product requests, children's disappointment when advertising-induced expectations are unmet, and unhappiness resulting from children's exposure to commercials portraying lifestyles more affluent than their own.[45] Research indicates that children's advertising does contribute to these outcomes,[46] though there is debate about whether such conflicts and unhappiness should be regarded as harmful.[47]

CONCLUSION

The problems of child-oriented advertising can best be dealt with if advertisers themselves recognize the inappropriateness of targeting children for commercial messages. I have tried to show why, within the context of a market economy, the responsibilities of advertisers to promote consumer satisfaction and not to discourage responsible consumer decisions should lead advertisers away from child-oriented advertising. The problem of what types of advertisements are appropriate and when they should be scheduled provides a challenging design problem for the many creative people in the advertising industry. With appropriate inspiration and incentives, I do not doubt that they can meet the challenge.

Whether appropriate inspiration and incentives will be forthcoming is more doubtful. Children's advertising seems well-entrenched and is backed by powerful economic forces.[48] It is clear that some advertisers do not recognize, or are unwilling to acknowledge, the ethical problems of child-focused advertising.[49] Even advertisers who for ethical reasons would favor the elimination of child-focused advertising may be reluctant to reorient their advertising campaigns because of the costs and risks of doing so. Theoretically, only advertisers whose products would not withstand the scrutiny of adult consumers should lose sales from such a reorientation. In the short run, a general retreat from children's advertising would involve risks of lost revenues for producers, advertisers, and retail sellers of products that would not sell as well when advertised to adults. It is also possible that television networks, stations, and producers of children's shows would lose revenues, and that children's programming might be jeopardized due to the lack of advertisers' interest in commercial time during children's programs.

On the other hand, a shift away from children's advertising to adult advertising could result in even more pressure on existing adult commercial time slots, driving up their prices to a level adequate to subsidize children's programming without loss to the networks. And there are alternative means of financing children's television that could be explored.[50] The extent to which lost revenues and diminished profits would result from recognizing the ethical ideals I have described is largely a question of the ability of all the beneficiaries of children's television advertising to respond creatively. Cooperation among competing advertisers also will be required. But the longer-term effect of relinquishing child-focused advertising would be to move manufacturers, advertisers, and retailers in the direction of products that would not depend for their success on the suggestibility and immaturity of children. In the longer run, the result could be a better use of society's scarce resources.

ENDNOTES

1. Richard P. Adler, "Children's Television Advertising: History of the Issue," in *Children and the Faces of Television*, ed. Edward L. Palmer and Aimee Dorr (New York: Academic Press, 1980), p. 241 (hereafter cited as Palmer and Dorr).

2. Ibid., p. 243.

3. The Children's Television Act of 1990 limits advertising during children's shows to 12 minutes per hour on weekdays and 10½ minutes per hour on weekends. Authorized by the Act to conduct an inquiry into "program-length commercials," the FCC is currently seeking public comment on its proposals. *Children's Television Act of 1990*, Pub. L. No. 101–437, §§102, 104, 104 Stat. 996 (1990) (codified at 47 U.S.C. §303 a-b).

4. For discussion of the constitutionality of banning children's advertising, see C. Edwin Baker, "Commercial Speech: A Problem in the Theory of Freedom," *Iowa Law Review* 62 (October 1976), p. 1; Martin H. Redish, "The First Amendment in the Marketplace: Commercial Speech and the Values of Free Expression," *George Washington Law Review* 39 (1970–1971), p. 429; Gerald J. Thain, "The 'Seven Dirty Words' Decision: A Potential Scrubbrush for Commercials on Children's Television?" *Kentucky Law Journal* 67 (1978–79), p. 947.

5. The FTC has defined "child-oriented television advertising" as "advertising which is in or adjacent to programs either directed to children or programs where children constitute a substantial portion of the audience." "FTC Final Staff Report and Recommendation," *In the Matter of Children's Advertising*, 43 *Fed. Reg.* 17967 (March 31, 1981), p. 2 (hereafter cited as "FTC Final Staff Report"). According to the report, the majority of children's advertising is targeted to children 2-to-11 or 6-to-11 years of age (p. 46).

6. One relevant ability is the ability to comprehend the persuasive intent of advertising. Research on the age at which children acquire this capacity has yielded varying results ranging from kindergarten age, to age 9 or 10. For example, M. Carole Macklin, "Do Children Understand TV Ads," *Journal of Advertising Research* 23 (February–March 1983), pp. 63–70; Thomas Robertson and John Rossiter, "Children and Commercial Persuasion: An Attribution Theory Analysis," *Journal of Consumer Research* 1 (June 1974), pp. 13–20. See also summaries of research in David Pillemer and Scott Ward, "Investigating the Effects of Television Advertising on Children: An Evaluation of the Empirical Studies," draft read to American Psychological Association, Division 23, San Francisco, California, August 1977; John R. Rossiter, "The Effects of Volume and Repetition of Television Commercials," in Richard P. Adler, Gerald S. Lesser, Laurene Krasny Meringoff, et al., *The Effects of Television Advertising on Children* (Lexington, Mass.: Lexington Books, 1980), pp. 160–62; Ellen Wartella, "Individual Differences in Children's Responses to Television Advertising," in Palmer and Dorr, pp. 312–14.

7. *Self-Regulatory Guidelines for Children's Advertising*, Children's Advertising Review Unit, Council of Better Business Bureaus, Inc., 3rd ed. (New York, 1983), p. 6.

8. F. Earle Barcus, "The Nature of Television Advertising to Children," in Palmer and Dorr, pp. 276–77.

9. Ibid., p. 275.

10. Research has been developed to assist advertisers in targeting child audiences. See, for example, Gene Reilly Group, Inc., *The Child* (Darien, Conn.: The Child, Inc., 1973), cited in Robert B. Choate, "The Politics of Change," in Palmer and Dorr, p. 329.

11. Submission before the FTC, 1978, quoted in Emilie Griffin, "The Future Is Inevitable: But Can It Be Shaped in the Interest of Children?" in Palmer and Dorr, p. 347.

12. Ibid., p. 344.

13. For example, Frances L. Ilg, Louise Bates Ames, Sidney M. Baker, *Child Behavior*, rev. ed. (New York: Harper & Row, 1981).

14. On the child's conception of time, see Jean Piaget, *The Child's Conception of Time* (New York: Basic Books, 1970).

15. One of my children at age five reasoned that, since five dollars was "too much" to pay for a toy car, it was "too much" to pay for a piano.

16. Research indicates that selling is a difficult concept for children. One study found that only 48 percent of six-and-a-half to seven-and-a-half year olds could develop an

understanding of the exocentric (as distinct from egocentric) verb "to sell." "FTC Final Staff Report," pp. 27–28, citing the work of Geis.

17. "FTC Final Staff Report," pp. 22–23, cites work of Roberts to support the notion that adults "counter-argue" when faced with commercial messages.

18. See Ibid., pp. 21–22, n. 51, for a description of studies by Atkin and White. Atkin found that 90 percent of the three-year-olds studied and 73 percent of the seven-year-olds thought that selling characters liked them. White found that 82 percent of a group of four- to seven-year-olds thought that the selling figures ate the products they advertised and wanted the children to do likewise.

19. Ibid. Atkin found in a group of three- to seven-year-olds that 70 percent of the three-year-olds and 60 percent of the seven-year-olds trusted the characters about as much as they trusted their mothers. See also T. G. Bever, M. L. Smith, B. Bengen, and T. G. Johnson, "Young Viewers' Troubling Response to TV Ads," *Harvard Business Review*, November–December 1975, pp. 109–20.

20. Charles K. Atkin, "Effects of Television Advertising on Children," in Palmer and Dorr, p. 300.

21. Supra, n. 11.

22. Toys, cereals, and candies are the products most heavily promoted to children. Studies show very limited use of product information in children's television advertising. Predominant are appeals to psychological states, associations with established values, and unsupported assertions about the product. Barcus, "The Nature of Television Advertising," pp. 275–79.

23. The FTC concluded from the literature that children tend to want whatever products are advertised. This is a further indication that they do not evaluate advertised products on the basis of their preferences and economic resources. "FTC Final Staff Report," p. 8. For data on the extent to which children actually want what they see advertised on television, see Atkin, in Palmer and Dorr, pp. 289–90.

24. The results of one study of children's understanding of television advertising messages suggested that, while "parents cannot 'force' early sophistication in children's reactions to television advertising, their attention and instruction can enhance the process." Focusing on children's capacities to understand advertising, rather than on their capacities to make decisions, the article supports the general proposition that the child's conceptual world differs in many ways from that of the adult. See John R. Rossiter and Thomas S. Robertson, "Canonical Analysis of Developmental, Social, and Experimental Factors in Children's Comprehension of Television Advertising," *The Journal of Genetic Psychology* 129 (1976), p. 326.

25. For discussion of consumer sovereignty, see Norman Bowie, *Business Ethics* (Englewood Cliffs, N.J.: Prentice Hall, 1982), pp. 80–88.

26. Supra, n. 11.

27. Gene Reilly Group, Inc., advising advertisers who target children, says that "the mother can simply be a 'purchasing agent' for the child." Quoted in Choate, "The Politics of Change," p. 329.

28. See generally "F.T.C. Final Staff Report."

29. Paul W. Farris and John A. Quelch, *Advertising and Promotion Management* (Radnor, Pa.: Chilton, 1983), p. 2.

30. Although toys, sweets, and fast-food restaurants are the staples of children's advertising, other snack foods and items like records are also targeted to children. It has even been suggested that child-oriented advertising may be more effective than adult advertising for some adult products. See Barcus, "The Nature of Television Ad-

vertising," pp. 275–76; William Melody, *Children's Television* (New Haven: Yale University Press, 1973), pp. 79–80.

31. Research shows a positive relationship between children's television viewing and purchase requests. Both experiments and surveys have found that exposure to advertising increases the number of requests children make: heavier viewers make more requests. See Atkin, "Effects of Television Advertising," pp. 290–91; Thomas S. Robertson, "Television Advertising and Parent-Child Relations," in Adler et al., "Children's Television Advertising," pp. 204–07. Some research indicates that the frequency of requests does not diminish as children become more aware of advertising's persuasive intent. Rossiter, "The Effects of Volume," pp. 163–65.

32. See Bever et al., "Young Viewers' Troubling Response."

33. One study found that a parent will pay 20 percent more for an advertised product with child appeal—even when a less-expensive, nonadvertised product is no different. Melody, *Children's Television*, p. 80.

34. Herbert Spencer cautioned against "the selfishness of affection which sacrifices the higher interests of a child to gain immediate pleasurable emotion." *The Principles of Ethics*, vol. II, sec. 434 (Indianapolis, Ind.: Liberty Classics, 1978; first published 1897), p. 361.

35. About one third to one half of the children involved in various research projects became unhappy, angry, or expressed disappointment after denials of food and toy requests. The rate was considerably higher among heavy television viewers. Toys and candies are denied more often than cereals. It is estimated that parents reject one third to one half of children's requests for products. Atkin, "Effects of Television Advertising," pp. 299–301.

36. For criticisms of the view that profit maximization signals maximal satisfaction of consumer wants, see Alan H. Goldman, *The Moral Foundations of Professional Ethics* (Totowa, N.J.: Rowman and Littlefield, 1980), pp. 247–57.

37. Supra, n. 23.

38. This is certainly the belief underlying advertisers' use of child-oriented advertising. See Melvin Helitzer and Carl Heyel, *The Youth Market: Its Dimensions, Influence and Opportunities for You* (New York: Media Books, 1970), cited in Melody, *Children's Television*, pp. 79–80.

39. *Comments of M & M/Mars, Children's Television Advertising Trade Regulation Rule-Making Proceeding*, Federal Trade Commission (November 1978), pp. 4–5 and 67.

40. They also have been called "intuitive level" ethical principles. R. M. Hare, *Moral Thinking* (Oxford: Clarendon Press, 1981).

41. Supra, notes 18, 19.

42. Quoted in Susan Bartlett Foote and Robert H. Mnookin, "The 'Kid Vid' Crusade," *The Public Interest* 61 (Fall 1980), p. 92.

43. For the view that children's special capacities and limitations should be respected but that children should not be "contained" in a special children's world isolated from that of adults, see Valerie Polakow Suransky, *The Erosion of Childhood* (Chicago: University of Chicago Press, 1982).

44. In response to the charge of unfairness, supporters of children's advertising sometimes point out that children are protected because their parents control the purse strings. June Esserman of Child Research Services, Inc., quoted in *Comments of M & M/Mars*, p. 4. This response misses the point. It is not potential economic harm that concerns these critics: it is the attitude toward children reflected in the use of children's advertising.

45. Atkin, "Effects of Television Advertising," pp. 298–301.

46. For example, one study found that heavy viewers of Saturday morning television got into more arguments with their parents over toy and cereal denials than did light viewers. Ibid., pp. 298–301. See also Scott Ward and Daniel B. Wackman, "Children's Purchase Influence Attempts and Parental Yielding," *Journal of Marketing Research*, August 1972, p. 318. But see Foote and Mnookin, "The 'Kid Vid' Crusade," p. 95 (harm not adequately documented.)

47. *Comments of M & M/Mars*, p. 64.

48. It was estimated that the coalition established to fight the FTC proceedings in 1978 put together a "war chest" of $15–$30 million. According to news reports the coalition included several huge law firms, the national advertising associations, broadcasters and their associations, the U.S. Chamber of Commerce, the Grocery Manufacturers of America, the sugar association, the chocolate and candy manufacturers, cereal companies and their associations, and more. See Choate, "The Politics of Change," p. 334.

49. "[I]n the area of children's products, the United States is an advertiser's paradise compared with many countries." Christopher Campbell, international marketing director at the Parker Brothers subsidiary of General Mills, quoted in Ronald Alsop, "Countries' Different Ad Rules Are Problem for Global Firms," *The Wall Street Journal*, September 27, 1984, p. 33. According to Alsop, "The other countries' aim is to protect kids from exploitation."

50. It is interesting to note that, in 1949, 42 percent of the children's programs broadcast were presented without advertiser sponsorship. Melody, *Children's Television*, p. 36.

Marketing Strategy and Implementation

Ethical Issues in Marketing Strategy and Implementation

John A. Quelch
N. Craig Smith

A broad range of ethical dilemmas confront the marketer on all elements of the marketing mix. This diversity of dilemmas exists because marketing deals with exchanges, both between functions within the corporation and between the corporation and its customers, suppliers, and competitors. Exchanges are messy and unpredictable. They involve relationships that require flexibility and nurturing. Achieving quality controls on marketing exchanges is much more challenging than in the closed loop world of the manufacturing plant.

In this chapter, we argue that ethical issues should be considered in the process of formulating marketing strategy. Doing so will reduce the chances of unforeseen ethical dilemmas surfacing during the design and implementation of marketing programs. For example, many industrial companies face the dilemma of whether to provide a lower level of customer service to smaller less-profitable customers. The company strategy may be to provide excellent service to all customers, but it must also give direction to field service personnel who, everyday, have to decide how to prioritize responses to customer service calls.

MARKETING STRATEGY FORMULATION

There are at least five reasons why it is essential to consider ethical issues when marketing strategy is being formulated:

- The range of stakeholders impacted by a company's marketing strategy is increasingly broad and diverse. It is the responsibility of the marketing strategist to weigh the relative importance of stakeholder groups and balance their interests, rather than abdicate this task to program managers and other subordinates who are less able to see the big picture.

- The late 1980s witnessed a reemergence of consumer activism and of boycotts directed at companies considered negligent in the areas of environmental protection or public health. This heightened consumerism stemmed from the perceived failure of government agencies to solve environmental and health problems or to regulate and discipline sufficiently the businesses that contribute to them. To avoid negative publicity and both the disruption of marketing plans and distraction of management time that can result from a consumer boycott, most major companies required, by the early 1990s, that environmental impacts be considered when marketing strategies are formulated.

- Adherence to what may in the past have been considered normal industry practice is less likely than ever to stand a company in good stead. Burroughs Wellcome, three-quarters owned by the largest charity in Great Britain, followed standard pharmaceutical industry practice by setting a steep price for AZT to recover its R&D investment. In so doing, it failed to anticipate fierce public criticism from advocacy groups representing HIV and AIDS sufferers.

- Recognizing ethical issues in marketing strategy formulation raises managers' sensitivity to the needs of customer segments with particular ethical concerns. This can result in new product ideas and motivate creative problem solving on the part of employees to conceive more ethical ways to satisfy customer needs.

- Those designing and executing the specific programs needed to implement a marketing strategy will be less likely to overlook ethical issues and commit ethical mistakes if the strategists have already taken them into account.

For ethical issues to be considered in marketing strategy formulation, it is necessary that a broad range of information from multiple sources be gathered by managers in their scanning of the external environment. It is equally necessary for managers to be alert to the ethical challenges that arise when the marketing strategy is translated into the marketing plan and budget. Questionable practices include: inflating sales forecasts to secure higher marketing budgets; loading distribution channels to meet fourth-quarter sales projections; and failing to reserve for sufficient dealer discounts, if sales are booked when products are shipped to dealers. As Henri Fayol pointed out in 1916, the compilation of a good business plan requires "moral courage," because "the public generally, and even shareholders best informed about the meaning of a business, are not kindly disposed toward a manager who has raised unfulfilled hopes, or allowed them to be raised."[1]

---

[1] Henri Fayol, *General and Industrial Management* (Toronto: Captus University Publications, 1991; first published 1916).

COMPETITIVE MARKETING STRATEGY

Competition is a cornerstone of the free enterprise system, and many federal and state laws have been written to encourage it. Yet competition raises a number of important ethical issues for the marketing manager. To name a few:

- Conspiring to fix prices is illegal. Yet, in oligopolistic industries, the players often follow the signals of a price leader; though relative market shares remain stable, profits for all parties remain much higher than if there were a price war. While consumers might be served by lower prices in the short term, higher prices provide funds for investment in new product development from which customers benefit in the long term. Under these circumstances, many managers have asked: Is price-signaling ethical?

- Companies often announce new products and their launch marketing budgets in advance, not only to attract customer interest but also to dissuade lesser competitors from introducing their new products at the same time. In the event, these announcements often prove exaggerated, especially regarding the size of the marketing budgets. Managers ask: Are such "strategic announcements" unethical? We would ask: Are they any different from price signals?

Competitive pressures often are used to justify questionable marketing strategies and tactics. If one company's sales force disparages a competitor's products to retail buyers, the second company can easily be tempted to respond either in kind or through engaging in other "dirty tricks," such as the deliberate disruption of a new-product test market. Meeting competition (sometimes abbreviated to "meetcomp") to secure orders can result in progressively less ethical business practices.

The preservation of confidential information is key to the trust on which business relationships depend. Any company with several competing customers has to be concerned about this. In South Korea, the contractors who make shoes for both Nike and Reebok have separated their factories and work forces with "Chinese walls" to preserve the secrecy of each customer's new product designs. In the advertising agency business, trust is in shorter supply; major clients refuse to hire agencies that do business with their competitors. As industry structures become more complex, it is increasingly likely that a company may be, at the same time, a customer, a competitor, and a partner in a strategic alliance. Drawing the boundaries between proprietary and nonproprietary market information under these circumstances is increasingly difficult.

THE INTERNATIONAL DIMENSION

The increasing globalization of markets has brought to prominence a number of ethical dilemmas that confront the international marketer:

- Business practices vary widely from one culture to another. Should an American manager follow U.S. business practices or those common to the country of the customer? U.S. legislation (such as the Foreign Corrupt Practices Act) may constrain the manager's options, to the extent that some contracts will be lost to foreign competitors with more "ethical flexibility."

- Legislation regulating the marketing of products also varies widely across countries. Given the constraints on the marketing of tobacco products in developed countries, is it ethical for Philip Morris and other tobacco companies to market these products aggressively in developing markets? Philip Morris managers might argue that they disagree with the legislative constraints in the United States (though they have to abide by them) and are being quite consistent in pursuing market opportunities where the constraints do not exist.

- Traditionally, international marketers have not sold the same product in all countries. The most technologically advanced products often are sold first in the developed world, while less complex and, in some cases, obsolete versions are sold at the same time in developing countries. This makes sense when the infrastructure or skills mix of the developing country is insufficient to take full advantage of the performance potential of the technologically advanced product. But, all too often, this practice has been based on the convenience of using the Third World as a dumping ground for obsolete product and production lines.

CORPORATE CULTURE AND VALUES

Ethical issues are more likely to be considered in the formulation of marketing strategy when the corporate culture and specific corporate values provide ethical guidance. A commitment to product or service quality, for example, is likely to discourage shipments of shoddy products to customers in order to meet delivery dates. The founder's own values often can become the easily understood centerpiece of a successful company's corporate culture. For example, the founder of Matsushita Electric Company stated that the company should be responsible for the products it sells until they are disposed of by the final customer—a long-term commitment far beyond the expiration date of the manufacturer's warranty that keeps Matsushita employees focused on making long-lasting, reliable products.

To be effective, corporate values must be limited in number, succinctly and unambiguously stated, and actionable. Though corporate values may sometimes seem inconvenient because they constrain the marketer's options in the face of less ethical competitors, they are helpful in several ways. First, a reputation for leadership in honest business practices within an industry can be a positive point of differentiation, as valuable a success factor in some cases as technology or market leadership. At the very least, such a company is more likely to attract and recruit employees of high integrity. Second, internal communications within an organization are facilitated when all departments and personnel share a common set of values. While interpretations may differ, the variance is likely to be less than in the absence of such shared values. A common approach can be especially helpful when an organization faces a crisis that requires many departments to work together quickly and effectively. Third, an organization with shared values is more likely to present itself consistently to outside suppliers and customers. The employees of an organization with a consistent reputation for integrity are less likely to have to contend with unethical propositions from third parties.

It is insufficient for an organization merely to acknowledge adherence to ethical business practices in a broad statement of corporate values. Some companies have developed a set of detailed yet manageable ethical principles applicable to executives in all business functions. A sample, developed by the Josephson Institute, is reproduced as Exhibit 1. Other companies rely alternatively, or in addition, on codes of conduct for each functional area (such as sales and marketing), taking care to ensure internal consistency among the various functional codes.

A code of conduct that provides very specific direction can help employees to avoid stepping over the line or at least sensitize them to the existence of a line and to consideration of where it lies. However, a code of conduct will quickly become the object of cynicism unless it is demonstrably followed by top management and unless adherence to the code is reflected in the reward system. In some companies, unfortunately, codes of conduct are used to protect top management against outside criticism when violations by lower level employees are uncovered. Yet, how many times has a salesperson been told by the regional manager, "Don't do anything illegal but, whatever you do, don't lose the order!" In such circumstances, the salesperson is likely to regard the existence of a code of conduct not as a helpful source of guidance but, rather, as an extra source of anguish.

Business and academic participants in the Woodstock Seminar in Business Ethics developed a checklist to consider in creating and maintaining an ethical corporate climate. This is shown as Exhibit 2.

MARKETING IMPLEMENTATION

Many organizations do not measure the success of their marketing implementation. Those that do typically focus on effectiveness (in meeting objectives) or efficiency (the ratio of output to input), or both; the most efficient marketing program is not always effective. If ethical considerations are included in the evaluation process, further complexity is added. For example, the marketing director of a private for-profit hospital operating well below capacity decides to provide coffee and donuts for ambulance drivers delivering

---

EXHIBIT 1 Ethical Principles for Business Executives

This list of principles incorporates the characteristics and values most people associate with ethical behavior. Ethical decision making systematically considers these principles.

I. Honesty. Ethical executives are honest and truthful in all their dealings, and they do not deliberately mislead or deceive others by misrepresentations, overstatements, partial truths, selective omissions, or any other means.

II. Integrity. Ethical executives demonstrate personal integrity and the courage of their convictions by doing what they think is right, even when there is great pressure to do otherwise; they are principled, honorable, and upright; they will fight for their beliefs. They will not sacrifice principle for expediency, be hypocritical or unscrupulous.

III. Promise-keeping and trustworthiness. Ethical executives are worthy of trust, they are candid and forthcoming in supplying relevant information and correcting misapprehensions of fact, and they make every reasonable effort to fulfill the letter and spirit of their promises and commitments. They do not interpret agreements in an unreasonably technical or legalistic manner in order to rationalize noncompliance or to create justifications for escaping their commitments.

IV. Loyalty. Ethical executives are worthy of trust, demonstrate fidelity and loyalty to persons and institutions by friendship in adversity, support and devotion to duty; they do not use or disclose information learned in confidence for personal advantage. They safeguard the ability to make independent professional judgments by scrupulously avoiding undue influences and conflicts of interest. They are loyal to their companies and colleagues and, if they decide to accept other employment, they provide reasonable notice, respect the proprietary information of their former employer, and refuse to engage in any activities that take undue advantage of their previous position.

V. Fairness. Ethical executives are fair and just in all dealings; they do not exercise power arbitrarily, and do not use overreaching nor indecent means to gain or maintain any advantage nor take undue advantage of another's mistakes or difficulties. Fair persons manifest a commitment to justice, the equal treatment of individuals, tolerance for and acceptance of diversity, and they are open-minded; they are willing to admit they are wrong and, where appropriate, change their positions and beliefs.

VI. Concern for others. Ethical executives are caring, compassionate, benevolent, and kind; they live the Golden Rule, they help those in need, and seek to accomplish their business objectives in a manner that causes the least harm and the greatest positive good.

VII. Respect for others. Ethical executives demonstrate respect for the human dignity, autonomy, privacy, rights, and interests of all those who have a stake in their decisions; they are courteous and treat all people with equal respect and dignity regardless of sex, race, or national origin.

VIII. Law-abiding. Ethical executives abide by laws, rules, and regulations relating to their business activities.

IX. Commitment to excellence. Ethical executives pursue excellence in performing their duties, are well

---

EXHIBIT 1 *(concluded)*

---

informed and prepared, and constantly endeavor to increase their proficiency in all areas of responsibility.

X. Leadership. Ethical executives are conscious of the responsibilities and opportunities of their position of leadership and seek to be positive ethical role models by their own conduct and by helping to create an environment in which principled reasoning and ethical decision making are highly prized.

XI. Reputation and morale. Ethical executives seek to protect and build the

company's good reputation and the morale of its employees by engaging in no conduct that might undermine respect, and by taking whatever actions are necessary to correct or prevent inappropriate conduct of others.

XII. Accountability. Ethical executives acknowledge and accept personal accountability for the ethical quality of their decisions and omissions to themselves, their colleagues, their companies, and their communities.

Source: Josephson Institute, *Ethics: Easier Said than Done*, 1989, p. 4.

---

patients to the hospital's emergency room. As a result, more patients are delivered; the program proves very cost efficient. However, a high percentage of the additional patients are poor people who do not have health insurance; admitting them will not contribute to the hospital's profit objective. Apart from debating the ethics of the hospital's for-profit strategy, is implementing the coffee and donuts program unethical?

According to Bonoma,[2] four activities characterize marketing implementation: interacting, allocating, organizing, and evaluating. Ethical dilemmas are common in all four areas. For example:

Interacting. A new salesperson for a sporting goods company is approached for free tickets to a baseball game by a major customer. He discovers that it is common practice in the industry to host important customers at sporting events. What should he do?

Allocating. A copier company guarantees total customer satisfaction as the cornerstone of its marketing strategy. However, the number of service and repair personnel is limited, so priorities have to be set about which service calls are answered first. Common practice is to give large customers priority over small customers, though the latter often depend entirely on a single machine. Is this an ethical allocation of service resources?

Organizing. A health and beauty aids manufacturer finds that certain products in its line are heavily purchased by Hispanic women. The vice president

---

[2] Thomas V. Bonoma, *The Marketing Edge* (New York: Free Press, 1987).

EXHIBIT 2   Checklist for Creating and Maintaining an Ethical Corporate Climate

A. Does top management have a common understanding of and strong commitment to ethical values?
1. Do the organization's purpose, responsibilities, and governing principles of conduct stress these values?
2. Are there forums for top managers to discuss the organization's ethical values?
3. Do top managers routinely discuss ethical questions and work out differences?
4. What are the ethical challenges currently facing top management?

B. Do management's actions and policies reflect the organization's ethical values?
1. Do individuals chosen for promotion and recognition exemplify those values?
2. Do management's strategic choices reflect those values?

C. Do employees throughout the firm share management's ethical values and commitment?
1. How does management communicate the ethical values that should guide employee conduct?
2. Are these communications clear and effective?
3. Is ethics included in orientation and training programs for new employees?
4. Does management monitor the ethical climate of the firm?
5. Is top management aware of the ethical concerns of employees at all levels?
6. Is top management aware of the barriers to ethical conduct that may exist at various levels of the organization?

D. Do managers at all levels work to build shared ethical values?
1. Does the firm hold seminars, workshops, and discussion groups on ethics?
2. Does the organization periodically revise and update its code of conduct, credo, or ethics statement? Does top management participate in this activity? Do rank-and-file employees participate?
3. Do employees in various functional areas meet to discuss ethical questions specific to their area?
4. Do ethical issues come up in informal discussions?
5. Do managers discuss ethical issues with their subordinates?
6. Are employees comfortable discussing ethical questions with their bosses?
7. Are ethical matters addressed in formal communications, such as newsletters, memoranda, and policy statements?

E. Does management provide employees with ethical guidance when needed?
1. Does management have a method for identifying and clarifying areas where ethical standards are unclear or in conflict with other objectives of the firm?
2. Does management monitor and report on ethical problems in the industry that may affect employees' ability and willingness to uphold the firm's standards?
3. Do employees have opportunities to raise ethical questions and concerns? Do they use these opportunities?
4. Does management communicate with employees concerning areas of ethical uncertainty or vulnerability?
5. Do supervisory personnel regard ethical guidance as part of their job?

EXHIBIT 2 *(concluded)*

F. Are ethical considerations included in personnel decisions?
  1. Are job candidates informed about ethical expectations and standards?
  2. Is commitment to the firm's stated values included among the organization's hiring criteria?
  3. Are ethical considerations built into personnel evaluations and promotion decisions?

G. Does the firm's system of rewards include ethical accountability?
  1. Does performance reporting include ethical performance?
  2. Do employees' goals and objectives include goals related to maintaining a strong ethical climate?
  3. Are compensation and bonuses affected by ethical performance?
  4. Does the organization identify and recognize individuals who make extraordinary contributions to maintaining the organization's ethical values?
  5. Does the compensation system avoid penalizing employees who are unable to achieve financial or other business objectives because of ethical constraints?
  6. Is management confident that employees will not be rewarded for financial accomplishments achieved using unethical methods?

H. Does the organization have a procedure for identifying and dealing with ethical violations?
  1. Does the organization have a hotline, ombudsman, ethics office, or other designated channel for employees to raise ethical questions about the conduct of their immediate supervisor?
  2. What are the designated channels for reporting, investigating, and sanctioning violations?
  3. Does the organization have adequate controls to prevent and detect ethical violations?
  4. Are reporting relationships structured to promote honest and accurate communication?

I. Does the organization have designated personnel whose job it is to monitor and promote an ethical climate?
  1. Does the board have a standing ethics committee or is the audit or other board committee charged with monitoring the ethical climate?
  2. Is there an ethics committee or office within the firm to handle day-to-day questions and activities related to ethics, such as conducting seminars and training programs, carrying on research, providing guidance to employees, investigating ethical violations, and reviewing the ethical impact of firm policies?

J. As a result of all the above, does every employee consider ethical conduct, supervision, and guidance part of the job?

Source: Woodstock Theological Center, *Creating and Maintaining an Ethical Corporate Climate* (Washington, D.C.: Georgetown University Press, 1990).

of marketing instructs the human resources department to hire Hispanic women as brand managers for these products and to terminate or transfer the existing managers. Is this appropriate?

Evaluating.   District sales managers in a U.S. food company are evaluated on total sales volume shipped to retail accounts in their districts. However, the national marketing manager implements different off-invoice allowances to the trade in high market share versus low market share districts. As a result, more volume is sold to accounts in high allowance districts, but some of the extra volume is diverted by the buyers into low allowance districts. What impact does this have on the fairness of the evaluation system for district managers?

As these examples indicate, ethical problems arise internally as well as externally when marketing programs are implemented. The boundary-spanning role of the marketing and sales functions places executives in frequent contact, not only with customers and suppliers but also with other functions and departments within the organization. Conflicts can result. For example, sales may have promised a specific delivery date to a customer that manufacturing finds itself unable to meet without compromising product quality. Such conflicts occur when different functions have different objectives and values, access to different information, or different interpretations of the information they do have.

Ensuring attention to ethics in marketing implementation is harder in some organizations than others. In particular, it is more challenging when the following circumstances apply:

1. Turnover in management or sales force, or both, is high, resulting in less continuity and uniformity of commitment to specific corporate values.

2. The company has recently been subject to a merger or acquisition, which has brought together organizations with different ethical standards—a recipe for misunderstanding and confusion.

3. The company operates in an industry subject to rapid technological change and frequent new-product introductions, which generate ethical dilemmas that have not been confronted previously.

4. The company does not sell direct to the final customer but, rather, through multiple intermediaries whose conduct cannot be monitored easily.

5. The company is a small player in a fragmented industry and, therefore, is tempted to cut corners out of a belief that it can escape regulatory scrutiny.

6. The company is a market follower and, therefore, sees itself as a hostage to industry practices, unable to unilaterally raise an industry's standards.

7. Industry trade associations do not exist, have not established standards of business conduct for the industry, or are too weak to enforce them.

Despite these differences, ethical considerations surface to some degree in the implementation of all marketing policies and programs. How can an organization ensure that its people take ethical issues into account before they act? There are four principal areas where managerial action can produce tangible results:

Corporate Strategy and Values.   As already discussed, doing what is right becomes much clearer if ethics have been taken into account in the strategy formulation process, if the organization clearly espouses honesty and integrity in its value systems, and if senior managers are strong role models for the rest of the organization.

Recruiting and Training.   Recruiting criteria must include an evaluation of each potential employee's ethical values, particularly as companies seek to delegate decision-making responsibility to field salespeople or to the factory shop floor. In-house training programs for all functions should include an ethical component. This can be best achieved through the use of role-playing scenarios based on situations that current and previous employees have had to confront. Such training typically highlights—to the surprise of most participants—the diversity of opinions within the organization about how ethical dilemmas should be addressed (or, indeed, whether they exist at all).

Reward Systems.   Employee compensation should not be based solely on the achievement of quantitative objectives. It should include qualitative factors, such as idea generation, development of subordinates, and the adherence to and promotion of corporate values and codes of conduct. In other words, rewards must be based not only on the achievement of ends but also on the means by which they are achieved. In this regard, it may be appropriate to ask customers and suppliers to rate the integrity of the company personnel with whom they come into contact.

Organization and Control.   Any company that wishes to incorporate an ethical component in its reward system must include individuals and organization structures that monitor and promote ethical attitudes and business behaviors. These individuals should preferably include not only the staff personnel from the human resources department but also the committed line managers in all functional areas who agree to spend a portion of their time championing ethical business behavior. At General Dynamics, for example, while an ethics program director is available to employees working on each major project, the director reports to a steering committee charged with ensuring implementation of the ethics program that includes two line vice presidents.

CONCLUSION

Ethical issues must be considered at all stages of the marketing process, from strategy formulation to implementation. If executives can be encouraged to consider ethical issues during the process, the end product (i.e., the marketing strategy itself) will be more robust. As a result, ethical problems, which might otherwise have been overlooked during strategy formulation, will less likely surface in crisis mode during implementation.

Sealed Air Corporation: Marketing Impacts of Eliminating CFCs

"Manufacturing, R&D, and marketing cannot reach separate conclusions on this issue; they have to work together."

Larry Chandler,
Sealed Air Corporation

In September 1988, Ray Meltvedt, polyethylene (PE) foam marketing manager at Sealed Air Corporation, was preparing for an important meeting with the company's executive vice president. At the meeting, he would present the commercial and environmental costs and benefits of removing chlorofluorocarbons (CFCs) from the production of PE foam.

Six months earlier, in March 1988, Meltvedt was in a hotel room in Chicago, where he was visiting one of Sealed Air's polyethylene foam production plants. He had recently been appointed PE foam marketing manager, responsible for Cell-Aire[1] and Cellu-Cushion protective packaging products (Exhibit 1 shows examples). Meltvedt had been in sales positions with Sealed Air on the West Coast since joining the company in 1984, but he had little experience with PE foam and was in Chicago to learn more. Yet it was not from the bundle of papers he'd been given and was casually reviewing that evening that he learned most, but from the television.

On the news it was reported that scientists had identified a significant ozone depletion in the mid-northern hemisphere, adding to fears of major environmental damage that had grown in recent months following the discovery of an ozone "hole" over Antarctica. CFCs were said to be largely to blame. Meltvedt then realized that his products were contributing to this problem. He recalled

This case was prepared by Professor N. Craig Smith with the assistance of Professor John A. Quelch.
Copyright © 1989 by the President and Fellows of Harvard College.
Harvard Business School case 9–589–107 (rev. 7/16/90).

[1] Cell-Aire, Cellu-Cushion, Sealed Air, Instapak, AirCap, PolyCap, Mail Lite, Jiffylite, Rigi Bag, Poly Mask, Bubble Mask, Kushion Kraft, and Dri-Loc are registered ® trademarks of Sealed Air Corporation. Jiffy is a ™ trademark of the same corporation.

EXHIBIT 1 Sample Applications of Cell-Aire and Cellu-Cushion Packaging Products

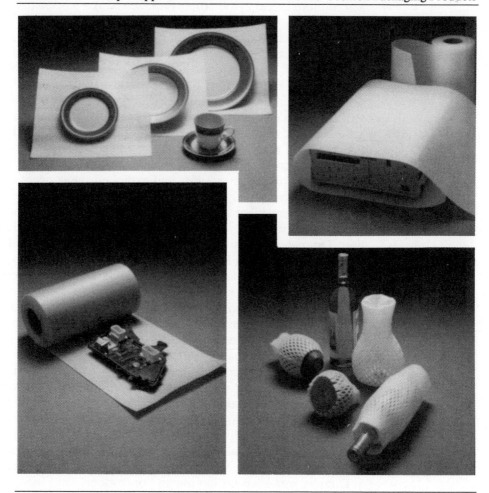

a company confidential memo written in February 1988, by Bill Armstrong, the technical development manager, which had covered a range of environmental issues and how they affected Sealed Air. This memo had been passed to Meltvedt by Paul Hogan, Sealed Air's vice president of marketing. Meltvedt had not had a chance to study the memo but remembered that, across the top, Hogan had written: "Very serious and important issue. Please handle."

SEALED AIR CORPORATION

In 1988, Sealed Air was the market leader in the manufacture and sale of protective packaging materials and systems. Its sales had grown threefold since

1980 to $303 million in 1987, with a similar growth in net pretax earnings to $34 million. It had 2,400 employees. Sealed Air's principal protective packaging products were Instapak foam-in-place packaging systems; AirCap and PolyCap Plus air cellular cushioning materials; Mail Lite, Jiffy Padded, Jiffylite, Jiffy Utility, and Jiffy Rigi Bag protective shipping mailers; Cell-Aire and Cellu-Cushion polyethylene foam; Poly Mask and Bubble Mask coated masking materials and Kushion Kraft cellulose wadding. Jiffy Packaging Corporation, a company with sales of $60 million in 1986, had been acquired in August 1987. Sealed Air also produced food packaging materials, such as Dri-Loc absorbent pads, for the retail packaging of meat, fish, and poultry; products that provided protection from electrostatic discharge and corrosion; and miscellaneous recreation and energy conservation products.

Sealed Air, founded in 1961, had exploited the concept of encapsulated air bubbles and eventually come to define its business as protective packaging. Sealed Air's president and CEO, T. J. Dermot Dunphy, had brought stability to Sealed Air when he joined the company in 1971. It then had sales of $5 million. Through innovation and technological leadership (Sealed Air committed 2.3 percent of sales to R&D, compared with an industry average below 1 percent) together with sound marketing and a selective acquisition strategy, Sealed Air achieved market leadership and substantial sales and earnings growth. Dunphy was aiming for sales of around $500 million by 1990 and, excluding any possible acquisitions, growth of around 15 percent per annum to realize sales of $1 billion by 1997.

Dunphy believed that "virtue is a competitive edge" and sought to combine high principles with economic reward. The old American saying "nice guys don't win ball games" was wrong in his opinion. In 1980 he had introduced a code of conduct to Sealed Air, which was regularly updated as a result of experience. Its provisions in 1988 covered employee relations, honesty in communications, dealing with competitors, product and worker safety, financial interests, bribery, political contributions, commercial confidentiality, and the importance of a customer orientation; Exhibit 2 summarizes the code.

Dunphy was keen on having an "open door," not least because employees tended to protect their subordinates or those they worked for. "Whistleblowing" was encouraged, despite fears in other companies that it undermined middle management; Dunphy had received several calls under this recent provision. Sealed Air did not recruit from competitors or interview employees with competitors and, thereby, obtain competitive information. This was prohibited by the code; it was also, in Dunphy's view, not something to be encouraged by an industry leader, as retaliation would make it a losing game. Dunphy was beginning to question the appropriateness of Sealed Air's policy of recruiting from companies with good training programs in other industries, because for a company of Sealed Air's size, even this might be seen as "poaching."

Dunphy was actively involved in and supportive of voluntary activities. He had, for example, developed companywide commitment to the "I Have a

---

EXHIBIT 2   Summary of Code of Conduct

Preamble

- Reputation: "Sealed Air Corporation has a reputation for conducting its business on a highly ethical level. It is important that we continue this record of integrity in the future." All employees are responsible for maintaining this reputation.
- List of rules no substitute: for "basic morality, common decency, high ethical standards, and respect for the law."
- Test to apply if in doubt: "Assuming full public disclosure of the action, should both the employee and the company feel comfortable from a moral, ethical, and legal standpoint? If the answer is 'yes,' then the action is very probably consistent with our corporate philosophy."
- Whistleblowing: "communication and 'whistleblowing' perform a valuable function in maintaining high ethical standards." If aware of circumstances or instructed to act contrary to the code, review with supervisor and, if matter not resolved, contact company's law department or president. Whistleblower protection ensured.
- Code violations: subject to disciplinary action, including dismissal.
- Guidelines apply worldwide

Guidelines

- Equal opportunity employer.
- Customer-oriented: "Everything a Sealed Air employee does on the job is ultimately related to satisfying a customer need within the framework of our Code of Conduct. Our advancement and job security, both as a company and as individuals, depend on our ability to satisfy properly the needs of our customers."
- High professional standards: in relationships with other employees, suppliers, customers, stockholders, and others having dealings with the company.
- Employee relations: treat each other with dignity and respect. Confidential employee information only used for proper purposes and available on "need to know" basis.
- Premium on honesty and fair dealing: information provided internally and externally is "expected to be truthful, accurate, and not misleading in any way."
- With competitors: compete vigorously and fairly, affording competitors respect we expect of them. Not using improper/illegal methods to obtain competitor information. Not encouraging actual/prospective employees to divulge confidential information gained as result of associations with other companies.
- Safety: committed to safe working conditions, product safety, compliance with laws relating to the protection of the environment.
- The law: policy to comply with laws affecting conduct of the business.
- Confidentiality: company assets, including confidential business information, not to be misused or made available to outsiders in ways detrimental to company interests.
- Employee financial interests: no divided loyalties through financial interests in competitors, suppliers, or customers.
- Bribery: illegal bribes or kickbacks intended to secure favored treatment for the company forbidden. Consult with supervisor if requested. Modest gratuities and tips are not encouraged but permissible if not violating local laws and expediting action, rather than securing influence.

EXHIBIT 2 *(concluded)*

- Gifts: acceptance of gifts "may involve a conflict of interest or create an appearance of impropriety." Acceptance of cash gifts forbidden; non-cash gifts of token or nominal value may be accepted if not intended/cannot be construed as bribe, kickback, or other form of compensation. Entertainment given or accepted in manner customary and necessary for business.
- Political contributions: none made worldwide. Employees encouraged to exercise individual rights to be active in local or national politics.
- Insider trading: employees reminded this is violation of U.S. law.

Source: Based on Sealed Air *Code of Conduct*, June 1988.

Dream" project, whereby a class at a local inner-city high school had been adopted, with its students visiting the company, and company employees in their spare time organizing social activities and helping the students develop study skills. The objective of the program was to prepare and encourage the students for a college education, which would be entirely funded by Dunphy and Sealed Air. Dunphy saw this as "a wonderful thing" that also had management development benefits—a good bonding activity involving people from different levels of the company. In 1986, Meltvedt had secured company support for a donation of 14 rolls of plastic (valued at $1,120) to the voluntary organization Survival. This gift was to be used to better equip the huts of Oaxacan Indians living on the Baja peninsula in California.

Dunphy's interest in social issues extended to the environment. He believed care for the environment was important—his daughter was an environmentalist by profession, working to protect the tropical rain forests. He also had identified a ground swell of opinion on these issues. His involvement with other companies had been helpful, particularly as a director of the New Jersey utility company for 10 years. Sealed Air was working on a company position statement on environmental issues and the environment was planned to be a major theme within the next annual report.

Working closely with Dunphy was Larry Chandler, executive vice president, reporting to whom were Jim Lyons, manufacturing vice president, Paul Hogan, vice president and director of marketing, and six other vice presidents. Meltvedt reported to Hogan (along with three other marketing managers).

SEALED AIR AND THE ENVIRONMENT

Armstrong's memo asked marketing managers to prepare product statements, delineating the various environmental assets and liabilities of Sealed Air products. The statements were to be used to prioritize future R&D activities and to provide a prepared set of responses (after appropriate review and approval) to questions from customers and others. Solid waste disposal and resource depletion were of most importance, as the statement developed for Jiffy padded mailers indicates (shown in Exhibit 3). However, Sealed Air's environmental concerns ranged from manufacturing, through customer use, to disposal of the product.

EXHIBIT 3　Jiffy Padded Mailers: Environmental Statement

1. How much recycled material is used to manufacture this product? How much can be used?

The Jiffy Padded Mailer is made with a 60 percent recycled content. This is believed to be the maximum content of recycled materials usable in this product because a recycled Kraft exterior or interior liners, or both, would not have sufficient strength to encapsulate the macerated padding.

2. How recyclable is the product itself?
   — Is it sortable from the general waste stream?
   — Are there sufficient quantities of this, or like products, to make segregation, accumulation, and recycling viable?

The Jiffy Padded Mailer could be sortable from the general waste stream along with newspapers and other paper products, such as paper grocery sacks and corrugated boxes. Segregation of this product for recycling is viable only where there are programs to recycle newspaper and other recyclable paper products.

3. What advantages does this product have over more recyclable alternatives?

This product is the most recyclable alternative available for a cushioned mailer. The disadvantage of this product is its relatively greater weight. As recycling becomes a more important issue throughout the community, the recyclable nature of the Jiffy Padded Mailer can be used greatly to our advantage.

4. What disposability assets does this product have, other than recyclability (i.e., reusable, compressible, bio- or photo-degradable, easily incineratable, etc.)?

The Jiffy Padded Mailer is biodegradable and is easily incinerated.

5. How can this product be made more: recyclable, reusable, degradable, etc.?

The Jiffy Padded Mailer can be made more recyclable through better education of the general public to include this product in the waste paper recycling stream. Many (most?) households are now recycling newspapers and this product should be included in that waste stream.

6. What are the recommended means by which this product should be properly disposed of, after use?

The best alternative for disposal is to recycle with the waste paper stream but other means, such as disposal in landfills and incineration, are acceptable.

Within manufacturing, emissions to the air and water and the production of hazardous as well as solid waste were the main concerns. Attached to Armstrong's memo was a note on CFC-related issues, identifying Sealed Air's Instapak and PE foams as responsible for CFC emissions at production plants. As early as 1981, water-blown formulations of Instapak had been developed in response to a request from Hewlett-Packard, the computer company. Few other customers were expressing an environmental interest at that time, but the development of the water-blown technology provided Sealed Air with a feasible alternative to the CFC blowing agent still largely used with the Instapak product line. A butane-based blowing agent seemed the best alternative for PE foam, Armstrong's memo suggested.

Sealed Air's problems in disposing of its own manufacturing waste had heightened awareness of environmental issues, alongside the extensive media coverage. There was a nationwide shortage of sanitary landfill. In New Jersey, there was no landfill capacity, and the trash from Sealed Air's Totowa plant had to be taken to Kentucky. As the plant manager commented, "We easily ship our garbage farther than we do our products." Waste removal costs at Totowa were rising dramatically. Sealed Air also was concerned about being associated with the litter problem, though litter and waste disposal were different issues in many respects.

An early statement, developed mid-1988, indicated Sealed Air's position on the environment:

> Sealed Air Corporation recognizes that there are problems creating public concern regarding packaging materials (both plastic and nonplastic) and the environment. We are committed to become part of the solution to these problems. We will act to educate our customers and consumers regarding the proper selection, use, reuse, disposal, and recycling of our materials. We are investigating potential solid waste issues to formulate rational and workable solutions and to identify potential business opportunities for the company in these areas.

CFCs AND THE OZONE LAYER

In July 1988, a *Newsweek* article observed: "For five decades, industrial societies have pumped potent chemicals into the atmosphere, unintentionally setting in motion the largest, longest, and most dangerous chemistry experiment in history." The unusually hot summer of 1988 brought to the fore public concerns about the environment. The greenhouse effect, depletion of the ozone layer, and other impacts on the environment of industrial pollutants, such as acid rain, received extensive media coverage. The drought in the Midwest was reminiscent of the 1930s and the sufferings of the dust-bowl states. Though this could not be blamed with any certainty on global warming due to the greenhouse effect, it had been reported that the average global temperature had risen by 0.9°F over the last century and was set to rise more dramatically. Experts were predicting an increase of 3–8°F before 2050, at least 0.6°F every 10 years. Days over 90°F in New York would increase from 15 to 48 by 2030.

While some scientists argued that the apparent global warming could not be unequivocally attributed to the greenhouse effect—rather than natural variations—until the year 2000, few disputed that industrial pollutants acted to trap solar heat in the atmosphere like the glass roof of a greenhouse. Carbon dioxide (CO_2), from the burning of fossil fuels, was the principal cause, estimated to be responsible for 40–45 percent of the problem, with increases in CO_2 due to deforestation responsible for a further 10–15 percent. CFCs, however, were said to be 20 percent to blame, with methane and other gases, such as nitrous oxide (N_2O), released by commercial agricultural fertilizers, responsible for the remaining 20 percent of the problem. The inundation of low-lying parts of the globe—due to rising sea levels as a result of water expansion and the melting of glaciers and some sea ice—was predicted, as well as a severe disruption of world agriculture. Global warming to date was said to have increased the level of the world's oceans by six inches, enough to push back America's sandy Atlantic coastline at an average rate of two to three feet a year. Sea levels were estimated to rise at least two to three feet over the next century, which some observers reported should be taken into account in long-term business investment decisions, along with other climatic changes.

A single CFC molecule could trap 20,000 times more heat than a single CO_2 molecule, but, fortunately, CFCs were more thinly dispersed through the atmosphere. Of greater concern was their separate effect on the ozone layer, a screen in the stratosphere protecting the Earth from the sun's harmful ultraviolet (UV) rays. Ozone (O_3), a gas composed of three oxygen atoms, is produced naturally when ultraviolet light from the sun breaks up molecules of oxygen (O_2) into single atoms (atomic oxygen), which then collide and combine with other molecules of two-atom oxygen to form O_3. Destroyed by natural processes, ozone levels would remain constant without CFCs. Ozone also was found in smog at lower levels, formed as a result of a complex chemical reaction involving hydrocarbons and nitrogen oxides released by cars, factories, and other sources, in the presence of sunlight. Close to ground level, this ozone impairs pulmonary functions, may cause premature aging of the lungs, and damages crops, trees, and other plants. Unfortunately, ozone depletion in the stratosphere was not compensated for by ozone creation in smog, and industrial manufacture of replacement ozone was not a realistic alternative.

Chlorofluorocarbons, developed in the 1930s as a coolant for refrigerators, soon found a wide range of applications because of their valuable properties as chemically inert, nontoxic, and easily liquefiable compounds. They were also long-lasting; CFC-12 had an atmospheric lifetime of 111 years. In 1974, however, University of California chemists Sherwood Rowland and Mario Molina theorized that ozone was being broken down by CFC chlorine atoms into chlorine monoxide (ClO) and regular oxygen (O_2). With free oxygen atoms then able to break up the chlorine monoxide, the chlorine atom could repeat the process, destroying upwards of 10,000 ozone molecules. Severe effects were predicted as a likely result of a thinner ozone layer. More UV would induce mutations in the plankton at the base of the food chain of the world's oceans, cause damage to the human immune system, and increase skin cancer. The Environmental Protection Agency (EPA) estimated a 1 percent loss of ozone in the upper atmosphere was likely to cause 3–5 percent more skin cancer worldwide. Crop damage was also likely, as well as uncertain climatic changes. David Doniger of the Natural Resources Defense Council commented: "It is no exaggeration to say that the health and safety of millions of people around the world are at stake."

Rowland and Molina's findings had prompted environmentalists to launch a boycott of aerosol products. More than half of the worldwide production of around 800,000 metric tons of CFCs was for aerosols. In 1978, when CFC production had fallen to 650,000 metric tons, legislation in the United States, Canada, Norway, and Sweden banned nonessential aerosols propelled by CFCs. In the scientific debate and ensuing confusion about the effects of CFCs, public interest waned and CFC production increased. U.S. industry sales of CFCs were around $750 million in the mid-1980s, used under trade names, such as "Freon," in refrigerants (45 percent by volume), blowing agents (30 percent), aerosols (5 percent), and cleaning agents and other applications (20 percent). This compared with worldwide use (excluding the United States) of aerosols (35 percent), blowing agents (25 percent), refrigerants (20 percent), and cleaning agents and other applications (20 percent).

In 1985, however, the British Antarctic Survey reported an ozone "hole" over the polar continent, confirmed by checks against data collected between 1978–85 by NASA's Nimbus 7 satellite. The discovery of this hole—technically a thinning of the ozone layer—led to unprecedented international action. In September 1987, building on negotiations under the United Nations Environment Program, agreement was reached to limit the production of five CFCs and three halons. The Montreal Protocol required ratifying governments to freeze CFC production and consumption at 1986 levels and achieve a 50 percent reduction by 1999. CFC–11, –12, –113, –114, and –115 were covered, as well as halon 1211, 1301, and 2402, production and consumption of which were to be reduced to 1986 levels by 1992. (The bromine in halons—mainly used in fire extinguishers—acted in a similar way to the chlorine in CFCs in attacking ozone.)

However, there were problems in securing worldwide support for the Montreal Protocol, as some developing countries, particularly India and China, felt that their industrialization was likely to be hampered by the higher costs of alternatives and by an agreement that limited them to a smaller use of CFCs per head of population than the developed nations. A further concern, noted by some experts in the United States, was that establishing a 50 percent reduction goal for CFC emissions by 1999 might encourage companies to hold their usage at current levels (or even increase it) in the interim, so the regulation, when implemented, would have minimal impact on their operations. In addition, companies that were able to reduce their emissions more than 50 percent in 1999 would conceivably be able to market the difference between their actual and allowed emissions to other companies in the same area who could not economically reduce their emissions by the required 50 percent.

More recent findings indicated that not only had there been an ozone depletion in the southern hemisphere of about 4 percent but also, as 100 scientists reported in March 1988, a depletion of 1.7–3.0 percent in the mid-northern hemisphere. This cast doubt over the claim by the Alliance for Responsible CFC Policy, a group of CFC users and producers, that ozone depletion was "within the range of previously observed variability." Alternatives to CFCs were available for most applications, but not, however, without drawbacks of impaired performance, increased cost, or reduced safety. Du Pont had developed CFC-134a, for example, a chlorine-free substance that deteriorated before reaching the upper atmosphere and was intended to be a direct replacement for some refrigeration and air-conditioning systems; but the automotive industry was estimating R&D costs of more than $1 billion for an air-conditioning system using an alternative refrigerant. However, the impact of CFCs on the ozone layer was no longer questioned. As atmospheric chemist James Anderson of Harvard University put it: "It is totally unequivocal and straightforward . . . there would be no ozone hole without fluorocarbons."

CELL-AIRE AND CELLU-CUSHION PACKAGING PRODUCTS

The Cell-Aire and Cellu-Cushion product range, which Sealed Air added when it acquired the company Cellu in 1984, comprised rolls of a variety of lengths, widths, and thicknesses of extruded polyethylene foam. Nonabrasive, lightweight, waterproof, and providing thermal insulation, Cell-Aire foam was used for the packaging of such products as injection molded parts for automobiles, china, circuit boards, furniture, pharmaceuticals, and optical lenses. Cellu-Cushion foam was of greater density and offered added protection with increased cushioning and durability. It was used for packaging wine and liquor bottles, exotic fruits, and machined parts and also was used in nonpackaging applications such as spa covers and as a lining for such items as attache cases and camera bags.

Table 1 shows PE foam sales since 1984. Sealed Air's main foam competitors were Sentinel (part of Packaging Industries, with a 20 percent market share in 1987), Ametek (30 percent), Astro/Richter (15 percent), and Dow (6 percent). The market was expected to grow at around 8 percent a year in real terms over the next three years, with Sealed Air and Astro/Richter securing a disproportionately larger share of the market, according to Sealed Air estimates. Sealed Air had continued to sell and support the PE foam line, despite losses, because of its strategic importance as an integral part of the company's product offering. However, it was hoped that manufacturing efficiencies (providing yield and density improvements), together with price increases, would

TABLE 1   PE Foam Sales

Year	$ Sales (000s)*	Market Share (percentage)	Net Income (Loss)†
1984	$15,600	29%	$ 50,400‡
1985	17,550	30	(339,300)
1986	24,050	27	(405,900)
1987	25,610	27	(674,100)
1988e	29,900	29	(351,000)

* Includes Jiffy sales from 1986.
† Fully costed.
‡ Based on Cellu accounting methods.
e Means estimated.

restore PE foam to profitability, as estimates for 1989 and beyond were beginning to indicate.

Sealed Air had considerable technological expertise. Armstrong had been very helpful in explaining to Meltvedt how the Cell-Aire and Cellu-Cushion product line was linked to the CFC issue; but his assessment of the situation was troubling. He explained that from a packaging point of view there were several alternatives to those products that depended wholly or in part on CFCs in their production:

- extruded, thermoformable expanded polystyrene;

- expanded polystyrene loose fills;

- expanded polyethylene—bun and sheet;

- polyurethane foams—prefoamed and foam-in-place;

- expanded polypropylene sheeting.

Replacement materials were available to a packaging engineer tasked with eliminating materials containing CFCs. Twenty years ago, protective packaging was dominated by nonplastic forms: cellulose wadding, corrugated inserts, rubberized hair (and vegetable fibers), glass fiber products, neoprene/rubber foams, vermiculite, shredded paper, crumpled kraft, and excelsior (wood wool). However, packages using these materials would be bigger, heavier, more costly, and provide less protection than packages using modern high-performance plastic foam materials. At one time, IBM shipped computers individually in padded vans. Plastic packaging materials provided the electronics industries, for example, with a way of protecting delicate products, such as hard disk drives or VCRs, while in transit by air, truck, train, or ship. Armstrong believed there was a link between the ability to protect these products through their distribution cycles and their success in penetrating mass consumer markets. Packaging and shipping were exceedingly small percentages of product costs, yet ensured low damage claim rates and high reliability of the delivered product. As plastic foams offered superior performance in most applications, nonplastic forms of packaging were unlikely to return.

Sealed Air's Cell-Aire and Cellu-Cushion products were blown with CFC-12 by injection during the extrusion process. A CFC-based blowing agent was used because it was safe, in terms of personnel exposure to the chemical and flammability; stable, with a long shelf life; relatively chemically inert; and cost effective. Alternatives to CFCs were available, but with cost or performance drawbacks. With aerosols, alternatives had, likewise, been available when CFC propellants were banned: other gases (nitrogen, CO_2, several hydrocarbons) or mechanical pumps. However, they only became viable when CFCs could not be used. Hydrocarbons, such as butane, presented flammability risks and reacted with ingredients used in the dispensed product. In some cases, internal mechanisms had to be designed, such as flexible pouches, to separate the propellant from the product. Mechanical dispensers could not provide control over mist sizing, and often the product had to be reformulated to compensate for this and similar problems. In nearly every case, the overall cost of the implemented alternative was more than the original CFC-based aerosol.

Armstrong was confident that Sealed Air could overcome manufacturing difficulties in switching to a non-CFC blowing agent, but he anticipated problems as well as increased costs and the possibility of reduced product performance. In his February 1988 memo on environmental issues, Armstrong stated that for Sealed Air's PE foams the most likely alternative to Freon would be butane, and that Sealed Air would be ahead of the competition because of in-house expertise available from its butane-based European foam lines. However, a new form of "environmentally safe" hydrochlorofluorocarbon (HCFC) had recently become available, which had, at most, only 5 percent of the ozone-depleting potential of CFCs, was nonregulated, and was being widely adopted as an alternative.

First and foremost among product performance concerns was cushioning properties: the packaging had to reduce external impact forces to levels below those which would cause product damage. Cushioning materials act as damped spring systems within the package to control the rate of deceleration of the packaged product during impacts, such as those that occur when the package is dropped. The required protection at minimal cushion thickness reduced package size requirements. Nonplastic forms of packaging needed to be two to three times thicker than plastic foam to provide the same performance, which would not only increase the package size and associated costs but also the amount of material to be disposed of after unpacking. Other performance concerns were:

- vibration transmissibility;

- general physical properties (tensile, tear, etc.);

- compatibility with the product to be packaged (i.e., corrosivity, tarnishing, abrasion, etc.);

- creep (loss of thickness over time, under load);

- aging properties;

- safety (flammability, off-gassing, etc.);

- aesthetic appearance.

Replacement alternatives had to be "transparent" to the user, replicating all significant properties of the original materials so no package redesign was required. They might, however, still need to be tested against military, industrial, or corporate standards and specifications, as required of the original material.

Armstrong's prognosis was that "customers will give preference to those materials and manufacturers that present them with the fewest problems." The Montreal Protocol was a factor but also legislation at federal, state, and particularly local levels, where there had been proposals to ban the sale or use of materials manufactured with CFCs. The Los Angeles mayor, for example, had directed city departments to stop buying products made of polystyrene foam, known as styrofoam, and asked attorneys to identify ways by which vendors leasing space from the city could be similarly prohibited. Armstrong was convinced that 100 percent elimination of CFCs would mean that "somewhere, someone will have to forfeit specific product attributes."

OPTIONS FOR SEALED AIR ON CFCs

There were five options Sealed Air could pursue on the CFC issue and the possible removal of CFCs from the manufacture of PE foam:

1. **Do nothing**: This would probably be the cheapest option. Sealed Air could wait for its suppliers of blowing agents (principally Du Pont) to develop a proven alternative or, indeed, for the theory on the cause of damage to the ozone layer to be shown to be wrong and public concern about CFCs to subside.

2. **Sit tight, but commit some resources to R&D**: This option would involve some costs in monitoring the situation, learning from suppliers, and conducting some exploratory research.

3. **Incremental change**: Develop alternative but only employ it gradually, seeking a reduction in the CFC content of the blowing agent rather than its elimination.

4. **Aggressive push**: All-out commitment to develop and employ a non-CFC blowing agent as soon as possible. This would be costly but might provide commercial advantages.

5. **Use known alternatives**: Switch to butane-based blowing agent, as used in Europe, but which had other known environmental problems and safety hazards.

Sealed Air was not, as yet, facing any restrictions on its use of CFCs. However, price increases of the existing blowing agent were foreseen in the years to come as suppliers passed on increases resulting from the reduced availability of CFCs in line with the Montreal Protocol. The PE foam mixture currently comprised 70 percent resin and 30 percent blowing agent by weight. R&D estimates indicated that an alternative blowing agent (SA-1), with an 85 percent reduction in CFCs, would require a PE foam mixture comprising 80 percent resin, 20 percent SA-1; it, therefore, would have an improved usage efficiency. Resin cost $0.52/lb., the existing blowing agent $0.54/lb., and SA-1 $0.81/lb. One pound of PE foam comprised 100 percent resin after the blowing agent had been injected and "aged out" of the foam (escaped). Labor inputs required would remain the same, but product densities were likely to be increased by 6–10 percent using SA-1; this would increase costs and affect product performance. Production output of PE foam in the 12 months to August 1988 was just over 18 million pounds.

In order to use butane in Europe, manufacturing facilities had to be "explosion-proofed." So, for example, rapid evacuation from the facility in the event of a leak had to be ensured; though some Sealed Air employees were still doubtful about whether a plant could be fully evacuated in the 30 seconds allowed. Butane-based extrusion was dependable, the technology certainly worked, and was largely viewed as safe. Additional safety equipment required consisted of a butane monitoring system for each plant at $75,000, a CO_2 fire extinguishing system ($20,000), and building conversion work in venting, automatic doors, rewiring, and the like ($100,000). On the other hand, there was a 21 percent cost saving in comparison with the cost of goods using the existing blowing agent. Additional factors to consider in a switch to butane were:

- Only the Hanover and Salem extruders would work on butane (new, compatible extruders would cost $800,000 each; conversion of other extruders would cost $400,000 each).

- Employee reluctance to work in a butane plant.

- Difficulty in getting V.O.C. (volatile organic compounds) permits in most states due to filled capacities.

- Butane contribution to air pollution (smog and the greenhouse effect).

- Extra "aging" required—for butane to "age out" from the foam before shipment.

- Increased insurance rates, estimated to rise from $400,000 a year for all plants to $600,000 (and as much as $800,000 if other producers in the industry did not also switch to butane).

- More complex safety problems relating to fires or employees.

- Extra supervisory personnel and safety engineers required on staff.

- Estimated additional scrap on conversion/acquisition of new extruders of 30 percent for first 30 days, 15 percent for second 30 days, budget thereafter.

- Costs (time and money) of obtaining appropriate permits from local fire departments.

Sealed Air produced PE foam on seven extruders located in different plants throughout the United States. Exhibit 4 shows extruder capacity and utilization in the 12 months to August 1988, labor requirement, whether the extruder was capable of using SA-1, and the associated costs. Changeover costs include extruder conversion and the costs of scrapping output of inferior quality as extruder operators learn to use the new blowing agent. The Salem and Hanover extruders could not be converted to CFC-free blowing agents. Based on scrap rates in a previous change of blowing agent, Meltvedt estimated total scrap costs at $557,000 for the five plants, assuming the scrap would have no value and assuming the continuation of 1988 capacity utilization levels. As Hanover would no longer produce PE foam, there would be additional freight costs by shipping from Totowa of $55,000 a year, storage costs of $10,000 a year, mothballing costs (extruder removal for storage) of $25,000, and a requirement to absorb the overhead costs of the plant over the remaining products produced there. Six employees would also have to go. Costs incurred at Salem would be $10,000 for mothballing (at the plant). PE foam employees could be allocated to other duties.

Advantages to the use of SA-1 were seen as:

- Marketing benefits, demonstrating environmental concern to customers.

- Avoid possible increases in cost of regulated blowing agent.

- Initial step to having a completely environmentally safe blowing agent.

- Improved employee morale, in the knowledge that Sealed Air was leading the industry on this issue.

The SA-1 blowing agent had been developed by Sealed Air by replacing a large proportion of the chlorofluorocarbon with a hydrochlorofluorocarbon (HCFC), known to be environmentally safe. A blowing agent known as SA-2 was under development that would entirely replace the CFC with HCFC and would, as a result, have only 5 percent of the ozone-depleting potential of CFC. The use of SA-2 would allow Sealed Air to claim its PE foam was 100 percent "CFC-free" and would protect the company against any outright bans on packaging applications of CFCs. However, the more volatile SA-2 would prove considerably more difficult to use and, while not involving further equipment costs after conversion to SA-1, would probably entail additional scrap rates of 15 percent on average, over the first 30 days. SA-2 cost $0.81/lb. and would have the same usage efficiency as SA-1 (i.e., require a mixture of 80 percent resin, 20 percent blowing agent). An immediate switch to SA-2 was viewed as too problematic by R&D.

EXHIBIT 4 PE Foam Production Plants

Plant*	Output M Lbs./Yr.	Extruder Capacity Lbs./Hr.	Percentage 5-Day Week Filled, Year to August 1988†	Hourly Number of Employees‡	Capable of SA-1 or SA-2 Blowing Agent	If Yes—Cost of Conversion: Scrap and Equipment§	Employee Lay-offs (If Any)
Totowa, New Jersey	1,950	650	50%	9	Yes	Scrap rate: 25% 1st 30 days. 20% 2nd 30 days. Budget thereafter. Equipment cost: negligible.	No
Hodgkins, Illinois	3,432	715	80	14	Yes	Scrap rate: 15% 1st 30 days. Budget thereafter. Equipment cost: negligible.	No
Hanover, Pennsylvania	1,800	300	100	8	No	N/A	Yes
Warrior, North Carolina	4,914	585×2‖	70	25	Yes	Scrap rate: 15% 1st 30 days. Budget thereafter. Equipment cost: negligible.	No
Grenada, Mississippi	3,334	585	95	12	Yes	Scrap rate: 25% 1st 30 days. 15% 2nd 30 days. Budget thereafter. Equipment cost: negligible.	No
Salem, Illinois	1,800	300	100	7	No	N/A	No
COI (City of Industry), California	819	455	30	11	Yes, but at high conversion cost.	Scrap rate: 15% 1st 30 days. 10% 2nd 30 days. Budget thereafter. Equipment cost: $80,000.	No

N/A means not applicable.
* The location of extruders was a result of historical factors (largely the result of acquisitions), rather than logistical demands; it was important to have a West Coast facility (COI), however.
† Average capacity utilization was 75 percent; extruders operate during all three shifts (24 hours a day).
‡ Different labor inputs reflect product differences in the output of the various extruders (e.g., specialty treatments), as well as efficiency differences.
§ R&D and labor costs excluded.
‖ Two extruders.

Source: Internal data, Sealed Air Corporation.

Price increases to cover the higher costs of alternative blowing agents would not be welcomed by customers. Resin cost increases had led to two price increases already in 1988 (9 percent in May, 7 percent in August), with a third price increase of 7 percent likely toward the end of the year. Price increases prompted some customers to trade down to a thinner foam. Sealed Air's competitors were generally price followers, raising their prices in line with increases by Sealed Air, the market leader.

Changes in product performance using SA-1 and SA-2 were not likely to be substantial. However, differences would be noticed, specifically the larger cell size of the foam, a rougher surface, and greater variations in thickness (the greater volatility of the blowing agent made quality control more difficult). Some specialty applications might be excluded as a consequence. The concern would be principally with consumer perceptions of differences and the requirement to reassure customers of continued performance standards and to encourage acceptance in the light of reduced environmental harm.

No customers as yet had to have CFC-free PE foam, but state legislation requiring this was a possibility in Vermont, Massachusetts, and Rhode Island. With PE foam often viewed as a commodity product, it could prove advantageous for the sales force to claim Sealed Air's product was ozone-friendly, providing a selling benefit in appeals to the good nature of customers. Positive PR stories in support were also likely, promoting a good public image of Sealed Air as a company that cares about the environment. However, the code of conduct prohibited competitive disparagement.

All of Sealed Air's competitors were using CFC-based blowing agents, with the exception of Astro, which was using butane. Ametek employed a CFC recovery system, but Sealed Air had doubts about its effectiveness in the Sealed Air manufacturing process. Sealed Air had inherited a similar system with the Jiffy acquisition, but found it would not work satisfactorily and, for this reason, had ruled out recovery systems as a possible solution to the CFC issue. No Sealed Air PE foam competitors were claiming, as yet, to be CFC-free—Astro, Ametek, or, indeed, indirect competitors supplying nonplastic forms of packaging. There were no indications that this claim would be forthcoming from these or other competitors. Instapak, the only other Sealed Air product manufactured using CFCs, was gradually, and without too much difficulty or expense, being switched to the water-blown technology. Instapak competitors also had yet to indicate any interest in CFC-free claims, where these could already be made, or, in other cases, in developing alternatives to CFCs.

Initial discussions with major distributors of PE foam had met with little enthusiasm for a CFC-free solution. Some were skeptical about its importance and commented: "We're supposed to be partners in this business." There was a concern about further price increases, which some viewed as "unnecessary and unjust." One distributor said, "We don't care whether it is safe for the environment or not; we can't survive further price increases."

"WHEN ARE WE GOING TO DO SOMETHING?"

As Meltvedt settled into his job as PE foam marketing manager, he had become increasingly frustrated by the lack of progress on the CFC issue. His July response to Armstrong's memo commented on Cell-Aire and Cellu-Cushion product disposability and recycling but said little about CFCs. He did report that a competitor (Packaging Industries of Hyannis, Massachusetts) had been charged with violating state CFC emission standards.

In June, Hogan asked the marketing managers to produce an R&D "wish list." At the top of Meltvedt's list of help requests from R&D was the request "switch to 100 percent nonregulated blowing agent at all plants." Meltvedt believed this was the right thing to do. R&D, in response, had been supportive, but cited difficulties. Some plant managers, meanwhile, were expressing grave doubts about using alternative blowing agents that would present production problems, and be more expensive on lines that were already losing money. As one regional plant manager put it in a meeting involving marketing, production, and R&D: "PE foam is losing enough money—don't you know that switching the blowing agent will cost us dollars and disrupt service to our customers? We can't afford that." Meltvedt sensed that he was being viewed as "the guy from California who was constantly trying to change things."

Industry delegates at a packaging association conference Meltvedt attended in September 1988 urged that a special case be made for the industry so it could continue its use of CFCs. One delegate, having explained that CFC-based blowing agents were the safest and most efficient available, urged that the industry wait until government forced a change or until chemical companies developed equally satisfactory alternatives. Meltvedt had come across a similar argument being made by another packaging trade association and was again unimpressed. On his return, and following a meeting involving R&D and production, where yet again obstacles to CFC elimination seemed insurmountable, Meltvedt decided to approach Chandler on the issue. R&D had estimated that total elimination of CFCs could be achieved by mid-1989 with sufficient commitment. Preparing for his meeting with Chandler that afternoon, Meltvedt went over the commercial and environmental costs and benefits of removing CFCs from the production of PE foam, including the marketing impacts of a likely price increase set against a "CFC-free" claim. He would ask Chandler, "How big a commitment to this issue is Sealed Air prepared to make?"

Reebok International Ltd.

In June 1988, executives of Reebok International Ltd.'s Reebok Footwear Division (RFD) met to review the company's U.S. marketing communications program for the second half of the year. In addition to category advertising to promote specific product lines, such as aerobic shoes, Reebok's vice president of advertising intended to pursue three multiproduct umbrella campaigns: television advertising during the 1988 Summer Olympics; television and print advertising with the tag line "Reeboks let U.B.U."; and print advertising to introduce Reebok's new performance feature, the Energy Return System.

In addition, Reebok executives had to review their marketing communications plan for the Human Rights Now! world concert tour. On March 29, Joe LaBonté, Reebok's president and chief operating officer, had announced that Reebok was joining Amnesty International (AI) in sponsoring this tour, which would celebrate the 40th anniversary of the United Nations' Universal Declaration of Human Rights. However, debate continued within Reebok about the merits of this sponsorship, about how aggressively Reebok should publicize its association with the tour, and about how the proposed communications program for the tour related to RFD's overall marketing communications plan.

COMPANY BACKGROUND AND STRATEGY

Reebok's antecedent, J. W. Foster and Sons, was founded in England in 1895 as a manufacturer of custom track shoes that were marketed by mail worldwide. The company was renamed Reebok in 1958. In 1979, Paul Fireman bought the North American distribution rights. In 1984, he and his backers, principally Pentland Industries plc, bought the parent company.

Fireman's first imports into the United States were three styles of hand-stitched, high-priced running shoes. In 1982, convinced that interest in running

This case was prepared by Tammy Bunn Hiller under the direction of Professor John A. Quelch. Copyright © 1988 by the President and Fellows of Harvard College. Harvard Business School case 9-589-027 (rev. 11/89).

would plateau and aerobics would become the next fitness craze, Fireman introduced the first aerobic/dance shoe, the Reebok Freestyle. The shoe was unique. It was made of garment leather. It was soft, supple, wrinkled at the toe, and comfortable to wear from day one. It was also more attractive than competitors' athletic shoes. Furthermore, it was the first athletic shoe specifically targeted at women.

With the introduction of aerobic shoes, Reebok began a period of phenomenal growth. Between 1982 and 1987, net sales grew from $3.5 million to $1.4 billion, and net income grew from $200,000 to $165 million. Reebok ranked first among major U.S. companies in sales growth, earnings growth, and return on equity for the years 1983 through 1987. Fireman's goal was for Reebok to become a $2 billion multinational by 1990.

Reebok's growth was accomplished through broadening of existing product lines, expansion into additional product categories, and acquisitions. Exhibit 1 presents a chronology of Reebok's new product line introductions and acquisitions. The company had five operating units: Reebok North America (which included RFD and the Reebok Apparel Division), Reebok International, Rockport, Avia, and Ellesse.

In 1987, RFD sold approximately 42.17 million pairs of shoes to its U.S. retailers. The shoes were sold to consumers for an average price of $43. RFD accounted for approximately 71 percent and 88 percent of Reebok's 1987 sales and operating profit, respectively. The division's sales and estimated operating income for 1983 through 1987 are shown in Table 1.

In the 1980s, RFD diversified its product offerings dramatically. In 1979 the division sold three shoes. In 1988 it sold more than 300 different shoes in 10 product categories. Aerobic shoes accounted for 56 percent of the division's sales in 1984. In 1987 they constituted only 29 percent.

The division sold its shoes direct to retailers through 17 independent sales organizations. This sales force sold only Reebok brand products and was paid on a commission basis. A staff of field service and promotion representatives, employed by Reebok, supported the sales force by traveling throughout the United States teaching retailers and consumers about the features and benefits of the division's shoes. RFD followed a limited distribution strategy. Its shoes were sold only through specialty athletic retailers, sporting goods stores, and department stores. They were not sold in low-margin mass merchandiser or discount stores.

RFD, like other major athletic shoe companies, contracted out all of its manufacturing. The shoes were made in eight countries. Most of them, 71 percent in 1987, were produced in South Korea. The division's large-volume needs, combined with labor disruptions in South Korea, caused supply problems in 1987. In late 1987, RFD added sourcing capacity in Taiwan, China, Thailand, the Philippines, and Indonesia. It also contracted to take all of the production of H.S. Corporation, a large South Korean footwear manufacturer that produced approximately 30 million pairs of shoes annually.

EXHIBIT 1   New Product Line Introductions and Acquisitions

Introductions	
Year	*Product Line Introduced*
1979	Reebok running shoes
1982	Reebok aerobic shoes
1983	Reebok tennis shoes
1983	Reebok fitness shoes
1984	Reebok children's athletic shoes
1985	Reebok apparel
1985	Reebok basketball shoes
1986	Reebok walking shoes
1987	Reebok volleyball/indoor court shoes
1987	Reebok sports conditioning shoes
1987	Reebok infants' and children's shoes
1987	Metaphors (women's casual comfort shoes)
1988	Reebok golf shoes
1988	Reebok cycling shoes

Acquisitions		
Date	*Company Acquired*	*Product Line*
October 1986	The Rockport Company	Casual, dress, and walking shoes.
April 1987	Avia Group International, Inc.	Athletic footwear for aerobics, basketball, tennis, running, walking, fitness/sports conditioning, and volleyball.
	Donner Mountain Corporation (subsidiary of Avia)	Walking and casual shoes and hiking boots.
May 1987	John A. Frye Corporation	Leather boots and casual and dress shoes.
June 1987	ESE Sports, Ltd.	Reebok's Canadian distributor.
January 1988	Ellesse USA, Inc.: exclusive rights to the Ellesse trademarks for the United States and Canada	Sportswear and athletic footwear.

THE ATHLETIC FOOTWEAR INDUSTRY

Growth of the Industry

Between 1981 and 1987, the U.S. athletic footwear market more than doubled in size. Wholesale sales of branded athletic footwear neared $3.1 billion in 1987. Nonbranded footwear added another $0.4 billion. Reebok held a 32.2 percent share of branded athletic footwear in 1987, up from 3.3 percent in 1984.

The industry's dynamic growth began in the early 1980s with the running craze. The running shoe was a new product that did not replace existing lines.

TABLE 1 RFD Sales and Estimated Operating Income ($ millions)

	1983	1984	1985	1986	1987
Net sales	$12.0	$64.0	$299.0	$841.0	$991.0
Cost of sales	6.8	37.9	171.0	475.0	562.0
Gross margin	5.2	26.1	128.0	366.0	429.0
SG&A expense	4.0	14.0	52.0	131.0	169.0
Operating income	$1.2	$12.1	$76.0	$235.0	$260.0

Compared with the sneakers of the 1970s, it was made of different materials, was more performance-oriented, and was more expensive. It also became a fashion item as Americans embraced more casual, health-conscious lifestyles.

In 1983 running shoe sales declined dramatically as Americans turned to other forms of exercise. New categories, such as aerobic and fitness shoes, however, continued to drive industry growth. The success of the aerobic shoe prompted many companies to develop women's shoes for traditionally male-dominated categories, such as basketball. By 1987, walking shoes, targeted largely at older females, were the fastest-growing line. Industry experts expected 8–12 percent growth in the U.S. athletic footwear market in 1988.

In 1987 Reebok also held a 4.4 percent share of the $4.5 billion foreign-branded athletic shoe market. Development of foreign markets lagged three or four years behind that of the U.S. market. In 1987 the aerobics boom was just taking off in Europe, and the women's athletic shoe market was largely untapped.

The Competition

Nike, in second place, had an 18.6 percent market share, down from 31.3 percent in 1984. Founded in 1964, Nike rose to prominence in the late 1970s thanks to high-tech innovations in running shoes. In 1984, however, Nike ignored the aerobics trend, wrongly counting on its running shoes to sustain company growth. Its warehouses became overstocked with running-shoe inventory, which Nike had to sell off through discount stores. This action tarnished Nike's reputation with the trade. From 1983 to 1985, its sales rose by only 9 percent. However, in 1985, the Air Jordan basketball shoe, named for Michael Jordan of the Chicago Bulls, generated sales of $100 million. In 1986 sales fell as quickly as they had risen when Jordan broke his foot early in the NBA season. That year Nike lost its number-one U.S. market share position to Reebok.

In 1987 Nike closed excess plant capacity, slashed overhead, and spent $23 million to promote its new Air line with a "Revolution in motion" advertising campaign that featured the Beatles' original recording of "Revolution." It also took advantage of Reebok's supply problems to revitalize its dealer relations.

Nike's expressed goal was to recapture the number-one spot from Reebok. For 1988, according to *Advertising Age* magazine, Nike was stepping up advertising spending by 36 percent to $34 million. Ten million dollars would be spent on network television for its new "Just do it" campaign, which would break in mid-August. In February 1988, Nike introduced a fashion-oriented nonathletic brand for women in an attempt to penetrate a market in which it was historically weak. The shoes, called IE, did not carry the Nike name.

Converse held an 8.1 percent share of the U.S. market in 1987, down from 11.2 percent in 1984. The Converse name was closely identified with canvas athletic shoes for children and teens, particularly for basketball. In 1988 the company introduced the Evolo line of leather athletic shoes, featuring upscale Italian styling and aimed at a more fashion-conscious customer.

Adidas, the world's largest athletic shoe company, had a 5.7 percent U.S. share and a 25 percent world share in 1987. Headquartered in West Germany, Adidas lost $30 million on its U.S. sales. Its 1988 U.S. advertising budget was estimated at only $3 million.

Avia, owned by Reebok, was the fifth-largest competitor in the U.S. branded athletic shoe market. Avia emphasized design technology and targeted active athletic participants who valued performance and functionality over other product features. With 1987 sales of $157 million, its share was 4.9 percent, up from 0.4 percent in 1984. Avia's 1988 advertising budget of $20 million was double 1987 expenditures.

Industry experts grouped Avia with LA Gear (2.3 percent share) and Asics Tiger (2.2 percent share) as small companies with innovative products and the potential to become significant players in the market. Twenty-five other companies competed in the branded athletic shoe market. Each had found a niche for itself, but none had been able to expand beyond it.

Competition remained keen in 1988. First, higher leather costs, increased labor rates, and a weakened dollar had increased the cost of Far East production by 10 percent in 1987. Further cost hikes, which would put pressure on the margins of all competitors, were expected in 1988. Second, to reduce inventory markdowns, retailers were narrowing their selections to only four or five brands and one or two lines of a few other brands. Third, athletic shoe product life cycles appeared to be shortening. By 1988 the life of a new model averaged only about nine months.

CONSUMER ATTITUDES AND BEHAVIOR

Paul Fireman credited Reebok's success to an ability to stay close to the consumer. "Consumer preferences are constantly changing," he contended, "and future progress is linked to our skill in understanding the messages sent from the marketplace so we can deliver the right products."

Industry experts segmented athletic shoe consumers into serious athletes, weekend warriors who used their shoes for sports but were not zealous athletes, and casual wearers who used athletic shoes only for streetwear. The "pyramid-of-influence" model, traditionally used in marketing athletic shoes, posited that the serious athlete was a very small segment of the market but an important opinion leader for both weekend warriors and casual wearers. Casual wearers accounted for 80 percent of athletic shoe purchases, wanted both style and comfort, and were thought to select shoes based on what they saw serious athletes wearing.

The pyramid model led athletic shoe marketers to emphasize technological and performance superiority in order to appeal to serious athletes. New shoes were first introduced in exclusive sports shops and gradually expanded into wider distribution.

The validity of the pyramid-of-influence model was questioned by some Reebok executives who believed that advertising directed at the serious athlete did not reach many consumers. They pointed to the results of a June 1986 survey that indicated that friends and relatives, not athletes, were the most important influence in athletic shoe users' brand decisions. Exhibit 2 shows the sources of information that athletic shoe purchasers used to decide which brand to buy. In addition, in a world where new athletic shoe styles could be knocked off in three months, the executives questioned the appropriateness of new product introductions not directed at the mass market.

In the 1986 survey, consumers were asked how important various attributes were when deciding which athletic shoes to buy. Fifty-eight percent of respondents rated comfort extremely important, followed by support/stability (43 percent), design (36 percent), quality (35 percent), price (30 percent), fashion (20 percent), and leadership (12 percent).

An October 1987 attitude and usage study indicated that 95 percent of athletic shoe owners were aware of Reebok shoes, up from 57 percent two years before. Ninety-eight percent of all teens, a segment that purchased more than three pairs of athletic shoes per year, were aware of the Reebok brand. Moreover, unaided awareness of Reebok had doubled over the past two years,

EXHIBIT 2 Sources of Information Used by Athletic Shoe Purchasers

		Reebok	
Information Source	*Total (Percentage)*	*Users (Percentage)*	*Nonusers (Percentage)*
Friend or relative	72%	69%	74%
Coach or instructor	65	64	65
Salesperson	54	53	54
Article in magazine	50	52	48
Advertisement	45	43	47

Note: All people included in the survey had bought athletic shoes for their own use within the 12 months prior to the survey and were aware of the Reebok brand. Reebok users were people who claimed to own and wear Reebok shoes fairly regularly. Reebok nonusers were people who did not.

whereas that of Nike had dropped. Fifty-three percent of teenagers surveyed considered Reebok the "in" shoe, compared with 38 percent for Nike. Reebok was also rated superior to its major competitors in both quality and comfort.

The brand had high penetration. Fifty-two percent of all people surveyed and 70 percent of the teens surveyed had owned Reebok shoes. Two years before, only 18 percent of people surveyed had ever owned Reebok shoes. Reebok's current ownership was 45 percent of those surveyed, higher than for any other brand. In addition, Reebok shoes were currently worn in 61 percent of the households in which athletic shoes were purchased in 1987. The owners claimed to be loyal as well. Two out of three of those who last purchased Reebok intended to make Reebok their next purchase, a repurchase rate higher than that for any competing brand. Finally, Reebok owners were significantly more likely to buy athletic shoes at regular price than were nonowners.

The results of the attitude and usage study were positive. But a series of focus group interviews in October 1987 uncovered some disturbing qualitative information.[1] In past focus groups, when participants were asked to describe Reebok shoes, the most commonly used adjectives were *innovative, vivid, adventurous, experimental, special, vibrant,* and *new.* The October 1987 focus group members, however, used such words as *comfortable, youthful, energy, fun, diverse, clean, leader, a standard,* and *middle class.* Teens said they were still buying Reeboks, but the way they talked about them had changed. They used to brag about their Reeboks. Now some teens apologized for them. At the same time, participants insisted that Reebok was not a badge brand. In other words, wearing Reeboks did not brand one as a jock or a yuppie or any other "type." "My Reeboks" meant something different to each person.

Sharon Cohen, vice president of advertising and public relations for Reebok North America since 1984, concluded: "When Reebok was new, just being discovered, we had a cult-like following. We were fresh and exciting and had brought new dimensions to the athletic shoe industry—style and comfort. Today we are a mass-appeal shoe, and this requires new strategic thinking. Now that everyone is wearing Reeboks, our job and the job of our advertising is to keep our brand exciting."

MARKETING COMMUNICATIONS

Before 1987

According to Cohen, Paul Fireman "always started with advertising. If he had only $100, he'd spend it on advertising." In the early years of the company, he made his own media buys. He bought astutely, making ad hoc print media

---

[1] A focus group brings together 6 to 10 individuals for an open-ended discussion led by a moderator.

purchases at low rates to make the brand as visible as possible even though sales were modest.

By the early 1980s, RFD's advertising program consisted of product-specific, sports-context print ads, heavy concentration in specialty periodicals targeted at serious athletes, lighter buys in related general-interest magazines, media-exposed use of the products by a select group of successful-athlete endorsers, and a great emphasis on grass-roots involvement.

Reebok paid star athletes to wear the Reebok label and to participate in Reebok-sponsored promotions, such as tennis clinics and autographing sessions. These athletes also could earn bonuses by winning specified tournaments/games/events or by winning specified honors within their sports, or both. In addition, lesser athletes, mostly promising youngsters, received free shoes and clothing from Reebok but were paid nothing. By supporting their training efforts in this way, Reebok increased the likelihood of signing them to endorsement contracts if they excelled later.

RFD's marketing of aerobic shoes exemplified its heavy grass-roots involvement in the sports addressed by its products. The division published aerobics newsletters, sponsored seminars and clinics, funded research on injury prevention, and created the sport's first certification program for instructors. It also offered aerobics instructors discounts on shoes and put Reebok shoes on the feet of many television aerobics instructors.

In addition, RFD communicated with its consumers through point-of-sale pieces and merchandising promotions in retail stores, outdoor advertising, radio, and, starting in 1986, television. RFD also advertised in trade publications, catalogues, and sales brochures to help its salespeople communicate better with their dealers.

As RFD's sales grew, so did its advertising, promotion, and public relations budgets. Combined, they grew from $2.7 million (4.2 percent of sales) in 1984 to $6.5 million (2.2 percent of sales) in 1985, $10 million (1.1 percent of sales) in 1986, and $34 million (3.4 percent of sales) in 1987.

In 1986, RFD began testing new approaches to advertising. It ran the advertisement shown in Exhibit 3, which featured a couple wearing Reebok shoes riding a motorcycle to brunch and was the first ad to feature an athletic shoe advertised outside of a sports context. It was followed by an 18-month-long campaign with the theme "Because life is not a spectator sport." Each print ad, an example of which is shown in Exhibit 4, emphasized the participant and the joy of the sport, not the shoe and its attributes. The ads used an unusual technique called prism color, in which photographs were transformed into pastel acrylic paintings. They ran in a balanced mix of 40 general-interest and specialty sport magazines.

The 1987 Program

Each year RFD developed a divisional marketing communications budget plus separate budgets for each category of sports shoe. Category managers were responsible for the decision making and management of their budgets, and

EXHIBIT 3   1986 Reebok "Motorcycle" Print Ad

Cohen was responsible for managing the divisional budget. Cohen and the category managers all reported to Frank O'Connell, the president of Reebok North America. Exhibit 5 presents the division's marketing organization in relation to the total corporation.

EXHIBIT 4 1986 Reebok "Spectator Sport" Print Ad

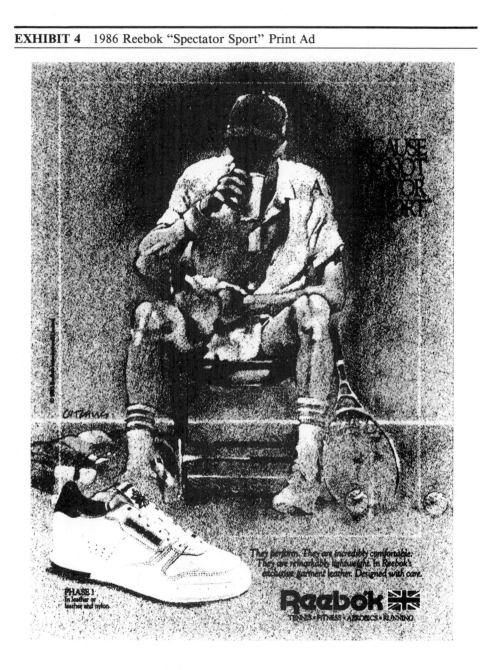

RFD's 1987 divisional advertising budget is outlined in Exhibit 6. In 1987 RFD advertised via print, radio, and television directed toward both the trade and consumers. Trade advertising, illustrated in Exhibit 7, emphasized that "Reebok is performance." Consumer advertising through July focused on the

EXHIBIT 5 Reebok Footwear Division Marketing Organization

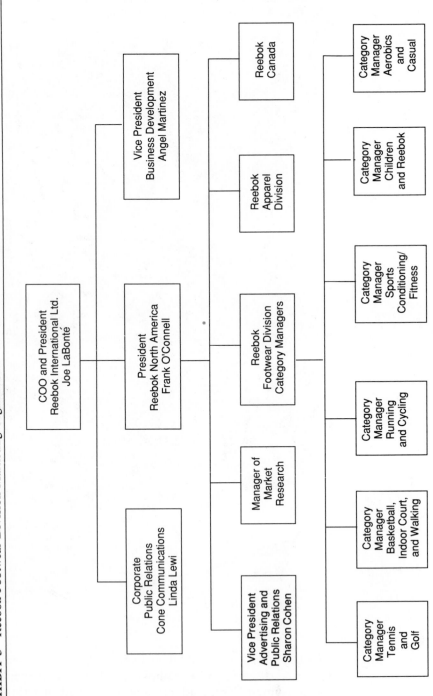

EXHIBIT 6 Reebok Footwear Division 1987 Advertising Budget ($ thousands)		
Television:		
Network	$6,354	
Spot	2,107	
Cable	222	
Total TV		$ 8,683
Radio Spot		179
Print:		
Magazines	$ 7,475	
Newspapers	166	
Total print		7,641
Outdoor and other		350
Total		$16,853

"Because life is not a spectator sport" campaign. In August the division began a new multi-themed campaign with different television and print ads designed for each sports category. Depending on the sport, print ads addressed one or more of four themes: performance, new technology, "classic" styling, and fashion. Exhibits 8 through 11 show ads for four sports categories. Five television ads each sold a different sports shoe, but all dramatically employed motion and featured "real people," not high-profile athletes. Radio was used to reinforce the television message.

The variety in RFD's 1987 advertising effort was exemplified by contrasting the second-half advertising of shoes in two sports categories, tennis and basketball. Tennis shoe advertising was targeted at 18- to 49-year-old adults. The category manager's $975,000 advertising budget was split nearly equally between television and magazines. Both the magazine and television copy evoked tennis tournaments. The television ads were shown only during the U.S. Open. The print ads ran in nine tennis magazines, including *Tennis* and *Racquet Quarterly*, and three general sports magazines, including *Sports Illustrated*.

Men's basketball shoe advertising was targeted at 12- to 24-year-old males. Approximately $1.2 million was spent, 60 percent on television, 24 percent on print, and the rest on radio. Ads in all media showed amateur players in action on neighborhood playground basketball courts. Television ads ran on network prime time and late night and during sports events. Magazines used were *Sports Illustrated*, *Boys' Life*, and *High School Sports*.

Women's basketball shoe advertising was targeted at female teens. The $960,000 women's basketball shoe budget, like that for tennis, was split evenly between television and print. Unlike the tennis ads, however, the basketball ads were fashion-oriented and did not show shoes being used in sports contexts. The television ad ran on early-fringe, weekend, and late-fringe network TV and on the MTV (music television) cable channel. The print ads ran in seven

EXHIBIT 7   1987 Reebok Trade Advertisement

EXHIBIT 8 1987 Reebok Tennis Shoe Print Ad

general-interest, fashion, and teen magazines, including *People, Glamour,* and *Seventeen.*

In addition to product-specific advertising, RFD sponsored a special insert in *Rolling Stone* magazine. The insert, titled "Artists of the Year 1967–1986," featured five Reebok shoe ads. These ads were one-offs; that is, they were used only once, in the *Rolling Stone* insert. Each ad featured someone giving a "Best performance in a pair of Reeboks" in a decidedly nonsports context. Exhibit 12 shows one of the ads.

Grass-roots promotions and athlete endorsements remained a large part of RFD's communications program in 1987, costing approximately $18 million. Promotional events included sponsorship of tennis tournaments for juniors and celebrities, the Reebok Teaching Pro Classic for tennis professionals, the Reebok Professional Aerobics Instructor Alliance, and the Reebok Racing Club. Shoe endorsers included basketball players Dennis Johnson, Danny Ainge, and Brad Daugherty, marathoner Steve Jones, tennis players Hana Mandlikova and Miloslav Mecir, aerobics expert Denise Austin, and the members of the U.S. National Cycling Team.

The 1988 Program

Category Advertising. The 1988 category budgets totaled approximately $22 million, $8 million of which was earmarked for category-specific print and

EXHIBIT 9   1987 Reebok Basketball Shoe Print Ad

television ads. The rest was allocated to athlete endorsements and grass-roots promotional events. The communications program for each category varied widely, as exemplified by the allocation of the 1988 budgets for tennis and basketball shown in Exhibit 13.

Almost 75 percent of the tennis category expenditures in 1988 were allocated to athlete endorsements and local and national tournament sponsorship. The objective was to maintain Reebok tennis shoes' credibility in the world of tennis. Reebok currently had a 40 percent share of the U.S. tennis shoe market and marketed the five best-selling tennis shoes in the world. Fewer than 10 percent of Reebok tennis shoes sold, however, were used on the tennis court; the rest were used for streetwear.

Tennis shoe print advertising in 1988 was geared toward casual usage. Thirty percent of the budget was allocated to hard-core performance-oriented ads. The rest was allocated to lifestyle/fashion-oriented ads, a departure from the strict performance orientation of the past.

Reebok basketball shoes, introduced in late 1985, were the best-selling basketball shoes in the United States. The category's 1988 television and radio ads featured people talking about the greatest basketball players they had ever seen, the "legends" of the old playgrounds. Print and outdoor ads showed "real" people engaged in playground basketball. Consumer promotions were of two types. First, a court-painting program sponsored renovation of basketball courts in low-income areas. Second, 10 local basketball tournaments, such

EXHIBIT 10 1987 Reebok Running Shoe Print Ad

as the Gus Macker 3-on-3 tournament in Belding, Michigan, were sponsored. Players under contract to Reebok attended the events to heighten their impact.

"U.B.U." Umbrella Advertising. From the 1987 consumer research, Frank O'Connell concluded that RFD needed a new umbrella campaign to rekindle the vitality of the Reebok name while ensuring its continuity as a mainstream brand. He charged Chiat/Day with developing advertising copy that was "on the edge, far out, with a unique look that would be new not only to footwear advertising, but to the whole advertising industry." Chiat/Day recommended that the new campaign stress freedom of expression and the individuality that one could achieve wearing a pair of Reeboks, but at the same time maintain the brand's mass appeal.

The result was an offbeat campaign with the tag line "Reeboks let U.B.U." The ads featured zany vignettes of people expressing their individual styles in their Reebok shoes: a three-legged man strutting in a baseball cap and raincoat, a girl dressed like a princess emerging from a subway exit wearing her crown and her Reeboks, a bevy of wood nymphs tiptoeing through a forest glade, a room full of pregnant women aerobic dancing, and a young couple rolling on the grass. Throughout the television commercials, "U.B.U." flashed on the screen in large, jagged, typewritten-style letters. In the final seconds of each ad, "Reeboks let U.B.U." appeared across the screen. The ads would be targeted

EXHIBIT 11 1987 Reebok Aerobic Shoe Print Ad

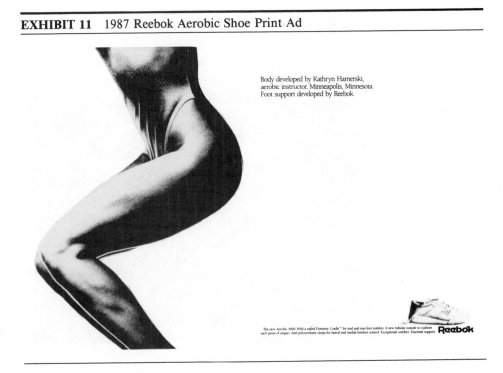

Body developed by Kathryn Hamerski, aerobic instructor, Minneapolis, Minnesota. Foot support developed by Reebok.

The new Aerobic 4000. With a raised Dynamic Cradle™ for mid and rear-foot stability. A new tubular outsole to cushion each point of impact. And polyurethane straps for lateral and medial forefoot control. Exceptional comfort. Essential support. **Reebok**

at 18- to 34-year-old adults, particularly women. They would be run on prime-time and late-night shows, such as "The Wonder Years," "Moonlighting," "LA Law," "thirtysomething," and "Late Night with David Letterman" and on cable channels, such as MTV, ESPN, and WTBS.

The proposed "U.B.U." print campaign used a revolutionary new colorization process. A marriage of photography and illustration, its finished product resembled that of colorized videos. The print ads, like the television ones, featured self-expression in Reebok shoes and used the same tag line. Exhibit 14 shows a sample print ad. The ads would run in fashion magazines, such as *Esquire* and *Glamour*, entertainment magazines, such as *People*, and life-style/special-interest magazines, such as *Rolling Stone, Self,* and *New York Woman*. Insertions would begin in August issues and run at least through December. In addition, ads would appear in July editions of five athletic shoe trade magazines.

Olympics Advertising. RFD purchased $6 million worth of television advertising time during NBC's coverage of the 1988 Summer Olympics, which spanned the last two weeks of September. Although Reebok shoes were not "Official Products of the 1988 Summer Olympics," this media purchase represented the largest concentrated spending level in the history of the athletic footwear industry and ensured the Reebok brand exclusivity in athletic foot-

EXHIBIT 12   Reebok Ad from 1987 *Rolling Stone* Magazine Insert

Best Performance in a pair of Reeboks February 12, 1982

wear advertising during NBC's coverage of the Summer Games. The Olympics advertising was expected to excite Reebok brand dealers, many of whom believed that the principal way to sell athletic shoes was through ads associating them with sports.

EXHIBIT 13   1988 Tennis and Basketball Category Allocation of Marketing Communications Budgets

Communications Program	Basketball(%)	Tennis(%)
Athlete endorsements	32%	59%
Magazine ads	3	15
Television ads	37	—
Newspaper ads	4	—
Radio	5	—
Consumer promotions	8	12
Associations and clubs	—	7
Outdoor	5	—
U.S. Open sponsorship	—	7
Merchandising aids	6	—
Total	100%	100%

The next step was to finalize copy for both the Olympics campaign and the umbrella campaign. The copy proposed by Chiat/Day for the Olympics ads featured "real" people wearing Reebok shoes frantically engaged in street or front-yard sports. Commercials began with the tag line "Summer Games, Bronx, New York" (or Baltimore, Maryland, and the like). At the end of each commercial, one person stopped his or her action and stated, "And you thought all the excitement was in Seoul."

ERS.   Both the Olympics and "U.B.U." ads would be targeted at style-conscious 18- to 34-year-old adults. To reach active sports participants, RFD also planned to run a performance-based print campaign featuring Reebok's new Energy Return System (ERS). ERS shoes were designed to compete with Nike's Air line in the $75–$90 per pair retail price range. Compressed air—sandwiched in four brightly colored tubes visible through the sole of the shoe—cushioned the foot when it hit the ground, captured some of the energy released, and returned it to the foot for extra bounce. The proposed ERS ads would carry the slogan "The revolution is over" in response to Nike's successful 1987 "Revolution" campaign. Exhibit 15 shows a sample ad. The ads would run from June to December in sports magazines, such as *Runner's World, Outside,* and *Sports Illustrated.*

RFD's divisional marketing communications budget would cover the $17 million combined cost of the "U.B.U.," Olympics, and ERS campaigns through the end of 1988. Exhibit 16 provides a breakdown of the proposed ad spending by campaign and media.

THE HUMAN RIGHTS NOW! TOUR

While O'Connell, Cohen, and Chiat/Day were developing copy for RFD's freedom-of-expression umbrella campaign, an opportunity arose to help fi-

EXHIBIT 14 1988 "Reeboks Let U.B.U." Print Ad

EXHIBIT 15   1988 Reebok ''Energy Return System'' Print Ad

EXHIBIT 16 Reebok Footwear Division, Proposed 1988 Advertising Budget Spending by Campaign ($ thousands)

Campaign	Television	Magazines	Outdoor	Total
"U.B.U."	$ 8,000	$1,900	$700	$10,600
Olympics	6,000	0	0	6,000
ERS	0	600	0	600
Total	$14,000	$2,500	$700	$17,200

Note: Budget excludes individual category communications budgets and Human Rights Now! tour budget.
An additional $1 million in sports-specific ERS print ads would be paid out of individual category manager budgets.

nance a world concert tour conceived by AI. The objective of the tour, later named the Human Rights Now! world concert tour, was to support AI's worldwide effort to develop awareness of the human rights guaranteed in the United Nations Universal Declaration of Human Rights.

Chiat/Day brought the idea to Reebok and suggested that it help underwrite the tour to reach young people with a positive message about the company. Before proceeding, Joe LaBonté commissioned a telephone survey of 1,000 U.S. adults to determine their awareness of and attitude toward AI. Awareness was highest (60 percent) among people 18 to 34 years old. Almost half of this age group (49 percent) had a favorable attitude toward AI, and only 7 percent had an unfavorable attitude. The rest were neutral or unaware.

Joe LaBonté decided to support the Human Rights Now! world concert tour, because he believed in the tour's cause and because it offered the opportunity to give something back to the young people who were responsible for the company's success. After discussions with Paul Fireman, he committed Reebok as sole underwriter of the tour. He felt that the time it would take for AI to enlist several sponsors would likely delay the concert tour until 1989. In addition, being sole corporate sponsor would give Reebok a greater voice in tour promotion decisions than if the job were shared.

LaBonté announced Reebok's underwriting of the tour at a press conference in Los Angeles on March 29. At the same time, telegrams announcing the sponsorship were sent to all of Reebok's retailers. Soon thereafter, letters explaining Reebok's involvement with the tour and the Reebok Human Rights Award were mailed to all Reebok employees, U.S. Reebok sales agencies, and Reebok International Division distributors.

Once committed to the tour, LaBonté formed a task force consisting of himself; Linda Lewi, vice president of Cone Communications, Reebok's public relations agency; and Angel Martinez, vice president of business development, to handle the public relations and advertising surrounding Reebok's involvement with the tour. Among their most important tasks was the management of relations between Reebok and AI.

AI was a nonpartisan organization with a worldwide grass-roots network that tried to ensure respect for human rights, the release of nonviolent prisoners of conscience, fair and prompt trials for all political prisoners, and an end to torture and executions. AI was funded by 700,000 members in 150 nations. It strove to be independent and impartial. The organization did not support or oppose any government or political system and accepted no financial contributions from governments. AI's activities included letter-writing campaigns in which AI members sent letters, cards, and telegrams on behalf of individual prisoners to government officials; publicizing of human rights abuse patterns; and meetings with government representatives. Members also organized public-awareness events, such as vigils outside government embassies. Since its founding in 1961, AI had worked on behalf of more than 25,000 prisoners around the world. In 1987, more than 150 of the prisoners of conscience "adopted" by AI groups in the United States were released.

Human Rights Day, December 10, 1988, would mark the 40th anniversary of the Universal Declaration of Human Rights. Adopted by the General Assembly of the United Nations in 1948, the declaration, based on the twin pillars of freedom from want and freedom from fear, proclaimed fundamental and equal rights for "all peoples and nations." On March 3, 1988, AI launched its most ambitious campaign ever, titled Human Rights Now! Its goals were to mobilize public opinion and pressure governments to honor the declaration. In March AI circulated copies of the declaration and petitions in support of it around the world. The combined petition would be presented to the United Nations on December 10.

In 1986 AI had sponsored an American rock music concert tour that brought AI 100,000 new members, most of whom were high school and college students. This success led AI to view music as an important vehicle to spread its message. Hence the Human Rights Now! world concert tour was conceived and scheduled to begin in September 1988. Although the venues and artists were not all finalized, AI hoped to include countries on five continents, including some with records of frequent human rights violations. Eighteen concerts were planned in 16 countries. Firm venues included Los Angeles, Philadelphia, London, and Brazil. Possibilities included Zimbabwe, the USSR, India, Thailand, Yugoslavia, Japan, Argentina, Italy, Spain, France, the Ivory Coast, Costa Rica, and Canada. The six-week tour would feature both international artists and national artists of each country in which the tour played. All artists would play for free. Sting, Peter Gabriel, Youssou N'Dour, and Tracy Chapman had committed themselves to the whole tour. Bruce Springsteen was considering joining the tour. If he did so, he would headline the event.

AI estimated that the tour would cost $22 million to produce. It expected to raise $12 million via ticket sales and broadcast rights. This left a $10 million shortfall. Therefore, for the first time in its history, AI sought corporate assistance.

In an agreement signed on April 22, Reebok made a commitment to provide $2 million seed money immediately and to finance the tour deficit to a maximum of $8 million. In addition, the nonprofit Reebok Foundation decided to fund up to $2 million.[2] The tour deficit was defined as the tour receipts received by AI from all sources other than Reebok and charitable contributions to AI minus all tour expenses.

AI had to consult with Reebok on all tour matters but had the final say on most aspects of the tour. Tour logo, name, and the design of tour merchandise required mutual approval. Reebok had certain rights to the tour name and logo as well as to photographs of the artists and audio and visual material created by AI and Reebok during the tour. Reebok could participate in the negotiation of the sale of television, radio, theatrical, and home video rights for any tour concert. The company also could create its own advertising with respect to the tour and its purposes. In addition, Reebok had the exclusive right to manufacture all tour merchandise, including clothing, posters, buttons, programs, videos, and books. The tour logo, advertising, promotional materials, and merchandise would all carry "Made possible by the Reebok Foundation" as a tag line. AI would be responsible for selling tour merchandise on the grounds of the concert on concert days. Reebok had the exclusive right to sell it through all other channels. Net profits from the sale of tour merchandise were considered tour receipts. In the unlikely event that merchandise net profits exceeded the tour deficit, the balance would be donated to AI.

To further emphasize Reebok's interest in human rights, the task force decided to establish the Reebok Human Rights Award, which was independent of AI. The $100,000 annual award, to be funded through the Reebok Foundation, would be split between two young people under 30 years of age, one male and one female. It would honor young people who, by circumstance or choice, acted against great odds to raise public awareness of and thereby help protect freedom of expression, or who suffered in their attempts to exercise their own freedom of expression.

In early June, the task force met to finalize a marketing communications program for the tour. Lewi proposed the $5 million plan shown in Exhibit 17. This expense would be in addition to the cost of underwriting the tour. The plan consisted of pre-event, event, and postevent advertising, promotions, and public relations.

The proposed pre-event plan included the following: advertising the tour on national and spot radio; advertising on network and cable television stations, via 20 public service announcements featuring celebrities talking about human rights abuses; advertising with spreads emphasizing a human rights theme in *Rolling Stone, Spin, L.A. Style, Details,* and *Interview* magazines and in the campus newspapers of the top 60 colleges and universities; speaking engagements by Reebok and AI executives before college leadership groups; interviews of AI executives and Human Rights Now! tour artists on "Good Morning

---

[2] The Reebok Foundation was a nonprofit organization set up in 1987 to seek out grant opportunities. In its first year the foundation awarded grants to 32 organizations in the fields of education, arts/culture, human/social services, health, and religion.

EXHIBIT 17 Proposed Marketing Communications Budget for Human Rights Now!
Concert Tour and Reebok Human Rights Award

Marketing Unit	Proposed 1988 Budget
Advertising:	
Media production	$ 50,000
Radio and campus media	1,575,000
Logo development	15,000
Merchandising brochures	25,000
Tour posters	100,000
Satellite network	375,000
Promotional materials	125,000
TV/video animated logo	15,000
Total advertising:	$2,280,000
Public relations:	
Press kits	$ 6,325
Clerk program/newsletters	65,000
Media relations	215,000
Parties	30,000
Ticket purchases	187,500
Press conferences	220,000
Radio	50,000
Human Rights Award	190,000
PR fees	250,000
Human rights education/campus program	251,000
Total public relations	$1,464,825
Promotions:	
Retail clerk premiums/contests	$ 200,000
Athletes program	60,000
Celebrity network TV, etc.	100,000
Internal support program	50,925
Distributors	3,000
Total promotions	$ 413,925
Merchandising:	
Product for tour musicians and VIPs	$ 92,650
Staff	175,000
Other:	
Contingency	250,000
Legal and accounting	260,000
	510,000
Total budget	$4,936,400

America" and similar programs to explain the tour and the award; newsletters and information meetings for employees, sales agencies, and international distributors; and premiums, such as T-shirts with the tour logo, to be given to retail store clerks to stimulate their awareness of and excitement about the tour. The radio and magazine ads would break on August 1, followed by the television ads in mid-August and the campus newspaper ads in early September.

Tentative plans for the event communications included the following: broadcasting at least one of the concerts via network television or cable; interviews to be given by the artists and by AI and Reebok executives on "Good Morning America" and similar shows; a radio petition drive to affirm support for the Universal Declaration of Human Rights; promotions through bookstores and record stores offering free concert tickets and tour merchandise to winning consumers; employee and retailer sweepstakes, with winners to be given free trips and tickets to concerts in Los Angeles or London; free tickets to be given to VIP customers in each country with a venue; hospitality suites set up at venues to entertain VIP customers; use of Reebok athletes to attend event parties and to give third-party endorsements of Reebok's underwriting of the tour; and invitations to all RFD employees to a closed-circuit viewing of one of the concerts.

The postevent plan included the following: stories released to leading newspapers, trade publications, and entertainment, lifestyle, and business magazines describing the tour's success and Reebok's charitable contribution to that success; sale of a tour documentary video and book; use of the video and book as retailer premiums; and the Reebok Human Rights Award ceremony.

The task force had to decide what changes, if any, to make to the proposed communications plan. Other Reebok executives were consulted before the meeting. Several sales managers queried, "How will this sell shoes?" They wished to explore opportunities for promotional tie-ins at the point of sale and advocated running "U.B.U." ads during the television broadcasts of the concerts. They thought that every opportunity to exploit Reebok's association with the tour should be used to sell more shoes.

Other executives disagreed. They cited risks to Reebok from association with the tour and advised that the company keep its involvement with the tour low-key in its retail outlets. Some executives also were wary of involving Reebok's athletes in the tour communications program. They feared that any negative tour publicity could rub off on the athletes and damage their influence as opinion leaders.

At the outset of the meeting, LaBonté stated: "The Human Rights Now! concert campaign promises to be the most exciting event this year in the athletic footwear industry. Our involvement with the tour must be perceived positively by our consumers, dealers, distributors, and employees. We must also ensure that the tour's advertising and promotion mesh with RFD's overall 1988 communications program."

Chapter 9.4

In the News

9.4.1 HOW A PR FIRM EXECUTED THE ALAR SCARE*

After this year's stir over use of the chemical Alar on apples, political publicist David Fenton celebrated the work of his firm in a lengthy memo to interested parties. He wrote of a "sea change in public opinion" that has "taken place because of a carefully planned media campaign, conceived and implemented by Fenton Communications with the Natural Resources Defense Council." Extracts are reprinted below:

In the past two months, the American public's knowledge of the dangers of pesticides in food has been greatly increased. Overnight, suppliers of organic produce cannot keep up with demand. Traditional supermarkets are opening pesticide-free produce sections. . . .

The campaign was based on NRDC's report "Intolerable Risk: Pesticides in Our Children's Food." Participation by the actress Meryl Streep was another essential element.

Usually, public interest groups release similar reports by holding a news conference, and the result is a few print stories. Television coverage is rarely sought or achieved. The intensity of exposure created by design for the NRDC pesticide story is uncommon in the nonprofit world.

Our goal was to create so many repetitions of NRDC's message that average American consumers (not just the policy elite in Washington) could not avoid hearing it—from many different media outlets within a short period of time. The idea was for the "story" to achieve a life of its own, and continue for weeks and months to affect policy and consumer habits. Of course, this had to be achieved with extremely limited resources.

In most regards, this goal was met. A modest investment by NRDC repaid itself manyfold in tremendous media exposure (and substantial, immediate revenue for future pesticide work). In this sense, we submit this campaign as a model for other nonprofit organizations.

Media coverage included two segments on CBS "60 Minutes," the covers of *Time* and *Newsweek* (two stories in each magazine), the "Phil Donahue" show, multiple appearances on "Today," "Good Morning America," and CBS "This Morning," several stories on each of the network evening newscasts, "MacNeil/Lehrer," multiple stories in the *New York Times, Washington Post, Los Angeles Times*, and newspapers around the country, three cover stories in *USA Today, People*, four women's magazines with a combined circulation of 17 million (*Redbook, Family Circle, Women's Day*, and *New Woman*), and thousands of repeat stories in local media around the nation and the world. . . .

Consumer feedback devices were built into the campaign, including self-published book sales and the first use of a 900 phone number by a nonprofit group. . . .

---

* By David Fenton, *The Wall Street Journal*, October 3, 1989. Reprinted by permission of *The Wall Street Journal*, © 1990 Dow Jones and Company, Inc. All Rights Reserved Worldwide.

Planning the Campaign

In October of 1988, NRDC hired Fenton Communications to undertake the media campaign for its report. . . . The report marked the first time anyone—inside government or out—had calculated children's actual exposure levels to carcinogenic and neurotoxic pesticides. The study showed one of the worst pesticides to be daminozide, or Alar, used primarily on apples and peanuts. . . .

[L]ast fall, Meryl Streep contacted NRDC, asking if she could assist with some environmental projects. Ms. Streep read the preliminary results of the study and agreed to serve as a spokesperson for it. . . .

It was agreed that one week after the study's release, Streep and other prominent citizens would announce the formation of NRDC's new project, Mothers and Others for Pesticide Limits. This group would direct citizen action at changing the pesticide laws, and help consumers lobby for pesticide-free produce at their grocery stores.

The separation of these two events was important in ensuring that the media would have two stories, not one, about this project. Thereby, more repetition of NRDC's message was guaranteed.

As the report was being finalized, Fenton Communications began contacting various media. An agreement was made with "60 Minutes" to "break" the story of the report in late February. Interviews also were arranged several months in advance with major women's magazines like *Family Circle, Women's Day*, and *Redbook* (to appear in mid-March). Appearance dates were set with the "Donahue Show," ABC's "Home Show," double appearances on NBC's "Today" show, and other programs.

Releasing the Report

On February 26, CBS "60 Minutes" broke the story to an audience of 40 million viewers. . . . The next morning, NRDC held a news conference attended by more than 70 journalists and 12 camera crews.

Concurrently, NRDC coordinated local news conferences in 12 cities around the country also releasing the report. . . .

Announcing Mothers and Others

On March 7, Meryl Streep held a Washington news conference to announce the formation of NRDC's Mothers and Others for Pesticide Limits. She was joined by board members, including pediatrician Dr. T. Berry Brazelton, National PTA president Manya Unger, and Wendy Gordon Rockefeller of NRDC.

Coverage of Mothers and Others that week included *USA Today* (cover); "The Today Show" on NBC; "The Phil Donahue Show" (10 million viewers); *Women's Day* (6 million copies sold); *Redbook* (4 million); *Family Circle* (6 million); *Organic Gardening* (1.5 million); *New Woman* (1.7 million); *People* magazine; *USA TODAY* television (200 markets); "Entertainment Tonight" (18 million viewers); ABC's "HOME Show" (3 million viewers); Cable News Network, and numerous radio networks, newspaper chains, broadcast chains, wire services, and other media around the nation.

In addition, we arranged for Meryl Streep and Janet Hathaway of NRDC to grant 16 interviews by satellite with local TV major market anchors. . . .

In the ensuing weeks, the controversy kept building. Articles appeared in food sections of newspapers around the country. Columnists and cartoonists took up the story. "MacNeil/Lehrer," the *New York Times*, and *Washington Post* did follow-up stories. . . .

Soon school systems began banning apples (which is not what NRDC intended or recommended). Three federal agencies (EPA, USDA, and FDA) issued an unusual joint statement assuring the public that apples were safe (although to children who consume a great deal, these assurances are not entirely true).

Then, by coincidence, two Chilean grapes were found laced with cyanide, and a story which had been building anyway went further. *Newsweek* and *Time* did additional stories—on both covers the same week—about the safety of the food system, with more coverage of the NRDC report.

And the industry struck back. NRDC's credibility was, as expected, questioned by industry "front groups," such as the American Council on Science and Health. A major corporate PR firm, Hill and Knowlton, was hired for $700,000 by the apple growers, which also put forward a $2 million advertising budget. Stories began appearing (including a *Washington Post* cover piece), saying that the levels of Alar in apples were below federal standards, and charging the media with exaggerating the story. This missed the whole point of the study—that children ingest so many apples for their size that the legal federal standard is unsafe. . . .

Usually, it takes a significant natural disaster to create this much sustained news attention for an environmental problem. We believe this experience proves there are other ways to raise public awareness for the purpose of moving the Congress and policymakers.

9.4.2 TETRIS GAME WINS BIG FOR NINTENDO BUT NOT FOR SOVIET INVENTORS—TO RUSSIA, A LESSON IN MARKETS*

MOSCOW—In the fall of 1985, two Soviet hackers sat down at a computer and devised an infuriatingly simple game that has taken the world by storm. Now a standard feature on Nintendo, the popular home video system, Tetris

* By Peter Gumbel, staff reporter of *The Wall Street Journal*, June 8, 1990. Reprinted by permission of *The Wall Street Journal*, © 1990 Dow Jones and Company, Inc. All Rights Reserved Worldwide.

is one of the hottest software games ever to hit the market. Four million copies have been sold in the United States alone so far.

But Alexei Pazhitnov and Vadim Gerasimov, the game's inventors, are only half celebrating. Although Tetris has won them international fame, the two hackers haven't received a penny of the profits the game has generated—and it isn't likely they ever will. Mr. Gerasimov, a 21-year-old student, can't even afford a computer of his own. "I don't worry about money very much," the thin, shy hacker says modestly, "but I hope that this mistake will be corrected."

As Soviet leader Mikhail Gorbachev battles to overhaul his nation's economy, he is counting on the talents of such people as Mr. Pazhitnov and Mr. Gerasimov. Mr. Gorbachev insists the U.S.S.R. has more to sell than just raw materials like oil and minerals, and he frequently talks about the nation's "huge scientific potential." Soviet officials hail the success of Tetris as proof.

Clumsy Efforts

But Tetris seems as much a testament to the chronic shortcomings of the Soviet economic system as an advertisement for Soviet science. Tetris's path from computer lab to international stardom was littered with obstacles. Its discovery owes more to chance than design. And clumsy Soviet efforts to market the game sparked acrimonious copyright lawsuits in the United States, giving the Soviets an unprecedented taste of American jurisprudence.

"Tetris has made history," says Nikolai E. Belikov, the Soviet trade specialist responsible for licensing the game. But he also concedes that the Soviet inexperience in trade hurt efforts to capitalize on Tetris. "This was our first contract with computer games and it was necessary to understand the market. We needed time," he says, adding that "we have learned very much from the experience."

Tetris is the brainchild of Mr. Pazhitnov, 35, a bearded expert in applied mathematics who works at the prestigious Soviet Academy of Sciences Computing Center, which studies, among other things, artificial intelligence. Like hackers the world over, he is often drawn to computer play. His passion happens to be puzzles.

A Primitive Game

While noodling around on his machine, Mr. Pazhitnov came up with a kind of computerized Rubik's Cube. In his version, a player races the clock to create orderly blocks out of squares, rectangles, and other shapes that drop from the top of a computer screen.

The Computing Center's clunky Soviet machines weren't equipped to handle graphics, so the first version of the game was fairly primitive. When the center purchased more sophisticated personal computers from IBM in 1985, Mr. Pazhitnov set about adapting his game to them. He got some help from Mr. Gerasimov, then a 17-year-old math whiz who frequently dropped by the center after school.

Fine-tuning Tetris became an obsession. "All the chiefs began to hate me because they wanted serious work," Mr. Pazhitnov recalls. But the two persisted, and over a period of months they came up with a game that was simple, elegant, and, according to its many fans, addictive.

Tetris was an instant hit among Soviet computer buffs, who copied it and passed it from hand to hand. "Within a couple of weeks, I found it in every corner of Moscow," Mr. Pazhitnov says.

State Ownership

For all their work, Mr. Pazhitnov and Mr. Gerasimov had only token rights to their invention and couldn't stop it from being pirated in the U.S.S.R., which doesn't have any effective copyright laws. The pair handed over the rights to Tetris to the computing center, which, as a state institution, is allowed to own inventions. The two knew it was the only chance they had to get the game on the market.

Soviet officials concede they probably wouldn't have done anything with the game had they not received a telegram in late 1987 from Robert Stein, a Hungarian refugee who runs a British company called Andromeda Software, seeking to acquire the rights to Tetris. Mr. Stein had spotted the game in 1986 while on a visit to Budapest. "I sat down and played it," Mr. Stein says. "I'm not a games player, and I knew that if I liked it, it must be a success."

Mr. Stein copied the game and took it back to London, where he sold the rights for an undisclosed amount to a British company called Mirrorsoft, a software unit of Maxwell Communication Corporation, the media conglomerate. Mr. Stein concedes he sold rights that weren't legally his, but he says he thought he would eventually be able to acquire the rights from the Soviets.

Mirrorsoft launched the game in Britain and Western Europe in January 1988, and, a few months later, in the United States, Mirrorsoft subsequently sublicensed the U.S. home-video rights to Tengen, Inc., a software unit of video-game manufacturer Atari Games Corporation of Milpitas, California.

Apparently concerned about his company's claim to Tetris—and its right to license it to Mirrorsoft—Mr. Stein went to Moscow in early 1988 to secure a license from Elorg, a Soviet state trading agency that acted on behalf of the computing center. Elorg gave Mr. Stein's company, Andromeda, a license to sell the personal computer version of the game.

Elorg officials say they discovered only by chance that Tetris was a big hit on the home-video market in the United States and elsewhere; they found out by reading computer trade magazines. Officials, who say they thought they had licensed only the personal computer version, not the home-video version, to Mr. Stein, were shocked. They complained to him, but didn't take any action to halt sales.

Elorg also claims Mr. Stein deliberately dragged his feet in paying them licensing fees, although the agency won't say how much it believes it is owed. Mr. Stein acknowledges some delays in paying the Soviets, but he says his customers were slow to pay him.

Meanwhile, another problem loomed. Rigid Soviet accounting rules make it almost impossible to reward people who think up marketable ideas. The computing center has earned hundreds of thousands of dollars so far from Tetris, but the money goes into a special fund that can be used only to buy new equipment. "It's part of our general stupidity in this country," says Vladimir Mazurik, a senior official at the center. "It's important to reward people who work hard."

Mr. Pazhitnov says he never expected to make a fortune off Tetris. He recalls telling his bosses at the computing center: "If you can pay me, please do. If you can't, it doesn't matter." Recently, he got a small bonus of 5,000 rubles. That's about $8,000 at the official exchange rate but, at the more realistic tourist rate, only $800.

The computing center also hopes to give IBM computers to Mr. Pazhitnov and Mr. Gerasimov. But "we can't without special agreement of the presidium of the Academy of Sciences," shrugs Yuri Yevtushenko, the center's director. "We are not a private organization, we are a state institute."

Evidently embarrassed by the situation, he says: "It's a new problem for the Soviet Union. We never even considered it before."

Hectic Negotiations

In any case, by early 1989, international interest in Tetris was soaring. Japanese, American, and British firms rushed to Moscow to vie for various rights to the game. Over several hectic days in February 1989, Elorg conducted parallel negotiations with Mr. Stein, who was trying to acquire the license for coin-operated arcade games, and Kevin Maxwell, Mirrorsoft's chairman and the son of British media tycoon Robert Maxwell, who thought he already held many of the licenses via Mr. Stein but came to Moscow to get more.

Nintendo of America, the U.S. unit of Nintendo Company of Kyoto, Japan, the video-game giant, also entered the fray—and ultimately walked off with one of the most valuable rights: an exclusive worldwide licensing agreement to use the game in its entertainment systems. (Mr. Stein got the arcade-game rights.)

Mirrorsoft's Mr. Maxwell was furious; he had hoped to receive all rights to the game. So apparently was his father, Robert Maxwell, chairman and chief executive of Maxwell Communication, whose publishing firm brought out the English version of Mr. Gorbachev's book, *Perestroika*. Mr. Belikov says the senior Mr. Maxwell fired off an angry letter to the Soviet government complaining about Elorg's negotiations with other companies. A spokesman for the senior Mr. Maxwell declines to comment on the matter.

Were it not for the tolerance of senior officials, who shrugged off the complaint, Mr. Belikov is convinced his career would have been ruined. "Thank heavens for *perestroika*," he beams.

When Nintendo of America, based in Redmond, Washington, returned to the United States in April, it was promptly sued for copyright infringement in federal court by Atari's Tengen, which thought it had acquired the video-game rights through Mirrorsoft. Nintendo filed a countersuit, also claiming its rights had been infringed upon. At issue was the question of whether Mr. Stein, the British businessman, had acquired the home-video rights along with the personal computer rights in 1988.

Under Oath

After an initial hearing in San Francisco in June, lawyers from both sides arranged a deposition in Moscow, believed to be the first such proceeding in the Soviet Union. For several hours, Mr. Pazhitnov and an Elorg official faced a barrage of questions in Moscow.

Meanwhile, an American lawyer for Tengen tracked Mr. Belikov down in Singapore, where he was on state business. The Soviet trade specialist wouldn't cooperate. Nintendo's lawyers had more luck. They persuaded Mr. Belikov to divulge many of the details of the commercial contracts with Mr. Stein. For the Soviet Union, long a closed and extremely secretive society, this was a major step into unknown territory. Mr. Belikov gave crucial details of the business transactions to the lawyers. Later, he went to the U.S. embassy in Moscow on six separate occasions to swear that his comments were true.

"It was the first time a Soviet trade organization had to swear an oath," says Mr. Belikov. "This is very unusual for us."

The final test of Soviet willingness to cooperate in the dispute came in November, when the case went to court in San Francisco. Mr. Belikov agreed to go and give evidence—"very apprehensively," says a lawyer for Nintendo. Because of extreme difficulties in getting a passport and U.S. visa, he just made it in the nick of time. But as it turned out, the judge issued a summary judgment against Tengen, and no evidence was heard. Tengen's lawyers say the company will appeal.

Elorg apparently decided it could play hardball, too. A few days before the hearing in San Francisco, the Soviet trading agency employed a U.S. accounting firm to audit Mr. Stein's books to determine exactly how much revenue the game had generated. The audit results weren't available.

Back in London, Mr. Stein is indignant. "Everybody hates me, and everyone is making a fortune out of Tetris," he says, though he declines to say how much he made off the game himself. "The Soviets didn't know they had this product. We told them they had a hot product. We made it famous."

Mr. Belikov concurs. "It's quite true what he says. We are grateful to Mr. Stein, because he did much to introduce the game," he says with a smile. "If he had just paid us adequately, he would have gained a million times more than he has earned now."

9.4.3 SALES JOB: AT NORDSTROM STORES, SERVICE COMES FIRST— BUT AT A BIG PRICE*

SEATTLE—Recently, a too-thin woman walked into employment counselor Alice Snyder's office here, slumped in a chair, and burst into tears. "I know this is going to sound strange," Ms. Snyder recalls the woman saying, "but I'm sure they're going to fire me." Never mind that she had worked for weeks without a day off, pulled 15-hour shifts without a break, and stockpiled stacks of service awards and customer thank-you letters. None of this mattered. She missed her sales quota, and now management was questioning her "commitment" to the company. She knew her days were numbered.

Ordinarily, Alice Snyder might classify such thinking as paranoid. But not in this case: The woman is a salesclerk at Nordstrom.

"You're not alone," Ms. Snyder says she told the woman. "You're the fourth person from that store I've seen this week." Nervous "Nordies," as they call themselves, have limped through her office so regularly—suffering from ulcers, colitis, hives, and hand tremors—that Ms. Snyder finally went to speak with Nordstrom, Inc.'s personnel office at the company's headquarters here. She says a manager insisted the company was one happy "family," then briskly showed her the door.

But if this prospering retailer is a family, then reports from some of the "children" suggest it's a dysfunctional one. The retailer, renowned for pampering its customers, expects its salesclerks

---

* By Susan C. Faludi, staff reporter of *The Wall Street Journal*, February 20, 1990. Reprinted by permission of *The Wall Street Journal*, © 1990 Dow Jones and Company, Inc. All Rights Reserved Worldwide.

to work many hours without pay in an environment of constant pressure and harassment that incites employees to prey on each other, according to nearly 500 complaints filed with the workers' union and interviews with several dozen employees in stores from Seattle to Los Angeles.

Last Thursday, a three-month investigation by the Washington state Department of Labor & Industries reached similar conclusions: The agency found the company systematically violated state law by failing to pay employees for a variety of duties, from delivering merchandise to inventory work, and by short-changing employees on overtime pay. The agency ordered Nordstrom to pay back wages—which the union estimates at $30 million to $40 million—or face possible legal action. (State authorities wouldn't confirm the union's estimate.)

"We're looking at what is likely to be the highest wage claim in the history of the state," says Mark McDermott, the agency's assistant director for employment standards. "These are employment-practice patterns the company engaged in, not isolated incidents."

Nordstrom's working conditions are the flip side of the company's phenomenal success as a retailer. In the past decade, low labor costs and a system that compels employees to compete for their paychecks have generally helped generate big earnings, a soaring stock price, and sales per square foot that are the envy of the industry. Though the company says it expects to report a drop in profit for its fiscal year ended January 31, its overall success in recent years has spurred the retailer to undertake a big national expansion.

Nordstrom's customers have been a major beneficiary of the exceptional service the department store chain demands. And, no doubt, thousands of salespeople have thrived in the Darwinian struggle on the sales floor. Pat McCarthy, a longtime salesman in the flagship store's men's clothing department, is one of them. He's turned two decades of cultivating

customers into commissions that yield an $80,000-plus yearly salary. "It's really a people job, which I love," says Mr. McCarthy. "Every year my sales have gotten progressively better."

But for thousands of other Nordstrom employees, the working arrangements aren't so congenial. Just as retail chains of all kinds—from Bloomingdale's to Macy's—are rushing to duplicate the Nordstrom commission system, the stories of unhappiness at the company are spreading.

Salespeople were reluctant to tell their story until recently, when the union representing Nordstrom workers in the Seattle area began looking into complaints that employees are told to punch out on their timeclock before turning to the many "non-sell" duties—such as stock work and deliveries to customers. Otherwise, they were warned, the hours would dilute their critical sales-per-hour performance. A low "SPH" is grounds for dismissal.

The union, the United Food and Commercial Workers, is in the midst of contract negotiations with five Nordstrom stores in the Seattle area and obviously has been scouting for damaging data. Of Nordstrom's 30,000 employees nationwide, only 1,500 are unionized, and the union is eager to win more members and boost its influence. When union leaders began an informal inquiry into working conditions, they say they struck a mother lode of discontent, with possibly big ramifications for Nordstrom. "Unionization of other stores easily could happen as an offshoot of these developments," says Joe Peterson, president of local 1001 of the union.

Within two months, the union had received certified letters from hundreds of Nordstrom employees who have worked, on average, 8 to 10 hours a week "off the clock." So many complaints came in, the union set up an 800 hotline to handle them all.

Nordstrom management says it will study the state's report and pay wage claims it considers legitimate. "We haven't seen any complaints" from the union, says Jim Nordstrom, co-chairman of the company with his brother John and cousin Bruce. He dismisses the labor board's findings as "simple record-keeping stuff" and the union's stack of claims as "a bargaining ploy." If employees are working without pay, breaks, or days off, then it's "isolated" or by "choice," he says.

"A lot of them say, 'I want to work every day.' I have as many people thank us for letting them work all these hours as complain." In fact, Jim Nordstrom suspects employees aren't putting in as much time as they might. "I think people don't put in enough hours during the busy time," he says. "We need to work harder."

Nordstrom's incentives, some employees say, tend to be more stick than carrot. While good customer service is rewarded with cheers at company meetings, occasional $5, $10, and $100 bonuses or "All-Star" honors, a steady flow of threatening management memos seems to be the preferred motivational tool. One August 29, 1989, memo, issued by a Nordstrom cosmetics manager in a California store, is typical. It set a long list of goals for the cosmetics counters and made clear that, "In the next 60 days if any of these areas are not met to our expectations you will be terminated." Another manager's memo reminds employees that it is considered "a lot" to call in sick once every three months and will bring into "question your dedication."

"It reminds me of a cult the way they program you to devote your life to Nordstrom," says Cherie Validi, a salesperson in the women's clothing department who has spent her share of days off making home deliveries and attending Nordstrom's pep rallies, where blond bathing beauties prance on stage, chanting "Vol-ume! Vol-ume!" "Granted, the customer gets treated like a hundred bucks. And Nordstrom gets rich off it. So nobody loses—except the employee," she says.

Ms. Validi, one of the top saleswomen in her department, came out the loser herself recently when she received a $100 paycheck for two weeks of work. Why? The commission on a customer's $6,000 return was deducted from her wages, standard practice at Nordstrom. Ms. Validi complained that the sale wasn't hers, that it took place on a day she didn't work. But the company held firm.

Nordstrom insists the system works. It says that employees get one of the highest base pay rates in the industry—as much as $10 an hour—and especially industrious employees can make as much as $80,000 a year. The company also says it only promotes from within and, under its corporate policy of decentralization, managers have unusual freedom to make decisions. "A lot of what comes out makes it sound like we're slave drivers," says Jim Nordstrom, or "Mr. Jim," as he is called by his employees. "If we were that kind of company, they wouldn't smile, they wouldn't work that hard. Our people smile because they want to."

But employees say Nordstrom's high base pay isn't much comfort. Workers only receive base pay if they don't sell enough to qualify for commission—and if they miss that sales quota several times, they're fired. Moreover, of the 1,500 salespeople in the union, the company lists only seven as having made more than $40,000 last year. (Nordstrom won't reveal the number for its roughly 20,000 non-union salespeople, but says union and non-union employees make an average of $20,000 to $24,000 a year. The national average, for all retail salesclerks, is $12,000 a year.)

Even the smiles aren't necessarily a reliable gauge of employee sentiment. Nordstrom periodically dispatches "secret shoppers," people hired to dress up as customers, to check on workers' demeanor. A frown can wind up as a demerit in an employee file. The company also encourages "smile contests." "They would go around and take pictures of whoever smiled the most" and then hang the photos in the lunchroom, recalls Andrea Barton, who worked for three years at a Nordstrom cosmetics counter in Seattle; she says she lost 20 pounds in the process. "I'd look at those pictures and go, 'Boy, some day I hope I'm up here.' " She groans. "I mean, the way I got when I was working there, it's just sickening."

She is only one of the more than 30 Nordstrom veterans, both current and former employees, who voiced such sentiments in interviews. Here are a few of their stories:

A divorced California homemaker who returned to the job market at 40, Patty Bemis joined Nordstrom in 1981, lured by the promise of a bigger income and the "status" of induction in the Nordie elite. She stayed for eight years.

"They came to me," she recalls of the Nordstrom recruiters. "I was working at The Broadway as Estee Lauder's counter manager and they said they had heard I had wonderful sales figures." Ms. Bemis was thrilled. "We'd all heard Nordstrom was the place to work. They told me how I would double my wages. They painted a great picture and I fell right into it."

She soon found herself working progressively harder—for less money and amid more fear.

"The managers were these little tin gods, always grilling you about your sales," she recalls. "You felt like your job was constantly in jeopardy. They'd write you up for anything, being sick, the way you dressed." Once, she had to get a doctor's note so she wouldn't get in trouble for wearing low-heel shoes to work. Sufficiently cowed, she reported to work even when she had strep throat.

Worn down by the pressure, "the girls around me were dropping like flies," she says. "Everyone was always in tears. You feel like an absolute nothing working for them."

Ms. Bemis was consistently one of her department's top sellers, but some years she only made $18,000, far below what she had expected she would earn. She won a companywide sales contest, and received "a pair of PJs," she recalls. "Whoopiedoo!" And she logged many unpaid hours, delivering cosmetics to customers and unpacking hundreds of boxes of makeup. The department rarely had more than one stock person and, in some of the stores, the salesclerks are expected to empty the trash. Jim Nordstrom explains: "Yes, we're always cutting back on stock people." He adds: "It may have happened that some people were asked to pitch in" and carry out the trash. "That would be great if that happened. If people don't want to, then obviously some people don't want to work hard."

Ms. Bemis recalls that "working off the clock was just standard," crucial to elevating sales per hour. "In the end, really serving the customer, being an all-star, meant nothing; if you had low sales per hour, you were forced out."

During a big Clinique sale, Ms. Bemis says she worked 12- and 15-hour shifts for a number of days without overtime pay or a day off. On the drive home at 10:30 on the 10th night, she passed out at the wheel and slammed into the freeway's center divider, she says. While she was at home recovering from head injuries, she recalls, "The manager kept calling me and saying, 'Patty, we can't hold your job much longer.' " Her doctor told her she should stay out a few more weeks, but she didn't dare. "Now, I know I have all these rights. But at the time all I knew was I had to have that job."

She finally left last spring. "I just couldn't take it anymore—the constant demands, the grueling hours. I just said one day, life's too short." She took a sales post at Scandia Down Shops, where she says she makes $400 more a month than at Nordstrom. "And I can sleep at night."

The first time Lori Lucas came to one of the many "mandatory" Saturday morning department meetings and saw the sign—"Do Not Punch the Clock"—she assumed the managers were telling the truth when they said the clock was temporarily out of order. But as weeks went by, she discovered the clock was always "broken" or the timecards were just missing.

Finally, she and several other employees just marked the hours down on their timecard manually. She and another employee recall that their manager whited-out the hours and accused the two of not being "team players." The employees took the tampered timecards to the California labor board. In response to the state agency's inquiry, the company reimbursed four employees for the time, according to a notification the company filed with the labor board.

The department meetings "were unbelievable," Ms. Lucas recalls. "There you'd be at seven in the morning and they had all these security guards dressed up like the California Raisins, with plastic garbage bags stuffed with M&Ms around their midriffs. And all you can hear is people chanting, 'We're number one!' and 'You want to do it for Nordstrom.' Finally I went up to the store manager and said, 'What is this all about?' and she said, 'You are here to learn the Nordstrom Way.' "

The Nordstrom Way involved an endless round of contests ("Who Looks More Nordstrom" was a popular one, intended to encourage employees to shop at the stores) and the daily recital of "affirmations" ("I only sell multiples," was one chanted by salespeople). And the Nordstrom Way, Ms. Lucas discovered, meant working for free. "My manager would say, 'You go clock out and come down and we'll talk.' That was her little trick way of saying there's non-sell work to do." Ms. Lucas's manager declines to comment.

Like most salesclerks at Nordstrom, Ms. Lucas also had daily quotas of thank-you letters to write, and monthly customer-service "books" to generate—photo albums that are supposed to be filled with letters from grateful customers. ("People would get so desperate they would have their friends and relatives write fake letters for them," Petra Rousu, a 10-year salesclerk veteran, recalls.) Such duties, Ms. Lucas says, were supposed to be tackled only after hours. "I'd be up until 3 A.M., doing my letters, and doing my manager's books," she says. "Before you know it, your whole life is Nordstrom. But you couldn't complain, because then your manager would schedule you for the bad hours,

your sales per hour would fall, and, next thing you know, you're out the door."

The pressure eventually gave Ms. Lucas an ulcer, she says. One day, after working 22 days without a day off, she demanded a lunch break. On her hour off, she applied for and got a new job elsewhere and gave notice as soon as she returned. "I remember thinking, I'm making less than $20,000 a year. Why am I killing myself? Nordstrom was the most unfair place I ever worked."

Every pay period, the Nordies gather around the bulletin board in the back room to view the chart. It ranks employees by sales per hour, and woe to anyone whose name falls below the red line.

Over the years, the need to stay above the line has inspired an ingenious set of scams and predatory maneuvers on the sales floor, some employees assert. "Sharking," as it's called, is so rampant that, at one pep rally, the saleswomen did a skit to the music from "Jaws" and presented a shark mask to an employee they considered particularly conniving.

Some Nordies boost their sales per hour by hogging the register and taking all the "walk-ups," or customers who haven't been helped, workers say. Some have been known to cut a deal with the few noncommission cashiers on the floor, who then ring up sales on the employee's identification number. Others get their rival's number and use it when accepting returns.

When all else fails, there's one way to push your name up the list: Bump off the number-one seller.

For nearly two years, Cindy Nelson had stayed on top of the chart in one of the Bellevue, Washington, stores. She was on her way to making "Pacesetter" again—a prestigious title bestowed upon the employees with the top sales. A clique of salesclerks on the floor—led by numbers two and three on the charts—held a powwow one day, decided that Ms. Nelson must be stealing their sales, and vowed to have her "watched," according to court depositions that later became part of a suit filed by Ms. Nelson against Nordstrom in Bellevue.

On September 29, 1986, Cindy Nelson reported for work and was immediately whisked into the personnel office. The department manager had before her five notes of complaint from the salesclerks, all unsigned, which claimed Ms. Nelson had been stealing sales.

Ms. Nelson asked to inspect the sales receipts in question and confront her accusers, but the manager, Rhoda Eakes, refused. "I just didn't feel that it was any of her business," Ms. Eakes explained later in a deposition. Then she told Ms. Nelson that she was fired. (All of the managers and employees involved in Ms. Nelson's firing declined comment, referring queries to Mr. Nordstrom, who said, "That gal wasn't a good employee.")

"I was totally stunned," recalls Ms. Nelson, who had a stack of customer-service citations in her file and had been told she was about to make manager. She was also, up until then, "your 100-percent gungho Nordie. This whole time I thought I was going to be this great Nordstrom person and now I was nothing, a nobody. I became an emotional wreck."

She tried applying to other Nordstrom stores but was repeatedly rejected. Finally, she took a job in a small dress shop—and filed suit. Last October, a King County Superior Court jury awarded her $180,000 in damages. The company and Ms. Nelson later settled out of court for an undisclosed sum.

In Ms. Nelson's court case, Nordstrom's Achilles heel proved to be its employee handbook, which outlined the terms and procedures for warning and firing employees. The company has subsequently replaced the 20-page rulebook with a one-page sheet, and one rule: "Use your good judgment in all situations," it says.

Jim Nordstrom says management chose to rewrite the manual after receiving a raft of lawsuits from ex-employees. "Our wrongful ter-

mination problems have gone way down since we got rid of that darn handbook," he says.

Part of becoming a Nordie, employees say, involves acquiring a certain look. Lupe Sakagawa, a top saleswoman, recalls that, on her first day on the job, her manager strong-armed her into buying $1,400 of the "right" clothes—all from the department. But that wasn't enough: The store manager then called her in and told her: "Correct your accent." Ms. Sakagawa is Mexican. "It was very hard for me to prove myself," she says, "because of that image of the Nordstrom Girl—blond hair, young, and cute."

For years, moreover, minority leaders in Seattle have complained of the company's failure to hire and promote blacks. In 1987, after the company was hit with seven discrimination complaints filed with the Equal Employment Opportunity Commission, Nordstrom hired a consulting firm to rebut the charges. But the consultant's confidential report—subsequently leaked—turned out to be a stinging attack on Nordstrom's "band-aid approach" to affirmative action. "The current lack of definitive personnel policies and procedures . . . perpetuates a system of institutional racism," the report said, "and has had little utility in preventing previous overt racist acts."

Since then, Jim Nordstrom says, the company has hired a black human resources officer, and "our minority numbers are outstanding." But he declines to reveal them. Charles Dudley, the human resource officer, won't supply the statistics, either: "You'll have to talk to Mr. Jim about that," he says. He did confirm that no company vice presidents are black or Hispanic.

Then there's the case of Sean Mulholland, a salesman who says he paid the price for failing to fit another aspect of the "Nordstrom image." He is gay.

In 1986, Mr. Mulholland started working in the men's clothing department in the Alderwood, Washington, store. He was careful to keep his private life a secret. A Nordie true believer, Mr. Mulholland accumulated a dozen company awards and a sales rating that never fell below No. 3 on the charts, according to records he has saved. "To me, Nordstrom was the Golden Fleece," he says. "I was so proud to work there. I strived to be what they wanted."

His faith remained unshaken in spite of some of the company's more bizarre rituals, like the time employees were sent outside for a "surprise." On the roof, a Nordie tossed down $1 bills tied in yellow ribbons. Mr. Mulholland recalls watching, dumbfounded, as fellow clerks scrambled for the cash. "I got this picture in my head: peasants groveling for the loaves of bread from the castle," he says.

But Mr. Mulholland stuck by the company until soon after he discovered he had AIDS. He told no one at the store about his illness. He had heard the jokes around the store about "fag" customers—"don't shake their hands."

When Mr. Mulholland contracted a lung infection, he had to call in sick. His manager phoned him repeatedly at home and demanded an explanation. After four days, Mr. Mulholland reported to work. He was at once summoned to personnel.

"They just dug into me, 'Why were you sick?' 'Where's your doctor's excuse?' " He told them he had an upper respiratory infection, but still they pressed him, he says.

"Finally I broke down crying. As a last resort to save my job, I told them I had AIDS," he says. Honesty backfired. The manager sent him home and told him to stay there. When he tried to return, he says, she told him the company had filled his job and there were no openings.

Nordstrom spokeswoman Kellie Tormey maintains that Mr. Mulholland "asked to leave. It was entirely his choice." Nordstrom made "numerous attempts to find something else for him, but he never once followed up on these opportunities."

But Mr. Mulholland has saved copies of the rejection letters he received from Nordstrom managers as he attempted—16 times in the course of the ensuing year and a half—to apply for job postings at four Nordstrom stores in the area. He was always turned away. "Finally I got the picture. They just cut the chain. One day I'm great; the next day I'm garbage."

Nordstrom officials brush aside such stories as the gripes of a few bad seeds. "Our people development is probably the most significant advantage our company has," Ms. Tormey says. "If you speak to employees in the stores, you'll see that it's a company that really values the team spirit." But an attempt to walk in the stores and do that is resisted. Ms. Tormey explains: "If you want to interview someone, we need to know ahead of time. That's just one of the things we're sensitive to." Finally, the public relations office picks a slate of employees for interviews. Kathleen Sargent is one of them.

"It's a feeling, it's family," Ms. Sargent says enthusiastically, as she settles into a vinyl chair in the employee cafeteria. A public relations official sits at her side.

"Sure, during the busy seasons, you do work six to seven days a week," Ms. Sargent says. "But being in the store with the Christmas tree here, you create your own memories." Ms. Sargent, who has worked for Nordstrom in Seattle for seven years, says she doesn't mind working for free. "When I go home and do follow-ups or write thank-yous, I think it's inappropriate to be charging the company for that."

It turns out that Ms. Sargent is also the goddaughter of Anne Nordstrom, Bruce Nordstrom's sister. "I don't see what that has to do with anything," Ms. Sargent says, when she is asked about it later. "I'm sure the advertising people didn't even know that when they picked me to talk to the press."

At the San Francisco store, another set of company-approved employees testify to the company's virtues. "Here at Nordstrom, I feel I can be the best that I can be," says Doris Quiros, a salesperson in the women's sportswear department. While other retailers "give you a big book of rules, when I came here, Nordstrom gave me one with only one rule: Use your best judgment. That's because they want me to be my own boss."

In the women's shoes department, Tim Snow, a former waiter, says people are impressed now when they learn where he works. "You can be at the grocery store and you show them your ID card and they'll start right off on how much they love to shop there."

The reasons people do love to shop at Nordstrom are plainly evident one recent Saturday afternoon in Mr. Snow's department. Sitar and tabla players serenade shoppers with soothing music as salesclerks proffer Nordstrom's much-vaunted service. But the scene isn't nearly so genteel back in the stockroom, where harried employees clang up and down metal stairs, balancing towers of shoeboxes. Lining the walls are the ubiquitous performance charts and sales contests. "Make Your Goal," instructs one sign. "Don't Let Us Down!" says another. "Be a Top Dog Pacesetter! Go for the Golden Milkbones!!" says a third. One salesclerk stops for a second to eye a visitor taking notes. Finally she asks, only half-joking, "Are you with the Nordstrom Secret Service?"

Corrections & Amplifications. Sean Mulholland, who is suing his former employer, Nordstrom, Inc., for allegedly unlawful discharge, says he has a written record of 16 contacts with Nordstrom managers, who allegedly orally rejected his efforts to seek reinstatement at Nordstrom. He didn't receive any letter of rejection, and Nordstrom denies that he was unlawfully discharged. A February 20 article mistakenly indicated that Nordstrom rejected Mr. Mulholland's applications in writing. (May 7, 1990)

A General Theory of Marketing Ethics[1]

Shelby D. Hunt
Scott J. Vitell

Almost all the theoretical efforts in the area of marketing ethics have been normative, not positive. That is, almost all theoretical works have focused on developing guidelines or rules to assist marketers in their efforts to behave in an ethical fashion. In contrast, the model developed in this chapter is descriptive, not prescriptive. It attempts to explain the decision-making process for problem situations having ethical content. The chapter begins with a discussion and evaluation of the two major normative ethical theories in moral philosophy: deontological theories and teleological theories. Although these theories are normative to the extent that people actually follow their prescriptions, any positive theory of marketing ethics must incorporate them. The chapter then develops a positive theory of marketing ethics and uses that theory to help explain some of the empirical research that has been conducted in the area of marketing ethics.

Research on ethical problems in marketing has hardly been a neglected area. Murphy and Laczniak (1981) list almost 100 articles dealing with the subject. Six major streams of research can be identified in these studies. First, some writers have attempted to show the relevance to marketing of formal ethical theories from philosophy. The works of Robin (1980) on ethical relativism and McMahon (1968) on situational ethics are examples of this approach. Second, some authors have attempted to develop models of ethical decision making in marketing. For example, Bartels (1967) suggested that the determinants of ethical decision making in marketing are economic implications,

[1] Shelby D. Hunt and Scott J. Vitell, "A General Theory of Marketing Ethics," *Journal of Macromarketing* 6 (Spring 1986), pp. 5–16. Reprinted by permission of the *Journal of Macromarketing*.

organizational expectations, and the effects of decisions on various constituencies. In the same vein, Pruden (1971) proposed that the determinants of ethical decision making are individual ethics, organization ethics, and professional ethics. A third stream of research examines specific practices within marketing and attempts to determine the extent to which various groups view the practices as being ethical or unethical. These practices can be within the areas of marketing research, marketing management, sales, advertising, or social marketing, among others. Very often "scenarios" are used as a research tool. Examples are Crawford's (1970) study of research directors; Ferrell and Weaver's (1978) study of marketing managers; Dubinsky, Berkowitz, and Rudelius's (1980) research on hypothetical sales practices; Krugman and Ferrell's (1981) investigation of the ethical perceptions of advertising practitioners; and Lusch, Laczniak, and Murphy's (1980) study of the ethical problems in social marketing.

The work of Bezilla, Haynes, and Elliott (1976) typifies a fourth stream of research: the mutual responsibilities between marketing research agencies and their clients. The work of Tybout and Zaltman (1974) exemplifies a fifth area: the responsibilities of marketing researchers to their respondents and subjects. The final line of research investigates the actions that corporate top management can take to help their employees make decisions in a more ethical fashion. Prominent among these suggested actions are the development of ethical codes (Coe and Coe, 1976), a prompt punishment of ethical violations (Kaikati and Label, 1980), and the use of consultants and ethical seminars (Murphy and Laczniak, 1981).

Murphy and Laczniak review the preceding research streams and conclude that research "related to marketing ethics has been less than innovative and systematic" (1981, p. 262). They also conclude that a major reason for the lack of systematic research in the area of marketing ethics is that "the field of marketing is without a global theory of ethics" (Murphy and Laczniak, 1981, p. 262). The classic *Journal of Marketing Research* article by Walker, Churchill, and Ford (1977) has served as the primary framework guiding empirical research in sales management. Similarly, the purpose of this article is to develop and present a general theory that can serve as a guide for empirical research in the important area of marketing ethics.

Departing from almost all previous theoretical efforts in marketing ethics, our model is *positive*, rather than normative. That is, almost all previous theoretical works have focused on developing guidelines or rules to assist marketers in their efforts to behave in an ethical fashion. A recent example is the framework developed by Laczniak (1983) suggesting that marketers should make their ethical decisions by paying attention to their "prima facie duties" and the principles of proportionality, liberty, and difference. In contrast, the model developed here is descriptive, rather than prescriptive. It purports to explain the decision-making process for situations involving an ethical problem. Since the model is grounded on two major frameworks in moral philosophy, a discussion of these two frameworks is necessary before the model is presented.

MORAL PHILOSOPHY

Ethics may be defined as "inquiry into the nature and grounds of morality where the term morality is taken to mean moral judgments, standards, and rules of conduct" (Taylor, 1975, p. 1). As Murphy and Laczniak (1981) have pointed out, almost all normative ethical theories in moral philosophy can be classified as either *deontological* or *teleological*. The fundamental difference is that deontological theories focus on the specific actions or behaviors of an individual, whereas teleological theories focus on the consequences of the actions or behaviors. In other words, the key issue in deontological theories is the inherent righteousness of a *behavior*, whereas the key issue in teleological theories is the amount of good or bad embodied in the *consequences* of the behaviors.

Deontologists believe that "certain features of the act itself other than the *value* it brings into existence" make an action or rule right (Frankena, 1963, p. 14). Teleologists, on the other hand, "believe that there is one and only one basic or ultimate right-making characteristic, namely, the comparative value (nonmoral) of what is, probably will be, or is intended to be brought into being" (Frankena, 1963, p. 14).

For deontologists, "the principle of maximizing the balance of good over evil, no matter for whom, is either not a moral criterion or standard at all, or, at least, it is not the basic or ultimate one" (Frankena, 1963, p. 14). Deontological views have a rich intellectual history dating back at least as far as Socrates. For deontologists the conundrum has been to determine the "best" set of rules to live by. Examples proposed have been the "golden rule" of "doing unto others as you would have them do unto you," and Sidgwick's principle of justice, which states "it cannot be right for A to treat B in a manner in which it would be wrong for B to treat A, merely on the ground that they are two different individuals, and without there being any difference between the natures or circumstances of the two which can be stated as a reasonable ground for difference of treatment" (Sidgwick, 1907, p. 380).

Laczniak (1983) has applied to marketing a framework developed by Ross (1930) proposing that marketers have certain "prima facie" (at first sight) *duties* which, under most circumstances, constitute moral obligations" (p. 11). These moral obligations include the duties of fidelity, gratitude, justice, beneficence, self-improvement, and noninjury.

Teleologists propose that people should determine the consequences of various behaviors in a situation and evaluate the goodness or badness of all the consequences. A behavior is then ethical if it produces a greater balance of good over evil than any available alternative. The various teleological theories differ on the question of whose good it is that one ought to try to promote.

Ethical egoism holds that individuals should always try to promote their own greatest good. That is, an act is "right" for an individual only if the consequences of that act for an individual are more favorable than the consequences of any other act. Philosophers such as Hobbes and Nietzsche were ethical egoists. Ethical universalism (utilitarianism), on the other hand, holds that an act is right only if it produces for *all* people a greater balance of good consequences over bad consequences than other available alternatives (i.e., "the greatest good for the greatest number"). Utilitarianism is often associated with such philosophers as G. E. Moore and John Stuart Mill.

There are two standard objections to deontological ethical theories. First, it seems impossible to develop a complete system of deontological rules that do not contain a potentially infinite number of exceptions. A hypothetical example would be, "Although it is wrong to tell a lie, it is ethical to tell a lie when to tell the truth would seriously hurt another person." Second, it seems impossible to formulate a set of rules that does not have conflicts among the rules. For example, in the previously mentioned Ross (1930) system, what does one do when a "duty of fidelity" conflicts with a "duty of justice"? A recognition of these problems, joined with a belief that deontological theories do not take the promotion of "the good" seriously enough, has led many ethicists to lean toward some form of utilitarianism. Yet it also has several major problems.

Three issues pose substantial problems for advocates of utilitarianism. First, as has been previously mentioned, is the issue of whose good is to be maximized. The good of the individual? Or the good of society in general? Or should it be some subset of society? Even if this issue could be resolved satisfactorily, utilitarianism poses massive measurement problems. In attempting to maximize the greatest good for the greatest number, how can an individual possibly measure the amount of good realized across many different kinds of outcomes and many different kinds of people, each having a different utility function. Third, even if the measurement problems could be overcome, many ethicists believe that maximizing the total good produced will not always yield the morally "correct" solution, because the total good may be distributed in an unjust fashion. Using an economic example, many ethicists would claim that it may be more ethically correct to have a smaller economic "pie" distributed widely among members of society, than to have a larger one with extreme income disparities.

Analyses like the preceding have led many moral philosophers to recommend a mixed deontological–teleological system of ethics. For example, Frankena (1963) advocates such a mixed system:

> This theory instructs us to determine what is right or wrong in particular situations, normally at least, by consulting rules such as we usually associate with morality; but it goes on to say that the way to tell what rules we should live by is to see which rules best fulfill the joint requirements of utility and justice. This view is still faced with the problem of measuring and balancing amounts of good and evil and, since it recognizes two basic principles, it must also face the problem of possible conflict between them.

The message to be gleaned from our discussion of normative theories of ethics is clear: any positive theory of ethics must account for both the deontological and teleological aspects of the evaluation process. That is, to the extent that people actually follow the normative theories previously discussed, these concepts should be incorporated into any positive theory purporting to explain their behavior. The ultimate underlying assumption of the positive theory to be developed in the next section is that people, in this case marketers, do in fact engage in both deontological and teleological evaluations in determining their ethical judgments and, ultimately, their behaviors. Although this is a fundamental assumption underlying the theory, we will show this assumption to be empirically testable.

DEVELOPMENT OF THE THEORY

The model displayed in Exhibit 1 addresses the situation where an individual confronts a problem perceived as having ethical content. This perception of an ethical problem situation triggers the whole process depicted by the model. If the individual does not perceive some ethical content in a problem situation, subsequent elements of the model do not come into play. Therefore, it is extremely important that any situations or scenarios used to test the model empirically be perceived by respondents as having ethical content. Why some situations are perceived as having an ethical dimension (and others not) will be examined later.

Given that an individual perceives a situation as having ethical content, the next step is the perception of various possible alternatives or actions that might be followed to resolve the ethical problem. It is unlikely that an individual will recognize the complete set of possible alternatives. Therefore, the evoked set of alternatives will be less than the universe. Indeed, ultimate differences in behaviors among individuals in situations that have ethical content may be traced, in part, to differences in their sets of perceived alternatives.

Once the individual perceives the evoked set of alternatives, our previous discussion on moral philosophy suggests that two kinds of evaluations will take place—a deontological evaluation and a teleological evaluation. In the deontological evaluation the individual evaluates the inherent rightness or wrongness of the behaviors implied by each alternative. The process involves comparing the behaviors with a set of predetermined deontological norms, representing personal values or rules of behavior. These norms range from general beliefs about such things as honesty, stealing, cheating, and treating people fairly to issue-specific beliefs about such things as deceptive advertising, product safety, sales "kickbacks," confidentiality of data, respondent anonymity, and interviewer dishonesty.

The teleological evaluation contains four constructs: (1) the perceived consequences of each alternative for various stakeholder groups, (2) the probability that each consequence will occur to each stakeholder group, (3) the desirability

EXHIBIT 1 General Theory of Marketing Ethics

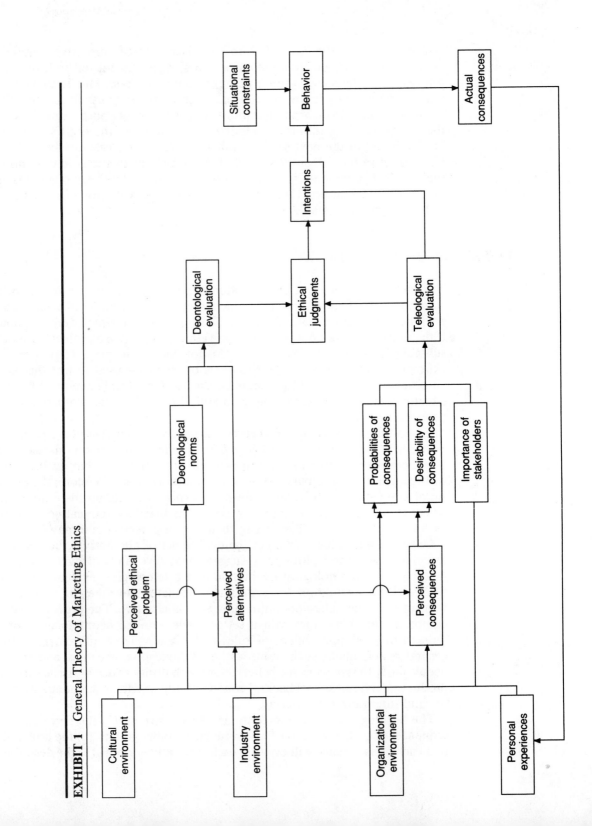

or undesirability of each consequence, and (4) the importance of each stakeholder group. Both the identity and importance of the stakeholder groups will vary across individuals and situations. For example, Brenner and Molander (1977) specifically identified customers, stockholders, and employees (in that order) as important groups for business executives. In marketing, Zey-Ferrell, Weaver, and Ferrell (1979) identified peers, interfacers, and managers as being salient. Further research by Zey-Ferrell and Ferrell (1982) indicated that the "organizational distance" between an individual and various other stakeholder groups has an impact on the relative importance of these groups in terms of influencing beliefs and behaviors in ethical situations.

Incorporating a probability construct in the model is consistent with the work of Dayton (1979), who proposed that an individual's preferences for alternatives in situations having an ethical content will be in proportion to the probability that the actions contribute to the individual's goal attainment. Although the model proposes that the teleological evaluation is influenced by the desirability and probability of consequences, as well as the importance of stakeholders, no specific information-processing rule (such as a lexicographic process) is postulated. The overall result of the teleological evaluation will be beliefs about the relative goodness versus badness brought about by each alternative as perceived by the individual.

The heart of the model comes next. The model postulates that an individual's ethical judgments (e.g., the belief that a particular alternative is the most ethical alternative) is a function of the individual's deontological evaluation (i.e., applying norms of behavior to each of the alternatives) and the individual's teleological evaluation (i.e., evaluating the sum total of goodness versus badness likely to be produced by each alternative). It is possible that *some* individuals in *some* situations will be strict deontologists and, therefore, will completely ignore the consequences of alternative actions. However, we believe it is unlikely that such a result would be found across many individuals for many different situations. Similarly, although it is possible that some individuals in some situations might be strict teleologists (completely ignoring deontological rules), such a situation is unlikely across many individuals for many situations.

Consistent with general theories in consumer behavior (e.g., Engel, Blackwell, and Kollat, 1978; Howard and Sheth, 1969) and the Fishbein and Ajzen (1975) model, we postulate that ethical judgments impact on behavior through the intervening variable of intentions. Following the recommendations of Reibstein (1978), we propose the intentions construct be conceptualized as the likelihood that any particular alternative will be chosen. Like Ryan (1976), we believe both ethical judgments and intentions should be better predictors of behavior in situations where the ethical issues are central, rather than peripheral. Supporting this view, research by Newstrom and Ruch (1975) found the ethical beliefs of a group of managers to be highly congruent with their claimed frequency of behavior.

The model proposes that ethical judgments often will differ from intentions because the teleological evaluation also independently affects the intentions construct. That is, an individual may perceive a particular alternative as the most ethical alternative and, nevertheless, intend to choose another alternative because of certain preferred consequences (e.g., there might be significant positive consequences to oneself as a result of choosing the "less ethical" alternative). The model suggests that, when behavior and intentions are inconsistent with ethical judgments, one of the consequences will be feelings of guilt. Therefore, two individuals may engage in the same behavior, yet only one may feel guilty, since the other's behavior was consistent with his or her ethical beliefs.

Situational constraints may also result in behaviors that are inconsistent with intentions and ethical judgments. One such situational constraint may be the *opportunity* to adopt a particular alternative. Zey-Ferrell, Weaver, and Ferrell (1979) empirically documented the influence of opportunity on behavior in situations having ethical content. Similarly, Mayer (1970) identified opportunity as being one of the three conditions impinging upon ethical behavior, and Newstrom and Ruch (1975) hypothesized that discrepancies between behavior and beliefs were largely a function of opportunity differences.

After behavior, there will be an evaluation of the actual consequences of the alternative selected. This is the major learning construct in the model. These actual consequences feed back into the construct of personal experiences. Hegarty and Sims (1978) examined whether a system of perceived rewards and punishments could change behaviors in a situation involving ethical content. They concluded that "the results lend support to the notion that many individuals can be conditioned (i.e., can 'learn') to behave unethically under appropriate contingencies" (p. 456).

Finally, the model proposes that the four constructs of (1) personal experiences, (2) organizational norms, (3) industry norms, and (4) cultural norms affect perceived ethical situations, perceived alternatives, perceived consequences, deontological norms, probabilities of consequences, desirability of consequences, and importance of stakeholders. The personal experiences construct has a number of dimensions, such as the individual's level of moral development as suggested by Kohlberg (1981), the individual's personality (Hegarty and Sims, 1978, 1979) as well as the individual's total life experiences.

Both industry and organizational norms are proposed as significant determinants of ethical judgments. The inclusion of these constructs is supported by the work of Newstrom and Ruch (1975), who found that "top executives actually serve as a key reference group to provide an important source of the managers' ethical standards" (p. 32). The extensive survey by Brenner and Molander (1977) of 1,200 business managers found that organizational norms, "industry ethical climate," and "society's moral climate" were major factors influencing ethical/unethical decisions (p. 56). Using a sample of 280 marketing managers, Ferrell and Weaver (1978) empirically documented the role of organizational norms in influencing ethical standards. Finally, a study by Dubinsky, Berkowitz, and Rudelius (1980) found that sales personnel "seem to want more guidelines [from the organization] to help them resolve ethical questions" (p. 15).

Bartels (1967) stressed the role of culture in influencing ethics. He identified such basic cultural factors as law, respect for individuality, rights of property, religion, national identity, and loyalty, and values and customs as being important factors. Bartels concluded, "Contrasting cultures of different societies produce different expectations and become expressed in the dissimilar ethical standards of those societies" (p. 23). Differences in cultural norms concerning bribery have been extensively noted in the marketing literature. For example, Kaikati and Label (1980) review the scope of the Foreign Corrupt Practices Act. They point out that "in many countries, not only are foreign payments not outlawed, but they are encouraged. In Germany, for example, tax manuals confirm that although bribes to domestic officials are not deductible as business expenses, bribes to foreign officials are" (p. 40).

TESTABLE PROPOSITIONS

Although there are many testable propositions implied by the model, the following seven seem particularly central to the claim that the model explains behavior in decision situations having ethical content:

1. EJ $= f(DE,TE)$
2. I $= f(EJ,TE)$
3. B $= f(I,SC)$
4. TE $= f(DC,IS,PC)$
5. DE $= f(DN,PA)$
6. DN $= f(PE,OE,IE,CE)$
7. IS $= f(PE,OE,IE,CE)$

Stated verbally, the *first* proposition proposes that in a situation involving ethical content where an individual perceives several alternatives, the ethical judgments (EJ) concerning each alternative are a function of deontological evaluation (DE) and teleological evaluation (TE). The *second* proposition states that the intention (I) to adopt a particular alternative is a function of ethical judgments (EJ) and teleological evaluation (TE). The *third* proposition states that the likelihood that an individual will engage in a particular behavior (B) is a function of the individual's intentions (I) and situational constraints (SC). The *fourth* proposition states that teleological evaluation (TE) for each alternative is a function of DC, PC, and IS, which are, respectively, the desirability or undesirability of the consequences of each alternative, the probabilities of the consequences associated with each alternative, and the importance of the stakeholders on whom the consequences fall. The *fifth* proposition states that the deontological evaluation (DE) is a function of deontological norms (DN) that are applied to each alternative (PA). The *sixth* proposition states that deontological norms (DN) are formed by the individual's personal experiences

(PE), organizational environment (OE), industry environment (IE), and cultural environment (CE). Similarly, the *seventh* proposition indicates that the importance of each stakeholder group (IS) is determined by the same environmental factors that form the deontological norms.

SUGGESTIONS FOR TESTING THE MODEL

As with all behavioral science theories, testing the model poses some research design and measurement problems. However, the problems seem tractable to normal research procedures. At least in the beginning, it would seem most appropriate to test portions of the model, rather than all the relationships in one large research design. The use of "scenario" techniques is well established in ethics research and would be a suitable vehicle for early research efforts.

We suggest that all scenarios be pretested to insure that respondents do in fact believe that there is an ethical issue involved in the scenario. The rough outlines of such a scenario might be as follows:

> You are a 52-year-old regional sales manager for a large industrial supply company. For several years sales have been declining dramatically in your region. After the vice president of sales expressed "grave concern" about this decline at the end of last year's sales meeting, you informed your salespeople that they had better increase their sales "or else drastic steps would be taken."
>
> Total sales for your region during the last six months have increased dramatically. However, you have just found out that several of your most successful salespeople have been providing excessive gifts to purchasing agents in order to increase sales. These gifts have been beyond the normal lunches, dinners, and small promotional items; the gifts were in the form of cash payments in amounts of $50 to $100. To the best of your knowledge, salespeople in your region have never before used excessive cash gifts. These gifts do not violate any laws.
>
> You must decide what to do about this situation (if anything). As regional sales manager, your pay raises and promotions will be based in large part upon the overall sales level in your region, and the vice president of sales has indicated that he is "very pleased with the sales increases."

In such a scenario as above, we would suggest that researchers provide the respondent several specific alternatives. For example, three alternatives for the sales manager might be to: (1) issue an order to the salespeople to stop the bribery and further punish them by reducing their compensation, (2) issue an order stopping the bribery but not reducing their compensation, and (3) say and do nothing at all. Ultimately, respondents would be asked to identify the degree to which they believe each alternative is ethical (Ethical Judgments) and the likelihood in a probability sense that they would actually adopt each alternative (Intentions).

Respondents could be probed about their general beliefs on the rightness or wrongness of the issues involved in the scenario (Deontological Norms). For example, respondents could be asked a series of questions concerning their beliefs about bribery and the ethical obligations of a supervisor to control the behaviors of subordinates. We suggest that a set of consequences be established and shown to each respondent (Perceived Consequences). These consequences should be both positive and negative for different sets of stakeholders. These stakeholders might be the salespeople themselves, the firm, the sales manager, and customers, among others. The value system of the respondent should be explored with respect to each set of stakeholders (Importance of Stakeholders). Questions could be used such as: "To what extent do you believe that the interests of your company should always be placed above your own personal self-interests?"

The construct labeled "Desirability of Consequences" could be measured by giving respondents the consequences in pairs and requesting that they indicate their degree of preference of each consequence compared with each other consequence. The construct labeled "Probabilities of Consequences" could be specified in the research design. For example, respondents could be told that, if they adopted the alternative of "doing nothing," there was a very "high likelihood" that there would be a further increase of 20 percent in total territory sales.

The preceding research design could be used to explore the extent to which the Intentions of respondents are consistent with their Ethical Judgments. Although we would anticipate a high positive correlation, we would not expect the two constructs to be perfectly correlated. Most importantly, the research design could explore the extent to which Ethical Judgments are consistent with the Deontological Evaluation (the Deontological Norms applied to each Perceived Alternative) and Teleological Evaluation (a combination of Probabilities of Consequences, Desirability of Consequences, and Importance of Stakeholders). The model suggests that Deontological Evaluation and Teleological Evaluation, taken collectively, would explain a higher percentage of the variance in ethical judgments than either construct taken separately. A research *program* could be developed through the use of a single scenario, such as the above, by manipulating the consequences of each alternative and their associated probabilities. This would enable the researcher to further explore how ethical judgments are formed within a particular population. Similarly, the same scenario and same set of consequences could be used on different populations (students versus marketers, for example) to deepen our understanding of the extent to which different populations have different ethical frameworks.

THE SOURCES OF ETHICAL VARIANCE

Although there are a few exceptions (e.g., Ferrell, Zey-Ferrell, and Krugman, 1983), most empirical research on marketing ethics follows a common pattern. First, the researcher develops several marketing scenarios, practices, or issues that ostensibly have ethical content. A questionnaire then is designed and administered to several different groups of respondents, such as students, homemakers, and marketers. These groups then are asked to evaluate the degree to which certain behaviors or decisions are ethical or unethical. Statistically significant differences are customarily found among the various groups, and the conclusion is drawn that an "ethics gap" exists between marketers and other relevant groups in society. The researcher then concludes that marketers should be concerned about this "ethics gap" and recommends a variety of actions to marketing academicians and practitioners. These actions include integrating discussions of marketing ethics into marketing courses, developing formal codes of ethics, hiring ethics consultants, and conducting ethics seminars to raise the level of ethics in marketing and bridge the ethics gap. Although these recommendations may have merit, the empirical research seldom provides sufficient grounds for accepting these recommendations because of research design artifacts and the lack of a theoretical framework.

Two research design artifacts severely limit the usefulness of most of the empirical studies on marketing ethics. First of all, most of the designs use "other party" questions. That is, a respondent is asked, "Do you think it was ethical (or unethical) for the marketer to have engaged in this behavior?" No one knows how the responses would have differed if the question had been, "What would you have done had you been in that same situation?" A second artifact is the presumption that the subject can respond meaningfully to the question. No consumer behavior researcher investigating brand loyalty among yacht owners would use a group like students as subjects. Nevertheless, in research on ethics we are often asked to have confidence in recommendations drawn from studies asking 18-year-old youths to pretend that they are the president of a $10 billion oil company facing some ethical problem. To what extent can groups such as students meaningfully place themselves in such a corporate position? Surely, we should be very careful in interpreting the meaningfulness of such studies.

The lack of a theoretical framework to guide research on marketing ethics has also resulted in empirical research that does not provide a suitable grounding for recommendations. Most empirical research simply documents the existence of different ethical judgments among different populations and does not investigate their causes. Recommendations for change may be misguided if the presumed causes of different ethical judgments are misidentified. The model proposed here suggests four major sources of variance in ethical judgments. First, perceptions of factual reality may differ. That is, respondents may differ in their perceptions of the available alternatives, the factual consequences of those alternatives to different groups, and the probability that the consequences will occur. Some respondents may perceive very favorable consequences of a particular alternative flowing to a particular stakeholder group. On the other hand, other respondents may perceive very negative consequences flowing from the same alternative to the same stakeholder group. In such a circumstance, a recommendation to "bridge the ethical gap" by devices like ethical seminars to change deontological norms would be misguided.

The model suggests that a second source of variance in ethical beliefs is a difference in teleological evaluation. Respondents may differ in how they perceive the probability and desirability of certain consequences, as well as the importance of different stakeholder groups. Some respondents may place high values on the "good of the corporation." Others may place high values on stakeholder groups such as self, family, co-workers, and consumers in general.

A third source of variance in ethical beliefs concerns differences in deontological evaluation. Individuals may apply different deontological rules to the problem situation or may differ in how they resolve the situation when two or more rules conflict. Referring back to the Ross (1930) theory of prima facie duties suggested by Laczniak (1983), suppose we have a situation where the duties of fidelity, gratitude, and justice might apply. Should these duties conflict, one individual might value fidelity over gratitude and justice; another might place gratitude over fidelity and justice; a third might place justice over the other two. Clearly, how one would go about changing the ethical beliefs of these three individuals in the same situation would differ dramatically.

The final source of variance in ethical beliefs suggested by the model involves differences in how people combine their deontological evaluations with their teleological evaluations. Some individuals may rely heavily on a deontological evaluation, ignoring the consequences of alternatives. Others may be primarily teleologists and decide their ethical judgments by focusing on the consequences of the alternatives. Obviously, recommendations for change that directly affect consequences would be relatively ineffective for deontologically oriented individuals. Similarly, admonishments to "always do the right thing" will be relatively unpersuasive to teleologists.

APPLYING THE THEORY TO PAST RESEARCH

A study by Sturdivant and Cocanougher (1973) on marketing ethics exemplified some common research findings. Respondents (executives, housewives, blue-collar workers, and students) were asked to evaluate the ethics of eight marketing practices on a seven-point scale ranging from completely ethical to completely unethical. The authors conclude that "it is clear, however, that in most cases a gap exists between the views of businessmen and other groups" (p. 176). Rather than recommend specific actions to reduce the gap, the authors ask, "to what extent should businessmen be concerned about the *differences in their ethical frameworks* versus that of students, housewives, workers, and other groups?" (p. 176, our emphasis). To what extent do such results suggest that the various groups have different "ethical frameworks"? If the "frameworks" differ, in exactly what way do they do so? Although sufficient data are not available to answer these questions conclusively, it is possible to make some reasonable conjectures from our ethics model.

As previously discussed, the model suggests that individuals or groups could have different ethical judgments because of four sources of variance: (1) perceptions of reality, (2) deontological evaluations, (3) teleological evaluations, and (4) combination rules. Yet, only sources two, three, and four would seem to qualify as different "ethical frameworks." That is, just because two people perceive different objective consequences of a behavior, their "ethical frameworks" may not differ. Therefore, people can have different ethical judgments and the same ethical frameworks. Similarly, individuals can have the same ethical judgments and different ethical frameworks.

For each of the eight marketing practices, Sturdivant and Cocanougher found that fewer executives viewed each practice as unethical. For example, consider the "automobile safety" scenario:

> A large auto manufacturer has developed a safety device that could reduce traffic injuries by as much as 50 percent. However, the device would increase the cost of each car by more than $300, which would undoubtedly cause the company to lose sales to competitors. Therefore, the company decided not to use the safety device unless all manufacturers are legally required to use it (Sturdivant and Cocanougher, 1973, p. 12).

Sixty-six percent of the blue-collar workers, 73 percent of the students, and 76 percent of the housewives perceived the decision as unethical. Yet only 51 percent of executives shared this view.

Do the preceding results imply that executives differ from other groups in their ethical framework? That is, did the sample of executives truly use different deontological norms in arriving at their judgments? We don't know. If they used the same norms, did they resolve conflict among the norms through a different procedure? We can't tell. Could it be that the students and housewives perceived that all the negative consequences would fall on people other than themselves or on those for whom they cared? Note that a smaller percentage of blue-collar workers viewed the decision as unethical, compared with the students. Were the workers perceiving negative consequences for the employees of the automobile company (with whom they could perhaps identify), whereas the students believed that all the negative consequences would be shouldered by stockholders (with whom they could not identify)? Unfortunately, these kinds of issues were not investigated. Nevertheless, our model suggests that these kinds of issues must be explored if we wish to test the hypothesis that marketing and/or other executives truly differ in their ethical frameworks. Stated succinctly, *different ethical judgments do not imply different ethical frameworks and similar ethical judgments do not imply similar ethical frameworks.*

An analysis similar to the preceding could be conducted on each of the eight scenarios examined by Cocanougher and Sturdivant. Likewise, the model could be used to examine (1) the differences reported by Crawford (1970) concerning the ethical beliefs of marketing executives contrasted with the beliefs of marketing researchers, (2) the research by Dubinsky and Rudelius (1980) comparing students with industrial salespeople, and (3) the findings of Schneider (1983) related to perceptions of consumers about common marketing research practices. Our purpose here is not to disparage the scholarship of these re-searchers, nor is it to claim that their conclusions related to different ethical frameworks are necessarily wrong. Rather, our objective is to suggest the next steps for research in marketing ethics: exploring the causes of differing ethical judgments.

A recent survey by the Gallup organization (*The Wall Street Journal*, November 1, 1983) provides indirect evidence of the potential merits of using the model to explore ethical issues. A survey of middle-level corporate exec-utives revealed that 39 percent of them had "ethical reservations" about "ac-cepting an invitation from a supplier for dinner at an expensive restaurant for self and spouse." However, further analysis of the data revealed that, whereas 31 percent of the executives who customarily receive invitations disapprove of the practice, 61 percent of the executives who do *not* receive these invitations disapprove. That is, a major determinant of whether the practice was perceived as unethical was whether the executive had an opportunity to share in the benefits. Such a finding is consistent with the issues the model proposes should be explored.

CONCLUSION

Many writers have pointed out that most of the research in marketing suffers from being scattered and fragmented (Jacoby, 1978; Sheth, 1967; Wind and Thomas, 1980). Anderson (1983, p. 28) contends that "what is required in marketing is a greater commitment to theory-driven, programmatic research, aimed at solving cognitively and socially significant problems." Not unlike other areas, research on ethical issues in marketing has similarly suffered. Lacking a model for guidance, past empirical research on this significant social issue often has produced more emotional heat than scholarly light.

The objective of this chapter has been to develop a theory of marketing ethics to guide empirical research and analysis. Consistent with the position taken by Bahm (1974), we believe that positive research should precede nor-mative writings. If one wished to make normative prescriptions about how other people should resolve their ethical conflicts, a useful starting point is to attempt to understand how these "others" do in fact arrive at their ethical judgments. Almost all of the theorizing concerning ethics in both moral phi-losophy and marketing has been normative in nature. To the extent that in-dividuals actually follow these prescriptions, any positive model of marketing ethics should include them. Therefore, to the extent that marketers use both deontological and teleological evaluations in resolving their ethical problems, the model must capture these processes.

This chapter has shown how the model can be used to analyze and explain some of the empirical findings of previous research on marketing ethics. The model also can be used by marketing management within a single firm. Levy and Dubinsky (1983) have highlighted the importance of marketing managers identifying the situations that pose ethical problems to sales personnel. They conclude that "being ethically troubled may result in salespeople experiencing increased levels of job-related tension, frustration, and anxiety, all of which can lead to lower job performance and higher job turnover" (p. 48). Therefore, the model should be useful in an intrafirm setting, where managers are interested in helping their personnel to identify, analyze, and (hopefully) resolve their ethical problems.

We do not claim that our model is "correct"; only empirical testing can justify the truth content of a model or theory. However, we can and do claim that the model is (1) consistent with moral philosophy and past research, (2) helpful in analyzing past research, and (3) amenable to empirical testing. The model's constructs and their interrelationships are sufficiently explicit to guide the empirical testing process. We offer it for that purpose.

REFERENCES

Anderson, Paul F. "Marketing Scientific Progress and Scientific Method." *Journal of Marketing* (Fall 1983), pp. 18–31.

Bahm, Archie J. *Ethics as a Behavioral Science* (Springfield, Ill.: Charles C Thomas), 1974.

Bartels, Robert. "A Model for Ethics in Marketing." *Journal of Marketing* (January 1967), pp. 20–26.

Bezilla, Robert; Joel B. Haynes; and Clifford Elliot. "Ethics in Marketing Research." *Business Horizons* (April 1976), pp. 83–86.

Brenner, Steven N., and Earl A. Molander. "Is the Ethics of Business Executives Changing?" *Harvard Business Review*, January–February 1977, pp. 57–71.

Coe, Ted L., and Barbara J. Coe. "Marketing Research the Search for Professionalism." In *Marketing 1776–1976 and Beyond*, ed. Kenneth L. Bernhardt, Chicago: American Marketing Association, 1976, pp. 257–95.

Crawford, C. Merle. "Attitudes of Marketing Executives toward Ethics in Marketing Research." *Journal of Marketing* (April 1970), pp. 46–52.

Dawson, L. M. "Toward a New Concept of Sales Management." *Journal of Marketing* 34 (April 1970), pp. 33–38.

Dayton, Eric, "Utility Maximizers and Cooperative Undertakings." *Ethics* (October 1979), pp. 130–41.

Dubinsky, Alan J.; Eric N. Berkowitz; and William Rudelius. "Ethical Problems of Field Sales Personnel." *MSU Business Topics* (Summer 1980), pp. 11–16.

Dubinsky, Alan J., and William Rudelius. "Ethical Beliefs: How Students Compare with Industrial Salespeople." In *Marketing in the 80's—Changes and Challenges*, ed. Richard Bagozzi, et al., Chicago: American Marketing Association, 1980, pp. 73–76.

Engel, James F.; Roger D. Blackwell; and David T. Kollat. *Consumer Behavior*, 3rd ed., Hinsdale, Ill.: Dryden, 1978.

Ferrell, O. C., and K. Mark Weaver. "Ethical Beliefs of Marketing Managers." *Journal of Marketing* (July 1978), pp. 69–73.

Ferrell, O. C.; Mary Zey-Ferrell; and Dean Krugman. "A Comparison of Predictors of Ethical and Unethical Behavior among Corporate and Agency Advertising Managers." *Journal of Macromarketing* (Spring 1983), pp. 19–27.

Fishbein, Martin, and Icek Ajzen. *Belief, Attitude, Intention and Behaviour: An Introduction to Theory and Research*, Reading, Mass.: Addison-Wesley, 1975.

Frankena, William. *Ethics*. Englewood Cliffs, N.J.: Prentice Hall, 1963.

Gross, C. W., and H. L. Verma. "Marketing and Social Responsibility." *Business Horizons* 20 (October 1977), pp. 75–82.

Hegarty, W. Harvey, and Henry P. Sims. "Some Determinants of Unethical Behavior: An Experiment." *Journal of Applied Psychology* (1978), pp. 451–57.

————. "Organizational Philosophy, Policies and Objectives Related to Unethical Decision Behavior: A Laboratory Experiment." *Journal of Applied Psychology* (1979), pp. 331–38.

Howard, John A., and Jagdish N. Sheth. *The Theory of Buyer Behavior*, New York: John Wiley & Sons, 1969.

Jacoby, Jacob. "Consumer Research: A State of the Art Review." *Journal of Marketing* 42 (April 1978), pp. 87–96.

Kaikati, Jack, and Wayne A. Label. "American Bribery Legislation: An Obstacle to International Marketing." *Journal of Marketing* (Fall 1980), pp. 38–43.

Kohlberg, Lawrence. *The Meaning and Measurement of Moral Development*. Worcester, Mass.: Clark University Press, 1981.

Krugman, Dean M., and O. C. Ferrell. "The Organizational Ethics of Advertising: Corporate and Agency Views." *Journal of Advertising* (1981), pp. 21–30.

Laczniak, Gene R. "Framework for Analyzing Marketing Ethics." *Journal of Macromarketing* (Spring 1983), pp. 7–18.

Lavidge, Robert J. "The Growing Responsibilities of Marketing." *Journal of Marketing* 34 (January 1970), pp. 25–28.

Levy, Michael, and Alan J. Dubinsky. "Identifying and Addressing Retail Salespeople's Ethical Problems: A Method and Application." *Journal of Retailing* (Spring 1983), pp. 46–66.

Lusch, Robert F.; Gene R. Laczniak; and Patrick E. Murphy. "The 'Ethics of Social Ideas' versus the 'Ethics of Marketing Social Ideas.' " *Journal of Consumer Affairs* (Summer 1980), pp. 156–63.

Mayer, R. R. "Management's Responsibility for Purchasing Ethics." *Journal of Purchasing* 4 (1970), pp. 13–20.

McMahon, Thomas V. "A Look at Marketing Ethics." *Atlantic Economic Review* 17 (March 1968).

Murphy, Patrick, and Gene R. Laczniak. "Marketing Ethics: A Review with Implications for Managers, Educators and Researchers." *Review of Marketing 1981* (1981), pp. 251–66.

Newstrom, John W., and William A. Ruch. "The Ethics of Management and the Management of Ethics." *MSU Business Topics* (Winter 1975), pp. 29–37.

Peter, J. Paul, and Jerry C. Olson. "Is Science Marketing?" *Journal of Marketing* 47 (Fall 1983), pp. 111–25.

Pruden, Henry O. "Which Ethics for Marketers?" In *Marketing and Social Issues*, ed. John R. Wish and Stephen H. Gamble. New York: John Wiley & Sons, 1971, pp. 98–104.

Reibstein, D. "The Prediction of Individual Probabilities of Brand Choice." *Journal of Consumer Research* 5 (December 1978), pp. 163–68.

Ricklefs, Roger. "On Many Ethical Issues, Executives Apply Stiffer Standards than Public." *The Wall Street Journal* (November 1, 1983).

Robin, Donald P. "Value Issues in Marketing." In *Theoretical Developments in Marketing*, ed. C. W. Lamb and P. M. Dunne. Chicago: American Marketing Association, 1980, pp. 142–45.

Ross, William David. *The Right and the Good.* Oxford: Clarendon Press, 1930.

Ryan, M. "Some Results from Programmatic Research Based on Fishbein's Extended Model." Paper presented at the Symposium on Consumer and Industrial Buying Behavior, University of South Carolina (March 1976).

Schneider, Kenneth C. "The Role of Ethics in Marketing Research." *The Mid-Atlantic Journal of Business* (Winter 1983), pp. 11–20.

Sheth, Jagdish N. "A Review of Buyer Behavior." *Management Science* 13 (August 1967), pp. B719–B56.

————. "Consumer Behavior: Surpluses and Shortages." In *Advances in Consumer Research.* Vol. 9, ed. A. A. Mitchell. Ann Arbor, Mich.: Association for Consumer Research, 1982, pp. 13–16.

Sidgwick, H. *The Methods of Ethics.* 7th ed. London: Macmillan, 1907.

Sturdivant, Frederick D., and A. Benton Cocanougher. "What Are Ethical Marketing Practices?" *Harvard Business Review* (November–December 1973), pp. 10–12, 176.

Takas, Andrew. "Societal Marketing—A Businessman's Perspective." *Journal of Marketing* 38 (October 1974), pp. 2–7.

Taylor, Paul W. *Principles of Ethics: An Introduction.* Encino, Calif.: Dickenson Publishing, 1975.

Tybout, Alice M., and Gerald Zaltman. "Ethics in Marketing Research: Their Practical Relevance." *Journal of Marketing Research* (November 1974), pp. 357–68.

Varble, D. L. "Social and Environmental Considerations in New Product Development." *Journal of Marketing* 36 (October 1972), pp. 11–15.

Walker, Orville C.; Gilbert A. Churchill, Jr.; and Neil M. Ford. "Motivation and Performance in Industrial Selling: Present Knowledge and Needed Research." *Journal of Marketing Research* 14 (May 1977), pp. 156–68.

Wind, Yoram, and Robert J. Thomas. "Conceptual and Methodological Issues in Organizational Buying Behavior." *European Journal of Marketing* 14 (1980), pp. 239–63.

Zey-Ferrell, Mary, and O. C. Ferrell. "Role-Set Configuration and Opportunities as Predictors of Unethical Behavior in Organizations." *Human Relations* 35 (1982), pp. 587–604.

Zey-Ferrell, Mary; K. Mark Weaver; and O. C. Ferrell. "Predicting Unethical Behavior among Marketing Practitioners." *Human Relations* 32 (1979), pp. 557–69.

The General Theory of Marketing Ethics: A Retrospective and Revision[1]

Shelby D. Hunt
Scott J. Vitell

Since its publication in 1986 in the *Journal of Macromarketing,* our general theory of marketing ethics has received much attention, not only from other marketing academicians but also from scholars in several other disciplines, including philosophy. A few scholars, apparently believing that our attempt to model ethical decision making was foolhardy at best or blasphemous at worst, reacted negatively to our theory. Gratifyingly, however, most scholars—including philosophers and professional ethicists—have been very supportive of our efforts at developing a better understanding of how marketers (and others) form their ethical judgments and determine what to do in ethically troublesome situations. These scholars, consistent with our original intentions, saw the model as being pedagogically useful in the classroom and valuable for guiding empirical research. Indeed, the efforts of those who have tested the model and our own use of it in classroom situations and workshops have led us to revise it (see Exhibit 1). Customarily, "retrospectives" focus on the historical origins of a particular article and "revisions" focus on the authors' current thinking. Therefore, in this "retrospective and revision," we briefly discuss the history of the development of the model, review some of the tests of it, and discuss the rationale for the revision.

---

[1] Copyright © by Shelby D. Hunt and Scott J. Vitell, September 1991.

EXHIBIT 1 Hunt-Vitell Theory of Ethics

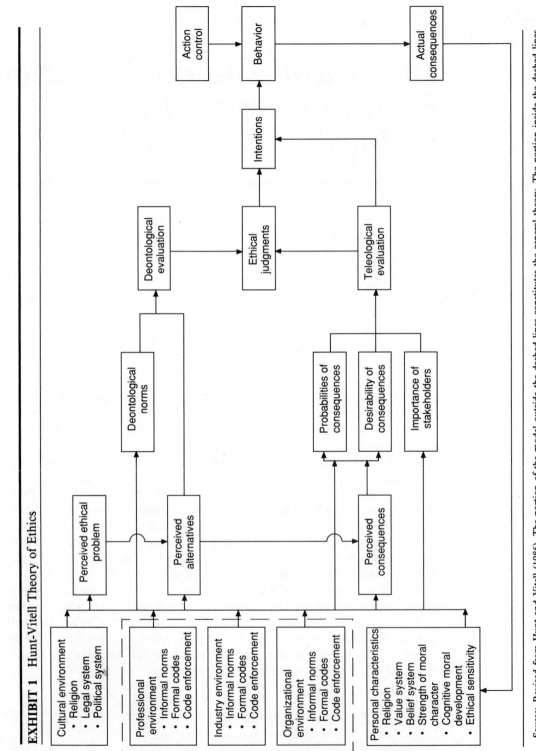

Source: Revised from Hunt and Vitell (1986). The portion of the model outside the dashed lines constitutes the general theory. The portion inside the dashed lines individuates the general model for professional and managerial contexts.

HISTORY

When the first author started teaching at the University of Wisconsin in January 1969, he assumed responsibility for developing a new course—later given the label "macromarketing"—that was to focus on subjects like ethics and social responsibility. In the early 1970s, marketing teaching materials in the area of ethics focused almost exclusively on the presumed existence of an "ethics gap" between marketers and other members of society that resulted from marketers having "different ethical frameworks." Using normative theories from moral philosophy, class discussion focused on what kinds of investigation would be appropriate for determining whether, in fact, there existed an ethics gap and whether this gap resulted from marketers having a different ethical framework. These discussions never seemed to get anywhere, because of the lack of a positive theory to guide our thinking on this topic (or so it seemed to the first author).

In preparation for teaching the class in the fall semester of 1974, a basic outline of a theory of ethical decision making was developed in an effort to make class discussion more productive. If people actually followed the suggestions and advice of moral philosophers, it was reasoned, then both deontological theories and teleological theories could provide a framework for a positive theory of ethics. Students responded favorably to the theory and, over a period of several years, it grew richer in detail. In 1980 the first author joined the faculty at Texas Tech University and, in the fall of 1981, the second author—then a doctoral student in Texas Tech's Ph.D. program—took Texas Tech's version of macromarketing. He became interested in testing the theory in his dissertation. Over the next few years, we jointly worked on the theory and our efforts resulted in the version of it published in the *Journal of Macromarketing* in 1986 and an empirical test of it.

TESTING THE THEORY

The research design of the first test of the theory (Vitell, 1986; Vitell and Hunt, 1990) explored how some 200 sales and marketing managers responded to the bribery scenario detailed in our 1986 paper. Briefly, the results showed that managers did tend to depend on both deontological and teleological factors when making ethical judgments, and they also tended to form their intentions for behaviors by relying both on their ethical judgments and teleological considerations. Moreover, we were able to conclude: "If one wants to foster more ethical behavior on the part of one's subordinates, the results of this study indicate that it would be better to reward ethical behavior than to punish unethical behavior" (1990, p. 262). However, the results also revealed a major shortcoming of the research design, to wit: many respondents simply did not see the bribery scenario as a true ethical *dilemma* (respondents seemed to clearly favor the alternative of issuing an order to the salespeople to stop giving excessive gifts, but not reducing their compensation). Therefore, we urged future researchers to create scenarios for testing the model that involved "true ethical dilemmas" (p. 261).

Since that original test, four other investigations have been conducted. First, Mayo and Marks (1990) explored how 100 marketing researchers would handle a marketing research ethical problem that centered on a study having questionable validity and reliability. Focusing on the "core" relationships of the model, they concluded: "The results provide substantial support for the relationships proposed in this part of the model, . . . ethical judgments to resolve dilemmas are found to be jointly determined by deontological and teleological evaluations, . . . [and] the relationship between judgments and intentions to adopt an ethical alternative is attenuated when its implementation does not result in a preferred consequence" (p. 163). However, as Mayo and Marks themselves point out, their measures of several of the model's constructs were problematical (p. 170).

In a commentary on the Mayo and Marks study, Hunt (1990, p. 175) also questioned the validity of several of their measures and asked: "In the process of coming to a summary ethical judgment in a situation, do people first come to an intermediate 'stopping point,' which may be referred to as 'deontological evaluation,' then combine this belief with their teleological evaluation?" He concluded that the best answer to this question was "no," viewing deontological evaluation and teleological evaluation as "processes," not "constructs." Therefore, direct measures of deontological evaluation and teleological evaluation are probably inappropriate. Instead of direct measures, empirical research should use "inferred" ones (p. 175).

A study by Singhapakdi and Vitell (1991) explored the relationship between several background variables, including "Machiavellianism" and "locus of control," and the deontological norms of 529 members of the American Marketing Association. Machiavellianism is a personality trait associated with a manipulative, unethical leadership style (Hunt and Chonko, 1984), and people who have a high "internal locus of control" believe that events that happen to them occur because of their own behavior or their own personal characteristics (Rotter, 1966). Using the marketers' agreement/disagreement with seven items drawn from codes of ethics of the American Marketing Association as a measure of "deontological norms," they found that those marketers scoring low on the Machiavellianism scale and those exhibiting a high "internal locus of control" had higher deontological norms.

Using the same American Marketing Association sample, Singhapakdi and Vitell (1990) also explored the relationships between various background factors and both "perceived ethical problem" and "perceived alternatives." They found that marketers scoring high on the Machiavellianism scale perceived ethical problems as less serious and were unlikely to view punishment of unethical behavior as a viable alternative. On the other hand, marketers in organizations enforcing a code of ethics perceived ethical problems as more serious and were more likely to view punishment of unethical behavior as an acceptable course of action.

Unlike all previous studies (which used cross-sectional research designs), the third study, by Hunt and Vasquez-Parraga (1992), used an experimental design to explore how 747 sales and marketing managers would handle ethical problems relating to salespeople (1) lying to their customers about plant capacity in order to negotiate better prices with purchasing agents and (2) recommending expensive products in their product lines even though less expensive products would better fit customer needs. This study represents the strongest test yet of our model, since it *(a)* employed an experimental design, *(b)* overcame some of the measurement problems associated with previous tests, and *(c)* used structural equations modeling techniques (LISREL). The results showed that goodness-of-fit indices were extremely high (.999 and .994), the squared multiple correlations for "ethical judgments" and "intervention" were large (.691 and .657, respectively), the total coefficient of determination for structural equations was impressive (.717), the signs of all the parameters were in the expected direction, and all hypothesized paths were statistically significant. In short, the study found the model to fit the data "like a glove." Equally important, it found that, at least in the situations investigated, marketers relied *primarily* on deontological factors and only secondarily on teleological factors in forming both their ethical judgments and their intentions to act. It also found that women marketers (compared with men) seemed to rely more heavily on deontological considerations in forming their ethical judgments and less heavily on teleological considerations in determining their intentions to act. Finally, those marketers who worked for companies that "strongly enforced" their codes of ethics (compared with those who did not) were more influenced by deontological considerations in forming their intentions to intervene and were less influenced by teleological considerations. However, Hunt and Vasquez-Parraga caution that the findings with respect to gender and codes of ethics should be viewed as very tentative, because of the small sample sizes involved.

THE REVISED THEORY

Exhibit 1 shows our current thinking about the model. Many scholars pointed out that most of the theory was really applicable to ethical decision making in general, not just to marketing or business. We agree and now point out the specific portion of the model (everything except the portion within the dashed lines) that constitutes what we believe is a general theory of ethical decision making in *all* contexts. Thus, all decision situations having ethical content will involve the process of deontological and teleological evaluation by individuals with varying personal characteristics and will occur within a particular cultural environment.

The purpose of our theory is to identify the reasoning process that individuals use when confronted with a decision situation having ethical content. All the evidence to date suggests that the core relationships in our model are correct. Therefore, our revised version does not change the basic model. The only exception is respecifying "situational constraints" as "action control." This is the extent to which an individual actually exerts control in the enactment of an intention in a particular situation (Ajzen, 1985; Tubbs and Ekeberg, 1991). We now discuss how our revision explicates in further detail some of the "background factors" that we believe may impinge on the overall process.

Many scholars are interested in investigating the subject of international ethics. An important question would be the extent to which cultural mores differ across societies and the extent to which those mores affect the deontological norms of individuals and how they value different stakeholders. Thus, scholars might explore the extent to which a society's religious tradition impacts individual decision processing. For example, are the deontological norms that are applied in a particular situation different in a predominantly Hindu nation, like India, when compared with a predominantly Judeo-Christian nation, like the United States? In conducting such research, we should keep in mind that even those individuals who do not subscribe to the predominant religious tradition in a society may be profoundly affected by the deontological norms associated with that religious tradition. In like manner, the impact of different societal legal systems and political systems would be worth exploring.

The revised model now identifies several personal characteristics that might influence the decision-making process. Unquestionably, an individual's personal religion influences ethical decision making. A priori, compared with nonreligious people, one might suspect that the highly religious people would have more clearly defined deontological norms and that such norms would play a stronger role in ethical judgments. Wilkes, Burnett, and Howell (1986) explore the meaning and measurement of "religiosity" in consumer research. The measures of religiosity that they developed would seem to be appropriate for exploring the extent to which strength of religious belief *per se* results in different decision processes.

An individual's value system would also unquestionably impact the decision process. In general, we urge researchers to explore many different values and the extent to which these values impact ethical decision making. Consider, for example, "organizational commitment" as one such value. Hunt, Wood, and Chonko (1989) found corporations that have high ethical values will, subsequently, have employees more committed to the organization's welfare. So far, so good. However, is it possible that individuals exhibiting high organizational commitment (even because of the organization's ethical values) will then place such great importance on the welfare of the organization that they may engage in questionable behavior if such behavior were thought to be beneficial to the organization? Only research can answer this question.

"Belief systems" focuses on the individual's set of beliefs about the world. For example, one might consider Machiavellianism as a belief system, as was explored by Singhapakdi and Vitell (1991). More generally, the kinds of beliefs we have in mind are those that reflect how the individual believes the world "works." To what extent does an individual believe that all people are solely self-interest motivated? In moral philosophy terms, to what extent does a person believe all others are guided by ethical egoism? The model suggests that, to the extent that an individual believes this is how the world actually "works," this belief will guide the individual's behavior by influencing the perceived consequences of alternatives and their probabilities.

Strength of moral character has been suggested as an important moderator of the relationship between intentions and behavior by Williams and Murphy (1990). Drawing on Aristotle's virtue ethics, Williams and Murphy emphasize, among other things, the important function of role models in developing a virtuous moral character (i.e., one having such virtues as perseverance, courage, integrity, compassion, candor, fidelity, prudence, justice, public-spiritedness, and humility). Thus, those individuals with high moral character would have the strength of will to behave consistently with their ethical judgments. To our knowledge, there are no measures available for moral character strength. In conducting empirical research, therefore, as surrogate measures one might consider (as does Trevino (1986)) using "ego strength" or Rotter's (1966) "inner-directedness versus outer-directedness."

The subject of cognitive moral development (Kohlberg, 1984; Rest, 1986; Trevino, 1986) has received much attention in the ethics literature. A recent study by Goolsby and Hunt (1992) found that marketing practitioners compare favorably with other social groups in their level of cognitive moral development. Moreover, they found that marketers scoring high on cognitive moral development tend to be female, highly educated, and high in social responsibility. Since stage of cognitive moral development implies a high capacity to reason through complex ethical situations, it would seem that individuals high in cognitive moral development would, among other things, bring in more deontological norms in any situation and would consider the interests of more stakeholders in their decision making.

As a final personal characteristic, some people are, quite simply, more *ethically sensitive* than others. That is, when placed in a decision-making situation having an ethical component, some people never recognize that there is an ethical issue involved at all. We must recall that the model starts with the perception that there is, indeed, some ethical problem involved in the situation. The systematic study of ethical sensitivity has begun in the areas of dentistry (Bebeau, Rest, and Yamoor, 1985), professional counseling (Volker, 1979), and accounting (Shaub, 1989). To date, no one has explored marketers' ethical sensitivity, but it would seem to be a fruitful area. For example, a principal value of ethics workshops and ethics training may well be a kind of "consciousness-raising," resulting in heightened ethical sensitivity.

The boxes in the model labeled "Industry Environment," "Professional Environment," and "Organizational Environment" specifically orient the model toward ethical situations for business people and the professions. We propose that all industries, professional associations, and organizations have complex sets of norms, some of which are often formalized in codes, but most of which are informal norms communicated in the processes whereby individuals are "socialized" into their respective organizations, professions, and industries. For example, as previously discussed, the study by Hunt and Vasquez-Parraga (1992) found it was not the existence of formal codes of ethics in organizations that impacted the decision process, but whether the formal codes were or were not perceived to be strictly enforced. Much work needs to be done in identifying the extant informal norms across different industries and professional associations. For example, to what extent do the norms related to personal selling in the steel industry differ from those in the chemical industry, or in advertising? It would seem that these differing sets of informal norms would play prominent roles in influencing which deontological norms an individual would consider as governing moral reasoning in specific decision contexts.

CONCLUDING NOTE

Nothing in our work is meant to disparage or deny the "is/ought" distinction or the "naturalistic fallacy" (i.e., the "fallacy of deriving (deducing) ethical statements from nonethical statements"; Angelas, 1981, p. 186).[2] Yet, it is our firm belief that understanding how ethical decisions are made ("is") can contribute to making those decisions better ("ought"). A major pedagogical objective of developing the model was to assist our students in understanding how different people can confront the (ostensibly) same situation, yet arrive at such disparate views about the moral appropriateness of alternative actions. Students' reactions to the theory have been uniformly positive—they claim to understand "others" better. Equally important, as a result of studying and discussing the model, many students report that they now have a deeper understanding of their *own* decision processes in ethically troublesome situations. As one student aptly put it, in any effort to follow the normative "to thine own self be true," it is helpful to "know thyself." We agree. Although "is" doesn't imply "ought," positive theories can contribute to reasoned, informed, and principled actions.

REFERENCES

Ajzen, I. "From Intentions to Actions: A Theory of Planned Behavior." In *Action Control: From Cognition to Behavior*, ed. J. Kuhl and J. Beckman. Berlin: Springer-Verlag, 1985, pp. 11–39.

---

[2] See Shelby D. Hunt, "The Three Dichotomies Model of Marketing Revisited: Is the Total Content of Marketing Thought Normative?" in *Marketing Theory Applications*, ed. Terry Childers et al., Chicago: American Marketing Association, 1991.

Angelas, Peter A. *Dictionary of Philosophy*. New York: Barnes and Noble, 1981.

Bebeau, M. J.; J. R. Rest; and C. M. Yamoor. "Measuring Dental Students' Ethical Sensitivity." *Journal of Dental Education* 49 (1985), pp. 225–35.

Goolsby, Jerry R., and Shelby D. Hunt. "Cognitive Moral Development and Marketing." *Journal of Marketing* 56 (January 1992), in press.

Hunt, Shelby D. "Commentary on an Empirical Investigation of a General Theory of Ethics." *Journal of the Academy of Marketing Science* 18 (Spring 1990), pp. 173–7.

Hunt, Shelby D., and Lawrence B. Chonko. "Marketing and Machiavellianism." *Journal of Marketing* 48 (Summer 1984), pp. 30–42.

Hunt, Shelby D., and Scott Vitell. "A General Theory of Marketing Ethics." *Journal of Macromarketing* 6 (Spring 1986), pp. 5–16.

Hunt, Shelby D.; Van R. Wood; and Lawrence B. Chonko. "Corporate Ethical Values and Organizational Commitment in Marketing." *Journal of Marketing* 53 (July 1989), pp. 79–90.

Hunt, Shelby D., and Arturo Z. Vasquez-Parraga. "Organizational Consequences and Marketing Ethics: Using the Hunt-Vitell Model to Explore Salesforce Supervision." Working paper (1992).

Kohlberg, Lawrence. *Essays on Moral Development: Vol. II. The Psychology of Moral Development*. New York: Harper & Row, 1984.

Mayo, Michael A., and Lawrence J. Marks. "An Empirical Investigation of a General Theory of Marketing Ethics." *Journal of the Academy of Marketing Science* 18 (Spring 1990), pp. 163–72.

Rest, James R. *Moral Development: Advances in Research and Theory*. New York: Praeger Publishers, 1986.

Rotter, Julian B. "Generalized Expectancies for Internal versus External Control of Reinforcement." *Psychological Monographs* 80, no. 1 (1966). Whole no. 609.

Shaub, Michael K. "An Empirical Examination of the Determinants of Auditors' Ethical Sensitivity." Doctoral dissertation, Texas Tech University, Lubbock (1989).

Singhapakdi, Anusorn, and Scott J. Vitell, Jr. "Marketing Ethics: Factors Influencing Perceptions of Ethical Problems and Alternatives." *Journal of Macromarketing* 10 (Spring 1990), pp. 4–18.

————. "Research Note: Selected Factors Influencing Marketers' Deontological Norms." *Journal of the Academy of Marketing Science* 19 (Winter 1991), pp. 37–42.

Trevino, Linda Klebe. "Ethical Decision-Making in Organizations: A Person-Situation Interactionist Model." *Academy of Management Review* 11, no. 3 (1986), pp. 601–17.

Tubbs, Mark E., and Steven E. Ekeberg. "The Role of Intentions in Work Motivation: Implications for Goal-Setting Theory and Research." *Academy of Management Review* 16, no. 1 (1991), pp. 180–99.

Vitell, Scott J. "Marketing Ethics: Conceptual and Empirical Foundations of a Positive Theory of Decision Making in Marketing Situations Having Ethical Content." Doctoral dissertation, Texas Tech University, Lubbock (1986).

Vitell, Scott J., and Shelby D. Hunt. "The General Theory of Marketing Ethics: A Partial Test of the Model." In *Research in Marketing*. Vol. 10. ed. Jagdish N. Sheth. Greenwich, Conn.: JAI Press, 1990, pp. 237–65.

Volker, J. M. "Moral Reasoning and College Experience." Manuscript, University of Minnesota, Minneapolis (1979).

Wilkes, Robert E.; John J. Burnett; and Roy D. Howell. "On the Meaning and Measurement of Religiosity in Consumer Research." *Journal of the Academy of Marketing Science* 14 (Spring 1986), pp. 47–56.

Williams, Oliver F., and Patrick E. Murphy. "The Ethics of Virtue: A Moral Theory for Marketing." *Journal of Macromarketing* 10 (Spring 1990), pp. 19–29.

Codes of Conduct

A. APPLE COMPUTER, INC.*

Understanding Parameters

Underlying the way we do business at Apple is one fundamental principle: good judgment. We deliberately keep policies to a minimum, and prefer to provide guidelines to assist Apple employees in selecting and evaluating appropriate actions. We believe it makes more sense to create an atmosphere that supports good judgment than to list pages and pages of directives and policies.

An understanding of our legal and ethical parameters enhances that judgment. Apple is a publicly held company, and, as such, has a responsibility to pay constant attention to all legal boundaries and to comply with all applicable laws. We have the same obligation to the communities in which we do business and to the customers with whom we do business.

Apple is also a company that cares deeply about its employees. For this reason, we strive to be constant and responsible in our dealings with one another. Although we realize that no two situations are alike, we aim for consistency and balance when encountering any ethical issues.

We also expect that those with whom we do business will adhere to the same standards, as appropriate.

Begin with the Fundamentals

All perceptions of good judgment revolve around a common ideal, a group of shared beliefs. At Apple, the way we do business is centered on five simple, general standards that apply to all Apple employees:

• Apple employees are expected to maintain the highest standards of business conduct.

---

* Apple's *Global Ethics Brochure* is reprinted by permission of Apple Computer, Inc. Copyright © 1991 Apple Computer, Inc. Reproduction of all, or any part, of this brochure requires permission of Apple Computer, Inc. Apple and the Apple logo are registered trademarks of Apple Computer, Inc.

- Apple employees are expected to be totally honest and ethical in all of the Company's business dealings.

- Apple's business will be conducted in accordance with applicable rules and laws and in such a way as to attain the highest standards of corporate citizenship.

- Each community in which Apple operates should benefit from our presence.

- It is expected that all Apple employees will respect appropriate confidentiality of information in their contacts with people outside of Apple, and will be especially vigilant in contacts with the press or competitors. All press inquiries should be directed to the Public Relations department or handled as directed by them. All inquiries from outside lawyers should be referred to Apple's Law department or handled as directed by them.

Putting the Customer First

We create, manufacture, and market computers for a simple reason: so people can use them to make their lives better. Our customers remain foremost in our minds. There is no upper limit on the quality of the products and service that we want to provide. We strive to understand our customers' needs, we provide customers with the tools and skills to enhance their use of Apple® products, and we are courteous and instructive.

Opportunity Is for Everyone

Apple encourages a creative, multiculturally diverse, and supportive work environment. No action could run more counter to Apple values than discrimination. Apple policy prohibits discrimination and harassment, and it is the responsibility of all Apple employees to conform to this policy. Discrimination, harassment, and slurs or jokes based on a person's race, sex, sexual orientation, religion, national origin, age, or handicap will not be tolerated concerning employees, applicants for employment, or others who may be present in the workplace.

Any Apple employee who feels he or she has been discriminated against or harassed, or feels he or she has witnessed such action, is strongly encouraged to report the incident to any member of the Human Resources department or to any manager, up to and including the Chairman and Chief Executive Officer.

Buying and Selling Apple Stock

Apple policy prohibits Apple employees from making transactions in Apple stock at a time when the employee may possess material information about Apple that has not been publicly disclosed. This policy is dictated by United States securities laws and is applicable worldwide. These securities laws and Apple policy also apply to members of the households of Apple employees or to others whose transactions may be attributable to Apple employees. Any violation can lead to criminal prosecution, civil penalties, and/or termination of employment.

Material information, in short, is any information that could affect the stock price. Material information may be either positive or negative in nature. Once a public announcement has been made of material Apple information, Apple employees should wait until the second business day after the announcement before engaging in any transactions. (For example, if an announcement is made on Monday, trade on Wednesday; if an announcement is made on Friday, trade on Tuesday.)

United States securities laws and Apple policy also apply to any material information that Apple employees may have regarding any Apple customer, vendor, or third party, if the information is not publicly available and a reasonable person might consider the information relevant to an investment decision.

Members of Apple's Board of Directors and certain officers are subject to more restrictions on the trading of stock. Any questions regarding insider trading should be directed to Apple's Law department.

Confidential Information

Information is the sum and substance of Apple's business relationships. Apple's business and business relationships center on the confidential and proprietary information of Apple and of those with whom we do business—customers, vendors, resellers, and others. Imperative upon each Apple employee is the duty to respect and protect the confidentiality of all such information.

The use of confidential and proprietary information—whether Apple's or a third party's—is usually covered by a written agreement. In addition to the obligations imposed by that agreement, all Apple employees should comply with the following requirements. First, confidential information should be received and disclosed only under the auspices of a written agreement. Second, confidential information should be disclosed only to those Apple employees who need to access such information to perform their jobs for Apple. For example, Apple's proprietary source code should not be disclosed to, or accessible by, anyone except the Apple engineers who need such source code to do their jobs. Third, confidential information of a third party should not be used or copied by any Apple employee except as permitted by the third-party owner (this permission is usually specified in a written agreement). Fourth, unsolicited third-party confidential information should be refused or, if inadvertently received by an Apple employee, returned unopened to the third party or transferred to the Apple Law department for appropriate disposition.

Using Third-Party Copyrighted Material

Apple employees may sometimes need to use third-party copyrighted material to perform their jobs or to prepare Apple products and promotional materials. Before such third-party material may be used, an appropriate license must be obtained. The need for such a license may exist whether or not the end product containing the third-party material is for personal use; for Apple internal, promotional, or demonstrational use; or for public or commercial distribution.

It is against Apple policy and it may be unlawful for any Apple employee to copy, reproduce, scan, digitize, broadcast, or modify third-party copyrighted material when preparing Apple products or promotional materials, unless written permission from the copyright holder has been obtained prior to the proposed use. Improper use could subject both the Company and the individuals involved to possible civil and criminal actions for copyright infringement.

It is also against Apple policy for Apple employees to use the Company's facilities for the purpose of making or distributing unauthorized copies of third-party copyrighted materials for personal use or for use by others.

Environmental Health and Safety

At Apple, meeting the challenges of rapidly expanding and changing technology means more than making the finest products. We strive to produce those products in a manner that conserves the environment and protects the safety and health of our employees, our customers, and the community.

Apple's objective in the environmental health and safety area is to assume a leadership position. To accomplish this objective, we will:

- Comply with all environmental, health, and safety laws and regulations in those countries in which we do business.

- Adopt our own corporate standards for protection of human health and the environment.

- Provide a safe work environment by integrating a comprehensive program of safety training and evaluation.

- Strive to anticipate future environmental, health, and safety risks and regulatory requirements, and have a proactive approach to dealing with them whenever appropriate.

Apple has proved to be a leader in technology, and believes that a comprehensive environmental health and safety program is an essential component of our forward-looking business approach. Our goal of providing a hazard-free work environment can be achieved by a conscientious effort and commitment to excellence from all Apple employees.

Keeping It Clean

Conflicts of interest can insidiously compromise employees' business ethics. At Apple, we perceive a conflict of interest to be any activity that is inconsistent with or opposed to Apple's best interests, or gives the appearance of impropriety. The way to identify a conflict is to decide if there is potential for even an appearance of a divided loyalty. To make things simpler, we've identified a few target areas:

Proper Payments.   All Apple employees are to pay for and receive only that which is proper. We will make no payments or promises to influence another's acts or decisions, and we will give no gifts beyond those extended in normal business. We will observe all government restrictions on gifts and entertainment.

Interest in Other Businesses.   Apple employees and members of their immediate families must avoid any direct or indirect financial relationship that could cause divided loyalty. Apple employees must receive written permission from the Apple vice president for their organization before beginning any employment, business, or consulting relationship with another company. This doesn't mean, however, that family members are precluded from being employed by one of Apple's customers, competitors, or suppliers.

Inventions.   Apple employees must receive the written permission of the Apple vice president for their organization before developing, outside of Apple, any products, software, or intellectual property that is or may be related to Apple's current or potential business.

Investments.   Passive investments of not more than 1 percent of total outstanding shares of companies listed on a national or international securities exchange, or quoted daily by NASDAQ or any other board, are permitted without Apple's approval—provided the investment is not so large financially that it creates the appearance of a conflict of interest or does not involve the use of confidential or proprietary information.

Market Intelligence.   Though market intelligence is important, only authorized Apple employees should obtain it, and only in straightforward ways. Apple and its employees must never accept or use information otherwise presented.

Family.   Apple employees should avoid conducting Apple business with members of their families—or others with whom they have significant relationships—in another business organization, unless they have prior written permission from the Apple vice president for their organization. Apple employees should avoid a direct reporting relationship with any member of their families or others with whom they have a significant relationship.

Tips, Gifts, and Entertainment.   Apple employees and members of their families must not give or receive valuable gifts—including gifts of equipment or money, discounts, or favored personal treatment—to or from any person associated with Apple vendors or customers. This is not intended to preclude Apple from receiving or evaluating appropriate complimentary products and services. It is also not intended to preclude Apple from making a gift of equipment to a company or organization, provided that the gift is given openly, with full knowledge by the company or organization, and is consistent with applicable law.

In rare circumstances, local custom in some countries may call for the exchange of gifts having more than nominal value as part of the business relationship. In these situations, gifts may be accepted only on behalf of Apple (not an individual) with the approval of the employee's managing director and the Apple Law department. Any gifts received are to be turned over to the Human Resources department for appropriate disposition. In all cases, the exchange of gifts must be conducted so there is no appearance of impropriety.

Honoraria.   Speaking at events, when it is determined to be in Apple's best interests, is considered part of an employee's normal job responsibilities. Because employees will be compensated by Apple for most or all of their time spent preparing for, attending, and delivering presentations approved by management, employees should not request or negotiate a fee or receive any form of compensation from the organization that requested the speech, unless the employee first receives express authorization from the Apple vice president for their organization.

Favors. Advertising novelties, favors, and entertainment are allowed when the following conditions are met:

- They're consistent with our business practices.
- They're of limited value ($50 U.S. dollars or less).
- They don't violate any applicable law.
- Public disclosure wouldn't embarrass Apple.

We can't, of course, list all the possible conflicts. These are examples of the types of conflicts of interest we expect Apple employees to avoid. Ultimately, it's the responsibility of each individual to avoid any situation that would even appear to be a conflict of interest or improper. Employees should feel free to discuss any potential conflict of interest situations with their supervisors and the Law department.

It's a Matter of Record

Records count. They are a vital part of maintaining a high level of ethical business transactions. All accounting transactions should be fully described in our records—there's never any reason for false or misleading entries—and payments on Apple's behalf should never be made other than as described in the records. At Apple, there is no place for undisclosed or unrecorded funds, payments, or receipts.

All Apple bank accounts that are to be established must first be approved by Apple's Treasury department. All payments to Apple should be made by recorded and traceable methods: checks (correctly dated), bank drafts, or bank transfers. No payments should be made in cash, except petty cash reimbursements.

Dealing with Government Contracts and Other Government Requirements

Apple employees should understand that special requirements may apply when contracting with any government body (including national, state, provincial, municipal, or other similar government divisions in local jurisdictions).

Disclosure and Certification Requirements. In addition to the general high standards imposed by these guidelines, government agencies often place special disclosure and certification requirements on firms with which they do business. These requirements impose on Apple employees the need to be especially vigilant to ensure that our general business practices conform to special government pricing, contracting, and certification needs.

In certain situations, for example, Apple may have to certify that it is supplying the government with its lowest commercial price. Apple may also have to certify that its prices have been arrived at independently.

Apple depends on all of its employees to make sure that these and other promises to the government are satisfied. Any doubts about such matters should be brought to the attention of the Law department.

Resellers.   Apple resellers throughout the world must retain the freedom to establish their resale prices for Apple products. Apple may publish suggested retail prices, but Apple may not require or attempt to influence any reseller into following any particular resale price. Because of the sensitivity of this topic, Apple employees should not discuss resale prices with any reseller. This applies whether discussing the prices of any reseller or of one of the reseller's competitors. Respecting the independence of the reseller to price Apple products for resale is a cornerstone of Apple's philosophy of product distribution.

Many countries have laws regarding the prices that manufacturers may charge resellers. For example, U.S. law prohibits the granting of discriminatory prices to competing purchasers of the same or similar products if the price difference affects competition. Similarly, promotional allowances and services need to be made available to all competing resellers, though the amounts can vary in proportion to the volume of Apple products purchased by the reseller. Some exceptions exist to both laws, but any exception must be carefully considered.

Competitors.   Apple needs to be equally careful when dealing with competitors. Agreements with competitors that affect product pricing or output, or allocation of customers or sales territories, may be prohibited, because they are counter to the principle of free competition. Apple employees should not discuss these topics with competitors, because no acceptable understanding could result. In some cases, the law may also view our resellers as our competitors.

Advice.   Whether they're termed antitrust, competition, or free trade laws, the rules are designed to keep the marketplace thriving and competitive. Understanding and applying these laws requires the involvement of Apple's lawyers. Apple is committed to compliance, and the consequences of errors are severe. If you have any questions or issues, you should contact the Law department for assistance.

Making Sure It Works

It's essential that we all keep an eye out for possible infringements of Apple's business ethics—whether these infringements occur in dealings with the government or the private sector, and whether they occur because of oversight or intention. Apple employees who have knowledge of possible violations should notify the Human Resources department and the Law department.

To assist employees in the day-to-day protection of our business ethics, we've compiled a list of some areas in which breaches could occur. We encourage you to keep an eye out for them.

Danger Areas.
1. Improper or excessive payments of any of the following:
   Consulting fees.

Public relations fees.
Advertising fees.
Legal fees.
Agents' fees.
Commissions.
Insurance premiums.
Other professional fees.
Expense reports.
Employee bonuses or compensation arrangements.
Employee loans.
Miscellaneous expenses.
Nondeductible expenses.
Director and officer payments.

2. Questionable payments to agents, consultants, or professionals whose backgrounds haven't been adequately investigated, who don't have signed contracts or letters of engagement, or whose association with Apple would be embarrassing if exposed.
3. Payroll-related expenditures, bonuses, awards, and noncash gifts given to or by Apple employees without proper approval and adequate documentation.
4. Payments made in cash.
5. Checks drawn payable to Cash or Bearer.
6. Transfers to or deposits in the bank account of an individual, rather than in the account of the company with which we are doing business.
7. Bank accounts or property titles not in Apple's name.
8. Billings made higher or lower than normal prices for fees, at a customer's request.
9. Payments made for any purpose other than that described in supporting documents.
10. Payments made to employees of customers or agencies through intermediary persons or organizations, or that seem to deviate from normal business transactions.
11. Any large, abnormal, unexplained, or individually approved contracts, or expenditures made without review of supporting documentation. Specific attention should also be given to large individual gifts.
12. Unusual transactions occurring with nonfunctional, inactive, or shell subsidiaries.
13. Undisclosed or unrecorded assets or liabilities.
14. Use of unethical or questionable means to obtain information, including information about competitors, or information concerning government acquisition plans or any procurement decision or action.
15. An employment, consulting, or business relationship between an Apple employee and another company, especially a company in the same or a related business as Apple.
16. Frequent trading (buying and selling over short intervals) in Apple stock or the stock of a company with which we do business.

Apple Compliance

Apple is committed to integrity in all of its dealings with employees, customers, and the general public.

Voluntary disclosures. In accordance with Apple's commitment to an effective relationship with its customers, it is the Company's policy to make voluntary disclosures, when appropriate, of problems affecting corporate relationships with any client, including any government body, and to cooperate with the appropriate government agency in any ensuing investigation or audit. Any employee who becomes aware of a problem or potential problem of the corporation should discuss the issue promptly with his or her manager and the Law department. The Law department should be notified immediately of any government inquiry, investigation, or audit.

Particularly in dealing with government customers, there are numerous rules and regulations about which employees should consult with their supervisors and the Law department to be sure Apple is meeting its obligations. Employees are also required to report to their supervisors and to the Law department any conduct they believe to be inconsistent with our obligations to the government. Reports will be handled with the strictest confidentiality within the Company to ensure that no employee suffers retaliation for bringing these matters to the attention of Apple management and its attorneys. An employee post office box, referred to as the Apple hotline, has been set up in the United States to receive such reports on an anonymous basis. These reports go directly to the Internal Audit department and are treated in a confidential manner. All information can be sent to:

Apple Computer, Inc.
P.O. Box 160444
Cupertino, California 95016-0444
USA

Consequences

Apple expects all of its employees, including those of Apple's subsidiary corporations, to comply with all provisions of these guidelines, to rely on their own high standards and reasoned evaluation in ambiguous situations, and to seek the advice and counsel of management and the Law department to clarify issues not covered by these guidelines or good judgment. These guidelines are based in part on various laws, and employees should be aware that violations of those laws may result in criminal fines and punishment of the Company and its employees, or adverse judgments in civil lawsuits.

Because of the severity of these issues, the Company may take action against any employee, contractor, or consultant whose actions have been found to violate these standards, policies, and guidelines. Such disciplinary action may include termination from employment or other working relationship.

B. QUAKER OATS COMPANY*

1/Introduction

This code has been developed to provide employees, shareholders, suppliers, and the public with an official statement on how Quaker conducts business.

---

* Reprinted by permission of the Quaker Oats Company.

The code specifies that each employee must conduct business in the full spirit of honest and lawful behavior and must not cause another employee or non-employee to act otherwise, either through inducement, suggestion, or coercion.

2/Who's Covered

The standards of this code apply to all Quaker employees. Key managers will be required to complete the signature card and will be responsible for reviewing the code with each of their employees. In addition, employees having regular involvement with the purchase or sale of goods or services, or the accounting thereof, should read this code annually, and some will be asked to complete the signature card. Also, at the discretion of the supervisor, additional individuals may be required to read the code and complete the signature card.

3/Conflict of Interest

No officer or employee can have any personal interest outside the Company that could conflict or appears to conflict with the interest of Quaker or its shareholders. Conflicts of interest may arise when an employee is in the position where he or she can use the Company connection for personal or family gain apart from normal compensation provided through employment.

It is impossible to enumerate all of the situations in which possible conflict might arise, but the following examples can be given:

Use of Corporate Funds and Assets.   The assets of Quaker are much more than our physical plants, equipment, or corporate funds. They include technologies and concepts, business strategies and plans, as well as information about our business. These assets may not be improperly used to provide personal gain for employees, nor may employees permit others to use Company assets, such as employees, materials, or equipment for personal purposes.

Confidential information.   As part of your job, you may have access to confidential information about Quaker, its customers, suppliers, and competitors. Until released to the public by a Company official, this information should not be disclosed to fellow employees who do not have a business need to know or to non-employees for any reason, without proper authorization. This includes information or data on products, financial data, business strategies, operating plans, corporate manuals, processes, systems, procedures, etc.

"Inside" Information.   Quaker is subject to a wide variety of complex laws and regulations governing transactions in corporate securities (stocks and bonds) and the securities industry. These laws are designed to protect the investing public by requiring disclosure of material information by the corporations whose securities are traded publicly. These laws are strictly enforced and violation can lead to civil and criminal actions against the individuals and the corporation involved.

Employees who know of any material fact about Quaker, which has not been disclosed to the general public, are said to have access to "inside" information. Some examples are: knowledge of significant new products or discoveries, sales and earnings figures, major contracts, plans for stock splits or acquisitions or mergers. Employees may not engage in any transactions in Quaker stocks or bonds until such information is disclosed to the public, nor may employees provide such information to others (family members, friends, brokers, etc.).

Personal Financial Gain. Employees should avoid any outside financial interest that could influence their corporate decisions or actions. Such actions could include, among other things:

- For an employee to have a personal or family interest, either direct or indirect, in an enterprise that does business or competes with Quaker or its subsidiaries. There are two exceptions to this rule. The first exception is when such interest is less than 1 percent of the capital shares (or other securities) of a corporation whose shares are publicly traded, and it is not a material part of the employee's income or net worth. The second exception is when the interest has been fully disclosed and approved by the Corporate Law Department.

- For an employee to loan or to borrow from individuals or concerns that do business with or compete with the Company or its subsidiaries, except banks and other financial institutions.

Outside Activities. Employees should avoid outside employment or activities that would have a negative impact on their job performance with Quaker, or conflict with their obligations to Quaker. Such actions might include, among other things:

- For an employee to serve as an officer, director, employee, or consultant of or receive income from any enterprise doing business with or competing with the Company or any of its subsidiaries, or seeking to do so, unless the relationship has been fully disclosed and approved by the Corporate Law Department.

- For an employee to accept compensation from outsiders for services or time for which he or she is being paid by the Company or its subsidiaries, unless the relationship has been fully disclosed and approved by the Corporate Law Department.

- For any member of management, or any employee in Marketing or Sales or the immediate family of such member or employee, to hold any interest in any advertising agency or other organization furnishing advertising, marketing, or sales promotion services, facilities, or materials to the Company or any of its subsidiaries. (This will not apply to ownership of less than 1 percent of the securities of a corporation engaged in operating an advertising medium, such as a broadcasting network or a magazine, if the securities are listed on a public securities exchange.)

- For a Company officer or any employee whose responsibilities involve commodity purchasing (or foreign exchange trading) to engage directly (or indirectly through family partners or associates) in personal trading in commodity futures in grains and commodities (or foreign currencies) used by the Company. The Company discourages all employees from engaging in commodity futures trading.

4/Dealing with Suppliers and Customers

Our business is built on integrity in dealing with customers and suppliers. Therefore, an employee or a member of an employee's immediate family must not benefit personally from any purchase of goods or services for the Company or its subsidiaries, or derive personal gain from transactions made as an employee of the Company.

The following guidelines are intended to help all employees make the proper decision in potentially difficult situations:

"Kickbacks" and Rebates. Purchase or sale of goods and services must not result in employees or their families receiving kickbacks or rebates.

Reciprocity. In many instances, Quaker may purchase goods and/or services from a supplier who buys products or services from us. This practice is normal and acceptable, but suppliers may not be asked to buy our products and services in order to become or continue to be a supplier.

Pricing Practices. All competing distributor customers within the same market area must be treated on an equitable basis with respect to prices, terms, trade promotion, and special packings offered, regardless of class of trade or type of format. Further details on Quaker pricing policies can be obtained from the Law Department's policy entitled "Antitrust Policy and Guidelines."

Gifts and Entertainment. To avoid both the reality and the appearance of improper business relations with suppliers or customers, the following standards will apply to receipt of gifts and entertainment by employees:

Gifts. Employees may not accept gifts of money under any circumstances nor may they solicit directly or indirectly non-money gifts, gratuities, or any other personal benefit or favor of any kind from suppliers, potential suppliers, or customers.

Employees and members of their immediate families may accept unsolicited, non-money gifts from a business firm or individual doing or seeking to do business with Quaker only if (1) the gift is of nominal intrinsic value or (2) the gift is advertising or promotional material.

Gifts of more than nominal intrinsic value may be accepted only if protocol, courtesy, or other special circumstances exist. However, all such gifts must be reported to the Corporate Law Department, which will determine whether the employee may keep the gift or must return it.

An employee cannot keep any gift sent directly to his or her home. Such gifts must be returned to the donor or turned in to the Corporate Law Department, which will maintain a log of such gifts and will determine whether the employee may keep the gift or must return it.

Entertainment. Employees may not encourage or solicit directly or indirectly entertainment from any individual or company with whom Quaker does business. From time to time, employees may offer and/or accept entertainment, but only if the entertainment is reasonable, occurs infrequently, and does not involve lavish expenditures.

5/Payments to Agents, Consultants, Distributors

Agreements with agents, sales representatives, distributors, and consultants must be in writing and must clearly and accurately set forth the services to be performed, the basis for earning the commission or fee involved, and the applicable discount, rate, or fee. The amount must not be excessive in light of the practice in the trade and be commensurate with the value of services rendered. The agent, sales representative, distributor, or consultant must be advised that the agreement may be publicly disclosed and must agree to such public disclosure. In some foreign countries, local laws may prohibit the use of agents or limit the rate of commission or fee.

Sales to third parties may not be billed at prices exceeding the established net price for the product. This ensures against overbilling and possible rebate abuses.

6/Payments to Countries Other than Payee's Residence

Requests by payees (third parties) for payment of fees or commissions to the payee's account in a country other than the payee's residence or place of business may not be made without prior approval of the Corporate Law Department.

7/Payments to Government Employees

No payment of money, gifts, services, entertainment, or anything of value may be offered or made available in any amount, directly or indirectly, to any government official or employee in any country. However, with prior approval of the Corporate Law Department, payments in nominal amounts may be made to low-level foreign government (non-U.S.) employees, whose duties are essentially ministerial or clerical, for the purpose of processing or expediting routine matters.

8/Import Restrictions

When traveling on Company business, employees must adhere to each country's laws regarding declaration and importation of money, negotiable instruments, and goods. Any goods for which an import license has not been obtained should not be carried into a country by an employee. Any questions regarding specific rules for each country should be referred to the Corporate Law Department.

9/Books and Records

All books and records throughout the Company must be accurate and fairly reflect the underlying transactions. It is each employee's responsibility to ensure that documents supporting the accounting records (receipts, disbursements, journal entries) contain wording which clearly describes the reason and purpose for the transaction.

It is each employee's responsibility to assure that all necessary accruals are made on a timely basis.

A complete description of guidelines for maintaining accounting records is contained in the Corporate Controller's Policy Manual (#01-01-017).

10/Competitive Practices

Collaboration with competitors in violation of the law on such things as pricing, production, marketing, inventories, product development, sales territories and goals, market studies, and proprietary or confidential information is prohibited.

Information about Competitors.   As a competitor in the marketplace, we continually seek economic knowledge about our competition. However, we will not engage in illegal or improper acts to acquire a competitor's trade secrets, customer lists, information about company facilities, technical developments, or operations. In addition, we will not hire competitors' employees to obtain confidential information or urge competitive personnel or customers to disclose confidential information.

11/Political Activities and Contributions

Quaker encourages each of its employees to be good citizens and to fully participate in the political process. Employees should, however, be aware that (1) laws in most countries prohibit Quaker from contributing to political candidates, political parties, or party officials; and (2) employees who participate in partisan political activities must make every effort to ensure that they do not leave the impression that they speak or act for Quaker. However, individual contributions to the Public Interest Committee of The Quaker Oats Company, a U.S. employee organization, are legal and an appropriate means for Quaker employees to support candidates for the U.S. Congress.

12/Implementation

Quaker Employees.   As a Quaker employee, you are required to report dishonest or illegal activities as well as probable violations of provisions of this code outlined above by other employees to your superior. If a satisfactory response is not received from your supervisor, you should contact either the Vice President–Corporate Controller and Planning, Terry G. Westbrook, (312) 222-8906; or the Senior Vice President–Law, Corporate Affairs, and Corporate Secretary, Luther C. McKinney, (312) 222-7855. Failure to submit such information or to submit facts which are known to be false is a violation of the code. Also, it is a serious violation for any Quaker manager to initiate or encourage reprisal action against any person who in good faith reports known or suspected code violations.

Board of Directors.   The Board is ultimately responsible to the shareholders for assuring that the business of Quaker is conducted in accordance with the code. The Board, through its own Audit Committee, will help assure that the code is properly administered. If willful violations are ascertained to have taken place, the Board shall ensure that the legal rights of individuals are protected, that Quaker's legal obligations are fulfilled, and that proper disciplinary and legal action is taken. The Board will further see that corrective measures and safeguards are instituted to prevent recurrence of violations.

Officers and Managers. All officers and managers are responsible for reviewing this code with each of their employees. New employees shall read, and some may be asked to complete, the signature card upon employment.

C. AMERICAN MARKETING ASSOCIATION*

Members of the American Marketing Association (AMA) are committed to ethical professional conduct. They have joined together in subscribing to this Code of Ethics embracing the following topics:

Responsibilities of the Marketer

Marketers must accept responsibility for the consequence of their activities and make every effort to ensure that their decisions, recommendations, and actions function to identify, serve, and satisfy all relevant publics: customers, organizations, and society.
Marketers' professional conduct must be guided by:

1. The basic rule of professional ethics: not knowingly to do harm.
2. The adherence to all applicable laws and regulations.
3. The accurate representation of their education, training, and experience.
4. The active support, practice, and promotion of this Code of Ethics.

Honesty and Fairness

Marketers shall uphold and advance the integrity, honor, and dignity of the marketing profession by:

1. Being honest in serving consumers, clients, employees, suppliers, distributors, and the public.
2. Not knowingly participating in conflict of interest without prior notice to all parties involved.
3. Establishing equitable fee schedules, including the payment or receipt of usual, customary, and/or legal compensation for marketing exchanges.

Rights and Duties of Parties in the Marketing Exchange Process

Participants in the marketing exchange process should be able to expect that:

1. Products and services offered are safe and fit for their intended uses.
2. Communications about offered products and services are not deceptive.
3. All parties intend to discharge their obligations, financial and otherwise, in good faith.

---

* Reprinted by permission of the American Marketing Association.

4. Appropriate internal methods exist for equitable adjustment and/or redress of grievances concerning purchases.

It is understood that the above would include, *but is not limited to*, the following responsibilities of the marketer:

In the Area of Product Development and Management.

- Disclosure of all substantial risks associated with product or service usage.
- Identification of any product component substitution that might materially change the product or impact on the buyer's purchase decision.
- Identification of extra-cost added features.

In the Area of Promotions.

- Avoidance of false and misleading advertising.
- Rejection of high-pressure manipulations, or misleading sales tactics.
- Avoidance of sales promotions that use deception or manipulation.

In the Area of Distribution.

- Not manipulating the availability of a product for purpose of exploitation.
- Not using coercion in the marketing channel.
- Not exerting undue influence over the reseller's choice to handle a product.

In the Area of Pricing.

- Not engaging in price-fixing.
- Not practicing predatory pricing.
- Disclosing the full price associated with any purchase.

In the Area of Marketing Research.

- Prohibiting selling or fund raising under the guise of conducting research.
- Maintaining research integrity by avoiding misrepresentation and omission of pertinent research data.
- Treating outside clients and suppliers fairly.

Organizational Relationships

Marketers should be aware of how their behavior may influence or impact on the behavior of others in organizational relationships. They should not demand, encourage, or apply coercion to obtain unethical behavior in their relationships with others, such as employees, suppliers, or customers.

1. Apply confidentiality and anonymity in professional relationships with regard to privileged information.
2. Meet their obligations and responsibilities in contracts and mutual agreements in a timely manner.
3. Avoid taking the work of others, in whole or in part, and represent this work as their own or directly benefit from it without compensation or consent of the originator or owner.
4. Avoid manipulation to take advantage of situations to maximize personal welfare in a way that unfairly deprives or damages the organization or others.

Any AMA members found to be in violation of any provision of this Code of Ethics may have his or her Association membership suspended or revoked.

Exercises

A. HOW DO YOUR ETHICS COMPARE WITH NEW YORK?*

This advertising ethics questionnaire was created by the Center for Communication of New York, for the Advertising Club of America (Adclub), which wanted to survey its members on the ethics of various business practices. *Advertising Age*, with the Adclub's permission, asked its readers the same questions. The journal wanted to determine whether the ethical standards of advertising people in New York differed from those of their fellow professionals elsewhere in the United States. More recently, this survey has been used in a variety of classroom situations to promote discussion of ethical marketing issues.

1. You are competing with three other agencies for the Magnasonic Consumer Electronics business. Its chief competitor is Rolavision, handled by XYZ Advertising. XYZ's account supervisor on Rolavision has interviewed with you recently for a job. You hire him, specifically to help with the Magnasonic pitch.

    1. Ethical   Unethical

2. A good friend of yours calls and says an associate of his is looking for a new advertising agency. His associate knows little about advertising and has asked for his advice. He offers to recommend your company, provided he will be paid a finder's fee of $20,000 if you land the business. You agree.

    2. Ethical   Unethical

3. Same as question 2, but your friend is in the business of consulting for clients looking for new advertising agencies, and he is being paid a fee by his client.

    3. Ethical   Unethical

4. Your agency is one of four semifinalists asked to participate in a competition for a new product assignment from a major toy marketer. While the agency has had experience in marketing to children, this assignment would be your agency's first in the toy category—and with a leading manufacturer. During a final briefing your prospective client discloses that the "new product" is a compatible set of war toys complete with

---

* Reprinted by permission of the Center for Communication, Inc., 570 Lexington Avenue, New York, NY 10022.

pseudo-ammunition, guns, and the like. Your agency decides that it will accept this assignment if it is awarded to them.

    4. Ethical   Unethical

5. You and two other agencies are in the final stages of a competition. Part of your pitch has to do with recommending and supporting a new marketing strategy. Late one evening, a few days before the scheduled presentation, you are proofing your slides at a slide supply house. By accident, you are handed a fairly complete set of slides put together for one of your competitors. You have enough time to examine and get the gist of it before returning the set to the supplier, who is embarrassed at his mistake. When you return to the office, you make significant changes in the way your agency presents itself so as to attack your competitor's recommended strategy in a direct and forceful manner without, of course, revealing to anyone that you have information on your competitor's actual recommendations.

    5. Ethical   Unethical

6. Same as question **5**, except your competitor's slides are in a file folder on the worktable next to you. You have to wait for the supplier to leave the room before you peek at them.

    6. Ethical   Unethical

7. You've been invited to compete for the business of a retail chain that has head-quarters in the Southeast. The chain is run autocratically by its 75-year-old founder. Every member of his senior management team is white, male, and more than 40 years old. In past discussions, you've come away with a clear impression that they are nar-rowminded, too. As it happens, a few months ago your agency lost the business of a large New York retail chain. You did excellent work for the chain and the account supervisor who knows all about the business still works for you but has been without an assignment for more than three months. The problem is, the account supervisor is a 35-year-old woman. You decide not to use her in your presentation.

    7. Ethical   Unethical

8. Same as question **7**, except that your account supervisor is male, 45 years old, and black. You decide not to include him in the presentation.

    8. Ethical   Unethical

9. Your agency is looking to hire a senior account management person. You interview a management supervisor, who promises to bring with him one of the accounts he is responsible for at his current agency—if you hire him at the salary he is asking. You hire him and the account comes to you.

    9. Ethical   Unethical

10. You and three other agencies are in a competition for a major airline account. As luck would have it, a good friend of yours is sleeping with the secretary for the airline's marketing VP. She's very indiscreet and tells your friend all about the exciting things going back and forth at the company during the review, including the individual views of the members of the airline's agency selection committee. Your friend gives you feedback on all your meetings and on your competitors' meetings with the airline.

    10. Ethical   Unethical

11. Same as question **10**, except your friend asks for a consulting fee, with a bonus if you get the business.

    11. Ethical   Unethical

12. Your agency is being considered by a group of restaurants that offers "good tasting" food at low prices. They ask your company to develop a better "price" story since they will soon begin cutting their prices even further. When the agency delves into the reasons why the company can continue to serve the same "good tasting" food at even lower prices, it learns that the group has found a supplier of slightly "off" food. While the food has not yet spoiled, it is close to that stage and requires additional seasonings and preservatives. Your agency accepts the assignment.

    12. Ethical   Unethical

B. MARKETING DILEMMAS*

These exercises were developed by Professor Charles S. Madden, Associate Dean for Graduate Programs at Baylor University. There are three exercises, each of which takes the reader through a scenario in several stages. The reader can stop after each stage to consider the ethics of the particular situation.

1. a.   Bill Mitchell, a newly hired sales rep for Amco Pharmaceuticals, was surprised to learn that there was a very extensive expense sheet to fill out after trips on the road. He spent almost an hour reading the instructions and filling out the first form after he finished training and made his first "solo" trip through his territory. After going through that, he realized that there were some expense categories that did not appear on the form. Among the expenses not listed was laundry. In his first draft of the expense account, he put laundry under miscellaneous. His sales manager examined the report and suggested that, rather than a large miscellaneous total, it would be better to classify laundry under meal expenses, because individual tickets were not required and he was under the daily per diem allowance. Bill was told that, while miscellaneous charges were usually examined very carefully, as long as meal totals were below the allowed limit, management never examined them.

    b.   A few months later, Bill was on the road dealing with the introduction of a new product when a good customer asked if he would like to attend a pro basketball game. Bill offered, because of his relationship with the customer, to obtain tickets and host a total of three customers from the same firm to the game. Upon returning from the trip, he asked about how he should deal with the basketball tickets and was again told to find a category in which he had not exceeded the limit and to "bury them there." By this time, he understood the process and felt pretty good about doing so.

    c.   Several months later, he called in from a long road trip and explained to his sales manager that, because of the difficulty in making appointments, he was

---

* Reprinted by permission of Charles S. Madden.

going to miss his wife's birthday. The sales manager told him he should do something really special for his wife to make it up to her. After talking with his wife on the telephone, he felt worse than ever. He wired her $150 worth of flowers and buried it in his expense account.

d. Several days after returning from the road trip, he was called into the marketing vice president's office and asked about the flower expense. Bill explained that he felt justified to have the company pay for the flowers. The marketing vice president listened carefully while Bill told the story of his wife's birthday. He went on to explain how it was commonly accepted practice among the sales force and sales managers.

e. Bill was fired for fraud on his expense account.

2. a. Jill McCarthy, a retail buyer for a large department store, was told during her training as a buyer that the company was very sensitive to any type of inducements given buyers beyond "modest tokens of friendship." The company felt that, as long as buyers were entertained or received tokens of appreciation of little or no value, their positions would not be compromised.

b. The first year of Jill's job involved nothing that could even be remotely linked to the "bribery policy." One salesperson for a large dress manufacturer had become good friends with Jill and offered to take her to dinner, so they could quietly discuss some of the emerging fashion trends that would be affecting the next season's lines. Jill was happy to go to dinner, because it was a good social opportunity to enjoy quiet conversations with her friend, Barbara, the sales representative. The dinner went very well and was very productive for both Jill and her store.

c. Later that year, Barbara invited Jill to attend an ice show with her, completely as a recreational activity. Jill remembered the dinner, felt that it would be very pleasant to attend anything with Barbara, and quickly accepted. On the date of the planned entertainment, Jill received a note from Barbara with four tickets, saying she was terribly sorry that she could not come to town but wanted Jill to invite other friends and enjoy the ice show.

d. A month later, with a note of apology, Jill received a smoked turkey and fruit cake from Barbara in the name of Barbara's company.

e. The following spring, Barbara contacted Jill and asked her to speak to the retail apparel manufacturers' sales trade association on the buyer's view of sales and service in retailing. Jill was very happy to receive the invitation to speak and was happier later to hear that there was an honorarium of $500 associated with the speaking engagement. She worked very hard on her speech and it was very well received. She felt she had earned every penny of the $500 in extra work.

f. In late summer, Barbara spent almost two days with Jill, acquainting her with some of the changes that would be made in the line and bringing her up to date on some new trends that were to be watched in the industry. Two weeks later, Jill received a $1,000 check from Barbara's company, with a notation that this was for her time and with great appreciation in advising Barbara on the needs of retailers such as herself.

g. Jill realized that she was in clear violation of the "bribery policy" but was not sure where she crossed the line.

3. a. Bob Smith, a field interviewer for a large marketing research company, was hired to do fairly lengthy interviews with consumers around the midwestern states. He was a very meticulous interviewer and turned in very complete answers to every open-ended research question. His recent survey forms were examined by a field supervisor and he received occasional questions on particularly unusual answers. On one set of questionnaires, he received a note asking him to "edit" the answers he received, so they would be more easily readable by a computer scanner and, at the same time, to make the most unusual answers conform more to the form.

b. Taking out some of these outlying answers, he found that more and more questionnaires had similar, if not identical, information after his interviews. He brought this to the attention of one of his supervisors, who reassured him that such patterns frequently happened on questionnaires and that he should not worry about it.

c. Later, because of an unrealistic deadline for interviewing, he decided that he would do half the interviews and then double them and copy the first half on the second half.

d. Bob's supervisor questioned the unusual pattern. Bob was asked to explain whether he followed procedure.

Bibliography*

Abratt, Russell, and Diane Sacks. "The Marketing Challenge: Toward Being Profitable and Socially Responsible." *Journal of Business Ethics* 7 (November 1988), pp. 497–507.

Achenbaum, Alvin A. "Can We Tolerate a Double Standard in Marketing Research?" *Journal of Advertising Research* 25 (June–July 1985), pp. RC3–RC7.

Ackerman, Norleen M., ed. *Ethics and the Consumer Interest.* American Council of Consumer Interests, 25th Annual Conference Proceedings, 1979, pp. 12–19.

Akaah, Ishmael P. "Differences in Research Ethics Judgments between Male and Female Marketing Professionals." *Journal of Business Ethics* 8 (May 1989), pp. 375–82.

————. "Attitudes of Marketing Professionals toward Ethics in Marketing Research: A Cross-National Comparison." *Journal of Business Ethics* 9 (January 1990), pp. 45–54.

Akaah, Ishmael P., and Edward A. Riordan. "Judgments of Marketing Professionals about Ethical Issues in Marketing Research: A Replication and Extension." *Journal of Marketing Research* 26 (February 1989), pp. 112–21.

Allmon, Dean E., and James Grant. "Real Estate Sales Agents and the Code of Ethics: A Voice Stress Analysis." *Journal of Business Ethics* 9 (October 1990), pp. 807–12.

Andreasen, Alan, and Arthur Best. "Consumers Complain—Does Business Respond?" *Harvard Business Review* (July–August 1977), pp. 93–101.

Armstrong, Robert W.; Bruce W. Stening; John K. Ryans; Larry Marks; and Michael Mayo. "International Marketing Ethics: Problems Encountered by Australian Firms." *European Journal of Marketing* 24 (October 1990), pp. 5–19.

Arrington, Robert L. "Advertising and Behavior Control." *Journal of Business Ethics* 1 (February 1982), pp. 3–12.

Baker, James C. "The International Infant Formula Controversy: A Dilemma in Corporate Social Responsibility." *Journal of Business Ethics* 4 (June 1985), pp. 181–90.

---

* Compiled by Edward S. Petry, Jr., Center for Business Ethics, Bentley College, Waltham, Massachusetts.

Barach, Jeffrey, A. "Simpson and Samson: Clues for Improving Public Service Advertising." In *The Individual, Business and Society*, ed. Jeffrey A. Barach. Englewood Cliffs, N.J.: Prentice Hall, 1977, pp. 157–64.

Barry, Vincent, ed. *Moral Issues in Business*. 3rd ed. Belmont, Calif.: Wadsworth, 1986, pp. 77–8 and 339–43.

Barry, Vincent. "Advertising and Corporate Ethics," In *Essentials of Business Ethics*, ed. Peter Madsen and Jay M. Shafritz. New York: Penguin, 1990, pp. 244–53.

Bartels, Robert. "A Model for Ethics in Marketing." *Journal of Marketing* 31 (January 1967), pp. 20–26.

Beauchamp, Tom L. "Manipulative Advertising." *Business and Professional Ethics Journal* 3, nos. 3 & 4 (Spring/Summer 1984), pp. 1–22. Comments by R. M. Hare, pp. 23–28, and Barry Biederman, pp. 29–30.

———. *Case Studies in Business, Society and Ethics*. Englewood Cliffs, N.J.: Prentice Hall, 1989, four case studies: pp. 63–98.

Beauchamp, Tom L., and Norman E. Bowie, eds. *Ethical Theory and Business*. 2nd ed. Englewood Cliffs, N.J.: Prentice Hall, 1983, pp. 334–57.

Bellizzi, Joseph A., and Robert E. Hite. "Supervising Unethical Salesforce Behavior." *Journal of Marketing* 53 (April 1989), pp. 36–48.

Beltramini, Richard F. "Ethics and the Use of Competitive Information Acquisition Strategies." *Journal of Business Ethics* 5 (August 1986), pp. 307–11.

Bennett, J. R. "*Saturday Review's* Annual Advertising Awards." *Journal of Business Ethics* 2 (May 1983), pp. 73–78.

Bezilla, Robert; Joel B. Haynes; and Clifford Elliott. "Ethics in Marketing Research." *Business Horizons* 19 (April 1976), pp. 83–86.

Blankenship, A. B. "Some Aspects of Ethics in Marketing Research." *Journal of Marketing Research* 1 (May 1964), pp. 26–31.

Boddewyn, J. J. "Advertising Regulation: Fiddling with the FTC While the World Burns." *Business Horizons* 28 (May–June 1985), pp. 32–40.

Bogart, Leo. "The Researcher's Dilemma." *Journal of Marketing* 26 (January 1962), pp. 6–11.

Bowie, Norman E., and Ronald F. Duska. "Applying the Moral Presuppositions of Business to Advertising and Hiring." In *Business Ethics*. 2nd ed., Norman E. Bowie and Ronald F. Duska. Englewood Cliffs, N.J.: Prentice Hall, 1990, pp. 53–57.

Braybrooke, David. *Ethics in the World of Business*. Totowa, N.J.: Rowman & Allanheld, 1983, pp. 63–104.

Brennan, Bernard F. "Remarks on Marketing Ethics." *Journal of Business Ethics* 10 (April 1991), pp. 255–58.

Camenisch, Paul F. "Marketing Ethics: Some Dimensions of the Challenge." *Journal of Business Ethics* 10 (April 1991), pp. 245–48.

Carroll, Archie B. "Consumer Stakeholders: Product Information Issues and Responses." In *Business & Society; Ethics and Stakeholder Management*, ed. Archie B. Carroll. Cincinnati: South-Western, 1989, pp. 222–51.

Carson, Thomas L.; Richard E. Wokutch; and James E. Cox, Jr. "An Ethical Analysis of Deception in Advertising." *Journal of Business Ethics* 4 (March 1985), pp. 93–104.

Cavanagh, Gerald F., and Arthur F. McGovern. "Advertising and Television." In *Ethical Dilemmas in the Modern Corporation*. Gerald F. Cavanagh and Arthur F. McGovern. Englewood Cliffs, N.J.: Prentice Hall, 1988, pp. 88–117.

Cheeseman, Henry R. "Ethical Considerations and Business; Advertising." In *The Legal and Regulatory Environment of Business*. Henry R. Cheeseman. New York: MacMillan, 1985, pp. 583–612.

Chonko, Lawrence B., and Shelby D. Hunt. "Ethics and Marketing Management: An Empirical Examination." *Journal of Business Research* 13 (1985), pp. 339–59.

Clasen, Earl A. "Marketing Ethics and the Consumer." *Harvard Business Review*, January–February 1967, pp. 79–86.

Conry, Edward J.; Gerald Ferrera; and Karla H. Fox. "Regulation of Advertising." In *The Legal Environment of Business*. Edward J. Conry, Gerald Ferrera, and Karla H. Fox. Dubuque: Wm. C. Brown, 1986, pp. 447–72.

Cragin, John P.; Y. K. Kwan; and Y. N. Ho. "Social Ethics and the Emergence of Advertising in China: Perceptions from within the Great Wall." *Journal of Business Ethics* 3 (May 1984), pp. 91–94.

Crawford, C. Merle. "Attitudes of Marketing Executives toward Ethics in Marketing Research." *Journal of Marketing* 34 (April 1970), pp. 46–52.

Crisp, Roger. "Persuasive Advertising, Autonomy, and the Creation of Desire." *Journal of Business Ethics* 6 (June 1987), pp. 413–18.

Day, Robert L. "A Comment on Ethics in Marketing Research.' " *Journal of Marketing Research* 12 (May 1975), pp. 232–33.

DeConinck, J. B., and D. J. Good. "Perceptual Differences of Sales Practitioners and Students Concerning Ethical Behavior." *Journal of Business Ethics* 8 (September 1989), pp. 667–76.

DeGeorge, Richard T. "Marketing, Truth and Advertising." In *Business Ethics*, 2nd ed., Richard T. DeGeorge. New York: MacMillan, 1986, pp. 265–90.

DesJardins, Joseph R., and John J. McCall, eds., *Contemporary Issues in Business Ethics*. Belmont, Calif.: Wadsworth, 1985, pp. 97–113, 122–57, and 175–97.

Dienhart, John W., and Saundra I. Foderick. "Ethical and Conceptual Issues in Charitable Investments, Cause-Related Marketing, and Advertising." *Business and Professional Ethics Journal* 7, nos. 3 & 4 (Fall–Winter 1988), pp. 47–60.

Dixon, D. F. "The Ethical Component of Marketing: An Eighteenth-Century View." *Journal of Macromarketing* 2 (Spring 1982), pp. 38–46.

Dixon, J. D., and B. G. S. James. "The Honesty of the Technical Salesman." *Management Decision* 22 (1984), pp. 47–52.

Dornoff, Donald J., and Clint B. Tankersley. "Do Retailers Practice Corporate Responsibility?" *Journal of Retailing* 51 (Winter 1975), pp. 33–42.

Dubinsky, Alan J. "Ethics in Industrial Selling: How Product and Service Salespeople Compare." *Journal of the Academy of Marketing Science* 13 (Winter 1985), pp. 160–70.

Dubinsky, Alan J.; Eric N. Berkowitz; and William Rudelius. "Ethical Problems of Field Sales Personnel." *MSU Business Topics* 28 (Summer 1980), pp. 11–16.

Dubinsky, Alan J., and Thomas N. Ingram. "Correlates of Salespeople's Ethical Conflict: An Exploratory Investigation." *Journal of Business Ethics* 3 (December 1984), pp. 343–53.

Dubinsky, Alan J., and M. Levy. "Ethics in Retailing: Perceptions of Retail Salespeople." *Journal of the Academy of Marketing Science* 13 (Winter 1985), pp. 1–16.

Dunfee, Thomas W. *Ethics and the M.B.A. Curriculum.* Philadelphia: The Wharton School of the University of Pennsylvania, 1986.

Durand, Richard M., and Zarrel V. Lambert. "Alienation and Criticisms of Advertising." *Journal of Advertising* 14, no. 3 (1985), pp. 9–17.

Durham, Taylor R. "Information, Persuasion, and Control in Moral Appraisal of Advertising Strategy." *Journal of Business Ethics* 3 (August 1984), pp. 173–80.

Dyllick, Thomas. "Ecological Marketing Strategy for Toni Yogurts in Switzerland." *Journal of Business Ethics* 8 (August 1989), pp. 657–62.

Ebejer, James M., and Michael J. Morden. "Paternalism in the Marketplace: Should a Salesman Be His Buyer's Keeper?" *Journal of Business Ethics* 7 (May 1988), pp. 337–39.

Emamalizadeh, Hossein. "The Informative and Persuasive Functions of Advertising: A Moral Appraisal—A Comment." *Journal of Business Ethics* 4 (Spring 1985), pp. 151–53.

Farmer, Richard N. "Would You Want Your Daughter to Marry a Marketing Man?" *Journal of Marketing* 31 (January 1967), pp. 1–3.

———. "Would You Want Your Son to Marry a Marketing Lady?" *Journal of Marketing* 41 (January 1977), pp. 15–18.

Farmer, Richard N., and W. Dickerson Hogue. *Corporate Social Responsibility.* 2nd ed. Lexington, Mass.: Lexington Books, 1985, pp. 148–51.

Ferrell, O. C., and Larry G. Gresham. "A Contingency Framework for Understanding Ethical Decision Making in Marketing." *Journal of Marketing* 49 (Summer 1985), pp. 87–96.

Ferrell, O. C., and Steven J. Skinner. "Ethical Behavior and Bureaucratic Structure in Marketing Research Organizations." *Journal of Marketing Research* 25 (February 1988), pp. 103–10.

Ferrell, O. C., and Mark Weaver. "Ethical Beliefs of Marketing Managers." *Journal of Marketing* 42 (July 1978), pp. 69–73.

Ferrell, O. C.; Mary Zey-Ferrell; and Dean Krugman. "A Comparison of Predictors of Ethical and Unethical Behavior Among Corporate and Agency Advertising Managers." *Journal of Macromarketing* 3 (Spring 1983), pp. 19–27.

Fraedrich, John; O. C. Ferrell; and William Pride. "An Empirical Examination of Three Machiavellian Concepts: Advertisers vs. the General Public." *Journal of Business Ethics* 8 (September 1989), pp. 687–94.

Frey, Cynthia J., and Thomas C. Kinnear. "Legal Constraints and Marketing Research: A Review and Call to Action." *Journal of Marketing Research* 16 (August 1979), pp. 295–302.

Fritzsche, David J. "An Examination of Marketing Ethics: Role of the Decision Maker, Consequences of the Decision, Management Position and Sex of Respondent." *Journal of Macromarketing*, Fall 1988, pp. 29–39.

Fritzsche, David J., and Helmut Becker. "Business Ethics of Future Marketing Managers." *Journal of Marketing Education,* Fall 1982, pp. 2–7.

————. "Ethical Behavior of Marketing Managers." *Journal of Business Ethics* 2 (November 1983), pp. 291–99.

Galbraith, John Kenneth. *The Affluent Society.* Boston: Houghton Mifflin, 1958.

Gardner, David M. "Deception in Advertising: A Conceptual Approach." *Journal of Marketing,* January 1975, pp. 40–46.

Gorlin, Rena A., ed. *Codes of Professional Responsibility.* 2nd ed. Washington, D.C.: Bureau of National Affairs, 1990, pp. 15–18 and 21–28. (Codes of American Association of Advertising Agencies and the Direct Marketing Association.)

Gratz, J. E. "The Ethics of Subliminal Communication." *Journal of Business Ethics* 3 (August 1984), pp. 181–84.

Greene, C. S., and Paul Miesing. "Public Policy, Technology, and Ethics: Marketing Decisions for NASA's Space Shuttle." *Journal of Marketing* 48 (Summer 1984), pp. 56–67.

Greenland, Leo. "Advertisers Must Stop Conning Consumers." *Harvard Business Review,* July–August 1974, pp. 18–28, 156.

Greyser, Stephen A. "Advertising Attacks and Counters." *Harvard Business Review,* March–April 1972, pp. 22–28, 140.

Greyser, Stephen A., and Bonnie Reece. "Businessmen Look Hard at Advertising." *Harvard Business Review,* May–June 1971, pp. 18–26, 157–65.

Grossbart, Sanford L., and Lawrence S. Crosby. "Understanding the Bases of Parental Concern and Reaction to Children's Food Advertising." *Journal of Marketing* 48 (Summer 1984), pp. 79–92.

Hardy, Kenneth G. "Time to Be Heard on Advocacy." *Canadian Business Review* 9 (Spring 1982), pp. 35–39.

Hawkins, Del I., and A. Benton Cocanougher. "Student Evaluations of the Ethics of Marketing Practices: The Role of Marketing Education." *Journal of Marketing* 36 (April 1972), pp. 61–72.

Henry, Jules. "Advertising as a Philosophical System." In *Business Ethics: A Philosophical Approach,* 3rd ed. Ed. by Kevin Funchion, Krishna Mallick, and Edward Meagher. Needham Heights, Mass.: Ginn, 1990, pp. 195–209.

Hite, Robert E.; Joseph A. Bellizzi; and Cynthia Fraser. "A Content Analysis of Ethical Policy Statements Regarding Marketing Activities." *Journal of Business Ethics* 7 (October 1988), pp. 771–76.

Hoffman, W. Michael, and Jennifer Mills Moore, eds. *Business Ethics; Readings and Cases in Corporate Morality.* 2nd ed. New York: McGraw-Hill, 1990, pp. 437–59 and 582–84.

Hollander, Sidney. "Ethics in Marketing Research." In *Handbook of Marketing Research.* ed. Robert Ferber. New York: McGraw-Hill, 1974, pp. 107–27.

Holley, David M. "A Moral Evaluation of Sales Practices." *Business and Professional Ethics Journal* 5, no. 1 (1987), pp. 3–21.

Humphrey, Ronald, and Howard Schuman. "The Portrayal of Blacks in Magazine Advertisements: 1950–1982." *Public Opinion Quarterly* 48 (Fall 1984), pp. 551–63.

Hunt, Shelby D., and Lawrence B. Chonko. "Marketing and Machiavellianism." *Journal of Marketing* 48 (Summer 1984), pp. 30–42.

Hunt, Shelby D., and John R. Nevin. "Why Consumers Believe They Are Being Ripped Off." *Business Horizons* 24 (May–June 1981), pp. 48–52.

Hunt, Shelby D.; Van R. Wood; and Lawrence B. Chonko. "Corporate Ethical Values and Organizational Commitment in Marketing." *Journal of Marketing* 53 (July 1989), pp. 79–91.

Hyman, Michael R., and Richard Tansey. "The Ethics of Psychoactive Ads." *Journal of Business Ethics* 9 (February 1990), pp. 105–14.

Iannone, A. Pablo, ed. *Contemporary Moral Controversies in Business.* New York: Oxford University Press, 1989, pp. 353–64 and 414–22.

Jones, Donald G., and Helen Troy. *A Bibliography of Business Ethics: 1976–1980.* Charlottesville: Colgate Darden Graduate School of Business Administration, University of Virginia; Edwin Mellen Press, 1986.

Jovanovic, B. "Truthful Disclosure of Information." *Bell Journal of Economics* 13 (Spring 1982), pp. 36–44.

Kaikati, Jack, and Wayne A. Label. "American Bribery Legislation: An Obstacle to International Marketing." *Journal of Marketing* 44 (Fall 1980), pp. 38–43.

Kelley, S. W.; O. C. Ferrell; and S. J. Skinner. "Ethical Behavior among Marketing Researchers: An Assessment of Selected Demographic Characteristics." *Journal of Business Ethics* 9 (August 1990), pp. 681–88.

Kelley, Scott W.; Stephen J. Skinner; and O. C. Ferrell; "Opportunistic Behavior in Marketing Research Organizations." *Journal of Business Research* 18 (June 1989), pp. 327–41.

Kizilbash, A. H.; William O. Hancock; Carlton A. Maile; and Peter Gillet. "Social Auditing for Marketing Managers." *Industrial Marketing Management* 8 (1979), pp. 1–6.

Kohn, Paul M.; Reginald G. Smart; and Alan C. Ogborne. "Effects of Two Kinds of Alcohol Advertising on Subsequent Consumption." *Journal of Advertising* 13, no. 1 (1984), pp. 34–40.

Krohn, Franklin B. "Teaching of Legal and Ethical Standards for Marketing Research." *Journal of Marketing Education* 4 (Spring 1982), pp. 31–34.

Krohn, Franklin B., and Laura M. Milner. "The AIDS Crisis: Unethical Marketing Leads to Negligent Homicide." *Journal of Business Ethics* 8 (October 1989), pp. 773–80.

Krugman, Dean O., and O. C. Ferrell. "Organizational Ethics of Advertising: Corporate and Agency Views." *Journal of Advertising* 10 (1981), pp. 21–30.

La Barbera, Priscilla. "The Shame of Magazine Advertising." *Journal of Advertising* 10, no. 1 (1981), pp. 31–37.

Laczniak, Gene R. "Framework for Analyzing Marketing Ethics." *Journal of Macromarketing* 1 (Spring 1983), pp. 7–18.

Laczniak, Gene R.; Robert F. Lusch; and John H. Murphy. "Social Marketing: Its Ethical Dimension." *Journal of Marketing* 43 (Spring 1979), pp. 29–36.

Laczniak, Gene R.; Robert F. Lusch; and William A. Strang. " 'Ethical Marketing' Perceptions of Economic Goods and Social Problems." *Journal of Macromarketing* 1 (Spring 1981), pp. 49–57.

Laczniak, Gene R., and Patrick E. Murphy. *Marketing Ethics: Guidelines for Managers.* Lexington, Mass.: Lexington Books, 1985.

_____. "Fostering Ethical Marketing Decisions." *Journal of Business Ethics* 10 (April 1991), pp. 259–72.

Lantos, Geoffrey P. "An Ethical Base for Marketing Decision Making." *The Journal of Business and Industrial Marketing* 2, no. 2 (Spring 1987), pp. 11–16.

Lee, Kam-Hon. "Ethical Beliefs in Marketing Management: A Cross Cultural Study." *European Journal of Marketing* 15, no. 1 (1981), pp. 58–67.

_____. "The Performative and Persuasive Functions of Advertising: A Moral Appraisal —A Further Comment." *Journal of Business Ethics* 6 (January 1987), pp. 55–58.

Leffler, K. B. "Persuasion or Information? The Economics of Prescription Drug Advertising." *Journal of Law and Economics* 24 (April 1981), pp. 45–74.

Leiser, Burton M. "Professional Advertising: Price Fixing and Professional Dignity versus the Public's Right to a Free Market." *Business and Professional Ethics Journal* 3 (Spring–Summer 1984), pp. 93–107. Comment, James E. Doughton, pp. 109–10 and Ruth Macklin, pp. 111–18.

Levitt, Theodore. "The Morality (?) of Advertising." *Harvard Business Review*, July–August 1970, pp. 84–92.

Levy, Michael, and Alan J. Dubinsky. "Identifying and Addressing Retail Salespersons' Ethical Problems: A Method of Application." *Journal of Retailing* 59 (Spring 1983), pp. 46–66.

Lippke, Richard L. "Advertising and the Social Conditions of Autonomy." *Business and Professional Ethics Journal* 8, no. 4 (Winter 1989), pp. 35–58.

Loken, Barbara, and Alan J. Dubinsky. "Analyzing Ethical Decision Making in Marketing." *Journal of Business Research* 19 (September 1989), pp. 83–108.

Lusch, Robert F.; Gene R. Laczniak; and Patrick E. Murphy. "The Ethics of Social Ideas versus the Ethics of Marketing Social Ideas." *Journal of Consumer Affairs* 14 (Summer 1980), pp. 156–63.

Mahler, Philip. "Corporate Espionage: When Market Research Goes Too Far." *Business Marketing* 69 (October 1984), pp. 50–66.

Mandel, Terry, and Marjorie Kelly. "Marketing with Integrity." *Business Ethics* 4, no. 5 (September/October 1990), pp. 21–23.

Manley, Walter W., II, and William A. Shrode. "Marketing and Advertising Issues for the 1990s." In *Critical Issues in Business Conduct; Legal, Ethical and Social Challenges for the 1990s*, ed. Walter W. Manley II and William A Shrode. New York: Quorum, 1990, pp. 183–94.

Mason, J. Barry; William O. Bearden; and Lynne Davis Richardson. "Perceived Conduct and Professional Ethics among Marketing Faculty." *Journal of the Academy of Marketing Science* 18 (Summer 1990), pp. 185–98.

Matthews, John B.; Kenneth E. Goodpaster; and Laura L. Nash, eds. *Policies and Persons: A Casebook in Business Ethics.* New York: McGraw-Hill, 1985. Three case studies: pp. 9–22, 250–78.

Mayo, Michael A. "Ethical Problems Encountered by U.S. Small Businesses in International Marketing." *Journal of Small Business Management,* April 1991, pp. 51–59.

Mayo, Michael, and Lawrence J. Marks. "An Empirical Investigation of a General Theory of Marketing Ethics." *Journal of the Academy of Marketing Science* 18 (Spring 1990), pp. 163–72. Comment by Shelby Hunt, pp. 173–78.

McGann, Anthony F. "Editorial: Off Pricing, Price Fixing and Advertising." *Journal of Advertising* 13, no. 1 (1984), p. 3.

Michelman, James H. "Deception in Commercial Negotiation." *Journal of Business Ethics,* November 1983, pp. 255–62.

Missner, Marshal, ed. *Ethics of the Business System.* Palo Alto, Calif.: Mayfield, 1980, pp. 235–60.

Molander, Earl A. "Marketing Ready-to-Eat Breakfast Cereals at the Kellogg Company." In *Responsive Capitalism; Case Studies in Corporate Social Conduct.* Earl A. Molander. New York: McGraw-Hill, 1980, pp. 128–43.

Moyer, Reed, ed. *Changing Marketing Systems.* Chicago: AMA, 1967, pp. 161–63.

Murdock, Gene W., and James M. Peterson. "Strict Product Liability for Advertisers: A Pro/Con Discussion." *Journal of Advertising* 10, no. 4 (1981), pp. 5–10.

Murphy, Patrick E., and Gene R. Laczniak. "Marketing Ethics: A Review with Implications for Managers, Educators, and Researchers." In *Review of Marketing,* ed. Ben M. Enis and Kenneth J. Roering. Chicago: American Marketing Association, 1981, pp. 251–66.

Murphy, Patrick E.; Gene R. Laczniak; and Robert F. Lusch. "Ethical Guidelines for Business and Social Marketing." *Journal of the Academy of Marketing Science* 6 (Summer 1978), pp. 195–204.

Nadelhaft, Marilyn. "An Issue of Trust: Ethics in Marketing Management." *Harvard Business School Bulletin* 66, no. 6 (December 1990), pp. 38–48.

Newton, Lisa H., and Maureen M. Ford, eds. *Taking Sides: Clashing Views on Controversial Issues in Business Ethics and Society.* Guilford: Dushkin, 1990, pp. 107–71.

Nevin, John R.; Shelby D. Hunt; and Michael G. Levas. "Legal Remedies for Deceptive and Unfair Practices in Franchising." *Journal of Macromarketing* 1 (Spring 1981), pp. 23–24.

Norris, Donald G., and John B. Gifford. "Retail Store Managers' and Students' Perceptions of Ethical Retail Practices: A Comparative and Longitudinal Analysis (1976–1986)." *Journal of Business Ethics* 7 (1988), pp. 515–24.

Oakes, Guy. *The Soul of the Salesman: The Moral Ethos of Personal Sales.* Atlantic Highlands, N.J.: Humanities Press International, 1990.

———. "The Sales Process and the Paradoxes of Trust." *Journal of Business Ethics* 9 (August 1990), pp. 671–80.

Offen, Neil H. "Commentary on Code of Ethics of Direct Selling Association." In *The Ethical Basis of Economic Freedom*, ed. Ivan Hill. Chapel Hill: American Viewpoint, 1976, pp. 263–82.

Packard, Vance. *The Hidden Persuaders*. New York: Pocket Books, 1957.

Partridge, Scott R., ed. *Cases in Business & Society*. 2nd ed. Englewood Cliffs, N.J.: Prentice Hall, 1989. Three case studies: pp. 221–34.

Patterson, James M. "What Are the Social and Ethical Responsibilities of Marketing Executives?" *Journal of Marketing* 30 (July 1966), pp. 12–15.

Perrien, Jean; Christian Dussart; and Paul Francorse. "Advertisers and the Factual Content of Advertising." *Journal of Advertising* 14, no. 1 (March 1985), pp. 30–35.

Pertschuk, Michael. "Confessions of an FTC Commissioner: Lessons Learned and Unlearned." *Across the Board* 20 (March 1983), pp. 26–33.

Peterson, Robin. "Physical Environment Television Advertisement Themes: 1979–1989." *Journal of Business Ethics* 10 (March 1991), pp. 221–28.

Pitts, Robert E., and Robert Allan Cooke. "A Realist View of Marketing Ethics." *Journal of Business Ethics* 10 (April 1991), pp. 243–44.

Post, James E., and Edward Baer. "Demarketing Infant Formula: Consumer Products in the Developing World." *Journal of Contemporary Business* 7 (Fall 1978), pp. 13–34.

Preston, Ivan L. "Reasonable Consumer or Ignorant Consumer? How the FTC Decides." *Journal of Consumer Affairs* 8, no. 2 (Winter 1974).

Pruden, Henry O. "Which Ethics for Marketers?" In *Marketing and Social Issues*, ed. John R. Wish and Stephen H. Gamble. New York: John Wiley & Sons, 1971, pp. 98–104.

Quinn, John F. "Moral Theory and Defective Tobacco Advertising and Warnings (The Business Ethics of Cipollone v. Liggett Group)." *Journal of Business Ethics* 8 (November 1989), pp. 831–40.

Reidenbach, Eric, and Donald P. Robin. "Some Initial Steps toward Improving the Measurement of Ethical Evaluations of Marketing Activities." *Journal of Business Ethics* 7 (November 1988), pp. 871–80.

————. "Epistemological Structures in Marketing: Paradigms, Metaphors and Marketing Ethics." *Business Ethics Quarterly*, April 1991, pp. 185–200.

Reidenbach, Eric; Donald P. Robin; and Lyndon Dawson. "An Application and Extension of a Multidimensional Ethics Scale to Selected Marketing Practices and Marketing Groups." *Journal of the Academy of Marketing Science* 19 (Spring 1991), pp. 83–93.

Robin, Donald P. "Value Issues in Marketing." In *Theoretical Developments in Marketing*, ed. C. W. Lamb and P. M. Dunne. Chicago: American Marketing Association, 1980, pp. 142–45.

Robin, Donald P., and R. Eric Reidenbach. "A Framework for Analyzing Issues in Marketing." *Business and Professional Ethics Journal* 5, no. 2 (1986), pp. 3–22. Comment by David J. Fritzsche, pp. 23–25.

————. "Social Responsibility, Ethics and Marketing Strategy: Closing the Gap between Concept and Application." *Journal of Marketing* 51 (January 1987), pp. 44–59.

Rodricks, Joseph V. "Risk Assessment and Product Misuse." *Chemical Times & Trends* 7 (April 1984), pp. 18–19.

Rudelius, William, and Rogene A. Buchholz. "Ethical Problems of Purchasing Managers." *Harvard Business Review* 57 (March–April 1979), pp. 11–14.

Sacks, Diane, and Russell Abratt. "The Marketing Challenge: Towards Being Profitable and Socially Responsible." *Journal of Business Ethics* 7 (July 1988), pp. 497–508.

Santilli, Paul C. "The Informative and Persuasive Functions of Advertising: A Moral Appraisal." *Journal of Business Ethics* 2 (February 1983), pp. 27–33.

Scherhorn, Gerhard. "The Goal of Consumer Advice: Transparency or Autonomy?" *Journal of Consumer Policy* 8 (June 1985), pp. 133–51.

Schneider, Kenneth C. "Subject and Respondent Abuse in Marketing Research." *MSU Business Topics* 25 (Spring 1977), pp. 13–20.

_____. "Teaching Ethics in Marketing Research: An Experiential Approach." *Journal of Marketing Education* 5 (Fall 1983), pp. 27–34.

_____. "The Role of Ethics in Marketing Research." *Mid-Atlantic Journal of Business* 22 (Winter 1983/84), pp. 11–20.

Schneider, Kenneth C., and Cynthia K. Holm. "Deceptive Practices in Marketing Research: The Consumer's Viewpoint." *California Management Review* 24 (Spring 1982), pp. 89–96.

Schudson, Michael. *Advertising, The Uneasy Persuasion.* New York: Basic Books, 1984.

Schultz, Q. J. "Professionalism in Advertising: The Origin of Ethical Codes." *Journal of Commerce* 31 (Spring 1981), pp. 64–71.

Sethi, S. Prakash. "Advocacy Advertising: A Novel Communications Approach to Building Effective Relations with External Constituencies," and "Business and the News Media: The Paradox of Informed Misunderstanding." In *Business and Society; Dimensions of Conflict and Cooperation,* ed. S. Prakash Sethi and Cecilia M. Falbe. Lexington, Mass.: Lexington Books, 1987, pp. 551–89 and 590–608.

Singhapakdi, Anusorn, and Scott J. Vitell, Jr. "Research Note: Selected Factors Influencing Marketers' Deontological Norms." *Journal of the Academy of Marketing Science* 19 (Winter 1991), pp. 37–43.

Sirgy, M. J., et al. "The Interface between Quality of Life and Marketing: A Theoretical Framework." *Journal of Marketing & Public Policy* 1 (1982), pp. 69–84.

_____. "The Question of Value in Social Marketing: Use of a Quality-of-Life Theory to Achieve Long-Term Life Satisfaction." *American Journal of Economics & Sociology* 44 (April 1985), pp. 215–28.

Skinner, Steven J.; O. C. Ferrell; and Alan J. Dubinsky. "Organizational Dimensions of Marketing-Research Ethics." *Journal of Business Research* 16, no. 3 (May 1988), pp. 209–24.

Smith, N. Craig. "Teaching Ethics in Marketing: One Approach and Some Caveats." *Quarterly Review of Marketing* 14 (1988), pp. 10–17.

_____. *Morality and the Market; Consumer Pressure for Corporate Accountability.* London: Routledge, 1990.

Smith, Scott M. "Marketing Research and Corporate Litigation . . . Where Is the Balance of Ethical Justice?" *Journal of Business Ethics* 3 (August 1984), pp. 185–94.

Snizek, William E., and Kenneth E. Crocker. "Professionalism and Attorney Attitudes toward Legal Service Advertising." *Journal of the Academy of Marketing Science* 13 (Fall 1985), pp. 101–19.

Snoeyenbos, Milton; Robert Almeder; and James Humber, eds. *Business Ethics; Corporate Values and Society.* Buffalo: Prometheus Books, 1983, pp. 398–401 and 421–24.

Snyder, James D. "Bribery in Selling: The Scandal Comes Home." *Sales and Marketing Management,* May 10, 1976, pp. 35–38.

Stern, Bruce L., and Robert R. Harmon. "Disclaimers in Children's Advertising." *Journal of Advertising* 13, no. 2 (1984), pp. 12–16.

Stewart, Robert M. "Morality and the Market in Blood." *Journal of Applied Philosophy* 1 (October 1984), pp. 227–38.

Storholm, Gordon, and Hershey Friedman. "Perceived Common Myths and Unethical Practices among Direct Marketing Professionals." *Journal of Business Ethics* 8 (December 1989), pp. 975–80.

Sturdivant, Frederick D., and A. Benton Cocanougher. "What Are Ethical Marketing Practices?" *Harvard Business Review* 51 (November–December 1973), pp. 10–12 and 176.

Timmerman, Ed, and Brad Reid. "The Doctrine of Invited Misuse: A Societal Response to Marketing Promotion." *Journal of Macromarketing* 4 (Fall 1984), pp. 40–48.

Trawick, F., and W. R. Darden. "Marketer's Perceptions of Ethical Standards in the Marketing Profession: Educators and Practitioners." *Review of Business and Economic Research* 16 (Fall 1980), pp. 1–17.

Trawick, I. Frederick; John E. Swan; and David R. Rink. "Back-Door Selling: Violation of Cultural versus Professional Ethics by Salespeople and Purchaser Choice of Supplier." *Journal of Business Research* 17 (November 1988), pp. 299–310.

Tsalikis, John, and David J. Fritzsche. "Business Ethics: A Literature Review with a Focus on Marketing Ethics." *Journal of Business Ethics* 8 (September 1989), pp. 695–743.

Tsalikis, John, and Osita Nwachukwu. "Cross-Cultural Marketing Ethics: An Investigation of the Ethical Beliefs' Differences between Greeks and Americans." *Journal of International Consumer Marketing* 1, no. 3 (Spring 1989).

Turk, Peter. "Children's Television Advertising: An Ethical Morass for Business and Government." *Journal of Advertising* 8 (1979), pp. 4–8.

Twedt, D. W. "Why a Marketing Research Code of Ethics?" *Journal of Marketing* 27 (1963), pp. 48–50.

Tybout, Alice M., and Gerald Zaltman. "Ethics in Marketing Research: Their Practical Relevance." *Journal of Marketing Research* 11 (November 1974), pp. 357–68.

—————. "A Reply to Comments on 'Ethics in Marketing Research: Their Practical Relevance.' " *Journal of Marketing Research* 12 (May 1975), pp. 234–37.

Velasquez, Manuel G. "Case Study—Toy Wars." In *Ethical Issues in Business: A Philosophical Approach.* 3rd ed. Ed. Thomas Donaldson and Patricia H. Werhane. Englewood Cliffs, N.J.: Prentice Hall, 1988, pp. 390–94.

Van Auken, Stuart, and Subhash C. Lonial. "Children's Perceptions of Human versus Animate Characters." *Journal of Advertising* 14, no. 2 (1985), pp. 13–22.

Vitell, Scott J., and Stephen J. Grove. "Marketing Ethics and the Techniques of Neutralization." *Journal of Business Ethics* 6 (August 1987), pp. 433–38.

Vitell, Scott J., and Shelby D. Hunt. "The General Theory of Marketing Ethics: A Partial Test of the Model." *Research in Marketing Annual* 10 (1990), pp. 237–66.

von Hayek, F. A. "The Non Sequitur of the 'Dependence Effect'." *Southern Economic Journal*, April 1961.

Waide, John. "The Making of Self and World in Advertising." *Journal of Business Ethics* 6 (February 1987), pp. 73–80.

Weigand, Robert E. "Buying into Market Control." *Harvard Business Review* 58 (November–December 1980), pp. 141–49.

Whalen, Joel; Robert E. Pitts; and John K. Wong. "Exploring the Structure of Ethical Attributes as a Component of the Consumer Decision Model: The Vicarious versus Personal Perspective." *Journal of Business Ethics* 10 (April 1991), pp. 285–94.

Whipple, Thomas W., and Alice E. Courtney. "Female Role Portrayals in Advertising and Communication Effectiveness: A Review." *Journal of Advertising* 14, no. 3 (1985), pp. 4–8.

Williams, John K. "And Now, a Pitch for Advertising." *Reason* 15 (September 1983), pp. 29–31.

Wyckham, Robert G.; Peter M. Banting; and Anthony K. Wensley. "The Language of Advertising: Who Controls Quality?" *Journal of Business Ethics* 3 (February 1984), pp. 47–53.

Yeo, Michael. "Marketing Ethics: The Bottom Line?" *Journal of Business Ethics* 7 (December 1988), pp. 929–33.

Zanot, Eric J.; J. D. Pincus; and E. J. Lamp. "Public Perceptions of Subliminal Advertising." *Journal of Advertising* 12, no. 1 (1983), pp. 39–45.

Zey-Ferrell, Mary K.; Mark Weaver; and O. C. Ferrell. "Predicting Unethical Behavior among Marketing Practitioners." *Human Relations* 32, no. 7 (1979), pp. 557–69.

Zinkhan, George M.; Michael Bisesi; and Mary Jane Saxton. "MBAs' Changing Attitudes toward Marketing Dilemmas: 1981–1987." *Journal of Business Ethics* 8 (December 1989), pp. 963–74.

Zinkhan, George M., and Betsy D. Gelb. "Competitive Intelligence Practices of Industrial Marketing." *Industrial Marketing Management* 14 (November 1985), pp. 269–75.

Index

A

A. H. Robins, 291
Abramson, Jill, 193n
Abt Associates, 63
Accreditation of marketing
  researchers, 186
Acid Rain Reduction Plan, 83
Action for Children's Television,
  672n
Adams, Beth, 296
Addiction Resources Center, 104
Adelson, Clifford, 243
Adidas, 722
Adler, Richard P., 612n, 682n,
  683n, 685n
Advertising; *see also* Children's television advertising
  annual expenditures for, 607–8
  bait-and-switch, 616–17
  bans on, 655–56
  deceptiveness law and, 662–71
  definition of, 607n
  endorsements and testimonials,
    615–16
  ethical issues in, 607–86
  implicit versus explicit meaning
    of ads, 664–69
  moral issues of, 619–23
  moral issues versus legal issues,
    624–25
  negative effects of, 621–23
  price-based advertising, 616–17
  regulation of, 610–18
  stereotyping in, 189–92, 622–23
Advertising Age, 268, 639, 647, 649
Advertising Times, 295
Advisory Committee on Shareholder Responsibility (Harvard
  University), 104–5
Advocacy Institute, 251, 252, 655–
  56
Adweek, 206–7, 633, 647
The Affluent Society (Galbraith),
  619

African National Congress (ANC),
  114
Airlines fare probe, 445–47
Ajzen, Icek, 763
Akaah, Ishmael P., 168
Akers, John, 121
Alar scare, 744–46
Allen, Anita L., 270n
Allgeir, Peter F., 103
Alliance for Responsible CFC
  Policy, 709
Allied Old English, 491–506
Aloha Airlines, 291–92
Alsop, Ronald, 686n
Amalgamated Aluminum, 428–31
American Advertising Federation,
  673–74
American Apparel Manufacturers
  Association, 407
American Association of Adver-
  tising Agencies, 668
  on children's television, 673–74
  Creative Code of, 624
American Association of Public
  Opinion Research code, of
  conduct, 146, 179
American Cancer Society, 94
American Civil Liberties Union,
  256
American Express, 246
American Family Association, 648
American Forest Council, 74
American Heart Association, 94
American Lung Association, 94
American Marketing Association,
  10–11
  code of conduct, 10, 146, 163,
    171–72, 179, 485–86, 778
  definition of advertising, 607n
American Psychological Association
  Committee for the Protection
    of Human Participants in
    Research, 174
  research guidelines, 173–76, 184,
    187